MW01043054

Research Methodology

To my wife Heidi, the most out-of-the-box thinker and caring person I've ever known. Thank you for a fantastic 30-year (and counting) journey together.

Research Methodology

Best Practices for Rigorous, Credible, and Impactful Research

Herman Aguinis

The George Washington University

 Sage

FOR INFORMATION:

2455 Teller Road
Thousand Oaks, California 91320
E-mail: order@sagepub.com

1 Oliver's Yard
55 City Road
London, EC1Y 1SP
United Kingdom

Unit No. 323-333, Third Floor, F-Block
International Trade Tower
Nehru Place, New Delhi – 110 019
India

18 Cross Street #10-10/11/12
China Square Central
Singapore 048423

Copyright © 2025 by Sage.

All rights reserved. Except as permitted by U.S. copyright law, no part of this work may be reproduced or distributed in any form or by any means, or stored in a database or retrieval system, without permission in writing from the publisher.

All third-party trademarks referenced or depicted herein are included solely for the purpose of illustration and are the property of their respective owners. Reference to these trademarks in no way indicates any relationship with, or endorsement by, the trademark owner.

Printed in the United States of America

Library of Congress Cataloging-in-Publication Data

ISBN: 978-1-0718-7194-2

Acquisitions Editor: Leah Fargotstein

Editorial Assistant: Jennifer Milewski

Production Editor: Syeda Aina Rahat Ali

Copy Editor: Michelle Ponce

Typesetter: diacriTech

Cover Designer: Candice Harman

Marketing Manager: Victoria Velasquez

This book is printed on acid-free paper.

24 25 26 27 28 10 9 8 7 6 5 4 3 2 1

BRIEF CONTENTS

DETAILED CONTENTS

LIST OF FIGURES

LIST OF TABLES

PREFACE

This textbook on methodological best practices takes a 360-degree view, covering topics pertinent to the authors, reviewers, and consumers of research alike. Its content is intended to serve undergraduate students, graduate students at the master's and doctoral level, junior as well as seasoned researchers (including journal reviewers and editors), and consumers of research (other researchers, organizational leaders, and policymakers).

The book is the product of my 30+ years of experience regarding research methodology as a researcher and research consumer. It is also the product of my experience as an evaluator of research quality in my capacity as former Editor-in-Chief of *Organizational Research Methods*, which is devoted entirely to research methodology, as well as having served as an editorial board member for more than 25 journals and evaluator for grant proposals in the United States and many other countries around the world (e.g., Belgium, Israel, Romania). Finally, it is also the result of my multiple professional roles addressing research methodology, such as having served as Chair of the Research Methods Division of the Academy of Management and member of the American Psychological Association Task Force on Increasing the Number of Quantitative Psychologists.

What did I learn as a result of these experiences? First, there are ways to do research right and ways to do research wrong, and we know this based on decades of accumulated knowledge. So, the first goal of this book is to synthesize this vast body of work on methodological best practices in a user-friendly manner. Second, I also learned that most social and behavioral scientists are not methodological specialists—nor do they want to take on such a role. Instead, most researchers are *methods users* as we conduct our own research and *methods consumers* as we read the research produced by others. So, the second goal of this book is to present material and best practices, mainly in the form of checklists. In other words, I wrote this book like a tutorial to include "how-to" and "dos and don'ts" guidelines so you can understand the extent to which methodological best practices are being followed—and so that you can follow best practices in your research. Each chapter includes figures and tables to make the material easier to digest. In addition, each chapter (a) describes why the particular methodological topic is important for doing rigorous, credible, and impactful research; (b) explains and expands upon the summaries, checklists, and steps in the figures and tables; and (c) provides examples and applications to demonstrate that the best-practice recommendations are actionable and implementable and not just wishful thinking. And, in case you are thinking about this, generative AI tools such as ChatGPT cannot tell you the best ways to do research. Indeed, they can provide some general and vague recommendations, but they are often overly general and flatly wrong due to "generative AI hallucination." In other words, ChatGPT often makes things up based on the information it picks up from the web.

The textbook covers the entire research process from the beginning (i.e., how to generate and test good theory) to the end (i.e., how to report results openly and transparently). In addition, it includes chapters on design, measurement, and quantitative and qualitative methods. Also, it contains chapters you will not find in other research methods books – for example, Chapter 16, titled "How to Enhance the Impact of Your Research." We conduct research for our satisfaction and, frankly, our career advancement, but we also research to hopefully improve individual well-being, organizational performance, and society. So, high-quality and rigorous research does not end with the publication of an article—it is followed by efforts to ensure our research reaches broad audiences who may benefit from it.

A unique pedagogical feature of this book is that it is modular. Think about how we listen to music. If we want to hear a specific song, we don't have to listen to all the other pieces in that "album" before we get to the one we want, right? We go straight to the song we want and listen to that specific one. So, as you read this book, if you are interested in a particular methodological topic, you don't have to read all the other chapters first. The book will be helpful to you based on your specific needs and interests because you can choose your level of depth depending on your needs. In other words, although the chapters are organized following the usual sequential stages of the research process, you can go directly to sections, chapters, and even chapter content (e.g., figure, table, example, "methods in practice" box) based on your particular needs at a particular time without the need to, for example, read Chapter 3 before you read Chapter 4. For instance, what if you read a published meta-analysis and want to learn whether the authors implemented best practices and results are credible and trustworthy? You would consult Chapter 11: How to Conduct Quantitative Analysis, Part III: Meta-analysis. In evaluating the meta-analysis you read, you may initially consult the checklist of best practices in Table 11.1 to see how many of the desirable features are present and which are absent. Then, suppose you are interested in a particular issue regarding the meta-analysis you are reading, such as the procedures implemented to code the primary-level studies. In that case, you can read that specific section in Chapter 11, which expands upon the summary in Table 11.1. Or, if you are unfamiliar with meta-analysis, you would take advantage of the entire chapter, which not only offers an overview of how to do a meta-analysis but also describes more advanced meta-analytic techniques such as meta-regression and meta-analytic structural equation modeling and a decision framework to understand whether a new meta-analysis on a topic that has already been meta-analyzed may be warranted. The table of contents is sufficiently detailed so you can jump to a specific topic you may be interested in based on your project or a paper you are reading.

If you are a social or behavioral science research methods course instructor, you would probably assign all or most chapters. This is why the book is organized following the usual research process stages and includes 16 chapters. As an instructor, you can assign approximately one chapter weekly throughout the quarter or semester. But, based on your course's specific goals and targeted audience, you may want to create a bundle of chapters that fit your specific needs. For example, for a more advanced course, you may want to include chapters addressing more advanced topics (e.g., Chapter 10: multilevel modeling, Chapter 11: meta-analysis). For courses that address qualitative topics, you may want to include content about qualitative research (Chapter 13). You will undoubtedly want to include Chapter 7 if you want your students to learn how to conduct experimental research. Also, for courses involving undergraduate and MBA students, you may want to assign a single chapter over two sessions: The first focused on conceptual issues, and the second focused on hands-on exercises and activities, in this way covering less content in a more applied and hands-on manner. The table of contents is sufficiently detailed to allow you, as an instructor, to assemble chapters that fit your course's learning goals and students regarding their specific backgrounds and learning goals.

In addition to a glossary of more than 600 terms, the book includes three additional pedagogical features that you will appreciate: 37 "Methods in Practice" boxes, 45 "Example" boxes, and 4 "Applied Methods" short case studies. These features will offer you an opportunity for hands-on engagement with the material.

Finally, Sage Publishing offers an exceptionally robust set of instructor resources accessible from each title's companion website, designed to save you time and to help you keep students engaged. To learn more, visit sagepub.com or contact your Sage representative at sagepub.com/findmyrep.

Sound research methods are now needed more than ever. Society demands it. Social and behavioral science researchers can and should deliver it. I sincerely hope this book will be helpful regarding this lofty goal if you are a student just getting started with research or a junior or seasoned researcher interested in "improving your research game."

Herman Aguinis
Washington, D.C.

ACKNOWLEDGMENTS

I thank my former doctoral students Professor Isabel Villamor (IESE Business School) and Professor Ravi S. Ramani (Morgan State University), for their invaluable assistance in compiling materials for this book. Also, I thank my current doctoral students, Amando Cope and Ursula Martin, for their help with the glossary, and Soolim Park and Urusha Thapa for reviewing page proofs. Finally, I am extremely thankful to Leah Fargotstein and Jennifer Milewski from SAGE, who have been champions for this book project since the beginning.

SAGE would like to thank the following reviewers who have taught research methods courses in business, communication and organizational leadership, human development and family science, international business, management, political science, psychology, sociology, and technology studies at the undergraduate, master's, and doctoral level courses and were kind enough to offer their suggestions for improvements and additions:

Anna Abelson, *USC Bovard College and Tisch Center of Hospitality*
Stuart Allen, *Robert Morris University*
Verl Anderson, *Dixie State University*
Ali Choudhry, *Rutgers University*
Ewa Golebiowska, *Wayne State University*
Stacy H. Haynes, *Mississippi State University*
Mindy Myers, *Midwestern State University*
Michael T. Moore, *Adelphi University*
Kristina M. Patterson, *Georgia Southern University*
Meghan Pfeiffer, *University of Memphis*
Pushkala Raman, *Texas Women's University*
Keivan Sadeghzadeh, *Northeastern University*
Scot Schraufnagel, *Northern Illinois University*
Craig Seidelson, *University of Indianapolis*
Amarjit Singh, *Hope International University*
Jordan Stalker, *DePaul University*
Tara Stoppa, *Eastern University*
Rachel R. Tambling, *University of Connecticut*
Mark Vrooman, *Utica University*
Haibo Wang, *Texas A&M International University*
Xuan Wang, *The University of Texas Rio Grande Valley*

H.A.

ABOUT THE AUTHOR

Herman Aguinis is the Avram Tucker Distinguished Scholar and Professor of Management at The George Washington University School of Business. His interdisciplinary research addresses research methods in the social and behavioral sciences and the acquisition and deployment of talent in organizations. In addition to his about 220 journal articles, 350 keynotes and presentations at professional conferences, and 200 invited presentations, he has published twelve books, including *Regression Analysis for Categorical Moderators, Performance Management*, and *Applied Psychology in Talent Management* (with W.F. Cascio). He served as Editor-in-Chief of *Organizational Research Methods* and received the Academy of Management Research Methods Division Distinguished Career Award for lifetime contributions. He is a three-time recipient of the Academy of Management Research Methods Division Robert McDonald Advancement of Organizational Research Methodology Award, recognizing the best article published in the preceding five years. Also, he received career awards for research contributions from the Society for Industrial and Organizational Psychology and the Society for Human Resource Management, served as President of the Academy of Management, and has been inducted into The PhD Project Hall of Fame. He is a Fellow of the Academy of Management, the American Psychological Association, the Association for Psychological Science, and the Society for Industrial and Organizational Psychology. He serves or has served on the editorial board of 26 journals. The Web of Science Highly Cited Researchers Report has ranked him among the world's 100 most impactful researchers in Economics and Business every year since 2018, and he has about 35,000 LinkedIn and X followers. For more information, please visit https://www.hermanaguinis.com.

1 HOW TO UNDERSTAND THE CURRENT METHODOLOGICAL LANDSCAPE

LEARNING GOALS

By the end of this chapter, you will be able to do the following:

1.1 Describe why you should care about research methods.

1.2 Explain the link between solid methods and the credibility of social and behavioral science research.

1.3 Compare the topics emphasized in each historical era to trace the development of research methodology.

1.4 Name the main design, measurement, and analysis categories of quantitative methods.

1.5 Name the main design, measurement, and analysis categories of qualitative methods.

1.6 Cite the trends for the most popular quantitative design, measurement, and analysis categories.

1.7 Cite the trends for the most popular qualitative design, measurement, and analysis categories.

1.8 Describe the five issues likely to have the most impact on the trustworthiness of future research methods.

IMPORTANCE OF RESEARCH METHODS

Richard Feynman is recognized as one of the most brilliant physicists ever. Born in 1918 in the USA, he was a theoretical physicist who made significant contributions in various fields such as quantum mechanics, quantum electrodynamics, and particle physics. He is credited with the beginning of nanotechnology, one of the most promising areas of physics today. Feynman popularized physics through lectures and books, making it more accessible to the general public. Among the honors he received for his research are the Nobel Prize and membership in the National Academy of Science, the American Association for the Advancement of Science, the American Physical Society, and the Royal Society of London.[1]

In explaining some reasons for his research success, Feynman insisted on using a rigorous scientific approach to seek the truth and warned us about how easy it is for pseudo-science to mislead us. In addition, Feynman often used the social sciences as an example of an area where the methods could and *should* be improved—and not doing so means knowledge will not be trustworthy, credible, or valuable.

The social and behavioral sciences are a broad group of academic disciplines that study the social life of individuals and human groups. This group of disciplines includes management, psychology, marketing, political science, anthropology, sociology, and education. These disciplines try to understand human relationships and analyze the complicated relationships between people, which involve a volatile and unpredictable human element. There is much room for improvement regarding research methodology in the social and behavioral sciences—hence the need for this book.

The social and behavioral sciences began with an interest in real-world problems such as how to improve employee performance and motivation, how to improve inter-group relations, how to enhance individual well-being, how to deliver better pedagogical techniques, and how to make products more attractive. As a result, the social and behavioral sciences were driven by problems and phenomena, similar to how other sciences were born. However, these problems were of a different kind than problems in physics. And because it was the first time these problems were studied, we needed to learn more about how to do so. We needed a set of valuable and innovative methods to guide basic questions, like: How should we collect data and what type of data? How do we measure things accurately? How do we analyze those data if we have collected the correct data type in the right way, using accurate measures? These questions reflect the three main areas of research methods: data collection, measurement, and data analysis, respectively. And the most critical questions, the ones that drive the research, follow from these: What legitimate conclusions can we draw from our results, and how do they address those fundamental organizational and societal challenges? It is unsurprising that since the birth of social science, much attention has been devoted to research methods—creating new ones, importing others from other sciences, and assessing their relative usefulness and accuracy.

But the initial enthusiasm for better research methodology evolved into the view that there was too much emphasis on research methods to the detriment of theory. Some believe we may suffer from "physics envy" and should not necessarily follow its lead in ensuring our methods are entirely trustworthy before making claims about a particular discovery. In fact, consider the fact that that articles describing the development and **validation** of new measures—a squarely methodological issue—have been among the most cited (i.e., influential) for decades. But more recently, social and behavioral science journals no longer publish these methodological articles. Why? There is a belief that the social and behavioral sciences have become too obsessed with methodology. Given what is published today in social and behavioral science journals, many methods-oriented papers published years ago would most certainly be rejected. Part of the backlash is because many social and behavioral scientists tend to think of research methods as mere details of the conscientious bookkeeper: methodological information needs to be in the report somewhere, but it should be tucked in a place that does not distract a reader from the heart of a paper.

Ironically, as methods seemed to become less of a focus in some academic circles, they are becoming more relevant than ever for the general public. In a post-pandemic world, we are now used to watching scientists debate data and graphs on TV and social media. Making sense of these opposing views boils down to details in research methodology that help determine whether a conclusion is trustworthy. How were the **variables** measured? What were the sources of data? How were the data analyzed? A researcher's decision about how to proceed for each of these will influence a study's results. A thorough understanding of research methods allows us to see the strengths and weaknesses of a particular methodological approach—and how they affect the legitimacy of a claim.

In 1968 eminent social scientist John Darley reviewed 50 years of social and behavioral science research.[2] He concluded that researchers had yet to learn from their methodological mistakes and were doomed to repeat them. But the 21st century marks the beginning of a sea change for the social and behavioral sciences. We have begun prioritizing research methods so they aren't sacrificed at the altar of "selling a good story." Instead, we are returning to the methodological preeminence that is the hallmark of credible and trustworthy science. This book provides tools for the next generation of social and behavioral scientists to avoid making the same mistakes Feynman noticed decades ago. But even as we look to the future, we must see it in the context of our past. As famously attributed to Italian-American historian of science George Santillana, "Those who do not remember their past are condemned to repeat their mistakes." So, your journey with me begins by tracing the history and trajectory of social and behavioral research.

RESEARCH METHODS: A BRIEF HISTORICAL JOURNEY

Research methodology in the past century can be organized around six periods. To allow you to visualize these periods more easily, Figure 1.1 includes a summary. The first period takes us through the mid-1920s, which, in many ways, set us on a methodological course that we sail to this day. The second period is through World War II, in which the roots of modern social and behavioral science methodological concepts and techniques were formed. The third takes us through roughly 1970, which saw the formation of many of our modern-day methodological concepts and techniques. The fourth, from 1970 through 1989, emphasized the development of good measures of critical **constructs**. The fifth period brings us through the recent past, marked by a plurality regarding data-analytic approaches. Finally, the sixth period is our future, offering a glimpse of possible and desirable research methodology.

FIGURE 1.1 ■ Historical Journey of Research Methodology in the Social and Behavioral Sciences: The Past Century

Source: Copyright © 2017 by American Psychological Association. Adapted with permission. J. M. Cortina, H. Aguinis, & R. P. DeShon, 2017, Twilight of dawn or of evening? A century of research methods in the Journal of Applied Psychology, *Journal of Applied Psychology, 102*(3), 274-290.

1917–1925: Who Are You?

The dominant **research paradigm** during these early years was atheoretical, as it had yet to amass evidence to assemble into theories. On the other hand, the first publications in the social and behavioral sciences showed a desire for objective methods that would lead us to appropriate and valuable conclusions. And indeed, researchers addressed this need through the methodology introduced in this period. Yet social scientists grappled with tension: the need to create a solid framework for social science research while remaining open to new ways of asking questions and finding answers. The case study method and measurement were the two focus areas reflecting this tension.

The case study method was a particularly effective tool for discovery. This method involved looking at cases out of the ordinary, such as with people who scored notably high and low on a given measure.[3]

There was great interest in measuring individual and group differences such as intelligence,[4] aptitudes,[5] traits such as aggressiveness,[6] and vocational interests.[7] This focus on measurement brought to bear the early treatment of various methodological topics that are now staples. Naturally, there was a burgeoning interest in the psychometric properties of measures; that is, researchers were focused on figuring out how to build tests of individual and group differences that were useful and trustworthy. Additionally, there was great interest in **correlational analysis, experience sampling methodology,** and the use of **inferential statistics.** Finally, multiple regression and the beginnings of more complex prediction models appeared. In sum, many of the most influential papers during this time were methodological, and they set the stage for future theory advancements made possible because of methodological advances.

The Roaring '20s, the Depression, and World War II

This period saw a dramatic expansion of methodology. Measurement focus expanded from measuring ability to measuring personality, and along with interest in assessing personality came questions about using **self-report** as a valid source of data. In addition, this period saw the seedlings of research methods topics that would become fundamental concepts in inferential statistics and psychometrics over the next half-century—words you will see again and again, including **distributions,**[8] **sampling error,**[9] **growth curves** in ability scores,[10] **discrimination parameters,**[11] and utility tables.[12] Another characteristic of this period is the beginning of the transition from a discovery model to a **hypothetico-deductive model.** As social and behavioral sciences found their footing, there was increased attention to verifying and using the knowledge it already had (e.g., using ability measures to sort individuals into appropriate military positions during World War II), with less focus on exploring new ways of uncovering knowledge. In other words, this period experienced a shift from discovery to hypothesis testing, which has continued to the present day.

The Baby Boom and Beyond: 1946 –1969

From the end of World War II (WWII) to the middle of the Vietnam conflict, we see the field begin to take the methodological shape into which it has since solidified. To be sure, methodological topics that had generated interest in the previous period continued to do so. But, measurement took center stage, and this period saw tremendous strides forward in developing, evaluating, and refining measures.

Importantly, two critical components of today's research methodology, theory development, and **statistical significance testing,**[13] came into their own. Also, many of our modern-day research practices were formed during this period, including one of the first extensive literature reviews in an empirical paper[14] and some of the first tests of formal theory.[15] Finally, it also included a growing appreciation of the limitations of self-report measures.

1970 –1989: Measurement and Its Discontents

The early 1970s produced highly influential measurement instruments, many still in use today. For example, the Job Diagnostic Survey (JDS) scores were related to absenteeism, performance, general satisfaction, and work motivation. As a second example, the Position Analysis Questionnaire (PAQ) identified dimensions of human behavior for specific jobs; these data help us understand the extent to which seemingly different jobs share common behavioral requirements (i.e., "job elements").[16] This has implications for human resources managers, career seekers, and organizations who design jobs. Not surprisingly, along with the emphasis on creating new measures came a focus on evaluating their trustworthiness.

The barrage of new measures led to the recognition that critical and thorny issues compromised the validity of those measures, most of which were self-reported. Studies questioned the accuracy of data collected using the available measures. This focus on evaluating the trustworthiness of measures produced seminal work on interrater reliability and agreement[17] but also culminated in articles that opened up new lines of research stretching into the following decade and beyond. These lines of research are seminal in today's understanding of how to do trustworthy research. They include topics such as **common method bias**[18] and **measurement invariance.**[19]

The development and improvement of measurement instruments were quickly followed by two immensely influential data-analytic innovations: **meta-analysis** and **structural equation modeling (SEM)**. First, **validity generalization**[20] (also called **psychometric meta-analysis**) represented a significant turning point, leading to a general belief that it is possible to draw conclusions about mean relations across studies,[21] even if these studies used unreliable measures. The second data-analytic innovation revolved around SEM. Particularly within the broader context of measurement development and improvement—and the assessment of overall measure quality—SEM was seen as a fundamental tool for understanding dimensionality,[22] hierarchical structures,[23] and relations between underlying constructs.[24]

At the end of the 1980s, the zeitgeist was that data-analytic solutions such as meta-analysis and SEM would mitigate research design and measurement challenges. The belief was augmented by the introduction of more powerful computers, which allowed researchers to conduct analyses at lightning speed compared with capabilities available just a few years earlier. Thus, a data-analytic solution (as opposed to a research design solution) was the practical and seemingly logical choice to address some of the evident measurement challenges.

1990 –Present: From One to Many

Novel methodological approaches such as meta-analysis and SEM were frequently used, were welcome, and became popular across substantive domains ranging from integrity testing[25] to job burnout[26] and leadership.[27] However, a fundamental realization remains true today: using any single methodological approach, no matter how potent, does not offer a silver-bullet answer to important theoretical and practical questions. Instead, each methodological approach has unique strengths and weaknesses, and tailoring the method to match the question is the most effective way to obtain trustworthy results. Thus, the period beginning in the 1990s was marked by an appreciation for many different methods, a movement that can be called "from one to many." This movement toward increased methodological plurality involved conceptual, design, measurement, and analysis topics described next.

New ways of obtaining information through study design emerged, such as in how, when, from where, and from whom data are gathered. For example, self-report data collected at only one point no longer provided a compelling basis for insights. Instead, researchers used more subtle ways of gathering information about people's thoughts, such as through **policy capturing**,[28] Second, they leveraged multiple data sources to go beyond information from the self-report, such as peers, customers, and supervisors.[29] Third, data were collected at two or more periods[30] in **longitudinal designs**. Fourth, they were gathered in multiple contexts, inside and outside the group or organization.[31] Finally, researchers broadened the scope of their study by focusing on individuals at lower levels of the organization and higher (e.g., top management teams[32]).

Not only is the approach to data collection more sophisticated, but from this era, we now have a more comprehensive understanding of measurement. Previous eras focused on how wording on a **survey** might affect the type of information produced. Still, this era added appreciation of other sources of error, like the passage of time and the use of multiple raters.[33] Previous eras heavily utilized one type of **scale**—i.e., **Likert-type scales** with answers ranging from "Strongly Agree" to "Strongly Disagree"—but different scale formats emerged in this era. Previous eras measured outcomes at one level of analysis only (i.e., employee), but now, we measure at many levels (e.g., the team level[34]).

Despite advances in measurement, this period also saw the gradual extinction of studies about measure development and validating measures. This is a strange occurrence given that so many of the most cited papers in the history of the social and behavioral sciences describe the development and validation of new measures. However, papers on data analysis continued to thrive. Many published papers addressed refinements and improvements in procedures and the estimation of parameters within the context of multiple regression,[35] meta-analysis,[36] **measurement equivalence**,[37] and **multilevel modeling**,[38] among many others.

The movement from one to many created unexpected challenges. First, researchers faced many choices regarding theory, design, measurement, and analysis. Second, there was an increased level of sophistication in the analytic repertoire. Moreover, a movement from one to many meant that methodological choices were not mutually exclusive and could be combined within the same study. But, there needed to be more guidance on how to go about implementing these integrative approaches so that the type of knowledge produced by one complemented the kind of knowledge produced by another. The challenges above opened up new opportunities. First, *Psychological Methods* and *Organizational Research Methods* were launched as new journals devoted to methodology in the mid to late 1990s. Second, some journals began to publish articles that reviewed methodological practices and offered specific guidelines and best-practice recommendations.[39]

The State of Social and Behavioral Science Methods

A few themes emerged over the past few decades. First, it became apparent that more than solutions based exclusively on data-analytic approaches would be necessary to address methodological challenges. Second, the adoption of novel data analytic approaches tended to happen rather quickly— the broader availability of statistical software packages accelerated the speed of the adoption process. Third, however, innovations regarding research design were slow and often were not implemented at all. Finally, in addition to the aforementioned methodological issues, there was a change in how methodological practices were reported. The trend toward longer Introduction sections seemed to shoot upward, placing more significant length constraints on Method sections.

Overall, the period including 1990 through 2014, involved the introduction of many methodological innovations and a staggering broadening of the methodological landscape to the point that the usual undergraduate and graduate training regarding methodology may need to catch up.

METHODS IN PRACTICE
THE NEED TO UPDATE RESEARCH METHODS EDUCATION

A study[40] involving graduate training in statistics, research design, and measurement in 222 psychology departments concluded that "statistical and methodological curriculum has advanced little [since the 1960s]" (p. 721) and that "new developments in statistics, measurement, and methodology are not being incorporated into most graduate training programs" (p. 730). Consequently, it is not surprising that editors of many journals have scrambled to find sufficiently knowledgeable reviewers to evaluate manuscripts using more novel methods. Given the proliferation of methodological techniques, the social and behavioral sciences may be forced to update research methods education.

I have just taken you through a brief historical review of methodological evolution in the last century. Now, let's learn about the types of methods currently in use. The following section addresses **quantitative methods**, and the following one discusses **qualitative** ones. This is useful for researchers who want to know what types of methods exist—and serve as a guide for particular methods you may want to learn in the future because they may be specifically suitable for your research questions and interests. Also, to learn about the relative popularity of various methods, we must consider a particular journal, *Organizational Research Methods* (ORM), as a case study. ORM is a natural choice for discussing social and behavioral science methodology given its broad coverage of methods: its papers span new methods in organizational research and existing methods in other fields; methods in **micro** areas of research (i.e., at the individual level of analysis), and **macro** (i.e., at the organizational, industry, and societal level of analysis); and, significantly, advancements in knowledge in both quantitative and qualitative methods of research.

MAPPING QUANTITATIVE RESEARCH METHODS

The late 1990s marked the beginning of a new era finally conducive to stand-alone methods journals. In contrast to journals devoted to methodology in specific social and behavioral science fields (e.g., *Applied Psychological Measurement, Psychological Methods, Sociological Methods & Research*) or journals devoted to particular methodological and data analytic approaches (e.g., *Multivariate Behavioral Research, Structural Equation Modeling*), ORM's mission is broader.

Based on a **content analysis** of the 193 articles published in ORM's first ten volumes (1998 to 2007), we now understand various research methodology topics in the social and behavioral sciences.

Quantitative Topics: Research Design

Regarding research design, the 24-category list includes:

- archival
- behavioral simulation
- case study
- control variables/statistical controls
- correlational/passive observation/non-experimental
- cross-cultural research
- electronic/ web research
- experimental
- experimental repeated measures
- exploratory
- external validity/ generalizability
- narrative literature review
- internal validity
- measurement design
- mixed methods (qualitative & quantitative)
- Monte Carlo / computer simulation
- multilevel research
- quantitative literature review/ meta-analysis
- quasi-experimental
- research setting
- sample size
- sampling
- survey
- temporal issues

Which are the most popular among these 24 topics? They are survey (32.35%), temporal issues (i.e., longitudinal designs) (13.24%), and electronic/web research (10.29%). If your goal is to be able to read and understand contemporary research, you should think about learning these approaches because you are likely to encounter them in published articles.

Quantitative Topics: Measurement

Below is the list of the categories in the quantitative-measurement group:

- archival data
- **banding**
- level of the dependent variable
- measurement invariance/equivalence
- reliability
- scale development
- source of measures
- test development
- test theory
- validity

Out of these, which are the most popular? They are validity (40.12%), reliability (23.26%), level of analysis of dependent variable (11.05%), scale development (9.88%), and measurement invariance/equivalence (8.72%). Again, these are topics you should be familiar with if your goal is to be able to read and understand contemporary research.

Quantitative Topics: Data Analysis

Below is the list of quantitative data analysis categories:

- **ANCOVA**
- **ANOVA**
- article citation/impact
- **average deviation scores**
- **Bayesian networks**
- **canonical correlation**
- categorical dependent variables
- **causal mapping**
- **chi-square**
- **cluster analysis**
- **coefficient beta**
- common method variance
- computational modeling
- computer simulation
- confidence intervals
- correlation

- critical ratio

- descriptive

- discriminant analysis

- effect size

- ethnostatistics

- factor analysis

- generalized estimating equations

- logistic regression

- longitudinal data analysis

- MANCOVA

- MANOVA

- meta-analysis

- missing data

- multidimensional scaling

- multilevel research

- multiple regression-correlation

- network analysis

- neural networks

- nonparametric techniques

- other

- outliers

- path analysis

- power analysis

- probable error

- probit regression

- simple linear regression – bivariate

- structural equation modeling

- t-tests

- z-tests

The most popular topics are as follows: multiple regression/correlation (17.03%), structural equation modeling (12.23%), multilevel research (10.92%), missing data (9.61%), factor analysis (6.68%), temporal issues (i.e., techniques for analyzing data collected throughout time) (6.55%).

In sum, the most popular quantitative topics are surveys, temporal issues, and electronic/web research (research design); validity, reliability, and level of analysis of the dependent variable (measurement); and multiple regression/correlation, structural equation modeling, and multilevel research (data analysis). Taken together, the lists in the following sections include a comprehensive list of quantitative methodological approaches used regularly regarding design, measurement, and data analysis. You can review these lists to set your own goals regarding which you would like to learn based on which ones are more closely related and helpful to your substantive research interests.

MAPPING QUALITATIVE RESEARCH METHODS: RESEARCH DESIGN, MEASUREMENT, AND DATA ANALYSIS

There are 21 popular approaches to qualitative research design:

- **action research**
- archival
- **biographical method**
- case studies
- clinical research
- direct estimates
- **document interpretation**
- ethnography
- **grounded theory**
- interviewing
- **interpretive**
- knowledge-based view
- narrative
- **observational techniques**
- **paper and pencil**
- **participant observation**
- **participative inquiry**
- **personal experience methods**
- policy capturing
- survey
- **visual method**

The most popular areas among these were: interpretive (26.67%), policy capturing (16.67%), and action research (13.33%).

In terms of qualitative measurement, there are four categories:

- archival data

- paper and pencil

- reliability

- survey

In terms of qualitative analysis, the popular topics include:

- **concept mapping**

- **conjoint analysis**

- content analysis

- interpretive

- **multisource ratings**

- narrative analysis

- policy capturing

- **semiotic analysis**

The most popular subcategories among the qualitative analysis topics were interpretive (26.32%), policy capturing (26.32%), and content analysis (21.05%).

Overall, the most popular qualitative topics are interpretive, policy capturing, and action research (research design), surveys and reliability (measurement), and interpretive, policy capturing, and content analysis (data analysis). If you are interested in qualitative methods, the list above is an excellent starting point to choose which methods you would like to learn in the future—those that would be most useful to your substantive research interests.

RESEARCH ON RESEARCH METHODS: BEST IN KIND

As mentioned earlier, a significant development was the creation of journals devoted to research methodology. As a researcher, you will want to know what the best research is on research methods. Why? Because this provides you with insights as the user of a method and, therefore, you should read these articles to ensure you follow their recommendations in your substantive research. Also, as a methodologist, you want to read these articles to do top-notch research on research methods.

The Academy of Management is a leading professional organization for social sciences related to organizations. Its members research organizational behavior, strategy, entrepreneurship, human resource management, conflict management, careers, diversity and inclusion, consulting, technology and innovation management, and many other topics. The Research Methods Division of the Academy of Management bestows a yearly award to the best article

TABLE 1.1 ■ Academy of Management Research Methods Division Best Article Awards Received by *Organizational Research Methods* Articles.	
Year	**Awarded Article**
2020	Newman, D. A. (2014). Missing data: Five practical guidelines. Organizational Research Methods, 17, 372-411.
2017	Gioia, D. A., Corley, K. G., & Hamilton, A. L. (2012). Seeking qualitative rigor in inductive research: Notes on the Gioia methodology. *Organizational Research Methods, 16*, 15-31.
2016	Carlson, K. D., & Wu, J. (2012). The illusion of statistical control: Control variable practice in management research. *Organizational Research Methods, 15*, 413-435.
2015	Aguinis, H., Pierce, C. A., Bosco, F. A., & Muslin, I. S. (2009). First decade of *Organizational Research Methods*: Trends in design, measurement, and data-analysis topics. *Organizational Research Methods, 12*, 69-112.
2014	LeBreton, J. M., & Senter, J. L. (2008). Answers to 20 questions about interrater reliability and interrater agreement. *Organizational Research Methods, 11*, 815-852.
2007	Edwards, J. R. (2001). Multidimensional constructs in organizational behavior research: An integrative analytical framework. *Organizational Research Methods, 4*, 144-192.
2005	Vandenberg, R. J., & Lance, C. E. (2000). A review and synthesis of the measurement invariance literature: Suggestions, practices, and recommendations for organizational research. *Organizational Research Methods, 3*, 4-69.
2004	Cortina, J. M., Chen, G., & Dunlap, W. P. (2001). Testing interaction effects in LISREL: Examination and illustration of available procedures. *Organizational Research Methods, 4*, 324-360.
2002	James, L. R. (1998). Measurement of personality via conditional reasoning. *Organizational Research Methods, 1*, 131-163.

Sources: Adapted from Aguinis, Ramani, & Villamor (2019) and Academy of Management Research Methods Division (https://rm.aom.org/awards/pastawardrecipients). Reproduced with permission.

on methodology published in any journal or book during the five preceding years. Table 1.1 lists ORM articles that received the Academy of Management Research Methods Division Best Article of the Year Award (RMD Award). We can learn a lot about the types of methods the field values by looking at which papers have received this prestigious award. This table shows that almost 50% of the awards have gone to ORM papers in the last twenty years and that these papers mostly pertain to quantitative methods.

Let's apply the same strategy of looking at award-winning papers to see what topics are deemed necessary by the field but specific to ORM. Instead of assessing the types of methods advancements most valued by the field, we can determine which methods advancements the experts at ORM value. Of note, the ORM award is not just a matter of opinion: year after year, the award-winning papers have been more impactful than non-award-winning papers (as judged by citation count using Web of Science). Like RMD Award winners, the majority (13/15) addressed quantitative issues. One noticeable difference, however, is that a majority (12/15) of these papers addressed issues related to analysis rather than measurement (Table 1.2).

Year	Article
TABLE 1.2 ■ _Organizational Research Methods_ Best Article of the Year Award Winners	
2020	2020: Certo, S. T., Busenbark, J. R., Kalm, M., & LePine, J. A. (2020). Divided we fall: How ratios undermine research in strategic management. _Organizational_ Research _Methods, 23_, 211-237.
2019	2019: Becker, T. E., Robertson, M. M., & Vandenberg, R. J. (2019). Nonlinear transformations in organizational research: Possible problems and potential solutions. _Organizational Research Methods, 22_, 831-866.
2018	2018: Putka, D. J., Beatty, A. S., & Reeder, M. C. (2018). Modern prediction methods: New perspectives on a common problem. Organizational Research Methods, 21, 689–732.
2017	2017: Cortina, J. M., Green, J. P., Keeler, K. R., & Vandenberg, R. J. (2017). Degrees of freedom in SEM: Are we testing the models that we claim to test? _Organizational Research Methods, 20_, 350–378.
2017	2017: Roulet, T. J., Gill, M. J., Stenger, S., & Gill, D. J. (2017). Reconsidering the value of covert research: The role of ambiguous consent in participant observation. _Organizational Research Methods, 20_, 487–517.
2016	2016: Shaffer, J. A., DeGeest, D., & Li, A. (2016). Tackling the problem of construct proliferation: A guide to assessing the discriminant validity of conceptually related constructs. _Organizational Research Methods, 19_, 80-110.
2015	2015: Cho, E., & Kim, S. (2015). Cronbach's coefficient alpha: Well- known but poorly understood. O_rganizational Research Methods, 18_, 207-230.
2015	2015: Walsh, I., Holton, J. A., Bailyn, L., Fernandez, W., Levina, N., & Glaser, B. (2015). What grounded theory is... A critically reflective conversation among scholars. _Organizational Research Methods, 18_, 581-599.
2014	2014: Newman, D. A. (2014). Missing data: Five practical guidelines. _Organizational Research Methods, 17_, 372-411.
2013	2013: Kozlowski, S. W. J., Chao, G. T., Grand, J. A., Braun, M. T., & Kuljanin, G. (2013). Advancing multilevel research design: Capturing the dynamics of emergence. _Organizational Research Methods, 16_, 581-615.
2012	2012: Kruschke, J. K., Aguinis, H., & Joo, H. (2012). The time has come: Bayesian methods for data analysis in the organizational sciences. _Organizational Research Methods, 15_, 722-752.
2011	2011: Cortina, J. M., & Landis, R. S. (2011). The earth is _not_ round (p = .00). _Organizational Research Methods, 14_, 332-349.
2011	2011: Edwards, J. R. (2011). The fallacy of formative measurement. _Organizational Research Methods, 14_, 370-388.
2010	2010: Leavitt, K., Mitchell, T. R., & Peterson, J. (2010). Theory pruning: Strategies to reduce our dense theoretical landscape. _Organizational Research Methods, 13_, 644-667.
2009	2009: Richardson, H. A., Simmering, M. J., & Sturman, M. C. (2009). A tale of three perspectives: Examining post hoc statistical techniques for detection and correction of common method variance. _Organizational Research Methods, 12_, 762-800.
2008	2008: Cheung, G. W. (2008). Testing equivalence in the structure, means, and variances of higher-order constructs with structural equation modeling. _Organizational Research Methods, 11_, 593-613.
2008	2008: LeBreton, J. M., & Senter, J. L. (2007). Answers to 20 questions about interrater reliability and interrater agreement. _Organizational Research Methods, 11_, 815-852.
2007	2007: Duriau, V. J., Reger, R. K., & Pfarrer, M. D. (2007). A content analysis of the content analysis literature in organization studies: Research themes, data sources, and methodological refinements. _Organizational Research Methods, 10_, 5-34.
2006	2006: Lance, C. E., Butts, M. M., & Michels, L. C. (2006). The sources of four commonly reported cutoff criteria: What did they really say? _Organizational Research Methods, 9_, 202-220.
2005	2005: Chen, G., Bliese, P. D., & Mathieu, J. E. (2005). Conceptual framework and statistical procedures for delineating and testing multilevel theories of homology. _Organizational Research Methods, 8_, 375-409.

Sources: Adapted from Aguinis, Ramani, & Villamor (2019) and Academy of Management Research Methods Division (https://rm.aom.org/awards/awardrecipients). Reproduced with permission.

This list is handy for social and behavioral science researchers because it provides an idea of the most current methodological topics, which will be addressed throughout this book. The award topics include:

- How **ratios** undermine research in strategic management (2020)[41]

- Possible problems and potential solutions for **nonlinear transformations** in organizational research (2019)[42]

- New perspectives on modern prediction methods (2018)[43]

- **Degrees of freedom** in SEM (2017)[44]

- Reconsidering the value of **covert research** and the role of ambiguous consent in participant observation (2016)[45]

- A guide to assessing the discriminant validity of conceptually related constructs to tackling the problem of construct proliferation (2015)[46]

- Cronbach's coefficient alpha (2015)[47]

- A critically reflective conversation among scholars on what grounded theory is (2015)[48]

- Five practical guidelines to address missing data (2014)[49]

- Advancing multilevel research design and capturing the dynamics of emergence (2013)[50]

- Bayesian methods for data analysis in the organizational sciences (2012)[51]

- The earth is not round (p = .00) (2011)[52]

- The fallacy of formative measurement (2011)[53]

- Strategies to reduce our dense theoretical landscape (**Theory pruning**) (2010)[54]

RESEARCH METHODS: THE PRESENT AND THE FUTURE

By now, you have a good idea of the historical journey of methods in the social and behavioral sciences, the wide variety of quantitative and qualitative approaches available, and the topics addressed by best-in-kind research on research methods. Next, this section addresses the future. Specifically: (1) Which methodological areas have been consistently popular? (2) Which are the methodological areas that are becoming increasingly popular? and (3) What will the future look like?

Which Are the Topical Areas That Have Been Consistently Popular over Time?

As a consumer of research, there are methodological approaches you should understand to be current on the latest literature. To give you a sense of the consistently popular methods topics, we look at a summary of the issues that were most typical (modal) of an article published in the first decade of ORM. Of note, the modal article addresses quantitative instead of qualitative topics. Popular topics are listed below, organized by research method area. Percentages denote the relative frequency of papers in each area of research methods—note how these differ across quantitative and qualitative papers.

Quantitative Articles

- Study design (15%): surveys, temporal issues, and electronic/Web research

- Measurement (49%): validity, reliability, and level of analysis of dependent variable

- Data analysis (49%): multiple regression/correlation, structural equation modeling, and multilevel research

Qualitative topics

- Study design (56%): interpretive, policy capturing, and action research

- Measurement (9%): surveys and reliability

- Data analysis (33%): interpretive, policy capturing, and content analysis

Which Are the Methodological Areas That Are Becoming Increasingly Popular?

As both a researcher and consumer of research, there are up-and-coming methodological topics you should aim to learn to stay current. As Figure 1.2 shows, in terms of quantitative topics, there are upward trends regarding surveys and electronic/Web research (design), level of analysis of the dependent variable and validity (measurement), and multilevel research (analysis). These trends can be explained by the availability of electronic data collection (rather than just paper and pencil) and the need to understand individuals and organizations within different levels and contexts (e.g., teams, organizations, and societies). Regarding qualitative topics, the attention devoted to interpretive and action research has increased with time (design). Still, trends in terms of measurement and analysis are difficult to identify, given that the overall number of articles is relatively small.

What Will the Future Look Like?

While this list could be extremely long, let's focus on five issues that may have the most significant impact in the years to come. These include (1) constructive **replication**; (2) embracing methods that allow us to study the exceptionally good and bad; (3) not allowing misguided or incomplete analyses to survive the review process; (4) shifting emphasis toward research design and measurement; and (5) increased theory specificity.

Constructive While Replication

More than a century ago, there was a call for a cooperative system in which social and organizational problems were assigned to a research group best suited to study them. The idea would be that a given research team would design studies, form hypotheses, test them, refine hypotheses, and retest until they had **triangulated** a solution. Although this and similar processes were reported early in the 20th century, they no longer happen in social and behavioral research. The reality is that the models offered in empirical papers are rarely tested again,[55] and those published in theoretical papers (i.e., offering a theoretical model without including data), such as *Academy of Management Review* articles, are rarely tested.[56] The reason is that to be published, an empirical paper must make a "theoretical contribution." In other words, it cannot test someone else's

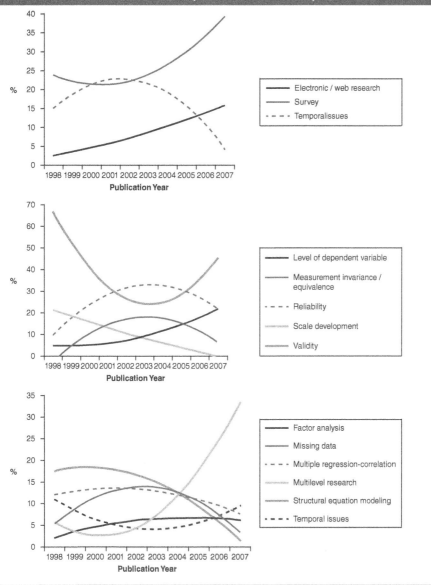

FIGURE 1.2 ■ Trends in Counts in Percentages for the Most Popular Quantitative Design (Top Panel), Quantitative Measurement (Center Panel), and Quantitative-Data Analysis (Bottom Panel) Topics

Source: Aguinis, Pierce, Bosco, & Muslin (2009). Reproduced with permission.

theory. If top journals are reluctant to publish constructive replications, then few researchers will conduct them. The solution here is simple. Our journals must encourage and publish high-quality constructive replications.

It bears mentioning that constructive replication and repetition are not the same thing. You may have heard that criticism regarding the lack of replication is unwarranted because the slack is picked up by meta-analyses (i.e., a method used to conduct a quantitative summary of the existing literature, as described in Chapter 11). But a meta-analysis is not constructive replication because it analyzes large numbers of studies rather than replicating a single study. A good replication involves testing either an entire theory or a portion of a theory already put forth in the literature. Such papers do exist, but they are rare. The social and behavioral sciences must embrace a model standard in other fields that involves independent verification of results through constructive replication.

Embracing Methods That Allow Us to Study the Exceptionally Good and Bad

The exceptional is, by definition, rare. In the sciences, we have moved toward a statistical significance model in which the probability of obtaining a particular value tells us how much stock to put in the results. However, statistical significance models require large samples to estimate probabilities reliably. Because exceptional cases are rare, finding large samples of the exceptional to use in statistical significance testing is impossible. Surely, there is value in understanding the exceptional and knowing why, for instance, some of the most influential and prolific scholars continue to work full-time, mostly pro bono, after retirement. Indeed, knowing why the employee with the perfect attendance record always attended every day is valuable. There is value, too, in studying people, units, and organizations that fail badly. Sometimes the best way to arrive at this understanding is through a case study of the exceptional.

EXAMPLE: Learning From Case Studies

Those who have read the book *Moneyball* know that making a case study of the Oakland A's was the only way to understand how they had one of the best records in baseball over several years with only one-third of other teams' payroll. At the other end of the spectrum, the National Transportation Safety Board officials had to use a case study approach in May of 2015 as they combed through the wreckage of an AMTRAK accident that killed 188 people in Philadelphia. So, while we need to know about the exceptionally good, we must also learn about the exceptionally bad. However, we may need to embrace qualitative methods such as case studies and grounded theory to do this. We might consider ourselves a science of the mean if we do not.[57]

Not Allowing Misguided or Incomplete Analyses to Survive the Review Process

Years ago, we could not conduct SEM analyses without knowing precisely what we were doing—an analyst had to understand the analysis to conduct it fully. The disadvantage of this was that very few people could conduct SEM analyses. The advantage was that only skilled analysts could engage in SEM. Today, SEM analyses are semiautomatic with a variety of software choices. Unfortunately, the result is that many such analyses are done incorrectly.

METHODS IN PRACTICE
CAN WE TRUST NUMERICAL RESULTS REPORTED IN PUBLISHED ARTICLES?

Nearly 40% of papers in the *Journal of Applied Psychology* (JAP) and *Academy of Management Journal* (AMJ) reported incorrect degrees of freedom for their SEMs, which means the authors of these papers were not testing the models that they claimed to be testing.[58] Similarly, models integrating **mediation** and **moderation** are quite common, and authors can access user-friendly scripts and programs that allow testing such models. Yet authors of papers in JAP, AMJ, and other top journals who hypothesize full mediation rarely defend full mediation and rarely test for it properly.[59] You may still need to learn what some of these words mean, so you may be tempted to gloss over this issue. But these are not merely the quibbles of stats geeks. These are problems that result in the wrong words going into the Results and Discussion sections of published articles.

These are problems that compromise the trustworthiness of research that we see used in media, politics, and law. The only solution to this problem is to ensure that every paper considered for publication has been evaluated carefully by someone with expertise in the methods described. However, a high level of knowledge and expertise is required to provide thorough, skilled reviews. Moreover, providing such reviews is time-consuming, and reviewers are volunteers who are not compensated for their work. So, given the strain on the reviewer pool, this won't be easy to do. Whether the solution is graduate training, continuing education, reviewer credentialing, reviewer compensation, or some combination, it will take work.

Shifting Emphasis Toward Research Design and Measurement

This may seem an odd point, given the previous section. Still, the hope is that the fascination with abstruse data analysis techniques gets replaced by a fascination with appropriate research design, including top-notch measurement. More researchers can perform advanced analyses as data analysis software becomes more accessible. As a result, our methodological rigor focus across fields has shifted from design and measurement, which was and is hard, to analysis, which has become easy to access. But the design comes first. Analysis can only fix data from a good design.

One possible means to achieving this end would be a Registered Reports model. In this publishing model, the Introduction and Method sections alone are subjected to a review process. Once these sections are approved, the author only needs to execute the design for the paper to be published. The paper's publication is not contingent on the resulting data's relationship with the introduction; data need only be collected consistent with the proposed method. An alternative would be to have reviewers and editors review only the Introduction and Method sections of completed papers before seeing the results. Either approach would go a long way toward eliminating the pervasive problem of **HARKing**—that is, hypothesizing after results are known.[60] Of course, ensuring that experts on a given design get a look at every viable submission to journals would help, too, but again, this would be difficult given the strain on the review system. The hope is that future methodology historians will look back upon the next few decades and observe that the review process rewarded researchers who made the difficult and time-consuming but appropriate design choices, even if that meant tolerating the study's limitations.

Increased Theory Specificity

Social and behavioral science theories tend to be vague.[61] They contain hypotheses that are, at best, directional (i.e., more of X is related to more of Y). Over time, we add boxes and arrows to our increasingly complex models rather than refining them. A model expanded this way "effectively closes it off from rebuttal or disconfirmation by anything in the world."[62] Other scientific fields move in the direction of parameterization of models—meaning that relations between variables are described in terms of direction and specific strength. But we do not do this, and we should, particularly given the availability of information on the current state of our knowledge, in the form of bivariate relations and their distributions, in the most popular domains in social and behavioral science research.[63] One way to shift emphasis to research design and measurement would be to embrace computational modeling, which involves detailed descriptions of processes complete with point estimates of parameters that can then be cross-validated and adjusted. Another way to move in this direction would be to embrace categorical shift models of human behavior. For example, approaches such as **catastrophe modeling** and **spline regression** involve identifying slope parameters and points along an axis of predictor values at which a dependent variable value and its relationship to the predictor changes suddenly.[64] The Bayesian methods described in Chapter 14 might help us here.[65] Specifically, suppose we were to evaluate study $k + 1$ not in isolation but as a mechanism for adjusting beliefs driven only by study k. In that case, **theory refinement** is more likely to move forward.

These are only a few examples of approaches that would help us to refine our theories. Whether through these or other mechanisms, the social and behavioral sciences would benefit from theoretical specificity. Next, in Chapter 2, we will focus on a critical aspect of research: ethics.

DISCUSSION QUESTIONS

1. Why should you care about research methods?

2. What are, in your opinion, the most important methodological developments in each of the six time periods described in Figure 1.1 that are still important today? Please explain your reasoning.

3. Is the balance between the relative popularity of quantitative and qualitative methods conducive to advancing social and behavioral science knowledge?

4. Do you see any typical pattern in the most recent articles that won the best AOM-RMD and ORM article of the year award?

5. Which topical areas have been consistently popular in the social and behavioral sciences? What do you think explains their popularity?

6. Which are the topical areas that have become increasingly popular? Why do you think this may be the case?

7. Do you think the predictions in this chapter about the future of research methods will come true in the coming years? Why? Why not?

8. What would, in your opinion, facilitate and impede the predictions in this chapter about the future of research methods?

KEY TERMS

action research
analysis of covariance (ANCOVA)
analysis of variance (ANOVA)
average deviation (AD)
banding
Bayesian networks

behavioral simulation
biographical method
canonical correlation analysis
case study
catastrophe theory
causal mapping

chi-square (χ^2) distribution

cluster analysis

coefficient beta

common method bias (CMB)

concept mapping

conjoint analysis

constructs

content analysis

control variable

correlational

correlational analysis

covert research

critical ratio

cross cultural research

degrees of freedom

discriminant analysis

distribution

document interpretation

effect size (ES)

experimental repeated measures

external validity

factor analysis

generalizability

generalized estimating equation (GEE)

grounded theory

growth curve

HARKing

hypothetico-deductive model

inferential statistics

internal validity

interpretive

logistic regression

longitudinal designs

macro organizational research

multivariate analysis of covariance (MANCOVA)

multivariate analysis of variance (MANOVA)

measurement equivalence

measurement invariance

mediation

meta-analysis

micro organizational research

mixed methods

moderation

Monte Carlo research

multidimensional scaling

multilevel modeling

multisource rating

network analysis

neural networks

non-experimental research

nonlinear transformations

nonparametric technique

observational technique

outliers

paper and pencil

participant observation

participative inquiry

passive observation

path analysis

personal experience methods

policy capturing

power analysis

probable error

probit regression

psychometric meta-analysis

qualitative methods

quantitative methods

quasi-experimental design

replication

research paradigm

sampling error

scale

self-report

semiotic analysis

simple linear regression – bivariate

spline regression

statistical control

statistical significance testing

structural equation modeling (SEM)

survey

theory pruning

theory refinement

triangulated

validity generalization (VG)

variables

visual method

Web of Science (WoS)

z-test

NOTES

This chapter is based to a large extent on the following sources:

Aguinis, H., Pierce, C. A., Bosco, F. A., & Muslin, I. S. (2009). First decade of Organizational Research Methods: Trends in design, measurement, and data-analysis topics. *Organizational Research Methods*, *12*(1), 69-112. https://doi.org/10.1177/1094428108322641

Aguinis, H., Ramani, R. S., & Villamor, I. (2019). The first 20 years of Organizational Research Methods: Trajectory, impact, and predictions for the future. *Organizational Research Methods*, *22*(2), 463-489. https://doi.org/10.1177/1094428118786564

Cortina, J. M., Aguinis, H., & DeShon, R. P. (2017). Twilight of dawn or of evening? A century of research methods in the Journal of Applied Psychology. *Journal of Applied Psychology*, *102*(3), 274-290. https://doi.org/10.1037/apl0000163

2 HOW TO CONDUCT ETHICAL RESEARCH

LEARNING GOALS

By the end of this chapter, you will be able to do the following:

2.1 Explain why you should care about ethical research.

2.2 Compare differences between two research philosophies: utilitarian and deontological.

2.3 Follow ethical standards in planning the purpose and study.

2.4 Execute ethical research that considers the rights of participants.

2.5 Consider special ethical requirements when conducting research in field settings.

2.6 Follow ethical standards in reporting your results.

2.7 Implement ethical standards when conducting research with online participants.

2.8 Enforce research ethics to prevent misconduct.

2.9 Apply your own ethical beliefs when considering ethical challenges and dilemmas.

IMPORTANCE OF ETHICAL RESEARCH

A key aspect of becoming a researcher is knowing the ethical guidelines that guide our work and what you should do to ensure the highest ethical standards in your research. Why? Of course, it is the right thing to do. But you will benefit from conducting ethical research because such research is more trustworthy, credible, and helpful.

Let's rewind to the middle of the 20th century to give you some history behind research ethics. At the end of World War II, the Allies responded to Nazi atrocities in concentration camps trials with The Nuremberg Trials. From these trials came the **Nuremberg Code**, which includes a **ten-point statement** delimiting permissible medical experimentation on human participants:[1]

1. **Voluntary consent** is essential

2. The results of any **experiment** must be for the greater good of society

3. Human experiments should be based on previous animal experimentation

4. Experiments should be conducted by avoiding physical/mental suffering and injury

5. No experiments should be conducted if it is believed to cause death/disability

6. The risks should never exceed the benefits

7. Adequate facilities should be used to protect **research participants**

8. Experiments should be conducted only by qualified scientists

9. Participants should be able to end their participation at any time

10. The scientist in charge must be prepared to terminate the experiment when injury, disability, or death is likely to occur

Still, interest in research ethics was virtually non-existent until the 1970s.[2] Practices such as deceiving participants, invading their privacy, and having little regard for participant confidentiality were common. This was not limited to social science research—there were also unethical studies in other fields. An alarming example is **The Tuskegee Syphilis Study**, which enrolled African Americans in a biomedical experiment on the long-term effects of untreated syphilis without their knowledge. As the public became aware of such studies in the late 1960s, legislators responded with the National Research Act establishing the **Institutional Review Boards** (IRBs) and spurring the interest in ethics we have today.

Ethical considerations now play a vital role in research by minimizing harm to participants, researchers, and the public. As current and future researchers, we must uphold these ethical guidelines and ensure they permeate our work's design, execution, analyses, and reporting. It is our responsibility to guarantee that our research is based on sound ethical standards that both protect the rights of research participants and the reputation of social and behavioral science as a field.

IRBs remain the presiding authority over institutions receiving federal funding for human participant research. We also have ethical codes[3] issued by professional organizations to offer protection mechanisms and prevent ethical violations. But what issues should you consider to ensure you adhere to ethical standards? This chapter will walk you through it, from planning to executing and reporting.

We will begin by defining ethics and explaining the basic concepts. Next, we go through how to plan ethical research and what you should consider when recruiting and selecting research participants. After that, you will learn how to execute ethical research once you have recruited your participants. This is where we cover participants' rights to **informed consent**: privacy, **confidentiality** and **anonymity**, **protection from deception**, and **debriefing**. It is also where we discuss field settings, which have special considerations for conducting ethical research. After discussing recruitment and execution, we focus on how to avoid unethical behaviors in reporting your results, implement best-in-kind ethical practices, and address ethical dilemmas and challenges while conducting the research. We will look at Amazon **Mechanical Turk** (MTurk) as a case study so you can see how to do this on one of the most popular online platforms for conducting research. The following section discusses research ethics enforcement, detailing how to prevent misconduct and resolve complaints. The chapter finishes with a case study that illustrates how ethical dilemmas play out in research. For this, we consider a methodological approach known for using deception to study sensitive topics: the **bogus pipeline**.

RESEARCH ETHICS: DEFINITION AND TWO APPROACHES

Interestingly, there are two approaches to ethics used in research, and how to decide what constitutes ethical research will depend on which one you follow.[4] The root of "**ethics**" comes from the Greek word *ethos*, which refers to one's character or disposition. Today, ethics is a branch of philosophy concerned with moral behavior. The study of ethics involves evaluating behavior in terms of right or wrong according to principles or guidelines.[5] Ethics consists of considering how people should act, judgments of those actions (e.g., right versus wrong, good versus bad), and rules for justifying actions.[6] So applied to the particular context of research, ethics focuses on providing guidelines for conducting, reviewing, and evaluating research. It also establishes enforcement mechanisms to ensure ethical standards are not violated. But this can be done in multiple ways, and they do not always agree.

Two main perspectives are used in determining whether research-related actions are ethical. The **utilitarian** perspective deems actions as ethical if they are likely to involve more benefits than harm and provide the greatest good for the largest number of individuals. Thus, utilitarians often conduct a cost/benefit analysis when faced with ethical dilemmas. For example, the American Psychological Association's (APA) Ethical principles of psychologists and code of conduct[7] espouse this philosophy. On the other hand, the **deontological approach** emphasizes strict adherence to universal rules of moral behavior regardless of the consequences of actions. For example, moral principles such as "do not tell a lie" and "always keep your promises" must be consistently followed. Thus, research involving deception or withholding information from participants is unethical, according to this perspective, even if the benefits of such research greatly outweigh the potential costs to research participants.

HOW TO PLAN ETHICAL RESEARCH

Table 2.1 summarizes recommendations for planning ethical research. This section will teach you that ethical considerations start before you begin your study. First, you should be capable of competently executing the proposed research.[8] Those who do not have the skills or expertise to conduct a particular study should be supervised by someone who does; otherwise, participants may be harmed, and results may be invalid. Next, you should know the relevant ethical guidelines[9] and federal and state legislation. These guidelines and laws can assist with designing an ethically sound study. Ignorance is not seen as a legitimate reason for unethical behavior arising from research, and certifications confirming your knowledge in this area may be required. For example, organizations such as **The Collaborative Institutional Training Initiative** (CITI Program) provide research ethics training and certifications at colleges and universities, healthcare institutions, technology and research organizations, and governmental agencies.[10]

After evaluating technical competence and knowledge of ethical guidelines, you must design a sound research study. Ethics and scientific quality are closely related: low-quality research designs are less likely to be ethically acceptable.[11] Furthermore, well-designed research will lead to accurate conclusions, which may help the populations it applies to. Thus, you need a good research design based on theory and previous work, using appropriate methods and samples.[12]

Finally, it would be best if you determined the ethical acceptability of your study. If you agree with a utilitarian perspective, benefits to participants, society, and science (e.g., increased knowledge) must outweigh costs and potential risks to research participants (e.g., wasted time, invasion of privacy, psychological or physical harm). In cases where participants are at risk (e.g., personality measures that unintentionally reveal personal information or cognitive ability measures that cause anxiety), steps must be taken to minimize potential harm (e.g., debriefing). You should obtain input from others who have a more impartial viewpoint. This can include peers, potential participants, or other similar sources regarding the ethical acceptability of your study.

TABLE 2.1 ■ Summary of Recommendations for Planning Ethical Research

Ethical Due Diligence

- Consider ethical issues before you even begin to conduct your study
- Evaluate your competence in conducting the research
- Become familiar with relevant ethical guidelines
- Design a sound research study
- Determine the ethical acceptability of your study
- Consider the costs of not conducting the research
- Evaluate if there are physical or psychological risks to participants
- Have your research approved by an institutional review board (IRB)

Recruiting and Selecting Research Participants

1. *University Participant Pools*
   - Consider that offering extra credit for participation can be perceived as coercive
   - Keep in mind that asking your students to participate in your research may be perceived as coercive
   - Justify participation by explaining that it involves a learning experience and a way to enhance, not hurt, grades

If students are minors:

- Obtain parental consent in addition to the minors' agreement
- Explain the purpose and requirements of the study to parents
- Get parents' consent to allow their child to participate
- Explain the nature of the research to minors in an age-appropriate manner
- Obtain their agreement to participate
- Highlight that participation is voluntary and can be terminated at any time
- Ensure minors do not feel coerced to participate because their parents have consented

2. *Volunteers*
   - Determine if inducements are excessive
   - Be careful when studying traditionally discriminated or exploited populations
   - Avoid falsely advertising what your study can realistically do
   - Do not unnecessarily raise the expectations of participants

Importantly and often overlooked, you must consider the costs of *not* conducting the research. Discarding a research idea that has the potential to benefit many others in meaningful ways because it involves some ethical concerns (e.g., not informing participants of the exact nature of the study) may not resolve ethical problems. Still, it may instead exchange one ethical dilemma for another.[13]

Suppose you choose to move forward with the study after determining its ethicality. In that case, you must adequately evaluate participants' physical or psychological risks to set up precautions that address and minimize the risks. This is done while designing and conducting the research (these risks are discussed in more detail later). As mentioned earlier, if you are affiliated with an institution that receives federal funding, you must have your research approved by an institutional review board (IRB) before it can be conducted. IRBs evaluate the research in comparison to designated ethical standards.

Recruiting and Selecting Research Participants

An essential part of planning your research study is determining if you can access participants and how you might do it. Again, ethical considerations are involved, particularly around the two types of participants we discuss in this section: (a) university student participant pools and (b) volunteers in general (e.g., employees, job applicants).

University Participant Pools

Historically, college students are the most frequently sampled group in social and behavioral science research in the United States[14] and elsewhere (e.g., Canada[15]; Australia[16]). This is because they are accessible. However, using university human participant pools creates ethical challenges. One concern involves the extent to which results from this sample can generalize to other populations, which is a broader question of ethicality that pertains to the actual benefit for the general public. But on top of this, many have argued that requiring student participation in research studies as part of the course they are taking may be **coercive**[17] because it restricts two essential participant rights: the freedom to refuse to participate and, in some cases, the freedom to withdraw without penalty. This is seen as coercive in a few ways. First, typically, students lose credit or have their grades lowered if they do not participate. Second, although alternatives to participation may be offered, they often need to be more attractive (e.g., writing an essay instead). Third, even offering extra credit for research participation can be perceived as coercive if students need the credit to raise or maintain their grades. Finally, students invited to participate in their instructor's research may believe their grades will be negatively affected if they disagree.

But is participation in a study coercive? Many have argued that coercive class requirements exist, such as examinations and term papers, but these are not considered unethical because their educational value justifies them.[18] Thus, participation may be justified if research involves a learning experience and a way to enhance rather than hurt grades.[19]

A final consideration regarding university participant pools is that they may include minors (i.e., individuals under 18). Special precautions must be taken with minors because they may not be mature enough or legally able to consent.[20] They may need help to weigh the risks of participation and may be unduly pressured by those with authority over them (e.g., faculty members, teaching assistants). To ensure the ethical treatment of minors, you should obtain parental consent in addition to the minors' agreement.[21] First, you should explain the purpose and requirements of the study to the parents or guardians and get their consent to allow the child to participate. Next, you should explain the nature of the research to minors in an age-appropriate manner, obtain agreement to participate, and tell minors that participation is voluntary and can be terminated at any time. You should also ensure minors are not coerced into participating because their parents have consented.

Volunteers

Using **volunteers** may seem like an obvious way to avoid coercing people into participation, but, as with college students, inducements may still exert subtle coercion.[22] While offering inducements such as monetary compensation increases participation rates and may seem appropriate to offer in exchange, ethical issues are raised when participants feel they cannot afford to refuse. For example, an inducement of $20 may be more coercive to part-time employees than full-time employees because the former may be unable to afford to refuse payment. To determine if inducements are excessive, you can offer the incentive to potential participants involving a varying amount of risk. If they acknowledge that they would participate even when considerable risk is involved, you will conclude that the inducement is probably too strong.[23]

You must also be careful when studying populations that have been exploited (e.g., African Americans and Latinx who have been exposed to discrimination in hiring practices or women who have been subjected to sexual harassment). A common issue is that ethnic minorities are underrepresented in research[24] or not treated with cultural sensitivity.[25] Another consideration is around what your research can offer exploited groups. For example, suppose you attract participants by promising to improve these groups' conditions. In that case, you must also consider the possibility that you may not be able to deliver on this promise: you may not find the results you anticipated, or you may find results that do not benefit the individuals studied and may pose harm to them. Thus, you must be careful to advertise what your study can do and not unnecessarily raise participants' expectations. Overall, there are particular precautions you should take when studying exploited groups, and the recruitment process must be thoughtful in reflecting this. For example, actively involving members of those groups in your research as assistants or co-investigators may help identify issues of concern to these groups.

HOW TO EXECUTE ETHICAL RESEARCH

Table 2.2 summarizes recommendations for executing your research following ethical standards. First, you must protect participants' rights from physical and psychological harm, whether your study is in laboratory or field settings. Although social and behavioral science research rarely involves physical and mental harm, it can happen. For instance, you might design experiments with various levels of stress (e.g., participants are told they have failed an employment test or are allowed to steal) or physical discomfort (e.g., physical ability tasks). In other cases, unanticipated harm can arise. For example, some participants may become upset when reading questions about their childhood on a pre-employment biodata questionnaire. Thus, taking every precaution to protect participants from harm includes weighing the ethics to ensure the benefits outweigh any potential harm; thoughtfully recruiting participants; and, if harm is determined to be ethically appropriate to obtain benefits, ensuring there are no other options for research methods that could get similarly helpful information without the potential for harm. In addition to protecting participants from harm, you must also protect their other rights. These rights include informed consent, **privacy, confidentiality, protection from deception**, and **debriefing**. For each of these rights, there are several steps that you should take to ensure that they are not violated in the conduct of your research. Much of the following discussion is based on existing codes and guidelines from the *Ethical Principles in the Conduct of Research with Human Participants*[26]; *Ethics for Psychologists: A Commentary on the APA Ethics Code*[27]; and *Planning Ethically Responsible Research: A Guide for Students and Internal Review Boards.*[28]

TABLE 2.2 ■ Summary of Recommendations for Executing Ethical Research

Ethical Due Diligence

- Take precautions to protect participants from harm

- Determine whether harm intentionally invoked is justified

- Ensure you respect all participants' rights

Participants' Rights

Right to Informed Consent and Informed Consent Form

- Provide all necessary information about the study at an appropriate reading level

- Ensure information is short

- Include an informed consent that covers (at a minimum):
  a. Description of the research
  b. Ability to decline or withdraw participation without negative consequences
  c. Information on conditions that might influence willingness to participate
  d. Additional information (e.g., participants should receive a paper or electronic version of the consent form)

Right to Privacy

- Respect participants' right to control the amount of information they reveal

- Avoid giving unwanted information, withholding information, or releasing information

Right to Confidentiality and Anonymity

- Allow participants to decide to whom they will reveal personal information

- State how participants' identities will be protected

- Decide whether participants are to be anonymous

- Use code names or numbering systems and destroy identifying information promptly

- Inform participants about limitations in confidentiality

Right to Protection from Deception

- Determine whether deception is justified (deception should be a last resort)

- Consider feasible alternatives

- Demonstrate that the value of the research outweighs the harm imposed on participants

- Inform participants and fully debrief them about the deception

Right to Debriefing

- Set aside time at the end of the study to debrief participants

- Include information about previous research, how the current study might add to this knowledge, how results might apply to other settings, and the importance of the research

- Gather input from participants and answer any questions they may have

- If the research involved deception, ensure that debriefing consists of both:
  a. *Dehoaxing:* explain the deception
  b. *Desensitizing:* help participants deal with new insights they received about themselves

Right to Informed Consent and Informed Consent Form

Social and behavioral science research often uses methods that do not require consent. This includes gathering data from **anonymous surveys**, observing people in natural settings (**naturalistic observation**), and examining existing data (**archival data**). Consent is also not required from individuals who behaviorally refuse to participate (i.e., by not responding to a recruitment advertisement). However, excepting the above circumstances, informed consent is required by law for all research conducted at institutions receiving federal funding for research on humans.

Potential **participants** must be provided with information about the study before deciding whether or not to participate. Study information can be communicated verbally or in writing, and participants should be asked to provide verbal or written consent (i.e., a signature) before beginning the study. The process of providing this information and receiving consent from the participant is known as informed consent. This information should be provided at an appropriate reading level and be short.[29] In addition, you must ensure that you answer any questions participants have after receiving the information and that they know whom to contact if they have questions or concerns about the research.

Participants signing a consent form should retain a paper or electronic copy. But note that while obtaining signed consent is essential for research involving many risks, it may only sometimes be necessary or appropriate. In addition, there are instances in which a participant's signature could harm the participants.[30] For example, individuals participating in a study examining how they conduct white-collar crime (e.g., embezzlement) would admit their guilt by participating, so it is best not to reveal their identity by receiving their signature. In these situations, however, participants still need to give consent and receive a copy of the consent form, even though they would not be required to sign it.

I have included a template for a consent form as an example. This form was created specifically for a study using MTurk participants (Amazon's MTurk is an online platform that allows you to recruit research participants), but it can be easily adapted for use in other contexts and with different types of participants.

Example: Sample Template of Consent Form for MTurk Research

The purpose of this study is to learn about (<u>goal of the study</u>). Your task is to (<u>action that MTurkers will be performing</u>).

To participate, you must be at least 18 years of age and have at least (<u>number of years</u>) of full-time work experience (<u>minimum 35 hours per week</u>). Your participation should take about (<u>estimated time of competition of the Human Intelligence Task or HIT</u>) minutes and you must complete it in one sitting.

Although it may not directly benefit you, this study may benefit society by improving our knowledge of (<u>study's practical implications</u>). There are no risks for participating in this study beyond those associated with normal computer use.

If you complete the study satisfactorily, you will receive (<u>compensation per HIT</u>) to compensate you for your participation. You will be paid via Amazon's payment system. Please note that this study contains several checks to make sure that participants are finishing the tasks honestly and completely. In accordance with the policies set by Amazon Mechanical Turk, we may reject your work if you do not complete the HIT correctly or if you do not follow the relevant instructions.

Please understand that your participation is voluntary, and you have the right to withdraw your consent or discontinue participation at any time without penalty. To stop, click on the "Return HIT" button, or close your browser window.

Your responses will be confidential and can be identified only by your Amazon Worker ID number, which will be kept confidential and will not appear in any reports or publications of this study. All your responses, including responses to demographic information (e.g., age, employment), will only be analyzed and reported at a group level. You may print this form for your records.

If you have questions about this research study or your participation, please contact (researcher posting the MTurk HIT), Department of (name of the department) at (name of university) by telephoning (researchers' phone number) or by email at (researchers' email). You may also contact (name of university) Office of Human Research with any questions about your rights as a participant in this study or any concerns or complaints by calling (phone number). This research and its procedures have been approved by (name of university)'s Institutional Research Board.

IRB Approval Number: (IRB number)

Thank you very much for your participation.

By clicking the "I consent" button below, you indicate that you are 18 years of age or older, that you have read and understood the description of the study, and that you agree to participate.

Source: Aguinis, Villamor, & Ramani (2021, Appendix G). Reproduced with permission.

Now that we have reviewed informed consent let's examine the issues the procedures should cover.

Description of the Research

This description should include the purpose of the study, what is expected of participants (e.g., tasks, time involved, inducements), and the importance or implications of the research. While you must describe the research, you do not have to disclose hypotheses or other information that would bias participants' responses or influence their behavior in the study. Still, enough information should be given so potential participants can decide if they wish to participate. Further, suppose it is necessary to withhold information about the study (i.e., deception). In that case, participants should be informed and assured that a full explanation will be provided at the end of the study.

Ability to Decline or Withdraw Participation Without Negative Consequences

Please remind participants of this right from the start, especially when students take part for class credit and might feel they have no right to withdraw. Likewise, participants may feel they have little right to withdraw when the researcher is in a position of authority (e.g., human resources manager, supervisor) or, as discussed earlier when study inducements are used (e.g., money or class credit). If you conduct research in organizational settings, you must prevent employees from perceiving that their employment status will be at risk if they do not participate. In addition, when you have authority over potential participants, using a third party to recruit participants may alleviate the pressure to participate.[31] Finally, some advocate that participants have a right to whatever benefits they were promised (e.g., money) if they withdraw due to feeling misinformed or misunderstanding the nature of the research study.[32]

Information on Conditions That Might Influence Willingness to Participate

This refers to providing a list of possible risks involved in the study, such as stress, physical exertion, and anxiety, and allowing participants to decide if they wish to be subjected to these risks. In addition to potential risks, participants should be informed of the benefits they can expect from participating. Benefits to participants may include scientific knowledge, learning or practice (e.g., mock job interviews), and inducements.

Right to Privacy

Participants have a right to privacy, which comes in different forms. First, the informed consent should contain any information participants might need to know when deciding to participate; specifically, it should describe the type of information that will be solicited from them. The study may ask for more sensitive information than potential participants would feel comfortable giving, and they should know what is being asked upfront. The right to privacy is also violated when participants are given unwanted information (e.g., graphic details of an incident involving sexual harassment between a supervisor and his direct report), when information that would normally be used to make decisions is withheld, or when information is released to unauthorized parties (e.g., a supervisor is shown the results of a study and uses it to make employment decisions). Finally, participants' right to privacy is upheld by their freedom to refuse to participate or withdraw once research has begun.

Right to Confidentiality and Anonymity

Participants have the right to decide who sees their personal information, and by guaranteeing participants' confidentiality, you may be able to obtain more cooperation and open and honest responses.[33] Researchers often promise confidentiality in exchange for participation, and ethical codes bind them to respect it.[34] Confidentiality differs from privacy in that it refers to data rather than individuals. At the same time, privacy concerns how the individual interacts with the study, and confidentiality refers to who interacts with identified data.

As with other rights, information regarding confidentiality should be given in informed consent. It should state how participants' identities will be protected and how unauthorized disclosures will be prevented. This entails information about who will access research data, how records will be maintained, and whether participants will remain anonymous.

If you decide the participants are to be anonymous, follow through by ensuring that no identifying information will be gathered (e.g., name, social security number, employee number). Ideally, you will want to guarantee anonymity because participants are likelier to participate and be honest when they know the results cannot be linked to them individually. Unfortunately, research often requires identifying information to link participants' data to another data set (e.g., supervisory ratings of performance, personnel records). In these cases, you can substitute code names or numbering systems and immediately destroy identifying information. Information describing this process, or others taken to protect their confidentiality, should be communicated in informed consent.

Further, it would be best to inform participants about confidentiality limitations. Exceptions to confidentiality are made when the participants may seem likely to endanger others' well-being. This would occur, for example, if an employee reveals to the researcher that "he just bought a gun and will teach his supervisor a lesson for giving him a low-performance rating."

Right to Protection from Deception

If you are considering deception, you must assess the feasibility of alternatives and the cost/benefit analysis to determine whether deception is justified. In these considerations and your application to the IRB, you must demonstrate that the value of the research outweighs the harm imposed on participants and the topic cannot be studied in any other way. If the deception is warranted and the study approved, you must address the fact that participants who may not be comfortable with this type of design have the right to opt out of participating. Of course, there are obvious challenges with informing participants that they will be deceived while maintaining the integrity of a study involving deception. To address this, communicate through informed consent that they might receive incomplete or misleading information about the research condition. If participants choose to complete the study, you are responsible for fully debriefing them afterward. Fortunately, debriefing seems to eliminate the adverse effects of deceptive research on participants.[35] Debriefing is covered in more detail below.

Although deception is the only possible way to study specific research topics, you should consider potential drawbacks. For example, some have argued that deception does not respect participants' rights, dignity, or privacy. However, steps are often taken and enforced by IRBs to ensure that participants' rights are upheld. Another potential drawback is the possibility of eliciting distrust in social and behavioral science research due to deception. However, on a perhaps more positive note, research has indicated that participants usually do not perceive deception as unethical.[36]

Overall, deception should only be used as a last resort. Examples of deception include using confederates posing as research participants, withholding information, producing false beliefs or assumptions, giving participants false feedback to determine how they react, or not paying the amount agreed upon before a study to examine participant reactions.

Right to Debriefing

After the study is completed, debriefing must take place to inform participants of the research purpose. Debriefing is the primary method used to ensure that participants receive the scientific knowledge that is often promised as a benefit of participating. Debriefing also removes any harmful effects brought on by the study, leaving participants with a sense of dignity and a perception that their time was not wasted.[37]

You should set aside time at the study's end to debrief participants individually if the research is sensitive. Debriefing should include information about previous research, how the current study might add to this knowledge, how study results might be applied to other settings, and the importance of this type of research. This time can also be used to gather input from participants and answer any questions they may have. For example, this might be an opportunity to ask participants what they thought of the study or why they responded or behaved the way they did. This is also an excellent time to collect the names and email addresses of those who wish to receive a copy of the study's findings. When conducting research within organizations, you should discuss the findings with study participants and any implications. Finally, if the research involved deception, debriefing should consist of both dehoaxing and desensitizing.

Dehoaxing

Dehoaxing refers to explaining the deception and removing any misinformation provided to participants as a part of the deception to alleviate any resulting negative emotions or feelings.[38] For example, a study may give falsely negative performance feedback to a participant despite good performance. Instead, the participant should be told that they received made-up negative performance feedback because the study aimed to examine their reactions and that their performance was good.

Desensitizing

Desensitizing entails helping participants deal with new insights they received about themselves due to their responses or actions in the study and removing any harm resulting from participation (e.g., hostile feelings towards those giving negative feedback[39]). Discussing feelings with participants and explaining their normal reactions can accomplish this goal.

SPECIAL CONSIDERATIONS FOR CONDUCTING ETHICAL RESEARCH IN FIELD SETTINGS

As discussed above, there are many ethical concerns to consider when conducting research. However, it may be challenging to resolve these ethical issues when research is conducted in field settings. This is particularly important to review because some have recently noted that ethical responsibilities in **field research** are a neglected topic.[40] Table 2.3 summarizes recommendations for conducting ethical research in field settings.

Most of these ethical concerns arise from navigating conflicting expectations from the organizations involved in the research,[41] such as in corporate, not-for-profit organizations, small businesses, or school settings. Indeed, you have your expectations and guidelines concerning research, while organizations, leaders, and employees may hold very different beliefs. An example might be when a researcher collaborates with an organization to develop a new measure of integrity using employee participants. The researcher may see it as selecting the most appropriate future job candidates. Alternatively, management may perceive it as a way, unbeknownst to employees, to weed out current employees who may be stealing. The researcher may argue that using research results violates participants' confidentiality. At the same time, management may counter that it will benefit the organization's bottom line to identify and terminate dishonest individuals. Thus, it is recommended that you clearly define your role when doing research in field settings and openly and honestly address conflicts between ethical norms with the organization before conducting the research. For example, have you been hired as a consultant by the organization's top leadership team?

Other ethical concerns revolve around the participants' rights that we discussed earlier. Participants' rights may be violated in organizational settings[42] due to a perception that research participation is simply part of the job. Indeed, some have argued that organizations are coercion systems, making it challenging to protect participants' rights as delineated by research ethics guidelines.[43] Thus, participants may feel pressured to participate in research studies sponsored

TABLE 2.3 ■ Summary of Special Considerations for Conducting Ethical Research in Field Settings
Ethical Due Diligence
• Clearly define your role when doing research in field settings
• Openly and honestly address conflicts between ethical norms with the organization before conducting the research
• Ensure the well-being of research participants (*committed-to-participant* approach)
• Follow applicable ethics codes and make it known to the organization that you will not violate ethical principles

by their employers.[44] In addition, you may not have sufficient control over the research to guarantee the ethical treatment of participants. Nevertheless, you have an ethical obligation to ensure the well-being of research participants in all settings. This is called a **committed-to-participant approach**, exemplified in a study examining the effects of different coping methods on diastolic blood pressure.[45] This study informed participants engaging in coping strategies likely to lead to high blood pressure about the risks of this behavior and recommended appropriate lifestyle changes. Thus, the researchers collected data to further their study aim, provided health improvement tools to participants, and created opportunities for organizations to benefit from healthier employees.

In sum, if organizations request that you act unethically, you must follow applicable ethics codes. You should make this known to the organization and reach a compromise that does not involve a violation of ethical principles.

HOW TO REPORT RESEARCH RESULTS ETHICALLY

Ethical considerations do not end with collecting data. This section discusses how to avoid ethical violations that can occur while writing up the research findings and submitting papers for publication. These violations include misrepresenting results, **censoring**, **plagiarism**, **unjustified authorship credit**, and refusing to provide data for replication. Table 2.4 contains a summary of the recommendations described next.

TABLE 2.4 ■ Summary of Recommendations for Reporting Research Results Ethically

Ethical Due Diligence

- Avoid ethical violations resulting from reporting research results unethically

Reporting Violations to Avoid

Misrepresentation of Research Results

- Honestly and accurately report results and not falsify, distort, or omit findings
- Never record data without being blind to the hypotheses or participants' treatment condition
- Avoid errors in data entry or data analyses and take immediate action to correct them

Censoring

- Honestly report data that contradict previous research, hypotheses, or beliefs
- Provide detailed reports of your methodology, data analyses, findings, and study limitations

Plagiarism and Authorship (Mis)Credit

- Avoid taking credit for work that is not yours (i.e., plagiarism)
- Prevent taking more credit than deserved (i.e., authorship order)
- Avoid self-plagiarism (making minor modifications to studies previously published)

Data Sharing

- Provide data when is requested by other researchers for reproducibility and replication

Misrepresentation of Research Results

To avoid misrepresenting research results, you must honestly and accurately report results and not falsify, distort, or omit findings. A classic case of manufacturing research results was Sir Cyril Burt's research on the inheritance of intelligence. See the Example box "Misrepresentation of Research Results: The Case of Sir Cyril Burt."

> **Example: Misrepresentation of Research Results: The Case of Sir Cyril Burt**
>
> Sir Cyril Burt conducted studies on twins and found substantial evidence of genetic influences on intelligence.[46] His findings were not questioned, but after he died in 1971, it was discovered that much of his data had been fabricated. In addition, co-authors listed in various research studies were fictitious. Although severe cases like this one appear to be the exception rather than the norm, falsifying data can have serious detrimental effects by providing false information as the basis for subsequent research. Less extreme forms of misrepresentation may include recording data without being blind to the hypotheses or participants' treatment conditions, which can lead to researcher bias. Other misrepresentations may occur due to errors in data entry or data analyses.[47] If honest data entry or analysis mistakes are found, immediate steps should be taken to correct them. For example, the website www.retractionwatch.org documents the many published articles that have been withdrawn due to errors and ethical violations, many of which were produced intentionally.

Censoring

Censoring data is especially prevalent when results reflect negatively on the organizations where the data were collected and that same organization has hired a researcher. However, failing to report data contradicting previous research, hypotheses, or beliefs is unethical.[48] In addition, you should provide detailed reports of your methodology, data analyses, findings, and study limitations so that other researchers, and research consumers (e.g., managers and policy-makers), can evaluate the research and determine its value and applicability. Likewise, not reporting findings of unpublished data, especially if the methods were sound, could be considered unethical because these findings may provide useful information.

Plagiarism and Authorship (Mis)Credit

You must avoid taking credit for work that is not yours (i.e., plagiarism) or taking more credit than deserved (i.e., first authorship when your contributions to a project were minimal). Plagiarism involves putting one's name on another's work, using a large part of someone else's work without citing it, or claiming others' ideas as one's own.[49] All these acts are considered stealing. The work of others must be acknowledged through direct quotations or citations so that readers understand the source of the information.[50] In addition, you should avoid self-plagiarism. This refers to making minor modifications to previously published studies to publish them again in another journal, which is considered unacceptable if data are published as original. However, data can be republished by another source if a previous publication is acknowledged. It is important to avoid self-plagiarism because this practice gives the impression that more evidence is available on a particular topic or view than there is.

Determining **authorship** credit can involve ethical concerns, primarily since most universities evaluate researchers in terms of their publications to assess a scholar's credibility, status, employment, promotions, and tenure.[51] Indeed, the American Psychological Association (APA) Ethics Committee stated that the most common problem regarding research was the determination of authorship credit.[52] The APA guidelines state that authorship credit should only be given to those who substantially contribute to the research effort. Thus, contributions involving conceptualization of the research idea, research design, data analysis, interpretation, and writing up the study would deserve credit. Seniority, status, power, and routine tasks such as data entry or typing would not, although minor contributions should be noted in a footnote or the acknowledgments section. Further, contributions made in the context of paid employment (e.g., research assistant) may deserve authorship credit if the contributions are substantial.[53]

After determining who should be included as an author, it is necessary to consider which name should come first. This person should have contributed the most in ideas, design, analyses, writing, and so forth. Significantly, this decision should be based on actual contributions and not merely reflect status or power.

Power differentials between authors are particularly salient between faculty and students. Unfortunately, studies on ethical concerns in research have found that authorship issues are increasingly salient among research projects by faculty and students.[54] Moreover, the APA ethical guidelines assert that a student should be named the first author of any article based mostly on their thesis or dissertation. However, some authors have pointed out instances where this may need to be revised.[55] Ethical issues arise when faculty or higher-status individuals take first-author credit they have yet to earn and when students are given unearned credit.[56] Giving students or others undeserved research credit misrepresents expertise and abilities and gives them an unfair advantage in employment, promotions, and tenure. A study using hypothetical vignettes involving authorship decisions found that faculty members were likelier than students to give authorship credit to the student in the scenario.[57]

Researchers should use the following steps to prevent ethical problems regarding authorship credit. First, the order of authorship, as well as the contributions expected of each, should be discussed early in the project.[58] Note that early agreements about authorship may need to be revised as the project progresses, responsibilities shift, or obligations still need to be fulfilled (e.g., missed deadlines). Initial disagreements on authorship order can be addressed using a point system in which more critical contributions are assigned more points. Authorship decisions follow point totals in this procedure, where the researcher with the most points becomes the first author.[59] Finally, third parties should be consulted if an agreement cannot be reached.[60]

Data Sharing

A final ethical issue regarding reporting research results involves the retention and provision of data. Replication protects against dishonesty, and data should be provided when other researchers request them for reproducibility and replication. Of course, as the earlier content of this chapter suggests, rigorous data take much work to come by. But, researchers are not obligated to share their data sets so others can conduct new studies. If a researcher requests existing data to replicate the study, the data should not be used for conducting new research on existing data. Exceptions to providing data are made if confidentiality would be violated or if data are owned by the organization in which they were collected. Most professional organizations and journals recommend that data be retained for five years after publication.

Example: Data Sharing

Unfortunately, numerous social and behavioral science researchers do not comply with the data-sharing principle. For example, a study reviewed articles on assessing test fairness published over three decades in leading management and industrial/organizational psychology journals. As part of their review, these researchers contacted 88 authors to solicit descriptive statistic information not reported in their articles. Of these, 65 responded saying that they did not have access to the source data, four indicated that they still possessed the source data but could not access them for various reasons (e.g., the senior author was on sabbatical leave), three authors indicated that they still possessed the source data but did not share the requested information, and 12 did not respond in any manner to three email requests sent to valid and current addresses. In short, fewer than five percent had access to their data and were willing to share descriptive statistic information not published in their original articles.[61]

APPLIED METHODS: ETHICAL RESEARCH CASE STUDY – THE USE OF MTURK

While we have described students and volunteers as the most common samples, a growing group is becoming the most used in social and behavioral science research: MTurk. The following case study examines ethical challenges associated with this sample population.

MTurk is a crowdsourcing website that hosts a wide-ranging array of digital tasks, uploaded by entities such as researchers and employers, for users to complete in exchange for monetary compensation. Web-based research using Amazon's Mechanical Turk (MTurk) has increased tenfold over the last decade, making it the most frequently used online data collection method.[62] For example, as shown in Figure 2.1, in management research alone, the use of MTurk has increased by over 2,117% in recent years, rising from 6 papers to 133 between 2012 – 2019.

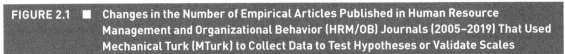

FIGURE 2.1 ■ Changes in the Number of Empirical Articles Published in Human Resource Management and Organizational Behavior (HRM/OB) Journals (2005–2019) That Used Mechanical Turk (MTurk) to Collect Data to Test Hypotheses or Validate Scales

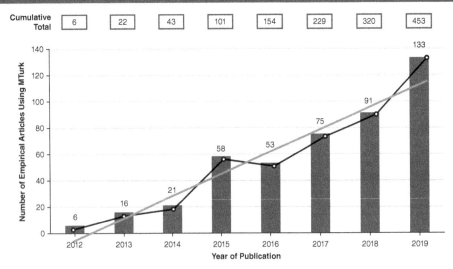

Source: Adapted from Aguinis, Villamor, & Ramani (2021, Appendix C). Reproduced with permission.

The reaction among researchers is a mixture of excitement and concern. There is excitement about the practical and logistical benefits of using MTurk, but despite its popularity, concerns call into question the ethicality of research based on MTurk.[63] The ethical challenges are (1) self-misrepresentation, (2) non-naiveté, (3) growth of MTurker communities, and (4) perceived researcher unfairness. Table 2.5 describes these four challenges in more detail.

So, what can you do to ensure that your research is based on the highest ethical standards when using MTurk or other online platforms? Table 2.6 summarizes the recommendations described below. While some of these best practices also apply to non-MTurk studies (online and in-person research), Table 2.6 's checklist focuses on mitigating ethical concerns when using MTurk.

Planning

DECIDE QUALIFICATIONS FOR SCREENING MTURKERS

Formulating study-appropriate protocols to screen MTurkers helps address ethical threats posed by self-misrepresentation, and MTurker non-naiveté. First, to address self-misrepresentation, there is a need to be explicit about the qualifications (e.g., age, experience, race) relevant to the study. Then, rather than explicitly listing desired qualifications, which can motivate self-misrepresentation, one can evaluate MTurkers using a screener study: pay everyone who participates, eliminate those who do not match desired criteria, and invite those who meet the qualifications/pass the screener to participate in the focal study.[64] This technique is beneficial when attempting to recruit unique populations (e.g., participants who identify as LGBTQ+[65]). Second, regarding MTurker non-naiveté, one must decide whether to use only highly qualified MTurkers (i.e., "Master Workers") who have considerable experience as an MTurker and therefore greater familiarity with common manipulations, attention check techniques, and experimental tasks and questions.[66] Alternatively, one can employ screening questions to gauge MTurker's familiarity with the research participant, **stimuli**, and, if applicable, manipulations.

TABLE 2.5 ■ Ethical Challenges in Conducting Research Using Amazon Mechanical Turk (MTurk)	
Ethical Challenge	**Description**
1. Self-misrepresentation	MTurkers may misrepresent self-reported demographic, personality, and other characteristics to meet a study's eligibility criteria. Estimates of the percentage of MTurkers who engage in such practices range from 10-13% to 24%-83%. The most misrepresented characteristics are income (38.2%), education (31.3%), age (22.6%), family status (14.8%), and gender (6.6%).
2. MTurker non-naiveté	MTurk's software does not track participant exposure to studies that examine particular topics or that use the same stimuli or manipulation. However, 10% of MTurkers account for over 40% of completed studies, and many "specialize" in studies that examine specific topics or are conducted by the same researchers. Many MTurkers are familiar with experimental settings and tasks or research materials, which can, on average, reduce effect size estimates by up to 40%.
3. Growth of MTurker communities	61% of MTurkers interact with other participants regarding their experience. Thus, MTurkers often know a study's purpose or the manipulations used.
4. Perceived researcher unfairness	In addition to concerns about the fairness of procedures used to make compensation decisions, ethical issues that cause MTurkers to perceive researchers as unfair include a lack of a process to communicate with researchers, unavailability of disability access features, and inaccurately stated time requirements. Furthermore, participants who feel treated unfairly can share their experiences in MTurker communities, leading to punitive actions such as a boycott of subsequent studies by that researcher.

Source: Adapted from Aguinis, Villamor, & Ramani (2021). Reproduced with permission.

TABLE 2.6 ■ Best-Practice Recommendations for Ensuring Ethical Research When Using Amazon Mechanical Turk (MTurk)			
Stage of Study	Recommendation	Question(s) to be Addressed (Do you...)	Ethical Challenges from Table 2.5 Addressed by Recommendation
Planning	**1.** Decide qualifications used to screen MTurkers	● ... decide the qualifications (e.g., age, experience, race) relevant to the study? ● ... evaluate MTurkers using a screener study, and eliminate those who do not match desired criteria before allowing the MTurker to participate in the focal study? ● ... determine a priori if they will only consider MTurkers from native-English-speaking countries (based on their IP addresses) or establish measurement equivalence across native and non-native English speakers? ● ... decide if they will only use highly qualified MTurkers (i.e., "Master Workers") or employ screening questions to gauge MTurker familiarity with the research participant, stimuli, and, if applicable, manipulations?	● Self-misrepresentation ● MTurker non-naiveté
	2. Formulate compensation rules	● ... pay U.S. minimum wage (approx. $7.25 per hour) when drawing on U.S. samples? ● ... consider criteria (if any) used to refuse payment to MTurkers and explain it in the consent form? ● ... use a consent form including details on compensation rules (see pages 30–31 for a customizable template)?	● Perceived researcher unfairness
	3. Design an ethical survey to gather responses	● ... require MTurkers to complete an informed consent form, including a "Captcha" verification? ● ... require MTurkers to provide their MTurk ID and maintain a reference database of past participants? ● ... use at least two attention checks? ● ... include a qualitative open-ended question? ● ... include "quit study" and "contact researcher" options on each study page?	● Self-misrepresentation ● Perceived researcher unfairness
	4. Craft the MTurk post or HIT (i.e., "Human Intelligence Task")	● ... provide a detailed description of the study, accurate estimated time commitment, what MTurkers will be asked to do, and specify compensation rules? ● ... avoid cues that might provide MTurkers with signals about the study's aims or that might motivate MTurkers to further engage in self-misrepresentation?	● Self-misrepresentation

Stage of Study	Recommendation	Question(s) to be Addressed (Do you...)	Ethical Challenges from Table 2.5 Addressed by Recommendation
Execution	**5.** Launch the study, monitor responses, and respond to concerns	● ... conduct a pilot test of the study that includes an open-ended question requesting feedback, with a minimum of 10 to 30 participants? ● ... monitor MTurker communities to gauge MTurkers reactions to the study? ● ... respond promptly to any questions or concerns raised by participants?	● Growth of MTurker communities ● Perceived researcher unfairness
	6. Screen data	● ... screen data promptly using at least two or more tools (e.g., MTurker self-reports of the response effort, answers to attention checks, response patterns and response times, statistical tools that evaluate inter-item correlations and respondent consistency within each measure and help identify potential outliers, IP address, and open qualitative question) to estimate likely percentage of unusable responses? ● ... adjust the number of potential participants to achieve desired sample size?	● Growth of MTurker communities
	7. Approve or deny compensation for completed responses	● ... approve or deny compensation for completed responses within 24 to 48 hours of the MTurker completing the study? ● ... specify the reason for rejecting compensation?	● Perceived researcher unfairness

Source: Adapted from Aguinis, Villamor, & Ramani (2021). Reproduced with permission.

FORMULATE COMPENSATION RULES

Clear rules regarding compensation help address the threat posed by the challenge of perceived researcher unfairness (see Table 2.5). Higher MTurker pay is linked to better performance on research tasks.[67] The recommendation is to pay a fair wage concerning the tasks required of the MTurker,[68] typically the minimum wage, when drawing on samples from the United States (U.S.).[69] In addition, you should decide a priori what criteria (if any) will be used to refuse payment to MTurkers,[70] and the payment schedule. Moreover, establishing codes of conduct, monitoring procedures, and penalties for fraudulent or untruthful reporting may help deter deceitful behavior, as levying economic penalties for violations can affect MTurkers' honesty.[71] These norms should be made explicit and shared with participants in the consent form. Recall that this chapter includes a template you can adapt for your studies.

DESIGN AN ETHICAL SURVEY TO GATHER RESPONSES

You can follow the next steps to design an MTurk survey that complies with ethical standards and addresses the self-misrepresentation and perceived researcher unfairness challenges.

MTurkers Should Complete an Informed Consent Form.[72] In addition to a consent form (see the template on pages 30-31), researchers should include a "**CAPTCHA**" verification at the beginning of the survey to thwart web robots—a "Completely Automated Public Turing Test to tell Computers and Humans Apart" that discerns human responses from web robots.[73] This is done by having respondents correctly answer a set of challenges (e.g., identify pictures and type in words) to proceed. In addition, it is useful to include procedures designed to capture an MTurkers' **IP address** and use features that prevent the same MTurker from completing the study more than once (i.e., avoiding "ballot box stuffing").[74]

Require MTurkers' IDs. It is helpful to require MTurkers to provide your MTurk ID and maintain a reference database of past participants. This helps identify MTurkers who attempt self-misrepresentation to qualify for a particular study.[75]

Use Attention Checks. It is helpful to use **attention checks**. While more is preferable, a minimum of two such checks should be employed.[76] Types of attention checks include instructed items that direct MTurkers to complete or abstain from a particular action, bogus items that ask MTurkers to answer obvious or ridiculous questions, self-reports of effort, and questions on which all or almost all respondents should provide the same response.[77] Specifically, for MTurk, it is necessary to include at least one open-ended question as an attention check to help address MTurker's inattention and vulnerability to web robots.[78] Using such items does not negatively affect data quality as long as items used are developed explicitly for this purpose, as opposed to being drawn from other sources or created ad-hoc.[79]

Include Options to "Quit Study" and "Contact Researcher." Including these options on each study page (as applicable) allows MTurkers to exit the study or ask questions, thereby addressing the threat posed by the challenge of perceived researcher unfairness.[80]

CRAFT THE MTURK TASK OR HIT (I.E., "HUMAN INTELLIGENCE TASK")

The last action of the planning stage is designing the HIT or job posting that MTurkers will see. Because one of the main complaints by MTurkers is that the HIT description and instructions need to be clarified,[81] the description should include details about the study. For example, details should include an accurate estimated time commitment, what MTurkers will be asked to do, and compensation rules.[82] At the same time, you must be careful to avoid cues that might provide MTurkers with signals about the study's aims, or motivate MTurkers to engage in self-misrepresentation.

Execution

LAUNCH THE STUDY, MONITOR RESPONSES, AND RESPOND TO CONCERNS

Pilot tests can be useful in refining the study before it goes out on a large scale. It is useful to administer a pilot test to a minimum of 10 to 30 participants, including an open-ended question requesting feedback.[83] Their feedback and responses will help you to ensure study instructions are clear and to identify and rectify potential data quality or programming problems before the data are collected. Once the study is launched, you can monitor MTurker communities (e.g., Turker Nation, MTurk Crowd) to gauge any reactions, check if pertinent information is being shared, and respond promptly to any questions or concerns raised by participants.[84] Together, these steps help address the threat posed by the growth of MTurker communities and perceived researcher unfairness.

SCREEN DATA

Screening MTurk data promptly helps estimate the likely percentage of unusable responses. This information informs the number of potential participants needed to achieve the required sample size. Unusable responses can usually be attributed to careless or insufficient effort responding (IER) or fraudulent and duplicate efforts. Available tools can be used to screen data for careless or IER. These include MTurker self-reports of effort, such as self-reported carelessness, rushed responding, skipping instructions, answers to attention checks, response times, and statistical tools that analyze answer choice response patterns.[85] Let's go through each in turn.

MTurkers who score higher on self-reports of response effort or fail to comply with directed questions are likelier to engage in careless responding or IER.[86] Thus, participant responses can be compared to those of other MTurkers before deciding to include or exclude them. When evaluating response times, a best practice is to exclude participants who complete the task in less than one or two seconds per item. Finally, the most effective statistical tools that can be employed include the **long-string index** (in which participant response patterns in choosing the same response for multiple items are analyzed for frequency and length, and a threshold is developed based on the data to indicate potentially invalid responses[87]) and **within-session response consistency** (which calculates the level of similarity in a participant's responses to items they have rated twice, and excludes responses that score below 0.25[88]). At least two of the recommendations should be used to screen data.[89]

Regarding fraudulent or duplicate efforts, the most commonly used method is to examine IP addresses and delete duplicates. However, the growing popularity of virtual private servers (VPS) that conceal the IP address of the device used to access the MTurk study makes it harder to rely solely on this screening procedure. Furthermore, if multiple MTurkers use the same device, their IP addresses will be the same, which can cause you to omit legitimate responses mistakenly. Accordingly, in addition to employing IP address screening (e.g., using software packages for R and Stata[90]), it is useful to examine the answer to the open-ended attention check question included in the study[91] before deciding to include or omit a particular response. Overall, these steps help address ethical threats posed by the challenges of the growth of MTurk communities.

APPROVE OR DENY COMPENSATION FOR COMPLETED RESPONSES

Based on data screening and using a priori rules, one can approve or deny compensation within 24 to 48 hours of the MTurker completing the study.[92] You can also specify the reason for rejecting compensation.[93] These steps help address the threat posed by perceived researcher unfairness.

HOW TO ENFORCE ETHICAL RESEARCH

Ethical guidelines regarding research are provided by professional organizations,[94] various state and federal laws, and state licensing boards. Yet, misconduct still occurs despite efforts to enforce ethical guidelines by IRBs, peers, and ethics committees in professional organizations and universities. So, this section first defines ethical misconduct and examines the prevalence of this behavior. It then discusses ways to prevent unethical treatment of participants, deter scientific misconduct, and resolve ethical complaints that arise in research.

Definition and Prevalence of Research Misconduct

As described earlier, ethical misconduct can occur in the planning, participant recruitment and selection, execution, and reporting stages of the research process. However, researchers have typically focused on studying ethical misconduct during the reporting stage. This is often labeled **scientific misconduct.**

Most scientific misconduct can be attributed to the intense pressure many researchers feel to have to find notable results that they can publish—the "publish or perish" pressures of academia given that publications are usually associated with important rewards (e.g., receiving an offer for a faculty position after earning a doctorate, receiving a promotion from assistant to associate and then to full professor).[95] Charles Babbage distinguished between three types of scientific misconduct: trimming, cooking, and forging.[96] **Trimming** is how much you edit or select data to eliminate inconsistent findings (e.g., omitting outliers and data dropping). **Cooking (the data)** refers to altering it to support researchers' hypotheses or expected outcomes. Finally, forging involves falsifying data instead of collecting data. These are in addition to the other types of scientific misconduct that have already been mentioned throughout this chapter (e.g., plagiarism, censoring conflicting data). These instances of misconduct, especially forging, have severe implications for science. Falsified research that enters the literature base, influences subsequent research, and is applied to organizational settings can cause irreparable harm because empirical findings did not substantiate the applications. Thus, it is critical to take steps to prevent and handle cases of scientific misconduct.

Example: Prevalence of Research Misconduct

Although extreme cases of misconduct may be rare, some do occur. For example, a survey of doctorate students and faculty in chemistry, microbiology, engineering, and sociology revealed that 43 percent of the students and 50 percent of the faculty had direct knowledge of acts of scientific misconduct.[97] These included falsifying results, plagiarism, withholding research results from competitors, and unjustified authorship credit. Unfortunately, the survey also found that 53 percent of students and 26 percent of faculty were unlikely to report or address the misconduct because they feared the consequences of doing so. This finding was supported by a survey of interns and faculty, which found that fear of retaliation was the primary reason for not reporting ethical violations.[98] Finally, researchers have noted that researchers' hesitancy in reporting ethical violations more generally (not just scientific misconduct) might be due to their close ties with colleagues and institutions; acting against them may result in negative repercussions.[99] However, they noted that this hesitancy in reporting could also result from simply lacking an understanding of ethical codes of conduct.

Preventing Misconduct

So, what can you do to prevent misconduct and not be involved in these scandals? There are several precautions that you can take. Here are four of the most critical ones.

Familiarize Yourself with Codes of Ethics

All researchers involved in a study must familiarize themselves with ethics codes and the guidelines that apply to their specific area of research. As mentioned at the beginning of this chapter, ignorance is not a legitimate excuse for ethical violations. Thus, you should periodically read ethical guidelines and understand how they apply to your research.

Obtain IRB Approval

IRBs assess potential risks and ethical concerns in human participant research. They also ensure that researchers follow procedures such as using informed consent to protect research participants' rights.[100] Thus, IRBs aim to guarantee that the potential benefits of research to participants, society, and science outweigh any risks or harm participants may incur. All institutions receiving federal funding for research (e.g., universities) must establish IRBs, and all research, including human participants, must pass your scrutiny. However, research may be exempt from IRB approval if it (a) examines certain educational practices, (b) uses tests, surveys, or interviews of a non-sensitive nature, (c) observes public behavior, or (d) analyzes archival data. Further, an expedited review is possible for research entailing minimal risk to participants. When evaluating research for approval, IRBs assess whether risks have been minimized, benefits outweigh the risks to participants, participants are selected, and informed consent will be obtained and documented. Despite their laudable purpose, IRBs have sustained criticism due to perceptions of inconsistency across institutions and overemphasis on policing researchers rather than protecting participants' rights.[101]

Participate in Replication Projects

A third mechanism to prevent ethical misconduct is through the replication of research. Replication determines whether previous findings can be duplicated and helps uncover errors and misconduct.[102] This is meant to deter unethical behavior in research. Unfortunately, replication is not common. Replication studies are not likely to be published, and onerous financial requirements are associated with large-scale replications. Also, many factors besides misconduct could explain the discrepant findings. Therefore, replication is not presently as effective in deterring unethicality as it could be.

Secure Feedback from an Expert in Your Area of Research

Peer review is critical to research and guards against error and misconduct. Peer review is just what it sounds like: fellow research experts review the work before publication. They check for quality in the theory, methodology, data analysis, conclusions, and overall paper. It is a necessary step in the publication process but can also be utilized early on. Journal reviewers often anonymously provide feedback on the research while screening for errors and ethical violations. While you will always get feedback from reviewers, if you know an expert in your area, you can also ask for feedback on each research step to ensure that you follow all the ethical standards that may apply to your research. In this case, the review process would not need to be anonymous.

The journal review process is typically anonymous to maintain objectivity in the knowledge development process. Authors are not told who reviews their papers, so relational tensions do not hinder using feedback effectively. Similarly, the author's identity is not disclosed to reviewers to reduce reviewer bias. If a reviewer knows the identity of the paper's authors, merely having this knowledge may influence how they interpret the work. Other steps to reduce potential bias include having multiple reviewers for one paper. This creates a platform for considering more than one point of view when evaluating a study. As a result, the feedback provided to authors is typically more comprehensive, and decisions about their work are made from multiple points of view. The final decision about whether the work will be accepted falls to the editor, who considers each reviewer's feedback and any subsequent revisions that authors have applied to their manuscripts when resubmitting the paper. Thus, between the authors' anonymity, having multiple reviewers, and leaving the final decision to the journal's editor, several mechanisms are in place with the peer-reviewed publication that helps reduce reviewer bias.

Although peer review is supposed to reduce ethical misconduct from the authors, it can often produce additional ethical concerns. For instance, despite the anonymity, reviewers can sometimes discern whose work they are reading and are more likely to accept work submitted by well-known names in the field. And then, there are intentional violations of ethicality: reviewers may steal ideas from studies they review, use their findings before the study is published, or unduly criticize work from authors researching similar topics to prevent them from publishing. This allows the reviewer to publish their work first and beat their peers for research funding.[103]

HOW TO RESOLVE ETHICS COMPLAINTS

The vulnerability of research to ethical violations may be disheartening, but we have discussed ways to prevent error and misconduct. Now we will discuss ways to address it once it has occurred. The first step is informal resolution, which does not involve formal procedures.[104] This should be used for minor violations and in situations where misconduct results from a lack of knowledge or sensitivity,[105] and it should not be used when serious ethical violations have occurred. Suppose a successful informal resolution cannot be achieved. In that case, the violation should be reported to the Ethics Committee or your relevant professional organization (e.g., American Psychological Association, American Sociological Association, Academy of Management, American Educational Research Association; International Political Science Association; National Association of Social Workers, National Economic Association, etc.). Those accused of ethical violations must cooperate fully with the agency reviewing the complaint. They will be asked to provide timely communication and adhere to any sanctions imposed for violations. The agency reviews the claim and sanctions those found guilty of violating ethical standards. Remember that frivolous complaints with the sole intention of harming another do not protect the public and are considered unethical.

Agencies can only hold accountable those who are members of the agency. But, both members and non-members of professional organizations can file complaints to its ethics committee. The committee may also file a complaint (i.e., *sua sponte* complaint). After the committee receives the complaint, the first step is typically for the Chair of the Ethics Committee to review it. They will determine whether there is sufficient evidence of a violation. If there is no cause for investigation, the complaint is dismissed. If evidence shows the alleged actions occurred, a formal case is opened, the investigation begins, and the accused cannot resign from the organization to avoid the charges. The accused is sent a charge letter and is given a chance to review and rebut the evidence provided against them.

A committee can impose one of several sanctions in response to ethical violations of differing severity. A reprimand is sufficient for minimal violations unlikely to harm others or the field. Censure is used when the violation is likely to cause some harm to others. It entails informing the violator that they committed an ethical violation and warning them that they are prohibited from making further violations.[106] The offenders are expelled from the organization for violations likely to cause substantial harm (although there are very few expulsions each year[107]). As an alternative to expulsion, the committee may offer stipulated resignation. The violator is allowed to resign on certain conditions. The violator is allowed to resign on certain conditions – for example, that the violation must be disclosed publicly for a certain period during which the violator is not allowed to reapply for membership. Further, stipulated resignation may require violators to be supervised, attend educational or training programs, seek treatment, or be placed on probation.

APPLIED METHODS: CASE STUDY – DEALING WITH ETHICAL DILEMMAS WHEN USING DECEPTION

Now let's explore and contextualize the ethical considerations we learned by considering a controversial method, the bogus pipeline.

The bogus pipeline (BPL) is a clever methodology[108] to decrease socially desirable responses in self-reported behaviors and opinions. Researchers show participants the BPL, a seemingly complex machine with several systems and electronic components. They tell the participants it is an infallible lie detector. Of course, the device is fake and cannot detect lies, but the researchers invest considerable resources in seemingly sophisticated equipment and time-consuming procedures to convince study participants otherwise. In effect, participants are deceived into thinking they are facing an authentic, sophisticated, and accurate lie detector, which may motivate them to provide more honest self-reports on sensitive research (e.g., racism and sexism,[109] cigarette[110] and marijuana[111] smoking, and alcohol consumption[112]).

Researchers have been enthusiastic about the effectiveness of the BPL procedure in collecting sensitive information. Meta-analytic reviews of the BPL literature[113] reflect an increased interest in and implementing the BPL. But there are some hesitations, too. First, some questioned the use of the BPL from an ethical standpoint shortly after the technique was introduced.[114] Using the BPL raises ethical issues beyond those present in more typical deception studies[115] in several ways. For example, in more typical deception studies, you may mislead participants by omission.[116] In contrast, using the BPL goes beyond passive concealment of the truth; researchers are actively lying to participants about the purpose of the study and the "lie detector's" nature and effectiveness. Additionally, participants in BPL studies may feel coerced into revealing sensitive personal information, including illegal behaviors. This means the information gathered in studies using the BPL may be self-incriminating, which poses a special threat to participants. Third, if study participants feel coerced into disclosing information they would otherwise avoid for their psychological well-being, they may experience significant distress. For example, participants may suddenly face truths about themselves (e.g., extreme racial prejudice) that they had previously denied to maintain psychological balance.[117] The typical deception research does not raise participants' awareness of these sensitive issues. Fourth, many BPL studies use samples of children instead of college students or adults, and children may be particularly susceptible to psychological harm. Finally, participants in BPL studies may feel coerced into providing the information requested (e.g., alcohol ingestion behavior) and effectively lose the freedom to avoid answering the question.

Given this background about the BPL, use the following debate between two researchers to consider the issues addressed in this chapter about planning, executing, and reporting ethical research.

A: Are there any practical benefits of using the BPL?

B: Certainly—there is a demonstrated need for the BPL, and there are practical benefits too. Due to social desirability, we need self-report information on various behaviors and attitudes that are hard to get information on. Think about things like cigarette smoking, drug, and alcohol consumption, and numerous variables such as racism,[118] interpersonal attraction,[119] and attitude change[120]— we need to know about it, and this information is used for research and interventions. Think about the utilitarian perspective: "good" is whatever produces the most benefit for the greatest number of people. We cannot know their antecedents, consequences, and correlations unless we use measures that capture these behaviors.

A: Of course, I agree that knowledge production is important, but your answer does raise questions about deception. And actually, I am taking a utilitarian perspective, too— except I am thinking of the damage caused to the research profession due to routinely lying to participants. This far outweighs the gains we make in knowledge,[121] mainly because correlations do not constitute strong evidence. So it is not worth giving researchers a reputation for routinely lying to find out interesting information. Plus, the BPL goes beyond the usual types of study deception since it involves lying to study participants about purposes and procedures.

B: That is an interesting comment, but it seems based on speculation. Are there any data showing that BPL procedures damage the profession, indicating how much damage is being done? Also, have you seen the empirical research on deception in general? It suggests that study participants are pretty accepting of deception procedures. They do not perceive them as aversive, undesirable, or unacceptable.[122] Plus, if any damage resulted from using the BPL (a question that needs to be empirically investigated), participants will likely understand why deception was necessary after proper debriefing.[123] There is evidence to back this up, too. For example, some researchers reported anecdotal data that participants in their BPL study were not distressed after being debriefed.[124] In another study, participants who had participated in a BPL experiment were just as willing to recommend the study to a friend as participants in an experiment with a much milder degree of deception,[125] like reading fake newspaper articles). And still, others said that participants were "amused by the deception!"[126] So I do not think the data available thus far suggest much "damage" done.

A: I am not convinced. Several studies have found that deceived experiment participants show lower trust,[127] lower compliance, and higher negativistic behavior,[128] even in the presence of debriefing procedures. Also, seminal work revealed that debriefing was not as effective as initially thought in mitigating negative attitudes caused by deceptive methodology.[129]

B: Sure, I am familiar with that work. But any damage the BPL might be doing to the profession (as opposed to other deceptive procedures used to conduct research[130]) must be measured and quantified before deciding if the damage is large or small. The truth is that we need to find out whether those results generalize to the BPL. While that is certainly an interesting hypothesis to be tested, it's an interesting question until we gather evidence. On the other hand, the benefit of using the BPL in research *is* empirically supported[131]: The effect size across many studies is almost half a standard deviation! So, we do know that using the BPL yields more veracious self-reports. But, again, this is quantified and empirically tested: there is a benefit to using the BPL.

A: We will get to the benefits issue, but first, can we agree that measuring the damage it may do before using the BPL is necessary? Let's leave it at this: would you want your children to be participants in these procedures? And would you feel comfortable telling your children's elementary school class that your job is to "lie to people so that they tell the truth about smoking"?

B: But think of the lives that can be saved and how much lower healthcare costs would be from not having to treat cancers and other diseases caused by smoking. And beyond that, think of the theories that valid self-reported information on these behaviors and attitudes will allow us to discover! Can some deception outweigh the fact that teenagers may quit smoking, thus preventing future health problems? Can't the potentially harmful effects of using the BPL be mitigated by a good debriefing procedure explaining why deception was needed? These empirical questions could be investigated before we write the procedure off as unethical. Similar studies regarding deception, in general, have been conducted in the past.

A: You're not wrong, but can we at least agree that the BPL should not be used when no demonstrated benefits exist?

B: Absolutely. Using the BPL to detect alcohol drinking and marijuana smoking is ineffective[132] if these behaviors are not considered socially undesirable. So, in this case, there is no reason why the BPL should yield more valid self-reports than regular paper-and-pencil questionnaires. But, again, you are correct that empirical evidence indicates no benefits to using the BPL in some areas, and in those cases, I agree that it does not make sense to use it. Regular self-reports are just as valid here.

A: Okay, so let me ask you this: given what we know about using the BPL in detecting smoking behavior, why not use self-reports without the BPL in these studies? We can predict with some degree of accuracy what the difference in scores will be from using self-reports alone versus self-reports accompanied by the BPL. You could add or multiply the obtained results by a constant. This would effectively avoid the ethical disadvantages.

B: It is an interesting idea, but we can only use this adjustment for aggregate data. For example, we could measure self-reported prejudice and then use an adjustment factor like the one you described to compute the number of respondents the BPL would have classified as "prejudiced." The problem is that we cannot use this to correct individual scores. So, it is a good solution, and we could utilize it in some areas, such as smoking. If we are interested in the number of smokers in a specific group (such as a high school), we could use self-report measures alone, make the appropriate adjustment, and then decide whether the number of smokers is large enough to warrant an intervention program. On the other hand, we cannot use this adjustment for further research because correlations are informative when examining individual scores on some socially undesirable variable with their scores on other variables. This would require individually "corrected" scores, which are unavailable with the method you describe.

A: Hmm. Okay, back to basic research. Your statements favoring the BPL assume that getting undistorted data about particular behaviors and attitudes is important. But is the juice worth the squeeze, so to speak? The value of pure information relative to the costs may not be worth it if we offer potentially ineffective treatment to smokers who might refuse. I am going to use a "slippery slope" argument here. Suppose the use of the BPL and deception, in general, continues. In that case, we will be unable to find the causes and correlates of anything because people will not trust researchers enough to provide good data.[133]

B: I see your slippery slope argument, and I raise a repeat answer: whether participants distrust research due to the BPL has yet to be specifically tested.

A: Since you believe that conducting more studies seems to be the solution for everything, let's do a study comparing "bogus information" with "real information." Given that we can get some of this information using "real lie detectors," such as biochemical measures like the number of carbon monoxide particles in saliva, we can compare BPL self-reports with the biochemical indicators. Of course, tests are imperfect, but they are more ethical than deception-based self-reports.

B: A review of methods to detect smoking behavior described several imperfect biological markers available, such as carbon monoxide and thiocyanate. However—and again, I am drawing on a utilitarian perspective—there are two arguments against using biochemical indicators. First, the BPL is less expensive to administer than biochemical markers. While biochemical markers like carbon monoxide can be assessed by collecting expired air samples from everyone, and thiocyanate can be measured by collecting saliva samples, these procedures require specialized equipment. Second and more importantly, you may use these indicators to (imperfectly) measure drug use, but there are no such things as biochemical markers to measure attitudes and prejudice. If these biological markers existed, years of research on measuring attitudes could have been spared!

Summary and Conclusion

B: We have covered much ground. We can summarize our basic positions now. First, I stand by the belief that the BPL can and should be used unless there are clear, empirically-based risks that outweigh the procedure's benefits.

A: And we should start with the assumption that the BPL procedure is inherently problematic because of ethical principles, including veracity, fidelity, privacy, and respect for autonomy. The BPL poses several ethical issues beyond more typical studies using deception. We didn't have a chance to review them before, so let me list them now. In BPL studies, (a) experimenters actively lie to participants, (b) the information gathered is personal and often self-incriminating, (c) participants could be forced to recognize truths about themselves (like prejudice) that may be psychologically destabilizing, (d) samples usually include children, and (e) participants effectively lose the ability to withdraw voluntarily from the experiment (by actions like providing false information). So, these unique ethical issues come with using the BPL and should not be used unless imperative. And this imperative need would have to be fully justified.

B: Yes, I appreciate you bringing all those to the fore before we wrap up. My arguments rest on some empirical assumptions, and we have agreed that more research is necessary before we can continue a productive discussion about these concerns. To recap, research needs to address several questions, including (a) Does using the BPL cause damage to the profession? (b) Can the harmful effects of the BPL be mitigated by debriefing? and (c) Will detecting smokers and offering them treatment increase the likelihood that they will accept treatment, or that they would benefit from it? Some of these questions have been posed regarding deception in general[134] rather than regarding the BPL.

A: Agreed, and I would add to that list a couple of additional questions: (a) Has the BPL led to any theoretical advances that might outweigh even minimal risks? and (b) What programs have been developed, or how many people have stopped smoking, as a result of using the BPL?

B: So, we agree that more research is necessary.

A: Yes, but let's acknowledge that more empirical data will not magically solve our disagreements. There are fundamental value questions that underlie our positions. So, even if we obtain information that the BPL has minimal costs, I would still say that my value on autonomy and privacy is greater than the value of new theory. And I am guessing you would disagree.

B: Correct, I would. I might be more willing to infringe on the rights of participants because I place more value on knowledge than on certain amounts and types of potential participant harm.

A: We will have to agree to disagree, then. All I would ask is that as we do the necessary research, we stay honest about our values and obligations. That is the only way we are going to move forward.

B: Indeed. Continuing debate from both utilitarian and deontological perspectives will create a better outcome and therefore is necessary from a utilitarian perspective!

A: I see what you did there. From a deontological perspective, an honest debate is also the right thing to do. These questions are not easily resolved, but I am glad we have begun the discussion.

We could summarize this debate in the following way. From most deontological (duty-based) perspectives, lying to study participants is wrong and never ethically justified. From this perspective, the ethics of the BPL and other deceptive techniques rest on the outcome of philosophical debates. This is outside the scope of much applied social and behavioral science. However, from a utilitarian (consequence-based) perspective, ethicality is determined by empirical consideration based on a cost-benefit analysis that determines whether the potential benefits may outweigh the potentially detrimental consequences of using the BPL. To conduct such an analysis, empirical evidence must be gathered regarding the benefits and costs of using the BPL.

This chapter has provided the tools to apply ethical standards in designing, carrying out, and reporting your research. Chapter 3 will focus on designing and implementing research that makes a sound theoretical contribution.

DISCUSSION QUESTIONS

1. Why should you care about ethical research?

2. What are the differences between the two research philosophies (utilitarian perspective and deontological approach)?

3. Can you explain the differences among research participant types and what ethical standards you should consider when recruiting and selecting each type of participant?

4. How can you ensure that you respect all participants' rights (e.g., right to informed consent, right to privacy, right to confidentiality and anonymity, right to protection from deception, right to debriefing) when executing your research?

5. Why should you consider special ethical requirements when conducting research in field settings? What are they?

6. How can you assess whether you have reported your results following the ethical standards of your field, thereby avoiding all potential problems related to reporting results?

7. What ethical recommendations must be implemented when using online participants (e.g., MTurk) and should also be considered when recruiting traditional samples (e.g., students)?

8. How can you ensure you report your results ethically to avoid misconduct?

9. What is your takeaway from the debate about the use of deception? Would you use deception, and the BPL in particular? Why or why not? On what side of the debate do you stand and why?

KEY TERMS

anonymity
anonymous survey
archival data
attention check
authorship
bogus pipeline (BPL)
CAPTCHA
censoring
coercive
committed-to-participant approach
confidentiality
cooking (the data)
debriefing
Dehoaxing
deontological approach

desensitizing
ethics
Human Intelligence Task (HIT)
informed consent
Institutional Review Board (IRB)
IP Address
long-string index
Mechanical Turk (MTurk)
naturalistic observation
Nuremberg Code
participants
plagiarism
Right to Confidentiality and Anonymity
Right to Debriefing
Right to Protection from Deception

Right to Privacy
scientific misconduct
stimuli
sua sponte
ten-point statement
The Collaborative Institutional
Training Initiative

trimming
Tuskegee Syphilis Study
unjustified authorship credit
utilitarian perspective
Voluntary consent
within-session response consistency

NOTES

This chapter is based to a large extent on the following sources:

Aguinis, H., & Handelsman, M. M. (1997a). Ethical issues in the use of the bogus pipeline. *Journal of Applied Social Psychology, 27(7)*, 557–573. https://doi.org/10.1111/j.1559-1816.1997.tb00647.x

Aguinis, H., & Handelsman, M. M. (1997b). The unique ethical challenges of the bogus pipeline methodology: Let the data speak. *Journal of Applied Social Psychology, 27(7)*, 582-587. https://doi.org/10.1111/j.1559-1816.1997.tb00649.x

Aguinis, H., & Henle, C. A. (2001). Empirical assessment of the ethics of the bogus pipeline. *Journal of Applied Social Psychology, 31(2)*, 352-375. https://doi.org/10.1111/j.1559-1816.2001.tb00201.x

Aguinis, H., & Henle, C.A. (2002). Ethics in research. In S.G. Rogelberg (Ed.), *Handbook of research methods in industrial and organizational psychology* (pp. 34-56). Blackwell.

Aguinis, H., Villamor, I., & Ramani, R. M. (2021). MTurk research: Review and recommendations. *Journal of Management, 47(4)*, 823–837. https://doi.org/10.1177/0149206320969787

3 HOW TO MAKE CONTRIBUTIONS TO THEORY

LEARNING GOALS

By the end of this chapter, you will be able to do the following:

3.1 Argue the criticality of theory for managers, researchers, students, and policymakers.

3.2 Articulate important distinctions in discerning good theory.

3.3 Evaluate when a new theory is needed from the unit and programmatic theory perspectives.

3.4 Devise how to prune the theoretical landscape by judging the importance of theory falsification, and distinguishing between falsification and failed confirmation.

3.5 Describe how theory elaboration improves theory and compare and contrast theory elaboration and other forms of theorizing.

3.6 Articulate the decision-making process for choosing a theory elaboration perspective.

3.7 Propose how to conduct a theory elaboration study by describing five ways to advance theory and explaining how the implementation approaches and tactics advance theory.

3.8 Articulate how bridging levels of analysis improves theory.

IMPORTANCE OF CONTRIBUTIONS TO THEORY

Theory is critical. If you look at the top journals' mission statements describing what they want from submissions, first and foremost, they want to see that your paper contributes to theory. The people involved in publishing your paper place primary importance on this: reviewers evaluate the contribution to theory, which weighs heavily in editors' decisions about a paper's publication worthiness. If the contribution to theory is not seen as sufficiently strong, your paper will unlikely be published.

Yet *why* theory is so critical isn't entirely clear, saying, "Because that is what makes a contribution worth publishing." This is problematic because the *why* of theory needs to be clear in a science that centers around it. Moreover, the demand for theoretical contribution often makes authors generate theory for theory's sake, clogging science with inconsistent theories of questionable validity.[1] This state of affairs has prompted some to claim we are too enamored with theory, advocate more emphasis on data, or even question how much theory is needed.[2] These writings reveal an ongoing debate about the criticality (or lack thereof) of theory in social and behavioral science and other fields.[3]

In this chapter, we walk through the reasons why theory is so critical. Thinking about theory can seem abstract at times, so throughout the chapter, we'll use the idea of **turnover** (when workers are separated from their jobs) as an example to make the concepts more concrete. We will cover answers to essential questions like: what does a good theory look like? How can you tell if a new theory helps or hinders our goals in science? What must you consider as you dissect the literature to interpret a body of knowledge, and how can you effectively contribute? These are all essential aspects of understanding how theory progresses science. But what is theory, and why do we care about it? This boils down to the idea that theory is a fancy word for "Do we understand what's going on?" And while the basic tenets of good theory hold across contexts, the understanding people want from a theory depends on the person's needs. So, first, let's look at the different users of theory to understand what we can offer to leaders and managers, researchers, students, and policymakers.

WHY THEORIES SHOULD BE USEFUL AND FOR WHOM

Criticality of Theory for Leaders and Managers

Leaders and managers wish to use theory to identify actions that effectively influence (i.e., improve) a situation and produce a desired outcome. For example, take the manager who notices high turnover. This manager seeks a theory that illuminates factors having direct and reliable causal effects. So, the theory should explain the factors most likely causing high-performing employees to leave. A validated theory on turnover would provide knowledge on factors the organization could influence, how those actions might reduce turnover, and to what extent. This knowledge would be *useful*. Yet, theories are critical for leaders and managers because they are useful and *usable*. This means that a theory's insights include information on factors that affect turnover, which the manager can influence.[4] A theory that posits that turnover is caused by some fixed and mostly inherited trait, such as employees' personality (i.e., something a manager cannot change), is less useful to the manager than a theory that posits that turnover is caused by a poorly-implemented performance management and compensation system (i.e., something a manager can change). Finally, while a **useful theory** on traits and turnover may not be immediately usable for managers, it may inform other theories that might be, such as theories on pre-employment selection. For example, potential employers wishing to reduce future turnover would measure the personality of job applicants and make employment decisions based on the resulting scores.

Criticality of Theory for Researchers

Theories are critical for researchers, but their needs and goals regarding theory are not necessarily the same as managers'. Using the same example, a theory relating personality to turnover is useful in improving researchers' understanding of turnover. It is even more useful if it leads to future research on turnover. For example, what other traits relate to turnover? Are there states (e.g., job dissatisfaction, tedious work) that may also be related to turnover? In sum, theory is critical to the researcher because it clarifies what is known and illuminates what researchers need to learn from future research.

Criticality of Theory for Students

Whether undergraduates, graduates, or enrolled in executive education courses, students are expected to parse complex problems. Theories are critical because they help students understand how to think about issues more accurately. Theories should encompass collections of validated findings woven into credible explanations for how and why phenomena operate. Thus, they provide the frameworks for thinking about problems. Let's use the turnover example. Many undergraduates may not realize how or why turnover happens or the processes involved; theories are useful because they combine these components into a coherent and valid framework that students can use to diagnose and respond to specific instances of turnover. While experienced executives may know all too well that turnover is expensive, they might not know how it happens or the extent of the problems it triggers, such as the departure of more high-performing employees in the near future.

Criticality of Theory for Policymakers

Finally, theories are also critical for yet another stakeholder group that, unfortunately, is overlooked in most social and behavioral science theories: policymakers.[5] Many policies and laws relate to theories on employee well-being and performance, leadership behavior, and firm structure and financial performance, among other highly relevant topics. So, many social and behavioral science theories are critical for policymakers because they address governance principles that guide organizations' and societies' actions.[6] Implications for policymaking are not the same as implications for practice, which are explicit actions managers should implement.[7] Instead, a good theory will provide clarity and credibility to two issues: writing a policy most likely to have the desired effects and the boundary conditions of a policy's effectiveness (i.e., when and where it will work, for whom, and to what degree).

As you can see, theory is critical because it provides the basis for understanding whatever you are trying to manage (i.e., improve), understand (i.e., study), or govern.[8] Your goal as a researcher is to understand individual and group behavior, organizations, how they function, and why individuals do certain things. You then teach these theories to students who will become leaders, managers, and possibly policymakers, who can make better choices and policies for how organizations will run. In the turnover example, managers armed with theory who notice high turnover in a unit within their firm can attribute this to the compensation system (or finding that applies to the case). They are then better equipped to diagnose and fix the problem. Such a theory comes from researchers, is taught to students, and can inform policy. While each role may use theory differently, they all use it for what it is: a credible and useful explanation.

IMPORTANT DISTINCTIONS IN DISCERNING GOOD THEORY

A theory should allow us to predict and explain. A theory explains why something has happened, allowing you to *predict what will happen*. This applies at two levels: in more narrow theory (**unit theory**) and within the broader context of the theory (**programmatic theory**). We will go over each in turn because there is an important distinction between *good unit theory* and *good programmatic theory*. We will also discuss the difference between a *good theory* and a *potentially good one,* which is essential because all theories are only potentially good until empirical evidence shows they are good.

Accurate Explanation

A good theory provides more than just an explanation. It should be *the most accurate* explanation given the knowledge at the time. So, explanations describe causes and effects while orienting you to the nature of the phenomenon. They involve the word "because." Good theory describes *what* happens and then explains *how* and *why* something happens.[9] Let's look at the turnover example again. Turnover is a common subject of study because it is costly for organizations that must recruit, select, and train new employees to replace the previous ones. So, suppose you seek to explain why skilled employees tend to be employed for shorter durations than unskilled ones (i.e., have higher turnover). In that case, a good theory doesn't just describe *what* is happening with turnover (e.g., using details to show who leaves and when). It also shows *how* this works (e.g., by elaborating on the process). Most importantly, it explains *why* higher skills cause people to switch jobs (this speaks to unit theory) and links these explanations to what is generally established about turnover in its numerous manifestations[10] (this addresses programmatic theory).

Insightful Prediction

It is not enough to make predictions that are relatively obvious extensions of what is known to be true, such as the idea that people who don't like their jobs are more likely to seek greener pastures. Instead, good theory makes predictions about a phenomenon by uncovering unrecognized causal relationships (e.g., is something else causing people to seek greener pastures?), enriching known ones (e.g., does dissatisfaction with supervisors lead to higher turnover than dissatisfaction with salary?), and discounting spurious ones[11] (e.g., is dissatisfaction with something within the organization the driving force?). The insights must be demonstrably correct in these cases, meaning they aren't just speculation but supported empirically. As we'll discuss, the ability to accurately reflect reality is what distinguishes a *good theory* from a *potentially good* theory, whose predictions *might* prove correct.

Good Theory Versus Potentially Good Theory

By definition, new theories are provisional (i.e., untested) and, hence, only potentially good. The theory's status change from potentially good to good comes from connecting theory and data. But verification is a two-way street. As much as the empirical data determine a theory's accuracy, the theory dictates the empirical evidence that best verifies its accuracy. In the turnover example, if the theory is that higher skills → employment options → decision to leave the organization, then you know that a test requires an understanding of what each concept entails to measure it and define its relationships to other parts of the theory. For testing higher skills and employment options, participants must be aware that their skill level opens up more options for employment. Participants must know they have alternative employment opportunities to test the relationship between employment options and the decision to leave for greener pastures. The match between theory and method is difficult or impossible without a clear theory.

Thus, to produce good unit theory, you must remember that *an ounce of theoretical prevention is worth a pound of methodological cure*.[12] The vast majority of papers rejected from journals suffer this fate because the methodology needs to validate the theory. When the measures have weak links to the theoretical argument, the design is inappropriate to the theoretical argument, or the hypotheses and research questions need to allow clear disconfirmation of what is false, there is a flaw that will prevent testing the theory.

In addition, unit theories have *potential* when they raise an interesting question. But a unit theory is *good* when it precisely explains something significant in the outcome of interest. Significance is a term often used to refer to the trustworthiness threshold in statistical tests. But it would be best if you also considered the *practical significance* outside the context of a particular statistical test. For example, you may often hear of practical significance as reflecting effect size in empirical work; the effect size typically calibrates the importance of a theory.[13] In other words, a large effect size determines how important the result is and how much it contributes to the theory. Yet practical significance also relates to the theory's user[14]: whom will this theory benefit, and what effect size result will produce meaningful information for them? This can't be discerned by a one-size-fits-all standard for interpreting effect sizes, which is fixed and often arbitrary. For example, a common rule of thumb for interpreting the importance of effect sizes is that a correlation of .10 is small and, therefore, trivial. In contrast, a correlation of .50 is large and, thus, very important. Many published articles praise results, including large effects, and dislike and lament those with small ones. Yet the importance of that correlation (i.e., effect size) is contextual. For example, take the finding that aspirin reduces the chance of a heart attack by .11%. Using rules of thumb, you might be tempted to dismiss this finding as unimportant. But considering the context, we see this would be unwise. Given the significance of heart attacks and the relative ease of taking aspirin,[15] this small effect makes a big difference. It's a small cost for a big benefit. Analogously, demonstrating that a manager saying, "How are you?" once a day to their employees decreases turnover by .1% would be useful from a practical significance standpoint given the cost/benefit ratio. In sum, the practical significance of effect size depends on its context, so you cannot evaluate the usefulness of a result—and hence the usefulness of the theory—by effect size alone.

Good Unit Theory and Good Programmatic Theory

A critical distinction increasingly at the fore of discussions about good theory is that of *unit theory* and *programmatic theory*. Most studies put forth a unit theory.[16] A unit theory explains the causal relationship of specific concepts; they are essential because they explain and predict empirical patterns.[17] Explaining how and why variables relate allows us to extend these explanations into accurate predictions. Let's look at our turnover example to see how understanding the relation between skills and job transitions constitutes a unit theory. Let's say a study shows that higher skills predict higher turnover because higher-skilled employees feel they have better options. This offers a feasible and testable rationale that, if supported, provides a means to prevent the departure of skilled employees (e.g., by offering better salary or benefits packages). Without the "because," if you just found skills to be associated with turnover, you could know neither what questions to ask (e.g., how much better does the offer need to be?) nor what steps to take to fix this organizational problem (e.g., re-arranging resources to provide a better offer).

Yet a unit theory's strength also depends on its relationship with what is known more broadly about a phenomenon – the programmatic theory.[18] Programmatic theory is "the context of interrelated theories within which unit theoretical work occurs."[19] In other words, programmatic theory is what we already know about the domain or topic more broadly; it's the "settled science" of verified and commonly accepted knowledge about the subject. And unit theories integrate into a body of programmatic theory. In our running example, programmatic theory would encompass what is known about turnover more generally, and a unit theory's explanation and prediction are considered within the broader context of programmatic theory.

For example, imagine someone seeking to discover some novel insight proposed a theory that turnover was good and should be encouraged. Such a unit theory could undoubtedly make an impact. Still, *only* if it were well argued concerning what the field already knows about turnover—and the settled science of turnover said that it's costly and problematic for organizations. Theorizing that it is actually good could only be taken seriously if the theory found a way to either discount or subvert the other (tested) unit theories that showed turnover to be bad.[20] This is precisely what occurred in the programmatic theory on turnover when the concept of "functional turnover" was introduced (an introduction that, of course, involved defining, differentiating, and testing it). Functional turnover is a unit theory that explains how and why organizations benefit from poor-performing employees leaving. Contrast functional turnover with dysfunctional turnover, which is when high-performing employees leave. Both concepts examine the broader research topic of turnover: employees leaving an organization. More specifically, the concepts look at the turnover of skilled workers. But a new unit theory was born by drilling down even further to look at the job performance of skilled workers. It differentiated poor-performing skilled workers from high-performing skilled workers, which led to a new understanding of when turnover might be beneficial (**functional turnover**) or detrimental (**dysfunctional turnover**) for organizations. This clarified, rather than muddled, what we know about turnover. Thus, both types of turnover could be integrated into the broader understanding (programmatic theory) of turnover.

Clear and coherent programmatic theory emerges from progressive research programs. Programmatic theory provides structure and support for unit theories. When a particular unit theory aligns with claims of other unit theories in their research domain, it supports the combined evidence of the broader body of knowledge (i.e., the programmatic theory of the domain). Conversely, if the unit theory claims don't explain how they fit in with (or challenge) the settled science of programmatic theory, the unit theory's claims appear weak. So in this way, the relationship of unit theory with programmatic theory bears strongly on the plausibility and importance of any new unit theory.

Let's dive into plausibility and importance with the functional turnover example. For it to be a plausible concept, you must explain how and why turnover benefits could outweigh its established costs. Even if there is empirical evidence supporting a theory of functional turnover, without a clear connection to the programmatic theory of turnover, it would be hard to understand what was incorrect about all the prior work on turnover that established it as harmful to organizations. This is why, besides being testable, a good unit theory needs to be coherent with (i.e., understandable in light of) the currently accepted programmatic theory. Otherwise, it risks creating confusion (and more need for theory pruning, as we'll get into later). In your research career, in developing a research idea, you will often be advised to look at what is already being discussed in the extant literature, which is referred to as "the conversation." Think of when you walk up to a group of people you want to join. What do you do first? Listen to the conversation to work your way in. It is far less effective to come up and speak to them with your thoughts without hearing what they are discussing first. Research works the same way. Sentences that do not relate to what else has been said do not add much to the conversation.[21] Statements that bring up issues that don't seem to connect to the conversation, or contradict others without a real explanation of why it makes sense to do so, only create confusion and muddle the topic at hand. The meaning and value of any new sentence (unit theory) depend on what those in the current conversation think (programmatic theory).

Finally, programmatic theory is also how you ultimately judge the theoretical contribution of any body of research—does it advance the settled science on a topic and allow you to make new claims that are likely to be true? You will learn in the next section that a good theory puts forth an idea and, at a more concrete level, clarifies which methods would be appropriate to test the relationships it proposes. Much in the same way, a good unit theory clarifies its relationships at a higher level, connecting to other unit theories within a programmatic theory.[22]

WHEN IS NEW THEORY NEEDED?

The Unit Theory Perspective

Creating any validated unit theory and even more time and energy to integrate multiple unit theories into a good programmatic theory will take resources. It must be worth the effort, which isn't always the case. Yet most journals imply or mandate that every empirical study needs to enrich or build theory with the omnipresent question, "What is a paper's theoretical contribution?" Most journals require reviewers to answer this question on manuscript evaluation forms. Some scholars are pushing back against this so-called obsession with theory[23] by saying that a theoretical contribution is not always needed. While this view has merit, it does not tell you when you do and when you do not need new theory. And while there are more and more papers on *how* to write about a theory,[24] even some that also help you decide *what kind* of theory to write,[25] we must consider whether there is a need for a new theory in the first place.

One way to understand whether a new theory is needed is by posing the "So what?" question from multiple perspectives. A research idea and its results can be interesting, but is the study relevant? Does it mean something to people who would use it? In other words, does it matter?

Practical Applications

From leaders' and managers' perspectives, the "So what?" would be, "Do results improve some problematic situation?" If not, a theory may not be needed. In addition, if the situations studied are rare or do not matter much in terms of individual well-being or organizational performance, maybe the benefit of developing a theory is not warranted by the cost of conducting the research. This argument sometimes emerges in discussions of the relevance of social and behavioral science research.[26]

Improved Predictions

Another way to answer the "So what?" question is to understand whether a new theory would improve predictions (which, as you'll recall, is one of the characteristics of good theory) or identify new and useful explanatory variables. For example, suppose a new theory offers the same predictions using an alternative explanation. In that case, the new theory is redundant and may cause confusion among the unit theories (hence muddling the programmatic theory). But it is useful if a new theory can improve existing theories' predictions. Alternatively, it may be useful by identifying new and useful explanatory variables. The comment, "Don't we know that already?" is often used to dismiss theory that explains known relationships (e.g., X has been shown to affect Y). But if a new theory makes it possible to predict Y using X by some practically significant margin more accurately, then the explanation for why that is should merit an investigation and, potentially, publication. Provided that the new explanation was sufficiently tested against the existing one (per **strong inference**'s "horse race"), a concept discussed in more detail later in this chapter, this is an occasion to remove the weaker theory and increase parsimony.

Relevant Questions

A related way to answer the "So what?" question is in the value of the predictions. There is a mistaken assumption that the value of a theory should always be clear when it is proposed. Most often, scientific discovery does not work this way.[27] In other words, a theory typically starts with a relevant question with no answer. A good example is asking, "Why do some people stay in miserable jobs?" It often takes time to realize the full value of a theory, especially when the theory is truly innovative because the current programmatic theory can get in the way.[28] For example, Kepler's new theory about how planets orbited at varying speeds and in an elliptical shape was not simply accepted when it was presented because the current programmatic theory (i.e., the "clockwork universe" model) could not accommodate such a theory, even though Kepler's questions were mathematically provable. New predictions are not valuable simply because they are new, so you must balance your need for the demonstrable utility of an explanation and predictions with the knowledge that such utility may not be fully realized for some time. New theory should not fix problems you do not have, but it can identify problems you did not even know you had. If a new theory might accelerate future research impacting both theory and practice,[29] then you should be patient.

The Programmatic Theory Perspective

For the author or reviewer weighing the need for a new unit theory among the existing ones, the question is about how the new unit theory fits with the existing ones. Suppose it cannot be connected to existing theory because it is overly complicated, circumscribed, or adds one more mediator or moderator to an already long laundry list. In that case, it is best to rework the theory until these problems are solved (or abandon it). Having too many unit theories obscures rather than clarifies predictions, as in the case of what types of leadership behaviors predict direct-report performance.[30] Parsimony is the antidote to this situation, and it comes from coherence within and among unit theories. With coherence, unit theory predictions are more easily comprehended. More importantly, coherence reconciles unit theories with each other to produce clarity on the settled science, which is the programmatic theory.

When programmatic theory is too complicated or doesn't point to a clear understanding of the issue, it can sometimes feel like there are "too much or too many theories" to make sense of a phenomenon. For example, explaining Y using many factors (X_1, X_2, X_3, X_4, and X_5) is fine if you can tell how each factor works separately and how they all work together. But if you can't tell which factor does what, or if the factors provide contradictory predictions that can't be adjudicated, we have a problem. We must clarify: can the user understand how to apply the theory, or is it unwieldy (i.e., too much)? Can the user discern precise predictions, or are there multiple possibilities (i.e., too many)? For example, one theory that proposes a four-way interaction mediated by three intervening variables is probably too much; two theories that explain Y irreconcilably are one too many. The following paragraphs discuss parsimony and coherence among unit theories and how they affect the theoretical landscape of programmatic theory.

Parsimony

More and more theories speak to a common underlying problem: the lack of **parsimony**. Parsimony uses **Occam's razor**—the simplest explanation is the best. Complicated and convoluted explanations are overwhelming and can easily feel like "too much." Even if explanations are not complicated, multiple explanations for the same thing feel like "too many" theories.

A modern objection is that parsimony is too reductionist because it bundles nuanced parts into some broader phenomenon. But in actuality, nuance is often superficial[31]—representing a change in what happens but not adding knowledge about how or why it happens—and counter-productive by adding non-essential information that reduces parsimony. A lack of parsimony, in either case, will limit a theory's usability in terms of guidance for research, practice, or policy-making[32] and can easily restrict or mislead rather than clarify understanding.[33]

Coherence

Coherence is about structure both within and among unit theories. Coherence *within* unit theories means that the concepts and their causal mechanisms make sense. Yet the unit theories must also make sense when considering them *together*, which makes programmatic theory coherent. Physics exemplifies coherence best. Specifically, one can study the topic of motion using different unit theories: classical Newtonian mechanics that measure the forces at play, Lagrangian mechanics that estimate potential and kinetic energy, or the Hamiltonian approach that makes different assumptions about the space in which the motion occurs. Each unit theory uses different constructs, but those constructs make it clear when each theory is appropriately applied, and all three are entirely consistent in the programmatic theory of motion; in fact, you can derive each unit theory from the others.

Consider the programmatic theory of group brainstorming as an example of coherence within and across unit theories. Three specific unit theories collectively explain why brainstorming in a group degrades the brainstorming process. Groups create (a) the capacity for **social loafing**,[34] (b) the fear of evaluation by others,[35] and (c) interference from what others are saying.[36] Each unit theory explains a distinct mechanism, but they do not contradict each other. On the contrary, they are unambiguous in their boundaries and integrate well with each other and what is known about groups more broadly. Because the programmatic theory of group brainstorming is so coherent, explaining why group brainstorming is ineffective seems like a small unit theory. The specific mechanisms within each theory seem like testable hypotheses. This is because the fit among the findings makes it easy for people to "chunk" the elements into a single structure that fits within the limits of human working memory.[37] Yet this coherent programmatic theory on group brainstorming represents decades of research and scores of studies that refined and tested dozens of alternative explanations[38] and fit these together coherently.

Achieving coherence helps reduce the stray theories that may be weaker than others and thus helps parsimony in the "less is more" sense by clarifying when theoretical explanations compete. In a famous *Science* article, "Strong Inference," the author explains how you can think of theoretical progress as a horse race.[39] You have two competing theories that predict some outcome of interest (e.g., is it social loafing or individual disengagement that makes people brainstorm less effectively in groups?). To learn which is better, you set up a study where both theories have the same chance of being right, but only one will be.[40] But for this to happen, the unit theories have to be comparable. They need to predict the same variables and use constructs and mechanisms to test against each other. This is less likely when, in an attempt to be novel, people write a new unit theory intending to maximize its difference from other unit theories (decreasing the coherence of the programmatic theory). The impetus to be novel is motivated by a hope for creativity and, frankly, by the desire to publish in prestigious journals (and receive accompanying rewards). But, when you let 1,000 flowers bloom, you get 10,000 weeds.[41] You need to do some theory pruning to cut down the vast number of theories by pitting comparable theories against each other.

> ### Example: Coherence
>
> Coherence does *not* mean that any new theory agrees with the established programmatic theory; if a new theory challenges some aspect of programmatic theory, the points of contention are clear and testable. For instance, some authors theorized how to overcome the problems that made group brainstorming ineffective, contradicting established programmatic theory.[42] Yet their theorization was framed and connected directly to the appropriate unit theories on group brainstorming. So when the data showed that group brainstorming could be better than individual brainstorming, they clarified rather than obscuring how it could work. Such clarity was useful and usable for both scholars and practitioners; this study has received more than 1,000 Google Scholar citations and appears in many management textbooks and practitioner publications.

PRUNING THE THEORETICAL LANDSCAPE

There are research approaches that researchers can take to prune the theoretical landscape and cut down on confusion. One way is through theory falsification. Another way is through improving theoretical precision. We will go through each in turn.

Theory Falsification

Unfortunately, most theories proposed are never tested,[43] partly because a proposal to test a theory is often not seen as a novel contribution. For example, a study testing a theory already published in conceptual journals such as *Organizational Psychology Review* or *Academy of Management Review* is unlikely to be published in a journal that publishes empirical research. Why? Because the theory has already been proposed elsewhere. To be blunt, this is absurd. Remember from earlier that all theories are provisional, meaning they start as *an* explanation among many potential explanations. To determine which theory offers the *best* explanation, theories need to be tested—often, they're not. Even more problematic is that a theory must be tested in many ways before it warrants inclusion in settled science. And so what happens is that proposed provisional theories accumulate, and it's undetermined which theory offers the *best* explanation—not just *an* explanation. This causes confusion (precisely, incoherence, as described earlier in this chapter) in programmatic theory that must be "pruned." Let's look at how contributions from unit theories that *are* empirically tested can avoid creating that confusion. This is achieved through falsification.

How Does Falsification Work with Theory?

Discovering the *best* explanation only happens when you try to falsify a theory rather than confirm (or fail to confirm).[44] But, of course, we need to aim for falsification to avoid ending up with too much theory or too many theories, Researchers often confuse the distinction between falsification and (dis)confirmation, so let's walk through it.

Falsification Versus Failed Confirmation

Falsification is the process of eliminating plausible alternative explanations to reveal what remains the best explanation. Karl Popper offered the following analogy: a theory is a fence around the truth, and every time you integrate more data, the fence gets smaller and closer to the truth. Of course, you can never get to that truth, but falsification brings you closer over time.

In practice, falsification seems to be mistaken for failed confirmation: "We tested this theory, and it didn't work; now it is falsified." This is actually what is known as failed confirmation, and unfortunately, it doesn't go far enough to provide grounds for falsification. Why not? Because inferences from disconfirming a result can't prove a theory is true, it can only prove that a theory is better than an alternative.[45] Moreover, failed confirmation often does not enlighten what is wrong with the theory.

Example: Falsification in the Task Conflict Literature

Task conflict arises between individuals who disagree about how a task should be performed instead of relationship conflict, which occurs in individuals' relationships. Task conflict was theorized to improve team performance, yet a meta-analysis showed that it typically did not.[46] While the meta-analysis was useful because it disconfirmed the theory, it did not explain what was wrong with the theory. Instead, it required the proposal of other unit theories to explain how and why task conflict was not helpful even though it seemed like it would be. Yet most of this research was confirmation, not falsification. In other words, research merely showed that whatever factor of interest was hypothesized to make task conflict helpful did so. This creates a lack of coherence and bloat at the level of programmatic theory because you end up with several disconnected ways to make task conflict productive. Despite all these ways, a subsequent meta-analysis supported the first prediction (i.e., most often, task conflict was not helpful).[47] So, while the unit theories were confirmed individually, they did not integrate into a proper understanding of how task conflict worked.

How to Falsify

What should have happened was that the various unit theories for what makes task conflict helpful should have each been seen as an alternative explanation for how task conflict works, and these could have been tested against or with each other to "shrink the fence." If task conflict is only helpful when there is a moderate amount, then falsification should encourage research that discounts the alternative explanations to this one. Such research would not, for example, confirm the curvilinear relationship between task conflict and performance; it would show that the amount of relationship conflict and trust predicted no variance above what the amount of task conflict explained. Falsification eliminates alternative explanations, and when these are guided by programmatic theory, it maintains the coherence of the programmatic theory.[48]

Theoretical Precision

Theories in social and behavioral science tend to progress in the following pattern of phases: (1) a period of enthusiasm about a new theory, (2) a period of attempted application to different domains, (3) a period of disappointment as the data do not always support it, (4) a period of confusion about inconsistent or unreplicable empirical results and several ad hoc excuses, and (5) finally, people lose interest in that specific theory and focus on other ones.[49] This all follows from imprecise theory.

Why Is Theoretical Precision Important?

Social and behavioral science research follows a cycle in which theories generate directional hypotheses, such as whether an effect will be positive or negative, and these hypotheses are empirically evaluated with null hypothesis significance testing, which determines whether an effect is likely to differ from zero. In other words, the system used in social and behavioral sciences only verifies if some effect exists without exploring other characteristics of the effect across contexts (e.g., size). Without understanding the magnitude and nature of the effect, we have a vague understanding of how the theory works, which is problematic for multiple reasons. First, because these theories are imprecise, they are difficult to refute, disconfirm, or falsify. Because science progresses by challenging and exploring a theory's predicted effects, an imprecise theory means we are just treading water instead of making strides. This stalls theoretical progress, and as the theory loses its potential for explanatory power, people lose interest and focus on other theories. Second, empirical results are rarely drawn upon to calibrate theoretical hypotheses to predict the magnitude of an effect. The directional hypotheses set forth by theories provide little reason to conduct statistical tests that detect anything other than differences from zero.[50] If you follow this cycle, you may be caught in a trap that yields little theoretical progress because theories are stated with such imprecision that they are difficult to refute.[51]

How to Be More Precise

To break this cycle, researchers can accelerate theoretical progress by developing more precise theories and exposing them to stringent tests that put them at genuine risk. So how can you do this in your research? First, you can enhance theoretical precision by moving beyond directional predictions.[52] For instance, specify lower and upper bounds within which a theoretical parameter should fall. Lower bounds would set a value below which an effect is considered trivial. Upper bounds would set the maximum value that could be reasonably attained on conceptual grounds, which could, for example, help distinguish if two constructs are conceptually distinct.[53]

You can also increase theoretical precision by making predictions that hypothesize results from comparisons (i.e., predicting that one effect will be larger or smaller than another).[54] Comparative predictions are consistent with the principle of strong inference,[55] a method for testing competing predictions that strengthen the logical conclusions yielded by empirical research.[56] As noted earlier, strong inference involves deriving competing hypotheses, then conducting empirical tests that produce evidence supporting one hypothesis while refuting another alternative hypothesis (or hypotheses). Other ways to refine theoretical predictions include identifying moderators influencing the strength and direction of relationships between constructs[57] and explicitly stating whether relationships are expected to be linear versus curvilinear.[58]

The most effective way to increase theoretical precision is to derive non-nil predictions, such that theories predict the presence of a nonzero effect rather than the absence of a zero effect.[59] Although you can find non-nil predictions in the hard sciences, such as physics and chemistry, they are rare in social and behavioral science. Moreover, predictions stated as point estimates can be challenging to justify, given the uncertainties inherent in the phenomena under investigation. However, it can be feasible to state predictions as ranges of values akin to the "good-enough" belt.[60] Values derived from non-nil predictions can be based on formal theorizing[61] or findings from previous empirical research, such as individual studies deemed relevant to the theory at hand[62] or meta-analyses that summarize effect sizes across multiple studies.[63]

HOW TO IMPROVE THEORY USING THEORY ELABORATION

Having discussed what we are looking for from theory, we turn to approaches to theorizing. First, recall that social and behavioral science research aims to explain and predict observable social processes that describe behaviors of individuals and groups, cultures, and organizations.[64] This is achieved through a complementary combination of theory and empirical data, which inform each other in the knowledge-creation process. This process has three facets: **theory generation**, **theory testing**, and **theory elaboration**.

Most studies include an element of theory generation, testing, and elaboration, but each study's primary focus is different. Some studies focus primarily on theory generation, some on theory testing, and some on theory elaboration. Yet, because of the interdependent nature of these facets, a study with a dominant focus on one facet may include other facets less prominently.

This section clarifies the three facets and discusses similarities and differences between different approaches to theorizing. Although theory elaboration is an important facet in the broader knowledge creation process, most of the literature on knowledge creation focuses on tools, perspectives, and insights about theory generation and theory testing.[65] Therefore, this section reviews theory generation (the deductive or inductive creation of a new theory) and theory testing (the analysis of whether and when a theory holds up empirical scrutiny). Still, it gives special attention to theory elaboration (improving an existing theory).

Approaches to Theorizing: Similarities and Differences

Theory Generation

As summarized in Table 3.1, theory generation provides new theoretical ideas. It begins with an unexplained phenomenon and then draws on data to induct new constructs and relationships

TABLE 3.1 ■ Contrasting Theory Generation, Theory Testing, and Theory Elaboration

	Theory Generation	Theory Testing	Theory Elaboration
Input	Unexplained phenomenon; little to no existing theory.	Formal hypotheses derived from extant theory.	Partially explained phenomenon; a current conceptual model and ideas.
Process and tactics	Induct constructs and relationships from data or develop and derive new concepts and relationships using logical, well-reasoned arguments.	Collect and analyze data to assess whether they provide evidence to support hypothesized relationships.	Use existing concepts and models to guide the collection and organization of data. Refine existing theory by contrasting, specifying, and structuring theoretical constructs and relations.
Output	New testable propositions; new constructs.	Accept or reject hypotheses derived from extant theory.	Refinement of existing theoretical ideas' contextual factors, constructs, and relationships.

Source: Adapted from Fisher & Aguinis (2017). Reproduced with permission.

(**inductive theory generation**) or derives new constructs and lays out relationships using well-reasoned arguments (**deductive theory generation**). New testable propositions or constructs stem from the theory generation process.

Theory Testing

Theory testing exposes theoretical ideas to empirical scrutiny. It begins with formal hypotheses derived from existing theory. You then collect and analyze data that may serve as evidence supporting the hypotheses. This allows you to accept or reject the derived hypotheses.

Theory Elaboration

Theory elaboration fosters the developing, expanding, and tightening of existing theoretical ideas. It begins with an existing conceptual model that partially explains a phenomenon. You then use the current concepts and model to collect and organize data to contrast, specify, and structure theoretical constructs and relations to refine existing theory. The output of such a process is a refined and elaborated theory that more accurately accounts for contextual factors, constructs, and relationships.

Before diving into the theory elaboration process, let's understand when to go this route. First, it would be best not to use theory elaboration in *all* research domains and under *all* circumstances. Moreover, there are specific decision criteria that you can use to help determine when a theory elaboration perspective may be particularly advantageous. The following section outlines a decision-making process you can use as a tool.

Decision Process for Choosing Whether to Adopt a Theory Elaboration Perspective

Theory elaboration is likely to be most beneficial under certain conditions. Accordingly, this section outlines a three-step decision process that serves as a guide when choosing whether or not to adopt a theory elaboration perspective. The decision process is based on three questions. If the answer to all three questions is affirmative, then theory elaboration is a viable and potentially beneficial research perspective. Conversely, other research approaches may be more helpful if the answer to any question is negative. Figure 3.1 summarizes this sequential decision process.

Question 1: Is There an Existing Theory and Access to Data That May Be Used to Explain or Offer Insight into the Focal Phenomenon?

Theory elaboration uses pre-existing conceptual ideas or a preliminary model as the starting point. Thus, the first decision involves conducting a comprehensive literature review to ascertain how some theory might provide a foundation for analyzing and understanding the phenomenon of interest and whether it is possible to access data you use to evaluate the phenomenon. If there is no prior theory that might provide a foundation for analyzing data about the issue of interest, or if it is difficult or impossible to access data to evaluate what is going on, other perspectives to theorizing, such as a deductive theory development approach, are more appropriate. Many articles published in the *Academy of Management Review* fit this scenario.[66]

On the other hand, if some existing theory may provide a basis for categorizing existing data and explaining focal relations and processes, and there is the potential to access data to evaluate focal relations and processes, then one can transition to question two. For example, the authors utilized the existing theory on organizational routines and team learning as a starting point to explain the adoption of new technology in hospitals.[67] As a result, they gained access to qualitative and quantitative data from cardiac surgery departments in 16 hospitals, allowing them to proceed to question two.

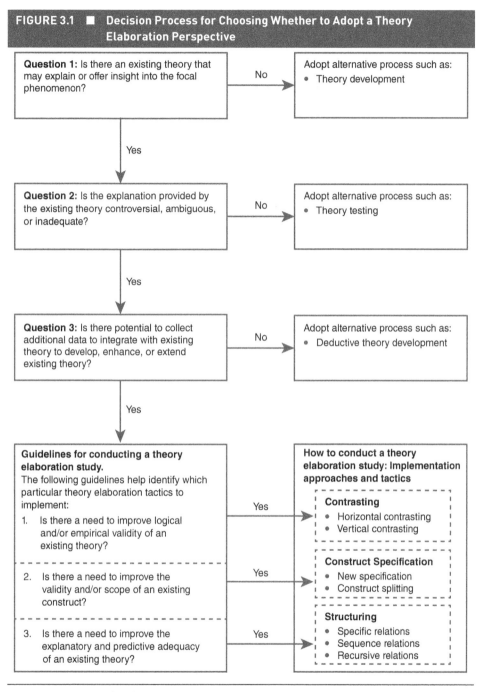

FIGURE 3.1 ■ Decision Process for Choosing Whether to Adopt a Theory Elaboration Perspective

Source: Fisher & Aguinis (2017). Reproduced with permission.

Question 2: Is the Explanation Provided by the Existing Theory Controversial, Ambiguous, or Inadequate?

Theory elaboration involves contrasting, specifying, or structuring theoretical constructs and relations. Thus, if the phenomenon of interest does not include some controversy, ambiguity, or inadequacy in explaining it, then other perspectives to theorizing, such as theory testing, are more likely to be appropriate. In such a case, hypotheses can be deductively developed and tested within the context of the existing data.[68] On the other hand, if there is some controversy, ambiguity, uncertainty, or inadequacy in the current theoretical explanation, you can transition to question three. For example, the controversy and ambiguity in research on workgroup diversity provided an opportunity for a theory elaboration study.[69] These authors summed up the existing literature. As per question three, the skepticism and mixed results provided a basis for them to consider collecting additional data to integrate with existing theory to develop, enhance, or extend existing theory.

Question 3: Is There Potential to Collect Additional Data to Integrate with Existing Theory to Develop, Enhance, or Extend Existing Theory?

Theory elaboration has a dual conceptual-empirical and inductive-deductive focus. Thus, if the research context is such that, for example, new data are unlikely to lead to inductive theorizing. You may be required to adopt a purely deductive theory development perspective. On the other hand, if there is the possibility of collecting new data that would allow for both inductive and deductive theorizing, theory elaboration will allow for contrasting, specifying, and structuring theoretical constructs and relations to more accurately account for and explain empirical observations to advance existing theory. For example, one author collected rich multi-source data (e.g., interviews, technology licensing office archives, patent records, financial records) to account for the opportunity identification processes adopted by eight entrepreneurial teams, all exploiting the same MIT invention (i.e., 3D printing technology).[70] His access to a novel setting (with eight different entrepreneurial teams, all with access to the same technology) and a contested theoretical base for entrepreneurial opportunity identification (i.e., neoclassical equilibrium, psychological, and Austrian theories) provided a valuable opportunity. He collected and analyzed data that allowed him to integrate empirical insights with existing theory on opportunity discovery to enhance and extend theory. This result could only have occurred with the theory elaboration approach. A more traditional theory testing approach couldn't be used due to the limited number of teams with access to the exact same technology and the intricacies of each team's opportunity discovery processes. Neither would theory generation have been appropriate, as there was already an established (albeit contested) theory base for explaining opportunity discovery. Hence, adopting a theory elaboration approach allowed for refining and clarifying the existing theory.

HOW TO CONDUCT A THEORY ELABORATION STUDY

Theory elaboration aims to improve existing theory's accuracy in *accounting for and explaining empirical observations*. It's a discovery process in which you *conceptualize* and *execute empirical research.* Like with theory testing, the process uses a pre-existing model. But rather than testing these ideas to (dis)confirm hypotheses, theory elaboration uses pre-existing conceptual ideas or a preliminary model to provide a foundation for a new study.[71] Accordingly, theory elaboration requires that you are familiar with the existing research and design to conduct a study that builds on what has been done before.

Five Ways to Advance Theory

There are five ways to advance theory as part of a theory elaboration study. Advancements may take place in one of five different forms.[72] First, you may improve theory through enhanced **construct validity** such that constructs are more clearly defined and distinguishable from similar constructs. Second, theory advancement occurs when construct scope is adequately captured to reflect the phenomenon in question. Third, theory may be improved when proposed relations have greater *logical adequacy* such that a relationship's implicit or explicit logic is specified. Fourth, you can improve theory if associations have greater *empirical adequacy* such that they better reflect realities. The final way you can improve theory is when theoretical relations have greater explanatory potential and **predictive adequacy** such that they can more accurately explain and predict outcomes of interest. A theory elaboration study should address at least one or more of these five criteria for theory advancement. All criteria involve specifying constructs, relations, and processes at the conceptual level and empirically assessing the fit of those relations.

Implementation Approaches and Tactics

This section identifies the three broad implementation approaches and seven specific tactics that you can use to elaborate theory. It also explains how each broad approach advances theory differently.[73] In addition, it offers "implementation guidelines" highlighting when each tactic will be most suitable and beneficial given a particular research context and purpose. In short, the material in this section offers concrete and actionable guidelines regarding how to conduct a theory elaboration study.

As a preview, here is a brief, high-level summary of the three implementation approaches and seven tactics to be described below. First, a **contrasting** approach to theory elaboration improves the logical and empirical adequacy of the theory. This is done by observing constructs and relations in different settings and levels of analysis. Specific tactics involve horizontal or vertical contrasting.

Second, a **construct specification** approach improves construct validity and scope. It involves identifying or refining theoretical constructs to reflect empirical realities more accurately. As a result, it creates more precise, more useful constructs and a better understanding of the nature of relations involving those constructs. Specific tactics entail creating new specifications or construct splitting.

Third, the **structuring** approach improves an existing theory's explanatory potential and predictive adequacy. It entails describing and explaining theoretical relations to align with empirical observations more accurately. Structuring tactics involve specifying or refining individual relations, sequences, or recursive structures. It may focus on identifying relations that have not previously been identified or explaining complex relations related to sequential or repeated interactions that have not been fully considered in prior theory.

Table 3.2 summarizes each approach and the tactics you can use as part of a theory elaboration study.

Contrasting

Contrasting is a theory elaboration approach in which the application of a theory in one setting is compared with the application in another. Contrasting theoretical constructs and relationships across different contexts allows you to understand better a theory's nature to determine which aspects are generalizable and context-specific. Contrasting may be done horizontally across different organizational, industry, or geographical contexts or vertically across varying levels of analysis.

TABLE 3.2 ■ How to Conduct a Theory Elaboration Study: Implementation Approaches and Tactics			
Implementation Approaches and Specific Tactics	**Graphical Representation**	**Fundamental Features**	**Primary Theory Advancement Purpose**
CONTRASTING			
Horizontal contrasting		Contrasting observations across different contexts	Improving logical and empirical adequacy
Vertical contrasting		Contrasting observations across different levels of analysis	Improving logical and empirical adequacy
CONSTRUCT SPECIFICATION			
New specification		Identifying and defining new constructs	Improving construct validity and scope
Construct splitting		Identifying a need to break a broad construct into specific constructs	Improving construct validity and scope
STRUCTURING			
Specific relations		Defining/redefining a specific relation between two constructs	Improving explanatory and predictive adequacy
Sequence relations		Explaining a sequence of events or relations	Improving explanatory and predictive adequacy
Recursive relations		Accounting for a recursive relation between two or more entities over repeated interactions	Improving explanatory and predictive adequacy

Source: Adapted from Fisher & Aguinis (2017). Reproduced with permission.

Horizontal Contrasting. Horizontal contrasting is the process of examining how an existing theoretical insight fits in a new context. For example, a theory is often developed inductively from data within a specific setting or deductively with a defined context as a boundary condition. One can examine how it fits with or explains data collected from a different context to advance that theory.[74] Replications and differences that emerge allow a theory to be advanced. In horizontal contrasting, the level of analysis (e.g., individual, team, organization, or field) remains constant across comparisons, but the context for comparison varies.

Example: Theory Elaboration on Institutional Change

Some authors used a theory elaboration perspective to compare and contrast theoretical insights based on prior research. The topic was institutional change initiated by organizations where the organization was at the center of a mature field. The authors of the elaboration study looked at that same outcome data—institutional change—but when it was initiated by actors (rather than organizations) on the periphery of an emerging field (rather than the center of a mature one).[75] The key output from horizontal contrasting is the generalization of aspects of a theory to a new context and a deeper understanding of how the elements of a theory vary when applied in a different context.

Vertical Contrasting. Vertical contrasting compares a theory developed at one level of analysis with data gathered at another to see if the theory can still describe the constructs and relations. Adapting theory developed for one level of analysis to examine phenomena at another level is prevalent in social and behavioral science research.[76] Examples include individual-level concepts adapted to explain organizational-level activities, including organizational learning,[77] organizational decision-making,[78] and organizational identity.[79] When transferring a theoretical perspective across levels of analysis, it is essential to consider which aspects of the theory function similarly in the new and old setting[80] and which elements of the theory change across levels.

Example: Theory Elaboration on Cognition

Some authors used the theory of cognition, traditionally an individual-level construct, to examine organizational responses to technological change.[81] The cognition literature provided an initial framework to examine how a top management team collectively interpreted external technological changes and how such interpretations constrained organizational behavior and impacted the development of a firm's capabilities. The output of vertical contrasting is new theoretical advancements that generalize a theory beyond prior applications and describe nuanced theoretical differences as the theory gets adapted across levels of analysis.

The horizontal or vertical contrasting tactics allow you to improve an existing theory's logical and empirical adequacy. Logical adequacy can be assessed by scrutinizing the fundamental nature of existing theoretical relations across different settings and varying levels of analysis. Do they make sense? Do they hold? Whether they hold or change may clarify the true mechanisms driving that relation. In terms of advancing the empirical adequacy of a theory, you will be able to ensure it applies the way it should. "There either must be more than one object of analysis, or that object of analysis must exist at more than one point in more than one point in time."[82] So, by examining whether a theory holds up empirically across different contexts through horizontal or vertical contrasting, theory elaboration can enhance the empirical adequacy of the theory. In sum,

Implementation Guideline #1: If the primary research focus is to improve an existing theory's logical and empirical validity, then a contrasting approach and tactics can be employed as part of a theory elaboration study.

Construct Specification

Construct specification is a theory elaboration approach in which a theoretical construct is specified or refined according to insights that emerge from the data. For example, based on empirical work, new constructs may emerge, or an existing construct may be split into two of more constructs. Both types of construct refinement can improve a theory.

New Specifications. You can advance existing theory by identifying and defining constructs that have yet to be considered. Constructs are the theoretical units approximated or observed in the empirical world. When you consider clear constructs, you can think of robust categories that extract a phenomenon into precise distinctions that a community of researchers can understand.[83] The more constructs we know, the more potential we have for uncovering their relationships—and theory is all about uncovering causal relationships between constructs. Therefore, identifying and defining previously unspecified constructs creates opportunities to recognize new theoretical relations that accurately depict reality. Conducting a theory elaboration study enables you to identify new constructs in an empirical setting. A grounded theory approach is one way to do so.[84]

Example: Construct Specification in Sensegiving

Some authors used theory elaboration to identify and describe the construct of sense giving—"the process of attempting to influence the sensemaking and meaning construction of others toward a preferred redefinition of [organizational] reality."[85] Sense-giving was inducted using a grounded theory approach to complement the existing theoretical concept of sensemaking in a strategic change context. Without applying the existing theory on sensemaking and strategic change, the recognition and specification of the sense-giving construct may never have come about.

Construct Splitting. Sometimes, theory can be advanced by splitting an existing construct into two more new ones. For example, scholars may initially propose and develop broad constructs to achieve theoretical parsimony,[86] but when examining how a construct behaves, you may see contradictory results. Digging in further, you may see these contradictions are due to differences in the construct's dimensions you did not previously see but are differentially affecting relationships and outcomes. By splitting the construct into two or more constructs, we distill differences that allow a more accurate portrayal of each. This enhances the validity and scope of the construct, and it may become easier to account for outcomes of interest.[87]

Example: Construct Splitting in Workgroup Diversity

Some authors used existing theories on workgroup diversity to examine diversity perspectives and workgroup effectiveness in three diverse professional services firms.[88] Through an in-depth analysis of individual interview data, they identified three distinct workforce diversity perspectives which each had implications for how well teams performed: the integration-and-learning perspective, the access-and-legitimacy view, and the discrimination-and-fairness perspective. Their research suggested that these different diversity perspectives impacted (1) the way people managed and expressed tensions related to diversity, (2) whether members of underrepresented groups felt respected and valued, and (3) how individuals interpreted the meaning of their racial identity in their workplaces. Therefore, by identifying and specifying different perspectives on workforce diversity, these authors were able to explain prior contradictions in the research on cultural diversity and workforce outcomes. This example illustrates how identifying and defining unique dimensions of an existing construct can refine theory. More accurate theoretical linkages can be proposed by specifying and splitting constructs, and previous social and behavioral science research inconsistencies can be resolved. This improves the validity and scope of the construct.

Adopting a construct specification approach to theory elaboration allows you to specify new constructs or split existing constructs based on observed empirical realities. Such tactics can enhance the construct validity and construct scope of existing theory. You enhance construct scope and validity when you clearly define a new or revised construct, and this construct is distinguishable from other similar constructs, increasing discriminant validity.[89] Construct splitting may enhance discriminant validity by more clearly distinguishing between different constructs. Theory is, therefore, advanced when constructs are refined such that they sufficiently but parsimoniously capture and reflect the phenomenon in question. The tactics of new construct specification or construct splitting empower you to improve the accuracy of existing constructs, advancing existing theory. In sum,

Implementation Guideline #2: If the primary focus is to improve a construct's validity and scope, then the construct specification approach and tactics can be employed as part of a theory elaboration study.

Structuring

Structuring is a theory elaboration implementation approach in which theoretical relations are elaborated upon to accurately describe and explain empirical observations. A structuring tactic to theory elaboration may focus on identifying relations that have not previously been identified or explaining complex relations related to sequential or repeated interactions that have not been fully considered in prior theory.

Specific Relations. One tactic to improve or advance a theory is identifying and describing specific relations between constructs that have not previously been described or identifying and describing the mechanisms that underlie known relations. You can see a theory as a system of constructs and variables where: (1) constructs are related to each other by propositions, and (2) variables are related by hypotheses.[90] Theory elaboration enables you to hone in on the relation between two (or more) constructs or variables to isolate and understand how variance in one accounts for variance in another.[91] Yet researchers seldom account for all the variance in an outcome variable, and the mechanisms driving key relations between variables often need to be better understood.[92] The structuring approach to theory elaboration enables you to use existing theory to move from a direct and linear relationship to moderation, mediation (through a new construct), and non-linear relationships. It also allows you to specify previously unspecified relations between constructs, or isolate and unpack the mechanisms driving known relations. For example, let's return to the stream of research on institutional change. Prior research had drawn attention to the relationship between a central field position and institutional change,[93] but the antecedents and mechanisms of this relation were poorly understood. The authors conducted a theory elaboration study to build on their prior understanding to specify which central actors in a field are more likely to institute change and isolate the mechanisms that drive such change.[94]

Sequence Relations. Another tactic for elaborating theory is through the examination of sequence effects. Many theories provide "explanations for phenomena in terms of relations among dependent and independent variables (e.g., more of X and more of Y produce more of Z)."[95] However, some situations must be understood considering the temporal ordering and probabilistic interaction between variables. Therefore, process theories that "provide explanations in terms of the sequence of events leading to an outcome (e.g., do A and then B to get C)" can provide an enriched and more valid perspective of reality.[96] Although conducting research that accounts for the temporal ordering of events is typically complex and challenging, theory elaboration is useful for examining such interactions over time and their effects on key outcome variables. Furthermore, when examining temporal processes, organizing data using existing theoretical constructs is often useful to gain new theoretical insights.[97] Hence, a theory elaboration tactic that utilizes existing theory to analyze data and develop new theoretical perspectives can be highly productive.

Example: Sequential Relations in Organizational Change

Some authors used theory elaboration to expand insights into organizational change by accounting for different sequential learning processes between organizations that successfully implemented new routines and those that did not.[98] They collected and analyzed qualitative and quantitative data on the learning and change processes and outcomes in multiple hospitals implementing innovative new cardiac surgery technology. Using extant theory on organizational learning and change as a theoretical base, they identified and categorized each hospital's learning and change processes. Their results reflect consistent differences in learning sequences between hospitals that successfully and unsuccessfully implemented the new technology. If the authors had not used extant theory to identify learning and change processes, their task of uncovering the temporal effects of organizational change would have been significantly more challenging. Similarly, if they had not collected and analyzed rich qualitative and quantitative data, they would not have accurately captured longitudinal effects. A sequence structuring tactic as part of a theory elaboration study provided them with the unique opportunity to integrate process and variance elements of organizational change.

Recursive Relations. A theory elaboration perspective can advance theory by accounting for and describing a theoretical model's recursive relations between different constructs. While the concept of interaction (i.e., moderating effects) is commonplace in theories, it is less common to examine what happens with repeated interaction between two constructs over some time. Using qualitative and quantitative data to capture and analyze an unfolding relation between two constructs as they interact repeatedly may enhance scholarly understanding of the nature of such a relation. For example, it is often the case that an existing theory may already reflect a relation between two constructs. Yet, the recursive nature of the relation between such constructs is often poorly understood or ignored. Therefore, a prior theoretical model can serve as a basis for designing and conducting a study to examine how a relation develops and evolves as two (or more) constructs repeatedly interact over time. Two kinds of recursive interactions can be examined in a theory elaboration study: dyadic interactions between actors or entities and multilevel interactions between constructs operating at different levels of analysis.

> **Example: Recursive Relations in Cognition and Capabilities**
>
> Research on cognition and capabilities exemplifies multiple, multilevel interactions between constructs over time.[99] The authors used a theory elaboration perspective to examine the relationship between managers' understanding of the changing world around them and the accumulation of organizational capabilities over time. Through their in-depth study of Polaroid, they identified that managerial cognitive representations direct organizational search processes, which influence the accumulation of organizational capabilities. Furthermore, accumulated organizational capabilities impact managerial cognitive representations and perceptions as they seek to make sense of a continually changing environment. Hence, a theoretical understanding of recursive relationships between managerial cognitions, organizational capabilities, and firm inertia was derived.

A structuring approach to theory elaboration allows you to improve an existing theory's explanatory and predictive adequacy. A theory's **explanatory adequacy** depends upon the specificity of assumptions regarding objects of analysis and the scope and parsimony of related propositions.[100] Predictive adequacy is the degree to which hypotheses and propositions approximate reality. These can be improved using a structuring approach better to understand specific, sequence, and recursive relations. With this understanding, the true nature of the interconnections between constructs, and the mechanisms driving those interconnections, can be more explicitly captured in social and behavioral science theories. With improved clarity on the true nature of construct relationships and mechanisms, the scope and parsimony of propositions can be improved. Qualitative research may be better suited to explain the adequacy of a theory than quantitative research (i.e., qualitative research may be better at finding and explaining causal relations, while quantitative methods may be better when you want to test these relations).[101] Hence, the structuring approach to theory elaboration can substantially enhance an existing theory's explanatory and predictive adequacy. In sum,

Implementation Guideline #3: If the primary focus is to improve an existing theory's explanatory and predictive adequacy, then the structuring approach and tactics can be employed as part of a theory elaboration study.

This section has described three broad approaches and seven specific tactics you can use as part of a theory elaboration study. Although each tactic is independently described, employing more than one in a single study is common and desirable. In other words, these tactics are not mutually exclusive because, as summarized in Table 3.2, they accomplish different yet complementary goals to advance theory.

Relation Between Theory Elaboration and Other Ways of Theorizing

We have gone through implementation tactics for various ways to consider data, constructs, and their relations. Theory elaboration is related to but differs from other methodological approaches as described next.

Theory Elaboration and Grounded Theory

First, consider the relationship between theory elaboration and grounded theory. Grounded theory may serve as a form of theory elaboration in well-done studies. It is an ongoing and recursive theory development, testing, and elaboration process. The development of grounded theory was an antidote to so-called "great man" sociological theories, which were so distant from empirical reality that they were virtually resistant to empirical testing or examination.[102] This approach sought a compromise between complete relativism and extreme empiricism. It tried to articulate a middle ground where you could use systematic data collection to develop theories that contribute to interpreting the reality of individuals in social settings.[103] In so doing, you should focus on linking empirical observations and interpretations with substantive (i.e., existing) theory in formulating and generating grounded theory.[104] Common misconceptions are that grounded theory allows you to ignore prior research in formulating a study or that grounded theory may be used to test predefined hypotheses.[105] Neither option is true. Just as theory elaboration requires you to be aware of existing theory and to build on but not explicitly test the existing theory, so does grounded theory. A grounded theory design is a potentially useful way to conduct a theory elaboration study,[106] yet not all theory elaboration studies necessarily use a grounded theory design. An **ethnomethodological study** of succession events in an emerging organization provides a salient example of how a grounded theory research design may be used to extend and elaborate prior theory.[107] Specifically, the author used a grounded theory design to examine and make sense of succession events in a university organization. This allowed the researcher to elaborate theory of organizational leadership succession in ways that would otherwise remain uncovered.

Theory Elaboration and Abductive Reasoning

Second, consider the relationship between theory elaboration and **abductive reasoning**. Abductive reasoning refers to reasoning that forms and evaluates hypotheses to make sense of puzzling facts.[108] You can find examples of abductive reasoning in medical diagnosis, fault diagnosis, and archaeological reconstruction.[109] Abduction was initially described as using known rules to explain a fact or observation but was later broadened to include making up new rules to explain surprising facts and observations.

Example: Theory Elaboration and Abductive Reasoning

Some authors contrasted abduction with other forms of reasoning by pointing out that "deduction proves that something *must* be; induction shows that something *is* operative; abduction merely suggests that something *may be*."[110] Even though abduction is a valuable way to advance theory,[111] its practical application for that purpose is less clear. Some have complained that this way of theorizing (abductive reasoning) is too permissive to extract theory from findings.[112] Theory elaboration, which may be viewed as abductive reasoning, provides an actionable and tangible set of guidelines to use abductive reasoning to advance theory.

Given the previous description, theory elaboration differs from abduction for theory advancement. Some authors described an interpretive abductive process for theory advancement that captures everyday common sense terms social actors use.[113] Those terms are then used with social actors' accounts of their experience to develop social scientific descriptions that provide the basis for new or revised theories. Theory elaboration differs from this interpretive abductive process in that theory elaboration starts with an existing theory, which is used to examine empirical realities to identify where such theory falls short so that it can be elaborated. So, although theory elaboration may be viewed as a type of abductive reasoning, it differs in its starting point from the interpretive approach to abductive reasoning.[114] This, however, does not preclude theory elaboration from fitting in with the broader philosophy of abductive reasoning and hence being viewed as a form of abduction.

HOW TO BRIDGE LEVELS OF ANALYSIS TO IMPROVE THEORY

In physics, one of the biggest challenges and critical issues is integrating the laws that explain the behavior of small objects (i.e., quantum theory) with the laws that explain the behavior of large objects (e.g., relativity theory).[115] Such integration would lead to a "grand relativistic quantum field theory." In this section, we use the discipline of management as an example to look at how the field of social and behavioral science, more broadly, faces a similar challenge to that of physics. As we review what this looks like for social and behavioral science, consider the parallels to your discipline. Are there discrepancies in the knowledge presented at different levels? Does this affect the implications for your domain? The question is how to integrate theories that explain phenomena at the individual or group level of analysis (e.g., goal setting) with theories that explain phenomena at the organizational level of analysis (e.g., the resource-based view of the firm) to create a "grand organization theory."

The modern social and behavioral science field began with an integrated focus as exemplified in Frederick Taylor's (1911) *The Principles of Scientific Management*, which examined how individual performance improvements could lead to great gains at the organizational (i.e., bottom line) level of analysis. Yet, as the field has developed, social and behavioral science specialization has led to a divide between what some label micro and macro research domains. Social and behavioral researchers typically specialize in either micro (e.g., individuals, teams) or macro (e.g., organizations, industries, countries) domains. This divide is further reflected by the preference to publish in either macro (e.g., *Strategic Management Journal*) or micro (e.g., *Journal of Applied Psychology*) journals. Not only do micro and macro scholars have differing areas of interest, but the disparities extend to the articles they write. For example, the journals publishing the articles differ in many characteristics, including average article length, acceptance rates, and even the average number of coauthors per article.[116]

Evidence of a divide between micro and macro domains is also reflected by the sometimes divergent research design, measurement, and data analysis techniques used across these domains.[117] This divergence can even appear when the methodological procedures are identical; yet researchers from different disciplines use different symbols and labels. This leads to a lack of communication between micro and macro researchers and even confusion and misunderstandings. For example, macro researchers, following econometrics and time-series terminology, refer to a "fixed effect," while micro researchers, following growth modeling language, refer to the same phenomenon using the label "random effect."[118]

The micro-macro divide may play a role in another important issue: the science-practice divide.[119] Practitioners who face day-to-day challenges are solving problems involving all levels of analysis. For example, a practitioner may be interested in performance issues at the organizational and individual levels of analysis. However, suppose social and behavioral science research addresses only the organizational or individual levels. In that case, practitioners will believe that social and behavioral science research lacks relevance and "does not matter."[120] This divide may be furthered by teaching focusing on individual (i.e., organizational behavior and human resources) or organizational (i.e., strategic management and entrepreneurship) issues.

It has been noted that researchers and practitioners have different goals,[121] and the same might be said of micro and macro researchers. But diversity research shows that going beyond surface-level differences with a more detailed and nuanced analysis can reveal more commonalities than differences,[122] and the same applies here: macro and micro research share significant similarities, which suggests bridging gaps between them is both possible and promising. Moreover, micro and macro domains are similar beyond a fundamental interest in organizations. For example, while a macro researcher may study CEO decisions and top management teams to understand the determinants of organizational survival, performance, and organizations, most introductory organizational behavior (OB) textbooks note in their first chapter that OB covers individual, group, and organizational levels. Also, a rich history concerning individual decision-making and group and team dynamics is reflected in OB research. The following section illustrates the micro-macro gaps across areas and what leading authors in each of these areas think about these gaps.

Examples of Micro-Macro Gaps in Need of Bridging: Useful, Specific, and Actionable Suggestions for Future Research

Corporate Governance

There is a need to improve theory in **corporate governance** research. There is an absence of multilevel research examining the relationship between the composition of a firm's board of directors, the dual role of serving as a firm's Chief Executive Officer (CEO) and board chairperson concurrently, and the firm's financial performance. The corporate governance literature does not provide evidence that board composition and board leadership are related to a firm's financial performance regardless of how performance is operationalized. To address this lack of evidence and bridge a micro-macro gap, multilevel research could examine the relationship between board composition (individual level), board leadership structure (group level), and firm performance (organizational level).[123]

Entrepreneurship

Entrepreneurship is another area that needs to bridge the micro-macro gap. Specifically, more multilevel theory on individuals' decision-making in an entrepreneurship context is required. To understand decisions about entrepreneurship tasks (e.g., firm emergence activities, hiring key personnel, selecting venture capitalists), conjoint analysis can capture individuals' decision processes and decompose them into underlying structures. For example, using metric conjoint analysis or policy capturing methodology along with hierarchical linear modeling, you could identify (a) common decision policies among samples of individual entrepreneurs and (b) individual differences as moderators of these common decision policies. Moreover, individuals are embedded within contexts (e.g., country). Entrepreneurs' decisions must therefore be examined across the following micro and macro levels: entrepreneurship decision (level 1), individuals' decision policies (level 2), and country (level 3). Finally, intraindividual differences (e.g., an entrepreneur's change in emotion) may exist when making entrepreneurship decisions. Thus, the relationship between situational context and an entrepreneur's decision policies must also be examined from a multilevel perspective.[124]

Applied Psychology and Human Resources Management

There is also a need to bridge a micro-macro gap in applied psychology and strategic HR management research. Workforce differentiation means the same job may contribute to strategic success in different ways within and across firms depending on its location within the firm's strategic capabilities. Strategic capabilities are bundles of information, technology, and people needed to implement a firm's strategy. To bridge a micro-macro gap, future multilevel theory could focus on workforce differentiation antecedents and consequences to understand the causal processes that link investments in HR management systems with a firm's performance. This multilevel research would include developing new measures of organizational strategy, strategic capabilities, strategic jobs, and workforce differentiation.[125]

Management

Organizational research is less divided along micro and macro lines than is currently assumed. Instead, the existing bridge between micro and macro domains needs regular maintenance. Furthermore, multilevel organizational thinking is native among organizational scientists, and there is a need to continue to train and develop a community of scholars who theorize and study multilevel aspects of organizations. Therefore, these actionable suggestions for bridging are refinements to existing processes. First, you can be explicit about the rationale and implications of using selected theoretical frameworks, allowing precision and clarity in integrating information across levels. Importantly, this clarity can prevent potential confusion with terminology and relationships between constructs. Another option is to conduct systematic literature reviews from a multilevel perspective. This synthesis helps to present a digestible, well-rounded understanding of a domain. Finally, you can conduct computer simulation studies to understand multilevel organizational processes that cannot be examined with other traditional research methods.[126]

Key Questions Related to Methodological Issues to Help Guide Bridging Efforts

While social and behavioral science theory has significantly progressed in bridging micro and macro domains, much work remains. In addition, future research could address other key theories that have the potential to bridge micro and macro management research areas but have yet to see such integration in the existing literature. The following critical questions related explicitly to methodological issues will help guide future micro-macro bridging efforts in social and behavioral science research:

- What are some best-practice recommendations in terms of research design, measurement, and data-analytic approaches that have the potential to bridge micro and macro research domains in social and behavioral science?

- What are some additional illustrations of how particular methodological approaches can effectively bridge micro and macro research domains?

- What unique epistemological approaches can be used to integrate micro and macro research domains?

- What are some novel methodological approaches for construct measurement that span a broad spectrum of micro and macro research?

- What are some ways of integrating qualitative and quantitative (or inductive and deductive) approaches with the potential to bridge micro and macro research domains?

This chapter has provided the tools to create new theories and ensure your research makes a relevant theoretical contribution. Chapter 4 will focus on how to plan your research.

DISCUSSION QUESTIONS

1. Why should you care about contributions to theory?

2. What are the critical distinctions in good theory?

3. Who are the main stakeholders you should consider when proposing a new theory, and how would each stakeholder use your theory?

4. When is a new theory needed from a unit theory perspective?

5. When is a new theory needed from a programmatic theory perspective?

6. How can you prune the theoretical landscape?

7. Why is falsification so relevant in theory? How is theory falsification different than failed confirmation?

8. Why is theoretical precision so important?

9. What are the similarities and differences between theory elaboration and other approaches for theorizing (i.e., grounded theory, abductive reasoning)?

10. How can you use theory elaboration to improve theory?

11. What should be your decision process for adopting a theory elaboration perspective? What questions should you answer before moving forward?

12. What are the five ways to advance theory?

13. What are the three implementation approaches and their seven associated tactics?

14. How can you contribute to bridging levels of analysis to improve theory?

15. In what way could methodological issues help you guide future micro-macro bridging efforts in social and behavioral science research?

KEY TERMS

abductive reasoning
construct specification
construct validity
contrasting
corporate governance
deductive theory generation
dysfunctional turnover
ethnomethodological study
explanatory adequacy
functional turnover
good theory
inductive theory generation
Occam's razor

predictive adequacy
programmatic theory
social loafing
strong inference
structuring
theory elaboration
theory generation
theory testing
turnover
unit theory
usable theory
useful theory

NOTES

This chapter is based to a large extent on the following sources:

Aguinis, H., & Cronin, M. A. (2022). It's the theory, stupid. *Organizational Psychology Review.* https://doi.org/10.1177/20413866221080629

Aguinis, H., Boyd, B. K., Pierce, C. A., & Short, J. C. (2011). Walking new avenues in management research methods and theories: Bridging micro and macro domains. *Journal of Management*, *37*(2), 395-403. https://doi.org/10.1177/0149206310382456

Aguinis, H., & Edwards, J. R. (2014). Methodological wishes for the next decade and how to make wishes come true. *Journal of Management Studies*, *51*(1), 143-174. https://doi.org/10.1111/joms.12058

Fisher, G., & Aguinis, H. (2017). Using theory elaboration to make theoretical advancements. *Organizational Research Methods*, *20*(3), 438-464. https://doi.org/10.1177/1094428116689707

4   HOW TO PLAN YOUR RESEARCH

LEARNING GOALS

By the end of this chapter, you will be able to do the following:

4.1   Assess how research planning addresses critical challenges you will face as a social and behavioral science researcher.

4.2   Plan relevant research to reduce science-practice and micro-macro gaps in social and behavioral science.

4.3   Design studies that strengthen causal inference.

4.4   Judiciously implement different procedures for strengthening causal inference in your studies (i.e., counterfactual thinking, matching, control variables, instrumental variables, and quasi-experiments).

4.5   Manage the internal versus external validity tradeoff in your research.

4.6   Judiciously implement methodological tools for managing the internal versus external validity tradeoff (i.e., experience sampling methodology, eLancing, virtual reality).

4.7   Appraise the appropriate use of control variables in your empirical work.

4.8   Formulate your research in a way that follows all required steps in the statistical control process, including when you draft your manuscript.

IMPORTANCE OF RESEARCH PLANNING

Social and behavioral science researchers face fundamental challenges. First, there is a need to produce new knowledge and disseminate it in high-quality journal articles, which today is more difficult than ever.[1] Indeed, you will compete globally for precious journal space, and journal rejection rates hover around 90%.[2] A second and closely related challenge is conducting rigorous research that produces knowledge relevant to individuals, organizations, and society.[3] For example, one of the Academy of Management's strategic objectives is professional impact, which "encourages our members to make a positive difference in the world by supporting scholarship that matters."[4] Similarly, the Society for Industrial and Organizational Psychology's (SIOP's) mission is to "enhance human well-being and performance in organizational and work settings."[5]

You will need more than technical knowledge and expertise on a particular topic to publish your research and ensure its positive impact. Selecting important research questions, adopting adequate research designs, choosing appropriate measures, and undertaking rigorous analyses pertinent to the focal questions are equally important. So, to produce rigorous and relevant results, you must properly plan your research.

When a journal rejects a manuscript, it's most often due to issues arising from poor planning. Sadly, these issues could have been foreseen before researchers went through the costly process of collecting data. Two reasons researchers don't prioritize research planning involve overreliance on data analysis and career incentives. Regarding analysis, there seems to be a belief that using the latest and most excellent statistical tools will overcome deficiencies in theory, design, and measurement. But a poor design cannot be fixed by analysis, however strong. Data analyses are rarely grounds for manuscript rejection from journals; weak analyses can often be improved if all other components are strong. Yet some consider data analysis the most critical aspect of research; perhaps this results from an overemphasis on analytical issues in social and behavioral sciences methodological journals. For instance, a review of almost 200 articles published in *Organizational Research Methods* (ORM) revealed that about half addressed data analysis. In contrast, only 15% addressed research design, and about 35% addressed measurement.[6] Another possible reason for overemphasizing data analysis is that future scholars' methodological training emphasizes data analysis over design. Very few doctoral-level courses address research planning thoroughly—a situation that has not changed much over the past three decades.[7]

Another likely contributing factor to insufficient research planning is related to faculty incentives for publishing a certain number of articles in top journals. Faculty are expected to publish as many articles as possible and as quickly as possible; therefore, the quantity of publications, rather than the quality of content, is sometimes the goal.[8] For a junior researcher whose goals in academia are to land a job, receive a promotion, and secure tenure, publishing in top-tier journals becomes a priority. Unfortunately, this often means cutting corners and not paying sufficient attention to research planning—ironically, leading to the manuscript being rejected.

Benjamin Franklin is credited for admonishing that an ounce of prevention is worth a pound of cure. This chapter applies this sage advice and offers insights that you can use to improve the quality of your empirical work *before data collection*. Each recommendation is accompanied by specific and actionable advice to implement as you strategize and plan empirical studies. The chapter starts by describing how to address an important issue and conduct research with a practical end. It then explains how to design studies that strengthen causal inference and rule out alternative explanations regarding causal relationships. Next, this chapter describes different procedures to enhance causal inference (i.e., counterfactual thinking, matching, control variables, instrumental variables, and quasi-experiments). The chapter then describes the internal versus external validity tradeoff, its implications, and the methodological tools that help you manage it (e.g., experience sampling methodology, eLancing, virtual reality). The final section focuses on choosing control variables appropriately, including an illustration of best-practice recommendations that can be implemented. All these are critical steps in the research planning process that prevent regrets after collecting data.

HOW TO ADDRESS AN IMPORTANT ISSUE AND CONDUCT RESEARCH WITH A PRACTICAL END IN MIND

The **science-practice gap** refers to more connections between the knowledge academics produce and the actionable knowledge organizational decision-makers and policymakers need to address their most pressing challenges.[9]

Example: Science-Practice Gap

The concern about the presence of a science-practice gap is not new.[10] For example, a content analysis of almost 6,000 articles published in the *Journal of Applied Psychology* and *Personnel Psychology* revealed that more research was needed to address issues concerning organizational decision-makers and society. The authors of this review concluded, "If we extrapolate past emphases in published research to the next ten years, we are confronted with one compelling conclusion, namely, that [the social and behavioral sciences]… will not be out front in influencing the debate on issues that are (or will be) of broad organizational and societal appeal."[11]

The science-practice gap is not unique to any social and behavioral sciences domain.[12] For example, in his Academy of Management presidential address, Hambrick (1994) lamented that social and behavioral science scholars have a "minimalist ethos: … minimal visibility, minimal impact." He noted, "Each August, we come to talk to each other [at the Academy of Management's annual meetings]; during the rest of the year, we read each other's papers in our journals and write our papers so that we may, in turn, have an audience the following August: an incestuous, closed loop."[13] The science-practice gap isn't arguing against the utility of basic research without immediate practical application. But if most social and behavioral science research falls into that category, it's unlikely to help fulfill professional associations' explicit mission statements about societal impact.

A study's contribution is amplified when there is a practical end in mind.[14] However, designing research with a practical end is not easy, and perhaps this is why it is infrequent.[15] Nevertheless, some steps increase the probability that a research study will have valuable implications for practice. One of those steps involves adopting a **design-science approach** proposed by Nobel laureate Herbert Simon.[16] Simon highlighted the need to recognize future orientation in applied science research. In other words, applied sciences are concerned with what already is and what *can be*. For example, applied disciplines such as medicine and engineering systematically go beyond describing the present to target creating preferred futures.[17] In the case of medicine, an example of a design-science approach is restoring health to a patient who has cancer. In the case of engineering, a design-science approach would involve creating a more fuel-efficient car. In social and behavioral science, a design-science approach may involve creating employee recruiting procedures that are equally fair for members of all ethnic groups.[18] It could also involve a performance management system that maximizes individual and firm performance and individual growth, personal development, and well-being.[19] Former Academy of Management President Bill Starbuck noted, "People should do [social and behavioral science]… research because they want to contribute to human welfare. Those who are professors… should use [their] abilities for purposes greater than themselves."[20]

What can we do to adopt a design-science approach? First, we should learn what this approach entails and how to implement it. Future generations of scholars must train in how to undertake a design science approach, and part of this training should involve choosing dependent (i.e., outcome) variables that interest organizational decision-makers and policy-makers[21] in addition to researchers. Second, researchers at all career stages can engage in boundary-spanning activities, such as spending sabbaticals in business practice and other organizations. This positions them to "translate" research and to understand research issues important to people outside of academia.[22] Third, students and instructors can participate in executive education to develop relationships with organizational decision-makers and policymakers. This allows a better understanding of the challenges these stakeholders face while working day-to-day in their jobs and organizations. Fourth, more senior scholars can become involved in managerial decision-making by serving on boards of directors.[23] Finally, scholars can target a non-academic audience by writing blogs and publishing articles in outlets such as *Business Horizons*. This can promote awareness of the issues stakeholders outside academic circles find essential.

Conducting relevant research does not mean that you chase contemporary trends. Instead, each action above will allow you to identify critical practical problems and offer valuable solutions for designing preferred futures. The resulting research will have multiple benefits. First, it will help accomplish the explicit strategic objectives of social and behavioral science professional organizations. Still, it will also help elevate the status and prestige of these fields in the eyes of outside stakeholders. These stakeholders include public policymakers, the media, and society at large. But research can't just be relevant; it must also be useful and address causal relations. Knowing causal relations allows organizational decision-makers to anticipate their initiatives' effects. The following section describes how to strengthen causal inferences.

HOW TO STRENGTHEN CAUSAL INFERENCES

Ideally, social and behavioral sciences' theories are causal, describing conditions and events believed to affect outcomes of interest and explaining mechanisms by which these effects occur.[24] To test causal claims, the conditions of empirical studies must justify **causal inferences**. In the philosophy of science, conditions for causality have been debated for centuries.[25]

In social and behavioral science research, three conditions must be satisfied to claim causation[26]: (a) the cause and effect must be associated, (b) the cause must precede the effect in time, and (c) alternative explanations for the presumed causal effect must be ruled out. The first of the three conditions for causality is most often satisfied, as this condition requires that the relationship between the presumed cause and effect differs from zero in the expected direction.[27] The second condition is satisfied less frequently because many studies rely on cross-sectional designs that need to establish the temporal precedence of a hypothesized cause relative to its effect.[28] This shortcoming can be overcome using longitudinal study designs that observe individuals, teams, or organizations on multiple occasions.[29] Finally, the third condition, regarding alternative explanations, is rarely satisfied. Nevertheless, it presents the most significant challenge for establishing causality due to the multitude of alternative explanations that can often account for the relationship between a presumed cause and effect. For this reason, we'll focus on addressing the third condition in this chapter.

You should design studies and implement procedures to strengthen inferences and rule out alternative explanations regarding causal relationships. Of course, implementing an experimental design is ideal for these two purposes, and we address this in detail in Chapter 7. But experiments are expensive and time-consuming, and for some types of social and behavioral science research, not feasible. For example, we cannot randomly assign people to conditions involving different levels of racial discrimination to study their reactions or randomly assign CEOs to firms to research leadership. Ultimately, demonstrating causality is only possible with critical research-design features (e.g., different levels of the independent variables[30]). In other words, "It is not possible to put right with statistics what has been done wrong by design."[31] Although we can't always employ the ideal design, alternative approaches to gathering evidence about causal relations exist. These involve counterfactual thinking, matching, control variables, instrumental variables, and quasi-experimental designs.

Counterfactual Thinking

One effective approach to ruling out alternative causal explanations is the counterfactual model of causation developed by Rubin and colleagues.[32] This model defines a causal effect as the difference in an outcome if the phenomenon had gone through different levels of the antecedent variable (i.e., what is causing the effect) simultaneously. For example, researchers conduct thought experiments to imagine different potential outcomes across levels of a causal variable,[33] such as how a firm's performance would vary with different strategies. This constitutes a **counterfactual** because the same observation unit cannot simultaneously exist at varying levels of a causal variable (e.g., a single firm cannot implement different strategies simultaneously). This approach to causation has become prevalent in psychology and education[34] and is gaining attention in other social and behavioral sciences.[35]

Matching

Matching involves units (e.g., employees, teams, organizations, industries, countries) with similar scores on one or more variables representing alternative explanations for the causal effect of interest.[36] When groups are similar in matching variables but differ on the causal variable, the phenomena represented by the matching variables can be ruled out as alternative explanations for the effect. Although matching has a long history in non-experimental research,[37] it presents several difficulties. These include losing information when continuous matching variables are categorized to form groups, introducing bias when matching variables are measured with error, and issues with forming matched groups when the number of matching variables is large.[38] This last difficulty can be addressed by combining variables into a multivariate composite, which is then used to create groups. This principle underlies propensity scores,[39] constructed using logistic regression to predict group membership based on the matching variables.

Control Variables

Controlling for variables involves accounting for those that could logically represent alternative explanations for the causal effect of interest.[40] The use of control variables is based on the premise that non-random sampling can be viewed as a type of omitted variables problem.[41] In particular, when units are not randomly assigned to levels of a causal variable, they can differ for reasons other than their standing on the causal variable. If these differences correlate with the causal variable and influence the dependent variable, the coefficient relating the causal variable to the dependent variable will be biased.

This situation is illustrated in Figure 4.1. In Figure 4.1a, X is specified as the sole cause of Y, whereas in Figure 4.1b, X and W are portrayed as two correlated causes of Y. If the correct model is shown in Figure 4.1b, the model in Figure 4.1a is estimated such that W is omitted, and the effect of X on Y will be biased by an amount equal to the product of the correlation between W and X times the path from W to Y (i.e., $b' = b + ac$). This bias is removed by controlling for W, as in Figure 4.1b. Note that the effectiveness of this approach depends on the availability of control variables that serve as proxies for the omitted causes of Y that are correlated with X. The choice of control variables should not be taken lightly because adding control variables effectively alter the causal model under investigation. Thus, the role of control variables in a model should be subject to the same conceptual scrutiny as that accorded to the focal causal variables.[42] Control variables are so relevant and used so pervasively that this topic is discussed in detail later in this chapter.

FIGURE 4.1 ■ Models Relating X to Y With and Without the Correlated Cause W: (a) X as a Cause of Y; (b) X and W as Correlated Causes of Y

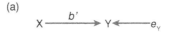
(a)

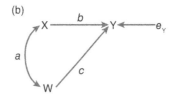
(b)

Source: Aguinis & Edwards (2014).

Instrumental Variables

Another approach to ruling out alternative causal explanations involves using instrumental variables,[43] typically through instrumental variable estimation. This approach is typically used to address endogeneity. **Endogeneity** is when one or more predictors in an equation are correlated with the residual—also called the error term (i.e., variance in the outcome variable that the predictors in the model do not explain).[44] Endogeneity can arise from several sources. One source is the aforementioned omitted variables problem, which occurs when predictor variables correlate with other outcome variable causes. Still, those other causes are not accounted for in the model (i.e., they are omitted). As a result, the variance from the other causes is effectively collapsed into the residual term under the umbrella of unexplained variance. This situation is depicted in Figure 4.2a, where the causal variable X is correlated with the residual e_Y, which includes the causes of Y not explicitly included in the model (the prime on b means this coefficient is biased). Endogeneity can be addressed by finding an instrumental variable for X, which needs to satisfy three conditions: (a) correlated with X, (b) uncorrelated with e_Y, and (c) correlated with Y only through its relationship with X. When an instrumental variable is located, it can be used in a two-stage analysis in which X is regressed on the instrumental variable, the predicted values of X are saved, and these values are then used to predict Y. This approach is depicted in Figure 4.2b, which shows the instrumental variable I as a cause of the predicted value of X (i.e., $\hat{X}$), which in turn is a predictor of Y. Although instrumental variable estimation provides a viable solution

FIGURE 4.2 ■ Models Depicting X as Endogenous and Adding the Instrumental Variable I to Address Endogeneity: (a) X as a Cause of Y That Is Correlated With e_Y; (b) Using I as an Instrumental Variable for X in Predicting Y

(a)

(b)
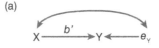

Source: Aguinis & Edwards (2014).

to the endogeneity problem, the conditions that instrumental variables must satisfy are stringent, and failure to meet the requirements can produce biased, inconsistent, and inefficient estimates.[45]

Quasi Experiments

Finally, another option is to use quasi-experimental designs.[46] A quasi-experimental design allows for the non-random assignment of units (again, e.g., employees, teams, organizations, industries, countries) to different conditions. It can also allow for the study of naturally occurring (as opposed to controlled) variation in the independent variable. Doing so combines non-experimental field studies and randomized experiments to improve confidence in causal inferences.[47] Quasi-experimental designs are particularly well-suited for social and behavioral science research that examines constructs such as changes in government policy, organizational expansion, innovation, and foreign direct investment decisions.[48] They are also useful when a difference in an outcome due to a change in an independent variable manifests only after some time. Examples of quasi-experiments include the study of risk propensity in foreign direct investment locations,[49] the investigation of the effect of organizational complexity on innovation,[50] and the examination of the impact of cross-cultural experience on opportunity recognition capabilities.[51] Additional examples include how monthly and quarterly earnings estimates might influence a multinational corporation's expansion plans,[52] how knowledge-sharing and innovation spread across local and foreign subsidiaries,[53] and the impact of home-country corporate social responsibility efforts on foreign operations.[54]

In summary, although randomized experiments are often impractical or unfeasible in social and behavioral science research, there are methods available that can help you draw more robust causal inferences from non-experimental research. Therefore, the following section focuses on planning your research to deal with the tradeoff between internal and external validity.

HOW TO BALANCE THE INTERNAL VERSUS EXTERNAL VALIDITY TRADEOFF

Internal validity refers to how conclusions can be made regarding whether one variable causes another. In other words, how confident are you that variable X causes outcome Y? External validity refers to the extent to which you can conclude that a particular effect or relationship generalizes across persons, settings, and time.[55] In other words, how confident are you about the generalizability of a particular relationship beyond, for example, a specific sample, research setting, and set of measures?

As a social and behavioral science researcher, you often face a dilemma. First, research designs that allow for researcher control, random assignment, and the manipulation of variables yield high confidence regarding internal validity but usually need to be stronger regarding external validity. Consider, for example, the limitations of using primarily students as research participants in university laboratory settings. Alternatively, research designs that involve collecting data in naturalistic (i.e., field) settings usually afford greater external validity but less confidence regarding internal validity. For example, consider all the noise in data drawn from larger databases and studies that lack researcher control. So, researchers are put in an uncomfortable position. You can design a causally strong study, but it will likely have a more dubious potential for generalizability across settings. Or, you can create a study capitalizing on large, presumably random, and generalizable samples, but there would be only weak and indirect evidence regarding causal relationships.[56]

The paragraph above used the word "presumably" to note that large sample size does not necessarily equate to generalizability. Reassuringly, the median sample size of articles published in *Strategic Management Journal* (SMJ) was N = 207 in the 1980–82 time period and N = 142 during 1990–92, but then increased substantially to N = 1,282 in the 2000–02 window.[57] However, a content analysis of 437 articles published in the *Academy of Management Journal* (AMJ), *Administrative Science Quarterly* (ASQ), *Journal of Management* (JOM), *Organization Science*, and SMJ found that fewer than one in five studies used a random sample.[58] In other words, the sampling strategy is typically based on data availability—known as *convenience sampling*—raising obvious questions regarding the generalizability of results.[59] As an illustration, even though samples may be large, using organizations drawn from different databases, such as COMPUSTAT versus TRINET, usually leads to different substantive conclusions.[60]

To address these challenges, you should plan studies that maximize internal and external validity and not one at the expense of the other. What can you do to balance tradeoffs between internal and external validity? The solution would have to involve experimental research design features (e.g., temporal sequencing, ability to manipulate variables) and naturalistic research design features (i.e., collecting data in naturally occurring environments instead of artificial settings). Technological advancements have allowed researchers in physics to implement novel research designs that resulted in important theoretical advances. Notable exemplars are the Large Hadron Collider and the James Webb space telescope. Similarly, technological advancements now allow social and behavioral science researchers to implement innovative research designs that will enable us to balance internal and external validity.

Methodological tools that help address the internal/external validity tradeoff include experience sampling methodology, eLancing, and virtual reality. These tools have great potential for advancing social and behavioral science theory because they also address the prominent issue of bridging the micro-macro gap discussed in Chapter 3. While the tools mainly apply to micro-level research, they can also advance theories in macro-level research in fields such as strategy, sociology, education, and political science.[61]

Example: Using Experience Sampling Methodology, eLancing, and Virtual Reality

As an example, these methods can be used to understand micro-foundations of corporate social responsibility—individual perceptions, attitudes, and behaviors that underlie the success or failure of corporate social responsibility policies and practices.[62] They can also be used to understand micro-foundations of human capital—individual behaviors serving as an intermediate mechanism between human resource management policies and practices and firm performance.[63] Similarly, they can be used for questions examining upper echelons, such as why and how top executives behave the way they do and the consequences of such behavior for their firms. Finally, these methods can be used in empirical research that sees strategy as something that people do in organizations, as opposed to something organizations have (i.e., the 'strategy-as-practice' perspective[64]).

Experience Sampling Methodology

Experience Sampling Methodology (ESM), also labeled ecological momentary assessment, allows you to gather detailed accounts of people's daily experiences over time and capture these experiences as they occur in a person's natural environment.[65] As such, ESM allows for a longitudinal examination of the nature and causal directions among the investigated constructs. As discussed above, **temporal sequencing** is necessary for inferring causal effects.[66] In addition, ESM studies have reasonable external validity because they are conducted in a participant's natural setting as they go about their daily activities. Therefore, participants' attitudes, emotions, and behaviors are captured as they occur naturally rather than in artificial laboratory settings that yield an uncertain degree of replicability outside the lab.

eLancing

eLancing, or internet freelancing, is a work arrangement that takes place through an eLancing 'marketplace,' a website that connects individuals seeking work and clients seeking workers. Each of these sites can be used to recruit participants and conduct research. Popular eLancing marketplaces include Amazon Mechanical Turk, Prolific, Upwork.com, freelancer.com, guru.com, and microworkers.com, and they involve millions of people worldwide.[67] Many studies illustrate using the eLancing environment to conduct field experimental research that maximizes internal and external validity.[68] Specifically, a researcher issues a call for work (i.e., experiment), then manipulates variables by changing the nature of the task, composition of teams, or amount and type of information shared with individuals and teams. Then dependent variables, such as team performance or individual job satisfaction with the team, are measured. Thus, eLancing allows you to use random assignment within a natural (i.e., eLancing) work environment.

Virtual Reality

Virtual reality (VR), often called a virtual environment, is a computer-generated, multi-sensory environment in which a user experiences telepresence. **Telepresence**, or full-immersion VR, means that users lose awareness of being present at the site of the human-computer interface and instead feel fully immersed in the VR environment experience.[69] For example, once immersed in a VR environment, users can perform surgery, walk on the surface of Mars, fly an aircraft, or stroll through the Sistine Chapel without being there.[70]

At present, VR is most often used for training (e.g., pilots and surgeons), architectural design (e.g., identifying design problems before actual construction), and entertainment (e.g., virtual worlds) purposes. Virtual reality technology allows us to infer causality by randomly assigning participants to conditions. Still, it also will enable inferences regarding external validity due to participants' immersion in natural (albeit virtual) environments.[71] Moreover, VR can be used to study sensitive topics such as workplace romance and unethical work behaviors. For example, when observed by a user immersed in a simulated organization, you could use VR to study affective and attitudinal reactions to different types of workplace romance (e.g., supervisor-subordinate and peer romances). VR also allows for manipulating other variables, such as a CEO's motives for engaging in unethical behavior (e.g., desire for personal gain versus protecting the company's reputation).

To summarize, technological advancements offer the opportunity to implement research designs that balance internal and external validity tradeoffs. Experience sampling methodology, eLancing, and VR are three examples of such innovative research tools. These innovations have allowed for important and meaningful theoretical progress in several research domains (e.g., stress, job satisfaction, personnel selection and placement, training and development, and team dynamics) and have great potential for domains such as **upper echelons**, micro-foundations, and **strategy-as-practice**,[72] among others.[73] In addition, these useful methodological tools for micro researchers can also be useful for macro researchers wishing to reinforce causal inferences.

The final topic discussed in this chapter has gathered much attention and is critical in research planning: the appropriate use of control variables.

HOW TO CHOOSE CONTROL VARIABLES

Because most social and behavioral science researchers use passive observation designs more frequently than any other type of design (i.e., data are collected without any type of researcher intervention or manipulation of independent variables), alternative explanations cannot be eliminated using study design features like they can with experimental and quasi-experimental designs. Instead, as mentioned earlier, observational methods rely on measuring and statistically controlling for alternative explanations. However, using controls is not effective "unless much is already known about which alternative interpretations are plausible, unless those that are plausible can be validly measured, and unless the substantive model used for statistical adjustment is well-specified. These are difficult conditions to meet in the real world of research practice, and therefore many commentators doubt the potential of such designs to support strong causal inferences in most cases."[74]

As illustrated in a comprehensive review of control variables,[75] researchers rarely fulfill the abovementioned criteria. Ironically, this is the same conclusion that other authors derived over 40 years ago when they stated that using control variables is "the commonest methodological vice in contemporary social sciences."[76] The concern then, as it remains today, is whether the observed findings are valid or simply artifacts of including invalidly specified control variables.

As a researcher and research consumer, you should adhere to and insist upon the following requirements. First, there should be (a) a solid conceptual explanation of why the control must be instituted; (b) a robust conceptual explanation of how it may come to influence the substantive variables of interest (both observed and latent), and the hypothesized relations among them; and (c) strong evidence regarding the psychometric properties of the measures used to assess controls—just as strong as the evidence for measures used to assess variables of substantive interest.

It is not infrequent for published social and behavioral science articles to justify the inclusion of one or more control variables with, "So-and-so authors did so in their previous publications, and thus, I must include them as well because I am studying similar phenomena." Another commonly-used rationale is, "We thought it would be prudent to include them just in case they had an unknown effect." However, these reasons are not a substitute for the conceptual evidence needed to indicate if and why the control variables would influence the variables of substantive interest and their associations.[77]

A typical assumption is that the inclusion of control variables, and in particular multiple control variables, is a safer and more statistically conservative approach than not including them.[78] This assumption relies on rather large inferential leaps, but the most significant and frequently violated assumption is that control variables hold theoretically meaningful relationships with predictors and outcomes.[79] Notably, several potential problems exist even if each of the assumptions above is met.[80] For example, the inclusion of control variables not only reduces available degrees of freedom and statistical power and can reduce the amount of explainable variance in outcomes of interest.[81] That is, when control variables are related to the predictor or outcome, results may give the appearance that the predictor is not related to the outcome or is related in an unexpected direction when, in fact, an examination of the **zero-order correlations** may suggest the opposite is true.[82] Such cases can lead to an incorrect conclusion that the predictor is not related to the outcome when, in fact, there is a clear bivariate relationship. On the other hand, by inflating the amount of explainable variance in the outcome, the exclusion of control variables can also lead to an incorrect conclusion that the predictor does relate to the outcome when, in fact, there is no such relationship. Accordingly, the inclusion or exclusion of control variables has important implications for theory and practice: such decisions can change substantive study results[83] and limit the ability to replicate, extend, and generalize a study's findings.[84]

Another potential problem with using control variables, often unacknowledged, is that they alter what is being measured or studied. Specifically, a model including control variables is no longer investigating the relationship between a predictor and an outcome but rather the relationship between a new **residual** predictor and the outcome. Because residual predictors isolate phenomena that typically coexist in reality, you need to be aware that you may be studying a relationship that either does not exist or deviates substantially from actual organizational realities.[85] For example, consider a study that controls for gender and weight when investigating the relationship between height and career earnings. In a published study, only 40% of the original height variance remained. As a result, in the final analysis, height did not represent height as one would typically think of it but rather something more closely aligned to physical proportionality. Consequently, the author of this study noted, "it is quite different to conclude that taller individuals earn more than it is to conclude physically well-proportioned individuals earn more."[86]

As mentioned, using control variables is integral to your methodological toolkit in addressing practical difficulties associated with implementing experimental designs. A review that relied on over 3,500 control variables in almost 600 articles drew useful conclusions: studies should explain how controls relate to focal variables and the theoretical justification for including them.[87]

Explain Why and How Controls Relate to Focal Variables

As evidenced in Tables 4.1 and 4.2, more effort is needed to explain why and how controls relate to focal variables of interest despite relevant and available theoretical options. For example, human capital and relational demography theories appeared explicitly or implicitly in more than two dozen justifications to explain relationships between popular social and behavioral science topics by looking at attitudes (e.g., job satisfaction, commitment) and behaviors (e.g., performance, organizational citizenship behaviors, turnover). **Human Capital theory**[88] proposes that specific individual characteristics such as tenure, education, and work experience positively affect attitudes and behaviors, resulting in accumulated knowledge. Individuals with this knowledge enjoy access to better jobs, more lucrative pay, additional resources necessary for successful task performance, and more significant incentives to remain once in an organization.[89] **Relational demography research**, on the other hand, suggests that employees who share similar qualities with other members of the organization enjoy more pleasant interactions, stronger social integration, and enhanced interpersonal attraction, all evident in work-related attitudes and behaviors.[90] As these theories explicitly reference many of the common statistical controls found in this review, there is an opportunity to improve current practices in control variable justifications.

Provide Theoretical Justifications for Each Control Variable

Instead of offering theoretically-based justifications for using a focal variable, researchers rely primarily on documenting previous empirical relationships or defaulting to the reasoning of "because they might relate." As seen in Table 4.1, established domains such as performance and job satisfaction were used to justify focal variables in roughly 75% of studies. In contrast, newer domains, such as burnout and **leader-member exchange** (LMX), were used to justify fewer than 65% of studies.

TABLE 4.1 ■ Types of Control Variable Justifications Offered Across Popular Social and Behavioral Science Domains

Research Domain	Justification	Citation	Previous	Anticipated	Found	Incremental	Eliminate	Theoretical	Analysis	Process	Multiple
Performance	76%	42%	6%	24%	31%	6%	17%	3%	11%	2%	17%
OCBs	75%	45%	8%	25%	22%	8%	18%	6%	12%	2%	18%
Turnover	79%	39%	11%	32%	24%	6%	18%	7%	13%	5%	21%
Job satisfaction	75%	40%	9%	22%	29%	4%	21%	3%	13%	3%	21%
Organizational commitment	71%	34%	9%	31%	18%	3%	15%	2%	13%	4%	15%
Burnout	60%	36%	1%	10%	31%	4%	20%	1%	13%	–	13%
Personality	75%	45%	1%	21%	30%	8%	17%	3%	10%	3%	11%
LMX	65%	46%	4%	36%	13%	3%	19%	2%	10%	4%	17%
Justice	64%	40%	10%	25%	22%	2%	9%	2%	8%	2%	13%
Affect	63%	37%	1%	34%	19%	6%	15%	5%	7%	2%	15%
Overall	72%	41%	7%	26%	25%	5%	17%	4%	11%	3%	17%

Note. The numbers in this table are not mutually exclusive. Some studies used the same justification for multiple control variables (within a research domain and across domains). The total % within each row only adds up to 100% because some studies used multiple justifications that were not mutually exclusive (except anticipated and found relationships, which were forced into a dichotomy for 99% of studies). Justification = the % of studies offering at least some rationale for the inclusion/exclusion of a control variable. Citation = the % of studies providing one source to justify a control variable. Previous = the % of studies referencing previous research using that variable as a control. Anticipated = the % of studies justifying the inclusion/exclusion of a control by describing an expected relationship between the control variable and a focal domain. Found = the % of studies citing previously found relationships between a control variable and a focal domain. Incremental = the % of studies employing a control variable for incremental and discriminant validity. Eliminate = the % of studies mentioning the desire to eliminate alternative explanations. Theoretical = the % of studies offering a justification that attempts to answer the how and the why control variables relate to a focal domain. Analysis = the % of studies that analyzed their study data to help determine control variable inclusion/exclusion. Process = the % of studies describing (at a minimum) a two-step process for deciding control variable inclusion/exclusion. Multiple = the % of studies using two or more justifications. OCBs: organizational citizenship behaviors, LMX: leader-member exchange.

Source: Adapted from Bernerth & Aguinis (2016).

TABLE 4.2 ■ Control Variable Justification Breakdown by Most Frequent Controls

Control	Justification	Citation	Previous	Anticipated	Found	Incremental	Eliminate	Theoretical	Analysis	Process	Multiple
Gender	63%	41%	6%	20%	24%	1%	13%	2%	13%	2%	12%
Age	63%	41%	7%	21%	25%	1%	14%	2%	11%	3%	14%
Organizational tenure	76%	41%	10%	26%	24%	2%	17%	1%	13%	2%	15%
Education	68%	44%	8%	19%	23%	2%	13%	2%	15%	2%	12%
Organization/group size	73%	38%	9%	32%	23%	5%	4%	4%	16%	5%	14%
Race	70%	50%	9%	25%	25%	1%	17%	6%	12%	6%	18%
Workload/hours	71%	28%	5%	30%	26%	4%	22%	3%	7%	2%	14%
Work experience	70%	31%	5%	35%	21%	2%	17%	5%	8%	4%	17%
Job tenure	68%	53%	9%	20%	33%	0%	22%	10%	5%	0%	18%
Dyadic tenure	66%	46%	9%	33%	13%	1%	11%	0%	7%	0%	5%
Negative affect	92%	66%	7%	25%	42%	8%	52%	8%	7%	0%	45%
Income-related controls	75%	38%	3%	41%	24%	6%	6%	3%	5%	0%	11%
Gender differences	78%	55%	12%	20%	33%	2%	14%	2%	12%	0%	8%
Positive affect	90%	77%	4%	27%	44%	6%	65%	13%	0%	0%	52%
Manager gender	38%	31%	17%	14%	5%	0%	17%	2%	7%	0%	21%

Note. Unless otherwise noted, all variables refer to employees (e.g., employee gender). The numbers in this table are not exclusive. Some studies used the same justification for multiple control variables (across domains). The control variables listed are in descending order starting with the most frequently used variable. Justification = the % of studies offering at least some rationale for the inclusion/exclusion of a control variable. Citation = the % of studies providing at least one source to justify a control variable. Previous = the % of studies referencing previous research using that variable as a control. Anticipated = the % of studies justifying the inclusion/exclusion of a control by describing an expected relationship between the control variable and a focal domain. Found = the % of studies citing previously found relationships between a control variable and a focal domain. Incremental = the % of studies employing a control variable for incremental and discriminant validity. Eliminate = the % of studies mentioning the desire to eliminate alternative explanations. Theoretical = the % of studies offering a justification that attempts to answer the how and the why control variables relate to a focal domain. Analysis = the % of studies that analyzed their study data to help determine control variable inclusion/exclusion. Process = the % of studies describing (at a minimum) a two-step process for deciding control variable inclusion/exclusion. Multiple = the % of studies using two or more justifications.

Source: Adapted from Bernerth & Aguinis (2016).

The information described above and summarized in Tables 4.1-4.2 suggests that the current usage of control variables could certainly improve. The following section describes a series of questions that you can use to plan which control variables to include or exclude. The steps in this process are summarized in Figure 4.3.

Required Steps in the Process of Statistical Control

At the most fundamental level, statistical control should start with a straightforward question: "Why do I want to use statistical controls or think I should use them?" The answer is essential and will guide subsequent questions and actions. The most common response to the crucial question says, "Because I suspect this variable relates to variables studied in my research." With this answer comes the follow-up question: "Is this the only reason for considering using this variable as a statistical control?" If so, without additional rationale, there's no justification for

FIGURE 4.3 ■ Decision-Making Tree Summarizing Sequential Steps in the Process of Selecting Control Variables

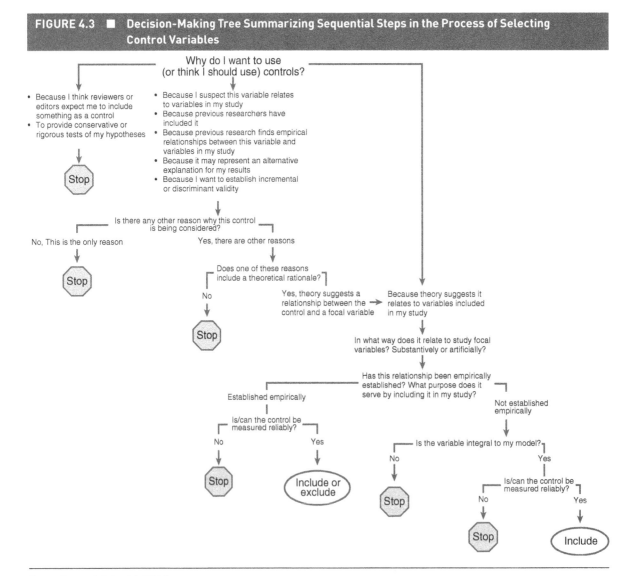

Source: Bernerth & Aguinis (2016).

including that particular control in the study. Other responses to the essential question that require this follow-up question are:

- "Because previous researchers have included such variables in their study."

- "Because previous research finds empirical relationships between this variable and a variable studied in my research."

- "Because it significantly correlates with other variables in my dataset."

- "Because it may represent an alternative explanation for my results."

- "Because it may contaminate my results."

- "Because I want to establish incremental or discriminant validity."

Again, if any of these are the reasons for the initial consideration of a control variable and you don't have an additional rationale, then including that variable as a statistical control is not justified. So, you must always ask the simple follow-up question, "What other reason(s) do I have for wanting to use controls or thinking I should use controls?" Keep asking this question and considering the answer until your justification is supported by theory, and if it can't be, those controls shouldn't be included in the analysis.

There's a response to the essential question that does not justify including a certain variable as a statistical control that's less often made explicit. However, there's reason to think it's familiar: "Because I think reviewers or editors expect me to include something as a control." If that's the reason, there's no need to proceed with the follow-up question; you should stop the process.

Another response is, "Because including these controls provides conservative, rigorous, or stringent tests" of a study's hypotheses. This fallacy was initially debunked years ago,[91] and there's enough accumulated evidence to conclude with certainty that there is nothing conservative or rigorous about including statistical controls.[92]

Suppose you identify a theory justifying the inclusion of control variables at some point during this sequence of questions and answers. In that case, you'll move on to a different set of follow-up questions that we'll discuss later. As shown in Figure 4.3, there's one last possible response, leading to the next set of questions. This response describes a theoretical relationship between a potential control and a focal study variable: "Because theory suggests it relates to variables included in my study." But here, still, you must keep asking follow-up questions: in what way does it relate substantively to your study variables? In what way does it relate artificially (i.e., introduce bias)? Both answers result in a similar follow-up question, but the distinction is important and must be reported explicitly in a manuscript. When theory suggests the control variable plays a role, three sequential questions follow: has this relationship been empirically established in existing research? (This can draw on a response from the earlier question set.) Does including it serves a purpose in the study? Can the variable be measured reliably, and is it? Suppose the potential control already has an empirically established relationship with a study focal variable. In that case, you can justifiably argue that its inclusion creates the opportunity for an incremental advance in theory. On the other hand, if evidence indicates the control variable represents an artificial relationship (e.g., third-party relationship), it would be justifiable, as it could help eliminate alternative explanations to reduce **contamination**[93] (as long as the variable is measured reliably). But note that here, if you want to exclude such variables to instead focus on previously unexplored relationships, that would make sense too. In the case of variables that lack established empirical relationships, these can be either included or excluded depending on how integral they are to your model (and again if they can be measured reliably). Integral variables should be included as either additional focal variables or exploratory variables. Nonintegral variables, and variables that cannot be measured reliably, should be excluded.

If your variables have passed the checks for inclusion, there's an important next step you need to take. In every manuscript you write, you need to clearly and unequivocally acknowledge the sequence of questions and answers you addressed (implicitly or explicitly) to get to this point. This is essential to move the control paradigm forward. It's necessary to describe a process for inclusion or exclusion that features a theoretical justification addressing the what, the how, and the why between controls and focal variables.[94] Similarly, it would be best to be diligent in reporting results. Reporting must include standard descriptive statistics for all controls, including reporting correlations and significance levels,[95] evaluating and describing results both with and without controls, and the reliability of controls. This information is increasingly important given the current variables and justifications existing research offers. That is, if controls (e.g., see positive affect in Table 4.2) are used to rule out alternative explanations, then their measurement needs to be reliable. Otherwise, researchers, reviewers, editors, and a healthily skeptical scientific readership, will not feel confident about parsed-out variance and the stability of regression weights. These practically feasible changes in publishing policy would help ensure that this paradigm shift for control variables begins and is ingrained into our research practices.

ILLUSTRATIONS OF BEST-PRACTICE RECOMMENDATIONS IMPLEMENTATION

Let's look at studies demonstrating how these recommendations might feasibly and practically take shape. Discussing the control variable inclusion or exclusion process openly and transparently is essential. For example, control variables might be introduced with a simple statement such as, "We identified several potentially relevant control variables."[96] That shows which controls were considered and why, and the authors can explain why they chose to either include or exclude those variables in their analysis. Here you would describe the specific reasons by answering the question in the decision tree shown in Figure 4.3 (i.e., "Why do I want to use, or think I should use controls?").

One type of rationale is a potential relationship between the control and a focal variable. You can see one way this might be phrased in the following example, which justifies including several demographic controls by acknowledging, "It was possible that nurses who worked full-time, had enhanced job responsibilities, and were more experienced (as reflected in their tenure or age) might have greater familiarity with hospital work processes that might enhance their confidence about speaking up at work."[97] In a second example of how this might be phrased, other authors noted that they controlled for employee pay "because pay influences turnover through desirability of movement; if the pay is high, alternative employment can be less attractive."[98]

An alternative (or potential additional rationale) refers to previously established empirical relationships. Examples include studies that controlled for employees' workload in the study of emotional exhaustion (and other variables), controlled for job performance and technical levels in the study of turnover,[99] and controlled for job tenure in the study of task performance.[100] These exemplars are particularly useful because, in each case, the authors described the existing relationships and explained why they are likely to exist, clarifying how they play into the study. For example, after describing previous meta-analytic findings, some authors noted, "This positive correlation may be explained by the fact that employees gain more job-relevant knowl-edge and skills as a result of longer job tenure, which thus leads to higher task performance."[101] Other authors continued their justification by explaining, "A heavy workload leads to these negative consequences partially because of the pressure and responsibility attendant on those with such workloads."[102] Finally, as another illustration, another group of researchers reasoned, "We controlled for job performance and technical levels, as the turnover literature highlights that competent and experienced employees have more alternative job opportunities and thus are more likely to quit their current jobs."[103]

Other types of rationale include the desire to eliminate alternative explanations and the desire to establish incremental or discriminant validity. An exemplar of how to describe an incremental/discriminant validity justification, a team of authors noted that the **Big Five traits** are thought to constitute the majority of the domain of personality, and several Big Five traits predict leadership and performance ratings. They noted that narcissism is related to some Big Five traits, so there is the question of concept redundancy. Specifically, narcissism correlates with Extraversion positively and Agreeableness and Neuroticism negatively, though these cor-relations are not especially strong. Moreover, the trait that is the best Big Five predictor of job performance and one of the best predictors of leadership (i.e., Conscientiousness) is generally unrelated to narcissism. For all these reasons, the authors of this study clearly and thoroughly explained why the Big Five personality traits should be statistically controlled in examining the relationships between narcissism, task performance, and contextual performance.[104] An exem-plar of how to explain the elimination of alternative explanations is the following description of why leader-member exchange (LMX) should be controlled for in the study of intelligence and job performance. These authors wrote:

> "We controlled for leader-member exchange to rule out an alternative explanation of any results. Leader-member exchange denotes the relationship quality between an employee and the employee's supervisor… Evidence linking emotional intelligence to the quality of social relationships … suggests that emotional intelligence may be related to leader-member exchange. Moreover, leader-member exchange [a positive relationship with the supervisor as perceived by the employee] is related to job performance…, and supervisors may provide lenient ratings to subordinates with good relationships. Thus, individuals with high emotional intelligence and low cognitive intelligence could have received high ratings because they developed good relationships with their supervisors."[105]

After offering some combination of the answers in the preceding paragraphs, in your manu-script, you must answer the question, "Do these reasons include a theoretical rationale?" This is because a sound control variable explanation necessitates examining and describing the relation-ship between potential controls and focal variables[106]; here, you'll describe the what, the how, and the why, like the examples listed earlier. This step does not need to be overly complex, but it does need to be included regardless of your ultimate decision. For example, a statement as simple as the following is appropriate: "In general, these variables were not significantly correlated with our dependent variables. As neither a strong theory nor previous empirical research suggested their inclusion, they were excluded from the analyses reported here. However, the same pattern of results is found if these variables are included."[107] As an additional illustration of phrasing, other authors state, "However, because tenure in either form was not correlated with withdrawal behaviors, and because the addition of tenure did not change the significance level of any of the results, the results were reported without controlling for tenure."[108]

In summary, combining the illustrations above into a single statement leads to the following template that you can use in your manuscripts:

"We considered several potentially relevant control variables including A, B, and C. Previous empirical research, including a recent meta-analysis by [insert text], suggests a relationship between A and X and between B and X. As theory explains, the relationship between A and X exists as a result of [insert text]. Moreover, B impacts X to the extent that [insert text]. Finally, researchers also suggest a relationship between C and X that is [insert text]. Given these relationships, X may relate to Y not because [insert text], as our theorizing suggests, but rather because [insert text]. Thus, it is important to parse out the variance between these controls and our predictor variable to eliminate alternative explanations and demonstrate the unique relationship between X and Y. That said, examination of the bivariate correlations found in Table XX indicates that A and B are not significantly correlated with X. C is not only significantly related to X, but it relates in a manner consistent with our theory-based expectation that comparison between our hypotheses tests with and without A and B yielded identical results. Thus, to maximize statistical power and offer the most interpretable results, we report the results without controlling for A and B. However, we control for C given the correlations in Table XX and the theory presented in our research."

Overall, you may be discouraged that this review on control variable usage details a need for progress in social and behavioral science over the past decade in this realm. Moreover, researchers often treat statistical controls as an afterthought rather than an integral part of research design and analysis. But on a more positive note, this review's in-depth and actionable nature provides you with direction and best-practice recommendations that will be a useful tool—whether as an author, journal editor, reviewer, or reader. Recent challenges to the credibility of research results[109] show the urgency of implementing research practices that abide by fundamental scientific principles, such as replicability and professional standards. We can continue to build trustworthy research by strengthening our approach to control variables in social and behavioral science research. The decisions for inclusion and exclusion and subsequent processes for implementing those decisions have significant consequences for substantive research conclusions. The recommendations just described will help provide theoretical bases and rationale for control variable usage in the future, which will systematize and increase transparency.

This chapter has provided the tools to plan your research properly. Chapter 5 will focus on the next critical step in the research process: how to collect your sample.

DISCUSSION QUESTIONS

1. What critical challenges will you face as a social and behavioral science researcher?

2. How much does research planning weigh into the reviewers' and editors' decision to reject or accept a manuscript?

3. What are some reasons researchers might not prioritize research planning?

4. How can you address these challenges by planning your study properly?

5. How can you plan research that bridges the science-practice gap in social and behavioral science?

6. What are the three conditions for determining causality?

7. What are the necessary steps in designing empirical studies that strengthen causal inference and rule out alternative explanations regarding causal relationships?

8. If you did not plan your study correctly, is there a way to address the lack of causal inference after collecting the data? Why or why not?

9. You can use different procedures to strengthen causal inference (e.g., counterfactual thinking, matching, control variables, instrumental variables, quasi-experiments). Under what conditions might each be most appropriate?

10. Which of the strategies discussed in this chapter (e.g., experience sampling methodology, eLancing, virtual reality) do you think would be most helpful in managing the tradeoff of internal versus external validity? How about in the context of your research?

11. What is the essential question to ask yourself in deciding whether to use variables as statistical controls in your analysis?

12. What are the typical responses to the essential question that do not sufficiently justify inclusion? What do they have in common?

13. What responses justify including control variables in your study? Which responses do not?

14. Which responses justify excluding potential control variables in your study?

15. What information regarding choosing control variables should you include in a manuscript? How might it be phrased?

16. How can you plan your study to implement all the best-practice recommendations for control variables? Which are the easiest and the most challenging recommendations to implement and why?

KEY TERMS

Big Five traits
causal inferences
COMPUSTAT
contamination
counterfactual
design-science approach
eLancing
endogeneity
Human Capital theory
leader-member exchange (LMX)
matching

relational demography research
residual
science-practice gap
strategy-as-practice
telepresence
temporal sequencing
TRINET
upper echelons
virtual reality (VR)
zero-order correlations

NOTES

This chapter is based to a large extent on the following sources:

Aguinis, H., Ramani, R. S., & Cascio, W. F. (2020). Methodological practices in international business research: An after-action review of challenges and solutions. *Journal of International Business Studies*, *51(9)*, 1593-1608. https://doi.org/10.1057/s41267-020-00353-7

Aguinis, H., & Edwards, J. R. (2014). Methodological wishes for the next decade and how to make wishes come true. *Journal of Management Studies*, *51(1)*, 143-174. https://doi.org/10.1111/joms.12058

Aguinis, H., & Vandenberg, R. J. (2014). An ounce of prevention is worth a pound of cure: Improving research quality before data collection. *Annual Review of Organizational Psychology and Organizational Behavior*, *1*, 569-595. https://doi.org/10.1146/annurev-orgpsych-031413-091231

Bernerth, J. & Aguinis, H. (2016). A critical review and best-practice recommendations for control variable usage. *Personnel Psychology*, *69(1)*, 229-283. https://doi.org/10.1111/peps.12103

5 HOW TO COLLECT YOUR SAMPLE USING SURVEYS AND OTHER MEANS

LEARNING GOALS

By the end of this chapter, you will be able to do the following:

5.1 Explain why a large sample size is only sometimes the best option.

5.2 Choose the appropriate effect size in conducting power analysis.

5.3 Determine an appropriate a priori Type I error (i.e., α) rate for hypothesis testing.

5.4 Use IP analysis to evaluate if your study participants are who you think they are.

5.5 Combine the data you collect with data from existing databases.

5.6 Recommend best practices for working with archival databases.

5.7 Implement a response rate validity framework to assess the appropriateness of your study's response rate.

5.8 Manage the publication bias and the file drawer problem.

IMPORTANCE OF SAMPLE SIZE

One of the most critical parts of your research is the samples you use and how you collect them. Specifically, if your goal is to draw conclusions from a population and not just a sample, you need to consider collecting sample data representative of the population. So, goal is to collect a **probability sample**, meaning that most population members have the same probability of being included in your sample. Doing so allows you to make strong statistical inferences about the whole group from which you draw the sample (i.e., your population). On the other hand, much of our research includes **non-probability samples**, meaning we collect data from a sample to which we have access (e.g., students) or those to sign up voluntarily to be part of our study (e.g., using an online platform). These types of samples are called *convenience samples*. For example, a commonly used type of **convenience sampling** is snowball sampling, which involves study participants recruiting more participants on your behalf (e.g., their friends and coworkers). This chapter gives you the necessary tools to ensure that your samples are appropriate for your research goals ideas and how to avoid common pitfalls.

The chapter starts by describing why a large sample size is not always the best option and addresses the truth and myths about two unwritten rules related to sample sizes. The chapter then explains how you can ensure your study participants are those you think they are. The following section focuses on combining data you collect with data from existing **databases**. This section takes you through the benefits of using archival databases for implementing methodological best practices such as research design and measurement control variables, missing data management, and outlier management. Toward the end of the chapter, you will learn how to evaluate your survey's **response rate (RR)**. We review why RR is important, RR trends over time, the difference between functional and dysfunctional RR, and a useful RR validity framework you can use in your research. Finally, the last section addresses how you can deal with **publication bias** and the **file drawer problem**, which are challenges directly related to the nature of your sample.

WHY LARGE SAMPLE SIZE IS NOT ALWAYS THE BEST OPTION

This section describes and critically analyzes two unwritten rules about sample size commonly used in social and behavioral science research. The unwritten rules were identified through an in-depth analysis of approximately 1,260 articles in journals that publish methodologically sophisticated and rigorous empirical research. These unwritten rules are not appropriate or misused in some way by researchers publishing in these journals. Thus, it is an important and prevalent problem.

This review searched the Method, Results, and Discussion sections for the 1,260 papers to identify authors' statements and justifications involving sample size. As a result, 102 articles (i.e., about 8.2% of all articles included in the review—not as many as one might hope) included a statement in which authors explained how they had chosen the study's sample size, described the consequences of their sample size; or explained or justified a result in relationship to their sample size. Two commonly invoked unwritten rules emerged: (a) determining whether the sample size is appropriate by conducting a power analysis using Cohen's definitions of small, medium, and large effect size; and (b) increasing the a priori Type I error rate for hypothesis testing to .10 because of a small sample size.

The following paragraphs critically analyze these unwritten rules by answering the following questions: Where did these rules come from? What did the attributed sources say about them? How much merit do these rules have? Finally, should you use these unwritten rules in your research?

Unwritten Rule #1: Determine Required Sample Size by Conducting a Power Analysis Using Cohen's Definitions of Small, Medium, and Large Effect Size

Statistical power is of primary concern in statistical analyses: it is the probability of detecting an effect in the population. Statistical power is $1 - \beta$: it determines your ability to find an effect. **Type I error rate** (α) is the probability of results showing an effect that does not exist. **Type II error rate** (β) is the probability of not detecting an effect that *does* exist. Note that Type I and Type II error have an inverse relationship.

Power is crucial because the purpose of conducting tests is to identify effects if they exist. Two key determinants of statistical power are sample size (N) and effect size. The larger the sample size, the higher the statistical power because more data allows more detection opportunities. Similarly, the larger the effect size, the higher the statistical power because a larger effect size is easier to find. A power analysis tells you the likelihood of finding an effect given the size of your sample and the size of your effect; it tells you what sample size is sufficiently large. So, the first step is to decide what effect size you think is appropriate and wish to target.[1]

A common unwritten rule in conducting a power analysis to assess whether one's sample size is sufficiently large is to use Cohen's definitions of small, medium, and large effect size.[2] For instance, a set of authors conducted a power analysis using **Cohen's values**. It concluded that a "power analysis indicated that the power to detect a medium effect with an α level of .05 was 46 percent, and the power to detect a large effect was 86 percent" (p. 394).[3] Others noted that "[s]tatistical power to detect a significant R^2 in the regression analysis was 35% for a small effect (R^2 = .0196, p < .05) and 99% for a medium effect (R^2 = .13, p < .05; Cohen, 1988)" (p. 598).[4] But what did Cohen recommend about the procedures to select a targeted effect size? Did he recommend that researchers use specific values for small, medium, and large effects? Did these values remain consistent over time? How did he come up with these values? Read the text below to learn the answers to these questions.

Cohen noted that "researchers find specifying ES [effect size] the most difficult part of power analysis" (p. 156).[5] To address this issue, Cohen and his coauthors outlined the following three strategies for identifying an appropriate effect size in power analysis: "(1) To the extent that studies that have been carried out by the current investigator or others are closely similar to the present investigation, the ESs found in these studies reflect the magnitude that can be expected; (2) In some research areas an investigator may posit some minimum **population effect** that would have either practical or theoretical significance; and (3) A third strategy is deciding what ES values to use in determining the power of a study is to use certain suggested conventional definitions of small, medium, and large effects… This option should be looked upon as the default option only if the earlier noted strategies are not feasible." (p. 52).[6]

Consider the history behind the conventional definitions of a small, medium, and large effect, which should be used *only if the other strategies are not feasible*. Cohen's first published description of specific magnitudes for effects appeared in his 1962 *Journal of Abnormal and Social Psychology* article. In this article, Cohen did a review and content analysis of articles published in the 1960 volume of the journal. When describing the effect sizes he used for his power analysis, Cohen noted that "the level of average population proportion at which the power of the test was computed as the average of the sample proportions found" and "the sample values were used to approximate the level of population correlation of the test" (p. 147).[7] For the correlation coefficient, Cohen defined .40 as medium because this seems to have been close to the average observed values in the *Journal of Abnormal and Social Psychology*'s articles from 1960. Then, he chose the value of .20 as small and .60 as large. In other words, Cohen's definitions of small, medium, and large effect sizes are based primarily on data from studies published over one year in that specific journal! A few years later, Cohen decided to lower these values to .10 (small), .30 (medium), and .50 (large) because the originally defined values seemed a bit too high.[8] Given the history behind the conventional values for small, medium, and large effects, it is unsurprising that Cohen acknowledged that these definitions "were made subjectively" (p. 156).[9] Yet these benchmarks are now used as an unwritten rule in assessing effect size. In light of the sources invoked to support its use, a critical analysis of this practice leads to the following conclusions:

1. Cohen mentioned that using his admittedly conventional values is only one of three procedures for identifying a targeted effect size for a power analysis to assess whether a study's sample size is sufficiently large.[10] Therefore, this strategy should be used only as

a last resort if the other two preferred strategies are not feasible. Unfortunately, many researchers focus on this procedure to exclude the other two.

2. Cohen noted that his small, medium, and large effect values are subjective. He changed the values for small, medium, and large effects over time with no apparent reason but his personal opinion that these values should be modified downward.

What Should You Keep in Mind About Unwritten Rule #1?

To recap, conducting a power analysis to determine whether a study's sample size is sufficiently large to detect an effect using Cohen's conventional definitions of effect sizes is common. Although Cohen and colleagues suggested three strategies for identifying the effect size for power analysis, most researchers use the effects that Cohen labeled small, medium, and large. Per Cohen's admission, these values are largely subjective. These values were initially derived from a narrow literature review of articles published in the 1960 *Journal of Abnormal and Social Psychology* volume. However, using these values is a pervasive practice, perhaps because it is more convenient than using the other two preferred strategies for identifying targeted effect sizes (i.e., an effect size derived from previous literature or an effect size that is scientifically or practically significant).

The two preferred strategies Cohen described involve the specific research context and domain rather than relying on broad-based conventions. Cohen himself recommended that context should be taken into account in choosing a targeted effect size in a power analysis when he wrote that effect sizes are relative not only to each other but also "to the area of behavioral science or even more particularly to the specific content and research methods being employed in any given investigation" (p. 25).[11] To his first point, Cohen wrote that, for the f^2 effect size, .02 is a "small effect."[12] However, a 30-year review of articles in three major social science journals found that the median effect size is only $f^2 = .002$ (i.e., ten times smaller than what Cohen labeled as a small effect).[13]

To his second point, it is generally not appropriate to equate Cohen's "small" (which requires a large n to be detected) effect with an "unimportant effect" and Cohen's "large" effect (which needs a smaller n to be detected) with "important effect." In some contexts, what seems to be a small effect can have significant consequences. For example, an effect size of 1% regarding male-female differences in performance appraisal scores led to only 35% of the highest-level positions being filled by women.[14] As these authors concluded, "relatively small sex bias effects in performance ratings led to substantially lower promotion rates for women, resulting in proportionately fewer women than men at the top levels of the organization" (p. 158).

Unwritten Rule #2: Increase the a Priori Type I Error Rate to .10 Because of Your Small Sample Size

Recall that statistical power is $1 - \beta$, where β is the Type II error rate and is inversely related to α (i.e., Type I error rate). In the presence of what is seen as a small N, a relatively common unwritten rule is to increase the a priori α from the usual .01 and .05 values to .10 or even .20 to increase statistical power. Here's an example of how this practice is justified from a published article: "[g]iven that the sample was now relatively small (i.e., 41 teams), an α level of .10 was used for all hypothesis testing" (p. 951).[15] Likewise, other authors increase their a priori α to .20 because their sample was small. For example, the justification is that "[t]he small sample required that we balance Type I and Type II error rates in statistical testing. At a traditional 95 percent confidence level, the power is only .20 (Cohen, 1977), given an average **cell size** of 12. Stevens (1996: 172) recommended a more 'lenient' α level to improve power. We chose an 80 percent confidence level to ensure at least a power of 0.50. Thus, we set the Type I error rate at 20 percent" (p. 399).[16]

As the above illustrations show, relaxing the a priori α level to .10 or even .20 is a methodological practice often implemented when a study includes a small sample. Increasing the α level increases statistical power and the chances of detecting an existing effect. Is this practice justified? In other words, is it justified to raise α to the specific value of .10 or even .20? Why not .15? Or .40, for that matter? Let's consider the evidence.

An article published in 1989 is often invoked as a source in support of the increase to .10. In discussing research studies with small samples, these authors noted that "when either sample size or anticipated effect size is small, a researcher should typically select a less conservative level of significance (e.g., .10 vs. .05)" (p. 340).[17] However, they also noted that there is no right or wrong level of significance. Blind adherence to the .05 significance level as the crucial value for differentiating publishable from unpublishable research cannot be justified.

METHODS IN PRACTICE
JUSTIFICATION FOR THE TYPE I ERROR RATE

"A researcher's selection of a significance level: (i.e., the Type I error rate or α)" should be treated as one more research parameter.[18] Rather than being set at a priori levels of .05, .01, or whatever, the appropriateness of a specific level of significance should be based upon considerations such as… sample size, effect size, measurement error, practical consequences of rejecting the **null hypothesis**, coherence of the underlying theory, degree of experimental control, and robustness" (p. 339). In another source often used as justification for an increase in the a priori α to .10, Stevens (1996) argued that when one has a small sample, "it might be prudent to abandon the traditional α levels of .01 or .05 to a more liberal α level to improve power sharply. But, of course, one does not get something for nothing. We are taking a greater risk of rejecting falsely, but that increased risk is more than balanced by the increase in power" (p. 137).[19]

The recommendation that we increase our a priori α level to .10 is fairly common in the literature. This is because it's meant to provide a means to increase statistical power in the presence of a small sample size. However, in light of the sources used to support this practice, a careful examination leads to the following conclusions:

1. Increasing the a priori α is reasonable and increases statistical power.

2. However, the practice of increasing α to the specific value of .10 or even .20 is subject to the criticism that these values are arbitrary, much like the values of .05 and .01 are also arbitrary.

3. Moreover, without taking into account the research context (e.g., negative consequences of incorrectly concluding there is an effect as a consequence of a Type I error), the practice of increasing the α level to an arbitrarily selected greater value may be equally as, or even more, detrimental to theory development and practice than having a small sample size, insufficient statistical power, and erroneously concluding that there is no effect.

What Should You Keep in Mind About Unwritten Rule #2?

Social and behavioral sciences researchers usually adopt the conventional .05 and .01 values for the a priori α (i.e., probability of erroneously concluding that there is an effect). As noted above, many authors choose to increase α to .10 or .20. However, this choice is seldom justified, and no discussion is usually provided regarding the trade-offs involved (i.e., an increase in the probability of committing a Type I error). Suppose you wish to increase power by increasing α. In that case, you should make an informed decision about the trade-off between Type I and Type II errors given their inverse relationship rather than choosing an arbitrarily larger value for α.

Let's consider a helpful way to weigh the pros and cons of increasing the Type I error rate for a specific research situation. Using this method, you can make a more informed decision regarding the value to give to α. The appropriate balance between Type I and Type II error rates can be achieved using a preset Type I error rate considering the **Desired Relative Seriousness (DRS)** of making a Type I versus a Type II error. Because Type II error = 1 - power, this strategy is also helpful in choosing an appropriate Type I error in relation to statistical power.[20] For example, consider the following situation: you are interested in testing the hypothesis that the effectiveness of a training program for unemployed individuals varies by region, such that the training program is more effective in areas where the unemployment rate is higher than 6%.[21] Assume you decide that the probability of making a Type II error (i.e., incorrectly concluding that the unemployment rate in a region is *not* a moderator) should not be greater than .15. You also decide that the seriousness of making a Type I error (i.e., incorrectly concluding that percentage of unemployment in a region *is* a moderator) is twice as serious as making a Type II error (i.e., DRS = 2). Assume you decide that DRS = 2 because a Type I error means that different versions of the training program would be needlessly developed for various regions, wasting the limited resources available. The desired preset Type I error can be computed as follows[22]:

$$\alpha_{desired} = \left[\frac{p(H_1)\beta}{1 - p(H_1)} \right] \left(\frac{1}{DRS} \right) \tag{5.1}$$

For this example, assume that based on a solid theory-based rationale and previous experience with similar training programs, you estimate that the probability that the moderator hypothesis is correct is $p(H_1) = .6$. Solving Equation 1 yields a desired α of .11. Thus, in this particular example, using a nominal (i.e., a priori) Type I error rate of .11 would yield the desired level of balance between Type I and Type II statistical errors. Implementing this procedure for choosing the specific a priori Type I error rate provides a more informed and better justification than using any arbitrary value. This strategy is also less likely to raise concerns among journal editors and reviewers.

Why are these unwritten rules used? One can suspect authors invoke them preemptively to counter a reviewer's potential criticism or respond to it when it is received. For example, criticism may arise when results do not turn out as predicted (e.g., a lack of support for a hypothesized effect). It may also come as reviewers stating, "Your sample size is not sufficient for a covariance structure analysis," and "Your small sample size led to insufficient statistical power to detect population effects." Sometimes the unwritten rules are even followed as a response to a reviewer or journal editor's request: "Given your small sample size, you must conduct a power analysis using Cohen's definitions of effect size." The recommendations above can help you use the most appropriate solution to adequately justify your sample size whenever you are tempted to rely on or as asked to these unwritten rules.

HOW TO MAKE SURE YOUR STUDY PARTICIPANTS ARE WHO YOU THINK THEY ARE

The use of web-based research (e.g., MTurk, StudyResponse, and Qualtrics) has increased 10-fold over the last decade.[23] While existing procedures are undoubtedly helpful in safeguarding the integrity of data, one important but overlooked aspect with implications for all types of web-based surveys and research is who completes the task: *is it the person whom you intended to include in the study, or is it perhaps someone who is not a member of the targeted population?* Of course, this is not a validity threat when collecting data in person. Still, it is highly relevant to web-based surveys and research that is hosted and often sourced online, as false identities are common online.[24] To this point, most existing research examining the quality of web-based data has focused on comparing web-based versus non-web-based participants or investigating the quality of web-based data against absolute standards. This section distinguishes between two types of web-based participants: those intentionally targeted for study inclusion; and those who are not (i.e., those using false identities). False identities can take various forms, including participants misrepresenting their background (e.g., giving false information), duplicating their participation (i.e., taking an online survey more than once), and being someone other than a targeted participant.

> ### Example: Identity of Web-Based Research Participants
>
> The identity of web-based participants is often in doubt, which poses a severe threat to theory and practice.[25] For example, one study found that over 50% of recruited participants were suspected of false identities.[26] Likewise, a series of experimental investigations of MTurk participants discovered that when a demographic screening question mentioned sexual orientation, 45.3% of participants identified as lesbian, gay, or bisexual (LGB) [sic]. Yet only 3.8% of participants identified as LGB [sic] in a duplicate study that did not post it as a screening question.[27] In an even more striking illustration, of the 900 MTurkers who began a study, "all but 33 dropped out when asked to provide a screenshot that verified their qualifications" (p. 212).[28]

The threat presented by misrepresented or outright false identities is that existing data-quality controls addressing other validity threats are less relevant. This is because the integrity of web-based research rests on the assumption that the data collected accurately represent the targeted population.[29] So, here are some best-practice suggestions for ensuring that your study participants are who you think they are.

Best-practice Recommendations for Improving the Validity of Web-Based Data Collection

Figure 5.1 offers a summary of best-practice recommendations, described as sequential steps. First, you should begin the process by checking for duplicate IP addresses. These would indicate that someone using the same computer-network configuration, or potentially the same proxied or spoofed IP address, completed the survey more than once. It could also mean someone took a survey more than once, perhaps to sway the organization's opinion of a particular manager or to influence organizational interventions/proposals favored by that specific employee. While either

FIGURE 5.1 ■ Decision-Making Tree for Implementing an IP Address Analysis for Improving the Validity of Web-Based Data Collection

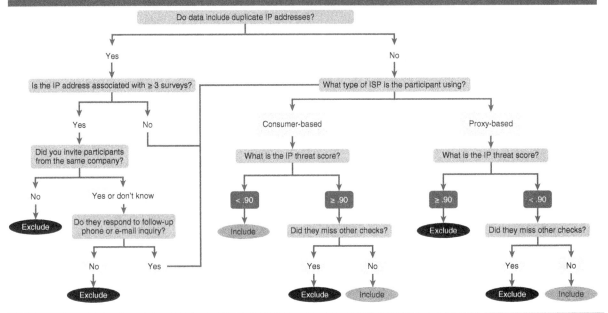

Source: Copyright © 2017 by American Psychological Association. Adapted/reprinted with permission. J. B. Bernerth, H. Aguinis, & E. Taylor, E., 2021, Detecting false identities: A solution to improve web-based surveys and research on leadership and health/well-being. *Journal of Occupational Health Psychology, 26*(6), 564–581.

scenario is plausible, sometimes a network uses a single public IP address for multiple devices within its network; when an organization's network is structured this way, multiple targeted individuals have the same IP address. For this reason, if the IP address appears multiple times but you did not invite multiple individuals from the same organization or group, these data should be excluded from final analyses. On the other hand, if duplicates exist and you did invite multiple individuals from the same organization or group or who's in the sample (e.g., if you used a snowball recruiting technique), you'll need to follow up to ascertain whether multiple individuals used the same computer (e.g., with a shared work computer or unit in a computer lab) to complete the survey. If attempts to verify the appropriateness of participants sharing IP addresses are unsuccessful, you should exclude those data from their analysis.

This recommendation is based on the evidence gathered in follow-up analyses investigating whether participants would respond to a direct email requesting verification information. The authors who performed these follow-up analyses used a subsample of 200 participants to record whether or not the person replied to the email (0 = no response, 1 = response) and subsequently conducted two separate **binary logistic regression** analyses with **IP threat score** and internet service provider (ISP) designation as the predictor variable, respectively. Both a high IP threat score and an ISP designation of proxy host reduced the odds of a participant responding to an email. So, if a user does not respond to a direct email, the likelihood of the data being tainted is higher. If email addresses were not collected, you must use all available information (e.g., how many **data-cleaning techniques** raise flags) in combination with your best judgment in deciding whether to retain or eliminate their data.

After ensuring no duplicates (or following up with any duplicate responses), you can employ an IP analysis. Suppose this analysis indicates a participant's ISP was consumer-based and their

IP threat score was less than .90. In that case, you should feel confident the participant is a member of the targeted population. If the analysis reveals a proxy-based ISP combined with an IP threat score greater than .90, likely, this respondent is not a member of the targeted population. Therefore, they can be removed from final analyses unless a follow-up inquiry provides information that justifies their inclusion. Note that the .90 value is based on a recommendation from threat prevention experts and is quite conservative. Regardless of the specific threshold used, it is critical that you report it explicitly so results can be replicated.

Suppose an IP analysis reveals a mixed identity (e.g., a consumer-based ISP with a high IP threat score). In that case, you should turn to other validity checks to help make ultimate inclusion or exclusion decisions (similar to best practices in defining and identifying outliers[30]). For example, many nontargeted individuals will likely disguise their true location; it is also likely that participants with a high IP threat score or those using a proxy-based ISP may not even know with which location their IP address is associated. Thus, you could ask a location demographic question on their survey and compare it with what an IP lookup indicates. When discrepancies exist or participants miss other checks, such as forced response items, removing those data would improve the validity of your conclusions.

How to Compute IP Threat Scores and Use Internet Service Provider (ISP) Designation to Identify Targeted and Non-targeted Participants

To compute each participant's IP threat score, you can use the publicly available analytic tool https://getipintel.net/. First, you enter the numeric IP address, then the tool tells you the probability of the associated device being flagged on lists of known masking or malicious hosts. The probability score ranges from 0 to 1, with numbers increasingly close to one indicating increased likelihood. This tool is dynamic and constantly updated in real-time.

To ascertain participants' ISP provider, you can use the publicly available IP address lookup tool https://www.infobyip.com/. First, you enter the numeric IP address, then the tool gives detailed information for each participant, including the ISP. You'll want more than one researcher to independently assess the ISP provider to designate each survey as 0 (targeted) or 1 (non-targeted). Example respondent ISPs designated as targeted include T-Mobile, Cox Communications, Xfinity, and the University of Washington. Example respondent ISPs designated as non-targeted include Psychz Networks, Vultr Holdings, Sharktech, CyberGhost, and Leaseweb.

Finally, it would be best to remember that due to the effects of the COVID-19 pandemic, the number of employees working from home has skyrocketed, likely increasing the number of individuals using a VPN. Because using a VPN may increase the chance of an individual mistakenly being classified as nontargeted, it is critical to remember that other tools can help ensure high-quality data and include the best practices for web-based samples. It is essential to consider multiple checks before removing a participant from a data set, as suggested in the decision-making tree displayed in Figure 5.1.

IMPLEMENTING BEST PRACTICES IN MERGING YOUR DATA WITH DATA FROM EXISTING DATABASES

Archival databases can provide significant methodological benefits because they contain large sample sizes and a broad range of variables. These benefits relate to standards for data collection (e.g., research design and measurement, control variables, and missing data management) and data preparation (e.g., outlier management)[31] that may be difficult to achieve when you collect the data yourself.

Benefits Regarding Research Design and Measurement

First, archival databases focus mainly on organizations, industries, and higher levels of analysis (i.e., macro research). They contain data collected over several periods, which can facilitate more effective testing of causal effects and the specific role of time.[32] Second, the broad set of variables allows for multiple measures of the same underlying construct (e.g., firm performance measured as both returns on assets and equity) for richer tests of hypothesized relations between constructs (i.e., tests across different operational definitions).

Benefits Regarding Control Variables

Using theoretically relevant statistical controls can strengthen causal inferences by allowing you to rule out alternative explanations for the hypothesized effects.[33] This leads to more robust results that enhance the ability to replicate, extend, and generalize a study's findings.[34] Databases offer contextual variables that can serve as theoretically justified controls in studies involving the upward expansion of your research. They can also be a more practical and feasible way to include statistical controls than other techniques like surveys, which must be distributed to many organizations, industries, and countries. Another benefit that large databases can offer is data on variables collected over time; this gives the ability to control for complex feedback loops that can exist in upwardly expanded research. For example, when studying how organizations' investment in education and training initiatives impacts performance, it is important to remember that organizational performance is also likely to impact investments in training and development. Archival databases allow you to test the impact of training and development investment at Time 1 on organizational performance at Time 2 and examine how this performance influences Time 3 training and development, controlling for Time 1 investment.

Benefits Regarding Missing Data Management

Large databases allow you to implement best practices for missing data effectively. First, they will enable you to use a straightforward approach by simply deleting missing data (e.g., through listwise or pairwise deletion). This strategy is feasible in large datasets when the percentage of missing data is small and the sample size needs to be bigger to ensure sufficient statistical power. [35] Under these circumstances, this strategy can be as effective as more complex missing data techniques, such as **multiple imputation (MI)** and **maximum likelihood (ML).** However, MI and ML can also be effective, as these techniques rely on large-sample assumptions and are less likely to produce results containing small-N bias.[36] Another best practice involves diagnosing patterns of missing data and testing assumptions depending on the pattern of missingness: completely at random, at random, or not at random.[37] The large number of variables in archival databases informs this. For example, due to the more comprehensive information in the database, you could test whether data are missing at random versus systematically by examining whether missing variables relate to other variables in the database.[38] Finally, replacing missing data in one database with data from another containing the same variable is possible.

Benefits Regarding Outlier Management

The presence of outliers—data points markedly different from others—can affect substantive conclusions in non-trivial ways. Best practice recommendations for outlier management include making informed decisions by first classifying these observations as either error, interesting, or influential outliers.[39] Unfortunately, it is sometimes tricky to retroactively determine the classification of an outlier once the data have already been collected (e.g., using surveys). However, when use a large database, you can use theory to guide further examination of the variables to find patterns that help to determine the cause (e.g., an extreme value on a financial statement might, on closer inspection, turn out to be accurate due to a particular event such as an acquisition, divestment, or sale of stock). You can also check for error outliers by systematically comparing extreme values with corresponding data for the same variable in other databases. Another tactic is to compare database data to the outlier observations across the same and different contexts (e.g., organization, industry, country) to see if they are typical or stand out in interesting ways. Finally, in large datasets, you can apply the **winsorizing approach** to outlier management, which involves transforming extreme values to a specified percentile of the data. While this approach reduces the influence of some observations, it retains all of them, which can be an advantage over approaches that outrightly eliminate extreme values.

Selecting Archival Databases and Variables

Table 5.1 summarizes six commonly used archival databases that contain data on organizations, industries, and countries (e.g., societal, economic, legal, and cultural data). As you can see, this table contains the following information: (1) vendor and website; (2) overall description; (3) unique characteristics; (4) level of analysis of the data; (5) geographic focus; (6) relevant categories of variables; and (7) subscription information. But many other databases are also very useful for social and behavioral research. Here is a partial list:

- Amadeus
- Bloomberg Professional Services
- BoardEx Academic
- Candid
- Capital IQ (CapIQ)
- Compustat
- Datastream
- Execucomp
- Factiva
- Lexis Nexis Academic
- Orbis
- Osiris
- Roper Center, Polling Data
- Thomson ONE
- Thomson Reuters ESG (Environmental, Social, and Governance; formerly known as Asset4)
- Wharton Research Data Services (WRDS)
- Worldscope
- Zephyr

TABLE 5.1 ■ Detailed Summaries of Six Commonly Used Databases

AMADEUS

Vendor and website	Bureau van Dijk at https://amadeus.bvdinfo.com/ and https://www.bvdinfo.com/en-gb/our-products/data/international/amadeus
Overall description	Amadeus provides data on approximately 21 million companies in Western and Eastern Europe, most of which are private. Data are only available through the web interface for the most recent ten years. Amadeus is a subset of Orbis (see below).
Unique characteristics	● Includes financial information for unlisted (private) and delisted firms. These data are usually hard to obtain, as most other databases focus primarily on publicly traded firms.
Level of analysis	Most variables are measured at the firm level. Individual-level data are available for board and management team members, auditors, and advisors. Market research data are at the industry level.
Geographic focus	Europe
Relevant variable categories	● Firm-level descriptive data (e.g., legal form, contacts, number of employees, location) ● Data on key individuals (e.g., characteristics of managers, board of directors, auditors, and advisers including gender, educational level, and an indicator for the level of independence) ● Financial data (e.g., firm performance, financial ratios, and stock data for listed companies, as well as the probability of default, the propensity to be sold, and other proprietary indicators) ● Ownership data (e.g., percent ownership by key shareholders, shareholders, detailed corporate structures) ● Market research, business, and company-related news, M&A deals, and rumors
Subscription information	● Standard is an annual subscription to the entire database, accessible through a web interface with export functions (e.g., for Excel) ● Most data are available through Wharton Research Data Services (WRDS) (e.g., company financials, stock information, ownership, and governance information). ● Archival data can also be purchased on DVDs from the vendor

BLOOMBERG PROFESSIONAL

Vendor and website	Bloomberg LP at https://www.bloomberg.com/professional/
Overall description	Bloomberg has long held the dominant market position in providing banks, traders, and researchers with real-time data on firms, industries, stocks, bonds, currencies, derivatives, and other financial products. Bloomberg also offers global and local economic data, news from various sources, and proprietary analysis.
Unique characteristics	● Newsfeeds from major business and national publications ● Country risk data from Bloomberg and the Economist Intelligence Unit. ● Extensive training and help functions
Level of analysis	Firm-level, country-level
Geographic focus	Global
Relevant variable categories	● Financial markets: equities, commodities, bonds (corporate, sovereign, and municipal), derivatives, mortgages, and currencies ● Economic: industrial production, capacity utilization, employment, trade, national accounts, and investment ● Environmental, social, and governance data on firms ● Industry-specific data on manufacturing, housing, retail, transportation, and logistics, and the public sector ● Legal and regulatory research and updates ● News about executives and other people with a name entry, including interviews, and feature stories

BLOOMBERG PROFESSIONAL

Subscription information	Many business schools have at least a handful of Bloomberg Terminals, discounted heavily from the prevailing corporate price. See https://www.bloomberg.com/professional for subscription information.

BOARDEX ACADEMIC

Vendor and website	BoardEx at https://boardex.com/
Overall description	BoardEx Academic contains information on company directors and top managers in public and private companies worldwide since 1999. Currently, there are over 750,000 people from over 18,000 firms. There is also basic information on the companies these people are associated with, including revenue, auditors, and bankers.
Unique characteristics	● Provides greater scope than some competitors, like Execucomp ● Global coverage, including ~10,000 firms outside the U.S. ● Includes non-company directorships and other activities ● Unique ID numbers enable researchers to follow executives' careers across companies
Level of analysis	Individual-level, with minimal firm-level data
Geographic focus	Global
Relevant variable categories	● Director profile includes biography, current and historic board and non-board positions, and other activities ● Compensation data from public filings (after 2009, availability is limited chiefly to major companies listed on exchanges in the U.S., U.K, Germany, and France) ● Details on committee service and committee chairships
Subscription information	BoardEx provides data and services to companies, but their Academic product is geared towards academic and non-profit researchers.

CAPITAL IQ (CapIQ)

Vendor and website	S&P Capital IQ (CapIQ) at https://www.capitaliq.com/
Overall description	Capital IQ (CapIQ) generally aims at investment professionals and allows for testing investment theses. Key Developments cover over 800,000 companies worldwide and are summaries compiled from company filings, conference calls, press releases, company surveys, and web mining. People Intelligence follows over 4.5 million executives, board members, key employees, and investment professionals like venture capitalists and private equity specialists. Finally, Capital Structure has detailed data on debt structure for 60,000+ companies (2001-present) and equity structure for 80,000+ companies (1994-present).
Unique characteristics	● People Intelligence is more detailed than many competitors and includes employees of private companies, non-profits, and other entities, not just senior managers of public firms. ● Individuals can be found by name and company but also by alma mater and other variables ● Often includes contact data for individuals, usually absent from company websites and challenging to find.
Level of analysis	Industry-level, firm-level and individual
Geographic focus	Global (>165 countries)
Relevant variable categories	● People Intelligence includes biographies, employment history, education, board memberships, and detailed compensation data for individuals ● "Potential Red Flags/Distress Indicators" such as labor-related announcements, lawsuits, regulatory compliance, and agency inquiries. ● Includes investor activism communications and changes in executives or board members ● Transcripts of conference calls, speeches, and other video and audio

(Continued)

TABLE 5.1 ■ Detailed Summaries of Six Commonly Used Databases (*Continued*)

CAPITAL IQ (CapIQ)

Subscription information	Subscriptions are available directly from S&P Capital IQ (CapIQ) or through WRDS. In addition, subscriptions are available to subsets of the data, like Person Professional (a smaller set of professionals and board members) or Compensation Detail (compensation data for executives).

CARBON DISCLOSURE PROJECT

Vendor and website	CDP (formerly Carbon Disclosure Project) at https://www.cdp.net/en Data are available at https://data.cdp.net
Overall description	The CDP gathers data on the environmental impact of public companies, cities, and regions, primarily related to greenhouse gases, water use, and supply chain activities. CDP releases datasets and reports from surveys, with information from 5600 companies, over 500 cities, and over 70 countries and regions. CDP is funded primarily with money from major institutional investors and charitable contributions but also makes some money from selling data. Data are from 2010-present.
Unique characteristics	● Self-reported environmental data from companies, cities, and regions. These data are often not available in other public files. ● Includes data about the impact on forests, water, and supply chain, as well as greenhouse gas emissions ● Companies are given scores for disclosure and performance
Level of analysis	Firm, city, and region
Geographic focus	Global
Relevant variable categories	Reports generally include emissions or resource usage data, with targets and reasons for change. Due to space limitations, we have only listed variables for climate change and water: ● Climate change: Company self-report data include the existence of internal incentives for climate targets (usually with qualitative descriptions), risk management strategy and procedures relating to climate change, prioritization of risks and opportunities, details about the integration of climate change into company strategy, and outcomes, carbon pricing, lobbying and sponsored research (including issues they engage with and proposed legislation), trade association membership and practices, targets, and initiatives, estimates of CO2 emissions saved, source, size, and location of emissions, fuel consumed (amounts and types), investments, mergers and divestitures, methods of engagement with customers, suppliers, and other partners ● Water: The amount of use and withdrawals, discharge and destination when tracked, supplier reporting requirements, risk assessment procedures, evaluation of water risks on growth strategy, contextual/stakeholder/ regulatory issues, level of direct responsibility, penalties, and enforcement orders, use targets, and linkages and tradeoffs with other environmental issues
Subscription information	● Offers selected open datasets online; users can register to download in Excel and other formats.

CENSUS BUREAU

Vendor and website	The United States Census Bureau at https://www.census.gov/ See https://factfinder.census.gov for a quick search by geography.
Overall description	Best known for conducting the national Decennial Census, the Census Bureau conducts many other regular and irregular surveys, including the American Community Survey (ACS) and the Economic Census. General data categories in the Decennial Census and the ACS include population, education, employment, income, health, language, families, and living arrangements. The Economic Census is carried out every five years for every industry, with statistics for cities, counties, metropolitan areas, states, and the U.S. The Census Bureau also publishes monthly and quarterly national economic indicators.

CENSUS BUREAU	
Unique characteristics	● The Longitudinal Business Database is confidential but accessible to qualified researchers through the Federal Statistical Research Data Centers.
	● For information on public use microdata, see: https://www.census.gov/programs-surveys/acs/data/pums.html
Level of analysis	People-centric data are aggregated at the following levels, from small to large: block level, block group, census tract, zip code, census place, town, city, metropolitan statistical area (MSA), congressional district, state, region, and national. Business-centric data are aggregated and reported for establishments (sub-firm), firms, and industry levels.
Geographic focus	U.S., including many different measures of geography
Relevant variable categories	Micro and macro researchers will be interested in the following surveys, datasets, and indicators available at various geographic levels.
	● The Survey of Business Owners: how businesses were acquired, primary functions in business, hours per week spent working, level of education, age, prior experience owning a business, service-disabled, and other veteran characteristics.
	● Business Dynamics Statistics: job creation and destruction, establishment births and deaths, firm startups, and shutdowns, with age and size of establishments down to the MSA
	● Other surveys and data series include: County Business Patterns, Statistics of U.S. Businesses, Non-employer statistics (sole proprietorships), R&D and Innovation Survey, Quarterly Workforce Indicators, and Retail and Wholesale Trade
Subscription information	Aggregated data and public-use microdata are freely available for download. In addition, access to restricted-use microdata is available for some approved researchers and projects. See https://www.census.gov/fsrdc for Federal Statistical Research Data Centers.

Source: Adapted from Hill, Aguinis, Drewry, Patnaik, & Griffin (2021, online supplement).

In addition, Table 5.2 shows several databases containing different variables useful for social and behavioral research. These variables reflect topics of interest, including organizational-level aggregations of variables typically measured at the individual and team levels.

A final resource, Table 5.3, shows different macro-contextual variables in the databases useful for social and behavioral research. These variables include characteristics of organizations (e.g., size, location, and product offerings) and their senior leadership team (e.g., career history, demographics), industries (e.g., competition, regulation, and growth), and countries (e.g., societal, economic, legal, and cultural). First, these variables are useful because they might predict macro-level constructs related to traditional micro phenomena (i.e., focused mainly on individuals and teams). For example, a researcher might be interested in examining how the characteristics of organizations co-vary with the types of performance management programs they implement. Second, these macro-contextual variables can be used as moderators. For example, a researcher might investigate how organizational, industry or country-level factors moderate the relation between organizational-level turnover and its outcomes. Finally, some macro-contextual variables in Table 5.3 can be used as macro-level statistical control variables that help rule out alternative explanations for hypothesized effects.

TABLE 5.2 ■ Types of Variables in Existing Databases Useful for Social and Behavioral Science Research

Databases	Performance management (e.g., hours of training per employee, total training spending, mentoring & development programs)	Employee health and well-being (e.g., health & safety policies and training, work/life balance, family-friendly policies)	Employee compensation (e.g., average salary, bonus plans, fringe benefits, CEO pay gap)	Workforce diversity & inclusion (e.g., % women, minority, disabled employees in the workforce and management and equal opportunity policies)	Business ethics & legal compliance (e.g., number of ethical & legal controversies, product responsibility policies, product recall(s))	Employee well-being (e.g., employee satisfaction, employee turnover)	Safety (e.g., accident rates, time lost, waste); and customer service (e.g., customer satisfaction, quality data)	Financial performance (e.g., revenue, profit, growth, return on capital); and productivity (e.g., efficiency, costs, output per worker)
Amadeus								
Bloomberg Professional	✓	✓	✓	✓	✓	✓	✓	✓
BoardEx Academic			✓					✓
Capital IQ (CapIQ)			✓					✓
Compustat								✓
Datastream								✓
Execucomp			✓		✓		✓	✓
Factiva			✓					✓
Foundation Center			✓					✓
LexisNexis Academic			✓		✓			✓
Orbis					✓			✓
Osiris								
Roper Center Polling Data								
Thomson ONE								✓

Databases	Performance management (e.g., hours of training per employee, total training spending, mentoring & development programs)	Employee health and well-being (e.g., health & safety policies and training, work/life balance, family-friendly policies)	Employee compensation (e.g., average salary, bonus plans, fringe benefits, CEO pay gap)	Workforce diversity & inclusion (e.g., % women, minority, disabled employees in the workforce and management and equal opportunity policies)	Business ethics & legal compliance (e.g., number of ethical & legal controversies, product responsibility policies, product recalls)	Employee well-being (e.g., employee satisfaction, employee turnover)	Safety (e.g., accident rates, time lost, waste); and customer service (e.g., customer satisfaction, quality data)	Financial performance (e.g., revenue, profit, growth, return on capital); and productivity (e.g., efficiency, costs, output per worker)
Thomson Reuters ESG (Environmental, Social, and Governance; formerly known as Asset4)	✓	✓	✓	✓	✓	✓	✓	✓
Wharton Research Data Services (WRDS)		✓	✓	✓	✓	✓		✓
Worldscope								✓
Zephyr								✓

Source: Hill, Aguinis, Drewry, Patnaik, & Griffin (2021).

Note: "✓" denotes the availability of variables in the specific database.

TABLE 5.3 ■ Types of Contextual Variables in Databases Useful for Social and Behavioral Science Research

Databases	Organizational characteristics (e.g., size, location, product offerings, supply chain relationships)	Senior leadership team (top mgt. team, & directors) characteristics (e.g., career history, demographic & functional diversity)	Industry characteristics (e.g., size, growth, innovation, alliances, competition, regulation)	Country characteristics (e.g., governance, politics, population, taxes, trade, culture)
Amadeus	✔	✔	✔	
Bloomberg Professional	✔	✔	✔	✔
BoardEx Academic		✔		
Capital IQ (CapIQ)	✔	✔	✔	✔
Carbon Disclosure Project	✔			
Census Bureau			✔	✔
Compustat	✔			
Database of Political Institutions				✔
Datastream	✔		✔	✔
Economist Intelligence Unit (EIU)			✔	✔
Execucomp		✔		
Factiva	✔	✔	✔	✔
Foundation Center		✔		
Gallup Analytics				✔
Global Leadership & Organizational Behavior Effectiveness (GLOBE)				✔
Hoover's	✔		✔	
ILOSTAT (and other International Labour Organization Data)				✔
LexisNexis Academic	✔	✔	✔	✔
Organisation for Economic Cooperation and Development (OECD) iLibrary			✔	✔
Open Secrets	✔		✔	✔
Orbis	✔	✔	✔	
Osiris	✔	✔	✔	✔
Polity IV				✔
Roper Center Polling Data				✔

Databases	Organizational characteristics (e.g., size, location, product offerings, supply chain relationships)	Senior leadership team (top mgt. team, & directors) characteristics (e.g., career history, demographic & functional diversity)	Industry characteristics (e.g., size, growth, innovation, alliances, competition, regulation)	Country characteristics (e.g., governance, politics, population, taxes, trade, culture)
Thomson Reuters ESG (Environmental, Social, and Governance; formerly known as Asset4)	✔	✔		
Thomson ONE	✔		✔	✔
Wharton Research Data Services (WRDS)	✔	✔	✔	✔
World Bank Data			✔	✔
Worldscope	✔	✔		
Worldwide Governance Indicators (WGI)				✔
Zephyr	✔	✔	✔	

Source: Hill, Aguinis, Drewry, Patnaik, & Griffin (2022).

Note: "✔" denotes the availability of variables in the specific database.

HOW TO EVALUATE THE APPROPRIATENESS OF YOUR STUDY'S RESPONSE RATE WHEN USING SURVEYS

This section summarizes why response rates (RRs) are important when conducting survey research. It shows RR trends over time, clearly explains how functional and dysfunctional RRs differ, and a validity framework you can use in your research. This section aims to critically assess survey RRs and describe a theory-based RR validity assessment framework that you can use to evaluate your sample's quality, appropriateness, and representativeness.

Importance of Response Rates and Their Trend Over Time

Researchers routinely rely on response-rate benchmarks to determine the quality and appropriateness of a particular sample.[40] A study's reported RR figures explicitly[41] or implicitly[42] in reviewers' and editors' assessments of rigor and validity. The importance of RR in the review process was highlighted in a study that examined the statistical and methodological issues raised in 304 reviewers' and editors' letters for 69 submitted manuscripts. They found that sampling, particularly a low RR, is one of the three most frequently raised concerns regarding research design. Thus, higher RRs influence editors' and reviewers' publication decisions, and we have seen a rise in RRs over time.[43] Although this is a positive development, you should know that the RR level alone is not necessarily an indicator of sample quality.

Two significant developments have influenced the nature of survey research and increased RRs in the past decade, both revolving around technological advances.[44] First, most survey data are collected electronically instead of paper-and-pencil methods.[45] In the past, most researchers recruited participants through a connection to a particular organization, which is often laborious and time-consuming.[46] Many of these studies faced external validity threats due to a limitation in sample diversity. This generated critiques of "**convenience sampling**,"[47] resulting in concerns about a low level of generalizability.[48] Electronic tools such as web-based platforms and the emergence of proprietary technologies have greatly facilitated survey construction and administration. Researchers used to invest effort in coding their survey into a user interface; now, survey vendors provide easy-to-use tools allowing researchers to design surveys with various scales. Further, they can be administered by simply emailing or texting links to potential respondents. Although outsourcing recruitment to panel administrators may threaten validity,[49] the practice allows researchers to address multiple facets of exciting questions with access to more extensive and diverse samples—and more quickly. Of course, the effectiveness of this method depends on the trustworthiness of the platform providing these participants.

Relatedly, another major factor changing the RR landscape is that of **professional respondents**—people who fill in questionnaires to make money. This occurs on the web-based platforms for electronic surveys that have emerged in recent years, such as MTurk, Qualtrics Panels, and Study Response Project. Such platforms enable researchers to administer more studies to more narrowly tailored samples.[50] However, although they allow a professional approach and user-friendly design and make it easy for respondents to complete surveys where and when they want, there are drawbacks. For example, MTurk by Amazon has become one of the most important sources for surveys using their cohorts of participants. Although MTurk enables the rapid collection of large amounts of worthy human subjects' data,[51] the expectation for participation compensation has risen, even for study participants outside these platforms. Another drawback is inattentiveness: participants may be less deliberate in reflecting upon and responding to survey items.

Another emerging issue is the difference in RRs in different parts of the world. For example, surveys administered in China tend to have higher RRs than those in the US. But more than knowledge of the RR values is required to understand the reasons for this difference.

How much have response rates changed over time? As shown in Figure 5.2, there has been a significant trend from 2010 to 2020[52] across 17 social and behavioral science journals. This figure shows that the overall average RR increased substantially from 48% in 2005 to 53% in 2010, 56% in 2015, and 68% in 2020.

Functional Response Rate and Dysfunctional Response Rate

It is critical to distinguish between two types of RRs. *Functional RR* is desirable; we can use it to derive conclusions with high confidence and make inferences about the targeted population (i.e., high validity). On the other hand, *dysfunctional RR* is undesirable because it leads to inaccurate conclusions and inferences about the targeted population (i.e., low validity).

A high RR may not always be functional, and a low RR is not always dysfunctional; you must consider the conditions of the study (summarized in Table 5.4). For example, a study with a RR of 85% in which respondents were coerced to participate fits in the High RR/Dysfunctional quadrant in Table 5.4. Similarly, a study with a high RR in which participants were inattentive is also categorized as High RR/Dysfunctional. Alternatively, a study with a low RR that involved random sampling and a careful check of responses, including cleaning the data to remove inattentive responses[53] or false identities (i.e., participation of nontargeted individuals),[54] would be

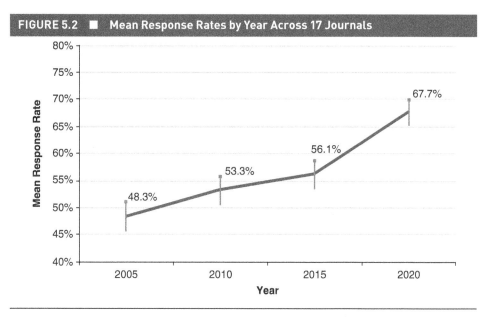

FIGURE 5.2 ■ Mean Response Rates by Year Across 17 Journals

Note: Journals included: *Academy of Management Journal, Administrative Science Quarterly, Career Development International, Human Relations, Human Resource Management, International Journal of Manpower, Journal of Applied Psychology, Journal of International Business Studies, Journal of Managerial Psychology, Journal of Management Studies, Journal of Vocational Behavior, Organizational Behavior and Human Decision Processes, Organization Studies, Personnel Psychology, Personnel Review, Strategic Management Journal,* and *Work and Occupation.*

Source: Holtom, Baruch, Aguinis, & Ballinger (2022). Reproduced with permission.

TABLE 5.4 ■ Functional RR and Dysfunctional RR

	High RR	Low RR
Functional RR	*Examples:* Either traditional research design that successfully followed 'best practice' or paid panel data collection of a representative population.	*Examples:* Random sampling, data cleaning procedures in place, data quality checks in place, and participant identity checks in place.
Dysfunctional RR	*Examples:* Participants were coerced into participating in the study or were inattentive.	*Examples: Only a* small proportion of the population responds, and the response rate varies widely across specific populations, with an unclear representation of the wider population.

Source: Holtom, Baruch, Aguinis, & Ballinger (2022). Reproduced with permission.

Note: RR = Response rate.

Low RR/Functional. There is a need to understand *why* a study has a low or high RR.[55] This supporting information allows us to be more or less confident about a study's conclusions in a way that looking at the RR value out of context cannot.

Response Rate Validity Framework

So, how can you address this critical point in your research? RRs are an "attention-driven" phenomenon,[56] and cognitive resources are finite. Therefore, response quality will reflect the amount of cognitive effort a participant is willing to invest in reflecting on and accurately responding to the survey. As attention increases, the validity of a response would be expected to increase; the inverse is also true. This should caution us against an exclusive focus on RR benchmarks; such a focus might cause researchers to take shortcuts—perhaps in the form of excessive reminders or excessively incentivizing respondents—that make the quality and validity of responses questionable. Excessive reminders and incentives are likely to yield participants whose primary motivation for responding is to generate an income stream through numerous studies. It is reasonable to assume such participants would have reduced reflection and attention to the questions on the survey.

How can we determine the validity of responses? This section presents a *response-rate validity assessment framework* that you can use, in conjunction with benchmarks, to judge the appropriateness of your sample. Evidence showing that the sample is appropriate will elicit more confidence in the RRs, strengthening the validity of generalization inferences.

But there is no definitive approach to determining the validity and no particular piece of evidence that wards off all validity threats. In the measurement theory of validity, more generally, validity is not a dichotomous variable (i.e., "valid vs. not valid"); instead, it is a matter of degree.[57] And so, we use several different types of evidence to gain valuable insights because each approach to evaluating validity has strengths and limitations. Converging through multiple pieces of evidence is what the measurement validation literature refers to as triangulation.[58] This same concept and approach to validity are how we assess RR validity; we must inspect different types of evidence to build the case for sample quality. Overall, this process can be viewed as subsuming a test validation strategy[59] and a nonresponse bias impact assessment strategy.[60]

Content validity is particularly relevant for the RR validation process. The framework suggests questions that will help you understand the appropriateness of inferences based on the RR. Below are the six factors that need to be balanced in evaluating a RR so readers of your work can determine the appropriateness of the inferences you have made in your study. Table 5.5 offers a summary.

Researcher-Participant Relationship

There are two concerns here. The first is that a power or status difference may lead to a participant feeling coerced to respond, and this coercion may impact both the likelihood and the nature of the response. The second concern is that participants may want to help the researcher and respond in a socially desirable rather than accurate way. Generally, a RR should be seen as more valid when the responses are freely given without fear of coercion and when participants are less aware of the specific hypotheses being tested.

Participant Qualifications

Sufficient information about who responds to a particular survey is essential in determining whether inferences from survey research are valid. For example, for surveys assessing personality or cognition, you can safely assume that the participant is qualified to respond. But there are other cases where some respondents may need to be more qualified, and that would make a RR less valid. As an example, if senior executives or top management team members are surveyed about a firm's strategic choices, and you can be sure that they respond, those responses would be more valid than cases where respondents cannot be verified (i.e., a firm-level response submitted by an unknown respondent) or where lower-level managers are the respondents. In addition, it is essential to know detailed information about team sizes, control span, and where the individuals sit within the organizational context. Suppose managers have 50 direct reports, for example. In that case, it is safe to assume that they cannot truly differentiate between their team members on scales of behaviors than managers with only ten direct reports.

TABLE 5.5 ■ A Validity Assessment Framework for Evaluating Response Rate	
Validity Evidence	**Questions to Ask in Gathering Validity Evidence**
Researcher-participant relationship	1. Do the researchers or their sponsoring institution have a relationship with the respondent? (e.g., no prior relationship whatsoever; alums of the researcher's university)
	2. What is the quality of that relationship? (e.g., low vs. high level of trust; low vs. high level of commitment)
	3. Is the pool of potential respondents drawn from a random sample?
	4. Are potential respondents representative of the population the research seeks to generalize?
	5. Are the participants students taught by the researcher?
Participant qualifications	1. Do potential respondents have first-hand knowledge of or experience with the phenomenon of interest?
	2. In what ways are potential respondents representative of incumbents in this domain?
	3. Are potential respondents qualified (e.g., possess requisite KSAs)?
Participant motivation	1. Is the participant being paid to complete the survey?
	2. How much is the payment? (compared to the country's minimum or average wage)
	3. How many other surveys has the person completed in the previous seven days or months?
	4. Is there evidence of careful attention to detail? (e.g., extensive attention checks)
Survey length and complexity	1. How cognitively demanding are the questions being asked on the survey? (e.g., simple facts vs. complex judgments)
	2. How many items are on the survey?
	3. How long does the average respondent take to answer all questions?
Number of times the survey is administered	1. Is the survey administered repeatedly?
	2. If so, what is the expected relationship between frequent response and quality?
Cultural and national context	1. What are the normative expectations for responding to surveys in the culture? (e.g., organizational culture, national culture)
	2. Is the response rate in line with the normative expectations?
	3. Is there a reason to expect a coercive or forced response?

Source: Adapted from Holtom, Baruch, Aguinis, & Ballinger (2022). Reproduced with permission.

Participant Motivation

A participant's motivation to complete the survey may increase or decrease the validity of the RR for that survey. You should be aware that providing tangible benefits as an incentive to participate may subtly coerce respondents, impacting responses to screening items and eligibility checks. Ideally, the participant reflects on and responds to survey questions thoughtfully. With pre-notification, reminders, nudges, additional incentives, and personalized feedback, participant responses may be motivated by the desire to alleviate the pressure from the researcher, generate income, or get a flattering piece of information back about themselves.

Participant motivation and incentives are particularly salient when those benefits are a high percentage of the income of the potential participant. While $0.50 or $5.00 may seem like a small amount of money in isolation or to someone based in a wealthy country, a subculture of professional participants uses platforms like MTurk heavily. These users often advise each other about how to clear qualification barriers[61] for MTurk tasks and surveys to generate significant income. Unfortunately, it is difficult to observe and report on these issues, which increases the potential risk to researchers and consumers of research. The most substantial evidence for a valid RR would be through methodology using high transparency and tight control over the participant recruitment, screening, and survey administration processes. In contrast, a reported RR for a survey study conducted with platforms like MTurk cannot offer equally strong evidence for validity.

Survey Length and Complexity

An association between survey length and measurement error has been documented, which creates tension between the amount of information that can be collected from respondents and the quality of these data.[62] Furthermore, long surveys raise concerns about fatigue because attention decreases when cognitive resources deplete. Additionally, in the case of longer surveys, some participants will pause and complete the survey later. This means they may respond to different parts of the same survey in different moods,[63] affecting responses.

Number of Times the Survey Is Administered

In general, a repeated measures design where the same scales are deployed more than once introduces the potential for some respondents to exhibit a psychological disposition to respond consistently.[64] While multi-wave data collection has many benefits (including but not limited to the reduction in common method variance), it is not a panacea. For example, temporal separation may allow contaminating factors to intervene and thus "could mask a relationship that really exists" (p. 888).[65]

Cultural and National Context

There is no such thing as a "correct" or "perfect" cultural context. However, the cultural characteristics of participants may shape RR validity under specific contexts and should therefore be reported. Indeed, research demonstrates that different cultural norms can impact response styles.[66] Furthermore, there are cultural contexts where a participant may feel more compelled to "help" a researcher by participating (e.g., high collectivism). Finally, there may also be organizational culture effects that influence the rate or authenticity of responses (e.g., where a participant desires to "help" you or where the survey is considered an essential part of voicing concerns).

HOW TO DEAL WITH PUBLICATION BIAS AND THE FILE DRAWER PROBLEM

This last section of this chapter focuses on explaining publication bias and the file drawer problem, and it provides a concrete strategy that you can use to address these problems. These issues are particularly relevant in conducting a research synthesis such as meta-analysis, but they also apply to many other types of data collection procedures and samples.

File Drawer Problem

The file drawer problem is a subset of a broader category of publication biases. The issue of publication bias potentially arises "whenever the research that appears in the published literature is systematically unrepresentative of the population of completed studies" (p. 1).[67] This is more than just a missing-at-random data problem. A missing-at-random data problem would be when, for example, a given study was randomly excluded from a meta-analysis. This would be of little consequence because the synthesis would rely on a sample of the available research/data. As noted by some authors, "If the missing studies are a random subset of all relevant studies, the failure to include these will certainly result in less information, wider confidence intervals, and less powerful tests, but will have no systematic impact on the effect size" (p. 277).[68]

But there is publication bias when research is systematically, not randomly omitted from a study. For example, a given array may be expected to have five to eight more correlations that are not statistically significant. What we cannot know, however, is whether 10%, 20%, 50%, or more of the entire body of reportable research relevant to any given synthesis is nonpublished.[69] If the general premise of the file drawer problem is correct, it is simply unknown how many statistically nonsignificant results there are. Without that information, the validity of the entire body of published research—primary research, narrative reviews, and meta-analyses—may be compromised.[70] This is because "readers and reviewers of that research are in danger of drawing the wrong conclusion about what that body of research shows" (p. 1).[71] Thus, the extant literature reflects an enduring and ubiquitous concern regarding the universality and consequences of the file drawer phenomenon on the research synthesis.[72] So, the basic notion of the file drawer problem is that research with statistically nonsignificant results is less likely to be published.[73] The file drawer problem can be summarized like this: "Research published in many journals is more likely to present statistically significant findings—that is, findings that reject the null hypothesis with a probability of $p < .05$ (or some other significance criterion)—than all research on the topic. This bias against null findings is present in the decisions made by reviewers and primary researchers" (p. 62).[74]

Example: Publication Bias

Publication bias via censoring studies has occurred for as long as research has been conducted and reported.[75] However, recent years have seen increased attention to that phenomenon alongside the widespread adoption of methodologies that summarize research. The general criticism is that meta-analyses and other types of research do not include a random sample (i.e., an unbiased set of all available scores or effect sizes). This prompted some authors to question the most widely accepted and implemented data-analytic methods, especially meta-analysis. As a result, a series of ingenious developments have been designed to ascertain whether a meta-analysis includes as many statistically nonsignificant results as one would expect from a given array of effect sizes.[76] These include "**Failsafe N**" approaches,[77] non-parametric/rank correlation tests,[78] linear-regression tests,[79] funnel plots,[80] and the trim and fill method.[81] In other words, an extensive methodological body of work was developed to mitigate the supposedly important biasing effects of the file drawer problem.

However, despite this distinguished body of work, there remains an apparent frustration. According to the Google Scholar database, Rosenthal's discussion of this phenomenon[82] has been cited about 9,700 times as of January 2024. As noted, techniques allow us to determine if elements of a given data array are potentially biased toward not including as many statistically nonsignificant results as expected. Once again, there is some direct and derivative evidence of publication bias,[83] but there is no estimate of its magnitude. Some authors captured this sentiment, who noted, "As might be expected, publication bias is easier to detect than to correct, at least to correct in a way that inspires great confidence" (p. 566).[84]

Recommendations to Address Publication Bias and the File Drawer Problem

So, how can you address publication bias and the file drawer problem? A common methodological practice is to discuss the implications of the file drawer problem regarding robust and trustworthy results. Specifically, substantive conclusions are interpreted more forcefully if a meta-analysis "passes" a file drawer problem test. Consider the following illustrations. Some authors noted that "in order to address potential 'file drawer' problems, Failsafe-N values were calculated for each of the variables, which estimates the number of unpublished studies with an average effect of zero that would be required to reduce a given meta-analytic coefficient to .10 (i.e., a small correlation with lower practical significance, as per Cohen, 1969). These results appear in Table …, demonstrating that these findings are unlikely to be significantly affected by publication bias" (p. 143).[85] Similarly, other authors have concluded that "a total of 73,415 unpublished studies containing null results would be required to invalidate the present study's conclusion that behavioral intentions and employee turnover are significantly related" (p. 681).[86] Finally, a study on the relationship between organizational culture and organizational performance illustrates the relevance of the file drawer problem. Specifically, this paper included a table listing failsafe *k*s for each of the 25 meta-analytically derived correlations. They did this because they wanted to evaluate the "robustness of their findings given that … meta-analytic results should consider the 'file drawer' problem … because effect sizes may be biased" (p. 688).[87]

This chapter has provided you with the tools to collect your sample properly. Chapter 6 will focus on the next critical step in the research process: How to measure your variables.

DISCUSSION QUESTIONS

1. What are the pros and cons of using a probability compared to a convenience sample?

2. Are large sample sizes always the best option? Why or why not?

3. What are two common unwritten rules? What is essential to know about them?

4. What are the consequences of choosing an (in)appropriately targeted effect size in your power analysis?

5. Do you agree that .05 should be the standard and only a priori Type I error rate used in all social and behavioral science research? Why or why not?

6. How can IP Threat scores and ISP Designation help you identify potential false identities?

7. What situations might contribute to inattentive responding?

8. What archival databases include variables that could be particularly useful for your research?

9. What are the most important benefits of combining your data with data from existing databases?

10. How are response rates and validity related?

11. If you conduct a study and find that your response rate is around 68%, can you conclude that your sample is high quality, appropriate, and representative? Why or why not?

12. What factors should be considered when implementing a response rate validity framework?

13. What is the file drawer problem? What is publication bias? How do they happen?

14. How can you minimize publication bias and file drawer problems generally? How about when conducting a research synthesis study (i.e., meta-analysis)?

KEY TERMS

binary logistic regression

cell size

coefficient of determination (R squared, or R^2)

Cohen's value (*d*)

convenience sampling

database

data-cleaning technique

Desired Relative Seriousness (DRS)

Failsafe N

file drawer problem

funnel plot

non-probability samples

IP threat score

maximum likelihood (ML)

multiple imputation (MI)

null hypothesis (H_0)

population effect

probability sample

professional respondents

publication bias

rank correlation test

response rate (RR)

Statistical power

trim and fill method

Type I error rate (α)

Type II error rate (β)

virtual private network (VPN)

winsorizing approach

NOTES

This chapter is based to a large extent on the following sources:

Aguinis, H., Beaty, J. C., Boik, R. J., & Pierce, C. A. (2005). Effect size and power in assessing moderating effects of categorical variables using multiple regression: A 30-year review. *Journal of Applied Psychology, 90*(1), 94-107. https://doi.org/10.1037/0021-9010.90.1.94

Aguinis, H., & Harden, E. E. (2009). Sample size rules of thumb: Evaluating three common practices. In C. E. Lance and R. J. Vandenberg (Eds.), *Statistical and methodological myths and urban legends* (pp. 269-288). Routledge.

Bernerth, J. B., Aguinis, H., & Taylor, E. C. (2021). Detecting false identities: A solution to improve web-based surveys and research on leadership and health/well-being. *Journal of Occupational Health Psychology*, *26*(6), 564–581. https://dx.doi.org/10.1037/ocp0000281.

Dalton, D. R., Aguinis, H., Dalton, C. M., Bosco, F. A., & Pierce, C. A. (2012). Revisiting the file drawer problem in meta-analysis: An assessment of published and nonpublished correlation matrices. *Personnel Psychology*, *65*(2), 221-249. https://doi.org/10.1111/j.1744-6570.2012.01243.x

Hill, N. S., Aguinis, H., Drewry, J. M., Patnaik, S., & Griffin, J. (2022). Using macro archival databases to expand micro research. *Journal of Management Studies*, *59*(3), 627-659. https://doi.org/10.1111/joms.12764

Holtom, B. C., Baruch, Y., Aguinis, H., & Ballinger, G. A. (2022). Survey response rates: Trends and a validity assessment framework. *Human Relations*, *75*(8):1560–1584. https://doi.org/10.1177/00187267211070769

6 HOW TO MEASURE YOUR VARIABLES

LEARNING GOALS

By the end of this chapter, you will be able to do the following:

6.1 Argue why you should care about measurement.

6.2 Defend the benefits of sound measurement.

6.3 Create different measurement scales, including nominal, ordinal, interval, and ratio scales.

6.4 Construct a new measure by determining a measure's purpose, defining the attribute, developing a measure plan, writing the measure's items, conducting a pilot study and item analysis, planning a distractor analysis, selecting the items, and establishing appropriate norms.

6.5 Evaluate and interpret the meaning of the reliability of your new measure using different estimation methods, including test-retest reliability, parallel forms, internal consistency, interrater reliability, and computing the standard error of measurement.

6.6 Gather validity evidence about your new measure, including content-related evidence, criterion-related evidence (i.e., predictive and concurrent), and construct-related evidence (i.e., convergent and divergent), and improve the estimation of validity coefficients by understanding the effects of range restriction.

6.7 Improve measures by enhancing construct validity, clarifying distinctions between reflective and formative measures, and minimizing psychometric deficiency and contamination.

6.8 Set up a five-step protocol to improve the accuracy of estimated relations between variables based on good measures.

IMPORTANCE OF MEASUREMENT

Measurement is pervasive in your everyday life. As you go through your daily activities, you glance at your watch to check the time, step on the scale to gauge your weight, and look at the speedometer to see how fast you drive. In addition, schools grade your knowledge, employers test your potential, and medical doctors evaluate your health. In sum, you are continually measuring and being measured by others. Not only does measurement influence your daily life, but social and behavioral science and practice rely on good measurement. Without good measurement as a foundation, this field could not advance or provide a valuable service to society.

As a researcher, you will continuously make decisions relying on accurate measurements. In practice, you will use your knowledge to make decisions, for example, employee selection and placement and a firm's strategic direction. These decisions should rely on a solid measurement of employee attributes, skills, and interests, and firm and contextual characteristics. If you do not have reliable and valid measures of employee characteristics, the decisions are unjustified, and numerous lives may be affected negatively. Thus, it would be best to base your recommendations and decisions on sound measurement.

Measurement is essential to research because it allows you to describe, predict, explain, diagnose, and decide the issues under investigation. If your research lacks good measurement, results will be meaningless and unable to inform the practice of social and behavioral science. In other words, measurement is the cornerstone of both the science and practice of social and behavioral science. Without solid measurement, your research is misleading, and your practice is haphazard. Thus, you must focus on measurement because it can provide accurate and relevant information that leads to informed decision-making.

This chapter is organized as follows. First, it defines measurement and discusses the benefits of sound measurement. It then describes the different **measurement scales**, including **nominal, ordinal, interval**, and **ratio scales**. The third section explains how to create a new measure by determining a measure's purpose, defining the attribute, developing a measure plan, writing the measure's items, conducting a **pilot study** and item analysis, planning a **distractor analysis**, selecting the items, and establishing appropriate **norms**. It also includes information on how you can evaluate the **reliability** of your new measure using different estimation methods such as **test-retest reliability, parallel forms, internal consistency**, and **inter-rater reliability** and gather validity evidence about your measure, including content-related evidence, criterion-related evidence, **construct-related evidence**, as well as how to improve the size of **validity coefficients**. The following section focuses on enhancing existing measures by improving their construct validity, distinguishing between reflective and formative measures, and minimizing **psychometric deficiency** and contamination. Finally, the last section describes a five-step protocol for improving the estimation of the relation between variables based on good measures. It illustrates how you can implement this five-step process with a case study of measurement in **corporate governance research**.

DEFINITION OF MEASUREMENT AND BENEFITS OF GOOD MEASUREMENT

Measurement is assigning numbers to attributes or properties of people, objects, or events based on rules.[1] From this definition, you can derive several characteristics of measurement. First, measurement focuses on *attributes* of people, things, or events, not actual people, things, or events. Second, measurement uses a set of rules to quantify these attributes. Rules must be standardized, clear, understandable, easy, and practical. Third, measurement consists of two components, scaling and classification. *Scaling* is assigning numbers to attributes of people, objects, or events to quantify them (i.e., determining how much of a particular attribute is present). *Classification* defines whether people, things, or events fall into the same or different categories based on a given attribute.

The above definition alludes to a process of measurement. First, you need to determine the purpose of measurement (e.g., prediction, classification, decision-making). Second, you must identify and define the attribute you intend to measure. A definition must be agreed upon before the attribute is measured, or different rules may be applied, resulting in varying numbers assigned to the attribute. The purpose of the measurement should guide the definition. Next, you determine a set of rules based on the definition to quantify the attribute. Finally, you apply the rules to translate the attribute into numerical terms.

As noted before, the science and practice of social and behavioral science can only exist with sound measurement. Following the abovementioned measurement processes, you can develop good measures to reap several benefits.[2] First, measurement contributes to objectivity. It minimizes subjective judgment in scientific observation and allows theories to be tested rigorously because the examined attributes can be adequately assessed and measured.[3] Second, measurement leads to quantification. By quantifying the attributes you are exploring, more detail can be gathered than with personal observations and judgments. In addition, more subtle effects can be observed, and more powerful statistical analysis methods can be used, enabling you to make precise statements about the patterns of attributes and their relationships with each other.[4] Third, standardized measures improve communication by creating a common language and understanding attributes. Thus, research can be compared. Fourth, sound measures save time and money by allowing researchers and practitioners to focus their energy elsewhere because these measures can be automated.

SCALES OF MEASUREMENT

As mentioned earlier, measurement uses a set of rules to quantify the attributes of people, objects, or events. The type of measurement scale limits the statistical analyses that can be applied to the quantification of attributes. Four measurement scales have been proposed[5]: Nominal, ordinal, interval, and ratio. As the measurement of attributes progresses from nominal to ratio, more sophisticated quantitative analyses can be implemented.

Nominal Scales

A nominal scale is the most basic, and it involves assigning numbers as labels to individual objects (e.g., telephone numbers) or categories of things (e.g., organizational unit). In addition, nominal scales determine whether objects belong in the same or different categories (e.g., US vs. Canada vs. Mexico) based on a given attribute (e.g., country of residence). Thus, nominal scales classify people or objects.

Data collected using nominal scales have limited transformations and statistics available. First, each category may be assigned any number as long as it is different from other category numbers. For example, US residents may be labeled 1 and Canadian residents 2, or US residents could be labeled 123 and Canadian residents 654. The categories are not ordered; one is not more than the other, but they are different. Second, the amount of difference between categories is unknown, and the only permissible statistics for nominal scales are those based on counting the number of subjects in each category (i.e., frequencies) and proportions.

Ordinal Scales

Ordinal scales involve assigning numbers to people or objects to determine their rank order. Ordinal scales help decide if one person is equal to, greater than, or less than another based on a given attribute. For example, a supervisor believes María is a better performer than Bob; thus, María is given a 2, while Bob is assigned a 1 to show María has a higher performance ranking than Bob. However, this does not indicate the magnitude of the difference between María's and Bob's performance levels, and you know that María is better than Bob.

Monotonic transformations are permissible for ordinal scales. This means that the transformation must maintain the rank order of individuals or categories. For example, categories labeled 1, 2, and 3 can be transformed into any numbers if their order is preserved (e.g., 4, 5, 6, or 10, 20, 30 is permissible, but 6, 5, 4 is not). Permissible statistics for data collected using ordinal scales include the **median** and the **mode**; the **mean** cannot be calculated because a different mean will be obtained whenever the categories are relabeled using different numbers, while the median and mode categories will stay the same. **Percentile ranks, correlation coefficients** based on ranks (e.g., Spearman's rho and Kendall's W), and **rank-order analysis of variance** can also be used.

Interval Scales

Interval, like ordinal scales, assign numbers to reflect whether individuals or objects are greater than, less than, or equal to each other. However, interval scales also indicate the difference between objects on a particular attribute. A typical example of an interval scale is Celsius temperature. If one city has a temperature of 20° and another has a temperature of 40°, you not only know that the second city has a warmer temperature than the first but that it is 20° warmer than the first. Thus, interval scales use constant units of measurement so that differences between objects on an attribute can be expressed and compared. However, the absolute magnitude of the attribute is not known because the zero point on an interval scale is arbitrarily determined (e.g., the zero point on the Celsius scale is set arbitrarily at the freezing point of water). Nevertheless, most measures used in social and behavioral science include interval scales.

Linear transformations (e.g., $X' = a + bX$) are permissible with interval scales where X' is the transformed score, X is the score to be transformed, and a and b are constants. For example, Celsius temperature can be converted to Fahrenheit using the following linear transformation: $F = 32 + 1.8C$. In addition**, arithmetic mean, variance,** and **Pearson product-moment correlation** are permissible on data collected using interval scales.

Ratio Scales

Ratio scales have a true zero point. The true zero point is when no amount of the attribute is present. Because a zero point can be determined, the ratio between the actual scores of an attribute can be examined. Weight and height are two good examples of ratio scales. Using length as an example, let's say three rulers have lengths of 10, 20, and 60 centimeters (i.e., approximately 3.94, 7.87, and 23.62 inches, respectively). You can state that the second ruler is twice as long as the first and the third is three times as long as the second because length is measured on a ratio scale. Unfortunately, ratio scales are rare in social and behavioral science, but they exist. One example is reaction time on performance tests.

A transformation allowed with ratio scales is $X' = bX$. Scores may be multiplied by a constant _b_, which changes the units of measurement, but not the ratio between two objects because this transformation does not change the zero point. Permissible statistics include the geometric mean.

So far, this chapter has defined measurement, discussed some of the benefits of measurement, and described the four types of measurement scales. The following section turns to the process of developing measures.

HOW TO CREATE A NEW MEASURE

While data can often be gathered using previously developed measures, you may face a situation in which a new measure needs to be developed. For example, this situation can happen because a previously developed measure lacks strong psychometric properties or there is no measure for a specific attribute you need to study. The careful construction of measures ensures that they are dependable and accurate assessments of the attributes examined. If you take precautions during measure development, you must make fewer revisions later to increase the measure's usefulness. This process involves determining the purpose of measurement, defining the attribute to be measured, developing a measurement plan, writing items, conducting a pilot study and item analysis, selecting items, establishing norms, and determining the reliability and validity of the measure.

Determining a Measure's Purpose

The first step in developing a measure is to determine its purpose. For example, measures may be designed to assess an attribute for research purposes (e.g., a measure of perceived social power and its relationship with various outcomes[6]), predict future performance (e.g., a measure of cognitive ability used to select applicants most likely to succeed on the job), evaluate performance adequacy (e.g., a measure of reading ability to assess proficiency), diagnose individual strengths and weaknesses (e.g., a measure of performance completed by supervisor),[7] evaluate programs (e.g., measurement of the degree of success of a new pedagogical approach), give guidance or feedback (e.g., a measure of vocational interests used for career development) or assess organizational success (e.g., a measure of a firm's financial performance). The intended use of the measure will guide the development by dictating factors like the thoroughness of attribute definition, types of items included, and length and complexity of the measure. Clearly stating the purpose before constructing the measure will help ensure it does what it was intended to do.

Defining the Attribute

The second step is to define precisely the attribute to be measured. Without a clear definition, it won't be easy to be sure the measure assesses the desired attribute.[8] To clarify the attribute, it is necessary to state what concepts are included in the attribute and what is excluded.

Example: Defining Social Power

As an example, a measure of perceived social power in dyadic relationships may include power bases such as expert, coercive, and legitimate power but exclude trustworthiness. Also, it is helpful to explain the processes underlying the attribute. Continuing with the social power example, a process may be that displaying specific nonverbal behaviors leads to supervisors being perceived as having high coercive power,[9] resulting in a dissatisfactory relationship with their subordinates, which, in turn, may adversely affect subordinate performance.[10] Further, it is important to state a theory describing the attribute's properties (e.g., overall or global social power may be broken down into various power bases[11]). A thorough attribute description provides a domain of content for writing items for the measure. With a precise and clear definition of the attribute in question, you know what will be measured and if it has been measured well.[12]

Developing a Measurement Plan

After you specify the measure's purpose and define the attribute, the next step is establishing the measurement plan. The measurement plan is a blueprint of the measure's content, format, items, and administrative conditions to ensure it will be well constructed. First, the measure plan must include an outline of content to be included in the measure derived from the attribute definition. It will enable adequate coverage of important aspects of the attribute. Next, a description of the target population responding to the measure, including their demographics and reading level, is needed. Then, based on the target population, a description of the types of items to be used (e.g., multiple choice, true/false, short answer, essay, verbal responses), number of items, and examples of the items are written. Further, administrative procedures like instructions, how long the measure will take to administer, how it will be administered and by whom, and how it will be scored and interpreted are outlined. Once you write the measurement plan, experts and potential users should review it. A well-thought-out plan enables appropriate items to be written and indicates intentions to design a good measure.

Writing Items

Next, you write the items using the definition of the attribute and the measure plan as guidelines. The more closely these guidelines are followed, the more likely items will measure the intended attribute. At this stage, you write twice the number of items desired for the final measure because items will be discarded or revised. Although it is hard to know ahead of time how many items you will need, it is advised that you have at least 30 items a measure to have high reliability, and, thus, you should write at least 60 items.[13] Note, however, that many measures in social and behavioral science include fewer than 30 items but estimates of their reliability still need to be revised. Thus, all other things being equal, although the number of items improves reliability, the number of items necessary to reliably measure an attribute depends on the attribute in question.

There are many guidelines for writing good items.[14] In general, you should write items as clearly as possible; they should not be vague or ambiguous, never contain double negatives, must have the appropriate level of complexity given the target population, avoid sexist or otherwise offensive language, and, when using negatively phrased items, the negative word should be capitalized, bolded, or underlined.

Conducting a Pilot Study and Item Analysis

After you write the items, they must be reviewed with the attribute definition and target population in mind for appropriateness, difficulty, and clarity. The measure is then administered, following the procedures outlined in the plan, to a sample representative of the target population in terms of age, gender, ability level, and so forth. Also, the sample must be large to sufficiently evaluate the measure (e.g., at least five times as many subjects as items).[15] Finally, you gather respondent reactions to assess the clarity of items and administrative procedures and determine if the time limit is adequate.

Gathering feedback from respondents will provide information about the clarity of items and procedures. In addition, an **item analysis** can be conducted to gather more in-depth information about the quality of the items. Item analysis helps eliminate items that are poorly written as well as items that are not relevant to the targeted attribute. Thus, item analysis can explain why a measure has a certain level of reliability or validity.[16] You can compute the following three types of indicators to understand item functioning better: (a) distractor analysis, (b) **item difficulty**, and (c) **item discrimination**. In addition, you can use **Item Response Theory** to conduct a comprehensive item analysis. These issues are discussed next.

Distractor Analysis

Distractor analysis evaluates multiple-choice items that may appear on measures of achievement or ability. You calculate the frequency that respondents choose each response to determine the effectiveness of distractors (i.e., incorrect responses). The frequencies for the distractors should be about equal. If a distractor is chosen less frequently than the others, it may be too transparent and should be replaced. Alternatively, if a distractor is selected more often than the others, it may be tapping partial knowledge of the item or indicating that the item is misleading.

Item Difficulty

Item difficulty evaluates how difficult it is to answer an item correctly. An indicator of item difficulty, known as the *p* **value**, (which is the same term but should not be confused with the *p* value use in hypothesis testing) can be calculated to determine the percent of respondents answering the item correctly. You compute the *p* value by dividing the number of individuals answering the item correctly by the total number responding to the item. A high *p* value indicates that most respondents answered the item correctly, and thus the item may be too easy. In contrast, a low *p* value indicates a difficult item since only some were able to answer the item correctly. Ideally, the mean item *p* value should be about .50, which indicates a moderate difficulty level for the measure. Extreme *p* values do not discriminate among individuals. Thus, items with extreme *p* values should be omitted or revised. However, an average *p* value of .50 may not be optimal for all measurement purposes (e.g., assessing the cognitive ability of applicants for an engineering position may require a measure with difficult items and thus a low mean *p* value).

Item Discrimination

Item discrimination analysis is appropriate for most measures, and it evaluates whether the response to a particular item is related to responses on the other items. It determines which items best measure the attribute and whether they differentiate between those who do well on the measure and those who do not. Those who do well on a measure overall should answer an item correctly, while those who do poorly should answer incorrectly. Several statistics serve this purpose. This section discusses the **discrimination index** and the **item-total score correlation** among them.

The discrimination index *d* compares the number of respondents who answered an item correctly in the high-scoring group with those who answered correctly in the low-scoring group. If an item discriminates adequately, more respondents with high scores should answer the item right compared to respondents with low scores. To calculate *d*, you select the top and bottom scoring groups (this can be done by taking the top and bottom quarters or thirds), and *d* is computed using Equation 6.1:

$$d = \frac{p_u}{n_u} - \frac{p_l}{n_l},\tag{6.1}$$

where p_u and p_l are the number of individuals passing the item in the upper and lower scoring groups, and n_u and n_l are the size of the upper and lower groups, respectively. Items with large, positive *d* scores are good discriminators; the item is harder for the lower-scoring group and easier for the higher-scoring group. An item with a negative *d* score should be discarded because negative scores indicate the item is easier for those who do poorly on the measure overall.

The second and most popular method for determining the ability of an item to discriminate is the correlation between an item and the total score on a measure. Items with high, positive item-total score correlations are related to the attribute the measure is examining and, thus, contribute to the measure's reliability. These items also have more variance than items with low item-total score correlations, which allows the measure to discriminate between individuals who do well on the measure and those who do not. Any items with item-total score correlations that are low or near zero should be revised, omitted, or replaced. Item-total score correlations above .30 are preferred.[17]

Implementing Item Response Theory (IRT)

In addition to the statistics described above, you can use IRT to conduct a comprehensive item analysis. IRT explains and analyzes the relationship between responses to individual items and the attribute being measured.[18] Specifically, IRT explains how individual differences regarding a particular attribute affect the behavior of individuals when they respond to an item. For example, individuals with a large amount of the attribute will be more likely to respond correctly to an item requiring more of that attribute. Thus, the amount of an attribute can be estimated based on how an individual responds to items on the measure.

IRT makes assumptions about the mathematical relationship between individuals' attribute level and the likelihood that they will answer an item in a certain way. These assumptions and responses to the measure combine to form an **item characteristic curve** (ICC) (which is the same acronym but should not be confused with the intra class correlation). ICC is a graphical representation of the probability of selecting the correct answer on an item due to an individual's level of the attribute. If an item assesses the attribute, the likelihood of choosing the correct response should increase as the attribute level does.[19]

By examining the ICC, you can determine item difficulty, discrimination, and the probability of answering correctly by guessing. Item difficulty is evaluated by examining the position of the curve. If the item is difficult, defined as requiring a large amount of the attribute to answer the item correctly, the curve starts to rise on the right side of the ICC plot. Alternatively, the curve rises for easy items on the plot's left side. The steepness of the ICC assesses item discrimination. The flatter the curve, the less the item discriminates among individuals. Finally, from the ICC, the probability of guessing the correct answer when an individual is low on the attribute can be determined. The lower asymptote of the curve is, the easier it is to guess correctly on that item. That is, the higher the curve begins on the y-axis, the higher the probability of guessing.

Consider the ICCs included in Figure 6.1. Items 2 and 3 are easier than 1 because their curves begin to rise further to the left on the plot. Item 1 is the most discriminating, while item 3 is the least because its curve is relatively flat. Finally, item 3 is the most susceptible to guessing because it begins higher on the y-axis.

Selecting Items

Based on the results of the pilot study and item analysis, you select and revise items. A standard method for selecting items uses the item analysis results to rank items based on their item-total score correlations from highest to lowest.[20] First, you choose a group of the top items (e.g., 30 items), and calculate reliability, for example, using **coefficient alpha** (reliability will be discussed more thoroughly in the next section). If the reliability of those items is high (e.g., ≥ .80), no more items are selected. If the reliability is not high enough, then five to ten more items are added, depending on the gap between current and desired reliability, and then reliability is re-computed for the new set of items. This iterative process is repeated until you reach the desired level of reliability. Note that items with low item-total score correlations (i.e., below .20) should not be

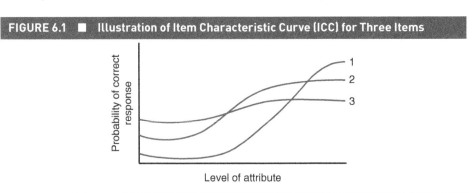

FIGURE 6.1 ■ Illustration of Item Characteristic Curve (ICC) for Three Items

Source: Aguinis, Henle, & Ostroff (2001). Reproduced with permission.

added because they do not improve reliability. Also, adding items should only continue if reliability is increasing or decreasing.

Once the desired reliability level is reached, you plot a frequency distribution of scores on the entire measure. A normal distribution is ideal, but adjustments can be made if the distribution is skewed. When the distribution is positively skewed (i.e., scores cluster at the lower end of the plot), the items are too hard. Thus, items with low p values should replace those with higher p values. Alternatively, when the distribution is negatively skewed (i.e., scores cluster at the high end of the plot), the items are too easy, and items with high p values should be replaced with ones with lower p values.

Establishing Norms

If the measure is used to make decisions about individuals (e.g., college admissions, employment, and job placement), norms should be established. Norms are used to provide standards for interpreting the scores of individuals. Norms are determined by gathering scores on the measure from a representative cross-section of individuals who are members of the target population (e.g., women and men, and various levels of socio-economic status[21]). Norms are typically expressed in either standard scores (i.e., z) or percentiles. Standard scores are scores on a measure referenced to the normal distribution (i.e., $z = [X\text{-}M]/SD$, where X is an individual's score on the measure, and M and SD are the measure's mean and standard deviation, respectively). Percentiles indicate the percentage of individuals in the sample who score below a particular cutoff.

Estimating Reliability

Reliability refers to the extent that a measure is dependable, stable, and consistent over time. If a measure is reliable, there is consistency between two sets of scores on a measure. For example, suppose a personality measure is administered to a job candidate, and the candidate does not get the job but applies for a similar position six months later and retakes the measure. In that case, the scores from the two administration periods should be similar if the measure is reliable. If the scores are considerably different, they may contain errors of measurement.

The concept of reliability assumes that scores obtained from a measure include a "true" score or an accurate representation of an individual's level of the attribute being measured. For example, suppose you administer a measure of research methods knowledge and skills to a group of students taking a methods course. In that case, you assume that the test assesses their research methods knowledge and skills. However, social and behavioral science measures contain error in addition to the true component. Errors of measurement are unsystematic or random and affect the obtained score on a measure but are unrelated to the measured attribute. For example, measurement errors can result from changes in individuals responding to the measure (e.g., fatigue, anxiety) that affect their scores at one administration but not at another or from changes in administrative conditions (e.g., noise, poor internet connection). These errors prevent direct measurement of true scores and force you to rely on obtained scores as estimates of true scores. Thus, a score obtained from a measure has a true score component and an error component. Equation 6.2 demonstrates this relationship:

$$X_{\text{obtained score}} = X_{\text{true score}} + X_{\text{error}} \qquad (6.2)$$

To improve a measure's reliability, measurement errors must be minimized. Ideally, they should be eliminated. By decreasing error and subsequently increasing reliability, it is more likely that the measure will reflect an individual's true possession of the attribute measured. If the measure contains a substantial amount of error, you cannot be confident that it measures the attribute. However, what constitutes measurement errors varies from one situation to another, depending on the purpose of measurement. In addition, different methods of estimating reliability treat some factors as errors while others do not. In sum, what is classified as measurement error depends on the purpose of measurement and, subsequently, the method used to estimate reliability.

Methods for Estimating Reliability

Methods for estimating the reliability of a measure use the correlation coefficient to assess the relationship or degree of consistency between two sets of scores. The **reliability coefficient** can range from 0 to 1, with numbers closer to one indicating high reliability and little measurement error and values closer to zero indicating low reliability and a large amount of measurement error.

There are four methods for estimating reliability: Test-retest, parallel forms, internal consistency, and interrater. Each method calculates a reliability coefficient. But, as summarized in Table 6.1., they differ regarding what they define as an error. Thus, choosing a way to estimate reliability depends on the measure's purpose and what is considered an important source of error.

Test-retest Reliability. Test-retest reliability involves giving the measure to the same group of individuals at different times. Scores are correlated from Time 1 and Time 2 to get a reliability coefficient called the **coefficient of stability**. The coefficient of stability assesses the amount of error due to random fluctuations in scores over time. Thus, an error is defined as changes in individuals (e.g., anxiety, fatigue, mood, health) and changes in measure administration (e.g., lighting, noise, distractions) that affect scores at one time but not at the other. The coefficient of stability can assess if a measure given now will be representative of the same individuals

TABLE 6.1 ■ Sources of Error in the Different Reliability Estimates	
Method of Estimating Reliability	**Source of Error**
Test-retest	
1. Test-retest	Time sampling
Parallel, Alternate, or Equivalent Forms	
1. Immediate	Content sampling
2. Delayed	Time and content sampling
Internal Consistency	
1. Split-half	Content sampling
2. Cronbach's α	Content sampling
3. Kuder-Richardson 20	Content sampling
Interrater Reliability	
1. Interrater agreement	Interrater consensus
2. Interclass correlation	Interrater consistency
3. Intraclass correlation	Interrater consistency

Source: Adapted from Aguinis, Henle, & Ostroff (2001). Reproduced with permission.

at a later time. In sum, you should use this method to estimate reliability when the measured attribute is believed to be stable over time. In addition, this method can determine if the measure is free from errors associated with time.

If the measure is reliable, scores should only change slightly from Time 1 to Time 2, and the rank order of individuals should stay the same. However, the reliability coefficient may differ depending on the length of time between administrations. If the period is too short, the effects of memory may inflate the reliability coefficient because respondents may be able to recall how they answered the measure the first time. However, learning may affect the reliability coefficient if the period is shorter. For example, suppose individuals learn the answers to the items on the measure or learn information that changes how they respond to the measure. In that case, reliability may be underestimated because their scores will have changed from one administration to another. Although there is no magical number for the interval between measure administrations, there should be at least eight weeks between administrations,[22] but not more than six months.

Parallel, Alternate, or Equivalent Forms. This method examines the consistency with which an attribute is measured across different measure versions. This is achieved by calculating the correlation between two forms (i.e., versions) to obtain a coefficient of equivalence. The two forms can be administered close together (i.e., *immediate parallel forms*). Still, to prevent order effects, half of those taking the measure should be given form A first and the other half form B. Error using this method is defined as content sampling or sample items that are nonequivalent. That is, high coefficients of equivalence indicate that the content sampled on the two versions of the measure are equivalent, thus, measuring the same attribute. This method can be modified to assess content and time sampling errors. For example, using *delayed parallel forms* estimates reliability by increasing the time between administrations (like test-retest) to get a coefficient of stability and equivalence by computing the correlation between one form given at Time 1 and the other form provided at Time 2.

Unfortunately, it is hard to design equivalent measures. To be equivalent, measures must have the same number and type of items and difficulty level, and the means and standard deviations of the scores obtained by respondents on both forms should be the same. Because it is hard to design equivalent forms of a measure, reliability coefficients determined by this method will be conservative reliability estimates. Despite the difficulties associated with this method, parallel forms are useful for measures likely to be administered repeatedly (e.g., achievement measures).

The above discussion of measurement equivalence focused on parallel forms.[23] Parallel measures have equal regressions of observed scores on true scores and equal error variances, and they can be used interchangeably. However, there are additional, less stringent types of measurement equivalence. First, Tau-equivalent measures have equal regressions of observed scores on true scores, but possibly different error variances.[24] Second, congeneric measures assess the same underlying construct (i.e., they are linearly related) but have different regressions of observed scores on true scores and error variances.[25]

Internal Consistency. Internal consistency determines the degree to which various items of a measure correlate. For example, the error is defined as item heterogeneity, so the more homogenous the items, the lower the error. This is important because highly intercorrelated items indicate they measure the same attribute. Three popular internal consistency methods are **split-half**, **Cronbach's coefficient alpha**, and **Kuder-Richardson 20**.

The *split-half method* estimates internal consistency by administering a measure once and splitting it into two equivalent halves after it has been given to get two scores for each individual. This method is based on the premise that any item or group should be equivalent to any other item or group. The correlation between the two halves is a coefficient of equivalence that demonstrates the similarity of responses between the two halves. Thus, an error is inconsistent content sampling between the haves for the measured attribute. However, this reliability coefficient is based on a single administration of the test, so it does not take into account errors of measurement that occur over time (e.g., changes in individuals or administration), and, thus, it provides a liberal estimate of reliability.

Like parallel forms, equivalent halves must be equal regarding content, difficulty, and means and standard deviations of responses. The measure can be divided by placing the odd items in one half and even items in the other or, preferably, by a random selection of items. The resulting coefficient of equivalence from the split halves is the reliability of a measure half the length of the original one, which underestimates reliability because reliability increases as the number of items does. Therefore, the **Spearman-Brown prophecy formula** shown in Equation 6.3 is used to determine the reliability of the entire measure:

$$r_{nn} = \frac{n\,r_{11}}{1 + (n-1)\,r_{11}}, \tag{6.3}$$

where n is the factor by which a measure is increased (e.g., $n = 2$ indicates the measure is doubled in size), r_{11} is the obtained reliability coefficient, and r_{nn} is the estimated reliability of a measure n times as long. For example, a mathematical ability measure is divided into two halves, with odd items in one and even in the other. The correlation between the two halves is .68, representing the reliability for a measure half the length of the original. If you use these values in Equation 6.3, the estimated reliability for the entire measure is:

$$r_{nn} = \frac{2(.68)}{1 + (2-1)(.68)} = .81. \tag{6.4}$$

Cronbach's α,[26] like split-half, indicates the degree to which items on a measure correlate. However, this method recognizes that there are many ways to divide a measure, so it takes the average of all possible split halves of a measure.[27] Cronbach's α is computed when there is a range of responses to items on a measure (e.g., "always," "sometimes," "occasionally," "never"). As noted above, this type of reliability coefficient is determined by taking the average of all the possible split halves of the measure to assess how similar items are to each other and, thus, whether they are measuring the same attribute. If reliability is low, the measure may be assessing more than one attribute. The equation for computing Cronbach's α is the following:

$$r_{tt} = \frac{k}{k-1}\left(\frac{\sigma_t^2 - \sum \sigma_i^2}{\sigma_t^2}\right), \tag{6.5}$$

where k is the number of items included in the measure, σ_t^2 is the variance of total scores on the measure, and $\sum \sigma_i^2$ is the sum of the variances of item scores.

A particular case of Equation 6.5 occurs when responses to items are binary (i.e., two responses, such as true or false and right or wrong). For this particular case, Kuder and Richardson developed the following variation of Equation 6.5 called *Kuder-Richardson 20*[28]:

$$r_{tt} = \frac{k}{k-1}\left(\frac{\sigma_t^2 - \sum pq}{\sigma_t^2}\right), \tag{6.6}$$

where k and σ_t^2 are defined in Equation 6.5 and $\sum pq$ is the sum of all the products of p and q for each item, with p representing the number of individuals who pass the item and q representing the number of individuals who fail the item.

Interrater Reliability. This method is useful when a measure is subjectively scored (e.g., observational data, ratings) and judgment is involved because raters' biases and inconsistencies (e.g., raters interpret rating standards differently or inconsistently) may influence ratings.[29] Interrater reliability determines the consistency among raters and whether the raters' characteristics determine the ratings instead of the attribute being measured.

Interrater reliability generally determines the degree of consistency across raters when rating objects or individuals. A distinction is made, however, between interrater consensus (i.e., the absolute agreement between raters on some dimension) and interrater consistency (i.e., interrater reliability or similarity in the ratings based on correlations or similarity in rank order).[30] The following three ways to calculate interrater reliability are discussed: **Interrater agreement, interclass correlation**, and **intraclass correlation**.

Interrater agreement focuses on the exact agreement between raters on their ratings of some dimension. The most commonly used statistics are (a) percentage of rater agreement, (b) index of agreement T, (c) coefficient of concordance W, and (d) kappa (K)[26]. In addition, when a group of judges rates a single attribute (e.g., organizational climate), the degree of rating similarity can be assessed using the r_{wg} index.[31] These indices focus on how much raters agree on the rating level or make the same ratings.[32]

Interclass and *intraclass correlations* are indices of consistency, are correlational, and refer to proportional consistency of variance among raters.[33] Interclass correlation is used when two raters rate multiple objects or individuals (e.g., performance ratings). Pearson product-moment correlation r and Cohen's weighted kappa (K)[29] are the most commonly used statistics. Intraclass correlation (ICC) is typically used when multiple raters rate objects or individuals. This method determines how much of the differences among raters are due to differences in individuals on the attribute being measured and how much is due to measurement errors.

There are six different forms of intraclass correlations. These different forms allow for situations including a group of raters and single and/or multiple dimensions. Intraclass correlation is typically expressed as the ratio of the variance associated with targets (e.g., objects or individuals being rated in performance evaluations) over the sum of the variance related to targets plus error variance based on the analysis of variance.[34] ICC (1,1) is used to evaluate the reliability of multiple raters judging multiple targets on a single dimension. ICC (2,1) is appropriate when the judges are randomly sampled from the larger population of judges, but each judge rates each target. ICC (3,1) is used when the same judges rate each target and there are no other possible judges of interest. ICC (2,1) differs from ICC (3,1) in that ICC (2,1) allows you to generalize reliability to other judges. At the same time, ICC (3,1) is used when there is an interest in the reliability of only a single judge or a fixed set of judges. The remaining three intraclass correlations are identical but include cases when multiple dimensions are rated for each target.

Interpreting Reliability and the Standard Error of Measurement

Reliability coefficients are the means to an end. The end is to produce scores that measure attributes consistently across time, forms of a measure, items within a measure, or raters. You compute a reliability coefficient to understand if your scores are consistent. But what exactly do the reliability coefficients tell you? What constitutes an acceptable level of reliability for your measure?

A reliability coefficient can be translated as the percent of score variance on a measure resulting from "true" differences in the measured attribute. For example, suppose a measure of entrepreneurial orientation has a reliability coefficient of .92. In that case, 92% of score variance can be accounted for by differences in entrepreneurial orientation among respondents, and 8% can be attributed to measurement errors.

The acceptable size of a reliability coefficient depends on the measure's purpose. For example, suppose the measure is used to compare individuals. In that case, the reliability coefficient should be greater than .90.[35] But .70 may be sufficient for most social and behavioral science measures, and even lower coefficients may be acceptable for research purposes.

Reliability estimates provide information about the consistency of most individuals' scores on a measure. However, they do not provide information about the consistency of a given individual's score on the measure.[36] Instead, reliability reflects the error associated with a particular measure. To gather information about how much error you can expect for an individual score on a measure, you can calculate the *standard error of measurement*. Standard error of measurement provides an estimate of the standard deviation of a normal distribution of scores that individuals would obtain if they responded to the measure an infinite number of times. The standard error of measurement σ_{Meas} is computed as follows:

$$\sigma_{Meas} = \sigma_x \sqrt{1 - r_{xx}},$$ (6.7)

where σ_x is the standard deviation of the distribution of obtained scores, and r_{xx} is the reliability estimate for the measure.

Using the standard error of measurement, you can derive confidence intervals that estimate the range of scores that will, at a certain probability level, include a true score (please see Equation 6.2 to refresh your memory). If the standard measurement error for a firm performance measure is 2.21 and an individual obtained a score of 60 on the measure, adding and subtracting the standard error from the obtained score (60 ± 2.21), a confidence interval of 57.79 to 62.21 is derived. This range of scores can be interpreted as if firm performance had been measured 100 times; the firm performance scores would fall between 57.79 and 62.21 about 68 times (i.e., 68% confidence interval). Note that the confidence level can be increased from 68% to 95% by adding and subtracting two standard errors from the obtained score (i.e., the interval would go from a low of 60 − 4.42 = 55.8 to a high of 60 + 4.42 = 64.42).

The standard error of measurement can inform decision-making about individuals, teams, and organizations in several ways. For example, if you decide whether to hire Hannah by comparing her score of 60 to a cutoff score of 65, the standard measurement error can help with this decision. Hannah's score is only five points away from the cutoff. Still, when you examine the 68% confidence interval calculated earlier (i.e., 57.79 to 62.21), you estimate that she will not likely meet this cutoff upon retesting. Further, the standard error can be used to assess whether two applicants' scores on the reading test differ.[37] For instance, Hannah scored a 60, and Naomi scored a 62. The standard error is 2.21, and the difference between the candidates is only 2 points; therefore, upon retesting, Hannah may score higher than Naomi. The standard error can also be used to evaluate scores between groups. For example, it can determine if scores for men and women differ significantly.

Improving Reliability

The reliability of your measures should be as large as possible to ensure that your measures are dependable, consistent, and stable over time. However, the size of the reliability coefficients may be limited by several factors. If you are unaware of these factors and need to consider them, you may overestimate reliability.

First, the method for estimating reliability can affect the size of the obtained coefficient. As described above, the various methods for assessing reliability define error differently; consequently, a measure's reliability coefficient differs depending on the method used. Some methods are more liberal (e.g., split-half), which may overestimate reliability, while others are more conservative (e.g., parallel forms), which may underestimate reliability.

Second, variability in scores can influence the size of reliability coefficients. For example, suppose you administer a measure of perceived social power (i.e., ability to influence) in a flat organization where all employees can influence each other. In that case, there will be no variance in scores because everyone will score very high. Variability among measure scores allows for differentiation among the individuals taking the measure. For example, if all respondents score 20, you cannot differentiate among them based on social power. However, if there is a wide range of scores (e.g., 20, 17, 13, 12, 9, 7, 6, 1), you can make many differentiations among pairs or groups of individuals. In addition, variability can be affected by individual differences. As individual differences (i.e., variability) among scores increase, so does the correlation between them, which makes it easier for the measure to differentiate among individuals. Thus, other things equal, the greater the variability, the greater the reliability.

Third, as the length of a measure increases, so does its reliability. If the number of items relevant to measuring a particular attribute increases, you can obtain a more accurate picture of an individual's true score. You can use Spearman-Brown's prophecy formula (i.e., see Eq. 6.3 as a reminder) to demonstrate the relationship between measure length and reliability. For example, assume you are using a measure of extroversion, which contains 15 items and has a reliability of .80, and you double the size of the measure. Entering these values in Equation 6.3 yields:

$$r_{nn} = \frac{2(.80)}{1 + (2 - 1)(.80)} = .89. \tag{6.8}$$

By doubling the number of items on the extraversion measure to 30, you increased its reliability from .80 to .89. However, a caveat must be made. Indiscriminately adding items will not increase reliability, especially internal consistency. Of course, additional items must be similar to previous ones and relevant to the measured attribute.

Fourth, the characteristics of the sample used also affect reliability. For example, the sample size will influence the magnitude of the reliability coefficients because larger samples will have less sampling error than small samples, thus providing a better reliability estimate. In addition, the sample must be representative of the population the measure will be used for reliability will be over or underestimated.

In sum, scores gathered using a measure are affected by numerous sources of error. As shown in Equation 6.2, observed scores have a true score and an error component. A reliability analysis allows you to estimate the extent to which observed scores are influenced by a random error component. A large reliability coefficient (i.e., small standard error of measurement) suggests that scores are consistent. However, consistency does not ensure accuracy. For example, a scale may be consistently off by 20 pounds. The scale lacks random measurement error; thus, scores are very consistent. However, scores do not represent the true weight, and thus, decisions made based on these scores (e.g., change patterns of eating behavior) may be incorrect. The issues of whether scores and decisions made based on scores are accurate are issues of validity. This topic is described next.

Gathering Validity Evidence

Validity refers to the utility of the inferences from a measure's scores. Inferences from measures can involve measurement issues (e.g., Does this measure of leadership effectiveness assess who is an effective leader?) or decisions (e.g., Can the measure of leadership effectiveness help predict who will be successful as a CEO?). Thus, the validation process evaluates whether a measure assesses the attribute it is supposed to and if it can be used to make accurate decisions. The measure itself is not validated; instead, the inferences about what the measure is assessing and decisions made from the scores are. Empirical investigations are conducted to gather evidence to support these inferences. Evidence is continually gathered to evaluate and revise a measure if it does not fulfill its intended purposes. Therefore, validation is an ongoing process. In sum, validity provides evidence attesting to what attributes a measure assesses, how well it measures that attribute, and what decisions can be made from a measure's scores.

Initially, it was posited that a particular type of validity was appropriate for a given measure. The specific measurement purpose dictated which type of validity was used to establish validity. However, validity is now viewed as a unitarian concept. There are no different types of validity but rather different types of evidence for describing the validity of a measure.[38] Thus, many types of evidence should be gathered to support the inferences and decisions based on a measure's scores. Next, three types of validity evidence are discussed: **Content**, **criterion**, and **construct**. Although they are discussed separately, they are interrelated, and a combination of them is necessary to determine what inferences can be made from a measure's scores.

Content-related Evidence

Content-related validity evidence examines the adequacy of domain sampling and whether a measure assesses the attribute it intends to measure. This is demonstrated when the content of a measure (i.e., items) is judged to be a representative sample of the attribute's content under consideration. Thus, this method of gathering validity evidence relies on the judgments of potential users and experts.

Establishing content-related evidence begins during the construction of a new measure. Developing a well-thought-out plan for measure construction (as described earlier in the chapter) and adhering to that plan provides evidence of content validity. When potential users of a measure and experts of the attribute being measured agree that the plan was well developed and implemented, the measure will most likely be a representative sample of the attribute's content. Thus, following the previously outlined plan for developing a measure will help establish content-related evidence.

The content-validation process starts with a description of the content domain. The content domain is the entire set of items that could be used to measure an attribute.[39] There are three parts to the content domain. First, a definition of the domain or attribute to be measured must be clarified. For example, if you are developing a measure of job satisfaction, a definition may be "Individual's affective reaction to their job." Next, the different areas or categories of the attribute to be included in the measure must be specified. For example, for this job satisfaction measure, you may include the following categories of satisfaction: Pay, supervision, coworkers, and the work itself. Finally, the relative importance of the categories must be established. For example, suppose you believe that satisfaction with pay and work is more important than satisfaction with supervision and coworkers. In that case, you must weigh them more heavily to comprise a more significant portion of the measure (e.g., pay = 30%, work itself = 30%, coworkers = 20%, supervision = 20%).

After you have described the content domain and written items following this description, you can compare the measure's content to the content domain to provide evidence of content validity. First, you evaluate each item on the measure against the definition and classified into a category to determine if it falls within the domain of the attribute. You also compare the measure as a whole to the content domain to evaluate if the measure samples all the areas of the attribute and if there are more items representing the areas that were ranked as more important. The closer the measure matches the content domain, the stronger the evidence regarding content validity.

The extent to which experts agree on the content validity of a measure can be calculated using **the Content Validity Ratio (CVR)**.[40] To compute CVR, experts familiar with the attribute measured (e.g., recognized researchers in the field of job satisfaction) rate whether each item is essential, useful but not essential, or not necessary for measuring the attribute. Their ratings are used in Equation 6.9:

$$\text{CVR} = \frac{n_e - N/2}{N/2}, \tag{6.9}$$

where n_e is the number of experts that rated the item as essential, and N is the total number of experts. The resulting CVR represents the overlap between the attribute's and measure's content. For example, if ten experts rate an item of a measure and eight of them believe the item is essential, CVR is:

$$\text{CVR} = \frac{8 - 10/2}{10/2} = .6. \tag{6.10}$$

CVR can range from –1 to +1, with values closer to +1 indicating that more experts agree that the item is essential. In the above example, CVR is .6, close to 1, so most experts believed there was an overlap between the item's content and the attribute's content. Further, CVRs for all the items on a measure can be averaged to determine the extent that experts believe the entire measure overlaps with the attribute content.

Criterion-related Evidence

As mentioned throughout this chapter, measurement is used to make important decisions. The second type of evidence, criterion-related, is particularly suited to determine if a measure can be used to make decisions and predictions. Thus, a measure demonstrates criterion-related evidence of validity if it can be used to make accurate decisions. Criterion-related evidence involves correlating scores on a predictor (i.e., the measure of an attribute) with some criterion (e.g., the measure of decision outcome or level of success) to determine if accurate decisions can be made from scores. Two types of studies, predictive and concurrent, can be designed to assess the relationship between a predictor and a criterion.

Predictive Validation Studies. These focus on the prediction of future behavior. Predictive studies begin with obtaining scores from a random sample of the population for which decisions will be made, thus ensuring that study results are generalizable. Next, you make decisions without using scores from the measure. Finally, after you have made the decision, you gather scores on a criterion and calculate the correlation between the measure and criterion.

> ### Example: Integrity Testing
>
> An example of a predictive validation study is when job applicants are given a measure of integrity and selected for the job without considering their scores. After applicants have been hired and are the job for some time, information on absenteeism, theft, and other counter-productive behaviors is gathered and correlated with the integrity measure to determine its predictive ability.

Concurrent Validation Studies. Predictive studies are less practical than concurrent studies because concurrent ones do not require using the measure to make decisions (eventually) and a time delay before the criterion data are collected. Thus, concurrent validation studies are more commonly implemented to determine whether using a measure leads to accurate decisions. Concurrent evidence evaluates if an individual's level of an attribute is adequate to achieve the criterion at present. Concurrent validation studies gather scores on the predictor and criterion at about the same time from a preselected population. Then, the correlation between predictor and criterion scores is obtained. For example, current employees could complete the integrity measure, and their employment files could be checked simultaneously to determine how often they are absent, if they have been disciplined for theft and any other information regarding counter-productive behaviors. The predictor and the criteria are then correlated to determine the predictive value of the integrity measure. Although concurrent studies are more practical than predictive, they may not be generalizable to the broad population because they rely on a preselected sample (i.e., individuals already employed in the organization) instead of randomly selecting from the target population.

Note that in both types of criterion-related validation studies (i.e., predictive and concurrent), there is an artificial reduction in the variance in one or more variables under consideration. This artificial reduction in variance, often labeled *range restriction* or *censorship*, deserves attention because it might impact correlation coefficients, **regression coefficients**, and means. For example, a reduction in variance decreases the size of validity coefficients so that results obtained using restricted samples may underestimate actual validity coefficients. There are three types of range restriction.[41] Cases I and II are often labeled "direct or explicit restriction," and Case III is often labeled "indirect or implicit restriction. Case I is a situation in which you are interested in the relationship (e.g., correlation) between predictor variable X and criterion variable Y, variable X's range is restricted. You have information regarding variable Y's variance in both the restricted (sample) and unrestricted (population) groups and information regarding variable X's variance in the restricted group only. You are not likely to encounter this situation. Case II involves a situation in which you are also interested in the correlation between X and Y, variable X's range is restricted, and you have information regarding X's variance in both the restricted (sample) and unrestricted (population) groups and information regarding variable Y's variance in the restricted group only. You are more likely to encounter this situation, as it is widespread in several research domains, such as human resource management, organizational behavior, and entrepreneurship. Finally, Case III involves a situation in which you are also interested in the correlation between X and Y. Still, range restriction has occurred on a third or more, often unknown variables (which are correlated with X and Y). Because of the correlations between X and the unknown variable(s) and Y and the unknown variable(s), you only have variance information regarding both X and Y for the restricted groups.

Construct-related Evidence

Construct-related evidence is the third type that describes whether inferences from a measure's scores are valid. Construct, like content-related evidence, is the process of accumulating evidence to establish whether the measure assesses the attribute it is intended to assess. However, instead of evaluating the measurement plan and determining whether the measure includes a representative sample of the attribute's content, construct-related evidence investigates hypothesized relationships between a construct and other constructs to assess if actual relationships are similar to predicted ones. A construct is an abstract characteristic or attribute that a measure is believed to be assessing. Examples of constructs include social power, job satisfaction, intelligence, entrepreneurial orientation, and firm performance. Because you cannot observe these constructs, you need measures to be concrete and operational indicators of them. Thus, construct-related evidence involves conducting studies to support that a measure is indeed assessing the proposed construct by relating a measure to measures of other constructs.

Gathering construct-related evidence begins with defining the construct and identifying observable indicators that operationally define the construct. After observable indicators of the construct are determined, relationships among the different indicators are investigated. If the observable indicators are good indicators of the construct, they should be highly intercorrelated, indicating that they measure the same concept. Once the internal consistency of the indicators has been established, you construct a *nomological network*.[42] A nomological network is a pattern of proposed relationships between the construct, its observable indicators, and other constructs and observable indicators. This network specifies variables the construct should and should not be related to. Studies are then conducted to determine the degree to which actual relationships match the expected ones delineated in the nomological network. The closer the match between the hypothesized nomological network and the actual relationships, the more substantial the evidence of construct validity.

Different studies can be designed to support the hypothesized relationships between the construct and other variables. The more evidence accumulated from various sources, the more confident you can be that the measure is assessing the construct. One type of study that examines several types of evidence of construct validity is the **multitrait-multimethod approach**.[43] To conduct a study using this approach, data must be gathered on at least two constructs, each measured using at least two methods (e.g., supervisor ratings, observations, self-reports). Correlations among the different constructs measured by different methods are calculated to form a multitrait-multimethod matrix. For example, the matrix shown in Figure 6.2 includes correlations among measures of teamwork, cognitive ability, and organizational commitment using supervisor ratings, self-ratings, and observer ratings.

FIGURE 6.2 ■ Illustration of Multitrait-Multimethod Matrix for Study on the Relationship Among Measures of Teamwork, Cognitive Ability, and Organizational Commitment

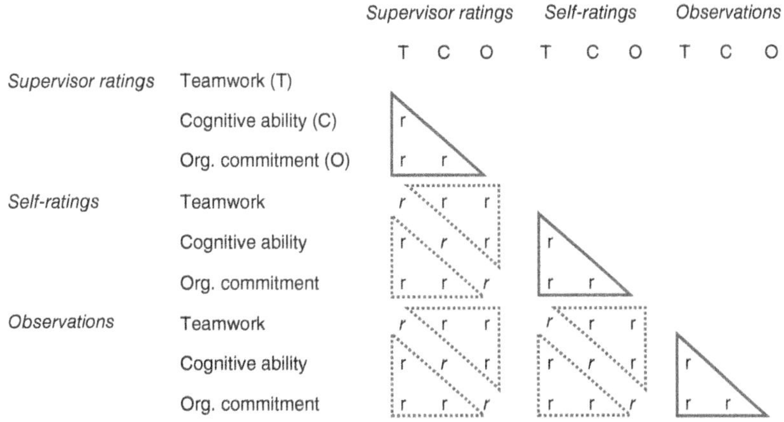

Source: Aguinis, Henle, & Ostroff (2001). Reproduced with permission.

The first type of evidence provided by the matrix is *convergent validity*. Convergent validity examines whether different methods of assessing the construct produce similar results. If results obtained using different methods are highly correlated, you can be more confident that your measures assess the intended construct. Convergent validity is determined by examining the italicized in the matrix.

Next, you can assess *divergent validity*; that is, whether measures hypothesized not to be related are not. Again, examining the correlations within the dashed triangles provides evidence regarding divergent validity.

Then, you can evaluate *method bias*, the inflation of correlations due to a common measurement method. This is determined by investigating the correlations between different constructs using the same method contained in the solid-lined triangles. Method bias exists if these correlations are higher than correlations between different constructs measured by different methods.

Improving Validity

Similar to the reliability coefficient, several factors affect the magnitude of the validity coefficient. First, there must be variability among the predictor and criterion scores to obtain high validity coefficients. If respondents have approximately the same scores, it will be hard for the measure to differentiate among individuals based on the criterion. Also, as described above, in many social and behavioral science situations, a sample's variability is artificially smaller than that in the population.[44] Range restriction can occur in the predictor when criterion data are available only for hired people. Low scorers on the predictor are not employed and thus are not represented in the sample. Likewise, restriction in the criterion may occur due to terminations, turnover, or transfers that occur before data on the criterion are gathered. Note that when a sample is affected by range restriction in the predictor, the criterion, or both, formulae and computer programs are available to determine the validity coefficient without range restriction.[45]

Second, you can enhance validity by minimizing the influence of factors unrelated to scores on the criterion. *Criterion contamination* occurs when factors that are unrelated to the criterion affect scores on the criterion and, consequently, lower validity. For example, an organization uses a general cognitive ability measure to predict job performance. However, if factors such as availability of resources, quality of equipment, or supervisory liking unduly influence supervisory ratings of performance, the validity of the cognitive ability measure will decrease. You are no longer just measuring job performance; you are also assessing differences in resources, equipment, and likeability.

Third, validity estimated using the correlation coefficient depends on the linear relationship between the measure and criterion. The predictor can accurately predict both high and low scores when the relationship is linear. The validity coefficient is underestimated if this statistical assumption is violated (e.g., the relationship between the predictor and criterion is curvilinear).

Finally, the measure is not similarly valid if the relationship between the measure and a criterion differs for various groups (e.g., men vs. women).[46] Thus, the prediction of outcomes based on a measure's scores will differ depending on group membership.[47] Consequently, the overall predictive accuracy of a measure will be diminished.[48]

In sum, this section reviewed the process of measure development. It discussed the determination of the purpose of measurement, the definition of the attribute to be measured, the measure development plan, writing items, conducting a pilot study and item analysis, selecting items, establishing norms, and assessing reliability and validity. Next, let's discuss how to improve existing measures.

HOW TO IMPROVE EXISTING MEASURES

How to Improve Construct Validity

Construct validity is a perennial concern in social and behavioral science research. In essence, construct validity refers to the extent to which a measure represents the intended construct.[49] Methodological reviews have repeatedly emphasized the importance of construct validity and the need to improve the measurement of theoretical constructs.[50] For instance, an old review on measurement practices published in the 1980s already identified several critical areas for improvement, including using categorical measures to represent complex constructs, relying on single indicators, inadequate assessment of reliability, and insufficient attention to levels of measurement.[51] Unfortunately, these issues were reexamined years later, and most studies continued to rely on single indicators, and those studies that used multiple indicators typically failed to report reliability estimates.[52] So, poor construct measurement continues to be one of the most severe threats to social and behavioral science research.[53]

Given all the concerns already described, you must actively strive to improve the construct validity of your measures. To this end, there are several recommendations you should take into account. First, at the conceptual level, it is essential to establish that measures meaningfully correspond to the intended constructs. This correspondence can be strengthened by clearly defining the construct of interest and selecting measures whose meaning unequivocally matches the construct's definition. Although this principle might seem obvious, there is plenty of studies in which the correspondence between constructs and measures is tenuous. For example, a review documented that many studies use the same archival measures to represent substantively different constructs.[54] You can evaluate the correspondence between constructs and measures by providing definitions of the constructs under investigation to informed judges and asking them to rate the extent to which each measure represents each construct. Good correspondence is evidenced by measures with high mean ratings on the intended construct, low mean ratings on other constructs, and low variance in ratings.[55] This pattern would indicate that the judges agree that the measure represents only the intended construct.

Second, you should specify the nature and direction of the relationships between constructs and measures.[56] Typically, constructs are treated as direct causes of their measures, consistent with the *reflective measurement model* in Figure 6.3a. This model underlies common factor analysis[57] and internal consistency reliability estimation[58] and captures the premise that variation in a construct produces variation in its observable indicators.[59] An alternative specification is shown in Figure 6.3b, which depicts a *formative measurement model*.[60] Although formative measurement has received increased attention in social and behavioral science research, it rests on several dubious assumptions, the foremost of which is that measures can cause constructs.[61] Stripped to their essence, measures are scores taken as empirical analogs of constructs. These scores have no causal potency in their own right but are visible traces of the unobserved phenomena to which constructs refer.[62] For these reasons, specifying models in which measures cause constructs makes little sense in most cases.[63]

Despite misgivings about formative measurement, we can understand their intuitive appeal. For instance, formative measurement models provide a succinct and convenient way to combine conceptually distinct measures into an overall composite. Indeed, guidelines for creating formative measures recommend selecting indicators that are conceptually distinct from one another.[64] However, when measures represent distinct dimensions, they should be conceived as constructs in their own right, and the relationship between each measure and its associated dimension should be carefully considered. In most cases, this process will yield a **multidimensional construct model** in

FIGURE 6.3 ■ Reflective and Formative Measurement Models

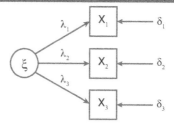

a. Reflective measurement model

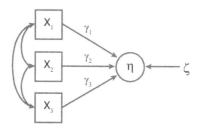

b. Formative measurement model

Source: Aguinis & Edwards (2014).

FIGURE 6.4 ■ Superordinate Multidimensional Construct Model

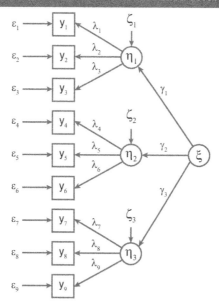

Source: Aguinis & Edwards (2014).

which the measures are reflective indicators of their dimensions, and the dimensions are reflective or formative indicators of a broader construct. A model that treats the dimensions as reflective relative to a broader construct is illustrated in Figure 6.4, which shows a superordinate multidimensional construct model.[65] This model is consistent with conventional second-order factor models, which have a long history in the factor analysis literature.[66] A model that specifies the dimensions as formative relative to a broader construct is depicted in Figure 6.5, which illustrates an aggregate multidimensional construct model.[67] The choice between these two models is a conceptual matter that depends on whether the broader construct is seen as producing its dimensions, as in Figure 6.4, or instead is a result of its dimensions, as in Figure 6.5.

Third, you should thoroughly evaluate measurement models using confirmatory factor analysis. When conducting a confirmatory factor analysis, an initial step is determining whether the data satisfy the estimation procedures' distributional assumptions (e.g., whether the data follow a multivariate normal distribution). When these assumptions are violated, alternative estimation methods can be used,[68] or remedial procedures can be applied, for example, to offset the effects of non-normality.[69] Next, the measurement model should be specified based on conceptual reasoning regarding the relationships between the constructs and their measures.[70] As part of specifying the model, it is essential to identify the measurement and structural portions of the model.[71] After the model is estimated, the resulting parameters should be examined to ensure they are consistent with the model and fall within logical bounds, such as item loadings that differ appreciably from zero and factor correlations that are significantly and substantively greater than -1.0 and less than 1.0.[72] In addition, sources of misfit should be examined, such as standardized residuals and modification indices that refer to constrained measurement errors and item cross-loadings. These results should not be used to empirically re-specify the model but instead to reveal where the sources of misfit are most pronounced. Finally, the target measurement model should be compared to alternative theoretically meaningful and justifiable models. For example, you should not follow the routine comparison of the target model to models that collapse factors, which has become commonplace in research because tests that compare these models merely indicate whether the correlations among the factors in the target model are less than unity. This condition can be assessed by determining whether the confidence intervals around the correlations exclude unity.

FIGURE 6.5 ■ Aggregate Multidimensional Construct Model

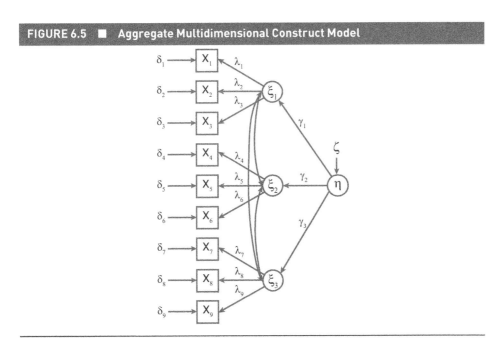

Source: Aguinis & Edwards (2014).

How to Improve Measurement Properties

A measure is considered psychometrically deficient if it fails to represent the desired construct comprehensively.[73] Using such measures provides an incomplete (i.e., deficient) understanding of the construct. Consequently, estimates of relations between the focal and other constructs are usually underestimated (i.e., observed effect size estimates are smaller than their true values). For example, measures of patent counts and patent citations are common in some research areas, such as International Business (IB) research. A recent review found that these measures have been used as proxies for constructs as diverse as knowledge sourcing and innovation performance. Furthermore, the articles using these measures mentioned that a crucial methodological challenge was the need for patent-based measures to represent the intended construct comprehensively. A similar challenge involving psychometrically deficient measures applies to data used to assess key IB constructs such as research and development (R&D) investment and R&D intensity. What can we do to improve psychometrically deficient measures?

First, consider that an ounce of prevention is worth a pound of cure.[74] In other words, the first solution is to evaluate whether the measure you are considering might be psychometrically deficient *before* you collect and analyze data. You can begin by examining the literature to determine if the measure has been employed previously to represent more than one construct. If so, it is necessary to provide one or more theoretical arguments to explain why using the measure to assess the focal construct is appropriate. It is also necessary to demonstrate why and how the conceptualization of the construct is accurate, given the context of the study.[75]

Second, for multidimensional constructs (e.g., organizational innovation), another solution for the psychometric-deficiency challenge is following the three-step process.[76] The first step is to specify whether the construct is reflective (i.e., measures are indicators of a superordinate construct) or formative (i.e., measures are aggregated to form the construct).

Example: Organizational Innovation Measured as Reflective or Formative

As an example, consider the construct of organizational innovation, which has been examined using measures such as product innovation, the total number of patent applications, the number of patents per employee, process innovation, and administrative innovation, among others. As described earlier (see Figure 6.3 as a reminder), reflective conceptualization implies an unobserved latent variable (i.e., organizational innovation) and that these measures are observable embodiments of this latent variable. In contrast, a formative conceptualization suggests that these measures are building blocks of an underlying latent variable (i.e., organizational innovation) defined by some combination of these measures.

The second step is to identify different dimensions of the construct and the implications of conceptualizing it in this manner. Because each measure in a reflective conceptualization captures all relevant information about the construct, different measures may be omitted as they provide interchangeable information.[77] Therefore, you may use just one measure to describe organizational innovation fully. However, in a formative conceptualization, each measure captures a different aspect of the construct, and omitting a measure detracts from the overall understanding of the construct. Therefore, you would use multiple measures and combine the scores to arrive at a composite value of organizational innovation.

The third and final step involves using analytical techniques to conceptualize the construct as reflective or formative.[78] For example, while reflective measures are expected to have high inter-correlations, formative measures do not need to demonstrate high internal consistency. You can take similar steps regarding measurement equivalence, measurement error, model identification, and model fit. Overall, following these three steps will provide evidence of whether the psychometric deficiency is a concern, regardless of how the construct is conceptualized.

Finally, another solution is to use multiple rather than single indicators. This is possible even when a particular database includes a single-item measure. Specifically, gaining a more comprehensive understanding of the construct is possible using two or more measures that provide alternative information. For example, in the case of organizational innovation, you may utilize multiple measures such as the number of new products introduced, the degree of "newness" of the products, the degree of technological advancement of products versus competitors' offerings, and process improvements to capture information about different facets of the construct. Another approach is to cross-reference measures of the construct across different databases.[79] For instance, returning to the example of patent-based measures, future research can use both when examining constructs related to innovation, knowledge, or technology rather than relying only on patent counts or citations.[80]

APPLIED METHODS: CASE STUDY – MEASUREMENT IN CORPORATE GOVERNANCE RESEARCH

The following section provides a five-step protocol to improve the accuracy of the estimates of relationships in your research. A case study illustrates the implementation of this protocol.

Strategic management studies is a relatively young field of inquiry. As expected of a nascent field of investigation, the development of strategic management studies was beset by a host of criticism and constructive commentary regarding its theoretical and methodological foundations and the robustness, or lack thereof, of its research. For example, some authors identified the need for more attention to measurement as an important challenge. Yet, there is little concern about measurement problems in many social and behavioral sciences fields.[81]

This section illustrates the increase in explanatory power achieved by improving the construct validity of independent and dependent variables. As a preview, Table 6.2 summarizes a five-step protocol described next.

TABLE 6.2 ■ Five-Step Protocol for Improving the Accuracy of Estimates of Relations Between Variables Based on Good Measures		
Step 1	Establish the base rate for the phenomenon in question.	Best base rate estimates for prior results derived from meta-analyses will likely be the most informative.
Step 2	Are the dependent variables germane?	Variables and their conceptual and operational definitions will be more credible if they reflect contemporary practice and appropriate construct validity.
Step 3	Are the independent variables germane?	Variables and their conceptual and operational definitions will be more credible if they reflect contemporary practice and appropriate construct validity.

(Continued)

TABLE 6.2 ■ Five-Step Protocol for Improving the Accuracy of Estimates of Relations Between Variables Based on Good Measures (*Continued*)		
Step 4	Do the relationships between the independent and dependent variables provide increased explanatory power compared to the base rate observed in Step 1?	If the answer is "No": If no such enhancements are observed, the contribution of the focal research may be gravely compromised. If the answer is "Yes": If such enhancements are observed, the contribution of the focal research is estimable.
Step 5	Given that estimable results are noted in Step 4, the base rate for the phenomenon of interest indicated in Step 1 may be revised for another iteration of research dedicated to the subject of interest.	

Source: Adapted from Dalton & Aguinis (2013). Reproduced with permission.

Step 1. Making Sense of Homogeneity of Results Using a Construct Validity Lens

Several authors have discussed methodological features that threaten the validity of conclusions.[82] For example, one specific threat to construct validity is the *less-than-ideal operationalization of constructs (LIOC)*.[83] This particular threat refers to issues described earlier in this chapter: contamination (i.e., a measure assesses issues that are not part of the construct) and deficiency (i.e., a measure does not assess issues that are part of the construct but should be assessed). A second threat is the *confounding constructs and levels of constructs (CCLC)*.[84] This occurs when a measure does not include the full range of possible values for a construct of interest.

Notably, most research published in corporate governance suffers from the LIOC and CCLC threats. These threats affect both outcomes (i.e., criteria) and predictors. First, consider the issue of less-than-ideal operationalization of constructs regarding the focal criterion of firm performance. For example, the meta-analytic evidence has relied on **return on assets (ROA)**, **return on equity (ROE)**, and **return on investment (ROI)**. Such measures might be calculated for 1, 3, 5- year periods and be hypothesized to be predicted by, for example, director independence or director equity. In these cases, however, none of these performance variables, irrespective of their magnitude or the extent of their relationship with other measures, indicate a direct benefit to shareholders, institutional or otherwise. For example, a company with a relatively high ROA may or may not present with a higher share price over the relevant period; that company may or may not elect to pay dividends. Accordingly, such variables do not provide a direct benefit to shareholders. Therefore, such measures of firm performance suffer from contamination (i.e., assess issues unrelated to shareholder benefit) and deficiency (i.e., do not assess issues directly related to shareholder benefit).

On the predictor side, corporate governance research relies on the "independence" of the board of directors. Independence is a critical construct in most corporate governance research, but, unfortunately, its measurement is subject to the CCLC construct validity threat. There has been concern about the board of directors' independence, or lack thereof, from the onset of agency theory. In addition, a recurring theme is whether the CEO should serve simultaneously as board chairperson.

By rule, the boards of all publicly traded firms must be comprised of 50% or more independent directors.[85] In addition, the average S&P 500 board presents with 84% independent directors.[86] For the Fortune 500, with data from 2012, the percentage of independent board members is 86.5. While these percentages are quite high, they are conceptually understated. Consider, for example, that the average number of board members for Fortune 500 firms is 10.7.[87] Moreover, all such firms have CEOs (who are not independent by rule) who always serve on their respective board.

In sum, although not acknowledged, less than ideal operationalization of constructs and confounding constructs and levels of constructs may be an important threat to the validity of conclusions in agency theory in particular and corporate governance research more broadly. Specifically, these construct validity issues should lead to small observed correlations between focal variables, regardless of the specific types of relationships examined. In other words, because of measurement contamination and deficiency as well as lack of sufficient variance (i.e., levels of the construct), effect size estimates (e.g., correlations, regression coefficients, the proportion of variance explained) involving independence and other variables—regardless of their nature—should be disappointingly small. A brief review of empirical results reported to date seems to underscore the conclusion that adopting a construct validity lens may allow us to re-interpret past findings. Next, several such relationships are re-examined, and this is done by offering a brief review of the meta-analytic evidence available, which is the standard for evidence in many scientific fields.[88]

BRIEF REVIEW OF EMPIRICAL RESEARCH REGARDING BOARD COMPOSITION

The extensive body of empirical research on board independence issues, including several meta-analyses and comprehensive narrative reviews, provides very modest or no support for hypothesized relationships between such constructs and firm performance[89]

Consistent with the guidelines outlined in Table 6.2, the first step is establishing a base rate for the body of prior research addressing the relationships between board independence issues and performance. For these data, relying on published meta-analyses (MAs) is critical for two reasons. First, the existence of a meta-analysis or several suggests that there is a relatively large body of research addressing such topics. Also, and critically for these purposes, MAs provide a summary mean which offers the best estimate of the relationship between the variables of interest. Accordingly, you can estimate the relationships between board independence and firm performance indicators by relying on several such MAs.

Consider the data of the meta-analysis of board independence and financial performance. The overall mean for their results was .015, with a 95% CI of .013 to .018. These authors also provided meta-analytic data on the relationship between CEO duality (i.e., whether the CEO serves simultaneously as board chairperson) and financial performance.[90] That mean estimate was −.041 with a CI of −.019 to −.057. Now, consider results reported by other authors regarding the relationship between board composition and financial performance. The mean effect size is .029, and the 95% CI for this mean estimate ranges from .027 to .030.[91] Next, additional triangulation is needed as it is important to gather evidence regarding a phenomenon of interest.[92] Yet another meta-analysis of board composition and financial performance[93] resulted in a slightly higher relative estimate of the summary mean: $r = .068$, CI .065 to .071. Even so, the variance explained is modest, less than 1 percent.

In fairness, however, these data and their analyses are based on articles published a while back. Accordingly, comparing these results with a more contemporary MA may be instructive. Some authors conducted a meta-analysis including 864 unique effect sizes based on a collective sample of 308,430 firms, as reported in 427 articles. A section of their work also addressed board composition and financial performance. The mean correlation is .035, and the 95% CI around this mean estimate ranges from .031 to .039.[94] The mean estimates of relationships between board independence and financial performance are very low. For the relationship over the four MAs described, these estimates ranged from a low of .015 to a high of .068, with variance explained of .0002 to .004.

Another basic independence notion derived from agency theory is how it might apply to the equity held by members of the board of directors, CEOs, senior executives of the firm, and other constituencies (e.g., institutional investors). One perspective suggests that shareholder and management interests can be aligned by providing an equity stake to executive officers and boards of directors.[95] The counter perspective provides that equity positions by management and boards often encourage improper and illegal behavior to maintain those managerial equity interests.[96]

The meta-analytic evidence thus far suggests that results are disappointedly homogeneous across studies and databases. Moreover, effect size estimates are vanishingly small. Nevertheless, these findings are quite consistent across various types of research questions. The only commonality across these diverse bodies of work is the reliance on the same measures for predictors (i.e., independence) and outcomes (i.e., firm performance) that suffer from the same threats to construct validity.

Step 2. Improving the Operationalization of Firm Performance: Total Shareholder Return and Shareholder Voice via "Withhold the Vote"

The previous section established the base rate for the phenomenon of interest (i.e., Step 1). In contrast, this section addresses whether the dependent variable(s) are germane, including issues about construct validity (i.e., Step 2). As an illustration, this section relies on a firm performance measure rarely relied on in macro studies that relate *directly* to the individual shareholder. It is referred to as **total shareholder return (TSR)**. A search of the Econlit and Business Source Premier databases found only one instance of its use in studies examining, for example, director independence, director equity, and board duality. So, although not used regularly by strategic management scholars, TSRs are now a common indicator of corporate performance and are included in annual reports to shareholders and **Securities and Exchange Commission** 10-K submissions. There is, then, no doubt that TSRs reflect contemporary practice. TSR is computed as follows:

Total Shareholder Return % = (Stock price at the end of the period − The stock price at the start of the period + Dividends paid or reinvested) ÷ The stock price at the start of the period

(6.11)

TSR data reported in corporate governance documents are usually displayed in a graphical format that includes 1, 3, 5, and, less often, 10-year periods. Beyond that, these data are generally compared to some reference group of companies or indices (for example, see AnnualReports.com, a comprehensive enablement providing full copies of annual reports and 10-Ks). But, again, TSR constitutes a metric of direct application to shareholders. It is the computation of the increase (or decrease) in the value of their shares plus whatever dividends have been paid or reinvested over the period.

Another development in corporate governance provides direct enablement for shareholders. This measure, too, provides another example of an operational connection between theory and practice. Shareholders have increasingly leveraged their statutory capability to "withhold" their vote(s) for directors in the proxy process (for an extended discussion of the development of these enablements, such as SEC rule 14a-11 and the Dodd-Frank Wall Street Reform and Consumer Protection Act[97]). This is a significant development. Consider that "In recent years, shareholders have relied increasingly on 'withhold the vote' or 'vote against' campaigns to signal disapproval of board candidates or board policies, instead of seeking to run and elect alternative nominees. These negative campaigns can be powerful catalysts for change" (p. 111).[98] This, too, is a significant development whereby shareholders, individuals who own relatively few shares in the enterprise or institutional investors who may hold the vast majority of the firm's equity, may directly register their disapproval by withholding their vote for the renewal of directors (including the CEO in their capacity as members of the board). This variable, too, reflects the contemporary practice and improved construct validity as well.

Step 3. Improving the Operationalization of Board Independence: Related Party Directors

To continue to follow the five-step protocol summarized in Table 6.2, the next step is to address whether the independent variable(s) are germane, including issues about construct validity (i.e., Step 3). Again, NYSE and NASDAQ guidelines provide interesting insight into the independence or otherwise of board members. These include having no material relationship with the company, not being an employee within the last three years, and not receiving more than $120,000 during any twelve months from the company (not including compensation as a director). Notably, what is omitted is a person referred to as a "related party" director (a.k.a, "constituent director," "constituency" director, a "designated" director, a "representative" director, or a "special interests" director[99]). Thus, the proportion of related party directors on a board can be an alternative measure of independence.

The earliest examples of such directors were agreements between U.S. automobile industries and their unions. In some cases, the union had bargained for a seat on the automobile company's board of directors. With regard to the "loyalty" issue, what would be most observers' intuition about whose loyalty was served by the union's representative on the board of directors? At this time, in fairness, such an arrangement was unusual. In later years, this phenomenon (potentially unaligned "outside" director loyalty) was often observed in venture capital (VC) backed company boards of directors.[100] Again, the basic issue was the extent to which such directors aligned their loyalty with the company on whose board they served or of the VC-backed company that arranged for their membership on the board. Do such directors have a parochial perspective, and will they advocate the views of the parties they represent? More recently, another interesting aspect of this phenomenon includes the U.S. Federal government, which under the authority of TARP (Troubled Asset Relief Program), named new directors for several benefitted companies.[101] This trend toward related party directors on various boards is no longer a curiosity. Indeed, mainly driven by activist investors, the number of such constituency directors has been estimated at 400.[102] This is yet another aspect of the contemporary publicly traded company and its intersection with board independence that has not been addressed.

Step 4. Re-examination of Substantive Construct-level Relationships Using Improved Measurements

This section refers to Table 6.2's Step 4, which suggests that relationships between independent and dependent variables that reflect contemporary practice and improved construct validity be compared to measures without that character. The issue is whether the former relationships provide increased explanatory power than the latter.

In addressing Step 1, meta-analytically derived mean estimates of hypothesized relationships between commonly relied-upon constructs in corporate governance research, mainly those grounded in agency theory, were reported. Moreover, it has been suggested that research based on contemporary operationalizations of these variables (e.g., total shareholder returns (TSRs), percentage of votes withheld, and related party directors) may provide better estimates of underlying construct-level relationships (i.e., Steps 2 and 3). The data on which the following sections rely are publicly available and drawn or derived from **Board Analyst** (board independence, CEO duality; officer and director's equity; institutionally held equity; outside related directors; votes withheld), **Wharton Research Data Services – WRDS** (total shareholder returns; https://wrds-web.wharton.upenn.edu/wrds/), and **AnnualReports.com**.

Duality: Should the CEO Serve Simultaneously as Chairperson of the Board?

As noted earlier, there is meta-analytic data on the relationship between CEO duality (i.e., whether the CEO serves simultaneously as chairperson of the board) and financial performance.[103] That mean estimate was –.041. However, when relying on the percentage of votes withheld, the relationship was .19. Regarding the ability to explain firm performance, analyses relying on traditional measures resulted in a .17% variance. In contrast, this re-analysis based on the percentage of votes withheld, a measure more proximal to shareholders, the percent of variance explained is increased to 3.61%.

Boards of Directors' Independence and Firm Performance

Prior meta-analyses of the relationship between board independence and firm performance resulted in mean estimates of .015,[104] .029,[105] .068,[106] and .035.[107] However, these analyses of the percentage of independent board members with total shareholder returns (TSRs) provided a substantially higher estimate of .133.

Officer and Directors Equity, Institutionally Held Equity, and Firm Performance

Prior meta-analyses provided estimates of the relationship between officer and director equity and firm performance. Such relationships have been uniformly modest—.028,[108] .053,[109] and .07.[110] The analyses presented in this chapter, relying on TSRs as the dependent variable, provide an interesting result. While the relationships between 1-year, 3-year, and 5-year TSRs and officer and director equity are unremarkable (.036, –.004, and .022 respectively), the relationship between officer and director equity and 10-year TSRs, however, is a comparatively notable, .18. In terms of proportion of variance explained, past research suggests that it ranges from .08% to .49%. Using TSR to measure firm performance leads to an estimate as high as 3.24%.

The prior meta-analyses did not address institutional equity. The analyses of 1-year, three-year, 5-year, and 10-year TSRs and institutional equity held in firms were not consequential—.02, –.046, .056, and .001. So, in this particular case, improving the construct validity of the outcome measure did not produce a substantial change in the results.

On the Bearing of Related Party Directors

An earlier section argued that related party directors constitute a far more robust threat to director independence than the commonly relied upon simple tally (usually the percentage of independent directors on the board). These results—consistent with prior results—suggest that director independence is not an issue concerning TSRs. Also, it is of no consequence concerning withheld votes.

The relationship between the percentage of related party directors on the board and TSRs was .029 (1-yr TSRs), .015 (3-yr TSRs), –.052 (5-yr TSRs), and –.064 (10-year TSRs). The relationship between the percentage of related party directors and withheld votes was –.039 (1-yr TSRs), .064 (3-year TSRs), –.054 (5-year TSRs), and –.001 (10-year TSRs). In other words, the proposed solution for improving the measurement of the independence construct did not lead to a substantial improvement in the effect size estimate.

Step 5. Revise for Another Iteration of Research Dedicated to the Subject of Interest

This section arrives at the last step of the protocol summarized in Table 6.2. Because substantially higher estimates of relationships were provided when relying on measures that reflect contemporary practice and improved construct validity, it can be believed – consistent with Step 5 – that the previous base rates for the phenomena in question have been exceeded. In addition, the meta-analyses reviewed resulted in bivariate correlations that are homogeneously low.

Step 5 also suggests that higher base rates warrant other iterations of research dedicated to the subject of interest. Given the demonstrated base rates, the relationships of interest may now be considered and included in further analyses, including those examining moderating and mediating effects and structural equation modeling.[111]

The potential advantages of this section's techniques are open to research relying on agency theory bases and the typical corporate governance variables reported in this section. Consider, for example, that any macro research could be driven, or at the least supplemented, by attention to corporate governance-dependent variables that are relied upon in contemporary practice. Fortunately, driven by the Securities and Exchange Commission (SEC) guidelines, such variables are easily identified. Also, it is notable that these indicators are now available to the SEC and constitute notice of reliance on such indicators to the filer's many constituencies.

Concerning contemporary practice and improved construct validity, this case study demonstrated some improvement in the scale of relationships associated with corporate governance. In addition, some initial work[112] provided an alert about the extant threats related to measurement problems in strategic management research, including construct validity. Based on data on MAs from 1980-2011,[113] this section examined the summary means of MAs in macro studies before and after 2005. The summary means for the prior period was .21; in the subsequent period, the summary mean was .22. Thus, unfortunately, not much progress has been made, and much work remains to be done. The five-step protocol will be instrumental in guiding your future efforts too.

This chapter has provided the tools to create and improve your measures. Chapter 7 will focus on how to design and conduct experimental research.

DISCUSSION QUESTIONS

1. Why should you care about measurement?

2. How could you defend the benefits of good measurement?

3. What are the differences between the various measurement scales (nominal, ordinal, interval, and ratio scales), and why are these differences significant?

4. How can you create a new measure (i.e., what are the critical steps to create a new measure)?

5. What happens if you ignore critical steps in formulating a new measure?

6. What reliability estimates can you use to learn which error affects your measures (hint: discuss test-retest reliability, parallel forms, internal consistency, and interrater reliability)?

7. You just created a new measure; the test-retest reliability estimate is .70, and Cronbach's α is .85. What is the meaning of these results regarding the amount and type of error in your measure? Would you use this particular measure, given these reliability estimates? Why? Why not?

8. By what means can you gather validity evidence about your measure (hint: discuss content-related evidence, criterion-related evidence, and construct-related evidence)?

9. What are two things you can do to improve the size of the validity coefficients?

10. What are two things you can do to improve your measure's construct validity?

11. How does range restriction (i.e., censorship) affect validity evidence, and what can you do?

12. What are two things you can do to minimize psychometric deficiency and contamination?

13. Do you agree that reflective measures are better than formative measures in most cases? Why? Why not?

14. What are the five steps in the protocol to improve the accuracy of estimated relations between variables? Describe a research domain of interest to you that would benefit from implementing this protocol.

KEY TERMS

annualreports.com
arithmetic mean
attributes
Board Analyst (Corporate Library's historical data)
censorship
classification
coefficient alpha
coefficient of stability
confounding constructs and levels of constructs (CCLC)
construct
construct-related evidence
the content validity ratio (CVR)
convergent validity
corporate governance research
correlation coefficients
criterion contamination
Cronbach's coefficient alpha
discrimination index
distractor analysis
divergent validity
interclass correlation
internal consistency
Interrater agreement
interrater reliability
interval scale
intraclass correlation (ICC) index
item analysis
item characteristic curve (ICC)
item difficulty

item discrimination
item response theory (IRT)
item-total score correlation
Kuder-Richardson 20 (KR-20)
less-than-ideal operationalization of constructs (LIOC)
linear transformations
mean
measurement scales
median
mode
monotonic transformations
multidimensional construct model
multitrait-multimethod approach
nominal scale
nomological network
norms
ordinal
p value
parallel forms
Pearson product-moment correlation
percentile ranks
pilot study
psychometric deficiency
range restriction
rank-order analysis of variance
ratio scales
reflective measurement model
regression coefficient
reliability
reliability coefficient

return on assets (ROA)

return on equity (ROE)

return on investment (ROI)

scaling

Securities and Exchange Commission

split-half method

standard error of measurement

test-retest reliability

Spearman-Brown prophecy formula

total shareholder returns (TSR)

validity

validity coefficients

variance

Wharton Research Data Services – WRDS

NOTES

This chapter is based to a large extent on the following sources:

Aguinis, H., & Edwards, J. R. (2014). Methodological wishes for the next decade and how to make wishes come true. *Journal of Management Studies*, *51*(1), 143-174. https://doi.org/10.1111/joms.12058

Aguinis, H., Henle, C.A., & Ostroff, C. (2001). Measurement in work and organizational psychology. In N., Anderson, D.S. Ones, H.K. Sinangil, and C. Viswesvaran (Eds.), *Handbook of industrial, work and organizational psychology* (vol. 1, pp. 27-50). Sage. https://doi.org/10.4135/9781848608320.n3

Dalton, D. R., & Aguinis, H. (2013). Measurement malaise in strategic management studies: The case of corporate governance research. *Organizational Research Methods*, *16*(1), 88-99. https://doi.org/10.4135/9781848608320.n3

7

HOW TO DESIGN AND CONDUCT EXPERIMENTAL RESEARCH

LEARNING GOALS

By the end of this chapter, you will be able to do the following:

7.1 Argue why you should care about experiments and how experiments provide evidence regarding causality.

7.2 Defend the usefulness of experimental vignette methodology (EVM) and describe the two main types of EVM.

7.3 Recommend how to conduct studies using experimental vignette methodology, including how to maximize internal and external validity and how to report results transparently to ensure replicability.

7.4 Compare the methodological approaches of online experiments, longitudinal surveys, and existing datasets, and identify the advantages of online experiments.

7.5 Diagram best-practice recommendations for using Amazon's Mechanical Turk (MTurk) in social and behavioral science research.

7.6 Critique the advantages and disadvantages of using virtual reality (VR) for conducting experiments.

7.7 Appraise the process of conducting thought experiments and identify when they will likely be particularly relevant.

7.8 Decide which type of thought experiment is most suitable given your research goals.

IMPORTANCE OF EXPERIMENTS

Understanding the direction and nature of causal relationships is the cornerstone of science.[1] However, while most social and behavioral science research provides evidence regarding covariation between antecedent and outcome variables, **covariation** alone (e.g., as X increases, Y also increases) does not answer two essential questions for establishing **causality**. First, did the antecedent occur temporally before the effect? Second, have other alternative explanations for covariation been ruled out?[2] A primary reason for the lack of clear answers to these questions is that much of social and behavioral science research consists of passive observation designs (i.e., the researcher does not manipulate the antecedent variables) and is **cross-sectional** (i.e., all data are collected simultaneously).[3] In contrast, understanding causal relationships requires experimental or quasi-experimental designs.[4]

Experimental studies provide essential advantages compared to passive observational designs, including those using self-reported questionnaires and **secondary data** sources (e.g., databases available in the public domain).[5] However, implementing experimental research includes challenges such as threats to external validity and logistical and practical implementation issues.[6] For example, experimental research often removes participants from their natural settings and takes place in a laboratory and highly controlled and isolated environment. Such a change of context puts into question the validity of results because it is impossible to know whether participants would behave in the same way in a natural compared to a laboratory setting. Other challenges of conducting experimental research are related to practical and logistical constraints. Specifically, it takes more time and effort to conduct an experiment involving creating experimental materials, recruiting participants, administering the **experimental treatments**, and addressing ethical challenges in administering the treatments compared to using archival data or an online survey.[7] These challenges can also make experimental studies more expensive and often difficult, if not impossible, to implement in naturally occurring contexts.

Thus, all of us social and behavioral science researchers seem to face a seemingly inescapable dilemma: (a) implement experimental designs that are more resource- and time-intensive, prone to ethical challenges, and challenged by difficulties regarding external validity (i.e., uncertainty regarding the generalizability of results), but yield high levels of confidence regarding internal validity, versus (b) implement non-experimental designs that often maximize external validity because they are conducted in natural settings, but whose conclusions are ambiguous in terms of the direction and nature of causal relationships.

This chapter will show you how using **vignettes**, online, virtual reality, and **thought experiments** can help you overcome some of the most pervasive methodological challenges associated with the design and implementation of experimental research. It begins with discussing experimental vignette studies, key steps and decision points, and best-practice recommendations for implementing this experimental methodology. The following section examines online experiments and how online platforms such as MTurk can help you overcome pervasive methodological challenges associated with experimental designs. The third section focuses on the advantages and challenges of using virtual reality-based experiments. Finally, the last section guides conducting thought experiments, including their unique features, a **taxonomy**, and best-practice recommendations for implementation.

HOW TO CONDUCT VIGNETTE EXPERIMENTS

Experimental vignette methodology (EVM) presents participants with carefully constructed and realistic scenarios. Thus, EVM enhances experimental realism and allows you to manipulate and control independent variables, simultaneously enhancing internal and external validity.[8]

Vignettes are a "short, carefully constructed description of a person, object, or situation, representing a systematic combination of characteristics" (p. 128).[9] An important characteristic of EVM is that it is not restricted to being presented solely in written format but can include images, videos, and other media.[10] There are two major types of EVM: Those assessing explicit (i.e., **paper people studies**) and those assessing implicit (i.e., **policy capturing** and **conjoint analysis**) processes and outcomes.

Paper People Studies

Paper people studies present participants with vignettes, typically written, and then ask participants to make explicit decisions, judgments, choices, or express behavioral preferences. This type of EVM has existed for many decades and has been used extensively.[11]

While this type of EVM has been popular in ethical decision-making contexts, it has also been applied in other areas. For example, a paper people study included employees in a law enforcement agency who read scenarios involving workplace romances that resulted in sexual harassment allegations. The results of this study provided evidence about the causal effects of type of workplace romance on subsequent attitudes about the romance participants.[12]

Policy Capturing and Conjoint Analysis Studies

Policy capturing and conjoint analysis studies present respondents with scenarios containing carefully manipulated variables.[13] In contrast to paper people studies, however, participants make decisions between scenarios for the researcher to capture participants' implicit processes.[14] In other words, in policy capturing and conjoint analysis studies, the goal is to understand the effects of the manipulated variables on implicit judgments through the ranking of vignettes or by asking participants to make choices and state preferences between them. Therefore, the specific purpose of this type of EVM is to assess participants' choices by capturing real-time processes and decisions—that are often not made openly and with the participants' full awareness. While policy capturing and conjoint analysis studies are often discussed separately,[15] and researchers in some fields use one or another label, policy capturing and conjoint analysis methods are virtually the same.

Based on a comprehensive review of EVM, we now have best-practice recommendations that address suggestions and trade-offs involved in each of the ten decision points associated with the planning, implementation, and reporting of results stages of EVM studies. A summary of these recommendations is presented in Figure 7.1.

Planning an EVM Study

Decision Point #1: Deciding Whether EVM Is a Suitable Approach

While EVM is valuable, there may be more appropriate methodological approaches for your specific needs. First, EVM is beneficial when you need to exercise control of independent variables to gather evidence regarding causation.[16] EVM allows you to include relevant factors to the research question while excluding those that might **confound** the results. This amount of control helps to test causal hypotheses that would otherwise be difficult. Therefore, EVM is particularly useful in research domains in which variables are known to correlate (i.e., covary), but there is a need to determine the nature and direction of causal relationships.

Second, EVM is also an appropriate method when facing ethical dilemmas in conducting experimental research. While it is challenging to manipulate sensitive topics ethically experimentally, EVM allows you to create hypothetical scenarios that address sensitive issues. For example, it would be ethically impossible to manipulate workplace romances in an experiment. However, as mentioned above, using EVM, some researchers have understood causal antecedents of perceptions and attributions of the blame of former workplace romance participants when the romance turns into a sexual harassment allegation.[17] In short, EVM is a good choice when the goal is to investigate sensitive topics in an experimentally controlled way.

It is also important to recognize issues that may lead to the decision *not to use* EVM. Specifically, because EVM requires participants to respond to hypothetical scenarios, there are some situations when those scenarios do not create the same context as would be encountered in naturally occurring settings (e.g., work, school).[18] This can make it difficult to use EVM when certain contextual pressures are difficult to reproduce. For instance, in some high-stakes decision-making scenarios (e.g., mergers and acquisitions of organizations), the presentation of hypothetical scenarios is likely to produce different responses than when those situations occur in real life.

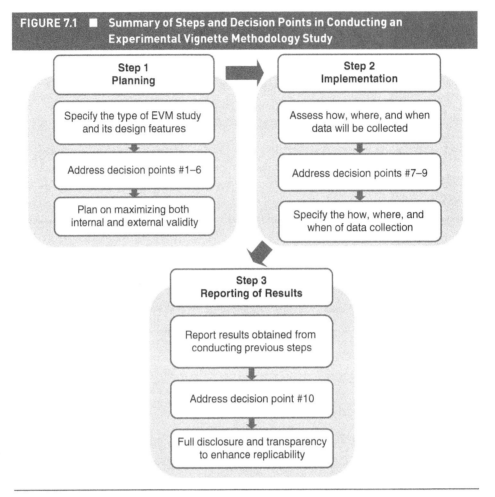

FIGURE 7.1 ■ Summary of Steps and Decision Points in Conducting an Experimental Vignette Methodology Study

Source: Aguinis & Bradley (2014). Reproduced with permission.

Decision Point #2: Choosing the Type of EVM

The next major decision is to choose the type of EVM. Again, the two primary options are paper people and policy capturing/conjoint analysis.

Paper People Studies.   Recall that paper people studies focus on explicit responses to hypothetical scenarios. Accordingly, this type of EVM is most appropriate when the goal is to assess explicit processes and outcomes—those about which participants are aware and on which they can provide valuable and accurate information.

Policy Capturing and Conjoint Analysis Studies.   Recall that policy capturing, and conjoint analysis studies capture implicit processes and outcomes.[19] In both types of EVM, it is assumed that important factors that make up the individual's decision process are known a priori. For this reason, these techniques are most useful in areas where theory provides a clear understanding of factors likely to influence processes and outcomes. However, suppose an area is relatively new or conceptually underdeveloped. In that case, knowing those factors may not be possible, making policy capturing and conjoint analysis less appropriate.

Additionally, policy capturing and conjoint analysis allow you to understand the decision-making process of a single individual. Because of this, these techniques can be used to collect large amounts of information, even from a relatively small group of participants,[20] and this is especially useful when the population of interest is small or inaccessible (i.e., highly successful entrepreneurs, CEOs).[21]

Decision Point #3: Choosing the Type of Research Design

The next decision involves choosing the type of research design. Choices include a **between-person, within-person, or mixed research design.**[22]

Between-person designs require that each participant read only one vignette, and comparisons are made across participants. True between-person designs are uncommon, especially when judgments are used as the dependent variable. For instance, because participants are only presented with a single rather than multiple vignettes, they lose any chance at the comparison that would help to ground responses contextually. Without other vignettes to serve as referent points for their judgments, answers may not accurately reflect the true judgments of each respondent. For this reason, it is important that in between-person designs, participants be provided with sufficient information to help provide as much context as possible. For instance, some researchers conducting a paper people EVM first presented participants with baseline information (i.e., a general description of the issues involved) to provide a similar contextual background for all participants.[23] Accordingly, the recommendation is to give the participants an adequate contextual background when using a between-subjects design or the within-person or mixed design options.

When using a within-person design, each participant views the same set of vignettes, and comparisons are made between vignettes within the same person. This type of design helps show the effects of a manipulation within one individual and helps uncover the judgment processes of a single individual.

Finally, in mixed designs, different participants receive different sets of vignettes; however, within each group, participants see the same vignettes. Accordingly, comparisons can be made across respondents because multiple respondents also offer responses regarding the same vignettes.

Decision Point #4: Choosing the Level of Immersion

One of the major criticisms regarding the use of EVM is that it is unrealistic, and results may need to be generalizable. In addition, EVM studies are criticized for only showing that specific outcomes *can* happen, but not necessarily that they *do* happen outside of the experimental situation. Accordingly, some researchers have called to improve the external validity of EVM by enhancing the level of realism present in the stimulus presentation.[24] Moreover, much like the training literature has demonstrated that transfer of training is improved by increasing the similarity between the training context and the context where what has been learned will be used,[25] improving realism is achieved by increasing the similarity between the experimental and natural settings.

One recommendation to improve realism is to increase the level of immersion experienced by participants—the subjective experience of being personally immersed in the situation described in the vignette. Technological advances have provided the means to do so by changing the method of presentation of scenarios. For example, audio, video, pictures, and other presentation methods can increase the realism of EVM studies instead of just written descriptions.[26] These types of presentation methods aim to engage participants' senses more fully. Indeed, as discussed later, virtual reality (VR) technology can be used to provide a higher level of immersion.

Increasing the immersion of participants has several benefits. First, observing actual behavior is more likely to engage participants to a greater extent, allowing them to remember and recall relevant information.[27] Additionally, as mentioned earlier, more immersive techniques enhance experimental realism. As some researchers showed, written presentations provide fewer distractors in scenarios than when behavior is directly observed.[28] But this is not necessarily an advantage. Using a more immersive medium makes scenarios lifelike, likely providing more "natural **noise**" in each scenario. If you control the distractors' "noise," more lifelike scenarios could be created without compromising the experiment's internal validity. For instance, some researchers observed voice behaviors using a video-vignette controlled presentation of one possible source of noise by using actors that were rated as equally attractive. This helped them rule out the effect that attractiveness could have on the study results.[29] Additionally, greater immersion is likely to help increase external validity as the scenarios more closely approximate experiences in the real world.[30] Finally, using techniques higher on immersion also allows you to explore sensitive topics that are difficult or unethical to manipulate in the real world.

While many benefits accompany immersive presentation techniques, there are also some trade-offs you should consider. For example, as vignette studies become more immersive, the cost associated with the experiment typically increases as well. On the other hand, creating a written vignette usually requires no more than your own time and creativity. But, in a study using video vignettes instead of written vignettes, you will need additional resources. For example, you may have to hire professional actors to role-play the various scenarios for the study participants.[31]

Decision Point #5: Specifying the Number and Levels of the Manipulated Factors

Theory plays a crucial role in planning an EVM study because it is the driving force in choosing the factors relevant to the research and the number of levels for each manipulated factor. This is often one of the criticisms against vignette methodologies[32]: because EVM requires pre-specified variables and levels, the threat of omitting important antecedent variables, especially in complex decision-making processes, is high. Some researchers noted that "the key is to identify what information is critical to the decision being studied" (p. 207).[33] Of course, the issue of model misspecification is a concern in all empirical research. Still, it is particularly important in the context of EVM and experimental research in general, given the criticism that that such research does not test "whether a hypothesis is true, but rather whether the experimenter is a sufficiently ingenious stage manager to produce the laboratory conditions which demonstrate that an obviously true hypothesis is correct" (p. 449).[34]

Two main approaches can be used in choosing which variables to include. The first involves an attribute-driven design, in which factors are considered orthogonal. This allows you to assess the independent effects of each manipulated factor more easily.[35] However, presenting orthogonal cues has limitations. For example, in some instances, combining orthogonal variables into a single vignette produces unrealistic scenarios. In this case, consider replacing the unrealistic scenarios with more realistic ones to help ensure balance in vignette representation.[36]

As a second recommendation, you can use the "actually derived cases" approach in which the variables chosen to be manipulated and the level of those variables are selected to represent concrete values found in actual settings.[37] Again, the recommendation is to ask individuals similar to the targeted sample to provide details as to realistic factor levels. One of the significant advantages of this approach is that it presents more realistic scenarios to respondents, which can help to increase the generalizability of results.

Decision Point #6: Choosing the Number of Vignettes

Presenting participants with the proper number of vignettes is crucial because too many vignettes can lead to participant information overload and fatigue. At the same time, not enough scenarios can limit your ability to manipulate critical variables and could result in biased responses because the scenarios included a few selective issues only.[38]

In choosing the number of vignettes, the first point to consider is that the study's purpose dictates this number. Thus, there is no exact answer to the question, "How many vignettes need to be presented?" Instead, a question to ask is, "What is the number of variables to be manipulated and the number of levels that each of those variables includes?"[39] The answer to this question will provide a full population of vignettes you can use in the study. While this full population of vignettes is available, using all the resulting vignettes may not be necessary. Regardless, the first step is to create a full population of vignettes. After the full population is constructed, you must decide how many vignettes to use. Here are two important recommendations. First, you should use at least five scenarios for every manipulated attribute.[40] Moreover, err on including more vignettes per respondent than fewer.[41] Second, including repeated vignettes allow you to assess reliability.[42] Thus, the recommendation is to have four or five duplicated scenarios.

Implementing an EVM Study

Decision Point #7: Specifying the Sample and Number of Participants

In EVM studies, "The quality of the data obtained is dependent upon the respondent" (p. 291).[43] This is especially true in considering the need to generalize results to a larger population. So, there is a need to match the sample to the larger population of interest.[44] Additionally, it is important that the situation presented to the participant be familiar to them. Otherwise, responses may be artificial. In short, the more the respondents can approximate a more generalized population, the higher the external validity of the results of an EVM study.

A frequent challenge in EVM studies is that accessing an appropriate sample can take time and effort. In this situation, you may turn to using student samples. Whether or not this is an appropriate practice has been debated for decades[45] due to concerns that student samples may not provide evidence that can be generalizable to broader populations.[46] This is especially the case in research that addresses issues associated with high-ranking employees (e.g., CEOs, board members, top management teams) or difficult-to-identify samples (e.g., early-stage entrepreneurs). Overall, there is a concern about the exclusive use of what is called a "WEIRD" sample: One consisting of White, educated, industrialized, rich, and democratic participants. An important advantage of EVM is that it can be used with samples outside the on-campus laboratory. However, when a suitable sample cannot be found, changing the vignettes to better match the abilities and knowledge of the sample used may be necessary.[47]

New technological advances have eased data collection from samples that match a study's purpose. For instance, Internet freelancing platforms, including prominent sites such as Amazon's Mechanical Turk (MTurk), provide you with access to large samples of working individuals at relatively low cost.[48] The next section of this chapter ("How to Conduct Experiments Online") provides more details and best-practice recommendations for using these online marketplaces. Overall, samples of working individuals can be collected almost as easily as college students, which can minimize concerns regarding external validity issues.[49]

Decision Point #8: Choosing the Setting and Timing for Administration

First, you should be aware of the conditions in which participants respond. The criticism that EVM lacks realism can be addressed, at least partly, by allowing respondents to participate in the study while located in their natural setting.[50]

Example: Using Video Vignettes to Conduct Experiments

Some researchers conducted a video vignette experiment investigating the effects of leadership status and style on perceptions of leadership effectiveness and team performance. But, instead of bringing participants to the university facilities, they were invited to watch the videos and participate remotely from their work environments.[51]

In addition to deciding on where to conduct the EVM study, timing is also important. It is best if participants can respond to the vignettes in a single session.[52] In some cases, such as video vignettes, presentation may require multiple sessions, but multiple sessions are more likely to be affected by history and other threats to validity.

Decision Point #9: Choosing the Best Method for Analyzing the Data

As noted earlier, the use of between-person designs is less than optimal. But, if such designs are used, data analytic techniques such as MANOVA, ANOVA, and ANCOVA are appropriate. When an EVM study includes the preferred within-person of mixed design types, there is a two-level data structure: vignette and respondent levels.[53] Because of the multilevel nature of the data, analyses that focus on both levels simultaneously need to be used. Specifically, you should use multilevel modeling.[54]

Reporting Results of an EVM Study

In the interest of replicability, you should describe the process of creating and administering the vignettes as transparently as possible.[55] A high level of detail is necessary given that research in the social and behavioral sciences is susceptible to numerous credibility issues regarding reporting results, including withholding or not accurately reporting procedures and results.[56]

Decision Point #10: Choosing How Transparent to Be in the Final Presentation of Methodology and Results

You should disclose as much information as possible about the vignettes used in the EVM study. In the case of text or picture vignettes studies, they should be included in the manuscript as this enhances the transparency of the research process.[57] When the vignettes cannot be physically included in the manuscript (such as in the case of video or virtual reality vignettes), you should make the materials available to others upon request or through the journal's website. Most social and behavioral science journals allow authors to post online supplements to accompany published articles. In the interest of furthering scientific knowledge, the recommendation is to make your vignettes available. As an illustration of transparency, some researchers included an appendix with the vignettes used in their study and the process used in creating and pilot testing them.[58] By providing the vignettes used in the experiment, future research now has a source to draw from in conducting work to extend theory while providing additional data to help validate the vignettes used.

Example: Enhancing Scientific Knowledge through Collaboration

While some may balk at making experimental materials accessible and available to others, scientific knowledge can be enhanced through collaboration. For example, the International Personality Item Pool (IPIP) was developed due to the slow development of the personality assessment field caused partly by constraints generated by copyrighted personality assessment tools.[59] Now consisting of over 2,000 individual personality-related items, the IPIP provides free access to a large set of items that you can use to further the field of personality testing.

Next, let's discuss the issue of how to conduct experiments online. The following material describes the advantages of doing so and best-practice recommendations regarding design, implementation, and reporting.

HOW TO CONDUCT EXPERIMENTS ONLINE

Online experiments can be conducted using "**online marketplaces**," websites where individuals interested in being hired and clients looking for individuals to perform some work meet. Using these online marketplaces can allow you to overcome some of the most pressing methodological challenges of conducting experiments. Table 7.1 compares online experiments with other methodologies, such as longitudinal surveys and existing datasets that include information collected by third parties.

METHODS IN PRACTICE
TAKING ADVANTAGE OF PUBLICLY AVAILABLE DATA

Keep in mind that databases refer to secondary data collected not through means of surveys but instead by garnering publicly available data. For example, public companies (companies listed on the stock exchange) are obligated to provide accounting and governance statements to the Securities and Exchange Commission, and these data are publicly available for shareholders to make decisions. Websites such as Hoover's or Market Line provide access to such databases. Also, longitudinal surveys refer to primary data sets collected by having individuals answer multiple surveys over set intervals (e.g., six months, 12 months, 18 months). The Panel Study of Entrepreneurial Dynamics (PSED) collected by the University of Michigan and much of the Census Data provided on self-employed individuals are two examples of longitudinal surveys.

TABLE 7.1 ■ Comparison of Online Experiments, Longitudinal Surveys, and Existing Datasets

	Control and Manipulation of Independent Variables	Realism	Operationalization of Variables / Internal Validity	Randomization	Ability to Measure the Effect of Independent Variable
Online experiments	Allows for control and manipulation	Very realistic situation and context	Control in the operationalization of variables	Allows for randomization	Great ability
Longitudinal Surveys	No control or manipulation	Potentially realistic situation and context	Some control in the operationalization of the dataset, but difficult to modify after the first wave of data collection	No randomization	Partial ability
Existing Datasets	No control or manipulation	Realistic situation and context	Little control in the operationalization of variables	No randomization	Partial ability

Source: Aguinis & Lawal (2012).

Next, let's discuss how conducting your experiment online has many benefits and allows you to overcome many of the difficult challenges involved in experimental research. The following section's material is general and broadly applicable to online research. But, it is also particularly applicable to research using the most popular online marketplace: MTurk.

Benefits of Online Experiments

Overcoming the Lack of Generalizability Challenge

Generalizability is a matter of degree, and there can always be an additional setting to which you would like to extrapolate a set of results. Online experiments allow you to overcome the lack of generalizability challenge because of the availability of highly heterogeneous participants worldwide. In this format, you can issue a call for work (i.e., an experiment) and require, for example, that study participants be from a particular region or industry and with specific experience and educational characteristics (including demographic characteristics). Online experiments also allow you to recruit study participants 24/7 worldwide. Moreover, the cost of recruiting and compensating study participants can be as low as a few cents of a U.S. dollar per task.

Overcoming the Omitted Measurement of an Important Variable Challenge

Another critical methodological challenge with experiments is that important variables might not be included in the study. Online experiments can overcome this methodological challenge because by conducting experiments, you have control over the research design and the variables included in the study. In other words, you collect all the necessary data to test a specific theory and hypotheses, including adding control,[60] moderator,[61] and mediator[62] variables.

Research in the social and behavioral sciences is multidimensional and multivariate in nature. But, it is only possible for any particular study to address a small subset of relevant questions and variables. However, online experiments provide you with the ability to include more variables compared to other types of field studies in which data collection efforts are more contextually determined by resources constraints (e.g., time, access to study participants) and the use of data collected by third parties (i.e., databases) which may not include all variables of theoretical interest.

Overcoming the Less-than-ideal Operationalization of Construct Challenge

Another methodological challenge you may face is that constructs are **operationalized** (i.e., measured) in a way that may be deficient (i.e., part of the construct domain is not measured) or contaminated (i.e., a measure includes a domain outside of the construct). Online experiments allow you to collect your data using your own measures. You can choose to use the best available instruments for each construct. Although other methods will enable you to use your measures, and it is difficult to think of an "ideal" measure in an absolute sense, online experiments reduce the practical burden and cost on researchers and also provide access to a vast number of highly diverse participants working in many different functions and industries.

Overcoming the Lack of Confidence Regarding Causality Challenge in Non-experimental Research

The frequent inability to make strong statements about causal relationships is due to the infrequent use of experimental research designs. The only way to truly determine causal relationships is to utilize experiments.[63] Online experiments can be designed that walk participants through several steps in the decision-making process. Thus, online experiments allow you to manipulate independent variables (e.g., number and type of team members) and then measure the effect of that precise manipulation on key outcome variables (e.g., team performance). Moreover, you can draw conclusions about the direction and strength of causal relationships by implementing random assignment of individuals to conditions (e.g., small versus large entrepreneurial teams, entrepreneurial teams with varying numbers of marketing experts).

Overcoming Additional Challenges: Participant Bias and Selective Survival

Participant bias can occur due to processes and beliefs such as **social desirability**. Online experiments can help mitigate this type of bias because participants are asked to do things instead of reporting their beliefs, perceptions, or hypothetical behaviors that might occur in hypothetical situations. Also, participants are asked to behave in ways they are quite familiar with and in situations they are very familiar with. Moreover, online experiment participants provide their consent to work on a particular set of tasks, which is actually a real job, and in many cases, are only aware they are part of a research study after the experiment.

Selective survival bias relates to selection issues due to non-desirable, non-random study participant selection. Online experiments help mitigate problems of selective survival bias because longitudinal experiments allow you more control. In addition, online experiments will enable you to follow participants through each process step until the outcome is achieved (or not).

Benefits of Using Amazon's Mechanical Turk (MTurk)

MTurk's popularity can be broadly attributed to four closely related benefits compared to research conducted using more traditional student or field samples: (1) Large and diverse participant pool, (2) ease of access and speed of data collection, (3) reasonable cost, and (4) flexibility regarding research design choice. As a preview, these benefits are summarized in Table 7.2.

Large and Diverse Participant Pool

MTurk allows you to access a more extensive and demographically diverse participant pool than traditional student samples and the United States (U.S.) population. For example, on average, compared to conventional student samples, MTurkers are older (M_{MTurk} = 32.93; $M_{Student}$ = 18.68), have more years of relevant work experience (M_{MTurk} = 5.11; $M_{Student}$ = 1.54), and report greater computer and internet knowledge.[64] On the other hand, compared to the general U.S. population, MTurkers are younger (50.9% are below 30 years of age compared to 14.5% of U.S. adults), more educated (47.1% have a college degree or higher compared to 37.8% of U.S. adults), and more likely to be female (61% are women compared to 49.5% of U.S. adults).[65] In addition, differences between MTurk respondents and nationally representative U.S. samples in demographics and political orientation can be eliminated by controlling for ten factors (i.e., age, gender, race, ethnicity, income, education, marital status, religion, ideology, and political partisanship).[66] Thus, MTurk also has the potential to complement laboratory studies by ensuring the transportability of laboratory results.[67]

Ease of Access and Speed of Data Collection

A second broad benefit of MTurk is that it allows you to recruit participants efficiently and gather data quickly. About 7,300 MTurkers are available for a study at any given time, and the time taken for half of these MTurkers to leave the pool and be replaced is about seven months.[68] By maintaining a relatively stable online pool of participants, MTurk significantly reduces recruitment efforts, making conducting, extending, replicating, or modifying a study easier. For example, most MTurk assignments, called Human Intelligence Tasks (i.e., HITs), are completed within 12 hours or less.

TABLE 7.2 ■ Summary of Main Benefits of Using Amazon Mechanical Turk (MTurk) for Conducting Social and Behavioral Sciences Research	
Benefit	**Description of Benefit**
1. Large and diverse participant pool	1. MTurk allows researchers access to a more extensive and demographically diverse participant pool than traditional student samples and the United States (U.S.) population. Compared to conventional student samples, MTurkers are older, have more relevant work experience, and report greater computer and internet knowledge. Compared to the general U.S. population, MTurkers are younger and more educated. In addition, demographic and political-affiliation differences can be eliminated by controlling for ten factors (i.e., age, gender, race, ethnicity, income, education, marital status, religion, ideology, and political partisanship). Thus, MTurk has the potential to complement laboratory studies by ensuring the transportability of results.
2. Ease of access and speed of data collection	2. About 7,300 MTurkers are available for a study at any time. By maintaining a relatively stable large online pool of participants, MTurk significantly reduces recruitment efforts, making it easier to conduct, extend, reproduce, replicate, or modify a study. Most MTurk assignments are completed within 12 hours or less.
3. Reasonable cost	3. Researchers can gather data at a lower cost than when using samples of students or working adults, or participants recruited through other online panel websites. MTurk's constant fee structure (i.e., the amount paid to Amazon to conduct a study) and integrated payment infrastructure reduces considerably the administrative costs associated with compensating participants.
4. Flexibility regarding research design choice	4. MTurk can implement experimental, passive observation, quasi-experimental, and longitudinal research designs and perform tasks such as content analysis. Furthermore, MTurk can be used to conduct cross-cultural and international research by restricting the participant pool to workers with specific cultural backgrounds or those living in particular countries. Together, these benefits allow researchers to advance theory by testing hypotheses in diverse samples about different effects and relations between variables (e.g., upward and downward, over time, dyadic).

Source: Aguinis, Villamor, & Ramani (2021). Reproduced with permission.

Reasonable Cost

MTurk's third significant advantage is that it allows researchers to gather data at a lower cost. This is particularly true when we compare the price of collecting data using MTurk to samples of students, working adults, or participants of other online panels such as Qualtrics.[69]

METHODS IN PRACTICE

COST OF USING MTURK COMPARED TO OTHER DATA COLLECTION OPTIONS

A team of researchers compared the total cost of MTurk studies to the amount they would have spent conducting the same five studies using laboratory samples. It concluded that laboratory samples were almost six times more expensive (i.e., $2,190 vs. only $367.77 for

MTurk).[70] In addition, MTurk's constant fee structure (i.e., the amount paid to Amazon to conduct a study) and integrated payment infrastructure considerably reduce the administrative costs associated with compensating participants.

Flexibility Regarding Research Design Choice

A fourth important advantage is that MTurk can be used to implement both experimental and passive observation, quasi-experimental, and longitudinal research designs. Furthermore, MTurk can be used to conduct cross-cultural and international research by restricting the participant pool to workers with specific cultural backgrounds or those living in particular countries. Together, these benefits allow you to advance theory by testing hypotheses in diverse samples about different effects and relations between variables (e.g., upward and downward, over time, dyadic). However, there's one important caveat: researchers from outside the U.S. or India may face challenges in creating researcher (i.e., requester) accounts on MTurk. These are typically restricted to users with U.S. billing addresses and U.S. social security or employer identification numbers. So, please keep this in mind as you think about using MTurk.

Although MTurk offers many advantages, it is no panacea. Several issues might threaten your MTurk research's validity, as described next.

Threats to Consider when Conducting Research Using Amazon's Mechanical Turk (MTurk)

Research using MTurk faces several threats that may compromise the validity of conclusions. These are the following: (1) MTurker inattention, (2) self-selection bias, (3) high attrition rates, (4) inconsistent English language fluency, (5) vulnerability to web robots, and (6) MTurker social desirability bias.

MTurker Inattention

MTurkers often complete their HITs in distracting environments and at rapid speed to maximize monetary returns, leading to careless or insufficient effort responses. About 15% of MTurkers fail attention and compliance checks.[71] Participant inattention is a frequently mentioned feature of MTurk research.[72] MTurkers are less likely to pay attention to study instructions and manipulations and more likely to engage in insufficient effort or careless responding than college student samples.[73]

METHODS IN PRACTICE
THE CHALLENGE OF PARTICIPANT DISTRACTION

A study found that, compared to student samples, online participants are significantly more likely to be distracted due to cell phone use (MTurker = 21% vs. student = 9%), internet surfing (MTurker = 11% vs. student = 1%), or conversing with another person (MTurker = 21% vs. student = 2%).[74] Failure to pay sufficient attention to study instructions or experimental stimuli threatens a study's internal validity (whether the stimulus or manipulation led to variation in outcome), construct validity (whether a measure accurately represents its intended construct), and statistical conclusion validity (i.e., the accuracy of inferences about covariation between variables).[75]

Self-selection Bias

Another salient feature is that MTurkers **self-select** into the potential participant pool. Unlike traditional student samples or field studies where the researcher defines the potential participant pool (e.g., first-line managers at a company), the decision to be an MTurker is based on an individual's personal and demographic characteristics such as monetary incentives, boredom, employment status, or country location.[76] These characteristics, which can serve as confounds and alternative explanations for observed relations, compromise the researchers' ability to randomly sample from their target population and threaten external validity.

High Attrition Rates

Another salient feature is the ease with which participants can withdraw from a study. Specifically, although attrition rates in MTurk studies often exceed 30% (31.9% to 51%), they are rarely reported.[77] And while attrition is also a concern when conducting laboratory or field research, the online nature of MTurk studies leads to higher attrition rates and even the possibility of differential attrition.[78] High attrition rates threaten internal validity by confounding the stimuli or manipulation that led to the observed effect. Although attrition due to factors unrelated to the study (e.g., Internet bandwidth challenges, work interruptions) does not compromise internal validity,[79] making that determination can be difficult in an online environment. Also, high attrition rates threaten the external validity of a study's results and conclusions, like self-selection bias.

Inconsistent English Language Fluency

A fourth feature is an inconsistency in the English language fluency of MTurkers. This feature is especially salient when studies use data collected in countries where English is not the primary language.[80] For instance, a comparison of measurement equivalence on the Big Five personality inventory for MTurkers, undergraduate students, and working adults found that data from MTurkers from countries where English is not the primary language displayed only **configural invariance** with data collected from both undergraduates as well as employed individuals from countries where English is the primary language. In other words, English language fluency influenced how participants interpreted the study's instructions, manipulations, and measures. Overall, inconsistency in MTurker English language fluency potentially threatens a study's internal, construct, and statistical conclusion validity.

Vulnerability to Web Robots (or "bots")

Bots are malicious software programs designed specifically to participate in online studies to receive compensation. These programs, often freely available and easy to use, generate data that follow a random or partially random distribution in response to a study's questions, making it harder to distinguish between bots and inattentive or careless participants.[81] For example, some authors reported that a plug-in for the web browser Google Chrome could be used to insert automated survey responses into an MTurk study.[82] While we currently lack estimates of the percentage of MTurk data attributable to bots, such programs represent a feature that can impact research conducted using MTurk. Overall, by substituting computer-generated responses instead of actual participants, these bots threaten the internal validity, construct validity, and statistical conclusion validity of MTurk studies.

MTurker Social Desirability Bias

Participants providing socially desirable or expected answers in response to your stimuli, manipulations, and questions represent another salient challenge. Because monetary compensation is one of the primary reasons for participating in a HIT, MTurkers are more likely to provide socially desirable responses than student samples.

METHODS IN PRACTICE
THE CHALLENGE OF SOCIAL DESIRABILITY BIAS

A study reported a statistically significant difference between undergraduate and MTurker responses on a social desirability scale.[83] In addition, the percentage of respondents who engage in this practice seems to vary across countries, with U.S. participants more likely to provide socially desirable responses than Indian participants.[84] Although some recent research[85] suggests that social desirability bias may not be as severe a threat when conducting experimental research on MTurk, overall MTurker social desirability bias threatens the internal and construct validity of MTurk studies.

Given the Methods in Practice box about challenges regarding social desirability bias, if you plan to use MTurk, you should consider implementing best-practice recommendations to address as many threats as possible. Let's discuss these recommendations next.

Best-practice Recommendations for Using Amazon's Mechanical Turk (MTurk)

The best-practice recommendations are organized around the three typical stages of an empirical study: planning, implementation, and reporting results. As a preview, Table 7.3 summarizes each of the recommendations.

Planning Stage

Evaluate the Appropriateness of MTurk to Develop or Test Theories. The first recommendation is to evaluate the alignment between the desired target population and that of MTurkers and collect and report detailed sample characteristics rather than assume similarity with earlier MTurk studies.[86] This helps address threats posed by unique challenges of MTurk—such as the inability to efficiently conduct cohort studies or collect nested (i.e., multilevel) data, differences in demographics from traditional student and field samples used in management research, and the influence of compensation and time of study posting on participation.[87]

Establish the Required Sample Size. Unfortunately, many MTurker responses are unusable due to high attrition rates and MTurker inattention. Therefore, in addition to the sample size determined through power analysis, it is helpful to collect data from at least an additional 15% to 30% of MTurkers[88] to compensate for likely participant attrition and failure to pass attention and compliance checks.[89]

Design a Data-collection Tool Used to Gather Responses. A well-designed data collection tool can help you address validity threats posed by the challenges of vulnerability to web robots, and MTurker inattention. There are five recommendations on how to accomplish this. First, MTurkers should complete an informed consent form,[90] which includes a "Captcha" verification to thwart web robots—a "Completely Automated Public Turing Test to tell Computers

TABLE 7.3 ■ Summary of Best-Practice Recommendations for Using Amazon Mechanical Turk (MTurk)		
Stage of Study	**Recommendation**	**Issues to be Addressed**
Planning	1. Evaluate the appropriateness of MTurk to develop or test theories	• Evaluating alignment between the desired target population and that of MTurkers • Collecting and reporting detailed sample characteristics rather than assuming similarity with earlier MTurk studies
	2. Establish the required sample size	• Planning to collect data from at least an additional 15%-30% of MTurkers to compensate for participant attrition and failure to pass attention checks
	3. Design a data-collection tool used to gather responses	• Requiring MTurkers to complete an informed consent form, including a "Captcha" verification to thwart web robots • Requiring MTurkers to provide their MTurk ID and maintaining a reference database of past participants to identify MTurkers who attempt self-misrepresentation • Using at least two attention checks (i.e., instructed items that direct MTurkers to complete or abstain from a particular action, bogus items that ask MTurkers to answer obvious or ridiculous questions, self-reports of effort, and questions on which all or almost all respondents should provide the same response) • Including a qualitative open-ended question as an attention check • Designing a short study (approximately 5 minutes) • Avoiding using scales that only have "end" points labeled
Implementation	4. Launch the study, monitor responses, and respond to concerns	• Conducting a pilot test with a minimum of 10 to 30 participants that includes an open-ended question requesting feedback • Monitoring MTurker communities to gauge MTurkers reactions to the study • Responding promptly to any questions or concerns raised by participants
	5. Screen data	• Screening data promptly using at least two or more tools (e.g., MTurker self-reports of the response effort, answers to attention checks, response times, statistical tools that analyze answer choice response patterns, IP addresses, and open-ended qualitative questions) to estimate likely percentage of unusable responses • Adjusting the number of participants to achieve a desired sample size
Reporting	6. Report details to ensure transparency	• Reporting information regarding all procedures followed, decisions made, and results obtained during each stage of the study • Providing all necessary data for future secondary analyses (e.g., meta-analyses) of findings (i.e., demographics, means, standard deviations, and effect sizes) • Reporting details regarding the posting of the HIT, qualifications used to restrict access to the HIT, and detailed sample characteristics • Explaining all decisions regarding the use of attention checks and screening techniques, including the number of participants excluded for each, decisions regarding sampling from particular countries, measurement equivalence when testing non-native English speakers, and non-naiveté

Source: Adapted from Aguinis, Villamor, & Ramani (2021). Reproduced with permission.

and Humans Apart" that discerns human responses from web robots.[91] This is done by having respondents correctly answer a set of challenges (e.g., identify pictures and type in words) to proceed. In addition, it is useful to include procedures designed to capture an MTurkers' IP address and use features that prevent the same MTurker from completing the study more than once (i.e., avoiding "ballot box stuffing").[92]

Second, it is helpful to require MTurkers to provide their MTurk ID and for you to maintain a reference database of past participants.

Third, to address the threat posed by MTurker inattention, it is helpful to use attention checks. While more is preferable, a minimum of two such checks should be employed.[93] Types of attention checks include instructed items that direct MTurkers to complete or abstain from a particular action, bogus items that ask MTurkers to answer obvious or ridiculous questions, self-reports of effort, and questions on which all or almost all respondents should provide the same response.[94] Specifically for MTurk, it is necessary to include at least one open-ended question as an attention check to help address MTurker's inattention and vulnerability to web robots.[95] Using such items does not negatively affect data quality as long as items used are developed explicitly for this purpose, as opposed to being drawn from other sources or created ad-hoc.

Fourth, designing short studies (i.e., no more than 5 minutes to complete) and avoiding using scales that only have the "end" points labeled (e.g., a Likert-type scale only labeling 1 = Strongly agree, 5 = Strongly disagree) can help minimize MTurker inattention.[96]

Fifth, to gauge social desirability, it is helpful to repeat pertinent questions at the end of the study that makes explicit the desired response and contrast participant answers to the same questions as when presented earlier.[97]

Implementation Stage

Launch the Study, Monitor Responses, and Respond to Concerns To ensure study instructions are clear and identify and rectify potential data quality or programming problems before the data are collected, conducting a pilot test with a minimum of 10 to 30 participants, including an open-ended question requesting feedback, is helpful.[98] In addition, once the study is launched, you can monitor MTurker communities (e.g., Turker Nation, MTurk Crowd) to gauge MTurkers reactions to the study (if any), check if pertinent information is being shared, and respond promptly to any questions or concerns raised by participants.[99]

Screen Data. Screening MTurk data promptly helps estimate the likely percentage of unusable responses. This information can help you adjust the number of potential participants to achieve the required sample size. Unusable responses can usually be attributed to careless or insufficient effort responding (IER) or fraudulent and duplicate efforts. Available tools that can be used to screen data for careless or IER include MTurker self-reports of effort (e.g., self-reported carelessness, rushed responding, skipping of instructions), answers to attention checks (e.g., directed questions), response times, and statistical tools that analyze answer choice response patterns.[100]

MTurkers who score higher on self-reports of response effort or fail to comply with directed questions are likelier to have engaged in careless responding or IER.[101] Thus, their responses can be compared to other MTurkers before including or excluding them. When evaluating response times, a best practice is to exclude participants who complete the task in less than one or two seconds per item. Finally, the most effective statistical tools that can be employed include a) long-string index (in which participant response patterns in choosing the same response for multiple items are analyzed for frequency and length, and a threshold is developed based on the data to indicate potentially invalid responses[102]); and b) within-session response consistency (which calculates the level of similarity in a participant's responses to items they have rated twice and excludes responses that score below 0.25[103]). You should use at least two of the recommendations above to screen data.[104]

Regarding fraudulent or duplicate efforts, the most commonly-used method is to examine IP addresses and delete duplicates. However, the growing popularity of **virtual private servers (VPS)** that conceal the IP address of the device used to access the MTurk study makes it harder to rely solely on this screening procedure.[105] Furthermore, suppose multiple MTurkers use the same device (e.g., a laptop in a dorm room or a computer laboratory, a shared phone or tablet). In that case, their IP addresses will be the same, which can cause researchers to omit legitimate responses mistakenly. Accordingly, in addition to employing IP address screening (e.g., using software packages for R and Stata),[106] examining the answer to the open-ended attention check question in the study before deciding to include or omit a particular response is helpful.

Reporting Stage

Report Details to Ensure Transparency. There are growing calls in the social and behavioral sciences about the need for greater transparency regarding specific procedures, judgment calls, and decisions made during a study.[107] These concerns are even more relevant for MTurk studies as participants are anonymous and often cannot be contacted for clarification. Accordingly, to address concerns about how different challenges may threaten the validity of results obtained and conclusions reached when using MTurk,[108] there is a need to describe all steps clearly.[109] First, studies should provide all necessary data for future secondary analyses (e.g., meta-analyses) of their findings (i.e., demographic data, means, standard deviations, and effect sizes). In addition, there is a need to report details regarding the posting of the HIT (i.e., were data collected in one batch or multiple batches, was the HIT reposted), qualifications used to restrict access to the HIT (e.g., age, country of residence, **Master Worker** status), and detailed sample characteristics (e.g., gender, race/ethnicity, employment status, work experience, educational qualifications). Furthermore, it is necessary to report details regarding the use of attention checks and screening techniques, including the number of participants excluded for each,[110] as well as decisions regarding sampling from particular countries, and measurement equivalence when testing non-native English speakers.[111]

Next, let's address another approach to conducting experiments. This involves the use of virtual reality.

HOW TO CONDUCT EXPERIMENTS USING VIRTUAL REALITY

Virtual reality (VR) is a computer-simulated, multi-sensory environment in which a perceiver, the user of the VR computer technology, experiences *telepresence*. Telepresence is a feeling in an environment generated by a communication medium.[112] Telepresence occurs when the VR user feels present and fully immersed in the VR environment.[113] The *vividness* and *interactivity* of the VR technology determine telepresence. The more vivid and interactive the VR system, the more captivating it is of the user's visual, aural, olfactory, tactile, and **proprioceptive** senses and, hence, the more apt it is to produce telepresence.[114] Highly immersive VR systems, or those able to deliver telepresence, typically consist of (a) a treadmill, motion platform, and position tracker; (b) tactile feedback, speech recognition, and spatial audio systems; and (c) an exoskeleton, data gloves, and head-mounted video display worn by the VR user.[115]

Benefits of Using Immersive VR Technology

There are several potential benefits to using highly immersive VR technology instead of a written vignette or videos to manipulate focal study variables as done with EVM. First, given that users can experience telepresence, VR technology can enhance the **experimental** and **mundane realism** and, consequently, the internal and external validity of an experiment. *Experimental realism* refers to the extent to which an experimental situation is perceived as realistic and believable by the study participants, and *mundane realism* refers to the extent to which events in an experiment are similar to those in the real world. Stimuli presented in a VR environment should be perceived as more realistic and similar to real-world events compared to less vivid, less interactive stimuli in written materials or videos.

Second, VR technology allows manipulating naturally occurring variables in a controlled laboratory setting. For example, given that a three-dimensional office environment with hallways, doors, rooms, and physical objects can be manipulated in VR,[116] and that multiple users can be simultaneously immersed in the same virtual world,[117] interpersonal processes that naturally occur in an organizational environment can now be manipulated using VR.

Third, VR technology can be used as a dynamic research method instead of static or one-time assessment methods (e.g., self-reports in a cross-sectional design) commonly used in social and behavioral research. By immersing VR users in a simulated organization and then measuring their reactions to dynamic stimuli at several time points rather than a single time point, you can study behavior that varies regularly.[118] As an illustration, a VR user's reaction to fluctuations in employee job performance could be assessed at multiple time points during a VR immersion.

Fourth, VR technology can foster a more sound investigation of sensitive topics that are difficult to study experimentally in the field (e.g., equity and inclusion, discrimination). If you are examining sensitive issues, traditionally, you may be limited to conducting passive observational studies or lab experiments using written vignettes or videos. Given VR technology's ability to manipulate naturally occurring field variables, however, you can conduct "field" experiments in a controlled VR environment. But using VR is no panacea. So, let's discuss potential pitfalls.

Potential Pitfalls of Using Immersive VR Technology

Highly immersive VR technology does have two potential disadvantages. First, immersive VR users sometimes experience **sopite syndrome**, which means they feel sick due to the display update lags and image jumps that occur with low-resolution head-mounted video displays. Symptoms are similar to motion sickness and include chronic fatigue, lethargy, headaches, eyestrain, lightheadedness, dizziness, and nausea, and this is why sopite syndrome is often called "VR motion sickness." For example, a study reported that 61% of 146 participants reported experiencing headaches, eyestrain, and nausea during a 20-minute immersion period, and 5% withdrew from the experiment because of nausea or dizziness.[119] However, you can use high-resolution displays and a high-bandwidth connection to reduce update lags, image flickers, and, in turn, VR motion sickness.

METHODS IN PRACTICE
COST OF VIRTUAL REALITY TECHNOLOGY

A potential disadvantage of highly immersive VR technology is its cost. For example, at the writing of this book, advanced high-resolution full-color head-mounted displays can cost over $1,000. In addition, exoskeletons, or whole-body suits, used to stimulate feelings in the muscles and joints to captivate the VR users' proprioceptive senses, can cost over $10,000. The good news for you is that immersive VR equipment costs continue to drop quickly, and even lower-end systems are beginning to include features previously available only on higher-end systems.

Another concern concerning highly immersive VR technology: Would its use require more stringent ethical standards than a written vignette or videos? It appears so, as you need to develop and use more thorough informed consent and debriefing procedures.[120]

Many of the limitations above can be addressed using another experimental approach: Thought experiments. Let's discuss this next.

HOW TO CONDUCT THOUGHT EXPERIMENTS

Thought experiments are judgments about what would happen if an imagined scenario were real.[121] Thought experiments are also called thought trials,[122] imaginary illustrations,[123] and meta-theorizing.[124] For decades, thought experiments have effectively created novel insights and advanced theories in numerous scientific fields. Overall, by presenting hypothesized alternate explanations, extending the extant theory to include new contexts, and providing counterexamples for prevailing theories, fields such as economics, public and international policy, physics, ethics, and others have utilized thought experiments to produce valuable theoretical insights. However, this methodology is relatively underutilized in social and behavioral science research.

There are at least two reasons for the underutilization of thought experiments. First, thought experiments are not usually taught in research methods courses.[125] Thus, social and behavioral science researchers may not have sufficient opportunities to acquire the competencies to conduct thought experiments. Second, most social and behavioral science researchers may not know what thought experiments are and their benefits. In addition, on a more pragmatic note, most researchers may need to be made aware that thought experiments are cost-efficient compared to vignette, online, and VR experiments and can be conducted for little to no financial cost.

Unique Defining Characteristics of Thought Experiments

Thought experiments take place in a unique setting: the laboratory of the mind.[126] As such, thought experiments are uniquely distinct from other types we have discussed. Specifically, thought experiments are unique regarding the: (1) nature of independent and dependent variables, (2) quantity of independent variables that can be manipulated, (3) type of and sample size, and (4) ethical and legal considerations associated with implementing the experiment.

First, the independent and dependent variables are imagined and not empirically manipulated or measured.[127] For example, you include empirical manipulations of independent variables in more traditional field and lab experiments (including vignette studies).[128] However, thought experiments do not have such empirical manipulations of independent variables. Instead, in thought experiments, you manipulate independent variables in imagined scenarios. For instance, some researchers expanded our understanding of how knowledge management theories are adopted by mentally manipulating the characteristics of routines that may influence this process.[129]

Second, thought experiments are unique because of their ability to include a virtually unlimited number of independent variables. In contrast, empirically-based experiments are limited due to sample size constraints[130] or participant issues such as fatigue.[131] Relatedly, traditional experiments are also limited by logistical and resource constraints, such as the cost and time involved in empirically manipulating too many independent variables. However, because thought experiments are conducted in your mind, they are uninhibited by such resource limitations.

Another key characteristic distinguishing thought experiments from other experiments is the study's sample. Traditional social and behavioral science experiments involve human participants, requiring significant time commitment through recruiting and compensation costs.[132] In addition, in conventional experiments, there is a need to obtain a sample size that is large enough to allow for data analyses at adequate levels of statistical power. None of these *sine qua non* requirements concern thought experiments because they occur within your mind and therefore do not require human participants.

Finally, experiments in social and behavioral sciences require ethical considerations due to the involvement of people as research participants. Understandably, experiments require appropriate approval from an institutional review board (IRB) that evaluates the potential risks. But, because thought experiments are imagined, they are not subject to the same ethical and legal considerations as traditional experiments requiring IRB approval. This feature is particularly attractive if you are interested in investigating socially sensitive phenomena[133] (e.g., racial discrimination, sexual harassment, workplace bullying) or other invasive inquiries for which traditional experiments pose a substantial risk to participants and therefore require understandably complex IRB approval processes, or are not possible at all.[134]

Taxonomy of Thought Experiments

Thought experiments can be classified along two dimensions: (a) the theory's development stage: early versus late,[135] and (b) the study's primary theoretical purpose: theory disconfirmation versus theory confirmation.[136] This taxonomy is useful for two purposes. First, it helps understand the different types of thought experiments conducted in the past and their distinct value-added contributions. Second, this taxonomy can be used to choose which kind of thought experiment would be most appropriate for a particular situation and particular theory-based goals. Accordingly, this taxonomy helps design choices in future research involving thought experiments. Figure 7.2 includes a summary of the four main types of thought experiments. Let's address each next.

Type I: Early Theory Stage and Theory Confirmation Purpose

Type I involves a situation where you want to build a theory and hope to confirm it rather than disconfirm it. A prominent example of this type of thought experiment is Newton's cannonball.[137] Early into his work on the theory of gravity and how it affects orbiting celestial bodies, Newton sought to confirm his ideas using a thought experiment. Newton imagined cannons firing cannonballs atop higher and higher mountains with increasing velocity. He surmised through this thought experiment that, eventually, the cannonballs would orbit the earth, confirming his nascent theoretical propositions on the nature of gravity.

Type II: Early Theory Stage and Theory Disconfirmation Purpose

Type II involves a thought experiment wherein a counterfactual or paradoxical situation is created in the early stages of theory development. Specifically, this type of thought experiment evaluates a nascent theory by reimagining an alternate explanation that must also be plausible. Schrödinger's cat[138] is an exemplar of this type of thought experiment. The fate of a (hypothesized) cat hinges on a subatomic event that may or may not occur according to the Copenhagen interpretation of quantum mechanics, which implies that the cat would be simultaneously alive and dead. However, someone observing the cat in the box would observe it to be alive or dead. Thus, Schrödinger conducted a thought experiment in which the theory he sought to question

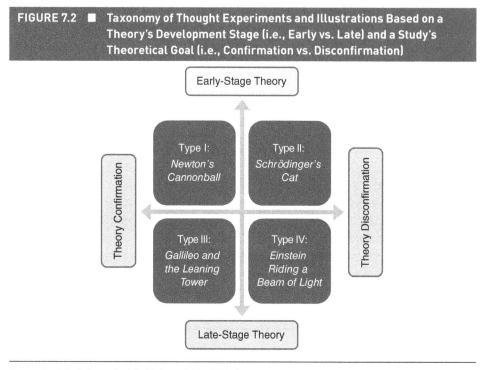

FIGURE 7.2 ■ Taxonomy of Thought Experiments and Illustrations Based on a Theory's Development Stage (i.e., Early vs. Late) and a Study's Theoretical Goal (i.e., Confirmation vs. Disconfirmation)

Source: Aguinis, Beltran, Archibold, Jean, & Rice (2023).

breaks down or results in a paradoxical event, thus disconfirming this early-stage theory and forcing theoretical refinement in the process of theory building.

Type III: Late Theory Stage and Theory Confirmation Purpose

A Type III thought experiment involves attempting to confirm a more developed theory. An example is Galileo's Leaning Tower of Pisa, in which he tested the more developed Aristotelian theory of gravity. As some researchers noted, this thought experiment occurred in 1589.[139] Galileo is said to have imagined dropping two bodies from the top of the Tower of Pisa to show that the times of their fall would be equal, although the objects differed regarding their weight. The story is that this thought experiment evolved into Galileo climbing to the top of the tower and dropping the objects. According to the researchers, this thought experiment is particularly noteworthy because it is paradigmatic in "the interpretation of the history of ideas" (p. 164). According to other theories, particularly Aristotle's theory of gravity, objects of varying mass were surmised to fall at different rates. Galileo's thought experiment helped to confirm his already-developed theoretical propositions.

Type IV: Late Theory Stage and Theory Disconfirmation Purpose

A Type IV thought experiment creates imaginary paradoxical situations to disconfirm a more developed theory. For example, Einstein famously imagined himself simultaneously riding a beam of light and observing that same beam of light from a distance. By imagining what both versions of himself would witness, he created a paradoxical situation given the parameters of the prevalent emission theory of light. Thus, he could disconfirm extant theory using what he termed a *Gedankenexperiment* (i.e., "thought experiment" in German). Eventually, he developed his theory of the nature of light and gravity.

If you are planning to conduct a thought experiment, then you should do so by implementing best-practice recommendations. So let's discuss these next.

Thought Experiments: Best-practice Recommendations

This section provides recommendations on deciding whether to use a thought experiment and which type, and how to plan, execute, report results, and discuss implications. These recommendations are organized into five steps and are summarized in Table 7.4.

TABLE 7.4 ■ Summary of Best-practice Recommendations for Deciding Whether to Conduct a Thought Experiment (and Which Type), Planning and Executing it, and Reporting Results and Discussing Implications	
Stage	**Recommendation**
1. Deciding whether to conduct a thought experiment and which type	● Use the decision tree in Figure 7.3 to decide whether a thought experiment (TE) is valuable and appropriate ● Determine the correct type of TE based on the taxonomy summarized in Figure 7.2
2. Planning a thought experiment: theory considerations	● Establish theoretical domain by reviewing key constructs, variables, and any relevant background information to create a mind model and set the scene for the experiment ● Target a specific theoretical proposition or assumption to be challenged or affirmed in the thought experiment ● Summarize theoretical assumptions to set the experimental boundaries of the TE ● Illustrate the dimensions of the theory used in the mind model by providing diagrams, tables, and figures
3. Executing a thought experiment: research design considerations	● Be a raconteur to theorize based on abstraction (use a narrative storylike structure) ● Choose an existing TE, alter a seminal TE to suit particular needs, or create a novel TE ● Use disciplined imagination (consistent internal and external logic) and specify why the proposed boundaries offered in the TE make sense ● Consider using multiple TEs to provide contrasting scenarios that test the theory ● Create *what-if* counterfactual scenarios to tie abstract theory to understandable situations based on events from the present, distant past, or imagined in the distant future
4. Reporting results of a thought experiment	● Report the type of TE used from Figure 7.2 to the reader ● Specify the usefulness of the thought experiment given the situational context ● Stipulate the meaning of the concepts used in the thought experiment, especially boundary conditions ● Include a figure or diagram to help illustrate the TE in the reader's mind ● Offer what the expected outcome(s) should be based on the proposed boundaries of the TE ● Bolster the results of the TE by combining them with supplemental data (e.g., archival)
5. Discussing implications of a thought experiment	● Present the proposed shift in thinking/perspective based on the TE ● Discuss obscure truths or biases illuminated by the TE and offer alternative explanations ● Discuss interdisciplinary linkages and the value of TE to other disciplines

Source: Adapted from Aguinis, Beltran, Archibold, Jean, & Rice (2023).

Deciding Whether to Conduct a Thought Experiment and Which Type

Although thought experiments have great potential for advancing social and behavioral sciences theory in many domains, they are only appropriate for some situations and contexts. Accordingly, the first step involves deciding the appropriateness of conducting a thought experiment based on the particular research situation and goals. Figure 7.3 summarizes a decision tree to determine whether conducting a thought experiment is potentially useful for making theory advancements and, if so, what type of thought experiment is most appropriate based on the taxonomy described earlier and summarized in Figure 7.2.

Decision Point #1: Is There a Need to Confirm or Disconfirm Theory? The first decision involves clarifying whether there is a need to confirm or disconfirm the theory.[140] In other words, is there a theoretical proposition or assumption to be confirmed or disconfirmed?[141] On the other hand, if the goal is primarily to conduct exploratory research, it is unlikely that using thought experiments will result in substantial theory advancements.

Decision Point #2: Can an Imagined Scenario Model the Theory? The second decision point asks whether you can conceive a scenario that succinctly and effectively models the theory to be tested. Scenarios should have a storylike narrative that brings the thought experiment to life in a manner that helps the reader follow your line of reasoning for their confirmation or disconfirmation assertion.[142] In this regard, the examples used to illustrate each of the four types in the taxonomy are useful exemplars that can be used as templates for future thought experiments. For example, Einstein effectively modeled complex concepts of physics for non-experts to understand. Likewise, Newton was able to model the highly abstract concept of gravity. In other words, you must be a storyteller who can theorize and connect the abstract and the concrete. Thought experiments can also arise from different situations, including real-life experiences and situations from the distant past or present[143] or completely new or novel situations.[144] This second decision point refers to whether and how the theory can be modeled in the thought experiment.

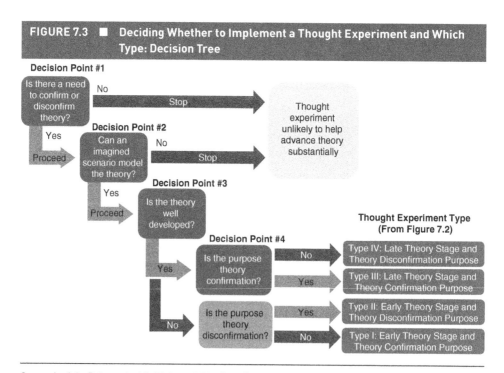

FIGURE 7.3 ■ Deciding Whether to Implement a Thought Experiment and Which Type: Decision Tree

Source: Aguinis, Beltran, Archibold, Jean, & Rice (2023).

Decision Point #3: Is the Theory Well Developed? The third decision point poses a question about the theory development stage. In other words, whether the theory is in the early (i.e., less developed) or late stage (i.e., more developed). For example, Newton's Cannonball and Schrödinger's Cat addressed early-stage theories, whereas Galileo and the Leaning Tower and Einstein Riding a Beam of Light addressed late-stage theories.

Decision Point #4: Is the Purpose Theory Confirmation or Disconfirmation? The fourth decision point asks if the goal is theory confirmation or disconfirmation. For example, Galileo and the Leaning Tower exemplifies a scenario where the purpose is theory confirmation (of a well-developed theory), leading to a Type III experiment. On the other hand, Schrödinger's Cat demonstrates a scenario where the purpose is theory disconfirmation (of an early-stage theory), leading to a Type II experiment. Thus, whereas Decision Point 1 should be answered as a simple "yes" or "no," Decision Point 4 should be answered explicitly as "theory confirmation" or "theory disconfirmation."

Planning a Thought Experiment: Theory Considerations

Once a decision has been made to conduct a thought experiment, the next step is planning it. Creating an engaging and convincing "mind model" for the experiment is crucial to facilitate a better understanding of complex abstractions.[145] This is done by understanding and relaying the tested theory, including its propositions, dimensions, and assumptions. Thus, planning a thought experiment requires identifying existing theory (either nascent or well-developed) and deciding to test the theory by confirming or disconfirming it. This can be achieved by specifying a point of dissension or agreement, whether from a debate in the literature or a commonly misunderstood relationship between similar concepts that justifies the need for a thought experiment. Early-stage theoretical testing relies on sparse or disparate studies, and later-stage theoretical testing relies on more abundant literature and better-developed and established ideas.

First, "setting the scene"[146] requires conjuring a "mind model" constructed by reviewing key constructs, variables, and relevant background information.[147] Of note, given sufficient knowledge of a theory, you can begin mentally experimenting without additional background research. For example, Einstein and Newton did not explicitly set out to do a thought experiment; however, they had sufficient knowledge to begin experimenting within their minds. Einstein performed many *Gedankenexperimente* in his idle time, which led to the development of his riding a beam of light experiment.

However, when performing a *Gedankenexperiment,* Einstein still made the theory tested explicit, as was the case with his beam of light experiment addressing how the emission theory of light was unfeasible. Another researcher clearly communicated to the reader that he explicitly sought to disconfirm the *employee productivity proposition* as a valid justification for mandatory drug testing.[148] The researcher noted that the **employee productivity proposition** "states that since the employer has purchased the employee's time, the employer has a proprietary right to ensure that the time purchased is used as efficiently and productively as possible" (p. 301). This study involved a thought experiment to demonstrate how the belief in this proposition as a valid justification for mandatory drug testing also commits one logically to morally repugnant consequences (e.g., employers having a proprietary right to mandate the use of a pain-inducing drug to increase employee efficiency).

The theoretical assumptions that form the boundaries of the experiment should also be explicit. For example, one researcher used an organized table to quickly summarize the assumptions of the key concepts relating to the experiment.[149] To facilitate creating an effective mental model and addressing assumptions, diagrams or figures can also help set the scene visually.

As an illustration, a researcher used several diagrams to explain the mind model of the experiment.[150] Alternatively, another researcher used two tables to ground the reader in the assumptions, logic, and domain characteristics of the thought experiment related to different theories under comparison.[151]

Executing a Thought Experiment: Research Design Considerations

The execution stage involves conducting the thought experiment in the laboratory of the mind with a well-defined model developed in the planning stage. Foremost, thought experiments should seek to test theory. Some researchers recommend that you be a *storyteller*, which involves "thinking in narrative, story like terms provides a route to theorizing via abstraction" (p. 754).[152] This recommendation is highlighted by others who argue that "narratives express the richness and diversity of human experiences and thus challenge simplistic analyses of managerial issues… Narrative is the expression of actual human experience" (p. 682).[153]

The narrative can take shape either by using an existing thought experiment,[154] altering one to suit the particular needs of a theory,[155] or creating an entirely new one.[156] Consider adopting thought experiments from completely different fields,[157] using multiple thought experiments,[158] basing a thought experiment on a real-life experience or situation,[159] and using metaphors.[160] For example, one researcher examined entrepreneurial ecosystems as organizational hybrids akin to biological hybrids.[161]

While thought experiments offer much freedom compared with other methods, you should use "disciplined imagination." As one researcher explained, 'discipline' in theorizing comes from consistent application of selection criteria to trial-and-error thinking, and the 'imagination' in theorizing comes from deliberate diversity introduced into the problem statements, thought trials, and selection criteria that comprise that thinking" (p. 516).[162] As such, disciplined imagination means that an underlying internal and external logic should make practical sense and can be conveyed to a reader.[163] Therefore, even the most fantastical thought experiments (e.g., Einstein riding a beam of light) are explained and grounded in natural and explainable phenomena that effectively convey abstract ideas.

To give a thought experiment more breadth, you may include multiple experiments or create new what-if counterfactual scenarios to apply and explain abstract theoretical mechanisms narratively.[164] For example, when considering behavioral solutions to the AIDS crisis, one researcher conducted multiple thought experiments with slight variations to contrast ideas.[165] Another helpful approach for including several thought experiments is adding *what-if* counterfactual scenarios to ground abstract theory narratively. For example, to demonstrate the effects of fiscal policy, some researchers used the Nazi seizure of power to create a counterfactual thought experiment.[166]

Reporting Results of a Thought Experiment

To report the results of a thought experiment, you must guide readers through the experiment and justify the choices made. First, the type of thought experiment used, from Figure 7.2, should be detailed to orient the reader to the thought experiment's nature (early vs. late stage, confirmation vs. disconfirmation).

Second, it is essential to justify why the method was used, given the situational context of the theory. For example, in examining whether prisoners have the right to die, one researcher explained how: "Few European jurisdictions are close to implementing a 'right to die' for citizens, and they are even further away from a 'right to die for prisoners'. But that does not mean we should not engage with the idea. When we engage in utopian thinking, considering what our society could and should look like, we can come across and highlight shortcomings and problems for the status quo" (p. 56).[167] Given the situational context, utopian thought is used and justified as there is no alternative to consider that particular situation.

Readers should be given a clear description of key concepts and definitions relevant to the thought experiment, given the abstract nature of thought experiments, particularly for boundary conditions.[168] As an illustration, some researchers explained that "often the concepts presented are suggestive, identifying the attributes of mentoring rather than stipulating the meaning of the concept itself and, in particular, its boundary conditions" (p. 721).[169] They cited several researchers who failed to define their focal construct. Similarly, some other researchers suggested the central concept of the thought experiment is to ensure the reader is clear on how they define stakeholders.[170]

To fully immerse the reader in the experiment and help detail what occurred in the researcher's imagination, consider including a figure or diagram to help ground the thought experiment and bring it to life.[171] Figures can help facilitate understanding as well as help to provide evidence for the explanations for each of the questions raised in the imagined scenario.[172] In other words, given the proposed specifications of the thought experiment, it should explain the outcome if the proposed boundaries are used.[173]

Finally, while thought experiments do not create empirical data, that is not to say that data should not inform thought experiments. For example, results can be supplemented and enhanced by connecting the experiment to historical evidence or archival data[174] or including qualitative information.[175] To this effect, part of the results reporting process includes incorporating lived experiences to enhance realism and fully immerse readers into the narrative scenario.[176]

Discussing Implications of a Thought Experiment

While the reporting stage is focused on a compelling narration of the thought experiment proper and its results, discussing the implications of the thought experiment considers the assertions the thought experiment makes and contextualizes them in terms of boundary conditions and alternate explanations. Discussing implications begins with presenting the proposed shift in thinking or perspective resulting from the thought experiment. For example, a researcher explained the difference between the original position before the thought experiment and the potential outcomes if the policy in the thought experiment was enacted.[177] Another researcher used the results of the thought experiment to consider how the focal construct, gender, affects an overall monastic framework.[178] In addition, the results of the thought experiment can be integrated or reconciled with other theories to create a new theory or framework.[179]

While many groundbreaking and paradigm-shifting results have come from thought experiments, "Thought experiments do not always reveal deep truths... there is always the possibility that the thought experiment might reveal a truth which would otherwise have remained obscure" (p. 15).[180] For example, a researcher used a thought experiment not to create a new grand theory on international trade but to raise key questions about how processes adapt to foreign environments.[181]

DISCUSSION QUESTIONS

1. What are the two critical considerations that must be met to establish causality, and how do experiments allow you to satisfy those considerations?

2. When is experimental vignette methodology (EVM) most likely to yield theoretical advancements? Give two examples of research questions that can be examined using EVM.

3. Compare the similarities and differences of between-person and within-person EVM studies. How would you analyze data from each type of study?

4. How do choices regarding the level of immersion, number, and levels of the manipulated factors relate to internal and external validity when using experimental vignette methodology (EVM)?

5. Describe three methodological challenges you might face when using longitudinal surveys or existing datasets and how online experiments can overcome these challenges.

6. Why has Amazon's Mechanical Turk (MTurk) become the most frequently used online data-collection method? List three best practices to consider when designing the data-collection tool used on MTurk.

7. How does virtual reality (VR) enable the study of sensitive topics? What potential ethical concerns might be raised using VR to study these topics?

8. How do thought experiments differ from online experiments?

9. Describe how a thought experiment can be used for theory disconfirmation and identify a theory in your field that would benefit from this approach.

10. What is "disciplined imagination," and why is it necessary for a successful thought experiment?

KEY TERMS

between-person research design
bots
causality
configural invariance
confound
conjoint analysis
covariation
cross-sectional research
employee productivity proposition
experimental realism
experimental treatment
Experimental vignette methodology (EVM)
Master Worker
mixed research design
mundane realism
noise

online marketplaces
operationalization
paper people studies
policy capturing
proprioceptive senses
secondary data
selective survival bias
self-selection bias
social desirability bias
sopite syndrome
taxonomy
thought experiment
vignette
virtual private servers (VPS)
within-person research design

NOTES

This chapter is based to a large extent on the following sources:

Aguinis, H., & Bradley, K. J. (2014). Best-practice recommendations for designing and implementing experimental vignette methodology studies. *Organizational Research Methods*, *17*(4), 351-371. https://doi.org/10.1177/1094428114547952

Aguinis, H., & Lawal, S. O. (2012). Conducting field experiments using eLancing's natural environment. *Journal of Business Venturing*, *27*(4), 493-505. https://doi.org/10.1016/j.jbusvent.2012.01.002

Aguinis, H., Beltran, J.R., Archibold, E. E., Jean, E. L., & Rice, D. B. (2023). Thought experiments: Review and recommendations. *Journal of Organizational Behavior*, 44(3), 544-560. https://doi.org/10.1002/job.2658

Aguinis, H., Villamor, I., & Ramani, R. M. (2021). MTurk research: Review and recommendations. *Journal of Management*, 47(4), 823–837. https://journals.sagepub.com/doi/10.1177/0149206320969787

Pierce, C. A., & Aguinis, H. (1997). Using virtual reality technology in organizational behavior research. *Journal of Organizational Behavior*, 18(5), 407-410. https://www.jstor.org/stable/3100211: 5%3C407:: AID-JOB869%3E3.0.CO;2-P

8 HOW TO PREPARE YOUR DATA FOR ANALYSIS

LEARNING GOALS

By the end of this chapter, you will be able to do the following:

8.1 Identify appropriate ways to address missing data, including assumptions considered, criteria for exclusion, and specific techniques used.

8.2 Choose the most suitable way to transform your data, if needed (e.g., nonlinear transformations to normalize scores).

8.3 Articulate how to define, identify, and handle the outliers in your data.

8.4 Plan how to identify and handle error outliers in your data.

8.5 Verify if your data contain interesting outliers and consider how you will deal with them.

8.6 Formulate your decision-making process for defining, identifying, and handling influential outliers in regression, structural equation modeling, and multilevel modeling.

8.7 Prepare your hypotheses while avoiding HARKing and consider how various forms of HARKing may affect your data.

8.8 Avoid unintentional cherry-picking and question trolling when implementing multivariate procedures.

IMPORTANCE OF CLEANING UP YOUR DATA

Once you have collected your data, a critical first step is properly cleaning and preparing them for analysis. This chapter focuses on data collection and preparation as these are foundational steps in all empirical research that precede data analysis, production of results, and drawing conclusions and implications for theory and practice.

This chapter offers recommendations in the form of checklists for your research's data collection and preparation stages. These recommendations are sufficiently broad that you can apply them to research adopting different epistemological and ontological perspectives—including quantitative and qualitative approaches—and across levels of analyses.

HOW TO HANDLE MISSING DATA AND DATA TRANSFORMATIONS

Missing Data

Let us start with a problem you will probably face in your research: your dataset includes missing data.[1] This is an issue not only in social and behavioral science research involving individual-level data collected using surveys[2] but also in macro research involving firm-level data available in archival sources and publicly or commercially available databases.[3]

There are several questions related to missing data management that you should address before you proceed with data analyses. For example, if you use data imputation approaches to create data that do not exist, what specific techniques are you implementing, and with which software package? What are the assumptions in implementing these procedures (e.g., data missing at random)? Are some of the initially collected data excluded from analysis, and if so, why? What is the approach to eliminating firms/individuals from the study based on missing data concerns (e.g., listwise, pairwise)?[4]

> **Example: Best Practices in Managing Missing Data: Two Illustrations**
>
> Let's consider research on when it is more beneficial to outsource customer-relationship management.[5] This is an interesting domain because it is typically the case that data on customer-relationship management is not available for all firms in a particular sample. For example, in a recently published study, the authors collected data on IT expenses for 119 of the 158 observations in the sample. So, how did they manage missing data? For the remaining 39 cases, where IT expenses are missing in a particular year, they searched the firm's 10-K statements and annual reports in previous and subsequent financial years. First, they replaced the missing value with IT expense from the previously available year. Then, for cases in which the IT expenses of a firm were not available for any financial year, they replaced the missing value with the average IT expense in the industry for the given year. This is an excellent example of how to manage missing data. In this study, the authors provided precise information on handling missing data and the justification for their procedures.
>
> As another illustration regarding best practices for missing data management, other authors studied whether the relation between intelligence and perceived leadership is curvilinear rather than linear.[6] Regarding missing data, they explained that they could not directly test the assumption of **missing completely at random (MCAR)** because data were missing only on one variable (IQ). To address this situation, using the full sample, they created a variable 'missing' code that was a "0" when data was complete and "1" otherwise. They then regressed the seven fully measured leader individual-difference characteristics (i.e., gender, age, age) on the variable 'missing' and fixed effects. The results confirmed that the variable 'missing' was unrelated individually and jointly to individual difference measures. Finally, as an additional test, they performed two Monte Carlo simulations to examine the MCAR assumption. The mean p-value of the MCAR test was .86 (SE .003; 95% CI [.85 to .87]), and the test was only significant 18 times out of 5,000 simulations (0.36%). Thus, they concluded that the listwise sample with full observations appeared to be MCAR. Yet, when they reported their results, they also included the results from the total sample using Stata's MLMV estimator (maximum likelihood estimator for missing data if data are **missing at random (MAR)**. So, these authors offered a detailed description of how they assessed the type of missing data pattern and how, based on their assessment, they chose a particular missing data management procedure.

Data Transformations

There is increased awareness that variables are not normally distributed in many research domains. That is, the data do not follow a **Gaussian pattern** in which scores are clustered around the mean, the mean and median are in the same location, and there are relatively small tails to the left and the right of the mean.[7] For example, recent research in individual performance has provided evidence regarding the prevalence of heavy-tailed distributions due to the presence of star performers.[8] Similarly, firm performance and firm size,[9] as well as firm revenue and growth,[10] also follow non-normal distributions.

A common practice is to implement nonlinear transformations to normalize scores.[11] Researchers also transform their data to reduce **heteroscedasticity**, linearize relations among variables, change relations between variables from multiplicative to additive, and promote analytical convenience (i.e., use familiar data-analytic techniques based on the general linear model[12]). However, a review of 323 articles showed that many articles do not adequately describe the transformation procedures, their justification, and their effects. So, there is a need to answer the following questions in your research: What were the effects of the transformation? Were hypotheses stated in terms of untransformed scores tested with transformed data? Which particular variables did the authors transform, what specific procedure did they use, and what is the justification for the particular procedure?

Example: Best Practices in Data Transformations: Two Illustrations

Consider a study on the relationship between ego depletion and abusive supervision as an example of best practices regarding data transformations.[13] Specifically, these authors noted that they squared the abusive supervision variable, which had a low mean level in their sample, and conducted an analysis with this transformed data as appropriate for their originally skewed data. After taking this approach, their results mirrored those of their original analysis, which means that the results remained statistically significant and supported the original hypotheses. Moreover, these authors reported the results of the standard linear regression analyses for parsimony in interpreting their results. In other words, these authors explained the rationale for the transformation and focused on the original scores because the results were similar to those based on the transformed data.

Another illustration of the procedure used and rationale for transformation is a study examining how firms' strategic reactions differ based on their reputation when consumer boycotts target them.[14] The authors of this study provided a detailed description of how they transformed the Fortune reputation ranking score as follows: They gave a 0 to 10 raw score to each organization included in the list. However, they faced a couple of challenges: (1) Fortune rankings did not report scores for 37 percent of the firms in their sample, which was an indicator that these firms were not key players in their field, and (2) the raw scores were unevenly distributed with most scores falling between 6 and 8. Thus, they followed prior research and adopted an ordinal transformation of the raw Fortune scores with the double goal of (1) demonstrating a firm's relative reputational position and (2) accounting for the skewed distribution of the scores. They used Stata's *xtile* function to evenly divide the raw scores into three quantiles and create an ordinal transformation of the reputation variable. Then, they used the scores of every firm in the reputation index to recalculate the tiers for each year. This way, raw scores varied in their distribution among the quantiles, depending on the shape of the raw scores that year. They could do this because they recalculated quantile membership for each year. Specifically, all companies in the top third received the highest value of "3," companies in the middle tier of the rankings in their year received a value of "2," and the lowest third of **Fortune's annual index** in a given year were given a "1." Finally, those firms that were not ranked received a "0" that reflected their marginal position in their fields. This data transformation allowed the authors to (1) assume that firms not covered in Fortune's Index had a lower reputational standing than those that appear in the ranking and (2) acknowledge the importance of the variation in the rankings. As you can see in this second example, these authors described their transformation procedure in detail, its rationale, and its assumptions. You should take a similar approach if you need to transform your data before analyzing them.

HOW TO HANDLE OUTLIERS

The presence of outliers, data points that deviate markedly from others, is one of the most enduring and pervasive methodological challenges in social and behavioral science research.[15] Outliers, by being different from other cases—be it other individuals, teams, or firms—usually disproportionately influence substantive conclusions regarding relationships among variables. Accordingly, the issue of outliers concerns research spanning all levels of analysis and ranging from individual and team[16] to firm, industry, and society.[17] Moreover, the topic of outliers has also caught widespread attention, as indicated by the book "Outliers," which occupied the number one position on the bestseller list for *The New York Times* for eleven consecutive weeks.[18] The fact that outliers are of concern to micro- and macro-level social and behavioral science and the public, in general, indicates that this is an important methodological topic.

Despite the importance of outliers, researchers need clear guidelines about how to deal with them appropriately. Further, although outliers are often seen as "data problems" that must be "fixed," outliers can also be of substantive interest and studied as unique phenomena that may lead to valuable theoretical insights.[19] Thus, there is a need for a better understanding and unambiguous guidelines regarding the following three issues: (1) how to define them (i.e., "What exactly is an outlier?"), (2) how to identify them (i.e., "How do I know whether a particular case is an outlier?"), and (3) how to handle them (i.e., "What do I do with a case that has been identified as an outlier?"). You may have read about multiple and often conflicting definitions of outliers, techniques to identify outliers, and suggestions on what to do with outliers once you find them. Moreover, the methodological literature on outliers seems fragmented and largely addresses outliers in specific contexts only; for example, most methodological sources only discuss outliers within a single data-analytic approach, such as **ordinary least squares (OLS)** regression.[20] In addition to the conflicting and fragmented methodological literature on outliers, there is little transparency surrounding how researchers define, identify, and handle outliers in published journal articles.

The main goal of this section is to offer best-practice recommendations for defining, identifying, and handling outliers within the context of three popular data-analytic techniques in social and behavioral sciences[21]: regression, structural equation modeling (SEM), and multilevel modeling. Note that because the general linear model serves as a common mathematical foundation for regression and ANOVA, the discussion of outliers in the context of regression also applies to the ANOVA context. As such, this section will serve as a useful guide as you engage in empirical research using these data-analytic techniques.

How to Identify Outliers

Table 8.1 shows several techniques for identifying potential outliers grouped into two categories: single construct techniques and multiple constructs (also labeled "distance") techniques. Single construct techniques examine extreme values within each construct. In contrast, multiple construct techniques assess how far an observation is from a centroid of data points computed from two or more constructs. It would be best if you used both single and multiple construct techniques.

For single construct techniques, the recommendation is to use visual tools first and then follow up with quantitative approaches, including standard deviation analysis or percentage analysis. The recommended cutoff for the quantitative techniques is that potential error

TABLE 8.1 ■ Outlier Identification Techniques Based on a Review of Social and Behavioral Science Research	
Single Construct Identification Techniques	
1. Box plot	A plot that depicts a summary of the smallest value of a construct (excluding outliers), lower quartile (Q1), median (Q2), upper quartile (Q3), and largest value (excluding outliers). Outliers can be identified as those points that lie beyond the plot's whiskers (i.e., the smallest and largest values, excluding outliers).
2. Stem and leaf plot	A plot that simultaneously rank-orders quantitative data and provides insight into the shape of a distribution. Stem-and-leaf pairs that are substantially far away from the rest of the pairs signal the presence of outliers.
3. Schematic plot analysis	Similar to a box plot but used specifically for effect sizes in the context of a meta-analysis.
4. Standard deviation analysis	Distance of a data point from the mean in standard deviation units.
5. Percentage analysis	The relative standing of a data point in a distribution of scores as indexed by its percentile.
Multiple Construct (i.e., "Distance") Identification Techniques	
6. Scatter plot	A plot of the values of two variables, with one variable on the X-axis (usually the independent variable) and the other on the Y-axis (usually the dependent variable). A potential outlier can be identified by a data point far away from the data centroid.
7. q-q plot	A plot (q stands for quantile) compares two probability distributions by charting their quantiles against each other. A non-linear trend indicates the possible presence of outlier(s).
8. p-p plot	A plot (p stands for probability) that assesses the degree of similarity of two datasets (usually the observed and expected) by plotting their two cumulative distribution functions against each other. A non-linear trend indicates the possible presence of outlier(s).
9. Standardized residual	A residual value is calculated by dividing the ith observation's residual value by a standard deviation term. Observations with high standardized residual values are likely to be outliers. However, an observation's standardized residual value does not measure an observation's outlyingness on the predictor variables.
10. Studentized residual	A residual value that measures *both* the outlyingness of the observation in terms of its standardized residual value (i.e., one type of distance) and the outlyingness of the observation on the predictor variables (i.e., a different kind of distance), such that a data point that is outlying in terms of both types of distance would have a studentized residual value that is greater than its standardized residual value. Observations with high studentized residual values are likely to be outliers.
11. Standardized deleted residual	A residual value is identical to a standardized residual, except that the predicted value for the focal observation is calculated without the observation itself. This exclusion prevents the focal observation from deflating the residual value and inflating the standard deviation term, where such deflation and inflation mask the existence of any outlyingness of the observation. Observations with high standardized deleted residual values are likely to be outliers.

(Continued)

TABLE 8.1 ■ Outlier Identification Techniques Based on a Review of Social and Behavioral Science Research (Continued)

Multiple Construct (i.e., "Distance") Identification Techniques

12.	Studentized deleted residual (i.e., externally studentized residual, jackknife residual)	A residual value that is identical to a studentized residual, except that the predicted value for the focal observation is calculated without the observation itself. This exclusion prevents the focal observation from deflating the residual value and inflating the standard deviation term, where such deflation and inflation mask the existence of any outlyingness of the observation. Observations with high studentized deleted residual values are likely to be outliers.
13.	Euclidean distance	Length of the line segment between two specified points in a one-, two-, or n-dimensional space. A large Euclidean distance between two data points may mean that one of the two data points is an outlier.
14.	Mahalanobis distance	Similar to Euclidean distance, but different in that Mahalanobis distance is the length of the line segment between a data point and the centroid (instead of another observation) of the remaining cases, where the centroid is the point created at the intersection of the means of all the predictor variables. A large Mahalanobis distance may mean that the corresponding observation is an outlier.
15.	K-clustering (with or without modified hat matrix) or other similar cluster analysis techniques	Yields different candidate subsets that one or more multiple-case diagnostics must evaluate.
16.	2- or 3-dimensional plots of the original and the principal component variables	A two- or three-dimensional plot of variables is produced as a result of principal component analysis. An isolated data point denotes a potential outlier.
17.	Autocorrelation function plot	A plot created by computing autocorrelations for data values at varying time lags. Potential outliers can be identified by data points that lie far from other data points.
18.	Time plot	A plot of the relationship between a particular variable and time. Potential outliers can be identified by data points that lie far from other data points.
19.	Extreme studentized deviate (i.e., Grubbs method)	Difference between a variable's mean and query value, divided by a standard deviation value.
20.	Hosmer and Lemeshow goodness-of-fit test	A Pearson Chi-squared statistic from a table of observed and expected (i.e., implied) frequencies.
21.	Leverage values	Also known as the diagonal elements of the hat matrix, leverage values measure the extent to which observations are outliers in the space of predictors.
22.	Centered leverage values	A centered index of leverage values. Specific statistical packages (e.g., SPSS) report centered leverage values instead of regular ones.
23.	Deletion standardized multivariate residual	A standardized residual term in the context of multilevel modeling. This allows for an assessment of the effect that a higher-level outlier has on model fit. Lower-level units should be investigated if an outlier is found at the higher level.

Influence Identification Techniques

24.	Cook's D_i	Assesses the influence that a data point i has on all regression coefficients.
25.	Modified Cook's D_i	It is similar to Cook's D_i but uses standardized deleted residuals rather than standardized residuals.
26.	Generalized Cook's D_i	Similar to Cook's D_i, but applied to structural equation modeling to assess whether a data point influences the parameter estimates.

Influence Identification Techniques	
27. Difference in fits, standardized (DFFITS$_i$)	Like Cook's D_i, this technique also assesses the influence that a data point i has on all regression coefficients as a whole. A large difference between the two techniques is that they produce information on different scales.
28. Difference in beta, standardized (DFBETAS$_{ij}$)	Indicates whether the inclusion of case i leads to an increase or decrease in a single regression coefficient j (i.e., a slope or intercept).
29. Chi-squared difference test	This method allows a researcher conducting structural equation modeling (SEM) to assess the difference in the model fit between two models, one with the outlier included and the other without the outlier.
30. Single parameter influence	Similar to DFBETAS$_{ij}$, this identification technique is used in SEM to assess the effect of an outlier on a specific parameter estimate, as opposed to the overall influence of an outlier on all parameter estimates in the model.
31. Average squared deviation technique	When conducting multilevel modeling, this method, a direct analog of Cook's D_i, investigates whether each group affects the fixed and random parameters, allowing for the identification of higher-level prediction outliers. In addition, lower-level units should be investigated if an outlier is found at the higher level.
32. Sample-adjusted meta-analytic deviancy (SAMD)	In a meta-analysis, this test statistic takes the difference between the value of each primary-level effect size estimate and the mean sample-weighted coefficient computed without that effect size in the analysis. Then it adjusts the difference value based on the sample size of the primary-level study. Outliers are identified by their extreme SAMD values.
33. Analyze with and without outliers	This technique refers to conducting the statistical analysis with and without a particular data point. The data point is an outlier if results differ across the two analyses.
34. Nearest neighbor techniques	Calculate the closest value to the query value using various distance metrics such as Euclidean or Mahalanobis distance. Techniques include K-nearest neighbor, optimized nearest neighbor, efficient Type 1 nearest neighbor, Type 2 nearest neighbor, the nearest neighbor with reduced features, dragon method, PAM (partitioning around medoids), CLARANS (Clustering Large Applications based upon randomized search), and graph connectivity method.
35. Non-parametric methods	Consist of fitting a smoothed curve without making any constraining assumptions about the data. For example, a lack of a linear trend in the relationship signals the presence of outliers.
36. Parametric methods	Unlike non-parametric methods, parametric methods make certain assumptions about the nature of the data. One such assumption is that the data come from a particular type of probability distribution (e.g., normal distribution). These techniques identify outliers as data points that fall outside the expectations about the nature of the data. Parametric methods include convex peeling, ellipsoidal peeling, iterative deletion, iterative trimming, depth trimming, least median of squares, least trimmed squares, and M-estimation.
37. Semi-parametric methods	These methods combine parametric methods' speed and complexity with non-parametric methods' flexibility to investigate local clusters or kernels rather than a single global distribution model. Outliers are identified as lying in regions of low density.
38. Iterative outlier identification procedure	In a sequence of steps, this procedure allows for estimating the residual standard deviation to identify data points sensitive to the estimation procedure used in a time series analysis. Such data points are subsequently identified as outliers.
39. Independent component analysis	A computation method separates independent components by maximizing their statistical independence. When found in a time series analysis, the separate independent components are identified as outliers.

Source: Adapted from Aguinis, Gottfredson, & Joo (2013). Reproduced with permission.

outliers are observations in the top and bottom 2.5% (two-tailed, α = .05) in a percentage analysis, or above or below ±2.24 SD units in a standard deviation analysis if you assume the underlying population distribution to be approximately normal.[22] This cutoff rule is because cases above or below the top and bottom 2.5% are considered sufficiently unlikely to be caused by substantive reasons assuming a "*t*-like" distribution. Further, the cutoff rule accounts for a study's particular research design by identifying a greater number of potential error outliers for studies with larger sample sizes.

For multiple construct techniques, the recommendation is to also begin with visual tools and then follow up with at least one quantitative approach in each of the following two categories: (a) outlyingness based on predictor scores (i.e., leverage, centered leverage, and **Mahalanobis distance** values), and (b) outlyingness based on residual scores (i.e., studentized deleted residuals, deletion standardized multivariate residuals). Regarding outlyingness based on predictor scores, researchers can use leverage, centered leverage, or Mahalanobis distance values because they produce the same type of information but on different scales.[23] Regarding outlyingness based on residual scores, you can use studentized deleted residuals for regression[24] and SEM,[25] and deletion standardized multivariate residuals for multilevel modeling.[26] Regarding multilevel modeling, identification techniques are first applied at the highest level of analysis. For example, in a 2-level model consisting of individuals nested in groups, single construct techniques are applied to the groups (a later section on influential outliers in multilevel modeling discusses when and how to check for error outliers in the lower level(s) of analysis). You should use this top-down approach as it allows you to pinpoint a smaller number of groups whose lower-level data points are worth examining.

Recommended cutoffs for leverage values are $2(k + 1)/n$ for large sample sizes and $3(k + 1)/n$ for small sample sizes, where k = number of predictors and n = sample size.[27] For centered leverage values, recommended cutoffs are $2k/n$ for large and $3k/n$ for small sample sizes. For Mahalanobis distance, recommended cutoffs are $\chi^2_{df = p; \text{ alpha level } = \alpha/n}$ for large sample sizes,[28]

and $\dfrac{p(n-1)^2 \left(F_{df=p, n-p-1; \text{alpha level}=\alpha/n}\right)}{n\left(n-p-1+p F_{df=p, n-p-1; \text{alpha level}=\alpha/n}\right)}$ for small sample sizes,[29] where p = number of variables, χ^2 = critical value in a Chi-squared distribution, F = critical value in an F distribution, and α = .05 or .01. Recommended cutoffs for studentized deleted residuals are $t_{df = n - k - 1; \text{ alpha level } = \alpha/n}$, where t = critical value in a t distribution, and α = .05 or .01. Finally, cutoffs for deletion standardized multivariate residuals for multilevel modeling are based on $\chi^2_{df = n \text{ of highest-level unit } j; \text{ alpha level } = \alpha/n}$, where α = .05 or .01.[30]

The rationale for the recommendations above is that they consider research design considerations by adjusting the cutoff value based on the sample size and number of predictors in the model.[31] From a practical standpoint, these recommendations are more readily available in widely used software packages for regression,[32] SEM,[33] and multilevel modeling.[34] Moreover, code that derives deletion-standardized multivariate residuals is available in MLwiN, R, and Stata (see https://www.stats.ox.ac.uk/~snijders/mlbook.htm).

Making Decisions on How to Define, Identify, and Handle Outliers

Recommendations on defining, identifying, and handling outliers rest on two overarching principles. The first states that you should describe the choices and procedures regarding the treatment (i.e., definition, identification, and handling) of outliers to ensure transparency—including a rationale for the particular procedures you implement. The second principle is that you should clearly and explicitly acknowledge the type of outlier you are interested in and then use an identification technique congruent with the outlier definition. Although this section focuses on regression, SEM, and multilevel modeling, these principles apply to outliers in other data-analytic contexts because their adoption will improve the replicability of substantive results—a requirement to advance science in general.[35] Moreover, using these two overarching principles will enhance the interpretability of substantive conclusions.

The more specific best-practice recommendations described next are built around steps involving three categories of outliers, as shown in Figure 8.1. The first category consists of *error outliers* or data points that lie far from other data points because they result from inaccuracies. The second category represents *interesting outliers*, accurate data points that lie far from other data points and may contain valuable or unexpected knowledge. The third category refers to **influential outliers**, which are accurate data points that lie far from other data points, are not error or interesting outliers, and affect substantive conclusions. The approaches to identifying and handling error and interesting outliers are similar across data-analytic techniques. However, how you identify and handle influential outliers depends on the particular technique—for example, regression versus SEM. Thus, this section offers a discussion regarding error and interesting

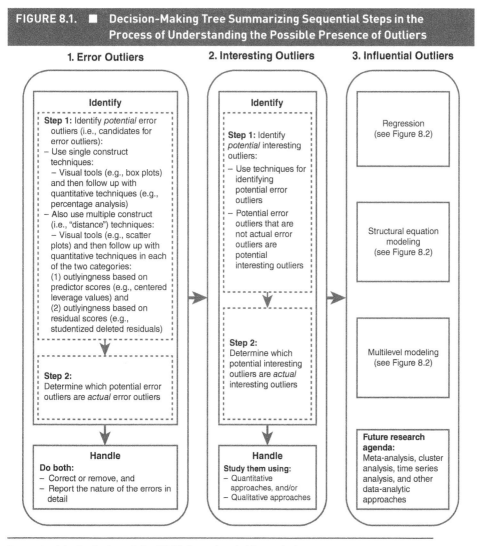

FIGURE 8.1. ■ Decision-Making Tree Summarizing Sequential Steps in the Process of Understanding the Possible Presence of Outliers

1. Error Outliers

Identify

Step 1: Identify *potential* error outliers (i.e., candidates for error outliers):
– Use single construct techniques:
  – Visual tools (e.g., box plots) and then follow up with quantitative techniques (e.g., percentage analysis)
– Also use multiple construct (i.e., "distance") techniques:
  – Visual tools (e.g., scatter plots) and then follow up with quantitative techniques in each of the two categories: (1) outlyingness based on predictor scores (e.g., centered leverage values) and (2) outlyingness based on residual scores (e.g., studentized deleted residuals)

Step 2: Determine which potential error outliers are *actual* error outliers

Handle
Do both:
– Correct or remove, and
– Report the nature of the errors in detail

2. Interesting Outliers

Identify

Step 1: Identify *potential* interesting outliers:
– Use techniques for identifying potential error outliers
– Potential error outliers that are not actual error outliers are potential interesting outliers

Step 2: Determine which potential interesting outliers are *actual* interesting outliers

Handle
Study them using:
– Quantitative approaches, and/or
– Qualitative approaches

3. Influential Outliers

Regression (see Figure 8.2)

Structural equation modeling (see Figure 8.2)

Multilevel modeling (see Figure 8.2)

Future research agenda: Meta-analysis, cluster analysis, time series analysis, and other data-analytic approaches

Source: Aguinis, Gottfredson, & Joo (2013). Reproduced with permission.

outliers and then a separate treatment of influential outliers within each of the specific contexts of regression, SEM, and multilevel modeling. As seen in Figure 8.1, the recommendation is that all empirical studies follow the same sequence of steps.

Table 8.2 includes examples of common situations researchers face regarding defining, identifying, and handling various types of outliers. For instance, regarding error outliers, this table illustrates a common situation when dealing with such outliers. A positive example of handling error outliers is a study identifying an outlying data point[36] (i.e., a potential error outlier). Then, to determine whether this was an error outlier, the authors called the respondent and found that this individual had misunderstood some of the questions. Subsequently, they corrected the error outlier based on the conversation. Each row in Table 8.2 includes illustrations of correct ways of dealing with outliers—including error, interesting, and influential outliers.

Institutional Review Boards (IRBs) vary concerning how they would view the practice of contacting participants to clarify outlying responses. Moreover, many IRBs may require data files to be anonymous as quickly as possible by stripping out identifying information, making

TABLE 8.2 ■ Common Research Situations Illustrating Correct Procedures for Defining, Identifying, and Handling Different Types of Outliers

	Correct Procedures	Rationale for Correct Procedures
Error Outlier	Some authors identified a potential error outlier. They investigated further and found that, after a phone call, the respondent had misunderstood some of the questions. Corrections were made to the data based on the telephone conversation.[37] Others eliminated some outliers, which they found were caused by coding errors.[38]	The amount of deviation of a data point from others does not necessarily mean that an error caused the data point. However, a potential error outlier is an actual error outlier when inaccuracies cause its deviation—and evidence must be provided regarding this issue.
Interesting Outlier	Treating unusually successful or unsuccessful acquisitions as potential sources of valuable knowledge, some authors identified the 12 most successful and the 12 least successful acquisitions as interesting outliers. Then, they applied a case study method to the 24 pairs of firms identified as interesting outliers.[39]	A study of interesting outliers may result in a generation of future-oriented knowledge that also informs practice.[40]
Influential Outliers When Conducting Regression	Multiple authorship teams clearly stated the identification techniques they used, which were appropriate (although authors did not use DFBETAS$_{ij}$).[41]	Correct identification techniques and their description are necessary to maximize transparency and ensure that influence outliers are properly detected.
Influential Outliers When Conducting Structural Equation Modeling	Some authors used a handling technique (i.e., deletion) and reported findings with and without the handling technique to ensure transparency.[42]	Reporting results with and without the handling technique ensures transparency and prevents readers from questioning whether the data were "manipulated" to confirm support for the hypotheses.
Influential Outliers When Conducting Multilevel Modeling	Some authors used a short footnote to clearly state that removing three influential outliers changed the statistical significance of two parameter estimates but ultimately failed to change the substantive conclusions.[43]	Even if influential outliers ultimately fail to change the substantive conclusions, the practice of reporting the results with and without the handling technique (e.g., deletion) prevents skeptical readers from suspecting that the researchers of a study manipulated data to maximize the chance of finding support for their hypotheses and then deliberately refrained from mentioning such a manipulation.

Source: Adapted from Aguinis, Gottfredson, & Joo (2013). Reproduced with permission.

it difficult to identify individual respondents. Thus, you need to keep diaries, logs, or journals during data collection that you can then use retrospectively to determine if something unusual happened with some particular case you can no longer trace.

Error Outliers

As shown in Figure 8.1, the first step in understanding the possible presence of outliers is to check for error outliers. For this particular type of outlier, no a priori theory is needed. The rationale for checking for the possible presence of error outliers is that this outlier type is always undesirable.[44]

Defining Error Outliers

Error outliers are data points that lie at a distance from other data points because they result from inaccuracies. More specifically, error outliers include outlying observations that are caused by: not being part of the targeted population of interest (i.e., an error in the sampling procedure), lying outside the possible range of values, errors in observation, errors in recording, errors in preparing data, errors in computation, errors in coding, or errors in data manipulation.[45] In short, error outliers are non-legitimate observations.

Identifying Error Outliers

Identifying error outliers involves the first step of locating outlying observations (i.e., identification of *potential* error outliers—candidates for error outliers) and then the second step of separately investigating whether the outlyingness of such data points results from errors (i.e., identification of *actual* error outliers). Identifying potential error outliers involves using various visual and quantitative techniques, which compensate for the relative weakness of each.[46] In other words, using more than one technique is necessary to identify as many potential error outliers as possible, even if some of these observations eventually do not turn out to be actual error outliers.

Once you identify the potential error outliers, concluding that the outlying data points are error outliers is premature. At this point, they are only candidates for error outliers. Instead, it is necessary to determine the cause of the identified outlying observations by, for example, checking whether original data entries (e.g., questionnaire responses) match the entries in the electronic data files. If they occur due to an error in recording, coding, or data collection (e.g., not part of the population of interest), then an outlying observation is an error outlier.[47] You should treat all remaining outlying data points with unclear causes as interesting outliers (as discussed later).

Handling Error Outliers

Once you identify the error outliers, the correct procedure is to either adjust the data points to their correct values or remove such observations from the dataset.[48] In addition, it is necessary to explain the reasoning behind classifying the outlier as an error outlier. For example, was it a coding error? A data entry error? A case that was inadvertently and incorrectly included in the database? As noted earlier, transparency is an essential overarching principle that is particularly critical in the case of error outliers. Finally, you must handle the error outlier by changing the data point's value or removing it, which can lead to important changes in substantive conclusions.

Interesting Outliers

As shown in Figure 8.1, the second step in understanding the possible presence of outliers is to examine interesting outliers. You should avoid automatically treating any outlying data point as harmful for two reasons.[49] First, defining outliers in a negative way most often leads to simply removing these cases, with the consequence that we reduce variability in a distribution of scores (i.e., "range restriction" because the range of scores has been restricted by deleting some extreme scores).[50] Second, whether you eventually exclude these outliers from the analysis, you must consider that simple removal and, thus, failure to study these outliers separately in detail can mean forgoing the discovery of valuable, future-oriented knowledge.[51]

Defining Interesting Outliers

Interesting outliers are outlying data points that are accurate and identified as outlying observations (i.e., potential error outliers) but not confirmed as actual error outliers. Also, these cases may contain potentially valuable or unexpected knowledge.[52]

Example: Defining Interesting Outliers: Three Illustrations

Consider the following three examples from different domains. First, some authors identified firms that were interesting outliers because they lost their superior economic performance.[53] Second, the positive psychology movement has focused on studying and analyzing individuals who are interesting outliers in terms of their feelings of happiness.[54] Finally, others encouraged the study of interesting outliers, defined as top performers.[55] For example, the best-selling book *Outliers* focuses on interesting outliers: unique individuals whose lives and career trajectories can be used in support of the contention that success in any field is primarily the result of practicing a specific task for a minimum of about 10,000 hours.[56]

Identifying Interesting Outliers

Identifying interesting outliers involves two steps. The first step is to identify potential interesting outliers, and the second is to identify which are actually interesting outliers. You have completed the first step by following the decision-making tree in Figure 8.1. The reason is that this step also involves using techniques that are the same as the techniques used to identify potential error outliers. Then any potential error outlier that is not an actual error outlier automatically becomes a potential interesting outlier. In the second step, the particular research domain influences how you identify interesting outliers from potential interesting outliers identified in the previous step. For example, if there is an interest in identifying specific individuals on more than ten corporate boards, then potential interesting outliers identified through single construct techniques would be considered interesting outliers. On the other hand, suppose you want to study the relationship between two constructs, such as firms that are outliers in annual profit and annual cost in research and development. In that case, you would identify potential interesting outliers through multiple construct identification techniques. Finally, note that interesting outliers can either be the focus of a study before data collection (i.e., a priori interesting outliers), or you can identify them after the data are collected (i.e., post hoc interesting outliers).

A case may be an error outlier, but the source of the error is not detected. Therefore, this case will likely be incorrectly treated as a potential interesting outlier in such situations. Moreover, pursuing potential interesting outliers is likely to include the examination of many error outliers that went undetected as errors. You can address such a situation by referring to the first of the two overarching principles mentioned earlier: Choices and procedures regarding the treatment of outliers should be described in detail to ensure transparency—including a rationale for the specific procedures you have implemented. In the situation involving possible undetected error outliers, because procedures were open and transparent, future research could attempt to replicate results (i.e., the presence of many potentially interesting outliers).

Handling Interesting Outliers

The recommendation for handling interesting outliers is to study them. You can do this using a quantitative approach similar to some authors who empirically analyzed differences between the manufacturing synergies of high and low outlier performers.[57] In addition, you can examine interesting outliers by adopting a qualitative approach similar to the one used in the book *Outliers,* where the author investigated the factors that contribute to high levels of individual success.[58]

Example: Handling Interesting Outliers

A positive example of handling interesting outliers is a study that examined firm acquisitions that were either highly successful or unsuccessful.[59] These authors identified highly successful acquisitions as 12 pairs of firms that showed increased industry-adjusted performance (i.e., return on assets) and industry-adjusted research and development intensity after the acquisition. In contrast, these authors identified highly unsuccessful acquisitions as 12 pairs of firms exhibiting the greatest reduction in the previously mentioned firm characteristics after the acquisition. They then applied a case study method on the 24 pairs of firms identified as interesting outliers. Doing so resulted in substantial theoretical implications whereby these authors derived potential predictors of outliers in the research domain of acquisitions. In contrast, failing to study numerous observations identified as interesting outliers constitutes an incorrect way of handling interesting outliers, as studying such outliers can produce valuable theoretical insights.

Influential Outliers

In contrast to the procedures for defining, identifying, and handling error and interesting outliers, which are relatively invariant across data-analytic approaches, *influential outliers* are addressed differently depending on particular statistical techniques. There are two types of influential outliers: (a) *model fit outliers* and (b) *prediction outliers*. Model fit outliers are data points whose presence alters the fit of a model, and prediction outliers are data points whose presence alters parameter estimates. The following paragraphs discuss influential outliers within the particular contexts of (a) regression, (b) SEM, and (c) multilevel modeling. Please refer to Figure 8.2 for decision-making charts showing the steps involved in defining, identifying, and handling model fit and prediction outliers within the context of these three popular data-analytic approaches.

Regression

Defining and Identifying Model Fit Outliers. Model fit outliers are cases that affect model fit (e.g., R^2). Depending on their location, they can either increase or decrease model fit. In practice, a model fit outlier often affects both model fit and parameter estimates (i.e., slope and intercept coefficients).

Figure 8.3 includes a simplified graphic illustration of a regression analysis on a hypothetical dataset involving one predictor and one criterion. Please note that this illustration uses an

FIGURE 8.2. ■ Decision-Making Tree Summarizing Sequential Steps in the Process of Defining, Identifying, and Handling Influential Outliers in the Context of Regression, Structural Equation Modeling, and Multilevel Modeling

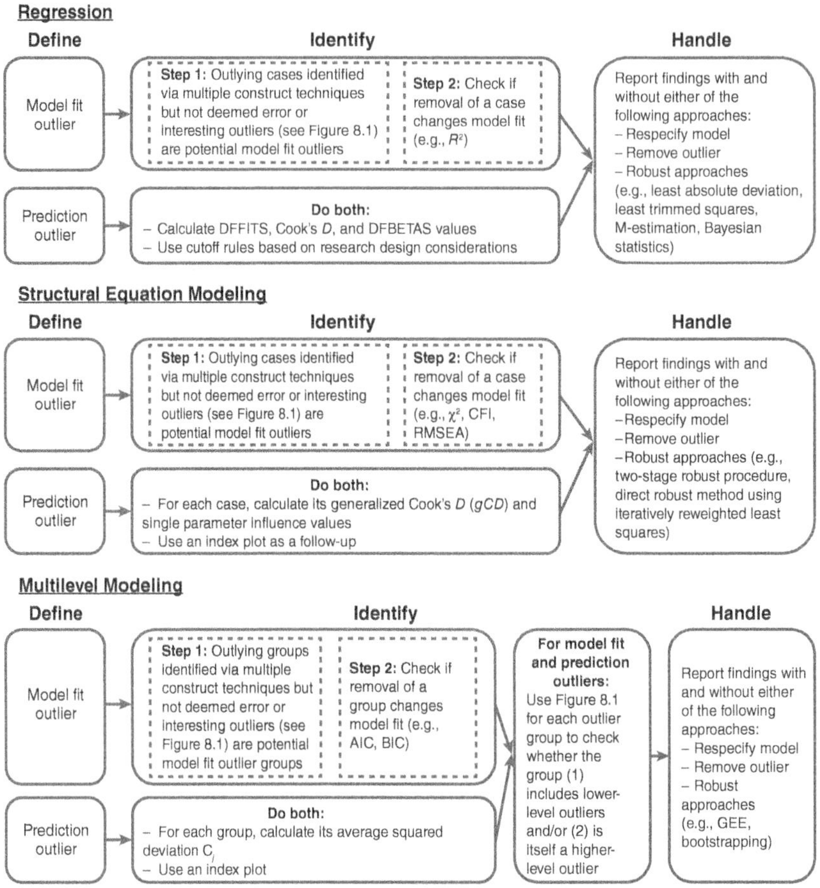

Source: Aguinis, Gottfredson, & Joo (2013). Reproduced with permission.

unusually small sample size for pedagogical purposes. The R^2 for the data in Figure 8.3 is .73 when we exclude Cases #1, #2, and #3 from the analysis. When Case #1, #2, or #3 is included, model fit changes to .11, .95, or .17, respectively. Further, including Case #1 or #3 reduces model fit and affects the parameter estimates (i.e., the intercept and slope). In contrast, Case #2 affects (i.e., improves) only model fit because of its location along the regression line.

Identifying model fit outliers involves a two-step process. The first step is identifying data points most likely to influence the model's fit because they deviate from other cases in the dataset. The second step involves investigating such cases to understand if they affect model fit. The rationale for the first step is a practical one because the first step reduces the number of cases to which the more time-consuming and effortful second step must be applied.

You automatically complete the first step after implementing the earlier recommendations regarding error and interesting outliers (see Figure 8.1). More specifically, cases identified with multiple construct techniques and subsequently determined not to be error or interesting outliers constitute candidates for model fit outliers.

FIGURE 8.3 ■ Graphic Illustration of Influential Outliers (i.e., Model Fit and Prediction Outliers) in the Context of Regression

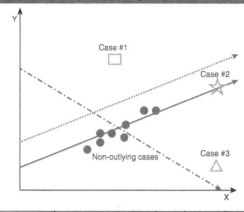

	Regression line	R^2	Slope	Intercept
With ● only	→	.73	.83	5.34
With ● only ☐	·····►	.11	.83	9.13
With ● only ☆	→	.95	.83	5.34
With ● only △	—·—·—►	.17	−.22	30.34

Source: Aguinis, Gottfredson, & Joo (2013). Reproduced with permission.

The second step is determining whether cases that differ markedly from the rest influence model fit (e.g., R^2). This involves checking whether removing an observation changes the statistical significance of a model fit index from statistically significant to statistically nonsignificant or vice versa.[60]

Defining and Identifying Prediction Outliers. Prediction outliers are cases that affect parameter estimates (i.e., slope and intercept coefficients). As illustrated in Figure 8.3, a data point can be a prediction outlier by either (1) having a sizeable residual value (e.g., Case #1) and (2) having both a sizeable residual value and extreme value(s) on the predictor(s) (e.g., Case #3). Note that having extreme values on the predictors but a small residual value will not make a data point a prediction outlier (see Case #2). However, as noted earlier, this case will likely be a model-fit outlier.

Three techniques are specifically designed to assess the presence of prediction outliers in the context of regression: **DFFITS**$_i$ (DIFFerence in FIT, Standardized—note that this an index of prediction and not model fit outliers despite its label), **Cook's D_i**, and **DFBETAS**$_{ij}$ (DIFFerence in BETA, Standardized). The subscript *i* refers to an observation, and *j* denotes a regression coefficient.[61] These prediction outlier identification techniques are available in most software packages and share two common characteristics. First, you calculate each for every observation. Second, each is a ratio, where the numerator quantifies the amount of change in the parameter estimates when the observation *i* is excluded from the sample. The denominator is a standard error term calculated without observation *i* in the sample.

Despite their similarities, these three techniques also have an important difference. DFFITS$_i$ and Cook's D_i are global indicators that assess the influence that a data point has on all regression coefficients as a whole. In contrast, DFBETAS$_{ij}$ is a more specific index that quantifies an observation's impact on a particular regression coefficient *j*. Given this difference, DFFITS$_i$, Cook's D_i, and DFBETAS$_{ij}$ do not always converge. A case may strongly influence just one regression coefficient but have a minimal influence on others. As a result, the observation's strong influence on the single regression coefficient may not be visible in a global measure of influence. Referring to Figure 8.3, DFFITS$_i$ and Cook's D_i could easily detect prediction outliers such as Case #3 because it disproportionately influences the slope and the intercept. However, these two global influence measures are less likely to detect Case #1 because this prediction outlier only exerts a disproportionate influence on the intercept. Using DFBETAS$_{ij}$ would increase the likelihood of identifying Case #1 as a prediction outlier. Therefore, it is important to investigate both specific and global prediction outliers.

It would be best if you used the following cutoffs.[62] For DFFITS$_i$, the recommended cutoff is $\pm 2\sqrt{(k + 1)/n}$ for observation i to be considered a prediction outlier, where k represents the number of predictors, and n represents the number of observations. For Cook's D_i, the recommendation is to use the F distribution, with $df = (k + 1, n - k - 1)$ and $\alpha = .50$, to determine the statistical significance of the values.[63] For DFBETAS$_{ij}$, the recommended cutoff is $\pm 2/\sqrt{n}$ for the observation i to be considered a prediction outlier regarding regression coefficient j. These recommendations adjust cutoff values depending on characteristics of the particular research context, such as the sample size and number of predictors.[64]

Handling Model Fit and Prediction Outliers.   The options for handling model fit and prediction outliers are the same. The framework consists of three courses of action: (a) **respecification**, (b) deletion, and (c) **robust approaches**.[65]

Respecification refers to adding additional terms to the regression equation. For example, these additional terms may carry information about non-linear effects (i.e., squared terms[66]) or moderating effects (i.e., product terms[67]). If the added variable adds incremental variance, there is a chance that the outlier may no longer be present. If the respecified model is supported (i.e., if the terms added post hoc significantly improve model fit or prediction), you can also build new theoretical models that can be tested, confirmed, or disconfirmed in future research. In other words, respecifying models post hoc is beneficial in helping you engage in theory-building, a type of contribution underutilized in many social and behavioral science domains.[68] Note that respecification capitalizes on chance—an element you should not use for theory testing due to generalizability and ethical concerns.[69] So, suppose you decide to report respecified model(s), along with a discussion about their implications for theory building. In that case, you should elaborate on the discussion in the "Future Research Directions" section of your manuscript.[70]

Regardless of whether you use respecification, other ways of handling influential outliers are to delete them or use robust approaches (which involve a non-OLS standard such as **least absolute deviation**, **least trimmed squares**, **M-estimation**, and **Bayesian statistics**).[71] It is important to report results with and without the chosen outlier handling technique, which includes explaining any differences in the results because the presence of influential outliers causes a dilemma in determining proper inference about a population based upon a sample. In other words, deletion or robust techniques remove or limit the information an actual data point provides, making the sample a potentially biased population representation. Because the absence or presence of a particular handling technique may lead to improper inferences about a population, you should report both results to (a) place the burden of determination for the most "accurate conclusions" on the reader and (b) ensure complete transparency so that the handling technique does not appear to have been chosen because it supported one's hypotheses. This recommendation is consistent with a customer-centric approach to reporting scientific results.[72]

On a positive note, a review of the substantive literature yielded examples of authorship teams that clearly stated the identification techniques used, and these identification techniques were appropriate (although authors did not use DFBETAS$_{ij}$).[73] However, on a less positive note, other authors did not clearly state the methods used to identify influential outliers. As a result, a skeptical scientific audience might question a study's substantive conclusions without describing the identification techniques.

Structural Equation Modeling

This section discusses influential outliers in SEM by addressing model fit and prediction outliers. Please refer to Figure 8.2 for a summary of the decision points involved.

Defining and Identifying Model Fit Outliers. Similar to regression, identifying model fit outliers in SEM is a two-step process. The first involves identifying model-fit outlier candidates. The second involves investigating which of the candidates influences the model's fit. As explained in the earlier section on regression, the first step helps researchers save time and effort, especially if the sample size is large.

As with regression, you complete the first step by implementing the recommendations regarding error and interesting outliers (see Figure 8.1). In other words, outliers identified with multiple construct techniques and subsequently determined not to be error or interesting outliers constitute candidates for model fit outliers. The second step in identifying model fit outliers in SEM is to check whether a candidate's removal changes the model's fit.[74] That is, excluding an observation may cause a change in the statistical significance of the overall model fit based on χ^2 or other fit indexes such as the **comparative fit index (CFI)** or **root mean square error of approximation (RMSEA)**.

Defining and Identifying Prediction Outliers. As with regression, there are two types of prediction outliers: **global prediction outliers** and **specific prediction outliers.** A global prediction outlier influences all parameter estimates in a particular model. On the other hand, a specific prediction outlier is a data point that influences a single parameter estimate. Thus, global prediction outlier methods in SEM are analogous to Cook's D_i and DFFITS$_i$ in regression, whereas specific prediction outlier techniques in SEM are analogous to DFBETAS$_{ij}$.

The recommendation is to use the generalized Cook's Distance (gCD_i) statistic to identify global prediction outliers, where i refers to a data point.[75] Calculating a gCD_i value for every observation is recommended for the following reasons. First, you calculate gCD_i values using a software package and, consequently, no additional effort is required in investigating all cases compared to just a few. Second, it is usually the case that there are no specific a priori predictions about which cases may be prediction outliers. Accordingly, it is beneficial to examine gCD_i values for all observations.

A gCD_i value is a ratio where the numerator quantifies the amount of change in a group of parameter estimates when an observation i is excluded from the sample. The denominator of this ratio is a standard error term that is also calculated without observation i in the sample. Note that gCD_i will always be positive because it indicates the absolute magnitude of change and not the direction of change. This is because gCD_i represents the change in multiple parameter estimates (not a single estimate), and it is not logically possible to show through a single value how multiple parameter estimates change in possibly different directions. Nonetheless, a single value of gCD_i summarizes the absolute magnitude of change: the greater the value of gCD_i, the greater the global influence of the corresponding data point on the parameter estimates.[76] There are no precise cutoffs regarding what gCD_i value indicates a global prediction outlier. Thus, you should use an index plot, which includes case numbers on the X axis and gCD_i values on the Y axis, to understand better which gCD_i values, and thus corresponding cases, markedly deviate from others. For example, some authors use index plots for various test statistics.[77]

Note that a case may strongly influence one parameter estimate but have a minimal influence on others. As a result, a global measure of influence may mask the observation's strong influence on the single parameter estimate. Therefore, it is important also to examine specific prediction outliers. Specific prediction outliers are identified by $\Delta\hat{\theta}_{ji}$, or the **single parameter influence,** which is the standardized change in the jth parameter resulting from the deletion of observation i.[78] Please note that positive values of $\Delta\hat{\theta}_{ji}$ indicate that excluding case i causes a smaller value of $\hat{\theta}_j$ (i.e., the estimate of the jth parameter), while negative values of $\Delta\hat{\theta}_{ji}$ indicate that excluding case i causes a larger value of $\hat{\theta}_j$. Thus, unlike a global prediction outlier represented by gCD_i, which expresses the absolute magnitude of change but not the direction of change, a specific prediction outlier identified by $\Delta\hat{\theta}_{ji}$ captures the magnitude and the direction of change. In addition, you should graph $\Delta\hat{\theta}_{ji}$ values in an index plot to identify $\Delta\hat{\theta}_{ji}$ values as influential because there are no clear cutoffs. Observations with $\Delta\hat{\theta}_{ji}$ values markedly deviating from other $\Delta\hat{\theta}_{ji}$ values are likely specific prediction outliers.[79] Finally, you can calculate $\Delta\hat{\theta}_{ji}$ using R code, MPlus batch runs, and SAS code.

Handling Model Fit and Prediction Outliers.   Overall, the recommendations for handling influential outliers in SEM are similar to those for regression. Regardless of whether or not you decide to respecify the model for theory-building purposes, it would be best if you used deletion or robust approaches. Regarding robust approaches, you should use a two-stage robust procedure[80] or a direct robust method using **iteratively reweighted least squares**.[81] Both methods use Mahalanobis distance to identify extreme cases and limit their influence in the analysis. Using either of these robust methods will lead to estimators that are less heavily affected by influential outliers.[82] Whether you use deletion or robust regression, you need to report the results obtained without the technique and with the technique. This practice also includes explaining any difference in substantive results. Implementing this recommendation will improve transparency in the eyes of a skeptical scientific audience.

Based on the substantive literature review, fewer than 5% of the 232 studies relied on SEM. One likely reason for this low frequency, compared to approximately 40% of the 232 studies that used regression, is that few studies or textbooks discuss the role of outliers when conducting SEM, as is the regression case. Therefore, if clearer guidelines for SEM exist, you can routinely address outliers and report your choices in future studies relying on SEM. At the same time, a common situation found across the studies that dealt with outliers when using SEM was how to handle influential outliers. For example, in a study, the authorship team addressed outliers correctly by reporting their findings with and without a specific handling technique (i.e., deletion).[83] On the other hand, multiple other authorship teams engaged in a particular handling technique (i.e., deletion) yet did not report their findings with and without the technique.

Multilevel Modeling

Multilevel modeling incorporates data at multiple levels of analysis and estimates parameters that reflect fixed and random effects. Given the complexity of the issues involved, it is not surprising that few resources discuss outliers in multilevel modeling, and many of those are highly technical.[84] Defining, identifying, and handling outliers in multilevel modeling becomes more complex than regression and SEM. For example, when using multilevel modeling and assuming a research design involving individuals nested within groups, you can plot the relationship between a lower-level predictor and a lower-level criterion for each group, representing as many lines of relations as there are groups. So, there could be model fit and prediction outliers for each of these groups. Also, groups could vastly differ from others in terms of their mean value, variance, intercept, and slope. Finally, there can be variation in sample sizes across groups, such that one group has many lower-level units and another has few lower-level units. Specifically, some authors reviewed 79 multilevel investigations published in the *Journal of Applied Psychology* between 2000 and 2010 and found that the level-2 sample size ranged from 12 to 708 (median = 51).[85]

Regardless of whether a multilevel study includes hypotheses about same-level direct effects (e.g., the effect of individual job satisfaction on individual job performance), cross-level direct effects (e.g., the effect of team-level cohesion on individual job performance), or cross-level interaction effects (e.g., moderating effect of team-level cohesion on the relationship between individual job satisfaction and individual job performance), the main goal of any analysis is to assess the size of the variance components and the sources of such variances. For example, consider the case where a data point in one group causes that group's intercept and slope to be vastly different from other groups. Such a point could lead you to believe there are between-group differences when such differences may not exist across most groups. Figure 8.2 summarizes the decision points involved in defining, identifying, and handling influential outliers in multilevel modeling, which the next section discusses.

Defining and Identifying Model Fit Outliers. From a practical standpoint, adopting a top-down approach to identifying model fit outliers in multilevel modeling is beneficial.[86] Thus, implementing outlier identification procedures begins at the highest level of analysis (i.e., level 3 in a 3-level model, level 2 in a 2-level model). The researcher then determines whether a group of observations affects the model fit due to: (1) the group itself and (2) a particular data point(s) in the group. If the former situation is correct, the focal group is a higher-level outlier (i.e., outlier group). If the latter case is correct, the individual observation(s) is a lower-level outlier. Again, the rationale for this top-down approach is practical because doing so is less time-consuming than using a bottom-up approach (i.e., examining lower-level outliers within each group first).

The identification of model fit outliers takes place through three steps: first, identifying model fit outlier group candidates; second, assessing whether the candidate groups truly affect model fit; and third, checking whether an actual model fit outlier group's outlyingness is driven by: (1) an outlying data point(s) in the group, and (2) the entire group. You automatically complete the first step after implementing the recommendations regarding error and interesting outliers discussed earlier (see Figure 8.1). In short, outlier groups identified with multiple construct techniques and subsequently determined not to be error or interesting outliers constitute candidates for model fit outlier groups. The second step involves checking whether removing a candidate group changes model fit from statistically significant to statistically nonsignificant or vice versa.[87] More specifically, the exclusion of a candidate group may cause a change in the statistical significance of the overall model fit (e.g., **Akaike Information Criterion [AIC]** or **Bayesian Information Criterion [BIC]**) or incremental variance explained.[88] If excluding a candidate group changes the statistical significance of a model fit index, then the group constitutes a model fit outlier group. The third step is to check whether the outlier group's effect on model fit is driven by: (1) an outlying data point(s) in the group (hence, an individual observation identified as a lower-level outlier) and (2) the entire group (hence, a group identified as a higher-level outlier). To determine exactly which one of the two situations is at hand for a model fit outlier group, follow the recommendations in Figure 8.1—those regarding error outliers, then interesting outliers, and finally influential outliers in the context of regression—for the lower-level cases in each model fit outlier group. The reason is that each group in a multilevel analysis constitutes a separate regression analysis. If one or more non-error, model fit outliers exist within the focal group, and if the exclusion of the model fit outliers within the group, in turn, makes the exclusion of the *group* no longer cause a statistically significant change in a model fit, then the model fit outliers within the focal group are lower-level outliers. In contrast, if no model-fit outliers exist within the focal group, or if the focal group's exclusion still causes a statistically significant change in a model-fit index even after removing the model-fit outlier(s), then the focal group itself is (also) considered a higher-level model fit outlier.

Defining and Identifying Prediction Outliers. As with model fit outliers, you can identify prediction outliers using a top-down approach.[89] First, the recommendation is to calculate the **average squared deviation**, or C_j, for each group of cases, where j[90] denotes the focal group. That is, C_j assesses the combined influence of a group j on both the fixed and random parameter estimates. Unfortunately, a statistical test for determining the significance of C_j has not yet been formally developed. Nevertheless, you can use an index plot to compare C_j values against one another. Some authors made statistical code available for this procedure in MLwiN, R, and Stata (see https://www.stats.ox.ac.uk/~snijders/mlbook.htm).

Next, for each group whose C_j is markedly deviant, you should check exactly what drives the group's particularly large value. As in the previous situation involving model fit outliers, a markedly large C_j may be caused by: (1) a prediction outlier(s) within the group and (2) the entire group as a prediction outlier. To determine which one of the two situations is at hand for a group with a markedly large C_j (i.e., prediction outlier group), you should examine any prediction outliers within each prediction outlier group by using procedures described in the discussion of prediction outliers in the context of regression. For example, if you identify one or more prediction outliers within the focal group, and if the exclusion of the prediction outlier(s) within the group makes the group's C_j value no longer notably different from those of other groups, then the prediction outlier(s) within the focal group are lower-level outliers. In contrast, if the prediction outlier identification procedure reveals no prediction outliers within the focal group, or if the focal group's C_j value remains notably different from other groups even after removing the prediction outlier(s), then the focal group itself is (also) considered a higher-level outlier.

Handling Model Fit and Prediction Outliers. Overall, approaches for handling influential outliers in multilevel modeling are similar to those used in regression and SEM. One option is to try respecifying the model for theory-building purposes. However, regardless of whether you use respecification, the recommendation is to use either deletion or robust techniques. Further, irrespective of whether you use deletion or robust regression, you should report results based on all of the approaches used—a practice that also includes explaining any differences in the results. This ensures transparency and empowers the reader to be more informed of the study's results.

The technique of respecification, as in the situation involving regression, can take the form of including another term in the model (e.g., cross-level interaction term). Once again, this inductive practice of respecifying models post hoc is beneficial in helping you engage in theory building. However, unlike in regression, the multilevel modeling context requires you to first decide on the level where you want to add any additional predictor(s). For example, in a two-level model, if the identified outliers (by following previously explained procedures) mainly consist of higher-level outliers (i.e., outlier groups), you may consider adding additional level 2 predictors. On the other hand, if the identified outliers mainly consist of lower-level outliers, consider adding additional level 1 predictors. In either case, if the added variable significantly adds incremental variance explained, a data point previously identified as an outlier may no longer be such after model respecification.

Options regarding robust techniques in the multilevel context include generalized estimating equations (GEE) methods and **bootstrapping** methods. GEE methods estimate the variances and covariances in the random part of the multilevel model directly from the residuals.[91] This approach estimates average population effects rather than modeling individual and group differences. The result of using GEE estimates is that they are less efficient than maximum likelihood estimates. Still, they need to make stronger assumptions about the structure of the random part of the multilevel model, which limits the effect of influential outliers. One drawback to this approach is that it only approximates the random effects, so you cannot analyze them in detail. Bootstrapping methods are another type of robust technique that you can use. These methods estimate the parameters of a model and their standard errors from the sample without reference to a theoretical sample distribution. A drawback of this approach is that it is only accurate for large sample sizes ($n > 150$).[92]

HOW TO NOT CLEAN UP YOUR HYPOTHESES BY HYPOTHESIZING AFTER RESULTS ARE KNOWN (HARKING)

Hypothesizing after results are known (HARKing[93]) refers to the questionable research practice of retroactive hypothesis, including an unexpected finding or exclusion of a "failed" prediction. The practice of HARKing, also referred to as accommodational hypothesizing[94] and presenting post-hoc hypotheses as a priori,[95] has been admitted by about 30% of researchers.[96]

Epistemological Background of HARKing

HARKing has long been a topic of debate among philosophers of science, who distinguish between hypotheses built as predictions (i.e., *a priori*) versus accommodations (i.e., *a posteriori*).[97] In fact, for some epistemologists,[98] whether you construct hypotheses before versus after examining the data is a crucial distinction. But, unfortunately, hypothesis origin information is rarely available to, and therefore seldom considered by, consumers of science.[99]

The following scenario illustrates the distinction between prediction (*a priori* hypothesizing) and accommodation (i.e., HARKing) with two hypothetical researchers: Penny Predictor and Annie Accommodator.[100] Imagine that Penny Predictor hypothesizes *a priori* (i.e., predicts) that openness to experience and employee turnover will be related. Penny tests and rejects the null hypothesis, and reports an effect size between the variable pair, r_{Penny}. The other researcher, Annie Accommodator, hypothesizes a relationship between extraversion and employee turnover. She also successfully rejects her null hypothesis. However, after analyzing the data, Annie discovers that a different variable, openness to experience, predicts turnover. Thus, she builds an accommodating hypothesis, a theoretical rationale for it, and reports an effect size between the accommodated pair, r_{Annie}. Still, other researchers might have removed the openness to experience-turnover hypothesis from their manuscript had they failed to observe a significant relation yet possibly reported the effect size (e.g., in a correlation matrix involving all study variables[101]). Is Penny's hypothesis or result about the openness to experience-turnover relation more credible than Annie's? Has Annie created a needlessly complex hypothesis or model, thus complicating the theoretical landscape unnecessarily?[102] Will Annie's hypothesis have less predictive success in the future? And, if so, what are the ramifications for scientific progress?

For philosophers of science, debate on Annie's and Penny's situation has ensued for over a century.[103] The view that Penny's hypothesis has an advantage over Annie's, by dint of having predicted the outcome, is labeled *predictivism* (also known as the *advantage thesis*). Proponents of this view[104] argue that hypothesis accommodation (i.e., HARKing) leads to the overfitting of data and impedes a theory's potential for predictive precision. In contrast, proponents of the alternative view, *accommodationism*, are agnostic to the difference between Penny's and Annie's hypotheses. Consequently, they argue that you should afford no privileged status to Penny's hypothesis.

HARKing Mechanisms

Prevalence of and Motivation for HARKing

A content analysis of hypothesis statements in doctoral dissertations and later published articles demonstrated HARKing's prevalence.[105] In this study, the supported-to-non-supported hypothesis ratio was significantly larger for published articles than the dissertations on which they relied, roughly 2 to 1 and 1 to 1, respectively. This finding represents the authors' removal of non-supported hypotheses (most common), the addition of new, supported hypotheses (less common), and reversing directional hypotheses (least common).

METHODS IN PRACTICE

HOW COMMON IS HARKING?

A study reported that 34% of scientists admitted to HARKing, and findings were "mined" until they reached a statistically significant relation. Then the authors presented them as if they were the original target of the study.[106] Similarly, other authors reported a HARKing frequency of 27%.[107] Further evidence indicates that researchers admit to knowledge of their colleagues' HARKing and, less frequently, "massaging" data.[108] Thus, the extant literature suggests that HARKing is quite common.

One reason why authors HARK involves reviewers' negative reactions to non-supported hypotheses.[109] Moreover, manuscript reviewers are the ones who often suggest that hypotheses be added *a posteriori* during the peer review process.[110] Although reviewer suggestions about the post hoc inclusion of hypotheses may be motivated by authors' implicit reference to them, this phenomenon is also likely attributable to the "theory fetish" in social and behavioral science.[111] In addition, other explanations for the prevalence of HARKing are specific to social and behavioral science, such as the infrequent implementation of experimental designs.[112] Indeed, compared to passive observational (i.e., correlational) research, relatively fewer HARKing opportunities are present in experimental research environments where hypotheses are often linked *a priori* to independent variable manipulations. Typically, an experiment involves one or two manipulations; dropping them from a manuscript would mean little information remaining to report. Finally, much social and behavioral science is conducted by those who seek to confirm their theories and use null tests.[113] In contrast, strong inference, which pits theories against each other,[114] is based on an experimental design paradigm, infrequent in social and behavioral science, and therefore offers relatively fewer opportunities for HARKing.

Overfitting, Complexity, and Predictive Precision

Some authors argued that the severity of HARKing's consequences depends on safeguards for overfitting data.[115] Overfitting refers to an increase in model complexity beyond some criterion of incremental variance explanation. For example, any set of data may be perfectly fit (e.g., $R^2 = 1.00$) with a model of n-1 parameters, where n represents the number of observations. However, you should draw a line between variance explained and parsimony. This is because overly complex models lack predictive precision.[116] As an illustration, imagine a researcher conducting a structural equation modeling analysis and sifting through a library of data containing several predictors of some outcome variable. Ritualistic tinkering might occur by adding some variables and removing others—the end of the exercise results in a model with n degrees of freedom and several fit statistics. However, as an author noted,[117] the researcher used several degrees of freedom during the selection process. Still, the reader may not realize these phantom degrees of freedom were hidden in the final model.

HARKing, Results Visibility, and Effect Size Estimates

Even if safeguards for overfitting were present, HARKing has another potential consequence. Specifically, HARKing emphasizes supported findings through retroactive hypothesis inclusion and de-emphasis of unsupported findings through retroactive hypothesis exclusion. If hypothesized relations are more likely to be mentioned in article titles and abstracts, such results become easier to locate and more prominent and visible than unsupported findings. Similarly, smaller effect size estimates associated with non-supported and removed hypotheses become more difficult to locate and also become less prominent and visible. Indeed, some authors were instructed[118] to recenter their article around the new findings supported by strong data while subordinating or even ignoring the original hypotheses. This presents a concern, particularly for subsequent narrative literature reviews and meta-analyses. Given that literature reviews often rely on electronic searches of titles, abstracts, and keywords, results run the risk of upward bias from HARKing's promotion of larger and significant findings and the demotion of smaller and nonsignificant ones. This is likely the case despite recent technological advancements and the recommendation that electronic searches involved in a meta-analysis rely on articles' full text,[119] which often returns more false positives than hits. Further, because results from narrative and meta-analytic literature reviews are reproduced in textbooks and reach a broad audience that includes practitioners, HARKing has the potential to widen the science-practice gap and hamper evidence-based management.[120]

Different Forms of HARKing

Many forms of author misconduct might lead to the publication of unrepresentative results, ranging from *p fishing* (i.e., trying multiple statistical tests to find one in which $p < .05$) to outright fabrication.[121] HARKing is often listed as an example of questionable research practice. But there are several forms of HARKing behavior, some of which might pose more significant concerns than others.

Table 8.3 summarizes a taxonomy including four types of HARKing. First, *hypothesis proliferation* occurs when authors add hypotheses to their study after the results have come in. This particular form of HARKing adds more luster to a result that was separate from the original conceptual design of a study. Still, it does not necessarily introduce bias into the research literature as long as the results in question would probably have been part of the descriptive statistics customarily included in research reports (e.g., table including correlations between all study variables). Thus, this type of HARKing may not distort the cumulative body of research in a field.

TABLE 8.3 ■ A Taxonomy of HARKing Behaviors
Less Problematic – Little Potential to Bias Cumulative Knowledge

1. *Hypothesis Proliferation:* An author adds hypotheses to a study after data are collected and analyzed to emphasize a result that was not part of the original conceptual design but was nevertheless going to be reported in the manuscript (e.g., correlation table).

2. *THARKing*: An author is likely to transparently HARK in the discussion section of a paper by forming new hypotheses based on results obtained.[122]

More Problematic – Great Potential to Bias Cumulative Knowledge

3. *Cherry-picking:* An author searches through data involving alternative measures or samples to find the results that offer the strongest possible support for a particular hypothesis or research question.

4. *Question Trolling*: An author searches through data involving several different constructs, measures of those constructs, interventions, or relationships to find seemingly notable results worth writing about.

Source: Murphy, K. R., & Aguinis, H. HARKing: How badly can cherry picking and question trolling produce bias in published results? *Journal of Business and Psychology, 34*(1), 1-17, 2019, Springer Nature.

Second, some might engage in ***THARKing*** (transparently HARKing[123]). For example, some authors may describe particular hypotheses in an article's discussion section based on the data they collected for their study. Some have argued that THARKing is ethical and likely beneficial, mainly if the hypotheses thus developed can subsequently be tested with an independent study.

Third, others may engage in ***cherry-picking***, which consists of searching through data involving alternative measures or samples to find the results that offer the strongest possible support for a particular hypothesis or research question a study investigated. Data snooping for statistically significant or noteworthy results are pervasive in many fields, including finance,[124] applied psychology,[125] international business,[126] strategic management studies,[127] and other psychology subfields.[128] Cherry-picking the best possible outcome out of multiple results aimed at the same research question or hypothesis certainly presents ethical concerns, but it is not clear how much bias it might introduce.

Finally, HARKing can take the form of ***question trolling***, which consists of searching through data involving several different constructs, measures of those constructs, interventions, or relationships to find seemingly notable results worth writing about. The question-trolling form of HARKing distorts the research process in two ways. First, rather than starting with a research question and proceeding to collect relevant data, researchers who engage in this form of HARKing allow the data to tell them which question is most likely to lead to a noteworthy result, thus bypassing the most important step in the research process—the conceptual development of a question that is worth attempting to answer. This type of HARKing will also introduce bias into the cumulative scientific literature, potentially more bias than cherry-picking.

Cherry-picking is a particular case of question trolling. Cherry-picking involves choosing the most favorable result from several sample statistics to estimate the same population parameter. In contrast, question trolling consists of selecting the most favorable result from several sample statistics that estimate several different population parameters (i.e., different relations among different sets of variables). In this sense, cherry-picking involves selectively choosing from a set of values in which there is variability between studies aimed at estimating the same underlying population value. On the other hand, question trolling involves selectively choosing among a set of values in which there is variability due to both differences in estimates of a population parameter in studies that all focus on the same question as well as differences in values of the population parameters that underlie the different questions, different variables, or different relationships.

Hypothesis proliferation and THARKing are not likely to introduce severe biases into the scientific literature, and hypothesis proliferation qualifies only as a questionable research practice due to a lack of transparency. However, cherry-picking and question trolling can be severe sources of bias due to systematically and proactively selecting the largest possible effect size estimates from several available.

Table 8.4 summarizes several conclusions about HARKing. First, it is important to recognize that different forms of HARKing differ regarding their effects. Specifically, they range from actually desirable (THARKing) to highly damaging to a field's cumulative knowledge and the credibility of science (e.g., some instances of question trolling). Second, cherry-picking's effect is overall small, but the impact of question trolling can be quite substantial. For example, question trolling is most damaging when there is greater variability in the population parameters underlying the results. Third, you can take several actions to minimize the detrimental effects of HARKing. For example, large sample sizes reduce the bias produced by cherry-picking.

TABLE 8.4 ■ Conclusions Regarding HARKing

Different Forms of HARKing

1. Not all forms of HARKing produce biased results. As summarized in Table 8.3, some forms of HARKing, such as THARKing, are desirable because they can lead to important discoveries.

2. Cherry-picking and question-trolling will always produce biased results. Because these both represent biased searches for the most favorable results, these forms of HARKing will, by definition, introduce biases. Moreover, under some circumstances (e.g., small samples, large sets of variables to be examined, heterogeneous population parameters), these biases can be substantial in absolute and relative terms.

3. HARKing is only sometimes a case of author misconduct. However, reviewers and editors often suggest substantial revisions to the paper they review, and they need to be on the lookout for pushing authors to create hypotheses that did not exist before submitting their manuscript.

Which Forms of HARKing Produce the Largest Bias

4. Cherry picking's impact is generally small. Except when HARKing is very prevalent, and the sample size is small, cherry-picking results have a small biasing impact on effect size estimates.

5. Question trolling's impact can be very large. Question trolling can have a large effect when this behavior is pervasive and if the set of results the author chooses from is highly heterogeneous (i.e., the variability in population parameters underlying the results that are scanned approaches the variability across the entire field of study of applied psychology).

6. How HARKing's bias is measured matters. Biases produced by cherry-picking and question trolling are generally small when measured in correlation units (i.e., usually in the .10s). But this same amount of bias seems to be much larger and impactful if measured in percent increase compared to the true effect sizes (i.e., 50% and even 100%).

Minimizing the Detrimental Forms of HARKing

7. Increase sample size. Large samples (e.g., samples larger than 200) help to minimize the biases associated with cherry-picking and question trolling. Some of the biases that are introduced by these HARKing behaviors are the result of taking systematic advantage of random fluctuations in data, and large samples help mitigate this concern.

8. Decrease the prevalence of HARKing. Decreasing the prevalence of HARKing may be sufficient to decrease its cumulative effects. The biases produced by cherry-picking or question trolling were generally small if the prevalence of HARKing was less than 40%. It may not be necessary to eliminate all HARKing to keep its detrimental effects in check.

(Continued)

TABLE 8.4 ■ Conclusions Regarding HARKing (*Continued*)
How Can You Detect and Deter Detrimental Forms of HARKing?

9. Use Occam's Razor. HARKed hypotheses often involve convoluted reasoning or counterfactual assumptions. Suppose the conceptual case for a hypothesis seems unlikely to hold up to scrutiny or does not seem to emerge organically from the literature and theory the author cites. In that case, this is one potential indicator of HARKing.

10. Have a healthily skeptical attitude. Stories that are too good to be true may not be true. It is unusual for every prediction and hypothesis to be supported in a study, and skepticism is warranted when reviewing a manuscript in which every prediction is supported.

11. Reduce the temptation to HARK. HARKing is not simply a problem of author misbehavior—reviewers and editors' requests that authors tidy up otherwise "messy" research by encouraging authors to drop or modify hypotheses that are not supported have the same detrimental effect as HARKing.

12. Encourage and reward replications. The temptation to artificially inflate one's results, including cherry-picking and question trolling, would be smaller if researchers believed that subsequent attempts at replication would quickly expose the unrepresentative nature of the results they published.

Source: Murphy, K. R., & Aguinis, H. HARKing: How badly can cherry picking and question trolling produce bias in published results? *Journal of Business and Psychology, 34*(1), 1-17, 2019, Springer Nature.

HARKing results from complex processes involving the current reward and incentive system, which motivates researchers to publish in particular journals.[129] Describing statistically significant effects that are as large as possible, which is done more easily by HARKing, helps in this regard. Also, another factor that leads to HARKing is researchers' and reviewers' lack of awareness regarding HARKing's detrimental effects.

Inadvertent Cherry-picking and Question Trolling: How Multivariate Procedures Produce Comparable Biases

Several widely-used statistical procedures involve the same forms of HARKing. Still, in these cases, the biases introduced by these statistical optimization procedures are not the result of a conscious choice by the researcher to use study results to present the most optimistic picture possible. Using these procedures is not in and of itself unethical. Still, the incautious use of statistical methods that maximize the fit of models to sample data or maximize the predictive power of statistical models can cause the same sorts of problems cherry-picking and question trolling cause. Again, the use of statistical maximization is not thought of as unethical. Therefore, little detail often is provided in published articles,[130] but its effects could, in the end, be considerably more insidious than the effects of HARKing. Consider, for example, statistical criteria to drive key decisions about the contents of regression models and structural models or relationships among constructs.

Multiple Regression. Suppose there are several variables that you might use to predict a criterion variable via multiple regression. In that case, it is not unusual to use some stepwise selection procedure to identify the subset of variables that yields the largest R^2, given the number of variables in the model. There are many variable selection methods available, including **forward selection algorithms** (where variables are added to a regression model until they fail to lead to incremental increases in R^2), **backward selection algorithms** (where one starts with a model with all p variables, then drops variables that make the smallest contribution to the predictive power of the model until one reaches the point where dropping the next variable will lead to a meaningful decrease in R^2), or true stepwise selection procedures in which you re-evaluate the decision to include specific variables in a model each time you add a new variable.

Although these variable-selection methods are widely used (e.g., forward selection is the default method in the SPSS Regression procedure), serious concerns exist about the effects of building prediction models based on statistical criteria. For example, these methods (1) over-estimate the values of both R^2 and the regression coefficients, (2) make unpredictable and potentially arbitrary choices of which variables to include and which to exclude from prediction models, (3) capitalize on chance fluctuations in sample data, and (4) produce results that do not reliably replicate.[131]

A prevalent yet not acknowledged instance of this mechanism is the choice of a particular set of control variables from several examined in a given study.[132] In most published studies, there needs to be more information on the specific rationale for including a set of control variables, and, in many cases, the authors likely examined several combinations of controls until a particular set leads to the largest possible R^2. But, the trial-and-error process that led to choosing the final set is usually not described in the published article. Selecting control variables is often the same process involved in question trolling.

These procedures combine potentially problematic cherry-picking and question-trolling features because authors choose the variables to include in a model and the weights assigned to those variables to maximize the model's predictive power. It is not uncommon for researchers to use formulas to estimate shrinkage when applying this sample equation to a broader population. Still, even when using these formulas, the distorting effects of selecting variables to study and assigning weights to those variables solely based on maximizing R^2 are potentially problematic.

Structural Equation Modeling. When evaluating structural equation models, it is common to use **modification indices** to decide which links between variables you should or should not include in a model. However, many authors have expressed serious reservations about using modification indices to guide important decisions about structural models.[133] In particular, if you use these indices at all, you should rely on them only when the changes they suggest are: (1) theoretically sensible, (2) minor, and (3) few in number.

As with stepwise selection procedures in multiple regression, using modification indices to alter the structure or meaning of structural models is problematic. First, it mindlessly elevates sample statistics to a position that is not warranted on conceptual grounds. Researchers using SEM may examine numerous possible relations involving dozens of indicators and their associations with other indicators and latent constructs—as well as relations among latent constructs and residual terms.[134] Reliance on statistical criteria to determine the structure and contents of models drive out logic, theory, past research, and even sound scientific judgment in the blind pursuit of improving results in your current sample.

Data Mining. The "big data" movement has given new life to an approach that you can find in social and behavioral sciences in one way or another for decades – i.e., **data mining**, in the form of using exploratory factor analysis of data with the hope of finding new insights into human behavior. Starting in the 1930s, this method became the basis for developing structural models in many domains, notably the structure of cognitive abilities.[135] As confirmatory factor analysis became more accessible (e.g., via LISREL, EQS, and other off-the-shelf software), factor-analytic studies increasingly shifted from an exploratory to confirmatory mode, in which *a prior*i theory rather than statistical results in a sample formed the basis for posing questions about underlying structures.[136] The decline of exploratory factor analysis can be considered the end of the first wave of fascination with data mining.

In recent years, data mining has come back with a vengeance. One of the fastest-growing occupations is "Data Scientist," and much of what data scientists do is search for patterns and regularities in data. Combining big data and emerging data mining techniques represents a revolution in the scientific method[137] that will replace the older method of forming hypotheses before analyzing data.

When paired with the very large data sets to which they are designed to be applied, contemporary data mining techniques avoid the problems with the instability of small-sample results. However, the shortcoming that big data and rigorous data-mining methods cannot overcome is that the results are necessarily driven by what is and is not measured. For example, some objective performance measures are relatively easy to collect but deficient measures of job performance (i.e., do not cover the entire performance domain).[138] Nevertheless, despite their questionable adequacy, a big-data approach to studying performance evaluations would depend on these objective measures. In general, reliance on big data and data mining can constrict research questions, where only those questions that can be answered by data easily collected and assembled into massive datasets are pursued.

Data mining explicitly capitalizes on one of the key principles of cherry-picking and question trolling. If researchers look at enough sample results, they will eventually find something interesting. Using very large samples solves one of the problems noted here (i.e., HARKing effects can be particularly large when N is small). But, in the end, its impact on science may be more pernicious than the damage done by the researcher who occasionally scans several results before arriving at a hypothesis. By driving deduction, scientific judgment, and considering existing research from any consideration of what to study or what it means, you risk magnifying every shortcoming of "dustbowl empiricism" to an unprecedented degree.

Detecting and Deterring HARKing

There are several suggestions for detecting and deterring HARKing. First, Occam's Razor is an essential tool for detecting HARKing. Second, HARKed hypotheses often involve convoluted reasoning or counterfactual assumptions. Finally, suppose the conceptual case for a hypothesis seems unlikely to hold up to scrutiny or does not seem to emerge organically from the literature and theory the author cites. In that case, this is one potential indicator of HARKing.[139]

Second, it is useful to have a healthily skeptical attitude; stories too good to be true may not be true. It is unusual for every prediction and hypothesis to be supported in a study, and skepticism is warranted when reviewing a manuscript in which every prediction is supported.

Third, another critical point is reducing the temptation to engage in HARKing. You can do this in two ways. First, HARKing is not simply a problem of author misbehavior. It is common for reviewers and editors to encourage authors to drop hypotheses and analyses that do not pan out, which creates problems that have a good deal in common with HARKing. Reviewers and editors must realize that their efforts to tidy up otherwise messy research (especially by encouraging authors to drop or modify hypotheses that are not supported) can have the same effect as HARKing. Editors and reviewers who encourage authors to change or drop hypotheses risk distorting the scientific enterprise in ways that present an overly optimistic and neat picture of what is inherently a complex discovery process. Thus, journal reviewers and particularly journal editors could help reduce the incidence of HARKing by resisting the urge to tidy up articles by trimming and modifying hypotheses. Hence, the resulting manuscript conveys a neater, more straightforward, more coherent, and even "interesting" story.[140]

Editors and reviewers can reduce the incentive to HARK by encouraging and rewarding replications. The temptation to artificially inflate one's results, including cherry-picking and question trolling, would be smaller if researchers believed that subsequent attempts at replication would quickly expose the unrepresentative nature of the results they published. Replication is a critical component of the standard scientific method. If authors saw a chance to publish their work in top journals by replicating previous studies, they would also know that if they published inflated results, the chances of detection would be high. So, as noted by some authors, solutions to "research performance problems" such as HARKing need to focus not only on what knowledge and skills researchers need to have to conduct replicable research but also their motivation to do so.[141]

Strategies for Reducing HARKing

HARKing likely makes summaries of findings appear larger than they are in actuality. Overfitting, lack of falsification, increased theoretical complexity,[142] and positively biased literature review conclusions slow scientific progress. Through modifications to literature search processes (e.g., relying less on the content of article abstracts), meta-analysts are likely to locate a larger sample of effect sizes and effect sizes that might have played ancillary study roles (e.g., control variables).

In addition, HARKing can lead to less-than-ideal management practices because effect size estimates are the primary input to estimates of practical significance.[143] For example, they are a key input value in utility calculations in the talent management acquisition literature. As effect sizes become increasingly inflated from HARKing, scientific understanding and practical significance estimates become overly optimistic. Unfortunate consequences for practitioners include failure to replicate findings in organizational settings, practitioners' unmet effectiveness expectations, and widening the science-practice gap.[144]

Recommendations for reducing HARKing at the individual (i.e., author) level include promoting the application of strong inference testing.[145] Moreover, increased application of strong inference is likely to foster scientific progress.[146] However, although individual solutions (e.g., research ethics education) may be intuitively appealing, such approaches are only marginally effective in research environments wherein reward structures make HARKing a "rational choice."[147] In addition, such interventions are likely futile without corresponding structural changes in university performance management systems.[148]

METHODS IN PRACTICE
CHALLENGES IN REDUCING HARKING THROUGH STRUCTURAL CHANGES

Suggestions for structural modifications are also numerous and exist at higher levels of the research community. For example, professional codes of conduct,[149] such as those set forth by the *Academy of Management* and the *American Psychological Association*, can address the effects of HARKing. Other promising solutions include a field's collective promotion of replication studies, decreasing the overemphasis on hypothesis and theory testing and legitimizing inductive research,[150] making HARKing a basis for manuscript rejection, legitimizing exploratory or descriptive research, delegitimizing admitted post-hoc hypotheses,[151] and insisting on the use of registries in which study details are posted before being conducted. Similarly, other authors argued that reviewers should resist negative[152] reactions to non-supported hypotheses.[153] However, these approaches rely on policing, policy setting, and attitude change. Further, if successful, these changes would ultimately require much time.

Perhaps the most promising route to reducing HARKing is modifying journals' manuscript peer review processes, which may be the ultimate impetus for the researcher's choice to HARK. Indeed, as described earlier, manuscript reviewers react negatively to non-supported hypotheses.[154] Some authors proposed that the peer review process proceeds in two stages.[155] In particular, preliminary editorial decisions (i.e., accept or reject) could be formed before reviewers' and editors' knowledge of results and discussion sections. The argument rests on the assumption that the purpose of the peer review process is to screen out poorly conducted or marginally relevant studies and not to judge whether the findings or conclusions are palatable to the prevailing zeitgeist. In addition, others argued that data could be collected by authors after a conditional acceptance by a journal, resulting in less time wasted with flawed methodologies or less critical research questions.[156] As another option, if a time lag between editorial decision and data collection were undesirable, results and discussion sections could be submitted simultaneously in a separate password-protected document. Following a favorable editorial decision, manuscript authors could submit the password. While you should focus on the individual level of analysis, you must also understand how the field can address these problems.

This chapter has provided the tools to clean your missing data, clean outliers in your data, and ensure you are appropriately developing your hypothesis. Chapter 9 will focus on how to conduct quantitative analysis and, in particular, regression-based approaches.

DISCUSSION QUESTIONS

1. Why should you care about cleaning up your data?

2. Which are the most appropriate ways to address missing data in your database (i.e., techniques, assumptions, criteria)?

3. If you need to transform your data, what is the most suitable way?

4. What sequential steps would you take to understand the possible presence of outliers in your data?

5. What would be your plan to identify and handle error outliers in your data?

6. How can you verify if your data contains interesting outliers? If you find interesting outliers, how will you deal with them?

7. What would your decision-making process for defining, identifying, and handling influential outliers in regression, SEM, and multilevel modeling be?

8. How can you clean up your hypotheses while avoiding HARKing?

9. What are the HARKing mechanisms you should always keep in mind?

10. In what way do the various forms of HARKing affect your data differently?

11. In the cases of unintentional cherry-picking and question trolling, how do multivariate procedures produce comparable biases in terms of multiple regression, structural equation modeling, and data mining?

12. How can you detect HARKing, and what strategies can you take to reduce it?

KEY TERMS

accommodationism

Akaike Information Criterion (AIC)

Bayesian Information Criterion (BIC)

Bayesian statistics

bootstrapping

cherry-picking

comparative fit index (CFI)

Cook's D_i

data mining

difference in beta, standardized (DFBETAS$_{ij}$)

difference in fits, standardized (DFFITS$_i$)

error outlier

Fortune's annual index (Fortune 500 index)

Gaussian pattern

heteroscedasticity

influential outlier

interesting outlier

least absolute deviation

least trimmed squares

Mahalanobis distance

M-estimation

missing at random (MAR)

missing completely at random (MCAR)

ordinary least squares (OLS)

p fishing

predictivism

question trolling

root mean square error of approximation
   (RMSEA)

single parameter influence

Structural Equation Modeling

THARKing

NOTES

Aguinis, H., Gottfredson, R. K., & Joo, H. (2013). Best-practice recommendations for defining, identifying, and handling outliers. *Organizational Research Methods*, *16*(2), 270-301. https://doi.org/10.1177/1094428112470848

Aguinis, H., Hill, N. S., & Bailey, J. R. (2019). Best practices in data collection and preparation: Recommendations for reviewers, editors, and authors. *Organizational Research Methods*, *24*(4), 678-693. https://doi.org/10.1177/1094428119836485

Bosco, F. A., Aguinis, H., Field, J. G., Pierce, C. A., & Dalton, D. R. (2016). HARKing's threat to organizational research: Evidence from primary and meta-analytic sources. *Personnel Psychology*, *69*(3), 709-750. https://doi.org/10.1111/peps.12111

Murphy, K. R., & Aguinis, H. (2019). HARKing: How badly can cherry-picking and question trolling produce bias in published results? *Journal of Business and Psychology*, *34*(1), 1-17. https://doi.org/10.1007/s10869-017-9524-7

9 HOW TO CONDUCT QUANTITATIVE ANALYSIS, PART I: REGRESSION-BASED APPROACHES

LEARNING GOALS

By the end of this chapter, you will be able to do the following:

9.1   Formulate why you should care about regression analysis.

9.2   Assess moderation effects in your research.

9.3   Manage the eight problems related to moderation: (1) lack of attention to measurement error, (2) variable distributions are assumed to include the full range of possible values, (3) unequal sample size across moderator-based categories, (4) insufficient statistical power, (5) artificial dichotomization of continuous moderators, (6) presumed effects of correlations between product term and its components, (7) interpreting first-order effects based on models excluding product terms, and (8) graphs that exaggerate the size of interaction effects.

9.4   Assess mediation effects in your research.

9.5   Manage the six problems related to mediation: (1) requiring a significant relation between the antecedent and the outcome, (2) disregarding the magnitude of the indirect effect, (3) testing the direct effect as a condition for mediation, (4) including a direct effect without conceptual justification, (5) testing mediation with cross-sectional data, and (6) lack of attention to measurement error.

9.6   Set up and perform Analysis of Covariance (ANCOVA) in your research.

9.7   Design studies that address nonlinear effects, including the too-much-of-a-good-thing (TMGT) effect: A formalized meta-theory used in several research domains.

9.8   Appraise the implications of the TMGT effect for your future research, including implications for theory development and theory testing (including statistical power and effect size, range restriction, advanced meta-analytic methods, and advanced growth modeling methods).

IMPORTANCE OF REGRESSION ANALYSIS

This chapter focuses on regression analysis, the most popular and fundamental data-analytic approach in social and behavioral science research. Mastering regression and regression-based approaches used to examine moderation, mediation, analysis of covariance, and the **too-much-of-a-good-thing effects** is critical because regression analysis is the building block for all other general linear model-based data analytic techniques, such as multilevel modeling and meta-analysis.

This chapter gives you all the tools you need to master four critical advanced regression analyses you may perform in your research. First, you will learn about moderation and consider the eight problems researchers encounter with this regression model. These include (1) lack of attention to measurement error, (2) variable distributions are assumed to include the full range of possible values, (3) unequal sample size across moderator-based categories, (4) insufficient statistical power, (5) artificial dichotomization of continuous moderators, (6) presumed effects of correlations between the product terms and its components, (7) interpreting first-order effects based on models excluding product terms, and (8) graphs that exaggerate the size of interaction effects. For each of these problems, you will also learn best-practice solutions. You will then learn about mediation and the six problems related to this, which include (1) requiring a significant relation between the antecedent and the outcome, (2) disregarding the magnitude of the indirect effect, (3) testing the direct effect as a condition for mediation, (4) including a direct effect without conceptual justification, (5) testing mediation with cross-sectional data, and (6) lack of attention to measurement error. Again, this chapter will give you all the necessary tools to address each of these problems. In the third section of the chapter, you will learn about ANCOVA and how to implement it in your research. The final section focuses on nonlinear effects. You will learn about the too-much-of-a-good-thing (TMGT) effect, a formalized **meta-theory** used in several research domains that you can use in future research. To illustrate how you can investigate the TMGT in your area of interest, this section includes a detailed description of implications for theory development and testing (including statistical power and effect size, restriction of range, advanced meta-analytic methods, and advanced growth modeling methods). This chapter will help you become familiar with best practices related to regression analysis and be ready to implement them in your research.

MODERATION

A moderator variable influences the nature (e.g., magnitude and direction) of the effect of an antecedent on an outcome. In other words, the relationship between two variables changes in size or direction when a third moderator variable's values change.

Moderation is illustrated graphically in Figure 9.1., which shows that the moderator variable Z influences the path relating X to Y. When the moderator variable is binary (i.e., two categories), Z can be **dummy coded** (i.e., 0 for members of one group and 1 for members of the other).[1]

FIGURE 9.1 ■ Graphic Representation of a Moderation Model

Source: Adapted from Aguinis, Edwards, & Bradley (2017). Reproduced with permission.

When the moderating effect is continuous (e.g., firm resources), studies typically rely on **moderated multiple regression**,[2] which consists of first creating a regression model that predicts the outcome based on a predictor X, a second predictor Z hypothesized to be a moderator:

$$Y = b_0 + b_1 X + b_2 Z + e, \tag{9.1}$$

where b_0 is the intercept.

As the second step, we add the product term between X and Z, which carries information on the moderating effect of Z on the X-Y relation:

$$Y = b_0 + b_1 X + b_2 Z + b_3 XZ + e \tag{9.2}$$

To assess the presence of a moderating effect, we calculate the differential or delta multiple coefficient of determination ΔR^2 from a model in Equation 9.1 (i.e., the additive model—first step) to a model that includes X, Z, and the product of X and Z (i.e., the multiplicative model—second step). ΔR^2 is an index of the proportion of variance in Y explained by the moderating effect of Z, or the interaction effect between X and Z, on Y. So, if $\Delta R^2 = .03$, it means that the interaction between X and Z explains 3% of the variance in Y above and beyond the variance already explained by the individual effects of X and Z.[3]

Moderation: Problems and Solutions

Problem #1: Lack of Attention to Measurement Error

A review of more than 200 papers showed that the most prevalent problem in studies that examine moderation concerns the effects of measurement error. A troubling finding is that around 62% of articles did not identify measurement error as a potential problem, as evidenced by the fact that they did not mention it at all. The results specific to moderation are consistent with the finding that articles in many journals do not report reliability estimates.[4] The reasons for this omission are unclear. It could reflect an implicit assumption that the effects of measurement error are negligible, a lack of knowledge regarding the biasing effects of measurement error on parameter estimates and hypothesis tests, or prevailing norms in the domains represented by the articles.

METHODS IN PRACTICE
IS LACK OF ATTENTION TO MEASUREMENT ERROR JUSTIFIED?

On the surface, the lack of attention to measurement error might seem understandable for certain constructs. For example, performance measures for public firms must go through an audit process, leaving little room for subjectivity that might introduce measurement error.[5] However, many other constructs involve ratings of beliefs and opinions collected using self-report surveys, measured with error.[6] Moreover, when independent and moderator variables are measured with error, unstandardized coefficient estimates will be biased, and this bias is particularly pronounced for moderating effects. In contrast, measurement error in outcome variables does not bias coefficient estimates. Still, it will attenuate estimates of explained variance, making it seem that predictors have less explanatory power than is the case.

The following expression estimates the reliability for the product term XZ based on the reliabilities of the predictor X and moderator Z variables when both are standardized[7]:

$$\rho_{XZ, XZ} = \frac{\rho_{XZ}^2 + \rho_{XX}\, \rho_{ZZ}}{\rho_{XZ}^2 + 1} \tag{9.3}$$

Equation 9.3 indicates that when predictor X and moderator Z are uncorrelated (i.e., $\rho_{XZ} = 0$), the reliability of the product term is reduced to the product of the reliabilities of the predictors. For example, if the reliability of X is .70 and the reliability of Z is also .70, the resulting reliability of the product term is only .49. It seems safe to assume that few, if any, social and behavioral sciences researchers would find it acceptable that 50% of the variance in a measure is simply random error (i.e., the numbers do not represent the underlying constructs but, instead, pure noise in the data).

There is a good reason to believe that the deleterious effects of measurement error are pervasive in articles reporting tests of moderation. Most of these articles report very small moderating effects across various domains, such as the moderating effect of headquarters embeddedness on the relation between subsidiary embeddedness and headquarters value-added or the moderating effect of a firm's resources and capabilities to deal with natural gas deregulation on the relation between managerial domain-specific experience and opportunity interpretation (i.e., ranging from threat to opportunity). In these examples, reliabilities for the product terms were not reported. Moreover, given that, when reported, reliabilities for the components are often in the .70s, about 50% of the variance in product terms is likely random error.

In short, tests of many moderator variable hypotheses have been undermined due to the deleterious impact of measurement error. In your future research, you should, at a minimum, report reliability estimates for all predictors, including product components. Reporting reliability is particularly important when a hypothesized moderating effect is not found because, if reliability is low, an existing moderating effect is likely underestimated and, in some cases, might go undetected.

Problem #2: Variable Distributions Are Assumed to Include the Full Range of Possible Values

The second important problem is that samples used in social and behavioral science research usually only represent part of the range of possible scores on the variables under consideration that might exist in the population.

METHODS IN PRACTICE
RANGE RESTRICTION AND ITS IMPACT

Studies regarding the resource-based theory of the firm rarely include the full range of resources.[8] Similarly, firms with poor performance in the population might not be represented in the sample, which could instead consist mainly of firms with high scores on performance and related variables.[9] These mechanisms lead to range restriction, meaning that the variance of variables is smaller in the sample than in the population.

Although rarely acknowledged, range restriction has an adverse impact on moderation tests (i.e., about 34% of articles include scores that do not span the entire possible range). Specifically, a Monte Carlo study revealed that the statistical power for detecting moderating effects is substantially diminished when sample variance is less than population variance, even by what may be considered a small amount.[10] For example, in a situation with a total sample size of 300 and no truncation on X scores, the statistical power to detect a medium-size moderating effect was an acceptable .81. However, when the scores were sampled from the top 80% of the distribution of the population scores, power decreased to .51. In other words, if moderation exists, the accuracy of the moderating effect test is tantamount to flipping a coin. Thus, given the realistic conditions in this Monte Carlo simulation, even a relatively mild degree of range restriction (i.e., just the bottom 20% of the distribution is truncated) can markedly decrease statistical power and threaten the validity of conclusions regarding moderating effect hypotheses. And, as with measurement error, even if a moderating effect is statistically significant, range restriction can bias the observed effect size downward.

In short, range restriction makes population-level moderating effects seem smaller than they are or might render them statistically nonsignificant. Therefore, in future research, you should capture the full range of scores of all variables involved in the analysis. When this is not feasible, and moderating effects are small or nonsignificant, you should provide the estimated population variance to rule out range restriction as a plausible alternative explanation for the results obtained.

Problem #3: Unequal Sample Size Across Moderator-based Categories

The third problem is that when the moderator variable is inherently categorical (e.g., industry type, firm type, college major), sample size across categories is usually unequal. This issue occurs in about 20% of articles. As a result, many samples include 25% or fewer observations in one category and 75% or more in the other.

> ### Example: Different Sample Sizes for Firm Ownership Types
>
> A study examined the type of firm ownership as a moderator of the relationship between media coverage and the subsequent entry of foreign firms. The moderator "type of firm ownership" included a minority (i.e., 20%) of firms owned by individuals, while the majority (i.e., 80%) were owned by at least one firm. Under these circumstances, moderating effects are underestimated and, in many cases, can even go undetected.

This problem arises because different sample size proportions across categorical moderator variables are akin to range restriction for continuous moderator variables. Specifically, the sample variance of the dichotomous categorical moderator Z is[11]:

$$S_Z^2 = \frac{\sum(Z_i - \bar{Z})}{N-1} = \frac{Np(1-p)}{N-1}, \tag{9.4}$$

where $N = n_1$ (i.e., the sample size in subgroup 1) + n_2 (i.e., the sample size in subgroup 2), and $p = n_1/N$. Equation 9.4 shows that holding N constant, the variance of a categorical moderator is maximized when p equals .50.

METHODS IN PRACTICE
REDUCED VARIABILITY DUE TO UNEQUAL SAMPLE SIZES ACROSS GROUPS

Consider a situation where N is held constant at 100. If $n_1 = 20$ and $n_2 = 80$ (i.e., total N = 100), the sample variance is 16/99 = .1616. However, if $n_1 = 35$ and $n_2 = 65$ (i.e., same total N = 100), the sample variance increases to 22.75/99 = .2298. Suppose there is an even split between the two subgroups so that $n_1 = 50$ and $n_2 = 50$; the sample variance is maximized at 25/99 = .2525.

An obvious solution to this problem is to sample a similar number of observations in each category. However, when the categorical moderator is unevenly distributed across the categories in the population, then oversampling from the smaller group improves statistical power at the cost of using a sample that might not be representative of the population. It would be best to consider these countervailing concerns when investigating categorical moderator variables.

Problem #4: Insufficient Statistical Power

Another important problem is insufficient statistical power or the probability of finding moderating effects in a sample when they exist in the population.[12] Given the previous discussion regarding measurement error, range restriction, and unequal sample sizes across categorical moderator variables, it should be apparent that much of the research assessing moderating effects are underpowered (i.e., about 43% of articles do not mention statistical power and seem underpowered given the presence of the several factors known to affect power adversely). Thus, it is unsurprising that so many moderation hypotheses are not empirically supported.

Sample sizes tend to be heavily right-skewed (i.e., few studies include a much larger sample size than the rest).[13] Thus, authors tend to focus on median rather than mean sample sizes. Yet, it is still too small to yield statistical power of .80 or higher to detect the typical moderating effect size.[14] Therefore, most moderation tests need more statistical power, meaning many moderating effects will likely go undetected. Statistical power can be increased by using larger samples and conducting research in settings that control for extraneous variables (i.e., experimental or simulation-based research). In all cases, you should compute and report statistical power to establish whether the absence of any moderating effects can be attributed to low statistical power instead of the absence of a true moderating effect.

Problem #5: Artificial Dichotomization of Continuous Moderators

A fifth problem relates to the nature of the moderator variable. Many theories include hypotheses about continuous moderator variables such as environmental dynamism, firm resources, and top management team characteristics (e.g., age, tenure, compensation). When testing hypotheses about continuous moderators, a common practice is to categorize these variables into subgroups such as "high" and "low" based on whether cases fall above or below the median of the moderator variable (this problem is present in about 10% of articles). An important shortcoming of this practice is the loss of information.[15]

METHODS IN PRACTICE
LOSING INFORMATION BECAUSE OF DICHOTOMIZATION

A recently published study included a measure of new ventures' variety in the repertoire of strategic actions using ratings of 34 different actions on a 5-point scale ranging from 1 (*not a part of our strategy at all*) to 5 (*a key part of our strategy*). Although each strategic action was rated on a 5-point scale, each firm's score was a count of the number of items rated three or higher. In this study, loss of information is evident because a firm that rated an action with a score of 5 and another that rated the same action with a score of 3 were both classified as being rated identically. This loss of information not only undermines the moderator's interpretation but also reduces the variance of the moderator variable, and the estimated moderating effects are biased downward.[16] In this illustration, the moderating effect of strategic variety on the relation between a firm's origin (i.e., whether independent entrepreneurs or established corporations created them) and sales growth was not statistically significant—possibly due to the artificial dichotomization of strategic variety.

Furthermore, artificial dichotomization can generate nonlinear nonrandom measurement errors.[17] For example, consider a moderator variable Z that ranges from 1 to 10 and is dichotomized, with scores of 1 through 5 placed in one group and 6 through 10 placed in the other group. In the first group, scores 1 and 2 will have negative measurement errors, whereas scores 4 and 5 will have positive ones. Likewise, in the second group, scores of 6 and 7 will have negative measurement errors, and scores of 9 and 10 will have positive ones. This pattern of measurement errors compounds any error in the measurement of Z as a continuous variable.

In short, the practice of artificially categorizing continuous moderator variables discards information, reduces statistical power to detect moderating effects, and attenuates the size of moderating effects. Hence, avoiding this practice in your research would be best.[18]

Problem #6: Presumed Effects of Correlations Between Product Term and Its Components

A sixth issue concerns the correlation between the product term XZ and its component variables X and Z. This correlation often generates concerns about **multicollinearity**, as expressed in about 44% of articles. Therefore, researchers often center the predictor and moderator variables at their means to address this concern. In other words, researchers create new "centered" X scores (i.e., $X - \overline{X}$) and centered Z scores (i.e., $Z = Z - \overline{Z}$) and conduct analyses using the centered rather than the original scores.

Contrary to common belief, any apparent multicollinearity created by the correlation of XZ with X and Z does not cause problems for moderation tests, provided such tests include X and Z along with XZ as predictors in the regression model (as shown in Equation 9.2). With this approach, the test for moderation does not involve XZ in its raw form but the partialed XZ product, which is necessarily uncorrelated with X and Z.[19] So, the test of the partialed XZ product is unchanged regardless of how X and Z are rescaled.[20] Thus, there is no need to center X and Z at their means to address this supposed "multicollinearity problem." Nonetheless, mean-centering can facilitate the interpretation of the X and Z coefficients because these coefficients represent the slope of each variable when the other variable equals zero.[21] When X and Z are mean-centered, the coefficient for X represents the slope of Y on X when Z is at its mean, and likewise, the coefficient on Z is the slope of Y on Z when X is at its mean. For example, if the coefficient for Z (i.e., b_3) is 2.00, this means that for a 1-point increase in Z, Y goes up by 2 points—at the mean value for X.

Also related to the interpretation of first-order effects, in the presence of an XZ interaction, first-order effects can be interpreted as an average across the full range of values of the other predictor.[22] Note that the presence of a significant interaction indicates that the effect of a predictor on the outcome depends on the value of the other predictor. Consequently, an average may only be meaningful in some contexts. For example, if there is a strong and positive X-Y relation for manufacturing firms (i.e., Z = 1) and a strong and negative X-Y relation for service firms (i.e., Z = 0), the coefficient associated with X in the full model including X, Z, and XZ would lead to the misleading conclusion that, overall, there is a zero X-Y relation. However, these crossover (i.e., disordinal) interactions involving effects in the opposite direction are not observed frequently.[23] Instead, noncrossover or ordinal interactions (i.e., the effect of one predictor on the outcome is in the same direction but stronger for some values of the other predictor compared to others) are more typical and, in these situations, interpreting first-order effects as an average across values of the other predictor may be informative.

In short, you should use mean-centering to facilitate the interpretation of coefficients on lower-order terms in the presence of interactions. But you should recognize that results regarding interaction effects remain unchanged if predictors are centered.

Problem #7: Interpreting First-order Effects Based on Models Excluding Product Terms

The seventh problem is that the coefficients of lower-order terms are often tested and interpreted before entering an interaction term, as evidenced in about 43% of studies. This practice is problematic because when an interaction exists, the predictor involved in the interaction does not have a single unique effect but instead has a range of effects that vary according to the level of the moderator variable. These effects are referred to as **simple slopes**[24] and can be used to interpret the form of an interaction. Because simple slopes represent a range of effects in most cases,[25] it is not meaningful to hypothesize or test a single effect for a predictor when that predictor interacts with a moderator variable.

METHODS IN PRACTICE
WHAT HAPPENS WHEN WE DON'T INCLUDE PRODUCT TERMS

Interpreting lower-order effects from models that exclude non-zero higher-ordering effects is a pervasive problem (i.e., 43% of articles). For example, one study hypothesized that informal control systems would enhance the performance of work units and further predicted that contextual factors, such as task interdependence, would moderate this relationship. The initial hypothesis was tested using a regression equation that excluded the moderator variables and their products with informal control systems. These terms were subsequently added to the equation to test the moderation hypotheses, which were supported. With this approach, the results for the initial hypothesis were inconclusive because the moderator effects indicated that informal control systems did not have a simple uniform relationship with performance but instead had an array of relationships that ranged from negative to positive, depending on the levels of the three moderator variables. You can avoid these situations by drawing conclusions based on equations that include first-order and interaction terms and simple slopes computed and tested at meaningful levels of the moderator variables.

Problem #8: Graphs That Exaggerate the Size of Interaction Effects

In principle, visualizations help readers understand and interpret the findings that they illustrate. But, a review of articles published in three journals showed that graphs of interactions did not provide this sort of help. Over two-thirds of the papers that presented graphs describing interactions (67.5%) offered incomplete visualizations of the interaction, and this approach often inadvertently magnified the apparent size and importance of the interaction effect by truncating the Y-axis. For example, this truncation from a seven-point range for the Y-scale to a two-point range for the Y-axis in a figure causes weak interaction effects to look stronger than they are.[26]

Truncation of the Y-axis is common, but the extent to which truncation occurs varies widely. In some papers, authors used a Y-axis that covered less than 10% of the range of Y values; in others, authors used a Y-axis that covered over 80%. Another 16.6% of the papers that tested interaction hypotheses did not present an interaction figure. Overall, only 25% of the papers included a figure that would make it reasonably easy for readers to accurately assess the strength of the interaction effect.

To demonstrate problems associated with using a truncated Y-axis, consider a study that examined the interaction effect between perspective-taking and self-efficacy on feedback seeking.[27] This exemplary study included easily interpretable figures. In Study 1, these authors reported self-efficacy by perspective-taking interaction, plotting the relation between self-efficacy and feedback seeking at − 1SD (low) and + 1SD (high) from the perspective-taking mean, using a Y-axis that spanned the full range of possible values (i.e., 7 points) for their dependent variable, feedback seeking.

Let's use the data from this same study to illustrate what would have happened if these authors had truncated the range of values for the dependent variable in their graph, as done in the vast majority of published articles. The top panel of Figure 9.2 uses the entire range of values of Y, closely mirroring the figure in the original study. In Figure 9.2's center panel, we plotted this same interaction using a shorter range of points for the Y-axis of 1.5 to 4.5 instead of the full range of 1 to 7, resulting in an apparent larger difference between the two slopes. In the bottom panel of Figure 9.2, we again plotted this same interaction using an even smaller range of two points for the Y-axis (i.e., 1.8 to 3.8), resulting in an apparent even more impressive difference between the slopes. The examples of Y-axis truncation in Figure 9.2's center and bottom panels are realistic and representative and show how truncation of the Y-axis can dramatically magnify the apparent strength of the interaction effect.

To address this problem, the recommendation is to present figures spanning the entire range of possible values for the Y scale. This common frame of reference will not exaggerate the size of interaction effects and make it easier to compare plots accurately across studies, even if they use different measurement scales for Y.

In sum, routinely presenting graphs in a way that magnifies their apparent strength and importance results in theory and practice derailment: Researchers, as well as managers and policymakers, can devote time and effort to the pursuit of dead-end interaction hypotheses, believing that they are chasing after interesting and exciting interaction possibilities. An incautious reader presented with the center or bottom panels of Figure 9.2 could easily assume that the interaction effect is strong.

Table 9.1 includes a brief description of each of the problems just described. Although this section addresses each issue separately, Monte Carlo simulation results demonstrate that the simultaneous presence of two or more of these problems usually will preclude you from reaching accurate conclusions about the existence of moderating effects.[28] Thus, you can use the information in this table as a resource for conducting moderation studies.

FIGURE 9.2 ■ Three Visualizations of the Same Interaction Effect

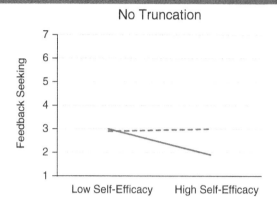

No Truncation

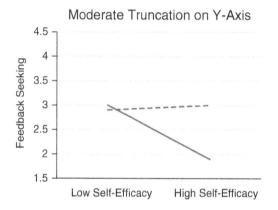

Moderate Truncation on Y-Axis

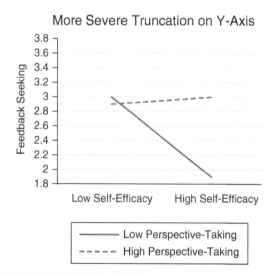

More Severe Truncation on Y-Axis

——— Low Perspective-Taking
----- High Perspective-Taking

Source: Murphy & Aguinis (2022) and Sherf & Morrison (2020). Reproduced with permission.

TABLE 9.1 ■ Summary of Problems Regarding Moderation Assessment, Detrimental Consequences for Substantive Conclusions, and Proposed Solutions		
Problems	**Detrimental Consequences for Substantive Conclusions**	**Proposed Solutions**
1. Lack of attention to measurement error in tests of moderation	● Less than perfect reliability can lead to incorrectly dismissing moderating effects and underestimating existing ones	● Report reliability estimates for all predictors (including those hypothesized to play the role of moderator variables); this practice is essential when a hypothesized moderating effect is not found
2. Tests of moderation assume that variable distributions include the full range of possible values	● Range restriction hurts the accuracy of substantive conclusions: Moderating effects can go undetected, and when detected, they are underestimated	● Attempt to capture the full range of population scores of all variables involved in the analysis and, if not feasible and moderating effects are not found or found to be small, information on sample and population variances should be provided to rule out range restriction as a plausible explanation for the results obtained
3. When testing hypotheses about categorical moderators, a large total sample size is assumed to be a sufficient condition for adequate statistical power even in the presence of unequal sample size across moderator-based categories	● Even if the total size is very large, unequal sample sizes across the moderator-based subgroups decrease statistical power and lead to an underestimation of moderating effects	● Collect data such that the number of firms within each moderator-based subgroup is similar (but keep in mind that this oversampling strategy may lead to an unrepresentative sample)
4. Statistical power is assumed to be adequate	● Statistical power is often insufficient due to small sample size, measurement error, range restriction, unequal sample size across moderator-based subgroups, and other artifacts and leads to false negative decisions regarding moderating effects	● A priori statistical power is necessary before collecting data to plan study design, and post hoc statistical power should be calculated in all cases when a moderating effect is not found to rule out the possibility that insufficient power has led to the no-moderator conclusion

(*Continued*)

TABLE 9.1 ■ Summary of Problems Regarding Moderation Assessment, Detrimental Consequences for Substantive Conclusions, and Proposed Solutions (*Continued*)		
Problems	**Detrimental Consequences for Substantive Conclusions**	**Proposed Solutions**
5. Moderator-based subgroups are created by categorizing continuous variables into subgroups such as "high" and "low" or categories below and below a distribution's median value (i.e., median split procedure)	• This practice results in information loss, reduced statistical power to detect moderating effects, and a downward bias in the size of estimated moderating effects	• The practice of artificially dichotomizing or polichotomizing continuous variables should be discontinued
6. Correlations between product terms and their components are believed to be a source of bias in terms of estimating and interpreting moderating effects	• Centering predictors to "reduce multicollinearity" creates additional procedures and steps that are unnecessary and create possible confusion when there is an interest in the moderating effect only and not in first-order effects	• First-order predictors should be centered only if there is an interest in interpreting them in the presence of moderating effects. Also, first-order effects can be interpreted as the average effect of a predictor across the full range of values of the other predictor, and their interpretation may be informative in the presence of ordinal (i.e., noncrossover) but not disordinal (i.e., crossover) interactions
7. First-order effects are interpreted based on partial models (i.e., models not including product terms)	• Because first-order coefficients are scale-dependent, their interpretation in partial models leads to misleading conclusions	• First-order effects should be based on centered predictors and interpreted based on full models (i.e., models including the predictor, moderator, and product terms)
8. Graphs that exaggerate the size of interaction effects	• Presenting graphs that focus on only a small portion of the outcome variable scale is deceiving because they lead to the impression that interaction effects are larger than they are	• Create graphs that include the full range of the Y scale on the Y axis

Source: Adapted from Aguinis, Edwards, & Bradley (2017) and Murphy & Aguinis (2022). Reproduced with permission.

MEDIATION

Mediation is the presence of an intervening variable or mechanism that transmits the effect of an antecedent variable on an outcome.[29] For instance, mediation is captured by the notion that the effect of the competitive environment on firm performance is transmitted by firm strategy, such that the environment influences strategic choices that, in turn, affect performance.[30] In the previous section, you learned that moderation refers to *the conditions under which* an effect varies in size. In contrast, mediation refers to *underlying mechanisms and processes* that connect antecedents and outcomes. Both processes are critical for advancing theory and practice.

A mediator variable transmits the effect of the antecedent on the outcome, either in part or whole.[31] Figure 9.3.a shows a no-mediation model in which there is only a direct effect of X on Y. Mediation is illustrated graphically in Figure 9.3.b, which shows that X affects Y both directly (i.e., path c') and indirectly (i.e., the combination of paths a and b) through the mediator M. The indirect effect represents that part of the effect of X on Y that is mediated by M, with the magnitude of this effect represented by the product of paths a and b. A full mediation model is one in which $ab \neq 0$ and $c' = 0$, whereas partial mediation exists when $ab \neq 0$ and $c' \neq 0$.

Mediation: Problems and Solutions

Consistent with the broader social and behavioral sciences research domain, most mediation studies rely on the causal-steps procedure.[32] This procedure can be expressed in terms of the three regression equations shown below[33]:

$$Y = cX + e_Y \tag{9.5}$$
$$M = aX + e_Z \tag{9.6}$$
$$Y = bM + c'X + e'_Y \tag{9.7}$$

In these equations, X, M, and Y are independent, mediator, and outcome variables, respectively, c, a, b, and c' are unstandardized regression coefficients, and e_Y, e_Z, and e'_Y are residual terms (to simplify notation, intercepts from the equations are omitted, as would be appropriate when M and Y are mean-centered). According to the causal-steps approach, mediation is indicated when: (a) c in Equation 9.5 is significant, (b) a in Equation 9.6 is significant, (c) b in Equation 9.7 is significant, and (d) c' in Equation 9.7 is not significant. The first condition is taken as evidence that there is a relation between X and Y to be mediated. The second and third conditions establish that the paths to and from the mediator variable M are significant. Finally, the fourth condition shows that M fully mediates the effect of X on Y. If the first three conditions are met, but the fourth condition is not, then mediation is considered partial rather than complete.

FIGURE 9.3 ■ Graphic Representation of a Mediation Model

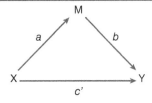

a: Direct effect (no mediation)   b: Direct and indirect mediation

---

Source: Adapted from Aguinis, Edwards, & Bradley (2017). Reproduced with permission.

Problem #1: Requiring a Significant Relation Between the Antecedent and the Outcome

Although the causal-steps approach is pervasive in mediation studies, it has several important drawbacks. First, requiring that c is significant in Equation 9.5 (as in about 52% of articles) can obscure cases in which a significant direct effect with the opposite sign accompanies a significant indirect effect.[34] For example, referring to Figure 9.3.b, the indirect effect of X on Y through M is the product ab, and the direct effect of X on Y is c'. The sum of these two effects is the total effect of X on Y, which is equivalent to c as shown in Figure 9.3.a. Thus, c can fail to reach significance when a significant indirect effect is offset by a countervailing direct effect, leading you to conclude that mediation is not present mistakenly. This issue is exemplified by a recent study of the resource-based view of the firm, which invoked the first condition of the causal-steps procedure to conclude that competitive advantage did not mediate the effects of resource value on firm performance, even though resource value was related to competitive advantage which, in turn, was related to firm performance.

The study above exemplifies a broader pattern exhibited by social and behavioral sciences studies that apply the causal-steps procedure, which routinely excludes mediation from consideration when c in Equation 9.5 is not significant. You can avoid this problem by focusing on the paths that constitute the mediated effect, which together is necessary and sufficient to establish mediation.[35]

Problem #2: Disregarding the Magnitude of the Indirect Effect

Although the procedures for testing the indirect effect represented by the ab product have been discussed,[36] this test is outside the conditions specified by the causal-steps approach. Nonetheless, this test is critical for evaluating the size of the mediating effect and comparing effects that describe alternative mediating mechanisms. Unfortunately, most studies that examine mediation do not test the mediated effect itself, and this tendency persists in recent research (i.e., 77% of articles).[37] For instance, a study examining decision speed as a mediator of the effects of six organizational and environmental factors on firm performance tested the individual paths of the model. Still, the mediating effects were not tested or compared. Consequently, this study missed a significant opportunity to weigh the mediating effects of the organizational and environmental factors under consideration, representing conceptually distinct determinants of strategic decision speed and firm performance. In the few studies that tested the mediated effect, most relied on the Sobel (1982) test and its variants, in which the product of the coefficients representing the mediated effect is divided by an estimate of its standard error and referred to as a z-distribution. Unfortunately, this test is inappropriate because it assumes that the product of the coefficients is normally distributed, which is different even when the coefficients themselves are normally distributed.[38] You can relax this assumption using nonparametric testing procedures, such as percentile-based confidence intervals derived using Bootstrap.[39] These procedures have been advocated in the methodological literature on mediation,[40] and you should choose them in your future mediation studies.

Problem #3: Testing the Direct Effect as a Condition for Mediation

A third problem concerns whether c' should be tested when assessing mediation (as reported in 39% of articles). Although this test was included in the original presentation of the causal-steps procedure,[41] subsequent revisions indicated that it is not required.[42] The rationale for this revision can be seen by returning to Figure 9.3.b, which shows that mediation relies on the paths from X to M and from M to Y (i.e., a and b). The path from X to Y that bypasses M (i.e., c') need not be considered when determining whether M mediates the effect of X on Y because this path is not part of the mediated effect. Moreover, requiring that c' is not significant can cause you to overlook meaningful mediating processes.

To illustrate, a study of differentiation as a mediator of the effects of imitation time lag on competitiveness inferred support for mediation based on whether the effects of time lag on competitiveness were no longer significant after controlling for differentiation. By imposing this condition, several mediating effects were dismissed even though the paths involved in the effects were significant. Thus, in your future research, you should conclude that mediation exists when the indirect effect is supported, regardless of the presence or absence of a direct effect.

Problem #4: Including a Direct Effect Without Conceptual Justification

Tests of mediation that follow the causal-steps procedure routinely include a direct path from X to Y that bypasses M regardless of whether mediation is hypothesized to be complete versus partial (37% of articles). This practice is likely due to the inclusion of X in Equation 9.7 and the test of c' as the fourth condition of the causal-steps procedure.

Although this practice is widespread, if the theory under investigation predicts complete mediation, you should test a model that specifies complete rather than partial mediation.[43] Referring to Figure 9.3, the causal-steps procedure prescribes the analysis of the model in Figure 9.3.b regardless of whether mediation is considered partial or complete. In contrast, others advised that you analyze the model in Figure 9.3.b for partial mediation and a **submodel** that omits path c' for complete mediation.[44] Following this approach, the model tested is aligned with the theory and hypotheses under consideration. Moreover, omitting path c' when complete mediation is hypothesized upholds the principle of parsimony and yields an estimate of path b consistent with the specified model.[45] Finally, the consequences of omitting path c' can be assessed by testing the fit of the complete mediation model using a chi-square statistic with one degree of freedom. This test effectively compares the complete mediation model to the partial mediation model because the chi-square test captures the improvement in fit if path c' were added to the model.

Routinely including direct effects violates the principle of parsimony and prompts you to test models unaligned with theory. If the theory under consideration predicts mediation, you should use the full mediation model as a baseline (i.e., $ab \neq 0$ and $c' = 0$ in Figure 9.3.b) and test the consequences of omitting the direct effect on the model's fit.

Problem #5: Testing Mediation With Cross-Sectional Data

Most studies investigating mediation rely on cross-sectional designs (58% of articles). However, mediated models contain causal paths that inherently involve the passage of time,[46] and testing these paths with cross-sectional data can produce biased estimates.[47] This bias can be ameliorated using longitudinal data in which X, M, and Y are measured sequentially on three occasions. Ideally, all three variables would be measured on each occasion, resulting in a panel model in which the hypothesized causal sequence of X → M → Y can be compared to alternative causal flows.[48] Longitudinal designs also provide a stronger basis than cross-sectional designs for drawing causal inferences, which are inherent in interpreting mediation models.[49]

Despite their strengths, longitudinal designs do not rule out the possibility of omitted variables that can account for the relations involved in mediated models,[50] which is a relevant source of endogeneity.[51] Nevertheless, it is encouraging that the importance of endogeneity is increasingly recognized in social and behavioral sciences studies. For example, the author guidelines for *Strategic Management Journal* (a leading journal in strategic management research) note that "SMJ strongly supports research that addresses interesting and important questions in strategic management that involve complicated causal processes. SMJ recognizes that statistical analyses relevant to these questions may raise the issue of endogeneity. If relevant, authors should acknowledge this issue in submitted manuscripts and make a good-faith effort to address it. In some cases, a causal inference may be impossible, but statistical correlations, especially if used to rule out some alternative hypotheses or mechanisms, may still be of interest."[52] The growing attention to endogeneity is a very positive development given that a review found that only 24 (about 4%) articles of about 580 analyzed reported using two-stage least squares for testing endogeneity.[53]

In short, mediated models contain causal paths that imply the passage of time, and testing these paths with cross-sectional data can produce biased estimates. Therefore, when possible and absent the possibility of implementing an experimental design,[54] you should assess mediation using longitudinal data in your research, preferably with panel models that allow the comparison of alternative causal flows.

Problem #6: Lack of Attention to Measurement Error

Finally, as with moderation, studies examining mediation rarely address measurement error's consequences (88.71% of articles). Measurement error in X and M can bias path estimates upward or downward. As a result, statistical tests of these paths can be either too liberal or too conservative, either of which would lead to incorrect conclusions. When mediation is examined using multiple regression, which the review indicated is usually the case,[55] measurement error is effectively disregarded, thereby introducing the bias mentioned above and its harmful consequences.

Creating and using more reliable measures is the best solution for addressing measurement error.[56] However, as a second-best option, some of the effects of measurement error can be offset by using structural equation modeling (SEM) with latent variables,[57] which has become increasingly prevalent.[58] This does not suggest that SEM is some magic cure for the many problems that can beset poor quality measures or that using SEM gives you an excuse to disregard fundamental measurement issues such as reliability and construct validity. Moreover, conventional applications of SEM only correct for certain sources of measurement error,[59] and other sources require more elaborate model specifications. Nevertheless, SEM offers important advantages over procedures that ignore measurement error completely.

Table 9.2 offers a summary of issues you should consider regarding mediation. This table summarizes each problem, the consequences of the problem, and solutions you can implement in your research to avoid each problem.

ANALYSIS OF COVARIANCE (ANCOVA)

ANCOVA is a statistical technique that combines the principles of ANOVA (Analysis of Variance) and linear regression. It is used primarily for comparing one or more means across different groups, while statistically controlling for the variability associated with one or more quantitative covariates that are not of primary interest but may influence the outcome variable. As such, ANCOVA is particularly useful for examining whether a particular intervention, decision, or action (e.g., training program, investment strategy) has worked as intended. Given the pervasive use of ANCOVA to address important theoretical and practical issues in social and behavioral science, this section considers both methodological and substantive issues you should consider when using this regression-based approach. Previous research has documented biases in ANCOVA treatment effects when **fallible covariates** (i.e., variables that are measured with at least some degree of error, which is every variable in social and behavioral research) are included in the model in non-experimental designs. This section provides new formulas describing the exact degree of bias under various conditions, the underlying mechanisms leading to inflation in Type I error rates, and subsequent erroneous substantive conclusions. You can use this analytic

TABLE 9.2 ■ Summary of Problems Regarding Mediation Assessment, Detrimental Consequences for Substantive Conclusions, and Proposed Solutions

Problems	Detrimental Consequences for Substantive Conclusions	Proposed Solutions
1. A significant relation between the antecedent and the outcome is a prerequisite for testing mediation	• This assumed prerequisite can lead you to overlook mediation when the direct and indirect effects in a model have opposite signs	• Conduct the mediation test without the precondition that the relation between the antecedent and the outcome should be significant
2. The causal-steps procedure yields information about the magnitude of the indirect effect transmitted through the mediator	• The causal-steps procedure does not involve the computation or test of the indirect effect and therefore does not indicate the magnitude of the mediating effect or allow its comparison with other effects (e.g., the indirect vs. the direct effect)	• Compute the size of the indirect effect by multiplying the paths to and from the mediator (i.e., paths a and b in Figure 9.3.b) and test this product using nonparametric procedures such as the bootstrap (rather than the Sobel test that assumes normality in the distribution of product coefficients)
3. The evaluation of mediation should include a test of the direct effect that bypasses the mediator	• Because the direct effect has no bearing on the presence of the indirect effect, this test can lead you to dismiss mediating effects inappropriately	• Conclude that mediation exists when the indirect effect is supported, regardless of the presence or absence of a direct effect
4. The causal-steps procedure routinely includes a direct path from the antecedent to the outcome, regardless of whether this path is conceptually justified	• Routinely including direct effects violates the principle of parsimony and prompts you to test models that are not aligned with the theory	• If the theory under consideration predicts mediation, then use the full mediation model as a baseline (i.e., $ab \neq 0$ and $c' = 0$ in Figure 9.3.b) and formally test the consequences of omitting the direct effect on the fit of the model
5. Mediation can be tested satisfactorily with cross-sectional data	• Mediated models contain causal paths that imply the passage of time, and testing these paths with cross-sectional data can produce biased estimates	• When possible, assess mediation using longitudinal data, preferably with panel models that allow the comparison of alternative causal flows
6. Lack of attention to measurement error in tests of mediation	• Measurement error can bias path estimates upward or downward, leading to unwarranted conclusions	• Create and use reliable measures. As a second-best option, use multiple-item measures for all constructs and analyze the data using structural equation modeling with latent variables

Source: Adapted from Aguinis, Edwards, & Bradley (2017). Reproduced with permission.

material when you attempt to replicate past studies (either for single studies or in a meta-analytic fashion) that may have committed Type I errors and reported possibly non-existent treatment effects.

You can also use ANCOVA to answer research questions, test theories, and evaluate treatments while implementing non-experimental research designs. Adjusting treatment effects for confounding variables in non-experimental designs is important for accurately determining the value and practical usefulness of treatments, interventions, and programs.[60]

Equation 9.8 shows an ANCOVA model with one treatment effect, α_j, and a single covariate, x_{ij}, centered by the average covariate value, $\bar{x}$:

$$y_{ij} = \mu + \alpha_j + \beta(x_{ij} - \bar{x}) + e_{ij} \tag{9.8}$$

where y_{ij} is the dependent variable of interest for subject i in group j, μ represents the grand mean, e_{ij} is a residual, β measures the effect of x_{ij} on y_{ij}, and using effect-coding requires $\Sigma_j \alpha_j = 0$. In this section, the case where $j = 0$ for the control group and $j = 1$ for the treatment group and $y_{ij} \sim N(\mu + \alpha_j + \beta(x_{ij} - \bar{x}), \sigma^2)$ is considered. Additionally, let $\mu_{1x} - \mu_{0x}$ represent the degree of covariate mean differences, or nonequivalence, between the treatment and control group on x_{ij} and let ρ_{xx} denote the reliability of x_{ij}. In general, ANCOVA makes the following assumptions: e_{ij} are identically and independently normally distributed; the slope, β, is equal across treatment and control groups; the relationship between y_{ij} and x_{ij} is linear conditioned on group membership (note that a more general polynomial function of x_{ij} could be modeled if the shape of the curve is the same across groups); and homogeneity of variance is satisfied across groups.

Another important assumption of ANCOVA is that covariates are measured without error. Controlling for fallible covariates leads to biased treatment effects.[61] Note that covariate measurement error is only a problem for non-experimental designs with groups that differ in average covariate values. More precisely, covariate measurement error (i.e., $\rho_{xx} < 1$) coupled with group average differences on the covariate (i.e., $\mu_{1x} - \mu_{0x} \neq 0$), which arises in non-experimental designs,[62] leads to biased treatment effects.

$$\Delta R_\alpha^2 = \frac{\rho_{xy}^2 \rho_{yy} (\mu_{1x} - \mu_{0x})^2 p(1 - p)(1 - \rho_{xx})^2}{\sigma_x^2 - \rho_{xx}(\mu_{1x} - \mu_{0x})^2 p(1 - p)} \tag{9.9}$$

Equation 9.9 represents the change in R^2 associated with the null hypothesis of no treatment effect after controlling for the covariate when H_0 is true. Also, note in Equation 9.9 that ρ_{xy} is the true score correlation between x_{ij} and y_{ij}, σ_x^2 is the variance of x_{ij}, p is the proportion of subjects in the treatment group, and ρ_{yy} is the reliability of the dependent variable scores. Equation 9.9 shows that ΔR_α^2 will be unbiased (i.e., $\Delta R_\alpha^2 = 0$.) when either $\rho_{xx} = 1$ or $\mu_{1x} - \mu_{0x} = 0$ and reaffirms concerns about employing ANCOVA in non-experimental settings when x_{ij} is measured with error and groups differ in covariate averages. Stated differently, testing the null hypothesis of no treatment effect with standard F-critical values (i.e., F^*) is inappropriate because F^* does not account for the biased effects when $\rho_{xx} < 1$ and $\mu_{1x} - \mu_{0x} \neq 0$[63]. Moreover, using F^* to test treatment effects frequently leads to incorrect statistical inferences and inflated Type I error rates. This leads to wrong substantive conclusions, such as concluding that a treatment works when it may not.

Figure 9.4 shows the exact degree of Type I error inflation across of set of illustrative conditions. For example, in Figure 9.4, a value of .05 represents a situation where α_r (i.e., actual Type I error rate) equals α (i.e., nominal Type I error rate). Figure 9.4 includes four panels with different values of ρ_{xy} and illustrates the degree of inflated Type I error rates as a function of $\mu_{1x} - \mu_{0x}$ and ρ_{xx} and holding sample size constant at 500. All four panels in Figure 9.4 show that Type I error rates are severely inflated as ρ_{xy} and $\mu_{1x} - \mu_{0x}$ increase and ρ_{xx} decreases. For instance, panel *b* shows that Type I error rates are nearly four times larger than the nominal level when $\rho_{xy} = 0.5$, $\mu_{1x} - \mu_{0x} = 0.5$, and $\rho_{xx} = 0.7$. The problem becomes even more severe for larger values of ρ_{xy}. For instance, as shown in panel *d*, even a small $\mu_{1x} - \mu_{0x}$ value and small amounts of covariate measurement error distort Type I errors when $\rho_{xy} = 0.9$.

Previous research has proposed methods for correcting biased treatment effects for covariate measurement error in non-experimental designs, and at least four methods have been developed in the statistics and econometrics literature: Errors-in-variables (EIV),[64] Lord's method,[65] Raaijmakers and Pieters' method (R&P),[66] and structural equation modeling (SEM) methods.[67] However, no research had evaluated the relative merits of these approaches. Therefore, if you were interested in using ANCOVA, you did not have guidelines regarding which approach works

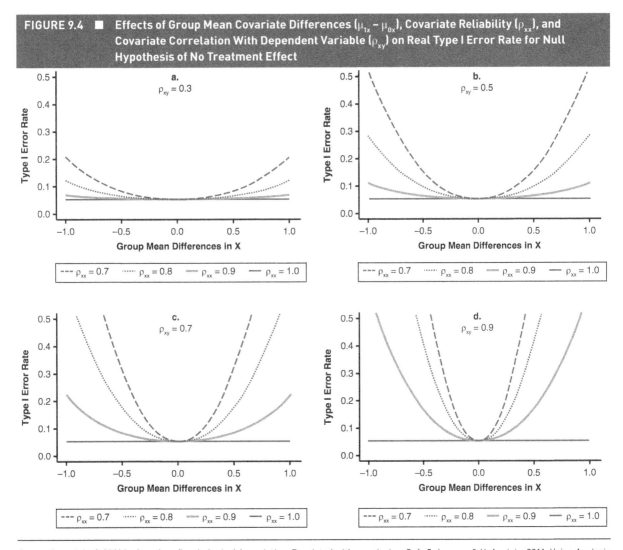

FIGURE 9.4 ■ Effects of Group Mean Covariate Differences ($\mu_{1x} - \mu_{0x}$), Covariate Reliability (ρ_{xx}), and Covariate Correlation With Dependent Variable (ρ_{xy}) on Real Type I Error Rate for Null Hypothesis of No Treatment Effect

Source: Copyright © 2011 by American Psychological Association. Reprinted with permission. S. A. Culpepper & H. Aguinis, 2011, Using Analysis of Covariance (ANCOVA) with fallible covariates, *Psychological Methods, 16*(2), 166-178.

Note. Sample size of 500, nominal rejection level of 0.05, and equal proportions of subjects in treatment and control groups (p = 0.5).

best and under what conditions. But, more recently, Monte Carlo simulations were implemented to evaluate the relative performance of existing approaches for adjusting treatment effects in non-experimental designs when the covariate is fallible.

Monte Carlo simulations offered new and comprehensive knowledge about the relative performance of existing methods for disattenuating parameter estimates in the presence of fallible covariates. An important implication is that EIV models are superior to their competitors (namely, SEM models, Lord's method, and Raaijmakers and Pieters's method). EIV methods produce accurate estimates of the true treatment effects, have greater levels of statistical power, and provide better control of Type I error rates. You may not have access to statistical software to implement EIV methods (in fact, Stata is the only widespread program able to conduct EIV analysis). But you can use a script in the open-source statistical software package R[68] to accurately assess treatment effects.

R Program for Errors-In-Variables (EIV) Regression

The following R code defines a function called 'eiv':

```
eiv<-function(formula,reliability,data){

mfx<-model.matrix(formula,data=data)

p<-length(mfx[1,])-1;n<-length(mfx[,1])

     mf <- match.call(expand.dots = FALSE)

     m <- match(c("formula", "data", "subset", "weights", "na.action",
          "offset"), names(mf), 0L)

     mf <- mf[c(1L, m)]

     mf$drop.unused.levels <- TRUE

     mf[[1L]] <- as.name("model.frame")

     mf <- eval(mf, parent.frame())

mf<-data.frame(mf)

MXX<-cov(mfx[,c(2:(p+1))]);MXY<-cov(mfx[,c(2:(p+1))],mf[,1])

Suu<-matrix(0,p,p);diag(Suu)<-(1-reliability)*diag(MXX)

Mxx<-MXX-(1-p/n)*Suu;Btilde<-solve(Mxx)%*%MXY

MSEtilde<-as.numeric(n*(1-2*t(Btilde)%*%MXY+t(Btilde)%*%MXX%*%Btilde)/
    (n-3))

Rhat<-matrix(0,p,p);diag(Rhat)<-(t(Btilde)%*%Suu)^2

VCtilde<-MSEtilde*(1/n)*solve(Mxx)+(1/n)*solve(Mxx)%*%(Suu*MSEtilde+Suu%
    *%Btilde%*%t(Btilde)%*%Suu+2*Rhat)%*%solve(Mxx)

ttilde<-Btilde/sqrt(diag(VCtilde))

output<-cbind(reliability,Btilde,sqrt(diag(VCtilde)),ttilde,
    2*(1-pt(ttilde,n-p)))

colnames(output)<-c('Reliability','Est.','S.E.','t','Prob.(>|t|)')

output

}
```

You can implement the eiv function by first submitting the code above to R. Once the eiv function is entered into R, you need to specify a statistical model, a vector of reliability coefficients for the predictors, and the name of the dataset. For example, the following code would compute an EIV analysis with a dependent variable (y), two covariates (x1 and x2), and a dichotomously coded treatment effect (treat):

```
eiv(y~x1+x2+treat, reliability=c(.8,.9,1), data=eivdata)
```

Also, note that the option 'reliability=' allows you to specify the reliability of the three predictors (in this case, the reliability coefficients for x1, x2, and treat are .8, .9, and 1.0, respectively). Finally, the option denoted by 'data=' specifies the name of the dataset containing the dependent and independent variables (the name of the dataset in this example is 'eivdata'). Submitting the eiv command will produce a regression output table with disattenuated estimates and parameter standard errors based upon Equation 9.9, t-values, and p-values.

In conclusion, the primary goal of this section is to assist you in addressing substantive questions by implementing more accurate data-analytic procedures. In addition to its value in basic research, ANCOVA is often used to assess treatment effects, which may determine the value and merit of programs, interventions, or organizational and social initiatives.[69] However, current applications of ANCOVA make it difficult to accurately assess and evaluate treatment effects given the normative presence of covariate measurement error. This section informs you that EIV is the best available procedure for estimating treatment effects accurately when using ANCOVA with non-experimental designs. Using EIV minimizes bias, maximizes statistical power, and keeps the Type I error rate close to its nominal level. In addition, the computer program allows you to implement EIV in the future to yield more accurate ANCOVA results, which, in turn, are likely to lead to more accurate assessments regarding the size of treatment effects and better decisions regarding interventions, practices and policy making.

USING REGRESSION TO UNDERSTAND NONLINEAR EFFECTS: THE TOO-MUCH-OF-A-GOOD-THING (TMGT) EFFECT

This section covers a type of nonlinear effect that is key in social and behavioral science: too-much-of-a-good-thing (TMGT). The TMGT effect occurs when ordinarily beneficial antecedents (i.e., predictor variables) reach inflection points, after which their relations with desired outcomes (i.e., criterion variables) cease to be linear and positive. Exceeding these inflection points is always undesirable because it leads to waste (no additional benefit) or undesirable outcomes (e.g., decreased individual or organizational performance). The philosophical tenet underlying the TMGT effect is that too much of any good thing is ultimately bad. This tenet permeates all aspects of life, from the physical (e.g., hydration[70]) to the social (e.g., power and politics).

Proverbs and aphorisms such as the Chinese "too much can be worse than too little" and its Western counterpart "everything in moderation; nothing in excess" suggest that this principle is widely accepted across cultures. In fact, these and similar sayings in both Eastern and Western cultures trace back to philosophers whose teachings have been highly influential in their respective regions (e.g., Aristotle and Confucius[71]). Modern scholars of philosophy have labeled this universal advocacy for proportionality over extremity the *doctrine of the mean*.[72] Pursuing the "**Golden Mean**," as it is also known, was a moral and practical imperative for its proponents.[73] In Confucius' words, "Perfect is the virtue which is according to the Mean!" (p. 2).[74]

Although influential philosophers have highlighted and promoted this concept, the social and behavioral science literature needs to include more discussions of the need for balance between deficiency and excess. Instead, researchers focus on addressing the former with less concern for the latter. Consequently, the assumption that "more is better" implicitly drives efforts to maximize desired outcomes through theory development and application. Researchers usually propose and test hypotheses describing linear relations between these criteria and their determinants in this quest to maximize individual, group, and organizational performance. Confirmation of such hypotheses reinforces the "more is better" assumption and leads many to conclude that linear relations best characterize important organizational relations (e.g., firm resources and performance[75]; conscientiousness and job performance[76]) when they may not. Through subsequent discourse, these theories become part of institutional logics, fashions, or fads[77] whose perceived legitimacy may perpetuate rather than mitigate against false understanding and misguided decisions.[78]

Theoretical progress occurs when scholars identify faulty logical or empirical inferences[79] and update or develop new theories to address them. Although new or updated theories must differ from their predecessors in some way, the decision-making process used to develop them is typically guided by some of the same or similar principles, presumptions, and perspectives. That is, theorists use the same widely accepted heuristics to update and revise earlier theories. However, a meta-theory is needed when the heuristics underlying the theory development process are deficient. For example, the common presumption of monotonic linear relations leads to the development and proliferation of theories with a common deficiency—failure to take the TMGT effect into account—making the introduction of a meta-theory necessary.

Meta-theories are theories of, or about, theories and are classified into one of two categories: (a) philosophical and (b) formalized. Philosophical meta-theories address theory in general and describe what theories are, what they should do, and how scholars should develop them.[80] Alternatively, formalized meta-theories are overarching principles that transcend specific topics or domains of study. Such formalized meta-theories describe and predict phenomena at more abstract or higher levels than specific theories.[81] In addition, formalized meta-theories extract what is generally consistent across theories, analogous to how meta-analysts extract what is generally consistent across primary-level studies.[82] Although meta-theories of both types have the potential to help advance the social and behavioral science field, researchers have focused more on philosophical meta-theories (e.g., deductive versus inductive theorizing[83]) than on formalized meta-theories. The challenge with formalized meta-theories involves a sacrifice of depth (specificity) for breadth (generality) because context-specific boundary conditions determine their relative explanatory power across contexts. Thus, the value of formalized meta-theories lies in their ability to account for various phenomena. The following section defines and describes a formalized meta-theory of the TMGT effect.

A Formalized Meta-theory of the TMGT Effect

As noted earlier, the TMGT effect occurs when ordinarily beneficial antecedents reach inflection points, after which their relations with desired outcomes cease to be linear and positive, yielding an overall curvilinear pattern. Though the TMGT effect involves a greater degree of complexity than simpler regression models, the TMGT effect provides an enhancement. Moreover, it contributes value-added to theory and practice because it accounts for a wide range of inconsistent and paradoxical findings in the literature. Researchers have produced several mixed and conflicting findings and theories which have yet to be reconciled. With the presumption of linear relations, such mixed findings present a paradox because they suggest that, although not possible, at least two of the following three mutually exclusive theses be true simultaneously:

Thesis A: Increases in beneficial antecedent X lead to increases in desired outcomes (i.e., $r_{xy} > 0$)

Thesis B: Increases in the same beneficial antecedent X have no impact on desired outcomes (i.e., $r_{xy} = 0$)

Thesis C: Increases in the same beneficial antecedent X lead to decreases in desired outcomes (i.e., $r_{xy} < 0$)

In other words, increasing X causes Y to increase (i.e., *Thesis A*), not change (i.e., *Thesis B*), and in some cases, decrease (i.e., *Thesis C*). This is a paradox because each possibility is tenable in isolation, but their combinations are not.[84] TMGT resolves this paradox[85] by separating levels of A and B, introducing a new perspective, and synthesizing a new theory.

First, due to the TMGT effect, each X-Y relation has a context-specific inflection point, after which further increases in the otherwise beneficial antecedent X lead to less desired outcomes. That is, it is necessary to separate the conflicting theses above according to levels of X. Stated differently, all seemingly positive monotonic causal relations (i.e., X→Y) reach a context-specific inflection point, I, after which they cease to be positive, resulting in an overall pattern of curvilinearity. In short, *Thesis A* holds when X is less than I, *Thesis B* holds when X is approximately equal to I, and *Thesis C* may hold when X is greater than I. The specific location of I on the X continuum depends on the context. The inflection points are context-specific because what is excessive in one context may be insufficient in another. Addressing the location of inflection points is the domain of relation-specific theorizing (e.g., at what specific point does too much organizational citizenship behavior leads to negative instead of positive individual performance, at what exact point does too much formal planning has no effect or even a negative instead of a positive effect on firm survival and success).

Second, confirming *Thesis C* means the relation follows an inverted U-shaped pattern. In contrast, the lack of confirmation of *Thesis C* means that the relation follows an asymptotic pattern. In either case, increases in the focal antecedent lead to undesired outcomes. As a best-case scenario, escalating the focal antecedent leads to wasted energy and resources because there are no improvements or additional beneficial outcomes despite the increase in inputs (i.e., higher levels of the predictor variables). Worse yet, when *Thesis C* does hold, such increases lead to detrimental consequences—just the opposite of what is hoped for and desired. Although curvilinear relations have been noted in some domains,[86] our meta-theory suggests that a paradigmatic shift from linear to curvilinear models is needed to improve theory and practice regardless of the level of analysis and sub-field of study.

Despite this conclusion, some have advocated the practical utility of linear models over curvilinear models. For instance, some authors concluded that linear decision-making models efficiently approximate curvilinear phenomena subject to diagnostic or predictive judgment because most such phenomena are monotonic.[87] Moreover, others have argued that ignoring nonlinearity simplifies the resulting models, and this simplification may improve practical utility.[88] While linear models may be more efficient and practical in specific cases (e.g., decision-making literature), understanding curvilinear relations is critical for research and applications.

Evidence and Explanation of the TMGT Effect

To illustrate how you can find examples of the TMGT effect across different disciplines, this section describes eight cases of TMGT in seemingly unrelated bodies of scholarly work in key areas in organizational behavior (OB), human resource management (HRM), entrepreneurship, and strategic management.

1. *Organizational Behavior Example A: Leadership.* Although effective leadership depends on initiating structure (i.e., instrumental command and control) and individualized consideration (i.e., concern for followers' needs), growing evidence[89] suggests that increasing them leads to positive outcomes up to an inflection point, after which they lead to detrimental outcomes for leaders, followers, and their organizations.

2. *Organizational Behavior Example B: Conscientiousness.* Conscientiousness has a positive relation with individual performance up to a point, after which increased conscientiousness can have a negative impact on performance.[90]

3. *Human Resource Management Example A: Enriched Job Design.* Enriching jobs positively impacts psychological outcomes and employee performance up to a point. However, after this inflection point, the effect approaches zero and becomes negative.[91]

4. *Human Resource Management Example B: Experience in Personnel Selection Decisions.* Recent evidence suggests that the TMGT effect applies to the relationship between experience and employee performance. That is, experience increases correspond to more desirable outcomes up to a point. However, after that inflection point, more experience does not lead to additional value and may lead to less desirable results.[92]

5. *Entrepreneurship Example A: New Venture Planning.* Recent evidence suggests that the relationship between formal planning and new venture survival and success should be conceptualized in light of an inflection point. Up to this point, increased formal planning contributes to the long-term survival and success of new firms, whereas, after it, increased planning has no benefit and may even have detrimental effects.[93]

6. *Entrepreneurship Example B: Firm Growth Rate.* Positive growth rates are beneficial because they are needed for firms to survive. As predicted by the TMGT effect, however, the evidence suggests that too much growth too fast leads to diminishing positive returns up to a point after which the growth rate has a negative impact on firm success.[94]

7. *Strategic Management Example A: Diversification.* Although a prevailing theoretical view is that diversification has a linear and positive relation with performance, a growing body of empirical evidence conforms to the TMGT effect. Too much diversification has a negative effect on firm performance.[95]

8. *Strategic Management Example B: Organizational Slack.* Organizational slack is also beneficial up to a point (i.e., an inflection point) but then turns negative. Consistent with a meta-theory of the TMGT effect, organizational slack (like body fat) is a necessary and good thing, but in high amounts, it can undermine rather than foster firm health.[96]

In summary, evidence supports the TMGT effect across levels of analysis (e.g., individual and firm level) and sub-fields of study (i.e., OB, HRM, entrepreneurship, and strategic management). Taken together, this evidence suggests that many supposedly positive and linear relations between beneficial antecedents and outcomes become asymptotic and even negative as values or levels of the antecedents increase. Moreover, in most cases, the inflection point where the relations cease to be linear falls within observable ranges of predictor scores and, hence, does not affect only extreme, unusual, or just a few cases or observations. Thus, the TMGT effect applies to a broad range of phenomena.

What Are the Implications of the TMGT Effect for Your Future Research?

Regardless of specialization, a common scientific objective is to develop theories that are as parsimonious, generalizable, and accurate as possible.[97] These guiding principles usually lead to hypothesized relations that take on their simplest possible form: linear and monotonic. This type of theorizing is common at the individual, group, and organizational levels of analysis. The prevailing theoretical perspective has been that more is better. However, growing bodies of seemingly anomalous empirical evidence contradict this dominant monotonic and linear paradigm established over the past few decades.

The TMGT effect is a meta-theoretical explanation for the counter-theoretical and seemingly anomalous findings based on linear and monotonic relations. Like more established principles in other scientific fields (e.g., Einstein's theory of relativity, $E = mc^2$), the TMGT suggests a curvilinear reality rather than linear relations. Due to the TMGT effect, positive monotonic relations reach context-specific inflection points, after which relations turn asymptotic or even negative, resulting in an overall pattern of curvilinearity. Stated differently, in addition to positive consequences, desirable antecedents may also lead to unanticipated consequences (i.e., neutral or even negative) when those antecedents reach high values or levels. The following section discusses the implications of the TMGT effect for future theory development and theory testing.

What Are the Implications for Theory Development?

An important implication of the TMGT effect for theory development concerns the location of context-specific inflection points. To make important advancements, theories should include a greater level of specificity.[98] Consistent with this notion, an implication of the TMGT effect is that future theory development efforts should not only predict whether X will be related to Y but also the precise points on the X continuum where the X-Y relation will turn asymptotic and, if applicable, negative. To this end, it may be possible to use various theoretical arguments and past empirical research to posit competing hypotheses regarding the approximate location of these inflection points.[99]

A second implication of the TMGT effect for theory development concerns reconsidering and expanding the role of moderating effects. A moderating, or interaction, effect implies that the relation between two variables depends on the value of a third (i.e., moderator) variable.[100] As such, moderator variables indicate a theory's boundary conditions (i.e., conditions under which the nature of an X-Y relation changes). In traditional regression terms, a model including a moderator variable is

$$Y = b_0 + b_1 X + b_2 Z + b_3 XZ + e, \qquad (9.10)$$

where the coefficient for the product term between the predictors X and Z carries information about the moderating effect of Z on the X-Y relation.

The TMGT effect suggests that the conceptualization of moderator variables should be expanded in future theory development efforts in two ways. First, an inflection point associated with the TMGT effect implies that the relation between predictor X and a desirable outcome Y is expected to change as values of the same predictor X vary. In other words, variable X is a predictor and moderator of the relation between itself and the outcome Y. Hence, the nonlinear relations predicted by the TMGT effect can be conceptualized as a particular case of the more general moderated relations. The resulting model is

$$Y = b_0 + b_1 X + b_2 XX + e, \qquad (9.11)$$

or, more simply,

$$Y = b_0 + b_1 X + b_2 X^2 + e, \qquad (9.12)$$

where the inflection point occurs precisely at the following value along the X continuum[101]: $-b_1/2 b_2$.

Second, the role of moderator variables is expanded in that they affect not only the location of the inflection point in the relation between X and Y but also the slope of this relation to the left and right of the inflection point along the X continuum. These moderating effects can be understood through a combination of Equations 9.10 and 9.12, which allows for the estimation of both linear interaction and curvilinear effects[102]:

$$Y = b_0 + b_1 X + b_2 Z + b_3 XZ + b_4 X^2 + e. \qquad (9.13)$$

A third implication of the TMGT effect also concerns a theory's degree of specificity. Stated differently, future theory development efforts guided by the TMGT effect should specify the presence of nonlinear relations, the location of inflection points, and the shape of such relations. For example, an X-Y relation will become asymptotic or negative once the inflection point is reached. Given these alternatives, it would be helpful to understand when the former or latter pattern is likely to emerge.

In the *Nicomachean Ethics* Books I and II,[103] Aristotle noted that three types of antecedents (i.e., predictors) can potentially lead to positive outcomes: "actions," "passions," and "things good in themselves." However, he was careful to qualify that the "mean" only applied to the former two. Only actions and passions could be problematic when taken too far. Following Aristotle's taxonomy, you can expect to find asymptotic relations for predictors that can be classified as being good in themselves (e.g., general mental ability, wisdom) but inverted-U-shaped associations between predictors and outcomes for predictors that can be classified as either actions or passions. The preceding section offers some examples of these types of relations. For example, the relation between "actions," such as diversification and its outcomes, and between "passions," such as conscientiousness and its outcomes, have been found to follow an inverted U-shaped pattern.

Equation 9.13 provides future theory development efforts with a conceptual framework to expand the meaning of moderating effects (i.e., X as a moderator of the relation between itself and Y), specify the location of the inflection points, and determine the nature of the X-Y relation to the left and the right of the inflection points, including whether the curvilinear relation is asymptotic (as indicated by a positive sign for b_4) or negative (as indicated by a negative sign for b_4).

Finally, considering the TMGT effect may lead to the need to rethink the nature of certain constructs. For example, in the case of some of the constructs discussed earlier, such as initiating structure and conscientiousness, too much of them may reflect psychopathology.[104] Stated differently, excessively high construct levels may constitute a different construct. Whether a particular construct is conceptualized differently when it reaches a high level, the TMGT is still helpful as a meta-theoretical principle to describe and explain relations involving that construct and other variables.

What Are the Implications for Theory Testing?

As an initial assessment of the TMGT effect, you can create graphs such as scatterplots to understand whether a data set may follow an asymptotic or inverted U-shaped pattern. However, more formal tests will often be required. When such formal tests are conducted, it will be necessary to consider statistical power and effect size, range restriction, and the possible use of advanced data analytic techniques, including meta-analysis and growth modeling. The following paragraphs describe each of these issues.

Statistical Power and Effect Size

Many scholars may have identified and tested but eventually not reported curvilinear relations as predicted by the TMGT effect because they did not achieve the standard .05 significance level.[105] Interaction effects are notoriously difficult to detect because methodological and statistical artifacts typically observed in research decrease statistical power.[106] Because the coefficient in Equation 9.11 is associated with a product term (XX), much like the coefficient associated with a product term (XZ) in Equation 9.13, tests of hypotheses regarding curvilinear effects as predicted by the TMGT effect are also likely to suffer from low statistical power.

Low statistical power means that even if the curvilinear effect exists in the population, there is a low probability that the effect will be found in any sample. Moreover, smaller effect sizes are harder to find compared to larger effects. Consequently, achieving sufficient statistical power to test hypotheses regarding asymptotic relations may be more challenging than inverted U-shaped relations. However, although an asymptotic relation is a smaller effect than a U-shaped one, this does not mean that an asymptotic relation is necessarily less important for science and practice.[107] For example, failing to recognize an asymptotic relation may lead decision-makers to escalate the focal antecedent, which can be costly and time-consuming. Still, in the end, the return on this increased investment will not pay off. In other words, not understanding the presence of an asymptotic relation can lead to wasted energy and resources.

Future tests of TMGT-effect hypotheses and theories should anticipate and mitigate the detrimental impact of factors known to decrease statistical power and, hence, the ability to find construct-level nonlinear relations. You can check recent reviews regarding statistical power issues to detect interaction effects in the context of regression.[108] Recommendations include issues related to research design, measurement, and analysis. For example, measures should be highly reliable and not coarse. Then after collecting data, you should avoid artificially dichotomizing continuous variables.

Restriction of Range

Selection artifacts primarily due to research design and measurement issues can prevent you from testing the presence of the TMGT effect in a valid manner. Specifically, selection effects in many social and behavioral sciences domains result when samples do not include scores representing the entire continuum of predictor scores.[109] In addition, selection effects are pervasive due to the use of non-experimental research designs. Indeed, these effects can occur at any level of analysis from the individual level (e.g., a sample of only those individuals whose scores are below a selection cutoff based on "theft proclivity" are included in the sample) to the firm level (e.g., only firms that are successful or are still in business are included in the sample) of analysis. This is an important issue to consider because assessing the presence of the TMGT effect requires a sufficient range of scores.

Figure 9.5 illustrates the need to include the full range of scores on the predictor variable. Concerning TMGT-effect-related inflection points, Figure 9.5 shows how researchers are likely to derive conflicting conclusions regarding the X-Y relation and overlook the TMGT effect when their data only include part of the range of predictor scores. For example, if a study contains predictor scores restricted to the range illustrated in Zone 2, the conclusion will be that there is a positive relation between X and Y. In contrast, a second study including the range of scores in Zone 3 would conclude that the relation is close to zero. However, including the full range of scores (i.e., Zones 1 through 4) would allow you to conduct a valid assessment of the presence of the TMGT effect and isolate the inflection point where the X-Y relation ceases to be linear. Note, however, that even if a study includes the full range of scores, failing to fit models that include nonlinear components, as described in the Implications for Theory Development section, could lead to the erroneous conclusion that a positive and linear trend best describes the data.

A common solution for addressing range restriction due to selection mechanisms is to apply statistical corrections that estimate the X-Y relations if the full range of X scores were available.[110] Unfortunately, although corrections for range restriction should allow you to test for the presence of the TMGT effect, these correction procedures ironically render such tests invalid because they assume a linear X-Y relation.[111] Using the available range restriction statistical correction procedures will prevent you from finding the inflection points (i.e., nonlinear relations) associated with the TMGT effect.[112]

A literature review led to the conclusion that there is an "unbalanced coverage of design, measurement, and analysis topics" and that "more attention is needed regarding the development of

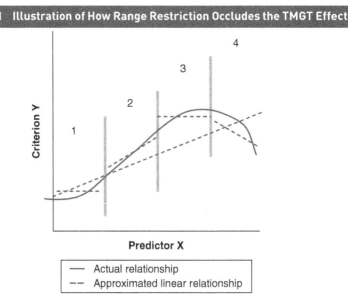

FIGURE 9.5 ■ Illustration of How Range Restriction Occludes the TMGT Effect

new as well as the improvement of existing research designs" (p. 106).[113] Thus, improvements in data-analytic tools alone will not likely lead to valid empirical tests of the TMGT effect in specific research domains. Instead, two solutions that include research design, measurement, and data analysis seem more promising. They are the following:

Advanced Meta-analytic Methods

Meta-analysis has become the methodological gold standard for conducting literature reviews in the social and behavioral sciences.[114] As a result, scholars give far more credence to meta-analytic results than they do to single-study findings—and with good reason. Meta-analytic techniques allow for estimating construct-level effect sizes through greater statistical power and the ability to correct several methodological and statistical artifacts, such as sampling and measurement error.

METHODS IN PRACTICE
USING META-ANALYSIS TO CAPTURE NON-LINEAR TRENDS

Despite the powerful influence of meta-analytic methods and findings in social and behavioral science research, the technique has far more potential than is currently being realized. For example, most meta-analysts report bivariate correlations computed under the usual assumption of linearity.[115] However, meta-analysis can be used to model curvilinear relations and test hypotheses and theories based on the TMGT effect. For example, some hypothesized that temporal variables (i.e., work experience and time on the job) would positively predict job performance up to inflection, after which the relation would turn negative.[116] This meta-analytic approach included the following three components. First, not making any corrections for range restriction because the presumption is about curvilinear rather than linear relations. Second, estimating but remaining skeptical of a linear model, even though the relation was statistically significant. Third, based on this skepticism, examining the data more closely. Because of this examination, results showed that the data followed an inverted U-shaped pattern similar to that shown in Figure 9.5. That is, results indicated positive correlations at low levels of the temporal variables (*Thesis A* above), zero-equivalent correlations relation at the middle-range (*Thesis B* above), and negative correlations at high levels (*Thesis C* above), thereby identifying the location of the inflection point along the X-variable continuum.

Advanced Growth Modeling Methods

Reexaminations of accepted relations with longitudinal methods have challenged some accepted relations in social and behavioral science theories[117] and suggest that traditional cross-sectional research designs and subsequent data-analytic approaches may need to be revised in many contexts. Compared with cross-sectional designs that can only test static relations at single points in time, longitudinal designs and analytic techniques such as growth modeling enable you to explicitly model dynamic relations (i.e., how X changes relate to Y over time).[118] The TMGT effect emerges over time. Hence, these techniques are suitable for testing TMGT-effect hypotheses.

You should note two qualifications to explore the TMGT effect using growth modeling techniques.[119] First, identifying and characterizing curvilinear relations with growth models requires careful theoretical planning of the number and intervals between the observations made over time. Though detecting a curvilinear pattern requires a minimum of three observations,[120] accurately characterizing growth curves may require more. Second, you have at least three growth modeling techniques from which to choose: (1) **latent growth modeling (LGM)**, (2) **random coefficients modeling (RCM)**, and (3) **latent class growth analysis (LCGA)**, also known as **latent class growth modeling (LCGM)** or **mixture modeling**. Each technique is better suited for certain types of tests and data than others. For instance, LCGA has a specific utility for identifying the categorical moderators (i.e., subpopulations) that determine inflection points' location.

In conclusion, this section explained how the TMGT effect is a meta-theoretical principle that allows you to account for and make sense of an increasing body of apparently paradoxical, counter-theoretical, and seemingly anomalous empirical findings across fields. It answers a call for improved theories that can explain phenomena at different levels of analysis, thereby mitigating the increased fragmentation of the field. The TMGT effect suggests that you hypothesize and test the possibility that relatively high levels of otherwise beneficial antecedents may lead to unexpected and undesired outcomes. Moreover, it is an admonition to practitioners that escalation of an initially positive action or organizational intervention may lead to negative results. It is key for you to understand the consideration of the TMGT effect, as this may open doors to groundbreaking theories and applications in your research.

This chapter has provided the tools for quantitative analysis, specifically regression-based approaches. Chapter 10 will continue to describe quantitative analysis, focusing on multilevel modeling.

DISCUSSION QUESTIONS

1. Why is it critical to master regression analysis, and how can your research improve by knowing more about this quantitative method?

2. How can moderation effects advance your research?

3. Which of the eight moderation-related problems may apply to your research, and how can you address them?

4. When would you consider testing for mediation effects in your research?

5. Which of the six problems related to mediation may affect your results, and what would you do to address each of them?

6. Why would you consider including ANCOVA as part of your methodology? What are its benefits?

7. How could you implement what you learn in this chapter to describe the exact degree of bias under various conditions and the underlying mechanisms that lead to inflation in Type I error rates and subsequent erroneous substantive conclusions?

8. How can you design studies that address nonlinear effects, including the too-much-of-a-good-thing (TMGT) effect?

9. What are some of the research questions in your area that the TMGT effect could explain?

10. What would be the implications for theory development and theory testing of pursuing that research and implementing the TMGT in your field?

KEY TERMS

dummy code
fallible covariates
Golden Mean
latent class growth analysis (LCGA)
latent class growth modeling (LCGM)
latent growth modeling (LGM)
meta-theory

mixture modeling
moderated multiple regression
multicollinearity
random coefficients modeling (RCM)
simple slope
submodel

NOTES

This chapter is based to a large extent on the following sources:

Aguinis, H., Edwards, J. R., & Bradley, K. J. (2017). Improving our understanding of moderation and mediation in strategic management research. *Organizational Research Methods*, *20*(4), 665-685. https://doi.org/10.1177/1094428115627498

Culpepper, S. A., & Aguinis, H. (2011). Using Analysis of Covariance (ANCOVA) with fallible covariates. *Psychological Methods*, *16*(2), 166-178. https://doi.org/10.1037/a0023355

Murphy, K. R., & Aguinis, H. (2022). Reporting interactions: Visualization, effect size, and interpretation. *Journal of Management*. https://doi.org/10.1177/01492063221088516

Pierce, J. R., & Aguinis, H. (2013). The too-much-of-a-good-thing effect in management. *Journal of Management*, *39*(2), 313-338. https://doi.org/10.1177/0149206311410060

Van Iddekinge, C. H., Aguinis, H., LeBreton, J. M., Mackey, J. D., & DeOrtentiis, P. S. (2021). Assessing and interpreting interaction effects: A reply to Vancouver, Carlson, Dhanani, and Colton (2021). *Journal of Applied Psychology*, *106*(3), 476-488. https://doi.org/10.1037/apl0000883

10 HOW TO CONDUCT QUANTITATIVE ANALYSIS, PART II: MULTILEVEL MODELING

LEARNING GOALS

By the end of this chapter, you will be able to do the following:

10.1 Argue why you should care about multilevel modeling and how it allows you to integrate micro and macro levels of analysis.

10.2 Diagram the three types of effects that can be examined using multilevel modeling.

10.3 Assess the different types of interaction effects you can test using multilevel modeling and their interpretation.

10.4 Appraise the issues that affect statistical power in multilevel designs.

10.5 Arrange the key steps in implementing multilevel modeling when addressing substantive questions of interest.

10.6 Recommend the best way to report the results of your multilevel research.

10.7 Critique the two sources of variance that affect whether or not to use multilevel modeling, and articulate the differences.

10.8 Articulate the best-practice steps involved in conducting and reporting multilevel modeling.

IMPORTANCE OF MULTILEVEL MODELING

Integrating micro and macro levels of analysis is one of the biggest challenges in the social and behavioral sciences.[1] Specifically, there is an interest in integrating theories that explain and predict phenomena at the individual, team, organizational, and higher **levels of analysis** (e.g., industry, country, economic bloc).[2] When conducting research that includes variables measured at different levels of analysis, you may often recognize that lower-level entities, such as individuals, are nested within higher-level collectives, such as teams. Note that lower-level entities do not have to be individuals. For example, lower-level entities can be organizations, and higher-level collectives can be industries, countries, or economic blocks (e.g., European Union). Regardless of the specific definition of entities and the collectives within which they reside, the multilevel nature of the resulting data requires that dependence among observations be considered both conceptually and analytically.[3]

Dependence is not solely a function of whether observations are formally clustered into larger units. Some researchers noted that "observations may be dependent, for instance, because they share some common feature, come from some common source, are affected by social interaction, or are arranged spatially or sequentially in time" (p. 138).[4] Thus, the dependence of observations also occurs when shared experiences and context affect lower-level units such as firms in the same industry facing similar market-based challenges, different branches of a bank being influenced by the same strategic priorities established for a particular geographic region, or employees within a team being similarly affected by the ineffective communication style of their leader. In other words, a higher-level variable may covary with relevant lower-level outcome variables, and entities within collectives may be more similar regarding certain variables than entities across collectives.[5] Consequently, dependence may occur "even if the variable of interest makes no reference to the group" (p. 358).[6] Covariation between higher-level variables and lower-level outcomes leads to gross errors of prediction if you use statistical approaches such as ordinary least squares (OLS) regression, which are not designed to model data structures that include dependence due to the clustering of entities.[7]

The essence of the multilevel approach is that an outcome of interest is conceptualized as resulting from a combination of influences emanating from the same level and higher levels of analysis. Moreover, the multilevel approach formally recognizes that entities (e.g., individuals) are typically nested in higher-level collectives (e.g., teams, organizations), which leads to nontrivial theoretical and analytical implications.

This chapter will show you how multilevel modeling can help you address the design, measurement, and analytical challenges associated with nested data. It begins by explaining the fundamentals of multilevel modeling, discusses interaction effects in multilevel modeling, outlines key considerations when conducting power analyses for multilevel designs, provides a step-by-step guide to conducting multilevel modeling, clarifies different sources of variance in multilevel models, and concludes with best-practice recommendations for conducting and reporting research involving multilevel analysis.

FUNDAMENTALS OF MULTILEVEL MODELING

In multilevel modeling, it is possible to test hypotheses regarding three types of relationships or effects. First, there are potential lower-level direct influences, such as between individuals' knowledge, skills, abilities, and other characteristics (KSAOs) and job performance. Second, there may be direct cross-level influences, such as the effects of group cohesion on group members' average job performance. And third, there may be cross-level interactions whereby the relationships between lower-level predictors and outcomes differ as a function of higher-level factors.

As an illustrative example, consider a study investigating whether the quality of leader-member exchange (LMX) (X) predicted individual empowerment (Y) using data collected across teams that differ regarding leadership climate (W).[8] One hypothesis is that employees who reported higher LMX (i.e., a better relationship with their leader) would feel more empowered (i.e., believe they have the autonomy and capability to perform meaningful work that can impact their organization). In addition, another hypothesis is that the team-level variable leadership climate (i.e., ambient leadership behaviors directed at the team as a whole) would also affect individual-level empowerment positively. Moreover, we can also expect that the relationship between LMX and empowerment would be moderated by leadership climate such that the relationship would be stronger for teams with a better leadership climate (i.e., an interaction between LMX and leadership climate on empowerment). Please remember this study because we will use it as an illustration throughout this chapter.

In the parlance of multilevel modeling, the questions that are answered by the hypotheses above refer to the following three types of effects:

1. *Lower-level direct effects.* Does a lower-level predictor X (i.e., Level 1 or L1 predictor) impact a lower-level outcome variable Y (i.e., L1 outcome)? Regarding our example, does LMX, as perceived by subordinates, predict individual empowerment? Note that LMX scores are collected for each worker (i.e., there is no aggregation of such scores to test the presence of a lower-level direct effect).

2. *Cross-level direct effects.* Does a higher-level predictor W (i.e., Level 2 or L2 predictor) impact an L1 outcome variable Y? Specifically, does the L2 variable of leadership climate predict L1 outcome individual empowerment?

3. *Cross-level interaction effects.* Does the nature or strength of the relationship between two lower-level variables (e.g., L1 predictor X and L1 outcome Y) change as a function of a higher-level variable W? Referring back to the example, does the relationship between LMX and individual empowerment vary as a function of (i.e., is moderated by) the degree of leadership climate such that the relationship will be stronger for teams with more positive leadership climate and weaker for teams with less positive leadership climate?

Overall, these same three questions are the focus of multilevel analyses regardless of the nature of the constructs and the particular measurement approach adopted to measure them.[9]

VISUAL REPRESENTATION OF TYPES OF VARIANCES MODELED IN MULTILEVEL ANALYSIS

The three types of effects described above can be measured using multilevel modeling because this approach can capture different sources of variance, as shown in Figure 10.1.[10] The dashed lines in Figure 10.1's top and bottom panels show that you can estimate an OLS regression equation for the relationship between LMX and empowerment within each team. Thus, each team has its own regression line defined by its own intercept and slope. Figure 10.1's panels also show a solid line, a **pooled regression line** between LMX scores and empowerment across all teams. This pooled regression line is defined by its intercept (i.e., γ_{00}; "gamma sub zero zero") and slope (i.e., γ_{10}; "gamma sub one zero"). Figure 10.1's Panel (a) also shows that regression lines differ across teams in terms of both intercepts and slopes. As shown in Figure 10.1's Panel (a), the variance of intercepts across teams is denoted by τ_{00} ("tau sub zero zero), and the variance of slopes across teams is denoted by τ_{11} ("tau sub one one"). In contrast, illustrating a different yet possible research scenario, Figure 10.1's Panel (b) shows that teams differ regarding slopes (i.e., $\tau_{11} > 0$) but not regarding intercepts (i.e., $\tau_{00} = 0$).

Figure 10.2 depicts individual data points within two illustrative teams: Team 1 in Panel (a) and Team 2 in Panel (b). Figure 10.2's Panel (c) shows data for all individuals from both teams combined. Similar to Figure 10.1, Figure 10.2's Panel (a) shows the OLS regression line for Team 1 (dashed line) as well as the pooled regression line for all teams (solid line). Also, Panel (a) shows the L1 residual or error scores r_{i1} (i.e., differences between observed and predicted scores for empowerment based on LMX scores within Team 1). Note that the variance of these residual scores within teams is symbolized by σ^2 in Figure 10.2's Panel (c). Figure 10.2's Panel (a) also shows the difference between the Team 1 intercept and the pooled (across all teams) intercept γ_{00} (i.e., L2 residual),

FIGURE 10.1 ■ Illustration of Variance of Intercepts (τ_{00}) and Slopes (τ_{11}) Across Teams

(a) Intercept and Slope Variance across Teams

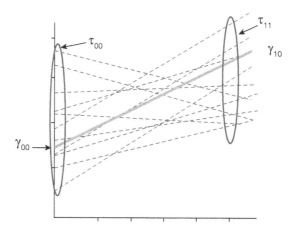

(b) Slope but No Intercept Variance across Teams

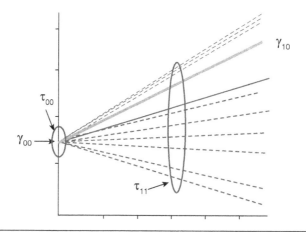

Source: Aguinis, Gottfredson, & Culpepper (2013). Reproduced with permission.

which is symbolized by u_{01}. In addition, Panel (a) shows the difference between the Team 1 slope and the pooled (across all teams) slope γ_{10} (i.e., L2 residual), which is symbolized by u_{11}. That is, u_{11} is nonzero when Team 1's prediction equation has a different slope than the pooled line. Similarly, Panel (b) also shows the OLS regression line. Figure 10.2 depicts individual data points within two illustrative teams: Team 1 in Panel (a) and of this particular team, the pooled regression line (across all teams), and the L1 and L2 residuals.

Panel (c) in Figure 10.2 shows combined individuals from Team 1 and Team 2. For clarity, this panel includes only Team 1 and Team 2 from the many teams in Figure 10.1. This panel shows the key sources of variance that we are interested in understanding using multilevel modeling: variance of the L1 residuals r_{ij} (i.e., σ^2, within-group variance), the variance of the L2 residuals u_{0j} (i.e., τ_{00}, intercept variance across teams), and variance of the L2 residuals u_{1j} (i.e., τ_{11}, slope variance across teams).

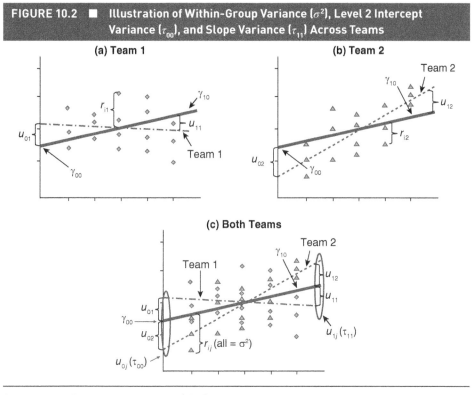

FIGURE 10.2 ■ Illustration of Within-Group Variance (σ^2), Level 2 Intercept Variance (τ_{00}), and Slope Variance (τ_{11}) Across Teams

Source: Aguinis, Gottfredson, & Culpepper (2013). Reproduced with permission.

ANALYTIC REPRESENTATION OF SOURCES OF VARIANCE MODELED IN MULTILEVEL ANALYSIS

In multilevel modeling, we always want to be able to orient ourselves as to what level we're dealing with. So, we use subscripts, with i tracking the individual level and j tracking the group level. As a preview of the technical material in the following sections, Table 10.1 includes definitions of key terms we will use throughout this chapter. You may want to keep this table handy as a "cheat sheet."

Analytically, Figure 10.2's Panel (c) can be described by the following L1 model[11]:

$$Y_{ij} = \beta_{0j} + \beta_{1j}\left(X_{ij} - \overline{X}_j\right) + r_{ij}. \tag{10.1}$$

Equation 10.1 takes on the familiar OLS regression equation form because it includes a predictor and a criterion residing at the same level of analysis (i.e., L1 in this case). Specifically, in the illustrative example, Y_{ij} is the predicted empowerment score for the ith person in team j, β_{0j} is the intercept parameter for team j, β_{1j} is the slope parameter for team j, X_{ij} is the individual LMX for the ith person in team j and is **re-scaled** (i.e., "centered") by the team average $\overline{X}_j$.

As discussed later in this chapter, this type of re-scaling, called "**group-mean centering**" or "**within-cluster centering**," is one of two approaches available. The term r_{ij} is the L1 residual term (i.e., randomly distributed error), reflecting individual-level differences in empowerment around the predicted empowerment score for employees within each team. In multilevel modeling, your interest is not in the residual scores per se, but in the variance of r_{ij}, denoted by σ^2, representing the amount of within-group variance for the criterion scores (i.e., individual empowerment).

TABLE 10.1 ■ Definitions of Technical Terms Used in Multilevel Analysis	
Term	**Definition**
Y_{ij}	Predicted (empowerment) score for the ith person in team j
β_{0j}	Intercept parameter for team j
β_{1j}	Slope parameter for team j
X_{ij}	The individual (LMX) for the ith person in team j re-scaled (i.e., "centered") by the team average $\bar{X}_j$.
r_{ij}	Level 1 residual term (i.e., randomly distributed error), reflecting individual-level differences (in empowerment) around the predicted (empowerment) score for employees within each team
σ^2	Amount of within-group variance for the criterion scores (i.e., individual empowerment), analogous to MS_{within} in analysis of variance (ANOVA)
τ_{00}	The variance of β_{0j}
τ_{11}	The variance of β_{1j}
τ_{01}	The covariance between β_{0j} and β_{1j}
W_j	Level 2 covariate
u_{0j} and u_{1j}	Residuals, or random effects, that capture group differences after controlling for Level 2 predictors
γ_{00}	The average Y_{ij} across Level 2 units
γ_{10}	The average relationship between $X_{ij} - \bar{X}_j$ and Y_{ij}
γ_{01}	The effect of $\bar{X}_j$ on β_{0j}
γ_{02}	The effect of W_j on β_{0j}

Note that σ^2 is analogous to MS_{within} in analysis of variance (ANOVA) and is illustrated graphically in Figure 10.2's Panel (c).

The interpretation of the parameter β_{0j} depends on the scaling of the predictor X_{ij}. Equation 10.1 re-scales the predictor by each team mean to establish a meaningful interpretation of this parameter. Consequently, the mean of $X_{ij} - \bar{X}_j$ is zero within teams, and β_{0j} is interpreted as the predicted level of empowerment for a typical (i.e., mean) LMX of members of a given team. Note that instead of re-scaling by the group mean, you could re-scale X_{ij} by any other value for LMX, say 4.5 on a 5-point scale. So, if you re-scale by 4.5, β_{0j} would be interpreted as the predicted level of empowerment for individuals in a given team with a team average LMX score of 4.5. Finally, based on Equation 10.1, the parameter β_{1j} is interpreted as the predicted increase in individual empowerment associated with a 1-unit increase in LMX for individuals within the jth team.

THE IMPORTANCE OF STATISTICAL POWER IN MULTILEVEL MODELING

Power refers to the ability of a test statistic to detect an existing effect of a certain magnitude with a specific degree of confidence.[12] Generally speaking, power increases to the extent that: 1) the population effect is larger; 2) sample size (i.e., degrees of freedom) increases; 3) the preset Type

I error rate α is higher; 4) predictors and criterion are measured with higher fidelity (e.g., degree of reliability in your measures); 5) variable distributions are not restricted; and 6) assumptions of statistical tests are not violated (e.g., homogeneity of error variances, linear relationships[13]). However, suppose you do not have sufficient statistical power. In that case, your research is susceptible to Type II errors or the likelihood that you will falsely conclude that given effects do not exist (i.e., false negatives). Such errors can lead to suboptimal use of resources, misguided interventions, deficient evaluation studies, and a wide variety of negative consequences resulting from an incorrect conclusion that the effect does not exist.

While challenges associated with achieving sufficient power in single-level investigations are relatively well understood,[14] multilevel investigations introduce additional complications. As some researchers noted, "Statistical power in multilevel designs is a complex combination of the number of higher-level units and lower-level units under investigation, the co-variances within and between units, and a slew of other factors that are still being investigated" (p. 631).[15] Stated differently, even when sample size and other design features are the same, power varies based on the parameter of interest—namely lower-level direct effects, cross-level direct effects, or cross-level interactions. Although some researchers have advocated general rules of thumb for multilevel samples, such as you should have at least 30 upper-level units with at least 30 lower-level entities in each (i.e., the so-called "**30-30 rule**"),[16] these rules are not likely to apply universally to the wide variety of situations that you will encounter.

To better understand issues associated with statistical power in multilevel designs, consider a typical design with individual employees nested in groups. Using conventional nomenclature, the relationship between a predictor and criterion at the lower level (i.e., Level 1) of a multilevel design can be shown as:

$$Y_{ij} = \beta_{0j} + \beta_{1j}\left(X_{ij} - \overline{X}_j\right) + r_{ij} \tag{10.2}$$

where Y_{ij} is the criterion score for the ith person in group j, β_{0j} is the intercept value for group j, β_{1j} is the slope for group j, X_{ij} is the predictor score for the ith person in group j and is centered by the group average, $\overline{X}_j$, and r_{ij} is the Level-1 residual term such that $r_{ij} \sim N(0, \sigma^2)$. In most applications, the regression coefficients are **distributed jointly** as random normal variables,

$$\begin{bmatrix} \beta_{0j} \\ \beta_{1j} \end{bmatrix} \sim N\left(\begin{bmatrix} \gamma_{00} \\ \gamma_{10} \end{bmatrix}, \begin{bmatrix} \tau_{00} & \tau_{01} \\ \tau_{01} & \tau_{11} \end{bmatrix} \right). \tag{10.3}$$

That is, τ_{00} measures the variance of β_{0j}, τ_{11} measures the variance of β_{1j}, and τ_{01} measures the covariance between β_{0j} and β_{1j}. In the single predictor case, one way to test for the presence of cross-level interactions is to estimate the following upper-level (i.e., Level 2) models[17]:

$$\beta_{0j} = \gamma_{00} + \gamma_{01}\left(\overline{X}_j - \overline{X}\right) + \gamma_{02}\left(W_j - \overline{W}\right) + \gamma_{03}\left(\overline{X}_j - \overline{X}\right)\left(W_j - \overline{W}\right) + u_{0j} \tag{10.4}$$
$$\beta_{1j} = \gamma_{10} + \gamma_{11}\left(W_j - \overline{W}\right) + u_{1j} \tag{10.5}$$

where u_{0j} and u_1j are residuals, or random effects, that capture group differences after controlling for Level 2 predictors $\overline{X}_j$ (group j's mean for X_{ij}), W_j (a Level 2 covariate), and the interaction between $\overline{X}_j$ and W_j. Note that $\overline{X}$ and $\overline{W}$ are the means for the entire sample for X and W, respectively. Additionally, the average Y_{ij} across level two units is represented by γ_{00}, and γ_{10}

measures the average relationship between $X_{ij} - \overline{X}_j$ and Y_{ij}. Furthermore, the effect of $\overline{X}_j$ and W_j on β_{0j} is captured by γ_{01} and γ_{02}, respectively. The interaction effect between $\overline{X}_j$ and W_j is represented by γ_{03}. In Equation 10.5, γ_{11} captures the extent to which W_j relates to group differences in β_{1j}. The Level 2 equations can be substituted into the Level 1 equation to yield:

$$
\begin{aligned}
Y_{ij} = \gamma_{00} &+ \gamma_{01}\left(\overline{X}_j - \overline{X}\right) + \gamma_{02}\left(W_j - \overline{W}\right) \\
&+ \gamma_{03}\left(\overline{X}_j - \overline{X}\right)\left(W_j - \overline{W}\right) \\
&+ \gamma_{10}\left(X_{ij} - \overline{X}_j\right) \\
&+ \gamma_{11}\left(X_{ij} - \overline{X}_j\right)\left(W_j - \overline{W}\right) \\
&+ u_{0j} + u_{1j}\left(X_{ij} - \overline{X}_j\right) + r_{ij}
\end{aligned}
\tag{10.6}
$$

Equation 10.6 shows that the effect of the cross-level interaction between W_j and X_{ij} is captured by τ_{11}. From Equation 10.6, we can also see that $Var\left(Y_{ij} \mid X_{ij}\right) = \tau_{00} + 2\,\tau_{01}\left(X_{ij} - \overline{X}_j\right) + \tau_{11}\left(X_{ij} - \overline{X}_j\right)^2 + \sigma^2$.[18]

It is important to appreciate the role of centering decisions in tests of cross-level interactions.[19] The observed variance in lower-level predictors (X_{ij}) may reflect lower- and upper-level influences, the relative extent to which can be expressed in terms of an **Intraclass Correlation Index (ICC)**. The ICC (ρ_x) is the ratio of between-group predictor variance (τ) relative to the total predictor variance [i.e., $\rho_x = \tau/(\tau+\sigma^2)$], where σ^2 is the variance component of the lower-level residual from a **null model**. In this fashion, ICCs can range from 0-1. At issue is that if lower-level predictor variance is used in its raw score form (X_{ij}) or centered on the basis of the total sample mean $\left(X_{ij} - \overline{X}\right)$, then it represents an intractable blend of upper- and lower-level influences. Consequently, it is unclear how much the interaction involving the lower-level predictor represents an interaction between the upper-level moderator and the *within-group variance of the lower-level predictor* versus an interaction between the upper-level moderator and the *between-group variance of the lower-level predictor*. For cases where you want to differentiate these two types of interactions, some researchers have advocated that the lower level predictor be centered within groups $\left(X_{ij} - \overline{X}_j\right)$ and the between-group variance $\left(\overline{X}_j - \overline{X}\right)$ be reintroduced as a Level 2 predictor.[20]

The number of lower-level entities and upper-level units plays a large role akin to the total sample size in single-level designs. Fortunately, you may have control over, for example, how many individuals you can sample versus how many groups you sample. Sampling more individuals from fewer groups is usually far less costly and logistically easier than sampling a larger number of groups; however, these decisions have implications regarding the resulting power to detect various effects. Generally speaking, there is a premium on the average number of lower-level entities for enhanced power to detect Level 1 direct effects. At the same time, there is a premium on the number of upper-level units for enhanced power to detect cross-level direct effects.[21] Because you may be interested in testing both effects, you are faced with a dilemma regarding how to proceed best.

Another key distinction for power in multi- versus single-level designs is the percentage of criterion variance that resides within versus between upper-level units, again typically expressed in terms of an ICC. Generally speaking, lower ICCs favor the power to detect Level 1 direct effects, whereas higher ICCs favor the power to detect cross-level direct effects.[22] Inevitably, specifying the number of parameter estimates and their complex relationships needed for conducting power analyses in multilevel designs can take time and effort. Although the calculations associated with weighing various tradeoffs are far from straightforward, available tools such as *Optimal Design*,[23] and *Power IN Two-level designs* (PINT)[24] make them more accessible to researchers while also permitting them to incorporate cost factors.[25] Unfortunately, *Optimal Design* is limited to estimating the power of treatment effects, and *PINT* requires users to provide estimates of many parameters that may be difficult to obtain a priori (e.g., variances and covariances of residuals). Moreover, neither tool incorporates the ability to consider the impact of variable reliabilities, nor can they provide power estimates for cross-level interactions.

In response to these challenges, simulation studies have shown that the power associated with tests of cross-level interactions is affected primarily by the magnitude of the direct cross-level effect (γ_{1w}) and the standard deviation of the Level 1 slope coefficients $(\sqrt{\tau_{11}})$, as well as by both average lower-level (n_i) and the upper-level (n_j) sample sizes. Moreover, these same four factors combined to drive power estimates, suggesting that compensatory factors can affect the power to detect cross-level interactions. These findings suggest that if you are interested in testing cross-level interactions, you should attempt to sample more thoroughly within units to enhance power, compared to sampling more units. However, many times in social and behavioral sciences there may be a natural limit to the sizes of certain groups (e.g., work teams, classrooms, nuclear families), which may preclude large numbers. Fortunately, in such instances, some additional power may be garnered by sampling more Level 2 units. Ultimately, the decision to focus on maximizing Level 1 versus Level 2 sample sizes may come down to what other parameters are of interest in your study. In other words, if you want to test a lower-level direct effect besides the cross-level interaction, then Level 1 sample sizes are most important. Alternatively, if you are also interested in testing cross-level direct effects, you should emphasize the number of sampled units.

You can conduct all calculations using a statistical power calculator available at https://hermanaguinis.com. To a priori calculate the power of a cross-level interaction test, you must estimate values for the various parameters in Equation 10.6. An ideal situation would be to conduct a pilot study with a representative sample from your target population and estimate values directly from those data. For consistency in these power calculations, the recommendation is to standardize (i.e., by converting to Z scores) all lower-level variables based on the total sample to provide a common metric.[26] These scores can then be used to derive the within-group centering and average Level 1 predictor scores for reintroduction at Level 2.[27] In addition, all Level 2 effects should be standardized at that level. While you may need more time or resources to conduct elaborate pilot studies every time, they may be helpful when the primary study represents an expensive endeavor or when it is vital to have high confidence that you are avoiding Type II errors.

If you cannot conduct a pilot study, several parameter values may be available from previous investigations. For example, previous work and perhaps even meta-analyses may provide insights regarding the magnitude of lower-level and cross-level direct effects. If ICCs for Level 1 predictors are unavailable, you may consider adopting values ranging from very small (e.g., .02) to relatively high (e.g., .75).

Values for the variability of slopes and the magnitude of the cross-level interaction are not likely to be available from previous research. Consequently, they are among the most challenging input values for power analysis. Generally speaking, the variability of slopes and the magnitude of cross-level interactions are likely higher when disordinal (i.e., cross-over) interactions are anticipated than ordinal (i.e., non-crossing) interactions. In the absence of information, however, you should consider a wide range of values. Note that the magnitudes of these parameters are influenced by standardization and centering techniques employed, as well as by substantive factors.

METHODS IN PRACTICE
WHAT ARE SMALL, MEDIUM, AND LARGE SLOPE VARIABILITY VALUES?

While some have advocated conventional small (.20), moderate (.30), and large (.40) average effect sizes,[28] others found that values of .10, .17, and .22 represented relatively little, moderate, and high variability, respectively.[29] However, if little is known about the true distributions of slopes, prior work in a substantive area and pilot studies can help you choose reasonable values for your applications. In many instances, values (or ranges) for various parameters should be chosen for their substantive importance. For example, effect sizes of certain magnitudes may be associated with strategic imperatives or goals, break-even analyses, valued impact of some social initiative, or points where an effort becomes cost prohibitive.

MULTILEVEL MODELING: STEP-BY-STEP ILLUSTRATION

The multilevel model-building process usually involves a sequence including four steps. The first step involves what is labeled an *unconditional means, one-way random-effects ANOVA*, or *null model*. The second step involves what is called a *random intercept and fixed slope model*. The third step involves the *random intercept and slope model*. Finally, the fourth step involves the *cross-level interaction model*. You can perform each step using the illustrative data file and the program available at https://hermanaguinis.com.

Step 1: Null Model

The *null model* begins by specifying the following relationship:

$$\text{Null model (Level 1)}: Y_{ij} = \beta_{0j} + r_{ij}, \tag{10.7}$$

which is identical to Equation 10.1 but excludes the L1 predictor. Due to the nested nature of the data, it is possible that both the intercept and slope in Equation 10.7 vary across teams. Specifically, teams likely differ in average empowerment (i.e., β_{0j} differs across the j teams), and individual team members' LMX levels may relate differently to empowerment across teams (i.e., β_{1j} differs across the j teams). This situation is illustrated in Panel (a) of Figure 10.1. However, in this first step in the model-building process, you omit predictors and only allow intercepts to vary across teams. Formally stated,

$$\text{Null model (Level 2)}: \beta_{0j} = \gamma_{00} + u_{0j} \tag{10.8}$$

In Equation 10.8, the team intercepts are shown to be a function of the **grand mean** (i.e., averaged across all teams) intercept γ_{00} and a residual term u_{0j} that describes how team intercepts deviate from the grand mean intercept. Substituting Equation 10.8 into Equation 10.7 leads to the following combined model:

$$\text{Null model (Combined)}: Y_{ij} = \gamma_{00} + u_{0j} + r_{ij} \tag{10.9}$$

Referring back to the illustrative example, the combined null model in Equation 10.9 shows that individual empowerment is a function of the grand mean LMX (i.e., γ_{00}), across-group differences in individual empowerment scores (i.e., L2 residuals u_{0j}), and within-group differences in individual empowerment scores (i.e., L1 residuals r_{ij}). As noted earlier, the variance of u_{0j}, denoted by τ_{00}, quantifies the heterogeneity in intercepts across teams. The variance of r_{ij}, denoted by σ^2, quantifies the within-group variance. Thus, compared to an ANOVA framework, σ^2 is analogous to MS_{within} and τ_{00} is analogous to $MS_{between}$. In terms of our illustration, τ_{00} quantifies the variation in mean empowerment scores across teams. A critical difference between ANOVA and multilevel modeling is that multilevel modeling conceptualizes the teams as a random sample from a larger population of teams (i.e., a random factor). In contrast, ANOVA conceptualizes the teams as qualitatively different (i.e., a fixed factor). Furthermore, the label *fixed effects* are reserved for multilevel modeling estimates that are constant across L2 units, such as γ_{00}, and the label *random effects* are used to denote the model estimates that vary across L2 units (e.g., u_{0j}).

As part of the first step in the model-building process, you should compute the intraclass correlation (ICC), which quantifies the proportion of the total variation in individual empowerment accounted for by team differences. An alternative interpretation is that the ICC is the expected correlation between empowerment scores for two individuals in the same team. ICC $= \tau_{00} / [\tau_{00} + \sigma^2]$ and it ranges from 0 to 1. A value near zero suggests that a model including L1 variables only is appropriate; hence, multilevel modeling may not be needed. Instead, a more straightforward OLS regression approach may be more parsimonious. On the other hand, ICC > 0, even as small as .10[30] suggests that an L2 variable W (e.g., leadership climate) may explain the heterogeneity of empowerment scores across teams (i.e., β_{0j}). Moreover, OLS standard errors and significance tests may be compromised in the presence of even smaller ICCs.

METHODS IN PRACTICE
WHAT ARE SMALL, MEDIUM, AND LARGE INTRACLASS CORRELATIONS?

Depending on the field, researchers have found that ICC values reported in multilevel studies usually range from .15 to .30,[31] from .10 to .25,[32] and from .05 to .20.[33] These results indicate that higher-level influences are more common than typically assumed or even considered in the social and behavioral sciences.[34]

Concerning the illustrative example, results presented in Table 10.2 indicate that ICC = .101, which means that differences across teams account for about 10% of the variability in individuals' empowerment levels. As shown in Table 10.2, the across-team variance in individual empowerment is τ_{00} .095, and the within-team variance is .714. In short, results provide evidence for a nested data structure that requires multilevel modeling rather than a single-level data analytic approach. Please note that you can also use a program at https://hermanaguinis.com/ to create a table like Table 10.2.

		Model		
		Random Intercept and Fixed Slope	Random Intercept and Random Slope	Cross-level Interaction
	Null			
Level and Variable	(Step 1)	(Step 2)	(Step 3)	(Step 4)
Level 1				
Intercept (γ_{00})	5.720 ** (0.045)	5.720 ** (0.038)	5.720 ** (0.038)	5.720 ** (0.038)
LMX (γ_{10})		0.279 ** (0.023)	0.270 ** (0.028)	0.269 ** (0.027)
Level 2				
Leadership Climate (γ_{01})		0.351 ** (0.055)	0.356 ** (0.055)	0.351 ** (0.055)
Cross-level Interaction				
LMX × Leadership Climate (γ_{11})				0.104 ** (0.037)
Variance Components				
Within-team (L1) variance (σ^2)	0.714	0.563	0.515	0.515
Intercept (L2) variance (τ_{00})	0.095	0.060	0.068	0.068
Slope (L2) variance (τ_{11})			0.025	0.019
Intercept-slope (L2) covariance (τ_{01})			−0.003	−0.004
Additional Information				
ICC	0.101			
−2Log likelihood (FIML)	1,637	1,478 **	1,469 *	1,462 **
Number of estimated parameters	3	5	7	8
Pseudo R^2	0	.23	.23	.24

TABLE 10.2 ■ Results of Multilevel Modeling Analysis with Illustrative Data

Source: Aguinis, Gottfredson, & Culpepper (2013). Reproduced by permission.

Note: L1 = Level 1, L2 = Level 2. FIML: Full information maximum likelihood estimation. Values in parentheses are standard errors, and *t*-statistics were computed as the ratio of each regression coefficient divided by its standard error.

*p < .05, **p < .01.

Step 2: Random Intercept and Fixed Slope Model

As a second step in the model-building process, you may be interested in understanding the factors that explain σ^2 and τ_{00}. This second step involves creating what is labeled a *random intercept and fixed slope model (RIFSM)*, which begins with the following equation:

$$\text{RIFSM (Level 1)} : Y_{ij} = \beta_{0j} + \beta_{1j}(X_{ij} - \bar{X}_j) + r_{ij}, \tag{10.10}$$

which is identical to Equation 10.1. The next step in the process of building the random intercept and fixed slope model involves adding the L2 equations as follows[35]:

$$\text{RIFSM (Level 2)}: \beta_{0j} = \gamma_{00} + \gamma_{01}\left(W_j - \overline{W}\right) + u_{0j}, \tag{10.11}$$

where the team intercepts are shown to be a function of the grand mean (i.e., averaged across all teams), intercept γ_{00}, and a residual term u_{0j} that describes how teams deviate from the grand mean, after controlling for team leadership. Also, γ_{01} is interpreted as the amount of change in a team's average empowerment score associated with a 1-unit increase in leadership climate. In this model, the slopes are not allowed to vary across teams, and hence,

$$\text{RIFSM (Level 2)}: \beta_{1j} = \gamma_{10}, \tag{10.12}$$

which leads to the following combined model:

$$\textit{RIFSM (Combined)}: Y_{ij} = \gamma_{00} + \gamma_{10}\left(X_{ij} - \overline{X}_j\right) + \gamma_{01}\left(W_j - \overline{W}\right) + u_{0j} + r_{ij} \tag{10.13}$$

Note that Equation 10.13 is called a random intercept and fixed slope model because it allows intercepts (i.e., mean scores) to vary across teams by the inclusion of u_{0j}. However, as shown in Equation 10.12, slopes cannot vary across teams. Instead, as shown in Equation 10.13, one fixed value for the slope of empowerment on LMX scores (i.e., γ_{10}) is used for all individuals regardless of team membership. In other words, the relationship between LMX and empowerment is assumed to be identical across all teams (similar to the assumption in ANCOVA.[36] In sum, Equation 10.13 predicts individual empowerment scores based on a common intercept γ_{00}, individual LMX scores (L1 predictor) reflected by the coefficient γ_{10}, and leadership climate (L2 predictor) reflected by the coefficient γ_{01}. In other words, γ_{01} assesses the possible presence of a cross-level direct effect (i.e., the effect of leadership climate on individual empowerment) controlling for individual-level LMX scores and, therefore, explains at least part of τ_{00} identified in the first step of the model building process.

In Equation 10.13, γ_{00} represents mean empowerment for a team with a leadership climate score at the mean $\overline{W}$, γ_{01} is the amount of change in a team's average empowerment score associated with a 1-unit increase in leadership climate, and u_{0j} is a residual term (i.e., errors) in predicting teams' average empowerment after controlling for L2 variable leadership climate. Note that W_j is re-scaled by the average team leadership climate ($\overline{W}$) to interpret γ_{00} in reference to $\overline{W}$. As in Equation 10.1, you can re-scale W_j using other values, leading to a different interpretation for γ_{00}. In this example, γ_{01} is the predicted slope for regressing empowerment on leadership climate for teams with a mean leadership climate score of $\overline{W}$.

With regard to the illustrative example, results presented in Table 10.2 indicate that mean empowerment for a team with a leadership climate score at the mean $\overline{W}$ is $\gamma_{00} = 5.72$. Table 10.2 also shows that a 1-unit increase in leadership climate is associated with a $\gamma_{01} = .351$ increase in a team's average empowerment score. Also, Table 10.2 shows that the predicted slope regressing empowerment on LMX is $\gamma_{10} = .279$. In short, results provide evidence in support of a direct single-level effect (i.e., individual LMX on individual empowerment) and a direct cross-level effect (i.e., team-level leadership climate on individual-level empowerment).

Step 3: Random Intercept and Random Slope Model

The third step in the model-building process involves examining whether the third key source of variance, the variance of slopes across groups (i.e., τ_{11}), differs from zero. In other words, you want to know if the relationship between LMX scores and empowerment varies across teams. If such variance is non-existent, there is no point in examining which moderators may explain slope variance across teams. To do so, you must build a *random intercept and random slope model (RIRSM)* that adds a random slope component so that β_{1j} can vary across teams.

First, as usual, you begin with the L1 equation (identical to Equation 10.1):

$$\text{RIRSM (Level 1):} Y_{ij} = \beta_{0j} + \beta_{1j}\left(X_{ij} - \overline{X}_j\right) + r_{ij}. \qquad (10.14)$$

Then, you allow both intercepts and slopes to vary across teams as follows:

$$\text{RIRSM (Level 2):} \beta_{0j} = \gamma_{00} + \gamma_{01}\left(W_j - \overline{W}\right) + u_{0j} \qquad (10.15)$$
$$\text{RIRSM (Level 2):} \beta_{1j} = \gamma_{10} + u_{1j}. \qquad (10.16)$$

In Equation 10.16, the slope of empowerment on LMX scores is a function of the grand mean (i.e., estimated across all teams) slope γ_{10} and a residual term u_{1j} that describes how team slopes differ from the pooled slope across teams. Substituting Equations 10.15 and 10.16 into Equation 10.14 yields the combined random intercept and random slope model as follows:

$$\begin{aligned}
&\text{RIRSM (Combined):}\\
&Y_{ij} = \gamma_{00} + \gamma_{01}\left(W_j - \overline{W}\right) + \gamma_{10}\left(X_{ij} - \overline{X}_j\right) + u_{0j} + u_{1j}\left(X_{ij} - \overline{X}_j\right) + r_{ij}
\end{aligned} \qquad (10.17)$$

A comparison of the combined random intercept and fixed slope model (Equation 10.13) with the random intercept and random slope model (Equation 10.17) seems to suggest that the only difference is that in the latter, you allow the slope of empowerment on LMX to vary across teams by the inclusion of u_{1j} and its variance τ_{11}. However, one additional parameter estimate must be more explicit in the model: The covariance between intercepts and slopes, denoted by τ_{01}. Thus, the random intercept and random slope model includes two parameters that are not part of the random intercept and fixed slope model: τ_{11} and τ_{01}. Referring to the illustrative example, a positive value of τ_{01} means that teams with steeper slopes (i.e., stronger relationship) of empowerment on LMX tend to have higher team empowerment levels.

Based on Equation 10.17, you can examine the standard error estimate, which is standard output in most software packages such as HLM and SAS, to answer whether the variance of the residuals u_{1j} (i.e., τ_{11}) is non-zero.[37] Specifically, the output file in some software packages includes a confidence interval computed based on the standard error for the estimate of τ_{11}. If the lower bound does not include zero, then you can conclude that the slope of empowerment on LMX scores varies across teams. However, despite its availability in many software packages, creating a confidence interval around τ_{11} can lead to incorrect conclusions. There are two reasons for this. First, standard errors for the variance components of the model, such as τ_{11}, are usually inaccurate. In fact, "The estimates of the variances are unbiased, but the standard errors are not always accurate" (p. 437).[38] Second, a confidence interval is created by adding and subtracting the same value, such as 1.96 for a 95% interval, and, therefore, the assumption is that the parameter estimate is normally distributed, which is "doubtful for estimated variances; for example, because these are necessarily nonnegative" (p. 100).[39] Accordingly, a better alternative for creating a confidence interval around τ_{11} is to implement a nonparametric residual bootstrap procedure.[40] This procedure to compute the confidence interval is also supported by theoretical evidence regarding its accuracy.[41]

A second option in understanding whether τ_{11} is different from zero is to compute a –2 log-likelihood ratio between Equation 10.17 (i.e., a model with a random slope component) and Equation 10.13 (i.e., a model without a random slope component).[42] A **log-likelihood value** quantifies the probability that the model being estimated produced the sample data.[43] Multiplying the log-likelihood value by –2 yields a value labeled "**deviance**," which can be used to compare the relative fit of two competing models. When **full information maximum likelihood (FIML)** is used, the deviance value shows how well the variance-covariance estimates (i.e., τ_{00}, τ_{01}, and τ_{11}) *and* the regression coefficients fit the sample data. However, when **restricted maximum likelihood (REML)** is used, the deviance value shows how well only the variance estimates fit the data, and the regression coefficients play no role in this computation. So, either FIML or REML can be used to assess whether τ_{11} is non-zero, but FIML should be used if there is an interest in comparing models regarding coefficients in addition to variance components.

Referring to the illustrative example, the researchers implemented the nonparametric bootstrap procedure and included 1,500 replications (i.e., 1,500 samples from the data with replacement). As a result, they found that the 95% bootstrap confidence interval for τ_{11} excluded zero and ranged from .004 to .046. Also, results shown in Table 10.2 indicate that, based on FIML, the model at Step 3 fits the data better than the model at Step 2, also suggesting a non-zero τ_{11} (i.e., deviance of 1,469; $p < .05$). Table 10.2 also includes deviance statistics comparing the model at Step 2 with the one at Step 1 (i.e., deviance of 1,478; $p < .01$), and the model at Step 4 compared to the model at Step 3 (i.e., deviance of 1,462; $p < .01$). The researchers also computed deviance statistics using REML, and found that the values became smaller (i.e., better fit) as they progressed through the models. However, as expected, the deviance statistics were overall larger (i.e., worse fit) than FIML because REML estimates compute fit based on differences in variance components only.

Note that each test above regarding the hypothesis that τ_{11} is zero relies on **null hypothesis significance testing**. Thus, like all such tests of significance, statistical power is an important consideration. In other words, to be informative, such tests need sufficient power to detect an existing non-zero value of τ_{11} in the population. Tests regarding τ_{11} rely on degrees of freedom determined by the number of L2 units (e.g., teams), which is usually much smaller than a study's total sample size regarding lower-level units (e.g., individual employees).

METHODS IN PRACTICE
CONSEQUENCES OF TYPICAL LEVEL 1 AND LEVEL 2 SAMPLE SIZES

The median L1 sample sizes in three social and behavioral science journals are 198, 204, and 161.[44] In contrast, multilevel research's median L2 sample size is only 51.[45] Given that most same-level research relying on degrees of freedom based on total sample size is notoriously underpowered[46] and that multilevel modeling is usually conducted with L2 sample sizes that are much smaller, many tests regarding τ_{11} may also be underpowered. In other words, there may be an incorrect conclusion that τ_{11} is not different from zero due to insufficient statistical power. To balance Type I and Type II error considerations, you should proceed with the cross-level interaction test even when the null hypothesis of no slope variance is retained when there is a solid theory-based rationale for a particular hypothesis. Also, the result that the null hypothesis that τ_{11} is zero was not rejected should be acknowledged explicitly so that future research can attempt to replicate the results obtained.

Using a typical χ^2 critical value with two degrees of freedom (one for τ_{11} and one for τ_{01}) to compare the models is overly conservative (i.e., likely to lead to a Type II error rate—not reject a false null hypothesis of no difference between the models). Accordingly, as a third option in understanding whether τ_{11} differs from zero, a more appropriate distribution for such tests is a mixture of two chi-square distributions.[47] Subsequently, some developed a method that simulates the deviance for the model with only a random intercept when testing whether the variance of slopes is significant.[48] Others demonstrated that the procedure is superior to competing tests (e.g., F-tests and tests that use critical values from a mixture of chi-square distributions) in terms of controlling Type I error rates and has similar statistical power.[49] This procedure evaluates whether the variance component differs from zero by calculating the proportion of simulated deviances that exceed the sample deviance (i.e., the p-value). Using the data from the illustrative example, results indicated that the p-value is 0.0013, and the bootstrap resampling results indicated that the 95% confidence interval for τ_{11} excludes zero and ranges from .004 to .046.

In sum, results based on the illustrative data file suggest that the relationship between LMX and individual empowerment varies depending on team membership. More precisely, results summarized in Table 10.2 shows that the variance in slopes across groups is τ_{11} = .025, and results based on the bootstrap confidence interval, the –2 log-likelihood, and the **Crainiceanu and Ruppert (2004)[50] test** suggest that this value is unlikely to be zero in the population. Therefore, these results provide evidence supporting team-level differences in the relationship between LMX and individual empowerment, suggesting the need to understand the variable(s) that explain such variability.

Step 4: Cross-level Interaction Model

The fourth and final step in the model-building process involves understanding whether a particular L2 variable can explain at least part of the slope variance across teams. Again, referring to the illustrative example, you may want to know whether leadership climate moderates the relationship between LMX and empowerment across teams. To do so, you begin building the *cross-level interaction model* with Equation 10.18 (identical to Equation 10.1):

$$\text{Cross-level Interaction Model (Level 1)}: Y_{ij} = \beta_{0j} + \beta_{1j}\left(X_{ij} - \overline{X}_j\right) + r_{ij} \qquad (10.18)$$

Then, you allow both intercepts and slopes to vary across teams as follows:

$$\text{Cross-level Interaction Model (Level 2)}: \beta_{0j} = \gamma_{00} + \gamma_{01}\left(W_j - \overline{W}\right) + u_{0j} \qquad (10.19)$$

$$\text{Cross-level Interaction Model (Level 2)}: \beta_{1j} = \gamma_{10} + \gamma_{11}\left(W_j - \overline{W}\right) + u_{1j} \qquad (10.20)$$

The difference between Equation 10.20 (cross-level interaction model) and Equation 10.16 (random intercept and random slope model) is that Equation 10.20 includes the L2 predictor hypothesized to play a moderating role. This is because you are no longer solely interested in whether there is variance in slopes across teams—that was the purpose of the previous step. Now, you are interested in understanding whether such variance can be explained by a particular L2 predictor (i.e., leadership climate).

In Equation 10.20, the moderating effect of leadership climate on the relationship between LMX and empowerment is captured by γ_{11}. Equivalently, γ_{11} is the cross-level interaction of LMX and leadership climate on empowerment. That is, γ_{11} represents the change in the slope of empowerment on LMX scores across teams when leadership climate increases by 1 point. For example, a result that γ_{11} is positive indicates that LMX is more strongly related to empowerment in teams with a more positive leadership climate than in teams with a less positive leadership climate.

Substituting the L2 Equations 10.19 and 10.20 into the L1 Equation 10.18 leads to a combined model as follows:

Cross-level Interaction Model (Combined):

$$
\begin{aligned}
Y_{ij} = \gamma_{00} &+ \gamma_{01}\left(W_j - \overline{W}\right) \\
&+ \gamma_{10}\left(X_{ij} - \overline{X}_j\right) \\
&+ \gamma_{11}\left(X_{ij} - \overline{X}_j\right)\left(W_j - \overline{W}\right) \\
&+ u_{0j} + u_{1j}\left(X_{ij} - \overline{X}_j\right) + r_{ij}
\end{aligned}
\tag{10.21}
$$

Equation 10.21 resembles the more familiar moderated multiple regression (MMR) model, which also includes the constituent linear terms. However, in contrast to the MMR model, Equation 10.21 includes the terms involving u_{0j} and u_{1j}, which vary across L2 units and, as mentioned earlier, this is why they are labeled *random effects*. On the other hand, γ_{00}, γ_{01}, γ_{10}, and γ_{11} are constant across L2 units, so they are labeled *fixed effects*.

Results using the illustrative data provide evidence in support of the cross-level interaction effect tested. Table 10.2 shows that the slope of individual empowerment on LMX is expected to equal γ_{10} = 0.269 for teams with an average leadership climate. However, the relationship between individual LMX and individual empowerment becomes stronger, by γ_{11} = .104 units, as a team's leadership climate increases by one unit.

Finally, an issue to consider is the possibility that as a result of implementing Step 2, results may suggest a nonsignificant L1 relationship between X and Y (i.e., γ_{10} = 0). In such instances, you may hesitate to proceed with Step 3 and investigate possible cross-level interactions. However, there could be variability in group slopes, although γ_{10} = 0. Accordingly, if there is a theory-based rationale for examining cross-level interaction effects, you should proceed with Step 3 regardless of the statistical significance of the direct effect for X. Moreover, standard practice when estimating interactions is to include lower-level effects, regardless of statistical significance, and this is a correct practice for the following reason. Consider the L2 equation for slopes for Step 3 (see Equation 10.16 above). In Equation 10.16, a nonsignificant relationship between X and Y implies that $\beta_{1j} = u_{1j}$ (i.e., on average, the relationship is zero, but groups deviate from zero by u_{1j}). Consider Equation 10.20, where the cross-level interaction effect is estimated by including $W_j - \overline{W}$. In Equation 10.20, γ_{11} is the cross-level interaction effect and γ_{10} is the relationship between X and Y for groups with $W_j = \overline{W}$. It is possible that γ_{10} = 0 for Model 3 in Equation 10.16, but $\gamma_{10} \neq 0$ after W_j is included in the equation and centered by the mean or some other value. Consequently, leaving X out of Step 4 will force $\gamma_{10} = 0$ at the point where $W_j = \overline{W}$. Accordingly, you should include X in the model to account for the fact that the relationship between X and Y may not be zero for the value at which W_j is centered.

WHY YOU NEED TO EXAMINE MORE THAN JUST THE TRADITIONAL INTRACLASS CORRELATION

In multilevel modeling, there is a need to assess empirically the extent to which shared experiences and context and, more generally, the clustering of entities within collectives have led to dependence. To do so, the consistent recommendation is to assess the degree of dependence by computing the intraclass correlation as discussed earlier, which assesses the proportion of between-group variance relative to the total variance in an outcome variable and is also interpreted as the correlation between two randomly selected members of the same group. The most influential and established textbooks addressing multilevel modeling offer this same recommendation.[51] As summarized by some researchers, "the first step in a multilevel analysis is partitioning the variance in an outcome variable into its within- and between-group components. If it turns out that there is little or no variation (perhaps less than 5%) in outcomes between groups, there would be no compelling need for conducting a multilevel analysis" (p. 6).[52] The reason for this recommendation is that the intraclass correlation ρ_α assesses the proportion of between-group variance relative to the total variance in an outcome variable, and, therefore, it signals the presence of nonindependence in the data structure.

Not surprisingly, given this consistent recommendation in the methodological literature, most social and behavioral sciences researchers compute and report results regarding ICC as evidence for the presence or absence of dependence and for justifying using multilevel modeling (or not) and subsequently testing cross-level interaction hypotheses. This pervasive and commonly implemented practice is reported in virtually all articles addressing multilevel issues.[53] Although some methodological sources have raised concerns about the sole reliance on ICC,[54] using it is a consensual and well-established procedure for determining the possible presence of dependence and deciding whether the data structure requires multilevel modeling. In the same vein, if the intraclass correlation is not sufficiently high, then multilevel modeling is not considered necessary, and there needs to be more justification for assessing cross-level interaction effect hypotheses.

However, relying on the traditional intraclass correlation only captures across-group variability due to intercept differences. Thus, the ICC is, using psychometric terminology, a deficient dependence index. In other words, across-group variability may also exist due to slope differences across groups, but this is not reflected in the intraclass correlation. To address this deficiency, we also need to consider the intraclass correlation ρ_β, which is the index of the proportion of variance in criterion scores due to group differences, but the source of this variability is a difference in slopes across groups.[55] There are a few differences between the traditional ICC, which we will now refer to as ρ_α, and ρ_β. First, ρ_α is a measure of between-group differences in criterion means, is orthogonal to within group deviations from the mean (i.e., $Y_{ij} - \overline{Y}_j$, where Y_{ij} is the criterion score for the ith person in group j and $\overline{Y}_j$ represents the overall sample mean), is a function of between-group variability in intercepts and slopes, and accounts for differences in slopes that only contribute to criterion mean differences. While ρ_α incorporates some variance attributed to slope differences when subgroups differ in average predictor values, because group-mean centering explicitly fixes subgroup predictor means to zero, group-mean centering removes group slope differences related variance from ρ_a. Second, slope variability across groups contributes to variability in $Y_{ij} - \overline{Y}_j$, which is a portion of variability attributed to between-group differences that is not quantified by ρ_a, and the extent to which slope differences affect differences in $\overline{Y}_j$ is a function of subgroup predictor mean differences. Third, the portion of the variance in $Y_{ij} - \overline{Y}_j$ attributed to slope differences is not a function of covariances between intercepts and slopes.

The differences between ρ_a and ρ_β have important implications for how you conduct data analysis and for model selection. For example, if you base your judgment about using multilevel modeling solely on ρ_a, you will mistakenly ignore important between-group slope variance. Consequently, you may incorrectly conclude that using OLS regression instead of multilevel modeling is appropriate. Moreover, this decision would also result in your not estimating cross-level interaction effects.

Another implication of this other source of variance is that relying solely on the traditional ICC can lead you to conclude that group differences only account for a marginal portion of the variance in the outcome. However, suppose you consider both ρ_a and ρ_β. In that case, you might find that group differences in means and slopes account for a significantly larger proportion of the dependent variable variance. Consequently, using only ρ_a as an index of group differences would miss the variance attributed to group slope differences and reduce the total reported variance attributed to group differences.

An additional consideration concerns the magnitude of ρ_β. Specifically, the ρ_β values may often seem small—perhaps leading to the conclusion that searching for cross-level interaction effects is futile. However, this conclusion is not warranted for the following reasons. First, ICC values of about .05 represent a small to medium effect and "values as small as .05 may provide prima facie evidence of a group effect" (p. 838).[56] Recent evidence reinforces this recommendation that traditional effect size guidelines overestimate the effects usually reported in social and behavioral science research.[57] Second, ICC values should be considered within specific contexts because small observed effects may result from inauspicious designs, studies involving phenomena leading to obscure consequences, and studies challenging fundamental assumptions.[58] Third, numerous methodological and statistical artifacts decrease the observed effect sizes compared to their true population counterparts.[59] Accordingly, it is likely that, in many cases, and due to methodological and statistical artifacts, observed variability in slopes as indicated by ρ_β is larger in the population than has been estimated. Fourth, in some cases, small effect sizes may be practically significant.[60] Thus, when the phenomena of interest have important implications for theory or practice, even small values for ρ_β may indicate the need to assess particular cross-level interaction hypotheses.

Because ρ_a and ρ_β index are different sources of group-based variance, you should compute both when conducting multilevel modeling or suspect non-independence in your data structure. Relying solely on ρ_a as the sole decision criterion may lead you to incorrectly use data-analytic approaches that require independence among observations and an opportunity cost in testing precise cross-level interaction effect hypotheses. In contrast, using both ρ_a and ρ_β improves the assessment of cross-level interaction effects, which play an important role in contemporary social and behavioral sciences theory and practice.

BEST-PRACTICE RECOMMENDATIONS FOR CONDUCTING AND REPORTING MULTILEVEL ANALYSIS AND CROSS-LEVEL INTERACTION EFFECTS

The final part of this chapter addresses important questions about what you should do before and after data collection to improve the accuracy of substantive conclusions regarding multilevel analysis and tests of cross-level interactions. Table 10.3 lists these recommendations, which are described in more detail next.

Pre-Data Collection Recommendations

Issue #1: What is the Operational Definition of a Cross-level Interaction Effect?

A frequently asked question regarding cross-level interaction effects refers to the very definition of this effect. First, there is a question of whether τ_{11} (i.e., the variance of slopes across groups) is the cross-level interaction effect. Second, there is a question of whether γ_{11} in the hierarchical linear model in Equation 10.20 can truly be called an interaction effect given that it is associated with a term that does not involve a product between two variables but with one variable only (i.e., W).

First, let's consider τ_{11}. A non-zero τ_{11} means that the slope of the L1 criterion on the L1 predictor varies across higher-level units (e.g., teams). Referring back to the illustrative example, a non-zero τ_{11} means that the effect of LMX on empowerment is not homogeneous across teams. However, this heterogeneity may be due to one or more potential L2 moderators. In this example, the researchers tested the potential moderating effect of leadership climate. However, they could have considered additional moderators instead or in addition to leadership climate. Thus, similar to the assessment of moderating effects in the context of meta-analysis, heterogeneity indicates that searching for particular moderators is warranted, but this is not the interaction effect *per se*.[61]

Now, consider the meaning of γ_{11} in the context of two extreme situations. First, assume that γ_{11} in Equation 10.20 is zero. This would mean that L2 variable W does not explain variance in the slope of the L1 *Y* outcome on the L1 X predictor across teams. Thus, for every unit increase in the higher-order variable (W), the relationship (slope) between L1 X and L1 Y remains unchanged. Now, assume that γ_{11} in Equation 10.20 is a very large and positive number, which implies that a small change in the value of W is associated with a large change in the slope of L1 outcome Y on L1 predictor X across teams. Thus, a non-zero γ_{11} means that the L1 effect of X on Y is distributed across L2 units—and this is the reason why some researchers used the term *distributive effect* to refer to the cross-level interaction effect.[62]

The fact that γ_{11} represents the cross-level interaction effect, also labeled the moderating effect of W on the X-Y relationship, is perhaps seen more easily by referring to the combined Equation 10.21. In Equation 10.21, which has a familiar form that closely matches that of MMR, γ_{11} is associated with the product term between re-scaled L1 predictor X and re-scaled L2 predictor W. In contrast, in the L2 Equation 10.20, γ_{11} is a coefficient predicting slope values, a model not as familiar to social and behavioral science researchers compared to a model that predicts criterion Y scores.

In sum, the coefficient γ_{11} is interpreted as the cross-level interaction effect regardless of whether it is obtained by using Equation 10.20 (i.e., predicting β_{1j} based on $\left(W_j - \overline{W}\right)$) or Equation 10.21 (i.e., predicting Y_{ij} based on $\left(X_{ij} - \overline{X}_j\right)\left(W_j - \overline{W}\right)$). The variance of slopes across groups τ_{11} is not the cross-level interaction effect because, although it provides information on

TABLE 10.3 ■ Summary of Best-Practice Recommendations for Conducting Multilevel Analysis and Estimating Cross-Level Interaction Effects

Pre-Data Collection Recommendations

- *Recommendation #1: Defining the Cross-level Interaction Effect.* Clearly and unambiguously identify and define the cross-level interaction effect. For example, in the combined Level 1 and Level 2 equation, the cross-level interaction effect is the coefficient associated with the product term between the Level 1 and Level 2 predictors.

- *Recommendation #2: Calculating Statistical Power.* Design the multilevel study to have sufficient statistical power to detect an existing cross-level interaction effect. Use the program at https://hermanaguinis.com to understand trade-offs in research design and measurement choices and allocate resources accordingly. Compute power after data collection if the cross-level interaction effect is not found. If power was sufficient, then you can have confidence that the effect does not exist in the population; if power was insufficient, then report the power value obtained and that results are inconclusive because of the possibility that the population effect exists but was not detected in the sample.

- *Recommendation #3: Testing Hypotheses about Different Types of Moderator Variables.* Plan to test hypotheses about cross-level interaction effects involving Level 2 continuous or categorical variables, but be aware of resulting differences in interpreting the observed effect.

Post Data Collection Recommendations

- *Recommendation #4: Determine Potential Sources of Variance in the Model.* Assess the degree of dependence by computing both the traditional intraclass correlation ρ_a (which assesses the proportion of between-group variance relative to the total variance in an outcome variable or the correlation between two randomly selected members of the same group) and ρ_β (which is the index of the proportion of variance in criterion scores due to group differences, but the source of this variability is a difference in slopes across groups).

- *Recommendation #5: Re-scaling (i.e., Centering) Predictor Variables.* In most cases, center the Level 1 predictor by team mean scores (i.e., group-mean centering) to improve the interpretation of the cross-level interaction effect. However, theory-based considerations should dictate the chosen approach to re-scaling.

- *Recommendation #6: Graphing the Cross-level Interaction.* Graph the cross-level interaction effect to understand its nature and direction. However, do not use the graph to draw conclusions about the size or importance of the effect. You can graph your interaction using a program available at https://hermanaguinis.com/

- *Recommendation #7: Interpreting Cross-level Interaction Effects.* Interpret the Level 1 or Level 2 predictor as the moderator based on substantive and conceptual interests because the cross-level interaction effect is symmetrical. In most cases, the Level 2 (or higher-level) predictor will serve the role of the moderator variable.

- *Recommendation #8: Estimating Multiple Cross-level Interaction Effects.* Include all cross-level interactions effects as part of the same model when testing more than one cross-level interaction effect. However, strong theory-based considerations and other situations (e.g., models may not converge, they may crash, or run out of degrees of freedom) may justify conducting a separate test with each interaction effect.

- *Recommendation #9: Testing Cross-level Interactions Involving Three or More Levels of Analysis.* Conduct tests of three-way and higher-order cross-level interaction effects following the same procedures as those for two-way interactions. However, be mindful that adequate sample sizes will be required for each level.

- *Recommendation #10: Assessing Practical Significance.* Compute the size of the cross-level interaction effect based on its predictive power and explanatory power. Then, place effect sizes within context to understand their importance for theory and practice.

Source: Adapted from Aguinis & Culpepper (2015); Aguinis, Gottfredson, & Culpepper (2013). Reproduced with permission.

the extent to which the slope of the L1 criterion on the L1 predictor varies across higher-level units (e.g., teams), it does not provide information on the particular variable(s) that are associated with this variability. The interpretation of the cross-level interaction effect γ_{11} will depend on the approach adopted regarding re-scaling, which is dictated by theory-based considerations. These problems are discussed in more detail in Issue #4.

Issue #2: What is the Statistical Power to Detect an Existing Cross-level Interaction Effect?

A second pre-data collection question refers to research design and statistical power. Specifically, you may want to know how large the sample size should be to detect existing cross-level interaction effects. As described earlier, the power to detect cross-level interactions is determined primarily by the magnitude of the cross-level interaction effect, the variance of L1 slopes across L2 units, and by L1 and L2 sample sizes. For the case of detecting cross-level interaction effects, the average L1 sample size has a relative premium of about 3:2 compared to the L2 sample size. Ultimately, the decision to focus on maximizing L1 versus L2 sample sizes may come down to what other parameters are of interest in your investigation. For example, if you want to test a lower-level direct effect along with the cross-level interaction, L1 sample sizes may be the most important. Alternatively, you can emphasize the number of L2 units sampled to test cross-level direct effects.

METHODS IN PRACTICE
CALCULATING STATISTICAL POWER

You can use a program available at https://hermanaguinis.com to estimate the power of your cross-level interaction test before data collection. The program can be used to gather important information to solve a dilemma regarding the decision to increase the number of L1 compared to L2 units. For example, you can use the program under two different scenarios. Hypothetical Scenario A could increase the number of individuals per team by 5. Hypothetical Scenario B would involve holding the number of individuals per team constant but increasing the number of teams from 50 to 80 instead. Using these different values as input in the power calculator allows for an understanding of the statistical power associated with each of these scenarios, and results can be used for design planning and as a guide in making more informed and better decisions about allocating resources before data collection. In addition, the power calculator can also be used to make better-informed decisions about substantive conclusions. Specifically, suppose a cross-level interaction effect hypothesis is not supported, and the power calculator suggests that power was sufficient. In that case, you can have confidence that the effect does not exist in the population. On the other hand, if power was insufficient, then you need to report the power value obtained and, unfortunately, report that results are inconclusive because of the possibility that the population effect exists but was not detected in the sample.

In sum, given the possible trade-offs between L1 and L2 sample sizes as well as interactive effects of the various factors on power (e.g., size of the cross-level interaction effect, the variance of L1 slopes across L2 units), you should not rely on popular rules of thumb such as the "30-30 rule,"[63] or assume that a particular sample size is sufficient to detect an existing effect.[64] Instead, it would be best to use the simulation-based power calculator[65] *a priori* to make decisions about research design features and post hoc to understand whether published studies reached sufficient levels of statistical power to detect existing effects.

Issue #3: Can Cross-level Interaction Effects Involving a Categorical L2 or Standardized Predictor Be Tested?

A third issue refers to the possibility that the multilevel model may include an L2 variable that is not continuous but has discrete categories (e.g., old vs. new compensation system). In other words, the question is whether you can test a hypothesis about cross-level interaction effects involving a L2 predictor that is categorical. Fortunately, this is possible. However, similar to using categorical predictors in the context of MMR,[66] the interpretation of the cross-level interaction effect is about differences in relationships between two or more groups. Specifically referring to Equation 10.21, γ_{11} is interpreted as a change in the slope of Y on X across teams associated with a 1-unit change in W. Now, assume that W is a binary variable that was coded as 1 = new compensation system and 0 = old compensation system. Referring to the illustrative example, the hypothesis is that the relationship between LMX scores and empowerment across teams will vary as a function of the compensation system. For example, if γ_{11} = 1.5, its interpretation is that the slope of Y on X is 1.5 points larger for teams in the new compensation system (i.e., coded as 1) compared to teams in the old compensation system (i.e., coded as 0). In other words, a stronger relationship exists between LMX and empowerment for individuals working in teams under the new compensation system. If the binary moderator is group-mean centered, the mean is a proportion of the category scored 1. Still, the interpretation is similar in that the coefficient refers to changes in the slope of Y on X for teams coded as 1 compared to teams coded as 0.

When the categorical L2 predictor includes more than k = 2 values, it is necessary to create $k - 1$ dummy codes added to Equation 10.21. The process is similar to creating dummy codes in the context of MMR. For example, assuming a L2 predictor with k = 3, the two dummy codes $W_{j(1)}$ (e.g., comparison of category 1 vs. 2) and $W_{j(2)}$ (e.g., comparison of category 1 vs. 3) are included in Equation 10.21 as follows:

$$
\begin{aligned}
Y_{ij} = \ & \gamma_{00} + \gamma_{01(1)}\left(W_{(1)j} - \overline{W}_{(1)}\right) \\
& + \gamma_{01(2)}\left(W_{(2)j} - \overline{W}_{(2)}\right) + \gamma_{10}\left(X_{ij} - \overline{X}_j\right) \\
& + \gamma_{11(1)}\left(X_{ij} - \overline{X}_j\right)\left(W_{j(1)} - \overline{W}_{(1)}\right) \\
& + \gamma_{11(2)}\left(X_{ij} - \overline{X}_j\right)\left(W_{j(2)} - \overline{W}_{(2)}\right) + u_{0j} \\
& + u_{1j}\left(X_{ij} - \overline{X}_j\right) + r_{ij}
\end{aligned}
\tag{10.22}
$$

Note that, similar to the situation involving two categories only, interpreting the cross-level interaction effect coefficients must consider which category was coded as 1 and 0 for each dummy variable. So, for example, assuming that the categories are three locations: (a) Colorado, (b) Indiana, and (c) Texas, and that $W_{j(1)}$ involves a comparison of Colorado (coded as 1) and Texas (coded as 0). A statistically significant $\gamma_{11(1)}$ = 2 would mean that the slope of empowerment on LMX is 2 points larger for teams in Colorado compared to teams in Texas.

Finally, you may choose to standardize predictors (i.e., re-scale raw scores so they have a mean of zero and standard deviation of one) to be able to interpret results referring to SD units instead of the units used in the original scales (e.g., 7-point Likert type scales) and in such situations, referring back to Equation 10.21, γ_{11} is the expected change in the size of the slope of LMX on empowerment in SD units that is associated with a 1-SD unit increase in the L2 predictor (i.e., leadership climate).

Post Data Collection Recommendations

Issue #4: What Sources of Potential Variance Should I Examine?

The appropriateness and usefulness of multilevel modeling rest on the presence of dependence among the data. In other words, the outcome of interest is affected by influences emanating from the same level and higher levels of analysis. As described earlier, in addition to the traditional ICC (i.e., ρ_α), which only captures variance due to intercept differences, you should also calculate ρ_β, which gives you information about the proportion of variance in criterion scores due to group differences, where the source of this variability is a difference in slopes across groups. Using both indices together helps you mitigate lost opportunity costs by testing precise cross-level interaction effect hypotheses, while improving the assessment of cross-level interaction effects, which play an important role in contemporary social and behavioral science theory and practice.

Issue #5: How Should I Re-scale (i.e., Center) Predictors and Why?

As noted earlier, re-scaling predictors is common when conducting multilevel analyses to help interpret results.[67] The two main re-scaling approaches are group-mean centering and **grand-mean centering**.[68] A third option is to not re-scale predictors at all, but this is not recommended because the resulting parameter estimates will be uninterpretable in many situations. Specifically, if you use raw (i.e., uncentered) scores instead of re-scaled scores, β_{0j} in Equation 1 represents the predicted level of empowerment for an LMX score of zero. But, this would be a meaningless interpretation because the LMX scale ranges from 1 to 7 and does not include zero as a possible value. Moreover, an LMX score of zero may not be meaningful at the construct level because it is possible to have a low or high LMX, but it is not possible to have no LMX. Most social and behavioral science measures do not have a true zero value because they are not ratio. Thus, re-scaling is needed in most studies in these domains. Alternatively, some financial measures do have a meaningful zero point (e.g., return on assets, return on investment[69]) so, in these cases, re-scaling may not be needed.

Group-mean centering changes the mean and correlation structure of the data, causing the L1 predictors to be uncorrelated with the L2 predictors. Alternatively, grand-mean centering involves using the mean of all scores at a particular level. In the illustrative example, using group-mean centering for the L1 predictor scores means interpreting the resulting coefficients in reference to team-level average LMX scores. However, grand-mean centering the L1 predictor would involve using the mean LMX scores across all individuals and grand-mean centering the L2 predictor would involve using the mean team leadership score across all teams. A significant concern regarding using grand-mean centering for the L1 predictor is that γ_{11} (i.e., cross-level interaction effect coefficient) conflates the between-team and within-team effects. In other words, using grand-mean centering for the L1 predictor leads to a cross-level interaction effect coefficient that is a "mixed bag" of two separate effects: (a) a true cross-level interaction involving the upper-level moderator and the within-group variance of the lower-level predictor (which is what you are interested in estimating), and (b) a between-level interaction (i.e., an interaction between the upper-level moderator and the between-group variance of the lower-level predictor). Thus, some have argued that using grand-mean centering for the L1 predictor does not allow for an accurate and meaningful interpretation of the cross-level interaction effect.[70] Accordingly, the recommendation is that group-mean centering leads to the most accurate estimates of within-group slopes and minimizes the possibility of finding spurious cross-level interaction effects.[71]

Although group-mean centering has been recommended, overall, as the best strategy for testing cross-level interaction hypotheses, it is important to recognize that such a choice needs to reflect theoretical processes related to deviations from a group average (e.g., social comparison effects in team research). Moreover, some researchers noted that "spurious cross-level interactions are rare, so one can generally use….grand-mean-centered variables to test for cross-level interactions as long as one runs an additional model with group-mean-centered variables to check for spurious interaction effects" (p. 433).[72] The alternative grand mean centering strategy would involve controlling for between-group variance by estimating the interaction between the L2 predictor and the group averages for the L1 constituent linear terms. One advantage of group-mean centering is that the resulting model includes fewer parameter estimates because there is no need to control for across-group variance (i.e., group-mean centering addresses this issue). However, estimating cross-level interactions using group-mean centering has a different substantive interpretation than estimating interactions using grand-mean centering. Specifically, using group-mean centering suggests that testing interactions needs to reflect theoretical processes addressing deviations from a group average such as in frog pond/social comparison effects in studies of teams. However, not all theories specifically refer to deviations from group averages or have reached that level of sophistication. In some situations, it may be more appropriate to use grand-mean centering with across-group variance controlled because a theory may address raw differences between L1 entities, not differences relative to a group average.

In short, group-mean centering the L1 predictor is the recommended approach in most situations when there is an interest in testing hypotheses about cross-level interaction effects. However, in some situations, it may be more appropriate to use grand-mean centering with across-group variance controlled because a particular conceptualization may address raw differences between L1 entities rather than differences relative to a group average. Thus, the choice for a re-scaling approach must be accompanied by a theory-based justification regarding the underlying process being modeled.

Issue #6: How Can I Graph a Cross-level Interaction Effect?

Another question is how to produce graphs to illustrate a cross-level interaction effect. Similar to the single-level context, graphs can illustrate the nature of the interaction effect, but should not be used to draw conclusions about the size or importance of the effect.[73] For example, considering the combined model in Equation 10.21, the expected value of Y_{ij} conditioned on values of X_{ij} and W_j can be written as:

$$E\left(Y_{ij}|X_{ij}, W_j\right) = \gamma_{00} + \gamma_{01}\left(W_j - \overline{W}\right) + \gamma_{10}\left(X_{ij} - \overline{X}_j\right) + \gamma_{11}\left(X_{ij} - \overline{X}_j\right)\left(W_j - \overline{W}\right) \quad (10.23)$$
$$= \gamma_{00} + \gamma_{01}\left(W_j - \overline{W}\right) + \left(\gamma_{10} + \gamma_{11}\left(W_j - \overline{W}\right)\right)\left(X_{ij} - \overline{X}_j\right) \quad (10.24)$$

In Equation 10.24, the relationship between X_{ij} and Y_{ij} is represented by the term preceding $X_{ij} - \overline{X}_j$, namely $\gamma_{10} + \gamma_{11}\left(W_j - \overline{W}\right)$. If W_j is a continuous variable, Equation 10.24 can be used to plot the X-Y relationship for any value for W_j. The equation describing the relationship between X and Y for a specific value of W_j is called a *simple regression equation* and the slope of Y on X at a single value of W_j is called a *simple slope*.

METHODS IN PRACTICE
PLOTTING INTERACTIONS

There are specific examples and a description of computer programs in SAS, SPSS, and R that allow the creation of plots to more easily understand the nature of the interaction effect, including plotting simple slopes.[74] These programs also allow for plotting **regions of significance**, which are values of W between which the simple slope of Y on X is statistically significant.

Equation 10.24 can also be used to plot the interaction effect in cases where W_j is a binary L2 variable that takes on the values of 0 and 1. Also, if W_j is a binary variable, it is easier to interpret the model coefficients if W_j is not re-scaled. Consequently, the predicted values of Y_{ij} for the two groups defined by W_j are:

$$E\left(Y_{ij}|X_{ij}, W_j = 0\right) = \gamma_{00} + \gamma_{10}\left(X_{ij} - \overline{X}_j\right) \tag{10.25}$$
$$E\left(Y_{ij}|X_{ij}, W_j = 1\right) = \gamma_{00} + \gamma_{01} + (\gamma_{10} + \gamma_{11})\left(X_{ij} - \overline{X}_j\right) \tag{10.26}$$

Now, the X-Y relationship can be plotted for each group. To do so, you can use values of 1 standard deviation below the mean, the mean, and one standard deviation above the mean for X. These particular values are recommended because they allow for an understanding of the nature of the relationship across a wide range of X scores.[75] Moreover, it may also be helpful to choose additional values that may be informative in specific contexts.

One important issue to when plotting interactions is to consider the axis for the Y scale. In many published articles, researchers use reduced scales for the Y axis (e.g., 4 scale points instead of 7). However, such reduction in the scale gives the false impression that the effect is more important because the slopes seem steeper and more different. So, it is acceptable to reduce the axis length to understand the interaction's nature. But, it is not acceptable to do so and then make statements about how "important" an effect is given the degree of steepness of the slope on the graph.

Issue #7: Are Cross-level Interaction Effects Symmetrical?

Another issue related to interpreting cross-level interaction effects is whether such effects are symmetrical. In other words, can you say that the L2 variable moderates the effect of the L1 predictor on the L1 criterion, and that the L1 predictor moderates the effect of the L2 predictor on the L1 criterion? From a statistical standpoint, it is just as appropriate to label the L2 predictor as the moderator of the effect of the L1 predictor X on the L1 outcome Y as it is to label the L1 predictor X as the moderator of the effect of the L2 predictor W on the L1 outcome Y because cross-level interactions are symmetrical. In multilevel modeling, it is usually the case that L2 is labeled as the moderator because, conceptually, it seems more appropriate to frame the higher-level variable as the contextual factor that affects the relationship between lower-level variables.

Specifically, in the discussion of how to graph cross-level interaction effects, the L2 variable was used as the moderator. However, referring back to Equation 10.21, the value for γ_{11} is the same whether it is associated with $\left(X_{ij} - \overline{X}_j\right)\left(W_j - \overline{W}\right)$ or with $\left(W_j - \overline{W}\right)\left(X_{ij} - \overline{X}_j\right)$. Thus, the choice to interpret W or X as the moderator is based on conceptual reasons.

Referring back to the illustrative example, the cross-level interaction effect hypothesis could be stated using either of the following forms:

Hypothesis 1a—L2 moderator: The effect of individual LMX on individual empowerment will be moderated by leadership climate such that higher levels of leadership climate will lead to a stronger LMX-empowerment relationship compared to lower values of leadership climate.

Hypothesis 1b—L1 moderator: The effect of leadership climate on individual empowerment will be moderated by individual LMX such that higher levels of LMX will lead to a stronger leadership climate-empowerment relationship compared to lower values of LMX.

In short, a substantive interest in studying either the L2 or the L1 predictor as a moderator dictates how you will conceptualize the nature of the cross-level interaction effect. However, L2 is usually labeled as the moderator due to conceptual reasons. Choices about how to phrase the cross-level interaction effect hypothesis and graph the effect will follow directly from the choice of which variable is labeled the moderator.

Issue #8: How Can I Estimate More Than One Cross-level Interaction Effect?

Also related to post data collection issues are questions about more complex models. For example, assume you are interested in testing two cross-level interactions: (a) interaction between L2 predictor W and L1 predictor X on Y, and (b) interaction between L2 predictor Z and L1 predictor X on Y. A frequent question is whether testing these hypotheses should be done sequentially in separate models or simultaneously in one single model including both $\left(X_{ij} - \overline{X}_j\right)\left(W_j - \overline{W}\right)$ and $\left(X_{ij} - \overline{X}_j\right)\left(Z_j - \overline{Z}\right)$.

Overall, the recommendation is to test both interaction effects as part of one combined model so that each estimated effect is adjusted for all the theoretically relevant components. For example, suppose the hypothesized cross-level interaction effects are evaluated in separate models. These effects may be upwardly biased due to possible non-zero intercorrelations between the various interaction effects. However, given that most cross-level interaction tests are likely to be insufficient regarding statistical power (see Issue #2), a strong theory-based rationale for the presence of such effects may justify conducting the tests separately. From the perspective of a tradeoff between Type I (i.e., false positive) and Type II (i.e., false negative) statistical errors, this approach would be equivalent to conducting follow-up comparisons in ANOVA without first conducting an omnibus test.

An additional consideration when testing both interaction effects as part of one combined model is that complex models may not converge, they may crash, or run out of degrees of freedom. In such situations, and absent a strong theory-based rationale for testing models separately, the recommendation is to proceed with testing models but then report results transparently and openly.[76] In other words, it is necessary to be clear about this limitation (i.e., models were tested separately), the reason why (e.g., the combined model crashed), and the consequences of the limitation (i.e., the need to replicate results in future research due to a possible inflation of Type I error rates).[77]

Finally, an issue related to complex models, in general, is that they may not converge. Several reasons may lead to this situation. For example, a model may not converge when certain algorithms are used,[78] the random effects are highly correlated, or the model needs to be clarified (e.g., the model may be too complex for the data). There are several possible courses of action when models do not converge. An initial course of action is to use a different software program.

If the model still does not converge, a second alternative is to center predictors because centering can help reduce correlations among random intercepts and slopes.[79] Ultimately, the source of the problem may be that the model is misspecified or too complex for the data in hand. In such cases, the only solution may be to simplify the random effects structure of the model.

Issue #9: How Can I Estimate Cross-level Interaction Effects Involving Variables at Three Different Levels of Analysis?

Another issue regarding more complex models involves the possibility of testing cross-level interactions involving more than two levels of nesting. As one illustration, you may be interested in testing a three-level interaction effect of LMX (Level 1, X), leadership climate (Level 2, W), and organizational culture (Level 3, Q) on individual empowerment. In such three-level models, team-level relationships can vary across higher-level units (e.g., organizations and geographic regions). Other situations that may involve three levels of analysis are studies that rely on experience sampling methodology or other types of diaries.[80] In such situations, there are observations of individuals over time (i.e., observations are nested within individuals), and individuals are nested within units (e.g., teams). So, in this situation, there are three levels of analysis with two levels of nesting. In other words, individual growth trajectories reside at L1, differences in growth rates across individuals within teams comprise the L2 model, and the variation across teams is the L3 model.[81]

Assuming that the three levels are individuals, teams, and organizations, a three-level model requires a subscript k to distinguish various organizations. For instance, X_{ijk} is the LMX score for the ith individual who is a member of team j within organization k. Similarly, W_{jk} is the leadership climate score for team j in organization k, and Q_k is the organizational culture value for organization k. Including a third-level variable also entails adding an additional residual value: (v_{0k}). This implies the potential of additional third-level variance components: intercept variance (φ_{00}), slope variance (φ_{11}), and intercept-slope covariance (φ_{01}).

Including additional variance components allows for several kinds of ICCs to be calculated.[82] First, the proportion of total variance is explained by the L3 variable, which is $\varphi_{00}/[\varphi_{00} + \tau_{00} + \sigma^2]$. Similar ICCs can be calculated for each level. Second, the proportion of total variance explained by the L3 and L2 variables, which is $[\varphi_{00} + \tau_{00}]/[\varphi_{00} + \tau_{00} + \sigma^2]$. Third, is the proportion of variance shared by the L3 and L2 variables, which is $\varphi_{00}/[\varphi_{00} + \tau_{00}]$.

In addition to various ICCs, several different regressions can be performed for a three-level analysis. For example, for each L1 variable, there are three types of regressions: within-L2 regression, within-L3/between-L2 regression, and between-L3 regression.

Testing for complex models, such as three-level cross-level interactions, involves expanding Equation 10.21 to include all first-order effects, all two-way cross-level interaction effects, and finally the term carrying information about the three-level interaction effect: $\left(X_{ijk} - \overline{X}_{jk}\right)$ $\left(W_{jk} - \overline{W}_k\right)\left(Q_k - \overline{Q}\right)$. All issues we discussed earlier regarding two-way cross-level interactions apply to the three-level interaction context. For example, model building and centering the variables can all be generalized from a two-level model. Further, there should be a clear definition of the cross-level interaction effect, all constituent terms should be included in the equation, and so forth.

A challenge regarding tests of three-way cross-level interaction effects is that it will be necessary to collect data from multiple higher-level units to capture possible variability of L1 and L2 intercepts and slopes across L3 units. As a result, you may have to abandon hypotheses involving three-level interaction effects in many cases due to insufficient evidence regarding variation in intercepts and slopes at the third level. For example, a study involved the following three levels: (L1) classes, (L2) teachers, and (L3) schools.[83] However, "because the number of schools was small and because there was little evidence of school-to-school variation, no level-3 predictors were specified" (p. 237).

Currently, no tool allows statistical power estimation to detect three-level interaction effects. Although some research has addressed statistical power in the context of three-level models, this work refers to statistical power computations specifically for a dummy-coded treatment effect (i.e., the main effect). Still, it does not address computations regarding three-level cross-level interaction effects.[84] Nevertheless, given the increased level of complexity of the model tested and results regarding the importance of the lower-level sample size for power, and other things being equal, statistical power for detecting a three-level interaction effect is unlikely to be greater than the power to detect a two-level cross-level interaction effect. Thus, it would be best to use the power calculator when making research design decisions to ensure sufficient power to detect each of the two-level cross-level interaction effects.[85] Although this will not guarantee sufficient power, this will at least produce some evidence about the probability of detecting a three-level interaction effect. Moreover, there should be a strong theory-based rationale to posit such a complex interaction effect.

Issue #10: What Is the Practical Significance of the Cross-level Interaction Effect?

An issue related to the interpretation of results refers to the practical significance of a cross-level interaction effect. A necessary step for understanding the practical significance of the cross-level interaction effect is to estimate the strength of the effect.[86] For example, OLS regression usually estimates effect sizes based on the extent to which a variable predicts outcomes of interest (i.e., regression coefficient associated with the product term) or based on fit (i.e., the proportion of variance explained by the interaction effect, usually assessed using R^2).[87] Similar options are available in multilevel modeling, each with advantages and disadvantages. Let's describe each of these options next.

The first option is to focus on the extent to which the cross-level interaction predicts the outcome of interest, which is indicated by γ_{11}. This indicator is useful because it refers to the original data collection metric. However, the other side of the coin is that, precisely because the coefficient is scale-specific, its size depends on the measures used to assess X, Y, and W. For example, referring back to the illustrative example, if a researcher uses a 100-point scale for empowerment, the resulting cross-level interaction effect γ_{11} will be much larger than if a researcher uses a 7-point scale. Because γ_{11} provides information regarding the prediction of Y scores, it is considered an index of an interaction's *predictive power*.

A second option for assessing effect size that has the advantage of scale independence consists of focusing on the cross-level interaction's *explanatory power*: the proportion of the total variability of the slope of Y on X across teams that is explained by the L2 predictor W. To do so, refer back to Equation 10.21, in which u_{1j} is the error term, and its variance, denoted by τ_{11}, represents the total across-team variance in slopes. Equation 10.20 also shows the error term u_{1j} (i.e., the β_{1j} portion independent of W). Note that u_{1j} in Equation 10.21 is left unexplained after controlling for the effect of W, and the symbol τ_{11w} refers to the variance of this error term. Accordingly, you can calculate the proportion of total across-team variance in slopes explained specifically by W as follows:

$$\frac{\tau_{11} - \tau_{11w}}{\tau_{11}}. \tag{10.27}$$

For the illustrative example, the proportion of the total slope variance explained by the moderating effect of leadership climate can be calculated using results shown in Table 10.2. These show that $\frac{\tau_{11} - \tau_{11w}}{\tau_{11}} = \frac{.025 - .019}{.025} = .24$. In other words, W accounts for 24% of the total variance of β_{1j} across teams. This is a useful indicator of practical significance because it can be used to understand the relative importance of effects within one study and across studies, given that the metric is the proportion of variance explained.

A third, commonly used option is to estimate the effect size using a "**pseudo R^2**" metric. In multilevel modeling, you can obtain a pseudo R^2 value for each step in the model-building process, which is reported in Table 10.2 for the illustrative data. For example, for Step 2, which involves the random intercept and fixed slope model, predicted criterion scores are obtained as follows:

$$\widehat{Y}_{ij} = \gamma_{00} + \gamma_{10}\left(X_{ij} - \overline{X}_j\right) + \gamma_{01}\left(W_j - \overline{W}\right) \tag{10.28}$$

which is the same as Equation 10.13, but excluding the error terms u_{0j} and r_{ij}. As shown in Table 10.2, pseudo R^2 increased from no variance explained by the null model to 23% of variance explained by the random intercept and fixed slope model. In other words, adding the coefficient associated with the L2 predictor increased variance explained by another 23%. The computation of pseudo R^2 for Step 3, which involves the random intercept and random slope model, involves calculating the squared correlation between observed and predicted Y_{ij} scores based on Equation 10.17 and excluding the error terms u_{0j}, $u_{1j}\left(X_{ij} - \overline{X}_j\right)$ and r_{ij} as follows:

$$\widehat{Y}_{ij} = \gamma_{00} + \gamma_{01}\left(W_j - \overline{W}\right) + \gamma_{10}\left(X_{ij} - \overline{X}_j\right). \tag{10.29}$$

Note that, because the variance component is not used in predicting Y_{ij} scores, Equations 10.28 and 10.29 are identical although they predict Y_{ij} scores for different steps in the model-building process. This is why pseudo R^2 values are nearly identical for Steps 2 and 3, although a comparison of Equations 10.13 and 10.17 shows that these models are quite different. The exclusion of variance components from the computation of pseudo R^2 values explains why some results can be counterintuitive. For example, pseudo R^2 values can be smaller when predictors are added to the model. Thus, this is why some researchers noted that the computation of pseudo R^2 values "now and then leads to unpleasant surprises" (p. 109).[88]

Table 10.2 also shows that adding the cross-product term in Step 4 increases about 1% of the variance explained. Once again, however, note that predicted Y_{ij} scores are obtained using an equation that excludes terms involving variance components as follows (which is Equation 10.21 without the variance component terms u_{0j}, $u_{1j}\left(X_{ij} - \overline{X}_j\right)$, and r_{ij}):

$$\widehat{Y}_{ij} = \gamma_{00} + \gamma_{01}\left(W_j - \overline{W}\right) + \gamma_{10}\left(X_{ij} - \overline{X}_j\right) + \gamma_{11}\left(X_{ij} - \overline{X}_j\right)\left(W_j - \overline{W}\right) \tag{10.30}$$

So, this result means that an additional 1% of variance is explained by adding the γ_{11} coefficient to the model. Still, there is no information regarding variance components and their effects on the proportion of variance explained in Y_{ij} scores. A primary advantage of multilevel modeling is the decomposition of various sources of variance based on the level at which each source of variance resides. However, the computation of pseudo R^2 values does not consider these different sources of variance. In other words, pseudo R^2 values are based on the fixed portion of the models only and ignore the random terms. This is why "the estimated values for R^2 usually change only very little when random regression coefficients are included in the model" (p. 113).[89] Another weakness to this approach is that there is the potential for you to obtain a negative pseudo R^2 value, but this likely means that the model is misspecified.[90] In sum, although Table 10.2 reports pseudo R^2, it is important to understand the meaning and interpretation of these values, specifically in the context of multilevel modeling.

In sum, each of the three options for reporting effect sizes and interpreting the practical significance of a cross-level interaction effect has advantages and disadvantages. So, the recommendation is that you report all three, together with statements about how each one should be interpreted. This recommendation follows the principle of full disclosure and, following a customer-centric approach, allows readers to interpret the meaningfulness of results themselves. Moreover, also related to the customer-centric approach to reporting significant results, effect sizes should be interpreted within specific contexts, and the fact that an effect seems small in terms of the proportion of variance explained does not automatically mean that it is unimportant in terms of theory or practice.

Issue #11: What Information Should Be Reported Based on Multilevel Modeling Analyses?

Many social and behavioral sciences need clearer reporting standards regarding multilevel modeling. As a result, there is wide variability in the type of information researchers choose to present in their tables—and how that information is presented. In contrast, the American Psychological Association (APA) clearly states what information should be reported when a study includes popular and long-established techniques such as multiple regression and ANOVA.[91] Although the APA Publication Manual does not refer to multilevel modeling at all, it does include a "Sample Multilevel Model Table" that can be used when reporting multilevel modeling results (p. 222).[92] Unfortunately, the APA Publication Manual does not include any text or rationale for why each piece of information should be included in this table. Therefore, the proposed template is not sufficiently comprehensive. For example, the APA template does not include information on ICC, the number of estimated parameters, and pseudo R^2. As mentioned earlier, ICC information is needed for readers to understand whether multilevel modeling was justified. Including the number of estimated parameters is also useful so that readers can quickly and accurately understand the nature of the model. Also as mentioned earlier, pseudo R^2 information is a useful, albeit imperfect, effect size metric. In addition, Table 10.2 is also more comprehensive than its APA counterpart because it includes sample size and clear labels for each model. Overall, reporting the information included in Table 10.2 is important because, absent this information, results based on multilevel modeling can be perceived as lacking transparency.

Table 10.2 can be used as a template for the information that needs to be reported when conducting a multilevel study regardless of the particular focus—L1 direct effects, L2 direct effects, or cross-level interactions. This table includes clear labels regarding the variables at which level, the sample size for each level, and the coefficients for each effect—including their standard errors and statistical significance. This table also includes a crucial piece of information often missing from published multilevel research: Complete information regarding the size of each variance component. This information is important for several reasons. First, as statistical software programs become increasingly available and easy to use, there are instances in which users may not fully understand the resulting output. Routinely reporting variance components will allow researchers to become more familiar with their data, results, and interpretation of results. Second, given increasing concerns about ethical violations and data "massaging,"[93] reporting variance components can allow a skeptical scientific audience to double-check results and possible misreporting (either by error or intention). Overall, multilevel research can benefit from greater standardization and openness regarding the reported information, and this format will be useful in this regard. Finally, Table 10.2 also shows all of this information for each step in the model-building process. Again, you can use a program at https://hermanaguinis.com to create a table like Table 10.2.

As multilevel modeling becomes a more popular approach in the social and behavioral sciences, results from such analyses must be reported in a detailed and comprehensive manner. Such clear and standardized reporting serves several purposes. First, it gives readers all the necessary information to understand and interpret results fully. Second, it allows future research to replicate the results of any particular study. Third, it makes results more useful and accurate regarding their future inclusion in subsequent qualitative and quantitative literature reviews (e.g., meta-analysis). Finally, the availability of information regarding the variability of slopes across groups allows for a more precise computation of statistical power. This is particularly important in cases when the evidence suggests the absence of a cross-level interaction effect.

DISCUSSION QUESTIONS

1. What does "dependence" mean when considering theories that integrate variables at different levels of analysis? Why is it important to consider?

2. Describe the three types of effects that can be examined using multilevel modeling.

3. Consider Equation 10.1. Which term's variance is of primary importance in multilevel modeling? Why?

4. What factors affect power in multilevel models? Why are "rules of thumb" (such as the "30-30 rule") not useful for the wide variety of situations that you will encounter?

5. How does the centering approach (i.e., group- versus grand-mean centering) affect statistical power in multilevel models?

6. Which two parameters of interest differ between Step 2 (i.e., Random intercept and fixed slope model) and Step 3 (i.e., Random intercept and random slope model) of the multilevel model building process? What is the substantive interpretation associated with these parameters?

7. Why is it important to report values of ICC, number of estimated parameters, and pseudo R^2 for your multilevel models?

8. Identify how the two sources of variance (i.e., ρ_α and ρ_β) contribute differentially to deciding when to use multilevel modeling. Moreover, what values of ρ_α and ρ_β should you use to decide whether or not to use a multilevel model?

9. How does the type of Level-2 moderator (i.e., continuous or categorical) affect the inferences drawn from the model?

10. When is it acceptable to conduct independent tests of each interaction effect for multiple interaction effects? What steps can you take to maximize the chance of testing a single model?

KEY TERMS

30-30 rule
Crainiceanu and Ruppert (2004) test
cross-level
cross-level interaction model
deviance
full information maximum likelihood (FIML)
grand mean
grand-mean centering
group-mean centering
intraclass correlation index (ICC)
joint distribution
levels of analysis
log-likelihood value
nonparametric bootstrap procedure

null hypothesis significance testing (NHST)
null model
omnibus test
pooled regression line
pseudo R^2
random intercept and fixed slope model (RIFSM)
random intercept and random slope model (RIRSM)
re-scale
regions of significance
restricted maximum likelihood (REML)
simple regression equation
within-cluster centering

NOTES

This chapter is based to a large extent on the following sources:

Aguinis, H., Gottfredson, R. K., & Culpepper, S. A. (2013). Best-practice recommendations for estimating cross-level interaction effects using multilevel modeling. *Journal of Management*, *39*(6), 1490–1528. https://doi.org/10.1177%2F0149206313478188

Aguinis, H., & Culpepper, S.A. (2015). An expanded decision making procedure for examining cross-level interaction effects with multilevel modeling. *Organizational Research Methods*, *18*(2), 155–176. https://doi.org/10.1177%2F1094428114563618

Mathieu, J. E., Aguinis, H., Culpepper, S. A., & Chen. G. (2012). Understanding and estimating the power to detect cross-level interaction effects in multilevel modeling. *Journal of Applied Psychology*, *97*(5), 951–966. https://psycnet.apa.org/doi/10.1037/a0028380

11

HOW TO CONDUCT QUANTITATIVE ANALYSIS, PART III: META-ANALYSIS

LEARNING GOALS

By the end of this chapter, you will be able to do the following:

11.1 Assess why you should care about meta-analysis, when and why it should be used, and the role of meta-analysis in producing comprehensive knowledge about the overall size of relations between variables, as well as when the size of the relation changes and why.

11.2 Formulate the critical choices and judgment calls you will face when conducting a meta-analysis and identify why they are important.

11.3 Propose the steps involved in conducting a state-of-the-science meta-analysis in each stage: data collection, data preparation, data analysis, and reporting.

11.4 Identify key considerations that influence whether meta-regression (MARA) is the appropriate methodology for a particular situation.

11.5 Arrange the key steps in the implementation of MARA and the various decision points you will encounter in conducting and reporting results.

11.6 Identify key considerations influencing whether using meta-analytic structural equation modeling (MASEM) is the appropriate methodology for a particular situation.

11.7 Arrange the key steps in implementing MASEM and the various decision points you will encounter in each stage: Specifying conceptual models, implementing meta-analytic procedures, implementing structural equation modeling procedures, and reporting results.

11.8 Evaluate whether conducting a new meta-analysis on a topic for which a meta-analysis already exists may be warranted.

IMPORTANCE OF META-ANALYSIS

It has been astutely suggested that "the goal of any empirical science is to pursue the construction of a cumulative base of knowledge upon which the future of the science may be built."[1] Meta-analysis is an extraordinary enablement to facilitate that journey. Often considered *the* definitive means of summarizing a body of empirical research, meta-analysis refers to a family of data collection and analysis techniques to produce a quantitative review of a body of literature. The word *meta* indicates that a meta-analysis occurs later than and transcends the original analysis. Conclusions based on meta-analytic findings set the standard for what is considered state-of-the-science, for what we know and do not know, and for which theory is considered valid and which is not.[2] These quantitative literature reviews have revolutionized social and behavioral science research and have been described as the "critical first step in the effective use of scientific evidence."[3]

A meta-analysis consists of extracting effect size estimates from previous studies and computing a summary across-study effect size and the variance of these estimates. Meta-analyzed effect sizes may be extracted from studies using experimental (i.e., providing evidence regarding causality) or passive observational (i.e., providing evidence regarding covariation) designs. So, based on gathering primary-level study effect sizes, a meta-analysis has two principal goals: (1) to estimate the overall strength and direction of an effect or relationship and (2) to estimate the across-study variance in the effect or relationship estimates and the factors (i.e., moderator variables) that explain this variance.[4] As some researchers noted, "the goal of a meta-analysis should be to synthesize the effect sizes and not simply (or necessarily) to report a summary effect. If the effects are consistent, then the analysis shows that the effect is robust across the range of the included studies. If there is modest dispersion, then this dispersion should serve to place the mean effect in context. If there is substantial dispersion, then the focus should shift from the summary effect to the dispersion itself. Researchers who report a summary effect and ignore heterogeneity are indeed missing the point of the synthesis."[5]

METHODS IN PRACTICE
POPULARITY AND IMPACT OF META-ANALYSIS

Not surprisingly, articles reporting meta-analyses are cited significantly more than primary-level studies. Accordingly, the reliance on and growth of meta-analytic applications for conducting quantitative literature reviews has been extraordinary. Consider, for example, the period from 1970 through 1985. Some researchers found that over those 15 years, the PsycINFO database included 224 articles with the expression "meta-analysis" or its derivatives in the title, the Academic/Business Source Premier (EBSCO) database had 55 such articles, and there were 55 such articles included in MEDLINE.[6] However, consider the substantial increase just a few years later (1994-2009): 3,481 articles in PsycINFO, 6,918 articles in EBSCO, and 11,373 articles in MEDLINE. Furthermore, based on evidence about the popularity of meta-analysis in the social and behavioral sciences, the use of this technique is expected to continue to grow exponentially.

This chapter is organized as follows. It begins with discussing the choices and judgment calls you will face and have to make when conducting a meta-analysis. The following section provides comprehensive guidance on how to conduct a meta-analysis. It includes a checklist of best-practice recommendations that you can use when conducting a meta-analysis or reviewing one in the future. Then, the chapter addresses **meta-regression**, a meta-analytic technique used to examine **boundary conditions** (i.e., whether meta-analytically derived effect sizes depend on methodological or substantive moderators). The following section is devoted to meta-analytical structural equation modeling, a fairly novel development consisting of conducting structural equation modeling using a meta-analytically derived correlation matrix as input. Finally, the chapter describes steps you can put in place to decide whether an updated meta-analysis on a topic that has already been meta-analyzed may be warranted.

META-ANALYSIS: CHOICES, CHOICES, CHOICES

You will face many methodological choices if you want to conduct a meta-analysis.[7] Each choice has important implications regarding the meta-analytic results you will obtain and the subsequent implications for theory and applications.[8] For example, some researchers used an improved correction for range restriction (i.e., when scores in a sample do not include the entire possible range) and found that previous meta-analyses had underestimated by 7% the validity of the Graduate Management Admission Test (GMAT) due to the application of sub-optimal range restriction corrections.[9] In other words, researchers' meta-analytic choices can affect substantive results regarding the obtained effect size estimates. In turn, these effect size estimates are used to make decisions about the relative validity of a theory (e.g., is personality related to job performance?) and the practical use of an intervention (e.g., is using subjective or objective measures for appraising employee performance equivalent?). Therefore, each meta-analytic choice has a direct impact on substantive theory-related conclusions as well as practical applications.[10]

A team of researchers conducted a comprehensive review of published meta-analyses in the social and behavioral sciences and identified 21 choices and judgment calls.[11] Of these 21, four are the most typical of published meta-analyses. First, regarding study design, most social and behavioral studies eliminated primary studies from their meta-analytic database based primarily on independence issues (i.e., when two or more effect sizes are computed using the same sample). And while the list of studies used in the meta-analysis was included in the article, the list of effect sizes used in the meta-analytic computations was not. Second, in terms of analysis, most studies relied on a random-effects model (i.e., the assumption is that multiple population effect sizes are estimated) and the Hunter and Schmidt (2004) procedures[12] that correct effect sizes for methodological and statistical artifacts (e.g., less than perfect reliability, rang restriction, sampling error). But, while most studies reported reliability estimates and effect sizes were corrected for measurement error, they did not report range restriction or corrected for it in the independent or dependent variables. Third, in terms of reporting results, the preferred effect-size metric was r, which was accompanied by a 95% confidence interval (i.e., an interval that would contain the true underlying effect size in 95% of the occasions if the study was repeated again and again) in about 50% of cases, but without a **credibility interval** (i.e., the interval that would contain a particular percent of the population values). Finally, regarding the robustness and replicability of results, the typical meta-analysis did not report tests of potential publication bias.

The following section offers a comprehensive and step-by-step description of how to conduct a meta-analysis. This section also describes the many choices and judgment calls you will likely have to make along the way, together with best-practice recommendations.

HOW TO CONDUCT A STATE-OF-THE-SCIENCE META-ANALYSIS

The fundamental components of a meta-analysis are as follows: (1) data collection (i.e., literature search and screening, coding), (2) data preparation (i.e., treatment of multiple effect sizes, outlier identification and management, publication bias), (3) data analysis (i.e., average effect sizes, heterogeneity of effect sizes, moderator search) and (4) reporting (i.e., transparency and reproducibility, future research directions). As a preview, a summary of the recommendations, which are described in detail next, is presented in Table 11.1.

TABLE 11.1 ■ Summary of Recommendations and Implementation Guidelines for Authors, Reviewers, and Readers of Meta-Analytic Reviews	
Recommendations	**Implementation Guidelines**
STAGE 1: DATA COLLECTION Organize and implement the search process and data extraction from primary-level studies	**Literature Search and Screening** ● Acknowledge that meta-analysis is increasingly becoming a "Big Science" project, requiring larger groups of collaborators ● Conduct a pre-meta-analysis scoping study to ensure that the research question is small enough to be manageable, large enough to be meaningful, there is a sufficient research base for analysis, and recent reviews have not already addressed the same topic ● Ensure authors' prolonged interest and deep knowledge of the topic to be meta-analyzed ● Avoid the construct identity fallacy: different measures are used for the same underlying construct (i.e., jingle), and the same construct is referred to using different labels (i.e., jangle) ● Avoid biases in the search process: availability bias by searching the "grey literature," cost bias by accessing paywalled journals, familiarity bias by consulting databases in other disciplines, language bias by searching non-English journals, and The Matthew Effect by not excluding low-citation sources ● Implement a variety of search strategies, including "snowballing" (a.k.a. ancestry searching or "pearl growing") ● To manage and document the search process, as per PRISMA, use recent software developments, such as www.covidence.org, www.hubmeta.com, or https://revtools.net/ ● Engage an information specialist (e.g., a librarian) in the search process **Coding of the Primary Studies** ● Implement procedures such as psychometric corrections and conversion of statistics to effect size estimates (e.g., rs, ds) using available and standardized tools such as R's *psychmeta* ● Consider trade-offs between increased measurement variance and using a larger meta-analytic database by teasing apart broad constructs into component dimensions or merging selected measures ● Archive the data perpetually through an Open Science repository rather than "making data available from the authors" ● Establish commensurability among measures, drawing on convergent and content validity as well as previous taxonomic work and expert opinion ● Reserve kappa for checking agreement on qualitative decisions ● Use a battery of measurement equivalence indexes to gather evidence that the different measures used assess the same underlying construct ● Include a transparent description of the search process and taxonomy of key constructs
STAGE 2: DATA PREPARATION Clean the data to perform the meta-analysis	**Treatment of Multiple Effect Sizes** ● Keep multiple correlations of the same relationship from the same sample statistically separate, preferably by using composite scores if intercorrelations among measures are available ● Consider alternative techniques to group measures, such as the Robust Error Variance (RVE) approach and a multilevel meta-analytic approach **Outlier Identification and Management** ● Do not use arbitrary cutoffs to identify and eliminate outliers ● Conduct analyses to determine whether outlying observations are error, influential, or interesting outliers ● Consider the possibility that some outliers may be legitimate observations ● Report results with and without outliers **Publication Bias** ● Complement or replace the fail-safe N procedure to detect publication bias with a selection-based method, such as published versus unpublished studies, symmetry methods such as Egger's regression, Trim-and-Fill technique, and the precision-effect test and estimate with standard errors (PET-PEESE)

Recommendations	Implementation Guidelines
STAGE 3: DATA ANALYSIS Assess heterogeneity of effect sizes	**Average Effect Sizes** ● Report the average association between variables as the initial stage of theory testing ● Report not only the average size but also its meaning and importance by placing it within a particular context and domain ● Use contemporary effect-size benchmarks such as small = 0.10, medium = 0.18, and large = 0.32 for correlations ● Adopt a random-effects and, if using psychometric corrections, Morris weights rather than a fixed-effects approach to calculating effect sizes ● Go beyond average effect sizes by using them as input for subsequent meta-analytic structural equation modeling (MASEM), which is described in more detail later in this chapter ● Extend or fill out the MASEM matrix with results derived from Individual Participant Data (IPD) ● Address nonsensical meta-analytically derived correlation matrices by excluding problematic cells and collapsing highly correlated variables into factors to avoid multicollinearity **Heterogeneity of Effect Sizes** ● Assess the degree of dispersion of effect sizes around the average ● Report heterogeneity of effect sizes by providing, at a minimum, credibility intervals, T^2 (i.e., SDr or the random-effects variance component), and I2 (i.e., percentage of total variance attributable to T^2) ● Employ a Bayesian approach that corrects for artificial homogeneity created by small samples ● Use asymmetric distributions in case of skewed credibility intervals **Moderator Search** ● Organize the search for moderators using Cattell's Data Cube: (a) sample, (b) variables, and (c) occasions ● Implement meta-regression (MARA) instead of subgrouping analysis when assessing continuous moderators, which is described in more detail later in this chapter
STAGE 4: REPORTING Ensure transparency and that meta-analytic progress continues	**Transparency and Reproducibility** ● Describe all procedures in sufficient detail so that others will be able to reproduce all data collection and analysis steps ● Make the meta-analytic database available in an Open Science archive ● If practical, turn your meta-analysis into a "living systematic review" that can be updated in real-time **Future Research Directions** ● Write future research directions as if you were in charge of the field and needed to direct subsequent studies, highlighting important understudied relationships ● Consider future meta-analyses focused on alternative construct definitions and measures ● Direct future projects towards understudied elements as well relationships that have been overly emphasized, perhaps to the point of recommending a moratorium ● Describe what moderators need to be considered in future research (e.g., sample characteristics, variables, contextual variation)

Source: Steel, Beugelsdijk, & Aguinis (2021).

Stage 1: Data Collection

Data collection is the creation of a database that enables a meta-analysis. Inherently, there is tension between making a meta-analysis manageable, small enough to be finished, and comprehensive enough to make a meaningful contribution. With the research base growing exponentially but research time and efficiency remaining relatively constant, the temptation is to limit the topic arbitrarily by journals, language, publication year, or how constructs are measured (e.g., a specific measure of cultural distance). The risk is that the meta-analysis is so narrowly conceived that it will only interest some. One solution is to acknowledge that meta-analysis is increasingly becoming a "Big Science" project, requiring larger groups of collaborators. Though well-funded meta-analytic labs exist, they are almost exclusively in medicine. In social and behavioral sciences, likely, influential reviews will increasingly become the purview of well-managed academic crowdsourcing projects (i.e., Massive Peer Production) whose leaders can tackle larger topics (i.e., community-augmented meta-analyses[13]), such as exemplified by Many Labs.[14]

With a large team or a smaller but more dedicated group, researchers have a freer hand in determining how to define the topic and the edges that define the literature. To this end, some researchers suggested that identifying a topic, described as Phase 0, may be an iterative definition, clarification, and refinement process.[15] Indeed, it may be helpful for you to conduct a pre-meta-analysis scoping study, ensuring that the research question is small enough to be manageable, large enough to be meaningful, there is a good research base for analysis, and that other recent or well-done reviews have not already addressed the same topic. Other researchers have stressed how the author's prior and prolonged interest in the topic is immensely helpful, exemplified by a history of publishing in a particular domain.[16] Deep familiarity with the nuances of a field assists in every step of a meta-analytic review.

Once a worthy topic within your capabilities has been established, the most challenging part of meta-analysis begins. First is the literature search and screening (i.e., locating and obtaining relevant studies), and second is coding (i.e., extracting the data within the primary studies).

Literature Search and Screening

The **construct identity fallacy** is the idea that there can be dozens of terms and scores of measures for the same construct (i.e., **jingle**), and different constructs can go by the same name (i.e., **jangle**).[17] Furthermore, the social and behavioral sciences have exploded almost exponentially, making a literature search more challenging. Then there are the numerous databases within which the targeted articles may be hidden due to their often flawed or archaic organization, mainly their keyword search functions.[18] One researcher noted that the keyword system had become so cumbersome and literal that it was practically worthless.[19]

Given this difficulty and that literature searches often occur iteratively as you learn the parameters of the search as it is conducted,[20] there is an incentive to filter or simplify the procedure and to not properly document such a fundamentally flawed process not to leave it open to critique from reviewers' potentially idealistic standards.[21] The result can be an **implicit selection bias**, where the body of articles is a subset of what is of interest.[22] Some researchers have suggested that there are four types of bias: **availability bias** (selective inclusion of studies that are easily accessible to the researcher), **cost bias** (selective inclusion of studies that are available free or at low costs), **familiarity bias** (selective inclusion of studies only from one's field or discipline), and **language bias** (selective inclusion of studies published in English).[23] Other researchers have also suggested citation bias due to *The Matthew Effect*, where initial citations beget further citations, resulting in cumulative advantages.[24]

With increased public information on citation structures thanks to software such as Google Scholar, there is the risk of selective inclusion of those studies that are heavily cited at the expense of studies that have not been picked up (yet). However, you can address these biases by searching the grey literature, finding access to paywalled scientific journals, including databases outside one's discipline, engaging in translation (at least those languages used in multiple sources), and not using a low citation rate as an exclusion criterion.

Presently, in efforts to increase transparency and replicability, the **PRISMA (Preferred Reporting Items for Systematic Reviews and Meta-Analyses)** method is recommended, which requires being extremely explicit about the exact databases, the exact search terms, and the exact results, including duplicates and filtering criteria.[25] Though more onerous, the **PRISMA-P** version goes even further in transparency, advocating for pre-registering the entire systematic review protocol encapsulated in a 17-item checklist.[26] In addition, the 2020 version of PRISMA recommends a 27-item checklist, not including numerous sub-items, to improve the trustworthiness of systematic reviews.[27] However, given the attempt to minimize decisions *in situ*, proper adherence to the PRISMA protocols can be difficult when searches are iterative, as you find new terms or measures as promising leads for relevant papers. When this happens, especially during the later stage of data preparation, you face the dilemma of either re-conducting the entire search process with the added criteria (substantively increasing the workload) or ignoring the new terms or measures (leading to a less-than-exhaustive search). New software has been developed to help address these challenges so search processes can be informed simultaneously with implementation, such as www.covidence.org, www.hubmeta.com, or https://revtools.net/ (with many more options curated at https://systematicreviewtools.com/, The Systematic Review Tool Box). These options provide a computer-assisted walk-through of the search and a screening process, which starts with deduplication and filtering on abstract or title, followed by full-text filtering (with annotated decisions). Furthermore, if you are reviewing an article, you should expect that this information is reported in a supplemental file, along with the final list of all articles coded and details regarding effect sizes, sample sizes, measures, moderators, and other specific details that would enable readers to readily reproduce the creation of the meta-analytic database.

Determining whether a search approach has been exhaustive is challenging, given that you may need a more complete understanding of the search criteria or how many articles can be expected. In other words, though the authors may have reported detailed inclusion and exclusion criteria, as per **Meta-Analytic Reporting Standards (MARS)**,[28] how can you, as a reviewer, evaluate their adequacy? Some researchers have suggested that this need for construct intimacy may be emphasized. A meta-analysis would require first drawing upon or publishing an in-depth review of the construct.[29] Once authors have demonstrated long and even affectionate familiarity with the topic (i.e., "immersion in the literature"[30]), reviewers may be further reassured that the technical aspects of the search were adequately carried out if a librarian (i.e., an information specialist) was reported to be involved.[31]

Coding of the Primary Studies

Extracting all the information from a preliminary study can be a lengthy procedure. Many materials are typically needed beyond sample size and the estimated size of a relation between variables (i.e., correlation coefficient). This includes details required for psychometric corrections, conversion from different statistical outputs to a standard effect size (e.g., r or d), and study conditions and context that permit later moderator analysis (i.e., conditions under which a relation between variables is weaker or stronger). Properly implementing procedures such as applying psychometric corrections for measurement error and range restriction is only sometimes straightforward.[32] But, while this used to be a manual process requiring intimate statistical knowledge (e.g., knowledge of how to correct various methodological and statistical artifacts), this process is increasingly semi-automated. For example, R's meta-analytic package *psychmeta* (the psychometric meta-analysis toolkit) provides conversion to correlations for Cohen's d, independent samples t values (or their p-values), two-group one-way ANOVA F values (or their *p*-values), 1df χ^2 values (or their *p*-values), **odds ratios**, **log odds ratios**, Fisher *z*, and the **common language effect size** (CLES, A, AUC).[33]

However, a pernicious coding challenge is related to the literature search and screening process described earlier. For initial forays into a topic, a certain degree of conceptual "clumping" is necessary to permit sufficient studies for meta-analytic summary, where you trade increased measurement variance for a more extensive database. As more studies become available, it is possible to make more refined choices and tease apart broad constructs into component dimensions or adeptly merge selected measures to minimize **mono-method bias**.[34]

Consequently, you may be expected to reassure reviewers that you grouped measures appropriately. This is not simply a case of using different indices of interrater agreement,[35] which often prove interchangeable themselves, but using a battery of options to show measurement equivalence, and these measures are tapping into approximately the same construct. Though few measures will be completely identical (i.e., parallel forms), there are the traditional choices of showing external validity, specifically convergent, and internal validity, specifically content.[36] For example, some researchers were faced with over 100 different measures of culture in their meta-analysis of Hofstede's Values Survey Module.[37] Their solution, which they documented over several pages, was to begin with the available *convergent validity* based on factor analysis or correlational studies. Given that the available associations were incomplete, they then proceeded to *content validation*, examining the definitions and survey items for consistency with the target constructs. Finally, for more contentious decisions, they drew on 14 raters to gather further evidence regarding content validity.

As can be seen, demonstrating that different measures tap into the same construct can be laborious, and preferably future meta-analyses could draw on previously established ontologies or taxonomic structures. As mentioned, there are some sources to rely on, such as work on organizational performance,[38] rule of law indices,[39] or a taxonomy of personality and cognitive ability.[40] Unfortunately, this work is still insufficient for many meta-analyses, and such a void is proving a major obstacle to advancing science. Furthermore, the multiplicity of overlapping terms and measures used by social and behavioral science researchers creates a knowledge management problem that is increasingly intractable for the individual researcher to solve. Some have argued that a solution is manageable but requires sustained collaboration between information systems, information science, computer science, and social and behavioral science researchers to develop information system artifacts to address the problem.[41]

Stage 2: Data Preparation

Literature search, screening, and coding provide the sample of primary studies and a preliminary meta-analytic database. Next, three aspects of the data preparation stage leave quite a bit of discretionary room for you, thus requiring explicit helpful discussion for meta-analysts, reviewers, and research consumers. First, there is the treatment of multiple effect sizes reported in a given primary-level study. Second, there is the identification and treatment of outliers. And third, the issue of publication bias.

Treatment of Multiple Effects Sizes

A single study may measure a construct in various ways, each producing its effect size estimate. In other words, effect sizes are calculated using the same sample and reported separately for each measure. Separately counting each result violates the principle of statistical independence, as all are based on the same sample.

Typically, the goal is to focus on the key construct, and so one option is for you to calculate composite scores, drawing on the correlations among the different measures.[42] Unless the measures are unrelated (which suggests they assess different constructs and should not be grouped), the resulting composite score will have better coverage of the underlying construct and higher reliability. Other techniques include the **Robust Error Variance** (**RVE**) approach, which considers the dependencies (i.e., covariation) among correlated effect sizes (i.e., from the same sample).[43] Another option is performing a multilevel meta-analytic approach, where Level 1 includes the effects sizes, Level 2 is the within-study variation, and Level 3 is the between-study variation.[44] A potential practical limitation is that these alternatives to composite scores pose large data demands as they typically require 40 to 80 studies per analysis to provide acceptable estimates.[45]

Outlier Identification and Management

Though rarely done, outlier analysis is strongly recommended for meta-analysis. Some choices include doing nothing, reducing the weight given to the outlier, or eliminating the outlier.[46] However, whatever the choice, it should be transparent, with the option of reporting results with and without outliers. To detect outliers, R's statistical package *metafor* provides a variety of influential case diagnostics ranging from externally standardized residuals to leave-one-out estimates.[47] As is the nature of outliers, their undue influence can substantially tilt results by their inclusion or exclusion.

Like the Black Swan effect, an outlier may be a legitimate effect size drawn by chance from the ends of a distribution, which would relinquish its outlier status as more effects reduce or balance its impact. Some researchers offered a decision tree involving steps to identify outliers (i.e., whether a particular observation is far from the rest), then decide whether specific outliers are errors, interesting, or influential.[48] Based on the answer, you can decide to eliminate it (i.e., if it is an error), retain it as is, or decrease its influence, and then, regardless of choice, report results with and without the outliers.

Publication Bias

Publication bias focuses on statistically significant or strong effect sizes rather than a representative sample of results. This can happen for various reasons, including underpowered studies and questionable research practices (QRPs) such as *p*-hacking, and it frequently occurs in various fields.[49] When it does occur, it can potentially distort findings severely.[50]

A few decades ago, the fail-safe N was a recommended component of a state-of-the-science meta-analysis, which consists of calculating the minimum number of undetected negative studies that would be needed to change the conclusions of a meta-analysis.[51] But, the fail-safe N has various problems, such as if the published literature indicates a lack of relationship, that is, the null itself, the equation becomes unworkable. Consequently, for decades a variety of researchers have recommended its disuse.[52] At the very least, the fail-safe N should be supplemented, and although there are no perfect methods to detect or correct publication bias, there is a wide variety of better options. For example, you can use selection-based methods and compare study sources, typically published versus unpublished, with the expectation that there should be little difference between the two. Also, there are various symmetry-based methods where the expectation is that sample size or standard error should be unrelated to effect sizes. **Egger's regression test** is one of the most popular symmetry techniques.[53]

You can also use **fixed-effect model** weighting to reduce the impact of errant heterogeneity to reduce the effect of publication bias.[54] Alternatively, the classic Trim-and-Fill technique can also be employed, imputing the "missing" correlates.[55] Finally, for a more sophisticated option, there is the **precision-effect test and precision-effect estimate with standard errors (PET-PEESE)**, which can detect and correct for publication.[56] Other researchers have provided guidance on when PET-PEESE becomes unreliable, typically when there are few studies, excessive heterogeneity, or small sample sizes, albeit often the same conditions that weaken the effectiveness of meta-analytic techniques in general.[57]

Stage 3: Data Analysis

Meta-analyses are overwhelmingly used to understand the overall (i.e., average) size of the relation between variables across primary-level studies.[58] But, meta-analysis is just as useful, if not more, to understand when and where a relation is likely to be stronger or weaker. Consequently, you should consider the three basic elements of the data analysis stage – average effect sizes, heterogeneity, and moderators – and their theoretical implications.

Average Effect Sizes

During the early years of meta-analysis, the main question of interest was: "Is there a consistent relation between two variables when examined across several primary-level studies that seemingly report contradictory results?" Showing association and connection represents the *initial* stages of theory testing, and most meta-analyses have some hypotheses attached to these estimates. Given that this is the lower-hanging empirical and theoretical fruit, much of it has already been plucked. Today, it is unlikely to satisfy social and behavioral science's demands for valuable theoretical contributions. An improved test of theory at this stage is not just positing that a relation exists and that it is unlikely to be zero, but how big it is.[59] To this end, some have drawn on Cohen (1962), who made rough benchmark estimates based on his review of articles published in the 1960 *Journal of Abnormal and Social Psychology* volume. Other researchers have compiled more current estimates and found that Cohen's categorizations of small, medium, and large effects do not accurately reflect today's social and behavioral science research.[60] Averaging across these studies suggests that a better generic distribution remains as per Cohen 0.10 for small (i.e., 25th percentile) but changes to 0.18 for medium (i.e., 50th percentile) and 0.32 for large (i.e., 75th percentile). Using these distributions of effect sizes, or those compiled from other analogous meta-analyses, you can go beyond the simple conclusion that a relationship is different from zero and, instead, critically evaluate the effect size within the context of a specific domain.

In terms of effect sizes, more than a single column is required. What is preferred is a grid of them. For example, **meta-analytic structural equation modeling (MASEM)** is based on expanding the scope of a meta-analysis from bivariate correlations to creating a full meta-analytic correlation matrix.[61] Given that this allows for additional theory testing options enabled by standard structural equation modeling, the publication of a meta-analysis can pivot on its use of MASEM. Options range from factor analysis to path analysis, such as determining the total variance provided by predictors or if a predictor is particularly important (e.g., dominance or relative weights analysis). It also allows for mediation tests, the "how" of theory, or "reasons for connections." It is even possible to use MASEM to test for interaction effects. Traditionally the correlation between the interaction term and other variables is not reported and often must be requested directly from the original authors. Doing so is a high-risk endeavor given researchers' traditionally low response rate.[62] Still, the rise of **Open Science** and the concomitant **Individual Participant Data (IPD)** means that this information is increasingly available. Amalgamating IPD across multiple studies is usually referred to as a mega-analysis and, as suggested here, can be used to supplement a standard meta-analysis.[63]

You should know that you can encounter incomplete and nonsensical matrices as you move from simply an average of bivariate relations toward MASEM. For incomplete matrices, some researchers provide recommendations for filling blank cells in a matrix, such as drawing on previously published meta-analytic values or expanding the meta-analysis to target missing correlations.[64] Nonsensical matrices (that occur increasingly as correlation matrices expand) create a non-positive definite "Frankenstein" matrix stitched together from incompatible moderator patches. Remedies such as excluding problematic cells or collapsing highly correlated variables into factors to avoid multicollinearity can be used.[65] In addition, you can employ more advanced methods that incorporate random effects and dovetail meta-regression with MASEM.[66] MASEM is described in detail later in this chapter.

Heterogeneity of Effect Sizes

Another concern is the degree of dispersion around the average effect. At a minimum, you should provide credibility intervals, T^2, SD_r, and I^2 (i.e., percentage of total variance attributable to T^2). Furthermore, you can use a Bayesian approach that corrects for artificial homogeneity created by small samples[67] and the use of asymmetric distributions in case of skewed credibility intervals.[68]

Moderator (i.e., Interaction-effect) Search

Interaction, or moderating effects, provides information on whether the relationship between two variables is contingent upon the value of a third variable.[69] Understanding a theory's moderators means that we understand a theory's boundary conditions. Therefore, understanding interaction effects is a key issue for theory development and testing, as well as practical applications of a theory.

A critical choice you face is the type of meta-analytic model to use. The two most established choices are (a) a **mixed-effects** or random-effects (ME) model and (b) a *fixed-effect* or **common-effect** (CE) model. These two models have different underlying assumptions, and as such, the choice for one or the other model can affect substantive conclusions regarding the presence of moderating effects. The ME model assumes that the studies in the meta-analysis are a random sample from a super-population of possible studies and that the super-population distribution of true effect sizes is normally distributed. In the ME model, the variance in the distribution of observed effects is attributed to (a) within-study variance (i.e., due mainly to sampling error) and (b) between-study variance (i.e., due to differences of true effect sizes in the super-population). In contrast, the CE model assumes that there is one common true effect underlying the distribution of observed effects. Hence, in the CE model, the variance in the distribution of observed effect sizes is attributed solely to within-study sampling variance. As a result, the confidence interval around the mean effect size is wider when using an RE model compared to a CE model because the ME confidence interval describes a large super-population of (most likely heterogeneous) effect sizes. In contrast, the CE confidence interval describes only a small subset of homogeneous super-population effect sizes.

Should you choose a random-effects or a common-effect model? In social and behavioral science research, an ME model is almost always the more appropriate choice. This is because an ME model allows the between-study variance to take on any value (including zero). In contrast, a CE model forces the between-study variance to be zero. Thus, the ME model can be conceptualized as the general case and the CE model as a specific case of the ME model in which the between-study variance in true effect sizes is assumed to be zero. However, to realize the full benefits of an ME meta-analysis, two critical assumptions must be satisfied:

(a) the observed effect sizes have been randomly sampled from a super-population of true effect sizes, and (b) the super-population of true effect sizes is normally distributed.[70] Furthermore, some researchers have warned that the random-studies assumption is a potentially serious limitation of the ME model.[71] In addition, the super-population normality assumption should not be taken lightly because ME inferential methods can perform poorly under minor deviations from normality.

METHODS IN PRACTICE
IS IT REALISTIC TO IMPLEMENT A COMMON-EFFECT MODEL?

The CE model would be appropriate when each of the primary-level studies included in a meta-analysis is functionally identical.[72] However, this condition rarely exists in social and behavioral science research because primary-level studies would have to include samples of participants from the same population, the same team of researchers, the same research design, the same measures for the independent and dependent variables, and the same procedures for all other aspects of the study. Therefore, this type of meta-analysis could occur in the biological, medical, and health sciences. For example, the same team of researchers could conduct 20 separate randomized trial studies examining the effect of a drug using samples from the same population of individuals and precisely the same procedures in each study and then conduct a subsequent meta-analysis using the 20 effect size estimates. But, this situation is almost impossible in the social and behavioral sciences. In short, a CE meta-analysis will be difficult to justify in social and behavioral science research.

Moderating effects, which account for substantive heterogeneity, can be organized around **Cattell's Data Cube** or the **Data Box**: (1) sample (e.g., firm or people characteristics), (2) variables (e.g., measurements), and (3) occasions (e.g., administration or setting).[73] Typical moderator variables include the country (e.g., developing versus developed), period (e.g., decade), and published versus unpublished status (where the comparison between the two can indicate the presence of publication bias). Theory is also often addressed as part of the moderator search.[74]

Two sets of statistical procedures are used to test for the presence of particular moderating effects depending upon whether the hypothesized moderator is categorical (i.e., variables for which values represent discrete categories – e.g., industry type) or continuous (i.e., variables for which, within the limits of the variable's range, any value is possible – e.g., job satisfaction, work motivation). In tests for hypothesized *categorical* moderating effects, each primary-level study is assigned a numerical value based upon the moderator (e.g., industry type: 1 = manufacturing, 2 = service) and subgrouped according to this coding scheme. In this so-called *subgroup analysis*, the goal is to examine whether effect sizes differ across the subgroups, while it is assumed that they do not differ within each subgroup. Although there are three types of subgroup analysis, they are algebraically equivalent and yield the same p value.

A type of subgroup analysis that resonates with most social and behavioral science researchers is analogous to ANOVA in primary-level research. This analysis involves computing a between-subgroup statistic Q_B to test that the difference between or among mean within-subgroup effect sizes is zero and a within-subgroup homogeneity statistic Q_W, which is obtained using an underlying CE model within each subgroup (i.e., assuming that all effect sizes within each group share a common population effect). A statistically significant Q_B, which follows a chi-square distribution with $df = p - 1$ (i.e., p is the number of subgroups), suggests that the subgrouping variable is a moderator. As a follow-up analysis, it is possible to use an RE model for each Q_W (i.e., within each subgroup) to test for further heterogeneity and subdivide subgroups further based on additional hypothesized moderators. In terms of the size of the moderating effect, you can compute an R^2 value, which indicates the proportion of variance of the total between-group variance (τ^2) explained by each moderator variable.

So, you should avoid using subgrouping methodology when testing continuous moderators because, as described above, subgrouping is usually reserved for categorical variables; otherwise, it requires dichotomizing continuous moderators, usually using a median split, which reduces statistical power.[75] As a superior alternative, you should use **meta-regression analysis (MARA)**.[76] MARA tests whether the size of the effects can be predicted by fluctuations in the values of the hypothesized moderators, which therefore are conceptualized as boundary conditions for the size of the effect. In addition, if there are enough studies, MARA enables simultaneous testing of several moderators. MARA is described in detail later in this chapter.

Stage 4: Reporting

A meta-analysis must be transparent and reproducible—meaning that all steps and procedures must be described so that a different team of researchers would obtain similar results with the same data. At present, this is among our most significant challenges. For example, half of the 500 effect sizes sampled from 33 meta-analyses in psychology were not reproducible based on the available information.[77] Also, a meta-analysis provides more than a summary of past findings and points toward the next steps. Consequently, you should consider future research directions, not just in terms of what studies should be conducted but when subsequent meta-analyses could be beneficial and what they should address.

Transparency and Reproducibility

Today, more than ever, it is important that meta-analytic work be reproducible, transparent, and can be subjected to rigorous scrutiny.[78] Therefore, you should not use your personal computers as an archive because data can often become challenging to obtain, lost, or incomplete. Instead, you should follow the Open Science, Open Data, Open Access, and Open Archive movement.[79] Along with the *complete* database, if the statistical process deviates from standard practice, you should make a copy of the analysis script available in an Open Science archive. Adopting an Open Science framework, choices can be examined and updated, improving the field as it encourages increased vigilance of the source authors. While this approach has several advantages, it does introduce considerable challenges.

Traditional reporting methods include flagging the extracted studies with an asterisk in the reference section or making a list available upon request from the authors. More is needed. Science is a social endeavor, and you need to be able to build on past meta-analyses to enable future ones; by making meta-analyses reproducible, that is, having access to the coding database, you are also making the process cumulative.[80] Open Science is a stepping stone towards **living systematic reviews (LSRs)**,[81] continuously updated in real-time. Having found traction in medicine, LSRs are based around critical topics that can enable broad collaborations (along with advances in technological innovations, such as online platforms and machine learning), though with their challenges.[82]

306   Research Methodology

METHODS IN PRACTICE
PERILS OF DATA SHARING

Data sharing is not without its perils, exacerbating the moral hazards associated with a common pool resource: the publication base.[83] Traditionally in a meta-analysis, the information becomes "consumed" once published or "extracted" in a meta-analysis, and the research base needs time to "regenerate," that is, grow sufficiently that a new summary is justified. Since there is no definitive point when regeneration occurs, we encounter a tragedy of the commons, where one instrumental strategy is to rush marginal meta-analyses to the academic market, shopping them to multiple venues in search of acceptance (i.e., science's first mover advantage[84]). Open Science will likely exacerbate this practice as the cost of updating meta-analyses would be substantially reduced. For example, in ecology, the authors of a meta-analysis on marine habitats admirably provided their complete database, which was rapidly re-analyzed by a subsequent group with a slightly different taxonomy.[85] In a charitable reply, these authors characterized this as an endorsement of Open Science, concluding, "Without transparent methods, explicitly defined models, and fully transparent data and code, this advancement in scientific knowledge would have been delayed if not unobtainable." However, as they noted, it took a team of ten authors over two years to create the original database, and posting it allowed others to supersede them with relatively minimal effort. If the original authors adopt an Open Science philosophy for their meta-analytic database (strongly recommended), subsequent free-riding or predatory authors could take advantage and publish by adding marginal updates.

Future Research Directions

A good section on "Future Research Directions," based on a close study of the entire field's findings, though perhaps sporadically used, can be as invaluable as the core results. This information allows meta-analysts to steer the field itself. It would be best to expound on the gap between what is already known and what is required for the field to move forward. The components of a good Future Research section touch on many of the very stages previously emphasized, especially Data Collection, Data Analysis, and Reporting.

During Data Collection, you had to be sensitive to inclusion and exclusion criteria and how constructs were defined and measured. This provides several insights. To begin with, the development of inclusion and exclusion criteria, along with addressing issues of commensurability, allows other researchers to consider construct definition and its measurement. Was the construct well-defined? Often, there are as many definitions as there are researchers, so this is an opportunity to provide some clarity. With an enhanced understanding, the measures can be evaluated, especially where they could be improved. How well do they assess the construct? Should some be favored and others abandoned?

During Data Analysis, you likely attempted to assemble a correlation matrix to conduct meta-analytic structural equation modeling and meta-regression. One of the more frustrating aspects of this endeavor is when the matrix is almost complete, but some cells are missing. Here is where other researchers can direct future projects towards understudied elements and point out that other relationships have been overly emphasized, perhaps to the point of recommending a moratorium. Similarly, the issue of heterogeneity and moderators comes up. The results may generalize, but this may be due to overly homogenous samples or settings. Also, some moderators likely needed to address theory, but the field did not report or contain them. Additionally, informing reviewers that the field cannot yet address such ambitions often helps curtail a critique of their absence. In short, you should stress how every future study should contextualize or describe itself (i.e., based on the likely major moderators).

Finally, the need for an Open Science framework was discussed during Reporting. For a meta-analyst, often the greatest challenge is not the choice of statistical technique but getting enough foundational studies, especially those that thoroughly report and are of unquestionable quality. The methodological techniques tend to converge at higher k (i.e., number of primary-level studies), and statistical legerdemain can mitigate but not overcome an inherent lack of data. Fortunately, the Open Science movement and the increased availability of a study's underlying data (i.e., IPD) open possibilities. Contextual and detailed information may not be reported in a study, often due to journal space limitations, but needed for meta-analytic moderator analyses. With Open Science, this information will be increasingly available, allowing for the improved application of many sophisticated techniques. Consequently, it would be best if you considered what new findings would be possible with a growing research base. As journal editors and reviewers, you should expect a synopsis of when a follow-up meta-analysis would be appropriate and what the next update could accomplish with a more varied database to rely on.

Next, let's address meta-regression in detail.

META-REGRESSION

Meta-regression is similar to but also different from traditional regression models. Specifically, it involves regressing meta-analytically derived effect sizes on several hypothesized predictors (i.e., boundary conditions) while weighting each effect size estimate by an indicator of its precision, such as the study's inverse of the within-study variance (i.e., sampling variance). Meta-regression offers two important benefits. The first significant benefit of meta-regression is that it capitalizes on a major advantage of meta-analysis, which involves relying on all available data to examine a particular phenomenon. Second, meta-regression avoids (a) artificial dichotomization of boundary conditions; and (b) the untenable assumption that reality includes only one boundary condition at a time.

The following equation[86] describes the extent to which boundary conditions x predict the relation between two variables, as indexed by the effect size y, in a sample of k studies:

$$y_i = B_0 + B_1 x_{i1} + \cdots B_j x_{ij} + u_i + e_i, \tag{11.1}$$

where y_i denotes the effect size estimate (e.g., rs or ds) in the ith study, x_{ij} denotes the value of the jth boundary condition in the ith study, B_j denotes the unstandardized regression coefficient associated with boundary condition j that indicates the extent to which the effect size y changes as a result of a one-unit change in x_{ij}, and B_0 is the model intercept. In addition, u_i denotes the random-effects (RE) variance components with distribution $N(0, \tau^2_{res})$, and e_i denotes the within-study variances with distribution $N(0, v_i)$. Further, τ^2_{res} denotes the residual heterogeneity, or the variability in the population of effect sizes not accounted for by the predictors (i.e., boundary conditions) in the model, and v_i represents the within-study variance of the studies.

Boundary conditions (i.e., x) are typically coded from information available or extracted from primary-level studies. For example, you may be interested in testing the hypothesis that the relation between cognitive ability and job performance is stronger in more complex jobs. To do so, you would code the level of job complexity in each study, which would be the operationalization of x by, for example, assigning a score from 1-5 to each sample based on the jobs the people in the sample occupy, with 1 indicating a lower level of complexity and 5 a high level of complexity.

As ordinary least squares (OLS) regression is one of the most frequently used data-analytic techniques in social and behavioral sciences and related fields, comparing and contrasting it with meta-regression is useful. First, meta-regression uses study-level rather than primary-level predictors. So, the predictors in Equation 11.1 are based on the characteristics of the studies included in the meta-analysis. In contrast to the typical primary study assessing boundary conditions, the meta-regression coefficients associated with the x variables provide information on the boundary conditions, and there is no need to include product terms in the equation. This is because the coefficients assess how much the relation between two variables, denoted by y in our model, changes as a function of x. In other words, positive (negative) coefficients indicate an increase (decrease) in effect size units with increasingly large values of x. Second, the criterion in meta-regression is the effect size of the relation between two variables from primary studies rather than scores on the criterion. Thus, whereas in OLS regression, the criterion consists of a column of scores for a particular variable (e.g., job performance), in meta-regression, there is a column of effect size estimates such as rs or ds (i.e., the relation between cognitive ability and job performance). Third, meta-regression assigns a weight to each study to account for its precision, with larger studies given a larger weight. This is an essential feature of meta-regression because it allows researchers to give more influence to studies providing more stable population estimates (i.e., those based on larger sample sizes). Fourth, it would be best if you made several method-ological choices and statistical adjustments that are non-existent in more traditional regression models,[87] such as deciding whether to pursue meta-regression analyses given the heterogeneity present in the studies as well as whether to adopt a fixed-effects (FE) or mixed-effects (ME) model and these choices have important implications for substantive conclusions.

Meta-regression: Best-practice Recommendations

The following best-practice recommendations are organized around the (a) conduct and (b) reporting of results of a study assessing boundary conditions with meta-regression. These recommendations focus on issues specific to meta-regression and not on additional decision points related to all types of meta-analysis. The recommendations are based on empirical and analytical evidence and are supported by results of simulation studies, analytical work, or both. In addition, if the evidence does not specify one correct way to proceed, the recommendations describe possible courses of action and the advantages and limitations of each alternative. A summary of the recommendations is presented in Table 11.2.

Conducting a Meta-regression Study

Calculation of Statistical Power. Statistical power is the probability that existing popula-tion boundary conditions will be detected. The power of the overall model is the probability that at least one of the boundary conditions will be detected. In contrast, the power of the individual coefficients refers to the probability that each specific boundary condition will be detected. Insufficient power means that substantive conclusions about boundary conditions will be incorrect because existing boundary conditions are unlikely to be found. Equations exist to calculate power under different conditions, including the estimation method used, the number of studies in the meta-analysis (i.e., the effective sample size for the meta-regression equation), whether moderators are continuous or categorical, the degree of heterogeneity in the sample of studies, the a priori Type I error rate, and the expected size of the boundary condition.[88]

TABLE 11.2 ■ Summary of Best-Practice Recommendations for Assessing Boundary Conditions Using Meta-Regression

Research Stage and Issue	Recommendation
Calculation of statistical power	
● Power is the probability that existing boundary conditions will be detected. In insufficient statistical power situations, substantive conclusions about boundary conditions may be incorrect because existing boundary conditions are unlikely to be detected.	● Calculate the statistical power for the overall model (i.e., the probability that at least one existing boundary condition will be detected) and each hypothesized boundary condition before using meta-regression. ● If power is low, do not use meta-regression or interpret results in the context of low power as non-significant results could be Type II errors (i.e., false negatives).
Calculation of heterogeneity	
● Heterogeneity is the systemic variability in the effect sizes across primary-level studies. In cases of low heterogeneity, boundary conditions are unlikely to be present. ● The presence of heterogeneity provides prima facie evidence to proceed with tests of boundary conditions.	● Calculate and report multiple heterogeneity indices and use several indices to decide whether to proceed with meta-regression analyses. ● Compare typical heterogeneity estimates (e.g., T^2) to estimates derived from Bayesian methods when informed priors are available. ● If the evidence suggests little heterogeneity, meta-regression will unlikely lead to meaningful theory advancements.
Choosing the type of meta-regression model	
● The two types of meta-regression models (ME and FE) have specific assumptions and computational considerations. This results in unique situations when their use is appropriate. ● The incorrect choice of model can increase Type I error rates, a decrease in power, and incorrect effect size estimates.	● Use the ME model except for the specific instances where an FE model may be appropriate. ● When using either model, provide a justification for the choice of model and, if using an FE model, show ME results and provide evidence that the assumptions of the FE model have been met.
Calculation of residual heterogeneity	
● Residual heterogeneity (i.e., τ^2_{res}) is the variability in effects not accounted for by the boundary conditions included in the model and can be estimated using either iterative or non-iterative estimators. ● Using a non-iterative estimator increases Type I error rates, decreases power, and reduces the model's predictive power.	● Use an iterative estimator of residual heterogeneity, such as the REML estimator. These estimators are more accurate than non-iterative estimators, especially when the number of studies is small (i.e., $k < 40$). ● The EB estimator can be used when sufficient data are available to generate an informed prior distribution.
Testing boundary condition hypotheses	
● The popular Wald-type method yields incorrect standard errors and false conclusions regarding boundary condition hypotheses because it makes incorrect sample size adjustments and, in ME models, does not allow for uncertainty in the estimate of τ^2_{res}. ● Using the Wald-type method results in Type I error rates up to four times the nominal level.	● Use the Hedges and Olkin (2014) method for FE models. ● Use the Knapp and Hartung (2003) method for ME models. ● Only use the robust standard errors produced by the HLM program (i.e., the Huber-White method) when $k > 80$.

(Continued)

TABLE 11.2 ■ Summary of Best-Practice Recommendations for Assessing Boundary Conditions Using Meta-Regression *(Continued)*	
Research Stage and Issue	**Recommendation**
Adjusting R^2 for known variance	
● Estimates of variance explained (i.e., R^2) obtained from meta-regression analyses are biased downwardly because R^2 treats within-study variance as unexplained variance. In contrast, in meta-regression, within-study variance can be quantified.	● Calculate R^2_{Meta} to adjust R^2 to consider the known within-study variance in a meta-regression context.
Explanation of methodological choices	
● It is essential to be transparent concerning all methodological choices.	● Follow an overarching principle of transparency concerning methodological reporting.
● Without transparency, there is a low likelihood that study findings can be reproduced and replicated, contributing to a decrease in the credibility and legitimacy of study findings.	● Explain and justify all methodological choices, including the model type, the residual heterogeneity estimator (for ME models), and the method used for statistical significance testing.
Reporting and interpreting meta-regression coefficients	
● Unstandardized regression coefficients can be used to communicate practical importance by calculating actual effect size values at different boundary condition values. In contrast, standardized regression coefficients provide a common metric of relative importance.	● Report both unstandardized and standardized regression coefficients.
● Reporting only one type of regression coefficient makes the practical significance of study results more challenging to interpret.	● Use unstandardized regression coefficients from the meta-regression analyses to generate effect size values at different theoretically or practically relevant values of the boundary condition under study.
Reporting variable intercorrelations and descriptive statistics	
● Most journals require reporting descriptive statistics and variable intercorrelations for primary studies.	● Report the intercorrelations and descriptive statistics of the boundary conditions and effect sizes.
● In the absence of this information, readers cannot fully evaluate meta-regression findings.	

Source: Adapted from Gonzalez-Mulé & Aguinis (2018). Reproduced with permission.

Note: T^2: between-studies variance, CrI: credibility interval, HLM: hierarchical linear modeling, REML: restricted maximum likelihood, EB: empirical Bayes, τ^2_{res}: residual heterogeneity, R^2: percent of variance explained by the regression equation, FE: fixed-effects model, ME: mixed-effects model.

Using these formulae, you can use a SAS macro that calculates the power of the overall meta-regression equation and individual boundary conditions.[89]

A simulation study found that the average power in meta-regression studies was closer to the result of a coin-flip than to the frequently cited recommended power level of at least .80.[90] Given that many studies likely have insufficient statistical power, it is likely that published meta-analyses have erroneously concluded that there are no statistically significant boundary conditions in the meta-regression analyses. So, the recommendation is to calculate the overall statistical power of your meta-regression model and the power to detect each hypothesized boundary condition before using meta-regression and reporting the analysis results. If power is found to be low, you should refrain from conducting meta-regression or, at the very least, be cautious when interpreting the results and conclusions of the study because non-significant results could be Type II errors (i.e., false negatives).

Calculation of Heterogeneity. Heterogeneity is the systemic variability (i.e., not attributable to sampling error) in the primary-level effect sizes. A large degree of heterogeneity indicates that boundary conditions are likely to present, and little heterogeneity indicates that boundary conditions are unlikely.[91] Thus, tests of heterogeneity provide prima facie evidence regarding the potential usefulness of investigating boundary conditions.

Heterogeneity can be calculated in five ways. First, the **Q statistic** is the weighted residual sum of squares between individual study effect sizes and the mean effect size across studies. The Q statistic follows a chi-square distribution and can be used to test the null hypothesis that heterogeneity is zero in the population. Q's statistical significance provides an easy-to-use decision rule as to whether to proceed with tests of boundary conditions.[92] However, the Q statistic does not provide an estimate of the amount of heterogeneity, and its statistical significance is largely based on sample size; further, because of its underlying basis in statistical significance testing, the Q statistic is underpowered with too few studies, and will also detect a trivial amount of heterogeneity with many studies. This increases the likelihood that you will identify a statistically significant boundary condition with minor importance for theory or practice.

Second, the credibility interval (CrI) provides a range that includes a particular percent of the population values (e.g., an 80% CrI includes 80% of the effect sizes in the population) after within-study variance and other study artifacts have been removed.[93] The CrI provides an absolute metric for evaluating the presence of heterogeneity as it is on the same scale as the effect size (e.g., r or d). Further, the CrI provides an upper and lower bound of the population effect size, with the typical decision rule being that if the CrI is sufficiently wide or includes zero, tests for boundary conditions are justified.[94] However, there is disagreement over what constitutes a narrow or wide CrI, and some have criticized the estimate of the variability in the true effects used to calculate the CrI as underestimating heterogeneity.[95]

Third, the **T^2 statistic** estimates the parameter τ^2 and denotes the between-study variance, computed as the Q statistic minus the degrees of freedom (i.e., $k - 1$) divided by a scaling factor. Thus, T^2 provides a direct estimate of the magnitude of heterogeneity. Like CrI, T^2 provides an absolute heterogeneity metric as it is on the same metric as the effect size (e.g., r or d), and its square root (i.e., T) can be used to compute a confidence interval around the population effect size. Researchers can proceed with their boundary condition tests if the confidence interval is sufficiently wide. However, like the CrI, it is unclear what constitutes a small or large value of T^2, and it cannot be used to compare heterogeneity across meta-analyses as it is a local estimate of heterogeneity.

Fourth, the **I^2 statistic** is a relative metric of heterogeneity.[96] Specifically, I^2 is the ratio of between-study variance to the total variance. While CrI and T^2 are on the same scale as the effect size analyzed in a meta-analysis, I^2 is on a 0 to 1 scale. Thus, although it does not provide information regarding the absolute amount of heterogeneity, the I^2 statistic can be used to compare heterogeneity across different meta-analyses by interpreting it as the percentage of variance attributable to between-study effects. Values of I^2 larger than .50 (i.e., more than 50% of the variance in effect sizes is attributable to between-study effects) indicate heterogeneity that should be explored further.

Finally, you may use a Bayesian method to estimate heterogeneity. Specifically, you can specify informed priors based on extant meta-analytic evidence and then use this data to build a probability density distribution of heterogeneity values. In this distribution, more likely values of heterogeneity (as determined by the informed priors) are given greater weight. Based on a Monte Carlo simulation and a re-analysis of several published studies, some researchers concluded that frequentist methods (e.g., T^2) underestimate heterogeneity and that the Bayesian method allows for more accurate estimation, mainly when the number of studies is small.[97] However, a challenge in all Bayesian analyses is the computation of a prior distribution.[98] Fortunately, you can use an existing database of about 150,000 effect sizes to calculate priors in the context of meta-regression.[99]

In sum, in terms of the calculation of heterogeneity, you should calculate, use, and report multiple indices of heterogeneity (i.e., the statistical significance of the heterogeneity, the absolute amount of heterogeneity, and the relative amount of heterogeneity) in deciding whether to proceed with meta-regression analyses. Another recommendation is to compare heterogeneity estimates (e.g., T^2) to estimates derived from Bayesian methods when the literature examined is sufficiently mature that informed priors are available. For example, suppose there is sufficient heterogeneity to justify using meta-regression based on examining multiple indices. In that case, you should explain your interpretation of the heterogeneity indices and provide a rationale for the analyses. On the other hand, if the body of evidence suggests more heterogeneity in the effect sizes, meta-regression is likely to lead to meaningful theory advancements.

Choosing the Type of Meta-Regression Model. As is the case in meta-analysis more generally, there are two types of meta-regression models: ME and FE models. Most meta-analysis programs with meta-regression capabilities, such as *Comprehensive Meta-Analysis*,[100] the *metafor* package in R,[101] and SPSS macros[102] can accommodate both models. As discussed earlier, each model has a specific set of assumptions, computational considerations, and situations when they should be used.

To compare the computational characteristics of the two models, the general weighting scheme for the studies analyzed in meta-regression is described by the following equation:

$$w_i = 1/\left[v_i + \tau_{\text{res}}^2 \right] \tag{11.2}$$

where w_i is the weight assigned to the ith study, v_i is the within-study variance of the ith study, and τ_{res}^2 is an estimate of the residual heterogeneity after accounting for the moderators included in the model. In the FE model, τ_{res}^2 is assumed to be zero. In contrast, in the ME model, τ_{res}^2 is assumed to be an unknown parameter (methods available to estimate τ_{res}^2 and the standard error of the regression coefficients are discussed below). As Equation 11.2 shows, ME models allow for both the residual heterogeneity and within-study variance to affect the weights of the effect sizes. This also affects the regression coefficients and results in larger standard errors, thus allowing for greater uncertainty in the estimates. This computational difference results in ME models assigning less weight to larger sample studies and more weight to smaller sample studies than FE models, which may result in effect size differences between the two.

METHODS IN PRACTICE
CONSEQUENCES OF CHOOSING A FIXED-EFFECTS (FE) VERSUS MIXED-EFFECTS (ME) META-REGRESSION MODEL

Whether to use the ME or FE model is a critical decision point because it affects Type I error rates, the power of the statistical tests, and the effect size estimate.[103] For example, some researchers found that although FE models are more powerful than ME models in detecting a true moderating effect, Type I error rates (i.e., false positives regarding the existence of boundary conditions) for FE models can exceed .50, which is ten times the usual .05 nominal level when there is moderate heterogeneity.[104] The high likelihood of false positive results may lead to the incorrect conclusion that there is a boundary condition, providing inaccurate information to organizational decision-makers. Therefore, FE models are appropriate only in mature fields of study when one is sufficiently confident that all possible moderators have been identified and included in the model and when the meta-analytic sample is sufficiently representative of the population. At the same time, ME models are appropriate in more nascent fields of study when the assumptions of the FE model are not satisfied.

In choosing the type of meta-regression model, you should use the ME model except for the specific instances where an FE model may be appropriate. Those instances include a mature field of study where all boundary conditions are included in the meta-regression model and when the sample of studies in the meta-analytic database is representative of the entire population of studies. When using either model, you should justify the model you use and, if using an FE model, also show ME results and provide evidence that the assumptions of the FE model have been met.

Calculation of Residual Heterogeneity. When using ME models, you must also decide how to estimate **residual heterogeneity,** τ^2_{res}. Residual heterogeneity is the variability in effects not accounted for by the boundary conditions included in the model (i.e., the variance that is "leftover") and, in conjunction with the within-study variance (v_i in Equation 11.2), is used to weigh the studies in the meta-regression analysis. This statistic is assumed to be zero in the FE model, and studies are only weighted by the inverse of the within-study variance. Note that τ^2_{res} is a population parameter that cannot be calculated precisely, and any estimate of τ^2_{res} includes some degree of error. Nevertheless, the choice of residual heterogeneity estimator has substantive consequences concerning Type I error rates, statistical power, and the predictive validity of the model because different estimators have different distributional assumptions, weigh studies differently, and vary in terms of their computational demands.[105]

Seven often-used residual heterogeneity estimators can be classified into iterative and non-iterative estimators. Both types estimate τ^2_{res} based on the heterogeneity in the studies and the covariance matrix of the proposed boundary conditions. Iterative estimators can be calculated using computer programs such as hierarchical linear modeling (HLM),[106] the *metafor* package in R, or macros designed for SPSS and other statistical software. Simulation studies show that iterative estimators such as the restricted maximum likelihood (REML) and **empirical Bayes (EB) estimators** perform best concerning accuracy and bias, which indicate the extent to which the estimator generates estimates that deviate from the population parameter and the extent to which the estimator systematically over- or underestimates τ^2_{res}, respectively.[107] This is especially true when the number of studies is small (i.e., $k < 40$), with iterative estimators being significantly more accurate than non-iterative estimates under these conditions.

In sum, you should use an iterative estimator of residual heterogeneity, such as the REML estimator. This is especially important if the number of studies is small ($k < 40$). The EB estimator can also be used when sufficient data are available to generate an informed prior distribution of residual heterogeneity, such as when conducting an updated meta-analysis to one published in the past.

Testing Boundary Condition Hypotheses. When used to test boundary condition hypotheses using meta-regression, the popular "**Wald-type**" **method** to estimate standard errors (i.e., the standard method used in WLS regression) yields incorrect estimates and false conclusions regarding the statistical significance of the regression coefficients. This is because the Wald-type method makes incorrect sample size adjustments to produce the standard errors of meta-regression coefficients,[108] and, in the context of ME models, the Wald-type method does not consider uncertainty in the estimate of τ^2_{res}. To address this issue when using FE models, you can use the Hedges and Olkin (2014) method to correct the standard error by dividing it by the square root of the mean-square residual and proceeding with hypothesis testing as usual while using a z-distribution. However, in ME models, the solution becomes more complex, as the method used to calculate the standard error of the regression coefficients has to consider uncertainty in the estimate of τ^2_{res}. As a result, using the Wald-type method in the ME model results in Type I error rates up to four times the nominal level, depending on sample size when the heterogeneity in the studies is greater than zero.[109]

Several alternative methods are available to calculate the standard error of the regression coefficient to address this problem. However, a comprehensive simulation study concluded that the Knapp and Hartung (2003) method provides the best statistical power and control of Type I error with accompanying ease of computation over other similarly effective methods and can be implemented using the *metafor* package in R and the *Comprehensive Meta-Analysis* computer program.[110]

Regarding testing boundary condition hypotheses, you should use the Hedges and Olkin (2014) method for FE models and the Knapp and Hartung (2003) method for ME models. Additionally, suppose you are using the HLM program for meta-regression. In that case, you should use robust standard errors (i.e., the Huber-White method) to test the statistical significance of the boundary conditions and only use this method when the sample size (k) is at least 80.

Adjusting R² for Known Variance. Estimates of variance explained (i.e., R^2) obtained from meta-regression analyses are biased downwardly because R^2 in a typical regression context treats within-study variance as unexplained.[111] In meta-regression, within-study variance can be quantified and used to calculate a more accurate estimate of R^2 as the percentage of between-studies variance explained by the model (i.e., R^2_{Meta}) in contrast to the typical method that calculates R^2 as the percentage of *total* variance accounted for by the model. The formula for R^2_{Meta} is the following:

$$R^2_{Meta} = 1 - \left[\tau^2_{res} / \tau^2 \right] \tag{11.3}$$

where τ^2_{res} is the residual heterogeneity after accounting for the boundary conditions, and τ^2 is the total heterogeneity. You can calculate R^2_{Meta} using estimates of τ^2_{res} and τ^2, as discussed previously. Typical regression models underestimate the amount of variance explained in the effect sizes by the boundary conditions included in the model. This is important because it suggests that meta-regression models have more explanatory power than typically reported and that published meta-regression studies underreported theories' explanatory power. In sum, you should calculate R^2_{Meta} to account for the known within-study variance in a meta-regression context.

Reporting Results of a Meta-regression Study

When reporting results, you should report your choices in detail to ensure transparency and maximize the likelihood of future results reproducibility. This is based on the same rationale for developing the MARS, as the American Psychological Association (APA) Publications and Communications board stated, "Without complete reporting of methods and results, the utility of studies for purposes of research synthesis and meta-analysis is diminished."[112]

Explanation of Methodological Choices. Many authors underreport key information regarding methodological choices. Thus, you should clearly explain and justify them. For example, suppose you want to use an FE model. In that case, you should clearly explain why it was used, including information about the heterogeneity of the studies, the maturity of the theory being examined, and the sampling population of studies.[113] Similarly, when using an ME model, you should provide a clear rationale as to why and an accompanying rationale to explain which estimator of residual heterogeneity was used. In either case, you should also report the specific method used to test the statistical significance of the regression coefficients.

Reporting and Interpreting Regression Coefficients. Most often, regression coefficients associated with a boundary condition are usually exclusively interpreted in terms of their statistical significance, as opposed to providing an interpretation that allows for assessing the magnitude and the importance of the effect size for theory and practice.[114] However, unstandardized and standardized regression coefficients can convey this information.

Unstandardized coefficients are useful in understanding practical importance because researchers can use unstandardized coefficients to generate meta-analytic effect size estimates under varying levels of the boundary condition.

> ### Example: Time as a Boundary Condition
>
> Some researchers examined time as a boundary condition, expecting that the temporal consistency and stability of job performance ratings would decline as the time between measurement episodes decreased.[115] Therefore, they chose practically relevant time gaps and entered these values into their meta-regression equation to provide actual estimates and accompanying confidence intervals of the temporal consistency and stability of job performance ratings at different time lags. When there is no particular interest in particular values of boundary conditions, a usual choice is to select values one SD below and above the mean. But, because unstandardized coefficients are scale-dependent, they cannot be used to compare the relative magnitude of effect sizes. Standardized coefficients allow for comparisons between boundary conditions within a meta-regression model and with a separately conducted meta-regression analysis. Thus, using standardized coefficients, you can compare the relative strength of one boundary condition over another. However, reporting only one coefficient type makes the practical significance of study results more difficult to interpret.

You should report unstandardized and standardized regression coefficients, as both sets provide important and complementary information. Further, using the unstandardized regression coefficients from meta-regression analyses to generate effect size values at different theoretically or practically relevant values of the boundary condition under study would be best.

Reporting Variable Intercorrelations and Descriptive Statistics. Finally, similar to reporting descriptive statistics (i.e., means, standard deviations) and variable intercorrelations in primary studies, in a meta-regression context, you should report the intercorrelations between effect sizes and boundary conditions as well as descriptive statistics to help readers and reviewers better evaluate meta-regression findings by identifying instances of high collinearity, redundancy between boundary conditions, or coding errors.[116]

Next, let's address a methodology that has rapidly gained ground: MASEM. MASEM combines meta-analysis (MA) and structural equation modeling (SEM). By incorporating the advantages of both tools, MASEM allows researchers to draw on accumulated findings to test the explanatory value of a theorized model against one or more competing models, thereby allowing researchers to conduct "horse races" between competing frameworks that cannot be carried out by meta-analysis alone. Moreover, the insights derived from such analyses can help inform theoretical models' boundaries, structure, and shortcomings while enabling researchers to determine theories' explanatory and predictive adequacy in advancing the field's knowledge.

META-ANALYTIC STRUCTURAL EQUATION MODELING

MASEM goes beyond meta-analysis by providing effect sizes that control for other variables in the model and information on the degree of fit of the entire model. In addition, MASEM can be used for testing intermediate mechanisms in a chain of relationships and pitting mediation hypotheses or models against one another regarding the existence, ordering, direction, and magnitudes of mediation (i.e., underlying) mechanism(s). Because mediating effects involve three or more variables, a meta-analysis focusing on bivariate relationships is ill-equipped to offer insights into important conceptual gaps. Furthermore, because it includes all the available data for a particular relationship, MASEM can maximize external validity.[117] MASEM can also integrate bivariate relationships from different primary-level studies. Finally, MASEM has a unique statistical power advantage.[118] Because the input for the SEM models is obtained via meta-analysis, which often pools thousands of individual-level effects, the sample size in MASEM is much larger than in a typical SEM study. Thus, findings from entire fields of study can be synthesized and tested using alternative model structures. MASEM provides a more powerful and in-depth basis for quantitatively synthesizing research findings than traditional meta-analysis or SEM.

As with any methodology, MASEM is subject to several boundary conditions. First, MASEM is less valuable for situations lacking competing hypotheses or models, such as when a research domain of interest is emergent. Second, MASEM is not practically feasible when there is limited availability of prior studies providing the needed meta-analytic correlations or primary study correlations to test one's specified models. Third, MASEM does not provide immunity to construct validity threats. Much like meta-analysis, there is the concern that the input (i.e., primary-level studies) can vary greatly in quality.[119] Fourth, MASEM will fail to produce useful results when missing data substitution, or imputation techniques are used excessively. For example, dealing with missing cells by replacing many existing variables with conceptually similar (i.e., surrogate) variables will not be very trustworthy to a practitioner interested in conclusions based on the actual variables of interest. Fifth, MASEM may have difficulties testing moderation due to the bivariate nature of the meta-analysis effect size data and limitations in conducting moderation tests within most SEM packages.

A sixth limitation of MASEM is the need for more conclusive causal inferences based on data from non-experimental studies. Unless all of the studies used as input to a MASEM rely on experimental designs, MASEM cannot provide unequivocal evidence regarding causality, even if the data come from studies using lagged/longitudinal research designs. Indeed, while the majority of social and behavioral science research provides evidence regarding covariation between antecedent and outcome variables, covariation alone does not address all three conditions needed to establish causality: (1) the cause preceded the effect, (2) the cause was related to the effect, and (3) there is no plausible alternative explanation for the effect other than the cause. One perspective is that it is simply impossible to make any claims about causality unless you are using the 'gold standard' of internal validity and causal evidence – experimental design.[120] Because the overwhelming majority of social and behavioral science research uses non-experimental designs, and the field is very likely to continue using such designs in the future, you should refrain from making strong causal statements when using MASEM and instead use the technique to evaluate the comparative fit of alternative models and provide guidance for future investigations, perhaps adopting an experimental design approach, in showing which models fit empirical reality best.

Finally, related to issues of causality, the data used in meta-analysis computations (i.e., means, standard deviations, sample sizes) could have been derived from research designs vulnerable to endogeneity. Endogeneity is a statistical bias that results from correlations between an independent variable and the error term in an ordinary least squares regression model. It can arise from several reasons: measurement error, autoregression, omitted variables, selection bias in collecting the sample, and simultaneous causality among the variables.[121] The possible presence of endogeneity may further narrow the studies that could be included in a MASEM, and you have to conduct additional logical argumentation and statistical procedures to help address it.

Despite these potential limitations, MASEM provides a stronger technique than traditional meta-analysis. MASEM allows you to take the findings from an entire stream of research and use them as the basis for testing complex models. Using a field's accumulated data, MASEM enables you to examine fundamentally important questions about the viability of theoretical and conceptual frameworks. Although MASEM does not allow conclusions about causal structures, it provides a vehicle for comparing alternative models and enables you to retain the empirically superior structure. This approach is consistent with the philosophy of science literature, which suggests that science aspires to retain the most plausible models given the available data and discard those that are inferior or falsified.[122]

MASEM: Implementation

Implementing MASEM requires four general steps. Figure 11.1 displays the process and shows where nine critical decision points arise. Of course, not all MASEM processes will include all the decision points, depending on the theoretical models to be tested and the data type available. However, this model provides a resource if you choose to conduct a MASEM study or evaluate a MASEM as a producer, consumer, or reviewer.

Step 1: Specify Variables and Conceptual Models

First, you must specify the variables and models to be evaluated. The nature of these models is driven by the research questions under investigation.

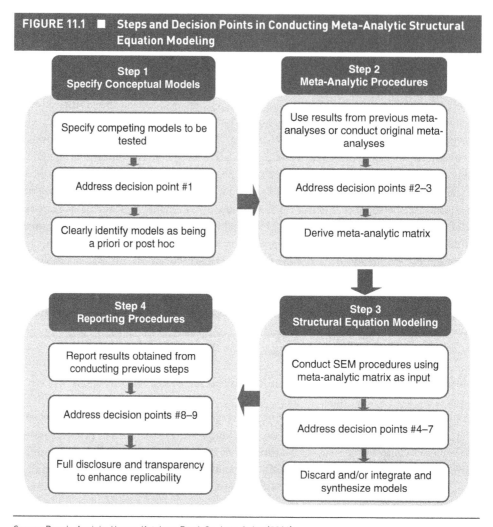

FIGURE 11.1 ■ Steps and Decision Points in Conducting Meta-Analytic Structural Equation Modeling

Source: Bergh, Aguinis, Heavy, Ketchen, Boyd, Su, Lau, & Joo (2016).

Decision Point #1. The first step in a MASEM involves specifying the study variables, models, and focal relationships. These models should be based on an exhaustive literature review of the pertinent theories and extant empirical studies to identify relevant variables and reduce the threat of omitted variables as a source of possible endogeneity. Endogeneity happens when the predictors correlate with the error term, resulting from several factors, such as missing variables from your model (i.e., omitted variables) and simultaneity (i.e., the predictor and outcome are both affected by a common underlying variable). This step involves specifying an outcome predicted by two or more antecedent variables, where all the predictors fully or partially co-vary. In addition, if a research question requires pitting mediation hypotheses or models against one another in terms of the existence, ordering, directions, or magnitudes of mediation mechanism(s), then the specified model can also take advantage of MASEM's ability to provide insight into a chain's intermediate mechanisms. For example, in a simple case involving four variables, this approach is realized by specifying A and B → C → D vs. A and C → B → D. Moreover, these models could be compared against a simpler one involving just one predictor such as A → C → D. At the end of this process, you can then present one or two superior models. In some cases, none of the pre-specified models may fit the data well, and you may offer post-hoc models created inductively based on the obtained results. Further, specifying competing models can present an opportunity for ruling out endogeneity as a threat to interpreting the findings. Thus, models' a priori or post-hoc nature should be made explicit.

Step 2: Meta-analytic Procedures

The second step is to collect meta-analytic data. This involves identifying meta-analytically derived effect sizes reported in prior meta-analyses or estimating these effects by performing a meta-analysis of the bivariate correlations from primary studies. As with all meta-analyses, effect size estimates must be converted to a common standardized metric across primary-level studies before being synthesized. This is why correlation coefficients are the most typical effect size metric rather than regression coefficients, given that the size and sometimes even the signs of regression coefficients are affected by the metrics of the particular measures used and the number of variables in a regression model.

Decision Point #2. When conducting meta-analyses, you will likely encounter situations whereby some meta-analytic effects cannot be computed due to missing studies. The possible solutions to this problem include: (1) search again for relevant studies based on the same and different search criteria; (2) contact other researchers to request correlation values[123]; (3) conduct original primary-level studies; (4) replace some existing variables with conceptually similar 'surrogate' variables; (5) group-specific constructs into a broader construct(s) by deriving composite correlations[124]; (6) use a two-stage structural equation modeling (TSSEM), which manages missing values automatically[125]; (7) implement advanced data imputation techniques such as full information maximum likelihood (FIML)[126]; (8) use the average effect size across all non-missing effect sizes; or (9) rely on subject matter experts or expertise to estimate the value for the missing effect sizes. The first three options are the most desirable because they involve using actual data without conceptual or empirical manipulation. If none of the above possible solutions are available, your remaining option is to limit the scope of inquiry.

Decision Point #3. When performing meta-analyses across several different pairs of variables, you will likely face a situation wherein a different sample size value is used to compute each meta-analytically derived correlation. The options to address this situation include using: (1) the **harmonic mean**[127]; (2) the smallest total sample size[128]; (3) the median[129]; or (4) the arithmetic mean.[130] The harmonic mean is calculated by $k/(1/N_1 + 1/N_2 + \ldots \ldots 1/N_k)$, where k equals the number of meta-analytic correlations and $N_1 \ldots N_k$ refers to the total sample sizes for each meta-analytically derived correlation.[131] The harmonic mean is the preferred option because it limits the influence of very large values and increases the influence of smaller values, in addition to being smaller in most cases than the arithmetic mean.[132]

Step 3: Structural Equation Modeling

Before discussing specific decision points, a general implementation issue is choosing a particular software package. Several alternatives are available, including IBM-SPSS Amos, EQS, Mplus, and R. Each of these packages offers similar capabilities, and the main difference is how the meta-analytic matrix used as input should be prepared for the analysis. This information is included in each of the packages' manuals. Given their similar capabilities, you should choose the package you already know.

Decision Point #4. It would be best to recognize that the likelihood of obtaining a non-positive definite meta-analytic matrix (i.e., ill-defined matrix including zero or negative eigen-values) increases in a MASEM study. This problem arises from several sources, including some meta-analytically derived matrixes that may have a small N for some cells, two variables may be very highly correlated, and the presence of empty cells may lead to an over-use of missing data imputation techniques. Some researchers suggested several possible solutions available in LISREL, such as choosing alternative global starting values or selecting more precise starting values for parameter estimates.[133] In addition, you can anticipate and address this problem by expanding the article pool and reducing the set of variables.

Decision Point #5. Within-study or within-sample dependency refers to an overrepresentation of the same study or sample, or very similar types of studies or samples, in estimating an effect size. Such dependencies (e.g., an effect size derived from a set of studies that rely on a single data-base) are problematic partly because they limit the generalizability of meta-analytic findings.[134] As noted by some researchers, "the data set to be [meta-analyzed] will invariably contain complicated patterns of statistical dependence . . . [because] each study is likely to yield more than one finding . . . the simple (but risky) solution . . . is to regard each finding as independent of the others" (p. 200).[135] When sample dependencies are present, you should follow these steps[136]: (1) include all substantively relevant correlations from each sample for further consideration; (2) derive a composite correlation from conceptually similar individual component correlations from each sample; and then (3) if multiple studies were based on completely or partially overlapping data sets, choose correlation(s) based on the larger sample size(s). You can also use a **generalized least squares (GLS)** procedure that accounts for the dependencies in effect sizes and may yield more accurate parameter estimates than the traditional ordinary least squares procedure.[137] Finally, another alternative is to apply random-effects meta-analyses or multilevel meta-analytic approaches in combination with MASEM.[138]

Decision Point #6. Apply multiple fit measures. While chi-square is a commonly used index of fit in SEM, it depends on sample size. Consequently, given the large number of observations usually seen in MASEM, the chi-square statistic might indicate poor fit, even if the discrepancy between the correlation matrix underlying the hypothesized model and the empirically obtained correlation matrix is very small.[139] Instead, it would be best if you used multiple fit indices, such as the comparative fit index (CFI), **goodness-of-fit index (GFI)**, and the **root mean square residual (RMSR)**. Although there are general guidelines regarding cutoffs for satisfactory fit, some recent analytical and simulation work demonstrated that many of the assumptions underlying these cutoff recommendations may need to be revised, and the cutoff is often context-specific.[140] So, you should be careful when specifying cutoff values and consider the relative fit of the compared models.

Decision Point #7. It would be best to distinguish between suitable and unsuitable meta-analytic correlations for a MASEM study. You can apply the following criteria: (1) choose meta-analytic correlations corresponding to variables whose operationalizations are consistent with a priori definitions of interest; (2) select meta-analytic correlations reported by meta-analyses that used pre-specified meta-analytic techniques (e.g., how unreliability was corrected); and (3) use meta-analytic correlations reported by meta-analyses based on the largest sample sizes.

Because MASEM is based on the syntheses of others' reported findings, it is important to recognize that those results may be based on designs vulnerable to endogeneity. Unfortunately, meta-analysis has no techniques to correct such issues retroactively. You should, therefore, recognize the possible threat of endogeneity to the population of correlations that could be used in the MASEM and choose to discard a study if its regression analyses indicate that endogeneity was a significant factor afflicting the relationships among the variables that would be used in the meta-analysis. Another alternative is to make logical arguments based on facts, rule out alternative explanations, provide evidence of theoretical mechanisms, and offer arguments that an instrument has a logical relationship with the endogenous variable, is correlated with the dependent variable only through the endogenous variable, and is not itself endogenous.[141]

In addition, you have options to help relieve the sources of endogeneity, including: (1) using lagged data models to help account for autocorrelation; (2) recognizing measurement error among the variables in the model; (3) expanding the variables in the model to help mitigate the omitted variables problem, and (4) and testing competing models that may reflect alternative and endogenous views. Finally, there may be multiple and often unknown reasons why endogeneity may exist (e.g., omitted variables). Still, based on current knowledge, you should rule out as many sources as possible.

Step 4: Reporting Procedures

Decision Point #8. In terms of reporting, you should follow the Meta-Analysis Reporting Standards (MARS) to maximize standardization, transparency, and replicability.[142] These standards include, for instance, the need to describe how studies were obtained and content-analyzed (e.g., decision point #2 regarding missing cells) and the nature of constructs or variables specified in the models. Consistent with standard practice, you should use ovals in figures to represent latent variables (i.e., underlying constructs) and rectangles for observable variables (i.e., indicators). Note that models including observed variables only would be drawn using rectangles for all variables, and the procedures involved would then be labeled meta-analytic path analysis rather than MASEM.

Decision Point #9. The MARS guidelines leave a few important issues unaddressed. So, in addition to following the MARS guidelines, you should: (1) create a table that includes all estimated bivariate meta-analytic correlations (including the 95% confidence interval for each correlation), the number of studies for each correlation (k), and total sample size (N); (2) report the results of each tested model by creating a figure including ovals representing latent factors (i.e., underlying constructs) and rectangles represent observable variables; (3) report coefficients (which are always standardized in MASEM), their statistical significance level, standard errors, and 95% confidence intervals; (4) report the results of each tested MASEM model by discussing the procedures used to address decision points #4-7; (5) if applicable, report formal tests of comparisons between coefficients in the model, and (6) clearly state that the reported results do not provide direct and unequivocal evidence regarding causality if the primary-level studies were not experimental in nature.

The last section in this chapter addresses a relevant question when planning to conduct a meta-analysis on a topic that has already been reviewed: "Is an updated meta-analysis warranted?"

IS THERE A NEED FOR AN UPDATED META-ANALYSIS?

The issue of meta-analytic currency has been intensely debated, culminating in a two-day international workshop by the Cochrane Collaboration's Panel for Updating Guidance for Systematic Review.[143] Drawing on this panel's work and similar recommendations by other researchers,[144] a revised set of guidelines is summarized in Figure 11.2.

FIGURE 11.2 ■ Decision Framework to Determine the Need to Conduct an Updated Meta-Analysis

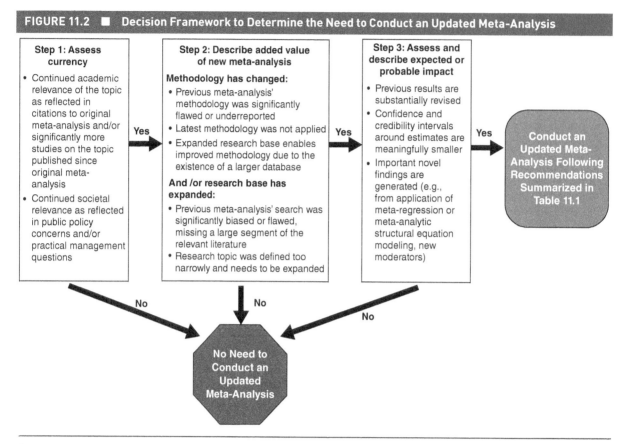

Source: Steel, Beugelsdijk, & Aguinis (2021).

Step one is the consideration of currency. Does the review still address a relevant question? Has the topic increased in relevance as reflected, for example, by frequent citations and the widespread concern about a particular topic (e.g., as reflected by media mentions)? *Step two* is to consider the methodology and the research base. Have any new relevant methods been developed? Did previously published meta-analyses miss any appropriate applications? Meta-analysis has rapidly developed, and as described in this chapter, numerous refinements could be applied, from outlier analysis to MASEM. Alternatively, have any new relevant studies been published or have new information? Also, an expanded research base enables the application of more sophisticated analysis techniques. *Step three* is the probable impact of the new methodology and studies. Can they be expected to change the findings or reduce uncertainty? For example, providing a previously unavailable complete meta-analytic database in an Open Science archive (enabling cumulative growth) can still be considered impactful (especially as it motivates all researchers to data-share or risk their meta-analysis being rapidly superseded).

Finally, if you decide an updated meta-analysis is warranted, you will implement the recommendations summarized in Table 11.1. The more of the elements expounded in Table 11.1 that your updated meta-analysis has compared to its predecessor, the more likely it is to deserve favorable treatment by journal reviewers and readers.

DISCUSSION QUESTIONS

1. What is a meta-analysis, and why is it important for advancing social and behavioral science research?

2. How do different choices and judgment calls affect the results of a meta-analytic study? Why?

3. Summarize the similarities and differences between the mixed-effects and fixed-effects meta-analytic models. When and why would you choose one or the other?

4. What are the critical steps you should take during each of the following stages in a state-of-the-science metanalysis: data collection, data preparation, data analysis, and reporting?

5. Choose a recently published meta-analysis. To what extent did it implement the best practices summarized in Table 11.1? Based on your critical examination, to what extent do you trust the results from this meta-analysis?

6. In what ways does meta-regression differ from ordinary least squares (OLS) regression?

7. What are the problems with using the subgrouping technique when examining continuous moderators with meta-regression?

8. Under what conditions is MASEM *not* an appropriate tool for meta-analysis?

9. Why is it important to identify models as a priori or post hoc when conducting MASEM?

10. Choose a substantive domain in which a meta-analysis has already been published. Then, based on examining Figure 11.2, what is your conclusion about whether an updated meta-analysis is warranted?

KEY TERMS

availability bias
boundary condition
Cattell's Data Cube
common language effect size
common-effect (CE) model
construct identity fallacy
cost bias
credibility interval
data box
Egger's regression test
empirical Bayes (EB) estimators
familiarity bias
fixed-effect model
generalized least squares (GLS)
goodness-of-fit index (GFI)
I^2 statistic

implicit selection bias
individual participant data (IPD)
jangle fallacy
jingle fallacy
language bias
living systematic review (LSR)
log odds ratio
meta-regression analysis (MARA)
Meta-Analytic Reporting Standards (MARS)
meta-analytic structural equation modeling (MASEM)
meta-regression
mixed-effects (ME) model
mono-method bias
odds ratio
Open Science

precision-effect test and precision-
  effect estimate with standard errors
  (PET-PEESE)
Preferred Reporting Items for Systematic
  Reviews and Meta-Analyses (PRISMA)
Preferred Reporting Items for Systematic
  Reviews and Meta-Analyses Protocols
  (PRISMA-P)

Q statistic
residual heterogeneity, τ^2_{res}
Robust Error Variance (RVE)
root mean square residual (RMSR)
T^2 statistic
The Matthew Effect
Wald-type method

NOTES

This chapter is based to a large extent on the following sources:

Aguinis, H., Dalton, D. R., Bosco, F. A., Pierce, C. A., & Dalton, C. M. (2011). Meta-analytic choices and judgment calls: Implications for theory building and testing, obtained effect sizes, and scholarly impact. *Journal of Management, 37*(1):5-38. https://doi.org/10.1177/0149206310377113

Aguinis, H., Gottfredson, R. K., & Wright, T. A. (2011). Best-practice recommendations for estimating interaction effects using meta-analysis. *Journal of Organizational Behavior, 32*(8), 1033-1043. https://doi.org/10.1002/job.719

Aguinis, H., Pierce, C. A., Bosco, F. A, Dalton, D. R., & Dalton, C. M. (2011). Debunking myths and urban legends about meta-analysis. *Organizational Research Methods, 14*(2), 306-331. https://doi.org/10.1177/1094428110375720

Bergh, D. D., Aguinis, H., Heavy, C., Ketchen, D. J., Boyd, B. K., Su, P., Lau, C., & Joo, H. (2016). Using meta-analytic structural equation modeling to advance strategic management research: Guidelines and an empirical illustration via the strategic leadership-performance relationship. *Strategic Management Journal, 37*(3), 477-497. https://doi.org/10.1002/smj.2338

Gonzalez-Mulé, E., & Aguinis, H. (2018). Advancing theory by assessing boundary conditions with meta-regression: A critical review and best-practice recommendations. *Journal of Management, 44*(6), 2246–2273. https://doi.org/10.1177/0149206317710723

Steel, P., Beugelsdijk S., & Aguinis, H. (2021). The anatomy of an award-winning meta-analysis: Recommendations for authors, reviewers, and users of meta-analytic reviews. *Journal of International Business Studies, 52*(1), 23-44. https://doi.org/10.1057/s41267-020-00385-z

12

HOW TO CONDUCT QUANTITATIVE ANALYSIS, PART IV: ADVANCED TECHNIQUES

LEARNING GOALS

By the end of this chapter, you will be able to do the following:

12.1 Formulate the goals of using market basket analysis (MBA).

12.2 Understand the benefits of using MBA, including how it allows for inductive theorizing, can address contingency relationships, does not rely on assumptions that are often violated when using regression-based techniques, allows for the use of data often considered "unusable" and "messy," can help build dynamic theories, is suited to examine relationships across levels of analysis, and is practitioner-friendly.

12.3 Arrange the steps involved in market basket analysis, including determining the suitability of MBA, defining the "transactions," collecting data, checking MBA requirements, and deriving association rules and their strength.

12.4 Formulate the goals of Experience Sampling Methodology (ESM).

12.5 Understand the benefits of ESM, including capturing dynamic person-by-situation interactions over time, enhancing ecological validity, and allowing for an examination of between- and within-person variability.

12.6 Describe the steps necessary to design and implement ESM, including determining the sample size, scheduling, signaling devices, recruiting participants, and data analysis.

12.7 Propose the advantages of Bayesian analysis over frequentist analysis, including using prior knowledge, the joint distribution of parameters, assessment of null hypothesis, ability to test complex models, unbalanced or small sample sizes, multiple comparisons, and power analysis and replication probability.

12.8 Set up the steps to implement Bayesian multiple linear regression, including establishing the prior distribution, computing the posterior distribution, accepting the null value, and summarizing Bayesian analysis's rich information.

IMPORTANCE OF ADVANCED QUANTITATIVE TECHNIQUES

The 21st century has marked the beginning of important changes in the social and behavioral sciences. The field decided to ensure that "selling a good story" was not prioritized over sound research methods, which are the hallmark of credible and trustworthy science. As a result, the last decade has been characterized by the introduction of many methodological innovations. This chapter describes three useful advanced quantitative social and behavioral sciences techniques: **Market Basket Analysis (MBA)**, Experience Sampling Methodology (ESM), and Bayesian Analysis. This chapter describes these three methods' main advantages and the steps needed to implement them in your research. Moreover, each section provides detailed examples of the steps you need to take. Finally, it illustrates how you would implement them across substantive domains such as marketing for MBA, entrepreneurship for ESM, and organizational research for Bayesian Analysis.

MARKET BASKET ANALYSIS

Market Basket Analysis (MBA) allows you to uncover non-obvious, usually hidden, and counterintuitive associations between products, items, or categories. This methodological approach allows you to identify those items that co-occur (i.e., appear together) frequently and assess the extent to which they co-occur. For example, MBA has been used to understand consumer behavior regarding types of books purchased together (as purchased on Amazon.com) and different types of wines the same individual is likely to purchase (as purchased on VirginWines.com).[1] Because MBA originated in the marketing field and was initially used to understand which supermarket items are purchased together (i.e., placed together in the same "basket"), the technique adopted the name *market basket analysis*.

IBM and Rutgers University researchers were the first to use MBA. These authors were computer scientists with access to an extensive repository of previously collected customer transaction data and discovered association rules between purchased items.[2] As a result, researchers in the field of marketing quickly adopted the method as a popular tool for numerous practical applications.

> ### Example: Are Cake Mix and Icing Purchased Together?
>
> Suppose that you use MBA to gather empirical support that cake mix and icing tend to be purchased together. You may then determine that cake mix and icing are **complementary items** (i.e., categories) such that lowering the price of only one is associated with increased demand for both goods.[3] Theoretically, you can use MBA to develop hypotheses and theories inductively. For example, these results suggest that consumers may have mental models that include associations among other complementary items regarding their activities and interests (e.g., running shoes and water bottles). From a practical standpoint, this study's results can be used to make decisions such as stocking the two items near each other, thereby increasing the likelihood that customers will easily find and purchase both products instead of just one.[4]

The applicability of an MBA is broader than analyzing archival data. You can also use this method with primary data. For example, researchers mailed out surveys where respondents completed open-choice checklists regarding common food allergens.[5] As a result, they found that specific food allergens tend to occur together in the same person. Another team of researchers collected responses from secondary-school students in Singapore about their preferences regarding school-based counseling services to illustrate the use of MBA with primary data.[6] Based on their responses to the administered questionnaires, students were separated into two groups—those willing to see a counselor and those unwilling—and others identified each group's main traits and concerns.[7] In short, although MBA has traditionally been used with archival data, it can also be used with primary data.

Categorical association rules are based on binary data. This is the most common type of association rule because MBA was initially developed to analyze shopping cart data in binary form: A customer bought or did not buy a particular product. However, it is possible to derive association rules involving continuous variables.[8] Association rules involving a continuous variable are called **quantitative association rules**. Categorical association rules relate a value of a categorical variable with the value of another categorical variable. Still, a quantitative association rule relates a value of a categorical variable with a summary statistic of a continuous variable (e.g., mean, median). For example, MBA has been used to derive quantitative association rules based on hotel customers.[9] The dataset included responses to Likert-type scales assessing behavioral and attitudinal constructs provided by customers of a large hotel chain. As a result, this study derived several quantitative association rules that related specific floor numbers with mean room satisfaction scores. In short, MBA allows for deriving association rules, including categorical and continuous variables, such as those measured using multiple-item scales.

Advantages of Using Market Basket Analysis

Advantage 1: MBA Allows for Inductive Theorizing

MBA is a powerful technique for inductive theorizing. More specifically, MBA allows you to use vast stores of data for theory-building purposes. Using MBA can lead to significant contributions by allowing you to implement an inductive approach to theory-building, which, despite its advantages, is underutilized in social and behavioral sciences research.[10]

Example: Using Market Basket Analysis for Theory Building

Using MBA for inductive theory-building has led to insights into marketing and other fields. For example, some authors pointed out that MBA has allowed marketing researchers to build theoretical models of purchasing decisions involving products in more than one category (i.e., multiple-category decision-making).[11] Others have used MBA inductively to study important questions outside the marketing field. And yet other authors used MBA to study patients with food allergies who present allergy symptoms to multiple food allergens.[12] MBA allowed them to inductively create models regarding which allergens are related to which (e.g., chicken with eggs, abalone with salmon eggs, and matsutake mushrooms with milk).

You can use MBA inductively to generate hypotheses to test deductively in follow-up work. For example, MBA has been used to collect archival data from a car rental company to derive association rules that related certain types of phrases uttered by customer service agents to whether customers later picked up reserved cars.[13] To test whether specific phrases improved the probability of pick-up, these researchers conducted a follow-up experiment to draw causal inferences. Customer service agents were randomly assigned to two groups—those trained on the recommendations based on the derived association rules (treatment) and those not (control). The dependent variable was the average pick-up ratio, defined as the number of actual pick-ups to the number of reservations. Results indicated that the average improvement in the pick-up ratio of the treatment group was greater than that of the control group. This study offers a good illustration of the possibility of first using MBA to generate hypotheses inductively and then conducting a follow-up study that is deductive in nature.

Advantage 2: MBA Can Address Contingency Relationships

You can use MBA to uncover contingency relationships, also labeled moderating or interaction effects.[14] Specifically, MBA can reveal the strength of a given relationship and the extent to which such relationships (i.e., association rules) vary across different contexts. For example, suppose that MBA yields the association rule linking variables A and B from a dataset. Once a binary moderator (consisting of groups G1 and G2) is added to the dataset, MBA may reveal that the *confidence* of [(A), (B)], or the association rule relating A and B, is weaker for group G1 and stronger for group G2. In addition, MBA may reveal that a distinct association, [(C), (B)], is also an association rule for group G1 but not for G2 and that yet another distinct association, [(F), (A)], constitutes an association rule for group G2 but not G1.

Example: Time and Place as Moderators in Market Basket Analysis

Some authors designed an algorithm that conducts MBA using a contingency approach, such that time and place were conceptualized as moderators.[15] Adding contextual information to an MBA analysis allows for identifying purchase patterns, considering whether they occur on particular days and regions. Although social and behavioral sciences scholars have relied primarily on methods such as moderated multiple regression to assess contingency relationships.[16] MBA is superior in many situations because it does not rely on often untenable assumptions.

Advantage 3: MBA Does Not Rely on Often Untenable Assumptions

MBA is not bound by assumptions such as the linearity, residual normality, and residual equal variance required by regression-based techniques, frequently used in social and behavioral science research.[17] MBA assesses relationships between items or categories instead of linear relationships between two or more variables. As a result, MBA is free from the strict assumptions often violated in social and behavioral sciences research.

Advantage 4: MBA Allows the Use of "Unusable" and "Messy" Data

MBA enables you to use data often seen as "unusable" for social and behavioral sciences research. Specifically, most organizations regularly collect data on many business functions, such as human resources.[18] For example, given the availability and affordability of data storage systems, organizations regularly collect data on employees (e.g., performance, absenteeism, benefits choices, training opportunities), customers (e.g., purchasing choices, frequency of visits), and many other issues. Moreover, such data are often collected unsystematically, sporadically, and without a particular scientific study in mind. MBA is ideally suited to be used inductively with such datasets to uncover association rules that may not be readily apparent.[19]

"Messy" data often involve issues such as missing values and outliers. This type of data is common and poses many challenges in social and behavioral sciences research, particularly at the organization and industry levels of analysis.[20] While MBA is not immune to the problem of missing values, it allows for the interpretation of missing data as indicating that no option was selected or preferred. MBA does this by deriving association rules with values of lift below 1.0, such that these association rules use the presence of one item to predict the absence of another item. *Lift* is the probability of all of the items in a rule occurring together (referred to as the *support*) divided by the product of the probabilities of the items occurring as if there was no association between them. Thus, MBA allows you to derive association rules such as the following: If a customer orders a tofu vegan meal as the main dish, there is a 65 percent chance that the customer will not order any dessert. A caveat to this advantage is that missing responses, or nonchoices, must be substantively meaningful, rather than caused by artifacts, for association rules that treat the absence of an item as a distinct item to be meaningful (see the section below titled "Step 4: Check MBA Requirements").

METHODS IN PRACTICE
MARKET BASKET ANALYSIS AND OUTLIERS

Another advantage of MBA related to messy data is that outliers influence association rules less than traditional data-analytic approaches. In the context of MBA, outliers result in infrequently occurring associations.[21] For example, results may indicate that only one customer's "basket" included a washing machine and a warranty for a computer. Whether the result of an error in data entry or extremely uncommon customer behavior, such a combination will have a lift value near unity and very small values for support and confidence. Consequently, this outlier will not influence overall substantive results to the extent that an outlier would influence regression results based on standard errors, correlation coefficients, and regression coefficients.[22]

While no method can overcome data collection or entry errors, MBA offers flexibility while attempting to use an extant dataset. However, suppose you are bound by regression's assumptions. In that case, you will find many datasets unusable, despite the value those datasets might offer as a window into social and behavioral science phenomena that may be otherwise unavailable.

Advantage 5: MBA Can Help Build Dynamic Theories

Social and behavioral science research increasingly acknowledges time's important role in theory-building.[23] Accordingly, there is a growing interest in understanding phenomena as they unfold longitudinally.[24] Accordingly, another advantage of MBA is that it can help you build theories from cross-sectional and longitudinal data. In other words, MBA allows for theory-building efforts that are both cross-sectional and longitudinal (i.e., dynamic) in nature.

Based on the nature of the available data, there are mainly two ways of building dynamic theories via MBA: (a) **multiple MBA** and (b) **sequential MBA (SMBA)**. You can use the multiple MBA approach when the available data include transactions over time (i.e., transactions at time 1, transactions at time 2, ..., transactions at time *k*). The multiple MBA approach involves treating each data wave as a single cross-sectional study and examining whether association rules' lift, support, and confidence vary over time, which can be done descriptively using graphs.[25] You can use SMBA when the available data describe individual events (i.e., items) as they have occurred over time. For example, a dataset may consist of employees' files since they were hired. So, the dataset may include information gathered during their first, second, third, and so forth month of employment. SMBA may uncover the presence of an association rule such as [(A), (B), (C)], suggesting that there is a pattern in which event A (e.g., being assigned to a formal mentor) occurs before B (e.g., volunteering to participate in a particular training and development program), which occurs before C (e.g., receiving higher performance evaluation scores).[26]

Advantage 6: MBA Can Be Used to Assess Multilevel Relationships

You can apply MBA across all levels of analysis ranging from within-individual to firm-, industry-, and country-level contexts. For example, MBA can simultaneously examine categories representing individual, group, team, or organizational characteristics. For example, in the field of marketing, if the organizational unit is used as the level of analysis, then you can derive association rules linking lower-level (e.g., individual SUBWAY restaurants) with higher-level units (e.g., the entire chain of SUBWAY restaurants within a particular state) and even higher levels of analysis (e.g., all SUBWAY restaurants within the United States).

Methods for assessing relationships between lower-level predictors and higher-level outcomes are nascent and in the early stages of development.[27] However, many social and behavioral sciences theories posit such effects.[28] Using MBA has excellent potential to lead to theoretical advancements regarding the presence of such relationships.

Advantage 7: MBA Is Practitioner-friendly

The widely documented science–practice divide in social and behavioral sciences is due, at least in part, to a lack of good communication between researchers and practitioners, who seem to speak different languages.[29] MBA is practitioner-friendly because of how results are presented. Numerical results produced by MBA are intuitive and easy to understand from a practical significance perspective. For example, *support* and *confidence* are based on a 0 to 100 percent probability scale, which facilitates the interpretation of association rules' practical significance. In other words, MBA relies on the strength of the association rules, which makes results more easily understandable by practitioners.

In short, MBA has excellent potential as a methodological approach in the social and behavioral sciences because it allows for inductive theorizing, can address contingency relationships, does not rely on assumptions that are often violated when using regression-based techniques, allows for the use of data often considered "unusable" and "messy," can help build dynamic theories, is suited to examine relationships across levels of analysis, and is practitioner-friendly. The following section provides a detailed description of how you can use MBA.

Steps Involved in Using Market Basket Analysis

This section describes the steps involved in conducting a study using MBA. The six steps cover the entire research process, which begins with assessing MBA's suitability to study the issue (Step 1) and the definition of the transactions (Step 2). Then, once data are collected (Step 3), there is a need to check whether some basic requirements for the use of MBA are met (Step 4). Then, association rules are derived (Step 5). Finally, results are interpreted (Step 6).

To make this description more vivid, let's use a dataset of 1,000 employees regarding their choices in terms of benefits. Although this dataset has been created for illustration purposes, these data are realistic because the distribution of benefits was patterned using results from a national compensation survey.[30] This illustrative dataset also includes information on other issues about each employee (e.g., gender, number of children). Such data are usually available to human resource management units of most organizations. In addition, they are of interest to researchers and practitioners wishing to study benefit bundles selected or preferred by different subgroups of employees based on demographic variables. Studying such data with MBA would be particularly helpful because the traditional one-size-fits-all approach to benefits is no longer tenable for the 21st century's increasingly diverse and global workforce.[31]

Step 1: Determine the Suitability of MBA

As noted earlier, MBA is typically used to examine associations based on data with binary variables. In addition, MBA can derive association rules that incorporate data collected from Likert-type or truly continuous scales.[32] However, it is not possible to apply MBA when the dataset consists of data collected from continuous or Likert-type scales only. There must be some categorical variables, among which there is some interest or meaningfulness for deriving categorical or quantitative association rules. Nonetheless, the majority of data routinely collected by organizations as part of their business analytics efforts and those collected by scholars for research purposes contain binary and continuous variables. Thus, MBA can be used with many types of data.

In addition, MBA has the most significant potential if the situation allows you to capitalize on one or more of the advantages mentioned in the previous section. In other words, if you are interested in theory-building; if applying regression-based techniques to the dataset will violate assumptions such as the linearity, residual normality, and residual equal variance; if the data seem unusable or too messy for use with traditional regression-based approaches; if you want to examine multilevel, contingency, and dynamic relationships; or if you are interested in producing results that can be communicated easily to a practitioner audience, then MBA is likely to be a good methodological alternative. On the other hand, MBA is not appropriate for theory-testing purposes due to its exploratory nature.

This illustration meets these criteria because it allows an inductively understanding of employees' choices in terms of their benefits. Also, this illustration reflects various issues and levels of analysis that can arise when using data collected via an organization's human resource planning software such as SAP SuccessFactors and Oracle HCM Cloud—data that would not typically be seen as "usable" and data that were not collected with a particular research study in mind.

Step 2: Define the "Transactions"

In marketing, a typical transaction consists of products purchased by a customer at a retail store or on a website. These transactions constitute the observations or cases that comprise the data entered into the MBA software. These items or categories can include information on individuals, teams, units, organizations, industries, or even countries. Also, transactions can occur at one point or over time and involve a day, a quarter, a fiscal year, or even more extended periods. Finally, transactions can be captured at any time because transactions are not limited to a particular event akin to stepping up to the register and checking out. In other words, transactions can involve multiple levels of analysis and be part of a cross-sectional or longitudinal data collection effort.

In social and behavioral science research, a transaction refers to a set of choices, resources, or other characteristics of a study's unit of analysis, such as an employee, entrepreneur, unit, or firm.

For example, a transaction in this specific dataset refers to the benefits and choices made available to an individual employee. As a supermarket customer might visit a store and fill a basket with a set of groceries (one example of a transaction), an employee selects a set of benefits when joining an organization and periodically updates these choices.

Step 3: Collect Data

MBA was initially designed with large datasets usually collected by others (i.e., not research team members). Thus, you can seek partnerships with organizations that will provide data in exchange for conducting analyses and presenting results to those who provided the data.[33] Of course, it is also possible for you to collect your data. However, given the effort and time involved and issues of accessibility to data sources, most MBA studies are likely to use data collected by other parties (e.g., non-profit organizations, chambers of commerce, and professional organizations). Given MBA's ability to produce results easily understood by practitioners, establishing partnerships to conduct social and behavioral sciences research should not be difficult.

Example: Conducting Market Basket Analysis Using Publicly Available Data

In addition to using data collected by organizations, you can implement a third-party data collection strategy consisting of reliance on publicly available information. For example, some authors investigated issues regarding individual performance by using data on academics, entertainers, politicians, and amateur and professional athletes.[34] Although they did not use MBA, all the data in five studies regarding 632,599 individuals in 198 separate samples were gathered from publicly available websites.

Step 4: Check MBA Requirements

The fourth step is to check two key requirements of MBA.[35] First, having a sufficiently large number of transactions is necessary because, otherwise, you would find few (if any) association rules with lift values meaningfully different from 1.0. Fortunately, it is relatively straightforward to meet the sample size requirement because of the vast stores of data being collected by firms in response to the analytics movement[36] and the sharp decrease in the cost of data storage technology.[37] As a result, some authors argued that firms are faced with the problem of too much data rather than too little.[38]

Note that it may be the case that the sample size is very large, but data are collected in only one context, such as a single organization with a unique culture. So, even a very large sample size would not mitigate concerns about the generalizability of results to other organizations (i.e., external validity evidence). In these situations, you need to explain in detail their data sources so that you can be fully informed regarding the extent to which association rules may generalize to other settings. Regarding specific sample sizes typically used in MBA studies in marketing and other fields, some authors noted that it is common for studies to include sample sizes ranging from tens of thousands to millions of transactions.[39] However, published MBA studies have used samples as small as a few hundred transactions.[40]

Regarding MBA's second requirement, you must verify that non-responses are substantively meaningful (e.g., an employee chose not to sign up for a benefit, thereby creating a non-choice), as opposed to being caused by artifacts (e.g., highly productive and busy employees did not have the time to fill out a questionnaire asking about their employee benefit options, thereby creating missing responses).[41] If it is clear that all non-responses are substantively meaningful, then you can proceed to interpret the association rules. Also, suppose it is possible to pinpoint which non-responses are not substantively meaningful. In that case, any association rule involving items with non-responses caused by artifacts should either be interpreted with special caution or discarded.

In some situations, it may be unclear whether the non-responses are substantively meaningful and, therefore, it will be difficult or impossible to tell from the dataset or a description of the dataset whether the lift, support, and confidence of association rules are inflated, deflated, or accurate. If so, checking whether non-responses are non-choices (i.e., substantively meaningful) or missing responses (i.e., caused by artifacts) is necessary. To do so, you can use exploratory data techniques such as frequency tables to identify binary-choice items to which no or few respondents responded and subsequently study the identified binary-choice items via the partnership forged with the organization that initially collected the data.[42] For example, with cooperation from the organization, you can examine the format of surveys used to collect the data (e.g., a binary-choice item was mistakenly excluded from the survey such that non-responses to the item are not substantively meaningful). Second, you can study the wording of items in the surveys (e.g., an item was worded in a particularly incomprehensible manner that discouraged responding). Third, you can also interview knowledgeable organizational members (e.g., a telephone conversation with a human resource manager reveals that an employee benefit option was unpopular with most employees).

Our illustrative dataset available at https://www.hermanaguinis.com meets both requirements. First, it has a sufficiently large number of transactions because it includes 1,000 employees. Also, all non-choices are substantively meaningful because they denote an employee's decision to sign up for one benefit option versus another. Thus, moving forward with deriving and interpreting association rules is appropriate.

Step 5: Derive Association Rules and Their Strength

As the next step, you enter all transactions into an appropriate software program to extract association rules and corresponding indexes. As defined earlier, the three most commonly used MBA indexes are lift, support, and confidence. In doing this, you will likely be asked by the software program to specify cutoff values for lift, given that it is a decision-making tool used to conclude whether the presence of an association cannot be explained by chance alone. This option can be useful in preventing the program from producing excessive associations (e.g., thousands or millions) from a very large and rich dataset. However, interpreting every association in such a scenario would be cumbersome. Thus, a histogram of all lift values is a useful tool to help decide on absolute or percent cutoff values for a lift in the given study.[43]

There are several MBA software packages commercially available such as IBM SPSS Modeler (formerly called *Clementine*) and SAS Enterprise Miner. As a third commercially available option, you can use Excel's pivot table function for a modified version of MBA.[44] In addition, an MBA software programs available free of charge include called *arule* (available online at https://www.kdnuggets.com/software/associations.html) and *arules* in R. Each of these software programs is accompanied by a tutorial. Because the goal in describing this fifth step is to provide an overview of the procedures involved, you can use the tutorials and datasets made available by the software packages because, as is the case with any new methodological approach, it will be difficult to fully understand how to use MBA and interpret the resulting software output without actually trying it.

These programs have similar capabilities, although they vary in terms of the particular labels used for specific procedures and results. Because of the similarities across software programs in terms of their overall capabilities, choosing one package over another is primarily an issue of personal preference and familiarity with each package. So, for example, the learning curve for IBM SPSS Modeler will be less steep for IBM SPSS users. Thus, using a software package with which you are already familiar would be best.

Step 6: Interpret Association Rules

The next and final step is to interpret the derived association rules. Using this dataset and for the pedagogical purpose of the illustration, this analysis was constrained to rules involving pairs of items only and positive associations only (i.e., as indicated by lift values larger than 1.0). Results indicated a total of 28 association rules, and they were sorted by lift value from highest to lowest.

From these results, the three rules with the highest lift values are (1) [(Dependent Care Reimbursement), (Wellness Programs)], with a lift of 2.42, support of 4 percent, and confidence (called "strength" by *Magnum Opus*), or the probability that the right-hand side item is chosen given that the left-hand side item is chosen, of 30.8 percent; (2) [(Holiday Pay), (Retirement Plans)], with a lift of 1.94, support of 11.1 percent, and confidence of 42.2 percent; and (3) [(Holiday Pay), (Healthcare Reimbursement)], with a lift of 1.85, support of 8.5 percent, and confidence of 32.3 percent.

Because all three association rules have lift values much higher than 1.0, it can be concluded that these rules exist in the form of positive relationships between the items and are not due to chance. Then the support values for these three rules can be considered, which range from 4 to 11.1 percent. Recall that support is the proportion of transactions in which two items appear together, so the items in these rules co-occur in 4 to 11.1 percent of the transactions in this dataset. [(Holiday Pay), (Retirement Plans)] and [(Holiday Pay), (Healthcare Reimbursement)] have the highest support values out of the 28 association rules returned by this criteria. In contrast, support for the association rule [(Dependent Care Reimbursement), (Wellness Programs)] is in the middle of the range of all support values (ranging from 1.8 to 11.1 percent). The confidence values for these three rules range from 30.8 to 42.2 percent, given that all confidence values (i.e., the probability that the right-hand side item is chosen given that the left-hand side item is chosen) in the dataset range from 13.8 to 51.2 percent.

Using these results for theory development purposes involves consideration of causal hypotheses, which is accomplished by examining the two confidence values of each rule (i.e., the presence of item B given the presence of item A, as well as the presence of item A given the presence of item B).[45] For example, [(Dependent Care Reimbursement; A), (Wellness Programs; B)] has confidence values of 30.8 (probability of B given A) and 31.5 percent (probability of A given B). [(Holiday Pay; A), (Retirement Plans; B)] has confidence values of 42.2 (probability of B given A) and 51.2 percent (probability of A given B). Finally, [(Holiday Pay; A), (Healthcare Reimbursement; B)] has confidence values of 32.3 (probability of B given A) and 48.6 percent (probability of A given B). Only the last example has widely divergent confidence values, such that you may wish to investigate whether the choice to have healthcare reimbursement leads to the choice to have holiday pay (rather than the other way around). One implication of this finding might be that using healthcare reimbursement makes employees pay more attention to and subsequently become more critical about their financial status, such that they seek additional forms of income, such as holiday pay.

You may also infer from the two rules with the highest support—[(Holiday Pay), (Retirement Plans)] and [(Holiday Pay), (Healthcare Reimbursement)]—that holiday pay is selected by employees who are seeking to maximize their income from the firm rather than focus on work-life balance. Specifically, these employees may be willing to forgo their holiday time for money because of financial pressures, leading them to seek security during retirement and protection from healthcare costs. These employees stand in contrast to others who do not select holiday pay and prefer to spend holidays with their families rather than earn additional income. In this sense, financial hardship may be a potential moderator.

Further, having dependents may moderate some derived associations, including the relationship between dependent care reimbursement and wellness programs. For example, the firm may discover that employees without dependents tend to choose dependent care reimbursement and wellness programs much less frequently together (e.g., support of 1 percent) than employees with dependents (e.g., support of 12 percent). Findings of contingency relationships from MBA can thus help form contingency theories and competing theories. Follow-up studies pitting such competing theories against one another can further advance employee benefits, compensation, motivation, and decision-making literature.

Such findings from MBA constitute actionable knowledge for practitioners as well, not just knowledge for theory-building, thereby narrowing the science–practice divide. Recall the previous example where the two association rules—[(Holiday Pay), (Retirement Plans)] and [(Holiday Pay), (Healthcare Reimbursement)]—applied more strongly to employees under financial pressure. Organizational leaders and human resource management unit members at the firm where the data were collected can use the finding to take several actions. For instance, if the firm's strategic objective is to support employees in areas outside of their work lives, practitioners may wish to promote a financial education program to struggling employees opting for holiday pay. They may also wish to encourage social outings among these employees, whose financial strain and forgone holidays may lead to burnout that could be ameliorated with greater social engagement with their peers.

The following section focuses on another advanced technique: Experience Sampling Methodology (ESM), and illustrates how you can implement it in your research using the case of entrepreneurship as an illustration.

EXPERIENCE SAMPLING METHODOLOGY

ESM is a methodological approach that allows you to gather detailed accounts of people's daily experiences over time and capture the ebb and flow of these experiences as they occur *in situ* (i.e., in the natural environment).[46] The three types of ESM protocols are (1) **interval contingent**, (2) **event contingent**, and (3) **signal contingent**.[47] In the *interval contingent* protocol, participants provide ESM responses at pre-determined intervals (e.g., every hour) or at the same time daily. An example of this protocol type is the study in which participants reported their mood and job satisfaction four times daily at fixed intervals for 19 working days.[48] In the *event contingent* protocol, participants respond only when the event of interest occurs. For example, some authors studied affect and interpersonal behavior by requiring participants to monitor their social interactions and report on features of their interactions for 20 consecutive days—i.e., participants completed ESM surveys immediately after the occurrence of significant interpersonal interactions (those lasting for at least 5 minutes).[49] Finally, in the *signal contingent* protocol, participants are prompted to respond by a signaling device at randomly selected time points in the day. As an illustration, some authors examined mood spillover among working parents by requiring participants to complete the experience sampling forms when prompted by the sound of the alarm watches eight times daily (randomly scheduled) for seven days.[50]

You can select from the three protocols to conduct ESM studies. Event-contingent ESM may be applicable for less frequently occurring phenomena such as opportunity discovery and evaluation. For example, you can ask entrepreneurs to report on independent variables such as their interactions (e.g., frequency and quality of interactions) and see how features of these encounters predict the types of business opportunities they recognize. Either interval-contingent or signal-contingent ESM may be used to examine the entrepreneurs' day-to-day venture efforts and how these efforts build up and influence their level of venture commitment and satisfaction. However, most ESM studies are signal contingent[51] because this protocol allows for random sampling of various events and avoids the systematic bias of fixed-time assessments and the expectancy effects associated with prior knowledge of the sampling period.[52]

Four Major Strengths of ESM

Strength 1: ESM Captures Dynamic Person-by-Situation Interactions Over Time

A methodological strength of ESM is its ability to capture the dynamic interplay of within-individual and situational variables over time.[53] Given ESM's ability to capture the dynamic person-by-situation interaction, you can use it to address questions on the individual-opportunity nexus. ESM studies can address aspects of the physical environment (e.g., venue, time), social context (e.g., number and descriptions of interactions), thoughts, feelings, actions, and motivational self-appraisals.[54] Key moments of interest, such as the "aha" or "eureka" experiences in opportunity discovery, can be matched with contextual variables such as the entrepreneur's location, time of day, and the people they were interacting with at that particular moment. You can investigate whether these situational features interact with individual-level variables (e.g., thoughts, feelings, actions) in influencing the types of opportunities that entrepreneurs discover.

Entrepreneurial motivation is another domain that incorporates person and situation factors and potential interactions between them. In many studies, entrepreneurs and other participants are asked to recall their goals to determine what predicts (entrepreneurial) behavior.[55] Such a one-time assessment assumes that person-situation factors that motivate entrepreneurs at the onset remain constant and influence all steps in the entrepreneurial process equally. This assumption may be questionable because the entrepreneurial process is dynamic and motivating factors in the nascent stage could differ from other venture stages.[56] With ESM, these concerns can be significantly reduced, if not circumvented, because it allows you to track motivational influences at different stages of the entrepreneurial process and analyze how outcome variables, such as changes in their venture goals (dependent variables), are predicted by individual and situational factors, such as their level of optimism and entrepreneurial self-efficacy (independent variables).

Strength 2: ESM Enhances Ecological Validity

Ecological validity is the extent to which findings can be generalized to the naturally occurring situations in which the investigated phenomenon occurs.[57] For example, existing studies on how entrepreneurs make decisions and evaluate opportunities are often scenario-based, where participants evaluate cases or vignettes based on the information available for each hypothetical situation.[58] Although scenarios provide study participants with standardized stimuli, the stakes are not real, and assumptions are often simplified; participants might underestimate the risks involved, and the decisions made might not reflect how entrepreneurs make such decisions. In a related vein, some studies that probe investors' decision-making processes use **verbal protocol analysis**, which requires participants to "think out loud" as they carry out a particular task as prompted by a hypothetical stimulus.[59] Participants' verbalizations are audio-recorded, transcribed, and content is analyzed through a coding scheme generated for particular research questions.[60] Notwithstanding the benefit of a much richer understanding of the process of interest that verbal protocols offer, the effect of the artificiality of the situation persists, much like in scenario-based studies.

You can use ESM to circumvent the limitations of scenario-based studies and examine entrepreneurs when they discover or evaluate opportunities together with factors that affected this discovery and evaluation. Furthermore, ESM can also capture dynamic factors in cognition that influence how entrepreneurs make decisions and act.[61] These include the entrepreneurs' temporal focus (i.e., the extent to which they think about the past, present, or future), their perceived goal progress, the degree to which they focus on maximizing gains or on avoiding losses, what they attend to at a particular moment (e.g., whether they are thinking about customers' needs, technological requirements, or new markets) and their emotional states at that moment.[62] All these cognitive factors can be examined as independent variables that could potentially impact the outcome of opportunity evaluation (whether the entrepreneur evaluates the business idea favorably or otherwise and the likelihood that the entrepreneur implements the idea).

Strength 3: ESM Allows for an Examination of Between- and Within-Person Variability

ESM allows you to examine within-person variations. Within-person variability provides a more in-depth understanding of the processes linking the predictor and criterion variables because within-person research can rule out spurious third variable explanations and coincident trends.[63] **Spurious variables**, such as personality factors, are relatively stable variables that can be measured at one point. Still, they can also be a slice of a coincident trend, such as satisfaction at one point.

More importantly, within-person processes provide insights beyond that of a between-person approach. Relationships analyzed using within- and between-individual approaches can vary dramatically in magnitude and direction[64] because inter-individual (between-person) and intra-individual (within-person) relationships are independent. For example, while momentary exercise increases momentary heart rate (within-individual), frequent exercises decrease chronic heart rate (across-individual). A study that required participants to engage in an analytic game found that self-efficacy was positively related to performance across individuals. Still, within individuals, self-efficacy was negatively related to performance over time, as high self-efficacy can lead to errors due to overconfidence.[65] Although beyond these findings, there may be nonlinear effects of self-efficacy on performance such that initial increases of self-efficacy improve performance, beyond a certain level, self-efficacy hurts performance. Such curvilinear effects can be modeled using ESM data.

Practically all empirical studies in entrepreneurship have examined between-person variability instead of within-individual variability.[66] Notwithstanding the contributions of studies focused on between-person variability, an intra-individual approach is worth pursuing because of the substantive insights you can obtain beyond inter-individual studies. For example, from a between-person analysis, you may expect fear of failure (predictor variable) and the level of entrepreneurial activity (outcome variable) to be negatively related. With the high failure rate among new ventures, those who are more fearful or have a greater fear of failure might be less likely to engage in entrepreneurial activities compared to the less fearful ones. However, fear might not reduce efforts if a within-individual approach is used as an entrepreneur can increase venture efforts for fear of losing the venture. You can also use ESM to examine the entrepreneur's emotional stability (a personality trait) and how this predicts their day-to-day stress levels and psychological well-being. Between-person analysis cannot control for all personality traits that account for the levels of the entrepreneur's well-being. ESM accommodates within-individual analysis, and differences in other personality and attitudinal variables can be ruled out as explanatory factors as they are constant within each individual.

Strength 4: ESM Mitigates Memory (i.e., Retrospective) Biases

Data collected using traditional one-time surveys and interviews are based on people's summaries of their experiences and behaviors prone to **recall errors**.[67] Traditional surveys that ask participants to reflect on their past behaviors or report on the nature and frequency of events generate data whose precision is compromised, as remembering these experiences is a fairly challenging memory-recall task.[68] It has been argued that memory works best when retrieval happens in the same context (time and place) as when the experience is encoded in the memory.[69] ESM minimizes the memory biases found in traditional surveys because ESM allows you to assess short-lived processes, states, and events in real-time.[70]

Example: Using Experience Sampling Methodology to Study the Opportunity Discovery Process

Entrepreneurs and people in many occupations function in environments that are usually unpredictable and ambiguous,[71] making it difficult for them to recall and describe details of what you aim to understand. For example, a researcher conducted in-depth interviews and demonstrated that individuals discover opportunities in areas related to their prior knowledge. However, because participants' interview responses are based on retrospection, they could have rationalized the discovery process and failed to include critical information about their experiences when the opportunity was discovered.[72] In yet another study, some authors asked entrepreneurs to describe the ideas on which their new ventures were based and why these ideas were worth pursuing.[73] Despite the study's contributions, because memory is subject to considerable distortions and changes over time, asking participants to recall events that happened in the past is indirect evidence at best.[74]

Researchers who probe processes using one-time questionnaires must be wary that entrepreneurs may need to distinguish between the actual event that occurred, their wishes, and social expectancies that could influence their reports. Asking entrepreneurs to summarize their experiences and behaviors might not accurately reflect the actual course of the entrepreneurial process. ESM can account for factors relevant to this process before they are altered by self-reflection,[75] and ESM achieves this by assessing experiences as they unfold *in situ*.[76]

Designing and Implementing ESM

The previous section explained the many benefits of using ESM and illustrated how to use it to advance theory and research. However, ESM studies can entail more time, energy, and resources from you and the participants than traditional methods (e.g., a one-time online survey). On your part, the high cost of implementing these studies could be seen as a significant difficulty. On the side of participants, they have to deal with the burden of response compliance imposed by this methodology, which can also be a practical hurdle. As with any proposal, implementation is crucial, including innovative and high-involvement research design approaches. You may only use ESM, or any other innovative methodological approach, with detailed practical guidelines. Accordingly, this section discusses some major issues in designing and implementing ESM in

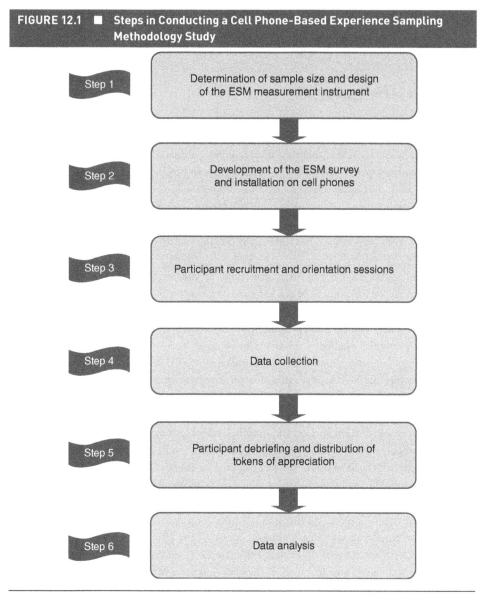

FIGURE 12.1   ■   Steps in Conducting a Cell Phone-Based Experience Sampling Methodology Study

Step 1 — Determination of sample size and design of the ESM measurement instrument

Step 2 — Development of the ESM survey and installation on cell phones

Step 3 — Participant recruitment and orientation sessions

Step 4 — Data collection

Step 5 — Participant debriefing and distribution of tokens of appreciation

Step 6 — Data analysis

Source: Uy, Foo, & Aguinis (2010). Reproduced with permission.

the illustrative case of entrepreneurship research using cell phone technology. These include sample size, the ESM survey, device and signaling schedules, and participant recruitment and orientation issues. Finally, it describes the resulting data structure and provides recommendations regarding data-analysis strategies. Figure 12.1 includes a flow chart summarizing the steps in implementing an ESM study. Although the example focuses on entrepreneurship, the steps equally apply to research in other social and behavioral science domains.

This section uses the research question "How does the entrepreneur's affect influence effort?" as a concrete example to explain the logistics of implementing an ESM study, from beginning (i.e., designing the ESM survey) to end (i.e., data analysis). This example is based on research showing that entrepreneurs who experience negative affect should exert more effort[77] because negative affect signals that things are not going well. Therefore, something needs to be done to correct the situation. Studying affect requires a methodological approach that can assess an entrepreneur's state at many points in time rather than assume that affect remains constant. ESM allows you to capture the impact of affect (independent variable) on the entrepreneur's effort (dependent variable).

Sample Size and the ESM Survey

Due to the amount of effort involved in the data collection process, most ESM studies have samples of participants that are considered modest in size by social and behavioral science research standards.[78] Nonetheless, because participants must respond multiple times during the study, the total N (i.e., the total number of data points) is usually sufficient to be reliable in statistical analyses that model within-individual relationships. In addition, the sampling involved in ESM studies pertains to sampling data from cases; in other words, gathering multiple reports on the experience of the same set of participants throughout the study. For example, the number of participants in a published study was only 27, but the authors obtained 1,907 ESM ratings of mood and job satisfaction.[79]

In designing the ESM survey, it is important to consider the research question being addressed and the variables examined. ESM surveys can capture internal and external dimensions of the phenomenon of interest. For example, in studying the affect and venture effort relationships over time, the ESM survey should have items that ask entrepreneurs to evaluate their affect at that particular moment and the extent to which they are engaged in venture-related tasks. In addition, if you are interested in knowing how external factors might impact the affect-effort relationship, the ESM surveys can also ask participants to provide information on elements of their current situation, such as where they are at that moment and whether they are alone or with other people.

Given the nature of ESM studies, you must balance obtaining enough information and not overburdening participants. Therefore, ESM surveys that can be completed in two minutes or less are reasonable.[80] In the example of affect and venture effort, the main items in the ESM survey are affect and effort assessments. So, we can use the shortened Positive and Negative Affect Scale (PANAS[81]) to measure affect. Shortened versions are routinely used in ESM studies to ease participant burden.[82] Moreover, although not without controversy,[83] the use of single-item scales is common in experience sampling studies[84] because of the effort required of participants to respond to each survey item multiple times. For example, in examining venture efforts, you can ask participants to report how much effort they put into venture tasks that are required immediately and how much effort they put into venture tasks beyond what is immediately required. Both affect and venture efforts are captured using Likert-type measures (based on a 5-point scale), which only imposes a little difficulty for participants to comply and provide sufficient range to minimize detrimental effects of scale coarseness.[85] Note that a measure is coarse when different true scores (e.g., 1.8 and 2.2) are collapsed into the same category (e.g., 2), as in the pervasive use of Likert-type scales including five scale points only. Figure 12.2 shows sample screenshots appearing on participants' cell phones (these screenshots show older phones on purpose to demonstrate the ESM's versatility).

Scheduling and Signaling Devices

The frequency and interval of the signals and the study duration depend on the research goals. There are no clear-cut rules for setting intervals. You should consider theory-related and practical issues, including the effect of time on the variables measured, participant burden, and the type of statistical analyses to use.[86] Signaling schedules are typically randomized within the day.[87]

FIGURE 12.2 ■ Experience Sampling Methodology Via Cell Phones: Sample Screenshots

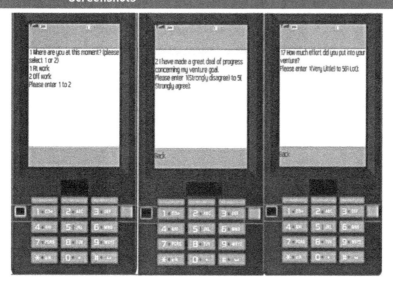

Source: Uy, Foo, & Aguinis (2010). Reproduced with permission. These screenshots show older phones on purpose to demonstrate ESM's versatility.

In other words, you generate the ESM schedule by determining the participants' working hours and reasonable periods to prompt them to respond without being too disruptive. For example, in examining the affective influences on venture efforts, you can adopt an ESM schedule between 10 AM to 10 PM because you want to survey entrepreneurs during their typical work hours. An ESM schedule with extremely late hours would be too intrusive, even though many entrepreneurs and people in many other occupations and industries might work irregular hours.

The earliest ESM studies were conducted using paper and pencil. Participants carried the questionnaire booklet and completed the required questions randomly as prompted by a portable electronic device such as beepers or programmable wristwatches.[88] A bit of trivia is that I was a study participant in one of the earliest ESM studies when I was a graduate student in the early 1990s. However, such procedures have several limitations, including the inability to assess compliance accurately, difficulty in data management (i.e., encoding data by hand introduces human error), and failure to rule out sampling bias because there is no foolproof way to check the time gap between the random prompts and when the participant responded.[89] So, you can use web-based ESM procedures, which require participants to go online and encode their responses on your website.[90] These computerized ESMs have several advantages, including precisely controlled signal timing, objective compliance tracking, and reduced human error in data management.[91] Computerized ESMs also allow you to obtain ancillary information, such as the time gaps between the prompt and response which could provide additional insights into the phenomenon of interest.

ESM and Cell Phones

A more recent development is the use of cell phone-based ESM. Cell phones have wireless application protocol (WAP) features, allowing you to embed survey items (usually as an application programmed in Java) on cell phones.[92] Cell phones in ESM studies have all the advantages of computerized ESM mentioned earlier—and more. For one, practically every entrepreneur owns a cell phone, and they rely on their cell phones as part of their day-to-day functioning.

With cell phones, participant responses are immediately transmitted, which allows you to track participant compliance in real-time. Moreover, this technology allows for real-time inter-active contact with entrepreneurs. For example, you can text or call the participants to get feed-back and resolve compliance issues. For example, suppose the entrepreneur accidentally deletes the survey application. In that case, the participant can inform you immediately, and the latter can transmit a new application at once (using the WAP), which could help boost response rates. In addition, the wireless networking feature in cell phones simplifies your task because responses can be directly transmitted to your computer or stored in the cloud.

In ESM with cell phones, you can prompt entrepreneurs to complete the survey by send-ing a text reminder (you pre-schedule these reminders). Entrepreneurs respond by opening the survey application on their cell phones, completing the survey, and sending it to a telephone number that receives all the responses ("system number"). Your computer receives their answers as a text message. A challenge of using cell phones involves phone compatibility because each phone model has a unique application programming interface (API), and there can be instances when the survey application cannot be launched on the entrepreneur's phone.[93] Fortunately, this problem can be resolved by adjusting the API to fit a particular phone model, which is a relatively simple programming task that a knowledgeable computer programmer can handle. Other issues, such as cell phone network traffic, can cause delays and even loss of information in sending and receiving texts, but these are not within your control. Nonetheless, telecommunication compa-nies have to adhere to strict service quality standards, and therefore the downside of congested network traffics are experienced rather infrequently.

Participant Recruitment and Orientation

Recruiting participants in ESM studies can be a challenging task because of the considerable effort required of them. An ideal situation to conduct ESM studies is when you can access a captive audience. To continue with our example, you can recruit participants in business incubators to examine the affective influences in venture efforts among start-up entrepreneurs. Because these entrepreneurs are housed in one location, it is easier for you to interact with them and, in the process, earn their trust and confidence and subsequently increase response rates.[94] Many incubators are high-tech business incubators that accommodate high-tech start-up entrepreneurs familiar with electronic gadgets (e.g., cell phones). While it is only sometimes possible to get a group of entrepreneurs housed in one location, the critical issue is recruiting entrepreneurs motivated to participate in the study. One such example is recruiting entrepre-neurs affiliated with entrepreneurship centers of universities and academic institutions and participating in business plan competitions. These individuals value entrepreneurship in an academic environment and might be more willing to be research participants. This approach of recruiting entrepreneurs has its drawbacks as the results may not be generalized to the popula-tion of entrepreneurs. Nonetheless, these entrepreneurs provide a good starting point to under-stand the process and within-individual issues in entrepreneurship. Moreover, this illustration is designed so that you can conduct similar research with limited time and monetary resources. A research team with greater resources may be able to conduct ESM on a random sample of entrepreneurs.

Prospective participants might be apprehensive of the inconvenience that ESM procedures inflict and the seemingly intrusive nature of the protocols.[95] You can overcome these potential difficulties through orientation. You should clarify the research goals, orient participants about the mechanics and duration of the study, and teach them how to complete the ESM surveys. Also, you should handle the orientation professionally but with a personal touch to make the entrepreneurs feel that their participation constitutes an integral part of the research endeavor. You must also be personally available for logistical and technical assistance and consistently provide verbal encouragement and support throughout the study.[96] Doing so will motivate participants to remain engaged until the end of the study, boost response rates, and ensure data quality. Past ESM studies provide evidence that recruiting busy people such as working parents with children[97] and hospital residents[98] is possible as long as you are diligent in establishing good relationships with their respective participants.

Using the cell phone-based ESM to study the affect and venture effort relationship would require you to assist participants in installing the ESM survey on their respective phones. You must explain every item in the ESM survey to prevent any confusion or misinterpretation. Participants are instructed to download and install the ESM survey on their phones and wait to delete it until the end of the study. Moreover, you can also administer background information surveys in the orientation by asking participants to provide demographic and venture-related information, which can be incorporated into the data analysis. For example, in the entrepreneurial affect-effort study, dispositional factors and venture information can be measured during the orientation before the start of the ESM study. It is also important to conduct a debriefing at the end of the study and ask participants about the overall experience of completing the ESM study—whether they had compliance difficulties or found the whole procedure too disruptive. Pilot tests and well-conducted orientation sessions can minimize unpleasant participant feedback in the debriefing.

While the steps listed above may seem logistically overwhelming initially, the resources needed to conduct ESM studies are reasonable. You will need to dedicate about two weeks to recruitment and orientation, and the next two weeks will involve implementing the study and closely monitoring the participants' compliance. You should constantly be available to assist participants and address their issues for four weeks to ensure smooth implementation and compliance with the research protocol. Regarding budget, the main costs include the development of the ESM survey and the tokens of appreciation for the participants. A quote of $800 was obtained from a company to program the ESM survey in a form that can be installed on the participants' cell phones. Given the 50-60 participants typical in ESM studies and an average of $100 per participant as a token of appreciation, the total cost, including survey development, is about $5,000-$6,000.

Data Structure and Analysis

Data collection using cell phone ESM is highly efficient because you can automatically transfer the ESM data to the statistical package without manual encoding. In addition, because all reminders and responses include the date and time stamps, you can determine which responses are valid. For example, consistent with other ESM studies,[99] a two-hour window can be a reasonable time frame such that responses received beyond two hours after the signal or text prompt has been sent are considered invalid.

For the example of affect predicting venture effort, you can have two data sets. The first set is the response-level data (or Level 1 data), including affect and venture efforts assessed via cell phone-based ESM. The second set consists of person-level data (or Level 2 data) such as gender, ethnicity/race, age, the industry of business venture, and other dispositional factors obtained from the background information survey administered in the orientation. The two sets can be merged using a unique identifier, the participant's ID number in most cases. The ESM data structure is stacked such that multiple observations for each participant are stacked on top of one another. Therefore, each ESM response occupies one data row, and the number of data rows for each participant equals the number of ESM responses for that participant. Table 12.1 illustrates what the stacked data structure might look like.

Given the hierarchical structure of the ESM data with multiple responses nested within individuals, multilevel modeling is an appropriate statistical methodology to analyze the data.[100] Multilevel modeling considers the correlated structure of the data as multiple reports are obtained from the same person throughout the ESM study.[101] It is also equipped to handle nested data with unequal observations across individuals and irregular intervals between observations.[102] Several statistical programs (e.g., HLM, MPlus, SAS, IBM SPSS, Stata, R) have multilevel modeling features that you can use to analyze ESM data. For example, a situational factor that might influence the affect-effort relationship among entrepreneurs is prior experience. Prior experience might weaken the relationship between affect and effort because the entrepreneur can draw from past experiences to determine the required effort and dilute the informational content of affect.[103] Table 12.1 includes some examples of commands in Stata 9 that you can use in conducting the analyses.

Moreover, because ESM accommodates temporal order, you can incorporate lagged effects to test the directionality of the relationships. Using the example of affect and venture effort, you can test whether affect predicts subsequent venture effort. You can also test whether venture effort influences the entrepreneur's affect the following day. Although ESM data can be used to test temporal effects, you must exercise caution in inferring causality because temporal sequencing is a necessary but insufficient condition, and causality can only be inferred if you can rule out other possible alternative explanations.

The steps in implementing ESM in Figure 12.1 refer to this specific example. You can apply these steps more broadly to other questions in your research. For example, for the question of

TABLE 12.1 ■ Hypothetical Example of Stacked ESM Data and Examples of Statistical Commands								
Participant ID#	Date	Reminder Sent	Response Received	Affect1	Affect2	Effort	Social Interactions	Prior Experience
1	08-01-23	10:00 AM	10:20 AM	2	3	4	2	2
1	08-01-23	7:45 PM	7:55 PM	3	2	3	1	2
1	08-02-23	11:15 AM	11:30 AM	3	2	3	3	2
1	08-02-23	6:20 PM	6:46 PM	2	5	3	0	2
2	08-01-23	10:50 AM	11:03 AM	4	3	2	2	1
2	08-01-23	8:03 PM	8:24 PM	5	5	4	1	1
2	08-02-23	10:03 AM	10:40 AM	5	4	5	1	1
2	08-02-23	4:55 PM	5:13 PM	4	3	3	0	1
3	08-01-23	11:07 AM	11:38 AM	3	3	3	3	0
3	08-01-23	5:28 PM	6:01 PM	2	1	4	2	0

Source: Uy, Foo, & Aguinis (2010). Adapted with permission.

Notes: To analyze the influence of affect on effort, the following xtmixed command can be used in Stata 9: *xtmixed effort affect | | participantID*. To analyze the moderating effect of prior experience on affect and effort, you can use the following command: *xtmixed effort affect experience affectX-experience | | participantID*.[104]

how the entrepreneurs' social interaction frequency predicts venture sales, similar steps as shown in Figure 12.1 can be used, except that this can be an event-contingent ESM in which entrepreneurs complete the ESM survey immediately after a significant social interaction occurs (e.g., meeting with investors, suppliers). Like this illustrative example, you can test direct and reverse relationships to ascertain the directionality of the relationships of these dynamic variables, and different lagged outcomes can be modeled in the analysis to examine the stability of the effects.

The following section focuses on the third advanced technique presented in this chapter: Bayesian Analysis.

BAYESIAN ANALYSIS

Bayesian analysis determines what parameter values (e.g., means, regression coefficients) can be inferred given the observed data. Bayesian analysis is the mathematically normative way to **reallocate credibility** across parameter values as new data arrive.

Reallocation of credibility across possible causes is common in everyday reasoning. For example, suppose there are two unaffiliated suspects for a crime, and strong evidence implicates one suspect. That the other suspect is exonerated can be inferred. Thus, data that increase the culpability of one suspect produce a reallocation of culpability away from the other suspect. The **complementary reallocation** is also common, as can be paraphrased from the fictional detective Sherlock Holmes: When you have eliminated all other possibilities, whatever remains, no matter how improbable, must be the truth.[105] In this case, data that reduce the credibility of some options increase the credibility of the remaining options, even if the prior credibility of those options was small. When the reallocation of credibility is done in the mathematically correct way, then it is Bayesian.

Formal Bayesian data analysis begins with a descriptive model, just as in classical statistics. The descriptive model has meaningful parameters that describe trends in the data. But, unlike classical methods, Bayesian analysis yields a complete distribution over the joint parameter space, revealing the relative credibility of all possible combinations of parameter values. Decisions about parameter values of particular interest, such as zero, can be made directly from the derived distribution.

Bayesian analysis is named after Thomas Bayes, who discovered a simple mathematical relation among conditional probabilities, now known as Bayes' rule.[106] When the rule is applied to parameters and data, it can be written as follows:

$$\underbrace{p(\theta|D)}_{\text{posterior}} = \underbrace{p(D|\theta)}_{\text{likelihood}} \underbrace{p(\theta)}_{\text{prior}} / \underbrace{p(D)}_{\text{evidence}} \tag{12.1}$$

where D is the observed data and θ is a vector of parameters in the descriptive model. The **posterior distribution,** $p(\theta|D)$, specifies the relative credibility of every combination of parameters given the data. Because the range of parameter values defines the complete space of possible descriptions, the distribution of credibility sums to 1 and is equivalent to a probability distribution. The posterior distribution provides the complete information that is mathematically possible about the parameter values given the data (unlike the point estimate and confidence interval in classical statistics, which provide no distributional information). To make this abstraction concrete, the following section describes the most common data-analytic application in organizational research over the past three decades: multiple linear regression.

Bayesian Multiple Linear Regression

Consider a common social and behavioral science research situation in which you are interested in predicting an outcome based on three predictors. For concreteness, the outcome is job performance, and the predictors are general mental ability (GMA), conscientiousness, and biodata (i.e., collected using a biographical inventory). To use a realistic illustration, data for 346 individual workers from meta-analytically derived population correlations reported are generated for each variable.[107] All four variables were generated from a multivariate normal distribution and rounded to the nearest Likert-scale value from 1 to 7.

Job performance, denoted y, is randomly distributed around a linear function of the other three variables, denoted x_1 (GMA), x_2 (conscientiousness), and x_3 (biodata). Formally, the relation is

$$p(y_i|\hat{y}_i, \sigma) = N(\hat{y}_i, \sigma) \text{ and } \hat{y}_i = \beta_0 + \beta_1 x_{1i} + \beta_2 x_{2i} + \beta_3 x_{3i} \tag{12.2}$$

where $\hat{y}_i$ is the predicted value of y_i.

Notice that five parameters must be estimated from the data: β_0 (i.e., the intercept), β_1 (i.e., the regression coefficient for GMA), β_2 (i.e., the regression coefficient for conscientiousness), β_3 (i.e., the regression coefficient for biodata), and σ (i.e., the standard deviation for job performance scores). Equation 12.2 expresses the probability of observed data values given any job applicant values of the parameters, constituting the likelihood function in the Bayes rule shown in Equation 12.1.

Establishing the Prior Distribution

Recall that Bayesian analysis reallocates credibility across candidate parameter values. Therefore, you should establish a prior distribution of credibility on the parameter values without the newly considered data. When there is little publicly agreed prior knowledge about the parameters, the prior distribution can be very broad so that no parameter value is given much more credence than any other parameter value. Suppose previous research provides clear guidance regarding plausible parameter values. In that case, the prior distribution can be specified to place more credibility on the plausible parameter values than on the implausible ones. The prior distribution cannot be set capriciously to favor your subjective and idiosyncratic opinion. The prior distribution is explicitly specified and justified for a skeptical scientific audience. When skeptics disagree about the appropriateness of a prior distribution, then a noncommittal broad prior distribution can be used. Another helpful procedure is to analyze with more than one prior distribution to demonstrate that the posterior distribution is essentially invariant under reasonable changes in the prior. In typical analyses, a noncommittal broad prior is used; therefore, the posterior distribution is very robust.

Even though the prior distribution is often deemed noncommittal, this does not imply that the prior distribution is an inconvenient nuisance for which you must apologize. On the contrary, a well-informed prior distribution can provide inferential leverage in many applications. As a simplistic example, consider the goal of estimating the possible bias of a coin. Suppose you flip the coin once, and it comes up heads. If you have little prior knowledge about the coin, then the single flip tells you only very *un*certainly that the coin might be somewhat head-biased. If, however, you have prior knowledge that the coin came from a magic shop and must be either an extremely head-biased coin or an extremely tail-biased coin, then the single flip tells us with high certainty that the coin is of the extremely head-biased type, because the extremely tail-biased coin would almost never exhibit even a single head. Because Bayesian analysis can incorporate prior knowledge when appropriate, it is consistent with the epistemological position that social and behavioral science theories will advance to the extent that you engage in empirical research that relies on the accumulation of knowledge.[108]

Not only can prior knowledge be useful but ignoring it can cause a derailment in accumulating knowledge and ineffective practical applications. For example, consider drug screening as part of the pre-employment testing process. Suppose you have a drug test that correctly detects drug use 95% of the time and gives false alarms only 5% of the time. Suppose you randomly select a job applicant, and the test result is positive. What is the probability that the person uses the drug? An answer that ignores the base rate of drug use might be near the detection rate of 95%. But the correct answer takes into account the base rate of drug usage. If the base rate in the population is 5%, then the probability of drug use in the randomly tested person is only 50%, not 95%. This follows directly from Bayes' rule:

$$p(\theta = user | D = +) = \frac{p(D = + | \theta = user)p(\theta = user)}{p(D = +)}$$
$$= \frac{p(D = + | \theta = user)p(\theta = user)}{p(D = + | \theta = user)p(\theta = user) + p(D = + | \theta = nonuser)p(\theta = nonuser)}$$
$$= \frac{0.95 \times 0.05}{0.95 \times 0.05 + 0.05 \times 0.95}$$
$$= 0.50$$

(12.3)

In this situation, the parameter θ being estimated is the person's drug use, which has two nominal values, θ = user or θ = non-user. The base rate is the prior distribution over the two values of the parameter, namely $p(\theta = user) = .05$ and $p(\theta = \text{non-user}) = .95$. The prior distribution in this scenario has been established from extensive previous research. Not using the well-informed prior would be a mistake because it would unfairly deny employment opportunities to job applicants. In any other domain of scientific inference, if you have a well-informed prior distribution, not using it could also be a costly mistake.

For this specific application to multiple linear regression, although the data are from an established substantive research domain (i.e., human resource selection), the goal is to provide a generic example without specific prior commitments (you can download the data file from https://www.hermanaguinis.com). Therefore, let's use a noncommittal, vague prior. For each regression coefficient, the prior distribution is a very broad normal distribution, with a mean of zero and a standard deviation that is extremely large relative to the scale of the data. The same assumption is made for the prior on the intercept. Finally, the prior on the standard deviation of the predicted value is merely a uniform distribution extending from zero to an extremely large value far beyond any realistic value for the scale of the data. In the specific analyses demonstrated in this section, the data were standardized so that the prior would be broad regardless of the original scale of the data. The analysis results were then algebraically transformed back to the original scale. For the standardized data, the prior on the intercept and regression coefficients was a normal distribution with a mean at zero and a standard deviation of 100. This normal distribution is virtually flat over the range of possible intercepts and regression coefficients for standardized data. The prior on the standard deviation parameter (σ in Eq. 12.2) was a uniform distribution from zero to 10, which again far exceeds any reasonable value for σ in standardized data. Thus, the prior places essentially no bias on the posterior distribution.

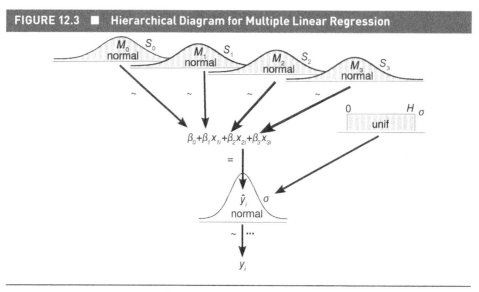

FIGURE 12.3 ■ Hierarchical Diagram for Multiple Linear Regression

Source: Kruschke, Aguinis, & Joo (2012). Reproduced with permission.

Note: The prior distribution has Histogram bars superimposed to indicate correspondence with posterior distributions shown in subsequent figures.

The full model is illustrated graphically in Figure 12.3 to facilitate this presentation. The lower part of the diagram illustrates the likelihood function of Equation 12.2: The arrow to y_i indicates that the data are normally distributed with mean $\hat{y}_i$ and standard deviation σ. The arrow pointing to $\hat{y}_i$ indicates that the predicted value equals a linear function of the predictors. The upper part of the diagram illustrates the prior distribution. For example, in the upper left it is shown that the intercept β_0 has a normal prior with mean M_0 and standard deviation S_0. The prior distribution is a joint distribution across the five-dimensional parameter space, defined here for convenience as the product of five independent distributions on the five parameters.

The prior distribution is a continuous mathematical function indicated by the black curves, but it is illustrated with superimposed histograms because the parameter distribution will be represented by using a very large (e.g., 250,000) representative random sample from the parameter space. Thus, the Bayesian analysis will reallocate the very large set of representative parameter values from the prior distribution to a posterior distribution, illustrated by histograms of the representative values. For any fixed data set and prior distribution, there is one true posterior distribution, represented by a very large representative sample of parameter values. The larger the representative sample, the higher resolution picture you have of the true posterior.

In summary, Bayesian inference involves reallocating credibility across the space of parameter values. The reallocation is based on the observed data, not on imagined data that might have been obtained from a null hypothesis if the intended sampling were repeated. Furthermore, the reallocation starts from a prior distribution. As noted earlier, the prior distribution is not capricious and must be explicitly reasonable to a skeptical scientific audience.

Computing the Posterior Distribution

The Bayes' rule in Equation 12.1 shows that the likelihood function and prior distribution have mathematical forms. The two mathematical forms are multiplied together in the numerator. The term *evidence* refers to the denominator of Bayes' rule, $p(D)$, also known as the marginal likelihood.

Computing the value of $p(D)$ can be difficult because it is an integral over the parameter space: $p(D) = \int p(D|\theta)p(\theta)d\theta$. For many years, Bayesian analysis was confined to mathematical forms that could be analytically integrated or analytically approximated. Fortunately, new computer-based methods allow Bayesian analysis to be computed flexibly and for very complex models.

The new method is called **Markov chain Monte Carlo (MCMC)**. The idea is to accurately approximate the posterior distribution by a very large representative random sample of parameter values drawn from the posterior distribution. From this very large sample of representative parameter values, you can determine the mean or modal parameter value, the quantiles of the parameter distribution, its detailed shape, and the forms of trade-offs between values of different parameters. What makes this approach possible is that MCMC methods generate the random sample without needing to compute the difficult integral for $p(D)$. Moreover, recent advances in algorithms and software have made it possible for you merely to specify the form of the likelihood function and prior distribution, and the software can apply MCMC methods.

The hierarchical diagram in Figure 12.3 contains all the information that must be communicated to a computer program to conduct MCMC sampling. Every arrow in the hierarchical diagram has a corresponding declaration in the software for Bayesian analysis. The program has been packaged so the user only needs to type three simple commands. One command loads the data, a second command creates the MCMC chain, and a third command creates graphs of the posterior distribution.

The MCMC chain provides a large sample of credible *combinations* of parameter values in the five-dimensional parameter space. This section will examine various one-dimensional projections of the posterior. Figure 12.4 shows the posterior distribution for data that have been standardized, and Figure 12.5 shows the posterior distribution on the original data scale. The middle row of Figure 12.4 shows the three regression coefficients. Notice that the posterior explicitly distributes each possible value's credibility (i.e., probability) for the regression coefficient. The upper right panel of Figure 12.4 shows the posterior for the intercept, and the upper middle panel shows the posterior for the standard deviation of the data around the linear prediction. By contrast, results from traditional analysis provide no distribution over parameter values.

Figure 12.4 shows additional information about the regression coefficients. The lower row shows the differences between standardized regression coefficients. This information is useful in understanding practical decisions regarding using each of the predictors in the model. While it is well known that standardized regression coefficients must be interpreted cautiously because the scales are brought into alignment only in terms of the sample-based standard deviations of the predictors,[109] a comparison of standardized coefficients can nevertheless be useful. For example, if it is equally costly to test a job applicant for GMA or conscientiousness, you would prefer to avoid the double cost of testing both. You may want to know which test yields higher predictiveness for job performance. The credible differences are determined by computing the difference between regression coefficients at every step in the MCMC chain and plotting the result.

Finally, the upper left panel of Figure 12.4 shows an entire distribution of credible values for the proportion of variance accounted for, denoted R^2. At each step in the MCMC chain, a credible value of R^2 is computed as simply a re-expression of the credible regression coefficients at that step: $R^2 = \sum_j \beta_j r_{y.x_j}$, where β_j is the standardized regression coefficient for the jth predictor at that step in the MCMC chain, and $r_{y.x_j}$ is the sample correlation of the criterion values, y, with the jth predictor values, x_j. The equation for expressing R^2 in terms of the regression coefficients

FIGURE 12.4 ■ Posterior Distribution for the Multiple Linear Regression Example, Showing Parameters for Standardized Data

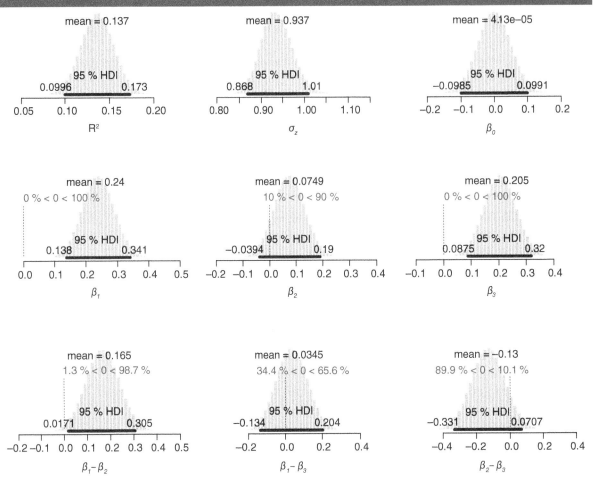

Source: Kruschke, Aguinis, & Joo (2012). Reproduced with permission.

Note: HDI = highest density interval.

is used by analogy to least-squares regression, in which the equation is exactly true.[110] The mean value in the distribution of R^2 is essentially the maximum-likelihood estimate when using vague priors and the least-squares estimate when using a normal likelihood function. The posterior distribution reveals the entire distribution of credible R^2 values. (The posterior distribution of R^2, defined this way, can exceed 1.0 or fall below 0.0, because R^2 here is a linear combination of credible regression coefficients, not the singular value that minimizes the squared deviations between predictions and data.)

The panels in Figure 12.4 show an interval marked as HDI, the *highest density interval.* Points inside an HDI have higher probability density (credibility) than points outside the HDI, and the points inside the 95% HDI include 95% of the distribution. Thus, the 95% HDI includes the most credible values of the parameter. The 95% HDI is useful as a summary of the distribution and decision tool. Specifically, the 95% HDI can help decide which parameter

FIGURE 12.5 ■ Posterior Distribution for the Multiple Linear Regression Example, Showing Original-Scale Parameters

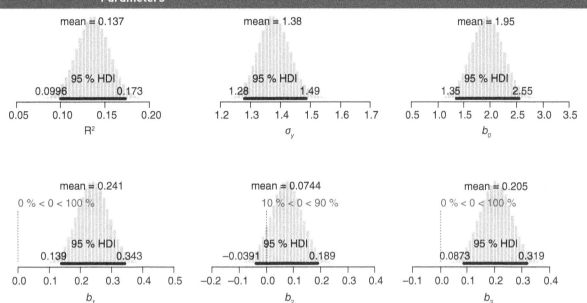

Source: Kruschke, Aguinis, & Joo (2012). Reproduced with permission.

Note: HDI = highest density interval.

values should be deemed not credible, that is, rejected. This decision process goes beyond probabilistic Bayesian inference *per se*, which generates the complete posterior distribution, not a discrete decision regarding which values can be accepted or rejected. A straightforward decision rule is rejecting any value outside the 95% HDI. In particular, to decide whether the regression coefficients are non-zero, consider whether zero is included in the 95% HDI. For example, Figure 12.4 shows that zero is excluded from the 95% HDI for predictor 1 and predictor 3. The lower left panel indicates that the regression coefficients on predictors 1 and 2 are credibly different (i.e., a difference of zero is not among the 95% most credible values). The upper left panel indicates that R^2 is well above zero.

Accepting the Null Value

A more sophisticated decision rule also has a way of accepting a (null) value, not merely rejecting it. This extended decision rule involves establishing a **region of practical equivalence (ROPE)** around the value of interest. For example, suppose you are interested in a particular regression coefficient's null value (i.e., zero). In that case, you establish slope values equivalent to zero for practical purposes in the particular application. For example, suppose you specify that slopes between −0.05 and +0.05 are practically equivalent to zero. You will *reject* the null value if the 95% HDI falls completely *outside* the ROPE because none of the 95% most credible values is practically equivalent to the null value. Moreover, you would *accept* the null value if the 95% HDI falls completely *inside* the ROPE because all 95% most credible values are practically equivalent to the null value. This is because the 95% HDI narrows as the sample size increases.

APPLIED METHODS: CASE STUDY – ACCEPTING THE NULL HYPOTHESIS WITH BAYESIAN ANALYSIS

To illustrate a case of accepting the null value, a larger sample (N = 1,730) of data from the linear regression model was simulated using true regression coefficients of .15, .00, and .15. The resulting posterior distribution is shown in Figure 12.6 for standardized parameters and in Figure 12.7 for original-scale parameters. Regarding Figure 12.6, notice in the middle panel that the posterior distribution for the regression coefficient on the second predictor has its 95% HDI entirely within the ROPE. Because most credible values are practically equivalent to zero, it was decided to accept the null value. The lower middle panel in Figure 12.6 shows that the difference between the first and third regression coefficients is centered on zero, but the 95% HDI of the difference only partially falls within the ROPE.

FIGURE 12.6 ■ **Posterior Distribution for a Large Illustrative Data Set (N = 1,730), Showing Standardized Parameters**

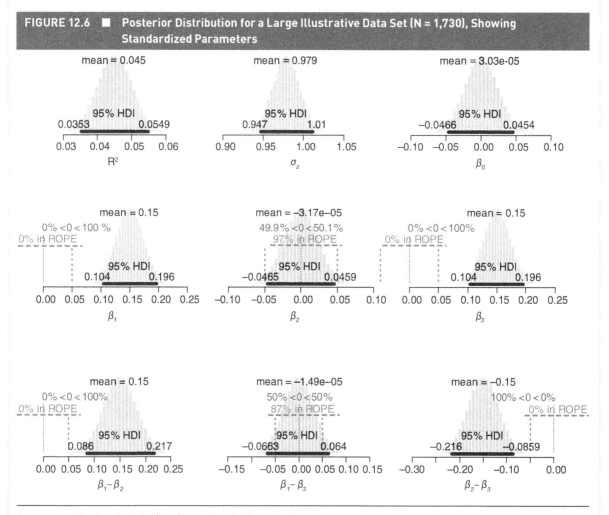

Source: Kruschke, Aguinis, & Joo (2012). Reproduced with permission.

Note: Notice that the 95% highest density interval (HDI) for the second regression coefficient (middle) falls within the region of practical equivalence (ROPE).

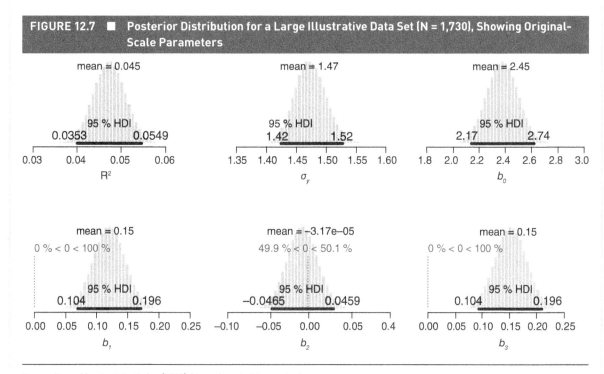

FIGURE 12.7 ■ Posterior Distribution for a Large Illustrative Data Set (N = 1,730), Showing Original-Scale Parameters

Source: Kruschke, Aguinis, & Joo (2012). Reproduced with permission.

Note: HDI = highest density interval.

Classical analysis based on null hypothesis significance testing (NHST) has no way of accepting the null hypothesis, which typically consists of specifying the absence of an effect or relationship.[111] Indeed, in NHST, because the null hypothesis can only be rejected, you are guaranteed to reject the null hypothesis, even when it is true, if the sample size is allowed to grow indefinitely. This is because you test with every additional datum collected.[112] This "sampling to reach a foregone conclusion" does not happen in a Bayesian approach. Instead, because the HDI narrows as the sample size increases, and therefore the null has a greater probability of being accepted when it is true, it is the case that the probability of false alarm asymptotes at a relatively small value (depending on the specific choice of ROPE). Illustrations of rates of false alarms and acceptances in sequential testing have been proposed.[113] Independently of its use as a decision tool for Bayesian analysis, the use of a ROPE has also been suggested to increase the predictive precision of theories in the social and behavioral sciences.[114]

Summary of Rich Information Provided by Bayesian Analysis

As shown in Figures 12.4 through 12.7, the posterior distribution reveals complete distributional information about which values of the parameters are more or less credible, including the standard deviation of the noise in the data. The posterior distribution simultaneously reveals the differences between standardized regression coefficients. Moreover, a complete distribution of credible R^2 values is provided.

A sampling distribution of parameter estimates from an assumed fixed parameter value differs from the parameter's posterior distribution. To create a sampling distribution of estimates, you start with an assumed fixed parameter value and then, analytically or through bootstrapping, create a sampling distribution of parameter estimates. The process is as follows:

1. Assume a fixed parameter value.

2. From a hypothetical population with that parameter value, repeatedly generate random samples according to an intended sampling design, the stopping rule.

3. For each randomly generated sample, compute a sample statistic that estimates the parameter value.

4. Create a sampling distribution of the estimator from the repeated random samples.

The result is a distribution that specifies the probability of each estimator value given the assumed parameter value and the sampling design. Notice that the distribution of sample estimates is not about the probability of a parameter value, given the data; the sampling process starts with a single assumed parameter value. Notice also that the estimator and the parameter are apples and oranges. The distinction between estimator and parameter is especially evident when the parameter of interest is the bias of a coin. The sample estimate is the number of "heads" in the sample divided by the sample size, N. The estimate can therefore take on any of the discrete values $0/N$, $1/N$, $2/N$, …, N/N (assuming that fixed N was the intended design). The estimator's sampling distribution is a distribution on those discrete proportions (specifically, a binomial distribution if N was fixed by design). In contrast, the posterior distribution on the underlying bias is a continuous distribution on the interval [0,1]. The posterior distribution is explicitly a probability distribution on parameter values, given the observed data. A significant advantage of the Bayesian approach is that the posterior distribution can be directly understood and interpreted: It reveals the relative credibility of every possible combination of parameter values given the data. From some assumed parameter value, a sampling distribution of parameter estimates has only a convoluted interpretation and little direct inferential relevance. Also, there is no unique sampling distribution because it depends on the design intention (a.k.a. stopping rule.)

From the posterior distribution, you can make decisions about landmark values of interest, such as null values. Using the HDI and ROPE, you can decide whether to reject or accept a candidate parameter value. And the decision is made without reference to p-values and sampling distributions as in NHST. Note that you need a Bayesian approach to implement the decision rule involving the ROPE. In particular, consider the decision to accept a (null) value if the 95% HDI falls entirely within the ROPE around the value. This decision rule only makes sense because the 95% HDI represents the bulk of the credible parameter values. The frequentist 95% confidence interval (CI) does not indicate the parameter's 95% most credible values. The CI is, by definition, different than the HDI. One clear illustration that the CI is not an HDI comes from multiple tests: The 95% CI grows much wider when you intend to conduct more tests, but the HDI is unchanged (because the posterior distribution is unchanged).

Although not illustrated by this multiple linear regression example, Bayesian analysis is exceptionally well suited for more complex applications. When the data are skewed or have outliers, it is easy to change the program to use a non-normal distribution, and interpretation of the posterior distribution proceeds seamlessly as before. By contrast, generating p-values for NHST can be challenging, especially for non-normal distributions in non-linear hierarchical models. When you are interested in non-linear trends in data, it is easy to change the program to model the trend of interest, whether it is polynomial, exponential, a power law, or sinusoidal, to name a few. Notably, a hierarchical structure is easily implemented in Bayesian software. For example, regression curves can be fit to each of many individuals, with higher-level parameters describing trends across groups or conditions, even for non-linear and non-normal models. Another example of a hierarchical structure includes a higher-level distribution to describe the distribution of the regression coefficients across predictors. This hierarchical structure allows each regression coefficient to inform the estimates of the other regression coefficients while simultaneously informing the higher-level estimates of their dispersion across predictors. The resulting shrinkage of estimated regression coefficients helps attenuate artificially extreme estimates caused by noisy data.

Synthesis of Advantages of Bayesian Data Analysis

Table 12.2 includes a summary of the advantages. This section also includes several examples of how specific published research based on frequentist analysis-based approaches failed to benefit from the advantages offered by a Bayesian approach—and how using Bayesian analyses would have led to richer and, in some cases, different substantive conclusions.

Advantage 1: Use of Prior Knowledge

The first advantage in Table 12.2 is that Bayesian data analysis incorporates the data and prior accumulated knowledge to generate parameter estimates that tend to be different and more accurate than those derived under frequentist methods. This is especially true when the prior accumulated knowledge corresponds to a distribution substantially different from a noncommittal broad prior distribution.

As an illustration of this advantage in a specific context,[115] consider a situation involving ten local validation studies (i.e., the correlation between test scores and performance) of a situation judgment test (i.e., including questions asking the job applicant to put themselves in situations and answer questions about what they would do). The ten corresponding correlations were calculated using frequentist analysis. Because of the nature of frequentist analysis, the calculation of each frequentist analysis-derived correlation does not involve prior knowledge, which in this example consists of correlations calculated from the other nine studies. As a result, one of the studies yielded a statistically non-significant correlation of .15 ($p > .05$). In contrast, when

Issue	Frequentist	Bayesian
1. Use of prior knowledge.	Does not incorporate prior knowledge into the estimation of parameters. Instead, it only uses the data at hand. As a result, the estimated parameters can be less precise.	Explicitly incorporates prior knowledge into the estimation of parameters by expressing the prior knowledge in terms of a prior distribution, which is then combined with the data to produce the posterior.
2. Joint distribution of parameters.	Creates only a local approximation.	Generates accurate joint distribution of parameter estimates.
3. Assessment of null hypotheses.	The null hypothesis cannot be accepted.	Null values can be accepted as well as rejected.
4. Ability to test complex models.	Often challenging to derive p-values, confidence intervals on parameters, and confidence intervals on predictions for new data.	Flexibility in adapting a model to diverse data structures and distributions (e.g., non-normal) with no change in inference method.
5. Unbalanced or small sample sizes.	In unbalanced ANOVA designs, users must choose "Type I" or "Type III" error terms. For example, a small sample violates assumptions for obtaining an accurate p-value in chi-square tests.	The posterior distribution reveals greater uncertainty in parameter estimates for cells with smaller sample sizes. However, the sample size does not affect the inference method.
6. Multiple comparisons.	Corrections are required for inflated Type I error rates (i.e., false positives), and correction depends on the comparisons you intend.	No reference to intended or post-hoc comparisons. The ease of hierarchical modeling allows rational sharing of information across groups to "shrink" estimates.
7. Power analysis and replication probability.	Virtually unknowable because of the lack of distributional information in a confidence interval.	Precisely estimated from the complete distribution of parameter values.

TABLE 12.2 ■ Brief Summary of Selected Advantages of Bayesian Analysis Over Frequentist Analysis

Source: Adapted from Kruschke, Aguinis, and Joo (2012). Reproduced with permission.

Bayesian analysis is employed such that prior knowledge regarding the other correlations is considered, the same study yields a Bayesian-based correlation of .18. Moreover, the corresponding 95% HDI does not contain the correlation value of .00. In short, the substantive conclusion based on a frequentist approach was that the correlation was not different from zero but using a Bayesian approach led to the conclusion that the correlation was different from zero.

A difference of less than .05 correlation units—about 33% change— in the estimated correlation magnitude might not seem impressive in several contexts. At the same time, in many other contexts, such as in the case of the ten local validation studies,[116] such a difference was practically significant enough for two local validation studies' correlations to be judged as different from zero (under Bayesian analysis) but statistically non-significant (under frequentist analysis). This is precisely the type of apparently small difference that has important practical consequences.[117] From a substantive perspective, the situation judgment test is now deemed valid in the two local contexts (i.e., a good predictor of performance). At the same time, the frequentist analysis may have concluded that the test should not be used because the relationship between test scores and performance was not statistically different from zero.

In summary, in practical applications, you benefit from using prior knowledge and the data to derive accurate parameter estimates. Bayesian data analysis does just that. By translating the prior knowledge into a prior distribution and then using Bayes' rule to combine the prior with the current data, the resulting posterior distribution gives you parameter estimates that are the best available, lacking further information.

Advantage 2: Joint Distribution of Parameters

As mentioned in issue #2 in Table 12.2, the second advantage of Bayesian data analysis is that the method produces a *joint* (i.e., simultaneous) distribution of credible parameter estimates across multiple predictors in a multi-dimensional parameter space, thereby allowing you to examine the trade-offs among values of different parameter estimates across the multiple predictors. The computer program produces scatter plots of jointly credible values for all pairs of parameters. For linear regression with normally distributed noise, the scatter plots tend to be simple oval shapes. Still, for other models, the scatter plots can be "banana" or S-shaped, indicating interesting trade-offs in credible parameter values. Frequentist analysis can use an asymptotic approximation to the likelihood function, but this approach generally fails to describe the posterior distribution. Although an illustration of this issue was not included in this chapter due to space constraints, the programs provide graphical displays of the posterior for all pairs of parameters.

Knowing the accurate trade-offs among credible parameter estimates across multiple predictors is more than a technical refinement. Consider the example from Figures 12.4 and 12.5, where Bayesian data analysis is used to fit a linear regression model to data, and job performance is predicted by GMA, conscientiousness, and biodata. Previous research indicates conscientiousness and biodata are fairly strongly correlated (r = .51). If you also know how strongly conscientiousness or biodata predicts job performance, you can use that prior knowledge to leverage a more precise estimation of the other predictor.[118] The inferential leverage derives from the trade-off in parameter estimates: The prior knowledge about one parameter narrows the estimate of the other parameter because of the trade-off.

Advantage 3: Assessment of Null Hypothesis

The third advantage summarized in Table 12.2 refers to assessing the null hypothesis. Within a Bayesian approach, as described earlier, accepting a null value involves establishing a region of practical equivalence (ROPE) around the value of interest. For example, suppose you are interested in the null value (i.e., zero) for a regression coefficient. In that case, you establish slope values equivalent to zero for practical purposes in the particular application. On the other hand, the classical frequentist framework cannot accept the null hypothesis.[119] The frequentist approach cannot incorporate an analogous decision rule involving a ROPE and CI (as opposed to HDI) because the CI, unlike the HDI, does not indicate which parameter values are credible, and the CI changes its size when the sampling and testing intentions change.

Further, in NHST, you are mathematically guaranteed to reject the null hypothesis even when it is true if the sample size is allowed to grow indefinitely and a test is conducted with every additional datum.[120] This "sampling to reach a foregone conclusion" does not happen in a Bayesian approach. Instead, because the HDI narrows as the sample size increases, and therefore the null has a greater probability of being accepted when it is true, it is the case that the probability of false alarm asymptotes at a relatively small value (depending on the specific choice of ROPE).

Advantage 4: Ability to Test Complex Models

Issue #4 in Table 12.2 refers to another important advantage of Bayesian methods: the ease of analyzing complex data structures and models. The model specification language is quite flexible in the Bayesian software JAGS. All the usual forms of the generalized linear model can be specified, including multiple linear regression, ANOVA, ANCOVA, logistic regression, ordinal regression, log-linear models for contingency tables, and many other data-analytic approaches that are the most frequently used.[121] A Bayesian approach can also be used to implement mixed models and nesting of variables in hierarchical models. Bayesian models are especially useful also for non-linear models. Moreover, you are not limited to normal distributions for describing metric data; you can use other distributions instead to accommodate outliers or skew in robust regression.[122] Bayesian approaches handle mixture models because data assignment to mixture components is probabilistic, and the estimated parameters are jointly distributed with the data assignments. In other words, instead of only a single data assignment to a mixture of components, multiple credible assignments are assessed simultaneously.

You can flexibly create a hierarchical non-linear model that reflects a structure appropriate to the data. The inference of credible parameter values occurs regardless of the model type. In all cases, a complete joint distribution of credible parameter values is created, even for dozens or hundreds of parameters, given the single set of actually observed data. Non-linear models are becoming more important in the social and behavioral sciences as researchers gain precision in specifying the functional forms of relations between variables.[123] Moreover, hierarchical models are becoming increasingly pervasive in many domains.[124] For example, in many applications, you measure aspects of individuals within different groups, and you want to estimate the effects of both individual-level variables (e.g., job satisfaction) and group-level variables (e.g., team cohesion) on individual-level outcomes (e.g., performance). Bayesian software allows the specification of any number of levels. Within each level, there can be complex models. For instance, you might have a multiple regression model for each individual and a higher-level model of how individual-level regression coefficients are distributed across groups.[125] Hierarchical modeling is also useful for meta-analysis, in which particular studies play the role of individuals, and higher-level model structure has parameters that describe overall tendencies across studies.[126] However, frequentist applications can be exceedingly difficult for complex applications, especially for non-linear or non-normal models, because generating sampling distributions and confidence intervals are often intractable.[127] Moreover, even in complex hierarchical applications, Bayesian methods straightforwardly generate predictions that accurately incorporate the full distribution of credible parameter values instead of just a single point estimate.

> **Example: Using a Bayesian Approach to Study Creativity, Organizational Innovation, and Competitiveness**
>
> As an example of how the flexibility of Bayesian methods might have impacted recent work, consider the extensive interest in how creativity and organizational innovation relate to competitiveness.[128] This study revealed a complex, polynomial-trend relationship between employee learning orientation and employee creativity moderated by a third factor, team learning behavior.[129] These researchers used frequentist hierarchical linear models. Despite the sophistication of their analysis, had they used a Bayesian approach, they would have discovered similar trends but with complete distributional information about the trade-offs between coefficients on different trend components. Moreover, they could have implemented non-normal distributions at any level in the hierarchical model to accommodate outliers, skewed data, or alternative assumptions about the distributions of trend parameters across different teams. Bayesian analyses like these have great potential to critically evaluate the robustness of recent conceptualizations involving non-normal[130] and non-linear[131] relationships.

Advantage 5: Unbalanced or Small Sample Sizes

Regarding issue #5 in Table 12.2, Bayesian methods can be used regardless of the overall sample size or relative sample sizes across conditions or groups. Essentially, in Bayesian analysis, the parameter estimates for every individual datum is updated, so it does not matter, computationally, wherein the design of each datum appears. By contrast, when different design cells include different sample sizes in frequentist ANOVA, you must decide between using Type I or Type III error terms in computing the best estimates and corresponding p-value. Similarly, in frequentist approaches to moderated multiple regression models with categorical moderator variables, an unequal number of individuals across groups (e.g., more men than women or more Whites than African Americans) leads to important errors in prediction.[132] These problems are irrelevant in the Bayesian analogs of multiple regression and ANOVA. As another example, in the frequentist chi-square tests of independence, the p-value is determined by approximating the sampling distribution of the discrete Pearson chi-square value with the continuous chi-square sampling distribution. Still, that approximation is reasonably good only when the expected cell frequency is about five or larger. Therefore, you must acknowledge that results and substantive conclusions might be incorrect. There is no such issue in Bayesian analogs of chi-square tests because the analysis estimates parameter values without relying on large-sample approximations.

Dynamic analyses of social networks in organizations are becoming an increasingly important research area in the social and behavioral sciences.[133] Recently, some authors used longitudinal data on friendship relations in the department of an organization to find that high self-monitors were more likely to appeal to new friends and to be in bridging networking positions than low self-monitors.[134] In doing so, these researchers used a frequentist procedure called **Quadratic Assignment Procedure (QAP)**. However, QAP assumes completely balanced sample sizes across distinct respondents, even when it is usually the case that individuals have different numbers of social network ties with other individuals, such that the assumption of completely balanced sample sizes is untrue.[135] Thus, it is likely that QAP's assumption of equal sample sizes biased the parameter estimates and the standard errors reported. Had these authors used a parametric descriptive model and Bayesian estimation, results would not have been susceptible to these problems.

Advantage 6: Multiple Comparisons

Issue #6 in Table 12.2 refers to another advantage of Bayesian methods that results from obviating *p*-values and confidence intervals. In frequentist analysis, the essential decision criterion is that alpha (i.e., Type I error rate) = .05 (or some other value such as .01), which means simply that the probability of falsely rejecting the null value is capped at the nominal level (i.e., typically 5%). However, a new problem arises when applying this decision criterion to situations with multiple tests. The problem is that every additional comparison presents an opportunity for a Type I error (i.e., false positive). Traditional analysts want to keep the overall probability of false positives, across the whole family of tests, at 5%. To do so, each individual comparison must be "corrected" to require a more stringent (i.e., smaller) *p*-value for a difference to be deemed statistically significant. This is a scientifically dubious practice because the difference between two groups can be declared significant or not entirely based on whether you are inquisitive and decide to conduct many comparisons or feign disinterest and run only a few comparisons.

In Bayesian analysis, there is no use of *p*-values and confidence intervals and no influence from which comparisons, and how many, you might or might not want to make. Instead, the distribution of credible parameter values is determined purely by the data and the structure of the model. Bayesian methods do not escape the possibility of false positives because they are caused by coincidences of rogue data that can arise in any random sample. But Bayesian methods do not try to control for inflation in Type I error rates based on your explicit or implicit intentions. Instead, Bayesian methods can incorporate rational constraints in a model's structure so that the data from different groups mutually inform each other's estimates, reducing the extremity of outlying estimates. For example, Bayesian approaches to ANOVA can use a hierarchical model structure such that group mean estimates shrink toward the overall mean. In other words, the data themselves dictate how much the estimates of outlying groups should be shrunken. This shrinkage in the estimates of the group means attenuates false positives.[136] The same approach applies to shrinking estimates of regression coefficients across multiple predictors.[137] Hierarchical models are not unique to Bayesian estimation but are especially straightforward to implement and evaluate in Bayesian software.

Advantage 7: Power Analysis and Replication Probability

The seventh issue summarized in Table 12.2 contrasts traditional and Bayesian approaches regarding statistical power analysis and replication probability. In traditional NHST, statistical power is the probability that a null hypothesis would be rejected if a particular alternative non-null effect were true and sampling proceeded a particular way. More generally, statistical power is the probability that an existing population effect will be detected in a sample of observed data. Determining a targeted non-zero effect size is the key prerequisite in any power analysis. In traditional power analysis, there is only one targeted effect size with no distribution of other reasonable values.[138] Because you have no sense of how uncertain the power estimate is, the traditional analysis yields estimates that have little stability and are, according to a recent analysis, "virtually unknowable".[139] This may be one of the reasons that published research is still underpowered[140] despite repeated calls that you conduct power analyses.[141]

In a Bayesian framework, the power estimate is robust because the hypothetical model uses the complete distribution of credible parameter values. Power is estimated using many credible parameter-value combinations and generating simulated data from each. The simulated data are analyzed by Bayesian methods and tallied concerning whether the effect was detected. Across many simulations, power is thereby estimated while considering the full uncertainty of the posterior parameter distribution. This method works for any model, regardless of hierarchical complexity or distributional assumptions.

METHODS IN PRACTICE
CAN WE TRUST FREQUENTIST RESEARCH ON THE SITUATIONAL INFLUENCES ON PERSONALITY?

As an example of the use of power analysis, consider a recent study of situational influences on personality states through time.[142] Because some of the observed effects trended in the predicted directions but did not reach statistical significance based on a traditional approach, the researchers conducted a power analysis to estimate the sample size that would have been needed to obtain a value of .80. The power and sample size estimates were based on the point estimate of an effect size in the frequentist analysis without considering the uncertainty of that point estimate. Therefore, researchers do not know whether the estimated power and needed sample size are stable. On the other hand, a Bayesian analysis would consider the uncertainty in the effect size estimate.

This chapter has provided the tools to implement three advanced quantitative techniques in your research. Chapter 13 will focus on conducting qualitative research.

DISCUSSION QUESTIONS

1. What do market basket analysis (MBA), Experience Sampling Methodology (ESM), and Bayesian analysis have in common?
2. Under what circumstances would you choose to implement MBA in your research?
3. What are the benefits of MBA over other quantitative analysis techniques?
4. How would you implement MBA in your research?
5. Why would you implement Experience Sampling Methodology (ESM) in your research?
6. Which of the advantages of ESM would tailor to your area of research?
7. In what way would you implement ESM in your research? What steps would you take?
8. What research questions in your field are more suitable for Bayesian analysis?
9. What are the main benefits of using Bayesian analysis over frequentist analysis?
10. How would you implement a Bayesian multiple linear regression in your research?

KEY TERMS

categorical association rules
complementary item
complementary reallocation
ecological validity
evidence
event contingent
highest density interval (HDI)

interval contingent experience sample methodology (ESM)
lift
Market Basket Analysis (MBA)
Markov chain Monte Carlo (MCMC)
multiple MBA
posterior distribution $p(\theta \mid D)$ term

Quadratic Assignment Procedure (QAP)

quantitative association rules

recall error

region of practical equivalence (ROPE)

sequential MBA (SMBA)

signal contingent experience sampling
 methodology

spurious variables

support

verbal protocol analysis

NOTES

This chapter is based to a large extent on the following sources:

Aguinis, H., Forcum, L. E., & Joo, H. (2013). Using market basket analysis in management research. *Journal of Management*, *39*(7), 1799-1824. https://doi.org/10.1177/0149206312466147

Kruschke, J. K., Aguinis, H., & Joo, H. (2012). The time has come: Bayesian methods for data analysis in the organizational sciences. *Organizational Research Methods*, *15*(4), 722-752. https://doi.org/10.1177/1094428112457829

Uy, M. A., Foo, M. D., & Aguinis, H. (2010). Using experience sampling methodology to advance entrepreneurship theory and research. *Organizational Research Methods*, *13*(1), 31-54. https://doi.org/10.1177/1094428109334977

13 HOW TO CONDUCT QUALITATIVE RESEARCH

LEARNING GOALS

By the end of this chapter, you will be able to do the following:

13.1 Assess the main challenges involved in interviewing key informants and plan questions regarding each research stage (i.e., research design, data collection, reporting of results).

13.2 Formulate the benefits of using Computer-Aided Text Analysis (CATA) in your research.

13.3 Describe best-practice recommendations for improving the accuracy of CATA measurement in your research (i.e., minimize transient error, specific factor error, and algorithm error).

13.4 Critically evaluate the trustworthiness of methodological literature reviews regarding the methods you are more interested in.

13.5 Implement best-practice recommendations for developing methodological literature reviews.

13.6 Verify that you are doing everything possible to improve transparency and replicability in your qualitative research.

13.7 Argue why mixed methods can lead to important theoretical advancements in the social and behavioral sciences.

13.8 Judge the transparency criteria in your qualitative research and asses the three types of replicability.

IMPORTANCE OF QUALITATIVE RESEARCH

Qualitative research examines written and spoken text. Given the wide availability of text, qualitative research has great potential to provide answers to pressing substantive questions. Accordingly, this chapter focuses on critical methodologies in qualitative research and best practice recommendations for each of them. The chapter starts with a type of qualitative research that is arguably one of the most popular and has yielded critical insights across several social and behavioral science fields: Interviews with **key informants (KIs)**. This section describes questions and challenges to address when conducting KI interviews, organized according to the research process: Research design, data collection, and reporting of results. The second section focuses on a more recently developed method in qualitative research that emerged due to technological innovations: **Computer-aided Text Analysis (CATA)**. After describing what this methodology is, when to use it, and why, this section describes best-practice recommendations for improving the accuracy of CATA measurement and research, focusing on how you can address three critical errors that those using CATA often face: **transient error, specific factor error,** and **algorithm error**. The third section of the chapter focuses on methodological literature reviews, which are becoming increasingly present and critical for developing social and behavioral sciences research. This section describes the best-practice recommendations you should implement when reading these literature reviews. Also, it provides a checklist you can use when writing a manuscript on a method you are interested in or when reviewing a methodological literature review in the future. The following section describes mixed methods and how social and behavioral science research would benefit from implementing more research that uses this approach, which combines qualitative and quantitative methods. Finally, the last section of this chapter focuses on how you could improve transparency and replicability in your qualitative research. To do so, this section focuses on transparency criteria in qualitative research, the three types of replicability, and implications for enhancing qualitative research transparency, emphasizing recommendations you can use to increase the transparency of your qualitative research.

INTERVIEWS WITH KEY INFORMANTS

The interest in key informants (KIs) lies in the power of these individuals to influence their organizations and communities.[1] There are several definitions of key informants, also referred to as "elite informants," ranging from top-ranking executives[2] to highly skilled professionals,[3] and people with substantial power and expertise not possessed by others.[4] Based on the existing literature, the following is a comprehensive definition of this concept[5]: "Key informants are key decision makers who have extensive and exclusive information and the ability to influence important organizational outcomes, either alone or jointly with others (e.g., a board of directors)."

Important differences create unique challenges and make interviewing KIs distinct from interviewing non-KIs. These distinctive aspects of KI interviewing include the researcher-informant power distribution, key informants' expectations, your role, the unique contribution of each interview, and outliers. In short, the differences between key and non-key informants and the issues involved in interviewing KIs create unique challenges in designing and conducting effective interviews. Therefore, the following section addresses best-practice recommendations for designing and conducting empirical research involving interviews with key informants.

Questions and Challenges to Address When Conducting Key Informant (KI) Interviews

This section offers recommendations in the usual sequential steps in the research process. To enhance the usefulness of these recommendations, they are described as critical questions you need to answer when conducting interviews with KIs. In asking and answering these questions, you follow the usual sequence of an empirical research study: Research design, data collection, and reporting results. As a preview, Table 13.1 includes each of the questions and their answers.

Research Stage	Project Question/Challenge
TABLE 13.1 ■	**Questions and Challenges to Address When Conducting Key Informant (KI) Interviews**

Research Stage	Project Question/Challenge
Research design	● Is interviewing KIs required or even necessary?
	● What is the best order for the interviews?
	● What is the right time in the research project to interview a KI?
Data collection	● How can you access KIs?
	● What is the best format for the interviews?
	● How should you manage power dynamics?
	● How can you obtain more honest responses?
	● How should you engage KIs?
	● Should you conduct remote interviews?
	● How should you conclude the interview?
	● How can you secure follow-up interviews?
	● How can you improve the trustworthiness of the resulting scholarly paper?
	a. How can you improve the credibility and dependability of the study?
	b. Should you seek disconfirming cases?
Reporting of results	● What information should you report and to whom?

Source: Solarino & Aguinis (2021).

Research Design

Is Interviewing KIs Required or Even Necessary? Suppose you are planning to conduct interviews with KIs. In that case, you must first consider whether your research questions may be answered more appropriately using other data sources that may also involve less time and effort.[6] To do so, it is necessary to understand the unique advantages that interviews with KIs offer because these advantages may not be applicable in all research contexts.

First, interviewing KIs allows for an in-depth understanding of decision-making processes, organizational narratives, and how specific individual characteristics, including attitudes, values, and preferences, may have shaped the informants' choices related to their organizations or communities. In other words, interviews with KIs offer a unique opportunity to explore the "**microfoundations**" (i.e., behavioral aspects) of the organization's strategy.[7] For instance, you can use interviews with KIs to explore the role of organizational narratives in enhancing or constraining new CEO or board-member decisions.

Second, the interviewer can learn about an informant's analysis and perspectives on a particular issue, event, or situation. For example, an author noted that some key informants embrace the opportunity to have their say on specific issues, particularly regarding any public criticism they have received, thereby enriching the research with multiple points of view that would not be available otherwise.[8]

In short, if the research domain and questions or hypotheses require either an in-depth understanding of the personalities and mindsets of KIs or knowledge of their analysis of a particular issue, interviewing KIs constitutes an appropriate and even necessary methodological approach. For instance, without interviews with KIs, you would have no information on what firms learn as they mature,[9] neither would we understand the importance of specific managerial choices in transferring complex knowledge from headquarters to firm subsidiaries successfully,[10] nor the role that heuristics play in shaping investments decisions under uncertain conditions.[11]

What Is the Best Order for the Interviews? In situations where the recruitment of KIs is highly successful, you face a decision on the order to conduct the interviews. Although the availability of participants is a significant factor in determining the order, you should interview the informants most capable of challenging your assumptions and preconceptions first if you have some choice. Assumptions are thoughts that cause you to predict an outcome. Thus, challenging your assumptions early in the study can create fresh thinking, allowing you to address novel emerging constructs or relationships between existing constructs that have previously gone unnoticed. Therefore, seeking informants outside your direct networks is helpful when scheduling the interviews. Indeed, while informants belonging to your network or the university alumni network are easier to access and can prove helpful in building up confidence and refining the interview protocol, these same informants tend to be "one's own kind of people." They share similar mindsets with you, posing the risk of relying too much on and for too long on shared and, therefore, unchallenged assumptions. This issue is further amplified by the **snowballing/referral approach** many use to access additional KIs with similar characteristics, further perpetuating your assumptions. So, by interviewing people outside of their networks early in the study, you are better positioned to challenge your initial assumptions and preconceptions.

What Is the Right Time in the Research Project to Interview a KI? For studies that also entail collecting data from sources other than KIs, you should conduct interviews with KIs later in the project. This approach is preferable for the following two reasons. First, accessing KIs is challenging. You risk long delays in securing an interview date and should plan accordingly. Second, interviews with KIs conducted later in the research project will benefit from your improved command of the subject matter. Such preparation includes but is not limited to knowing the details of the topics under investigation and the history of the informants and their firms, familiarity with specific jargon, finding specific examples to support ideas, and covering all the basic information that can be found in existing records.[12] Additionally, thorough preparation helps address the status imbalance between the interviewer and informant by highlighting the "seriousness of the interviewer"[13] and projecting a "positive image to gain their respect."[14] Being knowledgeable is important because it allows you to adapt your style to the KI. For instance, some authors commented, "like many other interviewers, we have sometimes been awarded additional information simply because we have appeared to know more than we actually did."[15] Being knowledgeable pays off also when you play their role as unknowing and "unthreatening"[16] because it allows guiding the interview in the desired direction.

Data Collection

How Can You Access KIs? The most pervasive challenge in interviewing KIs is gaining access to them in the first place. Indeed, you should expect limited access to KIs and a strong likelihood that gatekeepers will control access.[17] For example, an author needed "nearly two years of phone calls, screening meetings with executive assistants, and networking to interview two executives in a major manufacturing company."[18]

To recruit KIs' effectively, it is useful to frame your interview requests as a practical problem that would benefit the KIs or their organizations and communities. Another effective practice is to tell gatekeepers how the interviewee would benefit from participating and being explicit about the boundaries of the project's outputs.[19] Indeed, some qualitative researchers have convinced the gatekeeper and the informant that the project would offer value to them. This required preparing a proposal and asking broad questions to incorporate some of the informant's concerns about their business or industry and your goals. These investigators used a combination of the following approaches to overcome the access challenge. First, they leveraged the university's alum network and connections. Specifically, they relied on alum information at their universities to find and contact suitable informants. Others asked high-level university administrators (e.g., deans) to write an introduction letter for them. Overall, using academic credentials and institutional affiliations is useful to establish credibility in the eyes of the gatekeeper.[20]

Second, you can leverage other types of networks. For example, more experienced researchers relied on contacts developed during previous studies. Others can leverage personal and friendship-related connections, such as "one of the study's authors went to college with the son of one of the interviewed CEOs." One researcher reported having someone married to the CEO of a large venture capital as a student.

Third, there are ways to bypass the gatekeepers. One approach is to email the KIs directly. For example, you can use LinkedIn to contact informants with personalized emails. You can also exchange participation in the study with leadership workshops and training events. Specifically, the creation of an exclusive, selective event entices senior managers and makes them engage. And once they are in the room, they will speak and want to speak to you later. Executives are drawn by pairing with others and can be surprisingly frank in the right context. And yet another approach used to bypass the gatekeeper is to "walk up your interviewee." This includes starting by interviewing lower to mid-level managers to gain the credibility needed to convince the executives to meet you.

Fourth, you can fruitfully engage the gatekeeper. For example, you work with the CEO's executive assistant (EA). You can endear yourself to the EA, sometimes spending more time getting to know them. You could even meet them in person to make the connection. If you can personally meet the EA, they will become your advocate for your research. The EA would let you know the CEO's schedule and might follow up with information if you asked. Indeed, an author reported that once they satisfied all the inquiries of the gatekeeper, the latter subsequently contacted around 60 people for them.[21] In closing, gatekeepers can open doors to KIs as much as they can close them.

What Is the Best Format for the Interview? Accessibility to the informants and the time they are willing to dedicate to you determine the interview approaches you can use. If the informant can allocate a longer time to the interview or the KI can be accessed more than once, the recommendation is to start with an unstructured format (i.e., there is no set pattern, and questions are not arranged in advance). On the other hand, if the KI has limited time or can be interviewed only once, you should approach the KI with a **semi-structured format** (i.e., a few questions are predetermined, but other questions are not planned). Because follow-up interviews are not always possible, your initial approach should be that this will be a "one-shot opportunity." Therefore, you should prepare a detailed and flexible interview protocol. This approach offers the chance to cover all relevant topics without restricting the conversation.[22]

In addition, if you opt for a semi-structured interview, you let the KI speak freely. Specifically, you will let them say what they want without interrupting them. However, sometimes they may go too far away, and you must bring them back to the central theme. Also, you can keep the main questions to address during the interview in your notes to glance over them and check whether everything was covered during the interview. On the other hand, if you opt for an **unstructured approach,** you will not lead the interviews but let the informants talk about their experiences, thoughts, and ideas. In both cases, you must remain objective and ensure the informant's responses are dependable and trustworthy.

Finally, if you need to make closed-ended questions, these should come at the end of the interview after a succession of open-ended ones.[23] Again, the reason is that KIs can become irritated if not given a chance to explain precisely what they mean.[24]

How Should You Manage Power Dynamics? The power distribution is likely to favor the informant over you,[25] which can be intimidating. As professional communicators,[26] KIs may attempt to dominate the interview.[27] Be aware that it is easy to be drawn in by the articulateness and, in some cases, by the charm of organizational leaders without realizing it.[28] The risk of underestimating the power imbalance involves getting caught in the "**hostage syndrome.**" In such cases, you might suspend your judgment in the face of a KI's display of power by overestimating the importance of what the KI has to say.[29]

First, there are formal and informal strategies for reducing this power imbalance. Whether to leverage or minimize the power distance depends on the circumstance and the KI. On the formal side, you can seek endorsement from a prestigious organization, which will cast an aura of respectability on the interviewer. Regarding informal strategies, you should be acquainted with the habits, styles of dress, and rituals of interaction typical among KIs being interviewed.[30]

Second, you should be bold in asking sensitive questions because doing so challenges the researcher-informant power distribution. Asking such questions reduces the perceived status gap between you and the key informant.[31] But, it is important to wait until rapport has been established and enough discussion has occurred before asking any contentious or critical questions.[32] This caution is particularly relevant if you want to ask about potential mistakes the KI may have made. Moreover, asking potentially contentious questions can alienate the participant and lead to defensiveness. Before asking any threatening questions, it is important to know the jargon of the respondent to make the question clear and to be better informed than the KI when querying or challenging their knowledge or point of view.[33] The recommendation is to "stretch the bounds of etiquette," especially when the informant becomes uncomfortable. This can be done by advising the interviewee that a challenging question is coming and reminding them that all answers will remain anonymous. Furthermore, the power position of KIs allows them to choose which questions to answer and enables them to restrict access to information they might hold exclusively. To reduce the chance of this happening, you should build up trust in advance, stick to the facts, and ask and re-ask unanswered (or partially) questions in several ways to improve the study's dependability.

Finally, you can be respectful but also tactfully critical. You can use nonverbal cues to establish authority. For instance, you can fill a glass of water for your interviewee to signal that you welcome them into your space.[34] Nonverbal cues such as raising an eyebrow or a quick wide-eyed glance help maintain control over the interview process and show interest. Such cues can also convey that a deeper answer is needed, leading to key informant clarifications without verbal interruptions. These cues can also help prevent the informant from talking too much.[35]

How Can You Obtain More Honest Responses? KIs might be expressing an official organizational position rather than their own opinion,[36] and a common concern is that KIs might prefer to talk about how things ought to be rather than sharing detailed accounts of the challenges encountered and their coping strategies. Further, the challenge of obtaining honest responses is typical when interviewing KIs.

To obtain honest responses, you can rely on two interrelated principles: *confidentiality* and *neutrality*. Confidentiality is made explicit in the formal written agreement with the KI and implicit in your behavior during the interview. For example, not asking for specific names, focusing on the description of the issue, and not sharing what has been discussed during initial interviews are ways to communicate confidentiality. In other words, sometimes interviewees will test you and ask, "Who else have you talked to?" Your response can be: "I am very sorry; I cannot tell you any names. We guarantee anonymity to all our respondents." Typically, the interviewees are relaxed after getting this answer.

Regarding neutrality about the informants' answers, it encourages KIs to be more open. Adopting this approach shows that you understand the KI and encourages them to tell you more about the issue. As a result, KIs are more likely to open up and tell you their real attitudes and their organization's approach to issues. When the informant remains elusive, the suggestion is to stick to facts, ask and re-ask the questions differently, and clarify that the data are collected for research purposes only.

It is especially hard to discuss sensitive topics such as personal problems the KIs face (e.g., being fired from an organization), retiring, and other issues related to reputation concerns. To put the KI at ease, you can conduct the interview over dinner or during a walk after lunch, as some KIs feel less stressed talking about sensitive things outside of their office, which has the additional benefit of optimizing the informant's busy schedule. In addition, when interviewing KIs in neutral spaces, they are more likely to talk more freely.[37]

How Should You Engage KIs? Several practical solutions address the challenge of keeping your informants engaged. Three basic principles are the following: (1) *relevance*: it is better to ask questions that are both relevant to their recent concerns and bring a new perspective to them to keep KIs interested; (2) *being non-threatening*: you have to interview in a non-threatening way; and (c) *adaptability*: do not stick too closely to your pre-assigned questions, go with the flow of what they are talking about, and make it into a fascinating conversation.

Regarding relevance, you can empathize with the KI during the interview, imagining being in their shoes as the feeling of ease is important in generating informative responses and increasing the likelihood that KIs will provide referrals for additional interviews.[38] In addition, more seasoned researchers can enhance relevance by incorporating an intellectual debate in the interviews. Regarding being non-threatening, it is useful to position yourself as a learner. Moreover, you can use a KI's vanity to your advantage by emphasizing that they now have a chance to teach you, given that you are a "student" in their discipline.[39]

Finally, KIs occasionally give short or shallow responses. You can use several techniques to make the informant elaborate on their answers. These include eye glimpses, asking about hypothetical situations, and re-asking the question differently. Using nonverbal clues helps convey interest, express the need to deepen the answer, and clarify without directly interrupting the informant.[40] Hypothetical situations are imaginary but realistic cases, and the interviewer should ask the informant to describe or comment on how they would act in such a situation.[41]

Should You Conduct Remote Interviewing? When face-to-face interviewing is not an option, you can conduct the interview remotely (e.g., via Zoom). Moreover, you could find that a CEO is unwilling to grant a face-to-face interview but might agree to a phone interview on the way to the airport.[42]

Remote interviews are effective, far from the second-best option to in-person interviews, and can offer some advantages.[43] First, remote interviews are not limited by geography, so they help increase participation. In general, KIs appreciate the flexibility of a remote interview.[44] Second, in the case of phone interviews, the lack of visual contact can help reduce bias due to the similarity effect, as visual clues are removed. For example, you can benefit from phone interviews because this reduces the informant's perception of an age gap (i.e., you may be a lot younger than your interviewee), thereby disguising a factor that might have otherwise hurt your credibility.[45] Finally, while phone interviewing offers flexibility, it limits access to nonverbal cues. If you are a lot younger than the KI, depending on the research question and the scope of your study, this limitation could severely impact the quality of your research. Accordingly, video interviewing is a preferable option.

How Should You Conclude the Interview? Ending an interview is an important component of the process. The recommendation is to do so with an open-ended discussion, which is also an effective way to verify the completeness of the information acquired.[46] Typical questions to conclude the interview are: "Is there anything else you want to share?" Or "Are there any issues that you think are important that we did not cover?" The KI may reveal relevant information not covered in the previous answers or add new insights to a previous answer. Additionally, it is good practice to ask the informant for potential referrals[47] and describe how you will keep the KI informed and when they can expect to hear back from you on the study results.

Finally, you can use the end of the interview to set up the conditions for a follow-up interview by asking if you could come back later with the summary of findings to ask follow-up questions. Overall, ending the interview should set up expectations about the post-interview process because you can use this post-interview contact to leave a positive impression, facilitating further research.[48] Additionally, it can remind informants about documents they promised to share to check the accuracy and authenticate the transcript.[49]

How Can You Secure Follow-Up Interviews? Obtaining a follow-up interview with a KI can be very difficult. However, as part of the post-interview follow-up protocol, you can prepare short presentations of your findings and related topics and offer to share these presentations at a follow-up meeting.

Another good practice is sending thank-you notes and maintaining contact with the informant several times yearly to check on different issues and schedule additional interviews. Getting repeat conversations with them is a function of whether the topic is interesting, and if you did a decent job of engaging with them last time, then they are likely to meet you again as long as it is rare.

How Can You Improve the Trustworthiness of the Resulting Scholarly Paper? Credibility and dependability are necessary criteria for achieving trustworthiness in qualitative research.[50] This section addresses these issues in the specific context of KI interviewing and why it is useful to seek disconfirming cases.

How Can You Improve the Credibility and Dependability of the Study? Credibility is the degree of confidence in the findings and your interpretations.[51] Dependability is the degree to which you clearly explain the research process and carry it out in line with the rules and conventions of the chosen methodology and whether the results are stable over time and under different conditions.[52] A particular concern directly related to credibility is informant bias. Indeed, it is likely that there is something the interviewed person wants to get across. This could be some axe to grind or insights about what went wrong with a particular organizational event. Moreover, KIs might seek to manipulate you to write an article in their favor, and the most senior leaders tend to tell the story as being very much about them, while others have different recollections. In addition, KIs generally do not like talking about organizational failures, and, in such instances, they may express the official organizational position rather than their own opinion.[53] Given that these issues threaten credibility and dependability, you can adopt the following recommendations.

An effective strategy for addressing the credibility challenge is to use multiple sources to cross-check the same information, labeled *triangulation*.[54] You can use several complementary strategies to triangulate the answers you receive. You can ask for company data and files, which typically hint at what else was going on concurrently and reduce the chance of staying blinkered. You can also seek confirmation from lower-level managers, who often have an important alternative view. When data provided by the organization directly or by the KIs are unavailable, you can rely on archival records, public news, organization documents, and personal histories.[55]

The dependability challenge is conceptualized as within-respondent and between-respondent dependability. First, in quantitative research, within-respondent dependability is addressed using multi-item scales and estimating reliability (e.g., Cronbach's alpha) by asking multiple questions for each construct.[56] However, asking multiple questions on the same subject in KI research is not advisable because it gives the impression that you might not have understood the previous answer, diminishing your credibility.[57] To assess within-respondent dependability, a recommendation is to ask the informants to comment on their situations with questions such as "Why did [a news outlet] disagree with you?[58]" Using third parties to challenge the informant's view moves them away from their perspective without demonstrating skepticism and shows the interviewer's deep knowledge of the topic.

Furthermore, addressing between-respondent dependability in quantitative research involves estimating reliability across respondents by computing indexes of inter-rater reliability, such as **Cohen's Kappa**.[59] In the context of KI interviewing, you can ask informants to facilitate contact even with non-preferred colleagues and interview people from rival companies or customers. The degree of agreement across informants is evidence of dependability, like assessing inter-rater reliability in quantitative research.[60]

Should You Seek Disconfirming Cases? **Theoretical sampling** involves collecting and analyzing data to decide what to collect next to develop a theory as it emerges. **Purposive sampling** involves relying on your judgment when choosing population members to participate in your study. **Snowball sampling** consists of asking individuals in your study to recruit other participants. Finally, *convenience sampling* involves interviewing specific KIs because they are simply convenient (i.e., easily accessible to you).

Many studies involving KI interviews rely on snowball and convenience samples. As noted earlier, these sampling approaches will likely result in KIs from a population of similar-minded people. On a related note, if you are using purposive or theoretical sampling approaches, you should seek informants that could help better define the emergent patterns in the data. Access to KIs is often restricted, so you might have to access "second best" informants. Once the patterns in the data have been clarified and you have reached **theoretical saturation** (i.e., you believe that given the information you already received, no further data collection is necessary), you will stop the data collection, causing your findings to support biased results based on limited and homogenous information possibly.

To address the challenges, you should seek out "disconfirming cases" informants from different organizational conditions, statuses, and industries whose views on the phenomenon under investigation may differ from those of other KIs. Disconfirming cases do not necessarily fit emergent patterns[61] and serve to test the boundaries of the research. The general principle is the following: If you think your results are not generalizable or the existence of a particular kind of case will undermine all that you "know" to be true about a phenomenon, then look for that kind of case.[62] You should search for disconfirming cases, especially after you reach theoretical saturation, if you aim to generalize your findings, particularly in the presence of snowball or convenience samples, because they help assess the transferability of the study.[63]

Reporting of Results

Reporting results of interviews with KIs involves information in the resulting scholarly manuscript. But this issue also involves what should be reported back to the KIs.

What Information Should You Report, and to Whom? One particularly important issue regarding KI interviews is how to report direct statements. A challenge faced when reporting the interviews with KIs in a scholarly manuscript is conveying the context of quotes without violating confidentiality. Some authors offered examples of how you should report quotations from your informants. Specifically, their quotations are preceded by "the basic scene," which describes where the quotation was spoken under what circumstances.

In addition, you should also set up expectations early in interacting with KIs on what will be shared and when. First, you can prepare short presentations of your findings with illustrative graphs and figures or reports framing results in non-academic terms. Sometimes KIs ask whether they could describe your findings in their internal publications or blogs, and you must keep them patient until the article is published. Second, to prevent a premature and unintentional release of your research results, you can prepare practitioner reports that are primarily descriptive and focused on best practices for the KIs. Finally, you should keep the informants updated as the manuscript develops from its first draft to its final publication.

Next, let's address the topic of CATA, a relatively newer approach for analyzing the information you collect through your interviews and other methods aimed at gathering text rather than numbers. In a nutshell, computer-aided text analysis (CATA) is a form of content analysis that enables the measurement of constructs by processing text into quantitative data based on the frequency of words.[64]

COMPUTER-AIDED TEXT ANALYSIS (CATA)

Given the widespread availability of text that can be used to conduct social and behavioral sciences research across individual and firm levels of analysis, it is not surprising that CATA has recently been used to measure a wide range of constructs, such as organizational psychological capital,[65] blame,[66] and firmness of resolve.[67]

The availability of text makes CATA practically and logistically appealing. But, even more, critical from the perspective of theory advancement is that CATA offers psychometric advantages compared to more traditional measures such as self-reports and archival data.[68] Specifically, regarding internal validity, CATA frequently involves data collected in naturally-occurring organizational contexts, such as texts included in annual reports.[69] Thus, the data collected allow for greater confidence regarding relations among underlying constructs compared to other types of measures, such as self-reports and archival data.[70] Second, regarding external validity, using CATA allows for collecting a large amount of data across units, enhancing the generalizability of conclusions. In other words, collecting data across a larger sample of contexts, levels, and circumstances is easier than more traditional measures.[71] Third, regarding construct validity, CATA is less susceptible to threats such as standard method variance and endogeneity pervasive in more conventional measures because CATA facilitates data collection from different sources. Finally, regarding statistical conclusion validity, CATA facilitates the examination of extensive samples of texts, resulting in satisfactory statistical power to test hypotheses, which is different in social and behavioral sciences research that relies on more traditional measures.[72] In short, CATA offers advantages in terms of internal, external, construct, and statistical conclusion validity, which explains why it is seen as a nascent yet highly promising measurement approach.[73]

Although CATA holds considerable promise compared to more traditional measurement approaches, it is ironic that it lags in assessing measurement concerns. For instance, while there is considerable guidance regarding assessing and mitigating measurement error in survey research,[74] there is no such direction regarding CATA. This gap in measurement scrutiny between current CATA research and the standard for other approaches raises the question of how much measurement error exists in studies using CATA and the potential impact on the accuracy of substantive conclusions. So, although CATA is a promising and valuable measurement approach, there is a need to understand how to identify and minimize key sources of measurement error. The following section focuses on reducing measurement error by refining existing CATA measures and offering best-practice recommendations on assessing and minimizing measurement error in future CATA research to improve the accuracy of substantive conclusions.

Best-practice Recommendations for Improving the Accuracy of CATA

You should consider reliability concerns explicitly in interpreting past and future research using CATA because of measurement error. Transient and specific factor errors account for the vast majority of measurement error. And there is evidence that substantive relations reported in past research have been underestimated. The following section offers best-practice recommendations for improving the accuracy of CATA measurement and research. As a preview, Table 13.2 includes challenges that lead to each type of error and a summary of recommendations for addressing each.

It is always preferable to anticipate and attempt to mitigate measurement error *before* data collection.[75] Accordingly, if you are using CATA, you can consider the following actions to anticipate and minimize the effects of measurement error.

Transient Error

Two key challenges may drive transient error in CATA research. The first is where CATA scores demonstrate variability, but the language used in the texts is otherwise consistent over time. This may occur when there is a change in the construct being measured. It is not possible to parse out variability due to random error (i.e., noise) from substantive changes (i.e., true variability). Accordingly, a valuable assessment to be made is to refer to theory to identify whether the construct is likely to be stable over the assessment period.

TABLE 13.2 ■ Best-Practice Recommendations for Improving the Accuracy of Computer-Aided Text Analysis (CATA) Measurement and Research

Source of Error	Challenges	Best-Practice Recommendations
Transient error	CATA scores demonstrate variability over time.	Identify whether the construct is theorized to be stable over the assessment period. Decrease the lag between collected texts. Collect texts that are produced more frequently. Investigate the possibility of shocks within the sampling frame.
	The language used in texts varies significantly over time.	Identify whether texts with more standardized content are available. Identify whether the sampled texts are likely influenced by managerial attention rather than the salience of the measured construct. Confirm the author's identity and whether the author changed between texts for individual-level texts.
Specific factor error	Word lists are too inclusive or exclusive, resulting in words being used out of context or missed.	Iteratively compare the words identified by CATA and manual content analyses and refine the measure to improve alignment. Eliminate word stems and replace them with only the conjugations that fit the construct definition. Eliminate single words that are commonly used out of context and replace them with common short phrases. Identify omitted conjugations of words on the word list that are relevant to the construct. Generate a list of words used in your sampled texts and have judges evaluate whether words should be added to the measure.
	The measure was developed in a different context.	Iteratively compare the words identified by CATA and manual content analyses and refine the measure to improve alignment. Generate a deductive list of words to indicate the construct in the new context and have judges evaluate whether they should be included in the revised list. Generate a list of words used in your sampled texts and have judges evaluate whether the words reflect the construct in the new context.
Algorithm error	Two CATA software packages provide inconsistent scores.	Identify whether the measure uses features idiosyncratic to one package. Select a third package for comparison to both original packages. Recreate a CATA analysis using manual coding and compare results to both packages.

Source: McKenny, Aguinis, Short, & Anglin (2018). Reproduced with permission.

Example: Variability in State-Like Versus Trait-Like Constructs

State-like constructs such as optimism, affect, and mood change more frequently than trait-like constructs such as strategic orientation, personality, and values. If theory suggests that variability is likely, you should decrease the lag between the sampled texts. This can be accomplished by collecting the texts more frequently or, if the texts are only available at long intervals (e.g., annual reports), collecting texts that are produced more frequently (e.g., quarterly reports).

Transient error may also be influenced by variation in the construct from exogenous shocks. For instance, when economic conditions change between the creations of texts, the author's outlook may be affected, increasing the likelihood of changes in otherwise stable constructs. In addition, exogenous shocks such as the introduction of a lawsuit against the organization, the change of management teams/directors, or shareholder activism may also drive changes in the contents of organizational narratives over time and deflate test-retest reliability estimates. Accordingly, when transient error is significant, CATA users should examine whether any shocks that influenced the focal construct occurred during the assessment period.

Example: Transient Error and Variability in Language Over Time

Variability in the language used in the sampled texts over time is another key challenge associated with transient error. Consider the following example. In investigating three different constructs, two samples using CEO shareholder letters had a relatively high transient error: 49% of the observed variance for entrepreneurial orientation and 47% for market orientation. However, when ambidexterity was measured in Management Discussion and Analysis (MD&A) statements of 10-K filings, transient error only accounted for 20% of the observed variance. There were two likely reasons why the MD&A statements outperformed shareholder letters concerning transient error. First, the contents of the MD&A statements were more standardized, suggesting that if the underlying construct stayed the same over the assessment period, it was discussed approximately the same amount in both texts. Second, shareholder letters are considerably shorter and feature the voice of the CEO heavily, suggesting that the contents of these documents may be more subject to the attention of the CEO at the time of the text's creation. For instance, if innovation has been a priority for a firm for many years and this priority has not changed, the CEO may not emphasize this as much as other timelier strategic initiatives since they have limited space for communicating with shareholders.

The authors of these texts can also influence the language used in texts. While frequently attributed to the CEO, multiple individuals often produce shareholder letters.[76] The contributions of these individuals embed multiple perspectives of the organization into the text, reducing the likelihood that the idiosyncrasies of an individual contributor will bias construct measurement. However, having multiple contributors to a text increases the likelihood of measurement error when measuring individual-level constructs. For instance, the use of positive and negative language in a text is commonly used to measure the affective state of the text's author.[77] When a text has multiple authors, the presence of positive and negative language cannot be attributed to one individual. Accordingly, when measuring individual-level constructs, you should provide reasonable evidence that the only contributor to the text was the individual for whom the measurement is being made and that the author did not change.

Specific Factor Error

This type of error arises from two sources. First, the CATA measures include words and phrases frequently used out of context and omitted words and phrases consistently used to indicate the measured construct. This is addressed by iteratively removing words from the CATA measures frequently used out of context, adding words from the text consistently used in context, and recalculating parallel forms reliability estimates. This intervention of a human coder in CATA helps alleviate the threat of specific factor error introduced by the technique's inability to consider the context in which words are used.

Several key activities may help you to identify words to add or remove within the iterative word list refinement process. First, you can eliminate word stems and add the conjugated words appropriate for the measured construct to reduce the frequency of counting words used out of context. Illustrating how word stems can cause specific factor error, the original exploitation dictionary used "refine*" to capture how firms make small adjustments to improve existing products and processes. However, the words "refinery" and "refineries" were never used in the sample texts. Also, a way to decrease the number of counted words can be achieved by replacing single words with many meanings with short phrases with more targeted meanings. For example, the original innovativeness measure included the word "new." While "new" frequently signals innovation in shareholder letters, it is also commonly used to communicate phenomena unrelated to innovation (e.g., new regulations, New York). This suggests that replacing "new" with several short phrases, such as "new product" and "new technology," might provide a more reliable measurement of innovativeness. To capture omitted words, you should identify whether the measures include all conjugations of the words used in the measure and add any omitted conjugations that indicate the construct. You should also consider replicating the inductive word list development process to capture other relevant words used in the sample of narratives that reflect the measured construct.

A second challenge regarding specific factor error in CATA measures relates to the context in which the measure was developed. Different industries, texts, and individuals may use the same words to mean different things or use different words to mean the same thing. For example, the language used in CEO shareholder letters is likely different from that used in X (formerly Twitter) posts. Accordingly, measures developed for one context may need to be refined to be reliable in other contexts. An efficient way to refine the measure is to use the following two-phase CATA measure development process.[78] The first phase calls for words to be identified deductively from theory and existing measures.[79] You should include the words and phrases from existing CATA measures. The second phase calls for words to be identified inductively from the sample of texts.[80] At the end of each phase, judges evaluate whether these words indicate the construct in the new context. This two-phase process provides an initial refinement of the CATA measure. Further refinement can be accomplished by again iteratively removing words from the CATA measure frequently used out of context, adding words from the text consistently used in context, and recalculating parallel forms reliability estimates.

Algorithm Error

Algorithm error is driven by software design choices made by the CATA software developers, including each package's features and limitations. For instance, CAT Scanner can handle phrases with spaces, but DICTION 5.0 cannot. As a result, CATA measures that include phrases may produce different data across the two packages. Accordingly, you should identify whether your CATA measure uses features of one package not supported by the other. Other design choices the software developers make include handling punctuation and how words are defined. For example, should hyphenated words be treated as one word or two? These decisions are frequently less apparent than identifying whether features are consistent across packages. However, the impact of these algorithmic discrepancies can still be estimated by selecting a third CATA software package and triangulating the results. Alternatively, you could recreate a CATA analysis by manually coding texts for the words included in the CATA measure. Comparing these results with the CATA analysis may provide insight into the package algorithmic differences.

In the next section, we turn to methodological literature reviews, which provide a narrative (i.e., qualitative) description of a particular methodological approach. Methodological innovations are accelerating due to new software, the speed of computers, the availability of Big Data, and new sources of qualitative and quantitative data. Together, these innovations mean you must continuously expand your methodological toolkit. Accordingly, given the need to learn new methodological approaches, decreased resources invested in methodological training for students, and resources to retrain and retool more seasoned researchers, it is common that many journals regularly publish literature reviews on methodological issues.

METHODOLOGICAL LITERATURE REVIEWS

Methodological literature reviews are articles that formally or informally review the existing literature regarding practices about methodological issues, summarize the literature, and provide recommendations for improved practice. These reviews offer three main contributions. First, they help current and future researchers improve their methodological repertoire.[81] Second, by describing "how to do things right," methodological literature reviews help address the challenge of **questionable research practices (QRPs**[82]). That is, methodological literature reviews can be used by substantive researchers to learn how to apply a method and to check whether specific practices are appropriate or considered a QRP. Similarly, journal editors and reviewers can use methodological literature reviews to identify and attempt to minimize QRPs that exploit methodological gray areas in submitted manuscripts.[83] Third, methodological literature reviews help identify knowledge gaps and research needs, including methodological and substantive innovations resulting from improved methodology.[84]

Despite the contributions, there is room for improvement regarding literature reviews due to the need for more clarity and thoroughness in describing the procedures used to conduct the review and derive the recommendations presented therein.[85] The pressure to publish in key journals[86] is, to some extent, the culprit for insufficient clarity and thoroughness and the pervasiveness of QRPs in general and in literature reviews in particular, as the motivation to publish might, in some cases, supersede your motivation to be transparent and communicate judgment calls that take place during the research process.[87] However, given their role as authoritative "how-to" resources, methodological literature reviews must be clear about all procedures in presenting recommendations. In addition, given rapid technological advances, some journal editors, associate editors, and reviewers may not be fully equipped to evaluate submitted manuscripts describing methodological literature reviews, compounded by increased workloads due to the variety and quantity of submitted manuscripts.[88]

The purpose of this section is to provide recommendations on what components to include in a methodological literature review to enhance its thoroughness, clarity, and, ultimately, usefulness. Providing recommendations about what to include in a methodological literature review and how to present such information is of value for producers, evaluators, and users of methodological literature reviews.[89] Without this information, potential authors lack sufficient guidance on how to produce such reviews, journal editors and reviewers evaluating such efforts are left questioning the trustworthiness of submitted manuscripts, and users, including students and others interested in learning a new method, are unable to determine whether they can rely on the accuracy of the recommendations offered.

Best-practice Recommendations and Checklist

Table 13.3 summarizes these recommendations in the form of a checklist. The checklist organizes the broad and more specific issues around the following four questions: (1) How can a

TABLE 13.3 ■ Questions and Broad and Specific Issues to Enhance Thoroughness, Clarity, and Usefulness of Methodological Literature Reviews: Checklist for Producers, Evaluators, and Users		
Questions to Ask About the Review	**Broad Issue to be Addressed by the Review**	**Specific Issues to be Addressed by the Review**
		Does the review...
#1: Motivation and importance?	1. *Need for review*: Requirement for methodological literature review of the issues	1.1 Outline potential contributions of the methodological issue for substantive research? 1.2 Provide evidence of prior confusion about the methodological issue? 1.3 Demonstrate that researchers are incorrectly applying the methodology?
	2. *Criticality of issue*: Importance of the methodological issues	2.1 Provide evidence of growing interest or use of methodological issue? 2.2 Show that the issue is important for many (most) studies in the field? 2.3 Demonstrate that the issue is new or unfamiliar to most researchers? 2.4 Discuss the dangers of adopting incorrect approaches to knowledge generation and practice?
	3. *Implications of methodological issues reviewed*: Significance of methodological issues for different aspects of the research process	3.1 Explain how the methodological issue affects typical components of a paper (i.e., theory, design, measurement, analysis, and discussion/reporting)? 3.2 Discuss concerns regarding reporting transparency when describing analytical choices related to the methodological issue?
#2: Scope and data selection?	4. *Scope of review*: Breadth of issues addressed in the review	4.1 Provide a comprehensive "one-stop-shop" treatment on the issue? 4.2 Address the issue as manifested within specific fields? 4.3 Address a particular/narrower aspect of a larger issue?
#3: Transparency and replicability?	5. *Process of literature review*: Transparent reporting of procedure used to conduct the literature review	5.1 Transparently outline the process used to select journals, articles, and the period covered by the review? 5.2 Clearly specify the procedures used to code articles?
	6. *Source of recommendations*: Transparent reporting of procedure used to conduct the literature review	6.1 Rely on authors' expertise with methodological issues to derive recommendations? 6.2 Cite published research on best practices as evidence for recommendations? 6.3 Rely on simulations to derive recommendations? 6.4 Cite seminal papers/manuals as the source of recommendations?

Questions to Ask About the Review	Broad Issue to be Addressed by the Review	Specific Issues to be Addressed by the Review
		Does the review...
#4: Readability and usability?	7. *Structure of recommendations:* Compositional elements used to present recommendations	7.1 Organize recommendations by stage of the research process or as a step-by-step guideline? 7.2 Outline general best-practice recommendations when dealing with methodological issues? 7.3 Discuss context-specific best-practice recommendations or decisions? 7.4 Illustrate recommendations using an empirical example? 7.5 Identify published research that exemplifies best-practice recommendations?
	8. *Layout of recommendations:* Compositional elements used to present recommendations	8.1 Present recommendations in a separate section? 8.2 Present recommendations using a numbered list? 8.3 Summarize recommendations using tabular formats? 8.4 Employ graphical tools to present recommendations?
	9. *Readability of review:* Compositional elements used to present recommendations	9.1 Use simple and descriptive language?
	10. *Software guidelines:* Compositional elements used to present recommendations	10.1 Discuss software packages and options available to implement recommendations? 10.2 Provide software code to replicate procedures described in review?

Source: Adapted from Aguinis, Ramani, & Alabduljader (2020). Reproduced with permission.

methodological literature review's motivation for and importance be justified? (2) What strategies can be used to inform data selection decisions regarding the scope of a review? (3) How can the transparency and replicability of the process used to identify included articles and recommendations be enhanced? and (4) What features can be used to report results and improve the reliability and usability of a review's recommendations? This checklist informs you what to consider, include, and disclose when producing a methodological literature review. If you would like to produce a methodological literature review, you can proceed sequentially through these broad and specific issues as appropriate. In addition, evaluators (i.e., journal editors and reviewers) can use the knowledge in the checklist to evaluate submitted manuscripts and provide developmental feedback to potential authors on what components to include to increase transparency and reproducibility, thereby reducing QRPs.[90] Finally, users of methodological literature reviews, including students and researchers who are not methodologists, can utilize the checklist to understand whether a specific review can be trusted.

Next, let's discuss another important methodological approach: Mixed methods. Mixed-methods research includes at least one quantitative method (i.e., designed to examine numbers) and one qualitative method (i.e., designed to examine text).[91] This methodological approach has developed rapidly in the last few years, mainly in education and health sciences.[92]

MIXED METHODS

The central premise of mixed methods is that combining quantitative and qualitative approaches provides a better understanding of complex social and behavioral science phenomena than either approach alone. For example, a better understanding can be obtained by triangulating one set of results with another, thereby enhancing the validity of inferences.[93] Additional valuable features include complementarity (elaboration or clarification of the results from one method with the findings from the other method), development (when you use the results from one method to help develop the use of the other method), and expansion (seeking to extend the breadth and range of inquiry by using different methods for different inquiry components).[94]

Two main factors help you determine the type of mixed methods design best suited to your study[95]: *priority* and *implementation of data collection*. Regarding priority, as a mixed methods researcher, you can prioritize both quantitative and qualitative parts, emphasize qualitative more, or emphasize quantitative more. This emphasis results from the research question, practical constraints regarding data collection, and the presumed preference of the intended audience. Mixed methods designs can therefore be divided into (a) equivalent status designs (you conduct the study using both the quantitative and the qualitative approaches equally to understand the phenomenon under study) and (b) dominant studies or nested designs (you conduct the study with a dominant method and a small component of the other method). In addition, options regarding the data collection sequence consist of gathering the information simultaneously (i.e., concurrent or simultaneous design) or introducing the information in phases (i.e., sequential design). When qualitative data collection precedes quantitative data collection, the intention may be first to explore the problem being studied and then to follow up on this exploration with quantitative data that are amenable to studying a large sample.

METHODS IN PRACTICE
USING MIXED METHODS TO STUDY VARIABLES AT DIFFERENT LEVELS OF ANALYSIS

Mixed-methods research includes variables at different levels of analysis, such as leaders and the organization. For example, an important issue in social and behavioral sciences studies is the analysis of sources of heterogeneity and differences among organizations. As an illustration of the potential of mixed methods, you can select participants based on quantitative data (e.g., outliers or extreme data points in your sample) and then study these extreme members in depth using qualitative research.[96] Thus, if you are interested in studying organizations, you can use the following design that begins with a quantitative four-step firm selection process: 1) selecting a single industry, 2) clustering organizations by strategic type or group within this industry, 3) comparing performance indices within strategic groups, and 4) identifying those organizations within each strategic group that are the high and low performers. Then, these organizations would be studied using qualitative, in-depth fieldwork methods. This qualitative approach may help gain in-depth knowledge and understanding of the organization, its micro-processes, and individuals' specific characteristics, actions, and interactions.

Social and behavioral science research can benefit from greater integration of process- and outcome-oriented research through mixed methods, yielding important insights.[97] Giving more attention to process-related research can help improve understanding of content-related issues. Specifically, process studies can clarify the important variables and why they might influence relevant outcomes. For example, the quantitative portion of a mixed-methods study may focus on the statistical effects of several antecedent variables at different levels (e.g., individuals and organizational capabilities) on some outcome (e.g., competitive advantage or firm performance). Complementing and expanding upon this perspective, the qualitative portion may focus on process-related characteristics, such as how collective variables (organizational routines and capabilities) emerge through the social aggregation of individual variables.

Using mixed methods is about more than just stacking quantitative and qualitative methods. Instead, it is about integrating them to take advantage of the best features of each. Although mixed methods research is more institutionalized than quantitative and qualitative methods, they have great potential to help advance social and behavioral science theory.

Next, let's address the issue of transparency and replicability. Although transparency and replicability are usually discussed within quantitative research, the following section focuses on transparency and replicability in qualitative research. The perspective of this material is that of "**qualitative positivism**," also referred to as "**transcendental realism**." Specifically, this means that social phenomena exist in our minds and the objective world. Moreover, there are lawful and reasonably stable relationships that we aim to identify and study. This ontological perspective is fairly dominant in social and behavioral science research, and the goal is to produce replicable and cumulative knowledge. As such, the following section describes criteria that can be used to evaluate the extent to which qualitative research is transparent. If replication is a desirable goal, then transparency is required.

HOW TO IMPROVE TRANSPARENCY AND REPLICABILITY IN YOUR QUALITATIVE RESEARCH

Transparency Criteria in Qualitative Research

The transparency criteria in Table 13.4 cover the sequential aspects of the qualitative research process. They include research design (i.e., kind of qualitative method, research setting, your position along the insider-outsider continuum, sampling procedures, the relative importance of the participants/cases), measurement (documenting interactions with participants; saturation point; unexpected opportunities, challenges, and other events; management of power imbalance), data analysis (i.e., data coding and first-order codes; data analysis and second- and higher-order codes), and data disclosure (i.e., raw material availability).

An essential characteristic of the transparency criteria is that they are not mutually exclusive and, instead, have a cumulative effect on the trustworthiness and replicability of knowledge. In other words, transparency is a continuous variable of degree. So, the more the criteria that are fully met, the better.

Finally, the 12 criteria are applicable and sufficiently broad, so they can be used to assess transparency in many types of qualitative methods and across substantive domains. However, additional criteria could be added to the list as needed.

Transparency Criteria and Three Types of Replicability

As shown in Table 13.4, there are specific reasons why each transparency criterion is relevant for replicability. However, not all criteria are necessarily relevant for all three types of replicability. This is an important issue considering that not all types of replicability are always necessary—or even desirable—across ontological perspectives.

All the criteria are relevant for *exact replication* where a previous study is replicated using the same population and procedures. In an exact replication study, the goal is to assess whether the findings of a past study are reproducible.[98] Thus, the goal is to remain as close as possible to the original study regarding methodological approach, population and sampling criteria, data coding, analysis, and all other procedures to minimize possible sources of "disturbance" and falsify the original study's results.

In the case of **empirical replication**, a previous study is replicated using the same procedures but a different population. Again, the purpose is to assess how much results are generalizable to another population. In this second type of replication, the goal is to remain as close as possible to the original study regarding methodological procedures but not study participants. Accordingly, transparency criteria related to methodological procedures, but not necessarily about the sample and population characteristics, are most relevant (i.e., criteria 1, 6, 7, 8, 9, 10, and 11).

TABLE 13.4 ■ Transparency Criteria in Qualitative Research and Their Relevance for Exact, Empirical, and Conceptual Replication						
ID	Transparency Criterion	Definition	Criterion is necessary for replicability because…	Exact replication	Empirical replication	Conceptual replication
1	*Kind of qualitative method*	The qualitative methodology used in the study (e.g., action research, case study, grounded theory)	… a method's assumptions, beliefs, and values affect theory, design, measurement, analysis, and reporting choices, as well as the interpretation of results	✔	✔	
2	*Research setting*	The physical, social, and cultural milieu of the study (e.g., firm conditions, industry, participants' social status)	…it clarifies the structure, the sources, and the strength of the pre-existing conditions in the research setting	✔		✔
3	*Position of you along the insider-outsider continuum*	Your relationship with the organization and study participants; the closer the relationship, the more you are an insider rather than an outsider	… it allows for an understanding of your relationship with the organization and participants, which can alter the accessibility of data, what participants disclose, and how the collected information is interpreted	✔		✔
4	*Sampling procedures*	The procedures used to select participants or cases for the study (e.g., convenience, purposive, theoretical)	… given that samples are not probabilistic, it clarifies what kind of variability you are seeking (and along which specific dimensions), and the presence of possible biases in the sampling procedure	✔		✔

ID	Transparency Criterion	Definition	Criterion is necessary for replicability because...	Exact replication	Empirical replication	Conceptual replication
5	*The relative importance of the participants/ cases*	The study's sample and the relative importance of each participant or case	... it allows for the identification of participants and cases with similar characteristics as in the original study	✔		✔
6	*Documenting interactions with participants*	The documentation and transcription of the interviews and all other forms of observations (e.g., audio, video, notations)	...different means of documenting interactions may alter the willingness of participants to share information and therefore affect the type of information gathered	✔	✔	
7	*Saturation point*	It occurs when there are no new insights or themes in the process of collecting data and drawing conclusions	...identifying the saturation point can include judgment calls on your part (e.g. when a researcher believes that additional information will not result in discoveries or that new information will not add new categories to the coding scheme)	✔	✔	
8	*Unexpected opportunities, challenges, and other events*	Unexpected opportunities (e.g., access to additional sources of data), challenges (e.g., a firm's unit declines to participate in the last data collection stage and is replaced by a different one), and events (e.g., internal and external changes such as a new CEO or changes in market conditions during the study) that occur during all stages of the research process	... how researchers react and the actions they take in response to these unexpected events affect data collection and subsequent conclusions	✔	✔	
9	*Management of power imbalance*	The differential exercise of control, authority, or influence during the research process	... it allows other researchers to adopt similar strategies (e.g., endorsement from a prestigious institution, self-acquaintance, asking sensitive questions) that affect the type of information gathered as well as a study's conclusions	✔	✔	
10	*Data coding and first-order codes*	The process through which data are categorized to facilitate subsequent analysis (e.g., structural coding, descriptive coding, narrative coding)	... it allows other researchers to follow similar procedures and obtain similar conclusions	✔	✔	

(Continued)

ID	Transparency Criterion	Definition	Criterion is necessary for replicability because...	Exact replication	Empirical replication	Conceptual replication
	TABLE 13.4 ■ Transparency Criteria in Qualitative Research and Their Relevance for Exact, Empirical, and Conceptual Replication (Continued)					
11	*Data analysis and second and higher-order codes*	The classification and interpretation of linguistic or visual material to make statements about implicit and explicit dimensions and structures (Flick, 2014) and is generally done by identifying key relationships that tie the first-order codes together into a narrative or sequence (e.g., pattern coding, focused coding, axial coding)	... it allows other researchers to use a similar analytical approach and obtain similar conclusions	✔	✔	
12	*Data disclosure*	Raw material includes any information collected by you before any manipulation (i.e., analysis) (e.g., transcripts, video recordings)	... others can reuse the original material and attempt to obtain the same results and reach the same conclusions	✔		

Source: Aguinis & Solarino (2019). In the case of qualitative researchers who are not necessarily interested in empirical or conceptual replication, or believe that these two types are not necessary or even appropriate based on their ontological perspective, there is still an interest in transparency and perhaps in exact replication—which is about finding possible errors and the falsifiability of the knowledge produced.

Finally, a previous study is replicated using the same population but different procedures in a **conceptual replication**. This third kind of replication aims to assess whether findings, in terms of constructs and relationships among constructs, can be replicated using different methodological procedures and instruments. Because this replication study is based on the same theory as the original study,[99] transparency criteria related to population characteristics, but not necessarily methodological procedures, are most relevant (i.e., criteria 2-5).

Measures and Data Collection

How can you measure the extent to which a qualitative study is sufficiently transparent? The **behaviorally anchored rating scales (BARS)** described in Table 13.5 measure the extent to which an article meets each of the 12 transparency criteria in Table 13.4. BARS as a measurement instrument has been used extensively in social and behavioral sciences.[100] BARS is particularly suited for examining transparency because it includes anchors along an evaluative continuum with behavioral examples exemplifying outcomes at different levels of that continuum rather than unspecific and generic anchors such as "agree" and "disagree." In this way, BARS aims to reduce rater errors due to differing interpretations of scales by defining transparency in behavioral terms and offering concrete, specific examples of actions that exemplify transparency at different levels.

ID	Transparency Criterion	1 Criterion not mentioned complete absence of information on the specific criterion making replication not possible	2 Criterion mentioned but not elaborated criterion is mentioned, but no additional information is offered, making replication highly unlikely	3 Criterion partially met some elements are present, but the information is missing or incomplete, making replication unlikely	4 Criterion is met detailed or full disclosure of information on the specific criterionmaking replication possible
	TABLE 13.5 ■ Behaviorally Anchored Rating Scales (BARS) to Measure Transparency in Qualitative Research				
1	*Kind of qualitative method*	The authors do not describe the type of qualitative research approach they adopted in their study	The authors mention the use of a particular qualitative research approach but do not describe it	The authors describe the key elements of their qualitative research approach but fail to identify them by name	The authors clearly identify the type of qualitative research approach they adopted
2	*Research setting*	The authors do not describe the research setting of the study	The authors identify the setting without describing the pre-existing conditions that make the setting appropriate for the study	The authors describe only the key pre-existing conditions in the research setting that make it appropriate for the study	The authors offer a detailed and rich description of the research setting that goes beyond the description of the key pre-existing conditions (e.g., chronic excess capacity in a small competitive industry)
3	*Position of you along the insider-outsider continuum*	The authors do not disclose their position along the insider-outsider continuum	The authors mention but do not describe the existence of a relationship between them and the organization or the participants	The authors describe the type of relationship with the organization and the participants	The authors clearly position themselves on the insider-outsider continuum
4	*Sampling procedures*	The authors do not describe the sampling procedures	The authors describe the sampling procedure (e.g., snowball sampling, international sampling)	The authors describe the kind of variability sought through their sampling procedure	The authors describe the kind of variability they seek and how they identified the participants or cases
5	*Relative importance of the participants/cases*	The authors do not describe the final sample or the importance of specific types of participants	The authors describe the final sample	The authors describe the final sample and identify the key participants	The authors describe how each participant was instrumental in developing one or more themes

(Continued)

TABLE 13.5 ■ Behaviorally Anchored Rating Scales (BARS) to Measure Transparency in Qualitative Research (*Continued*)					
ID	Transparency Criterion	**1** **Criterion not mentioned** *complete absence of information on the specific criterion making replication not possible*	**2** **Criterion mentioned but not elaborated** *criterion is mentioned, but no additional information is offered, making replication highly unlikely*	**3** **Criterion partially met** *some elements are present, but the information is missing or incomplete, making replication unlikely*	**4** **Criterion is met** *detailed or full disclosure of information on the specific criterionmaking replication possible*
6	*Documenting interactions with participants*	The authors do not describe how the interactions with participants were documented	The authors describe how some of the interactions with participants were documented	The authors describe how each interaction was documented	The authors describe how each interaction was documented and the associated content
7	*Saturation point*	The authors do not describe when theoretical saturation was reached	The authors report whether they reached theoretical saturation or not	The authors describe how they reached theoretical saturation	The authors describe the precise criteria used to conclude that they have reached theoretical saturation
8	*Unexpected opportunities, challenges, and other events*	The authors do not describe whether any unexpected opportunities, challenges, and other events occurred during the research process	The authors report whether any unexpected opportunities, challenges, and other events occurred	The authors describe any unexpected opportunities, challenges, and other events that occurred and how they handled them	The authors describe any unexpected opportunities, challenges, and other events, how they were handled, and their impact on substantive conclusions
9	*Management of power imbalance*	The authors do not describe how they addressed the power imbalance between them and the participants	The authors report whether there was any power imbalance with the participants	The authors describe the strategies used to address a general power imbalance with participants	The authors describe specific strategies used to address power imbalance with specific participants
10	*Data coding and first-order codes*	The authors do not describe how they performed the first-order coding of the data nor disclose the first-order codes	The authors offer a general statement about how they conducted the first-order codes but do not specify a particular approach to doing so	The authors describe the first-order coding methodology (e.g., in vivo coding) and present the first-order code list	The authors describe the first-order coding methodology and present the full code list

ID	Transparency Criterion	1 Criterion not mentioned *complete absence of information on the specific criterion making replication not possible*	2 Criterion mentioned but not elaborated *criterion is mentioned, but no additional information is offered, making replication highly unlikely*	3 Criterion partially met *some elements are present, but the information is missing or incomplete, making replication unlikely*	4 Criterion is met *detailed or full disclosure of information on the specific criterionmaking replication possible*
11	*Data analysis and second or higher-order codes*	The authors do not disclose how they performed the data analysis nor disclose the second-order codes	The author describes how they approached the identification of key themes in generic terms	The authors describe the second-order coding methodology (e.g., axial coding) and present the second-order code list	The authors describe the second-order coding methodology and present the full code list
12	*Data disclosure*	The authors do not disclose the raw material (e.g., transcripts, video recordings) gathered and examined during the study	The authors identify the typology of sources gathered and examined during the study	The authors list or identify all the sources gathered and examined during the study	The authors disclose the raw material gathered and examined during the study

Source: Aguinis & Solarino (2019).

This BARS was developed following a best-practice deductive approach.[101] First, the domain of each transparency criterion was identified, then critical incidents were gathered to define those domains concretely.[102]

Recommendations for Enhancing Qualitative Research Transparency

As a preview of this section, Table 13.6 summarizes recommendations regarding each of the 12 transparency criteria. Again, transparency should be understood as a continuum. The higher the transparency level across the 12 criteria, the more the study becomes trustworthy and reproducible, and the higher the likelihood that future replication will be possible. In other words, the transparency criteria have a cumulative effect on the trustworthiness and replicability of results. Also, recommendations on what features or information to include are offered. Moreover, examples of published articles for which a particular criterion was fully met are offered to show that these recommendations are practical and actionable and not just wishful thinking.

Kind of Qualitative Method

You should be explicit about what specific qualitative method has been implemented (e.g., narrative research, grounded theory, ethnography, case study, phenomenological research). This is an important issue regarding transparency because different methodologies in qualitative studies have different goals, objectives, and implications for how the study is executed and how results are interpreted.[103] Moreover, explicitly stating the qualitative method clarifies your assumptions, beliefs, and values. For example, some authors clearly stated that they adopted a grounded theory approach,[104] and others noted that they implemented a longitudinal multiple-case study approach.[105]

TABLE 13.6 ■ Summary of Recommendations for Enhancing Transparency and Replicability in Your Qualitative Research	
Transparency Criterion	**Authors should...**
1. *Kind of qualitative method*	... be explicit about what specific kind of qualitative method has been implemented (e.g., narrative research, grounded theory, ethnography, case study, phenomenological research)
2. *Research setting*	... provide detailed information regarding contextual issues regarding the research setting (e.g., power structure, norms, heuristics, culture, economic conditions)
3. *Your position along the insider-outsider continuum*	... provide detailed information regarding your position along the insider-outsider continuum (e.g., the existence of a pre-existing relationship with study participants, the development of close relationships during data collection)
4. *Sampling procedures*	... be explicit about the sampling procedures (e.g., theoretical sample, purposive sample, snowballing sample, stratified sample)
5. *Relative importance of the participants/cases*	... be explicit about the contribution that key informants made to the study
6. *Documenting interactions with participants*	... document interactions with participants (e.g., specify which types of interactions led to developing a theme)
7. *Saturation point*	... identify the theoretical saturation point and describe the judgment calls you made in defining and measuring it
8. *Unexpected opportunities, challenges, and other events*	... report what unexpected opportunities, challenges, and other events occurred during the study, how they were handled (e.g., participants dropped out of the study, a new theoretical framework was necessary), and implications
9. *Management of power imbalance*	... report and describe whether power imbalance exists between you and the participants and how it was addressed (e.g., endorsement from a prestigious institution, self-acquaintance, asking sensitive questions)
10. *Data coding and first-order codes*	... be clear about the type of coding strategies adopted (e.g., structural, In vivo, open/initial, emotional, versus)
11. *Data analysis and second—or higher-order codes*	... how the data were analyzed (e.g., focused, axial, theoretical, elaborative, longitudinal)
12. *Data disclosure*	... make raw materials available (e.g., transcripts, video recordings)

Source: Aguinis & Solarino (2019).

Research Setting

You should provide detailed information regarding contextual issues regarding the research setting (e.g., power structure, norms, heuristics, culture, and economic conditions). In qualitative research, the research setting is a bundle of pre-existing conditions that alters how the data are collected and interpreted.[106] Given the increased use of less conventional settings, transparency about the research setting is critical in contemporary social and behavioral sciences studies.[107] An exemplar of a highly transparent research setting is an author who conducted a longitudinal case study on the British brick manufacturing industry, describing how the industry evolved, the industry's economic drivers, rivalry among manufacturers, the role of the institutions, and several other contextual issues.[108]

Your Position Along the Insider-Outsider Continuum

You should provide detailed information regarding your position along the insider-outsider continuum (e.g., the existence of a pre-existing relationship with study participants and developing close relationships during data collection). The presence or absence of these relationships can alter the accessibility of data, what participants disclose, and how the collected information is interpreted.[109] As an exemplar of a high degree of transparency regarding this criterion, some authors noted that they "employed both an 'insider' and an 'outsider' you" perspective and then described the role of each of them.[110]

Sampling Procedures

You should be explicit about sampling procedures (e.g., theoretical sample, purposive sample, snowballing sample, **stratified sample**). This is particularly relevant for qualitative research because samples are often non-probabilistic. An exemplar is a study by some authors who wrote: "We constructed a two-by-two cell design to explore effects of stronger/weaker scientific evidence and the degree of innovation complexity on spread pathways… We undertook theoretical rather than random sampling, choosing a pair of innovations in all four cells, giving us a total of eight cases."[111]

Relative Importance of the Participants/Cases

You should be explicit about key informants' contribution to the study. In qualitative research, not all cases are equally informative. There are circumstances in which some participants are more informative than others because they know and can better articulate how things are done.[112] For instance, some authors identified one of their key informants stating that "the primary interview subject was… who had experience in both state and federal government relations."[113]

Documenting Interactions with Participants

You should document interactions with participants (e.g., specify which types of interactions led to developing a theme). This issue is important because different means of documenting interactions (e.g., audio, video, notations) capture different types of information and alter the willingness of participants to share information.[114] An excellent example of transparency in documenting interactions with participants is a study where some authors described how each interview was documented and how the interviews with specific informants were instrumental in understanding how private and state-owned firms are managed in China.[115]

Saturation Point

You should identify the saturation point and describe your judgment calls in defining and measuring it. For example, the saturation point occurs when there are no new insights or themes in collecting data and drawing conclusions.[116] You should therefore report how you define the saturation point and how you decide that it is reached. As an illustration, some authors described how adding interviews resulted in novel codes and decided that theoretical saturation was reached (i.e., the codes generated after the 12th interview were variations of existing themes).[117]

Unexpected Opportunities, Challenges, and Other Events

You should report what unexpected opportunities, challenges, and other events occurred during the study and how they were handled (e.g., participants dropped out of the study, and a new theoretical framework was necessary). Because these unexpected events may affect data accessibility and substantive conclusions, you should report and describe any unexpected events and highlight whether they impacted the data collection and analysis. For instance, an author described how they took advantage of an unexpected request from their informants to "ask questions that would have been inappropriate [otherwise]."[118]

Management of Power Imbalance

It would be best to describe whether a power imbalance exists between you and the participants and how it has been addressed (e.g., endorsement from a prestigious institution, self-acquaintance, asking sensitive questions). This issue is important because it allows similar strategies to be adopted in future replication studies. One author, for instance, used the exchange of business cards with the informants to reduce the power differential,[119] and another used phone interviews not to reveal the age difference between them and their informants.[120]

Data Coding and First-Order Codes

You should be clear about the coding strategies adopted (e.g., **structural**, **in vivo**, **open/initial**, **emotional**, **versus**). This is an important issue because different coding procedures have different goals. An excellent example of transparency regarding data coding is the paper by some authors who clearly stated that they used in vivo coding to develop the first-order codes and then reported the full list of the codes in the paper.[121]

Data Analysis and Second- or Higher-Order Codes

You should be clear about how the data were analyzed (e.g., focused, axial, theoretical, elaborative, longitudinal). As an exemplar of transparency, some authors identified the methodologies adopted in data analysis (**axial** and **selective coding**) and reported the final higher-order and first-order codes that generated them.[122]

Data Disclosure

Future qualitative research should make raw materials available (e.g., transcripts and video recordings). While this criterion is necessary only for exact replication, disclosing the raw material is useful for error checking. You can make the data available to others directly, in data repositories, or by request. An example is a paper by some authors whose data are available for downloading from the Business History Initiative website.[123]

As an additional issue, the recommendations can also benefit future research adopting a mixed-methods approach, as described earlier in this chapter. Applying these recommendations to mixed-methods research can be particularly beneficial for two reasons. First, mixed-methods articles published have had more influence on subsequent research than articles adopting a single-method approach based on the average number of citations they received (i.e., the mean citation count is 59.13 for mixed-methods articles and 37.08 for single-methods articles[124]). Second, transparency issues in mixed-methods research require immediate attention. Specifically, some have argued that to move mixed methods forward and wrote that "to maximize the potential for subsequent research to be able to replicate a mixed methods study, researchers need to be as transparent as possible in reporting their methodological decisions and the rationale behind those choices... future researchers should be able to understand how ... data were collected, analyzed, and integrated such that similar methodological efforts could be recreated in different contexts collection and data analysis within a single study" (p. 186).[125]

DISCUSSION QUESTIONS

1. How are interviews with Key Informants (KIs) different from other types of interviews? What are the main challenges involved in interviewing KIs?

2. What are the key questions in each research stage (i.e., research design, data collection, reporting of results) you should address when conducting KI interviews?

3. When and why would you consider using computer-aided text analysis (CATA) in your research?

4. How can you improve the accuracy of your CATA measurement (i.e., how can you minimize transient error, specific factor error, and algorithm error)?

5. In what way would you design a methodological literature review about a method you are interested in?

6. How would you develop methodological literature reviews to ensure the highest quality standards?

7. Choose a recently published methodological literature review. Then, using the checklist in Table 13.3, to what extent is this published review thorough, clear, and useful?

8. Why can mixed methods lead to important theoretical advancements in social and behavioral sciences?

9. How can you verify that you are doing everything possible to improve transparency and replicability in your qualitative research?

10. How can you determine the transparency criteria in your qualitative research and assess whether you address the three replicability types?

11. Choose a recently published article that used qualitative methods. Then, using the BARS in Table 13.5, to what extent is this published article transparent?

12. What are the best practices for enhancing qualitative research transparency that you would implement in your qualitative research?

KEY TERMS

algorithm error	exact replication
axial coding	hostage syndrome
behaviorally anchored rating scales (BARS)	in vivo coding
Cohen's coefficient kappa	key informant (KI)
Computer-aided Text Analysis (CATA)	microfoundations
conceptual replication	open/initial coding
emotional coding	purposive sampling
empirical replication	qualitative positivism

questionable research practices (QRPs)
selective coding
semi-structured interview format
snowball sampling
specific factor error
stratified sample
structural coding

theoretical sampling
theoretical saturation
transcendental realism
transient error
unstructured approach
versus coding

NOTES

This chapter is based to a large extent on the following sources:

Aguinis, H., & Molina-Azorín, J. F. (2015). Using multilevel modeling and mixed methods to make theoretical progress in microfoundations for strategy research. *Strategic Organization*, *13*(4), 353-364. https://doi.org/10.1177/1476127015594622

Aguinis, H., & Solarino, A. M. (2019). Transparency and replicability in qualitative research: The case of interviews with key informants. *Strategic Management Journal*, *40*(8), 1291-1315. https://doi.org/10.1002/smj.3015

Aguinis, H., Ramani, R. S., & Alabduljader, N. (2022). Best-practice recommendations for producers, evaluators, and users of methodological literature reviews. *Organizational Research Methods*. https://doi.org/10.1177/1094428120943281

McKenny, A. F., Aguinis, H., Short, J. C., & Anglin, A. H. (2018). What doesn't get measured does exist: Improving the accuracy of computer-aided text analysis. *Journal of Management*, *44*(7), 2909-2933. https://doi.org/10.1177/0149206316657594

Solarino, A. M., & Aguinis, H. (2021). Challenges and best-practice recommendations for designing and conducting interviews with key informants. *Journal of Management Studies*, *58*(3), 649-672. https://doi.org/10.1111/joms.12620

14 HOW TO REPORT YOUR RESULTS

LEARNING GOALS

By the end of this chapter, you will be able to do the following:

14.1 Argue why you should care about how you report your results and how a lack of transparency harms social and behavioral science research's reproducibility, replicability, and credibility.

14.2 Judge why conventional methods of reporting p-values are arbitrary and misleading.

14.3 Recommend the correct ways to report p-values.

14.4 Assess how effect sizes capture information not included in statistical significance tests.

14.5 Compare your effect sizes to those reported in the social and behavioral sciences, and argue why effect sizes should be interpreted within a specific context.

14.6 Critique the differences between effect size estimates and the practical significance of your research results.

14.7 Appraise the correct way to report statistical results, including chi-squared (χ^2) and eta-squared (η^2).

14.8 Defend the importance of transparently and adequately reporting your study's limitations.

IMPORTANCE OF HOW YOU REPORT YOUR RESULTS

The social and behavioral sciences are currently debating the credibility, trustworthiness, and usefulness of the scholarly knowledge produced.[1] For example, some researchers found that between 25% to 50% of published articles have inconsistencies or errors.[2] Overall, there is a proliferation of evidence indicating substantial reasons to doubt the veracity and, justifiably, the conclusions and implications of scholarly work[3] because researchers are often unable to reproduce published results.[4] Regardless of whether this documented lack of reproducibility is a more recent phenomenon or one that has existed for a long time but has only recently gained prominence, it seems that we have reached a tipping point such that there is an urgency to understand this phenomenon, and find solutions to address it.

Concerns about lack of reproducibility are not entirely surprising considering the relative lack of methodological transparency about conducting empirical research in the social and behavioral sciences that eventually leads to a published article.[5] Low methodological transparency in how results are reported harms the credibility and trustworthiness of research results because it precludes inferential reproducibility. Inferential reproducibility is the ability of others to draw similar conclusions to those reached by the original authors regarding a study's results.[6] Note that this differs from results reproducibility, which is the ability of others to obtain the same results using the same data as in the original study.

From a measurement perspective, results reproducibility is conceptually analogous to reliability because it is about consistency. Specifically, do researchers other than those who authored a study find the same (i.e., consistent) results as reported in the original paper? On the other hand, inferential reproducibility is conceptually analogous to validity because it is about making similar inferences based on the results. Specifically, do researchers other than those who authored a study reach similar conclusions about relations between variables as described in the original study? Results reproducibility (i.e., reliability) is a necessary but insufficient precondition for inferential reproducibility (i.e., validity). In other words, inferences will be different if we cannot obtain the same results as in the published study using the same data. But it is possible to reproduce results (i.e., high reliability) but not inferences (i.e., low validity). Therefore, inferential reproducibility (i.e., the validity or relations between variables) is critical in building and testing theories and the credibility of the knowledge produced. In contrast, results reproducibility (i.e., reliability or consistency) is a means to an end.

In this chapter, you will learn how to report the results of your research to minimize problems related to insufficient reproducibility and replicability. This involves reporting significant results transparently and with impact in mind, which also means that research results are described in such a way as to be relevant for broader stakeholders (e.g., policymakers) and society at large. It begins with describing how to report p-values without relying on arbitrary benchmarks or crippling probability values. The following section discusses why effect sizes are useful when reporting results. The third section highlights how effect sizes vary across the social and behavioral sciences. The fourth section describes how to interpret effect sizes effectively and with practical significance. The fifth section provides an illustrative example of how to report two commonly used statistics (i.e., chi-square and **eta-square**). Finally, the last section provides guidance on reporting your study's limitations so they accurately reflect the challenges encountered in your research. Taken together, you will learn how to report results transparently to enhance reproducibility and replicability and explain the significance of your research for theory and practice.

HOW TO REPORT *P*-VALUES

Problems inherent in the conventional way statistical significance has been used and reported for hypothesis testing have been discussed across various social and behavioral sciences disciplines.[7] This section discusses the two most common challenges: 1) arbitrary and misleading a priori α values; and 2) reporting **crippled *p*-values**.

Conventional α Values Are Arbitrary and Misleading

The current convention in hypothesis testing is that you choose an a priori Type I error rate (α: the probability that the null hypothesis is rejected when it is true), compute the appropriate test statistic for the data in hand (e.g., t, F), and then obtain a probability value (p) associated with the test statistic that provides an estimate of the likelihood of obtaining these data if the null hypothesis is true. If $p < \alpha$ (the observed p-value is smaller than the a priori Type I error rate), then the null hypothesis is rejected (recall the null hypothesis usually states that there is no effect or relationship between variables).

The current zeitgeist in the social and behavioral sciences is to use α values of .10 (i.e., results are said to be "marginally significant"), .05 (i.e., results are "significant"), .01 (i.e., results are "highly significant"), or .001 (i.e., results are "very highly significant").[8] For example, if α = .05, you would consider an obtained p-value lower than .05 to be a significant result because, if the null were true, the probability of obtaining these data is less than 5% and, hence, the null is rejected.

The α values frequently chosen by social and behavioral science researchers are arbitrary. This conclusion becomes evident after closely examining the origin of these conventional cut-off scores.[9] For instance, the α = .05 value originated in the mid-1920s with a researcher who wrote that "The value for which $p = 0.05$ or 1 in 20 is 1.96 or nearly 2; it is convenient to take this point as the limit in judging whether a deviation is to be considered significant or not. Deviations exceeding twice the standard deviation are thus formally regarded as significant" (p. 47).[10] According to another researcher, the primary reason why the 5% cut-off was chosen was that Sir Ronald A. Fisher, the original proponent of the cut-off, "had no table for other significance levels, partly because his professional enemy, Karl Pearson, refused to let him reprint the tables Pearson had" (p. 200).[11] As some researchers sarcastically noted, "Surely, God loves the .06 nearly as much as the .05" (p. 1277).[12]

METHODS IN PRACTICE

WHY CONVENTIONAL VALUES FOR THE A PRIORI TYPE I ERROR RATE (α) ARE MISLEADING

In addition to being arbitrary, the conventional values for α are misleading. For example, when α = .05, obtaining a $p = 0.0499$ would lead to the conclusion that the null hypothesis should be rejected (i.e., there is an effect or relation), whereas obtaining a $p = .0501$ would lead to the conclusion that the null hypothesis should be retained (i.e., there is no effect or relation in the population). In other words, the conclusion of whether or not a variable is related to another or whether a manipulation has an effect can be entirely changed by a minuscule difference in the observed p-value. Using conventional cut-offs provides the illusion of an objective value against which to evaluate the veracity of the null hypothesis rather than using a researcher's subjective judgment and, therefore, "makes life tidier."[13] This convention, too, can lead to fundamental changes in a reader's interpretation of findings and the application and future development of those findings.

Another reason conventional cut-offs are misleading is that they are not based on considering the relative seriousness of making a Type I versus a Type II error. As noted earlier, a Type I error is the probability of rejecting the null hypothesis erroneously. In other words, concluding that there is an effect or relation when this is not true (i.e., false positive). The other side of the coin of a Type I error is a Type II error (β): the probability of retaining the null hypothesis erroneously. In other words, concluding the effect or relation does not exist when it does (i.e., false negative). Type I error is inversely related to Type II error. So, for the sake of the illustration, if you decided that you absolutely do not want to make a Type I error because you do not want to claim a finding that is not true and therefore set α at .000001 if you make an error most likely you will end up making a Type II error. That is, you will not reject the null hypothesis even if the null hypothesis is false. Alternatively, if you decide that you can relax the Type I error rate because you want to make sure you detect an effect if it exists and therefore set α at .80, if you make an error, most likely you will end up making a Type I error (i.e., there is an 80% chance you will "find" an effect or relation that does not exist). How many social and behavioral science researchers do you think make a conscious decision that a 5% chance of finding a "false" effect is acceptable? Moreover, how many compute the probability of not detecting an effect (Type II error rate) in their studies, and how many are comfortable with this level of risk? Some researchers calculated that when researchers set a Type I error rate at .05, they usually have a Type II error of about 60%.[14] This led to the conclusion that significance testing is a disaster because the actual error rate in the social sciences is 60% and not 5%.[15] How many researchers do you think are aware of their Type II error rates?

In short, although a conventional cut-off such as .05 or .01 aids you in simplifying the decision of whether or not a null hypothesis should be rejected, these values are arbitrary. Moreover, they are based on the untenable assumption that the relative seriousness of making a Type I and Type II error is identical across research domains, outcomes, and contexts.

Solution: Use α Values Based on the Relative Seriousness of Type I Versus Type II Error

Given the preceding section, we should question the conventional values for α. Instead, you should seek the right balance between risking a Type I in relation to a Type II error based on your assessment of the relative seriousness of making these two errors. You may recall we addressed this issue in Chapter 9 regarding the test of moderating (i.e., interaction) effects.

Consider the seriousness of making a Type I relative to a Type II error in the following two research situations. First, researchers studied the relationship between managerial incentives and CEO earnings manipulation behaviors.[16] In this case, a Type II error would be quite serious. Concluding that there was no such relation, when there is one, may lead some firms to introduce such incentives, given that they do not believe this would lead to negative consequences. Further, the finding would justify the incentive used by those using them. Using these incentives would then lead to greater earnings manipulation behaviors, resulting in some firms experiencing severe declines in their stock price, exposure to reputational damage, top management turnover, possible bankruptcies, and loss of general investor confidence. These costs are very high to the firms, investors, and society. On the other hand, a Type I error, where certain incentives are believed to lead to earnings manipulations when they do not, would cause some firms not to use those incentives, which may or may not have some negative consequences, depending on the other effects of the incentive. In this case, a Type II error would be more serious than a Type I error.

Example: Severity of Type I Versus Type II Error: Interdivisional Knowledge and Invention Impact

A team of researchers examined the relationship between the use of interdivisional knowledge and invention impact.[17] In this case, a Type I error would be more severe. Concluding that there is such a relation when there isn't one would lead to some firms investing a great deal of money, time, and other resources into facilitating knowledge transfer across divisions for no resultant gain. On the other hand, a Type II error would lead to some opportunity costs for firms because they did not invest in interdivisional knowledge transfers that could have led to a greater invention impact. In this case, a Type I error would be more serious than a Type II error.

Fortunately, there is a way to weigh the pros and cons of increasing the Type I error rate for a specific research situation.[18] The appropriate balance between Type I and Type II error rates can be achieved using a pre-set Type I error rate considering the Desired Relative Seriousness (DRS) of making a Type I versus a Type II error. Instead of increasing α to any arbitrary value, you can make a more informed decision regarding the specific value to give to α. Once the DRS of making a Type I versus a Type II error has been established, you can proceed to compute the Type I error rate.

METHODS IN PRACTICE

CASE STUDY: DETERMINING YOUR TYPE I ERROR RATE RATIONALLY RATHER THAN ARBITRARILY

Deciding on an appropriate DRS value could be considered an arbitrary process. Thus, this decision should be well thought out and argued and not determined by fiat. Consider the following illustration.[19] Dr. Gerardo is interested in testing the hypothesis that the effectiveness of a training program for unemployed individuals varies by region, such that the training program is more effective in regions where the unemployment rate is higher than 6%. Assume that Dr. Gerardo decides that the probability of making a Type II error (i.e., β, incorrectly concluding that the unemployment rate in a region is not a moderator) should not be greater than .15. He also decides that the seriousness of making a Type I error (i.e., incorrectly concluding that percentage of unemployment in a region is a moderator) is twice as serious as making a Type II error (i.e., DRS = 2). Assume Dr. Gerardo decides that DRS = 2 because a Type I error means that different versions of the training program would be needlessly developed for various regions, wasting the limited resources available. The desired pre-set Type I error can be computed as follows[20]:

$$\alpha_{desired} = \left[\frac{p(H_1)\beta}{1 - p(H_1)}\right]\left(\frac{1}{DRS}\right) \qquad (14.1)$$

where $p(H_1)$ is the estimated probability that the alternative hypothesis is valid (i.e., there is a moderating effect), and β is the Type II error rate. DRS is a judgment of the seriousness of a Type I error vis-à-vis the seriousness of a Type II error.

For this example, assume that based on a strong theory-based rationale and previous experience with similar training programs, Dr. Gerardo estimates that the probability that the hypothesis is correct is $p(H_1)$ = .6. Solving Equation 14.1 yields:

$$\alpha_{desired} = \left[\frac{(.6)(.15)}{1 - .6}\right]\left(\frac{1}{2}\right) = .11. \qquad (14.2)$$

Thus, a nominal Type I error rate of .11 would yield the desired balance between Type I and Type II statistical errors in this example.

Implementing the procedure described in "Case Study: Determining Your Type I Error Rate Rationally rather than Arbitrarily" for choosing the specific a priori Type I error rate provides a more informed and better justification than using any arbitrary value such as .05 or .01 without carefully considering the trade-offs and consequences of this choice. Moreover, researchers (including those reading a published article or report) can set their α level before deciding whether a particular null hypothesis should be rejected.

The Problem With Reporting Crippled *p*-values

Another problem related to the arbitrary way of reporting statistical significance is that you may note whether an observed *p*-value is below a conventional cutoff value instead of reporting the observed *p*-value. You alter a continuous probability scale from 0 to 1.0 by dichotomizing it.[21] For example, suppose you report whether p < .05, a significance test with a *p*-value of .000001 is reported the same as a significance test with a *p*-value of .049. In that case, both are smaller than .05. The problem with this practice is that valuable information is lost.[22] Knowing that the probability that the observed value would have occurred if the null hypothesis were true is 4.9% substantially differs from that probability being 1 in a million. Thus, by only reporting *p*-values relative to cut-offs, important information, which can fundamentally change a reader's (i.e., research consumer) interpretation of a study's findings, is lost.

Most social and behavioral science journal articles report observed *p*-values in relationship to cut-offs and not the actual *p*-values.[23] The irony of this situation is that the purported originator of the α = .05 cut-off, Sir Ronald A. Fisher, suggested that authors should also report actual *p*-values in addition to using cut-offs.[24] This position was echoed by practically every other eminent statistician of Fisher's time.[25] However, this recommendation has been ignored in the social and behavioral sciences.

Why is it that authors do not report observed *p*-values? One reason is that, decades ago, the lack of computers made it practically impossible to obtain actual *p*-values. Instead, researchers had no choice but to consult tables showing values for statistical tests large enough to reject the null hypothesis at the .01 or .05 level. Implementing this practice over decades likely resulted in the institutionalization of this convention because several generations of researchers were trained this way. Over time, using the .01 and .05 cut-offs without reporting the actual *p*-values became the standard practice, and researchers created their methodological comfort zones. Change is difficult, and researchers are resistant to change regarding methodological practices.[26] This is a likely reason for a "scientific community's persistence in the use of particular methods" (p. 433).[27] A second related reason for not reporting actual *p*-values is that, due to the institutionalization of reporting results in relationship to certain cut-offs only, some journal editors require that authors choose a specific value for α and use it for all tests of significance in a given study. A third reason editors and reviewers may require authors to use the conventional cut-offs and not report actual *p*-values is a generalized misunderstanding about significance testing and the meaning of the observed *p*-value. Many researchers have noted that significance testing is abused and misused; therefore, there seems to be a "human factors problem" (p. 371).[28] Significance testing allows researchers to infer whether the data obtained are unlikely to assume a true null hypothesis. On the other hand, significance testing is used incorrectly when conclusions are made regarding the magnitude of the effect, and, for example, a statistically-significant result at the .01 level is interpreted as a larger effect than a result at the .05 level.[29]

Solution: Report Precise *p*-values

You should report the actual observed *p*-values so that readers have this information available. Because actual *p*-values are now available in all statistical software packages, there is no impediment to including them in your research reports. Thus, you should report the precise *p*-value obtained (e.g., *p* = .052), and readers can decide whether the findings should be considered "statistically significant." Reporting should include a maximum of two or three decimal places because using more decimal places is unnecessary.[30]

By reporting actual *p*-values, valuable information is not lost by dichotomizing continuous variables.[31] First, readers know whether the *p*-value is .049 or .000001, and not just that it is < .05.

Second, the arbitrary cut-offs no longer exist; thus, 0.049 and 0.051 are treated as what they are and are not arbitrarily separated as opposed findings (i.e., there is an effect or relation vs. there is no effect or relation). Reporting actual p-values also helps solve an additional problem of statistical significance mentioned earlier: frequently occurring Type II errors. Many results are considered non-significant because they do not reach a conventional level for α. For example, if $\alpha = .05$, you may conclude that the finding is statistically non-significant, report $p > .05$, and provide no further information. Given the previous discussion about setting a value for α that considers the relative trade-offs between Type I and Type II errors, a reader may decide that if $\alpha = .08$, the null hypothesis should be rejected. However, this reader cannot decide the statistical significance of the result without knowing the actual p-value observed.

But, to better understand your research results and share this information with others, we need to go beyond p-values. Specifically, we need to also focus on effect size estimates. So, let's discuss this next.

WHY YOU SHOULD REPORT EFFECT SIZE ESTIMATES

Effect size (ES) estimates indicate relation strength (i.e., magnitude), are essential for the scientific enterprise, and are "almost always necessary" to report in primary studies.[32] However, reporting statistical significance says nothing about the strength of the effect (in the case of experiments in which causality can be inferred) or relation (in the case of non-experimental designs in which only covariation between variables can be inferred). The only conclusion we derive from a statistical significance test is whether the data obtained are unlikely, given a true null hypothesis. Moreover, effect size information is increasingly central in the scientific process, informing study design (e.g., *a priori* power analysis; hypothesis development), statistical analysis (e.g., meta-analysis; Bayesian techniques),[33] and assessing scientific progress[34] and practical significance.[35]

Confusion Between Statistical Significance and Magnitude of the Effect or Relation

As noted earlier, there is a human factors problem in the scientific community because many view the rejection of the null hypothesis as the ultimate goal of any empirical study. For example, a researcher noted that "the emphasis on tests of significance, and the consideration of the results of each experiment in isolation, have had the unfortunate consequence that scientific workers often have regarded the execution of a test of significance on an experiment as the ultimate objective" (pp. 32-33).[36]

Unfortunately, there are important problems with viewing the rejection of the null hypothesis as the ultimate research goal.[37] First, rejecting the null hypothesis does not tell you what you want to know. You want to know whether the null hypothesis is true given the data in hand—pHo/D. However, null hypothesis significance testing tells us the probability of obtaining the data in hand (or more extreme data) if the null hypothesis is true—pD/Ho. Unfortunately, $pHo/D \neq pD/Ho$. As succinctly noted by the late legendary methodologist Jacob Cohen, a test of statistical significance "does not tell us what we want to know, and we so much want to know what we want to know that, out of desperation, we nevertheless believe that it does!" (p. 997).[38]

Second, most null hypotheses are false at some level. As noted by some researchers, "the effects of A and B are always different—in some decimal place—for any A and B. Thus asking 'Are the effects different' is foolish" (p. 100).[39] From this perspective, finding that the null hypothesis should be rejected means that the sample size was large enough or, more generally, the research design was sufficiently adequate and had sufficient statistical power (i.e., probability of correctly rejecting the null hypothesis or 1 – Type II error). Some equate smaller p-values as though representing more meaningful effect sizes. Note that the larger the effect in the population, the more likely the null hypothesis will be rejected. In addition, the larger the sample size, the more likely the null hypothesis will be rejected, even if the population effect is miniscule.[40]

The confusion between statistical significance and the magnitude of the effect also has implications for theory development. Statistical significance is a necessary but not a sufficient yardstick to evaluate the precision and accuracy of a theory. Statistical significance does not tell you the extent to which the variables you investigated are sufficient to explain a particular phenomenon satisfactorily. For example, statistical significance does not tell you how much team collaboration relates to team performance. If the result is statistically significant, you conclude that these variables are related but do not know to what extent. To do so, you need to compute estimates of the magnitude of their relation.

METHODS IN PRACTICE
GUIDELINES FOR REPORTING STATISTICAL RESULTS

Because of the need to go beyond null hypothesis significance testing, journals in several disciplines require authors to report the significance test result and a measure of effect magnitude. For example, the American Psychological Association's Publication Manual notes that "it is almost always necessary to include some index of effect size or strength of relationship... The general principle to be followed... is to provide the reader not only with information about statistical significance but also with enough information to assess the magnitude of the observed effect or relationship" (p. 89).[41] In addition, several journals in the social and behavioral sciences require or strongly recommend that authors report estimates of effect magnitude.[42]

Solution: Report the Magnitude of the Effect

The convention in reporting statistical significance is a serious problem—so serious that some have suggested eliminating statistical significance. One journal, *The American Journal of Public Health*, once banned statistical significance tests altogether (although the ban only lasted two years). However, it is generally acknowledged that eliminating statistical significance will be challenging for two reasons. First, it does provide useful information that chance sampling influences are not a likely explanation of findings.[43] Second, many of the problems of significance testing can be solved by simple, incremental changes in design, reporting, and interpretation of statistical significance.[44]

Most critics of statistical significance believe that reporting effect sizes can mitigate some of the problems associated with sole reliance on null hypothesis significance testing. Several sources provide detailed guidelines and formulae for the computation of various effect magnitude estimates.[45] Table 14.1 includes formulae for the two most common types of effect magnitude estimates, which statistical analysis software packages include as part of the output. As shown in Table 14.1, effect magnitude estimates can be classified into two types: (a) group difference estimates and (b) variance-explained estimates. What these two types of effect magnitude estimates have in common is that they are standardized, independent of the metric used in any particular study (e.g., economic performance measured in US dollars or Euros; job satisfaction measured on a 3- or 7-point Likert-type scale), and can therefore be compared across studies.

Group difference estimates are useful when the null hypothesis refers to differences in mean scores across groups. For example, you may test the null hypothesis that a web-based training program will improve team collaboration. You may want to report the magnitude of the difference in average ratings between trained and non-trained groups.[46]

Variance-accounted-for estimates are usually reported in a squared metric (e.g., R^2). They are used when the null hypothesis refers to relations among variables and is interpreted as the proportion of variance in one variable explained by another. For example, if the relation between cognitive abilities and job performance is $r = .35$, cognitive abilities explain 12.25% of the variance in performance scores (i.e., $.35 \times .35$).[47]

Note that the formulae included in Table 14.1 allow you to compute sample-based estimates of effect magnitude. After all, you usually have a sample in hand only and not the entire population of scores. So, sampling error affects the accuracy of these estimates. When samples are small, and models include many predictors, there is more capitalization on chance, and hence, effect

TABLE 14.1 ■ Formulae for Computing Two Common Effect Size Types

	Effect Magnitude Estimate	Formula	Comments
Group Differences	Cohen's d	$\dfrac{\bar{X}_{GroupA} - \bar{X}_{GroupB}}{SD}$	One of the most common and frequently used estimates of differences between two groups. It denotes the difference between mean scores across groups in standard deviation units. SD is the common standard deviation. A value of 0 means no difference between the groups.
	Hedges's g	$\dfrac{\bar{X}_{GroupA} - \bar{X}_{GroupB}}{SD_{pooled}}$	This is a "corrected" d estimate based on a pooled SD across the groups.
Variance Explained	R^2	$SS_{regression}/SS_{total}$	One of the most common and frequently used estimates of variance explained. It denotes the proportion of variance in a criterion explained by the predictors given a linear predictor-criterion relation. A value of 0 means no variance explained.
	Adjusted R^2	$1 - (1 - R^2)\dfrac{N-1}{N-k-1}$	This "corrected" R^2 estimate considers capitalization on chance due to a small sample N and many predictors k.

Source: Adapted from Aguinis, Werner, Lanza-Abbott, Angert, Park, & Kohlhausen (2010). Reproduced with permission.

magnitude estimates are inflated. Thus, some researchers recommend "correcting" observed estimates, and some of these corrections are included in Table 14.1 as well. Most statistical packages include some of these corrected estimates and label them using the qualifier "adjusted" (e.g., adjusted R^2).

In addition to sample size and the number of predictors, the resulting estimates are also affected by the reliability of the measurement instruments used (i.e., lower reliability leads to smaller estimates), the type of scales used to measure each of the variables (i.e., fewer scale anchors lead to smaller estimates), heterogeneity of the sample used, variance in the scores (i.e., less heterogeneity and variance lead to smaller estimates), and research design (i.e., non-experimental designs usually lead to smaller estimates).[48] Thus, it is important that you include information on which specific estimate has been computed, whether it is an adjusted estimate or not, and a confidence interval around the estimate.[49]

In sum, you should report an estimate of the effect magnitude. Consumers of your research would benefit from knowing the probability that the data in hand would be obtained given a true null hypothesis and the estimated magnitude of the effect or relation. This type of reporting has important implications for theory building and evaluating a theory's quality.[50] For example, knowing that a particular set of variables explains only 5% of the variance in an outcome leads to the conclusion that a particular theoretical model is underspecified and more and better predictors should be investigated. On the other hand, knowing that a particular set of variables explains 80% of the variance in an outcome would conclude that the conceptual model is quite good.

HOW YOUR EFFECT SIZES COMPARE TO THOSE IN SOCIAL AND BEHAVIORAL RESEARCH

Now that you know the importance of reporting effect sizes (ES), let us examine how to understand how your results compare to those commonly reported in social and behavioral research. Traditionally, most social and behavioral science researchers have relied on effect size benchmarks as articulated by Cohen, who defined small, moderate (i.e., medium), and large $|r|$ as "about" .10, .30, and .50, respectively (p. 185).[51] However, the meaning of "about" is, unfortunately, quite ambiguous.

Example: Confusion and Lack of Consensus about Effect Size Cutoffs

One researcher interpreted Cohen's values as minimum cutoffs, which, for example, define the range of medium ES as $.30 \leq |r| < .50$.[52] Others classified effect sizes in terms of their surrounding anchors (e.g., $r = .39$ as medium-to-large).[53] Another interpretation is that Cohen's values represent range centroids. For example, some researchers interpreted Cohen's (1988) medium ES range, $.24 \leq |r| < .36$, as centered at .30.[54] Still, other approaches combine ranges and cutoffs.[55] And one researcher involved practical significance in a set of benchmarks, defining $r = .20$ as the minimum practically significant value, with minimum cutoffs for moderate and large ESs at $r = .50$ and $r = .80$, respectively.[56] As some recommended, "We must stress again that reporting and interpreting effect sizes in the context of previously reported effects is essential to good research. It enables readers to evaluate the stability of results across samples, designs, and analyses" (p. 599).[57]

To address these challenges, a team of researchers examined 147,328 ESs from 1,660 articles in the social and behavioral sciences.[58] Results showed a median ES of $|r|$ = .16, split into thirds (i.e., upper and lower boundaries for medium ES) at $|r|$ = .09 and .26. This medium ES range is similar to that obtained by other researchers[59] who split their ES distributions into thirds at $|r|$ = .10 and .22 (published ESs) and $|r|$ = .11 and .28 (non-published ESs), but substantially different (i.e., non-overlapping medium ES range) when compared to commonly used social and behavioral sciences benchmarks.[60] In addition, values of $|r|$ = .05, .07, .12, .21, .32, and .36 represent the 20th, 25th, 40th, 60th, 75th, and 80th percentiles of the ES distribution, respectively. Importantly, commonly used social and behavioral sciences benchmarks for small, medium, and large ESs (i.e., $|r|$ = .10, .30, .50) correspond to approximately the 33rd, 73rd, and 90th percentiles, respectively, of the distribution of 147,328 ESs. Finally, ESs in the center tertile of the distribution are classified as medium by commonly used social and behavioral sciences benchmarks in only 8.2% of cases (centroid interpretation) or 0% of the cases (cutoffs interpretation).

A meta-analysis using the 147,328 effect sizes (N = 325,218,877) found that the mean ES is small ($|r|$ = .222; 95% CI = .221, .223). The unweighted mean ES revealed a similar value, $|r|$ = .219. These results indicate that moderation is likely. Indeed, the I^2 statistic[61] approaches its maximum value of 100 (I^2 = 98.97), and the 80% credibility interval (-.03, .48) includes zero.[62] Furthermore, the median ES value $|r|$ = .16, is smaller than the mean meta-analytically derived ES, $|r|$ = .22, indicating that the distribution of ESs is positively skewed (skew $|r|$ = 1.27; skew$_r$ = 0.33). A positively skewed ES distribution is expected because large ESs are relatively rare in social and behavioral science research.[63]

Context-Specific Effect Size Benchmarks

Another issue you might face is that different major relation types exhibit distinct ES distributions. Distinct *within-discipline* benchmarks for relations of different types or in different research contexts have been suggested and provided in the social and behavioral sciences.[64] The study about effect sizes mentioned earlier identified 20 common, broad bivariate relation types and found substantial variance in ES distribution parameters. Specifically, results revealed medium ESs with partitions at $|r|$ = .18 and .39 (attitudes-attitudes), $|r|$ = .19 and .37 (attitudes-intentions), $|r|$ = .10 and .24 (attitudes-behaviors), and $|r|$ = .11 and .27 (intentions-behaviors). Thus, ES values greater than roughly $|r|$ = .25 exist for relations involving behaviors in the upper tertile of the ES distribution (i.e., a large ES). In contrast, for coarse relations not involving behaviors (i.e., attitudes-attitudes; attitudes-intentions), the corresponding value for a large ES is roughly $|r|$ = .40. Importantly, the distinction between broad relation types involving behaviors compared to those not involving behaviors is substantial. Indeed, achieving 6.50% variance explained (i.e., $|r|$ = .255) when predicting behavior represents a "large" ES in that context, but the corresponding value for a large ES among non-behavioral relations (i.e., attitudes-attitudes; attitudes-intentions) is 14.44% (i.e., $|r|$ = .380). Thus, in many contexts, traditional social and behavioral science benchmarks are non-applicable by a factor of two or more.

Values for fine relation types with employee performance reveal medium ES boundaries at $|r|$ = .13 and .31 (knowledge/skills/abilities-performance), $|r|$ = .10 and .23 (psychological characteristics-performance), $|r|$ = .05 and .14 (objective person characteristics-performance), and $|r|$ = .11 and .26 (attitudes-performance). While a global average may not be informative regarding attitudes, extra fine relations within the attitudes-performance relation type reveal medium ES partitions at $|r|$ = .10 and .22 (organization attitudes-performance), $|r|$ = .10 and .26 (job attitudes-performance), and $|r|$ = .13 and .32 (people attitudes-performance). Thus, although broad, knowledge-skills-abilities are more strongly related to performance than attitudes (broadly) and psychological characteristics. In addition, objective person characteristics exhibit relatively weak relations with performance.

Regarding the three fine relation types with employee movement behavior, medium ES boundaries are at $|r|$ = .07 and .17 (psychological characteristics-movement), $|r|$ = .04 and .11 (objective person characteristics-movement), and $|r|$ = .09 and .21 (attitudes-movement). In addition, two extra fine relation types for the attitudes-movement relation type revealed medium ES partitions at $|r|$ = .10 and .23 (organization attitudes-movement) and $|r|$ = .09 and .18 (job attitudes-movement). Finally, although the researchers located relatively few effect sizes for the people attitudes-movement relation type, they observed medium tertile partitions for this category at $|r|$ = .09 and .23. Thus, employee movement behavior is predicted relatively poorly compared to performance behavior. In addition, broadly, such relations with employee movement behavior larger than roughly $|r|$ = .20 exist within the top third of the ES distribution in that context (i.e., large ESs).

Also, center tertiles for coarse non-behavioral relations exhibit roughly 60% overlap with traditional social and behavioral science benchmarks (centroid interpretation) or 40% overlap (cutoffs interpretation).[65] Indeed, the centroid interpretation of traditional social and behavioral science benchmarks places $|r|$ = .30 at the *center* of the medium ES range. The corresponding centroid values found were $|r|$ = .28 (attitudes-attitudes) and $|r|$ = .27 (attitudes-intentions). Thus, medium ESs for these two particular bivariate relation types are about .30. However, medium ESs for coarse relation types involving behaviors (i.e., attitude-behavior; intention-behavior) are substantially smaller. For coarse behavioral relations, the overlap comparing traditional social and behavioral science benchmarks centroid-based medium ES range and what the researchers found ranged from 0-15% (0% for the cutoff interpretation). In addition, a meta-analysis of the data revealed that a medium ES centroid ($|r|$ = .30) seemed to depict non-behavioral relations (i.e., attitude-attitude; attitude-intention) but not behavioral relations (i.e., attitude-behavior; intention-behavior).

Finally, sample sizes required to achieve .80 *a priori* power vary considerably across content domains.[66] Indeed, sample sizes required to achieve .80 power for a 50th percentile ES vary between 97 and 150 (non-behavioral relations) and 215 and 304 (behavioral relations). In addition, in all cases where relation types are comparable, employee movement (e.g., turnover) studies require larger sample sizes than studies related to individual performance.

If your research involves attitudes and evaluations, you can use the information in Table 14.2 to compare them against existing research. If your research involves behaviors, you can compare your effect sizes with those in Table 14.3. Please note that this comparison is useful for you to understand the relative size of your effect sizes compared to others in a similar research domain. But, this does not necessarily mean that your effect is important. Let's discuss this vital distinction next.

HOW TO INTERPRET THE MEANING OF EFFECT SIZES

Reporting effect sizes compared to previously reported is important for the social and behavioral sciences. Another step that you need to take is to discuss the importance of these effects so consumers of research can understand its practical significance.

Confusion Between Magnitude of the Effect and Practical Significance

Calls for reporting the practical significance of research results are undoubtedly familiar. Several such calls have been made over the past few decades, such as one researcher's warning that "we must get over our obsession with null hypothesis significance tests and focus on the practical significance of our data" (p. 757).[67]

TABLE 14.2 ■ Effect Size Distribution Percentiles and Meta-Analytic Estimates for Illustrative Relations Between Attitudes/Evaluations and Behaviors											
Relation Type: Attitudes/ Evaluations with...	k	Med. N	Mean N	25th	33rd	50th	67th	75th	Unwt mean |r|	N-wtd mean |r|	SD_r
BEHAVIORS	7,958	220	483	.07	.10	.16	.24	.29	.21	.18	.18
A. Employee behaviors	7,736	217	479	.07	.10	.16	.24	.29	.21	.18	.18
1. Performance	3,224	190	284	.08	.11	.17	.26	.31	.22	.20	.17
1.1. Individual performance	2,737	192	276	.09	.11	.18	.26	.31	.22	.21	.17
1.1.1. Role performance	1,797	192	275	.08	.10	.17	.26	.31	.22	.22	.18
1.1.1.1. Subjective	1,205	185	276	.10	.12	.19	.29	.35	.25	.25	.19
1.1.1.1.1. Global	604	161	253	.10	.12	.19	.28	.33	.24	.24	.18
1.1.1.1.2. Facet/task	555	221	299	.10	.13	.21	.31	.37	.26	.27	.20
1.1.1.2. Objective	515	193	292	.05	.07	.12	.18	.21	.16	.14	.13
1.1.2. Extra-role performance	605	199	241	.11	.14	.20	.28	.32	.23	.22	.15
1.1.3. Goal performance	58	62	69	.13	.24	.43	.63	.72	.46	.46	.31
1.1.4. Training performance	167	182	402	.06	.08	.14	.22	.29	.19	.13	.13
1.1.5. Creative Performance	48	285	220	.09	.09	.13	.20	.26	.19	.15	.15
1.2. Group/team performance	147	92	257	.09	.12	.19	.37	.39	.26	.26	.21
2. Movement	866	309	1,093	.07	.09	.14	.21	.25	.17	.10	.12
2.1. Out of the organization	346	306	936	.07	.08	.12	.18	.21	.15	.10	.10
2.1.1. Turnover	270	306	1,045	.06	.07	.10	.14	.16	.11	.07	.07
2.1.1.1. Voluntary turnover	80	327	2,672	.05	.06	.09	.11	.14	.10	.06	.06
2.1.1.2. Involuntary turnover	12	785	699	.06	.07	.10	.10	.11	.08	.08	.04
2.1.2. Retention	73	861	562	.20	.24	.29	.32	.34	.27	.29	.09
2.2. Into the organization	17	354	320	.16	.22	.31	.37	.39	.32	.32	.18
2.3. Within organization	120	320	1,647	.04	.07	.15	.21	.25	.17	.05	.11
2.4. Job search behaviors	334	278	405	.07	.10	.17	.25	.28	.19	.20	.14
3. Absenteeism/tardiness	628	271	295	.05	.06	.11	.15	.17	.12	.11	.08
4. Interview behavior	79	266	387	.08	.10	.14	.23	.33	.23	.19	.22

(Continued)

TABLE 14.2 ■ Effect Size Distribution Percentiles and Meta-Analytic Estimates for Illustrative Relations Between Attitudes/Evaluations and Behaviors (Continued)

Relation Type: Attitudes/ Evaluations with...	k	Med. N	Mean N	25th	33rd	50th	67th	75th	Unwt mean |r|	N-wtd mean |r|	SD r
5. Leadership	689	416	693	.14	.17	.25	.33	.38	.28	.39	.25
6. Duration worked	143	196	788	.04	.05	.08	.14	.20	.14	.08	.09
7. Impression management	16	64	108	.16	.17	.20	.28	.64	.34	.28	.26
8. Participative behaviors	429	248	388	.09	.13	.21	.32	.38	.25	.24	.19
9. Counterproductive behaviors	546	374	1,120	.06	.08	.14	.20	.23	.17	.13	.12
10. Cognitive activities	293	171	205	.07	.10	.16	.26	.31	.22	.18	.16
11. Interaction behavior	563	182	211	.07	.09	.15	.24	.29	.19	.20	.17
B. Non-employee behavior	212	469	643	.04	.06	.10	.15	.20	.15	.12	.15
1. Socially valued behavior	43	242	264	.07	.09	.12	.18	.19	.15	.13	.10
2. Negative behaviors	127	470	797	.05	.06	.09	.14	.18	.14	.10	.13
2.1. Unhealthy behaviors	120	470	816	.05	.06	.09	.13	.16	.14	.09	.13

Source: Copyright © 2017 by American Psychological Association. Adapted with permission. F. A. Bosco, H. Aguinis, K. Singh, J. G. Field, & C. A. Pierce, 2015, Correlational effect size benchmarks, *Journal of Applied Psychology*, 100(2): 431-449.

Note: Percentiles show the distribution divided into 2, 3, and 4 equal partitions. *k* = number of effect sizes, Med. = median, unwt = unweighted, *N*-wtd = sample size weighted, and *SD_r* =standard deviation of *r*.

TABLE 14.3 ■ Effect Size Distribution Percentiles and Meta-Analytic Estimates for Illustrative Relations Between Behaviors and Attitudes/Evaluations

Relation Type: Behaviors with...	k	Med. N	Mean N	25th	33rd	50th	67th	75th	Unwt mean |r|	N-wtd mean |r|	SD r
ATTITUDES/EVALUATIONS	7,958	220	483	.07	.10	.16	.24	.29	.21	.18	.18
A. Object = Job/Task	2,972	224	674	.07	.09	.15	.22	.27	.19	.15	.17
1. Job characteristics	1,308	244	670	.07	.09	.14	.21	.25	.18	.13	.13
1.1 JCM	484	270	291	.07	.09	.15	.24	.29	.19	.19	.17
1.1.1. Identity	39	332	340	.09	.11	.15	.16	.17	.14	.15	.08
1.1.2. Significance	54	332	367	.03	.05	.07	.10	.14	.11	.08	.09
1.1.3. Autonomy	241	260	272	.11	.13	.21	.30	.36	.24	.25	.18
1.1.4. Feedback	122	279	297	.04	.06	.12	.19	.28	.17	.17	.18
1.2. Stressors	371	193	349	.06	.08	.14	.20	.24	.17	.16	.13

Relation Type: Behaviors with...	k	Med. N	Mean N	25th	33rd	50th	67th	75th	Unwt mean |r|	N-wtd mean |r|	SD_r
1.3. Job scope	42	332	341	.12	.15	.17	.18	.21	.18	.18	.09
1.4. Knowledge characteristics	166	332	3,146	.07	.09	.14	.22	.28	.17	.10	.07
1.5. Roles	130	240	280	.04	.07	.09	.15	.19	.15	.22	.23
2. General job affect	927	226	772	.07	.10	.16	.23	.27	.19	.16	.23
3. Compensation	201	271	687	.04	.06	.12	.16	.19	.14	.13	.11
4. Performance appraisal system	175	178	240	.07	.09	.15	.26	.34	.22	.22	.19
5. Goals	130	62	103	.10	.13	.23	.41	.53	.34	.27	.27
B. Object = Organization	1,456	241	407	.08	.10	.16	.23	.28	.20	.24	.20
1. Org policies/procedures	378	225	344	.08	.12	.18	.24	.28	.21	.20	.18
1.1. Justice	289	253	354	.08	.12	.18	.23	.27	.20	.19	.17
1.1.1. Interpersonal justice	23	231	724	.12	.14	.20	.29	.31	.23	.10	.14
1.1.2. Interactional justice	32	229	250	.08	.13	.20	.27	.30	.22	.20	.16
1.1.3. Distributive justice	85	270	326	.06	.07	.13	.19	.23	.17	.17	.16
1.1.4. Procedural justice	129	225	347	.09	.13	.19	.23	.28	.21	.22	.17
2. Employee-organization relationship	851	233	428	.08	.10	.15	.22	.27	.20	.27	.22
3. Perceived organizational performance	34	90	404	.06	.07	.10	.15	.19	.14	.11	.10
4. Embeddedness	51	310	295	.09	.10	.14	.24	.26	.17	.17	.12
5. Organizational image	36	612	616	.12	.14	.26	.31	.40	.26	.29	.16
6. Satisfaction towards organization	25	785	743	.05	.05	.08	.09	.11	.10	.11	.12
C. Object = People	1,338	199	290	.07	.10	.17	.27	.33	.23	.22	.19
1. Super/managers/leaders	626	237	342	.08	.11	.18	.27	.34	.23	.24	.20
1.1. Supervisor support	100	248	363	.07	.09	.12	.18	.23	.16	.17	.13
1.2. Supervisor Trust	22	124	185	.10	.11	.16	.22	.33	.23	.32	.23
1.3. Abusive supervision	29	216	248	.17	.17	.19	.26	.28	.23	.24	.15
1.4. Supervisor satisfaction	120	259	442	.09	.13	.19	.36	.47	.28	.34	.25
2. Coworkers	302	142	234	.08	.12	.19	.29	.37	.25	.20	.19

Source: Copyright © 2017 by American Psychological Association. Adapted with permission. F. A. Bosco, H. Aguinis, K. Singh, J. G. Field, & C. A. Pierce, 2015, Correlational effect size benchmarks, *Journal of Applied Psychology*, 100(2): 431-449.

However, there is confusion in the literature regarding the meaning of practical significance, and there is the general belief that reporting an estimate of the magnitude of the effect is the same as reporting a study's practical significance. Since the introduction of eta squared (η^2) as a measure of effect size, many have issued calls for reporting effect magnitude estimates as if it were a direct indicator of a study's practical significance. However, assume that a pre-employment test is correlated with future job performance at $r = .30$. How can a practitioner understand the practical significance of a pre-employment test that explains $.3 \times .3 = 9\%$ of the variance in future performance scores? Is this result practically significant? Should this practitioner recommend the use of the new pre-employment test to pre-screen job applicants in the future? Will using this pre-employment test lead to better hiring decisions? How much better? If you decide to use this test, what are the consequences of being unable to explain the remaining 91% of the variance in performance scores? As noted by some researchers, "the myth is that general statements such as 'X and Y are strongly related' are observation sentences vis-à-vis particular effect sizes irrespective of the contexts in which the values were generated" (p. 305).[68]

To answer the above questions and understand the practical significance of results, social and behavioral science researchers tend to use descriptive labels such as "strong" and "weak" in referring to effect sizes. As mentioned earlier, a well-known taxonomy suggested originally by Cohen uses the values of $r = .10$ as a "small" effect, $r = .30$ as a "medium" effect, and $r = .50$ as a "large" effect.[69]

METHODS IN PRACTICE

COHEN'S DEFINITIONS OF SMALL, MEDIUM, AND LARGE EFFECTS: WHERE DID THEY COME FROM?

Where did Cohen's values for small, medium, and large effect come from? How did Cohen determine that, for example, $r = .10$ is "small"? These definitions of small, medium, and large effect sizes are based partly on observed values as reported in the articles published in the 1960 volume of the *Journal of Abnormal and Social Psychology* and partly on Cohen's subjective opinion.[70] A few years later, Cohen decided to lower these values to .10 (small), .30 (medium), and .50 (large) because the originally defined values seemed a bit too high.[71] Given the history behind the conventional values for small, medium, and large effects, it is unsurprising that Cohen acknowledged that these definitions "were made subjectively" (p. 156).[72]

In short, the effect size values many social and behavioral sciences researchers use as benchmarks to understand whether their results are practically significant were originally derived from the observed effect sizes published more than 60 years ago in a single journal. This is why one researcher noted that using these values to determine practical significance "with the same rigidity that the $\alpha = .05$ criterion has been used... would merely be being stupid in a new metric" (p. 68).[73]

Solution: Report Practical Significance

As noted earlier, reporting effect magnitude estimates is essential to reporting results but insufficient to describe a study's practical significance. Also, using one-size-fits-all benchmark values to understand whether an effect is practically significant may be convenient for academics.

It may convey the impression of objectivity and standardization. However, this information is not necessarily valuable for those who make recommendations and decisions in organizations and other contexts (e.g., policymakers).

How often do social and behavioral science researchers discuss the issue of practical significance? A literature search for the phrase "practical significance" in the abstracts of several publications uncovered not a single article describing how to assess practical significance.[74] Instead, most articles described how a certain set of results had "practical significance."

For you to report results in a *customer-centric* way in terms of the needs of practitioners, you must contextualize and adequately interpret your results and conclusions. Practical significance involves a value judgment made by the consumer of research about the implications of a set of results and the consequences of a particular decision.[75] In addition, practical significance means asking whether results are noteworthy and whether they matter.[76] In other words, "data should be described in a way that fits with how practitioners would describe the situation being addressed in the study" (p. 1073).[77] Including a token section in an article's discussion section describing "implications for practice" has proven ineffective at bridging the science-practice gap and demonstrating the significance of research results in the eyes of practitioners. Also, including brief commentaries by individual executives as follow-ups to academic articles has been unsuccessful.[78]

To demonstrate a study's practical significance, there is a need to describe results in a way that makes sense for the potential beneficiaries of your research. You can achieve this by including potential beneficiaries and users in each research project as part of a qualitative study. Specifically, you can report the practical importance of results using practitioners' own discourse. In essence, you can use language and interpretation so that practitioners' voices are heard.[79] Qualitative methodology is particularly appropriate because its goal is to understand and describe phenomena. Also, qualitative research gives voice to the participants and emphasizes their understanding and interpretation of a given research study. Note that this does not mean that practitioners write a section of the resulting manuscript or that practitioners conduct the study but that they become participants in a qualitative study.

Several types of qualitative methods can be used to understand the extent to which a study's results are meaningful and valuable to practitioners.[80] These methods include case study, **cross-case analysis**, ethnography, **field notes analysis**, historical research, narrative inquiry, **practitioner inquiry**, **conversation analysis**, **focus groups**, **discourse analysis**, **social representation analysis**, and visual analysis. Next, let's discuss three approaches to demonstrate using qualitative methods to gather information regarding the practical significance of your research results.

Ethnography. Ethnography is a type of analysis that assumes the existence of shared cultural meaning in a social group.[81] It was initially developed in anthropology and is also used in sociology and education. It is a method that attempts to uncover meaning from the perspective of those involved. It involves studying a phenomenon in its natural setting and collecting data using several instruments, such as semi-structured interviews and diaries. If you conduct an ethnographic study, you will spend time in the field working alongside participants to immerse yourself in their world and become familiar with the participants' values, norms, and cultural environment. In addition, an ethnographic study aims to build bridges of understanding between groups of people who use different meanings and languages.[82] In short, ethnography can be used to understand the meaning of particular research results for individuals, such as human resource managers, employees, or consultants.

In terms of implementation, an ethnographic study should be seen as a conversation with a purpose. Your goal is to understand, from the participants' perspective, the extent to which research results matter and why this is so. What are the reactions of the participants to the research results? What do the results mean to them? How would they use the results in their work environments? How would the results be beneficial?

Conversation Analysis. Conversation analysis focuses on everyday conversations or institutional talk. Initially, the methodology was developed in psychology, sociology, linguistics, and communication studies. The participants usually collect the talk data using audio and video.[83] Conversation analysis focuses not only on what people say but also on how they say it.

For example, some researchers focused on what they labeled reaction tokens such as "Wow!" "My Goodness!" "Ooh!" and "That's amazing!" to answer the question of "what are these exclamatory imprecations doing?"[84] Conversation analysis involved first noticing a conversational phenomenon of interest (i.e., these "reaction tokens"), assembling a preliminary collection of instances of the phenomenon, and finally identifying the largest and most important subset within the collection, analyzing the clearest, less transparent, and deviant cases.

Conversation analysis allows for "a clearly specified, yet nuanced definition of intersubjectivity, depending on displayed understandings of prior talk" (p. 67).[85] One great practical advantage of this method is that you can rely on pre-existing data derived from various institutional contexts.

Narrative Inquiry. Narrative inquiry is a methodology used to think about experiences through the lens of stories and originates from the view that individuals have storied experiences.[86] Data used in narrative inquiry are collected using personal journals, stories, photographs, artifacts, annals, chronologies, interviews, and conversations to tell a narrative of people. Stated differently, these data are used to tell their stories. In this way, narrative inquiry can be used to tell a story of how and why a particular study results matter. You use storytelling to describe the practical significance of a result.

There are three important features of a narrative inquiry process.[87] First, the time dimension is important in narrative inquiry. A certain phenomenon is described in terms of its past, present, and future potential. Second, narrative inquiry pays attention to both personal and social conditions surrounding the phenomenon. Personal conditions include the individual's feelings, hopes, and desires; social conditions include the organizational environment and other social forces that form the individual's context. Third, it is important to identify the specific concrete, physical boundaries of where the phenomenon occurs. For generalizability, specifying location is crucial to understand the phenomenon of interest.

In sum, you can implement the aforementioned not-mutually-exclusive approaches to understand and explain your results to the intended consumer and beneficiaries. Furthermore, doing so will allow you to understand and describe the extent to which your research is practically significant.

Next, let's address two "case studies" of how to report statistical results. These two cases are particularly informative because one is a statistical test and the other an effect size measure. As such, many of the recommendations about these statistics also apply to other statistics and effect size measures.

HOW TO REPORT STATISTICAL RESULTS: THE CASE OF χ^2 AND η^2

Chi-Squared (χ^2)

In a covariance structure analysis, the underlying foundation for many data-analytic procedures such as factor analysis and structural equation modeling, the null hypothesis is H_0: $\Sigma = \Sigma\,(\theta)$.[88] In other words, this null hypothesis tests whether the covariance matrix implied in the hypothesized model and the observed covariance matrix fit identically in the population. The statistic used for testing this null hypothesis is χ^2.

However, you may have heard – or even been taught – a statistical and methodological myth and urban legend: *ignore results based on goodness-of-fit tests because the sample size is "too large."* A review uncovered that many authors argue that the χ^2 test is uninformative and should be ignored.[89] This is because the sample size was "too large" and, therefore, their χ^2 test had "too much statistical power," which made it too easy to reject the null hypothesis that the sample-based data provided evidence of a good fit. In other words, a common practice is to simply dismiss a statistically significant χ^2, which would suggest that the data do not fit a hypothesized model well. Note that it is true that if the null hypothesis is false, χ^2 will be more likely to be statistically significant as the sample size increases. This is an undisputed mathematical fact.[90] In contrast, a methodological myth and urban legend is the practice of routinely dismissing a statistically significant χ^2 because it is "uninformative."

There are at least two critical problems regarding this reporting practice. First, it has been used for many sample sizes, sometimes as low as the mid-100s. Second, the argument that N is too large, rendering the χ^2 test uninformative, is used when χ^2 is statistically significant (i.e., signaling poor fit). However, a literature review did not find *any* statements about N and statistical power (i.e., "statistical power may be insufficient to reject the null hypothesis") when the χ^2 is not statistically significant (i.e., signaling adequate fit). Thus, it seems that researchers may use a self-serving double standard regarding the interpretation of χ^2 test results: Sample size is too large, and the test should be ignored if results are statistically significant, suggesting that the data do not fit the hypothesized model well; whereas sample is just fine (and not "too small") if results are not statistically significant indicating that the data do fit the hypothesized model well.

Several important conclusions derive from this discussion. First, although most authors refer to the sample size as an issue to consider in interpreting χ^2 test results, some warn about having a sample that is *too small*. This is because large samples are needed not only for an accurate estimation of the fit of the data to the model but also for the accurate estimation of the model's parameters (especially for maximum likelihood estimation). Second, although some sources conclude that a "large" sample size may lead to a statistically significant χ^2 even when the difference between the sample-based and the implied covariance matrices is trivial, there is little conclusive information regarding what a "large" sample is. For example, some researchers refer to $N = 11{,}743$ as large and $N = 68$ as small.[91] But most published studies in social and behavioral sciences include sample sizes closer to 68 than 11,748, so the large sample size problem (i.e., rejecting good models) may not be as pervasive as the small sample size problem (i.e., accepting poor models).

Finally, although some authors refer to having "too much statistical power," this is not a problem of the χ^2 test. Instead, the problem is how to interpret statistical significance's meaning.[92] The p-value associated with the χ^2 statistic is the probability of observing the sample data, or data more deviant, given that the null hypothesis $\Sigma = \Sigma\,(\theta)$ is true. Thus, a statistically significant χ^2 does not tell us whether the difference (if any) between Σ and $\Sigma\,(\theta)$ is practically significant and only tells us that it is unlikely (usually at a probability of $p < .05$) that the null hypothesis is true, as discussed earlier in this chapter.

As with any statistical significance test, the probability of obtaining a statistically significant result increases as the sample size increases.[93] This is a mathematical fact and a desirable property for a test statistic. Therefore, the χ^2 is expected to vary directly with N even for incorrectly specified models.[94] Note, however, that if a study's sample is inordinately large, you may conclude that the sample-based covariance matrix is dissimilar to the covariance matrix implied by the hypothesized model in the population even if the difference between the matrices is miniscule and practically or scientifically insignificant. This characteristic is by no means unique to the χ^2 test.

So, the question is: Is it accurate to report that when samples are "large," using the χ^2 test to evaluate the fit of a model is uninformative and can be ignored? The answer is no. The χ^2 test is informative and should be reported regardless of sample size. This is due to the following four points. First, it is the only test to assess the statistical significance of the difference between the implied and the observed correlation matrices. Other goodness-of-fit indexes exist (e.g., comparative fit index, normed fit index, root mean square error of approximation) but do not assess statistical significance. Second, you do not know what a "large" sample is. It seems disingenuous to use the same "large N" argument regardless of a study's sample size. Third, the presence of samples that are too small (leading to incorrectly accepting a poor-fitting model) seems more common in social and behavioral sciences than in samples that are too large (leading to incorrectly rejecting model). Thus, it is likely that in published research in the social and behavioral sciences, some inappropriate models have been retained as adequate (due to the small sample size). Fourth, even if a sample is inordinately large, which is not the most typical scenario in the social and behavioral sciences, the χ^2 test is informative because, if interpreted correctly, it provides information regarding the fit between the observed covariance matrix in relation to the covariance matrix in the population underlying the hypothesized model. A statistically significant χ^2 tells you that the hypothesized and sample-based covariance matrices are not likely to be identical in the population but does not tell you whether this difference is practically or scientifically important. Unfortunately, the argument that sample size is "too large" and, therefore, a statistically significant χ^2 test should be ignored seems to be used sometimes as a rationalization for ignoring the result that the null hypothesis $\Sigma = \Sigma(\theta)$ (i.e., the hypothesized model is correct) has been rejected. In many cases, this argument is misused to avoid the inconvenient fact that (albeit small) differences between the observed and implied covariance matrices exist, and a researcher's proposed model may be incorrect.

Eta-Squared (η^2)

When using ANOVA to analyze data, several measures of strength of association are available. These include eta-squared (η^2), **epsilon-squared** (ε^2), and **omega-squared** (ω^2).[95]

As a descriptive index of the strength of association between an experimental factor (i.e., main or interaction effect) and a dependent variable, classical eta-squared is defined as the proportion of total variation attributable to the factor, and it ranges in value from 0 to 1.[96] From information typically reported in an ANOVA summary table, classical eta-squared for an experimental factor can be computed as follows:

$$\text{classical } \eta^2 = SS_{\text{factor}} / SS_{\text{total}} \tag{14.3}$$

where SS_{factor} is the amount of variation attributable to the experimental factor, and SS_{total} is the total variation.

In contrast to classical eta-squared, partial eta-squared for an experimental factor is defined as the proportion of total variation attributable to the factor, *partialling out or excluding other experimental factors from the total non-error variation*.[97] Like classical eta-squared values, partial eta-squared values range from 0 to 1. From information typically reported in an ANOVA summary table, partial eta-squared for an experimental factor can be computed as follows:

$$\text{partial } \eta^2 = SS_{factor} / (SS_{factor} + SS_{error}) \tag{14.4}$$

where SS_{factor} is the amount of variation attributable to the experimental factor, and SS_{error} is the amount of error or unexplained variation. Unlike classical eta-squared, partial eta-squared is an index of the proportion of total variation accounted for when the effects of all other non-error sources have been removed from the total variation. Thus, in a multifactor ANOVA, $SS_{factor} + SS_{error}$ in the denominator of Equation 14.4 is always less than or equal to the corresponding SS_{total} in the denominator of Equation 14.3. Consequently, partial eta-squared is typically greater than classical eta-squared for a source of variance.

When are classical eta-squared and partial eta-squared equivalent for a source of variance? Classical and partial eta-squared are identical in an experimental design with only one factor. In a one-way ANOVA, $SS_{total} = SS_{factor} + SS_{error}$. Thus, classical and partial eta-squared are equivalent.[98] In a multifactor ANOVA, classical and partial eta-squared are equivalent for a source of variance when that source is the only one contributing to the total non-error variation. For example, the potential sources of nonerror variance in a between-subjects A × B design are A, B, and A × B. If either A, B, or A × B is the only nonzero source of variance, and the two remaining sources of non-error variance have SS_{factor} values equal to 0. The classical eta-squared will be equal to the partial eta-squared for that factor. In this example, $SS_{total} = SS_A + SS_B + SS_{AB} + SS_{error}$. Suppose that SS_A and SS_B each equal 0. The SS_{total} would then be equal to $SS_{AB} + SS_{error}$; hence, classical eta-squared would equal partial eta-squared per Equations 14.3 and 14.4.

When are classical eta-squared and partial eta-squared not equivalent for a source of variance? In a multifactor ANOVA, they are not equivalent for a source of variance when other experimental factors have an SS_{factor} value greater than 0. Stated differently, classical and partial eta-squared are not equivalent when other factors in the analysis contribute to the total non-error variation. In practice, classical and partial eta-squared are almost always unequal.

With respect to multifactor between-subjects, within-subjects, or mixed-factor ANOVAs, only partial eta-squared values, and not classical eta-squared values, can sum to a value greater than 1.[99] Partial eta-squared values can sum to greater than one because each is computed using a different value for the "total variation" in the denominator of Equation 14.4. Thus, partial eta-squared is not a measure of unique variation in the dependent variable. Other factors in the analysis can also account for some of this nonerror variation. Unlike partial eta-squared values, classical eta-squared values cannot sum to greater than one because each is computed using the same value for SS_{total} in the denominator of Equation 14.3. Thus, classical eta-squared is a measure of unique variation in the dependent variable in that this nonerror variation cannot be accounted for by other factors in the analysis.

Why should this misreporting issue concern researchers in the social and behavioral sciences? First, for any multifactor ANOVA with more than one nonzero source of variance, partial eta-squared values are greater than the corresponding classical eta-squared values. Indeed, partial eta-squared values are often substantially greater than the corresponding classical ones. For instance, in a multifactor ANOVA, it is possible to have partial eta-squared values greater than .50 when the corresponding classical eta-squared values are less than .20. A review of classical and partial eta-squared in published articles revealed that the sum of reported classical eta-squared values ranged from 1.10 to 2.04 (M = 1.53 or 153% of the total variation), showing that the reported classical eta-squared values were inflated by 53% assuming the non-error sources in each analysis accounted for 100% of the total variation.[100] If, instead, you assume more realistically that the non-error sources accounted for between 10% and 75% of the total variation, then the reported classical eta-squared values were inflated by 78% and perhaps as much as 143%.

When considering implications of misreporting partial eta-squared values as representing classical eta-squared values from a multifactor ANOVA, note that they depend on (a) whether there was more than one experimental factor with an SS_{factor} value greater than 0 and (b) whether the magnitude of the disparity between the two values for a particular source of variance is small or large. The discrepancy can be quite large (e.g., a partial η^2 > .50 but the corresponding classical η^2 < .20). From a theory-testing standpoint, you may make misguided conclusions about your data because you misrepresent the strength of association between the variables you examined. These misguided conclusions may severely impact the further development and testing of a particular theory. Like a snowball effect, meta-analysts may then compute potentially inflated study-level effect size estimates (ds or rs) from classical eta-squared values that are actually partial eta-squared values. These study-level effect size estimates may result in misguided meta-analytic conclusions, which, in turn, may also impact the further development and testing of a particular theory. When conducting a meta-analysis, you should be especially cautious, preferably relying on other reported statistics such as means, standard deviations, sample sizes, or ds or rs instead of eta-squared values. Finally, you may make misguided or premature recommendations regarding using a costly treatment or intervention program about which the degree of success was misrepresented in empirical trials.

Next, let's address the critical issue of reporting the limitations in your research transparently and usefully.

HOW TO REPORT YOUR STUDY'S LIMITATIONS AND FUTURE RESEARCH DIRECTIONS

Limitation sections are useful for understanding the importance of the weaknesses of the specific research effort as reported by the authors, placing the study in context, and attributing a credibility level to it.[101] On the other hand, future research directions are less directly rooted in the presented research. Instead, they are forward-looking, pointing to theoretical and methodological areas where further development is desirable.

Self-reported limitations and directions for future research are also unique because they represent critical information that can affect the likelihood of a manuscript being published. The pressure stemming from the increasingly low acceptance rates for peer-reviewed journals[102] and emphasis on publications in academic reward structures[103] represent clear motives for not acknowledging limitations and for offering only benign directions for future research. At the very least, these pressures create a context for a tentative approach to disclosure. In the social and behavioral sciences, the recent attention to ethical issues in research communication[104] and the absence of established standards for reporting limitations and directions for future research highlights the need for a closer examination of these features. Accordingly, a team of researchers conducted a comprehensive review of the limitations and future directions sections of over 1,200 articles and devised recommendations that are discussed in detail below.[105]

Limitations

Disclosing Limitations

Guideline #1: Make it a Priority. Over a third of the articles report no limitations. While this percentage has decreased substantially over the years, all empirical research is flawed to some degree, and limitations should be reported in every published article. The presence of self-critical elements within research articles is consistent with the principles of falsificationism as a requirement for robust science and scientific progress.[106] Journal editors are best positioned to ensure certain limitations are mentioned in every empirically-based manuscript.

Guideline #2: Use a Separate Section. Half of the articles do not have a separate section identifying limitations. Accordingly, editorial guidelines of journals should require a separate heading for limitations. This recommendation goes beyond those from usual editorial guidelines such as, for example, the latest edition of the Publication Manual of the American Psychological Association (7th Edition), which only instructs authors to "Acknowledge the limitations of your research, and address alternative explanations of the results" (p. 90).[107] Also, more limitations are reported when located in separate sections, and there is significant variation in the presence of limitation sections across journal editors, indicating a certain amount of editorial control in this regard.[108] Insisting on a separate section allows journal editors to draw this information out, making limitations more salient for readers.

Guideline #3: Focus Specifically on Limitations. As mentioned earlier, publishing in top journals has become very competitive. In such a context, it is idealistic to expect authors to expand on the information that may jeopardize their publishing chances. Thus, the third recommendation is based on the belief that the reporting of limitations should be treated differently than other sections of manuscripts in the review process. Specifically, the onus of teasing out the main flaws of manuscripts should belong, for the most part, to reviewers. As stated by one researcher, "… the main purpose of the review process—to cull the best from the rest—inevitably focuses attention on a paper's weaknesses" (p. 1078).[109] Reviewers are not only particularly attentive to the adequacy of methods,[110] but, compared with authors and editors, they tend to the most critical issues in their evaluations of articles.[111] Moreover, reviewers are selected for their expertise in the study topic, and, with the protection provided by anonymity, they are in the best position to bring forward limitations. To channel this information systematically, if you are a reviewer, you can add a separate section in your evaluation and comments for authors. In this section, you can explicitly list limitations and the extent to which they affect the study regarding substantive conclusions.

Guideline #4: Focus on Those Weaknesses That Matter. Every research effort is limited in multiple ways, and for every manuscript deemed worthy of publication, a discerning set of reviewers will be able to point to multiple threats to every type of validity evidence. As stated, the review process's role is to bring forward these weaknesses and weigh their importance in light of the study's contribution. Self-reported limitations should not reflect a comprehensive inventory of a study's weaknesses but include those that matter most. As such, limitations that matter are not necessarily inherently linked to a methodological choice (e.g., external validity for laboratory study or causality for cross-sectional designs). The previous guideline suggested that reviewers bring forward limitations. The fourth guideline suggests that after considering the reviewers' opinions, editors are responsible for prioritizing limitations and directing authors as to which ones to include in their manuscripts.

The first four guidelines pertain to the identification of limitations. Next, let's discuss how they should be reported.

Describing Limitations

Guideline #5: Highlight the "So-What". In addition to describing the study's shortcomings, limitations statements should distinguish the "what" from the "so-what." It would be best if you did not use single-sentence descriptions of limitations that are not very informative. Limitations need to state not only the shortcomings of a study but also the implications of these shortcomings for the interpretation of the research and possibly for the area under study in general. For example, it is common to encounter statements that a particular sample characteristic (e.g., student-based, culture-specific) represents a limitation regarding the generalization of results. However, the precise nature of a sample is not inevitably related to external validity concerns.[112] For example, suppose using a student or a sample in a particular context relates to the phenomenon under study and influences the interpretation of the results. In that case, the relationship should be explained well.

Guideline #6: Describe Each Limitation, Do Not Justify. A prevalent rhetorical issue in reporting limitations consists of describing a weakness but immediately discounting it as a minor issue that does not threaten the interpretation of results. Most of you will recognize statements along the lines of: "The study had limitation X, but X does not really matter that much because of Y and Z." A study found that differences between reported and objectively coded limitations are quantitative and not qualitative in nature in that authors do seem to report limitations accurately but do so in a way that lessens their severity.[113] That the purpose of the vast number of limitations seems to be one of justification is problematic but not surprising. Again, authors must establish the credibility of their research endeavor and convince the reviewers (and other readers of your work) that their results stand despite being limited in some way. However, such a rhetorical exercise should not preclude the provision of a clear description of the impact of the limitation on the interpretation of the study.

Table 14.4 includes examples of how to formulate limitations better. This table includes typical ways self-reported limitations are described in current research. Each limitation in the column labeled "Currently Reported" suffers from the typical weaknesses described in the previous sections. In addition, Table 14.4 includes a separate column labeled "Reported following best-practice guidelines," in which each limitation is re-written following these recommendations. For example, the first limitation refers to internal validity. The text for the currently reported limitation indicates that you (a) cannot infer causality from cross-sectional designs but that (b) it is unlikely that the non-hypothesized directions of the effect has occurred. This information is not useful. In contrast, the same limitation written using best-practice guidelines has greater potential to educate readers, as it highlights. It explains the process by which reverse causality could occur in relative detail.

Future Directions

Describing Directions for Future Research

Guideline #7: Focus on Immediate and Incremental Opportunities. A literature review uncovered that many future research directions were essentially framed as limitations turned inside out. That is, limitations and directions for future research were presented as two sides of

TABLE 14.4 ■ Illustrations of How Limitations Are Currently Reported and How They Should Be Reported Based on Best-Practice Guidelines		
	Currently Reported	**Reported Following Best-Practice Guidelines**
Internal Validity	The cross-sectional nature of our design makes it difficult to infer a causal relation between job characteristics and employee well-being.	One limitation of our study is that we cannot rule out the possibility of fatigue influencing the self-report of work characteristics, a reversed causality effect. However, the influences of mental and physical fatigue on psychological states are pervasive and well-established in the literature. Therefore, it is likely that fatigue led to the emergence of some job characteristics.
External Validity	One limitation of our study is that we focus only on one interfirm collaboration type: collaborations in which firms share physical assets such as plants or distribution networks.	The fact that our study examines interfirm collaborations focusing on sharing physical assets (e.g., plants, distribution networks, etc.) is likely to affect the generalizability of our findings to interfirm collaborations that focus on learning or the exchange of skills and knowledge.
Construct Validity	One limitation of our study is that we proxied firm performance through the abnormal stock market return following merger announcements.	The interpretation of our results is constrained by our measure of firm performance (i.e., abnormal stock market return). Because post-merger integration tends to be complex and takes time, this measure does not allow drawing any conclusions about the long-term performance impact of such events.
Statistical Conclusion Validity	The regression analyses were sensitive to the effects of measurement error. However, the coefficients were statistically significant, supporting the hypothesized relations.	The regression analyses were sensitive to the effects of measurement error. Specifically, measurement error decreases observed coefficients in relationship to their true (population) counterparts. Thus, the fact that our results showed that the coefficients are statistically significant implies that the population effects are likely even larger than the ones we report in our tables.

Source: Brutus, Aguinis, & Wassmer (2013). Reproduced with permission.

the same coin. The weaknesses of a meaningful research effort will also point toward reasonable ways to address them or avenues for future investigations. It may come as no surprise that directions for future research almost perfectly mirror limitations. However, replicating the same information under both headings is redundant and not a good use of valuable journal space and reader time. This is not to say that these sections should be merged. Directions for future research are distinct in that they offer a unique opportunity for you to share where you believe immediate extensions are required. However, every published study can inspire dozens of ideas for future research, and you should frame your suggestions within a relatively short and proximal time frame. Including ideas that address current gaps in the literature instead of more distal ones would increase the instrumental value of these sections for readers. Constructive replications, often considered mundane, should be promoted as they accentuate the cumulative and incremental nature of progress in the behavioral sciences.[114] Suggestions that are projected into the distant future of a particular area are often interesting but not particularly useful if not complemented by actionable, incremental steps.

Guideline #8: Use Them as a Vehicle for Theoretical Advancement. Directions for future research offer an opportunity to advance theoretical issues—an opportunity of which few authors take advantage. Much attention has recently been given to enriching the theoretical landscape in the social and behavioral sciences.[115] Some authors have hinted that a lack of journal space hinders theoretical contribution. For example, one researcher stated that "a paper is usually too short to provide adequate space for a full accounting of 'why,' especially if the primitives, logic, corollaries, and implications of a theory are complex" (p. 18).[116] Therefore, directions for future research should be positioned in relation to theoretical development.[117] Ironically, introducing possible theoretical touchstones in directions for future research could help promote theoretical pruning. As one researcher stated, "Without head-to-head competition, there is little Darwinian selection on theories of organizations" (p. 692).[118] Sections devoted to directions for future research represent an ideal forum for such competition.

Table 14.5 summarizes the best-practice guidelines described in the previous sections. Also, the table identifies the different roles where you can make the most significant impact in implementing these recommendations: Author, reviewer, or editor. Overall, limitations and directions for future research need to be treated differently from other sections of manuscripts if they are genuinely informative. A best practice is to include a separate Limitations section in the Discussion sections of peer-reviewed publications rooted in the study's objective characteristics. In addition, exposing these limitations should be the shared responsibility of all participants in the peer review process.

TABLE 14.5 ■ Summary of Suggested Guidelines for Reporting Limitations and Directions for Future Research and Primary Agents for Each (i.e., Authors, Reviewers, and Editors)

Disclosing Limitations

1. **Guideline #1: Make it a priority**. Ensure that limitations are reported in every empirically-based article. (E)

2. **Guideline #2: Use a separate section.** Mandate headings for limitations in the journal editorial guidelines. (E)

3. **Guideline #3: Focus specifically on limitations.** List limitations and the extent to which they affect the study regarding substantive conclusions.(R)

4. **Guideline #4: Focus on those weaknesses that matter.** Self-reported limitations should reflect those weaknesses that matter most. (R, E)

Describing Limitations

5. **Guideline #5: Highlight the "so-what."** Limitations need to state not only the shortcomings of a study but also the implications of these shortcomings for the interpretation of the research. (A, E)

6. **Guideline #6: Describe each limitation, do not justify.** Limitations should clearly describe how they affect the interpretation of the results. (A, R, E)

Describing Directions for Future Research

7. **Guideline #7: Focus on immediate and incremental opportunities**. Directions for future research should be framed within a relatively short and proximal time frame. (A)

8. **Guideline #8: Use them for theoretical advancement**. Directions for future research should be positioned in relation to theoretical development. (A)

Source: Brutus, Aguinis, & Wassmer (2013). Reproduced with permission. E: editors, R: reviewers, A: authors.

In the Future Research Directions section, you should present forward-looking ideas that position the study within the context of the broader research domain. These should target incremental change and provide a unique opportunity to enrich the theoretical landscape. Incorporating the guidelines above with those proposed by other researchers[119] for Implications for Practice sections will lead to more informative and impactful Discussion sections.

DISCUSSION QUESTIONS

1. What is research reproducibility, and what is research replicability? Which one is most critical and why?

2. Why does a lack of transparency in how results of empirical studies are reported negatively affect the credibility of the social and behavioral sciences?

3. How can reporting p-values compared to statistical cutoffs (e.g., $p < .05$) mislead research consumers?

4. If a study reports p values based on cutoffs (e.g., $p < .05$) instead of actual p-values (e.g., $p = .03$), is it more or less credible, reproducible, and replicable? Why?

5. What is the process of selecting a priori α values based on comparing the relative seriousness of making a Type I versus a Type II error?

6. Do you think journal reviewers' evaluation of your research will be more or less positive based on whether you use conventional α values versus selecting α values based on your assessment of the seriousness of Type I versus Type II error? Why?

7. What is the difference between the information provided by tests of statistical significance and effect sizes?

8. Why do reporting results compared to context-specific effect sizes help others understand the importance of your research? Provide an example.

9. What is the difference between effect size estimates and the practical significance of your results?

10. How can ethnography, conversation analysis, and narrative inquiry help you explain the practical significance of your research?

11. Why should you not believe the methodological legend of dismissing models based on a statistically significant chi-squared (χ^2) test?

12. How can conflating classic eta-squared (η^2) with partial eta-squared when reporting results lead to misleading interpretations?

13. Why should you report your study's limitations without justifying them?

14. What are the similarities and differences between reporting limitations and directions for future research?

15. What is the role of authors, reviewers, and editors in improving how limitations are reported?

16. To improve the reporting of limitations, what can be done to minimize authors' conflict of interest (i.e., desire to publish their research)?

KEY TERMS

conversation analysis

cross-case analysis

discourse analysis

epsilon-squared (ε^2)

ethnography

field notes analysis

focus groups

omega-squared (ω^2)

practitioner inquiry

social representation analysis

NOTES

This chapter is based to a large extent on the following sources:

Aguinis, H., & Harden, E. E. (2009). Cautionary note on conveniently dismissing χ^2 goodness-of-fit test results: Implications for strategic management research. In D. D. Bergh and D. J. Ketchen (Eds.), *Research methodology in strategy and management*, Vol. 5 (pp. 111-120). Emerald Group Publishing.

Aguinis, H., Vassar, M., & Wayant, C. (2021). On reporting and interpreting statistical significance and *p*-values in medical research. *BMJ Evidence-Based Medicine*, *26*(2), 39-42. http://dx.doi.org/10.1136/bmjebm-2019-111264 (Reproduced with permission from BMJ Publishing Group Ltd.)

Aguinis, H., Werner, S., Abbott, J. L., Angert, C., Park, J. H., & Kohlhausen, D. (2010). Customer-centric science: Reporting significant research results with rigor, relevance, and practical impact in mind. *Organizational Research Methods*, *13*(3), 515-539. https://doi.org/10.1177%2F1094428109333339

Bosco, F. A., Aguinis, H. Singh, K., Field, J. G., & Pierce, C. A. (2015). Correlational effect size benchmarks. *Journal of Applied Psychology*, *100*(2), 431-449. https://psycnet.apa.org/doi/10.1037/a0038047

Brutus, S., Aguinis, H., & Wassmer, U. (2013). Self-reported limitations and future directions in scholarly reports: Analysis and recommendations. *Journal of Management*, *39*(1), 48-75. https://doi.org/10.1177%2F0149206312455245

Pierce, C. A., Block, R. A., & Aguinis, H. (2004). Cautionary note on reporting eta-squared values from multifactor ANOVA designs. *Educational and Psychological Measurement*, *64*(6), 916-924. https://doi.org/10.1177%2F0013164404264848

HOW TO IMPROVE THE TRANSPARENCY, REPRODUCIBILITY, AND REPLICABILITY OF YOUR RESEARCH

LEARNING GOALS

By the end of this chapter, you will be able to do the following:

15.1 Argue why you should care about the transparency, reproducibility, and replicability of your research and how a lack of transparency is detrimental to the credibility of social and behavioral science research.

15.2 Recommend how you can improve transparency about your theory and discuss the benefits of THARKing for theory development.

15.3 Appraise how to transparently report your research design choices, including the best way to report choices regarding control variables.

15.4 Critique, why you should transparently report all measures used in your study and how altering scale items affects the psychometric properties of the scales.

15.5 Assess how a lack of transparency in reporting data-analytical procedures impedes reproducibility and discuss best practices for reporting how you handled outliers.

15.6 Judge the importance of transparency when reporting results and describe why reporting results of all tests of assumptions increases transparency.

15.7 Defend how journals and publishers, editors, and reviewers play a crucial role in motivating authors to increase transparency.

15.8 Appraise how open-science training and promoting shared values can motivate authors to increase transparency.

IMPORTANCE OF TRANSPARENCY AND REPLICABILITY OF YOUR RESEARCH

Significant concerns exist about the credibility and usefulness of the scholarly knowledge produced in the social and behavioral sciences.[1] A critical issue in this debate is our inability to reproduce and replicate results described in published articles. *Reproducibility* means that someone other than a published study's authors can obtain the same results using the authors' data. In contrast, *replicability* means that someone other than the original authors can obtain substantially similar results by applying the same steps in a different context and with different data. It isn't easy to make the case that research results are credible and valuable if they are irreproducible and not replicable. In turn, the reproducibility of a study's findings is a vital prelude to meeting the conditions for repeatable cumulative knowledge development. Until a study's findings are reproduced, they cannot be assumed as a trustworthy benchmark for replication, comparison, and extension. Unfortunately, a proliferation of evidence indicates that lack of reproducibility and replicability are pervasive.[2] This has led some researchers to suggest a possible credibility crisis in science.[3]

Consequently, this chapter discusses the importance of improving the transparency of social and behavioral science research. In each of the first five sections, you will learn how to improve transparency about the steps of the typical research process: theory, design, measurement, analysis, and the reporting of results. Finally, the last section describes the open-science framework and suggestions for motivating authors to embrace open-science principles and practices.

HOW TO IMPROVE TRANSPARENCY ABOUT YOUR THEORY

The first transparency area refers to theory. The recommendation is to be explicit regarding research questions (e.g., theoretical goal, research strategy, epistemological assumptions) and **level of theory**, and congruence about levels with measurement and analysis (e.g., individual, dyadic, organizational), as well as specifying the a priori direction of hypotheses (e.g., linear, curvilinear), and distinguishing a priori versus post hoc hypotheses. These recommendations are summarized in Table 15.1.

TABLE 15.1 ■ Evidence-Based Best-Practice Recommendations to Enhance Methodological Transparency Regarding Theory	
Recommendations	**Improves Transparency by Allowing Others to...**
1. Specify the theoretical goal (e.g., creating a new theory, extending existing theory using a prescriptive or positivist approach, describing existing theory through interpretive approach); research strategy (e.g., inductive, deductive, abductive); and epistemological orientation (e.g., constructivism, objectivism)	1. Use the same theoretical lens to evaluate how your assumptions may affect the ability to achieve research goals (e.g., postpositivism assumes objective reality exists, focuses on hypothesis falsification; interpretative research assumes different meanings exist, focuses on describing meanings), and conclusions drawn (e.g., data-driven inductive approach versus theory-based deductive approach)
2. Specify the level of theory (e.g., individual, dyadic, organizational), and congruence with the level of measurement and analysis	2. Use the same levels to interpret implications for theory and understand whether theory, measurement, and analysis are congruent regarding levels of analysis
3. Acknowledge whether there was an expected a priori direction (e.g., positive, plateauing, curvilinear) for the nature of relations as derived from the theoretical framework used. Identify and report any post hoc hypotheses separately from a priori hypotheses. Report both supported and unsupported hypotheses.	3. Differentiate between inductive and deductive tests of theory and gather information regarding the precision, relevance, and boundaries of the theory tested (e.g., the match between theoretical predictions and results; the presence of contradictory findings; prediction of linear or curvilinear relations)

Source: Adapted from Aguinis, Ramani, & Alabduljader (2018).

For example, consider the recommendation regarding the **level of inquiry**. This recommendation applies to most studies because the explicit specification of the focal level of theory and congruence regarding levels with measurement and analysis facets of the study is necessary for drawing similar inferences across levels.[4] The level of the theory refers to the focal level (e.g., individual, team, firm) to which you seek to make generalizations.[5] On the other hand, the **level of measurement** refers to the level at which you collect data. Finally, the level of analysis refers to the level at which data is assigned for hypothesis testing and analysis. Transparency regarding the level of theory, measurement, and analysis allows others to recognize potential influences of such decisions on the research question and the meaning of results, such as whether constructs and results differ when conceptualized and tested at different levels or whether variables at different levels may affect the substantive conclusions reached.[6]

METHODS IN PRACTICE
THE IMPORTANCE OF DISCLOSING YOUR FOCAL LEVEL OF INQUIRY

Without transparency about the level of inquiry, it is difficult for reviewers and readers to reach similar conclusions about the meaning of results, compromising the credibility of your findings. For example, a retraction by some researchers was attributed to (among other things) the inappropriate use of levels of analysis, leading to the irreproducibility of the study's conclusions.[7] However, had the researchers reported the level of analysis, reviewers would have been able to use the same levels to interpret whether results were influenced by the alignment or lack thereof between the level of theory, measurement, and analysis. This may have helped reviewers identify incorrect inferences before publication, avoiding having to eventually retract the paper. Thus, low transparency when specifying levels of inquiry may help account for the difficulty in reproducing conclusions in some research. Furthermore, you must be transparent about your decisions even when the level of inquiry is explicit, such as when testing the relation between two individual-level variables. Being explicit about the level of inquiry is particularly important given the increased interest in developing and testing multilevel models and bridging the micro-macro gap, which adds to model complexities.[8]

Another recommendation is about including post hoc hypotheses separately from a priori ones.[9] Many researchers retroactively create hypotheses after determining the results supported by the data (i.e., HARKing).[10] HARKing implies that observed patterns were discovered from data analysis – an inductive approach. By crediting findings to a priori theory, readers assume the results are based on a random sample of the data and thus generalizable to a larger population. On the other hand, the truthful and transparent reporting of the use of HARKing is called THARKing—theorizing after results are known. THARKing, therefore, consists of inductive theorizing. THARKing can be a valuable investigative technique that provides interesting findings and discoveries.[11]

Consider the following exemplars of published articles that are highly transparent regarding theory. First, one researcher used an interpretive approach to examine social processes involved in organizational sensemaking (i.e., individuals' interpretations of cues from environments) among various organizational stakeholders.[12] The researcher explained the theoretical goal ("The aim of this study was theory elaboration," p. 24), the theoretical approach (i.e., describe theory using an interpretive qualitative approach), and the rationale for the choice ("Theory elaboration is often used when preexisting ideas can provide the foundation for a new study, obviating the need for theory generation through a purely inductive, grounded analysis," p. 24). High transparency in stating the theoretical goal, approach, and rationale allows researchers to use the same theoretical lens to evaluate how assumptions may affect the ability to achieve research goals and the conclusions drawn. As a second positive example, transparency about levels of inquiry was demonstrated in an article examining the effect of team personality and transformational leadership on proactive performance.[13] These researchers stated the level of theory ("Our focus in the current paper is on proactive teams rather than proactive individuals," p. 302), level of measurement ("Team members, excluding the lead technician, were asked to rate their lead technician, and these ratings were aggregated to produce the team-level transformational leadership score," p. 311), and level of analysis ("It is important to note that, because the analyses were conducted at the team level ($N = 43$), it was not appropriate to compute a full structural model," p. 313). Moreover, these researchers specified levels in their formal hypotheses (e.g., "The mean level of proactive personality in the team will be positively related to team proactive performance," p. 308), further enhancing transparency.

HOW TO IMPROVE TRANSPARENCY ABOUT YOUR RESEARCH DESIGN

The second area to address is research design, including choices about data collection procedures, sampling methods, power analysis, common method variance, and control variables. Information on issues such as sample size, sample type, conducting research using passive observation or experiments, and decisions on including or excluding control variables influence inferences drawn from these results and reproducibility.[14] These recommendations are summarized in Table 15.2.

Many of the recommendations included in Table 15.2 are related to the need to be transparent about specific steps taken to remedy often-encountered challenges and imperfections in the research design (e.g., common method variance, possible alternative explanations) and to note

TABLE 15.2 ■ Evidence-Based Best-Practice Recommendations to Enhance Methodological Transparency Regarding Research Design	
Recommendations	**Improves Transparency by Allowing Others to....**
1. Describe the type of research design (e.g., passive observation, experimental); data collection procedure (e.g., surveys, interviews); location of data collection (e.g., North America/China; at work/in a lab/at home); sampling method (e.g., purposeful, snowball, convenience); and sample characteristics (e.g., students versus full-time employees; employment status, hierarchical level in the organization; sex; age; race)	1. Determine the influence of study design and sample characteristics on research questions and inferences (e.g., use of cross-sectional versus experimental studies to assess causality) and overall internal and external validity of findings reported (e.g., if theoretical predictions may vary across groups and cultures; if the sample is not representative of the population of interest or the phenomenon manifests itself differently in sample)
2. If a power analysis was conducted before initiating the study or after the study's completion, report the results and explain if and how they affect the interpretation of the study's results	2. Draw independent conclusions about the effect of sample size on the ability to detect existing population effects given that low power increases the possibility of Type II error (i.e., incorrectly failing to reject the null hypothesis of no effect or relation)

Recommendations	Improves Transparency by Allowing Others to....
3. If common method variance was addressed, state the theoretical rationale (e.g., failure to correlate with other self-report variables) and study design (e.g., temporal separation, use of self- and other-report measures) or statistical remedies (e.g., Harman one-factor analysis) used to address it	**3.** Identify the influence, if any, of common method variance preemptive actions and remedies on error variance (i.e., variance attributable to methods rather than constructs of interest), which affects conclusions because it affects the size of obtained effects
4. Provide an explanation of which control variables were included and which were excluded and why, how they influenced the variables of interest, and their psychometric properties (e.g., validity, reliability)	**4.** Independently determine if conclusions drawn in the study were influenced by choice of control variables because a) including control variables changes the meaning of substantive conclusions to the part of predictor unrelated to the control variable rather than the total predictor; b) not specifying causal structure between control variables and focal constructs (e.g., main effect, moderator, mediator) can cause model misspecification and lead to different conclusions; and c) reporting measurement qualities provides evidence on whether control variables are conceptually valid and representative of the underlying construct

Source: Adapted from Aguinis, Ramani, & Alabduljader (2018).

the impact of these steps and choices on substantive conclusions, as they may amplify the flaws they are intended to remedy. Others cannot make similar inferences from the results without knowing which corrective actions were taken.[15]

METHODS IN PRACTICE
TRANSPARENCY AND CONTROL VARIABLES

Due to the practical difficulties associated with conducting experimental and quasi-experimental designs, researchers may include control variables (i.e., statistical controls) to account for the possibility of alternative explanations.[16] Including control variables reduces the degrees of freedom associated with a statistical test, statistical power, and the amount of explainable variance in the outcome.[17] On the other hand, excluding control variables can increase the amount of explainable variance and inflate the relation between the predictor and the outcome of interest. Therefore, the inclusion or exclusion of control variables affects the relation between the predictor and the outcome and the substantive conclusions drawn from your results. Yet, many researchers often do not disclose which control variables were initially considered for inclusion and why, which control variables were eventually included and which were excluded, and the psychometric properties (e.g., reliability) of those included.[18] As some researchers noted, many studies cite previous work or provide ambiguous or vague statements such as "it might relate" as a reason for control variable inclusion rather than providing a theoretical rationale for whether control variables have meaningful relations with criteria and predictors of interest.[19] Some researchers may include control variables simply because they suspect reviewers and editors expect such practice. Therefore, low transparency regarding the use of control variables reduces reproducibility because it is not known whether conclusions reached are simply an artifact of which specific control variables were included or excluded.[20]

A study by some researchers offers a good illustration of good practices for transparency in using control variables.[21] These researchers controlled for job tenure when testing the effect of positive moods on task performance. Furthermore, they provided an explanation of which control variables were included ("We included job tenure, in years, as a control variable") and why they were used ("…meta-analysis showed that the corrected correlation between work experience… and employee job performance was .27," p. 1575), and how the control variables might influence the variables of interest ("This positive correlation may be explained by the fact that employees gain more job-relevant knowledge and skills as a result of longer job tenure, which thus leads to higher task performance," p. 1575).

Example: Transparency and Common Method Variance

An example of high transparency about common method variance is a study by some researchers who examined how government directors' self-identification with both the focal firm and the government influences their self-reported governance behavior (managerial monitoring and resource provision).[22] These researchers noted why common method variance was a potential problem in their study ("As both the dependent and the independent variables were measured by self-report, common method variance could have influenced the results," p. 1800). Additionally, they were highly transparent in describing the techniques used to assess whether common method bias may have influenced their conclusions ("First, we conducted Harman's single factor test and found that three factors were present …also controlled for the effects of common method variance by partialling out a general factor score…we tested a model with a single method factor and examined a null model," p. 1800).

HOW TO IMPROVE TRANSPARENCY ABOUT YOUR MEASURES

The third transparency area you should pay attention to is measurement. In addition to unambiguous construct definitions, information about the psychometric properties of all the measures used (e.g., reliability, construct validity), statistics used to justify **aggregation,** and issues related to range restriction or measurement error are also important. The types of psychometric properties that need to be reported differ based on the conceptual definition of the construct and the precise scale used (e.g., original scale vs. scale in which some of the items have been revised or omitted). This is critically important because using a different set of items means that reliability and validity evidence based on the original set are no longer applicable because a revised scale is different.

In addition, when measuring higher-level constructs, transparency includes identifying the focal **unit of analysis,** whether it differs from the same construct at the lower level, the statistics used to justify aggregation, and the rationale for the choice of statistics used.[23] This allows others to more clearly understand the meaning of the focal construct of interest and whether aggregation might have influenced the definition of the construct and the meaning of results.

Transparency here also alleviates concerns about whether you cherry-picked aggregation statistics to support your decision to aggregate, enhancing reproducibility. These recommendations are summarized in Table 15.3.

Another important measurement transparency consideration is when no adequate measure exists for the focal constructs of interest. Questions regarding the impact of measurement error on results or the use of proxies of constructs are even more important when using a new or an existing measure that has been altered.[24] In these instances, transparency includes details on changes made to existing scales, such as which items were dropped or added and any changes in the wording or scale items. Without a clear discussion of the changes made, readers may doubt

TABLE 15.3 ■ Evidence-Based Best-Practice Recommendations to Enhance Methodological Transparency Regarding Measurement	
Recommendations	**Improves Transparency by Allowing Others to....**
1. Provide a conceptual definition of the construct; report all measures used; how indicators (e.g., reflective, formative) correspond to each construct; and evidence of construct validity (e.g., correlation tables including all variables, results of item and factor analysis)	1. Draw independent conclusions about a) overall construct validity (i.e., indicators assess underlying constructs); b) discriminant validity of constructs (i.e., constructs are distinguishable from one another); and c) discriminant validity of measures (i.e., indicators from different scales do not overlap). Absent such information, inferences have low reproducibility (e.g., small effects could be attributed to weak construct validity, large effects to low discriminant validity)
2. If scales were altered, report how and why (e.g., dropped items, changes in item referent). Provide psychometric evidence regarding the altered scales (e.g., criterion-related validity), and report the exact items used in the revised scale	2. Understand whether conclusions reached are due to scale alterations (e.g., cherry-picking items); independently reach conclusions about the validity of new and revised scales
3. If scores are aggregated, report measurement variability within and between units of analysis; statistics, if any, used to justify aggregation (e.g., r_{wg}, ICC); and results of all aggregation procedures	3. Reach similar conclusions regarding aggregated construct's meaning because different aggregation indices provide distinct information (e.g., r_{wg} represents interrater agreement and is used to justify aggregation of data to higher-level; ICC(1) represents interrater reliability and provides information on how lower-level data is affected by group membership, and if individuals are substitutable within a group)
4. If range restriction or measurement error were assessed, specify the type of range restriction, and provide a rationale for the decision to correct or not correct. If corrected, identify how (e.g., type of correction used, sequence, and formulas). Report observed effects and those corrected for range restriction and measurement error	4. Recognize how the method used to identify and correct for measurement error or range restriction (e.g., Pearson correlations corrected using the Spearman-Brown formula; Thorndike's Case 2) may have led to over- or under-estimated effect sizes

Source: Adapted from Aguinis, Ramani, & Alabduljader (2018).

Note: r_{wg} = Within-group inter-rater reliability; ICC = Intraclass Correlation Coefficient.

conclusions, as it might appear that you changed the scales to obtain the desired results, thereby reducing reproducibility.

An article on leadership offers an excellent example of transparency regarding score aggregation.[25] These researchers examined the consequences of differentiated leadership within groups and described why aggregation was necessary given their conceptualization of the theoretical relationships ("group-focused leadership fits… [the] referent shift consensus model in which within-group consensus of lower-level elements is required to form higher-level constructs," p. 95), provided details regarding within- and between-group variability, and reported both r_{wg} and ICC statistics.

> ### Example: Transparency and Conceptual Definitions
>
> An example of high transparency regarding conceptual definitions, choice of particular indicators, and construct validity is a study that used resource dependence and institutional theories to examine how firms respond to ecological uncertainty.[26] The authors of this study explained why they conceptualized ecological uncertainty as a formative construct ("to capture a resort's total efforts at adopting practices related to ecological mitigation") and how they assessed face and external validity ("we selected SACC ratings when there was a theoretical basis… we calculated variance inflation factors… assessed multicollinearity at the construct level with a condition index," p. 1513). Finally, they provided evidence of construct validity using correlation tables, including all variables.

HOW TO IMPROVE TRANSPARENCY ABOUT YOUR DATA ANALYSIS

The next transparency area is data analysis. Given the current level of sophistication of data-analytic approaches, offering detailed and specific recommendations on transparency regarding each of dozens of techniques such as meta-analysis, multilevel modeling, structural equation modeling, computational modeling, content analysis, regression, and many others would require an entire book. Accordingly, these recommendations are broad, generally applicable, and useful to various data analysis techniques. These recommendations are summarized in Table 15.4.

Researchers today have more degrees of freedom regarding data-analytic choices than ever before, and decisions made during analysis are rarely disclosed transparently.[27] So, noting the software employed and making available the syntax used to carry out the analyses facilitates readers' understanding of how the assumptions of the analytical approach affected results and conclusions.[28] For example, multiple scripts and packages are available within the R software to impute missing data. Two of these (MICE and Amelia) impute data assuming that the data are missing at random, while another (missForest) imputes data based on non-parametric assumptions. How data are imputed influences the values analyzed, affecting results and conclusions. Thus, not knowing which precise package was used contributes to inconsistency in results and the conclusions others draw about the meaning of results.

Another recommendation summarized in Table 15.4 relates to the topic of outliers. Outliers can affect parameter estimates (e.g., intercept or slope coefficients). Still, many studies fail to disclose whether a dataset included outliers, what procedures were used to identify and handle them, whether analyses were conducted with and without outliers, and whether results and inferences changed based on these decisions.[29] Consequently, low transparency about how outliers were defined, identified, and handle means that other researchers cannot reach similar conclusions (i.e., reduced reproducibility).

TABLE 15.4 ■ Evidence-Based Best-Practice Recommendations to Enhance Methodological Transparency Regarding Data Analysis	
Recommendations	**Improves Transparency by Allowing Others to....**
1. Report the specific analytical method used and why it was chosen (e.g., EFA versus CFA; repeated measures ANOVA using conventional univariate tests of significance versus univariate tests with adjusted degrees of freedom)	1. Independently verify whether the data analytical approach used influenced conclusions (e.g., using CFA instead of EFA to generate theory)
2. Report the software used, including which version, and make coding rules (for qualitative data) and data analysis syntax available	2. Check whether assumptions of data analytic procedures within the software used (e.g., REML versus FIML) affect conclusions
3. If tests for outliers were conducted, report methods and decision rules used to identify them; steps (if any) taken to manage outliers (e.g., deletion, Winsorization, transformation); the rationale for those steps; and report results with and without outliers	3. Infer if substantive conclusions drawn from results (e.g., intercept or slope coefficients; model fit) would differ based on how outliers were defined, identified, and managed

Source: Adapted from Aguinis, Ramani, & Alabduljader (2018).

Note: EFA = Exploratory Factor Analysis; CFA = Confirmatory Factor Analysis; ANOVA = Analysis of Variance; REML = Restricted Maximum Likelihood; FIML = Full Information Maximum Likelihood.

An illustration of a more specific and technical recommendation included in Table 15.4 relates to the usual practice of reporting that a study used a "repeated-measures ANOVA." Unfortunately, this type of reporting does not provide sufficient detail to others about whether you used a conventional F test, which assumes multisample sphericity, or a multivariate F test, which assumes homogeneity of between-subjects covariance matrices.[30] Without such information, which refers to providing a clear justification for a particular data-analytic choice, readers of your research attempting to reproduce results using the same general analytical method (e.g., ANOVA) may draw different inferences.

Example: Transparency and Outliers

An example of high transparency regarding outliers is studying the relationship between antecedents and outcomes of modular products and process architectures.[31] These researchers specified how they identified ("We also examined outliers and influential observations using indicators such as Cook's distance"), defined ("called up the respondent submitting these data, who said that he had misunderstood some of the questions in that he had considered"), and handled the outlier ("we subsequently corrected this company's score on one variable (product modularity)," p. 1132).

An illustration of a high degree of transparency in data analysis when using qualitative methods is a study that generated a theory on how affect relates to creativity at work.[32] These researchers detailed the coding rules they used when analyzing events ("A narrative content coding protocol was used to identify indicators of mood and creative thought in the daily diary narratives," p. 378).

In addition, they were highly transparent about what they coded to develop measures ("we also constructed a more indirect and less obtrusive measure of mood from the coding of the diary narrative, Coder-rated positive mood. Each specific event described in each diary narrative was coded on a valence dimension," p. 379), and how they coded measures ("defined for coders as "how the reporter [the participant] appeared to feel about the event or view the event"…"For each event, the coder chose a valence code of negative, neutral, positive, or ambivalent," p. 379).

HOW TO IMPROVE TRANSPARENCY ABOUT YOUR RESULTS

The next area is enhancing transparency about the final step of the typical empirical research study, that is, reporting results. The more transparent you are in reporting results, the better consumers of published work will be able to reach similar conclusions, and the more they will trust your work. These recommendations are summarized in Table 15.5.

The first issue in Table 15.5 relates to the need to provide sufficient detail on response patterns so others can assess how they may have affected inferences drawn from the results. While nonresponses are rarely the central focus of a study, it usually affects conclusions drawn from the analysis. Moreover, given the variety of techniques available for dealing with nonresponses by replacing missing data (e.g., deletion, imputation), absent precise reporting of results of missing data analysis and the analytical technique used, others are unable to judge whether your study's response rate and how you addressed this challenge because a source of research irreproducibility.[33] In short, insufficient transparency makes low reproducibility virtually guaranteed if this information is absent.

TABLE 15.5 ■ Evidence-Based Best-Practice Recommendations to Enhance Methodological Transparency Regarding Reporting of Results	
Recommendations	**Improves Inferential Reproducibility by Allowing Others to….**
1. Report results of missing-data analysis (e.g., sensitivity analysis); method (e.g., imputation, deletion) used to address missing data; information (even if speculative) as to why missing data occurred; response rate; and if conducted, results of non-response analyses	1. Have greater confidence in inferences and that you did not cherry-pick data to support preferred hypotheses; verify whether causes of missing data are related to variables of interest; and independently assess external validity (e.g., if survey respondents are representative of the population being studied)
2. Report results of all tests of assumptions associated with the analytical method. Examples include: Normality, heteroscedasticity, independence, covariance amongst levels of repeated measures, homogeneity of the treatment-difference variances, and group size differences in ANOVA	2. Verify whether possible violations of assumptions influenced study conclusions (e.g., based on chi-square statistic, standard errors) and tests of significance upwards or downwards, thereby affecting inferences drawn
3. Report complete descriptive statistics (e.g., mean, standard deviation, maximum, minimum) for all variables; correlation and (when appropriate) covariance matrices	3. Confirm that results support your claims (e.g., multicollinearity amongst predictors elevating probability of Type I errors; correlations exceeding maximum possible values); gauge if the number of respondents on which study statistics are based was sufficient to draw conclusions

Recommendations	Improves Inferential Reproducibility by Allowing Others to….
4. Report effect size estimates; confidence intervals (CI) for point estimates; and information used to compute effect sizes (e.g., within-group variances, degrees of freedom statistical tests)	**4.** Interpret accuracy (e.g., the width of CI reflects the degree of uncertainty of effect size; whether sampling error may have led to inflated effect estimates) and practical significance of study results (i.e., allowing for comparison of estimates across studies)
5. Report exact p-values to two decimal places; do not report p-values compared to cut-offs (e.g., $p < .05$ or $p < .01$)	**5.** Rule out whether conclusions are due to chance; judge the seriousness of making a Type I (incorrectly rejecting the null hypothesis) versus Type II (incorrectly failing to reject the null hypothesis) error within the context of the study
6. Use specific terms when reporting results. Examples include: ● Use "statistically significant" when referring to tests of significance; do not use terms such as "significant," "marginally/almost significant," or "highly significant." ● Identify precise estimate used when referring to "effect size" (e.g., Cohen's d, r, R^2, η^2, partial η^2, Cramer's V) ● Provide interpretations of effect sizes and confidence intervals regarding the study context, effect size measure used, and other studies examining similar relations. Do not use categories as absolute and context-free benchmarks	**6.** Understand that statistical significance is related to the probability of no relation, not effect size; comprehend what authors mean when referring to "effect size" (e.g., the strength of relation or variance explained); interpret evidence by comparing with previous findings and weigh the importance of effect size reported in light of the context of the study and its practical significance
7. Report the total number of tests of significance	**7.** Evaluate conclusions because conducting multiple tests of significance on the same dataset increases the probability of obtaining a statistically significant result solely due to chance and not because of a substantive relation between constructs
8. Report and identify both unstandardized and standardized coefficients	**8.** Understand the relative size of the relations examined (when using standardized coefficients); understand the predictive power and substantive impact of the explanatory variables (when using unstandardized coefficients)

Source: Adapted from Aguinis, Ramani, & Alabduljader (2018).

Note: ANOVA = Analysis of Variance; CI = Confidence Interval.

Another issue included in Table 15.5, which ties directly to transparency in data analytical choices, is reporting the results of any tests of assumptions that may have been conducted. Most analytic techniques include assumptions (e.g., linearity, normality, homoscedasticity, additivity), and many available software packages produce results of assumption tests without the need for additional calculations on your part. While the issue of assumptions might be seen as an issue that everyone should be paying attention to, most published articles do not report whether assumptions were assessed.[34]

METHODS IN PRACTICE
THE NORMALITY ASSUMPTION

Consider the assumption of normality of error distributions, which underlies most regression-based analyses. This assumption is violated frequently,[35] and many researchers are aware of this. Yet, many researchers continue to use software and analytical procedures that assume normality without openly reporting the results of tests of these assumptions. Reporting results of assumptions improves reproducibility by allowing others to independently assess whether the assumption may have been violated based on examining graphs or other information provided in the software output.

Another issue included in Table 15.5 is the need to report descriptive and inferential statistics clearly and precisely. This precision allows others to independently compare their results and conclusions with those reported. In addition, precision in reporting results allows others to confirm that you did not hide statistically non-significant results behind vague writing and incomplete tables. The most egregious example of a lack of precision is about p-values. Used to denote the probability that a null hypothesis (i.e., there is no effect or relation) is tenable, researchers use a variety of arbitrary cutoffs to report p-values (e.g., $p < .05$ or $p < .01$) as opposed to the exact p-value computed by default by most contemporary statistical packages.[36] Unfortunately, using these artificial cutoffs makes it more difficult to assess whether researchers made errors that obscured the true value of the probability (e.g., rounding .059 down to .05) or reported a statistically significant result when p-values do not match and to judge the seriousness of making a Type I (incorrectly rejecting the null hypothesis) versus Type II (incorrectly failing to reject the null hypothesis) error within the context of the study.[37]

An example of high transparency in reporting missing data is an article by some researchers that examined financial earning restatements and the appointment of CEO successors.[38] In addition to providing information as to why they had missing data ("lack of Securities and Exchange Commission (SEC) filings," p. 1765), the authors also reported how their sample size was affected by missing data ("our sample size experienced the following reduction"), the method used to address missing data ("deleted listwise"), how missing data may have affected results obtained ("model is very conservative, treating any missing data as non-random (if they are indeed random, it should not affect the analyses)," and the results of a non-response analysis ("we did compare the firms that were dropped for the reasons mentioned above with the remaining firms in terms of size, profitability, and year dummies. We found no significant difference," p. 1784). As a second illustration, a study on how skew and **heavy-tail distributions** influence firm performance is an example of high transparency regarding testing assumptions.[39] In answering their research question, these researchers explicitly noted why their data might violate the assumptions of homoscedasticity and independence required by their analytical method (i.e., OLS regression). They outlined the steps they took to account for these violations ("we add a lagged value of the dependent variable ($Y_i(t-1)$) to capture possible persistence (autocorrelation), heteroscedasticity"… "we use the generalized method of moments," p. 1732).

HOW TO MOTIVATE AUTHORS TO IMPROVE TRANSPARENCY

This final section describes how to motivate authors to improve transparency by making it a more salient requirement for publication. It begins by outlining general recommendations that can be implemented by journals and publishers, editors, and reviewers. Then it provides specific steps that can encourage authors to embrace open-science practices. This movement cuts across all scientific fields and does not only apply to social and behavioral science research. Open science consists of approaching the production and diffusion of scientific knowledge so that the process of conducting research, publications, and research data are publicly accessible in a digital format with no or minimal restrictions. As a preview, Table 15.6 includes a summary of recommendations.

General Recommendations

It is important to remember that transparency is a continuum and not a dichotomous variable. In other words, the larger the number of methodological practices reported transparently, the more likely the published study will have greater reproducibility and credibility. Therefore, the recommendations in Table 15.6 are not mutually exclusive. For example, while some address actions to be taken before submitting a manuscript and information authors must certify during the manuscript submission process, others can be used to give "badges" to accepted, exceptionally transparent manuscripts.[40] Moreover, implementing as many of these recommendations as possible will reduce the chance of future retractions and, perhaps, decrease the number of "risky" submissions, lowering the workload and current burden on editors and reviewers.

TABLE 15.6 ■ Recommendations for Journals and Publishers, Editors, and Reviewers to Motivate Authors to Enhance Methodological Transparency	
Transparency Issue	**Recommendations**
	Before submitting a manuscript for journal publication, authors could certify on the submission form that...
Data and Syntax Availability, Data Access, and Division of Labor	**1.** Data have been provided to the journal, along with coding rules (for qualitative data) and syntax used for analyses. If data cannot be made available, require authors to explain why
	2. All authors had access to data, and whether data analysis and results were verified by co-author(s)
Hypothesis Testing	**3.** Authors reported all hypotheses tested, even if they found statistically non-significant results
Power Analysis	**4.** If a power analysis was conducted, results were reported in the study
Measures	**5.** All measures used in the study were reported, along with evidence of validity and reliability
Response Rate	**6.** Response rate for surveys and how missing data were handled were reported
Statistical Assumptions	**7.** Results of tests of assumptions of the statistical model were reported
Outliers	**8.** If tests for outliers were conducted, the procedure used to identify and handle them was reported

(Continued)

TABLE 15.6 ■ Recommendations for Journals and Publishers, Editors, and Reviewers to Motivate Authors to Enhance Methodological Transparency (*Continued*)	
Transparency Issue	**Recommendations**
	Before submitting a manuscript for journal publication, authors could certify on the submission form that...
Control Variables	9. Justification of why particular control variables were included or excluded was made explicit, and results were reported with and without control variables
Aggregation	10. If scores were aggregated, variability within and across units of analysis and statistics used to justify aggregations were reported
Effect Size and Confidence Intervals	11. Effect sizes and confidence intervals around point estimates were reported
	12. Implications of observed effect size in the context of the study were explained
Reporting of *p*-values	13. Exact *p*-values rather than *p*-values compared to statistical significance cutoffs were reported
Precise Use of Terms when Reporting Results	14. Precise, unambiguous terms were used when reporting results. Examples include "split-half" or "coefficient alpha" instead of "internal consistency," and "statistically significant" as opposed to "significant," "highly significant," or "marginally significant
Limitations	15. The implications of the limitations on the results of the study were made explicit
Post hoc Analysis	16. Post hoc analyses were included in a separate section
	Reviewer evaluation forms could be revised to require reviewers to...
Competence	17. State level of comfort with and competence to evaluate the methodology used in the manuscript they are reviewing
Limitations	18. Identify limitations that impact the reproducibility of the study
Evaluating Transparency	19. Evaluate whether authors have provided all information required on the manuscript submission form
	The review process could be revised by...
Alternative/ Complementary Review Processes	20. Adopting a two-stage review process by requiring pre-registration of hypotheses, sample size, and data-analysis plan, with the results and discussion sections withheld from reviewers until the first revise/ reject decision is made
Availability of Data	21. Using online supplements that include detailed information such as complete data, coding procedures, specific analyses, and correlation tables
Auditing	22. Instituting a policy where some of the articles published each year are subject to communal audits, with data and programs made available and commentaries invited for publication

Source: Adapted from Aguinis, Ramani, & Alabduljader (2018).

Most recommendations in Table 15.6 can be implemented without incurring much cost, encountering practical hurdles, or fundamentally altering the manuscript submission and review process. Implementing many of these recommendations is now possible because of the availability of online supplemental files, which removes the important page limitation constraint. For example, due to page limitations, the *Journal of Applied Psychology* (JAP) decided to use a smaller font for the Method section (the same smaller size as the footnotes) from 1954 to 2007.[41] In addition, the page limitation constraint may have motivated editors and reviewers to ask authors to omit material from their manuscripts, resulting in low transparency for consumers of the research. Also, journal reviewers often require that you expand upon a study's "contributions to theory" at the expense of eliminating information on methodological details (e.g., tests of assumption checks, statistical power analysis, properties of measures).[42] Evidence of this phenomenon is that the average number of pages devoted to the Method and Results sections of articles in JAP remained virtually the same from the year 1994 to the year 2013. Still, the average number of pages devoted to the Introduction section increased from 2.49 to 3.90, and the Discussion section increased from 1.71 to 2.49.[43] Again, the availability of online supplements will hopefully facilitate the implementation of many of these recommendations that were not feasible in the past due to page limitations.

In hindsight, implementing some of the recommendations to enhance methodological transparency summarized in Table 15.6 could have prevented the publication of several articles that have subsequently been retracted. For example, an article submission requirement requesting that authors acknowledge that all research team members had access to the data might have prevented a retraction because, in this particular situation, not all authors had access to the data and could not detect problems before the paper was published.[44] Reassuringly, many journals are in the process of revising their manuscript submission policies. For example, some journals published by the American Psychological Association require that all data in their published articles be original.[45] But, although new policies implemented by journals such as *Strategic Management Journal* address important issues about "more appropriate knowledge and norms around the use and interpretation of statistics" (p. 257),[46] most are not directly related to transparency. Thus, although there is some progress in developing manuscript submission policies, transparency does not seem to be a central theme to date.

Regarding ease of implementation, recommendations #20 and #22 in Table 15.6 are broader in scope and, admittedly, may require substantial time, effort, and resources: Alternative/complementary review processes and auditing. Given resource constraints, some journals may implement these two recommendations but not both. Several journals offer alternative review processes (e.g., *Academy of Management Discoveries, Management and Organization Review, Organizational Research Methods, Journal of Business and Psychology, Journal of Management Scientific Reports*). The review involves a two-stage process. First, there is a "pre-registration" of hypotheses, sample size, and data analysis plan. If this pre-registered report is accepted, authors are invited to submit the full-length manuscript that includes results and discussion sections, and the paper is published regardless of statistical significance and size of effects.

Overall, recommendations in previous sections aim to enhance methodological transparency by addressing authors' knowledge and skills and motivation to be more transparent when publishing research. In addition to improving reproducibility, increased transparency also provides other benefits. For example, enhanced transparency can produce higher-quality studies and quality control.[47] Specifically, reviewers and editors can more easily evaluate if a study departs substantially from best-practice recommendations regarding particular design, measurement, and analytical processes and judge whether inaccurate judgment calls and decisions unduly influence the conclusions authors draw from results. In addition, when there are grey areas regarding specific methodological decisions and judgment calls, others can better evaluate your decisions and draw independent conclusions about the impact on the study's conclusions.[48]

Finally, enhanced transparency improves not just reproducibility but also the replicability of research. As described earlier, replicability is the ability of others to obtain substantially similar results as the original authors by applying the same steps in a different context and with different data. If there is low methodological transparency, low replicability may be attributed to differences in theorizing, design, measurement, and analysis rather than substantive differences, thereby decreasing the trust others can place in the robustness of our findings.[49]

Open-Science Recommendations

As mentioned earlier, open science is a different and more collaborative way of researching because it requires transparency and sharing of information (and data) throughout the research process. The recommendations below pertain specifically to improving transparency using an open-science framework. These recommendations are summarized in Table 15.7.

Changing the Incentive Structure

Introduce a Best-paper Award and Acknowledgement Based on Open-Science Criteria. Individual journals can identify specific criteria for the award. They might include categories such as study preregistration, open data, analytic code that facilitates reproducibility, or other research activities that seek to advance science by making innovative content open access. For instance, an award may be given to an author who develops a Shiny app in R or machine learning code that is user-friendly and helps others reproduce, replicate, and extend a research domain by learning from methodological techniques or study materials. This is similar to current practices at some journals (e.g., *Management and Organization Review, Strategic Management Journal*) for which articles that engage in open-science practices, such as

TABLE 15.7 ■ Recommendations for Improving Transparency Through Open Science: Changing the Incentive Structure, Improving Access to Training Resources, and Promoting Shared Values			
Recommendation	Benefits	Primary decision-makers involved in implementing the recommendations	Resources needed to implement and enforce the recommendations
Changing the incentive structure			
1. Introduce a best-paper award and acknowledgment based on open-science criteria	**Reporting and publishing** • Positive recognition for open-science efforts	Editors	• **Financial resources:** None • **Time:** 1 month from an ad-hoc committee of action editors • **Additional resources:** Offer guidelines to the awards committee • **Enforcement:** None

Recommendation	Benefits	Primary decision-makers involved in implementing the recommendations	Resources needed to implement and enforce the recommendations
Changing the incentive structure			
2. Encourage funding agencies to require open science practices (e.g., publicly posting all funded grants, supporting open-access publishing, preregistration, and data availability)	**Study design** ● Facilitation of replications and extensions of past studies **Data analyses** ● Improved analytic reproducibility ● Reduction in honest analytic mistakes	Funding agencies	● **Financial resources**: None ● **Time:** None ● **Additional resources**: Revisions to grant-submission guidelines ● **Enforcement**: Mandatory for those who receive funding
Improving access to training resources			
3. Provide access to open-science training	**Reporting and publishing** ● Improved quality of reviews ● Reduction of questionable research practices during the review process	Editors and reviewers	● **Financial resources**: None ● **Time:** None ● **Additional resources**: None ● **Enforcement**: Monitoring of training to designate a reviewer as an "open-science evaluator"
Promoting shared values			
4. Publish editorial statements that null results, outliers, "messy" findings, and exploratory analyses can advance scientific knowledge if a study's methodology is rigorous	**Reporting and publishing** ● Reduction in authors' incentives to engage in questionable research practices ● Reduction in potential reviewer bias against "messy" findings ● Promotion of more holistic evaluations of results	Editors	● **Financial resources**: None ● **Time:** Editor's time to write editorials ● **Additional resources**: Editor training ● **Enforcement**: None

Source: Adapted from Aguinis, Banks, Rogelberg, & Cascio (2020).

preregistration and open data, receive badges and which have been positive in terms of incentivizing open-science practices.[50]

The main benefit of taking this approach pertains to reporting and publishing. That is, awards and acknowledgments effectively promote positive recognition for open-science efforts.[51] The primary decision-makers in implementing this recommendation are editors, who must determine the award and recognition criteria. Editorial boards then need to form annual committees to evaluate published articles and to determine winners. While financial awards are powerful at signaling values, they are not required. However, virtually any kind of recognition will motivate authors to engage in such practices.

Encourage Funding Agencies to Promote Open-science Practices. This recommendation directly aligns open-science practices with financial incentives. Funding agencies can publicly post all funded grants, support open-access publishing, and encourage preregistration and data availability.

Numerous benefits might result from this recommendation. First, the open sharing of information allows for the facilitation of replications and extensions beyond previous studies.[52] Sharing data, analytic code, and other resources can reduce honest mistakes and improve analytic reproducibility. If data and analytic code are shared, it makes it easy to reproduce analyses perfectly and likely reduces honest mistakes by researchers.[53]

The primary decision-makers involved in this recommendation are funding agencies because of the power of the purse. Agencies can easily maximize taxpayer and donor dollars by implementing such changes. However, more resources are needed to implement them, either financial or time. The enforcement mechanism is that the changes are mandatory for those who receive funding. Hence, funding agencies can reward and incentivize those who develop and disseminate knowledge that benefits the broader scientific community.

Improving Access to Training Resources

Provide Access to Open-science Training. Many resources exist that could be used to implement this recommendation. For example, the cost of adding training resources to journal websites would be minimal. For instance, the Society for Industrial and Organizational Psychology's (SIOP) Education and Training committee has begun reviewer training to promote reviewer development.[54] This training is intended, in part, to educate reviewers about open science and to help reduce engagement in questionable research practices (QRPs) in the review process. Also, the journal Organizational Research Methods (ORM) published a special issue focusing on reviewer development. Some articles focus on transparency in collecting and handling data (e.g., missing data, outliers, control variables) before substantive analysis and checklists for authors, reviewers, and editors.[55] More generally, the Center for Open Science offers training on preregister studies and other related topics (see: https://cos.io/our-services/training-services).

The primary benefit of implementing this recommendation is improving the quality of peer reviews and reducing engagement in QRPs during the review process. Education for reviewers should also help reduce reviewer bias. This step can also encourage reviewers to accept transparent, exploratory analyses (e.g., THARKing, as discussed earlier).[56] The primary decision-makers involved in implementing this recommendation are editors and reviewers. As for enforcement, reviewers who complete specific training programs could receive badges and be qualified or even certified as "open-science evaluators."

Promoting Shared Values

There is evidence that researchers accept and support values related to open science.[57] So, emphasizing these shared values can be critical for open science. This gap means that although there is much research on reducing questionable research QRPs, many gatekeepers must adopt this knowledge in their practices. So, to narrow this gap, editors can publish editorial statements that null results, outliers, "messy" findings, and exploratory analyses can advance scientific knowledge if a study's methodology is rigorous.[58] There is a precedent for this combined effort: a group of editors collectively signaled important values (https://editorethics.uncc.edu/editor-ethics-2-0-code/). The primary benefit of supporting shared values is to influence reporting and publishing, for example, by encouraging authors to reduce their engagement in QRPs, to reduce potential reviewer bias against "messy findings," and to promote a more holistic evaluation of results.

The primary decision-makers involved in implementing this final recommendation are editors. The resource needed to implement this is the time of the editors to write editorials. An exemplar of this approach is the editorial published in *The Leadership Quarterly*.[59] This editorial not only signaled the values of the journal but discussed tangible changes to editorial practices. Since then, the journal has consistently improved its **impact factor** year after year relative to other journals in management and related disciplines. A journal's impact factor is based on the average number of citations received by articles, and it is used to rank journals in terms of their impact and influence; therefore, it is a critical measure to which most editors pay close attention.[60] A similar increase in impact factor was enjoyed by the *Journal of Business and Psychology*, which has been highly visible on the open-science front. Of course, these are just two illustrations, and it isn't easy to draw causal inferences. Yet these examples illustrate that engaging in open-science practices does not necessarily mean a journal's impact factor will decrease.

In closing, improving transparency has many benefits for authors, journals, and users of scientific knowledge. It is not enough to do good research; it is also essential to let others know precisely how you did your research. Reporting information transparently and openly regarding all stages of your research will enhance your research's reproducibility, replicability, trustworthiness, and usefulness.

DISCUSSION QUESTIONS

1. Why is a lack of transparency detrimental to the credibility of social and behavioral science research?

2. What is the difference between reproducibility and replicability? Can a study be reproducible but not replicable, or replicable but not reproducible? Why?

3. What steps can you take to increase transparency regarding your study's theory?

4. How do research design choices (e.g., sample location, data collection procedure) affect reproducibility?

5. How can choices regarding outliers' identification and handling affect results and substantive conclusions? Why does reporting results with and without outliers improve reproducibility?

6. Why does reporting results of all tests of assumptions increase replicability? Discuss the implications of violating the assumption of normality when conducting regression-based analyses.

7. How can we ensure that all authors have access to data, and whether data analysis and results were verified by co-author(s) can contribute to lowering the number of retractions and improving reproducibility?

8. Choose a recently published article in a journal of your choice. Compare the checklists in Tables 15.1-15.5 to what is reported in the article. To what extent did the authors describe their theory, design, measurement, analysis, and results transparently? What is your assessment of the extent to which you can replicate this study?

9. How can editors and reviewers motivate authors to increase transparency in social and behavioral science research?

10. What are some of the barriers that exist to the broader and universal adoption of open-science research? What are your suggestions for accelerating the adoption of open science in social and behavioral science research?

KEY TERMS

aggregation

heavy-tail distribution

impact factor

level of inquiry

level of measurement

level of theory

reproducibility

unit of analysis

NOTES

This chapter is based to a large extent on the following sources:

Aguinis, H., Banks, G. C., Rogelberg, S., & Cascio, W. F. (2020). Actionable recommendations for narrowing the science-practice gap in open science. *Organizational Behavior and Human Decision Processes*, *158*, 27-35. https://doi.org/10.1016/j.obhdp.2020.02.007

Aguinis, H., Cascio, W. F., & Ramani, R. S. (2017). Science's reproducibility and replicability crisis: International business is not immune. *Journal of International Business Studies*, *48*(6), 653-663. https://doi.org/10.1057/s41267-017-0081-0

Aguinis, H., Ramani, R. S., & Alabduljader, N. (2018). What you see is what you get? Enhancing methodological transparency in management research. *Academy of Management Annals*, *12*(1), 83-110. https://doi.org/10.5465/annals.2016.0011

Bergh, D. D., Sharp, B. M., Aguinis, H., & Li, M. (2017). Is there a credibility crisis in strategic management research? Evidence on the reproducibility of study findings. *Strategic Organization*, *15*(3), 423-436. https://doi.org/10.1177/1476127017701076

16 HOW TO ENHANCE THE IMPACT OF YOUR RESEARCH

LEARNING GOALS

By the end of this chapter, you will be able to do the following:

16.1 Defend why you should care about the impact of your research and why we need to broaden the definition of scholarly impact.

16.2 Discuss the use and misuse of journal lists and citations and the new bottom line for valuing academic research ("an A is an A").

16.3 Articulate the reasons for using journal lists in the social and behavioral sciences and the resulting positive and negative consequences.

16.4 Formulate how to broaden the meaning and measurement of scholarly impact and the need for a pluralist conceptualization of impact based on a multidimensional and multistakeholder model.

16.5 Propose how university administrators can enhance impact, including (1) aligning scholarly impact goals with actions and resource-allocation decisions, (2) ensuring that performance management and reward systems are consistent with impact goals, (3) being strategic in selecting a journal list, and (4) developing a strong doctoral program.

16.6 Arrange recommendations for researchers and educators to enhance scholarly impact, including (1) developing a personal scholarly impact plan, (2) becoming an academic decathlete, (3) finding ways to affect multiple impact dimensions simultaneously, and (4) leveraging social media to broaden impact on external stakeholders.

16.7 Asses how you can enhance your scholarly impact by creating a personal impact development plan.

16.8 Prepare your personal impact development plan, including the overall content, developmental activities, context, and university leaders' role in implementing it.

IMPORTANCE OF THE IMPACT OF YOUR RESEARCH

It is no exaggeration to state that the social and behavioral sciences are obsessed with assessing the impact of scholarly work.[1] As a result, most social and behavioral science professional organizations refer to impact in their mission statements and strategic plans.

> ### Example: What Do Professional Organizations Say About Impact?
>
> The strategic plan for the American Psychological Association is called "IMPACT APA."[2] As another example, one of the four Academy of Management strategic intent statements refers to "professional impact: The Academy of Management encourages our members to make a positive difference in the world by supporting scholarship that matters."[3] This strategic intent statement aims to "Define professional impact and for whom" and "engage our colleagues and relevant stakeholders in a reflexive consideration and conversation about the meaning of professional impact."[4]

Who are the scholars with the most significant impact? Which academic departments around the world have the most significant impact based on the aggregated research output of their members? What is the relative impact of individual articles and entire journals? We are very interested in answering these questions because performance management systems in universities, your chances of receiving an offer for an academic position (including admission into a doctoral program), and the allocation of resources and rewards to individuals and departments are determined, at least in part, by the impact of research.[5] But, answering these questions is also critical for consumers of research. As a reader of a research study, you want to know what is and what is not impactful research so you know what to pay attention to.

Accordingly, numerous articles have been written on the relative impact of individual scholars, individual articles, departments, universities, and even entire fields. For example, some authors ranked researchers based on their relative impact.[6] Other research has analyzed the factors that predict an article's impact.[7] Researchers have also provided an inductively-based framework for understanding why certain articles have more impact than others.[8] For example, studies have been conducted on whether meta-analyses focusing on theory building are more impactful than meta-analyses focusing on theory testing.[9] As another illustration, others examined whether specific methodological approaches are more impactful than others.[10] From the perspective of journals, journal editors continuously monitor and report their journals' impact.[11] Regarding the relative impact of different fields, a study showed that the field of management runs a significant "trade deficit" with economics, psychology, and sociology[12] because management journals are cited less frequently in those fields than those fields cite management journals. An alternative perspective notes that this deficit is a good thing because this "may account for what some allege is the parochial nature of the economics literature (reflected in a low level of interdisciplinary knowledge building) as well as an insular pattern of auto-erotic self-referencing (reflected in a high level of intradisciplinary citations)" (p. 154).[13] Overall, this voluminous amount of research shows that impact is one of the strongest currencies in the Academy.

SCHOLARLY IMPACT: INTERNAL AND EXTERNAL

At a surface level, it would seem that the voluminous body of work on the impact of research is quite diverse and heterogeneous. As mentioned in the previous section, some studies have produced rankings of scholars,[14] others have investigated factors likely to affect the impact of individual articles,[15] and some research has focused on the individual level of analysis (i.e., individual articles or individual researchers). In contrast, others addressed the department, university, or even field level of analysis.[16] But, despite the surface-level heterogeneity, this entire work has one important defining feature in common: The definition of "impact." These and many other articles have defined impact using the same conceptual and operational definition: Number of citations. More precisely, scholarly impact is consistently and uniformly assessed by counting the number of times a particular article, articles in a particular journal, an individual's entire body of work, the body of work of the faculty in a department or university, or the body of work produced by an entire field of study, has been cited in scholarly publications. In other words, all these measures of "impact" rely on whether other academics cite the article(s) in their scholarly work. Using **stakeholder theory** as a theoretical backdrop,[17] the social and behavioral science field seems to be primarily concerned with the impact of our scholarly work on *internal stakeholders* (i.e., other members of the Academy).

Many have expressed concern about a science-practice divide in social and behavioral science.[18] Specifically, the concern is that the research produced by scholars does not reach beyond the Academy and may not have a substantive impact on *external stakeholders*, including managers, organizations, policy-makers, and society.[19] So, there is a need to understand the impact on internal and external stakeholders. For example, could it be that researchers ranked highly in their impact on other academics, as assessed by citations, do not enjoy a similarly high degree of impact on other stakeholders—stakeholders outside of the Academy?

How can the impact of scholarship be assessed beyond the Academy? A study including 384 highly cited scholars was conducted to address this issue precisely. However, the measure of impact was more than just the number of citations. It also included a measure of impact at a much broader societal level: The number of pages on the Web as indexed by google.com, specifically residing on non-.edu domains.[20] The number of citations, as used in most research on impact, and the number of Web pages indexed by google.com, as used in this study on the impact on external stakeholders, are similar in that both are general measures of impact. Moreover, both are based on a simple, intuitively understandable, and unidimensional count. However, the big difference is that number of citations refers to the impact on a single stakeholder audience: academics—those writing academic publications. In contrast, the number of pages on google.com captures the impact on stakeholders inside and outside the Academy—academics and the media, public and private firms, governments, and non-profit organizations, among others.

Considering additional similarities between these two impact measures, the number of citations is general and broad and does not explain why a source has been cited. For example, it may be that an article is cited as exemplary research or as an example of the opposite—a poorly designed study. It could be that an article is cited in passing to support the importance and legitimacy of a particular research topic. Or, in contrast, an article may be analyzed and discussed in detail to generate important follow-up questions. In other words, the number of citations is a general measure that is not informative about the type of impact or reason for such impact.[21] Similarly, the number of pages on google.com is a general measure of impact that does not include information about the type of impact or reason for the impact.[22] For example, a researcher may be mentioned on the Web because the media has received their work positively or negatively. Or researchers may be mentioned because they have participated as expert witnesses in a high-profile United States Supreme Court case, an online executive education program, or a consulting project. Or it could be that a researcher has an important online presence because they have given an interview to a newspaper or a blogger has decided to write about a popular press book they have written. Like the number of citations, the number of pages on google.com is a measure of impact regardless of why a researcher is mentioned. Also, just like the number of citations indicates the level of impact on inside stakeholders (i.e., members of the Academy), having very few entries on google.com means that outside stakeholders (i.e., people outside of the Academy) are not paying much attention.[23]

Results of this study showed that the number of citations is very weakly related to the number of Google.com entries (considering the number of years since receiving a doctorate and the total number of articles). In other words, the number of Google entries, which reflects how much stakeholders outside the Academy pay attention to particular scholars, indicates a different type of impact. A constructive replication study, using h-index scores instead of the total number of citations, led to the same substantive conclusion.

Interestingly, when the 384 scholars were ranked based on both the number of citations and the number of Google entries, there were important changes in the rank ordering of individuals based on whether the impact was operationalized considering internal stakeholders (i.e., number of citations) or external stakeholders (i.e., number of Google entries). On average, there was a difference of 100.32 ranks between the lists based on citations and Google entries. Moreover, there were 19 scholars for whom there is a difference of more than 200 ranks across the two lists. A high rank based on citations can be associated with a much lower rank based on Google pages.

Are some scholars influential both on internal and external stakeholders? To do so, this study selected those in the top 100 ranks in terms of both citations and the number of Google entries. Interestingly, 20% (i.e., 8 out of 40) of these most influential individuals, both inside and outside the Academy, are affiliated with Stanford University. Harvard University accounted for 12.5% of such individuals (i.e., 5 out of 40), followed by the University of California (U.C.) Berkeley with 7.5% (i.e., 3 out of 40). Thus, three universities have been able to attract and retain 40% of the 40 individuals with the highest impact inside and outside the Academy. Not surprisingly, each university includes explicit statements about impact in its vision and mission statements.

The following sections will teach you about using and misusing journal lists and citations and the new bottom line for valuing academic research ("an A is an A"). The first section will also include the reasons for using journal lists in the social and behavioral sciences and the positive and negative consequences of this practice. You will then learn how the field can broaden the meaning and measurement of impact and the need for a pluralist conceptualization of impact based on a multidimensional and multistakeholder model. The following section proposes how university administrators can enhance impact, including (1) aligning scholarly impact goals with actions and resource-allocation decisions, (2) ensuring that performance management and reward systems are consistent with impact goals, (3) being strategic in selecting a **journal list**, and (4) developing a strong doctoral program. Next, the chapter describes recommendations for current and future researchers and educators, including (1) developing your **personal scholarly impact plan**, (2) becoming an **academic decathlete**, (3) finding ways to affect multiple impact dimensions simultaneously, and (4) leveraging social media to broaden impact on external stakeholders. The final section offers more detail on how you can enhance your impact by creating your **personal impact development plan (PIDP)**, as well as the steps to prepare your PIDP, including the overall content, developmental activities, as well as the role that context and university leaders will play in implementing it successfully. Following these recommendations will help you achieve the lofty goal that only a small minority of scholars have reached so far: Impact on internal and external stakeholders.

ON THE USE AND MISUSE OF JOURNAL LISTS AS AN INDICATOR OF SCHOLARLY IMPACT

Following a centuries-old tradition, modern research universities ground their legitimacy and authority in the value of published knowledge, which provides an objective and measurable standard for institutional performance and control.[24] This publication ethos has gradually become embedded in universities' growing managerialism and economic rationality,[25] or what some critics have referred to as the "McDonaldization" of academe,[26] the "market" university,[27] and the "managerial" university.[28] For example, university performance management and resource allocation systems are increasingly driven by a corporate-audit culture where resources and rewards are contingent on quantifiable research value and impact measures.[29]

"An A is an A": The New Bottom Line for Valuing Academic Research

An increasingly common method for measuring the value and impact of research derives from the quality of the academic journals within which the research is published.[30] In other words, the higher the judged quality of the journal, the higher the attributed quality and hence the value of its published articles.[31] The same procedure is used to measure the total value of research produced by a particular individual, which is done by simply adding all articles published in journals deemed high quality. This journal-proxy method provides a seemingly objective, standardized, and generalizable measure of research value that can apply across individual researchers, research disciplines, and academic organizations.

The growing use of journal-proxy measures of research value has increased pressure on academics to publish in elite journals to gain professional rewards and status.[32] In many universities around the world, these elite journals are identified by different labels, including "A," "top," "premiere," and other designations such as "A+," "A*," or even "A++" and "A**" that indicate their high status. This chapter refers to them simply as "**A-journals**."

The need to identify A-journals has led to many journal ranking lists that vary by disciplinary orientation and the metric used to rank journals.[33] These lists indicate the meritorious quality of the journals and, by extension, the respective scholarly publications included therein and the researchers who authored those publications. The use of such lists in assessing the bottom line for valuing academic research and its impact (i.e., how many A's) has spread across universities in Asia, Europe, North America, and South America,[34] and academic disciplines.[35]

The distinction between "A" and other journals emerged some time ago.[36] However, what is ominously different today is the *excessive* attention to journal lists that signal which journal articles count in promotion, tenure, and rewards decisions and which do not.[37] This "an A is an A" dictum is an expressive addendum to the general call to "publish or perish."

The institutional logic of universities has changed in the last two or three decades, forcing them to change how they operate and function.[38] Universities have undergone many transformations, making the issue of faculty evaluation and rewards suddenly more salient.[39] Indeed, the "an A is an A" phenomenon has now reached a point that, in many cases, faculty recruiting committees and promotion and tenure panels readily discuss "how many A's" a candidate has published and "how many A's" are needed for a favorable decision. At the same time, conversations about the distinctive intellectual value of a publication are often secondary to its categorical membership in journals.[40] For researchers, this categorization can translate into a stark dichotomy and imposed choice between scholarship that counts (i.e., published in A-journals) and scholarship that does not count (i.e., published anywhere else).[41] This phenomenon has daunting consequences for researchers, the scientific validity and usefulness of the knowledge they produce, and the sustainability of universities.

The Use of Journal Lists in the Social and Behavioral Sciences

Social and behavioral science scholars have typically addressed the use of journal lists informally among themselves in the literature addressing broader field assessments[42] or directly in professional presentations and publications devoted to the topic.[43]

> ### Example: A-Journal Counting and Chances of Landing an Academic Job
>
> A-journal counting has become routine and has taken on some of the trappings of a sports competition. For instance, publishing in an A-journal is often referred to as getting a "hit" to use a baseball analogy or a "goal" to use soccer (i.e., "football" outside the United States). As experienced by some authors after attending academic conferences, "people spoke in awe of 'big hits.'[44] Those whose work had made it into the 'top five' journals were paid homage by junior colleagues. If anything, this kind of language has become more prevalent." For example, a typical job posting for academic jobs will include: "Applicants for this position must have a Ph.D. in a [specific field] or related discipline and a strong record/potential for publication in the A journals."

In sports, the phrase "a win is a win" refers to the consensual bottom line in those competitions, which is that how the game was won is not as important as the fact that it was won. In many ways, it seems a point has been reached where the bottom line is that "an A is an A." Many other academic disciplines have reached a similar point.[45] Consistent with the principles of tournament theory,[46] faculty compete against each other for the finite number of pages available in the few A-journals. Just as individual faculty within a department compete, departments within a college are also engaged in the competition. At an even higher level, the different colleges are also occupied in cutthroat competition, as are the universities that house them. Many committees concerned with faculty recruiting, promotion and tenure, and performance appraisal are increasingly interested in faculty's research records regarding the "number of A's," which is equated with the "number of wins." Important academic rewards, such as intellectual status, job placement, tenure and promotion, salary, and research funds, are increasingly contingent on these "victories."[47] In an eloquent summary statement, some authors argued that "today's challenge to the integrity of scholarship does not come from external demands for ideological conformity, but rather from escalating competition for publication space in leading journals that is changing the internal dynamics of our community" (p. 413).[48]

This suggests that A-journal counting practices are sufficient to warrant analyzing its causes and effects and exploring possible solutions to their unintended negative outcomes. There is an instrumental value of A-journal counting in assessing research value and producing institutional and researcher hierarchies in the academe. After all, research institutions' rankings and prestige are determined at least to some extent by their members' A-journal publications.[49] And rankings are becoming the bottom line for many universities, schools/colleges, and departments.[50] Also, for many universities and schools trying to encourage more and higher-quality research, establishing lists of journals that should be targeted, albeit far from perfect, may be beneficial compared to no target. However, a concern is that using this singular measure in the results-only, the bottom-line approach reduces prized scholarship to a simple count of "number of A's." Furthermore, measuring research value by exclusively counting A-journal publications can perilously neglect how researchers cope with A-journal competition and progressively cultivate scholarship while remaining true to the meaning and value of their intellectual pursuit—and the impact of our research.

Reasons for the Use of Journal Lists

Explanations for the rise of A-journal counting practices include larger cultural, political, and economic forces shaping higher education globally, particularly universities' institutional arrangements for acquiring and allocating resources and controlling and rewarding performance.[51] However, two powerful mechanisms drive the "an A is an A" phenomenon: performance management systems and research accountability.

Performance Management Systems. Like many organizations, universities struggle with the need for performance management systems that distribute rewards in a systemic, standardized, and fair manner while not relying heavily on self-reported performance measures.[52] Consequently, journal lists have gradually become the arbiter for determining the value and impact of research. As some authors documented, the use of journal ranking lists to evaluate researcher productivity and quality of research began as an attempt by university administrators overseeing diverse departments to create a standard measure of the value of research performance across those units.[53] By instituting a journal ranking system, administrators sought to replace subjective evaluations of research quality with "common, intersubjective, verifiable standards, independent of human individuality" (p. 120).[54] Because researchers have considerable freedom in defining their research agenda and how to pursue it, many universities and their functional departments developed lists of A-journals to evaluate the quality of research output.[55] These journal lists enabled universities and departments to establish "quanta," a basis for measurement intended to be equitable and provide performance measurement guidelines for administrators.[56] These lists were intended to supplement, not replace, the more traditional qualitative assessment of research based on internal and external peer reviews of the research itself. Like many other quanta, however, journal ranking lists, initially a loosely-structured framework to aid administrators, have become reified and are now a taken-for-granted measure of the value of social and behavioral science research within the academic community.[57]

The compilation and analysis of journal ranking lists are now ubiquitous in the social and behavioral sciences and many other academic disciplines,[58] including marketing,[59] finance,[60] accounting,[61] and international business.[62] Interestingly, crystallization around the use of journal lists to gauge the value of social and behavioral science research has occurred despite growing evidence that so-called A-journals are not necessarily better at publishing insightful and influential articles than non-A journals or other sources of academic contribution, such as books or chapters in edited volumes.[63] Moreover, a bibliometric study of more than 85,000 papers published in 168 management and business journals found that top-rated journals strongly favor empirical studies that use quantitative methods applied to large datasets.[64] Thus, counting publications in A-journals means that "data that cannot be readily quantified are marginalized and rendered invisible, and proxy measures end up representing the thing itself" (p. 775),[65] thereby contributing to the new bottom line for valuing academic research.

Research Accountability. In addition to performance management systems, a second mechanism contributing to the "an A is an A" phenomenon is the growing pressure on universities to be accountable for the costs and benefits of their research. The issue of accountability is relevant not only to social and behavioral science but also to many other fields in the humanities and sciences.[66]

METHODS IN PRACTICE
THE PATH TOWARD SOCIAL AND BEHAVIORAL SCIENCE RESEARCH LEGITIMACY

Business schools house many social and behavioral scientists conducting research in psychology, sociology, political science, economics, and other disciplines. In the late 1950s, business schools began the long, arduous trek from vocational- or practitioner-oriented

trade schools to research-focused institutions.[67] Fueled by the demand for more professionally educated managers and the stinging rebukes of the quality of the research and teaching
of their faculty, business schools adopted the scholarly paradigm of the social sciences as
their path to legitimacy.[68] And this approach entailed defining and measuring the value or
quality of their research production.[69]

The need to quantify the value of research has become an urgent issue given the growing competitive pressures facing universities resulting from less government funding, greater
emphasis on rankings, mounting faculty shortage, and universities' entrenched research values.[70]
The dominance of the new bottom line for valuing academic research is an inevitable outcome of
this need to measure scholarly knowledge's value and link it to financial outcomes.[71] The practice of measuring and rewarding A-journal publications is starkly visible as many universities use
this metric to implement pay-for-article compensation systems,[72] provide faculty with summer
financial support (e.g., from 1/9th to 3/9ths of additional salary in many U.S. universities), reduce
teaching loads, and determine faculty base salary.[73] By enabling the measurement of what was
once the abstract concept of "desirable research productivity," universities can use A-journal
"hit" counts to determine whether the price they pay (in terms of faculty salary and research
funding) is commensurate with the value of the research output they receive, and then share
this information with external stakeholders including current and potential students, donors,
alumni, and funding agencies.

In addition to comparing individual researchers, journal lists can be used to compare departments or specific research domains across universities.[74] For example, deans and department
chairs can compute the number of A-journal articles published by their school's faculty and compare it to the number of A-journal publications by faculty at competing and aspiring institutions.
This information can be helpful for accreditation, fundraising, and other purposes.[75]

In sum, the new bottom line to measure the value of research follows naturally from the
practices used by universities to make evaluating research more standardized, transparent, and
fair. It is also the consequence of increasing pressures on universities to become more accountable and to provide evidence regarding the costs and benefits of the research they produce.

Positive and Negative Consequences of the New Bottom Line for Valuing Academic Research

This new bottom line for valuing academic research based on the "An A is an A" dictum has a
significant positive and negative impact on current and future researchers, the knowledge they
produce, and the universities that employ them.

Table 16.1 summarizes the positive and negative consequences of excessive A-journal counting practices for measuring the value of social and behavioral science research. Although journal
lists may initially have helped focus many universities and researchers on improving research
output and focusing their research efforts, their negative consequences currently outweigh their
positive effects. Like financial decisions in corporations, researchers and the universities that
employ them must show an adequate return on investment to remain viable. This bottom-line
and auditing mentality is at odds with the ethos of research that seeks to uncover important
truths having scholarly and practical significance.[76] Simply counting A-journal articles and
using this as the bottom line for valuing academic research places the integrity of our research
and our identity as researchers in conflict with the demands of exclusively results-oriented performance management systems.[77] Moreover, the new bottom line for valuing academic research

+/-	Consequence
TABLE 16.1 ■ **Summary of Positive and Negative Consequences of the New Bottom Line for Valuing Academic Research: "An A is an A"**	
Positive	1. Helps develop clear standards for judging the value of research and avoids having to translate subjective opinions about the quality of research into quantifiable ratings
	2. Increases the transparency of schools' performance management systems as well as the actual and perceived fairness of the procedures used to make decisions about the allocation of rewards
	3. Helps faculty effectively counter biased criticism of research by scholars in other fields that may adversely affect reward allocations
	4. Protects junior faculty members from biased decisions on the part of their department chairs (and other administrators), who, in many cases, are senior faculty members who are no longer research active and no longer have the necessary skills to evaluate the quality, rigor, and relevance of any given study
	5. Provides clear objectives and guidelines for training students and helping junior scholars establish and manage their careers
	6. Can serve as a self-selection mechanism for students and faculty
	7. Offers information and exemplars about the type of theorizing, methodology, and reporting that is required to publish in A-journals
Negative	1. Produces generalized negative effects on the field's research methods, knowledge generation, and social dynamics
	2. Increases the prevalence of questionable research practices (e.g., use and misuse of control variables, selective reporting of hypothesis tests, hypothesizing after results are known (HARKing), data transformations)
	3. Incentivizes researchers to produce as many A-journal articles as possible without necessarily considering whether results are reproducible and advance the broader conversation in the field or have meaningful, practical implications
	4. Results in an excessive division of labor and the proliferation of multi-author articles, which can lead to reciprocal systems of sham authorship and publication credit
	5. Contributes to the growing trend of doing and publishing research primarily for other researchers—not for other stakeholders, including the broader practice community
	6. Narrows the institutional base supporting field of social and behavioral science research, which can result in less variety in the field's knowledge
	7. Reduces heterogeneity and innovation in the field of social and behavioral science research through preferred methodological approaches less suited to the exploration of knowledge that seeks to discover novel phenomena and invent a new theory
	8. Decreases emphasis on what researchers care about in doing the field of social and behavioral science research because it moves the locus of control for social and behavioral science research from the researcher to the external market, thereby turning an intrinsically driven research process into one that is extrinsically motivated and controlled

Source: Adapted from Aguinis, Cummings, Ramani, & Cummings (2020).

means that research can become monetized: Each A-journal publication has a tangible monetary value.[78] The consequences of this conflict can have dire implications for the scientific validity and usefulness of our research and our careers as academics because, given that A-journal publications are readily monetizable, many faculty choose not to invest in activities that are nonmonetizable (e.g., mentoring a struggling student or junior faculty member) or not portable (e.g., institution building).

In conclusion, "An A is an A" is a common mantra, signaling the high value of articles published in A-journals. Although the phrase may seem a simple declaration, it has come to represent the decisive role that A-journal publications have come to play in the social and behavioral sciences and the new bottom line for valuing academic research. Indeed, an emphasis on A-journal publication, while laudable in certain respects, has had severely detrimental effects on the conduct, content, and reporting in social and behavioral science research; the behavior of social and behavioral science scholars; the implication of academic value; and the success of universities and the satisfaction of their stakeholders. This A-journal mindset has become institutionalized over the past few decades as universities responded to increasing pressure to measure the value of their research for performance management and accountability purposes. The realization of the dominance of this new bottom line for valuing academic research provides a foundation for moving the field of social and behavioral science research beyond A-journal strictures. So, there is a clear and urgent need to broaden how we conceptualize and measure scholarly impact, an issue addressed next.

HOW TO BROADEN THE MEANING AND MEASUREMENT OF IMPACT

Most current and future researchers and educators in the social and behavioral sciences want to and even *need* to have an impact.[79] That is, to have a significant or major effect on different types of stakeholders because making a difference is why most current and future scholars choose a research career.[80] Therefore, we must consider how our research affects other researchers and additional stakeholders.

Scholarly Impact: A Multidimensional and Multistakeholder Model

Figure 16.1 summarizes the **multidimensional and multistakeholder model of scholarly impact.** This figure shows that different impact dimensions are directly associated with specific and unique stakeholders. For the *theory and research dimension*, the key stakeholders are other researchers, and impact is usually measured using citations—the extent to which a scholar influences the thinking and work of other scholars. For the *education dimension*, the aspiration is to have a long-lasting influence on student development by disseminating relevant knowledge and its applications. For the *organizations dimension*, the aspiration is to influence practitioners: managers and consultants who use research-generated knowledge. Finally, for the *society dimension*, the goal is to influence policymakers (e.g., legislators, government officials).

An important aspect of the conceptual model in Figure 16.1 is that scholarly impact on one of the dimensions is not necessarily associated with impact on the others. For example, the study described at the beginning of this chapter found that citations (i.e., a measure of impact on theory and research) explained less than 3% of the variance in the number of mentions in Google pages (i.e., a measure of impact on organizations and society).[81] Therefore, the fact that a scholar has a high degree of influence on other scholars, based on their high citation count, does not necessarily mean that she has the same high degree of impact on other stakeholders, including students, organizations, and society.

FIGURE 16.1   ■   Scholarly Impact: Dimensions and Stakeholders

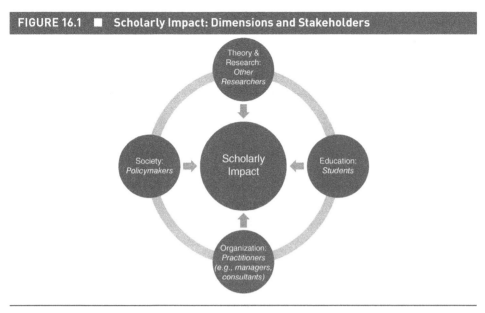

Source: Aguinis, Yu, & Tosun (2021).

The model in Figure 16.1 builds upon a pluralist conceptualization of scholarly impact.[82] Because it is multidimensional and multistakeholder, the model in Figure 16.1 makes it explicit that there is a need to (1) use different measures of impact depending on which dimension and stakeholder are the intended targets, (2) be locally sensitive as institutions may have different strategic priorities over time regarding their targeted dimensions and stakeholders, (3) understand that the impact dimensions can be complementary and should not be viewed as being mutually exclusive, and (4) consider the possibility that specific actions may affect more than one dimension and type of stakeholder simultaneously.

As an illustration of the broad applicability of this model, consider two studies that examined the views of university program heads for evaluating faculty's impact.[83] Specifically, these studies revealed that there had been a clear shift in emphasis toward the theory and research dimension because many universities focus on publications in top-tier and SSCI-indexed journals given their placement on rankings and impact indicators (e.g., the average number of citations received by articles published in those journals). These studies also revealed the increasing value of impacting organizations (i.e., practitioners, including managers and consultants) by highlighting the importance of, for example, organizing conferences for researchers and practitioners. Regarding the impact on education, there is also the expectation that faculty members will supervise doctoral and master's students and influence their careers.[84]

This model also allows us to uncover possible shifts from certain dimensions and stakeholders (e.g., organizations/practitioners) to others (e.g., theory and research/other researchers) and make explicit which ones are given more or less importance (e.g., publications in top-tier journals are given more value than publications in journals targeting practitioners). Another advantage of this model is that it makes these choices visible, which sometimes may be implicit or explicit. In other words, the model allows you to understand a university's actions and resource-allocation decisions about impact by classifying them in terms of their targeted dimensions and stakeholders (e.g., more resources and rewards on the theory and research compared to the organizations dimension). Finally, the model is value-free in that it does not dictate which dimension and type of stakeholders should be more relevant—but it allows you to understand quickly, based on observed actions and resource allocations, implicit underlying values about which dimensions and stakeholders are given more weight.

How can the model in Figure 16.1 be implemented in practice to assess scholarly impact in a pluralistic manner? What types of measures can we use? Let's address these issues next.

A Pluralist Conceptualization of Scholarly Impact: Multiple Stakeholders and Measures

As mentioned in the previous section, although measures relying on citations can serve as an indicator of impact on other researchers, and they are helpful for that purpose, they do not necessarily provide information about the impact on other stakeholders such as university students, corporate practitioners, non-governmental organizations, government policymakers, and society in general. There is an urgent need for a formal and broader conceptualization of impact that includes multiple stakeholders, particularly if you want your research to have impact beyond the Academy.[85]

In addition to multiple stakeholders, a pluralist conceptualization of scholarly impact includes multiple impact measures. Impact comes in different forms, and using a single measure of impact, such as citations, does not capture the multidimensional nature of this construct. For example, a social scientist can affect organizational practices by teaching executives. In contrast, another may impact that same stakeholder group by writing practitioner-oriented articles in such outlets as *Business Horizons* and *Organizational Dynamics*. Yet other scholars may influence practice through consulting, serving as an expert witness in high-profile court cases, media appearances, or by spending a sabbatical in business practice as translators of research results or as researchers of practitioner-oriented issues.[86]

Figure 16.2 includes a formal representation of a pluralist model of scholarly impact. Impact is viewed as a **superordinate** (i.e., higher-order) and multistakeholder factor ξ, which affects impact on various stakeholders labeled η_1 to η_k. In turn, the impact on each of these stakeholders is assessed by multiple measures (i.e., x_1 to x_N). For the sake of simplicity, Figure 16.2 includes

---

FIGURE 16.2 ■ **A Pluralist Conceptualization of Impact: Multiple Stakeholders and Multiple Measures**

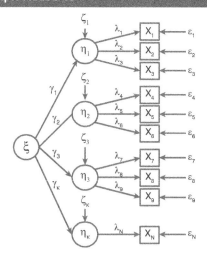

Source: Aguinis, Shapiro, Antonacopoulou, & Cummings (2014).

only three measures for each (i.e., three xs for each η), but there could be more or fewer indicators of impact on each.

A pluralist conceptualization views scholarly impact as a higher-order construct, including impact on various stakeholders inside and outside the Academy. In turn, multiple measures assess the impact on each of these stakeholders. For example, referring to Figure 16.2 and assuming an interest in conceptualizing and measuring impact on three types of stakeholders only, η_1 could represent academics, η_2 executive students, and η_3 the media. Given that these stakeholders are considered important by a particular university, measures can be used to assess the scholarly impact on each of them. For example, x_1 to x_3 would be three indicators of impact on academics: citations based on Web of Science, citations based on Google Scholar, and i10-index (i.e., the number of publications with at least ten citations each). Following this example, x_4 to x_6 would be three indicators of impact on executive students. These measures could include a combination of self-reported and third-party data. For example, these could include how executive students believe what they have learned will help them improve their effectiveness at work. Finally, regarding impact on the media (i.e., η_3), x_7 to x_9 would be measures of this latent construct. These could include, for example, the number of newspaper outlets (both online and print) that mention a scholar's research and youtube.com entries, both of which can be collected using Web-based tools generally referred to as "**altmetrics**." These measures have great potential and should be investigated as part of a future research agenda on this pluralist conceptualization because they allow for assessing impact on multiple stakeholders, not just academics.

As summarized in Table 16.2, this multistakeholder and multi-measure approach differs significantly from a traditional approach to scholarly impact. First, the prevailing impact model relies on citations, sometimes of various kinds. But even if multiple measures of citations are used, impact is considered from the perspective of one type of stakeholder only: researchers. In contrast, a pluralist conceptualization is *multistakeholder* because it involves assessing impact on researchers and other stakeholders interested in the knowledge we create. These stakeholders might include students at various levels (e.g., undergraduate, master's, doctoral, executive), corporate employees, unions, government policymakers, funding agencies, non-governmental organizations, accreditation organizations, and the media. The choice of which stakeholders to consider will vary, depending on the purpose for measuring scholarly impact. A pluralist conceptualization argues that *multiple* stakeholders should at least be considered explicitly in these decisions rather than habitual attention to only researchers.

A second significant difference between this proposed solution and the prevailing approach is that the former considers more than one operationalization or measure to assess each stakeholder's impact. Thus, a pluralist framework is *multi-measure* because it involves assessing impact via varying impact-related measures. Specifically, a pluralist conceptualization includes assessing citations as one indicator of impact on researchers, such as citations based on Web of Knowledge and Google Scholar and, for example, the i10-index. However, it does not assume that citation counting (in any of its varieties) is the only indicator. Equally importantly, it does not assume that citation count is a perfectly valid and reliable impact indicator. For example, other indicators of impact on researchers might include the number and types of scholarly awards received, the extent to which instructors at other institutions use an individual's work,[87] the number and quality of invited presentations at professional meetings (including keynote addresses), and workshops delivered at professional conferences and elsewhere that include researchers as the targeted audience, among others. Multiple measures can also be used to assess scholarly impact on other stakeholders.

TABLE 16.2 ■ Comparison of a Traditional and a Pluralist Approach to Conceptualizing and Measuring Scholarly Impact		
	Traditional Approach	**Pluralist Conceptualization**
Conceptualization of Scholarly Impact	• Impact is considered from the perspective of one type of stakeholder only: other academics.	• Impact is considered from the perspective of multiple stakeholders, including academics but also additional types of stakeholders having an interest in management knowledge, such as students at various levels (e.g., undergraduate, master's, doctoral, executive), executives, government policymakers, not-for-profit organizations, and the media, among others.
	• Zero-sum conceptualization of impact such that impact on researchers (i.e., via publications in "A-journals" and citations) is often assumed to be a detriment to impact on other stakeholders (i.e., teaching executive education courses), and vice versa.	• Allows for non-zero relationships between the overall impact on various stakeholder groups and non-zero relationships among impact indicators within and across stakeholder groups.
Measurement of Scholarly Impact	• Citation count, including the possibility of including multiple measures of citations (e.g., Web of Knowledge, Google Scholar, h-index).	• Considers more than one measure for assessing impact on each stakeholder and does not assume that citation count is a perfectly valid and reliable indicator of impact.
	• The same measures of citation counts are used in all contexts.	• Measures of impact can be adapted to a specific local context, and they can also be revised over time based on changes in strategic priorities.
	• Given the reliance on a single measure of impact, adjusting the relative weights of different impact indicators is impossible.	• The relative weight of impact measures can be adjusted based on the relative importance of different stakeholder groups. In addition, they can be used in a compensatory manner (i.e., a low score on a measure can be offset by a high score in another) or in a non-compensatory manner (i.e., a minimum threshold of impact required for each measure before computing an overall score of impact)

Source: Adapted from Aguinis, Shapiro, Antonacopoulou, & Cummings (2014).

The third distinction between this proposed solution and the traditional approach to impact is that a pluralist conceptualization can be adapted to a specific local context and revised over time based on changes in strategic priorities. As such, a pluralist conceptualization of impact can be *locally-sensitive*. For example, a university might target two key stakeholder groups regarding impact; another school might decide that there are five essential stakeholder groups. A pluralist conceptualization can accommodate such lofty goals as mitigating inequality and injustice within a particular societal context and even improving ecological viability by including non-profit organizations as stakeholders. Such a perspective would be consistent with a critical management worldview. These goals should be prioritized in defining and measuring impact because they are value-based and aligned with the goals of specific stakeholder groups, such as not-for-profit organizations and charities rather than business corporations. Thus, rather than focusing on the same type and number of stakeholders, this proposed solution enables changing them across and within schools over time based on an institution's strategic priorities. In short, a pluralist conceptualization is flexible and adaptive to changes in strategic priorities.

A fourth distinction is that a pluralist approach can be adjusted based on the relative importance of different stakeholder groups. As such, it can be *stakeholder-sensitive*. First and more specifically, a pluralist perspective on impact can be used in a compensatory manner. For example, the same overall impact score can be achieved by having a moderate score on one stakeholder and a very high score on another or reversing those scores between the two types of stakeholders. On the other hand, if there is a strategic decision that impacts a particular stakeholder group twice as important compared to the impact on another group, weights on measures of impact on those groups can be adjusted accordingly. Second, a pluralist conceptualization can be used in a non-compensatory manner. For example, suppose a particular stakeholder group is considered essential from a strategic standpoint. In that case, a minimum overall impact score for that group might be desired, combining more than one measure of impact. The use of a minimum threshold impact measure is illustrated by universities that encourage faculty members to focus research on publishing a certain number of "A-hits" to earn tenure and promotion, and only after doing so, to broaden their research goals and to publish outlets in ways that appeal to a broader readership, thus promoting a "sequential impact strategy."

Finally, a pluralist conceptualization departs from the assumption underlying the traditional model that the impact on one type of stakeholder is detrimental to the impact on other stakeholders. Specifically, a pluralist approach departs from the current win-lose or zero-sum conceptualization of research (i.e., publications in top-tier journals) at the expense of practice (i.e., assisting in changing the governance structure of a large multi-national corporation); research (i.e., producing knowledge) at the expense of service (i.e., devoting time and effort to the profession); and rigor (i.e., producing knowledge that mainly targets an academic audience) at the expense of relevance (i.e., producing knowledge that mainly targets a practitioner audience).[88] Instead of viewing each of these types of impact as inescapable tradeoffs, a pluralist conceptualization suggests that there can be *synergies across the various stakeholders* in terms of impact, such that more impact on one stakeholder leads to more impact on others—a possibility that again is illustrated by the sequential impact strategy described earlier. However, there is a potential problem with starting a career with an exclusive focus on basic research and then trying later to produce work that appeals to a broader audience. This career sequence can discourage scholars from seeking synergistic scholar-practitioner partnerships until later. By this time, synergies may be less possible because scholars' identities would be tied to their already-published worldview.

In summary, in contrast to the traditional zero-sum approach to assessing impact (which relies primarily, if not exclusively, on counting citations in various ways by only members of the Academy), a pluralist approach assesses the extent to which specific observable measures of impact are indicators for more than one stakeholder group. The extent to which impact on specific stakeholders is related to the impact on others.

ACTIONS THAT UNIVERSITY ADMINISTRATORS, RESEARCHERS, AND EDUCATORS CAN TAKE TO ENHANCE SCHOLARLY IMPACT

There are two key agents of scholarly impact. First, university administrators (e.g., department chairs, deans, research center directors, and vice presidents for research) play a critical role in leadership because they have decision-making authority over performance management and reward systems that influence faculty priorities and effort.[89] So, university administrators play a central role regarding which particular impact dimensions may be targeted for improvement. For example, a survey of university program heads mostly recognized the increased role of top-tier SSCI-indexed journals as highly valued and impactful contributions.[90]

Second, you, as current and future researchers and educators, are the agents who generate impact through your research, teaching, and service activities. Today's academic job market is hyper-competitive, and universities are increasingly interested in hiring and promoting impactful faculty. In addition, most academics are intrinsically motivated to do impactful work regardless of extrinsic rewards associated with impact (e.g., salary increases, promotion, research and teaching support, summer support).[91]

So, what can university administrators, researchers, and educators do to enhance scholarly impact? Let's address administrators first and then researchers and educators.

University Administrators

As a preview, Table 16.3 includes a summary of recommendations and implementation guidelines regarding actions that university administrators can take to enhance impact.

TABLE 16.3 ■ Enhancing Scholarly Impact: Recommendations for University Administrators	
Recommendations	**Implementation Guidelines**
1. **Align scholarly impact goals with actions and resource-allocation decisions**	As an implementation example, if a university's strategic impact priority is theory and research, then • Recruit senior faculty with known research records to fill endowed chairs and professorships • Engage in external fundraising to support research • Establish formal mentoring programs for early-career faculty • Provide methodological training so researchers' skills are updated on an ongoing basis • Provide clear guidelines to administrators of all levels on how to measure impact on theory and research (e.g., include an increase in endowed chairs and professorships through deans' fundraising efforts, research expenditure increase from both public and private funding sources, increased number of journal publications with desired visibility and impact as well as citation-based metrics)

Recommendations	Implementation Guidelines
2. **Ensure that performance management and reward systems are consistent with impact goals**	● Implement a portfolio approach to performance management because not all faculty members are typically able to influence all dimensions at a similarly high level ● Recognize that some faculty members may excel at one impact dimension, whereas others may excel at another ● Allocate different weights to different dimensions of impact ● Adjust the weights over time as faculty member's interests and trajectory change ● Acknowledge and reward impact dimensions important to the university
3. **Be strategic in selecting a journal list**	● Reexamine the journal list to motivate faculty to engage in research that can affect other researchers but also other stakeholders—the education, organizations, and society dimensions of impact ● Use a journal list as a tool to measure performance and allocate rewards and thereby enhance impact, but the selection of journals needs to be consistent with the type of impact a university desires ● In addition to theory and research, if the goal is to impact other dimensions, then include journals devoted to them, such as those focusing on the scholarship of teaching (i.e., influencing the education dimension and students as stakeholders)
4. **Develop a strong doctoral program**	● Consider that investing in the doctoral program is a long-term commitment critical for several impact dimensions because benefits include publications (i.e., theory and research dimension), but reputation as well ● Provide teaching opportunities so doctoral students develop their pedagogical skills ● Mentor and train students to write practitioner-oriented articles and learn how to bridge theory and practice early in their training ● Consider developing a doctorate of practice program to affect the organizations and society dimensions of impact
5. **Promote practical knowledge and applications**	● Coordinate with the development office, career center, and alum office to formulate a strategy for bridging the gap between education and research with industry so faculty can have broader industry exposure ● Forge a partnership with local private organizations and public agencies to provide access to faculty and students for experiential learning and applied research ● Institutionalize faculty consulting practice that combines with experiential learning projects because student involvement in consulting projects also enhances impact on the education dimension. ● Provide incentives for faculty to choose to spend part of their sabbaticals conducting applied research in an organization rather than another university

Source: Aguinis, Yu, & Tosun (2021).

Recommendation #1: Align Scholarly Impact Goals with Actions and Resource-Allocation Decisions

University administrators must ensure alignment among strategic impact priorities, actions, and resource allocation decisions. For example, suppose a university's strategic priority is to impact theory and research. In that case, actions may involve recruiting senior faculty with known research records to fill endowed chairs and professorships, engaging with external stakeholders to generate funds to be used for research, establishing formal mentoring programs for early-career faculty, and providing methodological training, so researchers' skills are updated on an ongoing basis. Given this particular illustration, and to ensure strategic alignment, this university would provide clear guidelines to administrators at all levels on measuring impact on theory and research. These measures can include an increase in endowed chairs and professorships through deans' fundraising efforts, research expenditure increase from both public and private funding sources, and an increased number of journal articles with desired visibility and impact as well as citations and its variants (e.g., total citations, h-index—as measured by different databases including Clarivate Web of Science, Google Scholar, and Scopus).

On the other hand, a lack of strategic alignment between the most critical impact dimensions and actions and resource-allocation decisions creates confusion and unintended effects. To continue with this illustration, if this university aspires to impact theory and research but does not offer necessary resources (e.g., reduced teaching loads for top researchers and summer support so faculty can allocate time to research), the most impactful research performers will likely leave.[92]

The recommendation is not necessarily to invest resources in one dimension. Instead, the point is to make resource allocations so that they are directly related to a unit's or university's strategic priorities regarding impact.

Recommendation #2: Ensure that Performance Management and Reward Systems Are Consistent with Impact Goals

University administrators must implement transparent performance management systems to incentivize faculty to focus on the targeted impact dimensions and stakeholders.[93] University administrators are fully aware of the idiosyncratic talent of the faculty. They should tap into their skills and talent accordingly, given that not all faculty members can typically influence all dimensions at a similarly high level. Therefore, as their citations demonstrate, some faculty members may excel at the theory and research dimension. On the other hand, others may excel at the society dimension—as demonstrated by their involvement as expert witness in a court case with implications for policy-making. Yet others may demonstrate their highest impact on education by, for example, writing a best-selling textbook or teaching case.

METHODS IN PRACTICE
USING A PORTFOLIO APPROACH FOR MEASURING (RESEARCH) PERFORMANCE

The recommendation is to implement a portfolio approach to performance management in which all the impact dimensions important to the university are acknowledged and rewarded. The scholarly impact model in Figure 16.2 allows universities to allocate different weights to different impact dimensions. Also, these weights can be adjusted over time as a faculty member's interests and career trajectory change. For example, suppose a faculty member is equally focused on theory and research, and education. Their overall performance score may be based on 50% for each of these two impact dimensions. But, this model is flexible in that, for example, another faculty member may weigh 30% for theory and research and 70% for education. Over time, such weight allocation can change across individuals and within an individual to consider that people's efforts and interests may change as they progress through the academic ranks. Accordingly, each faculty member's valuable contribution to the different impact dimensions can be recognized and rewarded based on their skills and interests.

Recommendation #3: Be Strategic in Selecting a Journal List

University administrators face increasing pressure from competing institutions to hire and retain faculty who publish in "A-journals."[94] Journal lists define what a top journal is and what is not. Moreover, the number of articles published in those top journals usually affects university rankings,[95] such as the popular QS World University Rankings.[96] Accordingly, it is unsurprising that many university administrators push faculty to publish in those journals because that helps improve rankings. Similarly, it is unsurprising that deans and other university administrators view other scholarly activities, such as writing books, chapters, and textbooks, as less important.[97]

As mentioned earlier, there are several advantages and disadvantages of relying on a journal list.[98] Some of these advantages include (1) setting standards for determining the value of research, (2) showing transparency and fairness of performance assessment and reward systems, (3) reducing possible bias held by researchers from other fields, (4) protecting junior faculty from biased decisions, and (5) establishing guidelines for doctoral student training and early career faculty development. However, chiefly relying on the A-journals for judging research impact has the following disadvantages[99]: (1) generalizing negative effects on the field's research methods, knowledge generation, and social dynamics; (2) increasing use of questionable research practices (QRPs); (3) motivating only counting the frequency of publications in A-journals without consideration for replication or contributions to a broader discourse engaging different stakeholders (e.g., managerial or policy implications); (4) increasing of multi-authorship which leads to reciprocal systems of sham authorship and publication credit; (5) a narrowing focus on impact on other researchers exclusively; (6) stifling innovative exploration for new phenomena and theorizing due to preferred use of certain methodologies; (8) discouraging researchers' communications with external stakeholders; and (9) incentivizing faculty to focus primarily on immediately monetizable (e.g., A-publications associated with summer support) versus nonmonetizable activities (e.g., mentoring a struggling junior faculty member and institution building).

Realizing the positive and negative effects of using A-journals to evaluate faculty impact and determine rewards, university administrators need to reexamine their journal list to motivate faculty to engage in research that can influence stakeholders that matter the most. A journal list is recommended to measure performance, allocate rewards, and enhance impact. But, like any tool, there is a need to be strategic in using it. Specifically, the selection of journals must be consistent with the type of impact a university desires. For example, schools strive for teaching excellence by linking theory and practice in classroom instructions. Many faculty, therefore, conduct pedagogical research to advance the scholarship of teaching (e.g., the effectiveness of various instructional methods, student learning behaviors, and online teaching and learning).

Recommendation #4: Develop a Strong Doctoral Program

University administrators face increasing pressure in managing doctoral programs due to budget constraints. The good news is that investing in a doctoral program is a long-term commitment critical for several impact dimensions. Benefits from the doctoral program are not just publications (i.e., theory and research dimension) but reputation. Schools with doctoral programs produce loyal alums. These alums become professors at other universities and spread the word about their alma mater, which eventually translates into good ratings based on reputation, given that alum ratings are influenced by the departments and programs they attended.[100] Also, well-trained doctoral students eventually become leaders in the field (e.g., journal editors, officers in professional organizations, and high-level university administrators). All these outcomes contribute to the impact of the school in the education, organizations, and society dimensions in addition to theory and research.

Therefore, university administrators must take a long-term strategic view to fund and support the doctoral program. In addition to research activities, university administrators and faculty mentors must provide teaching opportunities so doctoral students develop their pedagogical skills. Furthermore, doctoral students should be mentored and trained to write practitioner-oriented articles and learn how to bridge theory and practice early in their training.[101] If they do so, they will be inclined to broaden their scholarly impact from the beginning of their careers.

Lastly, university administrators could also consider developing a doctorate of practice program.[102] Such a program can be highly beneficial in terms of external impact because alums from this program are influential practitioner-scholars in organizations.

Recommendation #5: Promote Practical Knowledge and Applications

Lastly, university administrators should promote better integration of social and behavioral science education and research with industry practice to enhance impact on organizations and society. Unfortunately, these research-education and research-practice gaps are even wider in developing countries.

There are two challenges that administrators must address in terms of promoting practical knowledge and applications that will result in enhanced impact regarding the organizations and social dimensions. First, many schools recruit professors of practice. But, because practical industry skills are usually less valued than publications in top journals, those with practical skills face an entry barrier to pursuing an academic career. Another challenge is the need for opportunities for faculty to engage in practical industry experience, such as consulting activities.

University administrators should coordinate with the development office, career center, and alum office to formulate a strategy for bridging the research-education and research-practice gaps so faculty can have broader industry exposure. For example, one possibility is to partner with local private organizations and public agencies to provide access to faculty and students for experiential learning and applied research. Related to this point, university administrators can institutionalize faculty consulting practice that combines with experiential learning projects. The reason is that student involvement in consulting projects will also enhance the impact on the education dimension. Finally, administrators can incentivize faculty to spend part of their sabbaticals conducting applied research in an organization rather than another university. This would also help faculty enhance their impact on the organizations dimension.

Current and Future Researchers and Educators

As a preview of this section, Table 16.4 summarizes recommendations and implementation guidelines for current and future researchers and educators.

TABLE 16.4 ■ Enhancing Scholarly Impact: Recommendations for Researchers and Educators	
Recommendations	**Implementation Guidelines**

1. **Develop your personal scholarly impact plan**	● Ask yourself the following questions:
	  a) What is my personal scholarly impact plan for the near term (1-2 years), mid-range (3-6 years), and longer-term (6+ years)?
	  b) When do I want to impact which dimensions and stakeholders, and how exactly will I do so?
	● Receive top-notch research training, which is indispensable for producing high-quality and valid research that is trustworthy and credible
	● Be mindful that impact begins with minimizing questionable research practices and sharpening your skills to keep abreast with the theorizing and methodological requirements for high-impact research

2. **Become an academic decathlete**	● It is not sufficient to have a high impact on just one dimension ● Aspire to become an academic decathlete, though it is not necessary to excel in all the impact dimensions, but at least some of them ● Before tenure, a faculty member may focus on high-impact theory and research and education, but impact priorities may change over time
3. **Find ways to affect multiple impact dimensions simultaneously**	● Start with rigorous and high-quality research ● Do not wait until tenure to consider impact on dimensions other than theory and research because it may be then too late to adjust one's impact mindset ● Write bridging articles targeting students and practitioners ● Write a textbook integrating academic and applied sources ● Write cases for instructional use that influence other academics, students, and external stakeholders ● As inspiring exemplars, consider the cases of Professor Michael Hitt (Texas A&M University) and Professor Susan Jackson (Rutgers University).
4. **Leverage social media to broaden impact on external stakeholder**	● Use social media to interact with and impact a broader and global audience ● As inspiring exemplars, consider the cases of Professor Jeffrey Pfeffer (Stanford University).

Source: Aguinis, Yu, & Tosun (2021).

Recommendation #1: Develop Your Personal Scholarly Impact Plan

A critical question faculty members, as well as aspiring faculty members, need to ask is: What is my personal scholarly impact plan for the near term (1-2 years), mid-range (3-6 years), and longer-term (6+ years)? When do I want to impact which dimensions and stakeholders, and how exactly will I do so?

Later in this chapter, you will learn how to create your own Personal Impact Development Plan (PIDP) to answer each of these questions. But, the first step, particularly critical for students and junior scholars, is to receive top-notch research training, which is indispensable for producing high-quality and valid research.[103] Trustworthy and credible research is more likely to impact theory and research. In addition, it will be challenging to impact any of the four dimensions through untrustworthy and irreproducible scholarship.

Given the tremendous pressure to publish in prestigious journals (i.e., theory and research dimension), it is not surprising that questionable research practices (QRPs) are found in many different aspects of research practices dealing with data, hypotheses reporting, model construction, and statistical reporting.[104] Therefore, you must remember that impact begins with minimizing QRPs and sharpening your skills to keep abreast with high-impact research's theorizing and methodological requirements.

Recommendation #2: Become an Academic Decathlete

Faculty face higher and higher expectations to excel in multiple roles as educators and researchers and roles outside of the university walls. Thus, a point has been reached where faculty are expected to become "academic decathletes."[105] However, just like decathletes must excel in different events (e.g., long jump, javelin throw, 100 meters), it is not sufficient for faculty to have a high impact on just one dimension. Accordingly, faculty take on different roles and responsibilities, including teaching different types of students (e.g., undergraduate, graduate, doctoral, executive), engaging in both academic research and applied research, taking on administrative roles at the university, becoming members of journal editorial boards and associate editors or editor of journals, and engaging in consulting practice.

METHODS IN PRACTICE
CAN YOU BECOME AN ACADEMIC DECATHLETE?

Can you do it all? Becoming an academic decathlete is a daunting aspiration for all faculty, particularly for early career ones. However, this is the strategic direction faculty should consider, though this does not necessarily involve excelling in all dimensions, only some of them.[106] For example, a faculty member may focus on high-impact theory and research and education before tenure. Then, impact priorities may change over time. Later in the career, one can select other stakeholders as the main impact targets (e.g., practitioners). At that time, other high-impact activities can include a leadership role in the university and the Academy, becoming a journal editorial board member (and eventually associate editor and editor), focusing on executive education, continuing on research excellence both in academic and practice-focused publications and devoting time to consulting activities to disseminate knowledge to external stakeholders.

Recommendation #3: Find Ways to Affect Multiple Impact Dimensions Simultaneously

This pluralist scholarly impact model suggests that the multiple dimensions are not mutually exclusive. Therefore, faculty should find ways to affect more than one impact dimension simultaneously. First, faculty should start with rigorous and high-quality research. This is the first step in how faculty can establish a visible research identity and build a network of colleagues and collaborators. But faculty should not wait until tenure to consider activities that influence dimensions other than theory and research because it may be too late to adjust one's impact mindset.

Faculty should write practitioner-oriented articles targeting students and practitioners. Writing **bridging papers** is a natural off-shoot of more traditional scholarly articles. It has three benefits: making research relevant, making a difference, and improving teaching because students enjoy reading their professors' practical articles.[107]

On a related note, another synergistic activity is to write a textbook to influence students.[108] A textbook integrates academic and applied sources and offers students balanced science-practice knowledge for their education. In addition, a well-researched and structured textbook will make a long-lasting impact on the students after they become practitioners.

Writing cases for instructional use is another way of influencing several dimensions simultaneously. The annual listing of the most popular case studies, compiled by the Yale School of Management Case Research and Development Team based on sales, publishing data, Google analytics, and adoption information, provides insights into the multiple stakeholders positively influenced. Based on a database of over 300,000 users in 161 countries, two-thirds of the case adoptions came from outside the United States.[109] Case studies allow faculty to describe organizations' critical challenges and influence faculty and students regarding their teaching and learning.

The study described at the beginning of this chapter for measuring impact on internal and external stakeholders[110] (citations and Google web page mentions) uncovered exemplars of scholars who have had a high impact on internal and external stakeholders. For example, Professor Michael Hitt at Texas A&M University was ranked 16th regarding citations and ranked 9th based on 1,454,925 Google-indexed pages. Another example is Professor Susan Jackson at Rutgers University, who ranked 33rd in citation counts and 10th in Google-indexed pages (N = 1,205,200). These two examples demonstrate the high degree and broad influence some scholars have had regarding multiple dimensions of impact and set inspiring examples to emulate.

Recommendation #4: Leverage Social Media to Broaden Impact on External Stakeholders

Researchers and educators have traditionally used listservs, e-newsletters, and e-journals and attended annual conferences to disseminate research outcomes and teaching practices. All these interactions involve primarily internal stakeholders: other researchers and educators. These are effective strategies for engaging other researchers. But social media enables you to interact with and impact a broader global audience.[111] For example, many faculty share their expertise via LinkedIn, X (formerly Twitter), and Facebook. As an inspiring exemplar, Professor Jeffrey Pfeffer (Stanford University) is an active social media user and regularly shares his research, videos of keynote addresses, and evidence-based analyses of current events. His effective use of social media platforms and active community engagement has attracted large followings of scholars and practitioners alike on X (more than 14,000) and LinkedIn (more than 108,000) (as of January 2024). The effective use of social media can increase the reach and influence of research, especially on external stakeholders.

HOW TO CREATE YOUR OWN PERSONAL IMPACT DEVELOPMENT PLAN

The previous section included advice on enhancing your scholarly impact, including the specific recommendation about developing a personal scholarly impact plan. Theory and research in human resource management and performance management can help you do this. Specifically, a substantial body of evidence shows that personal development plans are effective tools for improving individual performance.[112] A typical individual performance development plan highlights strengths and areas needing development—and includes an action plan for further developing these strengths and improving weaknesses. Building upon this literature, this section teaches you how to create personal impact development plans (PIDPs). The following section describes why you need a PIDP, its content, activities, and the role of university leaders in your success in implementing it.

Personal Impact Development Plans: Why You Need Them

You can create your PIDP starting as a student, but PDIPs are just as useful for senior professors. Regardless of your position and career stage, as is the case for performance in general, PIDPs are needed because there is always room for improving impact. A good PIDP allows you to answer questions such as (1) How can I continually learn to increase my scholarly impact in the next year, and how can I increase it in the future? (2) How can I avoid unsatisfactory impact from the past, and what are the barriers to enhancing my scholarly impact? and (3) Where am I now, and where would I like to be regarding my impact journey? These questions are answered by targeting three pairs of impact competencies[113]:

Reflective Impact Competencies

Being aware of one's impact. First, *reflection on motivation for impact* refers to reflecting on values, passions, and motivations regarding one's impact. You should ask yourself: On whom do I want to have an impact and why? Second, *reflection on impact qualities* refers to reflection on strengths, shortcomings, and skills regarding one's impact. You should ask: What are my skills, or lack thereof, regarding my impact?

Communicative Impact Competencies

Being able to communicate with different stakeholders effectively. First, *networking for impact* refers to cultivating and leveraging a network of various stakeholders for impact-related purposes. Ask yourself: Do I interact with the people and groups I want to impact? Second, *impact circulating* refers to disseminating research through different channels such as social media, traditional media, and practitioner outlets. In other words, have I published and disseminated my research in outlets available beyond the academic community?

Behavioral Impact Competencies

Being able to shape one's impact by acting and being proactive. First, *impact exploration* refers to actively exploring and searching for impact opportunities inside and outside academic circles. You should ask yourself: Am I scanning the environment looking for ways to increase my impact? Second, *impact control* refers to actively influencing learning and work processes related to one's impact by setting goals and planning how to reach these goals. Finally, you should ask yourself: Am I learning new skills that will increase my impact in the future?

Now, pause for a few minutes and give yourself some time to think honestly about each of the six competencies by answering the questions above. Where do you stand regarding those impact competencies? What are your weakest competencies? Then, take a deep breath and realize that if you are serious about increasing your scholarly impact, creating, and implementing a PIDP will help you get there.

Personal Impact Development Plans: Overall Content

What does a PIDP look like? Figure 16.3 includes a template. First, it includes which specific impact competencies are targeted. Second, it includes illustrations of developmental activities to target each competency. Third, it includes examples of resources and support needed.

FIGURE 16.3 ■ Personal Impact Development Plan (PIDP): Template

Targeted Impact Competency	Question to Ask Yourself	Developmental Activity	Resources/Support Needed	Time Frame	Evidence of Development
Reflection on motivation for impact	On whom do I want to have impact and why?	Assess values, passions and motivations regarding one's impact.	Monthly one-on-one meetings with university leader.	Revisit these reflections with university leader in monthly one-on-one meetings.	Keeping a living document listing values, passions, motivations, and stakeholders for desired impact.
		"Mix with the best" to learn impactful scholars' motivations for impact.	Access to impactful scholars.	Meet with one impactful scholar per semester.	Gained insight into values, passions, and motivations for impact.
Reflection on impact qualities	What are my skills, or lack thereof, regarding my impact?	Assess strengths, shortcomings, and skills regarding one's impact.	Monthly one-on-one meetings with university leader.	Revisit these reflections with university leader in monthly one-on-one meetings.	Made a table of strengths, shortcomings, and skills regarding one's impact.
		Discuss impact qualities and what it takes to have impact on business and society with a mentor.	Access to senior mentors.	Meet with mentor once a semester.	Gained additional insight on impact qualities.
Networking for impact	Do I interact with the people and groups I want to impact?	Spend a sabbatical conducting applied research in an organization.	One-semester sabbatical.	Sabbatical will take place in [date].	Published a paper based on the study in a practitioner journal.
		Leverage social media channels to share expertise via LinkedIn, X (formerly Twitter), or Facebook.	Support creating a following on social media.	Share three posts about research over [date].	Increased following and engagement on posts.
Impact circulating	Have I published and disseminated my research in outlets available beyond the academic community?	Self-guided studying on how to write an article's "implications for practice" section.	Time and assistance finding sources (e.g., journal articles, videos) teaching the topic.	Self-guided studying to be completed by end of [date].	Applied learnings in subsequent paper's "implications for practice" sections.
		Write a case for instructional use.	Feedback on the written case.	Case will be written by [date].	Case used teaching and disseminated to external stakeholders via other outlets (e.g., news, blog).
Impact exploration	Am I scanning the environment looking for ways to increase my impact?	Attend a conference for researchers and practitioners.	University sponsorship of conference attendance.	Conference to take place on [date].	Provided written report and brief presentation after conference.
		Attend a workshop on how to enhance impact.	University sponsorship of workshop.	Workshop to be completed by [date].	Applied workshop skills.
Impact control	Am I learning new skills that will increase my impact in the future?	Self-guided studying to assess "prescriptive readiness" of research.	Time and assistance for finding sources and learning opportunities.	Self-guided studying to be completed by [date].	Used information derived from self-studying in subsequent research projects.
		On-the-job training with a more experienced and impactful peer.	Experienced impactful peer to design a "mini-training program" and time for training.	Five hours per week over a four-week period in [date].	On-the-job training influenced learning and work processes related to one's impact.

Source: Aguinis & Gabriel (2021). Reproduced with permission.

Finally, the PIDP includes a time frame for each developmental activity and evidence of development. To what extent has progress been made, and how to know if this is the case?

Personal Impact Development Plans: Developmental Activities

PIDP activities depend on a university's strategic goals, objectives, and resources that may or may not be available. The PIDP template in Figure 16.3 includes illustrative developmental activities such as the following:

- *On-the-job training.* Individuals are paired with a more experienced and impactful peer who designs a formal on-the-job training course. The design of these "mini-training programs" includes how many hours a day or week of training and specific impact learning objectives. For students, this can be a seminar or workshop on impact.

- *Assessing "prescriptive readiness" of research.* Not all research will be readily applicable and potentially impact societal issues and business relationships. For example, exploratory research is less likely to result in clear implications and prescriptions. Assessing prescriptive readiness involves researchers learning the different stages of prescriptive evidence: exploratory, preliminary, option, guideline, and standard.[114]

- *Mixing with the best.* Having an opportunity to meet or work with highly impactful scholars provides important learning opportunities.

The PIDP template in Figure 16.3 can be adapted based on an individual's context and needs. For example, a PIDP may include just two of the six competencies. Similarly, developmental activities, associated needed resources, time frames, and evidence of development can also be adapted and added given a particular context. Moreover, an individual's PIDP should be reviewed annually and updated based on having reached high levels of expertise in specific competencies but not others.

Personal Impact Development Plans: Role of Context and Profession and University Leaders

As the performance management literature demonstrates, development plans are unlikely to be effective or put in place in the first place without a supportive context. Thus, the successful implementation of PIDPs requires the active involvement of leaders in the profession (e.g., elected officers, journal editors). Intrinsic motivation to increase business researchers' and educators' impact is undoubtedly important, but there is a need for reward and compensation systems to acknowledge impact explicitly. Otherwise, one would fall into the proverbial folly of "rewarding A [exclusive impact on theory and research] while hoping for B [impact on societal issues and their business relation]." Accordingly, it will be difficult, if not impossible, to successfully implement PIDPs if professional organizations, journals, and faculty reward and promotion systems do not define, measure, and reward scholarly impact more broadly. For example, journal editors do not encourage authors to include text in their articles explaining their study's impact on societal issues and business relations. In that case, it is unlikely they will do so. Or authors will do so only in passing without too much detail or substance.[115]

At a local level, university leaders such as area heads, department chairs, associate deans, and deans have an important role in creating and implementing a faculty member's PIDP. This starts by serving as role models: university leaders should also have their own PIDPs. Doing so will also help university leaders understand the process from the faculty member's perspective, anticipate potential roadblocks and defensive attitudes, and create PIDPs for faculty members collaboratively.

University leaders play the following six roles in the development and implementation of PIDPs:

1. Explaining what is required of the individual to reach a required impact level

2. Referring to appropriate developmental activities

3. Reviewing and making suggestions about developmental objectives

4. Checking on the individual's progress toward developmental objective achievement (i.e., "evidence of development" in Figure 16.3)

5. Removing barriers to progress when possible

6. Offering the opportunity for regular check-ins and reinforcing positive behaviors

A helpful tool for university leaders to perform the functions above is the *feedforward interview (FFI)*, which involves a meeting between the faculty member and university leader to understand what competencies individuals possess that allow them to achieve a high level of impact and how to use these competencies in other contexts to make further improvements in the future. The FFI goes as follows[116]:

1. *Eliciting a success story.* The university leader asks, "A story about an event during which you felt you had a very high degree of impact on societal issues and their business relation."

2. *Uncover the underlying impact of success factors.* The second step involves understanding the factors that led to the success story: "What were some of the things you did or did not do, such as your specific personal strengths and capabilities, that made this impact success story possible?"

3. *Extrapolating the past into the future.* The third step involves asking questions that will identify an individual's ability to replicate the conditions that led to high impact from the past into the future: "Think about your current actions, priorities, and plans for the near future (e.g., next week, month, or quarter) and tell me how you think you may be able to replicate these conditions to be able to achieve the same level of impact as you did before."

University leaders play a key role in facilitating conditions for the successful implementation of PIDPs. But leaders will not be fully engaged in the process if they do not believe in the importance of impact. Also, leaders will only be fully engaged if acknowledged for helping faculty members increase their impact. Thus, evaluating leaders' performance should also include how they have been instrumental in helping faculty members increase their impact.

ENHANCING YOUR IMPACT: IT'S A JOURNEY

Achieving impact on societal issues will take time and effort. Using PIDPs, researchers and educators can engage in strategic and purposeful planning to increase their impact. The effective implementation of PIDPs will depend on whether professional organizations, journals, and universities implement rewards and other support systems that motivate individuals to engage in activities to increase their impact. Hopefully, given the increased demand for accountability and contributions to society, social and behavioral science will continue to work on improving its collective impact. Impact is not a destination – it's a journey. And hopefully, this book has provided you with tools to make the lofty aspiration of scholarly impact a reality.

DISCUSSION QUESTIONS

1. Why should you care about the impact of your research?

2. Why does scholarly impact need to be revisited?

3. What are the reasons for using journal lists in social and behavioral science?

4. What does the "an A is an A" mean, and why has it become the new bottom line for valuing academic research? What are the consequences of this approach to valuing research?

5. How do we need to broaden the meaning and measurement of impact?

6. What does it mean to consider a pluralist conceptualization of impact based on a multidimensional and multistakeholder model?

7. What are the advantages of journal lists? What are the disadvantages? Considering your responses, what is your view on whether we should have journal lists or abolish them?

8. In what way can university administrators contribute to enhancing impact?

9. How can current and future researchers and educators enhance their scholarly impact?

10. Create a personal impact development plan. Once done, compare it to a classmate's. What are you missing in your plan? What should you add (if anything)?

11. What should be the overall content, developmental activities, and role that context and university leaders will play in implementing your personal impact development plan?

KEY TERMS

academic decathlete
A-journal
altmetrics
bridging paper
feedforward interview (FFI)
i10-index
journal list
multidimensional and multistakeholder model
    of scholarly impact

personal impact development plan (PIDP)
personal scholarly impact plan
Social Sciences Citation Index (SSCI)
stakeholder theory
superordinate

NOTES

This chapter is based to a large extent on the following sources:

Aguinis, H., Cummings, C., Ramani, R. S., & Cummings, T. G. (2020). "An A is an A": The new bottom line for valuing academic research. *Academy of Management Perspectives*, *34*(1), 135-154. https://doi.org/10.5465/amp.2017.0193

Aguinis, H., & Gabriel, K. P. (2022). If you are serious about impact, create a personal impact development plan. *Business & Society*, *61*(4), 818–826. https://doi.org/10.1177/00076503211014482

Aguinis, H., Ramani, R. S., Alabduljader, N., Bailey, J. R., & Lee, J. (2019). A pluralist conceptualization of scholarly impact in management education: Students as stakeholders. *Academy of Management Learning & Education*, *18*(1), 11-42. https://doi.org/10.5465/amle.2017.0488

Aguinis, H., Shapiro, D. L., Antonacopoulou, E. P., & Cummings, T. G. (2014). Scholarly impact: A pluralist conceptualization. *Academy of Management Learning & Education*, *13*(4), 623-639. https://doi.org/10.5465/amle.2014.0121

Aguinis, H., Suárez-González, I., Lannelongue, G., & Joo, H. (2012). Scholarly impact revisited. *Academy of Management Perspectives*, *26*(2), 105-132. https://doi.org/10.5465/amp.2011.0088

Aguinis, H., Yu, L., & Tosun, C. (2021). How to enhance scholarly impact: recommendations for university administrators, researchers, and educators. *International Journal of Contemporary Hospitality Management*. https://doi.org/10.1108/IJCHM-10-2020-1189

GLOSSARY

30-30 rule: A rule of thumb for multilevel samples that recommends studies should have at least 30 upper-level units with at least 30 lower-level entities in each to demonstrate sufficient statistical power.

abductive reasoning: A type of reasoning that forms and evaluates hypotheses to make sense of puzzling facts by starting with a set of observations and then seeking the most straightforward and most likely conclusion.

academic decathlete: A faculty member's capacity to serve multiple roles to multiple stakeholders like teaching different types of students (e.g., undergraduate, graduate, doctoral, executive), engaging in both academic research and applied research, taking on administrative roles at the university, becoming members of journal editorial boards and associate editors or editor of journals, and engaging in consulting practice.

Accommodationism: Changing hypotheses based on knowledge of a study's results, but without making this process open and explicit and presenting the hypothesis as if results were not known in advance. See also "predictivism" and "HARKing."

action research: An investigative research approach that generates socially practical and theoretically meaningful research results to improve a social issue or problem.

aggregation: The practice of combining individual-level data to form higher-level data (e.g., using individual firms' outputs to describe an industry's output).

A-journal: A categorization of high-impact, elite journals primarily used as a proxy measure of research value. See also "journal list."

Akaike Information Criterion (AIC): An index of how well a model conforms to the data from which it was constructed,

given by $AIC = 2k - 2\ln\left(\hat{L}\right)$, where k is the number of estimated parameters in the model and $\hat{L}$ is the maximum value of the likelihood function for the model.

algorithm error: In computer-aided text analysis (CATA), a type of measurement error associated with the software design choices made by the developers of the CATA software.

altmetric: A non-traditional bibliographic metric to assess research impact that stands for "alternative metrics," which supplement traditional citation metrics like impact factor, such as the number of online or printed newspaper outlets that mention a scholar's research and youtube.com entries, whereby both collected using Web-based tools.

analysis of covariance (ANCOVA): A statistical method that determines response to different groups of independent variables that adjusts for the influence of variables not under investigation but still affect the results. ANCOVA is an extension of ANOVA that allows for the effects of a covariate on the dependent variable.

analysis of variance (ANOVA): A statistical method used for determining the variation between the mean scores of responses of two or more independent variables on a dependent variable.

annualreports.com: An online search database of business reports designed to inform shareholders and other interested parties about a company's operations and financial performance.

anonymity: When collecting data, researchers do not record any personal information that could identify participants. This way, the responses or data provided cannot be linked back to any specific individual.

anonymous survey: A confidential data collection method that does not require

participants to provide personally identifiable information such as name, email address, social security number, or physical address.

archival data: Information about past events collected before the beginning of a research project and stored in a stable form such as databases or videography.

arithmetic mean: A statistical formula expressed by the sum of the values divided by the number of values. See, "mean."

association rules: In market basket analysis, association rules are "if-then" statements in which correlation assumptions are inferred from the analysis of transaction sets. In the example: [graham cracker, chocolate] => [marshmallow], if a customer has a transaction that includes graham crackers and chocolate, then they are also likely to be interested in marshmallows. Association rules have two types, categorical and quantitative See also "categorical association rules," "quantitative association rules," and "Market Basket Analysis (MBA)."

attention and compliance check: A quality-control question inserted into online platforms (e.g., Amazon MTurk) to validate that the participant is not responding inattentively or carelessly.

attention check: A technique used to identify and filter uninspired respondents who can compromise the data quality by giving illogical or careless answers to open-ended questions, racing through surveys, skipping questions, or answering at random.

attributes: A quality or trait assessed for every observation and varies from one observation to the next.

authorship: Gives recognition for a person's efforts to a study and carries responsibility.

availability bias: In a meta-analysis, a type of implicit selection bias in the literature search related to the selective inclusion of studies that are easily accessible to the researcher. See "implicit selection bias."

average deviation (AD): A statistical measure of the spread of observations, which measures the distance of a deviation from the data set's mean, defined as, $average\ deviation = \frac{\sum_{i=1}^{n}|x_i - \bar{x}|}{n}$, where $x_1, x_2, ..., x_n$ represent sample values and $\bar{x}$ their mean.

average squared deviation: An assessment of the combined influence of a group j on both the fixed and random parameter estimates, notated as C_j, where j is the focal group among a set of cases.

axial coding: A grounded theory-based approach to coding that breaks down core themes from a document and relates them to one another through inductive and deductive analysis.

backward selection algorithm: See "stepwise selection procedure."

banding: A strategy typically used for hiring and referring candidates for selection whereby candidate employment test scores are divided into bands based on reliability, standard error of measurement, and standard error of the estimate.

Bayesian Information Criterion (BIC): A metric used in Bayesian statistics to select one model out of several alternatives, given by $BIC = k\ \ln(n) - 2\ \ln(\hat{L})$, where k is the number of estimated parameters in the model, n is the number of observations, and $\hat{L}$ is the maximum value of the likelihood function for the model. See also "Bayesian network."

Bayesian network: A probability estimation system represented by a graphical model of the probability relations where uncertainty is accounted for using Bayes' Theorem and sets of conditional probabilities. Bayes' Theorem provides a method to update the probability of an event occurrence given new evidence and is defined

as, $\underset{posterior}{p(\theta|D)} = \frac{\overset{likelihood}{p(D|\theta)}\ \overset{prior}{p(\theta)}}{\underset{evidence}{p(D)}}$, where D is the observed data and θ is a vector of parameters in the descriptive model.

Bayesian statistics: A statistical theory based on the Bayesian interpretation of probability, according to which probability indicates the degree of confidence in an event. See also "Bayesian network."

behavioral simulation: A computer-assisted analysis tool that investigates individual and group behavior by constructing and evaluating models.

behaviorally-anchored rating scales (BARS): A type of scale used extensively in social and behavioral sciences that includes examples of specific behaviors below the numerical values on the scale instead of generic labels such as "highly satisfied" or "strongly agree."

between-person research design: In experimental vignette methodology (EVM), a type of research design that requires that each participant read only one vignette, and comparisons are made across participants. See "experimental vignette methodology (EVM)."

Big Five traits: The psychological trait theory's classification of personality developed from the 1980s onward, which includes five traits: openness to experience, conscientiousness, extraversion, agreeableness, and neuroticism, also known as the Five-Factor Model, The Big Five Model, and The Big Five Personality Traits.

binary logistic regression: A regression model where the target variable is binary (e.g., it can take one of two values, 0 or 1).

biographical method: Using personal history collected using qualitative techniques such as interviews, focus groups, individual reflections, and other narratives in psychological research and analysis.

bivariate data: Data in which the units measure the paired value of two variables, such as the size and weight of a package in a set.

Board Analyst (Corporate Library's historical data): Dataset that includes independent information regarding corporate governance, executive compensation, and management performance of publicly traded US companies, in which much of the information was taken from publicly traded firms' proxy statements. The historical data, which started in 2001, represents a snapshot of the current database on June 30 of each year.

bogus pipeline (BPL): A method of data collection based on the idea that people might respond more honestly if they are afraid of being caught lying and consisting of using a fake lie detector. The phrase alludes to an alleged "pipeline to the soul" that is a fake.

bootstrapping: A robust method that estimates the parameters of a model and their standard errors from the sample without reference to a theoretical sample distribution. A drawback of this approach is that it is only accurate for large sample sizes ($n > 150$).

bots: Malicious software programs, known as "web robots," specifically designed to participate in online studies for "fake participants" to receive extra compensation. See also "Web robots."

boundary condition: A contingent relation that qualifies the relationship's nature and size between two variables.

bridging paper: A published article that connects (i.e., "bridges") previous research to practical advice.

Business Horizons: A bimonthly business journal targeting business academicians and practitioners and published by the Indiana University Kelley School of Business.

canonical correlation analysis: A method that infers information from a matrix that includes covariances between the variables and the variation. This method finds the linear functions of one set of variables that maximally correlate with the linear functions of a second set of variables.

CAPTCHA: A constructed abbreviation for "Completely Automated

Public Turing test to tell Computers and Humans Apart," which refers to a computer-generated challenge-response test used to determine whether a research participant is human.

case study: An in-depth, detailed examination of a particular case (such as an event, a family, an individual, a business, or another entity) in a real-world context. Case studies allow for intensive analysis but are limited by their generalizability.

catastrophe theory: An approach that uses methods to study the sudden and discontinuous effects on dependent variables resulting from small and continuous changes in independent variables (e.g., dam failure under slowly mounting pressure). See also "theory."

categorical association rules: In market basket analysis, association rules are based on binary data (e.g., a customer did or did not purchase an item). See "association rules."

categorical variable: A variable with a range of categories commonly assigned a fixed number of possible values, such as {upper, middle, lower} or {red, yellow, blue}.

Cattell's data cube: A representation of the three dimensions of data along three axes of a cube: the person (top to bottom dimension), the variable (left to right dimension), and the time (front to back dimension). Also known as a "data box."

causal inferences: Identifying a specific phenomenon's independent effect as part of a broader system.

causal mapping: A network consisting of links or relationships between nodes or participants such that a link between 'B' and 'D' indicates that 'B' has a causal influence on 'D.' See also "concept mapping."

causality: Information on the relationship between cause (i.e., interdependent variable) and effect (i.e., dependent variable).

cell size: The number of units that share a set of characteristics in a statistical table.

censoring: A situation in which some observations are missing from a data set due to those observations falling outside the limits of the scale of the measurement instrument.

censorship: A situation in which some observations are missing from a data set due to those observations falling outside the limits of the scale of the measurement instrument. See also "censoring."

cherry-picking: The practice of searching through data involving alternative measures or samples to find the results offering the strongest possible support for a particular hypothesis or research question that a study investigated. See also "HARKing."

chi-square (χ^2) distribution: A distribution of the sums of independent squared differences between the observed scores in a data set and the expected score for the set. The chi-square distribution is defined as,
$$f(x) = \begin{cases} \dfrac{x^{\frac{k}{2}-1} e^{-x/2}}{2^{\frac{k}{2}} \Gamma\left(\dfrac{k}{2}\right)} & \text{for } x \geq 0 \\ 0 & \text{otherwise} \end{cases},$$
where k is the degrees of freedom and $\Gamma(k/2)$ is the gamma function. This continuous probability distribution may be used to determine a number of statistical measures such as goodness of fit, homogeneity, trend, variance, or association/independence.

classification: Grouping data by similarity using an ordered collection of relevant categories.

cluster analysis: A statistical exploratory technique that groups cases based on shared similarities amongst a set of variables, often graphically, such as on a scatter plot. Because cluster analysis is an exploratory technique, it is not used for hypothesis testing.

coefficient alpha: An estimate of measurement reliability based on internal consistency that measures how closely related a set of data are as a group. See also "Cronbach's coefficient alpha."

coefficient beta: In a regression model, the degree of change in the dependent variable for every 1-unit change in the independent variable or each independent variable in the case of multiple independent variables (holding other variables in the model constant).

coefficient of determination (R squared, or R^2): The proportion of the variance in a dependent variable that is explained by the independent variable(s), defined as $R^2 = 1 - \dfrac{RSS}{TSS}$, where RSS is the residual sum of squares and TSS is the total sum of squares.

coefficient of stability: The degree to which scores fluctuate due to elements related to the specific time and occasion on which the measure was administered.

coercive: A practice applying intimidation tactics to get individuals to perform things they do not want.

Cohen's coefficient kappa: A statistic used to measure inter-rater reliability among qualitative items; critically, kappa accounts for the possibility of chance agreement.

Cohen's value (d): A measure of effect size for the comparison between two means, defined as
$$d = \frac{(\text{mean of the experimental group} - \text{mean of the control group})}{\text{pooled standard deviation}},$$

Collaborative Training Initiative (CITI program): A training program introduced by the National Institutes of Health (NIH) for Human Subjects Research Training that recognizes education and training gaps in the serviced communities and offers peer-reviewed, web-based instructional materials to fill those requirements.

committed-to-participant approach: A research approach in which researchers and research participants must be aware that their relationship is a result of research activity to play the participant as observer role.

common language effect size: A way to measure the size of an effect by computing the probability that a score sampled randomly from one distribution will be greater than a score sampled from another distribution.

common method bias (CMB): A systematic error variance attributable to the use of a common measurement method.

common-effect (CE) model: A meta-analytic model that assumes one true common effect is underlying the distribution of observed effects. Hence, in the CE model, the variance in the distribution of observed effect sizes is attributed solely to within-study sampling variance. Also called the "fixed-effect model." See also the "mixed-effects (ME) model."

comparative fit index (CFI): The analysis of the difference between the data and a hypothesized model to assess model fit while accounting for sample size. CFI values range from 0 to 1 and larger numbers indicate better fit.

complementary item: In market basket analysis, an item whose demand rises with the popularity of its complement, also called a "complementary good."

complementary reallocation: A form of Bayesian inference in which the addition of new data (i.e., evidence) that reduces the likelihood of one possibility will increase the likelihood of other remaining possibilities, even if the probability of those options is small.

COMPUSTAT: A well-known financial database and information source published by Standard and Poor (S&P).

Computer-aided Text Analysis (CATA): A family of software-driven methods to analyze a set of text by counting keywords, phrases, or other text-based markers; these used programs rely on researcher-developed dictionaries or word lists that the program then uses to analyze a document.

concept mapping: A diagram that visually represents relationships between ideas or concepts.

conceptual replication: An experiment in which a previous study is replicated using the same population but different procedures to assess whether findings, in terms of constructs and relationships among constructs, can be replicated using different methodological procedures and instruments.

concurrent validation studies: A study that shows the degree of agreement between two sets of measures, in which one set is generally brand-new, whereas the other is well-known and

has already been shown to be valid and reliable.

confederates: Individuals commonly employed in various experiments to secretly participate with actual research participants. Researchers use confederates to study participants in complex social settings and reliably capture naïve reactions.

confidentiality: A commitment of the researcher to keep participants' information private and ensuring it is not shared with others who are not authorized to see it.

confidence interval: A range of values derived from sample observations that are believed to contain the true parameter value with a stated probability level.

configural invariance: A statistical property that indicates that the same construct is being measured across multiple groups or across time.

confirmatory factor analysis (CFA): A statistical method for confirming a set of observed variables' factor structure, enabling the researcher to examine the idea that there is a connection between the variables seen and the latent constructs that underlie them using CFA.

confound: The presence of a variable that influences both independent and dependent variables causing a spurious association.

confounding constructs and levels of constructs (CCLC): A potential risk to the construct's validity if a measure does not account for the whole range of values for a given construct.

conjoint analysis: A survey-based statistical technique that investigates what people value in products or services and how they make decisions.

construct: A conceptual or theoretical entity derived from processes inferred - but not directly observable – from data rather than empirically verifiable and measurable events. Construct scope refers to the boundaries or limits of a construct's definition or descriptive validity.

construct identity fallacy: A term referring to discordant naming practices

revolving around the idea that there can be dozens of terms and scores of measures for the same construct (i.e., jingle), and different constructs can go by the same name (i.e., jangle).

construct scope: The boundaries or limits of a construct's definition. See also "construct."

construct specification: A theory elaboration approach in which a theoretical construct is specified or refined according to insights emerging from the data, wherein researchers can advance an existing theory by identifying and defining constructs that have not been considered or by splitting an existing construct into two more new constructs.

construct validity: Refers to how well a test or measure accurately assesses what it is intended or stated to, based on the accumulation of evidence to support the interpretation of that test or measure.

construct-related evidence: Evidence that shows whether a measure assesses the concept for which it intended to measure. A construct is a conceptual framework for understanding the latent variable, an unobservable element that affects scores on a particular measure.

contamination: A condition that occurs when unrelated constructs impact a response measure. See "criterion contamination."

content analysis: A method of analyzing a set of documents (such as research articles or news clippings) by sorting the content into categories and then quantifying the number of occurrences of a given entity, concept, or data in each category.

content validity: The extent to which a measure assesses every facet of the subject, concept, or behavior intended to measure.

content validity ratio (CVR): A measure that indicates the instrument's level of validity according to content validity expert ratings, given by $CVR = \frac{n_e - N/2}{N/2}$, where n_e is the number of experts that rated the item as essential, and N is the total number of experts.

contrasting: A theory elaboration approach in which the application of a theory in one setting is compared with the application of that same theory in another setting; it can be implemented in two ways (1) Horizontal contrasting, which is the process of examining how an existing theoretical insight fits in a new context, and (2) Vertical contrasting which compares a theory developed at one level of analysis with data gathered at another level of analysis, to see if the theory can still describe the constructs and relations.

control variable: Also called a "statistical control," is a variable thought to affect the response variable but is not of substantive interest to the study.

convenience sampling: A non-probabilistic sampling method that involves the sample being drawn from an easily accessible population.

convergent validity: The degree to which responses on one test or instrument strongly correlate with those on another test or instrument that uses a comparable concept.

conversation analysis: A qualitative research method focused on the verbal and non-verbal social interactions of everyday conversation or institutional talk.

Cook's D_i: An influence identification technique that assesses the influence a data point i has on all regression coefficients. Cook's D_i can be further used as follows: Modified Cook's D_i is similar to Cook's D_i, but it uses standardized deleted residuals rather than standardized residuals. Generalized Cook's D_i is applied to structural equation modeling to assess the influence that a data point has on the parameter estimates.

cooking (the data): Keeping the portions of the evidence supporting the theory and dismissing the rest of the data.

corporate governance: The policies, processes, procedures, structures, and mechanisms in place that influence the direction and control of a corporation.

corporate governance research: A domain that focuses on how corporate ownership and governance affect value creation and the welfare of stakeholders in companies.

correlational: statistical analysis to understand whether there is a relationship between two variables, usually not necessarily implying a causal relation—simply that the variables covary.

correlation coefficients: Indicators of how strongly two variables, x and y, covary.

correlational analysis: A statistical technique to determine the interdependence (i.e., relationship or covariation) between sets of variables.

cost bias: A type of implicit selection bias in the meta-analysis literature search related to the selective inclusion of studies available for free or at low costs. See "implicit selection bias."

counterfactual: An alternate result: consideration of what may have been seen if something had happened but did not.

covariation: Correlated variation; the measure of joint variability of two random variables, given by
$$cov_{x,y} = \frac{\sum (x_i - \bar{x})(y_i - \bar{y})}{N - 1},$$ where x_i is the ith data value of x, y_i is the ith data value of y, $\bar{x}$ is the mean of x, $\bar{y}$ is the mean of y, and N is the number of data values.

covert research: Research done without informing the participant(s) involved.

Crainiceanu and Ruppert (2004) test: A likelihood ratio test for the goodness-of-fit of linear regression models.

credibility interval (CrI): In a meta-analysis, the interval that includes a particular percent of the population values (e.g., an 80% CrI includes 80% of the effect sizes in the population), after within-study variance and other study artifacts have been removed. The CrI provides an absolute metric for evaluating the presence of heterogeneity as it is on the same scale as the effect size (e.g., r or d). Further, the CrI provides an upper and lower bound of the population effect size, with the typical decision rule being that if the CrI is sufficiently wide or includes zero, tests

for boundary conditions are justified. See also "confidence interval."

criterion contamination: A case where factors unrelated to the concept being measured nevertheless impact a measure (i.e., the criterion).

criterion validity: The evaluation of how effectively one measure can predict scores on another.

critical ratio: The quotient of any one deviation from the mean and the standard deviation.

Cronbach's coefficient alpha: An estimate of measurement reliability based on internal consistency that measures how closely related a set of data are as a group, also known as tau-equivalent reliability (ρ_T), given by
$$\rho_T = \frac{k^2 \bar{\sigma}_{ij}}{\sigma_x^2} = \frac{k}{k-1}\left(1 - \frac{\sum_{i=1}^{k}\sigma_i^2}{\sigma_x^2}\right),$$ where X_i denotes the score of item i, $X = X_1 + X_2 + ... + X_k$ is the sum of all items in a test of k items, σ_{ij} is the covariance between X_i and X_j, $\sigma_i^2 \left(= \sigma_{ij}\right)$ is the variance of X_i, σ_x^2 consists of variances and inter-item covariance (given by $\sigma_x^2 = \sum_{i=1}^{k}\sum_{j=1}^{k}\sigma_{ij} = \sum_{i=1}^{k}\sigma_i^2 + \sum_{i=1}^{k}\sum_{j\neq i}^{k}\sigma_{ij}$), and $\bar{\sigma}_{ij}$ is the average inter-item covariance $\left(\text{given by } \bar{\sigma}_{ij} = \frac{\sum_{i=1}^{k}\sum_{j\neq i}^{k}\sigma_{ij}}{k(k-1)}\right)$. See also "Kuder-Richardson 20 (KR-20)."

cross cultural research: The comparison of similar phenomena across multiple cultures; this method may involve secondary data or contrasting cases to provide a more robust analysis.

cross sectional research: A research design that involves collecting all data simultaneously rather than over multiple periods as done in longitudinal research.

cross-case analysis: A research method by which several case studies are compared and contrasted through in-depth analysis to produce new knowledge about themes, similarities, and differences across cases.

cross-level: In multilevel analysis, it refers to the influences and effects between variables residing at different levels of analysis (e.g., individuals, teams, firms). Lower numbers designate lower levels (e.g., individuals), such as Level-1 or L1. See also "level of analysis."

cross-level interaction model: The fourth and final step of multilevel modeling that determines whether a particular L2 variable is able to explain at least part of the variance in slopes across teams, given by the cross-level interaction model (combined) equation.

data box: See, "Cattell's data cube."

data mining: Discovering patterns among extremely large datasets (i.e., "big data") typically involves machine learning and database systems combined with statistics.

database: An organized collection of information (data) typically stored in a computer system.

data-cleaning: Finding and correcting corrupt, missing, incomplete, inaccurate, or irrelevant data in a record set, table, or database.

debriefing: A procedure that occurs after the study in which the participant is allowed to discuss with the researcher the study details.

deductive theory generation: An approach of theory generation that derives new constructs and lays out relationships using well-reasoned arguments. See also "theorizing" and "theory generation."

degrees of freedom (*df*): The number of independent information units in a sample, computed as the number of scores minus the number of mathematical restrictions.

dehoaxing: A procedure of debriefing participants involved in deception research to inform them that they were misled as part of the study.

deontological approach: An ethical theory proposing that an action is considered morally good because of some characteristic of the action itself, not because the product is good.

descriptive statistics: Summary numbers that summarize characteristics of a set of scores meaningfully and efficiently.

desensitizing: A procedure of detecting undesirable emotional consequences of the research and restoring

participants to a frame of mind at least as positive as before participation.

design-science approach: A research methodology focused on developing and validating prescriptive knowledge production.

desired relative seriousness (DRS): The researcher's evaluation of the relative importance of making a Type I versus Type II error. See also "Type I error rate."

deviance: A value used to compare the relative fit of two competing models given by multiplying the log-likelihood value by –2.

dichotomizing *p*-values: Reporting whether it is below a conventional cutoff (i.e., less than .05, less than .01) rather than reporting its precise value.

difference in beta, standardized (DFBETA-S_{ij}): An influence identification technique that indicates whether the inclusion of case *i* leads to an increase or decrease in a single regression coefficient *j* (i.e., a slope or intercept).

difference in fits, standardized (DFFITS$_i$): An influence identification technique that assesses the influence a data point *i* has on all regression coefficients; it is unique to Cook's D_i in that it produces information that exists on different scales.

discourse analysis: A qualitative method focused on analyzing the sequences of sentences, propositions, or speech within written or spoken language.

discriminant analysis: A statistical method that finds a linear combination of features that classifies data according to category (customer vs. non-customer).

discrimination index: A fundamental indicator of an item's validity. Given by $d = \dfrac{p_u}{n_u} - \dfrac{p_1}{n_1}$, where p_u and p_1 are the number of individuals passing the item in the upper and lower scoring groups, and n_u and n_1 are the size of the upper and lower groups, respectively.

disordinal: A type of interaction effect in which the direction of the relationship between an independent variable and the dependent variable changes across the levels of another independent variable (e.g., the lines cross).

distractor analysis: An analysis that evaluates the value that each false choice adds to the quality of a multiple-choice item.

distribution: One of several mathematical functions that give the probabilities of occurrence for different outcomes

divergent validity (also called discriminant validity): The extent to which a test or measurement differs from (i.e., does not correlate with) a measurement whose underlying idea is conceptually unrelated to it.

document interpretation: The process of determining the intended meaning of a written document.

dummy code: The practice of assigning 1 or 0 to the two states of a binary variable to represent one category or the other.

dysfunctional turnover: A type of employee turnover that replaces high-performing workers with poor-performing workers, which is detrimental to an organization overall. See "turnover."

ecological validity: The extent to which findings can be generalized to the naturally occurring situations in which the investigated phenomenon occurs.

effect size (ES): A measure of the magnitude of the relationship between variables.

Egger's regression test: A technique that assesses publication bias in meta-analyses by funnel plot symmetry. See also "funnel plot" and "publication bias."

eLancing: The practice of accepting freelance work through online job offers or e-lancing websites where employers post projects that freelancers from across the globe can bid on for contractual work (e.g., Upwork.com, MTurk.com).

emotional coding: In computer-aided text analysis (CATA), a coding method that reflects the participants' feelings and sentiments.

empirical Bayes (EB) estimator: A method to estimate the prior probability distribution using given data.

empirical replication: A study in which a previous study is conducted again using the same procedures but a different population to assess the extent to which results are generalizable. This type of replication aims to remain as close as possible to the original study regarding methodological procedures but not study participants (i.e., similar methods, different samples).

employee productivity proposition: An argument stating that since an employer has purchased their employee's time, the employer has a proprietary right to ensure that the time purchased is used as efficiently and productively as possible.

endogeneity: A statistical bias that results from correlations between an independent variable and the error term in an ordinary least squares regression model, which can arise from reasons such as measurement error, autoregression, omitted variables, selection bias in collecting the sample, and simultaneous causality among the variables.

epsilon-squared (ϵ^2): An infrequently used measure of effect size used in ANOVA.

error outlier: A data point that lies far from other data points because of inaccuracies.

eta-square (η^2): A measure of effect size used mostly in ANOVA. The classical eta-squared is defined as the proportion of total variation attributable to the factor, ranges in value from 0 to 1, and is given by the equation: classical $\eta^2 = SS_{factor} / SS_{total}$, where SS_{factor} is the amount of variation attributable to the experimental factor, and SS_{total} is the amount of total variation. The partial eta-squared for an experimental factor is defined as the proportion of total variation attributable to the factor, partialling out or excluding other experimental factors from the total nonerror variation, ranges in value from 0 to 1, and is given by the equation: partial $\eta^2 = SS_{factor} / (SS_{factor} + SS_{error})$, where SS_{factor} is the amount of variation attributable to the experimental factor and SS_{error} is the amount of error or unexplained variation.

ethics: Moral standards that guide a person's behavior or how an activity is carried out.

ethnography: The detailed study and analysis of a defined culture or society following qualitative methods of observation and participation for data collection.

ethnomethodological study: Explores how a society's normal social order is created through and from social interaction by focusing on practical reasoning rather than formal logic.

ethnostatistics: The study of statistics generation and use with a particular emphasis on the premise that statistics are influenced by the social biases inherent to the persons involved in their production.

event contingent experience sampling methodology: One of three types of ESM protocols, in the event contingent protocol, participants respond only when the event of interest occurs. See also "experience sampling methodology (ESM)."

evidence: Regarding Bayesian analysis, evidence refers to the denominator of Bayes' rule, $p(D)$, which is also known as the marginal likelihood; computing the value of $p(D)$ can be difficult because it is an integral over the parameter space: $p(D) = \int p(D|\theta)p(\theta)d\theta$.

exact replication: A study in which a previous study is replicated using the same population and procedures to assess whether the findings of a past study are trustworthy.

experience sampling methodology (ESM): A structured procedure that assesses detailed accounts of people's daily experiences over time and captures the ebb and flow of these experiences as they occur *in situ* (i.e., in the natural environment). See also "interval contingent experience sampling methodology," "event contingent experience sampling methodology," and "signal contingent experience sampling methodology captures."

experimental material: All objects, tools, equipment, and other materials required to conduct a given experiment.

experimental realism: The extent to which the study participants perceive an experimental situation as realistic and believable.

experimental repeated measures design: A research design wherein the researcher measures the same variable taken on the same participants in each condition of the independent variable. This repeated measures design may involve, for example, having a group of students take an exam while well-rested and having them then take the same exam when exhausted.

experimental treatment: A particular combination of conditions such that resultant effects may be compared.

experimental vignette methodology (EVM): A vignette-based research method that presents participants with carefully constructed and realistic scenarios; it enhances experimental realism and allows researchers to manipulate and control independent variables, thereby enhancing internal and external validity. There are two major types of EVM: paper people studies, and policy capturing and conjoint analysis. EVM also has three research designs: between-person, within-person, and mixed research designs. See also "paper people studies," "policy capturing and conjoint analysis," "between-person research designs," "within-person research designs," and "mixed research designs."

explanatory adequacy: The specificity of assumptions regarding objects of analysis and the scope and parsimony of related propositions.

exploratory research: Type of research conducted primarily into a phenomenon of which not much is known.

external validity: The extent to which the findings of a particular study can be generalized to other situations, people, and measures. See also "generalizability."

factor analysis: A statistical analysis method used to reduce the complexity of data by examining variance common among observed variables and forming a smaller number of unobserved latent (i.e., unobserved) factors.

failsafe N: The minimum number of hypothetical undetected no-effect studies (i.e., studies with no relationship between the independent and dependent variables) needed to change the conclusions of a meta-analysis that an effect or relationship exists.

fallible covariates: Predictor variables measured with at least some degree of error.

familiarity bias: In meta-analysis, a type of implicit selection bias literature search related to the selective inclusion of studies only from one's field or discipline. See "implicit selection bias."

feedforward interview (FFI): A meeting to understand an individual's competencies that enable achieving higher impact and performance and determining the best ways to use these competencies in other contexts to make further improvements in the future.

field notes analysis: A process of accumulating and analyzing field note data over time, starting when the field researcher begins in the field and beyond, to determine qualitatively what interactions and descriptive notes mean.

file drawer problem: A subset of the publication bias problem referring to the premise that there is no way to know how much reportable research in any given field is nonpublished. See "publication bias."

fixed-effect model: A meta-analytic model that assumes one true common effect is underlying the distribution of observed effects. Hence, in the fixed-effect model, the variance in the distribution of observed effect sizes is attributed solely to within-study sampling variance. See "common-effect (CE) model."

focus groups: A qualitative research method that relies on having informal group discussions focused on a particular topic or issue in a moderated setting.

formalized meta-theory: A category of meta-theories that refers to the overarching principles transcending specific topics or domains of study and describing and predicting phenomena in more abstract or higher levels than specific theories. Formalized meta-theories extract what is generally consistent across theories, similar to how meta-analysts extract what is

generally consistent across primary-level studies. See "meta-theory."

formative measurement model: A model in which measures cause constructs (as opposed to construct causing measures). See also "reflective measurement model."

Fortune's annual index (Fortune 500 Index): A stock market index based on Fortune magazine's annual ranking of the 500 largest publicly traded and privately held businesses in the United States that submit annual filings to the Securities and Exchange Commission, wherein the listed companies are ordered by revenue. The list is a market capitalization-weighted index; throughout the trading session, its value is calculated every 15 seconds. A base level of $1,000.00 was established using the closing price from December 31, 1999.

forward selection algorithm: A type of stepwise selection procedure that adds variables to a regression model until they fail to lead to incremental increases in R^2 (i.e., proportion of variance in the dependent variable explained by the set of independent variables). See "stepwise selection procedure."

F-test: A statistical test in which the outcome is expected to follow the F-distribution; typically used when comparing statistical models to determine which best fits the population from which test data have been drawn.

full information maximum likelihood (FIML): A missing data technique that attempts to estimate missing values by use of other known parameters.

functional turnover: A type of employee turnover that occurs by replacing poor-performing workers with high-performing skilled workers and is overall beneficial to a firm. See "turnover."

funnel plot: A simple scatter plot in meta-analysis that checks for publication bias by measuring the intervention effect estimates from individual studies against each study's size or precision; if done correctly, the plot looks like a tree or an inverted funnel. See also "publication bias."

Gaussian pattern: A bell-shaped curve, known as the normal distribution; with an approximately equal number of scores above and below the mean value.

generalizability: The extent to which statistical findings of a sample may be extrapolated to the population from which the sample was taken; a measure of how useful results are for a broader situation.

generalized estimating equation (GEE): A statistical method used to analyze correlated data that do not require one or more of the assumptions of the general linear model, such as linear relationship, multivariate normality, no or little multicollinearity, no auto-correlation, and homoscedasticity.

generalized least squares (GLS): A least squares approach to estimating the parameters of a linear regression model when there is some amount of correlation between the residuals. GLS is used instead of ordinary least squares or weighted least squares in cases where the latter could generate misleading inferences.

global prediction outlier: An outlier that influences all parameter estimates in a particular model.

Golden Mean: A Greek philosophy that emphasizes the desirable middle between two extremes (e.g., excess and deficit). Also called the "doctrine of the mean."

good theory: Empirically verified theory that provides the most accurate explanation given the knowledge at the time by describing what happens, then explaining how and why something happens, making insightful predictions, and explaining something significant in the outcome of interest.

goodness-of-fit index (GFI): A measure of fit between a model and the observed covariance matrix.

grand mean: The arithmetic average across all groups in a multilevel study.

grand-mean centering: In multilevel modeling, adjusting each score of a predictor variable by subtracting the overall mean (the grand mean) of that variable from each individual score, resulting in re-scaling the predictor variable around a mean of zero.

grounded theory: An inductive approach to qualitative data collection and interpretation that emphasizes recursive, open-ended exploration. In this inductive approach, a topic and sample are chosen, and empirical data are gathered and analyzed simultaneously to avoid the inception of a preconceived framework, leading to the generation of a theory grounded in these data.

group-mean centering: A method of re-scaling, also called "within-cluster centering," which changes the mean and correlation structure of multilevel data, causing the lower-level predictors to be uncorrelated with the higher-level predictors. See also "re-scale."

growth curve: A graphical representation of the change of a phenomenon over time.

HARKing: "Hypothesizing After Results are Known," presenting unexpected findings in research reports as a priori hypotheses. See also "accommodationism," "predictivism," "THARKing," "cherry-picking," and "question trolling."

harmonic mean: An average calculated by $k(1/N_1 + 1/N_2 + \ldots . 1/N_k)$, where k equals the number of meta-analytic correlations and $N_1...N_k$ refers to the total sample sizes used to compute each meta-analytically derived correlation.

heavy-tail distribution: A probability distribution whose tails are heavier than a normal (i.e., Gaussian) distribution.

heteroscedasticity: A situation when residual or error scores are not evenly distributed along the regression line, violating a regression assumption (i.e., homoscedasticity). Sometimes called "heteroskedasticity."

highest density interval (HDI): In Bayesian analysis, a way to summarize a distribution that indicates which points are most credible; the smallest interval on a distribution density curve for a given confidence level. HDI is typically evaluated against ROPE for equivalence

tests. See also "region of practical equivalence (ROPE)."

hostage syndrome: An effect of a power imbalance between an interviewer and a key informant (KI) wherein the interviewer might suspend their judgment in the face of a KI's display of power by overestimating the importance of what KIs have to say.

Human Capital theory: States that improving education and skill development can aid in increasing a person's lifelong productivity and success and benefit their organizations.

Human Intelligence Task (HIT): Represents a single, independent, virtual task that a worker can complete, submit an answer to, and receive payment for.

hypotheses: A testable claim or theory that will be investigated through empirical analysis.

hypothetical vignettes: A data-gathering technique that involves presenting hypothetical scenarios and asking research participants a series of pointed questions to get their beliefs and perspectives.

hypothetico-deductive method: A method that treats theory as a deductive system in which the explanatory power of a hypothesis is tested by making predictions on said hypothesis and comparing predictions against empirical data.

i10-index: A citation metric created by and maintained within Google Scholar that measures the number of publications with at least ten citations each.

I^2 statistic: A relative metric of heterogeneity calculated as the ratio of between-study variance to total variance.

impact factor: An measure of a journal's average impact based on citations generated by Clarivate, the analytics company operating Web of Science; it measures the frequency with which the average article in a journal has been cited in a particular year and it is calculated as: (total number of citations from JCR year to items in "year –2" + citations from JCR year to items in "year –1") ÷

(total number of citable items in "year –2" + citable items in "year –1").

implicit selection bias: In meta-analysis, an unconscious bias leads to a non-random or non-representative sample. There are four types of implicit selection bias in meta-analysis literature search, availability bias (selective inclusion of studies that are easily accessible to the researcher), cost bias (selective inclusion of studies that are available free or at low costs), familiarity bias (selective inclusion of studies only from one's field or discipline), and language bias (selective inclusion of studies published in English).

in vivo coding: A coding method in which a label is assigned to a passage of data using a word or short phrase from that same section of the passage.

incremental validity: A type of validity improvement occurs by incorporating a particular procedure into a current collection of assessment methods.

individual participant data (IPD): Raw data from individual participants; more useful than aggregated data for meta-analyses due to high precision and consistency.

inductive theory generation: An approach of theory generation that begins with an unexplained phenomenon and then draws on data to induct new constructs and relationships. See also "theorizing" and "theory generation."

inferential statistics: The use of data analysis techniques that allows for inferences about population characteristics based on sample data.

influential outlier: An accurate data point that lies far from other data points and affects substantive conclusions; it is not necessarily an error or interesting outlier.

informed consent: A research ethics principle; once a participant gives their informed permission, the researcher must explain the study's goals, their involvement in the study, and how it will operate. The informed consent form is a crucial component of the informed consent procedure.

Institutional Review Board (IRB): A regulatory organization designed to defend the rights and welfare of individuals recruited to participate in research projects carried out by the institution to which it is connected.

instrumental variables: A method to replace an independent variable with a new one when the latter relates to the error term.

Insufficient Effort Responding (IER): Refers to participants who pay insufficient attention to the item content of the research study conducted, which reduces the quality of data collected.

interclass correlation: A measure of the relation between two variables of different types (classes), most commonly measured using the Pearson product-moment correlation. See also "Pearson product-moment correlation."

interesting outlier: An accurate data point that lies far from other data points and may contain valuable or unexpected knowledge.

internal consistency: A measure of the degree to which various items of a measure correlate with each other; the more homogenous the items, the lower the error since the error is defined as item heterogeneity. See also "Cronbach's coefficient alpha."

internal validity: The extent to which we are confident about one variable's relation and causal effect on another.

interpretive: A qualitative method aimed at understanding (interpreting) people's meanings, purposes, and intentions for their actions and interactions with others.

interrater agreement: A measure of the agreement between raters on their ratings of some dimension. Tinsley and Weiss's index of agreement T is a popular method of calculating interrater agreement and is given by $T = \frac{N_1 - NP}{N - NP}$, where N_1 is the number of agreements, N is the number of individuals rated, and P is the probability of chance agreement on an individual.

interrater reliability: The level of consensus between different observers rating, coding, or evaluating the same phenomena.

interval contingent experience sampling methodology (ESM): One of three types of ESM protocols, in the interval contingent protocol, participants provide ESM responses at pre-determined intervals (e.g., every hour) or at the same time daily. See also "experience sampling methodology (ESM)."

interval scale: A type of scale that provides labels, order, and a specific interval between each variable option. See also "scale."

intraclass correlation (ICC) index: An index of consistency generally used when multiple raters are rating objects or individuals, typically expressed as the ratio of the variance associated with targets over the sum of the variance associated with targets plus error variance based on the results of an analysis of variance. This method determines how much of the differences among raters are due to differences in individuals on the attribute being measured and how much is due to measurement errors. Given by the ratio of between-group predictor variance (τ) relative to the total predictor variance [i.e., $\rho_x = \tau / (\tau + \sigma^2)$], where σ^2 is the variance component of the lower-level residual from a null model.

IP Address: Any network device uniquely identified by a series of assigned numbers, also known as "Internet Protocol address."

IP threat score: A tool used to help validate that web-based study participants are properly identifying themselves, wherein these tools return the probability of the user's associated device being flagged on lists of known masking or malicious hosts. The probability score ranges from 0 to 1, with numbers increasingly close to 1 indicating increased threat.

item analysis: An analysis that evaluates measures based on the value of individual items, item sets, and full sets using statistics and professional judgment.

item characteristic curve (ICC): A chart showing the relationship between the likelihood that a test question will be successfully answered and the test taker's true aptitude for the attribute being assessed.

item difficulty: An estimate of the proficiency required to answer a question correctly, frequently determined by calculating the percentage of those who pass it.

item discrimination: Refers to the degree to which an item on a measure can differentiate participants based on their knowledge, skills, or ability.

item response theory (IRT): A paradigm for creating, evaluating, and scoring exams, surveys, and other similar instruments used to gauge skills, attitudes, or other factors.

item-total score correlation: An indicator of the reliability of items on a measure. A high item-total correlation suggests that the item is consistent with the overall test and is measuring the same underlying construct as the other items.

iteratively reweighted least squares: A robust approach to model fit and outlier management, this method reiterates instances of weighted least squares (i.e., an ordinary least squares process that incorporates the known variance of observations) to find an estimate of a generalized linear model. See also "ordinary least squares."

jangle fallacy: A term that refers to discordant naming practices revolving around the assumption that different constructs can go by the same name. See "construct identity fallacy."

jingle fallacy: A term that refers to discordant naming practices revolving around the assumption that there can be dozens of terms and scores of measures for the same construct. See "construct identity fallacy."

Job Diagnostic Survey (JDS): A self-report tool specifically designed to evaluate how existing jobs may be redesigned for better employee results and to evaluate the effect of job changes on employees.

joint distribution: The pattern of values determined by the probability of occurrence of two or more random variables. A two-variable joint distribution, more specifically, may be called a bivariate distribution.

journal list: A ranked list of academic journals that indicates the meritorious quality of the journals and, by extension, the respective scholarly publications included therein and the researchers who authored those publications. Journal lists are often used as a measure of academic performance management systems. See also "A-journal."

key informant (KI): A key decision-maker with extensive and exclusive information and the ability to influence important organizational outcomes alone or jointly with others (e.g., on a board of directors).

Kuder-Richardson 20 (KR-20): Kuder-Richardson 20 (KR-20) is a special case of Cronbach's alpha in which the responses are binary in nature (i.e., there are just two possible outcomes for each question such as, correct or incorrect, true or false) given by $r_{tt} = \frac{k}{k-1}\left(\frac{\sigma_t^2 - \sum \sigma_i^2}{\sigma_t^2}\right)$, where k is number of items included in the measure, is the variance of total scores on the measure, and is the sum of the variances of item scores. See also "Cronbach's coefficient alpha."

language bias: In a meta-analysis, a type of implicit selection bias in the literature search related to the selective inclusion of studies published in English. See "implicit selection bias."

latent class growth analysis (LCGA): A person-centric longitudinal approach that models heterogeneity by classifying individuals into latent classes (i.e., unobserved groups) with similar characteristics. Also known as latent class growth modeling (LCGM) or mixture modeling.

latent class growth modeling (LCGM): A person-centric longitudinal approach that models heterogeneity by classifying individuals into latent classes (i.e., unobserved groups) with similar characteristics. See also "latent class growth analysis (LCGA)."

latent growth modeling (LGM): A longitudinal analysis technique used to estimate growth trajectories in structural equation modeling by representing repeated measures of dependent variables as a function of time. Also called latent growth curve analysis. See also "structural equation modeling (SEM)."

leader-member exchange (LMX): A theory that asserts that leaders and followers develop special relationships based on the quality of social exchanges, and perceptions of followers of that relationship affect employee and organizational outcomes.

least absolute deviation: A statistical optimization technique similar to least squares except that it uses absolute values instead of ordinary least squared values. The least absolute deviation minimizes the difference between points generated from the proposed function and the observed dependent variable data points. See also "ordinary least squares."

least trimmed squares: A statistical optimization technique similar to ordinary least squares except that it attempts to minimize the sum of squared error over a subset of the entire set; the unused points do not influence the fit of the function.

less than ideal operationalization of constructs (LIOC): A critical threat to the validity of conclusions specifically related to contamination (i.e., a measure assesses factors that are not part of the construct) and the deficiency (i.e., a measure does not assess factors that are part of the construct but should be assessed).

level of analysis: A study's focal level (e.g., individual, team, firm) at which data is assigned for hypothesis testing and analysis.

level of inquiry: Generally refers to the levels of theory, measurement, and analysis at which the researcher focuses a study. See also "level of theory," "level of measurement," and "level of analysis."

level of measurement: A study's focal level (e.g., individual, team, firm) at which the researcher collects data.

level of theory: A study's focal level (e.g., individual, team, firm) at which the researcher seeks to generalize.

leverage value: Also known as the diagonal elements of the hat matrix, leverage values measure the extent to which observations are outliers in the space of predictors. Recommended cutoffs for leverage values are $2(k+1)/n$ for large sample sizes and $3(k+1)/n$ for small sample sizes, where k = number of predictors and n = sample size. In addition, leverage values have a centered index measurement called "centered leverage values," recommended cutoffs for centered leverage values are $2k/n$ for large sample sizes and $3k/n$ for small sample sizes. Certain statistical packages (e.g., IBM SPSS) report centered leverage values instead of regular ones.

lift: In market basket analysis, the probability of all the items in a rule occurring together (i.e., "support") divided by the product of the probabilities of the items occurring as if there was no association between them. See also "Market Basket Analysis (MBA)" and "support."

Likert scale: A specialized scale consisting of statements that may indicate strong positive or negative responses.

linear transformations: Refers to adding a constant to the variable, subtracting a constant from the variable, multiplying a constant by the variable, and dividing a constant by the variable.

living systematic review (LSR): A review of literature or research continuously updated in real-time, incorporating new information as it becomes available.

log odds ratio: Refers to utilizing the natural logarithm of the odds ratio for large sample approximations. See "odds ratio."

logistic regression: A method of estimating the parameters of a logistic model.

log-likelihood value: A value that quantifies the probability that a model being estimated could be reproduced based on sample data.

longitudinal designs: A type of study where researchers observe participants over some time (e.g., days, weeks, or even years), allowing for an understanding of how things change over time and understand long-term effects or trends.

longitudinal study: A type of study in which participants are observed over time and compared against themselves at different times to determine any changing effect.

long-string index: The process of evaluating the frequency and length of participant response patterns while selecting the same response for several items and creating a threshold based on the data to flag potentially faulty responses.

macro organizational research: Organizational research done at the organizational level or social/economic environment analysis rather than the individual or team level.

Mahalanobis distance: A multiple construct (i.e., "distance") identification technique, which is the length of the line segment between a data point and the centroid (instead of another observation) of the remaining cases, where the centroid is the point created at the intersection of the means of all the predictor variables. A large Mahalanobis distance may mean that the corresponding observation is an outlier; recommended cutoffs are $\chi^2_{df=p;\ alpha\ level\ =\ \alpha/n}$ for large sample sizes, and $\dfrac{p(n-1)^2\left(F_{df=p,\ n-p-1;\ alpha\ level\ =\ \alpha/n}\right)}{n\left(n-p-1+pF_{df=p,\ n-p-1;\ alpha\ level\ =\ \alpha/n}\right)}$ for small sample sizes, where p = number of variables, χ^2 = critical value in a Chi-squared distribution, F = critical value in an F distribution, and α = .05 or .01. Recommended cutoffs for studentized deleted residuals are $t_{df=n-k-1;\ alpha\ level\ =\ \alpha/n}$, where t = critical value in a t distribution, and α = .05 or .01. Finally, cutoffs for deletion standardized multivariate residuals for multilevel modeling are based on $\chi^2_{df=n\ of\ highest-level\ unit\ j;\ alpha\ level\ =\ \alpha/n}$, where α = .05 or .01.

MARA: A meta-analytical technique that tests whether the size of the effects can be predicted by fluctuations in the hypothesized moderators' values. Also see "meta-regression analysis."

Market Basket Analysis (MBA): A data mining technique known as "affinity analysis," used to uncover preference-based covariation between items, traditionally in retail settings but gaining

popularity in other fields. MBA has two approaches: Multiple MBA and Sequential MBA. See also "multiple MBA" and "sequential MBA."

Markov chain Monte Carlo (MCMC): Used in Bayesian analysis, a Monte Carlo-style sampling method where the following sample drawn depends on the existing sample, known as a Markov chain. See also "Monte Carlo research."

Master Worker: A qualification granted to Amazon Mechanical Turk workers who consistently demonstrate a high degree of success in performing a wide breadth of HITs.

matching: A process for ensuring that participants in various study conditions are comparable at the start of the study on one or more important factors that could impact on results.

Matthew effect of accumulated advantage: A phenomenon in which those with an advantage accumulate more advantage and those disadvantaged become more disadvantaged over time; summarized by the adage, "the rich get richer while the poor get poorer."

maximum likelihood (ML): A method of estimating the parameters of an assumed probability distribution given some provided data.

mean: A summary statistic representing a data set's average. The arithmetic mean is the sum of the values divided by the number of values.

measurement equivalence: The event in which two measurement instruments are interchangeable as they produce the same results for the same sample.

measurement invariance: The notion that a measurement instrument should behave in the same way across varied conditions given that those conditions are irrelevant to the variable being measured.

measurement scales: A measurement classification of the values assigned to variables; there are four types of measurement scales: nominal, ordinal, interval, and ratio. See also "scale."

Mechanical Turk (MTurk): A marketplace for crowdsourcing that makes it simpler for people and companies to contract out their operations and

jobs to various organizations that can complete these tasks virtually.

mechanics: A set of physical theories describing the motion of macroscopic objects.

median: The number dividing a population, a probability distribution, or a data sample's upper and lower halves; a set's "middle" value.

mediation: Using an intermediary modeling variable that accounts for an observed relation between the independent and dependent variables. Mediation can be partial, which accounts for some of the relationships between the independent and dependent variables, or full in, which occurs when the inclusion of the mediation variable completely negates the relationship between the independent and dependent variables.

M-estimation: Statistical method used in the field of robust statistics, which deals with techniques for constructing estimators that are not unduly affected by small departures from model assumptions. The "M" in M-estimation stands for "maximum likelihood type" estimation.

meta-analysis: A family of analysis techniques and data collection to produce a quantitative review of a body of literature; it consists of a quantitative summary of the existing literature to arrive at an overall measure of the effect of a treatment as well as the variability of effects across primary-level studies and reasons for this variation (i.e., moderator variables).

Meta-Analytic Reporting Standards (MARS): A set of recommended information established by the American Psychological Association for inclusion in manuscripts reporting meta-analyses.

meta-analytic structural equation modeling (MASEM): A combination of meta-analysis (MA) and structural equation modeling (SEM) that incorporates the advantages of both approaches, allowing researchers to draw on accumulated findings to test the explanatory value of a theorized model against one or more competing models.

meta-regression: A meta-analytic technique that involves regressing meta-analytically derived effect sizes on several hypothesized predictors (i.e., boundary conditions) simultaneously while weighting each effect size estimate by an indicator of its precision, such as the inverse of the within-study variance (i.e., sampling variance) of the study. Meta-regression offers two important benefits: (1) it capitalizes on a major advantage of meta-analysis, which involves relying on all of the available data to examine a particular phenomenon, (2) avoids (a) artificial dichotomization of boundary conditions, and (b) the untenable assumption that reality includes only one boundary condition at a time.

meta-theory: Theories that are classified into two categories: (a) philosophical and (b) formalized. Philosophical meta-theories generally address theory and describe what theories are, what they should do, and how scholars should develop them. Alternatively, formalized meta-theories are overarching principles that transcend specific topics or domains of study and describe and predict phenomena in more abstract or higher levels than specific theories. Formalized meta-theories extract what is generally consistent across theories, similar to how meta-analysts extract what is generally consistent across primary-level studies.

micro organizational research: Organizational research done at the individual level of analysis, as opposed to the organizational level.

microfoundations: An area of study that relates macroeconomic phenomena in microeconomic contexts, specifically agents' behaviors, and interactions.

missing at random (MAR): An assumption that describes missing data that can be accounted for by variables with complete information.

missing completely at random (MCAR): An assumption describing missing data when there is no relationship between the absence of data and any observed or missing values; it occurs completely at random.

mixed methods: A research approach that uses several methods in a single research project, often blending quantitative and qualitative techniques in the same study.

mixed research design: In experimental vignette methodology (EVM), a type of research design that requires different groups of participants to receive different sets of vignettes; however, participants read the same vignettes within each group. Because multiple respondents also offer responses regarding the same vignettes, comparisons can be made across respondents. See also "experimental vignette methodology (EVM)."

mixed-effects (ME) model: A meta-analytic model that assumes that the studies in the meta-analysis are a random sample from a super-population of possible studies and that the super-population distribution of true effect sizes is normally distributed. In the ME model, the variance in the distribution of observed effects is attributed to: (a) within-study variance (i.e., due mainly to sampling error) and (b) between-study variance (i.e., due to differences of true effect sizes in the super-population). Also called "random-effects model." See also "common-effect (CE) model."

mixture modeling: A person-centric longitudinal approach that models heterogeneity by classifying individuals into latent classes (i.e., unobserved groups) with similar characteristics. Also known as latent class growth analysis (LCGA). See "latent class growth analysis (LCGA)."

mode: The number in a set of numbers that appears the most frequently and is, therefore, the value most likely to be sampled.

moderated multiple regression: A method of evaluating the effect of a moderator between an independent and a dependent variable by introducing a product term between the independent and moderating variables followed by a calculation of ΔR^2 (i.e., incremental proportion of variance explained in the dependent variable by including the product term in the regression equation).

moderation: A type of effect that serves as a contingency or boundary condition for the relations between two variables. Moderators variable can influence the size, direction, and strength of a relation or effect between two variables.

modification index: A method of respecification that estimates the amount by which the removal of a single parameter restriction would lower the chi-square, therefore indicating a better model fit. See also "respecification."

mono-method bias: The resultant bias due to utilizing a single method of measurement.

monotonic transformation: A process that converts one set of numbers into another while maintaining the order of the original numbers.

Monte Carlo research: A computer simulation technique that generates many well-defined random samples.

multicollinearity: High degree of covariation among some or all the predictors in a model.

multidimensional and multistakeholder model of scholarly impact: A pluralist conceptualization of scholarly impact that consists of four dimensions: Theory and Research, Education, Organizations, and Society. For the theory and research dimension, the key stakeholders are other researchers, and impact is usually measured using citations—the extent to which a scholar influences the thinking and work of other scholars. For the education dimension, the aspiration is to have a long-lasting influence on student development by disseminating relevant knowledge and its applications. For the organizations dimension, the aspiration is to influence practitioners: managers and consultants who use research-generated knowledge. For the society dimension, the goal is to influence policymakers such as legislators and government officials.

multidimensional construct model: A construct model in which the measures are reflective indicators of their dimensions, and the dimensions are reflective or formative indicators of a broader construct.

multidimensional scaling: A multivariate analysis technique that analyzes the structure of a data set by plotting points in one or two dimensions, for example, using space on a graph to map psychological distance as physical distance.

multilevel modeling: A method used with hierarchical data structures to assess the contribution of each level of analysis to the variance of the response variable.

multiple imputation (MI): An approach that minimizes the increased noise due to the process of replacing missing data values (i.e., statistical imputation) by drawing several imputed values from a distribution to create a number of new data sets, analyzing the data sets, and pooling the results into one result by calculating the mean, variance and confidence interval of the of concern.

multiple MBA: A market basket analysis (MBA) approach that is used when the available data include transactions that have occurred over time (i.e., transactions at time 1, transactions at time 2, ..., transactions at time *k*); each data wave is treated as a single cross-sectional study and then examining whether the lift, support, and confidence of association rules vary over time, which can be mainly done descriptively using graphs. See "Market Basket Analysis (MBA)."

multisource rating: A qualitative analysis technique that incorporates feedback ratings from multiple groups of assessors.

multitrait-multimethod approach: A data analysis approach used when responses must be gathered on at least two constructs, each measured by at least two different methods (e.g., supervisor ratings, observations, self-reports). Correlations among the different constructs measured by different methods are calculated to form a multitrait-multimethod matrix.

multivariate analysis of covariance (MAN-COVA): An extension of ANCOVA that covers cases where the experiment has more than one dependent variable and the control of covariates is required.

multivariate analysis of variance (MANOVA): A procedure that assesses possible group differences on a set of more than one dependent variables.

mundane realism: The extent to which events in an experiment are similar to those in the real world.

narrative analysis: The qualitative analysis of the stories individuals tell to themselves and others.

naturalistic observation: A qualitative research technique that involves watching participants in their natural setting.

network analysis: A technique used to analyze relationships among entities through networks and graph theory.

neural network: An algebraic process similar to the functioning neurons in the brain is used analytically in modeling and classification tasks; thus, an artificial neural network is composed of artificial neurons or nodes.

noise: Unexplained variability within a data sample caused by random irregularity in real-life data.

nominal scale: A specialized scale that uses labels to identify or categorize and has no specific order or quantitative value. See also "scale."

nomological network: In psychometrics, a conceptual framework that represents the relationships between a construct and other constructs.

non-experimental research: Research that measures variables as they naturally occur rather than manipulating independent variables. Also called "passive observation" research.

nonlinear transformation: A process where a variable is modified in a way that the relationship between the original and transformed variables is not a straight line (i.e., not linear).

nonparametric bootstrap procedure: A bootstrapping procedure that grows its sample via resampling via simulation (i.e., parametric bootstrapping). See also "bootstrapping."

nonparametric technique: A family of statistical procedures in which common assumptions about the distribution of attributes, such as normality or variance homogeneity, do not apply to the data under analysis.

non-probability sample: As sample including observations (e.g., individuals, firms) for which we have access (e.g., students) or those to sign up voluntarily to be part of our study (e.g.,

using an online platform). Also called "convenience samples."

norms: A statistical concept in psychometrics, where a test is created to measure a participant's performance in relation to the average replies of a standardized and representative group.

null hypothesis (H$_0$): The hypothesis that there is no effect or relationship between variables.

null hypothesis significance testing (NHST): A statistical inference approach based on assessing the probability that a null hypothesis (i.e., no effect) is false.

null model: In multilevel modeling, the first step specified by combining the ordinary least squares regression equations for Levels 1 and 2, given by the null model (combined) equation: $Y_{ij} = \gamma_{00} + u_{0j} + r_{ij}$, where Y_{ij} is the dependent variable for the ith person in team j, γ_{00} is the team-averaged intercept for all teams, u_{0j} is the L2 residual term, and r_{ij} is the L1 residual term (i.e., both residual terms are randomly distributed error).

null test: A formal process to statistically determine whether a relationship exists between cause and effect or if it is due to chance.

Nuremberg Code: A set of guidelines for research that were created after the atrocities committed by the Nazis and their allies in Germany and throughout Europe, particularly the cruel and frequently fatal experiments conducted on human victims without their consent during World War II. The created Code consists of a ten-point statement delimiting permissible medical experimentation on human participants. See "ten-point statement."

observational technique: An exploratory technique that emphasizes the direct observation of a scene, either by allowing the observer to mix in with the scene or by establishing an observation post such as a video camera.

Occam's razor: The principle that other things being equal, explanations that posit fewer entities should be preferred to explanations that posit more. See also "principle of parsimony."

odds ratio: A statistic used to quantify the strength of the association between two events, typically in a case-control study. It represents the odds that an event will occur given a particular exposure, compared to the odds of the event occurring without that exposure.

omega-squared (ω^2): A measure of effect size between a qualitative independent variable and quantitative dependent variable.

omnibus test: Any statistical significance test in which more than two conditions are simultaneously compared, such as when a model features two or more independent variables.

online marketplaces: Websites connecting individuals interested in being hired and clients looking for individuals to perform work meet.

open access: A practice of the open science academic movement that refers explicitly to distributing research results online free of charges or barriers (e.g., subscription or pay-per-view fees) as soon as it is published. See "open science."

open archive: A practice of the open science academic movement referring to making results available for free after some embargo period. See "open science."

open data: A practice of the open science academic movement specifically refers to that data open to everyone for access, use, and redistribution. See "open science."

Open Science: An academic movement and set of practices focused on making scientific research freely accessible for distribution, transparency, and collaboration; such practices include open access, open archive, and open data. See "open access," "open archive," and "open data."

open/initial coding: A grounded theory-based approach that divides data into discrete parts and labels observed phenomena during analysis.

operationalization: The practice of assigning explicit observations as representations of abstract constructs.

ordinal: A form of a interaction effect in which the lines do not cross.

ordinal scale: A type scale based on ranking but the intervals between values are not necessarily uniform or meaningful.

ordinary least squares (OLS): A linear regression technique that uses the principle of least squares (i.e., minimizing the sum of the squares of the difference between observed dependent variables and the outputs of the estimated function for the corresponding independent variable).

outlier: An observation that lies far from other data points in the same distribution. See also "winsorizing approach," and "error outlier," "interesting outlier," "influential outlier," "global prediction outlier," "respecification," and "specific prediction outlier."

outliers: data points that are markedly different from the rest of the data."

p fishing: The non-scientific practice of trying multiple statistical tests to find one in which $p < .05$, and such a practice is generally considered misconduct.

p value: In Item Response Theory (IRT), a measure of item difficulty that can be computed to determine the number of individuals that correctly responded to the query.

paper and pencil: A measure in which the questions are read, and the answers are written down.

paper people studies: Another way of referring to experimental vignette methodology (EVM) that presents participants with vignettes, typically in written form, and then ask participants to make explicit decisions, judgments, choices, or express behavioral preferences. See also "experimental vignette methodology (EVM)."

parallel forms: In psychometrics, a method used to assess the reliability of a measure, consisting of creating two different versions of the same measure (Form A and Form B) that are as similar as possible in terms of content, difficulty, and style. These parallel forms are then administered to the same group of people.

parameterization: Describing the relationship between variables in terms of specific strength and direction.

participant observation: An ethnographic method involving intensive fieldwork with a particular group of people to collect primary data whereby the observer lives among those under study and becomes a participating member to develop close relationships with the participants.

participants: The individuals who take part in a study whose behavior is recorded and analyzed by the researcher.

participative inquiry: A quasi-experimental research method in which the researcher studies a group by becoming a member of it.

passive observation: A research method in which researchers measure variables as they occur naturally without manipulating independent variables. See also "non-experimental research."

path analysis: A modeling technique that outlines paths of explanation from predictor variables to dependent variables.

Pearson product-moment correlation: A measure of the degree of linear covariation between two sets of data, also called Pearson correlation coefficient, Pearson's correlation, or Pearson's r, for short, symbolized by r for a sample and ρ for a population. It is given by
$$r = \frac{\sum_{i=1}^{n}(x_i - \bar{x})(y_i - \bar{y})}{\sqrt{\sum_{i=1}^{n}(x_i - \bar{x})^2}\sqrt{\sum_{i=1}^{n}(y_i - \bar{y})^2}},$$
where n is the sample size, x_i and y_i are individual values indexed by i, and $\bar{x}$ and $\bar{y}$ are sample means; or $\rho_{X,Y} = \frac{\text{cov}(X, Y)}{\sigma_X \sigma_Y}$, where cov is the covariance and σ_X and σ_Y are the standard deviations of X and Y, respectively.

peer review: A system to evaluate manuscripts describing research studies to assess the validity, correctness, and frequently the originality of publications before they are published.

percentile ranks: The proportion of scores in a frequency distribution that fall below that score.

personal experience method: A deep reflection in which a researcher writes about a topic of significant personal relevance and situates their experience within the societal context— also known as autoethnography.

personal impact development plan (PIDP): A self-reflective professional development plan focused on developing specific impact competencies over a predetermined period by setting developmental activities to target each competency.

personal scholarly impact plan: A multiphase, personalized plan that assists researchers in addressing specific dimensions of the multidimensional and multistakeholder model of scholarly impact.

p-hacking: The abuse of data analysis to manipulate results interpretation to find patterns that can be presented as statistically significant despite no actual relationship existing, thus dramatically increasing the likelihood (and underreporting) of Type I error (i.e., the probability of mistakenly reporting significant results).

philosophical meta-theory: A category of meta-theories that generally addresses theories and describe what they are, what they should do, and how scholars should develop them. See "meta-theory."

pilot study: A small-scale preliminary study carried out before any large-scale study to assess the likelihood of a later, full-scale project, also known as a "feasibility study."

plagiarism: Adopting someone else's ideas or efforts and passing them off as one's own.

policy capturing: A judgment analysis method used to describe the relationship between a research participant's decision and the information the participant used to make that decision. Also referred to as "conjoint analysis."

policy capturing: Another way of referring to experimental vignette methodology (EVM), in which the researcher presents scenarios and asks participants to make decisions to capture participants' implicit processes. See also "experimental vignette methodology (EVM)."

pooled regression line: A regression line that estimates the mean of a population of regression lines.

population effect: The effect or relationship between two variables in the population (i.e., "true" effect) rather than in any given sample.

posterior distribution, $p(\Theta|D)$ term: In Bayes' theorem, the posterior distribution specifies the relative credibility of every combination of parameters given the data. See also "Bayesian network."

power analysis: A method used to determine the required minimum sample size to ensure the detection of existing effects.

power of the purse: The ability of one entity to influence the actions of another positively or negatively by withholding or putting stipulations on the use of funds.

practitioner inquiry: A systematic and intentional analysis of one's professional practice to promote improvement; a method for "finding out."

precision-effect test and precision-effect estimate with standard errors (PET-PEESE): A step-wise combination of two methods for publication bias control, (1) PET method that uses the standard error of the effect sizes, and (2) PEESE method that uses the sampling variance as the predictor variables. PET-PEESE first tests whether PET is statistically significant, then uses PEESE if so, or PET if otherwise, to estimate the average effect size from a study with no sampling variance.

predictive adequacy: The degree to which hypotheses and propositions approximate reality.

predictive validation study: The degree to which results from a test or scale may be used to anticipate results from other criteria.

predictivism: A perspective on HARKing that argues that hypothesis accommodation leads to overfitting of data and impedes a theory's potential for predictive precision. See also "accommodationism" and "HARKing."

Preferred Reporting Items for Systematic reviews and Meta-Analyses (PRISMA): A minimum set (i.e., a 27-item checklist) of reportable items designed to assist authors to transparently report meta-analyses that requires authors to be explicit about the exact databases, the exact search terms, and the exact results, including duplicates and filtering criteria. Preferred Reporting Items for Systematic reviews and Meta-Analyses Protocols (PRISMA-P) requires authors to pre-register their study's entire systematic review protocol as encapsulated in a 17-item checklist.

principle of parsimony: The scientific principle that things typically behave or are connected in the simplest way. See also "Occam's razor."

probability sample: A sample in which most population members have the same probability of being included.

probable error: A statistical measure showing the half-range of an interval about the distribution center such that half of the values from the distribution lie within the interval and half outside.

probit regression: A regression model in which the outcome is a dichotomous or binary variable (e.g., "yes" or "no" options).

professional respondents: Questionnaire respondents (typically online based) who complete surveys primarily for monetary gain from response compensation.

programmatic theory: An umbrella theory that subsumes several unit theories in context to explain a phenomenon more broadly. See also "unit theory."

proprioceptive senses: Sensation referring to the feeling of movement, position, and/or on the body.

pseudo R^2: A measure of proportion of variance explained used for regression model comparison during instances where an R^2 value cannot be calculated.

psychometric deficiency: When a measure does not cover the entire construct domain.

psychometric meta-analysis: see "validity generalization."

psychometrics: A field of study concerned with testing, measurement, and assessment, especially within psychology and education.

publication bias: The practice of publishing research that is systematically unrepresentative of the completed studies population. A subset of the publication problem is the file drawer problem, which refers to the premise that there is no way to know how much reportable research in any given field is nonpublished. See also "funnel plot."

purposive sampling: A data collection methodology that relies on the researcher's judgment when choosing population members to participate in their study.

Q statistic: In a meta-analysis, a measure of heterogeneity is the weighted residual sum of squares between individual study effect sizes and the mean size across studies; the Q statistic, which follows a chi-square distribution, can be used to test the null hypothesis that heterogeneity is zero in the population. Larger Q values signal greater variability in primary-level effect sizes.

Quadratic Assignment Procedure (QAP): A non-parametric statistical test to evaluate the significance of regression coefficients.

qualitative methods: Research techniques that are largely inductive and rely on data obtained from participant observation, in-depth interviews, focus groups, document analysis, and other non-quantitative instruments.

qualitative positivism: A perspective that asserts that social phenomena exist not only in our minds, but also exist in the objective world, and there are lawful and reasonably stable relationships that we aim to identify and study. Also referred to as "transcendental realism."

quantitative association rules: In market basket analysis, association rules based on continuous data (e.g., summary statistics such as mean and median). See "association rules."

quantitative methods: Research techniques that focus on deductive approaches to data collection, analysis, and interpretation and an emphasis on hypothesis formation and testing.

quasi-experimental design: A type of research design in which the sample assignment for controlling or testing groups cannot be made random, either due to practical or ethical reasons.

question trolling: The practice of searching through data involving several different constructs, measures of those constructs, and interventions or relationships to find seemingly notable results worth writing about. See also "HARKing."

questionable research practices (QRPs): Research practices that fail to align with the principles of scientific integrity but fall short of "research misconduct."

random coefficients modeling (RCM): A linear modeling technique that models nested data (e.g., observations within individuals, individuals within teams, teams within organizations). Also called "hierarchical linear modeling" or "multilevel modeling."

random intercept and fixed slope model (RIFSM): The second step of multilevel modeling that explains σ^2 and τ_{00} and is given by the RIFSM (combined) equation.

random intercept and random slope model (RIRSM): The third step of multilevel modeling that adds a random slope component such that β_{1j}, the slope of an L2 variable, is allowed to vary across L2 variables and is given by the RIRSM (combined) equation.

random-effects model: A meta-analytic model that assumes the studies in the meta-analysis are a random sample from a super-population of possible studies and that the super-population distribution of true effect sizes is normally distributed. In the random-effects model, the variance in the distribution of observed effects is attributed to: (a) within-study variance (i.e., due mainly to sampling error) and (b) between-study variance (i.e., due to differences of true effect sizes in the super-population). Also called the "mixed-effects (ME) model." See "mixed-effects (ME) model."

range restriction: A term that refers to a situation when observed sample data are unavailable for the complete range of scores.

rank correlation test: Any of several methods that measure the relationship between different ordinal/ranked sets of variables (e.g., "first," "second," "third," so on).

rank-order analysis of variance: A type of analysis of variance based on the rank-based data (i.e., data collected using ordinal scales). See also "Analysis of Variance (ANOVA)."

ratio scale: A type of scale that includes a true zero value (i.e., the absence of the attribute being measured). See also "scale."

reallocation of credibility: A form of Bayesian inference in which the addition of new data (i.e., evidence) that increases the likelihood of one possibility will reduce the likelihood of other potential possibilities.

recall error: A cognitive bias wherein error is introduced when study participants are asked to recall past events.

reflective measurement model: A model such that the underlying construct drives their measures with positive and high intercorrelations. See also, "formative measurement model."

region of practical equivalence (ROPE): In Bayesian analysis, the region of practical equivalence corresponds to a "null" hypothesis in an equivalence test. ROPE is typically evaluated against HDI for equivalence tests. See also "highest density interval (HDI)."

region of significance: In moderator (i.e., interaction effect) analysis, the range of moderator values for which the regression shifts from non-significance to significance.

regression coefficient: A statistical measure of the average relationship between a dependent variable and an independent variable, thus, representing the extent to which the line slope representing the relation between the two goes upwards (i.e., positive coefficient) or downwards (i.e., negative coefficient). See also "coefficient beta."

relational demography research: An approach to researching the concept of "demographic similarity," which measures how much other people share a person's demographic characteristics in their social group.

reliability: Degree of consistency in the scores produced by a measure.

reliability coefficient: A measure of the consistency between two sets of scores that can range from 0 to 1, with numbers closer to one indicating high reliability and little measurement error and values closer to zero indicating low reliability and a large amount of measurement error

replication: The repetition of an original study using the same or similar methods and samples. See also "exact replication," "empirical replication," and "conceptual replication."

reprimand: A slight rebuke and only applied when relatively minimal infractions and wrongdoing occurs.

reproducibility: The condition of a study such that someone other than a published study's authors can obtain the same results using the original data.

re-scale: Group data centering techniques meant to provide reference points to give meaning to predictor variable values, particularly when the original scale does not include zero as a meaningful value; re-scaling often utilizes the arithmetic mean as a reference point, and it has two methods: group-mean centering and grand-mean centering. See "group-mean centering" and "grand-mean centering."

research paradigm: The set of generally accepted assumptions, concepts, procedures, and techniques within a discipline.

residual: The error in prediction; graphically represented by the vertical difference between a data point and the regression line.

residual heterogeneity (τ^2_{res})**:** The variability in effects not accounted for by the boundary conditions included in the model (i.e., the variance that is "leftover") and, in conjunction with the within-study variance, is used to weigh the studies in the meta-regression analysis.

respecification: Adding additional terms to the regression equation to manipulate model fit and account for outliers.

response rate (RR): The ratio of the number of completed surveys divided by the number of those surveyed. There are two types of RR: (1) Functional RR, which is desirable as it allows the researcher to derive conclusions with high confidence and make inferences about the targeted population (i.e., high validity), and (2) Dysfunctional RR, which is undesirable because it leads to inaccurate conclusions and inferences about the targeted population (i.e., low validity).

restricted maximum likelihood (REML): A maximum likelihood estimation that uses a function calculated from a transformed set of data such that nuisance parameters have no effect.

return on assets (ROA): A measure of company performance that shows how profitable a business is in relation to its assets' value.

return on equity (ROE): A measure of firm financial performance calculated by dividing a company's net income by its shareholders' equity.

return on investment (ROI): A profitability measurement used to determine how well an investment has done.

Right to Confidentiality and Anonymity: Confidentiality and anonymity are ethical practices used to safeguard the privacy of human participants when collecting, processing, and reporting data.

Right to Debriefing: A necessary step in the informed consent procedure that must be taken whenever deception is used in a research study. Participants receive a thorough explanation of the hypothesis being tested, the methods used to trick them, and the reason(s) why it was necessary to trick them during the debriefing.

Right to Privacy: The principle of protecting the individual's right to decide who can access their consent to participate in a study (i.e., extent, timing, circumstances).

Right to Protection from Deception: Research participants' right to be shielded from researchers purposely

misleading them about some important study aspects.

robust approaches: Statistics that work well with data derived from various probability distributions, particularly for atypical distributions.

Robust Error Variance (RVE): In a meta-analysis, RVE is a treatment of multiple effect sizes which considers the dependencies (i.e., covariation) among correlated effect sizes (i.e., from the same sample).

root mean square error of approximation (RMSEA): A measure of the estimated difference between the population's covariance matrices and those implied by the model per degree of freedom.

root mean square residual (RMSR): A measure used to assess the goodness of fit in models, particularly in the context of structural equation modeling (SEM) and other similar multivariate techniques.

sampling error: Fluctuations in statistical estimates due to data collected from a sample rather than the entire population.

scale: An ordered system of progressive test responses, of which there are several types: (1) Nominal scales use labels to identify or categorize and has no specific order or quantitative value (3) ordinal scales that uses labels and a specific order to represent non-mathematical ideas like the level of satisfaction or happiness and degree of pain (4) interval scale provide labels, order, and a specific interval between each variable option (5) ratio scales are an instance of an interval scale that accommodates a true zero value (i.e., complete absence of the attribute).

scaling: The categorization of different measurement scales: nominal scale, ordinal scale, interval scale, and ratio scale. See also "scale."

science-practice gap: A gap between the knowledge that academics produce and disseminate and the knowledge that practitioners consume and use.

scientific misconduct: Any action that violates accepted scientific practices and, as a result, compromises the integrity of the research process.

secondary data: Data collected not directly from the researcher, but by garnering publicly available data, such as publicly available firm performance (e.g., based on market performance).

Securities and Exchange Commission (SEC): A United States regulatory body responsible for maintaining the stock exchanges, brokers and dealers in securities, investment advisers, and mutual funds to support ethical business practices, release critical market data, and prevent fraud.

selective coding: A grounded theory-based approach to coding in which the researcher selects a main overarching category that connects and summarizes the core of the research.

selective survival bias: A type of sampling error or selection bias in which participants who achieve a particular milestone or point in the selection process are favored against those who did not.

self-plagiarism: The practice of reusing or recycling one's own precise words from previously published literature without attributing appropriate credit to the source.

self-report: Statements made by the participants about their state, feelings, beliefs, thoughts, and other personal statements.

self-selection bias: A type of selection bias introduced when participants elect to participate in a project, or not.

semiotic analysis: The study of social life as a system of signs that consist of a signifier (an observable event) and the signified (the concept associated with it).

semi-structured interview format: An interview technique wherein a few questions are predetermined, but other questions are not.

sequential MBA (SMBA): A market basket analysis (MBA) approach that is used when the available data describe individual events (i.e., items) as they have occurred over time. See "Market Basket Analysis (MBA)."

signal contingent experience sampling methodology: One of three types of

ESM protocols in which participants are prompted to respond by a signaling device at randomly selected time points in the day. See also "experience sampling methodology (ESM)."

simple linear regression: A type of regression model that describes the relationship between only one independent variable and one dependent variable using a straight line.

simple linear regression–bivariate: Type of statistical analysis that shows the relationship between two variables using a straight line.

simple regression: A type of regression analysis with only one independent variable and one dependent variable. Also called "simple linear regression."

simple slope: The regression of the outcome variable on the predictor variable at a specific value of the moderator variable; since simple slopes represent a range of effects in most cases, it is not meaningful to hypothesize or test a single effect for a predictor when that predictor interacts with a moderator variable.

single parameter influence: The standardized change in the jth parameter resulting from the deletion of observation i, symbolized by $\Delta \hat{\theta}_{ji}$. Positive values of $\Delta \hat{\theta}_{ji}$ indicate that excluding case i causes a smaller value of $\hat{\theta}_j$ (i.e., estimate of the jth parameter), while negative values of $\Delta \hat{\theta}_{ji}$ indicate that excluding case i causes a larger value of $\hat{\theta}_j$.

slope parameter: The increment response in the dependent variable per unit change in the independent variable.

snowball sampling: A procedure for collecting data in which study participants recruit more participants on behalf of the researcher (e.g., their friends, their coworkers). Also called "referral sampling."

social desirability bias: A type of response bias in which experiment participants answer questions in a way others will view favorably.

social loafing: The tendency that team members will put in less effort in a group setting.

social representation analysis: An area of research focused on the systems of values, beliefs, practices, ideas, and metaphors associated with how individuals think and interact with others to shape social constructs.

Social Sciences Citation Index (SSCI): A multidisciplinary citation index maintained by Clarivate Analytics.

sopite syndrome: A simulation sickness stemming from display update lags and image jumps that occur with some low-resolution head-mounted video displays; it has symptoms similar to motion sickness and includes chronic fatigue, lethargy, headaches, eyestrain, lightheadedness, dizziness, and nausea.

Spearman-Brown prophecy formula: A formula that links psychometric validity to measure length and is used to forecast validity after increasing the number of items.

specific factor error: A computer-aided text analysis-related measurement error associated with the choices made in creating word lists.

specific prediction outlier: An outlier that influences a single parameter estimate.

spline regression: A form of regression analysis that uses piecewise polynomial functions to model complex, non-linear relationships by dividing the data into segments (using points called knots) and fitting a smooth, continuous polynomial to each segment.

split-half method: A method for estimating internal consistency by administering a measure once and splitting it into two equivalent halves after it has been given to get two scores for each individual. This method is based on the premise that any item or group of items should be equivalent to any other item or group; the correlation between the two halves is a coefficient of equivalence that demonstrates the similarity of responses between the two halves. See "internal consistency."

spurious variables: A third variable that creates a false association between two other variables, leading to a misleading or incorrect interpretation of the relationship.

stakeholder theory: A perspective that emphasizes the interconnected relationships between an organization and the suppliers, customers, employees, investors, policymakers, communities, and others who hold a stake in the organization.

standard error of measurement: The degree to which measured test scores deviate from a "real" score. Given by $\sigma_{\text{Meas}} = \sigma_x\sqrt{1 - r_{xx}}$, where σ_x is the standard deviation of the distribution of obtained scores, and r_{xx} is the reliability estimate for the measure.

statistical control: A statistical technique used to regulate the extraneous variables to separate a variable's effect from the treatment effect to not confound it with the treatment. See also "control variable."

statistical power: The probability of detecting an effect in the population. Statistical power is defined as $1 - \beta$, where β is the Type II error rate (i.e., probability of mistakenly not detecting an existing effect). See also "power analysis" and "Type II error rate."

statistical significance testing: Assessment of the probability that a null hypothesis (i.e., no effect or relationship between variables) is false.

stepwise selection procedure: A method to systematically select variables used to predict a criterion via multiple regression, and it has two types: (1) Backward Selection Algorithms and (1) Forward Selection Algorithms. See "backward selection algorithms" and termforward selection algorithms."

stimuli: The items used to elicit a response from study participants or respondents.

strategy-as-practice: A unique method for researching strategic management, strategic decision-making, strategizing, strategy-making, and strategy work.

stratified sampling: A data collection approach that splits a population into multiple strata from which samples are drawn.

strong inference: A method for testing competing predictions that strengthen the logical conclusions yielded by

empirical research; it involves deriving competing hypotheses, then conducting empirical tests that produce evidence supporting one hypothesis while refuting another alternative hypothesis (or hypotheses).

structural coding: A first-round coding method in which data is codded according to research questions or topics.

structural equation modeling (SEM): Statistical technique that allows for the simultaneous analysis of complex relationships among multiple observed and latent variables.

structuring: A theory elaboration approach in which theoretical relations are expanded to describe and explain empirical observations accurately. See also "theorizing."

sua sponte: Latin that stands for "mutual consent; on one's own choice," which refers to a choice made with authority but without a formal request from another individual.

subject pools: A group of individuals from which study volunteers may be recruited.

subjects: Research participants whose behavior is recorded and analyzed by the researcher. See "participants."

submodel: A special case of a statistical model obtained by specifying certain parameters or certain relationships between parameters.

superordinate: A term used to describe a higher grade, status, or level within a hierarchical classification system.

support: In market basket analysis, the probability of all the items in a rule occurring together in market basket analysis (MBA). See "lift" and "Market Basket Analysis (MBA)."

survey: A study in which a group of participants is selected from a population, and a set of data, such as opinions or preferences, are collected (such as by questionnaire) and analyzed.

T^2 statistic: A measure of heterogeneity that estimates the parameter τ^2 and denotes the between-study variance, computed as the Q statistic minus the degrees of freedom (i.e., $k - 1$) divided by a scaling factor.

taxonomy: The classification of a system.

telepresence: Technology that makes it possible for someone to act as though they are physically present in a distant or virtual location.

temporal sequencing: An appropriate chronological sequence of events to establish causal relationships.

ten-point statement: A ten-point statement delimiting permissible medical experimentation on human participants: (1) Voluntary consent is essential, (2) The results of any experiment must be for the greater good of society, (3) Human experiments should be based on previous animal experimentation, (4) Experiments should be conducted by avoiding physical/mental suffering and injury, (5) No experiments should be conducted if it is believed to cause death/disability, (6) The risks should never exceed the benefits, (7) Adequate facilities should be used to protect participants, (8) Experiments should be conducted only by qualified scientists (9) Participants should be able to end their participation at any time, (10) The scientist in charge must be prepared to terminate the experiment when injury, disability, or death is likely to occur. See also "Nuremberg Code."

test-retest reliability: A measure that evaluates the consistency of scores across time, by administering the same measure to the same individuals repeatedly.

THARKing: The practice of "transparently HARKing," such as disclosing that a hypothesis was derived from and created after the data were collected. See also "HARKing."

The Collaborative Institutional Training Initiative: Commonly known as CITI Program, is a provider of research ethics, compliance, and professional development education--it focuses on providing training and education about human subject research, responsible conduct of research, and research administration.

The Matthew Effect: Refers to the idea that those who already have advantages or successes tend to receive more opportunities and rewards (i.e., "the rich get richer"), while those who have less get even less.

The National Research Act: The National Research Act created the National Commission for the Protection of Human Subjects of Biomedical and Behavioral Research, tasked with identifying the fundamental ethical principles that should direct the conduct of biomedical and behavioral research involving human participants and developing best practices to ensure that such research is conducted by those principles.

theoretical sampling: The process of collecting and analyzing data to decide what to collect next to develop a theory as it emerges.

theoretical saturation: In qualitative research, the point at which new information does not add new insights or changes conclusions.

theorizing: The process of developing a theory consists of three facets: theory generation, theory elaboration, and theory testing. See also "theory generation," "theory elaboration," "structuring," and "theory testing."

theory: A supposition intended to explain a phenomenon using scientific methods.

theory elaboration: A type of theorizing which uses existing concepts and models to guide the collection and organization of data by contrasting, specifying, and structuring theoretical constructs and relations. See also "theorizing" and "structuring."

theory generation: A facet of theorizing that provides new theoretical ideas, typically through inductive or deductive theory generation. See also "theorizing," "inductive theory generation," and "deductive theory generation."

theory pruning: The practice of enhancing hypothesis specification and study design to bound and reduce superfluous or overly grand theory.

theory refinement: The practice of updating theory in the light of on new data.

theory testing: A facet of theorizing in which data are collected and analyzed

to assess whether they provide evidence to support hypothesized relationships. See also "theorizing."

thought experiment: A judgment about what would happen if an imagined scenario were real, which can be used based on: (a) theory's development stage: early versus late, and (b) study's primary theoretical purpose: theory disconfirmation versus theory confirmation.

too-much-of-a-good-thing (TMGT) effect: An effect that is present when ordinarily beneficial antecedents (i.e., predictor variables) reach inflection points, after which their relations with desired outcomes (i.e., criterion variables) cease to be linear and positive.

total shareholder returns (TSRs): The overall total investment returns to the investor, which measure the performance of a company's several stocks and shares over time. TSR is frequently used by financial analysts and represented as an annualized percentage of the total capital gains and dividends that have been paid to investors, computed as Total Shareholder Return % = (Stock price at the end of the period – The stock price at the start of period) + Dividends paid or reinvested) ÷ Stock price at the start of the period.

transcendental realism: A perspective that asserts that social phenomena exist not only in our minds but they also exist in the objective world, and there are lawful and reasonably stable relationships that we aim to identify and study. Also referred to as "Qualitative positivism."

transient error: In computer-aided text analysis (CATA), a type of measurement error associated with differences in the language recorded at different times

triangulated: Using different methods, data, and other methodological procedures to investigate the same topic, hypothesis, question, or theory.

triangulation: The utilization of several research methods to analyze the same phenomenon with the intent of strengthening one's conclusions by converging multiple perspectives.

trim and fill method: A method in meta-analysis that minimizes publication

bias by trimming the studies that cause funnel plot asymmetry and filling imputed missing studies based on the bias-corrected overall estimate. See "funnel plot."

trimming: The act of manipulating research data and processes by changing and manipulating research outcomes.

TRINET: Database including information on public and private firms covering alternate (odd) years between 1981 and 1989.

turnover: The number or percent of individuals leaving an organization over a particular period. See also "functional turnover" and "dysfunctional turnover."

Tuskegee Syphilis Study: A study conducted by the U.S. Public Health Service (UPHS) Syphilis Study at Tuskegee Institute where informed consent was not given by the participants (600 low-income African American males) for 40 years; 400 of them had syphilis.

Type I error rate (α): The probability of sample results showing an effect that does not exist in the population.

Type II error rate (β): The probability of mistakenly not detecting an effect that does exist. Type II error has an inverse relationship with Type I error.

unit of analysis: The main entity described and analyzed in a study, such as the individuals, team, group, and organization.

unit theory: Theory that explains the causal relationship of specific concepts; it clarifies and predicts empirical patterns but is also narrower and can usually be subsumed within a programmatic theory. See also "programmatic theory."

unjustified authorship credit: the practice of awarding authorship to those who haven't contributed much effort or research content to important research publications.

unstructured interview format: A flexible interview technique wherein the interviewer allows the informant to take the lead and talk about their experience, thoughts, and ideas.

upper echelons: A person with significant leadership, power, or status.

usable theory: Theory that conveys insights that are actionable by practitioners to influence a relevant problem. See also "useful theory."

useful theory: Theory that conveys insights that provide knowledge about a problem relevant to theory consumers. See also "usable theory."

utilitarian perspective: An ethical theory that distinguishes between right and wrong by emphasizing results.

validity: The extent to which inferences made from a measure's scores are correct; the validation process evaluates whether a measure is assessing the attribute it is supposed to and if it can be used to make accurate decisions. The measure itself is not validated; instead, the inferences about what the measure is assessing, and the decisions made from the scores are. A validity indicator is validity coefficient, usually correlation coefficient, that shows how well a measurement tool forecasts a widely recognized indicator of a particular idea or criterion. See also "external validity" and "internal validity."

validity coefficients: A validity indicator, usually correlation coefficients, that shows how well a measurement tool forecasts a widely recognized indicator of a particular idea or criterion. See also "validity."

validity generalization (VG): The use of statistical procedures to assess a test's adequacy in multiple settings. Also called "psychometric meta-analysis."

variable: A measurable condition or characteristic that can take a different value.

variance: A measure of dispersion, it shows how far a set of numbers spreads from their average value and is given by $Var(X) = E[(X - \mu)^2]$ where X is a random variable with mean μ and $E[(X - \mu)^2]$ is the expected value of the squared deviation from the mean.

verbal protocol analysis: A methodology used to gain cognitive insights into complicated behaviors by requiring participants to "think out loud" as they carry out a particular task as prompted by a hypothetical stimulus. Participants' verbalizations are audio-recorded and transcribed, and content

is analyzed through a coding scheme generated for particular research questions.

versus coding: A coding method that focuses on processes and organizations in conflict by using binary terms to describe groups and processes.

vignette: A short, carefully constructed description of a person, object, or situation representing a systematic combination of characteristics. See also "experimental vignette methodology (EVM)."

virtual private network (VPN): A computer protocol that securely extends a private network (e.g., a university or employer intranet) across a public network (e.g., the internet) that allows users to access data as though their machine were directly connected to the private network.

virtual private servers (VPS): A virtual machine running an operating system connected to a private network. See also "virtual private network."

virtual reality (VR): The computer-generated simulation of a three-dimensional image or environment that may be interacted with by a person wearing specialized electronic equipment, such as a helmet with an internal screen or gloves with sensors, to make it seem real or tactile.

visual method: Any technique used to produce or transmit sociological knowledge visually, such as in photography or videography.

voluntary consent: A procedure that allows participants to make a free, educated decision about whether or not to participate in a project where they will be required to accept risks for the benefit of others.

Wald-type method: A test to determine if a model's explanatory variables are statistically significant and capable of use with continuous or binary variables.

Web of Science (WoS): A web-based platform that provides access to several databases housing reference data from academic sources in several academic fields.

web robots: Malicious software programs designed to participate in online

studies to receive compensation. Also known as "bots."

Wharton Research Data Services (WARDS): A data platform that enables historical analysis and insight into the most recent advancements in scholarly research by offering international institutions the top business intelligence, data analytics, and research platform.

winsorizing approach: A data outlier management technique that involves transforming extreme values to a specified percentile of the data. Although this approach reduces the influence of some observations, it retains all of them, which can be an advantage over approaches that outrightly eliminate extreme values.

within-cluster centering: In multilevel modeling, a method of re-scaling, also called "group-mean centering," changes the mean and correlation structure of multilevel data, causing the lower-level predictors to be uncorrelated with the higher-level predictors. See "re-scale."

within-person research design: In experimental vignette methodology (EVM), a type of research design that requires that each participant view the same set of vignettes, and comparisons are made between vignettes within the same person. See also "experimental vignette methodology (EVM)."

within-session response consistency: A statistical method meant to detect careless or insufficient effort responding by calculating the similarity level in a participant's responses to items they have rated twice and excluding responses that score below 0.25.

zero-order correlations: The correlation between variables without controlling for any other influence.

z-test: A statistical test based on approximating the probability histogram of the z-statistic under the null hypothesis by the normal distribution curve. A z-test is conducted by estimating the expected value (μ) and standard deviation (s), determining if the distribution is one-tailed or two-tailed, and calculating the standard score, given by

$$z = \frac{(\overline{X} - \mu_0)}{\sigma}.$$

ENDNOTES

CHAPTER 1

1. Glieck, J. (1993). *Genius: The life and science of Richard Feynman.* Vintage Books.

2. Darley, J. G. (1968). 1917: A journal is born. *Journal of Applied Psychology, 52*(1), 1–9. https://doi.org/10.1037/h0025256

3. Gates, A. I. (1918). The abilities of an expert marksman tested in the psychological laboratories. *Journal of Applied Psychology, 2*(1), 1–14. https://doi.org/10.1037/h0074646

4. Pintner, R. (1919). A non-language group intelligence test. *Journal of Applied Psychology, 3*(3), 199–214. https://doi.org/10.1037/h0072783

5. Henmon, V. A. C. (1919). Air service tests of aptitude for flying. *Journal of Applied Psychology, 3*(2), 103–109. https://doi.org/10.1037/h0070342

6. Moore, H. T., & Gilliland, A. R. (1921). The measurement of aggressiveness. *Journal of Applied Psychology, 5*(2), 97–118. https://doi.org/10.1037/h0073691

7. Freyd, M. (1922). A method for the study of vocational interests. *Journal of Applied Psychology, 6*(3), 243–254. https://doi.org/10.1037/h0072563

8. Cureton, E. E., & Dunlap, J. W. (1930). Note on the testing of departure from normality. *Journal of Applied Psychology, 14*(1), 91–94. https://doi.org/10.1037/h0072832

9. Edgerton, H. A. (1930). A table for finding the probable error of R obtained by use of the Spearman-Brown formula (n 2). *Journal of Applied Psychology, 14*(3), 296–302. https://doi.org/10.1037/h0075759

10. Jordan, A. M. (1930). Mental growth. *Journal of Applied Psychology, 14*(6), 517–531. https://doi.org/10.1037/h0074829

11. Anderson, J. E. (1935). The effect of item analysis upon the discriminative power of an examination. *Journal of Applied Psychology, 19*(3), 237–244. https://doi.org/10.1037/h0057233

12. Taylor, H. C., & Russell, J. T. (1939). The relationship of validity coefficients to the practical effectiveness of tests in selection: Discussion and tables. *Journal of Applied Psychology, 23*(5), 565–578. https://doi.org/10.1037/h0057079

13. Ghiselli, E. E., & Brown, C. W. (1948). The effectiveness of intelligence tests in the selection of workers. *Journal of Applied Psychology, 32*(6), 575–580. https://doi.org/10.1037/h0060336

14. Paterson, D. G., & Jenkins, J. J. (1948). Communication between management and workers. *Journal of Applied Psychology, 32*(1), 71–80. https://doi.org/10.1037/h0054451

15. Ziller, R. C., Behringer, R. D., & Goodchilds, J. D. (1962). Group creativity under conditions of success or failure and variations in group stability. *Journal of Applied Psychology, 46*(1), 43–49. https://doi.org/10.1037/h0045647

16. McCormick, E. J., Jeanneret, P. R., & Mecham, R. C. (1972). A study of job characteristics and job dimensions as based on the position analysis questionnaire (PAQ). *Journal of Applied Psychology, 56*(4), 347–368. https://doi.org/10.1037/h0033099

17. James, L. R., Demaree, R. G., & Wolf, G. (1984). Estimating within-group interrater reliability with and without response bias. *Journal of Applied Psychology, 69*(1), 85–98. https://doi.org/10.1037/0021-9010.69.1.85

18. Feldman, J. M., & Lynch, J. G. (1988). Self-generated validity and other effects of measurement on belief, attitude, intention, and behavior. *Journal of Applied Psychology, 73*(3), 421–435. https://doi.org/10.1037/0021-9010.73.3.421

19. Drasgow, F., & Kanfer, R. (1985). Equivalence of psychological measurement in heterogeneous populations. *Journal of Applied Psychology, 70*(4), 662–680. https://doi.org/10.1037/0021-9010.70.4.662

20. Schmidt, F. L., & Hunter, J. E. (1977). Development of a general solution to the problem of validity generalization. *Journal of Applied Psychology, 62*(5), 529–540. https://doi.org/10.1037/0021-9010.62.5.529

21. Aguinis, H., Pierce, C. A., Bosco, F. A., Dalton, D. R., & Dalton, C. M. (2011). Debunking myths and urban legends about meta-analysis. *Organizational Research Methods, 14*(2), 306–331. https://doi.org/10.1177/1094428110375720

22. Sackett, P. R., & Dreher, G. F. (1982). Constructs and assessment center dimensions: Some troubling empirical findings. *Journal of Applied Psychology, 67*(4), 401–410. https://doi.org/10.1037/0021-9010.67.4.401

23. James, L. A., & James, L. R. (1989). Integrating work environment perceptions: Explorations into the measurement of meaning. *Journal of Applied Psychology, 74*(5), 739–751. https://doi.org/10.1037/0021-9010.74.5.739

24. Williams, L. J., & Hazer, J. T. (1986). Antecedents and consequences of satisfaction and commitment in turnover models: A reanalysis using latent variable structural equation methods. *Journal of Applied Psychology, 71*(2), 219–231. https://doi.org/10.1037/0021-9010.71.2.219

25. Ones, D. S., Viswesvaran, C., & Schmidt, F. L. (1993). Comprehensive meta-analysis of integrity test validities: Findings and implications for personnel selection and theories of job performance. *Journal of Applied Psychology, 78*(4), 679–703. https://doi.org/10.1037/0021-9010.78.4.679

26. Lee, R. T., & Ashforth, B. E. (1996). A meta-analytic examination of the correlates of the three dimensions of job burnout. *Journal of Applied Psychology, 81*(2), 123–133. https://doi.org/10.1037/0021-9010.81.2.123

27. Gerstner, C. R., & Day, D. V. (1997). Meta-analytic review of leader–member exchange theory: Correlates and construct issues. *Journal of Applied Psychology, 82*(6), 827–844. https://doi.org/10.1037/0021-9010.82.6.827

28. Kristof-Brown, A. L., Jansen, K. J., & Colbert, A. E. (2002). A policy-capturing study of the simultaneous effects of fit with jobs, groups, and organizations. *Journal of Applied Psychology, 87*(5), 985–993. https://doi.org/10.1037/0021-9010.87.5.985

29. Chiaburu, D. S., & Harrison, D. A. (2008). Do peers make the place? Conceptual synthesis and meta-analysis of coworker effects on perceptions, attitudes, OCBs, and performance. *Journal of Applied Psychology, 93*(5), 1082–1103. https://doi.org/10.1037/0021-9010.93.5.1082

30. Liden, R. C., Wayne, S. J., & Stilwell, D. (1993). A longitudinal study on the early development of leader-member exchanges. *Journal of Applied Psychology, 78*(4), 662–674. https://doi.org/10.1037/0021-9010.78.4.662

31. Ahearne, M., Bhattacharya, C. B., & Gruen, T. (2005). Antecedents and consequences of customer-company identification: Expanding the role of relationship marketing. *Journal of Applied Psychology, 90*(3), 574–585. https://doi.org/10.1037/0021-9010.90.3.574

32. West, M. A., & Anderson, N. R. (1996). Innovation in top management teams. *Journal of Applied Psychology, 81*(6), 680–693. https://doi.org/10.1037/0021-9010.81.6.680

33. Cortina, J. M. (1993). What is coefficient alpha? An examination of theory and applications. *Journal of Applied Psychology, 78*(1), 98–04. https://doi.org/10.1037/0021-9010.78.1.98

34. Kearney, E., & Gebert, D. (2009). Managing diversity and enhancing team outcomes: The promise of transformational leadership. *Journal of Applied Psychology, 94*(1), 77–89. https://doi.org/10.1037/a0013077

35. Aguinis, H., & Stone-Romero, E. F. (1997). Methodological artifacts in moderated multiple regression and their effects on statistical power. *Journal of Applied Psychology, 82*(1), 192–206. https://doi.org/10.1037/0021-9010.82.1.192

36. Aguinis, H., & Whitehead, R. (1997). Sampling variance in the correlation coefficient under indirect range restriction: Implications for validity generalization. *Journal of Applied Psychology, 82*(4), 528–538. https://doi.org/10.1037/0021-9010.82.4.528

37. Raju, N. S., Laffitte, L. J., & Byrne, B. M. (2002). Measurement equivalence: A comparison of methods based on confirmatory factor analysis and item response theory. *Journal of Applied Psychology, 87*(3), 517–529. https://doi.org/10.1037/0021-9010.87.3.517

38. Mathieu, J. E., Aguinis, H., Culpepper, S. A., & Chen, G. (2012). Understanding and estimating the power to detect cross-level interaction effects in multilevel modeling. *Journal of Applied Psychology, 97*(5), 951–966. https://doi.org/10.1037/a0028380

39. Aguinis, H., Beaty, J. C., Boik, R. J., & Pierce, C. A. (2005). Effect size and power in assessing moderating effects of categorical variables using multiple regression: A 30-year review. *Journal of Applied Psychology, 90*(1), 94–107. https://doi.org/10.1037/0021-9010.90.1.94

40. Aiken, L. S., West, S. G., & Millsap, R. E. (2008). Doctoral training in statistics, measurement, and methodology in psychology: Replication and extension of Aiken, West, Sechrest, and Reno's (1990) survey of PhD programs in North America. *American Psychologist, 63*(1), 32–50. https://doi.org/10.1037/0003-066X.63.1.32

41. Certo, S. T., Busenbark, J. R., Kalm, M., & LePine, J. A. (2020). Divided we fall: How ratios undermine research in strategic management. *Organizational Research Methods, 23*(2), 211-237. https://doi.org/10.1177/1094428118773455

42. Becker, T. E., Robertson, M. M., & Vandenberg, R. J. (2019). Nonlinear transformations in organizational research: Possible problems and potential solutions. *Organizational Research Methods, 22*(4), 831-866. https://doi.org/10.1177/1094428118775205

43. Putka, D. J., Beatty, A. S., & Reeder, M. C. (2018). Modern prediction methods: New perspectives on a common problem. *Organizational Research Methods, 21*(3), 689-732. https://doi.org/10.1177/1094428117697041

44. Cortina, J. M., Green, J. P., Keeler, K. R., & Vandenberg, R. J. (2017). Degrees of freedom in SEM: Are we testing the models that we claim to test? *Organizational Research Methods, 20*(3), 350-378. https://doi.org/10.1177/1094428116676345

45. Roulet, T. J., Gill, M. J., Stenger, S., & Gill, D. J. (2017). Reconsidering

the value of covert research: The role of ambiguous consent in participant observation. *Organizational Research Methods, 20*(3), 487-517. https://doi.org/10.1177/1094428117698745

46. Shaffer, J. A., DeGeest, D., & Li, A. (2016). Tackling the problem of construct proliferation: A guide to assessing the discriminant validity of conceptually related constructs. *Organizational Research Methods, 19*(1), 80-110. https://doi.org/10.1177/1094428115598239

47. Cho, E., & Kim, S. (2015). Cronbach's coefficient alpha: Well known but poorly understood. *Organizational Research Methods, 18*(2), 207-230. https://doi.org/10.1177/1094428114555994

48. Walsh, I., Holton, J. A., Bailyn, L., Fernandez, W., Levina, N., & Glaser, B. (2015). What grounded theory is... A critically reflective conversation among scholars. *Organizational Research Methods, 18*(4), 581-599. https://doi.org/10.1177/1094428114565028

49. Newman, D. A. (2014). Missing data: Five practical guidelines. *Organizational Research Methods, 17*(4), 372-411. https://doi.org/10.1177/1094428114548590

50. Kozlowski, S. W. J., Chao, G. T., Grand, J. A., Braun, M. T., & Kuljanin, G. (2013). Advancing multilevel research design: Capturing the dynamics of emergence. *Organizational Research Methods, 16*(4), 581-615. https://doi.org/10.1177/1094428113493119

51. Kruschke, J. K., Aguinis, H., & Joo, H. (2012). The time has come: Bayesian methods for data analysis in the organizational sciences. *Organizational Research Methods, 15*(4), 722-752. https://doi.org/10.1177/1094428112457829

52. Cortina, J. M., & Landis, R. S. (2011). The earth is not round (p = .00). *Organizational Research Methods, 14*(2), 332-349. https://doi.org/10.1177/1094428110391542

53. Edwards, J. R. (2011). The fallacy of formative measurement. *Organizational Research Methods, 14*(2), 370-388. https://doi.org/10.1177/1094428110378369

54. Leavitt, K., Mitchell, T. R., & Peterson, J. (2010). Theory pruning: Strategies to reduce our dense theoretical landscape. *Organizational Research Methods, 13*(4), 644-667. https://doi.org/10.1177/1094428109345156

55. Colquitt, J. A., & Zapata-Phelan, C. P. (2007). Trends in theory building and theory testing: A five-decade study of the Academy of Management Journal. *Academy of Management Journal, 50*(6), 1281–1303. https://doi.org/10.5465/amj.2007.28165855

56. Edwards, J. R., Berry, J. W., & Kay, V. S. (2015). *Bridging the great divide between theoretical and empirical management research. Working paper, Kenan-Flagler Business School.* University of North Carolina. https://doi.org/10.5465/ambpp.2014.17696abstract

57. Aguinis, H., & O'Boyle, E., Jr. (2014). Star performers in twenty-first century organizations. *Personnel Psychology, 67*(2), 313–350. https://doi.org/10.1111/peps.12054

58. Cortina, J. M., Green, J. P., Keeler, K. R., & Vandenberg, R. J. (2017). Degrees of freedom in SEM: Are we testing the models that we claim to test? *Organizational Research Methods, 20*(3), 350-378. https://doi.org/10.1177/1094428116676345

59. Holland, S. J., Shore, D. B., & Cortina, J. M. (2016). Review and recommendations for integrated mediation and moderation. *Organizational Research Methods, 20*(4), *686-720*. https://doi.org/10.1177/1094428116658958

60. Murphy, K. R., & Aguinis, H. (2019). HARKing: How badly can cherry picking and question trolling produce bias in published results? *Journal of Business and Psychology, 34*(1), 1-17. https://doi.org/10.1007/s10869-017-9524-7

61. Edwards, M. (2010). *Organizational transformation for sustainability: An integral metatheory.* Routledge.

62. Healy, K. (2017). Fuck nuance. *Sociological Theory, 35*(2), 118-127. https://doi.org/10.1177/0735275117709046

63. Bosco, F. A., Aguinis, H., Singh, K., Field, J. G., & Pierce, C. A. (2015). Correlational effect size benchmarks. *Journal of Applied Psychology, 100*(2), 431– 449. https://doi.org/10.1037/a0038047

64. Pierce, J. R., & Aguinis, H. (2013). The too-much-of-a-good-thing effect in management. *Journal of Management, 39*(2), 313–338. https://doi.org/10.1177/0149206311410060

65. Kruschke, J. K., Aguinis, H., & Joo, H. (2012). The time has come: Bayesian methods for data analysis in the organizational sciences. *Organizational Research Methods, 15*(4), 722–752. https://doi.org/10.1177/1094428112457829

CHAPTER 2

1. Shuster, E. (1997). Fifty years later: The significance of the Nuremberg Code. *New England Journal of Medicine, 337(20)*,1436-1440. https://www.nejm.org/doi/full/10.1056/nejm199711133372006

2. McGaha, A. C., & Korn, J. H. (1995). The emergence of interest in the ethics of psychological research with humans. *Ethics & Behavior, 5*(2), 147-159. https://doi.org/10.1207/s15327019eb0502_3

3. American Psychological Association, Ethics Committee. (1992). Ethical Principles of Psychologists and Code of Conduct. *American Psychologist, 47*(12), 1597–1611. https://doi.org/10.1037/0003-066X.47.12.1597

4. Schlenker, B. R., & Forsyth, D. R. (1977). On the ethics of psychological research.

Journal of Experimental Social Psychology, *13*(4), 369-396. https://doi.org/10.1016/0022-1031(77)90006-3

5. Koocher, G. P., & Keith-Spiegel, P. (1998). *Ethics in psychology: Professional standards and cases.* (2nd edn). Crown Publishing Group/Random House.

6. Kitchener, K. S. (2000). Foundations of ethical practice, research, and teaching psychology. Lawrence Erlbaum. https://doi.org/10.4324/9781410601100

7. American Psychological Association, Ethics Committee. (1992). Ethical principles of psychologists and code of conduct. American Psychologist, 47(12), 1597–1611. https://doi.org/10.1037/0003-066X.47.12.1597

8. Sieber, J. E. (1992). Planning ethically responsible research: A guide for students and internal review boards. Sage. https://doi.org/10.4135/9781412985406

9. American Psychological Association (APA). (1987). *Ethical principles in the conduct of research with human participants.* American Psychological Association.

10. https://about.citiprogram.org/

11. Rosenthal, R. (1994). Science and ethics in conducting, analyzing, and reporting psychological research. *Psychological Science*, *5*(3), 127-134. https://doi.org/10.1111/j.1467-9280.1994.tb00646.x

12. National Commission for the Protection of Human Subjects in Biomedical and Behavioral Research. (1978). The Belmont Report: Ethical principles and guidelines for the protection of human subjects of research (DHEW Publication No. OS78-0012). US Government Printing Office.

13. Rosnow, R. L. (1997). Hedgehogs, foxes, and the evolving social contract in psychological science: Ethical challenges and methodological opportunities. Psychological Methods, 2(4), 345–356.

https://doi.org/10.1037/1082-989X.2.4.345

14. Sieber, J. E., & Saks, M. J. (1989). A census of subject pool characteristics and policies. *American Psychologist*, *44*(7), 1053-1061. https://doi.org/10.1037/0003-066X.44.7.1053

15. Lindsay, R. C., & Holden, R. R. (1987). The introductory psychology subject pool in Canadian universities. *Canadian Psychology*, *28*(1), 45-52. https://doi.org/10.1037/h0079868

16. Diamond, M. R., & Reidpath, D. D. (1992). Psychology ethics down under: A survey of student subject pools in Australia. *Ethics & Behavior*, *2*(2), 101-108. https://doi.org/10.1207/s15327019eb0202_3

17. McCord, D. M. (1991). Ethics-sensitive management of the university human subject pool. American Psychologist, 46(2), 151-152. https://doi.org/10.1037/0003-066X.46.2.151.a

18. Dalziel, J. R. (1996). Students as research subjects: Ethical and educational issues. *Australian Psychologist*, *31*(2), 119-123. https://doi.org/10.1080/00050069608260190

19. Keith-Spiegel, P., & Koocher, G. P. (1985). *Ethics in psychology: Professional standards and cases.* Crown Publishing Group/Random House.

20. Sieber, J. E. (1992). Planning ethically responsible research. SAGE Publications, Inc. https://www.doi.org/10.4135/9781412985406

21. Kimmel, A. J. (1996). *Ethical issues in behavioral research: A survey.* Blackwell Publishers.

22. Kimmel, A. J. (1996). *Ethical issues in behavioral research: A survey.* Blackwell Publishers.

23. Diener, E., & Crandall, R. (1978). *Ethics in social and behavioral research.* The University of Chicago Press.

24. Fisher, C. B. (1993). Joining science and application: Ethical challenges for you and practitioners. Professional Psychology: Research and Practice, 24(3), 378–381. https://doi.org/10.1037/0735-7028.24.3.378

25. Gil, E. F., & Bob, S. (1999). Culturally competent research: An ethical perspective. *Clinical Psychology Review*, *19*(1), 45-55. https://doi.org/10.1016/S0272-7358(98)00019-1

26. American Psychological Association (APA). (1987). Ethical principles in the conduct of research with human participants. American Psychological Association.

27. Canter, M. B., Bennett, B. E., Jones, S. E., & Nagy, T. F. (l994). Ethics far psychologists: A commentary on the APA Ethics Code. American Psychological Association.

28. Sieber, J. E. (1992). Planning ethically responsible research. SAGE Publications, Inc. https://www.doi.org/10.4135/9781412985406

29. Mann, T. (1994). Informed consent for psychological research: Do subjects comprehend consent forms and understand their legal rights?.*Psychological Science*, *5*(3), 140-143. https://doi.org/10.1111/j.1467-9280.1994.tb00650.x

30. Sieber, J. E. (1992). Planning ethically responsible research. SAGE Publications, Inc. https://www.doi.org/10.4135/9781412985406

31. American Psychological Association (APA). (1987). Ethical principles in the conduct of research with human participants. American Psychological Association.

32. Korn, J. H. (1988). Students' roles, rights, and responsibilities as research participants. *Teaching of Psychology*, *15*(2), 74-78. https://doi.org/10.1207/s15328023top1502_2

33. Singer, E., Von Thurn, D. R., & Miller, E. R. (1995). Confidentiality assurances and response: A quantitative review of the

experimental literature. *Public Opinion Quarterly*, 59(1), 66-77. https://doi.org/10.1086/269458

34. Bok, S. (1982). *Secrets: On the ethics of concealment and revelation.* Pantheon Books.

35. Smith, S. S., & Richardson, D. (1983). Amelioration of deception and harm in psychological research: The important role of debriefing. *Journal of Personality and Social Psychology*, 44(5), 1075-1082. https://doi.org/10.1037/0022-3514.44.5.1075

36. Smith, C. P., & Berard, S. P. (1982). Why are human subjects less concerned about ethically problematic research than human subjects committees? 1. *Journal of Applied Social Psychology*, 12(3), 209-221. https://doi.org/10.1111/j.1559-1816.1982.tb00860.x

37. Harris, B. (1988). Key words: A history of debriefing in social psychology. In J. Morawski (ed.), *The rise of experimentation in American psychology.* Oxford University Press, 188- 212.

38. Holmes, D. S. (1976). Debriefing after psychological experiments: I. Effectiveness of postdeception dehoaxing. *American Psychologist*, 31(12), 858–867. https://doi.org/10.1037/0003-066X.31.12.858

39. Holmes, D. S. (1976). Debriefing after psychological experiments: I. Effectiveness of postdeception dehoaxing. *American Psychologist*, 31(12), 858–867. https://doi.org/10.1037/0003-066X.31.12.858

40. Wright, T. A., & Wright, V. P. (1999). Ethical responsibility and the organizational researcher: A committed-to-participant research perspective. *Journal of Organizational Behavior*, 20(7), 1107-1112. https://www.jstor.org/stable/3100349

41. Mirvis, P. H., & Seashore, S. E. (1979). Being ethical in organizational research. *American Psychologist*, 34(9), 766–780. https://doi.org/10.1037/0003-066X.34.9.766

42. Harvey, S. (1994). Application of the CPA code of ethics in planning field research: An organizational case. *Canadian Psychology*, 35(2), 204–219. https://doi.org/10.1037/0708-5591.35.2.204

43. Mirvis, P. H., & Seashore, S. E. (1979). Being ethical in organizational research. *American Psychologist*, 34(9), 766–780. https://doi.org/10.1037/0003-066X.34.9.766

44. O'Neill, P. (1990). Ethical issues in field research: Balancing competing values. *Canadian Psychology*, 31(2), 147–154. https://doi.org/10.1037/h0078895

45. Wright, T. A., & Sweeney, D. (1990). Correctional institution workers' coping strategies and their effect on diastolic blood pressure. *Journal of Criminal Justice*, 18(2), 161-9. https://doi.org/10.1016/0047-2352(90)90033-8

46. Kimmel, A. J. (1996). *Ethical issues in behavioral research: A survey.* Blackwell Publishers.

47. Rosenthal, R. (1994). Science and ethics in conducting, analyzing, and reporting psychological research. *Psychological Science*, 5(3), 127-134. https://doi.org/10.1111/j.1467-9280.1994.tb00646.x

48. Rosenthal, R. (1994). Science and ethics in conducting, analyzing, and reporting psychological research. *Psychological Science*, 5(3), 127-134. https://doi.org/10.1111/j.1467-9280.1994.tb00646.x

49. Elliott, D., & Stern, J. E. (1997). *Research Ethics: A Reader.* University Press of New England.

50. Canter, M. B., Bennett, B. E., Jones, S. E., & Nagy, T. F. (1994). *Ethics far psychologists: A commentary on the APA Ethics Code.* American Psychological Association.

51. Costa, M. M., & Gatz, M. (1992). Determination of authorship credit in published dissertations. *Psychological Science*, 3(6), 354-357. https://doi.org/10.1111/j.1467-9280.1992.tb00046.x

52. American Psychological Association (APA). (1993). Report of the Ethics Committee, 1991 and 1992. American Psychologist, 48(7), 811–820. https://doi.org/10.1037/0003-066X.48.7.811

53. Fine, M. A., & Kurdek, L. A. (1993). Reflections on determining authorship credit and authorship order on faculty-student collaborations. *American Psychologist*, 48(11), 1141–1147. https://doi.org/10.1037/0003-066X.48.11.1141

54. Goodyear, R. K., Crego, C. A., & Johnston, M. W. (1992). Ethical issues in the supervision of student research: A study of critical incidents. *Professional Psychology: Research and Practice*, 23(3), 203–210. https://doi.org/10.1037/0735-7028.23.3.203

55. Shadish, W. R. (1994). APA ethics and student authorship on master's theses. *American Psychologist*, 49(12), 1096. https://doi.org/10.1037/0003-066X.49.12.1096

56. Fine, M. A., & Kurdek, L. A. (1993). Reflections on determining authorship credit and authorship order on faculty-student collaborations. *American Psychologist*, 48(11), 1141–1147. https://doi.org/10.1037/0003-066X.48.11.1141

57. Costa, M. M., & Gatz, M. (1992). Determination of authorship credit in published dissertations. *Psychological Science*, 3(6), 354-357. https://doi.org/10.1111/j.1467-9280.1992.tb00046.x

58. Koocher, G. P., & Keith-Spiegel, P. (1998). *Ethics in psychology: Professional standards and cases* (2nd edn). Oxford University Press.

59. Winston Jr, R. B. (1985). A suggested procedure for determining order of authorship in research publications. *Journal of Counseling & Development*, 63(8), 515-18. https://doi.org/10.1002/j.1556-6676.1985.tb02749.x

60. Fine, M. A., & Kurdek, L. A. (1993). Reflections on determining authorship credit and authorship

order on faculty-student collabo-rations. American Psychologist, 48(11), 1141–1147. https://doi.org/10.1037/0003-066X.48.11.1141

61. Aguinis, H., Beaty, J. C., Boik, R. J., & Pierce, C. A. (2000). *Statistical power of differential prediction analysis: A 30-year review.* In F. L. Oswald (Chair), Differential prediction in personnel selection: Past, present, and future. Symposium conducted at the meeting of the Society for Industrial and Organizational Psychology, New Orleans, LA.

62. Porter, C. O., Outlaw, R., Gale, J. P., & Cho, T. S. (2019). The use of online panel data in management research: A review and recommendations. *Journal of Management, 45*(1), 319-344. https://doi.org/10.1177/0149206318811569

63. Zack, E. S., Kennedy, J., & Long, J. S. (2019). Can nonprobability samples be used for social science research? A cautionary tale. *Survey Research Methods, 13*(2), 215-227. https://doi.org/10.18148/srm/2019.v13i2.7262

64. Wessling, K. S., Huber, J., & Netzer, O. (2017). MTurk character misrepresentation: Assessment and solutions. *Journal of Consumer Research, 44*(1), 211-230. https://doi.org/10.1093/jcr/ucx053

65. Casey, L. S., Chandler, J., Levine, A. S., Proctor, A., & Strolovitch, D. Z. (2017). Intertemporal differences among MTurk workers: Time-based sample variations and implications for online data collection. *SAGE Open, 7,* 2158244017712774. https://doi.org/10.1177/2158244017712774

66. Lovett, M., Bajaba, S., Lovett, M., & Simmering, M. J. (2018). Data quality from crowdsourced surveys: A mixed method inquiry into perceptions of Amazon's Mechanical Turk Masters. *Applied Psychology, 67*(2), 339-366. https://doi.org/10.1111/apps.12124

67. Casey, L. S., Chandler, J., Levine, A. S., Proctor, A., & Strolovitch,

D. Z. (2017). Intertemporal differences among MTurk workers: Time-based sample variations and implications for online data collection. *SAGE Open, 7,* 2158244017712774. https://doi.org/10.1177/2158244017712774

68. Crump, M. J., McDonnell, J. V., & Gureckis, T. M. (2013). Evaluating Amazon's Mechanical Turk as a tool for experimental behavioral research. *PloS One, 8,* e57410. https://doi.org/10.1371/journal.pone.0057410

69. Liu, B., & Sundar, S. S. (2018). Microworkers as research participants: Does underpaying Turkers lead to cognitive dissonance?. *Computers in Human Behavior, 24,* 89-101. https://doi.org/10.1016/j.chb.2018.06.017

70. Fieseler, C., Bucher, E., & Hoffmann, C. P. (2017). Unfairness by design? The perceived fairness of digital labor on crowdworking platforms. *Journal of Business Ethics, 156*(4), 987-1005. https://doi.org/10.1007/s10551-017-3607-2

71. Brink, W. D., Eaton, T. V., Grenier, J. H., & Reffett, A. (2019). Deterring unethical behavior in online labor markets. *Journal of Business Ethics, 156*(1), 71-88. https://doi.org/10.1007/s10551-017-3570-y

72. Bederson, B. B., & Quinn, A. J. (2011, May). Web workers unite! Addressing challenges of online laborers. ACM CHI'11 Extended Abstracts on Human Factors in Computing Systems (pp. 97-106). https://doi.org/10.1145/1979742.1979606

73. von Ahn, L., Blum, M., Hopper, N. J., & Langford, J. (2003). CAPTCHA: Using hard AI problems for security. Lecture Notes in Computer Science (pp. 294–311). Springer Nature. https://doi.org/10.1007/3-540-39200-9_18

74. Buhrmester, M. D., Talaifar, S., & Gosling, S. D. (2018). An evaluation of Amazon's Mechanical Turk, its rapid rise, and its effective use.

Perspectives on Psychological Science, 13(2), 149-154. https://doi.org/10.1177/1745691617706516

75. Stewart, N., Ungemach, C., Harris, A. J., Bartels, D. M., Newell, B. R., Paolacci, G., & Chandler, J. (2015). The average laboratory samples a population of 7,300 Amazon Mechanical Turk workers. *Judgment and Decision Making, 10*(5), 479-491.

76. Ramsey, S. R., Thompson, K. L., McKenzie, M., & Rosenbaum, A. (2016). Psychological research in the internet age: The quality of web-based data. *Computers in Human Behavior, 58,* 354-360. https://doi.org/10.1016/j.chb.2015.12.049

77. Huang, J. L., Bowling, N. A., Liu, M., & Li, Y. (2015). Detecting insufficient effort responding with an infrequency scale: Evaluating validity and participant reactions. *Journal of Business and Psychology, 30*(2), 299-311. https://doi.org/10.1007/s10869-014-9357-6

78. Dennis, S. A., Goodson, B. M., & Pearson, C. (2019). Virtual private servers and the limitations of IP-based screening procedures: Lessons from the MTurk quality crisis of 2018. SSRN 3233954. http://dx.doi.org/10.2139/ssrn.3233954

79. Huang, J. L., Bowling, N. A., Liu, M., & Li, Y. (2015). Detecting insufficient effort responding with an infrequency scale: Evaluating validity and participant reactions. *Journal of Business and Psychology, 30*(2), 299-311. https://doi.org/10.1007/s10869-014-9357-6

80. Mason, W., & Suri, S. (2012). Conducting behavioral research on Amazon's Mechanical Turk. *Behavior Research Methods, 44*(1), 1-23. https://doi.org/10.3758/s13428-011-0124-6

81. Schulze, T., Seedorf, S., Geiger, D., Kaufmann, N., & Schader, M. (2011). Exploring task properties in crowdsourcing–An empirical study on Mechanical Turk. *ECIS*

2011 Proceedings. http://aisel.aisn et.org/ecis2011/122

82. Zhou, H., & Fishbach, A. (2016). The threat of experimenting on the web: How unattended selective attrition leads to surprising (yet false) research conclusions. *Journal of Personality and Social Psychology, 111*(4), 493-504. https://doi.org/10.1037/pspa0000056

83. Kees, J., Berry, C., Burton, S., & Sheehan, K. (2017). An analysis of data quality: Professional panels, student subject pools, and Amazon's Mechanical Turk. *Journal of Advertising, 46,* 141-155. https://doi.org/10.1080/00913367.2016.1269304

84. Deng, X., Joshi, K. D., & Galliers, R. D. (2016). The duality of empowerment and marginalization in microtask crowdsourcing: Giving voice to the less powerful through value sensitive design. *MIS Quarterly, 40*(2), 279-302. https://doi.org/10.25300/MISQ/2016/40.2.01

85. Wood, D., Harms, P. D., Lowman, G. H., & DeSimone, J. A. (2017). Response speed and response consistency as mutually validating indicators of data quality in online samples. *Social Psychological and Personality Science, 8*(4), 454-464. https://doi.org/10.1177/194855061 7703168

86. Berinsky, A. J., Margolis, M. F., & Sances, M. W. (2014). Separating the shirkers from the workers? Making sure respondents pay attention on self-administered surveys. *American Journal of Political Science, 58*(3), 739-753. https://doi.org/10.1111/ajps.12081

87. Hong, M., Steedle, J. T., & Cheng, Y. (2020). Methods of detecting insufficient effort responding: Comparisons and practical recommendations. *Educational and Psychological Measurement, 80*(2), 312-345. https://doi.org/10.1177/0 013164419865316--

88. Wood, D., Harms, P. D., Lowman, G. H., & DeSimone, J. A. (2017). Response speed and response consistency as mutually validating

indicators of data quality in online samples. *Social Psychological and Personality Science, 8*(4), 454-464. https://doi.org/10.1177/194855061 7703168

89. Buchanan, E. M., & Scofield, J. E. (2018). Methods to detect low quality data and its implication for psychological research. *Behavior Research Methods, 50*(6), 1-11. https://doi.org/10.3758/s13428-018-1 035-6

90. Kennedy, R., Clifford, S., Burleigh, T., Jewell, R., & Waggoner, P. (2018). The shape of and solutions to the MTurk quality crisis. Available at SSRN 3272468. https://doi.org/10.2139/ssrn.3272468

91. Dennis, S. A., Goodson, B. M., & Pearson, C. (2019). Virtual private servers and the limitations of IP-based screening procedures: Lessons from the MTurk quality crisis of 2018. SSRN 3233954. http://dx.doi.org/10.2139/ssrn.32339 54

92. Bederson, B. B., & Quinn, A. J. (2011, May). Web workers unite! Addressing challenges of online laborers. ACM CHI'11 Extended Abstracts on Human Factors in Computing Systems (pp. 97-106). https://doi.org/10.1145/1979742.1 979606

93. Brawley, A. M., & Pury, C. L. (2016). Work experiences on MTurk: Job satisfaction, turnover, and information sharing. *Computers in Human Behavior, 54,* 531-546. https://doi.org/10.1016/j.chb.2015.08.031

94. American Psychological Association, Ethics Committee. (1992). Ethical Principles of Psychologists and Code of Conduct. *American Psychologist, 47*(12), 1597–1611. https://doi.org/10.1037/0003-066X.47.12.1597

95. Koocher, G. P., & Keith-Spiegel, P. (1985). *Ethics in psychology: Professional standards and cases.* Crown Publishing Group/Random House.

96. Kimmel, A. J. (1996). *Ethical issues in behavioral research: A survey.* Blackwell Publishers.

97. Swazey, J. P., Anderson, M. S., Lewis, K. S., & Louis, K. S. (1993). Ethical problems in academic research. *American Scientist, 81*(6), 542-553.

98. Holaday, M., & Yost, T. E. (1993). Publication ethics. *Journal of Social Behavior and Personality, 8*(4), 557.

99. Biaggio, M., Duffy, R., & Staffelbach, D. F. (1998). Obstacles to addressing professional misconduct. *Clinical Psychology Review, 18*(3), 273-285. https://doi.org/10.1016/S0272-7358(97)00109-8

100. Tanke, E. D., & Tanke, T. J. (1982). Regulation and education: The role of the institutional review board in social science research. In *The Ethics of Social Research* (pp. 131-149). Springer.

101. Rosnow, R. L., Rotheram-Borus, M. J., Ceci, S. J., Blanck, P. D., & Koocher, G. P. (1993). The Institutional Review Board as a mirror of scientific and ethical standards. American Psychologist, 48(7), 821–826. https://doi.org/10.1037/0003-066X.48.7.821

102. Kimmel, A. J. (1996). *Ethical issues in behavioral research: A survey.* Blackwell Publishers.

103. Kimmel, A. J. (1996). *Ethical issues in behavioral research: A survey.* Blackwell Publishers.

104. American Psychological Association, Ethics Committee. (1992). Ethical principles of psychologists and code of conduct. *American Psychologist, 47*(12), 1597–1611. https://doi.org/10.1037/0003-066X.47.12.1597

105. Hare-Mustin, R. T., & Hall, J. E. (1981). Procedures for responding to ethics complaints against psychologists. *American Psychologist, 36*(12), 1494–1505. https://doi.org/10.1037/0003-066X.36.12.1494

106. Hare-Mustin, R. T., & Hall, J. E. (1981). Procedures for responding to ethics complaints against psychologists. *American Psychologist*, 36(12), 1494–1505. https://doi.org/10.1037/0003-066X.36.12.1494

107. Koocher, G. P., & Keith-Spiegel, P. (1985). *Ethics in psychology: Professional standards and cases*. Crown Publishing Group/Random House.

108. Jones, E. E., & Sigall, H. (1971). The bogus pipeline: A new paradigm for measuring affect and attitude. *Psychological Bulletin, 76*, 349-364. https://doi.org/10.1037/h0031617

109. Roese, N. J., & Jamieson, D. W. (1993). Twenty years of bogus pipeline research: A critical review and meta-analysis. *Psychological Bulletin, 114*, 363-375. https://doi.org/10.1037/0033-2909.114.2.363

110. Aguinis, H., Pierce, C. A., & Quigley, B. M. (1993). Conditions under which a bogus pipeline procedure enhances the validity of self-reported cigarette smoking: A meta-analytic review. *Journal of Applied Social Psychology, 23*, 352-373. https://doi.org/10.1111/j.1559-1816.1993.tb01092.x

111. Aguinis, H., Pierce, C. A., & Quigley, B. M. (1995). Enhancing the validity of self-reported alcohol and marijuana consumption using a bogus pipeline procedure: A meta-analytic review. *Basic and Applied Social Psychology, 16*, 515-527. https://doi.org/10.1207/s15324834basp1604_8

112. Aguinis, H., Pierce, C. A., & Quigley, B. M. (1995). Enhancing the validity of self-reported alcohol and marijuana consumption using a bogus pipeline procedure: A meta-analytic review. *Basic and Applied Social Psychology, 16*, 515-527. https://doi.org/10.1207/s15324834basp1604_8

113. Aguinis, H., Pierce, C. A., & Quigley, B. M. (1995). Enhancing the validity of self-reported alcohol and marijuana consumption using a bogus pipeline procedure: A meta-analytic review. *Basic and Applied Social Psychology, 16*, 515-527. https://doi.org/10.1207/s15324834basp1604_8

114. Ostrom, T. M. (1973). The bogus pipeline: A new ignis fatuus? *Psychological Bulletin, 79*, 252-259. https://doi.org/10.1037/h0033861

115. Baumrind, D. (1985). Research using intentional deception: Ethical issues revisited. *American Psychologist, 40*, 165-174. https://doi.org/10.1037/0003-066X.40.2.165

116. Greenberg, J., & Folger, R. (1988). *Controversial issues in social research methods*. Springer-Verlag. https://doi.org/10.1007/978-1-4612-3756-3

117. Ostrom, T. M. (1973). The bogus pipeline: A new ignis fatuus? *Psychological Bulletin, 79*, 252-259. https://doi.org/10.1037/h0033861

118. Schlenker, B. R., Bonoma, T. V., Hutchinson, D., & Burns, L. (1976). The bogus pipeline and stereotypes toward Blacks. *Journal of Psychology, 93*, 319-329. https://doi.org/10.1080/00223980.1976.9915828

119. Page, R. A., & Moss, M. K. (1975). Attitude similarity and attraction: The effects of the bogus pipelint:. *Bulletin of the Psychonomic Society, 5*, 63-65. https://doi.org/10.3758/BF03336706

120. Gaes, G. G., Kalle, R. J., & Tedeschi, J. T. (1978). Impression management in the forced compliance situation: Two studies using the bogus pipeline. *Journal of Experimental Social Psychology, 14*, 493-510. https://doi.org/10.1016/0022-1031(78)90045-8

121. Orne, M. T. (1962). On the social psychology of the psychological experiment: With particular reference to demand characteristics and their implications. *American Psychologist, 17*, T16-783. https://doi.org/10.1037/h0043424

122. Christensen, L. (1988). Deception in social psychological research: When is its use justified? *Personality and Social Psychology Bulletin, 14*, 664-675. https://doi.org/10.1177/0146167288144002

123. Smith, S. S., & Richardson, D. (1983). Amelioration of deception and harm in psychological research: The important role of debriefing. *Journal of Personality and Social Psychology, 44*, 1075-1082. https://doi.org/10.1037/0022-3514.44.5.1075

124. Jones, E. E., & Sigall, H. (1971). The bogus pipeline: A new paradigm for measuring affect and attitude. *Psychological Bulletin, 76*, 349-364. https://doi.org/10.1037/h0031617

125. Gerdes, E. P. (1979). College students' reactions to social psychological experiments involving deception. *Journal of Social Psychology, 107*, 99-110. https://doi.org/10.1080/00224545.1979.9922678

126. Howard, G. S., Millham, J., Slaten, S., & O'Donnell, L. (l981). Influence of subject response style effects on retrospective measures. *Applied Psychological Measurement, 5*, 89-100. https://doi.org/10.1177/014662168100500113

127. Ring, K., Wallston, K., & Corey, M. (1970). Mode of debriefing as a factor affecting subjective reaction to a Milgram-type obedience experiment: An ethical inquiry. *Representative Research in Social Psychology, 1*, 67-88.

128. Silverman, I., Shulman, A. D., & Wiesenthal, D. L. (1970). Effects of deceiving and debriefing psychological subjects on performance in later experiments. *Journal of Personality and Social Psychology, 14*, 203-212. https://doi.org/10.1037/h0028852

129. Holmes, D. S. (1976). Debriefing after psychological experiments: II. Effectiveness of post-experimental desensitization. *American Psychologist, 31*, 868-875. https://doi.org/10.1037/0003-066X.31.12.868

130. Milgram, S. (1964). Issues in the study of obedience: A reply to Baumrind. *American Psychologist, 19*, 848-852. https://doi.org/10.10 37/h0044954

131. Roese, N. J., & Jamieson, D. W. (1993). Twenty years of bogus pipeline research: A critical review and meta-analysis. *Psychological Bulletin, 114*, 363-375. https://doi.org/10.1037/0033-290 9.114.2.363

132. Aguinis, H., Pierce, C. A., & Quigley, B. M. (1995). Enhancing the validity of self-reported alcohol and marijuana consumption using a bogus pipeline procedure: A meta-analytic review. *Basic and Applied Social Psychology, 16*, 515-527. https://doi.org/10.1207/s1532 4834basp1604_8

133. Orne, M. T. (1962). On the social psychology of the psychological experiment: With particular reference to demand characteristics and their implications. *American Psychologist, 17*, T16-783. https://d oi.org/10.1037/h0043424

134. Christensen, L. (1988). Deception in social psychological research: When is its use justified? *Personality and Social Psychology Bulletin, 14*, 664-675. https://doi.org/10.117 7/0146167288144002

CHAPTER 3

1. Antonakis, J. (2017). On doing better science: From thrill of discovery to policy implications. *The Leadership Quarterly, 28*(1), 5–21. https://doi.org/10.1016/j.leaqua.2 017.01.006

2. Hambrick, D. C. (2007). The field of management 's devotion to theory: Too much of a good thing? *Academy of Management Journal, 50*(6), 1346–1352. https://doi.org/1 0.5465/amj.2007.28166119

3. Cronin, M. A., Stouten, J., & van Knippenberg, D. (2021). The theory crisis in management research: Solving the right problem. *Academy of Management Review, 46*(4), 667–683. https://doi .org/10.5465/amr.2019.0294

4. Cronin, M. A., Stouten, J., & van Knippenberg, D. (2021). The theory crisis in management research: Solving the right problem. *Academy of Management Review, 46*(4), 667–683. https://doi .org/10.5465/amr.2019.0294

5. Aguinis, H., Jensen, S. H., & Kraus, S. (2021). Policy implications of organizational behavior and human resource management research. *Academy of Management Perspectives*. https://doi. org/10.5465/amp.2020.0093

6. Aguinis, H., Jensen, S. H., & Kraus, S. (2021). Policy implications of organizational behavior and human resource management research. *Academy of Management Perspectives*. https://doi. org/10.5465/amp.2020.0093

7. Bartunek, J., & Rynes, S. L. (2010). The construction and contributions of "implications for practice": What's in them and what might they offer? *Academy of Management Learning & Education, 9*(1), 100–117. https://doi.org/10.5 465/AMLE.2010.48661194

8. Whetten, D. A. (1989). What constitutes a theoretical contribution? *Academy of Management Review, 14*(4), 490–495. https://doi. org/10.5465/amr.1989.4308371

9. Sutton, R. I., & Staw, B. M. (1995). What theory is not. *Administrative Science Quarterly, 40*(3), 371–384. https://doi.org/10.2307/2393788

10. Lee, T. W., Hom, P. W., Eberly, M. B., Li, J. (Jason), & Mitchell, T. R. (2017). On the next decade of research in voluntary employee turnover. *Academy of Management Perspectives, 31*(3), 201–221. https ://doi.org/10.5465/amp.2016.0123

11. Cortina, J. M. (2016). Defining and operationalizing theory. *Journal of Organizational Behavior, 37*(8), 1142–1149. https://doi.org/10.1002 /job.2121

12. Aguinis, H., & Vandenberg, R. J. (2014). An ounce of prevention is worth a pound of cure: Improving research quality before data collection. *Annual Review of Organizational Psychology and Organizational Behavior, 1*(1), 569–595. http s://doi.org/10.1146/annurev-orgp sych-031413-091231

13. Bosco, F. A., Aguinis, H., Singh, K., Field, J. G., & Pierce, C. A. (2015). Correlational effect size benchmarks. *Journal of Applied Psychology, 100*(2), 431–449. https://doi.or g/10.1037/a0038047

14. Aguinis, H., Werner, S., Lanza Abbott, J., Angert, C., Park, J. H., & Kohlhausen, D. (2010). Customer-centric science: Reporting significant research results with rigor, relevance, and practical impact in mind. *Organizational Research Methods, 13*(3), 515–539. https://doi.org/10.1177/109442810 9333339

15. Rosenthal, R. (1990). How are we doing in soft psychology? *American Psychologist, 45*(6), 775. https:/ /doi.org/10.1037/0003-066X.45.6. 775

16. Cronin, M. A., Stouten, J., & van Knippenberg, D. (2021). The theory crisis in management research: Solving the right problem. *Academy of Management Review, 46*(4), 667–683. https://doi .org/10.5465/amr.2019.0294

17. Colquitt, J. A., & Zapata-Phelan, C. P. (2007). Trends in theory building and theory testing: A five-decade study of the Academy of Management Journal. *Academy of Management Journal, 50*(6), 1281–1303. https://doi.org/10.546 5/amj.2007.28165855

18. Cronin, M. A., Stouten, J., & van Knippenberg, D. (2021). The theory crisis in management research: Solving the right problem. *Academy of Management Review, 46*(4), 667–683. https://doi .org/10.5465/amr.2019.0294

19. Wagner, D. G., & Berger, J. (1985). Do sociological theories grow?

American Journal of Sociology, *90*(4), 697–728. https://doi.org/10.1086/228142

20. Park, H. Y., Ofori-Dankwa, J., & Bishop, D. R. (1994). Organizational and environmental determinants of functional and dysfunctional turnover: Practical and research implications. *Human Relations*, *47*(3), 353–366. https://doi.org/10.1177/001872679404700306

21. Huff, A. S. (2008). *Designing Research for Publication*. Sage.

22. Cronin, M. A., Stouten, J., & van Knippenberg, D. (2021). The theory crisis in management research: Solving the right problem. *Academy of Management Review*, *46*(4), 667–683. https://doi.org/10.5465/amr.2019.0294

23. Kim, P. H., Ployhart, R. E., & Gibson, C. B. (2018). Editors' Comments: Is organizational behavior overtheorized? *Academy of Management Review*, *43*(4), 541–545. https://doi.org/10.5465/amr.2018.0233

24. Makadok, R., Burton, R., & Barney, J. (2018). A practical guide for making theory contributions in strategic management. *Strategic Management Journal*, *39*(6), 1530–1545. https://doi.org/10.1002/smj.2789

25. Thatcher, S. M., & Fisher, G. (2021). The nuts and bolts of writing a theory paper: A practical guide to getting started. *Academy of Management Review*, *47*(1), 1–8. https://doi.org/10.5465/amr.2021.0483

26. Vermeulen, F. (2005). On rigor and relevance: Fostering dialectic progress in management research. *Academy of Management Journal*, *48*(6), 978–982. https://doi.org/10.5465/amj.2005.19573102

27. Cronin, M. A., & Loewenstein, J. (2018). *The Craft of Creativity*. Stanford University Press. https://doi.org/10.1515/9781503605510

28. Mathieu, J. E. (2016). The problem with [in] management theory.

29. Hambrick, D. C. (2007). The field of management's devotion to theory: Too much of a good thing? *Academy of Management Journal*, *50*(6), 1346–1352. https://doi.org/10.5465/amj.2007.28166119

30. Gottfredson Rosenthal, R. (1990). How are we doing in soft psychology? *American Psychologist*, *45*(6), 775. https://doi.org/10.1037/0003-066X.45.6.775

31. Healy, K. (2017). Fuck nuance. *Sociological Theory*, *35*(2), 118–127. https://doi.org/10.1177/0735275117709046

32. Antonakis, J. (2017). On doing better science: From thrill of discovery to policy implications. *The Leadership Quarterly*, *28*(1), 5–21. https://doi.org/10.1016/j.leaqua.2017.01.006

33. Tourish, D. (2019). The triumph of nonsense in management studies. *Academy of Management Learning & Education*, *19*(1), 99–109. https://doi.org/10.5465/amle.2019.0255

34. Comer, D. R. (1995). A model of social loafing in real work groups. *Human Relations*, *48*(6), 647–667. https://doi.org/10.1177/001872679504800603

35. Geen, R. G. (1983). Evaluation apprehension and the social facilitation/inhibition of learning. *Motivation and Emotion*, *7*(2), 203–212. https://doi.org/10.1007/BF00992903

36. Diehl, M., & Stroebe, W. (1987). Productivity loss in brainstorming groups: Toward the solution of a riddle. *Journal of Personality & Social Psychology*, *53*(3), 497–509. https://doi.org/10.1037/0022-3514.53.3.497

37. Gobet, F., Lane, P. C., Croker, S., Cheng, P. C., Jones, G., Oliver, I., & Pine, J. M. (2001). Chunking mechanisms in human learning. *Trends in Cognitive Sciences*, *5*(6),

236–243. https://doi.org/10.1016/S1364-6613(00)01662-4

38. Paulus, P. B., Dzindolet, M. T., Poletes, G., & Camacho, L. M. (1993). Perception of performance in group brainstorming: The illusion of group productivity. *Personality and Social Psychology Bulletin*, *19*(1), 78–89. https://doi.org/10.1177/0146167293191009

39. Platt, J. R. (1964). Strong Inference: Certain systematic methods of scientific thinking may produce much more rapid progress than others. *Science*, *146*(3642), 347–353. https://doi.org/10.1126/science.146.3642.347

40. Gottfredson, R. K., & Aguinis, H. (2017). Leadership behaviors and follower performance: Deductive and inductive examination of theoretical rationales and underlying mechanisms. *Journal of Organizational Behavior*, *38*(4), 558–591. https://doi.org/10.1002/job.2152

41. Leavitt, K., Mitchell, T. R., & Peterson, J. (2010). Theory pruning: Strategies to reduce our dense theoretical landscape. *Organizational Research Methods*, *13*(4), 644–667. https://doi.org/10.1177/1094428109345156

42. Paulus, P. B., & Yang, H.-C. (2000). Idea generation in groups: A basis for creativity in organizations. *Organizational Behavior and Human Decision Processes*, *82*(1), 76–87. https://doi.org/10.1006/obhd.2000.2888

43. Edwards, J. R. (2010). Reconsidering theoretical progress in organizational and management research. *Organizational Research Methods*, *13*(4), 615–619. https://doi.org/10.1177/1094428110380468

44. Greenwald, A. G., & Pratkanis, A. R. (1988). On the use of "theory" and the usefulness of theory. *Psychological Review*, *95*(4), 575–579. https://doi.org/10.1037/0033-295X.95.4.575

45. Gottfredson, R. K., & Aguinis, H. (2017). Leadership behaviors and follower performance: Deductive and inductive examination of

Journal of Organizational Behavior, *37*(8), 1132–1141. https://doi.org/10.1002/job.2114

of theoretical rationales and underlying mechanisms. *Journal of Organizational Behavior, 38*(4), 558–591. https://doi.org/10.1002/job.2152

46. De Dreu, C. K. W., & Weingart, L. R. (2003). Task versus relationship conflict, team performance, and team member satisfaction: A meta-analysis. *Journal of Applied Psychology, 88*, 741–749. https://doi.org/10.1037/0021-9010.88.4.741

47. De Wit, F., Greer, L. L., & Jehn, K. (2012). The paradox of intragroup conflict: A meta-analysis. *Journal of Applied Psychology, 97*(2), 360–390. https://doi.org/10.1037/a0024844

48. Gottfredson, R. K., & Aguinis, H. (2017). Leadership behaviors and follower performance: Deductive and inductive examination of theoretical rationales and underlying mechanisms. *Journal of Organizational Behavior, 38*(4), 558–591. https://doi.org/10.1002/job.2152

49. Meehl, P. E. (1978). Theoretical risks and tabular asterisks: Sir Karl, Sir Ronald, and the slow progress of soft psychology. *Journal of Consulting and Clinical Psychology, 46*(4), 806. https://doi.org/10.1037/0022-006X.46.4.806

50. Gigerenzer, G. (1998). Surrogates for theories. *Theory & Psychology, 8*(2), 195-204. https://doi.org/10.1177/0959354398082006

51. Edwards, J. R., & Berry, J. W. (2010). The presence of something or the absence of nothing: Increasing theoretical precision in management research. *Organizational Research Methods, 13*(4), 668-689. https://doi.org/10.1177/1094428110380467

52. Edwards, J. R., & Berry, J. W. (2010). The presence of something or the absence of nothing: Increasing theoretical precision in management research. *Organizational Research Methods, 13*(4), 668-689. https://doi.org/10.1177/1094428110380467

53. Bagozzi, R. P., Yi, Y., & Phillips, L. W. (1991). Assessing construct validity in organizational research. *Administrative Science Quarterly, 36*(3), 421-458. https://doi.org/10.2307/2393203

54. Edwards, J. R., & Berry, J. W. (2010). The presence of something or the absence of nothing: Increasing theoretical precision in management research. *Organizational Research Methods, 13*(4), 668-689. https://doi.org/10.1177/1094428110380467

55. Platt, J. R. (1964). Strong Inference: Certain systematic methods of scientific thinking may produce much more rapid progress than others. *Science, 146*(3642), 347-353. https://doi.org/10.1126/science.146.3642.347

56. Hitt, M. A., Gimeno, J., & Hoskisson, R. E. (1998). Current and future research methods in strategic management. *Organizational Research Methods, 1*(1), 6-44. https://doi.org/10.1177/109442819800100103

57. Edwards, J. R., & Berry, J. W. (2010). The presence of something or the absence of nothing: Increasing theoretical precision in management research. *Organizational Research Methods, 13*(4), 668-689. https://doi.org/10.1177/1094428110380467

58. Pierce, J. R., & Aguinis, H. (2013). The too-much-of-a-good-thing effect in management. *Journal of Management, 39*(2), 313-338. https://doi.org/10.1177/0149206311410060

59. Edwards, J. R., & Berry, J. W. (2010). The presence of something or the absence of nothing: Increasing theoretical precision in management research. *Organizational Research Methods, 13*(4), 668-689. https://doi.org/10.1177/1094428110380467

60. Serlin, R. C., & Lapsley, D. K. (1985). Rationality in psychological research: The good-enough principle. *American Psychologist, 40*, 73-83. https://doi.org/10.1037/0003-066X.40.1.73

61. Adner, R., Polos, L., Ryall, M., & Sorenson, O. (2009). The case for formal theory. *Academy of Management Review, 34*(2), 201-208. https://doi.org/10.5465/amr.2009.36982613

62. Mulaik, S. A., Raju, N. S., & Harshman, R. A. (2016). There is a time and a place for significance testing. In *What if there were no significance tests?*(pp. 109-154). Routledge.

63. Aguinis, H., Dalton, D. R., Bosco, F. A., Pierce, C. A., & Dalton, C. M. (2011). Meta-analytic choices and judgment calls: Implications for theory building and testing, obtained effect sizes, and scholarly impact. *Journal of Management, 37*(1), 5-38. https://doi.org/10.1177/0149206310377113

64. Lee, T. W., Mitchell, T. R., & Sablynski, C. J. (1999). Qualitative research in organizational and vocational psychology. *Journal of Vocational Behavior, 55*(2), 161–187. https://doi.org/10.1006/jvbe.1999.1707

65. Edmondson, A. C., & McManus, S. E. (2007). Methodological fit in management field research. *Academy of Management Review, 32*(4), 1246-1264. https://doi.org/10.5465/amr.2007.26586086

66. Navis, C., & Ozbek, O. V. (2016). The right people in the wrong places: The paradox of entrepreneurial entry and successful opportunity realization. *Academy of Management Review, 41*(1), 109-129. https://doi.org/10.5465/amr.2013.0175

67. Edmondson, A. C., Bohmer, R. M., & Pisano, G. P. (2001). Disrupted routines: Team learning and new technology implementation in hospitals. *Administrative Science Quarterly, 46*(4), 685-716. https://doi.org/10.2307/3094828

68. Lee, T. W., Mitchell, T. R., & Sablynski, C. J. (1999). Qualitative research in organizational and vocational psychology. *Journal of Vocational Behavior, 55*(2),

161– 187. https://doi.org/10.1006/j vbe.1999.1707

69. Ely, R. J., & Thomas, D. A. (2001). Cultural diversity at work: The effects of diversity perspectives on work group processes and outcomes. *Administrative Science Quarterly, 46*(2), 229-273. https://doi.org/10.2307/2667087

70. Shane, S. (2000). Prior knowledge and the discovery of entrepreneurial opportunities. *Organization Science, 11*(4), 448-469. https://doi.org/10.1287/orsc.11.4.448.14602

71. Lee, T. W., Mitchell, T. R., & Sablynski, C. J. (1999). Qualitative research in organizational and vocational psychology. *Journal of Vocational Behavior, 55*(2), 161– 187. https://doi.org/10.1006/jvbe.1999.1707

72. Bacharach, S. B. (1989). Organizational theories: Some criteria for evaluation. *Academy of Management Review, 14*(4), 496-515. https://doi.org/10.2307/258555

73. Bacharach, S. B. (1989). Organizational theories: Some criteria for evaluation. *Academy of Management Review, 14*(4), 496-515. https://doi.org/10.2307/258555

74. Vaughan, D. (1992). Theory elaboration: The heuristics of case analysis. In Ragin, C. C., & Becker, H. S. (Eds.), *What is a case? Exploring the foundations of social inquiry* (pp. 173-202). Cambridge University Press.

75. Maguire, S., Hardy, C., & Lawrence, T. B. (2004). Institutional entrepreneurship in emerging fields: HIV/AIDS treatment advocacy in Canada. *Academy of Management Journal, 47*(5), 657-679. https://doi.org/10.5465/20159610

76. Whetten, D. A., Felin, T., & King, B. G. (2009). The practice of theory borrowing in organizational studies: Current issues and future directions. *Journal of Management, 35*(3), 537-563. https://doi.org/10.1177/0149206308330556

77. Argote, L. (1999). *Organizational learning: Creating, retaining and transferring knowledge.* Springer.

78. Cyert, R. M. & March, J.G. (1963). *A behavioral theory of the firm.* Prentice-Hall.

79. Albert, S., & Whetten, D. A. (1985). Organizational identity. *Research in Organizational Behavior, 7*, 263-295.

80. Morgeson, F. P., & Hofmann, D. A. (1999). The structure and function of collective constructs: Implications for multilevel research and theory development. *Academy of Management Review, 24*(2), 249-265. https://doi.org/10.5465/amr.1999.1893935

81. Tripsas, M., & Gavetti, G. (2000). Capabilities, cognition, and inertia: Evidence from digital imaging. *Strategic Management Journal, 21*(10), 1147-1161. https://doi.org/10.1002/1097-0266(200010/11)21:10/11 < 1147::AID-SMJ128>3.0.CO;2-R

82. Bacharach, S. B. (1989). Organizational theories: Some criteria for evaluation. *Academy of Management Review, 14*(4), 496-515. https://doi.org/10.2307/258555

83. Suddaby, R. (2010). Editor's comments: Construct clarity in theories of management and organization. *Academy of Management Review, 35*(3), 346-357. https://doi.org/10.5465/AMR.2010.51141319

84. Strauss, A., & Corbin, J. (2007). *Basics of qualitative research: Techniques and procedures for developing grounded theory.* Sage.

85. Gioia, D. A., & Chittipeddi, K. (1991). Sensemaking and sensegiving in strategic change initiation. *Strategic Management Journal, 12*(6), 433-448. https://doi.org/10.1002/smj.4250120604

86. Eisenhardt, K. M. (1989). Building theories from case study research. *Academy of Management Review, 14*(4), 532-550. https://doi.org/10.2307/258557

87. Bacharach, S. B. (1989). Organizational theories: Some criteria for evaluation. *Academy of Management Review, 14*(4), 496-515. https://doi.org/10.2307/258555

88. Ely, R. J., & Thomas, D. A. (2001). Cultural diversity at work: The effects of diversity perspectives on work group processes and outcomes. *Administrative Science Quarterly, 46*(2), 229-273. https://doi.org/10.2307/2667087

89. Bacharach, S. B. (1989). Organizational theories: Some criteria for evaluation. *Academy of Management Review, 14*(4), 496-515. https://doi.org/10.2307/258555

90. Bacharach, S. B. (1989). Organizational theories: Some criteria for evaluation. *Academy of Management Review, 14*(4), 496-515. https://doi.org/10.2307/258555

91. Langley, A. (1999). Strategies for theorizing from process data. *Academy of Management Review, 24*(4), 691-710.

92. Anderson, P. J., Blatt, R., Christianson, M. K., Grant, A. M., Marquis, C., Neuman, E. J., Sonenshein, S. & Sutcliffe, K. M. (2006). Understanding mechanisms in organizational research: Reflections from a collective journey. *Journal of Management Inquiry, 15*(2), 102-113. https://doi.org/10.1177/1056492605280231

93. Greenwood, R., Suddaby, R., & Hinings, C. R. (2002). Theorizing change: The role of professional associations in the transformation of institutionalized fields. *Academy of Management Journal, 45*(1), 58-80. https://doi.org/10.5465/3069285

94. Greenwood, R., & Suddaby, R. (2006). Institutional entrepreneurship in mature fields: The big five accounting firms. *Academy of Management Journal, 49*(1), 27– 48. https://doi.org/10.5465/amj.2006.20785498

95. Langley, A. (1999). Strategies for theorizing from process

data. *Academy of Management Review, 24*(4), 691-710. https://doi.org/10.5465/amr.1999.2553248

96. Langley, A. (1999). Strategies for theorizing from process data. *Academy of Management Review, 24*(4), 691-710. https://doi.org/10.5465/amr.1999.2553248

97. Langley, A., & Truax, J. (1994). A process study of new technology adoption in smaller manufacturing firms. *Journal of Management Studies, 31*(5), 619-652. https://doi.org/10.1111/j.1467-6486.1994.tb00632.x

98. Edmondson, A. C., Bohmer, R. M., & Pisano, G. P. (2001). Disrupted routines: Team learning and new technology implementation in hospitals. *Administrative Science Quarterly, 46*(4), 685-716. https://doi.org/10.2307/3094828

99. Tripsas, M., & Gavetti, G. (2000). Capabilities, cognition, and inertia: Evidence from digital imaging. *Strategic Management Journal, 21*(10), 1147-1161. https://doi.org/10.1002/1097-0266(200010/11)21:10/11 < 1147::AID-SMJ128>3.0.CO;2-R

100. Bacharach, S. B. (1989). Organizational theories: Some criteria for evaluation. *Academy of Management Review, 14*(4), 496-515. https://doi.org/10.2307/258555

101. Bacharach, S. B. (1989). Organizational theories: Some criteria for evaluation. *Academy of Management Review, 14*(4), 496-515. https://doi.org/10.2307/258555

102. Glaser, B. G., & Strauss, A. (1967). *The discovery of grounded theory: Strategies for qualitative research.* Wiedenfeld and Nicholson. https://doi.org/10.1097/00006199-196807000-00014

103. Suddaby, R. (2010). Editor's comments: Construct clarity in theories of management and organization. *Academy of Management Review, 35*(3), 346-357. https://doi.org/10.5465/AMR.2010.51141319

104. Glaser, B. G., & Strauss, A. (1967). *The discovery of grounded theory: Strategies for qualitative research.* Wiedenfeld and Nicholson. https://doi.org/10.1097/00006199-196807000-00014

105. Suddaby, R. (2006). From the editors: What grounded theory is not. *Academy of Management Journal, 49*(4), 633-642. https://doi.org/10.5465/amj.2006.22083020

106. Bechky, B. A. (2003). Sharing meaning across occupational communities: The transformation of understanding on a production floor. *Organization Science, 14*(3), 312-330. https://doi.org/10.1287/orsc.14.3.312.15162

107. Gephart, R. P. (1978). Status degradation and organizational succession: An ethnomethodological approach. *Administrative Science Quarterly, 23*(4), 553-581. https://doi.org/10.2307/2392580

108. Thagard, P., & Shelley, C. P. (1997). Abductive reasoning: Logic, visual thinking, and coherence. In M. L. Dalla Chiara, K. Doets, D. Mundici, & J. van Benthem (Eds.), *Logic and scientific methods* (pp. 413–427). Kluwer. https://doi.org/10.1007/978-94-017-0487-8_22

109. Weick, K. E. (2005). Organizing and failures of imagination. *International Public Management Journal, 8*(3), 425–438. https://doi.org/10.1080/10967490500439883

110. Locke, K., Golden-Biddle, K., & Feldman, M. S. (2008). Perspective-making doubt generative: Rethinking the role of doubt in the research process. *Organization Science, 19*(6), 907-918. https://doi.org/10.1287/orsc.1080.0398

111. Locke, K., Golden-Biddle, K., & Feldman, M. S. (2008). Perspective-making doubt generative: Rethinking the role of doubt in the research process. *Organization Science, 19*(6), 907-918. https://doi.org/10.1287/orsc.1080.0398

112. Bamberger, P., & Ang, S. (2016). The quantitative discovery: What is it and how to get it published. *Academy of Management Discoveries, 2*(1), 1-6. https://doi.org/10.5465/amd.2015.0060

113. Gephart, R. P. (2018). Qualitative research as interpretive social science. *The SAGE handbook of qualitative business and management research methods.*

114. Blaikie, N. (2007). *Approaches to social enquiry (2nd Edition).* Polity Press.

115. Padmanabhan, T. (2006). Gravity: a new holographic perspective. *International Journal of Modern Physics D, 15*(10), 1659-1675. https://doi.org/10.1142/S0218271806009029

116. Wiseman, R. M., & Skilton, P. F. (1999). Divisions and differences: Exploring publication preferences and productivity across management subfields. *Journal of Management Inquiry, 8*(3), 299-320. https://doi.org/10.1177/105649269983008

117. Aguinis, H., Pierce, C. A., Bosco, F. A., & Muslin, I. S. (2009). First decade of Organizational Research Methods: Trends in design, measurement, and data-analysis topics. *Organizational Research Methods, 12*(1), 69-112. https://doi.org/10.1177/1094428108322641

118. Ployhart, R. E., & Vandenberg, R. J. (2010). Longitudinal research: The theory, design, and analysis of change. *Journal of Management, 36*(1), 94-120. https://doi.org/10.1177/0149206309352110

119. Cascio, W. F., & Aguinis, H. (2008). Research in industrial and organizational psychology from 1963 to 2007: Changes, choices, and trends. *Journal of Applied Psychology, 93*(5), 1062-1081. https://doi.org/10.1037/0021-9010.93.5.1062

120. Hambrick, D. C. (1994). What if the academy actually mattered?. *Academy of Management Review, 19*(1), 11-16. https://doi.org/10.5465/amr.1994.9410122006

121. Saari, L. (2007). Bridging the worlds. *Academy of Management Journal, 50*(5), 1043-1045. https://doi.org/10.5465/amj.2007.27156088

122. Harrison, D. A., Price, K. H., & Bell, M. P. (1998). Beyond relational demography: Time and the effects of surface-and deep-level diversity on work group cohesion. *Academy of Management Journal*, *41*(1), 96-107. https://doi.org/10.5465/256901

123. Dalton, D. R., & Dalton, C. M. (2011). Integration of micro and macro studies in governance research: CEO duality, board composition, and financial performance. *Journal of Management*, *37*(2), 404-411. https://doi.org/10.1177/0149206310373399

124. Shepherd, D. A. (2011). Multilevel entrepreneurship research: Opportunities for studying entrepreneurial decision making. *Journal of Management*, *37*(2), 412-420. https://doi.org/10.1177/0149206310369940

125. Huselid, M. A., & Becker, B. E. (2011). Bridging micro and macro domains: Workforce differentiation and strategic human resource management. *Journal of Management*, *37*(2), 421-428. https://doi.org/10.1177/0149206310373400

126. Rousseau, D. M. (2011). Reinforcing the micro/macro bridge: Organizational thinking and pluralistic vehicles. *Journal of Management*, *37*(2), 429-442. https://doi.org/10.1177/0149206310372414

CHAPTER 4

1. Ashkanasy, N. M. (2010). Publishing today is more difficult than ever. *Journal of Organizational Behavior*, *31*(1), 1-3. https://doi.org/10.1002/job.676

2. Certo, S. T., Sirmon, D. G., & Brymer, R. A. (2010). Competition and scholarly productivity in management: Investigating changes in scholarship from 1988 to 2008. *Academy of Management Learning & Education*, *9*(4), 591-606. https://doi.org/10.5465/amle.9.4.zqr591

3. Rynes, S. L., Colbert, A. E., & Brown, K. G. (2002). HR professionals' beliefs about effective human resource practices: Correspondence between research and practice. *Human Resource Management*, *41*(2), 149-174. https://doi.org/10.1002/hrm.10029

4. https://aom.org/about-aom/strategic-plan

5. Society for Industrial and Organizational Psychology. (n.d.). *SIOP Vision, Mission, Values, and Goals*. http://www.siop.org/mission.aspx

6. Aguinis, H., Pierce, C. A., Bosco, F. A., & Muslin, I. S. (2009). First decade of Organizational Research Methods: Trends in design, measurement, and data-analysis topics. *Organizational Research Methods*, *12*(1), 69-112. https://doi.org/10.1177/1094428108322641

7. Aiken, L. S., West, S. G., Sechrest, L., Reno, R. R., Roediger III, H. L., Scarr, S., ... & Sherman, S. J. (1990). Graduate training in statistics, methodology, and measurement in psychology: A survey of PhD programs in North America. *American Psychologist*, *45*(6), 721-734. https://doi.org/10.1037/0003-066X.45.6.721

8. Aguinis, H., Cummings, C., Ramani, R. S., & Cummings, T. G. (2020). "An A is an A": The new bottom line for valuing academic research. *Academy of Management Perspectives*, *34*(1), 135-154. https://doi.org/10.5465/amp.2017.0193

9. Rynes, S. L., Colbert, A. E., & Brown, K. G. (2002). HR professionals' beliefs about effective human resource practices: Correspondence between research and practice. *Human Resource Management*, *41*(2), 149-174. https://doi.org/10.1002/hrm.10029

10. Dunnette, M. D. (1990). *Blending the science and practice of industrial and organizational psychology: Where are we and where are we going?*. Consulting Psychologists Press.

11. Cascio, W. F., & Aguinis, H. (2008). Research in industrial and organizational psychology from 1963 to 2007: Changes, choices, and trends. *Journal of Applied Psychology*, *93*(5), 1062-1081. https://doi.org/10.1037/0021-9010.93.5.1062

12. Rousseau, D. M. (2007). A sticky, leveraging, and scalable strategy for high-quality connections between organizational practice and science. *Academy of Management Journal*, *50*(5), 1037-1042. https://doi.org/10.5465/amj.2007.27155539

13. Hambrick, D. C. (1994). What if the academy actually mattered?. *Academy of Management Review*, *19*(1), 11-16. https://doi.org/10.2307/258833

14. Hakel MD, Sorcher M, Beer M, Moses JL. 1982. Making It Happen: Designing Research with Implementation in Mind. Beverly Hills, CA: Sage Hakel, M. D. (1982). *Making it happen: Designing research with implementation in mind* (Vol. 3). SAGE Publications, Incorporated.

15. Cascio, W. F., & Aguinis, H. (2008). Research in industrial and organizational psychology from 1963 to 2007: Changes, choices, and trends. *Journal of Applied Psychology*, *93*(5), 1062-1081. https://doi.org/10.1037/0021-9010.93.5.1062

16. Simon H. 1996 (1969). *The Sciences of the Artificial*. MIT Press. (3rd ed).

17. Van Aken, J. E., & Romme, A. G. L. (2012). A design science approach to evidence-based management. *The Oxford handbook of evidence-based management*, pp. 43-57. Oxford University Press. https://doi.org/10.1093/oxfordhb/9780199763986.013.0003

18. Aguinis, H., Culpepper, S. A., & Pierce, C. A. (2010). Revival of test bias research in preemployment testing. *Journal of Applied Psychology*, *95*(4), 648. https://doi.org/10.1037/a0018714

19. Aguinis, H. (2023). *Performance management* (5th ed.). Chicago Business Press.

20. Barnett, M. L. (2007). (Un) learning and (mis) education through the eyes of bill Starbuck: An interview with pandora's playmate. *Academy of Management Learning & Education*, *6*(1), 114-127. https://doi.org/10.5465/amle.2007.24401709

21. Ruback, R. B., & Innes, C. A. (1988). The relevance and irrelevance of psychological research: The example of prison crowding. *American Psychologist*, *43*(9), 683. https://doi.org/10.1037/0003-066X.43.9.683

22. Shapiro, D. L., Kirkman, B. L., & Courtney, H. G. (2007). Perceived causes and solutions of the translation problem in management research. *Academy of Management Journal*, *50*(2), 249-266. https://doi.org/10.5465/amj.2007.24634433

23. Anderson, N. (2007). The practitioner-researcher divide revisited: Strategic-level bridges and the roles of IWO psychologists. *Journal of Occupational and Organizational Psychology*, *80*(2), 175-183. https://doi.org/10.1348/096317907X187237

24. Whetten, D. A. (1989). What constitutes a theoretical contribution?. *Academy of Management Review*, *14*(4), 490-495. https://doi.org/10.2307/258554

25. Illari, P. M., Russo, F., & Williamson, J. (Eds.). (2011). *Causality in the sciences*. Oxford University Press. https://doi.org/10.1093/acprof:oso/9780199574131.001.0001

26. Cook, T. D., Campbell, D. T., & `, W. (2002). *Experimental and quasi-experimental designs for generalized causal inference*. Houghton Mifflin.

27. Aguinis, H., & Vandenberg, R. J. (2014). An ounce of prevention is worth a pound of cure: Improving research quality before data collection. *Annual Review of Organizational Psychology and Organizational Behavior*, *1*(1), 569-595. https://doi.org/10.1146/annurev-orgpsych-031413-091231

28. Bowen, H. P., & Wiersema, M. F. (1999). Matching method to paradigm in strategy research: limitations of cross-sectional analysis and some methodological alternatives. *Strategic Management Journal*, *20*(7), 625-636. https://doi.org/10.1002/(SICI)1097-0266(199907)20:7 < 625::AID-SMJ45>3.0.CO;2-V

29. Ployhart, R. E., & Vandenberg, R. J. (2010). Longitudinal research: The theory, design, and analysis of change. *Journal of Management*, *36*(1), 94-120. https://doi.org/10.1177/0149206309352110

30. Lonati, S., Quiroga, B. F., Zehnder, C., & Antonakis, J. (2018). On doing relevant and rigorous experiments: Review and recommendations. *Journal of Operations Management*, *64*(1), 19-40. https://doi.org/10.1016/j.jom.2018.10.003

31. Cook, T. D., & Steiner, P. M. (2010). Case matching and the reduction of selection bias in quasi-experiments: The relative importance of pretest measures of outcome, of unreliable measurement, and of mode of data analysis. *Psychological Methods*, *15*(1), 56-68. https://doi.org/10.1037/a0018536

32. Rubin, D. B. (1978). Bayesian inference for causal effects: The role of randomization. *The Annals of Statistics*, 34-58. https://doi.org/10.1214/aos/1176344064

33. Little, R. J., & Rubin, D. B. (2000). Causal effects in clinical and epidemiological studies via potential outcomes: concepts and analytical approaches. *Annual Review of Public Health*, *21*(1), 121-145. https://doi.org/10.1146/annurev.publhealth.21.1.121

34. Collins, S. L., & Winship, C. (2007). *Counterfactuals and causal inference: Methods and principles for social research*. Cambridge University Press.

35. Edwards, J. R. (2008). To prosper, organizational psychology should... overcome methodological barriers to progress. *Journal of Organizational Behavior*, *29*(4), 469-491. https://doi.org/10.1002/job.529

36. Echambadi, R., Campbell, B., & Agarwal, R. (2006). Encouraging best practice in quantitative management research: An incomplete list of opportunities. *Journal of Management Studies*, *43*(8), 1801-1820. https://doi.org/10.1111/j.1467-6486.2006.00660.x

37. Cochran, W. G. (1968). The effectiveness of adjustment by subclassification in removing bias in observational studies. *Biometrics*, *24*, 295-313. https://doi.org/10.2307/2528036

38. Cook, T. D., Campbell, D. T., & Shadish, W. (2002). *Experimental and quasi-experimental designs for generalized causal inference*. Houghton Mifflin.

39. Li, M. (2013). Using the propensity score method to estimate causal effects: A review and practical guide. *Organizational Research Methods*, *16*(2), 188-226. https://doi.org/10.1177/1094428112447816

40. Atinc, G., Simmering, M. J., & Kroll, M. J. (2012). Control variable use and reporting in macro and micro management research. *Organizational Research Methods*, *15*(1), 57-74. https://doi.org/10.1177/1094428110397773

41. Hitt, M. A., Boyd, B. K., & Li, D. (2004). The state of strategic management research and a vision of the future. *Research methodology in strategy and management*. Emerald Group Publishing Limited. https://doi.org/10.1016/S1479-8387(04)01101-4

42. Carlson, K. D., & Wu, J. (2012). The illusion of statistical control: Control variable practice in management research. *Organizational Research Methods*, *15*(3), 413-435. https://doi.org/10.1177/1094428111428817

43. Bollen, K. A. (2012). Instrumental variables in sociology and the social sciences. *Annual Review of Sociology*, *38*, 37-72. https://doi.or

g/10.1146/annurev-soc-081309-1
50141

44. Hamilton, B. H., & Nickerson, J. A. (2003). Correcting for endogeneity in strategic management research. *Strategic Organization*, *1*(1), 51-78. https://doi.org/10.1177/1476127003001001218

45. Bollen, K. A. (2012). Instrumental variables in sociology and the social sciences. *Annual Review of Sociology*, *38*, 37-72. https://doi.org/10.1146/annurev-soc-081309-1 50141

46. Lonati, S., Quiroga, B. F., Zehnder, C., & Antonakis, J. (2018). On doing relevant and rigorous experiments: Review and recommendations. *Journal of Operations Management*, *64*, 19-40. https://doi.org/10.1016/j.jom.2018.10.003

47. Cuervo-Cazurra, A., Mudambi, R., Pedersen, T., & Piscitello, L. (2017). Research methodology in global strategy research. *Global Strategy Journal*, *7*(3), 233-240. https://doi.org/10.1002/gsj.1164

48. Castellani, D., Mariotti, I., & Piscitello, L. (2008). The impact of outward investments on parent company's employment and skill composition: Evidence from the Italian case. *Structural Change and Economic Dynamics*, *19*(1), 81-94. https://doi.org/10.1016/j.strueco.2007.11.006

49. Buckley, P. J., Chen, L., Clegg, L. J., & Voss, H. (2018). Risk propensity in the foreign direct investment location decision of emerging multinationals. *Journal of International Business Studies*, *49*(2), 153-171. https://doi.org/10.1057/s41267-017-0126-4

50. Huvaj, M. N., & Johnson, W. C. (2019). Organizational complexity and innovation portfolio decisions: Evidence from a quasi-natural experiment. *Journal of Business Research*, *98*, 153-165.

51. Vandor, P., & Franke, N. (2016). See Paris and... found a business? The impact of cross-cultural experience on opportunity recognition capabilities. *Journal of Business Venturing*, *31*(4), 388-407. https://doi.org/10.1016/j.jbusvent.2016.03.003

52. Irani, R. M., & Oesch, D. (2016). Analyst coverage and real earnings management: Quasi-experimental evidence. *Journal of Financial and Quantitative Analysis*, *51*(2), 589-627. https://doi.org/10.1017/S0022109016000156

53. Wang, S., Noe, R. A., & Wang, Z. M. (2014). Motivating knowledge sharing in knowledge management systems: A quasi-field experiment. *Journal of Management*, *40*(4), 978-1009. https://doi.org/10.1177/0149206311412192

54. Flammer, C., & Luo, J. (2017). Corporate social responsibility as an employee governance tool: Evidence from a quasi-experiment. *Strategic Management Journal*, *38*(2), 163-183. https://doi.org/10.1002/smj.2492

55. Campbell, D. T. (1979). *Quasi-experimentation: Design & analysis issues for field settings*. Boston.

56. Highhouse, S. (2009). Designing experiments that generalize. *Organizational Research Methods*, *12*(3), 554-566. https://doi.org/10.1177/1094428107300396

57. Ketchen Jr, D. J., Boyd, B. K., & Bergh, D. D. (2008). Research methodology in strategic management: Past accomplishments and future challenges. *Organizational Research Methods*, *11*(4), 643-658.

58. Short, J. C., Ketchen Jr, D. J., & Palmer, T. B. (2002). The role of sampling in strategic management research on performance: A two-study analysis. *Journal of Management*, *28*(3), 363-385.

59. Dipboye, R. L., & Flanagan, M. F. (1979). Research settings in industrial and organizational psychology: Are findings in the field more generalizable than in the laboratory?. *American Psychologist*, *34*(2), 141-150.

60. Davis, R., & Duhaime, I. M. (1992). Diversification, vertical integration, and industry analysis: New perspectives and measurement. *Strategic Management Journal*, *13*(7), 511-524. https://doi.org/10.1002/smj.4250130704

61. Floyd, S. W., & Sputtek, R. (2011). Rediscovering the individual in strategy: methodological challenges, strategies, and prospects. *Building Methodological Bridges*. Emerald Group Publishing Limited. https://doi.org/10.1108/S1479-8387(2011)0000006004

62. Morgeson, F. P., Aguinis, H., Waldman, D. A., & Siegel, D. S. (2013). Extending corporate social responsibility research to the human resource management and organizational behavior domains: A look to the future. *Personnel Psychology*, *66*(4), 805-824.

63. Foss, N. J. (2011). Invited editorial: Why micro-foundations for resource-based theory are needed and what they may look like. *Journal of Management*, *37*(5), 1413-1428. https://doi.org/10.1177/0149206310390218

64. Whittington, R. (2006). Completing the practice turn in strategy research. *Organization Studies*, *27*(5), 613-634. https://doi.org/10.1177/0170840606064101

65. Uy, M. A., Foo, M. D., & Aguinis, H. (2010). Using experience sampling methodology to advance entrepreneurship theory and research. *Organizational Research Methods*, *13*(1), 31-54. https://doi.org/10.1177/1094428109334977

66. Beal, D.J., & Weiss, H.M. (2003). Methods of ecological momentary assessment in organizational research. *Organizational Research Methods*, *6*(4), 440 - 464. https://doi.org/10.1177/1094428103257361

67. Aguinis, H., & Lawal, S. O. (2013). eLancing: A review and research agenda for bridging the science–practice gap. *Human Resource Management Review*, *23*(1), 6-17. https://doi.org/10.1016/j.hrmr.2012.06.003

68. Aguinis, H., & Lawal, S. O. (2012). Conducting field experiments using eLancing's natural environment. *Journal of Business Venturing, 27*(4), 493-505. https://doi.org/10.1016/j.jbusvent.2012.01.002

69. Stanney, K. M. (Ed.). (2002). Handbook of virtual environments: Design, implementation, and applications. Lawrence Erlbaum Associates Publishers.

70. Aguinis, H., Henle, C. A., & Beaty Jr, J. C. (2001). Virtual reality technology: A new tool for personnel selection. *International Journal of Selection and Assessment, 9*(1-2), 70-83.

71. Pierce, C. A., & Aguinis, H. (1997). Using virtual reality technology in organizational behavior research. *Journal of Organizational Behavior, 18*(5), 407-410. https://doi.org/10.1002/(SICI)1099-1379(199709)18:5 < 407::AID-JOB869>3.0.CO;2-P

72. Floyd, S. W., & Sputtek, R. (2011). Rediscovering the individual in strategy: Methodological challenges, strategies, and prospects. In *Building Methodological Bridges*. Emerald Group Publishing Limited. https://doi.org/10.1108/S1479-8387(2011)0000006004

73. Vergne, J. P., & Durand, R. (2010). The missing link between the theory and empirics of path dependence: conceptual clarification, testability issue, and methodological implications. *Journal of Management Studies, 47*(4), 736-759. https://doi.org/10.1111/j.1467-6486.2009.00913.x

74. Cook, T. D., Campbell, D. T., & Shadish, W. (2002). *Experimental and quasi-experimental designs for generalized causal inference*. Houghton Mifflin.

75. Edwards, J. R. (2008). To prosper, organizational psychology should... overcome methodological barriers to progress. *Journal of Organizational Behavior, 29*(4), 469-491. https://doi.org/10.1002/job.529

76. Meehl PE. (1971). High school yearbooks: A reply to Schwarz. *Journal of Abnormal Psychology, 77*, 143-148. http://dx.doi.org/10.1037/h0030750

77. Williams, L. J., Vandenberg, R. J., & Edwards, J. R. (2009). 12 structural equation modeling in management research: A guide for improved analysis. *Academy of Management Annals, 3*(1), 543-604. https://doi.org/10.5465/19416520903065683

78. Spector, P. E., & Brannick, M. T. (2011). Methodological urban legends: The misuse of statistical control variables. *Organizational Research Methods, 14*(2), 287-305. https://doi.org/10.1177/1094428110369842

79. Bono, J. E., & McNamara, G. (2011). From the editors: Publishing in AMJ- part 2: Research design. *Academy of Management Journal, 54*, 657-660. https://doi.org/10.5465/amj.2011.64869103

80. Aguinis, H., & Vandenberg, R. J. (2014). An ounce of prevention is worth a pound of cure: Improving research quality before data collection. *Annual Review of Organizational Psychology and Organizational Behavior, 1*(1), 569-595. https://doi.org/10.1146/annurev-orgpsych-031413-091231

81. Breaugh, J. A. (2008). Important considerations in using statistical procedures to control for nuisance variables in non-experimental studies. *Human Resource Management Review, 18*(4), 282-293. https://doi.org/10.1016/j.hrmr.2008.03.001

82. Spector, P. E., & Brannick, M. T. (2011). Methodological urban legends: The misuse of statistical control variables. *Organizational Research Methods, 14*(2), 287-305. https://doi.org/10.1177/1094428110369842

83. Rode, J. C., Mooney, C. H., Arthaud-Day, M. L., Near, J. P., Baldwin, T. T., Rubin, R. S., & Bommer, W. H. (2007). Emotional intelligence and individual performance: Evidence of direct and moderated effects. *Journal of Organizational Behavior, 28*(4), 399-421. https://doi.org/10.1002/job.429

84. Carlson, K. D., & Wu, J. (2012). The illusion of statistical control: Control variable practice in management research. *Organizational Research Methods, 15*(3), 413-435. https://doi.org/10.1177/1094428111428817

85. Newcombe, N. S. (2003). Some controls control too much. *Child Development, 74*(4), 1050-1052. https://doi.org/10.1111/1467-8624.00588

86. Breaugh, J. A. (2006). Rethinking the control of nuisance variables in theory testing. *Journal of Business and Psychology, 20*(3), 429-443. https://doi.org/10.1007/s10869-005-9009-y

87. Bernerth, J. & Aguinis, H. (2016). A critical review and best-practice recommendations for control variable usage. *Personnel Psychology, 69*(1), 229-283. https://doi.org/10.1111/peps.12103

88. Becker, G. (1964). *Human capital: A theoretical and empirical analysis with special reference to education*. Columbia University Press.

89. Ng, T. W., & Feldman, D. C. (2009). How broadly does education contribute to job performance?. *Personnel Psychology, 62*(1), 89-134. https://doi.org/10.1111/j.1744-6570.2008.01130.x

90. Horwitz, S. K., & Horwitz, I. B. (2007). The effects of team diversity on team outcomes: A meta-analytic review of team demography. *Journal of Management, 33*(6), 987-1015. https://doi.org/10.1177/0149206307308587

91. Meehl PE. (1971). High school yearbooks: A reply to Schwarz. *Journal of Abnormal Psychology, 77*(2), 143-148. http://dx.doi.org/10.1037/h0030750

92. Carlson, K. D., & Wu, J. (2012). The illusion of statistical control: Control variable practice in

management research. *Organizational Research Methods*, *15*(3), 413-435. https://doi.org/10.1177/1094428111428817

93. Spector, P. E., Zapf, D., Chen, P. Y., & Frese, M. (2000). Why negative affectivity should not be controlled in job stress research: Don't throw out the baby with the bath water. *Journal of Organizational Behavior*, *21*(1), 79-95. https://doi.org/10.1002/(SICI)1099-1379(200002)21:1 < 79::AID-JOB964>3.0.CO;2-G

94. Sutton, R. I., & Staw, B. M. (1995). What theory is not. *Administrative Science Quarterly*, 371-384. https://doi.org/10.2307/2393788

95. Carlson, K. D., & Wu, J. (2012). The illusion of statistical control: Control variable practice in management research. *Organizational Research Methods*, *15*(3), 413-435. https://doi.org/10.1177/1094428111428817

96. Bauer, T. N., Erdogan, B., Liden, R. C., & Wayne, S. J. (2006). A longitudinal study of the moderating role of extraversion: Leader-member exchange, performance, and turnover during new executive development. *Journal of Applied Psychology*, *91*(2), 298-310. https://doi.org/10.1037/0021-9010.91.2.298

97. Tangirala, S., & Ramanujam, R. (2008). Exploring nonlinearity in employee voice: The effects of personal control and organizational identification. *Academy of Management Journal*, *51*(6), 1189-1203. https://doi.org/10.5465/amj.2008.35732719

98. Maltarich, M. A., Nyberg, A. J., & Reilly, G. (2010). A conceptual and empirical analysis of the cognitive ability–voluntary turnover relationship. *Journal of Applied Psychology*, *95*(6), 1058. https://doi.org/10.1037/a0020331

99. Liu, D., Zhang, S., Wang, L., & Lee, T. W. (2011). The effects of autonomy and empowerment on employee turnover: Test of a multilevel model in teams. *Journal of*

Applied Psychology, *96*(6), 1305. https://doi.org/10.1037/a0024518

100. Tsai, W. C., Chen, C. C., & Liu, H. L. (2007). Test of a model linking employee positive moods and task performance. *Journal of Applied Psychology*, *92*(6), 1570. https://doi.org/10.1037/0021-9010.92.6.1570

101. Tsai, W. C., Chen, C. C., & Liu, H. L. (2007). Test of a model linking employee positive moods and task performance. *Journal of Applied Psychology*, *92*(6), 1570. https://doi.org/10.1037/0021-9010.92.6.1570

102. Kammeyer-Mueller, J. D., Simon, L. S., & Rich, B. L. (2012). The psychic cost of doing wrong: Ethical conflict, divestiture socialization, and emotional exhaustion. *Journal of Management*, *38*(3), 784-808. https://doi.org/10.1177/0149206310381133

103. Liu, D., Zhang, S., Wang, L., & Lee, T. W. (2011). The effects of autonomy and empowerment on employee turnover: Test of a multilevel model in teams. *Journal of Applied Psychology*, *96*(6), 1305-1316. https://doi.org/10.1037/a0024518

104. Judge, T. A., LePine, J. A., & Rich, B. L. (2006). Loving yourself abundantly: relationship of the narcissistic personality to self-and other perceptions of workplace deviance, leadership, and task and contextual performance. *Journal of Applied Psychology*, *91*(4), 762. https://doi.org/10.1037/0021-9010.91.4.762

105. Cote, S., & Miners, C. T. (2006). Emotional intelligence, cognitive intelligence, and job performance. *Administrative Science Quarterly*, *51*(1), 1-28. https://doi.org/10.2189/asqu.51.1.1

106. Becker TE. (2005). Potential problems in the statistical control of variables in organizational research: A qualitative analysis with recommendations. *Organizational Research Methods*, *8*(3), 274–289. https://doi.org/10.1177/1094428105278021

107. Ambrose, M. L., & Cropanzano, R. (2003). A longitudinal analysis of organizational fairness: An examination of reactions to tenure and promotion decisions. *Journal of Applied Psychology*, *88*(2), 266. https://doi.org/10.1037/0021-9010.88.2.266

108. Erdogan, B., & Bauer, T. N. (2010). Differentiated leader–member exchanges: the buffering role of justice climate. *Journal of Applied Psychology*, *95*(6), 1104-1120. https://doi.org/10.1037/a0020578

109. O'Boyle Jr, E. H., Banks, G. C., & Gonzalez-Mulé, E. (2017). The chrysalis effect: How ugly initial results metamorphosize into beautiful articles. *Journal of Management*, *43*(2), 376-399. https://doi.org/10.1177/0149206314527133

CHAPTER 5

1. Aguinis, H., Boik, R. J., & Pierce, C. A. (2001). A generalized solution for approximating the power to detect effects of categorical moderator variables using multiple regression. *Organizational Research Methods*, *4*(4), 291-323. https://doi.org/10.1177/109442810144001

2. Cohen, J. (1988). *Statistical power analysis for the behavioral sciences* (2nd ed.). Erlbaum.

3. Raver, J. L., & Gelfand, M. J. (2005). Beyond the individual victim: Linking sexual harassment, team processes, and team performance. *Academy of Management Journal*, *48*(3), 387-400. https://doi.org/10.5465/amj.2005.17407904

4. Morgeson, F. P., & Campion, M. A. (2002). Minimizing tradeoffs when redesigning work: Evidence from a longitudinal quasi-experiment. *Personnel Psychology*, *55*(3), 589-612. https://doi.org/10.1111/j.1744-6570.2002.tb00122.x

5. Cohen, J. (1992). A power primer. *Psychological Bulletin*, *112*(1), 155-159. https://doi.org/10.1037/0033-2909.112.1.155

6. Cohen, J., Cohen, P., West, S. G., & Aiken, L. S. (2003). *Applied multiple regression/correlation analysis for the behavioral sciences* (3rd ed.). Erlbaum.

7. Cohen, J. (1962). The statistical power of abnormal-social psychological research: A review. *The Journal of Abnormal and Social Psychology*, *65*(3), 145-153. https://doi.org/10.1037/h0045186

8. Cohen, J. (1988). *Statistical power analysis for the behavioral sciences* (2nd ed.). Erlbaum.

9. Cohen, J. (1992). A power primer. *Psychological Bulletin, 112*(1), 155-159. https://doi.org/10.1037/0033-2909.112.1.155

10. Cohen, J., & Cohen, P. (1983). *Applied multiple regression/Correlation analysis for the behavioral sciences*. Erlbaum.

11. Cohen, J. (1988). *Statistical power analysis for the behavioral sciences* (2nd ed.). Erlbaum.

12. Cohen, J. (1988). *Statistical power analysis for the behavioral sciences* (2nd ed.). Erlbaum.

13. Aguinis, H., Beaty, J. C., Boik, R. J., & Pierce, C. A. (2005). Effect size and power in assessing moderating effects of categorical variables using multiple regression: A 30-year review. *Journal of Applied Psychology, 90*(1), 94-107. https://doi.org/10.1037/0021-9010.90.1.94

14. Martell, R. F., Lane, D. M., & Emrich, C. (1996). Male-female differences: A computer simulation. American Psychologist, 51(2), 157-158. https://doi.org/10.1037/0003-066X.51.2.157

15. Brown, T. C. (2003). The effect of verbal self-guidance training on collective efficacy and team performance. *Personnel Psychology, 56*(4), 935-964. https://doi.org/10.1111/j.1744-6570.2003.tb00245.x

16. Boland Jr, R. J., Singh, J., Salipante, P., Aram, J. D., Fay, S. Y., & Kanawattanachai, P. (2001). Knowledge representations and knowledge transfer. *Academy of Management Journal*, *44*(2),

393-417. https://doi.org/10.5465/3069463

17. Sauley, K. S., & Bedeian, A. G. (1989). . 05: A case of the tail wagging the distribution. *Journal of Management*, *15*(2), 335-344. https://doi.org/10.1177/014920638901500209

18. Skipper, J. K., Guenther, A. L., & Nass, G. (1967). The sacredness of. 05: A note concerning the uses of statistical levels of significance in social science. *American Sociologist*, 16-18.

19. Stevens, J. (1996). *Applied multivariate statistics for the social sciences* (3rd ed.). Erlbaum

20. Murphy, K. R., & Myors, B. (1998). *Statistical power analysis: A simple and general model for traditional and modern hypothesis tests*. Lawrence Erlbaum.

21. Aguinis, H. (2004). *Regression analysis for categorical moderators*. Guilford.

22. Murphy, K. R., & Myors, B. (1998). *Statistical power analysis: A simple and general model for traditional and modern hypothesis tests*. Lawrence Erlbaum.

23. Aguinis, H., Villamor, I., & Ramani, R. M. (2021). MTurk research: Review and recommendations. *Journal of Management*, *47*(4), 823–837. https://doi.org/10.1177/0149206320969787

24. Lovett, M., Bajaba, S., Lovett, M., & Simmering, M. J. (2018). Data quality from crowdsourced surveys: A mixed method inquiry into perceptions of Amazon's Mechanical Turk Masters. *Applied Psychology*, *67*(2), 339–366. https://doi.org/10.1111/apps.12124

25. Chandler, J. J., & Paolacci, G. (2017). Lie for a dime: When most pre- screening responses are honest but most study participants are impostors. *Social Psychological & Personality Science*, *8*(5), 500–508. https://doi.org/10.1177/1948550617698203

26. Marcus, B., Weigelt, O., Hergert, J., Gurt, J., & Gelléri, P. (2017). The use of snowball sampling for multi source organizational research: Some cause for concern. *Personnel Psychology*, *70*(3), 635–673. https://doi.org/10.1111/peps.12169

27. Chandler, J. J., & Paolacci, G. (2017). Lie for a dime: When most pre- screening responses are honest but most study participants are impostors. *Social Psychological & Personality Science*, *8*(5), 500–508. https://doi.org/10.1177/1948550617698203

28. Sharpe Wessling, K., Huber, J., & Netzer, O. (2017). MTurk character misrepresentation: Assessment and solutions. *The Journal of Consumer Research*, *44*(1), 211–230. https://doi.org/10.1093/jcr/ucx053

29. DeSimone, J. A., DeSimone, A. J., Harms, P. D., & Wood, D. (2018). The differential impacts of two forms of insufficient effort responding. *Applied Psychology*, *67*(2), 309–338. https://doi.org/10.1111/apps.12117

30. Aguinis, H., Gottfredson, R. K., & Joo, H. (2013). Best-practice recommendations for defining, identifying, and handling outliers. *Organizational Research Methods*, *16*(2), 270–301. https://doi.org/10.1177/1094428112470848

31. Aguinis, H., Hill, N. S., & Bailey, J. R. (2021). Best practices in data collection and preparation: Recommendations for reviewers, editors, and authors. *Organizational Research Methods*, *24*(1), 678–693. https://doi.org/10.1177/1094428119836485

32. Aguinis, H., & Edwards, J. R. (2014). Methodological wishes for the next decade and how to make wishes come true. *Journal of Management Studies*, *51*(1), 143-174. https://doi.org/10.1111/joms.12058

33. Bernerth, J. B., & Aguinis, H. (2016). A critical review and best-practice recommendations for control variable usage. *Personnel*

Psychology, 69(1), 229-283. https://doi.org/10.1111/peps.12103

34. Nielsen, B. B., & Raswant, A. (2018). The selection, use, and reporting of control variables in international business research: A review and recommendations. *Journal of World Business, 53*(6), 958-968. https://doi.org/10.1016/j.jwb.2018.05.003

35. Cheema, J. R. (2014). Some general guidelines for choosing missing data handling methods in educational research. *Journal of Modern Applied Statistical Methods, 13*(2), 53–75. https://doi.org/10.22237/jmasm/1414814520

36. Schafer, J. L., & Graham, J. W. (2002). Missing data: Our view of the state of the art. *Psychological Methods, 7*(2), 147-177. https://doi.org/10.1037/1082-989X.7.2.147

37. Newman, D. A. (2014). Missing data: Five practical guidelines. *Organizational Research Methods, 17*(4), 372-411. https://doi.org/10.1177/1094428114548590

38. Schafer, J. L., & Graham, J. W. (2002). Missing data: Our view of the state of the art. *Psychological Methods, 7*(2), 147-177. https://doi.org/10.1037/1082-989X.7.2.147

39. Aguinis, H., Gottfredson, R. K., & Joo, H. (2013). Best-practice recommendations for defining, identifying, and handling outliers. *Organizational Research Methods, 16*(2), 270-301. https://doi.org/10.1177/1094428112470848

40. Bainbridge, H. T., Sanders, K., Cogin, J. A., & Lin, C. H. (2017). The pervasiveness and trajectory of methodological choices: A 20-year review of human resource management research. *Human Resource Management, 56*(6), 887-913. https://doi.org/10.1002/hrm.21807

41. Green, J. P., Tonidandel, S., & Cortina, J. M. (2016). Getting through the gate: Statistical and methodological issues raised in the reviewing process. *Organizational Research Methods, 19*(3), 402-432.

https://doi.org/10.1177/1094428116631417

42. Carley-Baxter, L. R., Hill, C. A., Roe, D. J., Twiddy, S. E., Baxter, R. K., & Ruppenkamp, J. (2013). Does Response Rate Matter? Journal Editors Use of Survey Quality Measures in Manuscript Publication Decisions. *Survey Practice, 2*(7). https://doi.org/10.29115/SP-2009-0033

43. Youk, S., & Park, H. S. (2019). Where and what do they publish? Editors' and editorial board members' affiliated institutions and the citation counts of their endogenous publications in the field of communication. *Scientometrics, 120*(3), 1237-1260. https://doi.org/10.1007/s11192-019-03169-x

44. Walter, S. L., Seibert, S. E., Goering, D., & O'Boyle, E. H. (2019). A tale of two sample sources: Do results from online panel data and conventional data converge?. *Journal of Business and Psychology, 34*(4), 425-452. https://doi.org/10.1007/s10869-018-9552-y

45. Coppock, A., & McClellan, O. A. (2019). Validating the demographic, political, psychological, and experimental results obtained from a new source of online survey respondents. *Research & Politics, 6*(1), 1-14. https://doi.org/10.1177/2053168018822174

46. Cunliffe, A. L., & Alcadipani, R. (2016). The politics of access in fieldwork: Immersion, backstage dramas, and deception. *Organizational Research Methods, 19*(4), 535-561. https://doi.org/10.1177/1094428116639134

47. Peterson, R. A., & Merunka, D. R. (2014). Convenience samples of college students and research reproducibility. *Journal of Business Research, 67*(5), 1035-1041. https://doi.org/10.1016/j.jbusres.2013.08.010

48. Berinsky, A. J., Huber, G. A., & Lenz, G. S. (2012). Evaluating

online labor markets for experimental research: Amazon. com's Mechanical Turk. *Political Analysis, 20*(3), 351-368. https://doi.org/10.1093/pan/mpr057

49. Aguinis, H., Villamor, I., & Ramani, R. S. (2021). MTurk research: Review and recommendations. *Journal of Management, 47*(4), 823-837. https://doi.org/10.1177/0149206320969787

50. Aguinis, H., Villamor, I., & Ramani, R. S. (2021). MTurk research: Review and recommendations. *Journal of Management, 47*(4), 823-837. https://doi.org/10.1177/0149206320969787

51. Aguinis, H., Villamor, I., & Ramani, R. S. (2021). MTurk research: Review and recommendations. *Journal of Management, 47*(4), 823-837. https://doi.org/10.1177/0149206320969787

52. Baruch, Y., & Holtom, B. C. (2008). Survey response rate levels and trends in organizational research. *Human Relations, 61*(8), 1139-1160. https://doi.org/10.1177/0018726708094863

53. DeSimone, J. A., & Harms, P. D. (2018). Dirty data: The effects of screening respondents who provide low-quality data in survey research. *Journal of Business and Psychology, 33*(5), 559-577. https://doi.org/10.1007/s10869-017-9514-9

54. Bernerth, J. B., Aguinis, H., & Taylor, E. C. (2021). Detecting false identities: A solution to improve web-based surveys and research on leadership and health/well-being. *Journal of Occupational Health Psychology, 26*(6), 564–581. https://doi.org/10.1037/ocp0000281

55. Rogelberg, S. G., & Stanton, J. M. (2007). Introduction: Understanding and dealing with organizational survey nonresponse. *Organizational research methods, 10*(2), 195-209. https://doi.org/10.1177/1094428106294693

56. Hobfoll, S. E., Shirom, A., & Golembiewski, R. (2000). Conservation of resources theory.

Handbook of organizational behavior. Jossey-Bass.

57. Aguinis, H., Villamor, I., & Ramani, R. S. (2021). MTurk research: Review and recommendations. *Journal of Management, 47*(4), 823-837. https://doi.org/10.1177/01492 06320969787

58. Scandura, T. A., & Williams, E. A. (2000). Research methodology in management: Current practices, trends, and implications for future research. *Academy of Management Journal, 43*(6), 1248-1264. https://doi.org/10.2307/1556348

59. Colquitt, J. A., Sabey, T. B., Rodell, J. B., & Hill, E. T. (2019). Content validation guidelines: Evaluation criteria for definitional correspondence and definitional distinctiveness. *Journal of Applied Psychology, 104*(10), 1243-1265. https://doi.org/10.1037/apl0000406

60. Rogelberg, S. G., & Stanton, J. M. (2007). Introduction: Understanding and dealing with organizational survey nonresponse. *Organizational research methods, 10*(2), 195-209. https://doi.org/10.1177/1094428106294693

61. Aguinis, H., Villamor, I., & Ramani, R. S. (2021). MTurk research: Review and recommendations. *Journal of Management, 47*(4), 823-837. https://doi.org/10.1177/01492 06320969787

62. Peytchev, A., & Peytcheva, E. (2017, December). Reduction of measurement error due to survey length: Evaluation of the split questionnaire design approach. *Survey Research Methods, 11*(4), 361-368.

63. Egloff, B., Tausch, A., Kohlmann, C. W., & Krohne, H. W. (1995). Relationships between time of day, day of the week, and positive mood: Exploring the role of the mood measure. *Motivation and Emotion, 19*(2), 99-110. https://doi.org/10.1007/BF02250565

64. Steenkamp, J. B. E., & Baumgartner, H. (1998). Assessing measurement invariance in cross-national consumer research. *Journal of Consumer Research, 25*(1), 78-90. https://doi.org/10.1086/209528

65. Podsakoff, P. M., MacKenzie, S. B., Lee, J. Y., & Podsakoff, N. P. (2003). Common method biases in behavioral research: A critical review of the literature and recommended remedies. *Journal of Applied Psychology, 88*(5), 879-903. https://doi.org/10.1037/0021-9010 .88.5.879

66. Ross, M., Xun, W. E., & Wilson, A. E. (2002). Language and the bicultural self. *Personality and Social Psychology Bulletin, 28*(8), 1040-1050. https://doi.org/10.1177/0146 1672022811003

67. Rothstein, H. R., Sutton, A. J., & Borenstein, M. (2005). *Publication bias in meta-analysis.* John Wiley & Sons. https://doi.org/10.1002/047 0870168

68. Borenstein, M. I., Hedges, L. V., Higgins, J. P. T., & Rothstein, H. R. (2009). *Introduction to meta-analysis.* John Wiley & Sons. https://doi.org/10.1002/9780470743386

69. Rothstein, H. R., Sutton, A. J., & Borenstein, M. (2005). *Publication bias in meta-analysis.* John Wiley & Sons. https://doi.org/10.1002/047 0870168

70. Fiedler, K. (2011). Voodoo correlations are everywhere—not only in neuroscience. *Perspectives on Psychological Science, 6*(2), 163-171. https://doi.org/10.1177/17456 91611400237

71. Rothstein, H. R., Sutton, A. J., & Borenstein, M. (2005). *Publication bias in meta-analysis.* John Wiley & Sons. https://doi.org/10.1002/047 0870168

72. Howard, G. S., Lau, M. Y., Maxwell, S. E., Venter, A., Lundy, R., & Sweeny, R. M. (2009). Do research literatures give correct answers?. *Review of General Psychology, 13*(2), 116-121. https://doi.org/10.1 037/a0015468

73. Borenstein, M. I., Hedges, L. V., Higgins, J. P. T., & Rothstein, H. R. (2009). *Introduction to meta-analysis.* John Wiley & Sons. https://doi.org/10.1002/9780470743386

74. Cooper HM. (2010). *Research synthesis and meta-analysis* (4th ed.). Sage.

75. Rothstein, H. R., Sutton, A. J., & Borenstein, M. (2005). *Publication bias in meta-analysis.* John Wiley & Sons. https://doi.org/10.1002/047 0870168

76. Sutton, A. J. (2009). Publication bias. In Cooper, H., Hedges, L. V., & Valentine, J. C. (Eds.), *The handbook of research synthesis and meta-analysis* (pp. 435–452). Russell Sage Foundation.

77. Becker, B, J. (2005). Failsafe N or file-drawer number. In Rothstein, H. R., Sutton, A. J., & Borenstein, M. (Eds.), *Publication bias in meta-analysis* (pp. 111–125). John Wiley & Sons. https://doi.org/10.1002/0 470870168.ch7

78. Begg, C. B., & Mazumdar, M. (1994). Operating characteristics of a rank correlation test for publication bias. *Biometrics, 50*(4), 1088-1101. https://doi.org/10.230 7/2533446

79. Sterne, J. A., & Egger, M. (2005). Regression methods to detect publication and other bias in meta-analysis. *Publication bias in meta-analysis: Prevention, assessment, and adjustments* (pp. 99–110). John Wiley & Sons. https://doi.org/10.10 02/0470870168.ch6

80. Sterne, J., A., Becker, B., J., & Egger M. (2005). The funnel plot. In Rothstein, H. R., Sutton, A. J., & Borenstein, M. (Eds.), *Publication bias in meta-analysis* (pp. 75–98). John Wiley & Sons. https://doi.org /10.1002/0470870168.ch5

81. Schwarzer, G., Carpenter, J., & Rücker, G. (2010). Empirical evaluation suggests Copas selection model preferable to trim-and-fill method for selection bias in meta-analysis. *Journal of Clinical Epidemiology, 63*(3), 282-288. https://doi.org/10.1016/j.jclinepi.200 9.05.008

82. Rosenthal, R. (1979). The file drawer problem and tolerance for null results. *Psychological Bulletin*, *86*(3), 638-641. https://doi.org/10.1037/0033-2909.86.3.638

83. Sutton, A. J. (2009). Publication bias. In Cooper, H., Hedges, L. V., & Valentine, J. C. (Eds.), *The handbook of research synthesis and meta-analysis* (pp. 435–452). Russell Sage Foundation.

84. Cooper, H., & Hedges, L, V. (2009). Potentials and limitations. In Cooper, H., Hedges, L. V., & Valentine, J. C. (Eds.), *The handbook of research synthesis and meta-analysis* (pp. 561–572). Russell Sage Foundation.

85. Willness, C. R., Steel, P., & Lee, K. (2007). A meta-analysis of the antecedents and consequences of workplace sexual harassment. *Personnel Psychology, 60*(1), 127-162. https://doi.org/10.1111/j.1744-6570.2007.00067.x

86. Steel, R. P., & Ovalle, N. K. (1984). A review and meta-analysis of research on the relationship between behavioral intentions and employee turnover. *Journal of Applied Psychology*, *69*(4), 673–686. https://doi.org/10.1037/0021-9010.69.4.673

87. Hartnell, C. A., Ou, A. Y., & Kinicki, A. (2011). Organizational culture and organizational effectiveness: A meta-analytic investigation of the competing values framework's theoretical suppositions. *Journal of Applied Psychology*, *96*(4), 677–694. https://doi.org/10.1037/a0021987

CHAPTER 6

1. Stevens, S. S. (1968). Measurement, statistics, and the schemapiric view. *Science*, *161*(3844), 849-856. https://doi.org/10.1126/science.161.3844.849

2. Nunnally, J.C. (1978) *Psychometric theory* (2nd ed). McGraw-Hill.

3. Aguinis, H. (1993). Action research and scientific method: Presumed discrepancies and actual similarities. *Journal of Applied Behavioral Science*, *29*(4), 416-431. https://doi.org/10.1177/0021886393294003

4. Pedhazur, E. J., & Pedhazur Schmelkin, L. (1991). Criterion-related validation. *Measurement, design and analysis: An integrated approach.* (pp. 30-32). Lawrence Erlbaum and Associates.

5. Stevens, S.S. (1951) Mathematics, measurement, and psychophysics, in S.S. Stevens (ed.), *Handbook of Experimental Psychology*. Wiley.

6. Nesler, M. S., Aguinis, H., Quigley, B. M., Lee, S. J., & Tedeschi, J. T. (1999). The development and validation of a scale measuring global social power based on french and Raven's power taxonomy. *Journal of Applied Social Psychology*, *29*(4), 750-769. https://doi.org/10.1111/j.1559-1816.1999.tb02022.x

7. Aguinis, H. (2023). *Performance management* (5th ed). Chicago Business Press.

8. Podsakoff, P. M., MacKenzie, S. B., & Podsakoff, N. P. (2016). Recommendations for creating better concept definitions in the organizational, behavioral, and social sciences. *Organizational Research Methods, 19*(2), 159-203. https://doi.org/10.1177/1094428115624965

9. Aguinis, H., & Henle, C. A. (2001). Effects of nonverbal behavior on perceptions of a female employee's power bases. *Journal of Social Psychology*, *141*(4), 537-549. https://doi.org/10.1080/00224540109600570

10. Aguinis, H., Nesler, M. S., Quigley, B. M., Lee, S. J., & Tedeschi, J. T. (1996). Power bases of faculty supervisors and educational outcomes for graduate students. *Journal of Higher Education*, *67*(3), 267-297. https://doi.org/10.2307/2943845

11. Aguinis, H., & Adams, S. K. (1998). Social-role versus structural models of gender and influence use in organizations: A strong inference approach. *Group & Organization Management*, *23*(4), 414-446. https://doi.org/10.1177/1059601198234005

12. Guion, R. M. (1998) *Assessment, measurement, and prediction for personnel decisions.* Lawrence Erlbaum. https://doi.org/10.4324/9781410602572

13. Nunnally, J.C. (1978) *Psychometric theory* (2nd ed). McGraw-Hill.

14. Thorndike, R. M., Cunningham, G. K., Thorndike, R. L., & Hagen, E. P. (1991). *Measurement and evaluation in psychology and education.* Macmillan Publishing Co, Inc.

15. Nunnally, J.C. (1978) *Psychometric theory* (2nd ed). McGraw-Hill.

16. Murphy, K.R., and Davidshofer, C.O. (1998) *Psychological Testing.* 4th edn. Prentice Hall.

17. Nunnally, J.C. (1978) *Psychometric theory* (2nd ed). McGraw-Hill.

18. Thissen, D., & Steinberg, L. (1988). Data analysis using item response theory. *Psychological Bulletin*, *104*(3), 385-395. https://doi.org/10.1037/0033-2909.104.3.385

19. Drasgow, F., & Hulin, C.L. (1991). Item response theory, in M. Dunnette and L. Hough (Eds.), *Handbook of Industrial and Organizational Psychology*. Consulting Psychologists Press. (vol. 1, pp. 577-636).

20. Nunnally, J. C., & Bernstein, I. H. (1994) *Psychometric theory* (3rd ed.). McGraw-Hill.

21. Angoff, W.H. (1971). Norms, scales, and equivalent scores, in R.L. Thorndike (Ed.), *Educational Measurement*. 2nd edn. American Council on Education.

22. Nunnally, J.C. (1978) *Psychometric theory* (2nd ed). McGraw-Hill.

23. Lord, F.M., & Novick, M.R. (1968) *Statistical theories of mental test scores*. Addison Wesley

24. Jöreskog, K. G. (1971). Statistical analysis of sets of congeneric tests. *Psychometrika*, *36*(2), 109-133. https://doi.org/10.1007/BF02291393

25. Vandenberg, R. J., & Lance, C. E. (2000). A review and synthesis of the measurement invariance literature: Suggestions, practices, and recommendations for organizational research. *Organizational Research Methods*, *3*(1), 4-70. https://doi.org/10.1177/109442810031002

26. Cortina, J. M. (1993). What is coefficient alpha? An examination of theory and applications. *Journal of Applied Psychology*, *78*(1), 98-104. https://doi.org/10.1037/0021-9010.78.1.98

27. Kuder, G. F., & Richardson, M. W. (1937). The theory of the estimation of test reliability. *Psychometrika*, *2*(3), 151-160. https://doi.org/10.1007/BF02288391

28. Kuder, G. F., & Richardson, M. W. (1937). The theory of the estimation of test reliability. *Psychometrika*, *2*(3), 151-160. https://doi.org/10.1007/BF02288391

29. Kraiger, K., & Aguinis, H. (2013). Training effectiveness: Assessing training needs, motivation, and accomplishments. In *How people evaluate others in organizations* (pp. 229-246). Psychology Press.

30. Kozlowski, S. W., & Hattrup, K. (1992). A disagreement about within-group agreement: disentangling issues of consistency versus consensus. *Journal of Applied Psychology*, *77*(2), 161-167. https://doi.org/10.1037/0021-9010.77.2.161

31. James, L. R., Demaree, R. G., & Wolf, G. (1993). rwg: An assessment of within-group inter rater agreement. Journal of applied psychology, 78(2), 306-309. https://doi.org/10.1037/0021-9010.78.2.306

32. LeBreton, J. M., & Senter, J. L. (2008). Answers to twenty questions about interrater reliability and interrater agreement. *Organizational Research Methods*, *11*(4), 815-852. https://doi.org/10.1177/1094428106296642

33. Kozlowski, S. W., & Klein, K. J. (2000). A multilevel approach to theory and research in organizations: Contextual, temporal, and emergent processes in K.J. Klein and S.W.J. Kozlowski (Eds.), *Multilevel Theory, Research, and Methods in Organizations* (pp. 512-553).

34. Lahey, M. A., Downey, R. G., & Saal, F. E. (1983). Intraclass correlations: There's more there than meets the eye. *Psychological Bulletin*, *93*(3), 586-595. https://doi.org/10.1037/0033-2909.93.3.586

35. Nunnally, J.C. (1978) *Psychometric theory* (2nd ed). McGraw-Hill.

36. Aguinis, H., Cortina, J. M., & Goldberg, E. (1998). A new procedure for computing equivalence bands in personnel selection. *Human Performance*, *11*(4), 351-365. https://doi.org/10.1207/s15327043hup1104_4

37. Aguinis, H., Cortina, J. M., & Goldberg, E. (2000). A clarifying note on differences between the WF Cascio, J. Outtz, S. Zedeck, and IL Goldstein (1991) and H. Aguinis, JM Cortina, and E. Goldberg (1998) banding procedures. *Human Performance*, *13*(2), 199-204. https://doi.org/10.1207/s15327043hup1302_5

38. Binning, J. F., & Barrett, G. V. (1989). Validity of personnel decisions: A conceptual analysis of the inferential and evidential bases. *Journal of Applied Psychology*, *74*(3), 478-494. https://doi.org/10.1037/0021-9010.74.3.478

39. Guion, R. M. (1977). Content validity—The source of my discontent. *Applied Psychological Measurement*, *1*(1), 1-10. https://doi.org/10.1177/014662167700100103

40. Lawshe, C. H. (1975). A quantitative approach to content validity. *Personnel Psychology*, *28*(4), 563-575. https://doi.org/10.1111/j.1744-6570.1975.tb01393.x

41. Thorndike, R.L. (1949) *Personnel selection*. John Wiley & Sons.

42. Cronbach, L. J., & Meehl, P. E. (1955). Construct validity in psychological tests. *Psychological Bulletin*, *52*(4), 281-302. https://doi.org/10.1037/h0040957

43. Campbell, D. T., & Fiske, D. W. (1959). Convergent and discriminant validation by the multitrait-multimethod matrix. *Psychological Bulletin*, *56*(2), 81-105. https://doi.org/10.1037/h0046016

44. Aguinis, H., & Stone-Romero, E. F. (1997). Methodological artifacts in moderated multiple regression and their effects on statistical power. *Journal of Applied Psychology*, *82*(1), 192-206. https://doi.org/10.1037/0021-9010.82.1.192

45. Johnson, J. T., & Ree, M. J. (1994). RANGEJ: A Pascal program to compute the multivariate correction for range restriction. *Educational and Psychological Measurement*, *54*(3), 693-695. https://doi.org/10.1177/0013164494054003014

46. Aguinis, H., & Stone-Romero, E. F. (1997). Methodological artifacts in moderated multiple regression and their effects on statistical power. *Journal of Applied Psychology*, *82*(1), 192-206. https://doi.org/10.1037/0021-9010.82.1.192

47. Aguinis, H., Petersen, S. A., & Pierce, C. A. (1999). Appraisal of the homogeneity of error variance assumption and alternatives to multiple regression for estimating moderating effects of categorical variables. *Organizational Research Methods*, *2*(4) 315-339. https://doi.org/10.1177/109442819924001

48. Aguinis, H., & Pierce, C. A. (1998). Heterogeneity of error variance and the assessment of moderating effects of categorical variables: A conceptual review. *Organizational Research Methods*, *1*(3), 296-314. https://doi.org/10.1177/109442819813002

49. Edwards, J. R. (2003). Construct validation in organizational behavior research. In J. Greenberg (Eds.), *Organizational Behavior: The state of the science* (2nd ed., pp. 327-371). Erlbaum.

50. Aguinis, H., & Vandenberg, R. J. (2014). An ounce of prevention is worth a pound of cure: Improving research quality before data collection. *Annual Review of Organizational Psychology and Organizational Behavior, 1*, 569-595. https://doi.org/10.1146/annurev-orgpsych-031413-091231

51. Venkatraman, N., & Grant, J. H. (1986). Construct measurement in organizational strategy research: A critique and proposal. *Academy of Management Review, 11*(1), 71-87. https://doi.org/10.5465/amr.1986.4282628

52. Boyd, B. K., Gove, S., & Hitt, M. A. (2005). Construct measurement in strategic management research: illusion or reality?. *Strategic Management Journal, 26*(3), 239-257. https://doi.org/10.1002/smj.444

53. Boyd, B. K., Bergh, D. D., Ireland, R. D., & Ketchen Jr, D. J. (2013). Constructs in strategic management. *Organizational Research Methods, 16*(1), 3-14. https://doi.org/10.1177/1094428112471298

54. Ketchen Jr, D. J., Ireland, R. D., & Baker, L. T. (2013). The use of archival proxies in strategic management studies: castles made of sand?. *Organizational Research Methods, 16*(1), 32-42. https://doi.org/10.1177/1094428112459911

55. Hinkin, T. R., & Tracey, J. B. (1999). An analysis of variance approach to content validation. *Organizational Research Methods, 2*, 175-186. https://doi.org/10.1177/109442819922004

56. Edwards, J. R., & Bagozzi, R. P. (2000). On the nature and direction of relationships between constructs and measures. *Psychological Methods, 5*(2), 155-174. https://doi.org/10.1037/1082-989X.5.2.155

57. Mulaik, S. A. (2009). *Foundations of Factor Analysis.* (2nd ed.). Taylor and Francis. https://doi.org/10.1201/b15851

58. Cronbach, L. J. (1951). Coefficient alpha and the internal structure of tests. *Psychometrika, 16*(3), 297-334. https://doi.org/10.1007/BF02310555

59. Borsboom, D., Mellenbergh, G. J., & Van Heerden, J. (2004). The concept of validity. *Psychological Review, 111*, 1061-1071. https://doi.org/10.1037/0033-295X.111.4.1061

60. Podsakoff, N. P., Shen, W., & Podsakoff, P. M. (2006). The role of formative measurement models in strategic management research: review, critique, and implications for future research. In D. J. Ketchen, and D. D. Bergh (Eds.), *Research methodology in strategy and management* (Vol. 3, pp. 197-252). Elsevier. https://doi.org/10.1016/S1479-8387(06)03008-6

61. Edwards, J. R. (2011). The fallacy of formative measurement. *Organizational Research Methods, 14*(2), 370-388. https://doi.org/10.1177/1094428110378369

62. Borsboom, D., Mellenbergh, G. J., & Van Heerden, J. (2004). The concept of validity. *Psychological Review, 111*(4), 1061-1071. https://doi.org/10.1037/0033-295X.111.4.1061

63. Edwards, J. R. (2011). The fallacy of formative measurement. *Organizational Research Methods, 14*(2), 370-388. https://doi.org/10.1177/1094428110378369

64. Diamantopoulos, A., & Siguaw, J. A. (2006). Formative versus reflective indicators in organizational measure development: A comparison and empirical illustration. *British Journal of Management, 17*(4), 263-282. https://doi.org/10.1111/j.1467-8551.2006.00500.x

65. Edwards, J. R. (2011). The fallacy of formative measurement. *Organizational Research Methods, 14*(2), 370-388. https://doi.org/10.1177/1094428110378369

66. Rindskopf, D., & Rose, T. (1988). Some theory and applications of confirmatory second-order factor analysis. *Multivariate Behavioral Research, 23*(1), 51-67. https://doi.org/10.1207/s15327906mbr2301_3

67. Edwards, J. R. (2001). Multidimensional constructs in organizational behavior research: An integrative analytical framework. *Organizational Research Methods, 4*(2), 144-192. https://doi.org/10.1177/109442810142004

68. Browne, M. W. (1984). Asymptotically distribution-free methods for the analysis of covariance structures. *British Journal of Mathematical and Statistical Psychology, 37*(1), 62-83. https://doi.org/10.1111/j.2044-8317.1984.tb00789.x

69. Satorra, A., & Bentler, P. M. (1994). Corrections to test statistics and standard errors in covariance structure analysis. In A. von Wye and C. C. Clogg (Eds.), *Latent variable analysis: Applications for developmental research* (pp. 399-419). Sage.

70. Edwards, J. R., & Bagozzi, R. P. (2000). On the nature and direction of relationships between constructs and measures. *Psychological Methods, 5*(2), 155-174. https://doi.org/10.1037/1082-989X.5.2.155

71. Bollen, K. A. (1989). *Structural equations with latent variables.* Wiley. https://doi.org/10.1002/9781118619179

72. Bagozzi, R. P., Yi, Y., & Phillips, L. W. (1991). Assessing construct validity in organizational research. *Administrative Science Quarterly, 36*(3), 421-458. https://doi.org/10.2307/2393203

73. Aguinis, H., Henle, C.A., & Ostroff, C. (2001). Measurement in work and organizational psychology. In N. Anderson, D.S. Ones, H.K. Sinangil, and C. Viswesvaran (Eds.), *Handbook of industrial, work and organizational psychology* (vol. 1,

pp. 27-50). Sage. https://doi.org/1 0.4135/9781848608320.n3

74. Aguinis, H., & Vandenberg, R. J. (2014). An ounce of prevention is worth a pound of cure: Improving research quality before data collection. *Annual Review of Organizational Psychology and Organizational Behavior, 1*, 569-595. https:// doi.org/10.1146/annurev-orgpsyc h-031413-091231

75. Ketchen Jr, D. J., Ireland, R. D., & Baker, L. T. (2013). The use of archival proxies in strategic management studies: castles made of sand?. *Organizational Research Methods, 16*(1), 32-42. ht tps://doi.org/10.1177/1094428112 459911

76. Edwards, J. R. (2001). Multidimensional constructs in organizational behavior research: An integrative analytical framework. *Organizational Research Methods, 4*(2), 144-192. https://doi.org/10.11 77/109442810142004

77. Edwards, J. R. (2011). The fallacy of formative measurement. *Organizational Research Methods, 14*(2), 370-388. https://doi.org/10.1177/1 094428110378369

78. Edwards, J. R. (2001). Multidimensional constructs in organizational behavior research: An integrative analytical framework. *Organizational Research Methods, 4*(2), 144-192. https://doi.org/10.11 77/109442810142004

79. Cascio, W. F. (2012). Methodological issues in international HR management research. *The International Journal of Human Resource Management, 23*(12), 2532-2545. https://doi.org/10.108 0/09585192.2011.561242

80. Ketchen Jr, D. J., Ireland, R. D., & Baker, L. T. (2013). The use of archival proxies in strategic management studies: castles made of sand?. *Organizational Research Methods, 16*(1), 32-42. https://doi.o rg/10.1177/1094428112459911

81. Hitt, M. A., Gimeno, J., & Hoskisson, R. E. (1998). Current and

future research methods in strategic management. *Organizational Research Methods, 1*(1), 6-44. https ://doi.org/10.1177/1094428198001 00103

82. Shadish, W.R., Cook, T.D., & Campbell, D.T. (2002). *Experimental and quasi-experimental designs for generalized causal inference.* Houghton Mifflin.

83. Cook, T. D., & Campbell, D. T. (1979). *Quasi-experimentation: Design and analysis issues for field settings.* Rand McNally.

84. Cook, T. D., & Campbell, D. T. (1979). *Quasi-experimentation: Design and analysis issues for field settings.* Rand McNally.

85. NASDAQ Membership. (2011). www w.nasdaq.com/screening/compa nies-by-industry.aspx?exchange= NASDAQ.

86. Spencer Stuart. (2011). *Spencer Stuart board index.*

87. BoardAnalyst. (2012). www.board analyst.com

88. Aguinis, H., Dalton, D. R., Bosco, F. A., Pierce, C. A., & Dalton, C. M. (2011). Meta-analytic choices and judgment calls: Implications for theory building and testing, obtained effect sizes, and scholarly impact. *Journal of Management, 37*(1), 5-38. https://doi.org/1 0.1177/0149206310377113

89. Dalton, D. R., Hitt, M. A., Certo, S. T., & Dalton, C. M. (2007). The fundamental agency problem and its mitigation. *Academy of Management Annals, 1*(1), 1-64. https://doi .org/10.5465/078559806

90. Dalton, D. R., Daily, C. M., Ellstrand, A. E., & Johnson, J. L. (1998). Meta-analytic reviews of board composition, leadership structure, and financial performance. *Strategic Management Journal, 19*(3), 269-290. https:// doi.org/10.1002/(SICI)1097-0266(199803)19:3 < 269::AID-SMJ950>3.0.CO;2-K

91. Rhoades, D. L., Rechner, P. L., & Sundaramurthy, C. (2000). Board composition and financial performance: A meta-analysis of the influence of outside directors. *Journal of Managerial Issues*, 76-91.

92. Scandura, T. A., & Williams, E. A. (2000). Research methodology in management: Current practices, trends, and implications for future research. *Academy of Management Journal, 43*(6), 1248-1264. https:// doi.org/10.2307/1556348

93. Wagner III, J. A., Stimpert, J. L., & Fubara, E. I. (1998). Board composition and organizational performance: Two studies of insider/ outsider effects. *Journal of Management Studies, 35*(5), 655-677. ht tps://doi.org/10.1111/1467-6486.0 0114

94. Bergh, D., Aguinis, H., & Heavey, C. (2011, November). *Does strategic leadership really matter? A meta-analysis of agency and upper-echelons research.* Paper presented at the meetings of the Strategic Management Society, Miami, FL.

95. Boone, J. P., Khurana, I. K., & Raman, K. K. (2011). Investor pricing of CEO equity incentives. *Review of Quantitative Finance and Accounting, 36*(3), 417-435. https:/ /doi.org/10.1007/s11156-010-018 3-2

96. Matta, E., & McGuire, J. (2008). Too risky to hold? The effect of downside risk, accumulated equity wealth, and firm performance on CEO equity reduction. *Organization Science, 19*(4), 567-580. https://doi.org/10.1287/orsc. 1070.0334

97. Goodman, L., Hing, V. A., & Ostrager, J. N. (2011). *Corporate governance and securities laws: A public handbook.* Curtis, Mallet-Prevost, Colt & Mosle LLP.

98. American Bar Association. (2011). *Corporate Directors' Guidebook.* American Bar Association.

99. Nathan, C. M. (2010). *Maintaining board confidentiality.* The Harvard

Law School Forum on Corporate Governance and Financial Regulation.

100. Director Accountability and Board Effectiveness. (2007). *The basic responsibilities of VC-backed company directors*. Available online at http://www.nvca.org

101. Directors Daily. (2009). Treasury names five new directors to GM's board. July, 24, p. 1.

102. Nathan, C. M. (2010). *Maintaining board confidentiality*. The Harvard Law School Forum on Corporate Governance and Financial Regulation.

103. Dalton, D. R., Daily, C. M., Ellstrand, A. E., & Johnson, J. L. (1998). Meta-analytic reviews of board composition, leadership structure, and financial performance. *Strategic Management Journal*, *19*(3), 269-290. https://doi.org/10.1002/(SICI)1097-0266(199803)19:3 < 269::AID-SMJ950>3.0.CO;2-K

104. Dalton, D. R., Daily, C. M., Ellstrand, A. E., & Johnson, J. L. (1998). Meta-analytic reviews of board composition, leadership structure, and financial performance. *Strategic Management Journal*, *19*(3), 269-290. https://doi.org/10.1002/(SICI)1097-0266(199803)19:3 < 269::AID-SMJ950>3.0.CO;2-K

105. Rhoades, D. L., Rechner, P. L., & Sundaramurthy, C. (2000). Board composition and financial performance: A meta-analysis of the influence of outside directors. *Journal of Managerial Issues*, 76-91.

106. Wagner III, J. A., Stimpert, J. L., & Fubara, E. I. (1998). Board composition and organizational performance: Two studies of insider/outsider effects. *Journal of Management Studies*, *35*(5), 655-677. https://doi.org/10.1111/1467-6486.00114

107. Bergh, D., Aguinis, H., & Heavey, C. (2011, November). *Does strategic leadership really matter? A meta-analysis of agency and*

upper-echelons research. Paper presented at the meetings of the Strategic Management Society, Miami, FL.

108. Dalton, D. R., Daily, C. M., Certo, S. T., & Roengpitya, R. (2003). Meta-analyses of financial performance and equity: fusion or confusion?.*Academy of Management Journal*, *46*(1), 13-26. https://doi.org/10.5465/30040673

109. Sundaramurthy, C., Rhoades, D. L., & Rechner, P. L. (2005). A meta-analysis of the effects of executive and institutional ownership on firm performance. *Journal of Managerial Issues*, 494-510.

110. Bergh, D., Aguinis, H., & Heavey, C. (2011, November). *Does strategic leadership really matter? A meta-analysis of agency and upper-echelons research*. Paper presented at the meetings of the Strategic Management Society, Miami, FL.

111. Aguinis, H., Bergh, D. D. & Joo, H. (2011, November). *Using meta-analytic structural equation modeling to advance strategic management theory*. Paper presented at the meeting of the Strategic Management Society, Miami, FL.

112. Boyd, B. K., Gove, S., & Hitt, M. A. (2005). Construct measurement in strategic management research: illusion or reality?.*Strategic Management Journal*, *26*(3), 239-257. https://doi.org/10.1002/smj.444

113. Aguinis, H., Dalton, D. R., Bosco, F. A., Pierce, C. A., & Dalton, C. M. (2011). Meta-analytic choices and judgment calls: Implications for theory building and testing, obtained effect sizes, and scholarly impact. *Journal of Management*, *37*(1), 5-38. https://doi.org/10.1177/0149206310377113

CHAPTER 7

1. Shadish, W. R., Cook, T. D., & Campbell, D. T. (2002). *Experimental and quasi-experimental designs*

for generalized causal inference. Houghton Mifflin.

2. Aguinis, H., & Vandenberg, R. J. (2014). An ounce of prevention is worth a pound of cure: Improving research quality before data collection. *Annual Review of Organizational Psychology and Organizational Behavior*, *1*, 569-595. https://doi.org/10.1146/annurev-orgpsych-031413-091231

3. Aguinis, H., & Edwards, J. R. (2014). Methodological wishes for the next decade and how to make wishes come true. *Journal of Management Studies*, *51*(1), 143–174. https://doi.org/10.1111/joms.12058

4. Grant, A. M., & Wall, T. D. (2009). The neglected science and art of quasi-experimentation: Why-to, when-to, and how-to advice for organizational researchers. *Organizational Research Methods*, *12*(4), 653-686. https://doi.org/10.1177/1094428108320737

5. Hill, N. S., Aguinis, H., Drewry, J. M., Patnaik, S., & Griffin, J. (2022). Using macro archival databases to expand theory in micro research. *Journal of Management Studies*. https://doi.org/10.1111/joms.12764

6. Highhouse, S. (2009). Designing experiments that generalize. *Organizational Research Methods* *12*(3), 554-566. https://doi.org/10.1177/1094428107300396

7. Aguinis, H., & Lawal, S. O. (2012). Conducting field experiments using eLancing's natural environment. *Journal of Business Venturing*, *27*(4), 493-505. https://doi.org/10.1016/j.jbusvent.2012.01.002

8. Hox, J. J., Kreft, I. G., & Hermkens, P. L. (1991). The analysis of factorial surveys. *Sociological Methods & Research*, *19*(4), 493-510. https://doi.org/10.1177/0049124191019004003

9. Atzmüller, C., & Steiner, P. M. (2010). Experimental vignette studies in survey research. *Methodology: European Journal of Research Methods for the Behavioral and Social Sciences*, *6*(3),

128-138. https://doi.org/10.1027/1614-2241/a000014

10. Hughes, R., & Huby, M. (2002). The application of vignettes in social and nursing research. *Journal of Advanced Nursing, 37*(4), 382-386. https://doi.org/10.1046/j.1365-2648.2002.02100.x

11. Hyman, M. R. & Steiner, S. D (1996). The vignette method in business research: Current uses, limitations and recommendations. In E. W. Stuart, D. J. Ortinau & E. M. Moore (Eds.), *Marketing: Moving toward the 21st century* (pp. 261-265). Winthrop University School of Business.

12. Pierce, C. A., Aguinis, H., & Adams, S. K. R. (2000). Effects of a dissolved workplace romance and rater characteristics on responses to a sexual harassment accusation. *Academy of Management Journal, 43*(5), 869-880. https://doi.org/10.5465/1556415

13. Carroll, J. S., & Johnson, E. J. (1990). *Decision research: A field guide.* Sage Publications.

14. Aiman-Smith, L., Scullen, S. E., & Barr, S. H. (2002). Conducting studies of decision making in organizational contexts: A tutorial for policy-capturing and other regression-based techniques. *Organizational Research Methods, 5*(4), 388-414. https://journals.sagepub.com/doi/10.1177/109442802237117

15. Priem, R. L., & Harrison, D. A. (1994). Exploring strategic judgment: Methods for testing the assumptions of prescriptive contingency theories. *Strategic Management Journal, 15*(4), 311-324. https://doi.org/10.1002/smj.4250150405

16. Cavanaugh, G. F., & Fritzsche, D. J. (1985). Using vignettes in business ethics research. In L. E. Preston (Ed.) *Research in corporate social performance and policy* (Vol. 7). Jai Press LTD.

17. Pierce, C. A., Aguinis, H., & Adams, S. K. R. (2000). Effects of a dissolved workplace romance and rater characteristics on responses to a sexual harassment accusation. *Academy of Management Journal, 43*(5), 869-880. https://doi.org/10.5465/1556415

18. Lohrke, F. T., Holloway, B. B., & Woolley, T. W. (2010). Conjoint analysis in entrepreneurship research a review and research agenda. *Organizational Research Methods, 13*(1), 16-30. https://journals.sagepub.com/doi/10.1177/1094428109341992

19. Shepherd, D. A., & Zacharakis, A. (1999). Conjoint analysis: A new methodological approach for researching the decision policies of venture capitalists. *Venture Capital: An International Journal of Entrepreneurial Finance, 1*(3), 197-217. https://doi.org/10.1080/136910699295866

20. Hughes, R., & Huby, M. (2002). The application of vignettes in social and nursing research. *Journal of Advanced Nursing, 37*(4), 382-386. https://doi.org/10.1046/j.1365-2648.2002.02100.x

21. Priem, R. L., & Harrison, D. A. (1994). Exploring strategic judgment: Methods for testing the assumptions of prescriptive contingency theories. *Strategic Management Journal, 15*(4), 311-324. https://doi.org/10.1002/smj.42501 50405

22. Atzmüller, C., & Steiner, P. M. (2010). Experimental vignette studies in survey research. *Methodology: European Journal of Research Methods for the Behavioral and Social Sciences, 6*(3), 128-138. https://doi.org/10.1027/1614-2241/a000014

23. Raaijmakers, A., Vermeulen, P., Meeus, M., & Zietsma, C. (2015). I need time! Exploring pathways to compliance under institutional complexity. *Academy of Management Journal, 58*(1), 85-110. https://doi.org/10.5465/amj.2011.0276

24. Woehr, D. J., & Lance, C. E. (1991). Paper people versus direct observation: An empirical examination of laboratory methodologies. *Journal of Organizational Behavior, 12*(5), 387-397. https://doi.org/10.1002/job.4030120504

25. Aguinis, H., & Kraiger, K. (2009). Benefits of training and development for individuals and teams, organizations, and society. *Annual Review of Psychology, 60,* 451-474. https://doi.org/10.1146/annurev.psych.60.110707.163505

26. Goldman, B. M., Gutek, B. A., Stein, J. H., & Lewis, K. (2006). Employment discrimination in organizations: Antecedents and consequences. *Journal of Management, 32*(6), 786-830. https://journals.sagepub.com/doi/10.1177/0149206306293544

27. Hughes, R., & Huby, M. (2002). The application of vignettes in social and nursing research. *Journal of Advanced Nursing, 37*(4), 382-386. https://doi.org/10.1046/j.1365-2648.2002.02100.x

28. Woehr, D. J., & Lance, C. E. (1991). Paper people versus direct observation: An empirical examination of laboratory methodologies. *Journal of Organizational Behavior, 12*(5), 387-397. https://doi.org/10.1002/job.4030120504

29. Whiting, S. W., Maynes, T. D., Podsakoff, N. P., & Podsakoff, P. M. (2012). Effects of message, source, and context on evaluations of employee voice behavior. *Journal of Applied Psychology, 97*(1), 159-182. https://psycnet.apa.org/doi/10.1037/a0024871

30. Heslin, P. A., Vandewalle, D., & Latham, G. P. (2006). Keen to help? Managers' implicit person theories and their subsequent employee coaching. *Personnel Psychology, 59*(4), 871-902. https://doi.org/10.1111/j.1744-6570.2006.00057.x

31. Taggar, S., & Neubert, M. (2004). The impact of poor performers on team outcomes: An empirical examination of attribution theory. *Personnel Psychology, 57*(4), 935-968. https://doi.org/10.1111/j.1744-6570.2004.00011.x

32. Lohrke, F. T., Holloway, B. B., & Woolley, T. W. (2010). Conjoint analysis in entrepreneurship research a review and research agenda. *Organizational Research Methods*, *13*(1), 16-30. https://journals.sagepub.com/doi/10.1177/1094428109341992

33. Shepherd, D. A., & Zacharakis, A. (1999). Conjoint analysis: A new methodological approach for researching the decision policies of venture capitalists. *Venture Capital: An International Journal of Entrepreneurial Finance*, *1*(3), 197-217. https://doi.org/10.1080/136910699295866

34. McGuire, W. J. (1973). The yin and yang of progress in social psychology: Seven koan. *Journal of Personality and Social Psychology*, *26*(3), 446-456. https://psycnet.apa.org/doi/10.1037/h0034345

35. Karren, R. J., & Barringer, M. W. (2002). A review and analysis of the policy-capturing methodology in organizational research: Guidelines for research and practice. *Organizational Research Methods*, *5*(4), 337-361. https://journals.sagepub.com/doi/10.1177/1094428022237115

36. Wason, K. D., Polonsky, M. J., & Hyman, M. R. (2002). Designing vignette studies in marketing. *Australasian Marketing Journal*, *10*(3), 41-58. https://doi.org/10.1016/S1441-3582(02)70157-2

37. Shepherd, D. A., & Zacharakis, A. (1999). Conjoint analysis: A new methodological approach for researching the decision policies of venture capitalists. *Venture Capital: An International Journal of Entrepreneurial Finance*, *1*(3), 197-217. https://doi.org/10.1080/136910699295866

38. Weber, J. (1992). Scenarios in business ethics research: Review, critical assessment, and recommendations. *Business Ethics Quarterly*, *2*(2), 137-160. https://doi.org/10.2307/3857568

39. Wason, K. D., Polonsky, M. J., & Hyman, M. R. (2002). Designing vignette studies in marketing. *Australasian Marketing Journal*, *10*(3), 41-58. https://doi.org/10.1016/S1441-3582(02)70157-2

40. Shepherd, D. A., & Zacharakis, A. (1999). Conjoint analysis: A new methodological approach for researching the decision policies of venture capitalists. *Venture Capital: An International Journal of Entrepreneurial Finance*, *1*(3), 197-217. https://doi.org/10.1080/136910699295866

41. Aiman-Smith, L., Scullen, S. E., & Barr, S. H. (2002). Conducting studies of decision making in organizational contexts: A tutorial for policy-capturing and other regression-based techniques. *Organizational Research Methods*, *5*(4), 388-414. https://journals.sagepub.com/doi/10.1177/109442802237117

42. Karren, R. J., & Barringer, M. W. (2002). A review and analysis of the policy-capturing methodology in organizational research: Guidelines for research and practice. *Organizational Research Methods*, *5*(4), 337-361. https://journals.sagepub.com/doi/10.1177/109442802237115

43. Cavanaugh, G. F., & Fritzsche, D. J. (1985). Using vignettes in business ethics research. In L. E. Preston (Ed.) *Research in corporate social performance and policy* (Vol. 7). Jai Press LTD.

44. Hughes, R., & Huby, M. (2002). The application of vignettes in social and nursing research. *Journal of Advanced Nursing*, *37*(4), 382-386. https://doi.org/10.1046/j.1365-2648.2002.02100.x

45. Gordon, M. E., Slade, L. A., & Schmitt, N. (1986). The "science of the sophomore" revisited: From conjecture to empiricism. *Academy of Management Review*, *11*(1), 191-207. https://doi.org/10.5465/amr.1986.4282666

46. Aguinis, H., Audretsch, D. B., Flammer, C., Meyer, K., Peng, M. W., & Teece, D. J. 2022. Bringing the manager back into management scholarship. *Journal of Management*. https://doi.org/10.1177/01492063221082555

47. Wason, K. D., Polonsky, M. J., & Hyman, M. R. (2002). Designing vignette studies in marketing. *Australasian Marketing Journal*, *10*(3), 41-58. https://doi.org/10.1016/S1441-3582(02)70157-2

48. Aguinis, H., & Lawal, S. O. (2013). eLancing: A review and research agenda for bridging the science–practice gap. *Human Resource Management Review*, *23*(1), 6-17. https://doi.org/10.1016/j.hrmr.2012.06.003

49. Aguinis, H., & Lawal, S. O. (2012). Conducting field experiments using eLancing's natural environment. *Journal of Business Venturing*, *27*(4), 493-505. https://doi.org/10.1016/j.jbusvent.2012.01.002

50. Grant, A. M., & Wall, T. D. (2009). The neglected science and art of quasi-experimentation: Why-to, when-to, and how-to advice for organizational researchers. *Organizational Research Methods*, *12*(4), 653-686. https://journals.sagepub.com/doi/abs/10.1177/1094428108320737

51. Sauer, S. J. (2011). Taking the reins: The effects of new leader status and leadership style on team performance. *Journal of Applied Psychology*, *96*(3), 574-587. https://psycnet.apa.org/doi/10.1037/a0022741

52. Aiman-Smith, L., Scullen, S. E., & Barr, S. H. (2002). Conducting studies of decision making in organizational contexts: A tutorial for policy-capturing and other regression-based techniques. *Organizational Research Methods*, *5*(4), 388-414. https://journals.sagepub.com/doi/10.1177/10944280 2237117

53. Atzmüller, C., & Steiner, P. M. (2010). Experimental vignette studies in survey research. *Methodology: European Journal of Research Methods for the Behavioral and Social Sciences*, *6*(3),

128-138. https://doi.org/10.1027/1614-2241/a000014

54. Aguinis, H., Gottfredson, R. K., & Culpepper, S. A. (2013). Best-practice recommendations for estimating cross-level interaction effects using multilevel modeling. *Journal of Management, 39*(6), 1490-1528. https://journals.sagepub.com/doi/10.1177/0149206313478188

55. Jasny, B. R., Chin, G., Chong, L., & Vignieri, S. (2011). Again, and again, and again…. *Science, 334*(6060), 1225-1225. https://doi.org/10.1126/science.334.6060.1225

56. Bedeian, A. G., Taylor, S. G., & Miller, A. N. (2010). Management science on the credibility bubble: Cardinal sins and various misdemeanors. *Academy of Management Learning & Education, 9*(4), 715-725. https://doi.org/10.5465/amle.9.4.zqr715

57. Asendorpf, J. B., Conner, M., De Fruyt, F., De Houwer, J., Denissen, J. J., Fiedler, K., Funder, D. C., Kliegl, R., Nosek, B. A., Perugini, M., Roberts, B. W., Schmitt, M., van Aken, M. A. G., Weber, H., & Wicherts, J. M. (2013). Recommendations for increasing replicability in psychology. *European Journal of Personality, 27*(2), 108-119. https://psycnet.apa.org/doi/10.1002/per.1919

58. Raaijmakers, A., Vermeulen, P., Meeus, M., & Zietsma, C. (2015). I need time! Exploring pathways to compliance under institutional complexity. *Academy of Management Journal, 58*(1), 85-110. https://doi.org/10.5465/amj.2011.0276

59. Goldberg, L. R., Johnson, J. A., Eber, H. W., Hogan, R., Ashton, M. C., Cloninger, C. R., & Gough, H. G. (2006). The international personality item pool and the future of public-domain personality measures. *Journal of Research in Personality, 40*(1), 84-96. https://doi.org/10.1016/j.jrp.2005.08.007

60. Atinc, G., Simmering, M. J., & Kroll, M. J. (2012). Control variable use and reporting in macro and micro management research. *Organizational Research Methods, 15*(1), 57-74. https://journals.sagepub.com/doi/10.1177/1094428110397773

61. Aguinis, H. (2004). *Regression analysis for categorical moderators.* Guilford.

62. Stone-Romero, E. F., & Rosopa, P. J. (2011). Experimental tests of mediation models: Prospects, problems, and some solutions. *Organizational Research Methods, 14*(4), 631-646. https://journals.sagepub.com/doi/10.1177/1094428110372673

63. Cook, T. D., Campbell, D. T., & Day, A. (1979). *Quasi-experimentation: Design & analysis issues for field settings* (Vol. 351). Houghton Mifflin.

64. Behrend, T. S., Sharek, D. J., Meade, A. W., & Wiebe, E. N. (2011). The viability of crowdsourcing for survey research. *Behavior Research Methods, 43*(3), 800-813. https://doi.org/10.3758/s13428-011-0081-0

65. Weinberg, J., Freese, J., & McElhattan, D. (2014). Comparing data characteristics and results of an online factorial survey between a population-based and a crowdsource-recruited sample. *Sociological Science, 1,* 292-310. https://doi.org/10.15195/v1.a19

66. Levay, K. E., Freese, J., & Druckman, J. N. (2016). The demographic and political composition of Mechanical Turk samples. *Sage Open,6*(1). https://doi.org/10.1177/2158244016636433

67. Bader, F., Baumeister, B., Berger, R., & Keuschnigg, M. (2021). On the transportability of laboratory results. *Sociological Methods & Research, 50*(3), 1452-1481. https://journals.sagepub.com/doi/full/10.1177/0049124119826151

68. Stewart, N., Ungemach, C., Harris, A. J., Bartels, D. M., Newell, B. R., Paolacci, G., & Chandler, J.

(2015). The average laboratory samples a population of 7,300 Amazon Mechanical Turk workers. *Judgment and Decision Making, 10*(5), 479-491. http://journal.sjdm.org/14/14725/jdm14725.pdf

69. Chandler, J., Rosenzweig, C., Moss, A. J., Robinson, J., & Litman, L. (2019). Online panels in social science research: Expanding sampling methods beyond Mechanical Turk. *Behavior Research Methods, 51*(5), 2022-2038. https://doi.org/10.3758/s13428-019-01273-7

70. Heer, J., & Bostock, M. (2010). Crowdsourcing graphical perception: Using Mechanical Turk to assess visualization design. In *ACM Proceedings of the SIGCHI Conference on Human Factors in Computing Systems,* 203-212. https://doi.org/10.1145/1753326.1753357

71. Barends, A. J., & de Vries, R. E. (2019). Noncompliant responding: Comparing exclusion criteria in MTurk personality research to improve data quality. *Personality and Individual Differences, 143,* 84-89. https://doi.org/10.1016/j.paid.2019.02.015

72. Buhrmester, M. D., Talaifar, S., & Gosling, S. D. (2018). An evaluation of Amazon's Mechanical Turk, its rapid rise, and its effective use. *Perspectives on Psychological Science, 13*(2), 149-154. https://journals.sagepub.com/doi/10.1177/1745691617706516

73. Goodman, J. K., Cryder, C. E., & Cheema, A. (2013). Data collection in a flat world: The advantages and weaknesses of Mechanical Turk samples. *Journal of Behavioral Decision Making, 26*(3), 213-224. https://doi.org/10.1002/bdm.1753

74. Clifford, S., & Jerit, J. (2014). Is there a cost to convenience? An experimental comparison of data quality in laboratory and online studies. *Journal of Experimental Political Science, 1*(2), 120-131. https://doi.org/10.1017/xps.2014.5

75. Cheung, J. H., Burns, D. K., Sinclair, R. R., & Sliter, M. (2017). Amazon Mechanical Turk in organizational psychology: An evaluation and practical recommendations. *Journal of Business and Psychology, 32*(4), 347-361. https://doi.org/10.1007/s10869-016-9458-5

76. Cheung, J. H., Burns, D. K., Sinclair, R. R., & Sliter, M. (2017). Amazon Mechanical Turk in organizational psychology: An evaluation and practical recommendations. *Journal of Business and Psychology, 32*(4), 347-361. https://doi.org/10.1007/s10869-016-9458-5

77. Zhou, H., & Fishbach, A. (2016). The threat of experimenting on the web: How unattended selective attrition leads to surprising yet false research conclusions. *Journal of Personality and Social Psychology, 111*(4), 493-504. https://psycnet.apa.org/doi/10.1037/pspa0000056

78. Buhrmester, M. D., Talaifar, S., & Gosling, S. D. (2018). An evaluation of Amazon's Mechanical Turk, its rapid rise, and its effective use. *Perspectives on Psychological Science, 13*(2), 149-154. https://journals.sagepub.com/doi/10.1177/1745691617706516

79. Arechar, A. A., Gächter, S., & Molleman, L. (2018). Conducting interactive experiments online. *Experimental Economics, 21*(1), 99-131. https://doi.org/10.1007/s10683-017-9527-2

80. Feitosa, J., Joseph, D. L., & Newman, D. A. (2015). Crowdsourcing and personality measurement equivalence: A warning about countries whose primary language is not English. *Personality and Individual Differences, 75*, 47-52. https://doi.org/10.1016/j.paid.2014.11.017

81. Dupuis, M., Meier, E., & Cuneo, F. (2019). Detecting computer-generated random responding in questionnaire-based data: A comparison of seven indices. *Behavior Research Methods, 51*(5),

2228-2237. https://doi.org/10.3758/s13428-018-1103-y

82. Buchanan, E. M., & Scofield, J. E. (2018). Methods to detect low quality data and its implication for psychological research. *Behavior Research Methods, 50*(6), 1-11. https://doi.org/10.3758/s13428-018-1035-6

83. Behrend, T. S., Sharek, D. J., Meade, A. W., & Wiebe, E. N. (2011). The viability of crowdsourcing for survey research. *Behavior Research Methods, 43*(3), 800-813. https://doi.org/10.3758/s13428-011-0081-0

84. Antin, J., & Shaw, A. (2012). Social desirability bias and self-reports of motivation: A study of Amazon Mechanical Turk in the US and India. *ACM Proceedings of the SIGCHI Conference on Human Factors in Computing Systems* (pp. 2925-2934). https://doi.org/10.1145/2207676.2208699

85. Mummolo, J., & Peterson, E. (2019). Demand effects in survey experiments: An empirical assessment. *American Political Science Review, 113*(2), 517-529. https://doi.org/10.1017/S0003055418000837

86. Chandler, J. J., & Paolacci, G. (2017). Lie for a dime: When most prescreening responses are honest but most study participants are impostors. *Social Psychological and Personality Science, 8*(5), 500-508. https://doi.org/10.1177/1948550617698203

87. Casey, L. S., Chandler, J., Levine, A. S., Proctor, A., & Strolovitch, D. Z. (2017). Intertemporal differences among MTurk workers: Time-based sample variations and implications for online data collection. *SAGE Open*. https://journals.sagepub.com/doi/10.1177/2158244017712774

88. Sprouse, J. (2011). A validation of Amazon Mechanical Turk for the collection of acceptability judgments in linguistic theory. *Behavior Research Methods, 43*(1),

155-167. https://doi.org/10.3758/s13428-010-0039-7

89. Barends, A. J., & de Vries, R. E. (2019). Noncompliant responding: Comparing exclusion criteria in MTurk personality research to improve data quality. *Personality and Individual Differences, 143*, 84-89. https://doi.org/10.1016/j.paid.2019.02.015

90. Bederson, B. B., & Quinn, A. J. (2011). Web workers unite! Addressing challenges of online laborers. *ACM CHI Extended Abstracts on Human Factors in Computing Systems* (pp. 97-106). https://doi.org/10.1145/1979742.1979606

91. von Ahn, L., Blum, M., Hopper, N. J., & Langford, J. (2003). CAPTCHA: Using hard AI problems for security. *Lecture Notes in Computer Science, 2656*, 294-311. https://doi.org/10.1007/3-540-39200-9_18

92. Buhrmester, M. D., Talaifar, S., & Gosling, S. D. (2018). An evaluation of Amazon's Mechanical Turk, its rapid rise, and its effective use. *Perspectives on Psychological Science, 13*(2), 149-154. https://journals.sagepub.com/doi/10.1177/1745691617706516

93. Thomas, K. A., & Clifford, S. (2017). Validity and Mechanical Turk: An assessment of exclusion methods and interactive experiments. *Computers in Human Behavior, 77*, 184-197. https://doi.org/10.1016/j.chb.2017.08.038

94. Huang, J. L., Bowling, N. A., Liu, M., & Li, Y. (2015). Detecting insufficient effort responding with an infrequency scale: Evaluating validity and participant reactions. *Journal of Business and Psychology, 30*(2), 299-311. https://doi.org/10.1007/s10869-014-9357-6

95. Dennis, S. A., Goodson, B. M., & Pearson, C. (2019). Virtual private servers and the limitations of IP-based screening procedures: Lessons from the MTurk quality crisis of 2018. *SSRN*, 3233954. htt

p://dx.doi.org/10.2139/ssrn.3233 954

96. Hamby, T., & Taylor, W. (2016). Survey satisficing inflates reliability and validity measures: An experimental comparison of college and Amazon Mechanical Turk samples. *Educational and Psychological Measurement, 76*(6), 912-932. https://doi.org/10.1177%2F0013164415627349

97. De Quidt, J., Haushofer, J., & Roth, C. (2018). Measuring and bounding experimenter demand. *American Economic Review, 108*(11), 3266-3302. https://doi.org/10.1257/aer.20171330

98. Kees, J., Berry, C., Burton, S., & Sheehan, K. (2017). An analysis of data quality: Professional panels, student subject pools, and Amazon's Mechanical Turk. *Journal of Advertising, 46*(1), 141-155. https://doi.org/10.1080/00913367.2016.1269304

99. Brawley, A. M., & Pury, C. L. (2016). Work experiences on MTurk: Job satisfaction, turnover, and information sharing. *Computers in Human Behavior, 54*, 531-546. https://doi.org/10.1016/j.chb.2015.08.031

100. Wood, D., Harms, P. D., Lowman, G. H., & DeSimone, J. A. (2017). Response speed and response consistency as mutually validating indicators of data quality in online samples. *Social Psychological and Personality Science, 8*(4), 454-464. https://journals.sagepub.com/doi/10.1177/1948550617703168

101. Berinsky, A. J., Margolis, M. F., & Sances, M. W. 2014. Separating the shirkers from the workers? Making sure respondents pay attention on self-administered surveys. *American Journal of Political Science, 58*(3), 739-753. https://doi.org/10.1111/ajps.12081

102. Hong, M., Steedle, J. T., & Cheng, Y. (2020). Methods of detecting insufficient effort responding: Comparisons and practical recommendations. *Educational and Psychological Measurement, 80*(2),

312-345. https://journals.sagepub.com/doi/10.1177/0013164419865316

103. Wood, D., Harms, P. D., Lowman, G. H., & DeSimone, J. A. (2017). Response speed and response consistency as mutually validating indicators of data quality in online samples. *Social Psychological and Personality Science, 8*(4), 454-464. https://journals.sagepub.com/doi/10.1177/1948550617703168

104. Buchanan, E. M., & Scofield, J. E. (2018). Methods to detect low quality data and its implication for psychological research. *Behavior Research Methods, 50*(6), 1-11. https://doi.org/10.3758/s13428-018-1035-6

105. Dennis, S. A., Goodson, B. M., & Pearson, C. (2019). Virtual private servers and the limitations of IP-based screening procedures: Lessons from the MTurk quality crisis of 2018. *SSRN*, 3233954. http://dx.doi.org/10.2139/ssrn.3233954

106. Kennedy, R., Clifford, S., Burleigh, T., Waggoner, P. D., Jewell, R., & Winter, N. J. (2020). The shape of and solutions to the MTurk quality crisis. *Political Science Research and Methods, 8*(4), 614-629. https://doi.org/10.1017/psrm.2020.6

107. Aguinis, H., Banks, G. C., Rogelberg, S. G., & Cascio, W. F. (2020). Actionable recommendations for narrowing the science-practice gap in open science. *Organizational Behavior and Human Decision Processes, 158*, 27-35. https://doi.org/10.1016/j.obhdp.2020.02.007

108. Hydock, C. (2018). Assessing and overcoming participant dishonesty in online data collection. *Behavior Research Methods, 50*(4), 1563-1567. https://doi.org/10.3758/s13428-017-0984-5

109. Thomas, K. A., & Clifford, S. (2017). Validity and Mechanical Turk: An assessment of exclusion methods and interactive experiments. *Computers in Human Behavior, 77*, 184-197. https://doi.org/10.1016/j.chb.2017.08.038

110. Cheung, J. H., Burns, D. K., Sinclair, R. R., & Sliter, M. (2017). Amazon Mechanical Turk in organizational psychology: An evaluation and practical recommendations. *Journal of Business and Psychology, 32*(4), 347-361. https://doi.org/10.1007/s10869-016-9458-5

111. Chandler, J., Mueller, P., & Paolacci, G. (2014). Nonnaïveté among Amazon Mechanical Turk workers: Consequences and solutions for behavioral researchers. *Behavior Research Methods, 46*(1), 112-130. https://doi.org/10.3758/s13428-013-0365-7

112. Steuer, J. (1992). Defining virtual reality: Dimensions determining telepresence. *Journal of Communication, 42*(4), 73-93. https://doi.org/10.1111/j.1460-2466.1992.tb00812.x

113. Durlach, N. I. & Mavor, A. S. (Eds.). (1995). *Virtual Reality: Scientific and Technological Challenges*. National Academy Press.

114. Vasser, M., & Aru, J. (2020). Guidelines for immersive virtual reality in psychological research. *Current Opinion in Psychology, 36*, 71-76. https://doi.org/10.1016/j.copsyc.2020.04.010

115. Biocca, F. (1992). Communication within virtual reality: Creating a space for research. *Journal of Communication, 42*(4), 5-22. https://psycnet.apa.org/doi/10.1111/j.1460-2466.1992.tb00810.x

116. Regan, E. C., & Price, K. R. (1994). The frequency of occurrence and severity of side-effects of immersion virtual reality. *Aviation, Space, and Environmental Medicine, 65*(6), 527-530.

117. Biocca, F. (1992). Virtual reality technology: A tutorial. *Journal of Communication, 42*(4), 23-72. https://psycnet.apa.org/doi/10.1111/j.1460-2466.1992.tb00811.x

118. Moustafa, F., & Steed, A. (2018). A longitudinal study of small group interaction in social virtual reality. In *Proceedings of the 24th ACM Symposium on Virtual Reality*

Software and Technology, 22, 1-10. https://doi.org/10.1145/3281505.3281527

119. Regan, E. C., & Price, K. R. (1994). The frequency of occurrence and severity of side-effects of immersion virtual reality. *Aviation, Space, and Environmental Medicine, 65*(6), 527-530.

120. Ramirez, E. J. (2019). Ecological and ethical issues in virtual reality research: A call for increased scrutiny. *Philosophical Psychology, 32*(2), 211-233. https://doi.org/10.1080/09515089.2018.1532073

121. Gendler, T. S. (2010). *Intuition, imagination, and philosophical methodology*. Oxford University Press. https://doi.org/DOI:10.1093/acprof:oso/9780199589760.001.0001

122. Dietrich, A., & Haider, H. (2015). Human creativity, evolutionary algorithms, and predictive representations: The mechanics of thought trials. *Psychonomic Bulletin & Review, 22*(4), 897-915. https://doi.org/10.3758/s13423-014-0743-x

123. Lennox, J. G. (1991). Darwinian thought experiments: A function for just-so stories. In T. Horowitz & G. J. Massey (Eds.), *Thought experiments in science and philosophy* (pp. 223-245). Rowman & Littlefield. https://doi.org/10.2307/2108510

124. Carr, A., & Zanetti, L. A. (1999). Metatheorizing the dialectic of self and other: The psychodynamics in work organizations. *American Behavioral Scientist, 43*(2), 324-345. https://doi.org/10.1177/00027649921955281

125. Tett, R., Walser, B., Brown, C., Simonet, D., & Tonidandel, S. (2013). The 2011 SIOP graduate program benchmarking survey part 3: Curriculum and competencies. *The Industrial-Organizational Psychologist, 50*(4), 69-90. https://www.siop.org/Membership/Surveys/Additional-Research

126. Brown, J. R. (2011). *The laboratory of the mind*. Routledge. https://doi.org/10.4324/9780203979150

127. Hatherly, D., Mitchell, R. K., Mitchell, J. R., & Lee, J. H. (2020). Reimagining profits and stakeholder capital to address tensions among stakeholders. *Business & Society, 59*(2), 322-350. https://doi.org/10.1177/0007650317745637

128. Eden, D. (2017). Field experiments in organizations. *Annual Review of Organizational Psychology and Organizational Behavior, 4*, 91-122. https://doi.org/10.1146/annurev-orgpsych-041015-062400

129. Hong, J. F. (2012). Glocalizing Nonaka's knowledge creation model: Issues and challenges. *Management Learning, 43*(2), 199-215. https://doi.org/10.1177/1350507611428853

130. Ferguson, T. D., & Ketchen, D. J. (1999). Organizational configurations and performance: The role of statistical power in extant research. *Strategic Management Journal, 20*(4), 385-395. https://doi.org/10.1002/(SICI)1097-0266(199904)20:4<385::AID-SMJ24>3.0.CO;2-X

131. Schwab, D. P. (2005). *Research methods for organizational studies*. Psychology Press.

132. Aguinis, H., Villamor, I., & Ramani, R. M. (2021). MTurk research: Review and recommendations. *Journal of Management, 47*(4), 823-837. https://doi.org/10.1177/0149206320969787

133. Barnes, C. M., Dang, C. T., Leavitt, K., Guarana, C. L., & Uhlmann, E. L. (2018). Archival data in micro-organizational research: A toolkit for moving to a broader set of topics. *Journal of Management, 44*(4), 1453-1478. https://doi.org/10.1177/0149206315604188

134. Liberale, A. P., & Kovach, J. V. (2017). Reducing the time for IRB reviews: A case study. *Journal of Research Administration, 48*(2), 37-50.

135. Colquitt, J. A., & Zapata-Phelan, C. P. (2007). Trends in theory building and theory testing: A five-decade study of the Academy of Management Journal. *Academy of Management Journal, 50*(6), 1281-1303. https://doi.org/10.5465/AMJ.2007.28165855

136. Brown, J. R. (1986). Thought experiments since the scientific revolution. *International Studies in the Philosophy of Science, 1*(1), 1-15. https://doi.org/10.1080/02698598608573279

137. Newton, I. (1728). *A treatise of the system of the world*. Kessinger Publishing, LLC.

138. Schrödinger, E. (1935). Die gegenwärtige situation in der quantenmechanik. *Naturwissenschaften, 23*(49), 823-828. https://doi.org/10.1007/BF01491914

139. Moody, E. A. (1951). Galileo and Avempace: The dynamics of the Leaning Tower experiment (I). *Journal of the History of Ideas, 12*(2), 163-193.

140. Wempe, B. (2008). Contractarian business ethics: Credentials and design criteria. *Organization Studies, 29*(10), 1337-1355. https://journals.sagepub.com/doi/10.1177/0170840608093546

141. Jalal, B., & Ramachandran, V. S. (2017). The twin vantage point paradox: A thought experiment. *The Journal of Mind and Behavior, 38*(2), 111-118. https://www.jstor.org/stable/44631533

142. Folger, R., & Turillo, C. J. (1999). Theorizing as the thickness of thin abstraction. *Academy of Management Review, 24*(4), 742-758. https://doi.org/10.2307/259352

143. Fisher, D. J. (2020). A psychoanalyst serves on a jury. *Canadian Journal of Psychoanalysis, 28*(2), 277-298.

144. Haukioja, J. (2020). Semantic burden-shifting and temporal externalism. *Inquiry, 63*(9-10), 919-929. https://doi.org/10.1080/0020174X.2020.1805704

145. Botha, A. P. (2019). A mind model for intelligent machine innovation

using future thinking principles. *Journal of Manufacturing Technology Management*, *30*(8), 1250-1264. https://doi.org/10.1108/JMTM-01-2018-0021

146. Reichstein, A. (2019). A right to die for prisoners? *International Journal of Prisoner Health. 16*(1), 56-66. https://doi.org/10.1108/ijph-07-2019-0036

147. Wempe, B. (2008). Contractarian business ethics: Credentials and design criteria. *Organization Studies, 29*(10), 1337-1355. https://journals.sagepub.com/doi/10.1177/0170840608093546

148. Caste, N. J. (1992). Drug testing and productivity. *Journal of Business Ethics, 11*(4), 301-306. https://doi.org/10.1007/BF00872172

149. Hong, J. F. (2012). Glocalizing Nonaka's knowledge creation model: Issues and challenges. *Management Learning, 43*(2), 199-215. https://doi.org/10.1177/1350507611428853

150. Botha, A. P. (2019). A mind model for intelligent machine innovation using future thinking principles. *Journal of Manufacturing Technology Management, 30*(8), 1250-1264. https://doi.org/10.1108/JMTM-01-2018-0021

151. Wempe, B. (2008). Contractarian business ethics: Credentials and design criteria. *Organization Studies, 29*(10), 1337-1355. https://journals.sagepub.com/doi/10.1177/0170840608093546

152. Folger, R., & Turillo, C. J. (1999). Theorizing as the thickness of thin abstraction. *Academy of Management Review, 24*(4), 742-758. https://doi.org/10.2307/259352

153. Jabri, M., & Pounder, J. S. (2001). The management of change: A narrative perspective on management development. *Journal of Management Development, 20*(8), 682-691. https://doi.org/10.1108/02621710110401400

154. Lucas, R. E. (2003). Macroeconomic priorities. *American Economic Review,*

93(1), 1-14. https://doi.org/10.1257/000282803321455133

155. Otero-Iglesias, M., & Weissenegger, M. (2020). Motivations, security threats and geopolitical implications of Chinese investment in the EU energy sector: The case of CDP Reti. *European Journal of International Relations, 26*(2), 594-620. https://journals.sagepub.com/doi/10.1177/1354066119871350

156. Elias, J. Z., & Gallagher, S. (2014). Word as object: A view of language at hand. *Journal of Cognition and Culture, 14*(5), 373-384. https://doi.org/10.1163/15685373-12342132

157. Vasileiou, E. (2021). Are markets efficient? A quantum mechanics view. *Journal of Behavioral Finance, 22*(2), 214-220. https://doi.org/10.1080/15427560.2020.1772260

158. Lachenicht, L. G. (1993). A skeptical argument concerning the value of a behavioural solution for AIDS. *South African Journal of Psychology, 23*(1), 15-20. https://journals.sagepub.com/doi/10.1177/008124639302300103

159. Fisher, D. J. (2020). A psychoanalyst serves on a jury. *Canadian Journal of Psychoanalysis, 28*(2), 277-298.

160. Wempe, B. (2008). Contractarian business ethics: Credentials and design criteria. *Organization Studies, 29*(10), 1337-1355. https://journals.sagepub.com/doi/10.1177/0170840608093546

161. McMullen, J. S. (2018). Organizational hybrids as biological hybrids: Insights for research on the relationship between social enterprise and the entrepreneurial ecosystem. *Journal of Business Venturing, 33*(5), 575-590. https://doi.org/10.1016/j.jbusvent.2018.06.001

162. Weick, K. E. (1989). Theory construction as disciplined imagination. *Academy of Management Review, 14*(4), 516-531. https://doi.org/10.2307/258556

163. Mankiw, N. G. (2013). Defending the one percent. *Journal of Economic*

Perspectives, 27(3), 21-34. https://doi.org/10.1257/jep.27.3.21

164. Stögbauer, C., & Komlos, J. (2004). Averting the Nazi seizure of power: A counterfactual thought experiment. *European Review of Economic History, 8*(2), 173-199. https://doi.org/10.1017/S1361491604001145

165. Lachenicht, L. G. (1993). A skeptical argument concerning the value of a behavioural solution for AIDS. *South African Journal of Psychology, 23*(1), 15-20. https://journals.sagepub.com/doi/10.1177/008124639302300103

166. Stögbauer, C., & Komlos, J. (2004). Averting the Nazi seizure of power: A counterfactual thought experiment. *European Review of Economic History, 8*(2), 173-199. https://doi.org/10.1017/S1361491604001145

167. Reichstein, A. (2019). A right to die for prisoners? *International Journal of Prisoner Health. 16*(1), 56-66. https://doi.org/10.1108/ijph-07-2019-0036

168. Nothhaft, H., & Stensson, H. (2019). Explaining the measurement and evaluation stasis: A thought experiment and a note on functional stupidity. *Journal of Communication Management, 23*(3), 213-227. https://doi.org/10.1108/JCOM-12-2018-0135

169. Bozeman, B., & Feeney, M. K. (2007). Toward a useful theory of mentoring: A conceptual analysis and critique. *Administration & Society, 39*(6), 719-739. https://journals.sagepub.com/doi/10.1177/0095399707304119

170. Hatherly, D., Mitchell, R. K., Mitchell, J. R., & Lee, J. H. (2020). Reimagining profits and stakeholder capital to address tensions among stakeholders. *Business & Society, 59*(2), 322-350. https://doi.org/10.1177/0007650317745637

171. Brown, J. R. (2011). *The laboratory of the mind*. Routledge. https://doi.org/10.4324/9780203979150

172. Botha, A. P. (2019). A mind model for intelligent machine innovation

using future thinking principles. *Journal of Manufacturing Technology Management, 30*(8), 1250-1264. https://doi.org/10.1108/JMTM-01-2018-0021

173. Mankiw, N. G. (2013). Defending the one percent. *Journal of Economic Perspectives, 27*(3), 21-34. https://doi.org/10.1257/jep.27.3.21

174. Kadvany, J. (2010). Indistinguishable from magic: Computation is cognitive technology. *Minds and Machines, 20*(1), 119-143. https://doi.org/10.1007/s11023-010-9185-z

175. Van Bockhaven, W., & Matthyssens, P. (2017). Mobilizing a network to develop a field: Enriching the business actor's mobilization analysis toolkit. *Industrial Marketing Management,67*, 70-87. https://doi.org/10.1016/j.indmarman.2017.08.001

176. Fisher, D. J. (2020). A psychoanalyst serves on a jury. *Canadian Journal of Psychoanalysis, 28*(2), 277-298.

177. Mankiw, N. G. (2013). Defending the one percent. *Journal of Economic Perspectives, 27*(3), 21-34. https://doi.org/10.1257/jep.27.3.21

178. Raverty, A. (2007). Are we monks, or are we men? The monastic masculine gender model according to the rule of Benedict. *The Journal of Men's Studies, 14*(3), 269-291. https://doi.org/10.3149/jms.1403.269

179. Sarmiento, R., & Shukla, V. (2011). Zero-sum and frontier trade-offs: An investigation on compromises and compatibilities amongst manufacturing capabilities. *International Journal of Production Research, 49*(7), 2001-2017. https://doi.org/10.1080/00207540903555544

180. Lachenicht, L. G. (1993). A skeptical argument concerning the value of a behavioural solution for AIDS. *South African Journal of Psychology, 23*(1), 15-20. https://doi.org/10.1177%2F008124639302300103

181. Hong, J. F. (2012). Glocalizing Nonaka's knowledge creation model: Issues and challenges.

Management Learning, 43(2), 199-215. https://doi.org/10.1177/1350507611428853

CHAPTER 8

1. Newman, D. A. (2014). Missing data: Five practical guidelines. *Organizational Research Methods, 17*(4), 372-411. https://doi.org/10.1177/1094428114548590

2. Aguinis, H., Pierce, C. A., Bosco, F. A., & Muslin, I. S. (2009). First decade of Organizational Research Methods: Trends in design, measurement, and data-analysis topics. *Organizational Research Methods, 12*(1), 69-112. https://doi.org/10.1177/1094428108322641

3. Ketchen, D. J., Ireland, R. D., & Baker, L. T. (2013). The use of archival proxies in strategic management studies: Castles made of sand? *Organizational Research Methods, 16*(1), 32-42 https://doi.org/10.1177/1094428112459911

4. Heggestad, E. D., Scheaf, D. J., Banks, G. C., Monroe Hausfeld, M., Tonidandel, S., & Williams, E. B. 2019. Scale adaptation in organizational science research: A review and best-practice recommendations. *Journal of Management, 45*(6), 2596–2627. https://doi/abs/10.1177/0149206319850280

5. Kalaignanam, K., Kushwaha, T., M. Steenkamp, J. E., & Tuli, K. R. (2013). The effect of CRM outsourcing on shareholder value: A contingency perspective. *Management Science, 59*(3), 748-769. https://doi.org/10.1287/mnsc.1120.1565

6. Antonakis, J., House, R. J., & Simonton, D. K. (2017). Can super smart leaders suffer from too much of a good thing? The curvilinear effect of intelligence on perceived leadership behavior. *Journal of Applied Psychology,*

102(5), 1003-1021. https://doi.org/10.1037/apl0000221

7. Aguinis, H., & O'Boyle Jr, E. (2014). Star performers in twenty-first century organizations. *Personnel Psychology, 67*(2), 313-350. https://doi.org/10.1111/peps.12054

8. Aguinis, H., Ji, Y. H., & Joo, H. (2018). Gender productivity gap among star performers in STEM and other scientific fields. *Journal of Applied Psychology, 103*(12), 1283. https://doi.org/10.1037/apl0000331

9. Stanley, M. H., Buldyrev, S. V., Havlin, S., Mantegna, R. N., Salinger, M. A., & Stanley, H. E. (1995). Zipf plots and the size distribution of firms. *Economics Letters, 49*(4), 453-457. https://doi.org/10.1016/0165-1765(95)00696-D

10. Crawford, G. C., Aguinis, H., Lichtenstein, B., Davidsson, P., & McKelvey, B. (2015). Power law distributions in entrepreneurship: Implications for theory and research. *Journal of Business Venturing, 30*(5), 696-713. https://doi.org/10.1016/j.jbusvent.2015.01.001

11. Becker, T. E., Robertson, M. M., & Vandenberg, R. J. (2019). Nonlinear transformations in organizational research: Possible problems and potential solutions. *Organizational Research Methods, 22*(4), 831-866. https://doi.org/10.1177/1094428118775205

12. Cohen, J., Cohen, P., West, S. G., & Aiken, L. S. (2013). *Applied multiple regression/correlation analysis for the behavioral sciences.* Routledge. https://doi.org/10.4324/9780203774441

13. Courtright, S. H., Gardner, R. G., Smith, T. A., McCormick, B. W., & Colbert, A. E. (2016). My family made me do it: A cross-domain, self-regulatory perspective on antecedents to abusive supervision. *Academy of Management Journal, 59*(5), 1630-1652. https://doi.org/10.5465/amj.2013.1009

14. McDonnell, M. H., & King, B. (2013). Keeping up appearances:

Reputational threat and impression management after social movement boycotts. *Administrative Science Quarterly, 58*(3), 387-419. https://doi.org/10.1177/00018 39213500032

15. Hunter, J. E., & Schmidt, F. L. (2004). *Methods of meta-analysis: Correcting error and bias in research findings* (2nd ed.). Sage.

16. Orr, J. M., Sackett, P. R., & DuBois, C. L. Z. (1991). Outlier detection and treatment in I/O psychology: A survey of researcher beliefs and an empirical illustration. *Personnel Psychology, 44*(3), 473-486. https://doi.org/10.1111/j.1744-6570.1 991.tb02401.x

17. Hitt, M. A., Harrison, J. S., Ireland, R. D., & Best, A. (1998). Attributes of successful and unsuccessful acquisitions of US firms. *British Journal of Management, 9*(2), 91-114. https://doi.org/10.1111/1467-8551.00077

18. Gladwell, M. (2008). *Outliers: The story of success.* Little, Brown and Company.

19. Hitt, M. A., Harrison, J. S., Ireland, R. D., & Best, A. (1998). Attributes of successful and unsuccessful acquisitions of US firms. *British Journal of Management, 9*(2), 91-114. https://doi.org/10.1111/14 67-8551.00077

20. Cohen, J., Cohen, P., West, S. G., & Aiken, L. S. (2003). *Applied multiple regression/correlation analysis for the behavioral sciences* (3rd ed.). Erlbaum.

21. Aguinis, H., Pierce, C. A., Bosco, F. A., & Muslin, I. S. (2009). First decade of Organizational Research Methods: Trends in design, measurement, and data-analysis topics. *Organizational Research Methods, 12*(1), 69-112. https://doi.org/10.1177/ 1094428108322641

22. Martin, M. A., & Roberts, S. (2010). Jackknife-after-bootstrap regression influence diagnostics. *Journal of Nonparametric Statistics, 22*(2), 257-269. https://doi.org /10.1080/10485250903287906

23. Fidell, L. S., & Tabachnick, B. G. (2003). Preparatory data analysis. In J. A. Schinka & W. F. Velicer (Eds.), *Handbook of psychology: Research methods in psychology* (Vol. 2, pp. 115-141). John Wiley & Sons. https://doi.org/10.1002/047 1264385.wei0205

24. Cohen, J., Cohen, P., West, S. G., & Aiken, L. S. (2003). *Applied multiple regression/correlation analysis for the behavioral sciences* (3rd ed.). Erlbaum.

25. Tabachnick, B. G., & Fidell, L. S. (2007). *Using multivariate statistics* (5th ed.). Pearson.

26. Snijders, T. A. B., & Bosker, R. J. (2012). *Multilevel analysis: An introduction to basic and advanced multilevel modeling* (2nd ed.). Sage Publications.

27. Cohen, J., Cohen, P., West, S. G., & Aiken, L. S. (2003). *Applied multiple regression/correlation analysis for the behavioral sciences* (3rd ed.). Erlbaum.

28. Becker, C., & Gather, U. (1999). The masking breakdown point of multivariate outlier identification rules. *Journal of the American Statistical Association, 94*(447), 947-955. https://doi.org/10.1080/0162 1459.1999.10474199

29. Barnett, V., & Lewis, T. (1994). *Outliers in statistical data* (3rd ed.). Wiley.

30. Snijders, T. A. B., & Bosker, R. J. (2012). *Multilevel analysis: An introduction to basic and advanced multilevel modeling* (2nd ed.). Sage Publications.

31. Martin, M. A., & Roberts, S. (2010). Jackknife-after-bootstrap regression influence diagnostics. *Journal of Nonparametric Statistics, 22*(2), 257-269. https://doi.org /10.1080/10485250903287906

32. Cohen, J., Cohen, P., West, S. G., & Aiken, L. S. (2003). *Applied multiple regression/correlation analysis for the behavioral sciences* (3rd ed.). Erlbaum.

33. Zhang, Z., & Yuan, K.-H. (2012). semdiag: Structural equation modeling diagnostics (R package version 0.1.2) [Computer software manual]. http://cran.at.r-project. org/web/packages/semdiag/sem diag.pdf

34. Raudenbush, S. W., Bryk, A. S., Cheong, Y. F., Congdon, R. T., Jr., & Du Toit, M. (2004). *HLM 6: Hierarchical linear and nonlinear modeling.* Scientific Software International.

35. Brutus, S., Aguinis, H., & Wassmer, U. (2013). Self-reported limitations and future directions in scholarly reports: Analysis and recommendations. *Journal of Management, 39*(1), 48-75. https://doi.org/10.117 7/0149206312455245

36. Worren, N., Moore, K., & Cardona, P. (2002). Modularity, strategic flexibility, and firm performance: A study of the home appliance industry. *Strategic Management Journal, 23*(12), 1123-1140. https:// doi.org/10.1002/smj.276

37. Worren, N., Moore, K., & Cardona, P. (2002). Modularity, strategic flexibility, and firm performance: A study of the home appliance industry. *Strategic Management Journal, 23*(12), 1123-1140. https:// doi.org/10.1002/smj.276

38. Huffman, M. L., Cohen, P. N., & Pearlman, J. (2010). Engendering change: Organizational dynamics and workplace gender desegregation, 1975-2005. *Administrative Science Quarterly, 55*(2), 255-277. https://doi.org/10.2189/asqu.2010. 55.2.255

39. Hitt, M., Harrison, J., Ireland, R. D., & Best, A. (1998). Attributes of successful and unsuccessful acquisitions of US firms. *British Journal of Management, 9*(2), 91-114. https://doi.org/10.1111/14 67-8551.00077

40. Mohrman, S. A., & Lawler, E. E., III. (2012). Generating knowledge that drives change. *Academy of Management Perspectives, 26*(1), 41-51. https://doi.org/10.5465/am p.2011.0141

41. Colbert, A. E., Kristof-Brown, A. L., Bradley, B. H., & Barrick, M. R.

[2008]. CEO transformational leadership: The role of goal importance congruence in top management teams. *Academy of Management Journal, 51*(1), 81-96. https://doi.org/10.5465/amj.2008.30717744

42. Goerzen, A., & Beamish, P. W. (2005). The effect of alliance network diversity on multinational enterprise performance. *Strategic Management Journal, 26*(4), 333-354. https://doi.org/10.1002/smj.447

43. Smillie, L. D., Yeo, G. B., Furnham, A. F., & Jackson, C. J. (2006). Benefits of all work and no play: The relationship between neuroticism and performance as a function of resource allocation. *Journal of Applied Psychology, 91*(1), 139-155. https://doi.org/10.1037/0021-9010.91.1.139

44. Huffman, M. L., Cohen, P. N., & Pearlman, J. (2010). Engendering change: Organizational dynamics and workplace gender desegregation, 1975-2005. *Administrative Science Quarterly, 55*(2), 255-277. https://doi.org/10.2189/asqu.2010.55.2.255

45. Tabachnick, B. G., & Fidell, L. S. (2007). *Using multivariate statistics* (5th ed.). Pearson.

46. Edwards, J. R., & Cable, D. M. (2009). The value of value congruence. *Journal of Applied Psychology, 94*(3), 654-677. https://doi.org/10.1037/a0014891

47. Huffman, M. L., Cohen, P. N., & Pearlman, J. (2010). Engendering change: Organizational dynamics and workplace gender desegregation, 1975-2005. *Administrative Science Quarterly, 55*(2), 255-277. https://doi.org/10.2189/asqu.2010.55.2.255

48. Kutner, M. H., Nachtsheim, C. J., Neter, J., & Li, W. (2004). *Applied linear statistical models* (5th ed.). McGraw-Hill/Irwin.

49. Hawawini, G., Subramanian, V., & Verdin, P. (2003). Is performance driven by industry- or firm-specific factors? A new look at the evidence. *Strategic Management Journal, 24*(1), 1-16. https://doi.org/10.1002/smj.278

50. McNamara, G., Aime, F., & Vaaler, P. M. (2005). Is performance driven by industry- or firm-specific factors? A response to Hawawini, Subramanian, and Verdin. *Strategic Management Journal, 26*(11), 1075-1081. https://doi.org/10.1002/smj.496

51. Mohrman, S. A., & Lawler, E. E., III. (2012). Generating knowledge that drives change. *Academy of Management Perspectives, 26*(1), 41-51. https://doi.org/10.5465/amp.2011.0141

52. Mohrman, S. A., & Lawler, E. E., III. (2012). Generating knowledge that drives change. *Academy of Management Perspectives, 26*(1), 41-51. https://doi.org/10.5465/amp.2011.0141

53. Wiggins, R. R., & Ruefli, T. W. (2005). Schumpeter's ghost: Is hypercompetition making the best of times shorter? *Strategic Management Journal, 26*(10), 887-911. https://doi.org/10.1002/smj.492

54. Diener, E. (2000). Subjective well-being: The science of happiness and a proposal for a national index. *American Psychologist, 55*(1), 34-43. https://doi.org/10.1037/0003-066X.55.1.34

55. O'Boyle, E., Jr., & Aguinis, H. (2012). The best and the rest: Revisiting the norm of normality of individual performance. *Personnel Psychology, 65*(1), 79-119. https://doi.org/10.1111/j.1744-6570.2011.01239.x

56. Gladwell, M. (2008). *Outliers: The story of success*. Little, Brown and Company.

57. St. John, C. H., & Harrison, J. S. (1999). Manufacturing-based relatedness, synergy, and coordination. *Strategic Management Journal, 20*(2), 129-145. https://doi.org/10.1002/(SICI)1097-0266(199902)20:2 < 129::AID-SMJ16>3.0.CO;2-F

58. Gladwell, M. (2008). *Outliers: The story of success*. Little, Brown and Company.

59. Hitt, M. A., Harrison, J. S., Ireland, R. D., & Best, A. (1998). Attributes of successful and unsuccessful acquisitions of US firms. *British Journal of Management, 9*(2), 91-114. https://doi.org/10.1111/1467-8551.00077

60. Yuan, K.-H., & Bentler, P. M. (1998). Structural equation modeling with robust covariances. *Sociological Methodology, 28*(1), 363-396. https://doi.org/10.1111/0081-1750.00052

61. Cohen, J., Cohen, P., West, S. G., & Aiken, L. S. (2003). *Applied multiple regression/correlation analysis for the behavioral sciences* (3rd ed.). Erlbaum.

62. Belsley, D. A., Kuh, E., & Welsh, R. E. (1980). *Regression diagnostics: Identifying influential data and sources of collinearity*. John Wiley.

63. Cohen, J., Cohen, P., West, S. G., & Aiken, L. S. (2003). *Applied multiple regression/correlation analysis for the behavioral sciences* (3rd ed.). Erlbaum.

64. Cohen, J., Cohen, P., West, S. G., & Aiken, L. S. (2003). *Applied multiple regression/correlation analysis for the behavioral sciences* (3rd ed.). Erlbaum.

65. Cohen, J., Cohen, P., West, S. G., & Aiken, L. S. (2003). *Applied multiple regression/correlation analysis for the behavioral sciences* (3rd ed.). Erlbaum.

66. Pierce, J. R., & Aguinis, H. (2013). The too-much-of-a-good-thing effect in management. *Journal of Management, 39*(2), 313-338. https://doi.org/10.1177/0149206311410060

67. Aguinis, H. (2004). *Regression analysis for categorical moderators*. Guilford.

68. Aguinis, H., Forcum, L. E., & Joo, H. (2013). Using market basket analysis in management research. *Journal of Management, 39*(7), 1799-1824. https://doi.org/10.1177/0149206312466147

69. Leung, K. (2011). Presenting post hoc hypotheses as a priori: Ethical and theoretical issues. *Management and Organization Review, 7*(3), 471-479. https://doi.org/10.1111/j.1740-8784.2011.00222.x

70. Brutus, S., Aguinis, H., & Wassmer, U. (2013). Self-reported limitations and future directions in scholarly reports: Analysis and recommendations. *Journal of Management, 39*(1), 48-75. https://doi.org/10.1177/0149206312455245

71. Kruschke, J. K., Aguinis, H., & Joo, H. (2012). The time has come: Bayesian methods for data analysis in the organizational sciences. *Organizational Research Methods, 15*(4), 722-752. https://doi.org/10.1177/1094428112457829

72. Aguinis, H., Werner, S., Abbott, J. L., Angert, C., Park, J. H., & Kohlhausen, D. (2010). Customer-centric science: Reporting significant research results with rigor, relevance, and practical impact in mind. *Organizational Research Methods, 13*(3), 515-539. https://doi.org/10.1177/1094428109333339

73. Colbert, A. E., Kristof-Brown, A. L., Bradley, B. H., & Barrick, M. R. (2008). CEO transformational leadership: The role of goal importance congruence in top management teams. *Academy of Management Journal, 51*(1), 81-96. https://doi.org/10.5465/amj.2008.30717744

74. Yuan, K.-H., & Bentler, P. M. (1998). Structural equation modeling with robust covariances. *Sociological Methodology, 28*(1), 363-396. https://doi.org/10.1111/0081-1750.00052

75. Pek, J., & MacCallum, R. C. (2011). Sensitivity analysis in structural equation models: Cases and their influence. *Multivariate Behavioral Research, 46*(2), 202-228. https://doi.org/10.1080/00273171.2011.561068

76. Pek, J., & MacCallum, R. C. (2011). Sensitivity analysis in structural equation models: Cases and their influence. *Multivariate Behavioral Research, 46*(2), 202-228. https://doi.org/10.1080/00273171.2011.561068

77. Martín, N., & Pardo, L. (2009). On the asymptotic distribution of Cook's distance in logistic regression models. *Journal of Applied Statistics, 36*(10), 1119-1146. https://doi.org/10.1080/02664760802562498

78. Pek, J., & MacCallum, R. C. (2011). Sensitivity analysis in structural equation models: Cases and their influence. *Multivariate Behavioral Research, 46*(2), 202-228. https://doi.org/10.1080/00273171.2011.561068

79. Pek, J., & MacCallum, R. C. (2011). Sensitivity analysis in structural equation models: Cases and their influence. *Multivariate Behavioral Research, 46*(2), 202-228. https://doi.org/10.1080/00273171.2011.561068

80. Yuan, K.-H., & Bentler, P. M. (1998). Structural equation modeling with robust covariances. *Sociological Methodology, 28*(1), 363-396. https://doi.org/10.1111/0081-1750.00052

81. Zhong, X., & Yuan, K.-H. (2011). Bias and efficiency in structural equation modeling: Maximum likelihood versus robust methods. *Multivariate Behavioral Research, 46*(2), 229-265. https://doi.org/10.1080/00273171.2011.558736

82. Zhong, X., & Yuan, K.-H. (2011). Bias and efficiency in structural equation modeling: Maximum likelihood versus robust methods. *Multivariate Behavioral Research, 46*(2), 229-265.

83. Goerzen, A., & Beamish, P. W. (2005). The effect of alliance network diversity on multinational enterprise performance. *Strategic Management Journal, 26*(4), 333-354. https://doi.org/10.1002/smj.447

84. Shi, L., & Chen, G. (2008). Detection of outliers in multilevel models. *Journal of Statistical Planning and Inference, 138*(10), 3189-3199. https://doi.org/10.1016/j.jspi.2008.01.004

85. Mathieu, J. E., Aguinis, H., Culpepper, S. A., & Chen. G. (2012). Understanding and estimating the power to detect cross-level interaction effects in multilevel modeling. *Journal of Applied Psychology, 97*(5), 951-966. https://doi.org/10.1037/a0028380

86. Langford, I. H., & Lewis, T. (1998). Outliers in multilevel data. *Journal of the Royal Statistical Society, Series A, 161*(2), 121-160. https://doi.org/10.1111/1467-985X.00094

87. Yuan, K.-H., & Bentler, P. M. (1998). Structural equation modeling with robust covariances. *Sociological Methodology, 28*(1), 363-396. https://doi.org/10.1111/0081-1750.00052

88. Van Dick, R., Van Knippenberg, D., Kerschreiter, R., Hertel, G., & Wieseke, J. (2008). Interactive effects of work group and organizational identification on job satisfaction and extra-role behavior. *Journal of Vocational Behavior, 72*(3), 388-399. https://doi.org/10.1016/j.jvb.2007.11.009

89. Langford, I. H., & Lewis, T. (1998). Outliers in multilevel data. *Journal of the Royal Statistical Society, Series A, 161*(2), 121-160. https://doi.org/10.1111/1467-985X.00094

90. Snijders, T. A. B., & Bosker, R. J. (2012). *Multilevel analysis: An introduction to basic and advanced multilevel modeling* (2nd ed.). Sage Publications.

91. Hox, J. J. (2010). *Multilevel analysis: Techniques and applications* (2nd ed.). Routledge.

92. Hox, J. J. (2010). *Multilevel analysis: Techniques and applications* (2nd ed.). Routledge.

93. Kerr, N. L. (1998). HARKing: Hypothesizing after the results are known. *Personality & Social Psychology* Review, *2*(3), 196-217. https://doi.org/10.1207/s15327957pspr0203_4

94. Hitchcock, C., & Sober, E. (2004). Prediction versus accommodation and the risk of overfitting. *British Journal for the Philosophy of*

Science, 55(1), 1-34. https://doi.or g/10.1093/bjps/55.1.1

95. Leung, K. (2011). Presenting post hoc hypotheses as a priori: Ethical and theoretical issues. *Management and Organization Review, 7*(3), 471-479. https://doi.org/10.1111/j. 1740-8784.2011.00222.x

96. John, L. K., Loewenstein, G., & Prelec, D. (2012). Measuring the prevalence of questionable research practices with incentives for truth-telling. *Psychological Science, 23*(5), 524-532. https://doi.org/10.1177/0956797611430 953

97. Harker, D. (2008). On the predilections for predictions. *British Journal for the Philosophy of Science, 59*(3), 429-453. https://doi.org/10. 1093/bjps/axn017

98. Lipton, P. (2005). Testing hypotheses: Prediction and prejudice. *Science, 307*(5707), 219-221. https://doi.org/10.1126/science.1103024

99. Gardner, M. R. (1982). Predicting novel facts. *The British Journal for the Philosophy of Science, 33*(1), 1-15. https://doi.org/10.1093/bjps /33.1.1

100. Hitchcock, C., & Sober, E. (2004). Prediction versus accommodation and the risk of overfitting. *British Journal for the Philosophy of Science, 55*(1), 1-34. https://doi.org/1 0.1093/bjps/55.1.1

101. Dalton, D. R., Aguinis, H., Dalton, C. M., Bosco, F. A., & Pierce, C. A. (2012). Revisiting the file drawer problem in meta-analysis: An empirical assessment of published and nonpublished correlation matrices. *Personnel Psychology, 65*(2), 221-249. https://doi.org/10.1111/j.1744-6570.2012. 01243.x

102. Leavitt, K., Mitchell, T. R., & Peterson, J. (2010). Theory pruning: Strategies to reduce our dense theoretical landscape. *Organizational Research Methods, 13*(4), 644-667. https://doi.org/10. 1177/1094428109345156

103. Mill, J. S. (1843). *A System of Logic.* George Routledge and Sons.

104. Hitchcock, C., & Sober, E. (2004). Prediction versus accommodation and the risk of overfitting. *British Journal for the Philosophy of Science, 55*(1), 1-34. https://doi.org/1 0.1093/bjps/55.1.1

105. O'Boyle Jr, E. H., Banks, G. C., & Gonzalez-Mulé, E. (2017). The chrysalis effect: How ugly initial results metamorphosize into beautiful articles. *Journal of Management, 43*(2), 376-399. http s://doi.org/10.1177/01492063145 27133

106. Fanelli, D. (2009). How many scientists fabricate and falsify research? A systematic review and meta-analysis of survey data. *PLoS ONE, 4*, e5738. https://doi.or g/10.1371/journal.pone.0005738

107. John, L. K., Loewenstein, G., & Prelec, D. (2012). Measuring the prevalence of questionable research practices with incentives for truth-telling. *Psychological Science, 23*(5), 524-532. https://doi.org/10.1177/0956797 611430953

108. De Vries, R., Anderson, M. S., & Martinson, B. C. (2006). Normal misbehaviour: Scientists talk about the ethics of research. *Journal of Empirical Research on Human Research Ethics: An International Journal, 1*(1), 43-50. https://doi.or g/10.1525/jer.2006.1.1.43

109. Orlitzky, M. (2012). How can significance tests be deinstitutionalized? *Organizational Research Methods, 15*(2), 199-228. https://doi.org/10.1177/1094428111428356

110. Bedeian, A. G., Taylor, S. G., & Miller, A. N. (2010). Management science on the credibility bubble: Cardinal sins and various misdemeanors. *Academy of Management Learning & Education, 9*(4), 715-725. https://doi.org/10.5465/AML E.2010.56659889

111. Hambrick, D. C. (2007). The field of management's devotion to theory: Too much of a good thing? *Academy of Management Journal,*

50(6), 1346-1352. https://doi.org/1 0.2307/20159476

112. Scandura, T. A., & Williams, E. A. (2000). Research methodology in management: Current practices, trends, and implications for future research. *Academy of Management Journal, 43*(6), 1248-1264. https:// doi.org/10.2307/1556348

113. Leavitt, K., Mitchell, T. R., & Peterson, J. (2010). Theory pruning: Strategies to reduce our dense theoretical landscape. *Organizational Research Methods, 13*(4), 644-667. https://doi.org/10. 1177/1094428109345156

114. Edwards, J. R., & Berry, J. W. (2010). The presence of something or the absence of nothing: Increasing theoretical precision in management research. *Organizational Research Methods, 13*(4), 668-689. https://doi.org/10.1177/1 094428110380467

115. Hitchcock, C., & Sober, E. (2004). Prediction versus accommodation and the risk of overfitting. *British Journal for the Philosophy of Science, 55*(1), 1-34. https://doi.org/1 0.1093/bjps/55.1.1

116. Hitchcock, C., & Sober, E. (2004). Prediction versus accommodation and the risk of overfitting. *British Journal for the Philosophy of Science, 55*(1), 1-34. https://doi.org/1 0.1093/bjps/55.1.1

117. Babyak, M. A. (2004). What you see may not be what you get: A brief, nontechnical introduction to overfitting in regression-type models. *Psychosomatic Medicine, 66*(3), 411-421. https://doi.org/10.1 097/00006842-200405000-00021

118. Bem, D. J. (2002). Writing the empirical journal article. In J. M. Darley, M. P. Zanna & Roediger III. H. L. (Eds.), *The compleat academic: A career guide* (pp. 3-26). American Psychological Association.

119. Dalton, D. R., Aguinis, H., Dalton, C. M., Bosco, F. A., & Pierce, C. A. (2012). Revisiting the file drawer problem in meta-analysis: An empirical assessment of

published and nonpublished correlation matrices. *Personnel Psychology, 65*(2), 221-249. https://doi.org/10.1111/j.1744-6570.2012.01243.x

120. Cascio, W. F., & Aguinis, H. (2008). Research in industrial and organizational psychology from 1963 to 2007: Changes, choices, and trends. *Journal of Applied Psychology, 93*(5), 1062-1081. https://doi.org/10.1037/0021-9010.93.5.1062

121. Banks, G.C., Rogelberg, S.G., Woznyj, H.M., Landis, R.S. & Rupp, D.E. (2016). Editorial: Evidence on questionable research practices: The good, the bad and the ugly. *Journal of Business and Psychology, 31*, 323-338. https://doi.org/10.1007/s10869-016-9456-7

122. Hollenbeck, J. H. & Wright, P. M. (2017). Harking, sharking, and tharking: Making the case for post hoc analysis of scientific data. *Journal of Management, 43*(1), 5-18. https://doi.org/10.1177/0149206316679487

123. Hollenbeck, J. H. & Wright, P. M. (2017). Harking, sharking, and tharking: Making the case for post hoc analysis of scientific data. *Journal of Management, 43*(1), 5-18. https://doi.org/10.1177/0149206316679487

124. Lo, A. W., & MacKinlay, A. C. (1990). Data-snooping biases in tests of financial asset pricing models. *Review of Financial Studies, 3*(3), 431–467. https://doi.org/10.1093/rfs/3.3.431

125. Wing, H. (1982). Statistical hazards in the determination of adverse impact with small samples. *Personnel Psychology, 35*(1), 153-162. https://doi.org/10.1111/j.1744-6570.1982.tb02191.x

126. Aguinis, H., Cascio, W. F., & Ramani, R. S. (2017). Science's reproducibility and replicability crisis: International business is not immune. *Journal of International Business Studies, 48*(6), 653-663. https://doi.org/10.1057/s41267-017-0081-0

127. Bergh, D. D., Sharp, B. M., Aguinis, H., & Li, M. (2017). Is there a credibility crisis in strategic management research? Evidence on the reproducibility of study findings. *Strategic Organization,15*(3), 423-436. https://doi.org/10.1177/1476127017701076

128. Wilkinson, L., & Task Force on Statistical Inference. (1999). Statistical methods in psychology journals: Guidelines and explanations. *American Psychologist, 54*(8), 594-604. https://doi.org/10.1037/0003-066X.54.8.594

129. Aguinis, H., Shapiro, D. L., Antonacopoulou, E., & Cummings, T. G. (2014). Scholarly impact: A pluralist conceptualization. *Academy of Management Learning and Education, 13*(4), 623-639. https://doi.org/10.5465/amle.2014.0121

130. Aguinis, H., Ramani, R. S., & Villamor, I. (2019). The first 20 years of Organizational Research Methods: Trajectory, impact, and predictions for the future. *Organizational Research Methods, 22*(2), 463-489. https://doi.org/10.1177/1094428118786564

131. Harrell, H. (2011). *Regression modeling strategies with applications to linear models, logistic regression and survival analysis*. Springer-Verlag.

132. Bernerth, J. & Aguinis, H. (2016). A critical review and best-practice recommendations for control variable usage. *Personnel Psychology, 69*(1), 229-283. https://doi.org/10.1111/peps.12103

133. Kline, R. B. (2005). *Principles and practice of structural equation modeling* (2nd ed.). Guilford Press.

134. Landis, R. S., Edwards, B. D., & Cortina, J. M. (2009). On the practice of allowing correlated residuals among indicators in structural equation models. In C. E. Lance & R. J. Vandenberg (Eds.), *Statistical and methodological myths and urban legends: Doctrine, verity and fable in the organizational and social sciences* (pp. 193-214). Routledge/Taylor & Francis Group.

135. Thurstone, L.L. (1934). The vectors of the mind. *American Psychologist, 41*(1), 1-32. https://doi.org/10.1037/h0075959

136. Cortina, J. M., Aguinis, H., & DeShon, R. P. (2017). Twilight of dawn or of evening? A century of research methods in the Journal of Applied Psychology. *Journal of Applied Psychology, 102*(3), 274-290. https://doi.org/10.1037/apl0000163

137. Pigliucci, M. (2009). The end of theory in science? *EMBO Reports, 10*(6), 534. https://doi.org/10.1038/embor.2009.111

138. Murphy, K.R. & Cleveland, J.N. (1995). *Understanding performance appraisal: Social, organizational and goal-oriented perspectives*. Sage.

139. Hollenbeck, J. H. & Wright, P. M. (2017). Harking, sharking, and tharking: Making the case for post hoc analysis of scientific data. *Journal of Management, 43*(1), 5-18. https://doi.org/10.1177/0149206316679487

140. Aguinis, H., Ramani, R. S., & Villamor, I. (2019). The first 20 years of Organizational Research Methods: Trajectory, impact, and predictions for the future. *Organizational Research Methods, 22*(2), 463-489. https://doi.org/10.1177/1094428118786564

141. Aguinis, H., Ramani, R. S., & Villamor, I. (2019). The first 20 years of Organizational Research Methods: Trajectory, impact, and predictions for the future. *Organizational Research Methods, 22*(2), 463-489. https://doi.org/10.1177/1094428118786564

142. Hitchcock, C., & Sober, E. (2004). Prediction versus accommodation and the risk of overfitting. *British Journal for the Philosophy of Science, 55*(1), 1-34. https://doi.org/10.1093/bjps/55.1.1

143. Bosco, F. A., Aguinis, H., Singh, K., Field, J. G., & Pierce, C. A. (2015). Correlational effect size benchmarks. *Journal of Applied Psychology, 100*(2), 431-449. https://doi.org/10.1037/a0038047

144. Cascio, W. F., & Aguinis, H. (2008). Research in industrial and organizational psychology from 1963 to 2007: Changes, choices, and trends. *Journal of Applied Psychology, 93*(5), 1062-1081. https://doi.org/10.1037/0021-9010.93.5.1062

145. Leung, K. (2011). Presenting post hoc hypotheses as a priori: Ethical and theoretical issues. *Management and Organization Review, 7*(3), 471-479. https://doi.org/10.1111/j.1740-8784.2011.00222.x

146. Leavitt, K., Mitchell, T. R., & Peterson, J. (2010). Theory pruning: Strategies to reduce our dense theoretical landscape. *Organizational Research Methods, 13*(4), 644-667. https://doi.org/10.1177/1094428109345156

147. Kerr, N. L. (1998). HARKing: Hypothesizing after the results are known. *Personality & Social Psychology* Review, 2(3), 196-217. https://doi.org/10.1207/s15327957pspr0203_4

148. Aguinis, H., Shapiro, D. L., Antonacopoulou, E. P., & Cummings, T. G. (2014). Scholarly impact: A pluralist conceptualization. *Academy of Management Learning & Education, 13*(4), 623-639. https://doi.org/10.5465/amle.2014.0121

149. Colquitt, J. A., Kozlowski, S. W. J., Morgeson, F. P., Rogelberg, S. G., & Rupp, D. E. (2012). Journal Editor Ethics. https://editorethics.charlotte.edu/editor-ethics-2-0-code

150. Aguinis, H., & Vandenberg, R. J. (2014). An ounce of prevention is worth a pound of cure: Improving research quality before data collection. *Annual Review of Organizational Psychology and Organizational Behavior, 1*, 569-595. https://doi.org/10.1146/annurev-orgpsych-031413-091231

151. Kerr, N. L. (1998). HARKing: Hypothesizing after the results are known. *Personality & Social Psychology* Review, 2(3), 196-217. https://doi.org/10.1207/s15327957pspr0203_4

152. Brandt, M. J., Ijzerman, H., Dijksterhuis, A., Farach, F. J., Geller, J., Giner-Sorolla, R., Grange, J. A., Perugini, M., Spies, J. R., & van 't Veer, A. (2014). The replication recipe: What makes for a convincing replication? *Journal of Experimental Social Psychology, 50*, 217-224. https://doi.org/10.1016/j.jesp.2013.10.005

153. Leung, K. (2011). Presenting post hoc hypotheses as a priori: Ethical and theoretical issues. *Management and Organization Review, 7*(3), 471-479. https://doi.org/10.1111/j.1740-8784.2011.00222.x

154. Bedeian, A. G., Taylor, S. G., & Miller, A. N. (2010). Management science on the credibility bubble: Cardinal sins and various misdemeanors. *Academy of Management Learning & Education, 9*(4), 715-725. https://doi.org/10.5465/AMLE.2010.56659889

155. Kepes, S., McDaniel, M., Brannick, M., & Banks, G. (2013). Meta-analytic reviews in the organizational sciences: Two meta-analytic schools on the way to MARS (the Meta-analytic Reporting Standards). *Journal of Business & Psychology, 28*(2), 123-143. https://doi.org/10.1007/s10869-013-9300-2

156. Schminke, M. (2010, October). Enhancing research integrity: A modest proposal. Presented at the annual conference of the Society for Organizational Behavior, Binghamton, NY.

CHAPTER 9

1. Aguinis, H. (2004). *Regression analysis for categorical moderators*. Guilford.

2. Aiken, L. A., & West, S. G. (1991). *Multiple regression: Testing and interpreting interactions*. Sage.

3. Murphy, K. R., & Aguinis, H. (2022). Reporting interactions: Visualization, effect size, and interpretation. *Journal of Management*. https://doi.org/10.1177/01492063221088516

4. Boyd, B. K., Gove, S., & Hitt, M. A. (2005). Construct measurement in strategic management research: Illusion or reality? *Strategic Management Journal, 26*(3), 239-257. https://doi.org/10.1002/smj.444

5. Boyd, B. K., Bergh, D. D., Ireland, R. D., & Ketchen, D. J. (2013). Constructs in strategic management. *Organizational Research Methods, 16*(1), 3-14. https://doi.org/10.1177/1094428112471298

6. Boyd, B. K., Gove, S., & Hitt, M. A. (2005). Construct measurement in strategic management research: Illusion or reality? *Strategic Management Journal, 26*(3), 239-257. https://doi.org/10.1002/smj.444

7. Busemeyer, J. R., & Jones, L. E. (1983). Analysis of multiplicative combination rules when the causal variables are measured with error. *Psychological Bulletin, 93*(3), 549-562. https://doi.org/10.1037/0033-2909.93.3.549

8. Crook, T. R., Ketchen, D. J., Combs, J. G., & Todd, S. Y. (2008). Strategic resources and performance: A meta-analysis. *Strategic Management Journal, 29*(3), 1141-1154. https://doi.org/10.1002/smj.703

9. Bergh, D. D., Aguinis, H., Heavey, C. Ketchen, D. J., Boyd, B. K., Su, P., Lau, C., & Joo, H. (2016). Using meta-analytic structural equation modeling to advance strategic management research: Guidelines and an empirical illustration via the strategic leadership-performance relationship. *Strategic Management Journal, 37*(3), 477-497. https://doi.org/10.1002/smj.2338

10. Aguinis, H., & Stone-Romero, E. F. (1997). Methodological artifacts in moderated multiple regression and their effects on statistical power. *Journal of*

Applied Psychology, 82(1), 192-206. https://doi.org/10.1037/0021-9010.82.1.192

11. Aguinis, H., Boik, R. J., & Pierce, C. A. (2001). A generalized solution for approximating the power to detect effects of categorical moderator variables using multiple regression. *Organizational Research Methods, 4*(4), 291-323. https://doi.org/10.1177/109442810144001

12. Aguinis H. (2004). *Regression analysis for categorical moderators.* Guilford.

13. Shen, W., Kiger, T. B., Davies, S. E., Rasch, R. L., Simon, K. M., & Ones, D. (2011). Samples in applied psychology: Over a decade of research in review. *Journal of Applied Psychology, 96*(5), 1055-1064. https://doi.org/10.1037/a0023322

14. Aguinis, H., Beaty, J. C., Boik, R. J., & Pierce, C. A. (2005). Effect size and power in assessing moderating effects of categorical variables using multiple regression: A 30-year review. *Journal of Applied Psychology, 90*(1), 94-107. https://doi.org/10.1037/0021-9010.90.1.94

15. MacCallum, R., Zhang, S., Preacher, K. J., & Rucker, D. D. (2002). On the practice of dichotomization of quantitative variables. *Psychological Methods, 7*(1), 19-40. https://doi.org/10.1037/1082-989X.7.1.19

16. Aguinis, H. (1995). Statistical power problems with moderated multiple regression in management research. *Journal of Management, 21*(6), 1141-1158. https://doi.org/10.1016/0149-2063(95)90026-8

17. Maxwell, S. E., & Delaney, H. D. (1993). Bivariate median splits and spurious statistical significance. *Psychological Bulletin, 113*(1), 181-190. https://doi.org/10.1037/0033-2909.113.1.181

18. Aguinis H., & Gottfredson, R. K. (2010). Best-practice recommendations for estimating interaction effects using moderated multiple regression. *Journal of Organizational Behavior, 31*(6), 776-786. https://doi.org/10.1002/job.686

19. Dalal, D. K., & Zickar, M. J. (2012). Some common myths about centering predictor variables in moderated multiple regression and polynomial regression. *Organizational Research Methods, 15*(3), 339-362. https://doi.org/10.1177/1094428111430540

20. Cohen, J. (1978). Partialed products *are* interactions; Partialed powers *are* curve components. *Psychological Bulletin, 85*(4), 858-866. https://doi.org/10.1037/0033-2909.85.4.858

21. Aiken, L. A., & West, S. G. (1991). *Multiple regression: Testing and interpreting interactions.* Sage.

22. Aiken, L. A., & West, S. G. (1991). *Multiple regression: Testing and interpreting interactions.* Sage.

23. Rogers, W. M. (2002). Theoretical and mathematical constraints of interaction regression models. *Organizational Research Methods, 5*(3), 212-230. https://doi.org/10.1177/1094428102005003002

24. Aiken, L. A., & West, S. G. (1991). *Multiple regression: Testing and interpreting interactions.* Sage.

25. Aguinis H. (2004). *Regression analysis for categorical moderators.* Guilford.

26. Murphy, K. R., & Aguinis, H. (2022). Reporting interactions: Visualization, effect size, and interpretation. *Journal of Management.* https://doi.org/10.1177/01492063221088516

27. Sherf, E. N. & Morrison, E. W. (2020). I do not need feedback! Or do I? Self-efficacy, perspective taking, and feedback seeking. *Journal of Applied Psychology, 105*(2), 146-165. https://doi.org/10.1037/apl0000432

28. Aguinis, H., Culpepper, S. A., & Pierce, C. A. (2010). Revival of test bias research in preemployment testing. *Journal of Applied Psychology, 95*(4), 648-680. https://doi.org/10.1037/a0018714

29. Ndofor, H. A., Sirmon, D. G., & He, X. (2011). Firm resources, competitive actions and performance: Investigating a mediated model with evidence from in-vitro diagnostics industry. *Strategic Management Journal, 32*(6), 640-657. https://doi.org/10.1002/smj.901

30. Child, J. (1972). Organizational structure, environment and performance: The role of strategic choice. *Sociology, 6*(1), 1-22. https://doi.org/10.1177/003803857200600101

31. MacKinnon, D. P. (2008). *Introduction to statistical mediation analysis.* Erlbaum.

32. Miller, T. L., Triana, M., Reutzel, C. R., & Certo, S. T. (2007). Mediation in strategic management research: Conceptual beginnings, current application, and future recommendations. In D. Ketchen & D. D. Bergh (Eds.), *Research methodology in strategy and management* (pp. 295-318). Emerald Group. https://doi.org/10.1016/S1479-8387(07)04010-6

33. Baron, R. M., & Kenny, D. A. (1986). The moderator-mediator variable distinction in social psychological research: Conceptual, strategic, and statistical considerations. *Journal of Personality and Social Psychology, 51*(6), 1173-1182. https://doi.org/10.1037/0022-3514.51.6.1173

34. MacKinnon, D. P., Lockwood, C. M., Hoffman, J. M., West, S. G., & Sheets, V. (2002). A comparison of methods to test mediation and other intervening variable effects. *Psychological Methods, 7*(1), 83-104. https://doi.org/10.1037/1082-989X.7.1.83

35. Kenny, D. A., Kashy, D. A., & Bolger, N. (1998). Data analysis in social psychology. *The Handbook of Social Psychology, 1*, 233-265.

36. Baron, R. M., & Kenny, D. A. (1986). The moderator-mediator variable distinction in social psychological research: Conceptual, strategic, and statistical considerations.

Journal of Personality and Social Psychology, 51(6), 1173-1182. https://doi.org/10.1037/0022-3514.51.6.1173

37. Miller, T. L., Triana, M., Reutzel, C. R., & Certo, S. T. (2007). Mediation in strategic management research: Conceptual beginnings, current application, and future recommendations. In D. Ketchen & D. D. Bergh (Eds.), *Research methodology in strategy and management* (pp. 295-318). Emerald Group. https://doi.org/10.1016/S1479-8387(07)04010-6

38. Anderson, T. W. (1984). *An introduction to multivariate statistical analysis* (2nd ed.). Wiley. https://doi.org/10.2307/2531310

39. Mooney, C. Z., & Duval, R. D. (1993). *Bootstrapping: A nonparametric approach to statistical inference.* Sage. https://doi.org/10.4135/9781412983532

40. MacKinnon, D. P., Lockwood, C. M., Hoffman, J. M., West, S. G., & Sheets, V. (2002). A comparison of methods to test mediation and other intervening variable effects. *Psychological Methods,7*(1), 83-104. https://doi.org/10.1037/1082-989X.7.1.83

41. Baron, R. M., & Kenny, D. A. (1986). The moderator-mediator variable distinction in social psychological research: Conceptual, strategic, and statistical considerations. *Journal of Personality and Social Psychology, 51*(6), 1173-1182. https://doi.org/10.1037/0022-3514.51.6.1173

42. Kenny, D. A., Kashy, D. A., & Bolger, N. (1998). Data analysis in social psychology. *The Handbook of Social Psychology, 1*, 233-265.

43. LeBreton, J. M., Wu, J., & Bing, M. N. (2008). The truth(s) on testing for mediation in the social and organizational sciences. In C. E. Lance & R. J. Vandenberg (Eds.), *Statistical and methodological myths and urban legends: Received doctrine, verity, and fable in the organizational and social sciences* (pp. 107-141). Routledge.

44. James, L. R., Mulaik, S. A., & Brett, J. M. (2006). A tale of two methods. *Organizational Research Methods, 9*(2), 233-244. https://doi.org/10.1177/1094428105285144

45. LeBreton, J. M., Wu, J., & Bing, M. N. (2008). The truth(s) on testing for mediation in the social and organizational sciences. In C. E. Lance & R. J. Vandenberg (Eds.), *Statistical and methodological myths and urban legends: Received doctrine, verity, and fable in the organizational and social sciences* (pp. 107-141). Routledge.

46. LeBreton, J. M., Wu, J., & Bing, M. N. (2008). The truth(s) on testing for mediation in the social and organizational sciences. In C. E. Lance & R. J. Vandenberg (Eds.), *Statistical and methodological myths and urban legends: Received doctrine, verity, and fable in the organizational and social sciences* (pp. 107-141). Routledge.

47. Maxwell, S. E., & Cole, D. A. (2007). Bias in cross-sectional analyses of longitudinal mediation. *Psychological Methods,12*(1), 23-44. https://doi.org/10.1037/1082-989X.12.1.23

48. Hom, P., & Haynes, K. T. (2007). Applying advanced panel methods to strategic management research: A tutorial. In D. J. Ketchen & D. D. Bergh (Eds.), *Research methodology in strategy and management* (Vol. 4, pp. 193-272). Emerald. https://doi.org/10.1016/S1479-8387(07)04008-8

49. Stone-Romero, E. F., & Rosopa, P. J. (2011). Experimental tests of mediation: Prospects, problems, and some solutions. *Organizational Research Methods, 14*(4), 631-646. https://doi.org/10.1177/1094428110372673

50. Holland, P. W. (1988). Causal inference, path analysis, and recursive structural equations models. In C. C. Clogg (Ed.), *Sociological methodology* (pp. 449-484). American Sociological Association. https://doi.org/10.2307/271055

51. Hamilton, B. H., & Nickerson, J. A. (2003). Correcting for endogeneity in strategic management research. *Strategic Organization, 1*(1), 51-78. https://doi.org/10.1177/1476127003001001218

52. Guidelines Regarding Empirical Research in SMJ (2022). https://onlinelibrary.wiley.com/pb-assets/assets/10970266/SMJ_Author_Instructions_January_2022-1641850654740.pdf

53. Semadeni, M., Withers, M.C., & Certo T. (2014). The perils of endogeneity and instrumental variables in strategy research: Understanding through simulation. *Strategic Management Journal, 35*(7), 1070-1079. https://doi.org/10.1002/smj.2136

54. Eden, D., Stone-Romero, E. F., & Rothstein, H. R. (2015). Synthesizing results of multiple randomized experiments to establish causality in mediation testing. *Human Resource Management Review, 25*(4), 342-351. https://doi.org/10.1016/j.hrmr.2015.02.001

55. Miller, T. L., Triana, M., Reutzel, C. R., & Certo, S. T. (2007). Mediation in strategic management research: Conceptual beginnings, current application, and future recommendations. In D. Ketchen & D. D. Bergh (Eds.), *Research methodology in strategy and management* (pp. 295-318). Emerald Group. https://doi.org/10.1016/S1479-8387(07)04010-6

56. Aguinis, H., & Edwards, J. R. (2014). Methodological wishes for the next decade and how to make wishes come true. *Journal of Management Studies,51*(1), 143-174. https://doi.org/10.1111/joms.12058

57. Bollen, K. A. (1989). *Structural equations with latent variables.* Wiley. https://doi.org/10.1002/9781118619179

58. Shook, C. L., Ketchen, D. J., Jr., Hult, G. T. M., & Kacmar, K. M. (2004). An assessment of the use of structural equation modeling in strategic management research. *Strategic Management Journal,*

25(4), 397-404. https://doi.org/10.1002/smj.385

59. DeShon, R.P. (1998). A cautionary note on measurement error corrections in structural equation models. *Psychological Methods, 3*(4), 412-423. https://doi.org/10.1037/1082-989X.3.4.412

60. Grant, A. M., & Wall, T. D. (2009). The neglected science and art of quasi-experimentation: Why-to, when-to, and how-to advice for organizational researchers. *Organizational Research Methods, 12*(4), 653-686. https://doi.org/10.1177/1094428108320737

61. Ree, M. J., & Carretta, T. R. (2006). The role of measurement error in familiar statistics. *Organizational Research Methods, 9*(1), 99-112. https://doi.org/10.1177/1094428105283192

62. Porter, A. C., & Raudenbush, S. W. (1987). Analysis of covariance: Its model and use in psychological research. *Journal of Counseling Psychology, 34*(4), 383-392. https://doi.org/10.1037/0022-0167.34.4.383

63. Raaijmakers, J. G. W., & Pieters, L. P. M. (1987). Measurement error and ANCOVA: Functional and structural relationship approaches. *Psychometrika, 52*, 521-538. https://doi.org/10.1007/BF02294817

64. Warren, R. D., White, J. K., & Fuller, W. A. (1974). An errors-in-variables analysis of managerial role performance. *Journal of the American Statistical Association, 69*(348), 886-893. https://doi.org/10.1080/01621459.1974.10480223

65. Lord, F. M. (1960). Large-sample covariance analysis when the control variable is fallible. *Journal of the American Statistical Association, 55*(290), 307-321. https://doi.org/10.1080/01621459.1960.10482065

66. Raaijmakers, J. G. W., & Pieters, L. P. M. (1987). Measurement error and ANCOVA: Functional and structural relationship approaches. *Psychometrika, 52*,

521-538. https://doi.org/10.1007/BF02294817

67. Hayduk, L. A. (1996). *LISREL Issues, Debates, and Strategies*. Johns Hopkins University Press.

68. Culpepper, S. A., & Aguinis, H. (2011). R is for revolution: A cutting-edge, free, open source statistical package. *Organizational Research Methods, 14*(4), 735-740. https://doi.org/10.1177/1094428109355485

69. Arvey, R. D., Cole, D. A., Hazucha, J. F., & Hartanto, F. M. (1985). Statistical power of training evaluation designs. *Personnel Psychology, 38*(3), 493-507. https://doi.org/10.1111/j.1744-6570.1985.tb00556.x

70. Kim, W. C., Hwang, P., & Burgers, W. P. (1993). Multinationals' diversification and the risk-return trade-off. *Strategic Management Journal, 14*(4), 275-286. https://doi.org/10.1002/smj.4250140404

71. Phillips, C. (2011). *Six questions of Socrates: A modern-day journey of discovery through world philosophy*. WW Norton & Company.

72. Confucius. (2004). *The doctrine of the mean*. Kessinger Publishing.

73. Hamburger, M. (1959). Aristotle and Confucius: A comparison. *Journal of the History of Ideas*, 236-249. https://doi.org/10.2307/2707821

74. Confucius. (2004). *The doctrine of the mean*. Kessinger Publishing.

75. Barney, J. (1991). Firm resources and sustained competitive advantage. *Journal of Management, 17*(1), 99-120. https://doi.org/10.1177/014920639101700108

76. Barrick, M. R., & Mount, M. K. (1991). The big five personality dimensions and job performance: a meta-analysis. *Personnel Psychology, 44*(1), 1-26. https://doi.org/10.1111/j.1744-6570.1991.tb00688.x

77. Abrahamson, E., & Fairchild, G. (1999). Management fashion: Life-cycles, triggers, and collective

learning processes. *Administrative Science Quarterly, 44*(4), 708-740. https://doi.org/10.2307/2667053

78. David, R. J., & Strang, D. (2006). When fashion is fleeting: Transitory collective beliefs and the dynamics of TQM consulting. *Academy of Management Journal, 49*(2), 215-233. https://doi.org/10.5465/amj.2006.20786058

79. Platt, J. R. (1964). Strong Inference: Certain systematic methods of scientific thinking may produce much more rapid progress than others. *Science, 146*(3642), 347-353. https://doi.org/10.1126/science.146.3642.347

80. Bacharach, S. B. (1989). Organizational theories: Some criteria for evaluation. *Academy of Management Review, 14*(4), 496-515. https://doi.org/10.2307/258555

81. Richter, F. M. (1986). Heuristics and the study of human behavior. In D. W. Fiske, & R. A. Shweder (Eds.), *Metatheory in social science: Pluralisms and subjectivities* (pp. 271-283). University of Chicago Press.

82. Aguinis, H., Dalton, D. R., Bosco, F. A., Pierce, C. A., & Dalton, C. M. (2011). Meta-analytic choices and judgment calls: Implications for theory building and testing, obtained effect sizes, and scholarly impact. *Journal of Management, 37*(1), 5-38. https://doi.org/10.1177/0149206310377113

83. Locke, E. A. (2007). The case for inductive theory building. *Journal of Management, 33*(6), 867-890. https://doi.org/10.1177/0149206307307636

84. Lewis, M. W. (2000). Exploring paradox: Toward a more comprehensive guide. *Academy of Management Review, 25*(4), 760-776. https://doi.org/10.5465/amr.2000.3707712

85. Poole, M. S., & Van de Ven, A. H. (1989). Using paradox to build management and organization theories. *Academy of Management*

Review, 14(4), 562-578. https://doi.org/10.2307/258559

86. Richter, F. M. (1986). Heuristics and the study of human behavior. In D. W. Fiske, & R. A. Shweder (Eds.), *Metatheory in social science: Pluralisms and subjectivities* (pp. 271-283). University of Chicago Press.

87. Hastie, R. K., & Dawes, R. M. (2001). *Rational choice in an uncertain world: The psychology of judgment and decision making.* Sage Publications.

88. Einhorn, H. J., & Hogarth, R. M. (1975). Unit weighting schemes for decision making. *Organizational Behavior and Human Performance, 13*(2), 171-192. https://doi.org/10.1016/0030-5073(75)90044-6

89. Harris, K. J., & Kacmar, K. M. (2006). Too much of a good thing: The curvilinear effect of leader-member exchange on stress. *The Journal of Social Psychology, 146*(1), 65-84. https://doi.org/10.3200/SOCP.146.1.65-84

90. Whetzel, D. L., McDaniel, M. A., Yost, A. P., & Kim, N. (2010). Linearity of personality–performance relationships: A large-scale examination. *International Journal of Selection and Assessment, 18*(3), 310-320. https://doi.org/10.1111/j.1468-2389.2010.00514.x

91. Xie, J. L., & Johns, G. (1995). Job scope and stress: Can job scope be too high?. *Academy of Management Journal, 38*(5), 1288-1309. https://doi.org/10.5465/256858

92. Sturman, M. C. (2003). Searching for the inverted U-shaped relationship between time and performance: Meta-analyses of the experience/performance, tenure/performance, and age/performance relationships. *Journal of Management, 29*(5), 609-640. https://doi.org/10.1016/S0149-2063(03)00028-X

93. Chrisman, J. J., McMullan, E., & Hall, J. (2005). The influence of guided preparation on the long-term performance of new ventures. *Journal of Business*

Venturing, 20(6), 769-791. https://doi.org/10.1016/j.jbusvent.2004.10.001

94. Ramezani, C. A., Soenen, L., & Jung, A. (2002). Growth, corporate profitability, and value creation. *Financial Analysts Journal, 58*(6), 56-67. https://doi.org/10.2469/faj.v58.n6.2486

95. Qian, G., Li, L., Li, J., & Qian, Z. (2008). Regional diversification and firm performance. *Journal of International Business Studies, 39*(2), 197-214. https://doi.org/10.1057/palgrave.jibs.8400346

96. Tseng, C. H., Tansuhaj, P., Hallagan, W., & McCullough, J. (2007). Effects of firm resources on growth in multinationality. *Journal of International Business Studies, 38*(6), 961-974. https://doi.org/10.1057/palgrave.jibs.8400305

97. Einstein, A. (1934). On the method of theoretical physics. *Philosophy of Science, 1*(2), 163-169. https://doi.org/10.1086/286316

98. Edwards, J. R., & Berry, J. W. (2010). The presence of something or the absence of nothing: Increasing theoretical precision in management research. *Organizational Research Methods, 13*(4), 668-689. https://doi.org/10.1177/1094428110380467

99. Gray, P. H., & Cooper, W. H. (2010). Pursuing failure. *Organizational Research Methods, 13*(4), 620-643. https://doi.org/10.1177/1094428109356114

100. Aguinis, H. (2004). *Regression analysis for categorical moderators.* The Guilford Press.

101. Weisberg, S. (2005). *Applied linear regression.* (3rd ed.). Wiley. https://doi.org/10.1002/0471704091

102. Aguinis, H. (2004). *Regression analysis for categorical moderators.* The Guilford Press.

103. Aristotle. (2000). *Nicomachean ethics, Book I* (Translated by, R. Crisp) (Electronic edition). Cambridge University Press. http://www.netlibrary.com/urlapi.asp?

action=summary&v=1bookid=112436.

104. Le, H., Oh, I. S., Robbins, S. B., Ilies, R., Holland, E., & Westrick, P. (2011). Too much of a good thing: Curvilinear relationships between personality traits and job performance. *Journal of Applied Psychology, 96*(1), 113-133. https://doi.org/10.1037/a0021016

105. Aguinis, H., Werner, S., Lanza Abbott, J., Angert, C., Park, J. H., & Kohlhausen, D. (2010). Customer-centric science: Reporting significant research results with rigor, relevance, and practical impact in mind. *Organizational Research Methods, 13*(3), 515-539. https://doi.org/10.1177/1094428109333339

106. Aguinis, H. (2004). *Regression analysis for categorical moderators.* The Guilford Press.

107. Cortina, J. M., & Landis, R. S. (2009). When small effect sizes tell a big story, and when large effect sizes don't. In C. E. Lance, & R. J. Vandenberg (Eds.), *Statistical and methodological myths and urban legends: Doctrine, verity and fable in the organizational and social sciences* (pp. 287-308). Routledge.

108. Aguinis, H., & Gottfredson, R. K. (2010). Best-practice recommendations for estimating interaction effects using moderated multiple regression. *Journal of Organizational Behavior, 31*(6), 776-786. https://doi.org/10.1002/job.686

109. Heckman, J. J. (1979). Sample selection bias as a specification error. *Econometrica: Journal of the Econometric Society*, 153-161. https://doi.org/10.2307/1912352

110. Thorndike, R. L. (1949). *Personnel selection: Test and measurement techniques.* Wiley.

111. Hunter, J. E., Schmidt, F. L., & Le, H. (2006). Implications of direct and indirect range restriction for meta-analysis methods and findings. *Journal of Applied Psychology, 91*(3), 594. https://doi.org/10.1037/0021-9010.91.3.594

112. Sturman, M. C. (2003). Searching for the inverted U-shaped relationship between time and performance: Meta-analyses of the experience/performance, tenure/performance, and age/performance relationships. *Journal of Management*, *29*(5), 609-640. https://doi.org/10.1016/S0149-2063(03)00028-X

113. Aguinis, H., Pierce, C. A., Bosco, F. A., & Muslin, I. S. (2009). First decade of Organizational Research Methods: Trends in design, measurement, and data-analysis topics. *Organizational Research Methods*, *12*(1), 69-112. https://doi.org/10.1177/1094428108322641

114. Rousseau, D. M., Manning, J., & Denyer, D. (2008). 11 Evidence in management and organizational science: assembling the field's full weight of scientific knowledge through syntheses. *Academy of Management Annals*, *2*(1), 475-515. https://doi.org/10.5465/19416520802211651

115. Rousseau, D. M., Manning, J., & Denyer, D. (2008). 11 Evidence in management and organizational science: assembling the field's full weight of scientific knowledge through syntheses. *Academy of Management Annals*, *2*(1), 475-515. https://doi.org/10.5465/19416520802211651

116. Sturman, M. C. (2003). Searching for the inverted U-shaped relationship between time and performance: Meta-analyses of the experience/performance, tenure/performance, and age/performance relationships. *Journal of Management*, *29*(5), 609-640. https://doi.org/10.1016/S0149-2063(03)00028-X

117. Ilies, R., Scott, B. A., & Judge, T. A. (2006). The interactive effects of personal traits and experienced states on intraindividual patterns of citizenship behavior. *Academy of Management Journal*, *49*(3), 561-575. https://doi.org/10.5465/amj.2006.21794672

118. Ployhart, R. E., & Vandenberg, R. J. (2010). Longitudinal research: The theory, design, and analysis of change. *Journal of Management*, *36*(1), 94-120. https://doi.org/10.1177/0149206309352110

119. Ployhart, R. E., & Vandenberg, R. J. (2010). Longitudinal research: The theory, design, and analysis of change. *Journal of Management*, *36*(1), 94-120. https://doi.org/10.1177/0149206309352110

120. Chan, D. (1998). The conceptualization and analysis of change over time: An integrative approach incorporating longitudinal mean and covariance structures analysis (LMACS) and multiple indicator latent growth modeling (MLGM). *Organizational Research Methods*, *1*(4), 421-483. https://doi.org/10.1177/109442819814004

CHAPTER 10

1. Aguinis, H., Boyd, B. K., Pierce, C. A., & Short, J. C. (2011). Walking new avenues in management research methods and theories: Bridging micro and macro domains. *Journal of Management*, *37*(2), 395-403. https://journals.sagepub.com/doi/10.1177/0149206310382456

2. Molloy, J. C., Ployhart, R. E., & Wright, P. M. (2011). The myth of "the" micro-macro divide: Bridging system-level and disciplinary divides. *Journal of Management*, *37*(2), 581-609. https://journals.sagepub.com/doi/10.1177/0149206310365000

3. Snijders, T. A. B., & Bosker, R. J. (2012). *Multilevel analysis: An introduction to basic and advanced multilevel modeling* (2nd edition). Sage.

4. Kenny, D. A., & Judd, C. M. (1996). A general procedure for the estimation of interdependence. *Psychological Bulletin*, *119*(1), 138-148. https://psycnet.apa.org/doi/10.1037/0033-2909.119.1.138

5. Bliese, P. D., & Hanges, P. J. (2004). Being both too liberal and too conservative: The perils of treating grouped data as though they were independent. *Organizational Research Methods*, *7*(4), 400-417. https://journals.sagepub.com/doi/10.1177/1094428104268542

6. Bliese, P. D. (2000). Within-group agreement, non-independence, and reliability: Implications for data aggregation and analysis. In K. J. Klein & S. W. J. Kozlowski (Eds.), *Multilevel theory, research, and methods in organizations: Foundations, extensions, and new directions* (pp. 349-381). Jossey-Bass.

7. Hox, J. (2010). *Multilevel analysis: Techniques and applications* (2nd edition). Routledge.

8. Chen, G., Kirkman, B. L., Kanfer, R., Allen, D., & Rosen, B. (2007). A multilevel study of leadership, empowerment, and performance in teams. *Journal of Applied Psychology*, *92*(2), 331-346. https://psycnet.apa.org/doi/10.1037/0021-9010.92.2.331

9. Preacher, K. J., Zyphur, M. J., & Zhang, Z. (2010). A general multilevel SEM framework for assessing multilevel mediation. *Psychological Methods*, *15*(3), 209-233. https://psycnet.apa.org/doi/10.1037/a0020141

10. Aguinis, H., Gottfredson, R. K., & Culpepper, S. A. (2013). Best-practice recommendations for estimating cross-level interaction effects using multilevel modeling. *Journal of Management*, *39*(6), 1490-1528. https://journals.sagepub.com/doi/10.1177/0149206313478188

11. Raudenbush, S. W., & Bryk, A. S. (2002). *Hierarchical linear models: Applications and data analysis methods* (2nd edition). Sage.

12. Mathieu, J. E., Aguinis, H., Culpepper, S. A., & Chen, G. (2012). Understanding and estimating the power to detect cross-level interaction effects in multilevel modeling. *Journal of Applied Psychology*, *97*(5), 951-966. https://psycnet.apa.org/doi/10.1037/a0028380

13. Culpepper, S. A. (2010). Studying individual differences in predictability with gamma regression and nonlinear multilevel models. *Multivariate Behavioral Research, 45*(1), 153-185. https://doi.org/10.1080/00273170903504885

14. Aguinis, H., Beaty, J. C., Boik, R. J., & Pierce, C. A. (2005). Effect size and power in assessing moderating effects of categorical variables using multiple regression: A 30-year review. *Journal of Applied Psychology, 90*(1), 94-107. https://psycnet.apa.org/doi/10.1037/0021-9010.90.1.94

15. Mathieu, J. E., & Chen, G. (2011). The etiology of the multilevel paradigm in management research. *Journal of Management, 37*(2), 610-641. https://journals.sagepub.com/doi/10.1177/0149206310364663

16. Kreft, I., & De Leeuw, J. (1998). *Introducing multilevel modeling.* Sage.

17. Enders, C. K., & Tofighi, D. (2007). Centering predictor variables in cross-sectional multilevel models: A new look at an old issue. *Psychological Methods, 12*(2), 121-138. https://psycnet.apa.org/doi/10.1037/1082-989X.12.2.121

18. Clarke, P., & Wheaton, B. (2007). Addressing data sparseness in contextual population research. *Sociological Methods & Research, 35*(3), 311-351. https://journals.sagepub.com/doi/10.1177/0049124106292362

19. Hofmann, D. A., & Gavin, M. B. (1998). Centering decisions in hierarchical linear models: Theoretical and methodological implications for organizational science. *Journal of Management, 24*(5), 623-641. https://doi.org/10.1177%2F014920639802400504

20. Enders, C. K., & Tofighi, D. (2007). Centering predictor variables in cross-sectional multilevel models: A new look at an old issue. *Psychological Methods, 12*(2), 121-138. https://psycnet.apa.org/doi/10.1037/1082-989X.12.2.121

21. Raudenbush, S. W., & Liu, X. (2000). Statistical power and optimal design for multisite randomized trials. *Psychological Methods, 5*(2), 199-213. https://psycnet.apa.org/doi/10.1037/1082-989X.5.2.199

22. Raudenbush, S. W., & Liu, X. (2000). Statistical power and optimal design for multisite randomized trials. *Psychological Methods, 5*(2), 199-213. https://psycnet.apa.org/doi/10.1037/1082-989X.5.2.199

23. Spybrook, J., Raudenbush, S. W., Congdon, R., & Martinez, A. (2009). *Optimal design for longitudinal and multilevel research: Documentation for the "Optimal Design" Software* (Version 2.0).

24. Bosker, R. J., Snijders, T. A. B., & Guldemond. (2003). *PINT (Power IN Two-level designs): Estimating standard errors of regression coefficients in hierarchical linear models for power calculations*. User's manual. (Version 2.1).

25. Scherbaum, C. A., & Ferreter, J. M. (2009). Estimating statistical power and required sample sizes for organizational research using multilevel modeling. *Organizational Research Methods, 12*(2), 347-367. https://journals.sagepub.com/doi/10.1177/1094428107308906

26. Hox, J. J. (2010). *Multilevel analysis: Techniques and Applications* (2nd edition). Routledge.

27. Enders, C. K., & Tofighi, D. (2007). Centering predictor variables in cross-sectional multilevel models: A new look at an old issue. *Psychological Methods, 12*(2), 121-138. https://psycnet.apa.org/doi/10.1037/1082-989X.12.2.121

28. Snijders, T. A. B., & Bosker, R. J. (1993). Standard errors and sample sizes for two-level research. *Journal of Educational Statistics, 18*(3), 237-259. https://journals.sagepub.com/doi/10.3102/10769986018003237

29. Mathieu, J. E., Aguinis, H., Culpepper, S. A., & Chen, G. (2012). Understanding and estimating the power to detect cross-level interaction effects in multilevel modeling. *Journal of Applied Psychology, 97*(5), 951-966. https://psycnet.apa.org/doi/10.1037/a0028380

30. Kahn, J. H. (2011). Multilevel modeling: Overview and applications to research in counseling psychology. *Journal of Counseling Psychology, 58*(2), 257-271. https://psycnet.apa.org/doi/10.1037/a0022680

31. Mathieu, J. E., Aguinis, H., Culpepper, S. A., & Chen, G. (2012). Understanding and estimating the power to detect cross-level interaction effects in multilevel modeling. *Journal of Applied Psychology, 97*(5), 951-966. https://psycnet.apa.org/doi/10.1037/a0028380

32. Hedges, L. V., & Hedberg, E. C. (2007). Intraclass correlation values for planning group-randomized trials in education. *Educational Evaluation and Policy Analysis, 29*(1), 60-87. https://journals.sagepub.com/doi/10.3102/0162373707299706

33. Peugh, J. L. (2010). A practical guide to multilevel modeling. *Journal of School Psychology, 48*(1), 85-112. https://doi.org/10.1016/j.jsp.2009.09.002

34. Liden, R. C., & Antonakis, J. (2009). Considering context in psychological leadership research. *Human Relations, 62*(11), 1587-1605. https://journals.sagepub.com/doi/abs/10.1177/0018726709346374

35. Enders, C. K., & Tofighi, D. (2007). Centering predictor variables in cross-sectional multilevel models: A new look at an old issue. *Psychological Methods, 12*(2), 121-138. https://psycnet.apa.org/doi/10.1037/1082-989X.12.2.121

36. Culpepper, S. A., & Aguinis, H. (2011). Using analysis of covariance (ANCOVA) with fallible covariates. *Psychological Methods, 16*(2), 166-178. https://psycnet.apa.org/doi/10.1037/a0023355

37. Bliese, P. D. (2002). Multilevel random coefficient modeling in organizational research: Examples using SAS and S-PLUS. In

F. Drasgow & N. Schmitt (Eds.), *Measuring and analyzing behavior in organizations: Advances in measurement and data analysis* (pp. 401-445). Jossey-Bass.

38. Maas, C. J. M., & Hox, J. J. (2004). The influence of violations of assumptions on multilevel parameter estimates and their standard errors. *Computational Statistics & Data Analysis, 46*(3), 427-440. https://doi.org/10.1016/j.csda.2003.08.006

39. Snijders, T. A. B., & Bosker, R. J. (2012). *Multilevel analysis: An introduction to basic and advanced multilevel modeling* (2nd edition). Sage.

40. Carpenter, J. R., Goldstein, H., & Rasbash, J. (2003). A novel bootstrap procedure for assessing the relationship between class size and achievement. *Applied Statistics, 52*(4), 431-443. https://doi.org/10.1111/1467-9876.00415

41. Field, C. A., & Welsh, A. H. (2007). Bootstrapping clustered data. *Journal of the Royal Statistical Society-B, 69*(3), 369-390. https://doi.org/10.1111/j.1467-9868.2007.00593.x

42. Bliese, P. D. (2002). Multilevel random coefficient modeling in organizational research: Examples using SAS and S-PLUS. In F. Drasgow & N. Schmitt (Eds.), *Measuring and analyzing behavior in organizations: Advances in measurement and data analysis* (pp. 401-445). Jossey-Bass.

43. Peugh, J. L. (2010). A practical guide to multilevel modeling. *Journal of School Psychology, 48*(1), 85-112. https://doi.org/10.1016/j.jsp.2009.09.002

44. Dalton, D. R., Aguinis, H., Dalton, C. A., Bosco, F. A., & Pierce, C. A. (2012). Revisiting the file drawer problem in meta-analysis: An empirical assessment of published and non-published correlation matrices. *Personnel Psychology, 65*(2), 221-249. https://doi.org/10.1111/j.1744-6570.2012.01243.x

45. Mathieu, J. E., Aguinis, H., Culpepper, S. A., & Chen, G. (2012). Understanding and estimating the power to detect cross-level interaction effects in multilevel modeling. *Journal of Applied Psychology, 97*(5), 951-966. https://psycnet.apa.org/doi/10.1037/a0028380

46. Maxwell, S. E. (2004). The persistence of underpowered studies in psychological research: Causes, consequences, and remedies. *Psychological Methods, 9*(2), 147-163. https://psycnet.apa.org/doi/10.1037/1082-989X.9.2.147

47. Stram, D., & Lee, J.W. (1994). Variance components testing in the longitudinal mixed effects model. *Biometrics, 50*(4), 1171-1177. https://doi.org/10.2307/2533455

48. Crainiceanu, C., & Ruppert, D. (2004). Likelihood ratio tests in linear mixed models with one variance component. *Journal of the Royal Statistical Society-B, 66*(1), 165-185. https://doi.org/10.1111/j.1467-9868.2004.00438.x

49. Scheipl, F., Greven, S., & Kuechenhoff, H. (2008). Size and power of tests for a zero random effect variance or polynomial regression in additive and linear mixed models. *Computational Statistics & Data Analysis, 52*(7), 3283-3299. https://doi.org/10.1016/j.csda.2007.10.022

50. Crainiceanu, C., & Ruppert, D. (2004). Likelihood ratio tests in linear mixed models with one variance component. *Journal of the Royal Statistical Society-B, 66*(1), 165-185. https://doi.org/10.1111/j.1467-9868.2004.00438.x

51. Hox, J. J. (2010). *Multilevel analysis: Techniques and applications* (2nd edition). Routledge.

52. Heck, R. H., Thomas, S. L., & Tabata, L. N. (2010). *Multilevel and longitudinal modeling with IBM SPSS*. Routledge.

53. Hülsheger, U. R., Alberts, H. J. E. M., Feinholdt, A., & Lang, J. W. B. (2013). Benefits of mindfulness at work: The role of mindfulness in emotion regulation, emotional exhaustion, and job satisfaction. *Journal of Applied Psychology, 98*(2), 310-325. https://psycnet.apa.org/doi/10.1037/a0031313

54. Snijders, T. A. B., & Bosker, R. J. (2012). *Multilevel analysis: An introduction to basic and advanced multilevel modeling* (2nd edition). Sage.

55. Aguinis, H., & Culpepper, S. A. (2015). An expanded decision-making procedure for examining cross-level interaction effects with multilevel modeling. *Organizational Research Methods, 18*(2), 155-176. https://journals.sagepub.com/doi/10.1177/1094428114563618

56. LeBreton, J. M., & Senter, J. L. (2008). Answers to 20 questions about interrater reliability and interrater agreement. *Organizational Research Methods, 11*(4), 815-852. https://journals.sagepub.com/doi/10.1177/1094428106296642

57. Bosco, F. A., Aguinis, H., Singh, K., Field, J. G., & Pierce, C. A. (2014). Correlational effect size benchmarks. *Journal of Applied Psychology, 100*(2), 431-449. https://psycnet.apa.org/doi/10.1037/a0038047

58. Cortina, J.M. & Landis, R.S. (2009). When small effect sizes tell a big story, and when large effect sizes don't. In C. E. Lance & R. J. Vandenberg (Eds.), *Statistical and methodological myths and urban legends: Doctrine, verity, and fable in the organizational and social sciences* (pp. 287-308). Routledge.

59. Aguinis, H., Beaty, J. C., Boik, R. J., & Pierce, C. A. (2005). Effect size and power in assessing moderating effects of categorical variables using multiple regression: A 30-year review. *Journal of Applied Psychology, 90*(1), 94-107. https://psycnet.apa.org/doi/10.1037/0021-9010.90.1.94

60. Aguinis, H., Werner, S., Abbott, J. L., Angert, C., Park, J. H., & Kohlhausen, D. (2010). Customer-centric science: Reporting significant research results with rigor, relevance, and practical impact

in mind. *Organizational Research Methods, 13*(3), 515-539. https://journals.sagepub.com/doi/10.1177/1094428109333339

61. Aguinis, H., Gottfredson, R. K., & Wright, T. A. (2011). Best-practice recommendations for estimating interaction effects using meta-analysis. *Journal of Organizational Behavior, 32*(8), 1033-1043. https://doi.org/10.1002/job.719

62. Raudenbush, S. W., & Bryk, A. S. (2002). *Hierarchical linear models: Applications and data analysis methods* (2nd edition). Sage.

63. Kreft, I., & De Leeuw, J. (1998). *Introducing multilevel modeling.* Sage.

64. Liden, R. C., & Antonakis, J. (2009). Considering context in psychological leadership research. *Human Relations, 62*(11), 1587-1605. https://journals.sagepub.com/doi/10.1177/0018726709346374

65. Mathieu, J. E., Aguinis, H., Culpepper, S. A., & Chen, G. (2012). Understanding and estimating the power to detect cross-level interaction effects in multilevel modeling. *Journal of Applied Psychology, 97*(5), 951-966. https://psycnet.apa.org/doi/10.1037/a0028380

66. Aguinis, H. (2004). *Regression analysis for categorical moderators.* Guilford.

67. Dalal, D. K., & Zickar, M. J. (2012). Some common myths about centering predictor variables in moderated multiple regression and polynomial regression. *Organizational Research Methods, 15*(3), 339-362. https://journals.sagepub.com/doi/10.1177/1094428111430540

68. Enders, C. K., & Tofighi, D. (2007). Centering predictor variables in cross-sectional multilevel models: A new look at an old issue. *Psychological Methods, 12*(2), 121-138. https://psycnet.apa.org/doi/10.1037/1082-989X.12.2.121

69. Dalton, D. R., & Aguinis, H. (2013). Measurement malaise in strategic management studies: The case of corporate governance research. *Organizational Research Methods,*

16(1), 88-99. https://journals.sagepub.com/doi/abs/10.1177/1094428112470846

70. Enders, C. K., & Tofighi, D. (2007). Centering predictor variables in cross-sectional multilevel models: A new look at an old issue. *Psychological Methods, 12*(2), 121-138. https://psycnet.apa.org/doi/10.1037/1082-989X.12.2.121

71. Hofmann, D. A., & Gavin, M. B. (1998). Centering decisions in hierarchical linear models: Theoretical and methodological implications for organizational science. *Journal of Management, 24*(5), 623-641. https://journals.sagepub.com/doi/10.1177/014920639802400504

72. Bliese, P. D. (2002). Multilevel random coefficient modeling in organizational research: Examples using SAS and S-PLUS. In F. Drasgow & N. Schmitt (Eds.), *Measuring and analyzing behavior in organizations: Advances in measurement and data analysis* (p. 401-445). Jossey-Bass.

73. Aguinis, H. (2004). *Regression analysis for categorical moderators.* Guilford.

74. Preacher, K. J., Curran, P. J., & Bauer, D. J. (2006). Computational tools for probing interaction effects in multiple linear regression, multilevel modeling, and latent curve analysis. *Journal of Educational and Behavioral Statistics, 31*(4), 437-448. https://journals.sagepub.com/doi/10.3102/10769986031004437

75. Aiken, L. S., & West, S. G. (1991). *Multiple regression: Testing and interpreting interactions.* Sage.

76. Aytug, Z. G., Rothstein, H. R., Zhou, W., & Kern, M. C. (2012). Revealed or concealed? Transparency of procedures, decisions, and judgment calls in meta-analyses. *Organizational Research Methods, 15*(1), 103-133. https://journals.sagepub.com/doi/10.1177/1094428111403495

77. Brutus, S., Aguinis, H., & Wassmer, U. (2013). Self-reported limitations and future directions in scholarly reports: Analysis and recommendations. *Journal of Management, 39*(1), 48-75. https://journals.sagepub.com/doi/10.1177/0149206312455245

78. Wolfinger, R. & O'Connell, M. (2007). Generalized linear mixed models: A pseudo-likelihood approach. *Journal of Statistical Computation and Simulation, 48*(3-4), 233-243. https://doi.org/10.1080/00949659308811554

79. Gelfand, A. E., Sahu, S. K., & Carlin, B. P. (1995). Efficient parametrisations for normal linear mixed models. *Biometrika, 82*(3), 479-488. https://doi.org/10.1093/biomet/82.3.479

80. Uy, M. A., Foo, M. D., & Aguinis, H. (2010). Using event sampling methodology to advance entrepreneurship theory and research. *Organizational Research Methods, 13*(1), 31-54. https://journals.sagepub.com/doi/10.1177/1094428109334977

81. Raudenbush, S. W., & Bryk, A. S. (2002). *Hierarchical linear models: Applications and data analysis methods* (2nd edition). Sage.

82. Snijders, T. A. B., & Bosker, R. J. (2012). *Multilevel analysis: An introduction to basic and advanced multilevel modeling* (2nd edition). Sage.

83. Raudenbush, S. W., Rowan, B., & Cheong, Y. F. (1993). Higher Order Instructional Goals in Secondary Schools: Class, Teacher, and School Influences. *American Educational Research Journal, 30*(3), 523-553. https://journals.sagepub.com/doi/10.3102/00028312030003523

84. Konstantopolous, S. (2008). The power of the test for treatment effects in three-level cluster randomized designs. *Journal of Research on Educational Effectiveness, 1*(1), 66-88. https://doi.org/10.1080/19345740701692522

85. Mathieu, J. E., Aguinis, H., Culpepper, S. A., & Chen, G. (2012).

Understanding and estimating the power to detect cross-level interaction effects in multilevel modeling. *Journal of Applied Psychology, 97*(5), 951-966. https://psycnet.apa.org/doi/10.1037/a0028380

86. Aguinis, H., Werner, S., Abbott, J. L., Angert, C., Park, J. H., & Kohlhausen, D. (2010). Customer-centric science: Reporting significant research results with rigor, relevance, and practical impact in mind. *Organizational Research Methods, 13*(3), 515-539. https://journals.sagepub.com/doi/10.1177/1094428109333339

87. Aguinis, H. (2004). *Regression analysis for categorical moderators.* Guilford.

88. Snijders, T. A. B., & Bosker, R. J. (2012). *Multilevel analysis: An introduction to basic and advanced multilevel modeling* (2nd edition). Sage.

89. Snijders, T. A. B., & Bosker, R. J. (2012). *Multilevel analysis: An introduction to basic and advanced multilevel modeling* (2nd edition). Sage.

90. Hox, J. (2010). *Multilevel analysis: Techniques and applications* (2nd edition). Routledge.

91. APA Publications and Communications Board Working Group on Journal Article Reporting Standards. (2008). Reporting standards for research in psychology: Why do we need them? What might they be? *American Psychologist, 63*(9), 839-851. https://doi.apa.org/10.1037/0003-066X.63.9.839

92. American Psychological Association. (2019). *Publication manual of the American Psychological Association* (7th edition). American Psychological Association.

93. Bedeian, A. G., Taylor, S. G., & Miller, A. N. (2010). Management science on the credibility bubble: Cardinal sins and various misdemeanors. *Academy of Management Learning and Education, 9*(4), 715-725. https://doi.org/10.5465/amle.9.4.zqr715

CHAPTER 11

1. Curran, P. J. (2009). The seemingly quixotic pursuit of a cumulative psychological science. *Psychological Methods, 14*(2), 77-80. https://psycnet.apa.org/doi/10.1037/a0015972

2. Schmidt, F. L. (1992). What do data really mean? Research findings, meta-analysis, and cumulative knowledge in psychology. *American Psychologist, 47*(10), 1173-1181. https://psycnet.apa.org/doi/10.1037/0003-066X.47.10.1173

3. Rousseau, D. M., Manning, J., & Denyer, D. (2008). Evidence in management and organizational science: Assembling the full weight of scientific knowledge through synthesis. *Academy of Management Annals, 2*(1), 475-515. https://doi.org/10.5465/19416520802211651

4. Aguinis, H., Dalton, D. R., Bosco, F. A., Pierce, C. A., & Dalton, C. M. (2011). Meta-analytic choices and judgment calls: Implications for theory building and testing, obtained effect sizes, and scholarly impact. *Journal of Management, 37*(1), 5-38. https://journals.sagepub.com/doi/abs/10.1177/0149206310377113

5. Borenstein, M., Hedges, L. V., Higgins, J. P. T., & Rothstein, H. R. (2009). *Introduction to meta-analysis.* John Wiley & Sons.

6. Aguinis, H., Pierce, C. A., Bosco, F. A., Dalton, D. R., & Dalton, C. M. (2011). Debunking myths and urban legends about meta-analysis. *Organizational Research Methods, 14*(2), 306-331. https://journals.sagepub.com/doi/10.1177/1094428110375720

7. Kulinskaya, E., Morgenthaler, S., & Staudte, R. G. (2008). *Meta analysis: A guide to calibrating and combining statistical evidence.* John Wiley & Sons.

8. Schmidt, F. L. (2008). Meta-analysis: A constantly evolving research integration tool. *Organizational Research Methods, 11*(1), 96-113. https://journals.sagepub.com/doi/10.1177/1094428107303161

9. Oh, I., Schmidt, F. L., Shaffer, J. A., & Le, H. (2008). The Graduate Management Admission Test (GMAT) is even more valid than we thought: A new development in meta-analysis and its implications for the validity of the GMAT. *Academy of Management Learning and Education, 7*(4), 563-570. https://doi.org/10.5465/amle.2008.35882196

10. Schulze, R., Holling, H., & Bohning, D. (2003). *Meta-analysis: New developments and applications in medical and social sciences.* Hogreffe & Huber Publishers.

11. Aguinis, H., Dalton, D. R., Bosco, F. A., Pierce, C. A., & Dalton, C. M. (2011). Meta-analytic choices and judgment calls: Implications for theory building and testing, obtained effect sizes, and scholarly impact. *Journal of Management, 37*(1), 5-38. https://doi.org/10.1177/0149206310377113

12. Hunter, J. E., & Schmidt, F. L. (2004). *Methods of meta-analysis: Correcting error and bias in research findings* (2nd edition). Sage.

13. Tsuji, S., Bergmann, C., & Cristia, A. (2014). Community-augmented meta-analyses: Toward cumulative data assessment. *Perspectives on Psychological Science, 9*(6), 661-665. https://journals.sagepub.com/doi/10.1177/1745691614552498

14. Klein, R. A., Vianello, M., Hasselman, F., Adams, B. G., Adams Jr, R. B., Alper, S., ... & Batra, R. (2018). Many Labs 2: Investigating variation in replicability across samples and settings. *Advances in Methods and Practices in Psychological Science, 1*(4), 443-490. https://journals.sagepub.com/doi/10.1177/2515245918810225

15. Tranfield, D., Denyer, D., & Smart, P. (2003). Towards a methodology for developing evidence-informed management knowledge by means of systematic review. *British Journal of Management, 14*(3), 207-222. https://doi.org/10.1111/1467-8551.00375

16. Denyer, D. & Tranfield, D. (2008). Producing a systematic review. In D. Buchanan (Ed.), *The Sage handbook of organizational research methods* (pp. 671–689). Sage.

17. Larsen, K. R., & Bong, C. H. (2016). A tool for addressing construct identity in literature reviews and meta-analyses. *MIS Quarterly, 40*(3), 529-551. https://www.jstor.org/stable/26629026

18. Gusenbauer, M. & Haddaway, N. R. (2020). Which academic search systems are suitable for systematic reviews or meta-analyses? Evaluating retrieval qualities of Google Scholar, PubMed, and 26 other resources. *Research Synthesis Methods, 11*(2), 181-217. https://doi.org/10.1002/jrsm.1378

19. Spellman, B. A. (2015). A short (personal) future history of revolution 2.0. *Perspectives onPsychological Science,* 10(6), 886-889. https://journals.sagepub.com/doi/full/10.1177/1745691615609918

20. Booth, A., Briscoe, S., & Wright, J. M. (2020). The "realist search": A systematic scoping review of current practice and reporting. *Research Synthesis Methods, 11*(1), 14-35. https://doi.org/10.1002/jrsm.1386

21. Aguinis, H., Ramani, R. S., & Alabduljader, N. (2018). What you see is what you get? Enhancing methodological transparency in management research. *Academy of Management Annals, 12*(1), 83-110. https://doi.org/10.5465/annals.2016.0011

22. Lee, C. I., Bosco, F. A., Steel, P., & Uggerslev, K. L. (2017). A metaBUS-enabled meta-analysis of career satisfaction. *Career Development International, 22*(5), 565-582. https://doi.org/10.1108/CDI-08-2017-0137

23. Rothstein, H. R., Sutton, A. J., & Borenstein, M. (2005). *Publication bias in meta-analysis: Prevention, assessment, and adjustments.* Wiley & Sons, Ltd.

24. Merton, R. K. (1968). The Matthew effect in science: The reward and communication systems of science are considered. *Science, 159*(3810), 56-63. https://doi.org/10.1126/science.159.3810.56

25. Moher, D., Liberati, A., Tetzlaff, J., & Altman, D. G. (2009). Preferred reporting items for systematic reviews and meta-analyses: the PRISMA statement. *Annals of Internal Medicine, 151*(4), 264-269. https://doi.org/10.7326/0003-4819-151-4-200908180-00135

26. Moher, D., Shamseer, L., Clarke, M., Ghersi, D., Liberati, A., Petticrew, M., Shekelle, P., & Stewart, L. A. (2015). Preferred reporting items for systematic review and meta-analysis protocols (PRISMA-P) 2015 statement. *Systematic Reviews, 4*(1), 1. https://doi.org/10.1186/2046-4053-4-1

27. Page, M. J., McKenzie, J. E., Bossuyt, P. M., Boutron, I., Hoffmann, T. C., Mulrow, C. D., ... & Moher, D. (2021). The PRISMA 2020 statement: An updated guideline for reporting systematic reviews. *International Journal of Surgery,* 88, 105906. https://doi.org/10.1016/j.ijsu.2021.105906

28. Kepes, S., McDaniel, M. A., Brannick, M. T., & Banks, G. C. (2013). Meta-analytic reviews in the organizational sciences: Two meta-analytic schools on the way to MARS (the Meta-analytic Reporting Standards). *Journal of Business and Psychology, 28*(2), 123-143. https://doi.org/10.1007/s10869-013-9300-2

29. Steel, P., Beugelsdijk, S., & Aguinis, H. (2021). The anatomy of an award-winning meta-analysis: Recommendations for authors, reviewers, and readers of meta-analytic reviews. *Journal of International Business Studies, 52*(1), 23-44. https://doi.org/10.1057/s41267-020-00385-z

30. DeSimone, J. A., Köhler, T., & Schoen, J. L. (2019). If it were only that easy: The use of meta-analytic research by organizational scholars. *Organizational Research Methods,* 22(4), 867-891. https://j

ournals.sagepub.com/doi/abs/10.1177/1094428118756743

31. Johnson, B.T., & Hennessy, E.A. (2019). Systematic reviews and meta-analyses in the health sciences: Best practice methods for research syntheses. *Social Science & Medicine, 233,* 237-251. https://doi.org/10.1016/j.socscimed.2019.05.035

32. Aguinis, H., Hill, N. S., & Bailey, J. R. (2021). Best practices in data collection and preparation: Recommendations for reviewers, editors, and authors. *Organizational Research Methods, 24*(4), 678-693. https://doi.org/10.1177/1094428119836485

33. Dahlke, J. A., & Wiernik, B. M. (2019). Psychmeta: An R package for psychometric meta-analysis. *Applied Psychological Measurement, 43*(5), 415-416. https://journals.sagepub.com/doi/10.1177/0146621618795933

34. Podsakoff, P. M., MacKenzie, S. B., & Podsakoff, N. P. (2012). Sources of method bias in social science research and recommendations on how to control it. *Annual Review of Psychology, 63,* 539-569. https://doi.org/10.1146/annurev-psych-120710-100452

35. LeBreton, J. M., & Senter, J. L. (2008). Answers to 20 questions about interrater reliability and interrater agreement. *Organizational Research Methods, 11*(4), 815–852. https://journals.sagepub.com/doi/10.1177/1094428106296642

36. Wasserman, J. D., & Bracken, B. A. (2003). Psychometric characteristics of assessment procedures. In J. R. Graham & J. A. Naglieri (Eds.), *Handbook of psychology* (pp. 43–66). Wiley.

37. Taras, V., Kirkman, B. L., & Steel, P. (2010). Examining the impact of culture's consequences: A three-decade, multilevel, meta-analytic review of Hofstede's cultural value dimensions. *Journal of Applied Psychology,* 95(3), 405-439. https://psycnet.apa.org/doi/10.1037/a0018938

38. Richard, P. J., Devinney, T. M., Yip, G. S., & Johnson, G. (2009). Measuring organizational performance: Towards methodological best practice. *Journal of Management, 35*(3), 718-804. https://doi.org/10.1177/0149206308330560

39. Versteeg, M., & Ginsburg, T. (2017). Measuring the rule of law: a comparison of indicators. *Law & Social Inquiry, 42*(1), 100-137. https://doi.org/10.1111/lsi.12175

40. Stanek, K. C., & Ones, D. S. (2018). Taxonomies and compendia of cognitive ability and personality constructs and measures relevant to industrial, work, and organizational psychology. In D. S. Ones, N. Anderson, C. Viswesvaran, & H. K. Sinangil (Eds.), *The SAGE handbook of industrial, work and organizational psychology* (2nd ed.) (pp. 366–407). Sage.

41. Larsen, K. R., Hekler, E. B., Paul, M. J., & Gibson, B. S. (2020). Improving usability of social and behavioral sciences' evidence: A call to action for a national infrastructure project for mining our knowledge. *Communications of the Association for Information Systems, 46*(1), 1. https://doi.org/10.17705/1CAIS.04601

42. Schmidt, F. L., & Hunter, J. E. (2015). *Methods of meta-analysis* (3rd ed.). Sage.

43. Tanner-Smith, E. E., & Tipton, E. (2014). Robust variance estimation with dependent effect sizes: Practical considerations including a software tutorial in Stata and SPSS. *Research Synthesis Methods, 5*(1), 13-30. https://doi.org/10.1002/jrsm.1091

44. Pastor, D. A., & Lazowski, R. A. (2018). On the multilevel nature of meta-analysis: A tutorial, comparison of software programs, and discussion of analytic choices. *Multivariate Behavioral Research, 53*(1), 74-89. https://doi.org/10.1080/00273171.2017.1365684

45. Viechtbauer, W., Lopez-Lopez, J. A., Sanchez-Meca, J., & Marin-Martinez, F. (2015). A comparison of procedures to test for moderators in mixed-effects meta-regression models. *Psychological Methods, 20*(3), 360-374. https://psycnet.apa.org/doi/10.1037/met0000023

46. Tabachnick, B. G., & Fidell, L. S. (2014). *Using multivariate statistics*. Pearson Education Limited.

47. Viechtbauer, W. (2010). Conducting meta-analyses in R with the metafor package. *Journal of Statistical Software, 36*(3), 1-48. https://doi.org/10.18637/jss.v036.i03

48. Aguinis, H., Gottfredson, R. K., & Joo, H. (2013). Best-practice recommendations for defining, identifying, and handling outliers. *Organizational Research Methods, 16*(2), 270-301. https://journals.sagepub.com/doi/10.1177/1094428112470848

49. Ioannidis, J. P., Munafò, M. R., Fusar-Poli, P., Nosek, B. A., & David, S. P. (2014). Publication and other reporting biases in cognitive sciences: Detection, prevalence, and prevention. *Trends in Cognitive Sciences, 18*(5), 235-241. https://doi.org/10.1016/j.tics.2014.02.010

50. Friese, M., & Frankenbach, J. (2020). *p*-Hacking and publication bias interact to distort meta-analytic effect size estimates. *Psychological Methods, 25*(4), 456–471. https://psycnet.apa.org/doi/10.1037/met0000246

51. Rosenthal, R. (1979). The file drawer problem and tolerance for null results. *Psychological Bulletin, 86*(3), 638–641. https://doi.org/10.1037/0033-2909.86.3.638

52. Scargle, J. D. (2000). Publication bias: The "File Drawer" problem in scientific inference. *Journal of Scientific Exploration, 14*(1), 91-106. https://doi.org/10.48550/arXiv.physics/9909033

53. Dalton, D. R., Aguinis, H., Dalton, C. A., Bosco, F. A., & Pierce, C. A. (2012). Revisiting the file drawer problem in meta-analysis: An empirical assessment of published and non-published correlation matrices. *Personnel Psychology, 65*(2), 221-249. https://doi.org/10.1111/j.1744-6570.2012.01243.x

54. Henmi, M., & Copas, J. B. (2010). Confidence intervals for random effects meta-analysis and robustness to publication bias. *Statistics in Medicine, 29*(29), 2969-2983. https://doi.org/10.1002/sim.4029

55. Duval, S. J. (2005). The trim and fill method. In H. R. Rothstein, A. J. Sutton, & M. Borenstein (Eds.) Publication bias in meta-analysis: Prevention, assessment, and adjustments (pp. 127–144). Wiley.

56. Stanley, T. D., & Doucouliagos, H. (2014). Meta-regression approximations to reduce publication selection bias. *Research Synthesis Methods, 5*(1), 60-78. https://doi.org/10.1002/jrsm.1095

57. Stanley, T. D. (2017). Limitations of PET-PEESE and other meta-analysis methods. *Social Psychological and Personality Science, 8*(5), 581-591. https://journals.sagepub.com/doi/abs/10.1177/1948550617693062

58. Carlson, K. D., & Ji, F. X. (2011). Citing and building on meta-analytic findings: A review and recommendations. *Organizational Research Methods, 14*(4), 696-717. https://journals.sagepub.com/doi/10.1177/1094428110384272

59. Meehl, P. E. (1990). Appraising and amending theories: The strategy of Lakatosian defense and two principles that warrant it. *Psychological Inquiry, 1*(2), 108-141. https://doi.org/10.1207/s15327965pli0102_1

60. Paterson, T. A., Harms, P. D., Steel, P., & Credé, M. (2016). An assessment of the magnitude of effect sizes: Evidence from 30 years of meta-analysis in management. *Journal of Leadership & Organizational Studies, 23*(1), 66-81. https://journals.sagepub.com/doi/10.1177/1548051815614321

61. Oh, I. S. (2020). Beyond meta-analysis: Secondary uses of

meta-analytic data. *Annual Review of Organizational Psychology and Organizational Behavior, 7*, 125-153. https://doi.org/10.1146/annurev-orgpsych-012119-045006

62. Polanin, J. R., Espelage, D. L., Grotpeter, J. K., Valido, A., Ingram, K. M., Torgal, C., El Sheikh, A. m & Robinson, L. E. (2020). Locating unregistered and unreported data for use in a social science systematic review and meta-analysis. *Systematic Reviews, 9*, 116. https://doi.org/10.1186/s13643-020-01376-9

63. Boedhoe, P. S., Heymans, M. W., Schmaal, L., Abe, Y., Alonso, P., Ameis, S. H., Anticevic, A., Arnold, P. D., Batistuzzo, M. C., Benedetti, F., & Beucke, J. C. (2019). An empirical comparison of meta- and mega-analysis with data from the ENIGMA obsessive-compulsive disorder working group. *Frontiers in Neuroinformatics, 12*, 102. https://doi.org/10.3389/fninf.2018.00102

64. Landis, R.S., (2013). Successfully combining meta-analysis and structural equation modeling: Recommendations and strategies. *Journal of Business and Psychology, 28*(3), 251-261. https://doi.org/10.1007/s10869-013-9285-x

65. Sheng, Z., Kong, W., Cortina, J. M., & Hou, S. (2016). Analyzing matrices of meta-analytic correlations: Current practices and recommendations. *Research Synthesis Methods, 7*(2), 187-208. https://doi.org/10.1002/jrsm.1206

66. Jak, S., & Cheung, M. W. L. (2020). Meta-analytic structural equation modeling with moderating effects on SEM parameters. *Psychological Methods, 25*(4), 430-455. https://psycnet.apa.org/doi/10.1037/met0000245

67. Steel, P., Kammeyer-Mueller, J., & Paterson, T. A. (2015). Improving the meta-analytic assessment of effect size variance with an informed Bayesian prior. *Journal of Management, 41*(2), 718-743. https://journals.sagepub.com/doi/10.1177/0149206314551964

68. Possolo, A., Merkatas, C., & Bodnar, O. (2019). Asymmetrical uncertainties. *Metrologia, 56*(4), 045009. https://doi.org/10.1088/1681-7575/ab2a8d

69. Aguinis, H., & Gottfredson, R. K. (2010). Best-practice recommendations for estimating interaction effects using moderated multiple regression. *Journal of Organizational Behavior, 31*(6), 776-786. https://doi.org/10.1002/job.686

70. Bonett, D. G. (2010). Varying coefficient meta-analytic methods for alpha reliability. *Psychological Methods, 15*(4), 368-385. https://psycnet.apa.org/doi/10.1037/a0020142

71. Schulze, R. (2004). *Meta-analysis: A comparison of approaches*. Hogrefe & Humber.

72. Borenstein, M., Hedges, L. V., Higgins, J. P. T., & Rothstein, H. R. (2009). *Introduction to meta-analysis*. John Wiley & Sons.

73. Revelle, W., & Wilt, J. (2019). Analyzing dynamic data: A tutorial. *Personality and Individual Differences, 136*, 38-51. https://doi.org/10.1016/j.paid.2017.08.020

74. Cortina, J. M. (2016). Defining and operationalizing theory. *Journal of Organizational Behavior, 37*(8), 1142-1149. https://doi.org/10.1002/job.2121

75. Steel, P. D., & Kammeyer-Mueller, J. D. (2002). Comparing meta-analytic moderator estimation techniques under realistic conditions. *Journal of Applied Psychology, 87*(1), 96-111. https://psycnet.apa.org/doi/10.1037/0021-9010.87.1.96

76. Aguinis, H., Gottfredson, R. K., & Wright, T. A. (2011). Best-practice recommendations for estimating interaction effects using meta-analysis. *Journal of Organizational Behavior, 32*(8), 1033-1043. https://doi.org/10.1002/job.719

77. Maassen, E., van Assen, M. A., Nuijten, M. B., Olsson-Collentine, A., & Wicherts, J. M. (2020). Reproducibility of individual effect sizes in meta-analyses in psychology. *PloS one, 15*(5), e0233107. https://doi.org/10.1371/journal.pone.0233107

78. Hohn, R. E., Slaney, K. L., & Tafreshi, D. (2020). An empirical review of research and reporting practices in psychological meta-analyses. *Review of General Psychology, 24*(3), 195-209. https://journals.sagepub.com/doi/10.1177/1089268020918844

79. Aguinis, H., Banks, G. C., Rogelberg, S., & Cascio, W. F. (2020). Actionable recommendations for narrowing the science-practice gap in open science. *Organizational Behavior and Human Decision Processes, 158*, 27-35. https://doi.org/10.1016/j.obhdp.2020.02.007

80. Polanin, J. R., Hennessy, E. A., & Tsuji, S. (2020). Transparency and reproducibility of meta-analysis in psychology: A meta-review. *Perspectives on Psychological Science, 15*(4), 1026-1041. https://journals.sagepub.com/doi/10.1177/1745691620906416

81. Elliott, J. H., Synnot, A., Turner, T., Simmonds, M., Akl, E. A., McDonald, S., Salanti, G., Meerpohl, J., MacLehose, H., Hilton, J., & Tovey, D. (2017). Living systematic review: 1. Introduction—the why, what, when, and how. *Journal of Clinical Epidemiology, 91*, 23-30. https://doi.org/10.1016/j.jclinepi.2017.08.010

82. Millard, T., Synnot, A., Elliott, J., Green, S., McDonald, S., & Turner, T. (2019). Feasibility and acceptability of living systematic reviews: Results from a mixed-methods evaluation. *Systematic Reviews, 8*(1), 1-14. https://doi.org/10.1186/s13643-019-1248-5

83. Alter, G., & Gonzalez, R. (2018). Responsible practices for data sharing. *American Psychologist, 73*(2), 146-156. https://psycnet.apa.org/doi/10.1037/amp0000258

84. Newman, M. E. (2009). The first-mover advantage in scientific publication. *Europhysics*

Letters, 86(6), 68001. https://doi: 10.1209/0295-5075/86/68001

85. Kinlock, N. L., Prowant, L., Herstoff, E. M., Foley, C. M., Akin-Fajiye, M., Bender, N., Umarani, M., Ryu, H. Y., Şen, B., & Gurevitch, J. (2019). Open science and meta-analysis allow for rapid advances in ecology: A response to Menegotto et al. (2019). *Global Ecology and Biogeography, 28*(10), 1533-1534. https://doi.org/10.1111/geb.12964

86. Viechtbauer, W., López-López, J. A., Sánchez-Meca, J., & Marín-Martínez, F. (2015). A comparison of procedures to test for moderators in mixed-effects meta-regression models. *Psychological Methods, 20*(3), 360-374. https://psycnet.apa.org/doi/10.1037/met0000023

87. Borenstein, M., Hedges, L. V., Higgins, J., & Rothstein, H. R. (2009). *Introduction to meta-analysis.* John Wiley & Sons.

88. Hedges, L. V., & Pigott, T. D. (2004). The power of statistical tests for moderators in meta-analysis. *Psychological Methods, 9*(4), 426-445. https://psycnet.apa.org/doi/10.1037/1082-989X.9.4.426

89. Cafri, G., Kromrey, J. D., & Brannick, M. T. (2009). A SAS macro for statistical power calculations in meta-analysis. *Behavior Research Methods, 41*(1), 35-46. https://doi.org/10.3758/BRM.41.1.35

90. Gonzalez-Mulé, E., & Aguinis, H. (2018). Advancing theory by assessing boundary conditions with meta-regression: A critical review and best-practice recommendations. *Journal of Management, 44*(6), 2246-2273. https://journals.sagepub.com/doi/10.1177/0149206317710723

91. Aguinis, H., & Pierce, C. A. (1998). Testing moderator variable hypotheses meta-analytically. *Journal of Management, 24*(5), 577-592. https://doi.org/10.1016/S0149-2063(99)80074-9

92. Hedges, L. V., & Olkin, I. (2014). *Statistical methods for meta-analysis.* Academic Press.

93. Schmidt, F. L., & Hunter, J. E. (2014). *Methods of meta-analysis: Correcting error and bias in research findings.* Sage.

94. Whitener, E. M. (1990). Confusion of confidence intervals and credibility intervals in meta-analysis. *Journal of Applied Psychology, 75*(3), 315-321.

95. Erez, A., Bloom, M. C., & Wells, M. T. (1996). Using random rather than fixed effects models in meta-analysis: Implications for situational specificity and validity generalization. *Personnel Psychology, 49*(2), 275-306. https://doi.org/10.1111/j.1744-6570.1996.tb01801.x

96. Higgins, J., & Thompson, S. G. (2002). Quantifying heterogeneity in a meta-analysis. *Statistics in Medicine, 21*(11), 1539-1558. https://doi.org/10.1002/sim.1186

97. Steel, P., Kammeyer-Mueller, J., & Paterson, T. A. (2015). Improving the meta-analytic assessment of effect size variance with an informed Bayesian prior. *Journal of Management, 41*(2), 718-743. https://journals.sagepub.com/doi/10.1177/0149206314551964

98. Zyphur, M. J., & Oswald, F. L. (2015). Bayesian estimation and inference: A user's guide. *Journal of Management, 41*(2), 390-420. https://journals.sagepub.com/doi/abs/10.1177/0149206313501200

99. Bosco, F. A., Aguinis, H., Singh, K., Field, J. G., & Pierce, C. A. (2015). Correlational effect size benchmarks. *Journal of Applied Psychology, 100*(2), 431-449. https://psycnet.apa.org/doi/10.1037/a0038047

100. Borenstein, M., Hedges, L. V., Higgins, J., & Rothstein, H. R. (2009). *Introduction to meta-analysis.* John Wiley & Sons.

101. Viechtbauer, W. (2010). Conducting meta-analyses in R with the metafor package. *Journal of Statistical. Software, 36*(3), 1–48. https://doi.org/10.18637/jss.v036.i03

102. Wilson, D. B. (2005). *Meta-analysis macros for SAS, SPSS, and Stata.* http://mason.gmu.edu/~dwilson/ma.html.

103. Viechtbauer, W., López-López, J. A., Sánchez-Meca, J., & Marín-Martínez, F. (2015). A comparison of procedures to test for moderators in mixed-effects meta-regression models. *Psychological Methods, 20*(3), 360-374. https://psycnet.apa.org/doi/10.1037/met0000023

104. Overton, R. C. (1998). A comparison of fixed-effects and mixed (random-effects) models for meta-analysis tests of moderator variable effects. *Psychological Methods, 3*(3), 354-379. https://psycnet.apa.org/doi/10.1037/1082-989X.3.3.354

105. López-López, J. A., Marín-Martínez, F., Sánchez-Meca, J., Van den Noortgate, W., & Viechtbauer, W. (2014). Estimation of the predictive power of the model in mixed-effects meta-regression: A simulation study. *British Journal of Mathematical and Statistical Psychology, 67*(1), 30-48. https://doi.org/10.1111/bmsp.12002

106. Raudenbush, S. W. (2009). Analyzing effect sizes: Random-effects models. In H. Cooper, L. V. Hedges, & J. C. Valentine (Eds.), *The handbook of research synthesis and meta-analysis* (pp. 296-314). Russell Sage Foundation.

107. Van den Noortgate, W., & Onghena, P. (2003). Hierarchical linear models for the quantitative integration of effect sizes in single-case research. *Behavior Research Methods, Instruments, & Computers, 35*(1), 1-10. https://doi.org/10.3758/BF03195492

108. Hedges, L. V., & Olkin, I. (2014). *Statistical methods for meta-analysis.* Academic Press.

109. Knapp, G., & Hartung, J. (2003). Improved tests for a random effects meta-regression with a single covariate. *Statistics in Medicine*, *22*(17), 2693-2710.

110. Viechtbauer, W., López-López, J. A., Sánchez-Meca, J., & Marín-Martínez, F. (2015). A comparison of procedures to test for moderators in mixed-effects meta-regression models. *Psychological Methods*, *20*(3), 360-374. https://psycnet.apa.org/doi/10.1037/met0000023

111. Aloe, A. M., Becker, B. J., & Pigott, T. D. (2010). An alternative to R^2 for assessing linear models of effect size. *Research Synthesis Methods*, *1*(3-4), 272-283. https://doi.org/10.1002/jrsm.23

112. APA Publications and Communications Board Working Group on Journal Article Reporting Standards. (2008). Reporting standards for research in psychology: Why do we need them? What might they be? *American Psychologist*, *63*(9), 839-851. https://doi.apa.org/doi/10.1037/0003-066X.63.9.839.

113. Overton, R. C. (1998). A comparison of fixed-effects and mixed (random-effects) models for meta-analysis tests of moderator variable effects. *Psychological Methods*, *3*(3), 354-379. https://psycnet.apa.org/doi/10.1037/1082-989X.3.3.354

114. Murphy, K. R., & Aguinis, H. (2022). Reporting interactions: Visualization, effect size, and interpretation. *Journal of Management*. https://doi.org/10.1177/01492063221088516

115. Sturman, M. C., Cheramie, R. A., & Cashen, L. H. (2005). The impact of job complexity and performance measurement on the temporal consistency, stability, and test-retest reliability of employee job performance ratings. *Journal of Applied Psychology*, *90*(2), 269-283.

116. Bedeian, A. G. (2013). "More than meets the eye": A guide to interpreting the descriptive statistics and correlation matrices reported in management research. *Academy of Management Learning & Education*, *13*(1), 121-135. https://doi.org/10.5465/amle.2013.0001

117. Shadish, W. R, Cook, T. D., & Campbell, D. T. (2002). *Experimental and quasi-experimental designs for generalized causal inference*. Houghton Mifflin.

118. Cheung, M. W. L., & Chan, W. (2005). Meta-analytic structural equation modeling: A two-stage approach. *Psychological Methods*, *10*(1), 40-64. https://psycnet.apa.org/doi/10.1037/1082-989X.10.1.40

119. Eysenck, H. J. (1978). An exercise in mega-silliness. *American Psychologist*, *33*(5): 517. https://psycnet.apa.org/doi/10.1037/0003-066X.33.5.517.a

120. Antonakis, J., Bendahan, S., Jacquart, P., & Lalive, R. (2010). On making causal claims: A review and recommendations. *Leadership Quarterly*, *21*(6), 1086-1120. https://doi.org/10.1016/j.leaqua.2010.10.010

121. Semadeni, M., Withers, M. C., Certo, T. (2014). The perils of endogeneity and instrumental variables in strategy research: Understanding through simulation. *Strategic Management Journal*, *35*(7), 1070-1079. https://doi.org/10.1002/smj.2136

122. Popper, K. (1963). *Science as falsification*. Mayfield Publishing Company.

123. Shadish, W. R. (1996). Meta-analysis and the exploration of association mediating processes: A primer of examples, methods, and issues. *Psychological Methods*, *1*(1), 47-65. https://psycnet.apa.org/doi/10.1037/1082-989X.1.1.47

124. Viswesvaran, C. & Ones, D. S. (1995). Theory testing: Combining psychometric meta-analysis and structural equations modelling. *Personnel Psychology*, *48*(4), 865-885. https://doi.org/10.1111/j.1744-6570.1995.tb01784.x

125. Fan, H., Jackson, T., Yang, X., Tang, W., & Zhang, J. (2010). The factor structure of the Mayer–Salovey–Caruso Emotional Intelligence Test V 2.0 (MSCEIT): A meta-analytic structural equation modeling approach. *Personality and Individual Differences*, *48*(7), 781-785. https://doi.org/10.1016/j.paid.2010.02.004

126. Cheung, M.W. L. (2008). A model for integrating fixed-, random-, and mixed-effects meta-analyses into structural equation modeling. *Psychological Methods*, *13*(3), 182-202. https://psycnet.apa.org/doi/10.1037/a0013163

127. Burke, M. J. & Landis, R. S. (2003). Methodological and conceptual challenges in conducting and interpreting meta-analyses. In *Validity generalization: A critical review*, K. R. Murphy (Ed). (pp. 287-309). Erlbaum.

128. Roesch, S. C. & Weiner, B. (2001). A meta-analytic review of coping with illness: Do causal attributions matter? *Journal of Psychosomatic Research*, *50*(4), 205-219. https://doi.org/10.1016/S0022-3999(01)00188-X

129. Tokunaga, R. S., & Rains, S. A. (2010). An evaluation of two characterizations of the relationships between problematic Internet use, time spent using the Internet, and psychosocial problems. *Human Communication Research*, *36*(4), 512-545. https://doi.org/10.1111/j.1468-2958.2010.01386.x

130. Graham, J. M. (2011). Measuring love in romantic relationships: A meta-analysis. *Journal of Social and Personal Relationships*, *28*(6), 748-771. https://journals.sagepub.com/doi/10.1177/0265407510389126

131. Brown, S. D., Tramayne, S., Hoxha, D., Telander, K., Fan, X., & Lent, R. W. (2008). Social cognitive predictors of college students' academic performance and persistence: A meta-analytic path analysis. *Journal of Vocational*

Behavior, 72(3), 298-308. https://doi.org/10.1016/j.jvb.2007.09.003

132. Landis, R. S. (2013). Successfully combining meta-analysis and structural equation modeling: Recommendations and strategies. *Journal of Business and Psychology, 28*(3), 251-261. https://doi.org/10.1007/s10869-013-9285-x

133. Eby, L. T., Freeman, D. M., Rush, M. C., & Lance, C. E. (1999). Motivational bases of affective organizational commitment: A partial test of an integrative theoretical model. *Journal of Occupational and Organizational Psychology, 72*(4), 463-483. https://doi.org/10.1348/096317999166798

134. Combs, J. G., Ketchen, Jr, D. J., Crook, T. R., & Roth, P. L. (2011). Assessing cumulative evidence within 'macro' research: Why meta-analysis should be preferred over vote counting. *Journal of Management Studies, 48*(1), 178-197. https://doi.org/10.1111/j.1467-6486.2009.00899.x

135. Glass, G. V, McGaw, B., & Smith, M. L. (1981). *Meta-analysis in social research*. Academic Press.

136. Geyskens, I., Steenkamp, J. B. E., & Kumar, N. (2006). Make, buy, or ally: A transaction cost theory meta-analysis. *Academy of Management Journal, 49*(3), 519-543. https://doi.org/10.5465/amj.2006.21794670

137. Furlow, C. F., & Beretvas, S. N. (2005). Meta-analytic methods of pooling correlation matrices for structural equation modelling under different patterns of missing data. *Psychological Methods, 10*(2), 227-254. https://psycnet.apa.org/doi/10.1037/1082-989X.10.2.227

138. Van Den Noortgate, W., & Onghena, P. (2003). Multilevel meta-analysis: A comparison with traditional meta-analytical procedures. *Educational and Psychological Measurement 63*(5), 765-790. https://journals.sagepub.com/doi/10.1177/0013164403251027

139. Aguinis, H. & Harden, E. E. (2009). Sample size rules of thumb. In C. E. Lance & R. J. Vandenberg (Eds.), *Statistical and methodological myths and urban legends* (pp. 267-286). Routledge.

140. Nye, C. D., & Drasgow, F. (2011). Assessing goodness of fit: Simple rules of thumb simply don't work. *Organizational Research Methods, 14*(4), 548-570. https://journals.sagepub.com/doi/10.1177/1094428110368562

141. Bettis, R., Gambardella, A., Helfat, C., & Mitchell, W. (2014). Quantitative empirical analysis in strategic management. *Strategic Management Journal, 35*(7), 949-953. https://www.jstor.org/stable/24037327

142. Kepes, S., McDaniel, M. A., Brannick, M. T., & Banks, G. C. (2013). Meta-analytic reviews in the organizational sciences: Two meta-analytic schools on the way to MARS (the Meta-Analytic Reporting Standards) *Journal of Business and Psychology, 28*(2), 123-143. https://doi.org/10.1007/s10869-013-9300-2

143. Garner, P., Hopewell, S., Chandler, J., MacLehose, H., Akl, E. A., Beyene, J., Chang, S., Churchill, R., Dearness, K., Guyatt, G., ... & Lefebvre, C. (2016). When and how to update systematic reviews: Consensus and checklist. *British Medical Journal, 354*, i3507. https://doi.org/10.1136/bmj.i3507

144. Mendes, E., Wohlin, C., Felizardo, K. & Kalinowski, M. (2020). When to update systematic literature reviews in software engineering. *Journal of Systems and Software, 167*, 110607. https://doi.org/10.1016/j.jss.2020.110607

CHAPTER 12

1. Berry, M. J. A., & Linoff, G. S. (2004). *Data mining techniques for marketing, sales, and customer relationship management* (2nd ed.). Wiley Publishing.

2. Agrawal, R., Imieliński, T., & Swami, A. (1993). Mining association rules between sets of items in large databases. In P. Buneman & S. Jajodia (Eds.), *Proceedings of the 1993 ACM SIGMOD International Conference on Management of Data*. Association for Computing Machinery (ACM). https://doi.org/10.1145/170036.170072

3. Chen, Y. L., Tang, K., Shen, R. J., & Hu, Y. H. (2005). Market basket analysis in a multiple store environment. *Decision Support Systems, 40*(2), 339-354. https://doi.org/10.1016/j.dss.2004.04.009

4. Russell, G. J., & Petersen, A. (2000). Analysis of cross category dependence in market basket selection. *Journal of Retailing, 76*(3), 367-392. https://doi.org/10.1016/S0022-4359(00)00030-0

5. Kanagawa, Y., Matsumoto, S., Koike, S., & Imamura, T. (2009). Association analysis of food allergens. *Pediatric Allergy and Immunology, 20*(4), 347-352. https://doi.org/10.1111/j.1399-3038.2008.00791.x

6. Goh, D. H., & Ang, R. P. (2007). An introduction to association rule mining: An application in counseling and help-seeking behavior of adolescents. *Behavior Research Methods, 39*(2), 259-266. https://doi.org/10.3758/BF03193156

7. Goh, D. H., & Ang, R. P. (2007). An introduction to association rule mining: An application in counseling and help-seeking behavior of adolescents. *Behavior Research Methods, 39*(2), 259-266. https://doi.org/10.3758/BF03193156

8. Bennedich, M. (2009). *Mining survey data*. Unpublished master's thesis in computer science, School of Engineering and Business Management, Royal Institute of Technology, Stockholm, Sweden.

9. Bennedich, M. (2009). *Mining survey data*. Unpublished master's thesis in computer science, School of Engineering and Business Management, Royal Institute of Technology, Stockholm, Sweden.

10. Shepherd, D. A., & Sutcliffe, K. M. (2011). Inductive top-down theorizing: A source of new theories of organization. *Academy of Management Review, 36*(2), 361-380. https://doi.org/10.5465/AMR.2011.59330952

11. Russell, G. J., Ratneshwar, S., Shocker, A. D., Bell, D., Bodapati, A., Degeratu, A., .. & Shankar, V. H. (1999). Multiple-category decision-making: Review and synthesis. *Marketing Letters, 10*(3), 319-332. https://doi.org/10.1023/A:1008143526174

12. Kanagawa, Y., Matsumoto, S., Koike, S., & Imamura, T. (2009). Association analysis of food allergens. *Pediatric Allergy and Immunology, 20*(4), 347-352. https://doi.org/10.1111/j.1399-3038.2008.00791.x

13. Takeuchi, H., Subramaniam, L. V., Nasukawa, T., Roy, S., & Balakrishnan, S. (2007). *A conversation-mining system for gathering insights to improve agent productivity.* Paper presented at the IEEE International Conference, Tokyo, Japan. https://doi.org/10.1109/CEC-EEE.2007.3

14. Boyd, B. K., Takacs Haynes, K., Hitt, M. A., Bergh, D. D., & Ketchen Jr, D. J. (2012). Contingency hypotheses in strategic management research: Use, disuse, or misuse?. *Journal of Management, 38*(1), 278-313. https://doi.org/10.1177/0149206311418662

15. Tang, K., Chen, Y. L., & Hu, H. W. (2008). Context-based market basket analysis in a multiple-store environment. *Decision Support Systems, 45*(1), 150-163. https://doi.org/10.1016/j.dss.2007.12.016

16. Aguinis, H., Beaty, J. C., Boik, R. J., & Pierce, C. A. (2005). Effect size and power in assessing moderating effects of categorical variables using multiple regression: a 30-year review. *Journal of Applied Psychology, 90*(1), 94-107. https://doi.org/10.1037/0021-9010.90.1.94

17. Weinzimmer, L. G., Mone, M. A., & Alwan, L. C. (1994). An examination of perceptions and usage of regression diagnostics in organization studies. *Journal of Management, 20*(1), 179-192. https://doi.org/10.1177/014920639402000110

18. Davenport, T. H., Harris, J., & Shapiro, J. (2010). Competing on talent analytics. *Harvard Business Review, 88*(10), 52-58.

19. Shmueli, G., Patel, N. R., & Bruce, P. C. (2010). *Data mining for business intelligence: Concepts, techniques, and applications in Microsoft Office Excel with XLMiner.* Wiley.

20. Mcdonald, R. A., Thurston, P. W., & Nelson, M. R. (2000). A Monte Carlo study of missing item methods. *Organizational Research Methods, 3*(1), 71-92. https://doi.org/10.1177/109442810031003

21. He, Z., Xu, X., Huang, J. Z., & Deng, S. (2004). Mining class outliers: concepts, algorithms and applications in CRM. *Expert Systems with Applications, 27*(4), 681-697. https://doi.org/10.1016/j.eswa.2004.07.002

22. Cohen, J., Cohen, P., West, S. G., & Aiken, L. S. (2003). *Applied multiple regression/correlation analysis for the behavioral sciences* (3rd ed.). Routledge.

23. Mitchell, T. R., & James, L. R. (2001). Building better theory: Time and the specification of when things happen. *Academy of Management Review, 26*(4), 530-547. https://doi.org/10.2307/3560240

24. Ployhart, R. E., & Vandenberg, R. J. (2010). Longitudinal research: The theory, design, and analysis of change. *Journal of Management, 36*(1), 94-120. https://doi.org/10.1177/0149206309352110

25. Tang, K., Chen, Y. L., & Hu, H. W. (2008). Context-based market basket analysis in a multiple-store environment. *Decision Support Systems, 45*(1), 150-163. https://doi.org/10.1016/j.dss.2007.12.016

26. Han, H. K., Kim, H. S., & Sohn, S. Y. (2009). Sequential association rules for forecasting failure patterns of aircrafts in Korean airforce. *Expert Systems with Applications, 36*(2), 1129-1133. https://doi.org/10.1016/j.eswa.2007.10.012

27. Croon, M. A., & van Veldhoven, M. J. (2007). Predicting group-level outcome variables from variables measured at the individual level: a latent variable multilevel model. *Psychological Methods, 12*(1), 45. https://doi.org/10.1037/1082-989X.12.1.45

28. Coff, R., & Kryscynski, D. (2011). Invited editorial: Drilling for micro-foundations of human capital–based competitive advantages. *Journal of Management, 37*(5), 1429-1443. https://doi.org/10.1177/0149206310397772

29. Aguinis, H., Werner, S., Lanza Abbott, J., Angert, C., Park, J. H., & Kohlhausen, D. (2010). Customer-centric science: Reporting significant research results with rigor, relevance, and practical impact in mind. *Organizational Research Methods, 13*(3), 515-539. https://doi.org/10.1177/1094428109333339

30. U.S. Bureau of Labor Statistics. (2006). *National compensation survey.* U.S. Government Printing Office.

31. Martocchio, J. J. (2011). Strategic reward and compensation plans. In S. Zedeck (Ed.), *APA handbook of industrial and organizational psychology: Building and developing the organization* (pp. 343-372). APA. https://doi.org/10.1037/12169-011

32. Bennedich, M. (2009). *Mining survey data.* Unpublished master's thesis in computer science, School of Engineering and Business Management, Royal Institute of Technology, Stockholm, Sweden.

33. Cunliffe, A. L., & Alcadipani, R. (2016). The politics of access in fieldwork: Immersion, backstage

dramas, and deception. *Organizational Research Methods, 19*(4), 535-561. https://doi.org/10.1177/1094428116639134

34. O'Boyle Jr, E., & Aguinis, H. (2012). The best and the rest: Revisiting the norm of normality of individual performance. *Personnel Psychology, 65*(1), 79-119. https://doi.org/10.1111/j.1744-6570.2011.01239.x

35. Marakas, G. M. (2003). *Modern data warehousing, mining, and visualization: Core concepts.* Prentice Hall.

36. Davenport, T. H., Harris, J., & Shapiro, J. (2010). Competing on talent analytics. *Harvard business review, 88*(10), 52-58.

37. Shmueli, G., Patel, N. R., & Bruce, P. C. (2010). *Data mining for business intelligence: Concepts, techniques, and applications in Microsoft Office Excel with XLMiner.* Wiley.

38. Berry, M. J. A., & Linoff, G. S. (2004). *Data mining techniques for marketing, sales, and customer relationship management* (2nd ed.). Wiley Publishing.

39. Berry, M. J. A., & Linoff, G. S. (2004). *Data mining techniques for marketing, sales, and customer relationship management* (2nd ed.). Wiley Publishing.

40. Goh, D. H., & Ang, R. P. (2007). An introduction to association rule mining: An application in counseling and help-seeking behavior of adolescents. *Behavior Research Methods, 39*(2), 259-266. https://doi.org/10.3758/BF03193156

41. Holtom, B. C., Baruch, Y., Aguinis, H., & Ballinger, G. A. 2022. Survey response rates: Trends and a validity assessment framework. *Human Relations.* https://doi.org/10.1177/00187267211070769

42. Chiu, S., & Tavella, D. (2008). *Data mining and market intelligence for optimal marketing returns.* Butterworth-Heinemann. https://doi.org/10.4324/9780080878096

43. Baralis, E., Cagliero, L., Cerquitelli, T., Garza, P., & Marchetti, M. (2011). CAS-Mine: providing personalized services in context-aware applications by means of generalized rules. *Knowledge and Information Systems, 28*(2), 283-310. https://doi.org/10.1007/s10115-010-0359-z

44. Ting, P. H., Pan, S., & Chou, S. S. (2010). Finding ideal menu items assortments: An empirical application of market basket analysis. *Cornell Hospitality Quarterly, 51*(4), 492-501. https://doi.org/10.1177/1938965510378254

45. Gu, L., Li, J., He, H., Williams, G., Hawkins, S., & Kelman, C. (2003, December). Association rule discovery with unbalanced class distributions. In *Australasian Joint Conference on Artificial Intelligence* (pp. 221-232). Heidelberg. https://doi.org/10.1007/978-3-540-24581-0_19

46. Hormuth, S. E. (1986). The sampling of experiences in situ. *Journal of Personality, 54*(1), 262-293. https://doi.org/10.1111/j.1467-6494.1986.tb00395.x

47. Wheeler, L., & Reis, H. T. (1991). Self-recording of everyday life events: Origins, types, and uses. Journal of Personality, 59(3), 339-354. https://doi.org/10.1111/j.1467-6494.1991.tb00252.x

48. Ilies, R., & Judge, T. A. (2002). Understanding the dynamic relationships among personality, mood, and job satisfaction: A field experience sampling study. *Organizational Behavior and Human Decision Processes, 89*(2), 1119-1139. https://doi.org/10.1016/S0749-5978(02)00018-3

49. Côté, S., & Moskowitz, D. S. (1998). On the dynamic covariation between interpersonal behavior and affect: prediction from neuroticism, extraversion, and agreeableness. *Journal of Personality and Social Psychology, 75*(4), 1032-1046. https://doi.org/10.1037/0022-3514.75.4.1032

50. Williams, K. J., & Alliger, G. M. (1994). Role stressors, mood spillover, and perceptions of work-family conflict in employed parents. *Academy of Management Journal, 37*(4), 837-868. https://doi.org/10.5465/256602

51. Hektner, J. M., Schmidt, J. A., & Csikszentmihalyi, M. (2007). *Experience sampling method: Measuring the quality of everyday life.* Sage Publications. https://doi.org/10.4135/9781412984201

52. Alliger, G. M., & Williams, K. J. (1993). Using signal-contingent experience sampling methodology to study work in the field: A discussion and illustration examining task perceptions and mood. *Personnel Psychology, 46*(3), 525-549. https://doi.org/10.1111/j.1744-6570.1993.tb00883.x

53. Scollon, C. N., Kim-Prieto, C., & Diener, E. (2003). Experience sampling: Promises and pitfalls, strengths and weaknesses. *Journal of Happiness Studies, 4,* 5-34. https://doi.org/10.1023/A:1023605205115

54. Hektner, J. M., Schmidt, J. A., & Csikszentmihalyi, M. (2007). *Experience sampling method: Measuring the quality of everyday life.* Sage Publications. https://doi.org/10.4135/9781412984201

55. Kuratko, D. F., Hornsby, J. S., & Naffziger, D. W. (1997). An examination of owner's goals in sustaining entrepreneurship. *Journal of Small Business Management, 35*(1), 24-33. https://doi.org/10.1016/S1053-4822(03)00017-2

56. Shane, S., Locke, E. A., & Collins, C. J. (2003). Entrepreneurial motivation. *Human Resource Management Review, 13*(2), 257-279.

57. Brunswick, E. (1949). *Systematic and representative design of psychological experiments.* University of California Press.

58. Choi, Y. R., & Shepherd, D. A. (2004). Entrepreneurs' decisions to exploit opportunities. *Journal of Management, 30*(3), 377-395. https

://doi.org/10.1016/j.jm.2003.04.002

59. Mason, C., & Stark, M. (2004). What do investors look for in a business plan? A comparison of the investment criteria of bankers, venture capitalists and business angels. *International Small Business Journal, 22*(3), 227-248. https://doi.org/10.1177/0266242604042377

60. Sarasvathy, D. K., Simon, H. A., & Lave, L. (1998). Perceiving and managing business risks: Differences between entrepreneurs and bankers. *Journal of Economic Behavior & Organization, 33*(2), 207-225. https://doi.org/10.1016/S0167-2681(97)00092-9

61. Baron, R. A. (2008). The role of affect in the entrepreneurial process. *Academy of Management Review, 33*(2), 328-340. https://doi.org/10.5465/amr.2008.31193166

62. Uy, M. A. (2009). *The roller coaster ride: Affective influences in entrepreneurial goal pursuit.* Unpublished doctoral dissertation, University of Colorado, Boulder.

63. Beal, D. J., & Weiss, H. M. (2003). Methods of ecological momentary assessment in organizational research. *Organizational Research Methods, 6*(4), 440-464. https://doi.org/10.1177/1094428103257361

64. Tennen, H., & Affleck, G. (1996). Daily processes in coping with chronic pain: methods and analytic strategies. In M. Zeidner & N. S. Endler (Eds.), *Handbook of coping: Theory, research, applications* (pp. 151-177). Wiley & Sons.

65. Vancouver, J. B., Thompson, C. M., Tischner, E. C., & Putka, D. J. (2002). Two studies examining the negative effect of self-efficacy on performance. *Journal of Applied Psychology, 87*(3), 506-516. https://doi.org/10.1037/0021-9010.87.3.506

66. Zhao, H., Seibert, S. E., & Hills, G. E. (2005). The mediating role of self-efficacy in the development of entrepreneurial intentions.

Journal of Applied Psychology, 90(6), 1265-1272. https://doi.org/10.1037/0021-9010.90.6.1265

67. Kraiger, K., & Aguinis, H. (2001). Training effectiveness: Assessing training needs, motivation, and accomplishments. In M. London (Ed.), *How people evaluate others in organizations* (pp. 203-220). Lawrence Erlbaum.

68. Robinson, M. D., & Clore, G. L. (2002). Belief and feeling: evidence for an accessibility model of emotional self-report. *Psychological Bulletin, 128*(6), 934-960. https://doi.org/10.1037/0033-2909.128.6.934

69. Rugg, M. D., & Wilding, E. L. (2000). Retrieval processing and episodic memory. *Trends in Cognitive Science, 4 (3)*, 108-115. https://doi.org/10.1016/S1364-6613(00)01445-5

70. Beal, D. J., & Weiss, H. M. (2003). Methods of ecological momentary assessment in organizational research. *Organizational Research Methods, 6*(4), 440-464. https://doi.org/10.1177/1094428103257361

71. Lichtenstein, B. B., Dooley, K. J., & Lumpkin, G. T. (2006). Measuring emergence in the dynamics of new venture creation. *Journal of Business Venturing, 21*(2), 153-175. https://doi.org/10.1016/j.jbusvent.2005.04.002

72. Shane, S. (2000). Prior knowledge and the discovery of entrepreneurial opportunities. *Organization Science, 11*(4), 448-469. https://doi.org/10.1287/orsc.11.4.448.14602

73. Baron, R. A., & Ensley, M. D. (2006). Opportunity recognition as the detection of meaningful patterns: Evidence from comparisons of novice and experienced entrepreneurs. *Management Science, 52*(9), 1331-1344. https://doi.org/10.1287/mnsc.1060.0538

74. Schacter, D. L., Norman, K. A., & Koutstaal, W. (1998). The cognitive neuroscience of constructive memory. *Annual Review of*

Psychology, 49(1), 289-318. https://doi.org/10.1146/annurev.psych.49.1.289

75. Hektner, J. M., Schmidt, J. A., & Csikszentmihalyi, M. (2007). *Experience sampling method: Measuring the quality of everyday life.* Sage Publications. https://doi.org/10.4135/9781412984201

76. Beal, D. J., & Weiss, H. M. (2003). Methods of ecological momentary assessment in organizational research. *Organizational Research Methods, 6*(4), 440-464. https://doi.org/10.1177/1094428103257361

77. Carver, C. (2003). Pleasure as a sign you can attend to something else: Placing positive feelings within a general model of affect. *Cognition and Emotion, 17*(2), 241-261. https://doi.org/10.1080/0269993030.2294

78. Aguinis, H., & Harden, E. E. (2009). Sample size rules of thumb: Evaluating three common practices. In C. E. Lance and R. J. Vandenberg (Eds.), *Statistical and methodological myths and urban legends: Received doctrine, verity, and fable in the organizational and social sciences* (pp. 269-288). Routledge.

79. Ilies, R., & Judge, T. A. (2002). Understanding the dynamic relationships among personality, mood, and job satisfaction: A field experience sampling study. *Organizational Behavior and Human Decision Processes, 89*(2), 1119-1139. https://doi.org/10.1016/S0749-5978(02)00018-3

80. Hektner, J. M., Schmidt, J. A., & Csikszentmihalyi, M. (2007). *Experience sampling method: Measuring the quality of everyday life.* Sage Publications. https://doi.org/10.4135/9781412984201

81. Watson, D., Clark, L. A., & Tellegen, A. (1988). Development and validation of brief measures of positive and negative affect: the PANAS scales. *Journal of Personality and Social Psychology, 54*(6), 1063-1070. https://doi.org/10.1037/0022-3514.54.6.1063

82. Zohar, D., Tzischinski, O., & Epstein, R. (2003). Effects of energy availability on immediate and delayed emotional reactions to work events. *Journal of Applied Psychology*, *88*(6), 1082-1093. https://doi.org/10.1037/0021-9010.88.6.1082

83. Warren, C. R., & Landis, R. S. (2007). One is the loneliest number: a meta-analytic investigation on single-item measure fidelity. *Ergometrika*, *4*(1), 32-53.

84. Ong, A. D., Bergeman, C. S., Bisconti, T. L., & Wallace, K. A. (2006). Psychological resilience, positive emotions, and successful adaptation to stress in later life. *Journal of Personality and Social Psychology*, *91*(4), 730-749. https://doi.org/10.1037/0022-3514.91.4.730

85. Aguinis, H., Pierce, C. A., & Culpepper, S. A. (2009). Scale coarseness as a methodological artifact: Correcting correlation coefficients attenuated from using coarse scales. *Organizational Research Methods*, *12*(4), 623-652. https://doi.org/10.1177/1094428108318065

86. Hektner, J. M., Schmidt, J. A., & Csikszentmihalyi, M. (2007). *Experience sampling method: Measuring the quality of everyday life*. Sage Publications. https://doi.org/10.4135/9781412984201

87. Larson, R. W., & Richards, M. H. (1994). *Divergent realities: The emotional lives of mothers, fathers, and adolescents*. Basic Books.

88. Fisher, C. D. (2002). Antecedents and consequences of real-time affective reactions at work. *Motivation and Emotion*, *26*(1), 3-30. https://doi.org/10.1023/A:1015190007468

89. Barrett, L. F., & Barrett, D. J. (2001). An introduction to computerized experience sampling in psychology. *Social Science Computer Review*, *19*(2), 175-185. https://doi.org/10.1177/089443930101900204

90. Judge, T. A., & Ilies, R. (2004). Affect and job satisfaction: a study of their relationship at work and at home. *Journal of Applied Psychology*, *89*(4), 661-673. https://doi.org/10.1037/0021-9010.89.4.661

91. Barrett, L. F., & Barrett, D. J. (2001). An introduction to computerized experience sampling in psychology. *Social Science Computer Review*, *19*(2), 175-185. https://doi.org/10.1177/089443930101900204

92. Vos, I., & de Klein, P. (2002). *The Essential Guide to Mobile Business*. Prentice Hall.

93. Chu, H. H., Song, H., Wong, C., Kurakake, S., & Katagiri, M. (2004). Roam, a seamless application framework. *Journal of Systems and Software*, *69*(3), 209-226. https://doi.org/10.1016/S0164-1212(03)00052-9

94. Uy, M. A. (2009). *The roller coaster ride: Affective influences in entrepreneurial goal pursuit*. Unpublished doctoral dissertation, University of Colorado, Boulder.

95. Hektner, J. M., Schmidt, J. A., & Csikszentmihalyi, M. (2007). *Experience sampling method: Measuring the quality of everyday life*. Sage Publications. https://doi.org/10.4135/9781412984201

96. Alliger, G. M., & Williams, K. J. (1993). Using signal-contingent experience sampling methodology to study work in the field: A discussion and illustration examining task perceptions and mood. *Personnel Psychology*, *46*(3), 525-549. https://doi.org/10.1111/j.1744-6570.1993.tb00883.x

97. Williams, K. J., & Alliger, G. M. (1994). Role stressors, mood spillover, and perceptions of work-family conflict in employed parents. *Academy of Management Journal*, *37*(4), 837-868. https://doi.org/10.5465/256602

98. Zohar, D., Tzischinski, O., & Epstein, R. (2003). Effects of energy availability on immediate and delayed emotional reactions to work events. *Journal of Applied Psychology*, *88*(6), 1082-1093. https://doi.org/10.1037/0021-9010.88.6.1082

99. Judge, T. A., & Ilies, R. (2004). Affect and job satisfaction: a study of their relationship at work and at home. *Journal of Applied Psychology*, *89*(4), 661-673. https://doi.org/10.1037/0021-9010.89.4.661

100. Bliese, P. D., Chan, D., & Ployhart, R. E. (2007). Multilevel methods: Future directions in measurement, longitudinal analyses, and nonnormal outcomes. *Organizational Research Methods*, *10*(4), 551-563. https://doi.org/10.1177/1094428107301102

101. Walls, T. & Schafer, J. (2006). *Models for intensive longitudinal data*. Oxford University Press. https://doi.org/10.1093/acprof:oso/9780195173444.001.0001

102. Nezlek, J. B. (2001). Multilevel random coefficient analyses of event-and interval-contingent data in social and personality psychology research. *Personality and Social Psychology Bulletin*, *27*(7), 771-785. https://doi.org/10.1177/0146167201277001

103. Forgas, J. P. (1995). Mood and judgment: the affect infusion model (AIM). *Psychological Bulletin*, *117*(1), 39-66. https://doi.org/10.1037/0033-2909.117.1.39

104. Rabe-Hesketh, S., & Skrondal, A. (2008). *Multilevel and longitudinal modeling using Stata*. STATA press.

105. Doyle, A. C. (1890). *The sign of four*. Spencer Blackett.

106. Bayes, T. (1763). LII. An essay towards solving a problem in the doctrine of chances. By the late Rev. Mr. Bayes, FRS communicated by Mr. Price, in a letter to John Canton, AMFR S. *Philosophical transactions of the Royal Society of London*, *53*, 370-418. https://doi.org/10.1098/rstl.1763.0053

107. Roth, P. L, Switzer, F. S., Van Iddekinge, C. H., & Oh, I. S. (2011). Toward better meta-analytic matrices: How input values can

affect research conclusions in human resource management simulations. *Personnel Psychology*, *64*(4), 899-935. https://doi.org/10.1111/j.1744-6570.2011.01231.x

108. Schmidt, F. (2008). Meta-analysis: A constantly evolving research integration tool. *Organizational Research Methods*, *11*(1), 96-113. https://doi.org/10.1177/1094428107303161

109. King, G. (1986). How not to lie with statistics: Avoiding common mistakes in quantitative political science. *American Journal of Political Science*, *30*(3), 666-687. https://doi.org/10.2307/2111095

110. Hays, W. L. (1994). *Statistics*, Fifth Edition. Harcourt Brace.

111. Cortina, J. M., & Folger, R. G. (1998). When is it acceptable to accept a null hypothesis: No way, Jose?. *Organizational Research Methods*, *1*(3), 334-350. https://doi.org/10.1177/109442819813004

112. Aguinis, H., & Harden, E. E. (2009). Sample size rules of thumb: Evaluating three common practices. In C. E. Lance and R. J. Vandenberg (Eds.), *Statistical and methodological myths and urban legends: Received doctrine, verity, and fable in the organizational and social sciences* (pp. 269-288). Routledge.

113. Kruschke, J. K. (2013). Bayesian estimation supersedes the t test. *Journal of Experimental Psychology: General*, *142*(2), 573-603. https://doi.org/10.1037/a0029146

114. Edwards, J. R., & Berry, J. W. (2010). The presence of something or the absence of nothing: Increasing theoretical precision in management research. *Organizational Research Methods*, *13*(4), 668-689. https://doi.org/10.1177/1094428110380467

115. Brannick, M. T. (2001). Implications of empirical Bayes meta-analysis for test validation. *Journal of Applied Psychology*, *86*(3), 468-480. https://doi.org/10.1037/0021-9010.86.3.468

116. Brannick, M. T. (2001). Implications of empirical Bayes meta-analysis for test validation. *Journal of Applied Psychology*, *86*(3), 468-480. https://doi.org/10.1037/0021-9010.86.3.468

117. Cortina, J. M., & Landis, R. S. (2009). When small effect sizes tell a big story, and when large effect sizes don't. In C. E. Lance & R. J. Vandenberg (Eds.), *Statistical and methodological myths and urban legends: Doctrine, verity and fable in the organizational and social sciences* (pp. 287-308). Routledge.

118. Western, B., & Jackman, S. (1994). Bayesian inference for comparative research. *American Political Science Review*, *88*(2), 412-423. https://doi.org/10.2307/2944713

119. Cortina, J. M., & Folger, R. G. (1998). When is it acceptable to accept a null hypothesis: No way, Jose?. *Organizational Research Methods*, *1*(3), 334-350. https://doi.org/10.1177/109442819813004

120. Kruschke, J. K. (2013). Bayesian estimation supersedes the t test. *Journal of Experimental Psychology: General*, *142*(2), 573-603. https://doi.org/10.1037/a0029146

121. Kruschke, J. K. (2011). *Doing Bayesian data analysis: A tutorial with R and BUGS*. Academic Press / Elsevier.

122. O'Boyle Jr, E., & Aguinis, H. (2012). The best and the rest: Revisiting the norm of normality of individual performance. *Personnel Psychology*, *65*(1), 79-119. https://doi.org/10.1111/j.1744-6570.2011.01239.x

123. Pierce, J. R., & Aguinis, H. (2013). The too-much-of-a-good-thing effect in management. *Journal of Management*, *39*(2), 313-338. https://doi.org/10.1177/0149206311410060

124. Aguinis, H., Pierce, C. A., Bosco, F. A., & Muslin, I. S. (2009). First decade of Organizational Research Methods: Trends in design, measurement, and data-analysis topics. *Organizational Research Methods*, *12*(1), 69-112. ht

125. Lykou, A., & Ntzoufras, I. (2011). WinBUGS: A tutorial. *Wiley interdisciplinary reviews: Computational statistics*, *3*(5), 385-396. https://doi.org/10.1002/wics.176

126. Kruschke, J. K. (2011c, August 1). Extrasensory Perception (ESP): Bayesian estimation approach to meta-analysis. Message posted to http://doingbayesiandataanalysis.blogspot.com/2011/08/extrasensory-perception-esp-bayesian.html

127. O'Boyle Jr, E., & Aguinis, H. (2012). The best and the rest: Revisiting the norm of normality of individual performance. *Personnel Psychology*, *65*(1), 79-119. https://doi.org/10.1111/j.1744-6570.2011.01239.x

128. Zhou, J. (2003). When the presence of creative coworkers is related to creativity: role of supervisor close monitoring, developmental feedback, and creative personality. *Journal of Applied Psychology*, *88*(3), 413-422. https://doi.org/10.1037/0021-9010.88.3.413

129. Hirst, G., Van Knippenberg, D., & Zhou, J. (2009). A cross-level perspective on employee creativity: Goal orientation, team learning behavior, and individual creativity. *Academy of Management Journal*, *52*(2), 280-293. https://doi.org/10.5465/amj.2009.37308035

130. O'Boyle Jr, E., & Aguinis, H. (2012). The best and the rest: Revisiting the norm of normality of individual performance. *Personnel Psychology*, *65*(1), 79-119. https://doi.org/10.1111/j.1744-6570.2011.01239.x

131. Pierce, J. R., & Aguinis, H. (2013). The too-much-of-a-good-thing effect in management. *Journal of Management*, *39*(2), 313-338. https://doi.org/10.1177/0149206311410060

132. Aguinis, H., Culpepper, S. A., & Pierce, C. A. (2010). Revival of test bias research in preemployment testing. *Journal of Applied*

Psychology, 95(4), 648-680. https://doi.org/10.1037/a0018714

133. Newman, M. E. J., Barabasi, A. L., & Watts, D. J. (2006). *The structure and function of dynamic networks*. Princeton University Press.

134. Sasovova, Z., Mehra, A., Borgatti, S. P., & Schippers, M. C. (2010). Network churn: The effects of self-monitoring personality on brokerage dynamics. *Administrative Science Quarterly, 55*(4), 639-670. https://doi.org/10.2189/asqu.2010.55.4.639

135. Casciaro, T., & Lobo, M. S. (2008). When competence is irrelevant: The role of interpersonal affect in task-related ties. *Administrative Science Quarterly, 53*(4), 655-684. https://doi.org/10.2189/asqu.53.4.655

136. Gelman, A., Hill, J., & Yajima, M. (2009). *Why we (usually) don't have to worry about multiple comparisons (Technical Report)*. Department of Statistics, Columbia University.

137. Kruschke, J. K. (2011). *Doing Bayesian data analysis: A tutorial with R and BUGS*. Academic Press / Elsevier.

138. Scherbaum, C. A., & Ferreter, J. M. (2009). Estimating statistical power and required sample sizes for organizational research using multilevel modeling. *Organizational Research Methods, 12*(2), 347-367. https://doi.org/10.1177/1094428107308906

139. Miller, J. (2009). What is the probability of replicating a statistically significant effect?.*Psychonomic Bulletin & Review, 16*(4), 617-640. https://doi.org/10.3758/PBR.16.4.617

140. Maxwell, S. E. (2004). The persistence of underpowered studies in psychological research: causes, consequences, and remedies. *Psychological Methods, 9*(2), 147-163. https://doi.org/10.1037/1082-989X.9.2.147

141. Aguinis, H., Beaty, J. C., Boik, R. J., & Pierce, C. A. (2005). Effect size and power in assessing moderating effects of categorical variables using multiple regression: a 30-year review. *Journal of Applied Psychology, 90*(1), 94-107. https://doi.org/10.1037/0021-9010.90.1.94

142. Huang, J. L., & Ryan, A. M. (2011). Beyond personality traits: A study of personality states and situational contingencies in customer service jobs. *Personnel Psychology, 64*(2), 451-488. https://doi.org/10.1111/j.1744-6570.2011.01216.x

CHAPTER 13

1. Bergh, D. D., Aguinis, H., Heavey, C., Ketchen, D. J., Boyd, B. K., Su, P., ... & Joo, H. (2016). Using meta-analytic structural equation modeling to advance strategic management research: Guidelines and an empirical illustration via the strategic leadership-performance relationship. *Strategic Management Journal, 37*(3), 477-497. https://doi.org/10.1002/smj.2338

2. Giddens, A. (1972). Elites in the British class structure. *Sociological Review, 20*(3), 345-372. https://doi.org/10.1111/j.1467-954X.1972.tb00214.x

3. McDowell, L. (1998). Elites in the City of London: some methodological considerations. *Environment and Planning, 30*(12), 2133-2146. https://doi.org/10.1068/a302133

4. Vaughan, S. (2013). Elite and elite-lite interviewing: Managing our industrial legacy. *Researching sustainability: A guide to social science methods, practice and engagement*, 105-119.

5. Aguinis, H., & Solarino, A. M. (2019). Transparency and replicability in qualitative research: The case of interviews with elite informants. *Strategic Management Journal, 40*(8), 1291-1315. https://doi.org/10.1002/smj.3015

6. Richards, D. (1996). Elite interviewing: Approaches and pitfalls. *Politics, 16*(3), 199-204. https://doi.org/10.1111/j.1467-9256.1996.tb00039.x

7. Contractor, F., Foss, N. J., Kundu, S., & Lahiri, S. (2019). Viewing global strategy through a microfoundations lens. *Global Strategy Journal, 9*(1), 3-18. https://doi.org/10.1002/gsj.1329

8. Ostrander, S. A. (1993). "Surely you're not in this just to be helpful" Access, Rapport, and Interviews in Three Studies of Elites. *Journal of Contemporary Ethnography, 22*(1), 7-27. https://doi.org/10.1177/089124193022001002

9. Bingham, C. B., & Eisenhardt, K. M. (2011). Rational heuristics: The 'simple rules' that strategists learn from process experience. *Strategic Management Journal, 32*(13), 1437-1464. https://doi.org/10.1002/smj.965

10. Szulanski, G., & Jensen, R. J. (2006). Presumptive adaptation and the effectiveness of knowledge transfer. *Strategic Management Journal, 27*(10), 937-957. https://doi.org/10.1002/smj.551

11. Maitland, E., & Sammartino, A. (2015). Decision making and uncertainty: The role of heuristics and experience in assessing a politically hazardous environment. *Strategic Management Journal, 36*(10), 1554-1578. https://doi.org/10.1002/smj.2297

12. Harvey, W. S. (2011). Strategies for conducting elite interviews. *Qualitative Research, 11*(4), 431-441. https://doi.org/10.1177/1468794111404329

13. Zuckerman, H. (1972). Interviewing an ultra-elite. *Public Opinion Quarterly, 36*(2), 159-175. https://doi.org/10.1086/267989

14. Harvey, W. S. (2011). Strategies for conducting elite interviews. *Qualitative Research, 11*(4), 431-441. https://doi.org/10.1177/1468794111404329

15. Pollitt, C., Harrison, S., Hunter, D. J., & Marnoch, G. (1990). No hiding place: On the discomforts of researching the contemporary

policy process. *Journal of Social Policy, 19*(2), 169-190. https://doi.org/10.1017/S0047279400001987

16. Desmond, M. (2004). Methodological challenges posed in studying an elite in the field. *Area, 36*(3), 262-269. https://doi.org/10.1111/j.0004-0894.2004.00223.x

17. Shenton, A. K., & Hayter, S. (2004). Strategies for gaining access to organisations and informants in qualitative studies. *Education for Information, 22*(3-4), 223-231. https://doi.org/10.3233/EFI-2004-223-404

18. Thomas, R. J. (1993). Interviewing important people in big companies. *Journal of Contemporary Ethnography, 22*(1), 80-96. https://doi.org/10.1177/089124193022001006

19. Ostrander, S. A. (1993). "Surely you're not in this just to be helpful": Access, rapport, and interviews in three studies of elites. *Journal of Contemporary Ethnography, 22*(1), 7-27. https://doi.org/10.1177/089124193022001002

20. Welch, C., Marschan-Piekkari, R., Penttinen, H., & Tahvanainen, M. (2002). Corporate elites as informants in qualitative international business research. *International Business Review, 11*(5), 611-628. https://doi.org/10.1016/S0969-5931(02)00039-2

21. Harvey, W. S. (2009). Methodological approaches for junior yous interviewing elites: A multidisciplinary perspective. *Economic Geography Research Group.* Working Paper Series No. 01.09

22. Bernard, H. R. (2011). *Research methods in anthropology: Qualitative and quantitative approaches.* Rowman Altamira Press.

23. Rivera, S. W., Kozyreva, P. M., & Sarovskii, E. G. (2002). Interviewing political elites: Lessons from Russia. *PS: Political Science & Politics, 35*(4), 683-688. https://doi.org/10.1017/S1049096502001178

24. Schoenberger, E. (1991). The corporate interview as a research method in economic geography. *The Professional Geographer, 43*(2), 180-189. https://doi.org/10.1111/j.0033-0124.1991.00180.x

25. Welch, C., Marschan-Piekkari, R., Penttinen, H., & Tahvanainen, M. (2002). Corporate elites as informants in qualitative international business research. *International Business Review, 11*(5), 611-628. https://doi.org/10.1016/S0969-5931(02)00039-2

26. Fitz, J., and Halpin, D. (1995). '"Brief encounters": Researching education policy-making in elite' settings. In J. Salisbury, and S. Delamont (Eds.), *Qualitative Studies in Education.* Avebury (pp. 65-86).

27. Ostrander, S. A. (1993). "Surely you're not in this just to be helpful" Access, Rapport, and Interviews in Three Studies of Elites. *Journal of Contemporary Ethnography, 22*(1), 7-27. https://doi.org/10.1177/089124193022001002

28. Thomas, R. J. (1993). Interviewing important people in big companies. *Journal of Contemporary Ethnography, 22*(1), 80-96. https://doi.org/10.1177/089124193022001006

29. Ostrander, S. A. (1993). "Surely you're not in this just to be helpful" Access, Rapport, and Interviews in Three Studies of Elites. *Journal of Contemporary Ethnography, 22*(1), 7-27. https://doi.org/10.1177/089124193022001002

30. Thomas, R. J. (1993). Interviewing important people in big companies. *Journal of Contemporary Ethnography, 22*(1), 80-96. https://doi.org/10.1177/089124193022001002

31. Ostrander, S. A. (1993). "Surely you're not in this just to be helpful" Access, Rapport, and Interviews in Three Studies of Elites. *Journal of Contemporary Ethnography, 22*(1), 7-27. https://doi.org/10.1177/089124193022001002

32. Richards, D. (1996). Elite interviewing: Approaches and pitfalls. *Politics, 16*(3), 199-204. https://doi.org/10.1111/j.1467-9256.1996.tb00039.x

33. Ostrander, S. A. (1993). "Surely you're not in this just to be helpful" Access, Rapport, and Interviews in Three Studies of Elites. *Journal of Contemporary Ethnography, 22*(1), 7-27. https://doi.org/10.1177/089124193022001002

34. Empson, L. (2018). Elite interviewing in professional organizations. *Journal of Professions and Organization, 5*(1), 58-69. https://doi.org/10.1093/jpo/jox010

35. Ostrander, S. A. (1993). "Surely you're not in this just to be helpful" Access, Rapport, and Interviews in Three Studies of Elites. *Journal of Contemporary Ethnography, 22*(1), 7-27. https://doi.org/10.1177/089124193022001002

36. Harvey, W. S. (2010). Methodological approaches for interviewing elites. *Geography Compass, 4*(3), 193-205. https://doi.org/10.1177/1468794111404329

37. Elwood, S. A., & Martin, D. G. (2000). "Placing" interviews: Location and scales of power in qualitative research. *The Professional Geographer, 52*(4), 649-657. https://doi.org/10.1111/0033-0124.00253

38. Harvey, W. S. (2011). Strategies for conducting elite interviews. *Qualitative Research, 11*(4), 431-441. https://doi.org/10.1177/1468794111404329

39. Laurila, J. (1997). Promoting research access and informant rapport in corporate settings: Notes from research on a crisis company. *Scandinavian Journal of Management, 13*(4), 407-418. https://doi.org/10.1016/S0956-5221(97)00026-2

40. Ostrander, S. A. (1993). "Surely you're not in this just to be helpful" Access, Rapport, and Interviews in Three Studies of Elites. *Journal of Contemporary Ethnography, 22*(1), 7-27. https://doi.org/10.1177/089124193022001002

41. Smigel, E. O. (1958). Interviewing a legal elite: The Wall Street lawyer. *American Journal of Sociology,*

64(2), 159-164. https://doi.org/10.1086/222423

42. Undheim, T. A. (2003). Getting connected: How sociologists can access the high tech elite. *The Qualitative Report*, 8(1), 104-128.

43. Holt, A. (2010). Using the telephone for narrative interviewing: A research note. *Qualitative Research*, 10(1), 113-121. https://doi.org/10.1177/1468794109348686

44. Stephens, N. (2007). Collecting data from elites and ultra elites: Telephone and face-to-face interviews with macroeconomists. *Qualitative Research*, 7(2), 203-216. https://doi.org/10.1177/1468794107076020

45. Odendahl, T., & Shaw, A. M. (2002). 'Interviewing elites'. In Gubrium, J. and Holstein J. (Eds.), *Handbook of interview research: Context and methodology*. SAGE Publications (pp. 299-316). https://doi.org/10.4135/9781412973588.n19

46. Richards, D. (1996). Elite interviewing: Approaches and pitfalls. *Politics*, 16(3), 199-204. https://doi.org/10.1111/j.1467-9256.1996.tb00039.x

47. Thomas, R. J. (1993). Interviewing important people in big companies. *Journal of Contemporary Ethnography*, 22(1), 80-96. https://doi.org/10.1177/089124193022001006

48. Healey, M. J., & Rawlinson, M. B. (1993). Interviewing business owners and managers: A review of methods and techniques. *Geoforum*, 24(3), 339-355. https://doi.org/10.1016/0016-7185(93)90026-E

49. Welch, C., Marschan-Piekkari, R., Penttinen, H., & Tahvanainen, M. (2002). Corporate elites as informants in qualitative international business research. *International Business Review*, 11(5), 611-628. https://doi.org/10.1016/S0969-5931(02)00039-2

50. Lincoln, Y.S., & Guba, E. G. (1985). *Naturalistic Inquiry*. SAGE Publications. https://doi.org/10.1016/0147-1767(85)90062-8

51. Gill, M. J., Gill, D. J., & Roulet, T. J. (2018). Constructing trustworthy historical narratives: Criteria, principles and techniques. *British Journal of Management*, 29(1), 191-205. https://doi.org/10.1111/1467-8551.12262

52. Elo, S., Kääriäinen, M., Kanste, O., Pölkki, T., Utriainen, K., & Kyngäs, H. (2014). Qualitative content analysis: A focus on trustworthiness. *Sage Open*, 4(1), 2158244014522633. https://doi.org/10.1177/2158244014522633

53. Harvey, W. S. (2010). Methodological approaches for interviewing elites. *Geography Compass*, 4(3), 193-205. https://doi.org/10.1111/j.1749-8198.2009.00313.x

54. Inkpen, A. C. (2008). Knowledge transfer and international joint ventures: The case of NUMMI and General Motors. *Strategic Management Journal*, 29(4), 447-453. https://doi.org/10.1002/smj.663

55. Hoffmann, W. H. (2007). Strategies for managing a portfolio of alliances. *Strategic Management Journal*, 28(8), 827-856. https://doi.org/10.1002/smj.607

56. Aguinis, H., Henle, C., & Ostroff, C. (2001). Measurement in work and organizational psychology. In N. Anderson, D. S. Ones, & H. K. Sinangil. *Handbook of industrial, work & organizational psychology* (Vol. 2, pp. 27-50). SAGE Publications. https://doi.org/10.4135/9781848608320.n3

57. King, N. (1998). The Qualitative Research Interview. In Gillian, S. and Cassell, C. (Eds.), *Qualitative Methods and Analysis in Organizational Research: A Practical Guide*. SAGE Publications (pp. 118-1340).

58. Berry, J. M. (2002). Validity and reliability issues in elite interviewing. *PS: Political Science & Politics*, 35(4), 679-682. https://doi.org/10.1017/S1049096502001166

59. Aguinis, H., Henle, C., & Ostroff, C. (2001). Measurement in work and organizational psychology. In N. Anderson, D. S. Ones, & H. K. Sinangil. *Handbook of industrial, work & organizational psychology* (Vol. 2, pp. 27-50). SAGE Publications. https://doi.org/10.4135/9781848608320.n3

60. LeBreton, J. M., & Senter, J. L. (2008). Answers to 20 questions about interrater reliability and interrater agreement. *Organizational Research Methods*, 11(4), 815-852. https://doi.org/10.1177/1094428106296642

61. Patton, M. Q. (1990). *Qualitative Evaluations and Research Methods*. SAGE Publications.

62. Given, L. M. (Ed.). (2008). *The Sage encyclopedia of qualitative research methods*. SAGE Publications. https://doi.org/10.4135/9781412963909

63. Lincoln, Y.S., & Guba, E. G. (1985). *Naturalistic Inquiry*. SAGE Publications. https://doi.org/10.1016/0147-1767(85)90062-8

64. Short, J. C., Broberg, J. C., Cogliser, C. C., & Brigham, K. H. (2010). Construct validation using computer-aided text analysis (CATA) an illustration using entrepreneurial orientation. *Organizational Research Methods*, 13(2), 320-347. https://doi.org/10.1177/1094428109335949

65. McKenny, A. F., Short, J. C., & Payne, G. T. (2013). Using computer-aided text analysis to elevate constructs: An illustration using psychological capital. *Organizational Research Methods*, 16(1), 152-184. https://doi.org/10.1177/1094428112459910

66. Gangloff, K. A., Connelly, B. L., & Shook, C. L. (2016). Of scapegoats and signals: Investor reactions to CEO succession in the aftermath of wrongdoing. *Journal of Management*, 42(6), 1614-1634. https://doi.org/10.1177/0149206313515521

67. Brett, J. M., Olekalns, M., Friedman, R., Goates, N., Anderson, C., & Lisco, C. C. (2007). Sticks and stones: Language, face, and online dispute resolution. *Academy of Management Journal*, 50(1),

85-99. https://doi.org/10.5465/am j.2007.24161853

68. Aguinis, H., & Edwards, J. R. (2014). Methodological wishes for the next decade and how to make wishes come true. *Journal of Management Studies*, *51*(1), 143-174. https://doi.org/10.1111/joms.12058

69. Short, J. C., Broberg, J. C., Cogliser, C. C., & Brigham, K. H. (2010). Construct validation using computer-aided text analysis (CATA) an illustration using entrepreneurial orientation. *Organizational Research Methods*, *13*(2), 320-347. https://doi.org/10.1177/1094428109335949

70. Dalton, D. R., & Aguinis, H. (2013). Measurement malaise in strategic management studies: The case of corporate governance research. *Organizational Research Methods*, *16*(1), 88-99. https://doi.org/10.1177/1094428112470846

71. McKenny, A. F., Short, J. C., Zachary, M. A., & Payne, G. T. (2012). Assessing espoused goals in private family firms using content analysis. *Family Business Review*, *25*(3), 298-317. https://doi.org/10.1177/0894486511420422

72. Aguinis, H. (1995). Statistical power problems with moderated multiple regression in management research. *Journal of Management*, *21*(6), 1141-1158. https://doi.org/10.1016/0149-2063(95)90026-8

73. Aguinis, H., & Vandenberg, R. J. (2014). An ounce of prevention is worth a pound of cure: Improving research quality before data collection. *Annual Review of Organizational Psychology and Organizational Behavior*, *1*(1), 569-595. https://doi.org/10.1146/annurev-orgpsych-031413-091231

74. Schmidt, F. L., Le, H., & Ilies, R. (2003). Beyond alpha: An empirical examination of the effects of different sources of measurement error on reliability estimates for measures of individual-differences constructs. *Psychological*

Methods, *8*(2), 206. https://doi.org/10.1037/1082-989X.8.2.206

75. Aguinis, H., & Vandenberg, R. J. (2014). An ounce of prevention is worth a pound of cure: Improving research quality before data collection. *Annual Review of Organizational Psychology and Organizational Behavior*, *1*(1), 569-595. https://doi.org/10.1146/annurev-orgpsych-031413-091231

76. Barr, P. S., Stimpert, J. L., & Huff, A. S. (1992). Cognitive change, strategic action, and organizational renewal. *Strategic Management Journal*, *13*(S1), 15-36. https://doi.org/10.1002/smj.4250131004

77. Savani, K., & King, D. (2015). Perceiving outcomes as determined by external forces: The role of event construal in attenuating the outcome bias. *Organizational Behavior and Human Decision Processes*, *130*, 136-146. https://doi.org/10.1016/j.obhdp.2015.05.002

78. Short, J. C., Broberg, J. C., Cogliser, C. C., & Brigham, K. H. (2010). Construct validation using computer-aided text analysis (CATA) an illustration using entrepreneurial orientation. *Organizational Research Methods*, *13*(2), 320-347. https://doi.org/10.1177/1094428109335949

79. Short, J. C., Broberg, J. C., Cogliser, C. C., & Brigham, K. H. (2010). Construct validation using computer-aided text analysis (CATA) an illustration using entrepreneurial orientation. *Organizational Research Methods*, *13*(2), 320-347. https://doi.org/10.1177/1094428109335949

80. Short, J. C., Broberg, J. C., Cogliser, C. C., & Brigham, K. H. (2010). Construct validation using computer-aided text analysis (CATA) an illustration using entrepreneurial orientation. *Organizational Research Methods*, *13*(2), 320-347. https://doi.org/10.1177/1094428109335949

81. Wright, P. M. (2016). Ensuring research integrity: An editor's perspective. *Journal of*

Management, *42*(5), 1037-1043. https://doi.org/10.1177/0149206316643931

82. Butler, N., Delaney, H., & Spoelstra, S. (2017). The gray zone: Questionable research practices in the business school. *Academy of Management Learning & Education*, *16*(1), 94-109. https://doi.org/10.5465/amle.2015.0201

83. Aguinis, H., Hill, N. S., & Bailey, J. R. (2021). Best practices in data collection and preparation: Recommendations for reviewers, editors, and authors. *Organizational Research Methods*, *24*(4), 678-693. https://doi.org/10.1177/1094428119836485

84. Kunisch, S., Menz, M., Bartunek, J. M., Cardinal, L. B., & Denyer, D. (2018). Feature topic at organizational research methods: how to conduct rigorous and impactful literature reviews?. *Organizational Research Methods*, *21*(3), 519-523. https://doi.org/10.1177/1094428118770750

85. Adams, R. J., Smart, P., & Huff, A. S. (2017). Shades of grey: Guidelines for working with the grey literature in systematic reviews for management and organizational studies. *International Journal of Management Reviews*, *19*(4), 432-454. https://doi.org/10.1111/ijmr.12102

86. Aguinis, H., Cummings, C., Ramani, R. S., & Cummings, T. G. (2020). "An A is an A": The new bottom line for valuing academic research. *Academy of Management Perspectives*, *34*(1), 135-154. https://doi.org/10.5465/amp.2017.0193

87. Murphy, K. R., & Aguinis, H. (2019). HARKing: How badly can cherry-picking and question trolling produce bias in published results?. *Journal of Business and Psychology*, *34*(1), 1-17. https://doi.org/10.1007/s10869-017-9524-7

88. Corley, K. G., & Schinoff, B. S. (2017). Who, me? An inductive study of novice experts in the context of how editors come to understand theoretical contribution.

Academy of Management Perspectives, 31(1), 4-27. https://doi.org/10.5465/amp.2015.0131

89. Jones, O., & Gatrell, C. (2014). The future of writing and reviewing for IJMR. *International Journal of Management Reviews, 16*(3), 249-264. https://doi.org/10.1111/ijmr.12038

90. Aguinis, H., Hill, N. S., & Bailey, J. R. (2021). Best practices in data collection and preparation: Recommendations for reviewers, editors, and authors. *Organizational Research Methods, 24*(4), 678-693. https://doi.org/10.1177/1094428119836485

91. Greene, J. C., Caracelli, V. J., & Graham, W. F. (1989). Toward a conceptual framework for mixed-method evaluation designs. *Educational Evaluation and Policy Analysis, 11*(3), 255-274. https://doi.org/10.3102/01623737011003255

92. Denscombe, M. (2008). Communities of practice: A research paradigm for the mixed methods approach. *Journal of Mixed Methods Research, 2*(3), 270-283. https://doi.org/10.1177/1558689808316807

93. Jick, T. D. (1979). Mixing qualitative and quantitative methods: Triangulation in action. *Administrative Science Quarterly, 24*(4), 602-611. https://doi.org/10.2307/2392366

94. Greene, J. C., Caracelli, V. J., & Graham, W. F. (1989). Toward a conceptual framework for mixed-method evaluation designs. *Educational Evaluation and Policy Analysis, 11*(3), 255-274. https://doi.org/10.3102/01623737011003255

95. Morgan, D. L. (1998). Practical strategies for combining qualitative and quantitative methods: Applications to health research. *Qualitative Health Research, 8*(3), 362-376. https://doi.org/10.1177/104973239800800307

96. Rouse, M. J., & Daellenbach, U. S. (1999). Rethinking research methods for the resource-based perspective: isolating sources of sustainable competitive advantage. *Strategic Management Journal, 20*(5), 487-494. https://doi.org/10.1002/(SICI)1097-0266(199905)20:5 < 487::AID-SMJ26>3.0.CO;2-K

97. Molina-Azorin, J. F. (2012). Mixed methods research in strategic management: Impact and applications. *Organizational Research Methods, 15*(1), 33-56. https://doi.org/10.1177/1094428110393023

98. Bergh, D. D., Sharp, B. M., Aguinis, H., & Li, M. (2017). Is there a credibility crisis in strategic management research? Evidence on the reproducibility of study findings. *Strategic Organization, 15*(3), 423-436. https://doi.org/10.1177/1476127017701076

99. Tsang, E. W., & Kwan, K. M. (1999). Replication and theory development in organizational science: A critical realist perspective. *Academy of Management Review, 24*(4), 759-780. https://doi.org/10.5465/amr.1999.2553252

100. Cascio, W. F., & Aguinis, H. (2018). *Applied psychology in talent management* (8th edition). SAGE Publications. https://doi.org/10.4135/9781506375953

101. Guion, R. M. (2011). *Assessment, measurement, and prediction for personnel decisions*. Routledge. https://doi.org/10.4324/9780203836767

102. Kell, H. J., Martin-Raugh, M. P., Carney, L. M., Inglese, P. A., Chen, L., & Feng, G. (2017). Exploring methods for developing behaviorally anchored rating scales for evaluating structured interview performance. *ETS Research Report Series, 2017*(1), 1-26. https://doi.org/10.1002/ets2.12152

103. Creswell, J. W., & Poth, C. N. (2016). *Qualitative inquiry and research design: Choosing among five approaches*. SAGE Publications.

104. Monteiro, F., & Birkinshaw, J. (2017). The external knowledge sourcing process in multinational corporations. *Strategic Management Journal, 38*(2), 342-362. https://doi.org/10.1002/smj.2487

105. Ma, S., & Seidl, D. (2018). New CEOs and their collaborators: Divergence and convergence between the strategic leadership constellation and the top management team. *Strategic Management Journal, 39*(3), 606-638. https://doi.org/10.1002/smj.2721

106. Van Bavel, J. J., Mende-Siedlecki, P., Brady, W. J., & Reinero, D. A. (2016). Contextual sensitivity in scientific reproducibility. *Proceedings of the National Academy of Sciences, 113*(23), 6454-6459. https://doi.org/10.1073/pnas.1521897113

107. Boyd, B. K., & Solarino, A. M. (2016). Ownership of corporations: A review, synthesis, and research agenda. *Journal of Management, 42*(5), 1282-1314. https://doi.org/10.1177/0149206316633746

108. Wood, A. (2009). Capacity rationalization and exit strategies. *Strategic Management Journal, 30*(1), 25-44. https://doi.org/10.1002/smj.725

109. Berger, R. (2015). Now I see it, now I don't: You's position and reflexivity in qualitative research. *Qualitative Research, 15*(2), 219-234. https://doi.org/10.1177/1468794112468475

110. Gioia, D. A., & Chittipeddi, K. (1991). Sensemaking and sensegiving in strategic change initiation. *Strategic Management Journal, 12*(6), 433-448. ttps://doi.org/10.1002/smj.4250120604

111. Ferlie, E., Fitzgerald, L., Wood, M., & Hawkins, C. (2005). The non-spread of innovations: the mediating role of professionals. *Academy of Management Journal, 48*(1), 117-134. https://doi.org/10.5465/amj.2005.15993150

112. Aguinis, H., Gottfredson, R. K., & Joo, H. (2013). Best-practice recommendations for defining, identifying, and handling outliers. *Organizational Research Methods,*

16(2), 270-301. https://doi.org/10.1177/1094428112470848

113. Shaffer, B., & Hillman, A. J. (2000). The development of business–government strategies by diversified firms. *Strategic Management Journal*, *21*(2), 175-190. https://doi.org/10.1002/(SICI)1097-0266(200002)21:2 < 175::AID-SMJ86>3.0.CO;2-L

114. Opdenakker, R. (2006, September). Advantages and disadvantages of four interview techniques in qualitative research. In *Forum Qualitative Sozialforschung/Forum: Qualitative Social Research* 7(4). https://doi.org/10.17169/fqs-7.4.175

115. Bruton, G. D., Ahlstrom, D., & Wan, J. C. (2003). Turnaround in East Asian firms: Evidence from ethnic overseas Chinese communities. *Strategic Management Journal*, *24*(6), 519-540. https://doi.org/10.1002/smj.312

116. Bowen, G. A. (2008). Naturalistic inquiry and the saturation concept: a research note. *Qualitative Research*, *8*(1), 137-152. https://doi.org/10.1177/1468794107085301

117. Guest, G., Bunce, A., & Johnson, L. (2006). How many interviews are enough? An experiment with data saturation and variability. *Field Methods*, *18*(1), 59-82. https://doi.org/10.1177/1525822X05279903

118. Michel, A. (2014). The mutual constitution of persons and organizations: An ontological perspective on organizational change. *Organization Science*, *25*(4), 1082-1110. https://doi.org/10.1287/orsc.2013.0887

119. Yeung, H. W. C. (1995). Qualitative personal interviews in international business research: some lessons from a study of Hong Kong transnational corporations. *International Business Review*, *4*(3), 313-339. https://doi.org/10.1016/0969-5931(95)00012-O

120. Stephens, N. (2007). Collecting data from elites and ultra elites: telephone and face-to-face interviews with macroeconomists. *Qualitative Research*, *7*(2), 203-216.

https://doi.org/10.1177/1468794107076020

121. Dacin, M. T., Munir, K., & Tracey, P. (2010). Formal dining at Cambridge colleges: Linking ritual performance and institutional maintenance. *Academy of Management Journal*, *53*(6), 1393-1418. https://doi.org/10.5465/amj.2010.57318388

122. Klingebiel, R., & Joseph, J. (2016). Entry timing and innovation strategy in feature phones. *Strategic Management Journal*, *37*(6), 1002-1020. https://doi.org/10.1002/smj.2385

123. Gao, C., Zuzul, T., Jones, G., & Khanna, T. (2017). Overcoming institutional voids: A reputation-based view of long-run survival. *Strategic Management Journal*, *38*(11), 2147-2167. https://doi.org/10.1002/smj.2649

124. Molina-Azorin, J. F. (2012). Mixed methods research in strategic management: Impact and applications. *Organizational Research Methods*, *15*(1), 33-56. https://doi.org/10.1177/1094428110393023

125. Molina-Azorin, J. F., Bergh, D. D., Corley, K. G., & Ketchen Jr, D. J. (2017). Mixed methods in the organizational sciences: Taking stock and moving forward. *Organizational Research Methods*, *20*(2), 179-192. https://doi.org/10.1177/1094428116687026

CHAPTER 14

1. Grand, J. A., Rogelberg, S. G., Allen, T. D., Landis, R. S., Reynolds, D. H., Scott, J. C., Tonidandel, S., & Truxillo, D. M. (2018). A systems-based approach to fostering robust science in industrial-organizational psychology. *Industrial and Organizational Psychology*, *11*(1), 4-42. https://doi.org/10.1017/iop.2017.55

2. Nuijten, M. B., Hartgerink, C. H., Assen, M. A., Epskamp, S., & Wicherts, J. M. (2016). The prevalence of statistical reporting

errors in psychology (1985–2013). *Behavior Research Methods*, *48*(4), 1205-1226. https://doi.org/10.3758/s13428-015-0664-2

3. Banks, G. C., Rogelberg, S. G., Woznyj, H. M., Landis, R. S., & Rupp, D. E. (2016). Editorial: Evidence on questionable research practices: The good, the bad, and the ugly. *Journal of Business and Psychology, 31*(3), 323-338. https://doi.org/10.1007/s10869-016-9456-7

4. Cortina, J. M., Green, J. P., Keeler, K. R., & Vandenberg, R. J. (2017). Degrees of freedom in SEM: Are we testing the models that we claim to test? *Organizational Research Methods, 20*(3), 350-378. https://journals.sagepub.com/doi/10.1177/1094428116676345

5. O'Boyle, E. H., Banks, G. C., & Gonzalez-Mulé, E. (2017). The chrysalis effect: How ugly initial results metamorphosize into beautiful articles. *Journal of Management, 43*(2), 376-399. https://journals.sagepub.com/doi/abs/10.1177/0149206314527133

6. Goodman, S. N., Fanelli, D., & Ioannidis, J. P. (2016). What does research reproducibility mean?. *Science Translational Medicine, 8*(341), 341-353. https://doi.org/10.1126/scitranslmed.aaf5027

7. Cascio, W. F., & Aguinis, H. (2001).The Federal Uniform Guidelines on Employee Selection Procedures (1978): An update on selected issues. *Review of Public Personnel Administration, 21*(3), 200-218. https://journals.sagepub.com/doi/10.1177/0734371X0102100303

8. Aguinis, H., & Harden, E. E. (2009). Sample size rules of thumb: Evaluating three common practices. In C. E. Lance and R. J. Vandenberg (Eds.), *Statistical and methodological myths and urban legends: Received doctrine, verity, and fable in the organizational and social sciences* (pp. 269-288). Routledge.

9. Little, J. (2001). Understanding statistical significance: A

conceptual history. *Journal of Technical Writing and Communication, 31*(4), 363-372. https://journals.sagepub.com/doi/10.2190/TUL8-X9N5-N000-8LKV

10. Fisher, R. A. (1925). *Statistical methods for research workers*. Oliver and Boyd.

11. Gigerenzer, G. (1998). We need statistical thinking, not statistical rituals. *Behavioral and Brain Sciences, 21*(2), 199-200. https://doi.org/10.1017/S0140525X98281167

12. Rosnow, R. L., & Rosenthal, R. (1989). Statistical procedures and the justification of knowledge in psychological science. *American Psychologist, 44*(10), 1276-1284. https://psycnet.apa.org/doi/10.1037/10109-027

13. Hubbard, R. & Ryan, P. A. (2000). The historical grown of statistical significance testing in psychology—and its future prospects. *Educational and Psychological Measurement, 60*(5), 661-681. https://psycnet.apa.org/doi/10.1177/00131640021970808

14. Sedlmeier, P., & Gigerenzer, G. (1989). Do studies of statistical power have an effect on the power of studies? *Psychological Bulletin, 105*(2), 309-316. https://psycnet.apa.org/doi/10.1037/10109-032

15. Hunter, J. E. (1997). Needed: A ban on the significance test. *Psychological Science, 8*(1), 3-7. https://journals.sagepub.com/doi/10.1111/j.1467-9280.1997.tb00534.x

16. Zhang, X., Bartol, K. M., Smith, K. G., Pfarrer, M. D., & Khanin, D. M. (2008). CEOs on the edge: Earnings manipulation and stock-based incentive misalignment. *Academy of Management Journal, 51*(2), 241-258. https://doi.org/10.5465/amj.2008.31767230

17. Miller, D. J., Fern, M. J., & Cardinal, L. B. (2007). The use of knowledge for technological innovation within diversified firms. *Academy of Management Journal, 50*(2), 308-326. https://doi.org/10.5465/amj.2007.24634437

18. Murphy, K. R., & Myors, B. (1998). *Statistical power analysis: A simple and general model for traditional and modern hypothesis tests.* Erlbaum.

19. Aguinis, H. (2004). *Regression analysis for categorical moderators.* Guilford.

20. Murphy, K.R., & Myors, B. (1998). *Statistical power analysis: A simple and general model for traditional and modern hypothesis tests.* Erlbaum.

21. Aguinis, H., Pierce, C. A., & Culpepper, S. A. (2009). Scale coarseness as a methodological artifact: Correcting correlation coefficients attenuated from using coarse scales. *Organizational Research Methods, 12*(4), 623-652. https://journals.sagepub.com/doi/10.1177/1094428108318065

22. Cohen, J. (1983). The cost of dichotomization. *Applied Psychological Measurement, 7*(3), 249-253. https://journals.sagepub.com/doi/10.1177/014662168300700301

23. Aguinis, H., Werner, S., Lanza Abbott, J., Angert, C., Park, J. H., & Kohlhausen, D. (2010). Customer-centric science: Reporting significant research results with rigor, relevance, and practical impact in mind. *Organizational Research Methods, 13*(3), 515-539. https://journals.sagepub.com/doi/10.1177/1094428109333339

24. Fisher, R. A. (1959). *Statistical methods and scientific inference* (2nd edition). Hafner.

25. Gigerenzer, G. (1998). We need statistical thinking, not statistical rituals. *Behavioral and Brain Sciences, 21*(2), 199-200. https://doi.org/10.1017/S0140525X98281167

26. Aguinis, H., Pierce, C. A., Bosco, F. A., & Muslin, I. S (2009). First decade of Organizational Research Methods: Trends in design, measurement, and data-analysis topics. *Organizational Research Methods, 12*(1), 69-112. ht

tps://journals.sagepub.com/doi/10.1177/1094428108322641

27. Podsakoff, P. M., & Dalton, D. R. (1987). Research methodology in organizational studies. *Journal of Management, 13*(2), 419-441. https://journals.sagepub.com/doi/10.1177/014920638701300213

28. Tryon, W. W. (2001). Evaluating statistical difference, equivalence, and indeterminacy using inferential confidence intervals: An integrated alternative method of conducting null hypothesis statistical tests. *Psychological Methods, 6*(4), 371-386. https://psycnet.apa.org/doi/10.1037/1082-989X.6.4.371

29. Aguinis, H. (2004). *Regression analysis for categorical moderators.* Guilford.

30. Bedeian, A. G., Sturman, M. C., & Streiner, D. L. (2009). Decimal dust, significant digits, and the search for stars. *Organizational Research Methods, 12*(4), 687-694. https://journals.sagepub.com/doi/10.1177/1094428108321153.

31. Aguinis, H., Pierce, C. A., & Culpepper, S. A. (2009). Scale coarseness as a methodological artifact: Correcting correlation coefficients attenuated from using coarse scales. *Organizational Research Methods, 12*(4), 623-652. https://journals.sagepub.com/doi/10.1177/1094428108318065

32. Kelley, K., & Preacher, K. J. (2012). On effect size. *Psychological Methods, 17*(2), 137–152. https://psycnet.apa.org/doi/10.1037/a0028086

33. Kruschke, J. K., Aguinis, H., & Joo, H. (2012). The time has come: Bayesian methods for data analysis in the organizational sciences. *Organizational Research Methods, 15*(4), 722-752. https://journals.sagepub.com/doi/10.1177/1094428112457829

34. Grissom, R. J., & Kim, J. J. (2012). *Effect sizes for research: Univariate and multivariate applications* (2nd edition). Routledge.

35. Brooks, M. E., Dalal, D. K., & Nolan, K. P. (2014). Are common language effect sizes easier to understand than traditional effect sizes? *Journal of Applied Psychology, 99*(2), 332-340. https://psycnet.apa.org/doi/10.1037/a0034745

36. Yates, F. (1951). The influence of "statistical methods for research workers" on the development of the science of statistics. *Journal of the American Statistical Association, 46*(253), 19-34. https://doi.org/10.1080/01621459.1951.10500764

37. Schmidt, F. L. (1996). Statistical significance testing and cumulative knowledge in psychology: Implications for training of researchers. *Psychological Methods, 1*(2), 115-129. https://psycnet.apa.org/doi/10.1037/1082-989X.1.2.115

38. Cohen, J. (1994). The earth is round (*p*< 0.05). *American Psychologist, 49*(12), 997-1003. https://psycnet.apa.org/doi/10.1037/0003-066X.49.12.997

39. Tukey, J. W. (1991). The philosophy of multiple comparisons. *Statistical Science, 6*(1), 100-116. https://www.jstor.org/stable/2245714

40. Aguinis, H., & Harden, E. E. (2009). Cautionary note on conveniently dismissing χ^2 goodness-of-fit test results: Implications for strategic management research. In D. D. Bergh and D. J. Ketchen (Eds.), *Research methodology in strategy and management*, Vol. 5 (pp. 111-120). Emerald Group Publishing.

41. American Psychological Association. (2020). *Publication manual of the American Psychological Association* (7th edition). American Psychological Association. https://doi.org/10.1037 /0000165-000

42. Thompson, B. (2006). Role of effect sizes in contemporary research in counseling. *Counseling and Values, 50*(3), 176-186. https://doi.org/10.1002/j.2161-007X.2006.tb00054.x

43. Chow, S. L. (1998). Précis of statistical significance: Rationale, validity, and utility. *Behavioral and Brain Sciences, 21*(2), 169-239. https://doi.org/10.1017/S0140525X98001162

44. Abelson, R. P. (1997). On the surprising longevity of flogged horses: Why there is a case for the significance test. *Psychological Science, 8*(1), 12-15. https://journals.sagepub.com/doi/10.1111/j.1467-9280.1997.tb00536.x

45. Sink, C. A., & Stroh, H. R. (2006). Practical significance: The use of effect sizes in school counseling research. *Professional School Counseling, 9*(5), 401-411. https://www.jstor.org/stable/42732713

46. Aguinis, H., Mazurkiewicz, M. D., & Heggestad, E. D. (2009). Using Web-based frame-of-reference training to decrease biases in personality-based job analysis: An experimental field study. *Personnel Psychology, 62*(2), 405-438. https://doi.org/10.1111/j.1744-6570.2009.01144.x

47. Aguinis, H., & Smith, M. A. (2007). Understanding the impact of test validity and bias on selection errors and adverse impact in human resource selection. *Personnel Psychology, 60*(1), 165-199. https://doi.org/10.1111/j.1744-6570.2007.00069.x

48. Vacha-Haase, T., & Thompson, B. (2004). How to estimate and interpret various effect sizes. *Journal of Counseling Psychology, 51*(4), 473-481. https://psycnet.apa.org/doi/10.1037/0022-0167.51.4.473

49. Algina, J., & Keselman, H. J. (2003). Approximate confidence intervals for effect sizes. *Educational and Psychological Measurement, 63*(4), 537-553. https://journals.sagepub.com/doi/10.1177/0013164403256358

50. Bacharach, S. B. (1989). Organizational theories: Some criteria for evaluation. *Academy of Management Review, 14*(4), 496-515.

51. Cohen, J. (1988). *Statistical power analysis for the behavioral sciences* (2nd edition). Lawrence Erlbaum Associates.

52. Ellis, P. D. (2010). *The essential guide to effect sizes: Statistical power, meta-analysis, and the interpretation of research results.* Cambridge University Press.

53. Rosnow, R. L., & Rosenthal, R. (2003). Effect sizes for experimenting psychologists. *Canadian Journal of Experimental Psychology, 57*(3), 221-237. https://psycnet.apa.org/doi/10.1037/h0087427

54. Rhoades, L., & Eisenberger, R. (2002). Perceived organizational support: a review of the literature. *Journal of Applied Psychology, 87*(4), 698-714. https://doi.org/10.1037/0021-9010.87.4.698

55. Rudolph, C. W., Wells, C. L., Weller, M. D., & Baltes, B. B. (2009). A meta-analysis of empirical studies of weight-based bias in the workplace. *Journal of Vocational Behavior, 74*(1), 1-10. https://doi.org/10.1016/j.jvb.2008.09.008

56. Ferguson, C. J. (2009). An effect size primer: A guide for clinicians and researchers. *Professional Psychology: Research and Practice, 40*(5), 532-538. https://psycnet.apa.org/doi/10.1037/a0015808

57. Wilkinson, L., & APA Task Force on Statistical Inference. (1999). Statistical methods in psychology journals: Guidelines and explanations. *American Psychologist, 54*(8), 594–604. https://psycnet.apa.org/doi/10.1037/0003-066X.54.8.594

58. Bosco, F. A., Aguinis, H., Singh, K., Field, J. G., & Pierce, C. A. (2015). Correlational effect size benchmarks. *Journal of Applied Psychology, 100*(2), 431-449. https://psycnet.apa.org/doi/10.1037/a0038047

59. Dalton, D. R., Aguinis, H., Dalton, C. A., Bosco, F. A., & Pierce, C. A. (2012). Revisiting the file drawer problem in meta-analysis: An empirical assessment of published and non-published correlation matrices. *Personnel Psychology, 65*(2), 221-249. https://

doi.org/10.1111/j.1744-6570.2012
.01243.x

60. Cohen, J. (1988). *Statistical power
analysis for the behavioral sciences*
(2nd edition). Lawrence Erlbaum
Associates.

61. Higgins, J. P. T., &Thompson, S. G.
(2002). Quantifying heterogeneity
in a meta-analysis. *Statistics in
Medicine, 21*(11), 1539-1558. https:
//doi.org/10.1002/sim.1186

62. Hunter, J. E., & Schmidt, F. L.
(2004*). Methods of meta-analysis:
Correcting error and bias in
research findings* (2nd edition).
Academic Press.

63. Cohen, J. (1988). *Statistical power
analysis for the behavioral sciences*
(2nd edition). Lawrence Erlbaum
Associates.

64. Hill, C. J., Bloom, H. S., Black, A.
R., & Lipsey, M. W. (2008). (2008).
Empirical benchmarks for inter-
preting effect sizes in research.
*Child Development Perspectives,
2*(3), 172-177.

65. Cohen, J. (1988). *Statistical power
analysis for the behavioral sciences*
(2nd edition). Lawrence Erlbaum
Associates.

66. Faul, F., Erdfelder, E., Buchner, A.,
& Lang, A.-G. (2009). Statistical
power analyses using G*Power
3.1: Tests for correlation and
regression analyses. *Behavior
Research Methods, 41*(4), 1149-
1160. https://doi.org/10.3758/BR
M.41.4.1149

67. Kirk, R. E. (1996). Practical significance: A concept whose time has
come. *Educational and Psychological Measurement, 56*(5), 746-759. h
ttps://journals.sagepub.com/doi/
10.1177/0013164496056005002

68. Cortina, J. M., & Landis, R. S.
(2009). When small effect sizes
tell a big story, and when large
effect sizes don't. In C. E. Lance
and R. J. Vandenberg (Eds.), *Statistical and methodological myths
and urban legends: Received doctrine, verity, and fable in the organizational and social sciences* (pp.
287-308). Routledge.

69. Cohen, J. (1962). The statistical
power of abnormal-social psychological research: A review. *Journal
of Abnormal and Social Psychology,
65*(3), 145-153. https://psycnet.ap
a.org/doi/10.1037/h0045186

70. Aguinis, H., Beaty, J. C., Boik, R.
J., & Pierce, C. A. (2005). Effect
size and power in assessing moderating effects of categorical variables using multiple regression: A
30-year review. *Journal of Applied
Psychology, 90*(1), 94-107. https://
psycnet.apa.org/doi/10.1037/002
1-9010.90.1.94

71. Cohen, J. (1988). *Statistical power
analysis for the behavioral sciences*
(2nd edition). Lawrence Erlbaum
Associates.

72. Cohen, J. (1992). A power primer.
Psychological Bulletin, 112(1),
155-159. https://psycnet.apa.org/
doi/10.1037/0033-2909.112.1.155

73. Thompson, B. (2002). "Statistical," "practical," and "clinical":
How many kinds of significance
do counselors need to consider?
*Journal of Counseling & Develop-
ment, 80*(1), 64-71. https://doi.or
g/10.1002/j.1556-6678.2002.tb00
167.x

74. Aguinis, H., Werner, S., Lanza
Abbott, J., Angert, C., Park, J. H.,
& Kohlhausen, D. (2010). Customer-centric science: Reporting
significant research results with
rigor, relevance, and practical
impact in mind. *Organizational
Research Methods, 13*(3), 515-539.
https://journals.sagepub.com/doi
/10.1177/1094428109333339

75. Vaske, J. J., Gliner, J. A., & Morgan, G. A. (2002). Communicating
judgements about practical significance: effect size, confidence
intervals and odds ratios. *Human
Dimensions of Wildlife, 7*(4), 287-
300. https://doi.org/10.1080/1087
1200214752

76. Armstrong, S. A., & Henson, R.
K. (2004). Statistical and practical significance in the IJPT: A
research review from 1993-2003.
International Journal of Play

Therapy, 13(2), 9-30. https://psycn
et.apa.org/doi/10.1037/h0088888

77. Baldridge, D. C., Floyd, S. W., &
Markóczy, L. (2004). Are managers from Mars and academicians from Venus? Toward an
understanding of the relationship
between academic quality and
practical relevance. *Strategic
Management Journal, 25*(11), 1063-
1074. https://doi.org/10.1002/smj.
406

78. Rynes, S. L., Colbert, A. E., &
Brown, K. G. (2002). HR professionals' beliefs about effective
human resource practices: Correspondence between research
and practice. *Human Resource
Management, 41*(2), 149-174. https:
//doi.org/10.1002/hrm.10029

79. Willig, C., & Stainton-Rogers, W.
(2008). Introduction. In C. Willig
and W. Sainton-Rogers (Eds.),
*Sage handbook of qualitative
research in psychology* (pp. 1-12).
Sage.

80. Green, J. L., Camilli, G., & Elmore,
P. B. Eds. (2006). *Handbook of
complementary methods in education research.* Lawrence Erlbaum.

81. Griffin, C., & Bengry-Howell, A.
(2008). Ethnography. In C. Willig
and W. Sainton-Rogers (Eds.),
*Sage handbook of qualitative
research in psychology* (pp. 15-31).
Sage.

82. Steier, F. (Ed.). (1991). *Research
and reflexivity.* Sage.

83. Wilkinson, S., & Kitzinger, C.
(2008). Conversation analysis. In
C. Willig and W. Sainton-Rogers
(Eds.), *Sage handbook of qualitative
research in psychology* (pp. 54-71).
Sage.

84. Wilkinson, S., & Kitzinger, C.
(2006). Surprise as an interac-
tional achievement: Reaction
tokens in conversation. *Social Psychology Quarterly, 69*(2), 150-182. h
ttps://journals.sagepub.com/doi/
10.1177/019027250606900203

85. Wilkinson, S., & Kitzinger, C.
(2008). Conversation analysis. In
C. Willig and W. Sainton-Rogers

(Eds.), *Sage handbook of qualitative research in psychology* (pp. 54-71). Sage.

86. Phillips, N., Sewell, G., & Jaynes, S. (2008). Applying critical discourse analysis in strategic management research. *Organizational Research Methods, 11*(4), 770-789. https://journals.sagepub.com/doi/10.1177/1094428107310837

87. Connelly, F. M., & Clandinin, D. J. (2006). Narrative inquiry. In J. L. Green, G. Camilli, & P. B. Elmore (Eds.), *Handbook of complementary methods in education research* (pp. 477-488). Lawrence Erlbaum.

88. Cheung, G. W., & Rensvold, R. B. (2001). The effects of model parsimony and sampling error on the fit of structural equation models. *Organizational Research Methods, 4*(3), 236-264. https://journals.sagepub.com/doi/10.1177/109442810143004

89. Aguinis, H., & Harden, E. E. (2009). Cautionary note on conveniently dismissing χ^2 goodness-of-fit test results: Implications for strategic management research. In D. D. Bergh and D. J. Ketchen (Eds.), *Research methodology in strategy and management*, Vol. 5 (pp. 111-120). Emerald Group Publishing.

90. Marsh, H. W., Hau, K., & Wen, Z. (2004). In search of golden rules: Comment on hypothesis-testing approaches to setting cutoff values for fit indexes and dangers in overgeneralizing Hu and Bentler's (1999) findings. *Structural Equation Modeling, 11*(3), 320-341. https://doi.org/10.1207/s15328007sem1103_2

91. Bentler, P. M., & Bonett, D. G. (1980). Significance tests and goodness of fit in the analysis of covariance structures. *Psychological Bulletin, 88*(3), 588-606. https://psycnet.apa.org/doi/10.1037/0033-2909.88.3.588

92. Cascio, W. F., & Aguinis, H. (2005). Test development and use: New twists on old questions. *Human Resource Management, 44*(3),

219-235. https://doi.org/10.1002/hrm.20068

93. Aguinis, H., Beaty, J. C., Boik, R. J., & Pierce, C. A. (2005). Effect size and power in assessing moderating effects of categorical variables using multiple regression: A 30-year review. *Journal of Applied Psychology, 90*(1), 94-107. https://psycnet.apa.org/doi/10.1037/0021-9010.90.1.94

94. Marsh, H. W., Hau, K., & Wen, Z. (2004). In search of golden rules: Comment on hypothesis-testing approaches to setting cutoff values for fit indexes and dangers in overgeneralizing Hu and Bentler's (1999) findings. *Structural Equation Modeling, 11*(3), 320-341. https://doi.org/10.1207/s15328007sem1103_2

95. Cohen, J., Cohen, P., West, S. G., & Aiken, L. S. (2003). *Applied multiple regression/correlation analysis for the behavioral sciences* (3rd edition). Erlbaum.

96. Maxwell, S. E., & Delaney, H. D. (2000). *Designing experiments and analyzing data: A model comparison perspective*. Erlbaum.

97. Tabachnick, B. G., & Fidell, L. S. (2001). *Using multivariate statistics* (4th edition). Allyn & Bacon.

98. Haase, R. F. (1983). Classical and partial eta square in multifactor ANOVA designs. *Educational and Psychological Measurement, 43*(1), 35-39. https://journals.sagepub.com/doi/10.1177/001316448304300105

99. Cohen, J. (1973). Eta-squared and partial eta-squared in fixed factor ANOVA designs. *Educational and Psychological Measurement, 33*(1), 107-112. https://journals.sagepub.com/doi/10.1177/001316448304300105

100. Pierce, C. A., Block, R. A., & Aguinis, H. (2004). Cautionary note on reporting eta-squared values from multifactor ANOVA designs. *Educational and Psychological Measurement, 64*(6), 916-924. https://journals.sagepub.com/doi/10.1177/0013164404264848

101. Ioannidis, J. P. A. (2007). Limitations are not properly acknowledged in the scientific literature. *Journal of Clinical Epidemiology, 60*(4), 324–329. https://doi.org/10.1016/j.jclinepi.2006.09.011

102. Ashkanasy, N. M. (2010). Publishing today is more difficult than ever. *Journal of Organizational Behavior, 31*(1), 1-3. https://www.jstor.org/stable/41683890

103. Aguinis, H., Cummings, C., Ramani, R. S., & Cummings, T. G. (2020). "An A is an A": The new bottom line for valuing academic research. *Academy of Management Perspectives, 34*(1), 135-154. https://doi.org/10.5465/amp.2017.0193

104. Honig, B., & Bedi, A. (2012). The fox in the hen house: A critical examination of plagiarism among members of the Academy of Management authors. *Academy of Management Learning and Education, 11*(1), 101-123. https://doi.org/10.5465/amle.2010.0084

105. Brutus, S., Aguinis, H., & Wassmer, U. (2013). Self-reported limitations and future directions in scholarly reports: Analysis and recommendations. *Journal of Management, 39*(1), 48-75. https://journals.sagepub.com/doi/10.1177/0149206312455245

106. Popper, K. R. (1959). *The logic of scientific discovery*. Basic Books.

107. American Psychological Association. (2020). *Publication manual of the American Psychological Association* (7th edition). American Psychological Association. https://doi.org/10.1037/0000165-000

108. Brutus, S., Gill, H., & Duniewicz, K. (2010). Self-reported limitations in industrial and organizational psychology. *Personnel Psychology, 63*(4), 907-936. https://doi.org/10.1111/j.1744-6570.2010.01192.x

109. Harrison, D. A. (2002). From the editors: Obligations and obfuscations in the review process. *Academy of Management Journal, 45*(6), 1079-1084. https://doi.org/10.5465/amj.2002.9265944

110. Gilliland, S. W., & Cortina, J. M. (1997). Reviewer and editor decision making in the journal review process. *Personnel Psychology*, *50*(2), 427-452. https://doi.org/10.1111/j.1744-6570.1997.tb00914.x

111. Van Lange, P. A. M. (1999). Why authors believe that reviewers stress limiting aspects of manuscripts: The SLAM effect in peer review. *Journal of Applied Social Psychology*, *29*(12), 2550-2566. https://doi.org/10.1111/j.1559-1816.1999.tb00125.x

112. Highhouse, S. (2009). Designing experiments that generalize. *Organizational Research Methods*, *12*(3), 554–566. https://journals.sagepub.com/doi/10.1177/1094428107300396

113. Aguinis, H., & Lawal, S. O. (2012). Conducting field experiments using eLancing's natural environment. *Journal of Business Venturing*, *27*(4), 493-505. https://doi.org/10.1016/j.jbusvent.2012.01.002

114. Shen, W., Kiger, T. B., Davies, S. E., Rasch, R. L., Simon, K. M., & Ones, D. (2011). Samples in applied psychology: Over a decade of research in review. *Journal of Applied Psychology*, *96*(5), 1055-1064. https://psycnet.apa.org/doi/10.1037/a0023322

115. Glynn, M. A., & Rafaelli, R. (2010). Uncovering mechanisms of theory development in an academic field: Lessons from leadership research. *Academy of Management Annals*, *4*(1), 359-401. https://doi.org/10.5465/19416520.2010.495530

116. Barley, S. R. (2006). When I write my masterpiece: Thoughts on what makes a paper interesting. *Academy of Management Journal*, *49*(1), 16–20. https://doi.org/10.5465/amj.2006.20785495

117. Aguinis, H., & Cronin, M. A. 2022. It's the theory, stupid. *Organizational Psychology Review*. https://doi.org/10.1177/20413866221080629

118. Davis, G. F. (2010). Do theories of organizations progress? *Organizational Research Methods*, *13*(4), 690–709. https://journals.sagepub.com/doi/10.1177/1094428110376995

119. Bartunek, J. M., & Rynes, S. L. (2010). The construction and contributions of "implications for practice": What's in them and what might they offer? *Academy of Management Learning and Education*, *9*(1), 10–117. https://doi.org/10.5465/amle.9.1.zqr100

CHAPTER 15

1. Bosco, F. A., Aguinis, H., Field, J. G., Pierce, C. A., & Dalton, D. R. (2016). HARKing's threat to organizational research: Evidence from primary and meta-analytic sources. *Personnel Psychology*, *69*(3), 709-750. https://doi.org/10.1111/peps.12111

2. Banks, G. C., Rogelberg, S. G., Woznyj, H. M., Landis, R. S., & Rupp, D. E. (2016). Evidence on questionable research practices: The good, the bad, and the ugly. *Journal of Business and Psychology*, *31*(3), 323-338. https://doi.org/10.1007/s10869-016-9456-7

3. Cortina, J. M., Aguinis, H., & DeShon, R. P. (2017). Twilight of dawn or of evening? A century of research methods in the Journal of Applied Psychology. *Journal of Applied Psychology*, *102*(3), 274-290. https://psycnet.apa.org/doi/10.1037/apl0000163

4. Dionne, S. D., Gupta, A., Sotak, K. L., Shirreffs, K. A., Serban, A., Hao, C., Kim, D. H., & Yammarino, F. J. (2014). A 25-year perspective on levels of analysis in leadership research. *Leadership Quarterly*, *25*(1), 6-35. https://doi.org/10.1016/j.leaqua.2013.11.002

5. Rousseau, D. M. (1985). Issues of level in organizational research: Multi-level and cross-level perspectives. *Research in Organizational Behavior*, *7*, 1-37.

6. Hitt, M. A., Beamish, P. W., Jackson, S. E., & Mathieu, J. E. (2007). Building theoretical and empirical bridges across levels: Multilevel research in management. *Academy of Management Journal*, *50*(6), 1385-1399. https://doi.org/10.5465/amj.2007.28166219

7. Walumbwa, F. O., Luthans, F., Avey, J. B., & Oke, A. (2011). Retraction. Authentically leading groups: The mediating role of collective psychological capital and trust. *Journal of Organizational Behavior*, *32*(1), 4-24 (Retraction published 2014, *Journal of Organizational Behavior*, *35*(5), 746). https://doi.org/10.1002/job.1936

8. Aguinis, H., Boyd, B. K., Pierce, C. A., & Short, J. C. (2011). Walking new avenues in management research methods and theories: Bridging micro and macro domains. *Journal of Management*, *37*(2), 395-403. https://journals.sagepub.com/doi/10.1177/0149206310382456

9. Hollenbeck, J. R. & Wright, P. M. (2017). Harking, sharking, and tharking: Making the case for post hoc analysis of scientific data. *Journal of Management*, *43*(1), 5-18. https://journals.sagepub.com/doi/10.1177/0149206316679487

10. Bosco, F. A., Aguinis, H., Field, J. G., Pierce, C. A., & Dalton, D. R. (2016). HARKing's threat to organizational research: Evidence from primary and meta-analytic sources. *Personnel Psychology*, *69*(3), 709-750. https://doi.org/10.1111/peps.12111

11. Murphy, K. R., & Aguinis, H. (2019). HARKing: How badly can cherry-picking and question trolling produce bias in published results?. *Journal of Business and Psychology*, *34*(1), 1-17. https://doi.org/10.1007/s10869-017-9524-7

12. Maitlis, S. (2005). The social processes of organizational sensemaking. *Academy of Management Journal*, *48*(1), 21-49. https://doi.org/10.5465/amj.2005.15993111

13. Williams, H. M., Parker, S. K., & Turner, N. (2010). Proactively performing teams: The role of work design, transformational leadership, and team composition.

Journal of Occupational and Organizational Psychology, 83(2), 301-324. https://doi.org/10.1348/096317910X502494

14. Aguinis, H., & Vandenberg, R. J. (2014). An ounce of prevention is worth a pound of cure: Improving research quality before data collection. *Annual Review of Organizational Psychology and Organizational Behavior,1*, 569-595. https://doi.org/10.1146/annurev-orgpsych-031413-091231

15. Becker, T. E. (2005). Potential problems in the statistical control of variables in organizational research: A qualitative analysis with recommendations. *Organizational Research Methods, 8*(3), 274-289. https://journals.sagepub.com/doi/10.1177/1094428105278021

16. Bernerth, J. B., & Aguinis, H. (2016). A critical review and best-practice recommendations for control variable usage. *Personnel Psychology, 69*(1), 229-283. https://doi.org/10.1111/peps.12103

17. Edwards, J. R. (2008). To prosper, organizational psychology should... Overcome methodological barriers to progress. *Journal of Organizational Behavior, 29*(4), 469-491. https://doi.org/10.1002/job.529

18. Becker, T. E. (2005). Potential problems in the statistical control of variables in organizational research: A qualitative analysis with recommendations. *Organizational Research Methods, 8*(3), 274-289. https://doi.org/10.1177/1094428105278021

19. Bernerth, J. B., & Aguinis, H. (2016). A critical review and best-practice recommendations for control variable usage. *Personnel Psychology, 69*(1), 229-283. https://doi.org/10.1111/peps.12103

20. Edwards, J. R. (2008). To prosper, organizational psychology should... Overcome methodological barriers to progress. *Journal of Organizational Behavior, 29*(4), 469-491. https://doi.org/10.1002/job.529

21. Tsai, W. C., Chen, C. C., & Liu, H. L. (2007). Test of a model linking employee positive moods and task performance. *Journal of Applied Psychology, 92*(6), 1570-1583. https://psycnet.apa.org/doi/10.1037/0021-9010.92.6.1570

22. Zhu, H., & Yoshikawa, T. (2016). Contingent value of director identification: The role of government directors in monitoring and resource provision in an emerging economy. *Strategic Management Journal, 37*(8), 1787-1807. https://doi.org/10.1002/smj.2408

23. Yammarino, F. J., Dionne, S. D., Chun, J. U., & Dansereau, F. (2005). Leadership and levels of analysis: A state-of-the-science review. *Leadership Quarterly, 16*(6), 879-919. https://doi.org/10.1016/j.leaqua.2005.09.002

24. Zhang, Y., & Shaw, J. D. (2012). From the editors: Publishing in AMJ-part 5: Crafting the methods and results. *Academy of Management Journal, 55*(1), 8-12. https://doi.org/10.5465/amj.2012.4001

25. Wu, J. B., Tsui, A. S., & Kinicki, A. J. (2010). Consequences of differentiated leadership in groups. *Academy of Management Journal, 53*(1), 90-106. https://doi.org/10.5465/amj.2010.48037079

26. Tashman, P., & Rivera, J. (2016). Ecological uncertainty, adaptation, and mitigation in the US ski resort industry: Managing resource dependence and institutional pressures. *Strategic Management Journal, 37*(7), 1507-1525. https://doi.org/10.1002/smj.2384

27. Freese, J. (2007). Replication standards for quantitative social science: Why not sociology. *Sociological Methods & Research, 36*(2), 153-172. https://journals.sagepub.com/doi/10.1177/0049124107306659

28. Waldman, I. D., & Lilienfeld, S. O. (2016). Thinking about data, research methods, and statistical analyses: Commentary on Sijtsma's (2014) "Playing with Data." *Psychometrika, 81*(1), 16-26. https://doi.org/10.1007/s11336-015-9447-z

29. Aguinis, H., Gottfredson R. K., & Joo, H. (2013). Best-practice recommendations for defining, identifying, and handling outliers. *Organizational Research Methods, 16*(2), 270–301. https://journals.sagepub.com/doi/10.1177/1094428112470848

30. Keselman, H. J., Algina, J., & Kowalchuk, R. K. (2001). The analysis of repeated measures designs: A review. *British Journal of Mathematical and Statistical Psychology, 54*(1), 1-20. https://doi.org/10.1348/000711001159357

31. Worren, N., Moore, K., & Cardona, P. (2002). Modularity, strategic flexibility, and firm performance: a study of the home appliance industry. *Strategic Management Journal, 23*(12), 1123-1140. https://doi.org/10.1002/smj.276

32. Amabile, T. M., Barsade, S. G., Mueller, J. S., & Staw, B. M. (2005). Affect and creativity at work. *Administrative Science Quarterly, 50*(3), 367-403. https://journals.sagepub.com/doi/10.2189/asqu.2005.50.3.367

33. Holtom, B. C., Baruch, Y., Aguinis, H., & Ballinger, G. A. (2022). Survey response rates: Trends and a validity assessment framework. *Human Relations.* https://doi.org/10.1177/00187267211070769

34. Weinzimmer, L. G., Mone, M. A., & Alwan, L. C. (1994). An examination of perceptions and usage of regression diagnostics in organization studies. *Journal of Management, 20*(1), 179-192. https://journals.sagepub.com/doi/10.1177/014920639402000110

35. Aguinis, H., O'Boyle, E. H., Gonzalez-Mulé, E., & Joo, H. (2016). Cumulative advantage: Conductors and insulators of heavy-tailed productivity distributions and productivity stars. *Personnel Psychology, 69*(1), 3-66. https://doi.org/10.1111/peps.12095

36. Bakker, M., & Wicherts, J. M. (2011). The (mis) reporting of statistical results in psychology journals. *Behavior Research Methods,*

43(3), 666-678. https://doi.org/10.3758/s13428-011-0089-5

37. Aguinis, H., Werner, S., Abbott, J. L., Angert, C., Park, J. H., & Kohlhausen, D. (2010). Customer-centric science: Reporting significant research results with rigor, relevance, and practical impact in mind. *Organizational Research Methods, 13*(3), 515-539. https://journals.sagepub.com/doi/10.1177/1094428109333339

38. Gomulya, D., & Boeker, W. (2014). How firms respond to financial restatement: CEO successors and external reactions. *Academy of Management Journal, 57*(6), 1759-1785. https://doi.org/10.5465/amj.2012.0491

39. Makino, S. and Chan, C. M. (2017). Skew and heavy-tail effects on firm performance. *Strategic Management Journal, 38*(8), 1721–1740. https://doi.org/10.1002/smj.2632

40. Kidwell, M. C., Lazarević, L. B., Baranski, E., Hardwicke, T. E., Piechowski, S., Falkenberg, L. S., ... & Errington, T. M. (2016). Badges to acknowledge open practices: A simple, low-cost, effective method for increasing transparency. *PLoS Biol, 14*(5), e1002456. https://doi.org/10.1371/journal.pbio.1002456

41. Cortina, J. M., Aguinis, H., & DeShon, R. P. (2017). Twilight of dawn or of evening? A century of research methods in the Journal of Applied Psychology. *Journal of Applied Psychology, 102*(3), 274-290. https://psycnet.apa.org/doi/10.1037/apl0000163

42. Hambrick, D. C. (2007). The field of management's devotion to theory: Too much of a good thing? *Academy of Management Journal, 50*(6), 1346–1352. https://doi.org/10.5465/amj.2007.28166119

43. Schmitt, N. (2017). Reflections on the *Journal of Applied Psychology* for 1989 to 1994: Changes in major research themes and practices over 25 years. *Journal of Applied Psychology, 102*(3), 564-568. https:

//psycnet.apa.org/doi/10.1037/apl0000053

44. Walumbwa, F. O., Luthans, F., Avey, J. B., & Oke, A. (2011). Retraction. Authentically leading groups: The mediating role of collective psychological capital and trust. *Journal of Organizational Behavior, 32*(1), 4-24 (Retraction published 2014, *Journal of Organizational Behavior, 35*(5), 746). https://doi.org/10.1002/job.1936

45. Journal of Applied Psychology. (2022). *Original use of data.* Retrieved on April 27, 2022 https://www.apa.org/pubs/journals/apl/?tab=1

46. Bettis, R. A., Ethiraj, S., Gambardella, A., Helfat, C., & Mitchell, W. (2016). Creating repeatable cumulative knowledge in strategic management. *Strategic Management Journal, 37*(2), 257-261. http://www.jstor.org/stable/43897939

47. Chenail, R. J. (2009). Communicating your qualitative research better. *Family Business Review, 22*(2), 105-108. https://journals.sagepub.com/doi/10.1177/0894486509334795

48. Tsui, A. S. (2013). The spirit of science and socially responsible scholarship. *Management and Organization Review, 9*(3), 375-394. https://doi.org/10.1111/more.12035

49. Cuervo-Cazurral, A., Andersson, U., Brannen, M. Y., Nielsen, B. B., & Reuber, A. R. (2016). From the Editors: Can I trust your findings? Ruling out alternative explanations in international business research. *Journal of International Business Studies, 47*(8), 881-897. https://doi.org/10.1057/s41267-016-0005-4

50. Kidwell, M. C., Lazarević, L. B., Baranski, E., Hardwicke, T. E., Piechowski, S., Falkenberg, L. S., ... & Errington, T. M. (2016). Badges to acknowledge open practices: A simple, low-cost, effective method for increasing

transparency. *PLoS Biol, 14*(5), e1002456. https://doi.org/10.1371/journal.pbio.1002456

51. Nosek, B. A., Spies, J. R., & Motyl, M. (2012). Scientific utopia II: Restructuring incentives and practices to promote truth over publishability. *Perspectives on Psychological Science, 7*(6), 615-631. https://journals.sagepub.com/doi/10.1177/1745691612459058

52. Köhler, T., & Cortina, J. M. (2021). Play it again, Sam! An analysis of constructive replication in the organizational sciences. *Journal of Management, 47*(2), 488-518. https://journals.sagepub.com/doi/abs/10.1177/0149206319843985

53. Hardwicke, T. E., Mathur, M. B., MacDonald, K., Nilsonne, G., Banks, G. C., Kidwell, M. C., Hofelich Mohr, A., Clayton, E., Yoon, E. J., & Henry Tessler, M. (2018). Data availability, reusability, and analytic reproducibility: Evaluating the impact of a mandatory open data policy at the journal Cognition. *Royal Society Open Science, 5*(8), 180448. https://doi.org/10.1098/rsos.180448

54. Köhler, T., Gonzàlez-Morales, M. G., Banks, G. C., O'Boyle, E., Allen, J., Sinha, R., Woo, S. E., & Gulick, L. (2020). Supporting robust, rigorous, and reliable reviewing as the cornerstone of our profession: Introducing a competency model for peer review. *Industrial and Organizational Psychology: Perspectives on Science and Practice, 13*(1), 1-27. https://doi.org/10.1017/iop.2019.121

55. Aguinis, H., Hill, N. S., & Bailey, J. R. (2021). Best practices in data collection and preparation: Recommendations for reviewers, editors, and authors. *Organizational Research Methods, 24*(4), 678-693. https://journals.sagepub.com/doi/10.1177/1094428119836485

56. Murphy, K. R., & Aguinis, H. (2019). HARKing: how badly can cherry-picking and question trolling produce bias in published results? *Journal of Business and*

Psychology, 34(1), 1-17. https://doi.org/10.1007/s10869-017-9524-7

57. Anderson, M. S., Martinson, B. C., & De Vries, R. (2007). Normative dissonance in science: Results from a national survey of US scientists. *Journal of Empirical Research on Human Research Ethics, 2*(4), 3-14. https://journals.sagepub.com/doi/10.1525/jer.2007.2.4.3

58. Hill, A. D., Bolton, J. F., & White, M. A. (2020). A call to find knowledge in our non-findings. *Strategic Organization, 18*(4), 645-654. https://journals.sagepub.com/doi/10.1177/1476127019867860

59. Antonakis, J. (2017). On doing better science: From thrill of discovery to policy implications. *The Leadership Quarterly, 28*(1), 5-21. https://doi.org/10.1016/j.leaqua.2017.01.006

60. Ramani, R. S., Aguinis, H., & Coyle-Shapiro, J. A. (2022). Defining, measuring, and rewarding scholarly impact: Mind the level of analysis. *Academy of Management Learning and Education, 21*(3). https://doi.org/10.5465/amle.2021.0177

CHAPTER 16

1. Adler, N. J., & Harzing, A. W. (2009). When knowledge wins: Transcending the sense and nonsense of academic rankings. *Academy of Management Learning & Education, 8*(1), 72-95. https://doi.org/10.5465/amle.2009.37012181

2. IMPACT APA: American Psychological Association strategic plan. 2022. Available at https://www.apa.org/about/apa/strategic-plan

3. Academy of Management Strategic Plan. (2012). *Explore the full plan.* http://strategicplan.aomonline.org/plan/full

4. Academy of Management Strategic Plan. (2012). *Explore the full plan.* http://strategicplan.aomonline.org/plan/full

5. Gomez-Mejia, L. R., & Balkin, D. B. (1992). Determinants of faculty pay: An agency theory perspective. *Academy of Management Journal, 35*(5), 921-955. https://doi.org/10.5465/256535

6. Podsakoff, P. M., MacKenzie, S. B., Podsakoff, N. P., & Bachrach, D. G. (2008). Scholarly influence in the field of management: A bibliometric analysis of the determinants of university and author impact in the management literature in the past quarter century. *Journal of Management, 34*(4), 641-720. https://doi.org/10.1177/0149206308319533

7. Judge, T. A., Cable, D. M., Colbert, A. E., & Rynes, S. L. (2007). What causes a management article to be cited—article, author, or journal?. *Academy of Management Journal, 50*(3), 491-506. https://doi.org/10.5465/amj.2007.25525577

8. Partington, D., & Jenkins, M. (2007). Deconstructing scholarship: An analysis of research methods citations in the organizational sciences. *Organizational Research Methods, 10*(3), 399-416. https://doi.org/10.1177/1094428107300202

9. Aguinis, H., Dalton, D. R., Bosco, F. A., Pierce, C. A., & Dalton, C. M. (2011). Meta-analytic choices and judgment calls: Implications for theory building and testing, obtained effect sizes, and scholarly impact. *Journal of Management, 37*(1), 5-38. https://doi.org/10.1177/0149206310377113

10. Molina-Azorin, J. F. (2012). Mixed methods research in strategic management: Impact and applications. *Organizational Research Methods, 15*(1), 33-56. https://doi.org/10.1177/1094428110393023

11. Colquitt, J. A. (2011). The next three years at AMJ—Maintaining the mission while expanding the journal. *Academy of Management Journal, 54*(1), 9-14. https://doi.org/10.5465/amj.2011.59215082

12. Lockett, A., & McWilliams, A. (2005). The balance of trade between disciplines: Do we effectively manage knowledge?. *Journal of Management Inquiry, 14*(2), 139-150. https://doi.org/10.1177/1056492605276645

13. Bedeian, A. G. (2005). Crossing disciplinary boundaries: A epilegomenon for Lockett and McWilliams. *Journal of Management Inquiry, 14*(2), 151-155. https://doi.org/10.1177/1056492605276647

14. Podsakoff, P. M., MacKenzie, S. B., Podsakoff, N. P., & Bachrach, D. G. (2008). Scholarly influence in the field of management: A bibliometric analysis of the determinants of university and author impact in the management literature in the past quarter century. *Journal of Management, 34*(4), 641-720. https://doi.org/10.1177/0149206308319533

15. Aguinis, H., Dalton, D. R., Bosco, F. A., Pierce, C. A., & Dalton, C. M. (2011). Meta-analytic choices and judgment calls: Implications for theory building and testing, obtained effect sizes, and scholarly impact. *Journal of Management, 37*(1), 5-38. https://doi.org/10.1177/0149206310377113

16. Certo, S. T., Sirmon, D. G., & Brymer, R. A. (2010). Competition and scholarly productivity in management: Investigating changes in scholarship from 1988 to 2008. *Academy of Management Learning & Education, 9*(4), 591-606. https://doi.org/10.5465/AMLE.2010.56659878

17. Freeman, R. E. (2010). *Strategic management: A stakeholder approach.* Cambridge university press. https://doi.org/10.1017/CBO9781139192675

18. Bansal, P., Bertels, S., Ewart, T., MacConnachie, P., & O'Brien, J. (2012). Bridging the research–practice gap. *Academy of Management Perspectives, 26*(1), 73-92. https://doi.org/10.5465/amp.2011.0140

19. Cascio, W. F., & Aguinis, H. (2008). Research in industrial and organizational psychology from 1963 to 2007: Changes, choices, and trends. *Journal of Applied Psychology*, *93*(5), 1062-1081. https://doi.org/10.1037/0021-9010.93.5.1062

20. Aguinis, H., Suárez-González, I., Lannelongue, G., & Joo, H. (2012). Scholarly impact revisited. *Academy of Management Perspectives*, *26*(2), 105-132. https://doi.org/10.5465/amp.2011.0088

21. Kacmar, K. M., & Whitfield, J. M. (2000). An additional rating method for journal articles in the field of management. *Organizational Research Methods*, *3*(4), 392-406. https://doi.org/10.1177/109442810034005

22. Barjak, F., Li, X., & Thelwall, M. (2007). Which factors explain the Web impact of scientists' personal homepages?. *Journal of the American Society for Information Science and Technology*, *58*(2), 200-211. https://doi.org/10.1002/asi.20476

23. Thelwall, M., & Sud, P. (2011). A comparison of methods for collecting web citation data for academic organizations. *Journal of the American Society for information Science and Technology*, *62*(8), 1488-1497. https://doi.org/10.1002/asi.21571

24. Wellmon, C. & Piper, A. (2017). Publication, power, and patronage: On inequality and academic publishing. *Critical Inquiry*. https://criticalinquiry.uchicago.edu/publication_power_and_patronage_on_inequality_and_academic_publishing/

25. Callahan, J. L. (2018). The retrospective (im) moralization of self-plagiarism: Power interests in the social construction of new norms for publishing. *Organization*, *25*(3), 305-319. https://doi.org/10.1177/1350508417734926

26. Hays, D. & Wynyard, R. (2002). *The McDonaldization of higher education*. Praeger.

27. Berman, E. (2012). *Creating the market university: How academic science became an economic engine*. Princeton University Press. https://doi.org/10.23943/princeton/9780691147086.001.0001

28. Anderson, G. (2008). Mapping academic resistance in the managerial university. *Organization*, *15*(2), 251-270. https://doi.org/10.1177/1350508407086583

29. Lorenz, C. (2012). If you're so smart, why are you under surveillance? Universities, neoliberalism, and new public management. *Critical Inquiry*, *38*(3), 599-629. https://doi.org/10.1086/664553

30. Garfield, E. (2005). *The agony and the ecstasy—The history and meaning of the Journal Impact Factor.* Paper presented at the International Congress on Peer Review and Biomedical Publication; Chicago, IL.

31. Bedeian, A. G. (1996). Lessons learned along the way: Twelve suggestions for optimizing career success. In P. J. Frost & M. S. Taylor (Eds.), *Rhythms of academic life: Personal accounts of careers in academi*a (pp. 3-10). Sage. https://doi.org/10.4135/9781452231570.n1

32. Shapiro, D. L. (2017). 2016 Presidential Address: Making the Academy Full-Voice Meaningful. *Academy of Management Review*, *42*(2), 165-173. https://doi.org/10.5465/amr.2016.0539

33. Ryazanova, O., McNamara, P., & Aguinis, H. (2017). Research performance as a quality signal in international labor markets: Visibility of business schools worldwide through a global research performance system. *Journal of World Business*, *52*(6), 831-841. https://doi.org/10.1016/j.jwb.2017.09.003

34. Ryazanova, O., McNamara, P., & Aguinis, H. (2017). Research performance as a quality signal in international labor markets: Visibility of business schools worldwide through a global research performance system. *Journal of World Business*, *52*(6), 831-841. https://doi.org/10.1016/j.jwb.2017.09.003

35. Deegan, C. (2016). So, who really is a "noted author" within the accounting literature? A reflection on Benson et al. (2015). *Accounting, Auditing & Accountability Journal*, 29, 483-490. https://doi.org/10.1108/AAAJ-05-2015-2052

36. Van Fleet, D. D., McWilliams, A., & Siegel, D. S. (2000). A theoretical and empirical analysis of journal rankings: The case of formal lists. *Journal of Management*, *26*(5), 839-861. https://doi.org/10.1177/014920630002600505

37. Honig, B., Lampel, J., Baum, J. A., Glynn, M. A., Jing, R., Lounsbury, M., ... & Van Witteloostuijn, A. (2018). Reflections on scientific misconduct in management: Unfortunate incidents or a normative crisis?. *Academy of Management Perspectives*, *32*(4), 412-442. https://doi.org/10.5465/amp.2015.0167

38. Edwards, M. A., & Roy, S. (2017). Academic research in the 21st century: Maintaining scientific integrity in a climate of perverse incentives and hypercompetition. *Environmental Engineering Science*, *34*(1), 51-61. https://doi.org/10.1089/ees.2016.0223

39. Certo, S. T., Sirmon, D. G., & Brymer, R. A. (2010). Competition and scholarly productivity in management: Investigating changes in scholarship from 1988 to 2008. *Academy of Management Learning & Education*, *9*(4), 591-606. https://doi.org/10.5465/AMLE.2010.56659878

40. Edwards, M. A., & Roy, S. (2017). Academic research in the 21st century: Maintaining scientific integrity in a climate of perverse incentives and hypercompetition. *Environmental Engineering Science*, *34*(1), 51-61. https://doi.org/10.1089/ees.2016.0223

41. Aguinis, H., Shapiro, D. L., Antonacopoulou, E. P., & Cummings, T. G. (2014). Scholarly impact: A pluralist conceptualization. *Academy of Management Learning & Education*, *13*(4), 623-639. https://doi.org/10.5465/amle.2014.0121

42. Tsui, A. S. (2013). The spirit of science and socially responsible scholarship. *Management and Organization Review*, *9*(3), 375-394. https://doi.org/10.1111/more.12035

43. Adler, N. J., & Harzing, A. W. (2009). When knowledge wins: Transcending the sense and nonsense of academic rankings. *Academy of Management Learning & Education*, *8*(1), 72-95. https://doi.org/10.5465/amle.2009.37012181

44. Harley, B. (2019). Confronting the crisis of confidence in management studies: Why senior scholars need to stop setting a bad example. *Academy of Management Learning & Education*, *18*(2), 286-297. https://doi.org/10.5465/amle.2018.0107

45. Carpenter, C. R., Cone, D. C., & Sarli, C. C. (2014). Using publication metrics to highlight academic productivity and research impact. *Academic Emergency Medicine*, *21*(10), 1160-1172. https://doi.org/10.1111/acem.12482

46. Connelly, B. L., Tihanyi, L., Crook, T. R., & Gangloff, K. A. (2014). Tournament theory: Thirty years of contests and competitions. *Journal of Management*, *40*(1), 16-47. https://doi.org/10.1177/0149206313498902

47. Shapiro, D. L., & Kirkman, B. L. (2018). It's time to make business school research more relevant. *Harvard Business Review*. https://hbr.org/2018/07/its-time-to-make-business-school-research-more-relevant

48. Honig, B., Lampel, J., Baum, J. A., Glynn, M. A., Jing, R., Lounsbury, M., ... & Van Witteloostuijn, A. (2018). Reflections on scientific misconduct in management:

Unfortunate incidents or a normative crisis?. *Academy of Management Perspectives*, *32*(4), 412-442. https://doi.org/10.5465/amp.2015.0167

49. Edwards, M. A., & Roy, S. (2017). Academic research in the 21st century: Maintaining scientific integrity in a climate of perverse incentives and hypercompetition. *Environmental Engineering Science*, *34*(1), 51-61. https://doi.org/10.1089/ees.2016.0223

50. Ryazanova, O., McNamara, P., & Aguinis, H. (2017). Research performance as a quality signal in international labor markets: Visibility of business schools worldwide through a global research performance system. *Journal of World Business*, *52*(6), 831-841. https://doi.org/10.1016/j.jwb.2017.09.003

51. Edwards, M. A., & Roy, S. (2017). Academic research in the 21st century: Maintaining scientific integrity in a climate of perverse incentives and hypercompetition. *Environmental Engineering Science*, *34*(1), 51-61. https://doi.org/10.1089/ees.2016.0223

52. Aguinis, H. (2023). *Performance management* (5th edition). Chicago Business Press.

53. Gomez-Mejia, L. R., & Balkin, D. B. (1992). Determinants of faculty pay: An agency theory perspective. *Academy of Management Journal*, *35*(5), 921-955. https://doi.org/10.5465/256535

54. Kula, W. (1986). *Measures and men*. Princeton University Press. https://doi.org/10.1515/9781400857739

55. Van Fleet, D. D., McWilliams, A., & Siegel, D. S. (2000). A theoretical and empirical analysis of journal rankings: The case of formal lists. *Journal of Management*, *26*(5), 839-861. https://doi.org/10.1177/014920630002600505

56. Van Fleet, D. D., McWilliams, A., & Siegel, D. S. (2000). A theoretical and empirical analysis of journal rankings: The case of formal lists.

Journal of Management, *26*(5), 839-861. https://doi.org/10.1177/014920630002600505

57. Adler, N. J., & Harzing, A. W. (2009). When knowledge wins: Transcending the sense and nonsense of academic rankings. *Academy of Management Learning & Education*, *8*(1), 72-95. https://doi.org/10.5465/amle.2009.37012181

58. Pontille, D., & Torny, D. (2010). The controversial policies of journal ratings: Evaluating social sciences and humanities. *Research Evaluation*, *19*(5), 347-360. https://doi.org/10.3152/095820210X12809191250889

59. Tadajewski, M. (2016). Academic labour, journal ranking lists and the politics of knowledge production in marketing. *Journal of Marketing Management*, *32*(1-2), 1-18. https://doi.org/10.1080/0267257X.2015.1120508

60. Guo, H., Wang, B., Qiao, X., & Liu, R. (2016). A review of studies on citations and journal ranking in finance. *Managerial Finance*, *42*, 303-311. https://doi.org/10.1108/MF-04-2015-0123

61. Deegan, C. (2016). So, who really is a "noted author" within the accounting literature? A reflection on Benson et al. (2015). *Accounting, Auditing & Accountability Journal*, 29, 483-490. https://doi.org/10.1108/AAAJ-05-2015-2052

62. Tüselmann, H., Sinkovics, R. R., & Pishchulov, G. (2016). Revisiting the standing of international business journals in the competitive landscape. *Journal of World Business*, *51*(4), 487-498. https://doi.org/10.1016/j.jwb.2016.01.006

63. Wang, J., Veugelers, R. & Stephan, P. (2016). Bias against novelty in science: A cautionary tale for users of bibliometric indicators. *National Bureau of Economic Research Working Paper Series*, No. 22180. http://www.nber.org/papers/w22180https://doi.org/10.3386/w22180

64. Vogel, R., Hattke, F., & Petersen, J. (2017). Journal rankings in management and business studies: What rules do we play by?. *Research Policy*, *46*(10), 1707-1722. https://doi.org/10.1016/j.respol.2017.07.001

65. Power, M. (2004). Counting, control and calculation: Reflections on measuring and management. *Human Relations*, *57*(6), 765-783. https://doi.org/10.1177/0018726704044955

66. Lorenz, C. (2012). If you're so smart, why are you under surveillance? Universities, neoliberalism, and new public management. *Critical Inquiry*, *38*(3), 599-629. https://doi.org/10.1086/664553

67. McLaren, P. G. (2019). Stop blaming Gordon and Howell: Unpacking the complex history behind the research-based model of education. *Academy of Management Learning & Education*, *18*(1), 43-58. https://doi.org/10.5465/amle.2017.0311

68. Pfeffer, J., & Fong, C. T. (2002). The end of business schools? Less success than meets the eye. *Academy of Management Learning & Education*, *1*(1), 78-95. https://doi.org/10.5465/amle.2002.7373679

69. Bennis, W. G., & O'Toole, J. (2005). How business schools have lost their way. *Harvard Business Review*, *83*(5), 96-104.

70. Cummings, T. G. (2011). How business schools shape (misshape) management research. In S. A. Mohrman & E. E. Lawler, (Eds.), *Useful research: Advancing theory and practice* (pp. 331–350). Berrett-Koehler.

71. O'Brien, J. P., Drnevich, P. L., Crook, T. R., & Armstrong, C. E. (2010). Does business school research add economic value for students?. *Academy of Management Learning & Education*, *9*(4), 638-651. https://doi.org/10.5465/amle.9.4.zqr638

72. Honig, B., Lampel, J., Baum, J. A., Glynn, M. A., Jing, R., Lounsbury, M., ... & Van Witteloostuijn, A. (2018). Reflections on scientific misconduct in management: Unfortunate incidents or a normative crisis?. *Academy of Management Perspectives*, *32*(4), 412-442. https://doi.org/10.5465/amp.2015.0167

73. Gomez-Mejia, L. R., & Balkin, D. B. (1992). Determinants of faculty pay: An agency theory perspective. *Academy of Management Journal*, *35*(5), 921-955. https://doi.org/10.5465/256535

74. Trieschmann, J. S., Dennis, A. R., Northcraft, G. B., & Nieme Jr, A. W. (2000). Serving constituencies in business schools: MBA program versus research performance. *Academy of Management Journal*, *43*(6), 1130-1141. https://doi.org/10.5465/1556341

75. Ryazanova, O., McNamara, P., & Aguinis, H. (2017). Research performance as a quality signal in international labor markets: Visibility of business schools worldwide through a global research performance system. *Journal of World Business*, *52*(6), 831-841. https://doi.org/10.1016/j.jwb.2017.09.003

76. Walsh, J. P. (2011). Presidential address: Embracing the sacred in our secular scholarly world. *Academy of Management Review*, *36*(2), 215-234. https://doi.org/10.5465/amr.36.2.zok215

77. Edwards, M. A., & Roy, S. (2017). Academic research in the 21st century: Maintaining scientific integrity in a climate of perverse incentives and hypercompetition. *Environmental Engineering Science*, *34*(1), 51-61. https://doi.org/10.1089/ees.2016.0223

78. Connelly, C. E., & Gallagher, D. G. (2010). Making" The List": The Business School Rankings and the Commodification of Business Research. *Journal of Curriculum Theorizing*, *26*(3), 86-99.

79. Walsh, J. P. (2011). Embracing the sacred in our scholarly secular world. *Academy of Management Review*, *36* (2), 215-234. https://doi.org/10.5465/AMR.2011.59330756

80. Walsh, J. P. (2011). Embracing the sacred in our scholarly secular world. *Academy of Management Review*, *36* (2), 215-234. https://doi.org/10.5465/AMR.2011.59330756

81. Aguinis, H., Suárez-González, I., Lannelongue, G., & Joo, H. (2012). Scholarly impact revisited. *Academy of Management Perspectives*, *26*(2), 105-132. https://doi.org/10.5465/amp.2011.0088

82. Aguinis, H., Suárez-González, I., Lannelongue, G., & Joo, H. (2012). Scholarly impact revisited. *Academy of Management Perspectives*, *26*(2), 105-132. https://doi.org/10.5465/amp.2011.0088

83. Tung, V. W. S., Law, R., & Chon, K. (2018). Changing proxies for evaluating research performance: What matters to university programme heads?. *Tourism Recreation Research*, *43*(3), 346-355. https://doi.org/10.1080/02508281.2017.1415654

84. Tung, V. W. S., Law, R., & Chon, K. (2018). Changing proxies for evaluating research performance: What matters to university programme heads?. *Tourism Recreation Research*, *43*(3), 346-355. https://doi.org/10.1080/02508281.2017.1415654

85. DeTienne, D. R. (2013). From the Editors: Assessing Scholarly Impact in the World of Google. *Academy of Management Learning & Education*, *12*(1), 1-3. https://doi.org/10.5465/amle.2013.0013

86. Shapiro, D. L., Kirkman, B. L., & Courtney, H. G. (2007). Perceived causes and solutions of the translation problem in management research. *Academy of Management Journal*, *50*(2), 249-266. https://doi.org/10.5465/amj.2007.24634433

87. Ashford, S. J. (2013). Having scholarly impact: The art of hitting academic home runs. *Academy of Management Learning & Education*, *12*(4), 623-633. https://doi.org/10.5465/amle.2013.0090

88. Aguinis, H., Gottfredson, R. K., Culpepper, S. A., Dalton, D. R., & De Bruin, G. P. (2013). Doing good

and doing well: On the multiple contributions of journal editors. *Academy of Management Learning & Education, 12*(4), 564-578. https://doi.org/10.5465/amle.2012.0066

89. Tracey, J. B. (2018). Moving the impact dial. *Cornell Hospitality Quarterly, 59*(3), 200-200. https://doi.org/10.1177/1938965518784676

90. Tung, V. W. S., Law, R., & Chon, K. (2018). Changing proxies for evaluating research performance: What matters to university programme heads?. *Tourism Recreation Research, 43*(3), 346-355. https://doi.org/10.1080/02508281.2017.1415654

91. Aguinis, H., Joo, H., & Gottfredson, R. K. (2013). What monetary rewards can and cannot do: How to show employees the money. *Business Horizons, 56*(2), 241-249. https://doi.org/10.1016/j.bushor.2012.11.007

92. Aguinis, H., & O'Boyle Jr, E. (2014). Star performers in twenty-first century organizations. *Personnel Psychology, 67*(2), 313-350. https://doi.org/10.1111/peps.12054

93. Aguinis, H. (2019). *Performance management for dummies*. John Wiley & Sons.

94. Aguinis, H., Cummings, C., Ramani, R. S., & Cummings, T. G. (2020). "An A is an A": The new bottom line for valuing academic research. *Academy of Management Perspectives, 34*(1), 135-154. https://doi.org/10.5465/amp.2017.0193

95. Aguinis, H., Cummings, C., Ramani, R. S., & Cummings, T. G. (2020). "An A is an A": The new bottom line for valuing academic research. *Academy of Management Perspectives, 34*(1), 135-154. https://doi.org/10.5465/amp.2017.0193

96. Tung, V. W. S., Law, R., & Chon, K. (2018). Changing proxies for evaluating research performance: What matters to university programme heads?. *Tourism Recreation Research, 43*(3), 346-355. https://doi.org/10.1080/02508281.2017.1415654

97. Tung, V. W. S., Law, R., & Chon, K. (2018). Changing proxies for evaluating research performance: What matters to university programme heads?. *Tourism Recreation Research, 43*(3), 346-355. https://doi.org/10.1080/02508281.2017.1415654

98. Aguinis, H., Cummings, C., Ramani, R. S., & Cummings, T. G. (2020). "An A is an A": The new bottom line for valuing academic research. *Academy of Management Perspectives, 34*(1), 135-154. https://doi.org/10.5465/amp.2017.0193

99. Law, R., Chan, I. C. C., & Zhao, X. (2019). Ranking hospitality and tourism journals. *Journal of Hospitality & Tourism Research, 43*(5), 754-761. https://doi.org/10.1177/1096348019838028

100. Ryazanova, O., & McNamara, P. (2016). Socialization and proactive behavior: Multilevel exploration of research productivity drivers in U.S. business schools. *Academy of Management Learning & Education, 15*(3), 525-548. https://doi.org/10.5465/amle.2015.0084

101. Fisher, G. (2020). Why every business professor should write practitioner-focused articles. *Business Horizons, 63*(4), 417-419. https://doi.org/10.1016/j.bushor.2020.03.004

102. Banerjee, S., & Morley, C. (2013). Professional doctorates in management: Toward a practice-based approach to doctoral education. *Academy of Management Learning & Education, 12*(2), 173-193. https://doi.org/10.5465/amle.2012.0159

103. Aguinis, H., Banks, G. C., Rogelberg, S. G., & Cascio, W. F. (2020). Actionable recommendations for narrowing the science-practice gap in open science. *Organizational Behavior and Human Decision Processes, 158*, 27-35. https://doi.org/10.1016/j.obhdp.2020.02.007

104. Tourish, D., & Craig, R. (2020). Research misconduct in business and management studies: Causes, consequences, and possible remedies. *Journal of Management Inquiry, 29*(2), 174-187. https://doi.org/10.1177/1056492618792621

105. Kovoor-Misra, S. (2012). Academic decathletes: Insights from the metaphor and an exemplar. *Journal of Management Inquiry, 21*(3), 279-286. https://doi.org/10.1177/1056492611428749

106. Kovoor-Misra, S. (2012). Academic decathletes: Insights from the metaphor and an exemplar. *Journal of Management Inquiry, 21*(3), 279-286. https://doi.org/10.1177/1056492611428749

107. Fisher, G. (2020). Why every business professor should write practitioner-focused articles. *Business Horizons, 63*(4), 417-419. https://doi.org/10.1016/j.bushor.2020.03.004

108. Aguinis, H. (2019), *Performance Management for Dummies*, Wiley.

109. Yale School of Management. (2020). *Top 40 Most Popular Case Studies of 2019*. https://som.yale.edu/news/2020/02/top-40-most-popular-case-studies-of-2019

110. Aguinis, H., Suárez-González, I., Lannelongue, G., & Joo, H. (2012). Scholarly impact revisited. *Academy of Management Perspectives, 26*(2), 105-132. https://doi.org/10.5465/amp.2011.0088

111. Dauenhauer, P. J. (2020). Expand your academic impact with social media best practices. *Matter, 2*(4), 789-793. https://doi.org/10.1016/j.matt.2020.02.017

112. Aguinis, H. (2023). *Performance management* (5th ed.). Chicago Business Press.

113. Akkermans, J., Brenninkmeijer, V., Schaufeli, W. B., & Blonk, R. B. (2015). It's all about CareerSKILLS: Effectiveness of a career development intervention for young employees. *Human Resource Management, 54*(4),

533–551. https://doi.org/10.1002/hrm.21633

114. Banks, G. C., Barnes, C. M., & Jiang, K. (2021). Changing the conversation on the science–practice gap: An adherence-based approach. *Journal of Management*, *47*(6), 1347–1356. htt

ps://doi.org/10.1177/01492063219 93546

115. Bartunek, J. M., & Rynes, S. L. (2010). The construction and contributions of "implications for practice": What's in them and what might they offer? *Academy of Management Learning & Education*,

9(1), 100-117. https://doi.org/10.54 65/amle.9.1.zqr100

116. Kluger, A. N., & Nir, D. (2010). The feedforward interview. *Human Resource Management Review*, *20*(3), 235–246. https://doi.org/10. 1016/j.hrmr.2009.08.002

INDEX